The Best Known Works

of

Anton Chekhov

One Volume Edition

BLUE RIBBON BOOKS, INC.

NEW YORK CITY

PRINTED AND BOUND BY THE CORNWALL PRESS, INC., FOR
BLUE RIBBON BOOKS, INC., 386 FOURTH AVE., NEW YORK CITY
Printed in the United States of America

Contents

VOLUME I
TALES

VOLUME II
TALES

CONTENTS

VOLUME III
TALES

CONTENTS

VOLUME IV
NOVEL

CONTENTS

VOLUME V
TALES

VOLUME VI
TALES

CONTENTS

VOLUME VII

TALES

CONTENTS

VOLUME VIII

PLAYS

VOLUME IX

PLAYS

VOLUME I

The Kiss

On the twentieth of May, at eight o'clock in the evening, six batteries of the N Artillery Brigade arrived at the village of Miestetchki to spend the night, before going to their camp.

The confusion was at its height—some officers at the guns, others in the church square with the quartermaster—when a civilian upon a remarkable horse rode from the rear of the church. The small cob with well-shaped neck wobbled along all the time dancing on its legs as if some one were whipping them. Reaching the officers the rider doffed his cap with ceremony and said—

"His Excellency, General von Rabbek, requests the honour of the officers' company at tea in his house nearby. . . ."

The horse shook its head, danced, and wobbled backwards; its rider again took off his cap, and turning around disappeared behind the church.

"The devil!" the general exclaimed, the officers dispersing to their quarters. "We are almost asleep, yet along comes this von Rabbek with his tea! That tea! I remember it!"

The officers of the six batteries had vivid recollections of a past invitation. During recent manœuvres they had been asked, with their Cossack comrades, to tea at the house of a local country gentleman, a Count, retired from military service and this hearty, old Count overwhelmed them with attentions, fed them like gourmands, poured vodka into them and made them stay the night. All this, of course, was fine. The trouble was that the old soldier entertained his guests too well. He kept them up till daybreak while he poured forth tales of past adventures and pointed out valuable paintings, engravings, arms, and letters from celebrated men. And the tired officers listened, by force until he ended, only to find out then the time for sleep had gone.

Was von Rabbek another old Count? It might easily be. But there was no neglecting his invitation. The officers washed and dressed, and set out for von Rabbek's house. At the church square they learnt that they must descend the hill to the river, and follow the bank till they reached the general's gardens, where they would find a path direct to the house. Or, if they chose to go up hill, they would reach the general's barns half a verst from Miestetchki. It was this route they chose.

"But who is this von Rabbek?" asked one. "The man who commanded the N Cavalry Division at Plevna?"

"No, that was not von Rabbek, but simply Rabbe—without the von."

"What glorious weather!"

At the first barn they came to. two roads diverged; one ran straight forward and faded in the dusk; the other turning to the right led to the general's house. As the officers drew near they talked less loudly. To right and to left stretched rows of red-roofed brick barns, in aspect heavy and morose as the barracks of provincial towns. In front gleamed the lighted windows of von Rabbek's house.

"A good omen, gentlemen!" cried a young officer. Our setter runs in advance. There is game ahead!"

1

On the face of Lieutenant Lobuitko, the tall stout officer referred to, there was not one trace of hair though he was twenty-five years old. He was famed among comrades for the instinct which told him of the presence of women in the neighborhood. On hearing his comrade's remark, he turned his head and said—

"Yes. There are women there. My instinct tells me."

A handsome, well-preserved man of sixty, in mufti, came to the hall door to greet his guests. It was von Rabbek. As he pressed their hands, he explained that though he was delighted to see them, he must beg pardon for not asking them to spend the night; as guests he already had his two sisters, their children, his brother, and several neighbours—in fact, he had not one spare room. And though he shook their hands and apologised and smiled, it was plain that he was not half as glad to see them as was last year's Count, and that he had invited them merely because good manners demanded it. The officers climbing the soft-carpeted steps and listening to their host understood this perfectly well; and realised that they carried into the house an atmosphere of intrusion and alarm. Would any man—they asked themselves—who had gathered his two sisters and their children, his brother and his neighbours, to celebrate, no doubt, some family festival, find pleasure in the invasion of nineteen officers whom he had never seen before?

A tall elderly lady, with a good figure, and a long face with black eyebrows, who resembled closely the ex-Empress Eugenie, greeted them at the drawing-room door. Smiling courteously and with dignity, she affirmed that she was delighted to see the officers, and only regretted that she could not ask them to stay the night. But the courteous. dignified smile disappeared when she turned away, and it was quite plain that she had seen many officers in her day, that they caused not the slightest interest, and that she had invited them merely because an invitation was dictated by good breeding and by her position in the world.

In a big dining-room seated at a big table sat ten men and women, drinking tea. Behind them, veiled in cigar-smoke, stood several young men, among them one, red-whiskered and extremely thin, who spoke English loudly with a lisp. Through an open door the officers saw into a brightly lighted room with blue wall-paper.

"You are too many to introduce singly, gentlemen!" said the general loudly, with affected joviality. "Make one another's acquaintance, please— without formalities!"

The visitors, some with serious, even severe faces, some smiling constrainedly, all with a feeling of awkwardness, bowed, and took their seats at the table. Most awkward of all felt Staff-Captain Riabovitch, a short, round-shouldered. spectacled officer, whiskered like a lynx. While his brother officers looked serious or smiled constrainedly, his face, his lynx whiskers, and his spectacles seemed to explain: "I am the most timid, modest, undistinguished officer in the whole brigade." For some time after he took his seat at the table he could not fix his attention on any single thing. Faces, dresses, the cut-glass cognac bottles, the steaming tumblers, the moulded cornices—all merged in a single, overwhelming sentiment which caused him intense fright and made him wish to hide his head. Like an inexperienced lecturer he saw everything before him, but could distinguish nothing, and was in fact the victim of what men of science diagnose as "physical blindness."

But, slowly conquering his diffidence, Riabovitch began to distinguish and observe. As became a man both timid and unsocial, he remárked first of all the amazing temerity of his new friends. Von Rabbek, his wife, two elderly ladies, a girl in lilac, and the red-whiskered youth who, it appeared, was a young von Rabbek, sat down among the officers as unconcernedly as if they had held rehearsals, and at once plunged into various heated arguments in which they soon involved their guests. That artillerists have a much better time than cavalrymen or infantrymen was proved conclusively by the lilac girl, while von Rabbek and the elderly ladies affirmed the converse. The conversation became desultory. Riabovitch listened to the lilac girl fiercely debating themes she knew nothing about and took no interest in, and watched the insincere smiles which appeared on and disappeared from her face.

While the von Rabbek family with amazing strategy inveigled their guests into the dispute, they kept their eyes on every glass and mouth. Had every one tea, was it sweet enough, why didn't one eat biscuits, was another fond of cognac? And the longer Riabovitch listened and looked, the more pleased he was with this disingenuous, disciplined family.

After tea the guests repaired to the drawing-room. Instinct had not cheated Lobuitko. The room was packed with young women and girls, and ere a minute had passed the setter-lieutenant stood beside a very young, fair-haired girl in black, and, bending down as if resting on an invisible sword, shrugged his shoulders coquettishly. He was uttering, no doubt, most unentertaining nonsense, for the fair girl looked indulgently at his sated face, and exclaimed indifferently, "Indeed!" And this indifferent "Indeed!" might have quickly convinced the setter that he was on a wrong scent.

Music began. As the notes of a mournful valse throbbed out of the open window, through the heads of all flashed the feeling that outside that window it was spring-time, a night of May. The air was odorous of young poplar leaves, of roses and lilacs—and the valse and the spring were sincere. Riabovitch, with valse and cognac mingling tipsily in his head, gazed at the window with a smile; then began to follow the movements of the women; and it seemed that the smell of roses, poplars, and lilacs came not from the gardens outside, but from the women's faces and dresses.

They began to dance. Young von Rabbek valsed twice round the room with a very thin girl; and Lobuitko, slipping on the parquetted floor, went up to the girl in lilac, and was granted a dance. But Riabovitch stood near the door with the wall-flowers, and looked silently on. Amazed at the daring of men who in sight of a crowd could take unknown women by the waist, he tried in vain to picture himself doing the same. A time had been when he envied his comrades their courage and dash, suffered from painful heart-searchings, and was hurt by the knowledge that he was timid, round-shouldered, and undistinguished, that he had lynx whiskers, and that his waist was much too long. But with years he had grown reconciled to his own insignificance, and now looking at the dancers and loud talkers, he felt no envy, but only mournful emotions.

At the first quadrille von Rabbek junior approached and invited two non-dancing officers to a game of billiards. The three left the room; and Riabovitch, who stood idle, and felt impelled to join in the general movement, followed. They passed the dining-room, traversed a narrow glazed corridor, and a room where three sleepy footmen jumped from a sofa with a start; and after walking, it seemed, through a whole houseful of rooms, entered a small billiard-room.

Von Rabbek and the two officers began their game. Riabovitch, whose only game was cards, stood near the table and looked indifferently on, as the players, with unbuttoned coats, wielded their cues, moved about, joked, and shouted obscure technical terms. Riabovitch was ignored, save when one of the players jostled him or caught his cue, and turning towards him said briefly, "Pardon!" so that before the game was over he was thoroughly bored, and, impressed by a sense of his superfluity, resolved to return to the drawing-room, and turned away.

It was on the way back that his adventure took place. Before he had gone far he saw that he had missed his way. He remembered distinctly the room with the three sleepy footmen; and after passing through five or six rooms entirely vacant, he saw his mistake. Retracing his steps, he turned to the left, and found himself in an almost dark room which he had not seen before; and after hesitating a minute, he boldly opened the first door he saw, and found himself in complete darkness. Through a chink of the door in front peered a bright light; from afar throbbed the dullest music of a mournful mazurka. Here, as in the drawing-room, the windows were open wide, and the smell of poplars, lilacs, and roses flooded the air.

Riabovitch paused in irresolution. For a moment all was still. Then came the sound of hasty footsteps; then, without any warning of what was to come, a dress rustled, a woman's breathless voice whispered "At last!" and two soft, scented, unmistakably womanly arms met round his neck, a warm cheek impinged on his, and he received a sounding kiss. But hardly had the kiss echoed through the silence when the unknown shrieked loudly, and fled away—as it seemed to Riabovitch—in disgust. Riabovitch himself nearly screamed, and rushed headlong towards the bright beam in the door-chink.

As he entered the drawing-room his heart beat violently, and his hands trembled so perceptibly that he clasped them behind his back. His first emotion was shame, as if every one in the room already knew that he had just been embraced and kissed. He retired into his shell, and looked fearfully around. But finding that hosts and guests were calmly dancing or talking, he regained courage, and surrendered himself to sensations experienced for the first time in life. The unexampled had happened. His neck, fresh from the embrace of two soft, scented arms, seemed anointed with oil; near his left moustache, where the kiss had fallen, trembled a slight, delightful chill, as from peppermint drops; and from head to foot he was soaked in new and extraordinary sensations, which continued to grow and grow.

He felt that he must dance, talk, run into the garden, laugh unrestrainedly. He forgot altogether that he was round-shouldered, undistinguished, lynx-whiskered, that he had an "indefinite exterior"—a description from the lips of a woman he had happened to overhear. As Madame von Rabbek passed him he smiled so broadly and graciously that she came up and looked at him questioningly.

"What a charming house you have!" he said, straightening his spectacles.

And Madame von Rabbek smiled back, said that the house still belonged to her father, and asked were his parents still alive, how long he had been in the Army, and why he was so thin. After hearing his answers she departed. But though the conversation was over, he continued to smile benevolently, and think what charming people were his new acquaintances.

At supper Riabovitch ate and drank mechanically what was put before him, heard not a word of the conversation, and devoted all his powers to the unravelling of his mysterious, romantic adventure. What was the explanation? It was plain that one of the girls, he reasoned, had arranged a meeting in the dark room, and after waiting some time in vain had, in her nervous tension, mistaken Riabovitch for her hero. The mistake was likely enough, for on entering the dark room Riabovitch had stopped irresolutely as if he, too, were waiting for some one. So far the mystery was explained.

"But which of them was it?" he asked, searching the women's faces. She certainly was young, for old women do not indulge in such romances. Secondly, she was not a servant. That was proved unmistakably by the rustle of her dress, the scent, the voice. . . .

When at first he looked at the girl in lilac she pleased him; she had pretty shoulders and arms, a clever face, a charming voice. Riabovitch piously prayed that it was she. But, smiling insincerely, she wrinkled her long nose, and that at once gave her an elderly air. So Riabovitch turned his eyes on the blonde in black. The blonde was younger, simpler, sincerer; she had charming kiss-curls, and drank from her tumbler with inexpressible grace. Riabovitch hoped it was she—but soon he noticed that her face was flat, and bent his eyes on her neighbour.

"It is a hopeless puzzle," he reflected. "If you take the arms and shoulders of the lilac girl, add the blonde's curls, and the eyes of the girl on Lobuitko's left, then——"

He composed a portrait of all these charms, and had a clear vision of the girl who had kissed him. But she was nowhere to be seen.

Supper over, the visitors, sated and tipsy, bade their entertainers good-bye. Both host and hostess again apologised for not asking them to spend the night.

"I am very glad, gentlemen!" said the general, and this time seemed to speak sincerely, no doubt because speeding the parting guest is a kindlier office than welcoming him unwelcomed. "I am very glad indeed! I hope you will visit me on your way back. Without ceremony, please! Which way will you go? Up the hill? No, go down the hill and through the garden. That way is shorter."

The officers took his advice. After the noise and glaring illumination within doors, the garden seemed dark and still. Until they reached the wicket-gate all kept silence. Merry, half tipsy, and content, as they were, the night's obscurity and stillness inspired pensive thought. Through their brains, as though Riabovitch's, sped probably the same question: "Will the time ever come when I, like von Rabbek, shall have a big house, a family. a garden, the chance of being gracious—even insincerely—to others, of making them sated, tipsy, and content?"

But once the garden lay behind them, all spoke at once, and burst into causeless laughter. The path they followed led straight to the river, and then ran beside it, winding around bushes, ravines, and over-hanging willow-trees. The track was barely visible; the other bank was lost entirely in gloom. Sometimes the black water imaged stars, and this was the only indication of the river's speed. From beyond it sighed a drowsy snipe, and beside them in a bush, heedless of the crowd, a nightingale chanted loudly. The officers gathered in a group, and swayed the bush, but the nightingale continued his song.

"I like his cheek!" they echoed admiringly. "He doesn't care a kopeck! The old rogue!"

Near their journey's end the path turned up the hill, and joined the road not far from the church enclosure; and there the officers, breathless from climbing, sat on the grass and smoked. Across the river gleamed a dull red light, and for want of a subject they argued the problem, whether it was a bonfire, a window-light, or something else. Riabovitch looked also at the light, and felt that it smiled and winked at him as if it knew about the kiss.

On reaching home, he undressed without delay, and lay upon his bed. He shared the cabin with Lobuitko and a Lieutenant Merzliakoff, a staid, silent little man, by repute highly cultivated, who took with him everywhere *The Messenger of Europe,* and read it eternally. Lobuitko undressed. tramped impatiently from corner to corner, and sent his servant for beer. Merzliakoff lay down, balanced the candle on his pillow, and hid his head behind *The Messenger of Europe.*

"Where is she now?" muttered Riabovitch, looking at the soot-blacked ceiling.

His neck still seemed anointed with oil, near his mouth still trembled the speck of peppermint chill. Through his brain twinkled successively the shoulders and arms of the lilac girl, the kiss-curls and honest eyes of the girl in black, the waists, dresses. brooches. But though he tried his best to fix these vagrant images, they glimmered, winked, and dissolved; and as they faded finally into the vast black curtain which hangs before the closed eyes of all men, he began to hear hurried footsteps, the rustle of petticoats, the sound of a kiss. A strong, causeless joy possessed him. But as he surrendered himself to this joy, Lobuitko's servant returned with the news that no beer was obtainable. The lieutenant resumed his impatient march up and down the room.

"The fellow's an idiot," he exclaimed, stopping first near Riabovitch and then near Merzliakoff. "Only the worst numbskull and blockhead can't get beer!" *Canaille!"*

"Every one knows there's no beer here," said Merzliakoff. without lifting his eyes from *The Messenger of Europe.*

"You believe that!" exclaimed Lobuitko. "Lord in heaven, drop me on the moon, and in five minutes I'll find both beer and women! I will find them myself! Call me a rascal if I don't!"

He dressed slowly, silently lighted a cigarette, and went out.

"Rabbek, Grabbek, Labbek," he muttered, stopping in the hall. "I won't go alone, devil take me! Riabovitch, come for a walk! What?"

As he got no answer, he returned, undressed slowly, and lay down. Merzliakoff sighed, dropped *The Messenger of Europe,* and put out the light. "Well?" muttered Lobuitko, puffing his cigarette in the dark.

Riabovitch pulled the bed-clothes up to his chin, curled himself into a roll, and strained his imagination to join the twinkling images into one coherent whole. But the vision fled him. He soon fell asleep, and his last impression was that he had been caressed and gladdened, that into his life had crept something strange, and indeed ridiculous, but uncommonly good and radiant. And this thought did not forsake him even in his dreams.

When he awoke the feeling of anointment and peppermint chill were gone. But joy, as on the night before, filled every vein. He looked entranced at the window-panes gilded by the rising sun, and listened to the noises outside. Some one spoke loudly under the very window. It was Lebedietsky, commander of his battery, who had just overtaken the brigade. He was talking to the sergeant-major, loudly, owing to lack of practice in soft speech.

"And what next?" he roared.

"During yesterday's shoeing, your honour, *Golubtchik* was pricked. The *feldscher* ordered clay and vinegar. And last night, your honour, mechanic Artemieff was drunk, and the lieutenant ordered him to be put on the limber of the reserve gun-carriage."

The sergeant-major added that Karpoff had forgotten the tent-pegs and the new lanyards for the friction-tubes, and that the officers had spent the evening at General von Rabbek's. But here at the window appeared Lebedietsky's red-bearded face. He blinked his short-sighted eyes at the drowsy men in bed, and greeted them.

"Is everything all right?"

"The saddle wheeler galled his withers with the new yoke," answered Lobuitko.

The commander sighed, mused a moment, and shouted—

"I am thinking of calling on Alexandra Yegorovna. I want to see her. Good-bye! I will catch you up before night."

Fifteen minutes later the brigade resumed its march. As he passed von Rabbek's barns Riabovitch turned his head and looked at the house. The venetian blinds were down; evidently all still slept. And among them slept she— she who had kissed him but a few hours before. He tried to visualise her asleep. He projected the bedroom window opened wide with green branches peering in, the freshness of the morning air, the smell of poplars, lilacs, and roses, the bed, a chair, the dress which rustled last night, a pair of tiny slippers, a ticking watch on the table—all these came to him clearly with every detail. But the features, the kind, sleepy smile—all, in short, that was essential and characteristic—fled his imagination as quicksilver flees the hand. When he had covered half a verst he again turned back. The yellow church, the house, gardens, and river were bathed in light. Imaging an azure sky, the green-banked river specked with silver sunshine flakes was inexpressibly fair; and, looking at Miestetchki for the last time. Riabovitch felt sad, as if parting forever with something very near and dear.

By the road before him stretched familiar, uninteresting scenes; to the right and left, fields of young rye and buckwheat with hopping rooks; in front, dust and the napes of human necks; behind, the same dust and faces. Ahead of the column marched four soldiers with swords—that was the advance guard Next came the bandsmen. Advance guard and bandsmen, like mutes in a funeral procession, ignored the regulation intervals and marched too far ahead. Riabovitch, with the first gun of Battery No. 5, could see four batteries ahead.

To a layman, the long, lumbering march of an artillery brigade is novel, interesting, inexplicable. It is hard to understand why a single gun needs so many men; why so many, such strangely harnessed horses are needed to drag it. But to Riabovitch, a master of all these things, it was profoundly dull. He had learned years ago why a solid sergeant-major rides beside the officer in front of each battery: why the sergeant-major is called the *unosni*, and why the drivers of leaders and wheelers ride behind him. Riabovitch knew why the near horses are called saddle-horses, and why the off horses are called led-horses—and all of this was uninteresting beyond words. On one of the wheelers rode a soldier still covered with yesterday's dust, and with a cumbersome, ridiculous guard on his right leg. But Riabovitch, knowing the use of this leg-guard, found it in no way ridiculous. The drivers, mechanically and with occasional cries, flourished their whips. The guns in them-selves were unimpressive. The limbers were packed with tarpaulin-covered sacks of oats; and the guns themselves, hung round with tea-pots and satchels, looked like harmless animals, guarded for some obscure reason by men and horses. In the lee of the gun tramped six gunners, swinging their arms, and behind each gun came more *unosniye*, leaders, wheelers; and yet more guns, each as ugly and uninspiring as the one in front. And as every one of the six batteries in the brigade had four guns, the procession stretched along the road at least half a verst. It ended with a waggon train, with which, its head bent in thought, walked the donkey Magar, brought from Turkey by a battery commander.

Dead to his surroundings, Riabovitch marched onward, looking at the napes ahead or at the faces behind. Had it not been for last night's event. he would have been half asleep. But now he was absorbed in novel, entrancing thoughts. When the brigade set out that morning he had tried to argue that the kiss had no significance save as a trivial though mysterious adventure; that it was without real import; and that to think of it seriously was to behave himself absurdly. But logic soon flew away and surrendered him to his vivid imaginings. At times he saw himself in von Rabbek's dining-room, *tête-à-tête* with a composite being, formed of the girl in lilac and the blonde in black. At times he closed his eyes, and pictured himself with a different, this time quite an unknown, girl of cloudy feature; he spoke to her, caressed her. bent over her shoulder; he imagined war and parting . . . then reunion, the first supper together, children. . . .

"To the brakes!" rang the command as they topped the brow of each hill.

Riabovitch also cried "To the brakes!" and each time dreaded that the cry would break the magic spell. and recall him to realities.

They passed a big country house. Riabovitch looked across the fence into the garden, and saw a long path, straight as a ruler, carpeted with yellow sand, and shaded by young birches. In an ecstasy of enchantment, he pictured little feminine feet treading the yellow sand; and, in a flash. imagination restored the woman who had kissed him, the woman he had visualised after supper the night before. The image settled in his brain and never afterwards forsook him.

The spell reigned until midday, when a loud command came from the rear of the column.

"Attention! Eyes right! Officers!"

In a *calèche* drawn by a pair of white horses appeared the general of brigade. He stopped at the second battery, and called out something which no one understood. Up galloped several officers, among them Riabovitch.

"Well, how goes it?" The general blinked his red eyes, and continued, "Are there any sick?"

Hearing the answer, the little skinny general mused a moment, turned to an officer, and said—

"The driver of your third-gun wheeler has taken off his leg-guard and hung it on the limber. *Canaille!* Punish him!"

Then raising his eyes to Riabovitch, he added—

"And in your battery, I think, the harness is too loose."

Having made several other equally tiresome remarks, he looked at Lobuitko, and laughed.

"Why do you look so downcast, Lieutenant Lobuitko? You are sighing for Madame Lopukhoff, eh? Gentlemen, he is pining for Madame Lopukhoff!"

Madame Lopukhoff was a tall, stout lady, long past forty. Being partial to big women, regardless of age, the general ascribed the same taste to his subordinates. The officers smiled respectfully; and the general, pleased that he had said something caustic and laughable, touched the coachman's back and saluted. The *calèche* whirled away.

"All this, though it seems to me impossible and unearthly, is in reality very commonplace," thought Riabovitch, watching the clouds of dust raised by the general's carriage. "It is an everyday event, and within every one's experience. . . . This old general, for instance, must have loved in his day; he is married now, and has children. Captain Wachter is also married. and his wife loves him, though he has an ugly red neck and no waist. . . Salmanoff is coarse, and a typical Tartar. but he has had a romance ending in marriage. . . . I. like the rest, must go through it all sooner or later."

And the thought that he was an ordinary man. and that his life was ordinary, rejoiced and consoled him. He boldly visualized *her* and his happiness, and let his imagination run mad.

Towards evening the brigade ended its march. While the other officers sprawled in their tents, Riabovitch. Merzliakoff, and Lobuitko sat round a packing-case and supped. Merzliakoff ate slowly, and, resting *The Messenger of Europe* on his knees, read on steadily. Lobuitko, chattering without cease, poured beer into his glass. But Riabovitch, whose head was dizzy from uninterrupted day-dreams, ate in silence. When he had drunk three glasses he felt tipsy and weak; and an overmastering impulse forced him to relate his adventure to his comrades.

"A most extraordinary thing happened to me at von Rabbek's," he began, doing his best to speak in an indifferent. ironical tone. "I was on my way, you understand, from the billiard-room . . ."

And he attempted to give a very detailed history of the kiss. But in a minute he had told the whole story. In that minute he had exhausted every detail; and it seemed to him terrible that the story required such a short time. It ought, he felt, to have lasted all the night. As he finished, Lobuitko, who as a liar himself believed in no one. laughed incredulously. Merzliakoff frowned, and, with his eyes still glued to *The Messenger of Europe*, said indifferently—

"God knows who it was! She threw herself on your neck, you say, and didn't cry out! Some lunatic, I expect!"

"It must have been a lunatic," agreed Riabovitch.

"I, too, have had adventures of that kind," began Lobuitko, making a frightened face. "I was on my way to Kovno. I travelled second class. The carriage was packed, and I couldn't sleep. So I gave the guard a rouble, and he took my bag, and put me in a *coupé*. I lay down, and pulled my rug over me. It was pitch dark, you understand. Suddenly I felt some one tapping my shoulder and breathing in my face. I stretched out my hand, and felt an elbow. Then I opened my eyes. Imagine! A woman! Coal-black eyes, lips red as good coral,

nostrils breathing passion, breasts—buffers!"

"Draw it mild!" interrupted Merzliakoff in his quiet voice. "I can believe about the breasts, but if it was pitch dark how could you see the lips?"

By laughing at Merzliakoff's lack of understanding, Lobuitko tried to shuffle out of the dilemma. The story annoyed Riabovitch. He rose from the box, lay on his bed, and swore that he would never again take any one into his confidence.

Life in camp passed without event. The days flew by, each like the one before. But on every one of these days Riabovitch felt, thought, and acted as a man in love. When at daybreak his servant brought him cold water, and poured it over his head, it flashed at once into his half-awakened brain that something good and warm and caressing had crept into his life.

At night when his comrades talked of love and of women, he drew in his chair, and his face was the face of an old soldier who talks of battles in which he has taken part. And when the rowdy officers, led by setter Lobuitko, made Don Juanesque raids upon the neighbouring "suburb," Riabovitch, though he accompanied them, was morose and conscience-struck, and mentally asked *her* forgiveness. In free hours and sleepless nights, when his brain was obsessed by memories of childhood, of his father, his mother, of everything akin and dear, he remembered always Miestetchki, the dancing horse, von Rabbek, von Rabbek's wife, so like the ex-Empress Eugenie, the dark room, the chink in the door.

On the thirty-first of August he left camp, this time not with the whole brigade but with only two batteries. As an exile returning to his native land, he was agitated and enthralled by daydreams. He longed passionately for the queer-looking horse, the church, the insincere von Rabbeks. the dark room; and that internal voice which cheats so often the love-lorn whispered an assurance that he should see *her* again. But doubt tortured him. How should he meet her? What must he say? Would she have forgotten the kiss? If it came to the worst—he consoled himself—if he never saw her again, he might walk once more through the dark room, and remember. . . .

Towards evening the white barns and well-known church rose on the horizon. Riabovitch's heart beat wildly. He ignored the remark of an officer who rode by, he forgot the whole world, and he gazed greedily at the river glimmering afar, at the green roofs, at the dove-cote, over which fluttered birds, dyed golden by the setting sun.

As he rode towards the church. and heard again the quartermaster's raucous voice, he expected every second a horseman to appear from behind the fence and invite the officers to tea. . . . But the quartermaster ended his harangue, the officers hastened to the village, and no horseman appeared.

"When Rabbek hears from the peasants that we are back he will send for us," thought Riabovitch. And so assured was he of this, that when he entered the hut he failed to understand why his comrades had lighted a candle, and why the servants were preparing the samovar.

A painful agitation oppressed him. He lay on his bed. A moment later he rose to look for the horseman. But no horseman was in sight. Again he lay down; again he rose; and this time, impelled by restlessness, went into the street. and walked towards the church. The square was dark and deserted. On the hill stood three silent soldiers. When they saw Riabovitch they started and saluted, and he, returning their salute, began to descend the well-remembered path.

Beyond the stream, in a sky stained with purple, the moon slowly rose. Two chattering peasant women walked in a kitchen garden and pulled cabbage leaves; behind them their log cabins stood out black against the sky. The river bank was as it had been in May; the bushes were the same; things differed only in that the nightingale no longer sang. that it smelt no longer of poplars and young grass.

When he reached von Rabbek's garden Riabovitch peered through the wicketgate. Silence and darkness reigned. Save only the white birch trunks and patches of pathway, the whole garden merged in a black, impenetrable shade. Riabovitch listened greedily, and gazed intent. For a quarter of an hour he loitered; then hearing no sound, and seeing no light, he walked wearily towards home.

He went down to the river. In front rose the general's bathing-box; and white towels hung on the rail of the bridge. He climbed on to the bridge and stood still; then, for no reason whatever, touched a towel. It was clammy and cold. He looked down at the river which sped past swiftly, murmuring almost inaudibly against the bathing-box piles. Near the left bank glowed the moon's ruddy reflection, overrun by ripples which stretched it, tore it in two. and, it seemed, would sweep it away as twigs and shavings are swept.

"How stupid! How stupid!" thought

Riabovitch, watching the hurrying ripples. "How stupid everything is!"

Now that hope was dead, the history of the kiss, his impatience. his ardour, his vague aspirations and disillusion appeared in a clear light. It no longer seemed strange that the general's horseman had not come, and that he would never again see *her* who had kissed him by accident instead of another. On the contrary, he felt, it would be strange if he did ever see her again. . . .

The water flew past him, whither and why no one knew. It had flown past in May; it had sped a stream into a great river; a river, into the sea; it had floated on high in mist and fallen again in rain; it might be. the water of May was again speeding past under Riabovitch's eyes. For what purpose? Why?

And the whole world—life itself—seemed to Riabovitch an inscrutable, aimless mystification. . . . Raising his eyes from the stream and gazing at the sky, he recalled how Fate in the shape of an unknown woman had once caressed him; he recalled his summer fantasies and images—and his whole life seemed to him unnaturally thin and colourless and wretched. . . .

When he reached the cabin his comrades had disappeared. His servant informed him that all had set out to visit "General Fonrabbkin," who had sent a horseman to bring them. . . . For a moment Riabovitch's heart thrilled with joy. But that joy he extinguished. He cast himself upon his bed, and wroth with his evil fate, as if he wished to spite it, ignored the invitation.

The Chorus Girl

ALL this happened long ago. She was younger and nicer in those days. Nikolai Petrowitch Kolpakow, her admirer, was visiting her in her country home. It was unbearably hot and humid. Kolpakow had finished his noonday meal, and had drunk a whole bottle of bad port wine; he did not feel very well and was in bad mood. Both were bored, waiting for the cooler evening to take a walk.

Suddenly the doorbell rang. Kolpakow was in his shirt sleeves. He jumped up from his seat and looked questioningly at Pasha.

"Maybe it is the letter carrier, or perhaps a girl friend," said the actress.

Kolpakow didn't mind in the least Pasha's girl friends nor the letter carrier. But to be sure he picked up his coat and went into the next room while Pasha went out to open the door.

To her great surprise it was not the letter carrier, nor one of her friends, but a young and beautiful lady, handsomely dressed in a refined style; she looked like a "good" woman.

The stranger was pale and breathing heavily as if she had ascended several flights of stairs.

"What is it you wish?" asked Pasha.

The lady did not answer immediately. She entered the room, glanced with curious looks over the furniture. She appeared to be in pain. It was some time before she had composed herself and was able to speak. She took a seat.

"Is my husband here?" she asked

finally, raising her eyes which were red from crying.

"Whose husband?" asked Pasha, and she became suddenly so frightened that her hands and feet grew cold. "Whose husband?" she repeated, trembling with emotion.

"My husband, Nikolai Petrowitch Kolpakow."

"No, . . . madam . . . I . . . I never knew a husband."

A few minutes of silence elapsed. The lady repeatedly wiped her eyes with a lace handkerchief. Pasha had not dared to sit down. She looked at her visitor, frightened and helpless.

"You maintain then that he is not here?" asked the lady with a firm voice and a curious smile.

"I . . I do not know what you mean."

"You vulgar low woman . . ." murmured the lady, looking with hatred and contempt at Pasha. "Yes, yes . . . you are a vulgar woman and I am happy, very happy that I have finally a chance to tell you so face to face!"

Pasha felt that she must have impressed this lady in black very vulgarly and she began to be ashamed of her painted red cheeks, of the freckles that covered her nose and the bangs flowing gaily over her forehead. It seemed to her that if she had happened to be slender without paint and powder and bangs it would have been easier for her to conceal that she was a "bad" woman. She could have met her on equal terms, and she would even have dared to sit on the chair on the other side of the table.

"Where is my husband?" asked the lady again. "But it does not matter whether he is here or not. I simply want to tell you that embezzlements have been discovered and that they are looking for Nikolai Petrowitch. They are going to arrest him. And that is your work!"

The lady arose and paced the room in great excitement. Pasha looked at her in astonishment. She could not grasp what all this meant.

"Today he will be found and arrested," said the lady, crying and sobbing. "I know who led him on to all this, you vulgar ugly woman! You low creature," her face expressed the contempt she felt for Pasha. It looked as if she would spit in her face the next moment. "I am powerless . . . Do you hear me, you beastly woman? . . . I am helpless, you are stronger than I am, but there is One who is going to take care of me and my children! God sees everything! He is just! He will repay you for all my tears, all my sleepless nights! The time will come when you will remember me!"

Again there was a long silence. The lady walked up and down while Pasha stared at her! she could not understand and expected momently that something dreadful would happen.

"I know nothing of all this, madam," she said, and commenced to cry heartbreakingly.

"You lie!" cried the lady. "I know everything. I have known you for a long while. I know that there has not been a day during the last four months that he did not spend with you!"

"Yes? And what of is? What is there wrong in that? A good many come to see me and to visit with me. I do not urge them to come. They come of their own free will."

"I am telling you that they have discovered an embezzlement. He stole money from his office. For your sake . . . for the sake of such a woman as you are he committed a crime. Listen," resumed the lady very decisively stopping squarely in front of Pasha. "You cannot have principles, you who live only to wrong others. That is all that you desire. But I cannot believe that you are such a low woman that you have even lost your last spark of humanity. He has a wife, he has children . . . If they sentence him and send him to Siberia, I and the children must starve . . . try to understand this! But still there remains one way to save us from misery and dishonor. If I can make good and deposit today nine hundred rubles, he will not be prosecuted. Nine hundred rubles only!"

"Nine hundred rubles?" asked Pasha quietly. "I don't know anything about nine hundred rubles. I haven't received them."

"I do not beg of you nine hundred rubles. You have no money and I do not need your money. I ask for something entirely different. . . . Men are in the habit of giving girls like you jewelry. Return to me the things my husband gave you!"

"He never gave me jewelry, madam," cried Pasha, who had begun to understand

"Where is the money? He has squandered his own, mine and other people's money. . . Listen, I beg of you! I have been overcome by all this and I called you a great many unpleasant things but I beg you to forgive me. You must hate me, I know it. And if you are capable of pity, try to put yourself into my own place I implore you, give me back those things!"

"Hm . . ." said Pasha, and shrugged her shoulders. "I would do so with pleasure but may God punish me if he

ever gave me presents. Please do believe me. But you are right," the actress corrected herself embarrassedly, "once he brought me these two things—I gladly give them back to you if you wish them. . . ."

Pasha opened the drawer of her dresser and handed to her visitor a thin gold bracelet and a little ring with a red stone.

The lady flushed and every muscle in her face seemed to vibrate. She was offended.

"What are you giving me?" she said. "I do not ask for alms, but for that which is not yours, what you induced my husband, the poor unhappy creature, to give you, you who know how to take advantage of such situations. Thursday as I met you with my husband on the Avenue, you wore expensive brooches and rings. You don't need to play for my benefit the part of an innocent lamb. For the last time I ask of you, will you return those things to me or not?"

"How comical you are . . ." said Pasha, who felt quite offended. "I assure you that your Nikolai Petrowitch never gave me anything but this bracelet and this ring. He brought only cake——"

"Cake . . ." laughed the lady in strangely shrill voice, "at home the children have nothing to bite and here you feast on cake. So you refuse to return to me those things?"

She did not receive an answer. She seated herself in a comfortable rocking-chair and looked fixedly at one point evidently thinking rapidly.

"What shall I do?" she said, "if I don't get this nine hundred rubles he is lost and I and the children with him. Shall I kill this monster, or shall I throw myself on my knees before her?"

The lady pressed the handkerchief to her face and started to cry.

"I beg of you," she sobbed, "you have ruined my husband and wrecked his life, do save him. . . . I know you do not feel pity for him, but the children, think of the children. . . . Why should those innocent children suffer so?"

Pasha thought of those little children, standing on a street corner crying with hunger, and she herself started to cry.

"What can I do, dear lady?" she asked with a gesture of helplessness. "You say that I am a beast, and that I wrecked Nikolai Petrowitch. But I swear to you before God that I never had any financial advantages from him. In our chorus Motja is the only one who has a rich lover. We others are starving half the time. Nikolai Petrowitch is a fine and well dressed gentleman, and so I received him. We cannot be very fastidious in our choice. . . ."

"I am asking you for those things! Give them to me. I am crying . . . I am lowering myself. If you wish me to do so, I will throw myself at your feet. Please! . . . Please?"

Pasha screamed in fright. She felt that this beautiful lady who was talking like the leading woman in the theater was ready to kneel before her in her pride, in her nobility, in order to humiliate herself and to humiliate the actress

"Very well, then, I shall give you the things!" exclaimed Pasha huskily, drying her tears. "Here, please. They are not from Nikolai Petrowitch. I received them from other gentlemen. But as you please. . ."

Pasha again opened the drawer of her dresser and handed to the lady a diamond brooch, several rings and several necklaces.

"Take this, take these too, and take these, though from your husband I have never received anything. Here, take them all, and make yourself rich!" continued Pasha, offended by the threatened prostration at her feet.

"But if you are such a fine lady . . . his own wife, better try to keep him with you. I surely did not call him. He came himself."

The lady looked through her tears over the jewelry spread on the table and said: "This is not all . . . these things are not even worth five hundred rubles."

Pasha went again to the dresser and quickly threw a gold watch, a cigarette case and a pair of cuff buttons with the other things. She spoke now very resolutely: "I have no more . . . you can look for yourself!"

The lady sighed, gathered the things with trembling hands in her handkerchief, and walked out. She did not say a word, she did not even nod her head.

The door to the next room opened and in came Kolpakow. He was pale and he shook his head nervously as if he had taken a bitter drink. In his eyes glistened tears.

"What are those things that you are supposed to have given me?" Pasha turned on him. "When, if I may ask, did you give me these things?"

"Things. . . . Nonsense!" answered Kolpakow, shaking his head. "My God, she has cried before you; she has humiliated herself. . . .

"I ask you, what are these presents that you are supposed to have given me?" screamed Pasha.

"My God, she, the pure, the noble,

the proud woman. . . . at the feet of this creature she would even have thrown herself! My doings have brought her to this! I have permitted it."

He grasped his head with his hands and groaned:

"Never, never shall I forgive myself. Never. Begone, you beast," and he looked with contempt at Pasha, while his trembling hands thrust her far away from him. "She wanted to throw her- self upon her knees and . . . before whom? 'Before you! Oh, my God!"

He dressed himself quickly. He care- fully avoided touching Pasha and left the house.

Pasha threw herself in a chair and cried loudly. She was sorry that she had given away her jewelry. The whole scene was offensive. She recalled how a mer- chant had beaten her three years ago, for no reason, and she cried much louder.

La Cigale

CHAPTER I

OLGA'S HUSBAND

At Olga Ivanovna's wedding, all who knew her were present.

"Look at him. He has something about him!" she said to her friends, pointing to her husband, seeming to wish to explain why she had married an ordi- nary man, who had nothing about him.

Her husband, Osip Stepanovich Dymov, was a doctor and had the title of titular councillor. On the staffs of two hos- pitals: in one a supernumerary house- surgeon and in the other the dissector. From nine o'clock until midday he was daily occupied in his ward or in receiv- ing patients, and after he went by tram to the other hospital, where he dissected corpses. A small private practice pro- duced about five hundred roubles per year. That was all. What else can be said about him? While Olga Ivanovna and her good friends and acquaintances were remarkable in some manner, they all were considered celebrities, or if they were not so in fact, they all showed bril- liant potentialities. There was an actor from the dramatic theatre, a man of great, and long since recognized, talent, an elegant, clever and modest man, an excellent reader, who taught Olga Ivan- ovna elocution; a singer from the opera, a fat, good-natured man, who with a sigh told Olga Ivanovna that she was ruining herself: "If she were not so lazy, and only took herself properly in hand, she would become a remarkable singer"; then there were several painters, headed by Ryabovsky, who painted genre, ani- mal and landscape pictures. He was a very good-looking, fair-haired young man of about twenty-five. who had had success at exhibitions and had sold his last picture for five hundred roubles. He corrected Olga Ivanovna's sketches and said perhaps something could be made of her; then there was also the violoncellist whose instrument wailed, and who asserted quite openly that of all the women of his acquaintance only

Olga Ivanovna knew how to accompany him; then there was the literary man, who was already well known for the novels, tales and plays he had written. Who was there besides? Well, yes, there was also Vasily Vasilich, a gentleman-landowner, a dilettante illustrator and maker of vignettes, who felt acutely the ancient Russian style of the Byliny and Epics, and who produced really wonderful things on paper, china and smoked plates. For this group of artistic and free young people—all so spoiled by fate, but who still were delicate and modest, and who only remembered the existence of doctors at the time of illness—the name of Dymov sounded as meaningless as Sidorov or Tarasov. In the midst of this society Dymov himself felt strange, superfluous and small, though he was tall and broad-shouldered. It appeared to them as if he were in another man's dress-coat, and that he had the beard of an office clerk. However, if he had been a writer or an artist, they would have said that with his beard he reminded them of Zola.

The artist told Olga Ivanovna that with her flaxen hair and her bridal attire she was very like a graceful cherry tree, when in spring it is entirely covered with delicate white blossoms.

"No, just listen!" Olga Ivanovna said, seizing his hand. "How do you think all this happened? Listen, listen! . . . I must tell you that my father worked together with Dymov in the same hospital. When my poor father fell ill, Dymov passed whole days and nights beside his bed. What self-sacrifice! Listen, Ryabovsky. . . . And you, author, listen too, it is quite interesting. Come nearer. What self-sacrifice, what sincere interest! I also did not sleep at night, but sat near father's bed, and suddenly, lo and behold, the good young man was conquered! My Dymov fell over head and ears in love. Truly fate is very strange! Well, after my father's death he came to see me from time to time, we met in the street, and one fine evening suddenly—bang!—he proposed. . . . It was quite unexpected. . . . I cried all night and fell desperately in love. And as you see, I've become a wife. Isn't it true there's something strong, powerful, bearlike in him? Now his face is turned only three-quarters towards us, and it's badly lighted, but when he turns quite this way just notice his forehead. Ryabovsky, what do you think of that forehead? Dymov, we are talking about you!" she called to him. "Come here. Stretch out your honest hand to Ryabovsky. . . . So. Be friends. . . ."

Dymov, smiling good-humouredly and naïvely, held out his hand to Ryabovsky and said:

"Very pleased. A certain Ryabovsky finished his course of study with me. Was he a relation of yours?"

CHAPTER II

TWO CUT FINGERS

OLGA IVANOVNA was twenty-two years of age, Dymov thirty-one. They began housekeeping splendidly. Olga Ivanovna covered all the walls of the drawing-room with her own and other people's sketches, in frames and without frames, near the piano and the furniture she made all sorts of cosy arrangements with Chinese umbrellas, easels, variegated coloured rags, daggers, little busts, photographs and so on. . . . She glued on the walls of the dining-room all sorts of popular coloured woodcuts, she hung up birch bark shoes and sickles, placed a scythe and a rake in one corner and obtained in that way a dining-room in the Russian style. In order to make the bedroom look like a cavern she draped the ceiling and the walls with dark-coloured cloth, she hung up a Venetian lantern over the bed, and placed a figure with a halberd at the door. Everybody found that the young couple had a very charming nook.

Every day rising about eleven Olga Ivanovna would play on the piano, or if there was sun she would paint something in oils. Then at about twelve she would go to her dressmaker. As she and Dymov had but little money, only just enough, she and her dressmaker were obliged to have recourse to cunning, in order that she might often appear in new dresses and surprise people by her elegance. Very often out of old dyed dresses, out of bits of tulle that cost next to nothing or with the addition of lace, plush or silk a wonderful garment was produced, something quite enchanting—not a dress, but a dream. From her dressmaker's Olga Ivanovna usually drove to visit some actress of her acquaintance; to hear the news of the theatre, and at the same time to solicit a ticket for the first performance of a new play, or for some benefit night. From the actress's it was necessary to go to the studio of some artist or to some picture show, then to one or other of the celebrities she knew to invite them to her house, to pay them a visit or simply to gossip. Everywhere she was greeted gaily and cordially, and she was assured that she was pretty, charming and quite uncommon. . . . The people she called celebrities and great received

her as one of themselves, as their equal, and everybody with one voice prophesied that with her talents, taste and cleverness, if she did not fritter them away, great things might be expected. She sang, she played on the piano, she painted in oils, she modelled, she took part in amateur theatricals, and all this she did not in an ordinary way, but with talent; if she made little paper lanterns for illuminations, dressed herself out, or tied somebody's tie—she did it all in an uncommonly artistic manner, gracefully and charmingly. But in nothing were her talents more clearly evident than in her skill in rapidly making acquaintance and soon becoming intimate with famous people. It was only necessary for somebody to become a little famous, and cause himself to be talked about, for her to get acquainted with him, and the same day she would be on quite friendly terms and invite him to her house. To make a new acquaintance was for her a real holiday. She idolized celebrated men, she was proud of them, and dreamed of them every night. She thirsted for them and she was never able to quench her thirst. The old ones left and were forgotten, others came in their place, but she soon became accustomed to these, or became disenchanted with them, and then she began eagerly to seek out new men, new great men; she found them, and again searched for others. Why?

At five she dined at home with her husband. His simplicity, his good sense and good-nature caused her emotion and delight. She would constantly jump up, embrace his head impetuously and cover it with kisses.

"Dymov, you are a clever, a noble man," she would say; "but you have one very serious deficiency. You take not the slightest interest in art. You have no taste for music and painting."

"I don't understand them," he said meekly. "All my life I've been occupied with natural science and with medicine, and I had no time to interest myself in art."

"But, Dymov, that is terrible!"

"Why? Your friends don't know anything about natural science or medicine, and you don't blame them for it. Every man has his own sphere. I don't understand landscapes and operas, but I think if certain clever people devote their whole lives to them and other clever people pay great sums of money for them, it means that they are necessary. I don't understand them, but not to understand does not mean to reject them."

"Let me press your honest hand!"

After dinner she went to her friends, then to the theatre or to a concert and only returned home after midnight. And so it was every day.

On Wednesdays she gave small evening parties. At these parties the mistress of the house and her guests did not play at cards nor did they dance, but they amused themselves in various artistic ways. The actor from the dramatic theatre recited, the singer sang, the artists drew in the albums, of which Olga Ivanovna had a great number, the violoncellist played and their hostess herself also drew, modelled, sang and accompanied. In the intervals between the recitations, music and singing, they talked and argued about literature, the theatre and painting. There were never any ladies, because Olga Ivanovna considered that all ladies, with the exception of actresses and her dressmaker, were dull and commonplace. There was never

a single party that passed without the mistress of the house having little thrills whenever the bell rang, nor without her saying with a triumphant expression of countenance, "There he is!" meaning by the word "he" some new celebrity she had invited to her house. Dymov never appeared in the drawing-room, and nobody remembered his existence. But exactly at half-past eleven the door that led into the dining-room opened and Dymov appeared in the doorway with his meek good-natured smile, and rubbing his hands he would say:

"Gentlemen, come to supper, please."

Everybody went into the dining-room and they saw on the table exactly the same things: a dish of oysters, a piece of ham or veal, sardines, cheese, caviar, pickled mushrooms, vodka and two decanters of wine.

"My dear *maître d'hôtel!*" Olga Ivanovna exclaimed, clasping her hands with delight. "You are positively enchanting! Gentlemen, look at his forehead! Dymov, turn so that we can see your profile. Gentlemen, just look: isn't it the face of a Bengal tiger, and the expression is kind and mild as a deer's. Oh, you darling!"

The guests ate, and looking at Dymov they thought: "Indeed, he is a very good fellow!" but they soon forgot him and continued to talk about the theatre, music and painting.

The young couple were happy, and their life flowed on smoothly, though the third week of their honeymoon was not quite a happy one—it might be called even sad. Dymov caught the erysipelas in the hospital. He was confined to his bed for six days, and was obliged to have his beautiful black locks shaved off. Olga Ivanovna sat by his bedside and cried bitterly, but when he was on the mend she tied a white handkerchief round his shaven head and began to paint him as a Bedouin. And they both were gay. Four days after he had recovered and had resumed his work in the hospital he again had another mishap.

"I have no luck, mama!" he said to her one day at dinner. "To-day I had four dissections, and I cut two of my fingers. And it was only when I got'home that I noticed it."

Olga Ivanovna was alarmed. He smiled and said it was a trifle and that he often cut his hands slightly while making dissections.

"I become absorbed in my work, mama, and get absent-minded."

Olga Ivanovna waited with anxiety, fearing that he might get infected by the corpses, and she prayed to God at night, but all passed off well. And again their life flowed on peacefully and happily without sorrow or alarm. The present was beautiful, and to improve it spring was approaching, already smiling from afar and giving promise of a thousand joys. There would be no end to happiness! In April, May and June a country house far away from town—walks, sketches, fishing, nightingales, and then from July to the late autumn an excursion of artists to the Volga, and in this excursion as an indispensable member of the society Olga Ivanovna would naturally take part. She had already had two linen costumes made for the journey, she had bought colours, paint-brushes, canvas and a new palette. Ryabovsky came almost every day to see what progress she had made in painting. When she showed him her painting he would thrust his hands deep into his pockets,

press his lips firmly together, sniff and say:

"So . . . this cloud jumps at you. It is not lighted up as it would be in the evening. The foreground is somewhat muddled, and there is something not quite right, you understand. . . . Your log hut has been squashed by something and squeaks piteously. . . . You ought to make this corner darker. But in general it's not so bad . . . quite praise-worthy."

And the more unintelligible he was the better Olga Ivanovna was able to understand him.

CHAPTER III

NO, MY DARLING!

Two days after Whit-Sunday, having had his dinner, Dymov bought various *hors d'œuvres* and sweetmeats, and went to visit his wife in the country. He had not seen her for more than two weeks, and he was very dull without her. While sitting in the railway coach and afterwards when he was looking for his *dacha* in the large wood, he felt hungry and tired and thought how he would have supper quietly with his wife, and then tumble into bed. And he looked gaily at the parcel in which he had caviar, cheese and smoked salmon.

When at last he found his house the sun was already setting. The old maid-servant said that her mistress was not at home, but that she would soon come in. The *dacha*, which was uninviting in appearance, with low ceilings and walls that had writing-paper glued on them and uneven floors full of chinks, consisted of only three rooms. In one room there was a bed, in another there were canvases, paint-brushes, dirty paper and men's overcoats and hats lying about on the chairs and window-sills, and in the third room Dymov found three unknown men. Two of them were dark-haired and bearded, while the third was clean shaven and fat, evidently an actor. A samovar was boiling on the table.

"What do you want?" the actor asked in a deep bass voice, looking round at Dymov unsociably. "Do you want to see Olga Ivanovna? Wait, she will be in soon."

Dymov sat down and waited. One of the dark men, looking at him sleepily and lazily, poured out some tea and asked:

"Perhaps you would like some tea too?"

Dymov wanted both to eat and to drink, but in order not to spoil his appetite he refused the tea. Soon footsteps and a familiar laugh were heard; a door was slammed and Olga Ivanovna entered the room, in a broad-brimmed hat, carrying a box in her hand; she was followed by merry, rosy-cheeked Ryabovsky carrying a large umbrella and a camp stool.

"Dymov!" Olga Ivanovna cried, and she blushed with delight. "Dymov!" she repeated, laying her head and both her hands on his breast. "It's you! Why haven't you been for so long? Why? Why?"

"When have I time, mama? I am always occupied, and when I was free it always happened that the trains did not suit."

"How happy I am to see you! I dreamed about you the whole of the night. I was afraid you were ill. Oh, if you only knew how charming you are and now you have come exactly at the right moment! You will be my saviour! You alone can save me! To-morrow

there is to be a most original wedding here," she continued, laughing and tying her husband's cravat. "A young telegraphist from the station is getting married, a certain Chikeldéev. A good-looking young fellow; besides he's not stupid, and, you know, he has something in his face strong and bearlike. . . . He'd make a good model for a young Viking. We, *dachniki*, all take a great interest in him, and we gave him our word of honour to come to his wedding. He's not a rich man, solitary and shy, and, of course, it would be a sin not to stand by him at such a moment. Just imagine, they'll be married after the liturgy, and from church we all go on foot to the bride's house . . . can you understand, through the wood, birds singing, sun spots on the grass, and all of us forming variously coloured patches on a bright green ground—most original, in the style of the French expressionists. But, Dymov, in what am I to go to the wedding?" Olga Ivanovna said, and she looked as if she was going to cry. "I have nothing with me here, literally nothing! No dress, no flowers, no gloves. . . . You must save me. As you have come it's quite clear fate destines you as my saviour. My dear, take these keys, go home and take out of my wardrobe my pink frock. You remember it; it hangs quite in front. . . . Then in the lumber room, to the right, you'll find on the floor two band-boxes. When you open the upper one you'll find tulle, tulle, tulle, and all sorts of scraps and below them flowers. Take all the flowers out very carefully; try, darling, not to crush them. I shall choose what I want afterwards . . . and buy me a pair of gloves. . . ."

'All right," Dymov said, "I'll go back to-morrow and send them down."

'To-morrow, how is that possible?" Olga Ivanovna exclaimed, and she looked at him with astonishment. "When will you have time to-morrow? The first train leaves here at nine o'clock and the wedding is at eleven. No, my darling, you must go to-day, positively to-day! If you can't come back to-morrow, send the things by a messenger. Well, or else . . . a passenger train is just due. Don't miss it, darling!"

"All right."

"Oh, how sorry I am to let you go!" Olga Ivanovna said, and tears rose to her eyes. "What a fool I was to promise the telegraphist!"

Dymov hurriedly swallowed a glass of tea, took a couple of cracknels and, smiling, meekly went back to the station. And the caviar, the cheese and the smoked salmon were eaten by the two dark men and the fat actor.

CHAPTER IV

PASSIONATELY

On a calm moonlit July night Olga Ivanovna was standing on the deck of a Volga steamboat looking at the water or at the beautiful banks. Ryabovsky, who stood beside her, was telling her that the black shadows on the water were not shadows, but a dream, and when gazing at those bewitching waters, with their fantastic glitter, when looking at that fathomless sky and those gloomy pensive banks, which spoke to them of the troubles of life and of the existence of something higher, something eternal and glorious, it would be well to forget oneself—to die—to become a memory. The past was mean and uninteresting, the future was insignificant, but this beautiful night, unique in a lifetime, would soon be over, it would be blended with eternity—why live at all?

And Olga Ivanovna listened now to Ryabovsky's voice, now to the stillness of the night, and she thought that she too was immortal and would never die. The turquoise-coloured water, such as she had never seen before, the sky, the river's banks, the black shadows and the unaccountable delight that filled her soul, told her that she too would become a great artist, and that somewhere in the distant future, beyond the moonlit night in boundless space, success, fame, the love of the people awaited her. When, without blinking, she looked long into the distance there appeared before her a crowd of people, lights, the solemn sounds of music, shouts of enthusiasm— she herself was in a white dress with flowers, flowers were shed on her from all sides. She also thought that a really great man, a genius, the chosen of God, was standing beside her, leaning over the bulwarks. . . . All that he had created so far was excellent, novel, uncommon, and what he would create in time, when with years his rare talents would increase in strength, and he would become astonishingly, immeasurably great, this could be read in his face, by the way he expressed himself and by his regard for nature. He had quite a special way of talking about shadows, evening tones and brilliant moonlight, in a language quite his own, so that you involuntarily felt the witchery of his power over nature. He himself was very handsome, original, and his life was independent, free, avoiding anything worldly, it was like the life of a bird.

"It is getting chilly," Olga Ivanovna said, shivering.

Ryabovsky wrapped her up in his cloak, and said sadly:

"I feel I am in your power. I am a slave. Why are you so bewitching to-night?"

The whole time he gazed at her without removing his eyes from her: his eyes were terrible, and she feared to look at him.

"I am madly in love with you . . ." he whispered, breathing upon her cheek. "Say but one word and I will cease to live. I will give up art . . ." he murmured, greatly excited. "Love me, love . . ."

"Don't say such things." Olga Ivanovna said, closing her eyes. "It is terrible. And Dymov?"

"What of Dymov? Why Dymov? What have I to do with Dymov? There's the Volga, the moon, beauty, my love, my rapture, but there's no such thing as Dymov. . . . Oh, I know nothing. . . . I don't want the past, give me but one moment . . . one instant!"

Olga Ivanovna's heart went pit-a-pat. She wanted to think of her husband, but all her past with her wedding, with Dymov and her evening parties, seemed to her small, insignificant, dim, unnecessary and far, far away. Really, what was Dymov? Why Dymov? What was Dymov to her? Does he really exist in nature, or is he merely a dream?

"For him, a common and ordinary man, the happiness he had already had was sufficient," she thought as she covered her face with her hands. "Let them judge me *there*, let them curse me, but I, to spite them all, will just go and perish . . . go and perish. . . . One must try everything in life. Good Lord, how painful, but how nice!" . .

"Well, what? What?" the artist murmured, putting his arm rond her and greedily kissing the hands with which she was feebly trying to push him away. "You love me? Yes? Yes? Oh, what a night! What a glorious night!"

"Yes, what a night!" she whispered, looking into his eyes that were glistening with tears; then having rapidly looked round, she put her arms round him and kissed him passionately on the lips.

"We're arriving at Kineshma," somebody said on the other side of the deck.

Heavy footsteps could be heard. It was one of the waiters who was passing by.

"Listen," Olga Ivanovna said to him, laughing and crying with happiness, "bring us some wine."

The artist, pale with excitement, sat down on a bench and looked at Olga Ivanovna with adoring and grateful eyes, then he closed them and said with a languid smile:

"I am tired!"

And rested his head on the bulwarks.

CHAPTER V

RED WITH SHAME

THE second of September was a calm and warm but dull day. Early in the morning a light fog had hovered about the Volga, and after nine o'clock it had begun to drizzle. There was no hope of the sky's clearing. At breakfast Ryabovsky had said to Olga Ivanovna that painting was the most ungrateful, the most tiresome art, that he was no artist, that only fools thought he had talent, and suddenly, without any cause, he seized a knife and scraped out his very best sketch.

After breakfast he sat gloomily at the window looking out at the Volga. The Volga was already without brilliancy, dim, dull and cold in appearance. Everything foretold the approach of sad, gloomy autumn. It seemed as if the sumptuous green carpets that were spread on the banks, the reflections of diamond rays, the transparent blue distance and the whole of the elegance of stately nature had been stripped off the Volga and packed away in a trunk till the next spring, and the ravens flew along the Volga mocking her: "Bare! bare!" Ryabovsky listened to their cawing and thought that he was done for, and had lost his talent, that everything in this world was conditional, relative and stupid, and that he ought never to have got entangled with this woman. . . . In a word, he was in a bad humour and in low spirits.

Olga Ivanovna sat behind the partition on her bed passing her beautiful flaxen hair between her fingers, and imagining herself in her own drawing-room, her bedroom or her husband's study; her imagination bore her to the theatre, to her dressmaker's and to her celebrated friends. What were they doing now? Did they remember her? The season had already begun and it was time to think about her little parties. And Dymov? Dear Dymov! How meekly and childishly—complainingly, he begged her in his letters to come home quickly! Every month he sent her seventy-five roubles, and when she wrote to him that she had run into debt to the artists to the amount of one hundred roubles he sent her that too. What a kind, generous man he was! The

journey had tired Olga Ivanovna, she felt dull and she wanted to get away as soon as possible from these peasants, from the smell of the river's damp and to cast off from herself that feeling of physical impurity that she had been experiencing the whole time that she had been living in peasants' huts and wandering from village to village. If Ryabovsky had not given his word of honour to the artists to remain with them until the twentieth of September, it would be quite possible to go away that very day. And how nice that would be!

"Good God!" Ryabovsky sighed. "When will the sun come out again? I can't finish my sunlit landscape without the sun!"

"But you have also a sketch with a cloudy sky," Olga Ivanovna said, coming from behind the partition. "You remember in the right foreground there is a wood and to the left a herd of cows and geese. You could finish it now."

"Eh?" the artist said, frowning. "Finish! Do you really think I am so stupid, that I don't know what I am to do!"

"How changed you are with me!" Olga Ivanovna sighed.

"Well, so much the better!"

Olga Ivanovna's lips trembled as she sat down near the stove and began to cry.

"Yes, we only wanted tears. Stop crying! I have a thousand causes for tears, but I don't cry."

"A thousand causes!" Olga Ivanovna sighed. "The chief cause is you're tired of me. Yes!" she said and began to sob. "In truth you are ashamed of our love. You are always trying that the artists should not notice anything, though it is impossible to conceal it, and it has been known to them all long ago."

"Olga, there's one thing I ask you," the artist said, in an imploring tone, and he pressed his hand to his heart, "only one thing: don't torment me! That is all I require of you!"

"But swear that you still love me!"

"This is torment!" the artist hissed through his clenched teeth, jumping up from his seat. "It will end by my throwing myself into the Volga or going mad! Leave me in peace!"

"Well then, kill me, kill me!" Olga Ivanovna cried. "Kill me!"

She again began to sob and went behind the partition. The rain continued to spatter on the thatched roof of the log-hut. Ryabovsky, seizing his head in both hands, began to pace up and down, from corner to corner, then with a determined face, looking as if he wanted to prove something to somebody, he pressed his cap on his head and taking his gun over his shoulder he left the house.

For long after he had gone Olga Ivanovna lay on the bed and cried. At first she thought it would be a good thing to take poison, that when he returned Ryabovsky might find her dead; then her thoughts carried her mentally into her own drawing-room, or into her husband's study, and she imagined herself sitting motionless at Dymov's side and enjoying physical peace and cleanliness, or else in the evening sitting in the theatre listening to Masini. And the longing for civilization, for the noise of towns and of celebrated people oppressed her heart. A peasant woman entered the hut and began leisurely to light the stove and prepare dinner. There was a smell of burning and the air became blue with smoke. The artists came in dirty top-boots, and with faces wet with rain; they examined their sketches, and to console themselves said that even in bad weather the Volga had certain charms. The cheap clock on the wall went: "tick-tick-tick." . . . The flies feeling cold crowded together in the front corner near the icons and buzzed; and the movements of cockroaches could be heard among the thick cardboards beneath the benches. . . .

Ryabovsky only returned home when the sun came out again. He threw his cap on the table, and looking pale and worn out, he sank on to a bench in his dirty boots, and closed his eyes.

"I am tired," and knitting his brows he made an effort to raise his eyelids.

In order to prove that she was not angry, Olga Ivanovna came up to him and silently kissed him, and then caressingly passed a comb through his light hair. She wanted to comb his hair.

"What is it?" he asked, shuddering, as if something cold had touched him, and he opened his eyes. "What is it? Leave me in peace, I beg of you."

He pushed her aside with his hand and went away from her, and it appeared to her that the expression on his face was one of aversion and vexation. At that moment the peasant woman brought him a plate of cabbage soup, carrying it in both hands, and Olga Ivanovna saw that both her thumbs were wetted by the soup, and the dirty peasant woman with her large stomach, the cabbage soup, which Ryabovsky began to eat quickly, the log-hut and the whole of this life, which she had liked so much at first, for its simplicity and artistic disorder, appeared horrible to her now.

She suddenly felt herself insulted, and she said coldly:

"We must separate for some time, or else from sheer dullness we may have a serious quarrel. All this is boring me. I'm going away to-day."

"On what? Ride-a-cock-horse on a walking-stick?"

"To-day is Thursday, and at half-past nine the steamboat will arrive here."

"Eh? Yes, yes. . . . Well, what's to be done, go . . ." Ryabovsky said gently as he wiped his mouth with a towel in lieu of a napkin. "You are dull here, you have nothing to do, and I would be a great egoist to try to keep you here. Go, and after the twentieth we shall meet again."

Olga Ivanovna packed up her things gaily, even her cheeks began to glow with pleasure.

"Was it really possible," she asked herself, "that soon she would be able to write in a drawing-room, to sleep in a bedroom and to dine off a tablecloth?" Her heart was relieved and she was no longer angry with the artists.

"The colours and the paint-brushes I leave you, Ryabovsky," she said. "If anything remains you will bring it. . . . Mind, don't be lazy without me, don't mope, but work. You're my own good boy!"

At ten o'clock Ryabovsky kissed her, to take leave, so as not to kiss her on the boat, she thought, in the presence of the other artists, and then conducted her to the landing-place. The steamer soon arrived and bore her away.

She reached her home on the third day. Without taking off her hat and waterproof and breathing heavily from excitement she passed through the drawing-room into the dining-room. Dymov, without a coat and with his waistcoat unbuttoned, was sitting at the table sharpening a knife against a fork; a partridge was on a dish before him. When Olga Ivanovna entered the flat she was quite certain that it was necessary to hide everything from him, and that she had sufficient skill and strength to do so; but now, when she saw his broad, good-natured, happy smile and his sparkling joyful eyes, she felt to hide anything from this man would be as mean and horrid, and also as impossible and beyond her strength as it would be to calumniate, to steal or to murder, and in a moment she decided to tell him all that had happened. Having allowed him to embrace and kiss her, she sank on her knees before him and covered her face with her hands.

"What? What is it, mama?" he asked tenderly. "You've been dull?"

She raised her face, red with shame, and looked up at him in a guilty and imploring manner, but fear and shame prevented her from telling him the truth.

"It was nothing," she said. I only . . ."

"Let's sit down," he said, lifting her up and seating her at the table. "There we are . . . Have some partridge? Poor little thing, you are hungry."

She drew in her native air greedily, and ate the partridge, while he looked at her with affection and laughed joyfully.

CHAPTER VI

PAIN IN THE TEMPLES

TOWARDS the middle of winter it was evident that Dymov began to suspect that he was being deceived. As if his own conscience were not clean, he was no longer able to look his wife straight in the eyes, nor did he smile joyfully when they met and, in order to remain less alone with her, he often brought home to dinner his colleague, Dr. Korostelev, a little closely cropped man with a wrinkled face who, when he talked to Olga Ivanovna, was so confused that he either buttoned and unbuttoned his jacket the whole time, or twirled the left side of his moustache with his right hand. During dinner the two doctors would talk of the possibility of heart troubles being produced by the displacement of the diaphragm, or that of late large numbers of neurotic complaints had come under their observation, or that on the previous day while making the dissection of a patient, who according to the diagnosis had died of "malignant anæmia," Dymov had discovered a cancer in the pancreas. And it seemed that they both carried on these medical discussions only in order to permit Olga Ivanovna to remain silent, that is, not to lie. After dinner Korostelev would sit down to the piano, and Dymov would say to him with a sigh:

"Ech, brother! Well, well! Play us something sad."

Raising his shoulders, and spreading his fingers wide, Korostelev took several accords and began to sing in a tenor voice: "Show me a single dwelling, where the Russian peasant does not groan," and Dymov, sighing again, rested his head on his fist and sank into meditation.

Of late Olga Ivanovna had been extremely imprudent. Every morning she awoke in the very worst of humours, and with the thought that she no longer loved Ryabovsky, and that all was finished, thank God! But while she drank her coffee she thought that

Ryabovsky had taken her husband from her, and that now she remained without her husband and without Ryabovsky; then she remembered that her acquaintances had said that Ryabovsky was preparing for the exhibition some thing astonishing, a mixture of a landscape and a genre painting, in Polenov's style, and that everybody who had seen it in his studio was enthusiastic about it; but this, she thought, he had created under her influence, and in general, thanks to her influence, he had greatly changed for the better. Her influence was so beneficial and so essential that if she left him he might possibly perish. And she also remembered that the last time he had come to see her in a grey speckled frock-coat and a new tie and had asked her:

"Am I not handsome?"

He really was elegant; with his long curls and blue eyes he looked very handsome, and (or perhaps she had only imagined it) he was very affectionate with her too.

Remembernig many things and pondering over them, Olga Ivanovna dressed, and drove to Ryabovsky's studio in great agitation. She found him gay and in raptures with his really magnificent picture; he jumped about, played the fool and answered serious questions with jokes. Olga Ivanovna was jealous of Ryabovsky's picture and hated it, but out of politness she stood before it for about five minutes in silence, sighing, as one sighs before a holy shrine, and at last she said in a low voice:

"Yes, you have never painted anything like it. Do you know, it is terrible!"

Then she began to implore him to love her, not to desert her, to have pity on her, poor unhappy thing. She wept, she kissed his hands, demanded that he should swear he loved her, proved to him that without her good influence he would stray from the right path and perish. And, having spoiled his good-humour and feeling that she had humiliated herself, she drove off to her dressmaker, or to an actress she knew, to try to obtain tickets.

If she did not find him in his studio she would leave a letter in which she swore that unless he came to her that very day she would certainly take poison. He was afraid, went to her and remained to dinner. Unrestrained by the presence of her husband, he was insolent to her, she returned insolence with insolence. Both felt they were a drag on each other, that they were despots and enemies and were angry, and owing to their anger they never noticed that they were both behaving in an unseemly manner, and that even closely cropped Korostelev understood everything. After dinner Ryabovsky hastily took leave and went away.

"Where are you going?" Olga Ivanovna asked him in the ante-room, and she looked at him with hatred.

Frowning and screwing up his eyes he named one of the ladies of their acquaintance, and it was evident he was laughing at her jealousy and did it on purpose to vex her. She went into her bedroom and lay down on the bed; from jealousy, vexation, a feeling of humiliation and shame she bit the pillow and began to sob aloud. Dymov left Korostelev in the drawing-room, went into the bedroom and quite confused and perplexed he said to her softly:

"Don't cry aloud, mama. . . . Why? One must be silent about it. . . . One must not let people notice it. . . . You know, what's done can't be undone."

Not knowing how she could quell the terrible jealousy she felt within her, which already caused her to have pain in the temples, and thinking she might still improve matters, she washed, powdered her tear-stained face and flew off to the lady of her acquaintance. Not finding Ryabovsky with her, she drove to another and then to a third. . . . At first she was ashamed of driving about in that way; but after a time she became used to it, and it sometimes happened that in one evening she went to all the women she knew, to look for Ryabovsky, and they all understood why she had come.

One day she said to Ryabovsky about her husband:

"That man crushes me with his magnanimity."

This phrase pleased her so much that whenever she met the artists who knew of her romance with Ryabovsky she said each time, referring to her husband, and making an energetic gesture with her hand:

"That man crushes me with his magnanimity!"

The order of their life was the same as in the previous year. On Wednesdays there were small evening parties. The actor recited, the artists drew, the violoncellist played, the singer sang, and invariably at half-past eleven the door that led into the dining-room was opened, and Dymov with a smile on his face said:

"Gentlemen, come to supper, please."

As formerly, Olga Ivanovna looked out for great men, found them, was dissatisfied with them and looked for others. As formerly, she returned home late at night, but now Dymov was not asleep as he used to be the year before, but was sitting in his study working. He never went to bed till about three o'clock and he rose at eight.

One evening when she was preparing to go to the theatre, she was standing before the pier-glass when Dymov, clad in a dress-coat and a white tie, came into her bedroom; he smiled meekly, and as formerly he looked his wife joyfully straight in the eyes. His face beamed.

"I have just been defending my thesis," he said, sitting down and stroking his knees.

."Defending?" Olga Ivanovna asked.

"Ogo!" he laughed, and he stretched his neck in order to see his wife's face in the mirror, as she was still standing before it with her back towards him arranging her hair. "Ogo!" he repeated. "Do you know it is very probable I shall be offered the post of professor's substitute on general pathology. It looks very like it."

It was evident by his delight and his beaming face that if Olga Ivanovna had shared his happiness and triumph he would have forgiven her everything, the present and the future, and he would have forgotten everything, but she did not understand what the post of professor's substitute or general pathology meant; besides, she was afraid of being late for the theatre and said nothing.

He sat for two minutes, smiled culpably and then left the room.

CHAPTER VII

SEND!

IT was a most agitating day.

Dymov had a very bad headache: in the morning he would not have any breakfast and he did not go to the hospital, but passed the whole day in his study lying on the Turkish divan. At one o'clock Olga Ivanovna went as usual to Ryabovsky's, in order to show him her new sketch of still-life, and to ask him why he had not been to see her on the previous day. The sketch appeared to her insignificant, and she had only painted it in order to have an extra excuse for going to the artist's.

She entered the house without ringing, and while she was taking off her galoshes in the ante-room it seemed to her as if somebody had run quietly across the studio with a womanlike rustle of skirts, and when she hastened to look into the studio she saw for a moment a bit of a brown petticoat disappearing behind a large picture that, as well as the easel on which it stood, was covered with a long black linen that reached to the floor. She could not doubt that it was a woman. How often had Olga Ivanovna herself found a hiding-place behind that picture! Ryabovsky, evidently very much confused and seeming to be surprised at her arrival, held out both his hands to her and said with a forced smile:

"Ah, ah, ah, ah! So pleased to see you. What good news do you bring me?"

Olga Ivanovna's eyes filled with tears. She felt shame and bitterness. and not for a million could she have spoken in the presence of that strange woman, that rival. that liar. who was now standing behind the picture, and was probably giggling malevolently.

"I have brought you a sketch . . ." she said timidly, in a faltering voice and her lips trembled—"a nature morte."

"Ah, ah, ah! a sketch?"

The artist took the sketch into his hand and while examining it he went as if mechanically into the next room.

Olga Ivanovna followed him submissively.

"Nature morte . . . first class," he muttered, as if he was searching for rhymes "sport. . . port kurort. . . ."

Hasty steps and the rustle of a dress were heard in the studio. That meant *she* had gone away. Olga Ivanovna wanted to scream, to hit the artist with something heavy across the head and then go away, but she could see nothing through her tears; she was crushed by her shame and she felt not like Olga Ivanovna, the artist, but like a small insect.

"I am tired . . ." the artist said languidly, looking at the sketch, and he shook his head in order to conquer his drowsiness. "This is pretty, of course, but to-day it is a sketch, and last year it was a sketch, and in a month's time it will be a sketch. . . . Doesn't it bore you? In your place I would chuck painting and give up my whole time to music or something else. Why, you are no painter but a musician. If you only knew how tired I am! I'll go and order tea. . . . Eh?"

He left the room, and Olga Ivanovna heard him give some order to his man-servant. So as not to take leave, not to have an explanation, but chiefly not to begin sobbing, she hastened into the ante-room, put on her galoshes before Ryabovsky returned and ran into the street. Here she sighed lightly and felt she was for ever free, not only from Ryabovsky, but from painting, and from the great shame that had weighed on her so heavily in the studio. All was finished!

She drove to her dressmaker's and then called on Barnay (the famous German tragedian), who had only arrived the day before, then to a music shop, and the whole time she was thinking how she was to write to Ryabovsky a cold, severe letter full of dignity, and then how in the spring or the summer she would go with Dymov to the Crimea, where she would free herself entirely from all the past and would begin quite a new life.

When she returned home late at night she did not redress, but sat down in the drawing-room to write her letter. Ryabovsky had told her she was not an artist, and she, to revenge herself on him, would write that every year he painted the same thing over and over again, and every day he said the same thing, that he was stagnating and that he would do nothing better than what he had already produced. She wanted to write that he owed much to her good influence, and if he acted badly it was only because her influence was paralyzed by various equivocal individuals, like the one who that day had hidden behind the picture.

"Mama!" Dymov called to her from his study without opening the door, "Mama!"

"What do you want?"

"Mama, don't come in here, but only come to the door. This is what has happened. . . . Three days ago I was infected with diphtheria in the hospital . . . and now I am feeling queer. Send quickly for Korostelev."

Olga Ivanovna called her husband like all her other male friends by their family names; his name Osip did not please her, because it reminded her of Gogol's Osip. Now she called out:

"Osip, this cannot be!"

"Send. I'm feeling bad," Dymov said behind the closed door, and she heard him go to the divan and lie down. "Send," his voice came to her hoarsely.

"What can this be?" Olga Ivanovna thought, and she grew cold with terror. "Why, it is dangerous!"

Without any necessity for doing it, she took up a candle and went into her bedroom, and there while thinking what she ought to do, she unintentionally looked at herself in the pier-glass. In her pale, frightened face, in the jacket with long sleeves and yellow frills at the throat and the striped skirt made in an unusual fashion, she appeared to be frightful—to be bad. Suddenly she became painfully sorry for Dymov, his unbounded love for her, his young life and even his widowed bed, on which for long he had not slept, and she remembered his usual meek, submissive smile. She began to cry bitterly, and wrote an imploring letter to Korostelev. It was two o'clock in the night.

CHAPTER VIII

NEVER TO AWAKEN

At past seven o'clock next morning, when Olga Ivanovna came out of her bedroom with a head heavy from want of sleep, unkempt and unbeautiful, and with a guilty expression on her face, an unknown gentleman with a black beard (probably a doctor) passed her and went into the lobby. There was a smell of medicine about the house. Korostelev was standing near the door that led into the study, twirling the left side of his moustache with his right hand.

"Excuse me, I cannot let you go to him." he said gloomily to Olga Iva-nova. "You might catch the infection. And really, why should you? And all the same it would do no good, as he is delirious."

"Has he the real diphtheria?" Olga Ivanovna asked in a whisper.

"People who rush into danger ought really to be prosecuted," Korostelev continued without replying to Olga Ivanovna's question. "Do you know how he caught the infection? Last Tuesday he sucked the diphtheria membrane out of a boy's throat through a glass tube. What good could that do? It was stupid . . . sheer folly. . . ."

"Is there danger? Is there much danger?" Olga Ivanovna asked.

"Yes. They say it's a bad form. One ought really to send for Shrek."

First a little red-haired man with a long nose and a Jewish accent came, then a tall, stooping man with long dishevelled hair, who looked like an archdeacon, took his place; he was followed by a very stout young man in spectacles with a red face. They were doctors, who came to watch at their colleague's bedside. Korostelev, though he had finished his time of watching, remained in the house and wandered about the rooms like a ghost. The housemaid served tea to the doctor on duty, and she had often to run to the chemist's, so there was nobody to do out the rooms. The house was quiet and dreary.

Olga Ivanovna sat in her bedroom and thought that God was punishing her for being unfaithful to her husband. A silent, resigned creature, depersonalized by his own meekness, characterless and weak from a superfluity of goodness, was dully suffering there on his sofa, and did not complain. And had he complained, even if it had been in his delirium, the doctors, who were attending on him, would know that it was not alone the diphtheria that was to blame. If they asked Korostelev . . . he knew everything, and it was not without cause that he looked on his friend's wife with those eyes that seemed to say she was the chief and the real miscreant, and that the diphtheria was only her accomplice. She no longer remembered the moonlit night on the Volga, nor the declaration of love, nor the poetical life in the *isba;* she only remembered that from idle caprice, from mere indulgence she had soiled herself entirely—body, legs and arms—in something dirty, something sticky, which she could never again wash off.

"Oh, how terribly I lied!" she thought when she remembered the troubled love she had had with Ryabovsky. "May it all be accursed! . . ."

At four o'clock she dined with Korostelev. He ate nothing, he only drank claret and scowled. She also ate nothing. At times she prayed mentally and vowed to God that if Dymov only recovered she would love him again and be his faithful wife. At others, forgetting herself for a moment, she would look at Korostelev and think: "How tiresome it must be to be an ordinary, in no way remarkable, and quite an unknown man, with such a wrinkled face and such bad manners too!" Then again she thought, that at that very moment God would kill her because she, fearing the infection, had not once been in her husband's study. And in general she had a dull dejected feeling and a conviction that her life was spoilt and there was no way of mending it.

After dinner darkness came on. When Olga Ivanovna went into the drawing-room she found Korostelev asleep on the couch with a gold embroidered silk cushion under his head. "Kri-pua," he snored, "Kri-pua."

The doctors, who came to watch at his bedside and went away again, did not notice this disorder. They did not notice that a strange man was asleep in the drawing-room and snoring, nor that there were sketches on the walls, nor that the room was furnished fantastically, nor that the mistress of the house was unkempt and slovenly—all this did not arouse the slightest interest now. One of the doctors suddenly laughed at something, and this laugh sounded strange and timid and it produced a weird effect.

Shortly after, when Olga Ivanovna went into the drawing-room again, Korostelev was no longer asleep. He was sitting up smoking.

"He has the diphtheria of the nasal cavity," he said in a whisper. "The heart is also not working well. It's really a bad job."

"Have you sent for Shrek?" Olga Ivanovna asked.

"He has been already. He noticed that the diphtheria had attacked the nose. Eh, after all, who is Shrek? There's nothing really special about Shrek. He's Shrek and I'm Korostelev—that's all."

Time went on terribly slowly. Olga Ivanovna lay on her bed, which had not been made since the morning, and dozed. It appeared to her that from floor to ceiling the whole house was filled with a huge piece of iron, and that it was only necessary to carry the iron out for everybody to become gay and relieved again. Awaking she remembered that this iron was Dymov's illness.

"Nature morte—port," she thought,

sinking into drowsiness again, ". . . sport . . . Kurort. . . . And how is Shrek . . . trek . . . wreck. . . ? Where are my friends now? Do they know that we are in trouble? Lord save us . . . remove it . . . Shrek— trek. . . ."

And again there was the iron weight. . . . Time dragged on slowly and the clocks in the lower story struck very often. There was constant ringing of the door bell . . . doctors kept coming. . . . The housemaid came into the room with an empty glass on a tray and asked:

"Madam, do you wish me to make the bed?"

Receiving no answer she went out again. The clock below struck the hour. She dreamed of rain on the Volga, and then again somebody came into the bedroom. It appeared to be a stranger. Olga Ivanovna jumped up and recognized Korostelev.

"What o'clock is it?" she asked.

"About three."

"Well, how is he?"

"How, indeed! I have come to say he is passing away . . ."

He sobbed and sat down on the bed next to her, brushing away his tears with his sleeve. At first she did not understand, but she felt cold all over and began to cross herself slowly.

"Passing away . . ." he repeated in a shrill voice, and he sobbed again. "Dying, because he has sacrificed himself. . . . What a loss for science!" he said bitterly. "He was a great, an extraordinary man. . . . None of us can be compared with him. What gifts! What hopes we all had of him!" Korostelev continued, wringing his hands. "My God, my God, what a man

of science the world has lost; we shall never see his like again. Osip Dymov, Osip Dymov, what have you done? Oh! oh! My God! My God!"

Korostelev buried his face in his hands and rocked to and fro.

"And what moral force!" he continued, becoming more and more incensed with someone. "A kind, honest, loving soul, not a man, but glass! He served science and he died for science. He worked like an ox—day and night— nobody spared him; a young scientist, a future professor, he had to look out for private practice—to work all night at translations in order to pay for these . . . wretched rags!"

Korostelev looked with hatred at Olga Ivanovna, and he seized the sheet with both hands and shook it angrily as if it were in fault.

"He did not spare himself and he was not spared by others. But what is the use of talking now!"

"Yes, he was a rare man!" somebody with a deep bass voice said in the drawing-room.

Olga Ivanovna remembered all her past life with him, from the beginning to the end, with all its details, and she suddenly understood that he really was a rare, an uncommon man who, compared with all those she knew, was really a great man. And remembering how her late father and all his colleagues had treated him, she understood that they all looked upon him as a future celebrity. The walls, the ceiling, the lamp and the carpet on the floor winked at her mockingly, as if they wanted to say: "Lost your chance, lost your chance!" With a cry she fled from the bedroom, rushed through the drawing-room, passing some strange man, and ran into her husband's study. He was lying, motionless on the Turkish divan, covered up to the waist with a quilt. His face was sunken and terribly emaciated, and it had the greyish yellow colour that is never seen in the living. It was only by his forehead, by his dark eyebrows, and by his well-known smile that it was possible to recognize Dymov. Olga Ivanovna hastily felt his breast. his forehead and his hands. His breast was still warm, but his forehead and his hands were unpleasantly cold. and the half-open eyes did not look at Olga Ivanovna, but at the quilt.

"Dymov," she called to him in a loud voice. "Dymov!"

She wanted to explain to him that all had been a mistake, that not everything was lost, that life could yet be beautiful and happy, that he was an exceptional, an extraordinary, a great man, and that for her whole life she would revere him, pray to him and feel a sacred veneration for him.

"Dymov," she called aloud, shaking him by the shoulder, not being able to believe that he would never awaken again. "Dymov, Dymov, listen!"

At the same time Korostelev was saying to the housemaid:

"What is the use of asking? Go to the Church beadle and ask him where the old women live; they will wash and lay out the body—they will do all that is necessary."

Verotchka

IVAN ALEXEIEVITCH OGNEFF well recollects an August evening when he opened noisily the hall door and went out on the terrace with a light cloak and a wide-brimmed straw hat—the very hat which now, beside his top-boots, lies in the dust underneath his bed. He then carried in one hand heavy books and manuscripts, and in his other a heavy cane.

In the doorway, stood his host, Kuznetsoff, aged and bald, with his long grey beard, and his white cotton jacket, lantern held aloft. And Kuznetsoff smiled kindly and nodded his head.

"Good-bye, old fellow!" cried Ogneff.

Kuznetsoff laid the lamp on the hall table, and followed Ogneff to the terrace. Their faint shadows swept down the steps, across the flower-beds, and came to a stop against the lime-trees.

"Good-bye, and again thank you, old fellow," said Ogneff. "Thanks for your heartiness, your kindness, your love. . . . Never . . . never in my whole life shall I forget your goodness. . . . You have been so kind . . . and your daughter has been so kind . . . all of you have been so kind, so gay, so hearty. . . . So good, indeed, that I cannot express my gratitude."

Under stress of feeling, under influence of the parting glass, Ogneff's voice sounded like a seminarist's, and his feeling showed not only in his words but in the nervous twitching of eyes and shoulders. And Kuznetsoff, touched also by emotion and wine, bent over the young man and kissed him.

"I have grown as used to you as if I were your dog," continued Ogneff. "I have been with you day after day. I have spent the night at your house a dozen times, and drunk so much of your liqueurs that it frightens me to think of it. . . . But, most of all, Gavriil Petrovitch, I thank you for your co-operation and help. Without you, I should have been worrying over my statistics till October. But I will put in my preface: "It is my duty to express to M. Kuznetsoff, President of the N. District Zemstvo Executive, my gratitude for his kind assistance." Statistics have a brilliant future! Give my deepest regards to Vera Gavriilovna! And tell the doctors, the two magistrates, and your secretary that I shall never forget their kindness. . . . And now, old friend, let us embrace and kiss for the last time!"

Ogneff again kissed the old man. When he reached the last step. he turned his head and said—

"I wonder shall we ever meet again."

"God knows," answered Kuznetsoff. "Probably never."

"I fear so. Nothing will lure you to Petersburg, and it is not likely that I shall ever return to these parts. Good-bye!"

"But leave your books," called Kuznetsoff after him. "Why carry such a weight? My man will bring them to-morrow."

But Ogneff, who had not heard him, walked quickly away. Warmed with wine, his heart was full at the same time of sorrow and joy. He walked forward reflecting how often in life we meet such kindly men and women, how sad it is that they leave but memories behind. It is as on a journey. The

traveller sees on the flat horizon the outline of a crane; the weak wind bears its plaintive cry; yet in a moment it is gone; and strain his eyes as he may towards the blue distance, he sees no bird, and hears no sound. So in the affairs of men, faces and voices tremble a moment before use, and slip away into the gone-before, leaving behind them nothing but the vain records of memory. Having been every day at hearty Kuznetsoff's house since he arrived that spring at N., Ogneff had come to know and love as kinsmen the old man, his daughter, their servants. He knew every spot in the old house, the cosy terrace, the turns in the garden paths, the trees outlined against garden and bathing-box. And now in a few seconds when he had passed the wicket-gate, all these would be memories, void for evermore of real significance. A year—two years—would pass. and all these kindly images, dulled beyond restoring, would recur only in memory as the shapeless impressions of a dream.

"In life," thought Ogneff, as he approached the gate, "there is nothing better than men. Nothing!"

It was warm and still. The whole world smelt of heliotropes, mignonette, and tobacco-plants which had not yet shed their blooms. Around shrubs and tree-trunks flowed a sea of thin, moonlight-soaked mist; and—what long remained in Ogneff's memory—wisps of vapour, white as ghosts, floated with motion imperceptibly slow across the garden path. Near the moon, shining high in heaven. swam transparent patches of cloud. The whole world, it seemed, was built of coal-black shadows and wandering wisps of white; and, to Ogneff, it seemed as if he were looking not at Nature, but at a decorate scene, as if clumsy pyrotechnists, illuminating the garden with white Bengal fire, had flooded the air with a sea of snowy smoke.

As Ogneff approached the wicket-gate a black shadow moved from the low palisade and came to meet him.

"Vera Gavriilovna," he exclaimed joyfully "You here! After I had looked for you everywhere to say good-bye! . . . Good-bye, I am going."

"So early—it is barely eleven o'clock."

"But late for me. I have a five-verst walk, and I must pack up tonight. I leave early tomorrow. . . ."

Before Ogneff stood Kuznetsoff's daughter, twenty-one-year-old Vera, whom he had seen so often, pensive and carelessly-dressed and interesting. Day-dreaming girls who spend the whole days lying down or in desultory reading, who suffer from tedium and melancholy, usually dress without care. But if Nature has given them taste and the instinct of beauty, this negligence in dress has often a charm of its own. And, indeed, Ogneff, recalling the vision of pretty Vera, cannot imagine her without a loose jacket, hanging in folds away from her waist, without untidy curls on her forehead, without the red, shaggy-tasselled shawl which all day long lay in the hall among the men's caps, or on the chest in the dining-room, where the old cat used it unceremoniously as bed. The shawl and the creased jacket seemed to express the easy-going indolence of a sedentary life. But perhaps it was because Ogneff liked Vera, that every button and fold exhaled to him goodness and poetry, something foreign to women insincere, void of the instinct of beauty, and cold. . . . And Vera, too, had a

good figure, regular features, and pretty wavy hair. To Ogneff, who knew few women, she seemed beautiful.

"I am going away," he said again, bidding her good-bye at the wicket-gate. "Think well of me! And thanks for everything!"

And again twitching his shoulders, and speaking in the sing-song seminarist's voice which he had used to the old man, he thanked Vera for her hospitality, her kindness, her heartiness.

"I wrote about you to my mother in every letter," he said. "If all men were like you and your father, life on earth would be paradise. Every one in your house in the same. So simple, so hearty, so sincere. . . ."

"Where are you going?"

"First to my mother, in Oriol. I shall spend two days there. Then to St. Petersburg to work."

"And then?"

"Then? I shall work all winter, and in spring go somewhere in the country to collect material. Well . . . be happy, live a hundred years, and think well of me! This is the last time we meet."

Ogneff bowed his head and kissed Verotchka's hand; then in silent confusion straightened his cloak, rearranged his package of books, and said—

"What a thick mist to-night!"

"Yes. Have you not forgotten anything?"

"Nothing . . . I think."

For a moment Ogneff stood silently. Then he turned awkwardly to the gate and went out of the garden.

"Wait! Let me go with you as far as the wood," said Vera, running after him.

They followed the road. Trees no longer obscured the view, and they could see the sky, and the country far ahead. Through breaks in the veil of semi-transparent smoke, the world exposed its fairness; the white mist lay unevenly around bushes and hayricks, or wandered in tiny cloudlets, clinging tò the surface as if not to cut off the view. The road could be seen all the way to the wood, and in the ditches beside it rose little bushes which trapped and hindered the vagabond mist wisps. Half a verst away rose a dark belt of forest.

"Why has she come? I shall have to see her home," Ogneff asked himself. But looking at Vera's profile, he smiled kindly, and said—

"I hate going away in weather like this. This evening is quite romantic, what with the moonlight, the silence . . . and all the honours! Do you know what, Vera Gavriilovna? I am now twenty-nine years old, yet have never had a single romance! In all my life so far, not one! So of trysts, paths of sighs, and kisses, I know only by hearsay. It is abnormal. Sitting in my own room in town, I never notice the void. But here in the open air I somehow feel it . . . strongly . . . it is almost annoying."

"But what is the cause?"

"I can't say. Perhaps it is because so far I have never had time, perhaps simply because I have never yet met a woman who . . . But I have few friends, and seldom go anywhere."

They walked three hundred yards in silence. As Ogneff looked at Vera's shawl and uncovered head, he recalled the past spring and summer days, when far from his grey St. Petersburg rooms, caressed by kindly Nature and by kindly friends, pursuing his much-loved work, he had seen slip by, uncounted, sunset

after dawn, day after day, nor noticed how, foreshadowing summer's end, the nightingale first, the quail, and then the corncrake ceased their songs. Time had passed unseen; and that, he supposed, meant that life had spun out pleasantly and without jar. He recalled how at the end of April he had arrived at N., a poor man, unused to society; and expected nothing but tedium, solitude, and contempt for statistics—which in his opinion took a high place among the useful sciences. He remembered the April evening of his arrival at the inn of Old-Believer Riabukhin, where for twenty kopecks a day he was given a bright, clean room, with only one restriction, that he should smoke out of doors. He remembered how he had rested a few hours, and, asking for the address of the President of the Zemstvo Executive, had set out on foot to Gavriil Petrovitch's house; how he had tramped through four versts of rich meadows and young plantations; how high under a veil of cloud trembled a lark, filling the world with silver sounds, while above the green pastures, with a stolid, pompous flapping of wings, the rooks flew up and down.

"Is it possible?" Ogneff asked himself, "that they breathe this air every day, or is it perfumed only this evening in honour of me?"

He remembered how, expecting a dry, business-like reception, he had entered Kuznetsoff's study timidly, with averted face, and shyly stroked his beard. And how the old man contracted his brows, and failed utterly to understand what this young man with his statistics wanted with the Zemstvo Executive. But as he began to understand what statistics really mean, and how they are collected, Gavriil Petrovitch woke up, smiled, and with infantile curiosity began to examine his visitor's note-books. . . . And on the evening of the same day, Ogneff sat at Kuznetsoff's supper-table, grew tipsy on strong liqueurs, and, watching the placid faces and lazy gestures of his new acquaintances, felt spreading through his whole body that sweet, drowsy indolence of one who, wanting to continue his sleep, stretches himself and smiles. And his new-found friends looked at him lovingly, asked were his father and mother alive, how much he earned a month, and whether he often went to the theatre.

Ogneff recalled the long drives through the cantons, the picnics, the fishing parties, the trip to the convent when the Mother Superior presented each visitor with a bead-purse; he recalled the endless, heated, truly Russian arguments in which the disputants, banging their fists on the table, misunderstood and interrupted without knowing what they meant to say, wandered from the subject, and after arguing fiercely a couple of hours, exclaimed with a laugh, "The devil knows what this dispute is about. We began about health, and are now arguing about rest in the grave!"

"Do you remember when you and I rode to Shestovo with the doctor?" asked Ogneff as they drew near to the wood. "We met a lunatic. I gave him five kopecks, and he crossed himself thrice, and threw the money in my face. What hosts of impressions I carry away—if fused in a compact mass, I should have a big ingot of gold! I never understood why clever, sensitive men crowd into big cities instead of living in the country. Is there more space and truth on the Nevsky, and in the big damp houses? My house, for instance, which is packed from top to bottom with artists, students, and journalists, always seems to me to embody an absurd prejudice."

Some twenty paces from the wood the road crossed a narrow bridge with posts at the corners. During their spring walks, this bridge was a stopping place for the Kuznetsoffs and their visitors. Thence they could draw echoes from the wood, and watch the road as it vanished in a black drive.

"We are at the bridge," said Ogneff. "You must return."

Vera stopped, and drew a deep breath.

"Let us sit down for a minute," she said, seating herself on a pillar. "When we say good-bye to friends we always sit down here."

Ogneff sat beside her on his parcel of books, and continued to speak. Vera breathed heavily, and looked straight into the distance, so that he could not see her face.

"Perhaps some day, in ten years' time, we'll meet somewhere again," he said. "Things will be different. You will be the honoured mother of a family, and I the author of a respectable, useless book of statistics, fat as forty thousand albums put together . . . To-night, the present counts, it absorbs and agitates us. But ten years hence we shall remember neither the date nor the month, nor even the year, when we sat on this bridge together for the last time. You, of course, will be changed. You will change."

"I asked you just now. . . ."

"I did not hear."

Only now did Ogneff notice the change that had come over Vera. She was pale and breathless; her hands and lips trembled; and instead of the usual single lock of hair falling on her forehead, there were two. She did her best to mask her agitation and avoid looking him in the face; and to help in this, she first straightened her collar as if it were cutting her neck, and then drew the red shawl from one side to the other.

"You are cold, I am afraid," began Ogneff. "You must not sit in the mist. Let me see you home."

Vera did not answer.

"What is the matter?" resumed Ogneff. "You do not answer my questions. You are ill?"

Vera pressed her hand firmly to her cheek, and suddenly drew it away.

It is too awful," she whispered, with a look of intense agony. "Too awful!"

"What is too awful?" asked Ogneff, shrugging his shoulders, and making no attempt to conceal his surprise. "What is the matter?"

Still breathing heavily and twitching her shoulders, Vera turned away from him, and after looking a moment at the sky, began—

"I have to speak to you, Ivan Alexeievitch. . . ."

"I am listening."

"I know it will seem strange to you . . . you will be astonished, but I do not care. . . ."

Ogneff again shrugged his shoulders and prepared to listen.

"It is this . . . ," began Vera, averting her eyes, and twirling the shawl-tassels in her fingers. "You see, this is . . . that is what I wanted to say. . . . It will seem absurd to you . . . and stupid . . . but I cannot bear it!"

Vera's words, half smothered in incoherent stammering, were suddenly interrupted by tears. She hid her face in the shawl, and wept bitterly. Ogneff, confused and stupefied, coughed, and, having no idea what to say or do, looked helplessly around. He was unused to tears, and Vera's breakdown seemed to make his own eyes water.

"Come, come!" he stammered helplessly. "Vera Gavriilovna! What does this mean? Are you ill? Some one has annoyed you? Tell me what it is . . . and perhaps I can help you."

And when, in a last attempt to console her, he drew her hands cautiously from her face, she smiled at him through her tears, and said—

"I . . . I love you!"

The words, simple and ordinary, were spoken in a simple and ordinary voice. But Ogneff, covered with intense confusion, turned his face away.

His confusion was followed by fright. The atmosphere of mournfulness, warmth, and sentiment, inspired by liqueurs and leave-takings, suddenly made way for a sharp, unpleasant feeling of awkwardness. Feeling that his whole soul had been turned inside out, he looked shyly at Vera; and she, having avowed her love, and cast for ever away her woman's enhancing inaccessibility, seemed smaller, simpler, meaner.

"What does it all mean?" he asked himself in terror. "And then . . . do I love her . . . or not?—that is the problem."

But she, now that the hardest, painfullest part was ended, breathed easily and freely. She rose from her seat, and, looking straight into Ogneff's eyes, spoke quickly, warmly, without constraint.

Those who have been overtaken by sudden terror seldom remember details, and Ogneff to-day recalls not one of Vera's words. He remembers only their import and the emotions they brought forth. He remembers her voice, which seemed to come from a strangled throat. a voice hoarse with emotion, and the magic passion and harmony in its intonations. Crying, smiling, scattering tear-drops from her eyes, she confessed that since the first days of their friendship she had been won by his originality, his intellect, his kind, clever eyes, and by the aims and aspirations of his life. That she loved him devoutly, passionately, madly; that in summer when she went from the garden into the house and saw his coat in the hall, or heard his voice. her heart thrilled with a presage of intense joy; that his most trivial jokes had made her laugh; that every figure in his note-books exhaled to her wisdom and majesty; that even his cane standing in the hall had seemed to her lovelier than the trees.

The wood, the patches of mist, even the black roadside ditches were charmed. it seemed, as they listened. But Ogneff's heart felt only estrangement and pain. Avowing her love, Vera was entrancingly fair; her words were noble' and impassioned. But Ogneff felt not the pleasure or vital joy which he himself yearned for, but only sympathy with Vera, and pain that a fellow-creature should suffer so for his sake. Heaven only knows why it was so! But whether the cause was book-learned reason, or merely that impregnable objectivity which forbids some men to live as men, the ecstasy and passion of Vera seemed to him affected and unreal. Yet even while he felt this, something whispered that, in the light of Nature and personal happiness, that which he listened to then was a thousand times more vital than all his books, his statistics, his eternal verities. And he was angry, and

reproached himself, though he had no idea wherein he was at fault.

What increased his confusion was that he knew he must reply. An answer was inevitable. To say to Vera plainly "I do not love you!" he had not the strength. But he could not say "I do," for with all his searchings he could not find in his heart a single spark.

And he listened silently while she said that she could know no greater happiness than to see him, to follow him, to go with him wheresoever he might go, to be his wife and helper . . . and that if he abandoned her she would die of grief.

"I cannot stay here," she exclaimed, wringing her hands. "I have come to detest this house, and this wood, and this air. I am tired of this changeless restfulness and aimless life; I can stand no longer our colourless, pale people, as like one another as two drops of water! They are genial and kind . . . because they are contented, because they have never suffered and never struggled. But I can stand it no more. . . . I want to go to the big grey houses, where people suffer, embittered by labour and need. . . ."

And all this seemed to Ogneff affected and unreal. When Vera ceased to speak he was still without an answer. But silence was impossible, and he stammered out—

"I . . . Vera Gavriilovna . . . I am very grateful to you, although I feel that I deserve no such . . . such feelings. In the second place, as an honest man, I must say that . . . happiness is based on mutuality . . . that is. when both parties . . . when they love equally."

Ogneff suddenly felt ashamed of his

stammering speech, and was silent. He felt that his expression was guilty, stupid, and dull, and that his face was strained and drawn out. And Vera, it seemed, could read the truth in his look, for she paled, looked at him with terror, and averted her eyes.

"You will forgive me," stammered Ogneff, feeling the silence past bearing. "I respect you so very, very much that . . . that I am sorry . . ."

Vera suddenly turned away, and walked rapidly towards the house. Ogneff followed her.

"No, there is no need!" she said. waving her hand. "Do not come! I will go alone. . . ."

But still . . . I must see you home."

All that Ogneff had said, even his last words, seemed to him flat and hateful. The feeling increased with each step. He raged at himself and, clenching his fists, cursed his coldness and awkwardness with women. In a last vain effort to stir his own feelings he looked at Vera's pretty figure, at her hair, at the imprints of her little feet on the dusty road. He remembered her words and her tears. But all this filled him only with pain, and left his feelings dead.

"Yes. . . . A man cannot force himself to love!" he reasoned, and at the same time thought, "When shall I ever love except by force? I am nearly thirty. Better than Verotchka among women I have never met . . . and never shall meet. Oh, accursed old age. Old age at thirty!"

Vera walked before him, each moment quickening her steps. Her face was bowed to the ground, and she did not look round once. It seemed to Ogneff that she had suddenly grown slighter and that her shoulders were narrower.

"I can imagine her feelings," he said to himself. "Shame . . . and such pain as to make her wish for death! . . . And in her words there was life and poetry, and meaning enough to have melted a stone! But I . . . I am senseless and blind."

"Listen, Vera Gavriilovna." This cry burst from him against his will. "You must not think that I . . . that I . . ."

Agneff hesitated and said nothing more. At the wicket-gate Vera turned, looked at him for an instant, and, wrapping her shawl tightly around her shoulders, walked quickly up the path.

Ogneff remained alone. He turned back to the wood, and walked slowly, stopping now and then and looking towards the gate. His movements expressed doubt of himself. He searched the road for the imprints of Verotchka's feet. He refused to credit that one whom he liked so much had avowed to him her love, and that he had awkwardly, boorishly scorned her. For the first time in life he realised how little one's actions depend from mere goodwill; and he felt as feels every honourable, kindly man who, despite his intentions, has caused his nearest and dearest unmeant and unmerited suffering.

His conscience stung him. When Verotchka vanished in the garden he felt that he had lost something very dear which he would never find again. With Vera, it seemed to him, a part of his youth had passed away, and he knew that the precious moments he had let slip away without profit would never return.

When he reached the bridge he stopped in thought, and sought the cause of his unnatural coldness. That it lay not outside himself, but within, he saw clearly. And he frankly confessed that this was not the rational calmness boasted by clever men, not the coldness of inflated egoism, but simply impotence of soul, dull insensibility to all that is beautiful, old age before its day—the fruit, perhaps, of his training, his grim struggle for bread, his friendless, bachelor life.

He walked slowly, as if against his own will, from the bridge to the wood. There where on a pall of impenetrable black the moonlight shone in jagged patches he remained alone with his thoughts; and he passionately longed to regain all that he had lost.

And Ogneff remembers that he returned to the house. Goading himself forward with memories of what had passed, straining his imagination to paint Vera's face, he walked quickly as far as the garden. From road and garden the mist had melted away, and a bright, newly washed moon looked down from an unflecked sky; the east alone frowned with clouds. Ogneff remembers his cautious steps, the black windows, the drowsy scent of heliotropes and mignonette. He remembers how old friend Karpo, wagging genially his tail, came up and snuffed at his hand. But no other living thing did he see. He remembers how he walked twice around the house, stood awhile before the black window of Vera's room: and abandoning his quest with a sigh returned to the road.

An hour later he was back in town; and, weary, broken, leaning his body and hot face against the gate, knocked at the inn. In the distance barked a sleepy dog; and the night watchman at the church beat an iron shield.

"Still gadding about at night!" grumbled the Old-Believer, as in a long, woman's night-dress he opened the door. "What do you gain by it? It would be better for you if you stayed at home and prayed to God!"

When he entered his room Ogneff threw himself upon the bed, and long gazed steadily at the fire. At last he rose, shook his head, and began to pack his trunk.

The Match

CHAPTER I

COMMITTED

ON the morning of October 6, 1885, in the office of the Inspector of Police of the second division of S—— District, there appeared a respectably dressed young man, who announced that his master, Marcus Ivanovitch Klausoff, a retired officer of the Horse Guards, separated from his wife, had been murdered. While making this announcement the young man was white and terribly agitated. His hands trembled and his eyes were full of terror.

"Whom have I the honor of addressing?" asked the inspector.

"Psyekoff, Lieutenant Klausoff's agent: agriculturist and mechanician!"

The inspector and his deputy, on visiting the scene of the occurence in company with Psyekoff, found the following: Near the wing in which Klausoff had lived was gathered a dense crowd. The news of the murder had sped swift as lightning through the neighborhood, and the peasantry, thanks to the fact that the day was a holiday, had hurried together from all the neighboring villages. There was much commotion and talk. Here and there, pale, tear-stained faces were seen. The door of Klausoff's bedroom was found locked. The key was inside.

"It is quite clear that the scoundrels got in by the window!" said Psyekoff as they examined the door.

They went to the garden, into which the bedroom window opened. The window looked dark and ominous. It was covered by a faded green curtain. One corner of the curtain was slightly turned up, which made it possible to look into the bedroom.

"Did any of you look into the window?" asked the inspector.

"Certainly not, your worship!" answered Ephraim, the gardener, a little gray-haired old man, who looked like a retired sergeant. "Who's going to look in, if all their bones are shaking?"

"Ah, Marcus Ivanovitch, Marcus Ivanovitch!" sighed the inspector, looking at the window, "I told you you would come to a bad end! I told the dear man, but he wouldn't listen! Dissipation doesn't bring any good!"

"Thanks to Ephraim," said Psyekoff; "but for him, we would never have guessed. He was the first to guess that something was wrong. He comes to me this morning, and says: 'Why is the master so long getting up? He hasn't left his bedroom for a whole week!' The moment he said that, it was just as if some one had hit me with an ax. The thought flashed through my mind, 'We haven't had a sight of him since last Saturday, and to-day is Sunday'! Seven whole days—not a doubt of it!"

"Ay, poor fellow!" again sighed the inspector. "He was a clever fellow, finely educated, and kind-hearted at that! And in society, nobody could touch him! But he was a waster, God rest his soul! I was prepared for anything since he refused to live with Olga Petrovna. Poor thing, a good wife, but a sharp tongue! Stephen!" the inspector called to one of his deputies, "go over to my house this minute, and send Andrew to the captain to lodge an information with him! Tell him that Marcus Ivanovitch has been murdered. And run over to the orderly; why should he sit there, kicking his heels? Let him come here! And go as fast as you can to the examining magistrate, Nicholas Yermolaïyevitch. Tell him to come over here! Wait; I'll write him a note!"

The inspector posted sentinels around the wing, wrote a letter to the examining magistrate, and then went over to the director's for a glass of tea. Ten minutes later he was sitting on a stool, carefully nibbling a lump of sugar, and swallowing the scalding tea.

"There you are!" he was saying to Psyekoff; "there you are! A noble by birth! a rich man—a favorite of the gods, you may say, as Pushkin has it, and what did he come to? He drank and dissipated and—there you are— he's murdered."

After a couple of hours the examining magistrate drove up. Nicholas Yermolaïyevitch Chubikoff—for that was the magistrate's name—was a tall, fleshy old man of sixty, who had been wrestling with the duties of his office for a quarter of a century. Everybody in the district knew him as an honest man, wise, energetic, and in love with his work. He was accompanied to the scene of the murder by his inveterate companion, fellow worker, and secretary, Dukovski, a tall young fellow of twenty-six.

"Is it possible, gentlemen?" cried Chubikoff, entering Psyekoff's room, and quickly shaking hands with everyone. Is it possible? Marcus Ivanovitch? Murdered? No! It is impossible! Im-poss-i-ble!"

"Go in there!" sighed the inspector.

"Lord, have mercy on us! Only last Friday I saw him at the fair in Farabankoff. I had a drink of vodka with him, save the mark!"

"Go in there!" again sighed the inspector.

They sighed, uttered exclamations of horror, drank a glass of tea each, and went to the wing.

"Get back!" the orderly cried to the peasants.

Going to the wing, the examining magistrate began his work by examining the bedroom door. The door proved to be of pine, painted yellow, and was uninjured. Nothing was found which could serve as a clew. They had to break in the door.

"Everyone not here on business is requested to keep away!" said the magistrate, when, after much hammering and shaking, the door yielded to ax and chisel. "I request this, in the interest of the investigation. Orderly, don't let anyone in!"

Chubikoff, his assistant, and the inspector opened the door, and hesitatingly, one after the other, entered the room. Their eyes met the following sight: Beside the single window stood the big wooden bed with a huge feather mattress. On the crumpled feather bed lay a tumbled, crumpled quilt. The pillow, in a cotton pillow-case, also much crumped, was dragging on the floor. On the table beside the bed lay a silver watch and a silver twenty-kopeck piece. Beside them lay some sulphur matches. Beside the bed, the little table, and the single chair, there was no furniture in the room. Looking under the bed, the inspector saw a couple of dozen empty bottles, an old straw hat. and a quart of vodka. Under the table lay one top boot, covered with dust. Casting a glance around the room, the magistrate frowned and grew red in the face.

"Scoundrels!" he muttered, clenching his fists.

"And where is Marcus Ivanovitch?" asked Dukovski in a low voice.

"Mind your own business!" Chubikoff answered roughly. "Be good enough to examine the floor! This is not the first case of the kind I have had to deal with! Eugraph Kuzmitch," he said, turning to the inspector, and lowering his voice, "in 1870 I had another case like this. But you must remember it—the murder of the merchant Portraitoff. It was just the same there. The scoundrels murdered him, and dragged the corpse out through the window——"

Chubikoff went up to the window, pulled the curtain to one side, and carefully pushed the window. The window opened.

"It opens, you see! It wasn't fastened. Hm! There are tracks under the window. Look! There is the track of a knee! Somebody got in there. We must examine the window thoroughly."

"There is nothing special to be found on the floor," said Dukovski. "No stains or scratches. The only thing I found was a struck safety match. Here it is! So far as I remember, Marcus Ivanovitch did not smoke. And he always used sulphur matches, never safety matches. Perhaps this safety match may serve as a clew!"

"Oh, do shut up!" cried the magistrate deprecatingly. "You go on about your match! I can't abide these dreamers! Instead of chasing matches, you had better examine the bed!"

After a thorough examination of the bed, Dukovski reported:

"There are no spots, either of blood or of anything else. There are likewise no new torn places. On the pillow there are signs of teeth. The quilt is stained with something which looks like beer and smells like beer. The general aspect of the bed gives grounds for thinking that a struggle took place on it."

"I know there was a struggle, without your telling me! You are not being asked about a struggle. Instead of looking for struggles, you had better——"

"Here is one top boot, but there is no sign of the other."

"Well, and what of that?"

"It proves that they strangled him, while he was taking his boots off. He hadn't time to take the second boot off when——"

"There you go!—and how do you know they strangled him?"

"There are marks of teeth on the pillow. The pillow itself is badly crumpled, and thrown a couple of yards from the bed."

"Listen to his foolishness! Better come into the garden. You would be better employed examining the garden than digging around here. I can do that without you!"

When they reached the garden they began by examining the grass. The grass under the window was crushed and trampled. A bushy burdock growing under the window close to the wall was also trampled. Dukovski succeeded in finding on it some broken twigs and a piece of cotton wool. On the upper branches were found some fine hairs of dark blue wool.

"What color was his last suit?" Dukovski asked Psyekoff.

"Yellow crash."

"Excellent! You see they wore blue!"

A few twigs of the burdock were cut off, and carefully wrapped in paper by the investigators. At this point Police Captain Artsuybasheff Svistakovski and Dr. Tyutyeff arrived. The captain bade them "Good day!" and immediately began to satisfy his curiosity. The doctor, a tall, very lean man, with dull eyes, a long nose, and a pointed chin, without greeting anyone or asking about anything, sat down on a log, sighed, and began:

"The Servians are at war again! What in heaven's name can they want now? Austria, it's all your doing!"

The examination of the window from the outside did not supply any conclusive data. The examination of the grass and the bushes nearest to the window yielded a series of useful clews. For example, Dukovski succeeded in discovering a long, dark streak, made up of spots, on the grass, which led some distance into the center of the garden. The streak ended under one of the lilac bushes in a dark brown stain. Under this same lilac bush was found a top boot, which turned out to be the fellow of the boot already found in the bedroom

"That is a blood stain made some time ago," said Dukovski, examining the spot.

At the word "blood" the doctor rose, and going over lazily, looked at the spot.

"Yes, it is blood!" he muttered.

"That shows he wasn't strangled, if there was blood," said Chubikoff, looking sarcastically at Dukovski.

"They strangled him in the bedroom; and here, fearing he might come round again, they struck him a blow with some sharp-pointed instrument. The stain under the bush proves that he lay there a considerable time, while they were looking about for some way of carrying him out of the garden.

"Well, and how about the boot?"

"The boot confirms completely my idea that they murdered him while he was taking his boots off before going to bed. He had already taken off one boot, and the other, this one here, he had only had time to take half off. The half-off boot came off of itself, while the body was dragged over, and fell——"

"There's a lively imagination for you!" laughed Chubikoff. "He goes on and on like that! When will you learn enough to drop your deductions? Instead of arguing and deducing, it would be much better if you took some of the blood-stained grass for analysis!"

When they had finished their exam-

ination, and drawn a plan of the locality, the investigators went to the director's office to write their report and have breakfast. While they were breakfasting they went on talking:

"The watch, the money, and so on— all untouched—" Chubikoff began, leading off the talk, "show as clearly as that two and two are four that the murder was not committed for the purpose of robbery."

"The murder was committed by an educated man!" insisted Dukovski.

"What evidence have you of that?"

"The safety match proves that to me, for the peasants hereabouts are not yet acquainted with safety matches. Only the landowners use them, and by no means all of them. And it is evident that there was not one murderer, but at least three. Two held him, while one killed him. Klausoff was strong, and the murderers must have known it!"

"What good would his strength be, supposing he was asleep?"

"The murderers came on him while he was taking off his boots. If he was taking off his boots, that proves that he wasn't asleep!"

"Stop inventing your deductions! Better eat!"

"In my opinion, your worship," said the gardener Ephraim, setting the samovar on the table, "it was nobody but Nicholas who did this dirty trick!"

"Quite possible," said Psyekoff.

"And who is Nicholas?"

"The master's valet, your worship," answered Ephraim. "Who else could it be? He's a rascal, your worship! He's a drunkard and a blackguard, the like of which Heaven should not permit! He always took the master his vodka and put the master to bed. Who else could it be? And I also venture to point out to your worship. he once boasted at the public house that he would kill the master! It happened on account of Aquilina. the woman, you know. He was making up to a soldier's widow. She pleased the master; the master made friends with her himself, and Nicholas—naturally, he was mad! He is rolling about drunk in the kitchen now. He is crying, and telling lies, saying he is sorry for the master——"

The examining magistrate ordered Nicholas to be brought. Nicholas, a lanky young fellow, with a long, freckled nose, narrow-chested, and wearing an old jacket of his master's, entered Psyekoff's room, and bowed low before the magistrate. His face was sleepy and tear-stained. He was tipsy and could hardly keep his feet.

"Where is your master?" Chubikoff asked him.

"Murdered! your worship!"

As he said this, Nicholas blinked and began to weep.

"We know he was murdered. But where is he now? Where is his body?"

"They say he was dragged out of the window and buried in the garden!"

"Hum! The results of the investigation are known in the kitchen already! —That's bad! Where were you, my good fellow, the night the master was murdered? Saturday night, that is."

Nicholas raised his head, stretched his neck, and began to think.

"I don't know, your worship," he said. "I was drunk and don't remember."

"An alibi!" whispered Dukovski, smiling, and rubbing his hands.

"So-o! And why is there blood under the master's window?"

Nicholas jerked his head up and considered.

"Hurry up!" said the Captain of Police.

"Right away! That blood doesn't amount to anything, your worship! I was cutting a chicken's throat. I was doing it quite simply, in the usual way, when all of a sudden it broke away and started to run. That is where the blood came from."

Ephraim declared that Nicholas did kill a chicken every evening, and always in some new place, but that nobody ever heard of a half-killed chicken running about the garden, though of course it wasn't impossible.

"An alibi," sneered Dukovski; "and what an asinine alibi!"

"Did you know Aquilina?"

"Yes, your worship, I know her."

"And the master cut you out with her?"

"Not at all. He cut me out—Mr. Psyekoff there, Ivan Mikhailovitch; and the master cut Ivan Mikhailovitch out. That is how it was."

Psyekoff grew confused and began to scratch his left eye. Dukovski looked at him attentively, noted his confusion, and started. He noticed that the director had dark blue trousers, which he had not observed before. The trousers reminded him of the dark blue threads found on the burdock. Chubikoff in his turn glanced suspiciously at Psyekoff.

"Go!" he said to Nicholas. "And now permit me to put a question to you, Mr. Psyekoff. Of course you were here last Saturday evening?"

"Yes! I had supper with Marcus Ivanovitch about ten o'clock."

"And afterwards?"

"Afterwards—afterwards— Really, I do not remember," stammered Psyekoff. "I had a good deal to drink at supper. I don't remember when or where I went to sleep. Why are you all looking at me like that, as if I was the murderer?"

"Where were you when you woke up?"

"I was in the servants' kitchen, lying behind the stove! They can all confirm it. How I got behind the stove I don't know——"

"Do not get agitated. Did you know Aquilina?"

"There's nothing extraordinary about that——"

"She first liked you and then preferred Klausoff?"

"Yes. Ephraim, give us some more mushrooms! Do you want some more tea, Eugraph Kuzmitch?"

A heavy, oppressive silence began and lasted fully five minutes. Dukovski silently kept his piercing eyes fixed on Psyekoff's pale face. The silence was finally broken by the examining magistrate:

"We must go to the house and talk with Maria Ivanovna, the sister of the deceased. Perhaps she may be able to supply some clews."

Chubikoff and his assistant expressed their thanks for the breakfast, and went toward the house. They found Klausoff's sister, Maria Ivanovna, an old maid of forty-five, at prayer before the big case of family icons. When she saw the portfolios in her guests' hands, and their official caps, she grew pale.

"Let me begin by apoligizing for disturbing, so to speak, your devotions." began the gallant Chubikoff, bowing and scraping. "We have come to you with a request. Of course, you have heard already. There is a suspicion that your dear brother, in some way or other, has been murdered. The will of God, you know. No one can escape death, neither czar nor plowman. Could you not help us with some clew, some explanation——?"

"Oh, don't ask me!" said Maria Ivanovna, growing still paler. and covering her face with her hands. "I can tell you nothing. Nothing! I beg you! I know nothing—What can I do? Oh, no! no!—not a word about my brother! If I die, I won't say anything!"

Maria Ivanovna began to weep, and left the room. The investigators looked at each other, shrugged their shoulders, and beat a retreat.

"Confound the woman!" scolded Dukovski, going out of the house. "It is clear she knows something, and is concealing it! And the chambermaid has a queer expression too! Wait, you wretches! We'll ferret it all out!"

In the evening Chubikoff and his deputy, lit on their road by the pale moon, wended their way homeward. They sat in their carriage and thought over the results of the day. Both were tired and kept silent. Chubikoff was always unwilling to talk while traveling, and the talkative Dukovski remained silent, to fall in with the elder man's humor. But at the end of their journey the deputy could hold in no longer, and said:

"It is quite certain," he said, "that Nicholas had something to do with the matter. *Non dubitandum est!* You can see by his face what sort of a case he is! His alibi betrays him, body and bones. But it is also certain that he did not set the thing going. He was only the stupid hired tool. You agree? And the humble Psyekoff was not without some slight share in the matter. His dark blue breeches, his agitation, his lying behind the stove in terror after the murder, his alibi and—Aquilina——"

"'Grind away, Emilian; it's your week!' So, according to you, whoever knew Aquilina is the murderer! Hot-head! You ought to be sucking a bottle, and not handling affairs! You were one of Aquilina's admirers yourself—does it follow that you are implicated too?"

"Aquilina was cook in your house for a month. I am saying nothing about that! The night before that Saturday I was playing cards with you, and saw you, otherwise I should be after you too! It isn't the woman that matters, old chap! It is the mean, nasty, low spirit of jealousy that matters. The retiring young man was not pleased when they got the better of him, you see! His vanity, don't you see? He wanted revenge. Then, those thick lips of his suggest passion. So there you have it: wounded self-love and passion. That is quite enough motive for a murder. We have two of them in our hands; but who is the third? Nicholas and Psyekoff held him, but who smothered him? Psyekoff is shy, timid, an all-round coward. And Nicholas would not know how to smother with a pillow. His sort use an ax or a club. Some third person did the smothering; but who was it?"

Dukovski crammed his hat down over his eyes and pondered. He remained silent until the carriage rolled up to the magistrate's door.

"Eureka!" he said, entering the little house and throwing off his overcoat. "Eureka, Nicholas Yermolaïyevitch!

The only thing I can't understand is, how it did not occur to me sooner! Do you know who the third person was?"

"Oh, for goodness sake, shut up! There is supper! Sit down to your evening meal!"

The magistrate and Dukovski sat down to supper. Dukovski poured himself out a glass of vodka, rose, drew himself up, and said, with sparkling eyes:

"Well, learn that the third person, who acted in concert with that scoundrel Psyekoff, and did the smothering, was a woman! Yes-s! I mean—the murdered man's sister, Maria Ivanovna!"

Chubikoff choked over his vodka, and fixed his eyes on Dukovski.

"You aren't—what's-its-name? Your head isn't what-do-you-call-it? You haven't a pain in it?"

"I am perfectly well! Very well, let us say that I am crazy; but how do you explain her confusion when we appeared? How do you explain her unwillingness to give us any information? Let us admit that these are trifles. Very well! All right! But remember their relations. She detested her brother. She never forgave him for living apart from his wife. She is of the Old Faith, while in her eyes he is a godless profligate. There is where the germ of her hate was hatched. They say he succeeded in making her believe that he was an angel of Satan. He even went in for spiritualism in her presence!"

"Well, what of that?"

"You don't understand? She, as a member of the Old Faith, murdered him through fanaticism. It was not only that she was putting to death a weed, a profligate—she was freeing the world of an antichrist!—and there in her opinion, was her service, her religious achievement! Oh, you don't know those old maids of the Old Faith. Read Dostoyevsky! And what does Lyeskoff say about them, or Petcherski? It was she, and nobody else, even if you cut me open. She smothered him! O treacherous woman! wasn't that the reason why she was kneeling before the icons, when we came in, just to take our attention away? 'Let me kneel down and pray,' she said to herself, 'and they will think I am tranquil and did not expect them!' That is the plan of all novices in crime, Nicholas Yermolaïyevitch, old pal! My dear old man, won't you intrust this business to me? Let me personally bring it through! Friend. I began it and I will finish it!"

Chubikoff shook his head and frowned.

"We know how to manage difficult matters ourselves," he said; "and your business is not to push yourself in where you don't belong. Write from dictation when you are dictated to; that is your job!"

Dukovski flared up, banged the door, and disappeared.

"Clever rascal!" muttered Chubikoff, glancing after him. "Awfully clever! But too much of a hothead. I must buy him a cigar case at the fair as a present."

The next day, early in the morning, a young man with a big head and a pursed-up mouth, who came from Klausoff's place, was introduced to the magistrate's office. He said he was the shepherd Daniel, and brought a very interesting piece of information.

"I was a bit drunk," he said. "I was with my pal till midnight. On my way home, as I was drunk, I went into the river for a bath. I was taking a bath, when I looked up. Two men were walking along the dam, carrying something black. 'Shoo!' I cried at them. They got scared, and went off like the wind toward Makareff's cabbage garden. Strike me dead, if they weren't carrying away the master!"

That same day, toward evening, Psyekoff and Nicholas were arrested and brought under guard to the district town. In the town they were committed to the cells of the prison.

CHAPTER II

CONFESSION

A FORTNIGHT passed.

It was morning. The magistrate Nicholas Yermolaïyevitch was sitting in his office before a green table, turning over the papers of the "Klausoff case"; Dukovski was striding restlessly up and down, like a wolf in a cage.

"You are convinced of the guilt of Nicholas and Psyekoff," he said, nervously plucking at his young beard. "Why will you not believe in the guilt of Maria Ivanovna? Are there not proofs enough for you?"

"I don't say I am not convinced. I am convinced, but somehow I don't believe it! There are no real proofs, but just a kind of philosophizing—fanaticism, this and that——"

"You can't do without an ax and bloodstained sheets. Those jurists! Very well, I'll prove it to you! You will stop sneering at the psychological side of the affair! To Siberia with your Maria Ivanovna! I will prove it! If philosophy is not enough for you, I have something substantial for you. It will show you how correct my philosophy is. Just give me permission——"

"What are you going on about?"

"About the safety match! Have you forgotten it? I haven't! I am going to find out who struck it in the murdered man's room. It was not Nicholas that struck it; it was not Psyekoff, for neither of them had any matches when they were examined; it was the third person, Maria Ivanovna. I will prove it to you. Just give me permission to go through the district to find out."

"That's enough! Sit down. Let us go on with the examination."

Dukovski sat down at a little table, and plunged his long nose in a bundle of papers.

"Bring in Nicholas Tetekhoff!" cried the examining magistrate.

They brought Nicholas in. Nicholas was pale and thin as a rail. He was trembling.

"Tetekhoff!" began Chubikoff. "In 1879 you were tried in the Court of the First Division, convicted of theft, and sentenced to imprisonment. In 1882 you were tried a second time for theft, and were again imprisoned. We know all——"

Astonishment was depicted on Nicholas's face. The examining magistrate's omniscience startled him. But soon his expression of astonishment changed to extreme indignation. He began to cry and requested permission to go and wash his face and quiet down. They led him away.

"Bring in Psyekoff!" ordered the examining magistrate.

They brought in Psyekoff. The young man had changed greatly during the last few days. He had grown thin and pale, and looked haggard. His eyes had an apathetic expression.

"Sit down, Psyekoff," said Chubikoff. "I hope that today you are going to be reasonable, and will not tell lies, as you did before. All these days you have denied that you had anything to do with the murder of Klausoff, in spite of all the proofs that testify against you. That is foolish. Confession will lighten your guilt. This is the last time I am going to talk to you. If you do not confess to-day, to-morrow it will be too late. Come, tell me all——"

"I know nothing about it. I know nothing about your proofs," answered Psyekoff, almost inaudibly.

"It's no use! Well, let me relate to you how the matter took place. On Saturday evening you were sitting in Klausoff's sleeping room, and drinking vodka and beer with him." (Dukovski fixed his eyes on Psyekoff's face, and kept them there all through the examination.) "Nicholas was waiting on you. At one o'clock, Marcus Ivanovitch announced his intention of going to bed. He always went to bed at one o'clock. When he was taking off his boots, and was giving you direction about details of management, you and Nicholas, at a given signal, seized your drunken master and threw him on the bed. One of you sat on his legs, the other on his head. Then a third person came in from the passage—a woman in a black dress, whom you know well, and who had previously arranged with you as to her share in your criminal deed. She seized a pillow and began to smother him. While the struggle was going on the candle went out. The woman took a box of safety matches from her pocket, and lit the candle.

Was it not so? I see by your face that I am speaking the truth. But to go on. After you had smothered him, and saw that he had ceased breathing, you and Nicholas pulled him out through the window and laid him down near the burdock. Fearing that he might come round again, you struck him with something sharp. Then you carried him away, and laid him down under a lilac bush for a short time. After resting awhile and considering, you carried him across the fence. Then you entered the road. After that comes the dam. Near the dam, a peasant frightened you. Well, what is the matter with you?"

"I am suffocating!" replied Psyekoff. "Very well—have it so. Only let me go out, please!"

They led Psyekoff away.

"At last! He has confessed!" cried Chubikoff, stretching himself luxuriously. "He has betrayed himself! And didn't I get round him cleverly! Regularly caught him napping——"

"And he doesn't deny the woman in the black dress!" exulted Dukovski. "But all the same, that safety match is tormenting me frightfully. I can't stand it any longer. Good-by! I am off!"

Dukovski put on his cap and drove off. Chubikoff began to examine Aquilina. Acquilina declared that she knew nothing whatever about it.

At six that evening Dukovski returned. He was more agitated than he had ever been before. His hands trembled so that he could not even unbutton his greatcoat. His cheeks glowed. It was clear that he did not come empty-handed.

"Veni, vidi, vici!" he cried, rushing into Chubikoff's room, and falling into an armchair. "I swear to you on my honor, I begin to believe that I am a genius! Listen, devil take us all! It is funny, and it is sad. We have caught three already—isn't that so? Well, I have found the fourth, and a woman at that. You will never believe who it is! But listen. I went to Klausoff's village, and began to make a spiral round it. I visited all the little shops, public houses, dram shops on the road, everywhere asking for safety matches. Everywhere they said they hadn't any. I made a wide round. Twenty times I lost faith, and twenty times I got it back again. I knocked about the whole day, and only an hour ago I got on the track. Three versts from here. They gave me a packet of ten boxes. One box was missing. Immediately: 'Who bought the other box?' 'Such-a-one! She was pleased with them!' Old man! Nicholas Yermolaïyevitch! See what a fellow who was expelled from the seminary and who has read Gaboriau can do! From to-day on I begin to respect myself! Oof! Well, come!"

"Come where?"

"To her, to number four! We must hurry, otherwise—otherwise I'll burst with impatience! Do you know who she is? You'll never guess! Olga Petrovna, Marcus Ivanovitch's wife—his own wife—that's who it is! She is the person who bought the matchbox!"

"You—you—you are out of your mind!"

"It's quite simple! To begin with, she smokes. Secondly, she was head and ears in love with Klausoff, even after he refused to live in the same house with her, because she was always scolding his head off. Why, they say she used to beat him because she loved him so much. And then he positively refused to stay in the same house. Love turned sour. 'Hell hath no fury like a woman scorned.' But come along! Quick, or it will be dark. Come!"

"I am not yet sufficiently crazy to go and disturb a respectable honorable woman in the middle of the night for a crazy boy!"

"Respectable, honorable! Do honorable women murder their husbands? After that you are a rag, and not an examining magistrate! I never ventured to call you names before, but now you compel me to. Rag! Dressing-gown!— Dear Nicholas Yermolaïyevitch, do come, I beg of you——!"

The magistrate made a deprecating motion with his hand.

"I beg of you! I ask, not for myself, but in the interests of justice. I beg you! I implore you! Do what I ask you to, just this once!"

Dukovski went down on his knees.

"Nicholas Yermolaïyevitch! Be kind! Call me a blackguard, a ne'er-do-well, if I am mistaken about this woman. You see what an affair it is. What a case it is. A romance! A woman murdering her own husband for love! The fame of it will go all over Russia. They will make you investigator in all important cases. Understand, O foolish old man!"

The magistrate frowned, and undecidedly stretched his hand toward his cap.

"Oh, the devil take you!" he said. "Let us go!"

It was dark when the magistrate's carriage rolled up to the porch of the old country house in which Olga Petrovna had taken refuge with her brother.

"What pigs we are," said Chubikoff, taking hold of the bell, "to disturb a poor woman like this!"

"It's all right! It's all right! Don't get frightened! We can say that we have broken a spring."

Chubikoff and Dukovski were met at the threshold by a tall buxom woman of three and twenty, with pitch-black brows and juicy red lips. It was Olga Petrovna herself, apparently not the least distressed by the recent tragedy.

"Oh, what a pleasant surprise!" she said, smiling broadly. "You are just in time for supper. Kuzma Petrovitch is not at home. He is visiting the priest, and has stayed late. But we'll get on without him! Be seated. You have come from the examination?"

"Yes. We broke a spring, you know," began Chubikoff, entering the sitting room and sinking into an armchair.

"Take her unawares—at once!" whispered Dukovski; "take her unawares!"

"A spring—hum—yes—so we came in."

"Take her unawares, I tell you! She will guess what the matter is if you drag things out like that."

"Well, do it yourself as you want. But let me get out of it," muttered Chubikoff, rising and going to the window.

"Yes, a spring," began Dukovski, going close to Olga Petrovna and wrinkling his long nose. "We did not drive over here —to take supper with you or—to see Kuzma Petrovitch. We came here to ask you, respected madam, where Marcus Ivanovitch is, whom you murdered!"

"What? Marcus Ivanovitch murdered?" stammered Olga Petrovna, and her broad face suddenly and instantaneously flushed bright scarlet. "I don't —understand!"

"I ask you in the name of the law! Where in Klausoff? We know all!"

"Who told you?" Olga Petrovna asked in a low voice, unable to endure Dukovski's glance.

"Be so good as to show us where he is!"

"But how did you find out? Who told you?"

"We know all! I demand it in the name of the law!"

The examining magistrate, emboldened by her confusion, came forward and said:

"Show us, and we will go away. Otherwise, we——"

What do you want with him?"

"Madam, what is the use of these questions? We ask you to show us! You tremble, you are agitated. Yes, he has been murdered, and, if you must have it, murdered by you. Your accomplices have betrayed you!"

Olga Petrovna grew pale.

Come!" she said in a low voice, wringing her hands. "I have him—hid—in the bath house! Only for heaven's sake, do not tell Kuzma Petrovitch. I beg and implore you! He will never forgive me!"

Olga Petrovna took down a big key from the wall, and led her guests through the kitchen and passage to the courtyard. The courtyard was in darkness. Fine rain was falling. Olga Petrovna walked in advance of them. Chubikoff and Dukovski strode behind her through the long grass, as the odor of wild hemp and dishwater splashing under their feet reached them. The courtyard was wide. Soon the dishwater ceased, and they felt freshly broken earth under their feet. In the darkness appeared the shadowy outlines of trees, and among the trees a little house with a crooked chimney.

"That is the bath house," said Olga Petrovna. "But I implore you, do not tell my brother! If you do, I'll never hear the end of it!"

Going up to the bath house, Chubikoff and Dukovski saw a huge padlock on the door.

"Get your candle and matches ready," whispered the examining magistrate to his deputy.

Olga Petrovna unfastened the padlock, and let her guests into the bath house. Dukovski struck a match and lit up the anteroom. In the middle of the anteroom stood a table. On the table, beside a sturdy little samovar, stood a soup tureen with cold cabbage soup and a plate with the remnants of some sauce.

"Forward!"

They went into the next room, where the bath was. There was a table there also. On the table was a dish with some ham, a bottle of vodka, plates, knives, forks.

"But where is it—where is the murdered man?" asked the examining magistrate.

"On the top tier." whispered Olga Petrovna, still pale and trembling.

Dukovski took the candle in his hand and climbed up to the top tier of the sweating frame. There he saw a long human body lying motionless on a large feather bed. A slight snore came from the body.

"You are making fun of us, devil take it!" cried Dukovski. "That is not the murdered man! Some live fool is lying here. Here, whoever you are, the devil take you!"

The body drew in a quick breath and stirred. Dukovski stuck his elbow into it. It raised a hand, stretched itself, and lifted its head.

"Who is sneaking in here?" asked a

hoarse, heavy bass. "What do you want?"

Dukovski raised the candle to the face of the unknown, and cried out. In the red nose, disheveled, unkempt hair, the pitch-black mustaches, one of which was jauntily twisted and pointed insolently toward the ceiling, he recognized the gallant cavalryman Klausoff.

"You—Marcus—Ivanovitch? Is it possible?"

The examining magistrate glanced sharply up at him, and stood spellbound.

"Yes, it is I. That's you, Dukovski? What the devil do you want here? And who's that other mug down there? Great snakes; It is the examining magistrate! What fate has brought him here?"

Klausoff rushed down and threw his arms round Chubikoff in a cordial embrace. Olga Petrovna slipped through the door.

"How did you come here? Let's have a drink, devil take it! Tra-ta-ti-to-tum —let us drink! But who brought you here? How did you find out that I was here? But it doesn't matter! Let's have a drink!"

Klausoff lit the lamp and poured out three glasses of vodka.

"That is—I don't understand you," said the examining magistrate, running his hands over him. "Is this you or not you!"

"Oh, shut up! You want to preach me a sermon? Don't trouble yourself! Young Dukovski, empty your glass! Friends, let us bring this—What are you looking at? Drink!"

"All the same, I do not understand!" said the examining magistrate, mechanically drinking off the vodka. "What are you here for?"

"Why shouldn't I be here, if I am all right here?"

Klausoff drained his glass and took a bite of ham.

"I am in captivity here, as you see. In solitude, in a cavern, like a ghost or a bogey. Drink! She carried me off and locked me up, and—well, I am living here, in the deserted bath house, like a hermit. I am fed. Next week I think I'll try to get out. I'm tired of it here!"

"Incomprehensible!" said Dukovski.

"What is incomprehensible about it?"

"Incomprehensible! For Heaven's sake, how did your boot get into the garden?"

"What boot?"

"We found one boot in the sleeping room and the other in the garden."

"And what do you want to know that for? It's none of your business. Why don't you drink, devil take you? If you wakened me, then drink with me! It is an interesting tale, brother, that of the boot! I didn't want to go with Olga. I don't like to be bossed. She came under the window and began to abuse me. She always was a termagant. You know what women are like, all of them. I was a bit drunk, so I took a boot and heaved it at her. Ha-ha-ha! Teach her not to scold another time! But it didn't! Not a bit of it! She climbed in at the window, lit the lamp, and began to hammer poor tipsy me. She thrashed me, dragged me over here, and locked me in. She feeds me now—on love, vodka, and ham! But where are you off to, Chubikoff? Where are you going?"

The examining magistrate swore, and left the bath house. Dukovski followed him, crestfallen. They silently took their seats in the carriage and drove off. The road never seemed to them so long and disagreeable as it did that time. Both remained silent. Chubikoff trembled with rage all the way. Dukovski hid his nose in the collar of his overcoat, as if he was afraid that the darkness and the drizzling rain might read the shame in his face.

When they reached home, the examining magistrate found Dr. Tyutyeff awaiting him. The doctor was sitting at the table, and, sighing deeply, was turning over the pages of the *Neva*.

"Such goings-on there are in the world!" he said, meeting the examining magistrate with a sad smile. "Austria is at it again! And Gladstone also to some extent——"

Chubikoff threw his cap under the table, and shook himself.

"Devils' skeletons! Don't plague me! A thousand times I have told you not to bother me with your politics! This is no question of politics! And you," said Chubikoff, turning to Dukovski and shaking his fist, "I won't forget this in a thousand years!"

"But the safety match? How could I know?"

"Choke yourself with your safety match! Get out of my way! Don't make me mad, or the devil only knows what I'll do to you! Don't let me see a trace of you!"

Dukovski sighed, took his hat, and went out.

"I'll go and get drunk," he decided, going through the door, and gloomily wending his way to the public house.

Excellent People

ONCE upon a time there lived in Moscow a man called Vladimir Semyonitch Liadovsky. He took his degree at the university in the faculty of law and had a post on the board of management of some railway; but if you had asked him what his work was, he would look candidly and openly at you with his large bright eyes through his gold pince-nez, and would answer in a soft, velvety, lisping baritone:

"My work is literature."

After completing his course at the university, Vladimir Semyonitch had had a paragraph of theatrical criticism accepted by a newspaper. From this paragraph he passed on to reviewing, and a year later he had advanced to writing a weekly article on literary matters for the same paper. But it does not follow from these facts that he was an amateur, that his literary work was of an ephemeral, haphazard character. Whenever I saw his neat spare figure, his high forehead and long mane of hair, when I listened to his speeches, it always seemed to me that his writing, quite apart from what and how he wrote, was something organically part of him, like the beating of his heart, and that his whole literary programme must have been an integral part of his brain while he was a baby in his mother's womb. Even in his walk, his gestures, his manner of shaking off the ash from his cigarette, I could read this whole programme from A to Z, with all its claptrap, dullness, and honorable sentiments. He was a literary man all over when with an inspired face he laid a wreath on the coffin of some celebrity, or with a grave and solemn face collected signatures for some address; his passion for making the acquaintance of distinguished literary men, his faculty for finding talent even where it was absent, his perpetual enthusiasm, his pulse that went at one hundred and twenty a minute, his ignorance of life, the genuinely feminine flutter with which he threw himself into concerts and literary evenings for the benefit of destitute students, the way in which he gravitated towards the young—all this would have created for him the reputation of a writer even if he had not written his articles.

He was one of those writers to whom phrases like, "We are but few," or "What would life be without strife? Forward!" were pre-eminently becoming, though he never strove with any one and never did go forward. It did not even sound mawkish when he fell to discoursing of ideals. Every anniversary of the University on St. Tatiana's Day, he got drunk, chanted *Gaudeamus* out of tune, and his beaming and perspiring countenance seemed to say: "See, I'm drunk; I'm keeping it up!" But even that suited him.

Vladimir Semyonitch had genuine faith in his literary vocation and his whole programme. He had no doubts, and was evidently very well pleased with himself. Only one thing grieved him—the paper for which he worked had a limited circulation and was not very influential. But Vladimir Semyonitch believed that sooner or later he would succeed in getting on to a solid magazine where he would have scope and could display himself—and what little distress he felt on this score was pale beside the brilliance of his hopes.

Visiting this charming man, I made the acquaintance of his sister, Vera Semyonovna, a woman doctor. At first sight, what struck me about this woman was her look of exhaustion and extreme ill-health. She was young, with a good figure and regular, rather large features, but in comparison with her agile, elegant, and talkative brother she seemed angular, listless, slovenly, and sullen. There was something strained, cold, apathetic in her movements, smiles, and words; she was not liked, and was thought proud and not very intelligent.

In reality, I fancy, she was resting.

"My dear friend," her brother would often say to me, sighing and flinging back his hair in his picturesque literary way, "one must never judge by appearances! Look at this book: it has long ago been read. It is warped, tattered, and lies in the dust uncared for; but open it, and it will make you weep and turn pale. My sister is like that book. Lift the cover and peep into her soul, and you will be horror-stricken. Vera passed in some three months through experiences that would have been ample for a whole lifetime!"

Vladimir Semyonitch looked round him, took me by the sleeve, and began to whisper:

"You know, after taking her degree she married, for love, an architect. It's a complete tragedy! They had hardly been married a month when—whew— her husband died of typhus. But that was not all. She caught typhus from him, and when, on her recovery, she learnt that her Ivan was dead, she took a good dose of morphia. If it had not been for vigorous measures taken by her friends, my Vera would have been by now in Paradise. Tell me, isn't it a tragedy? And is not my sister like an *ingénue*, who has played already all the five acts of her life? The audience may stay for the farce, but the *ingénue* must go home to rest."

After three months of misery Vera Semyonovna had come to live with her brother. She was not fitted for the practice of medicine, which exhausted her and did not satisfy her; she did not give one the impression of knowing her subject, and I never once heard her say anything referring to her medical studies.

She gave up medicine, and, silent and unoccupied, as though she were a prisoner, spent the remainder of her youth in colorless apathy, with bowed head and hanging hands. The only thing to which she was not completely indifferent, and which brought some brightness into the twilight of her life, was the presence of her brother, whom she loved. She loved him himself and his programme; she was full of reverence for his articles; and when she was asked what her brother was doing, she would answer in a subdued voice as though afraid of waking or distracting him: "He is writing. . . ." Usually when he was at his work she used to sit beside him, her eyes fixed on his writing hand. She used at such moments to look like a sick animal warming itself in the sun. . . .

One winter evening Vladimir Semyonitch was sitting at his table writing a critical article for his newspaper: Vera Semyonovna was sitting beside him, staring as usual at his writing

hand. The critic wrote rapidly, without erasures or corrections. The pen scratched and squeaked. On the table near the writing hand there lay open a freshly-cut volume of a thick magazine, containing a story of peasant life, signed with two initials. Vladimir Semyonitch was enthusiastic; he thought the author was admirable in his handling of the subject, suggested Turgenev in his descriptions of nature, was truthful, and had an excellent knowledge of the life of the peasantry. The critic himself knew nothing of peasant life except from books and hearsay, but his feelings and his inner convictions forced him to believe the story. He foretold a brilliant future for the author, assured him he should await the conclusion of the story with great impatience, and so on.

"Fine story!" he said, flinging himself back in his chair and closing his eyes with pleasure. "The tone is extremely good."

Vera Semyonovna looked at him, yawned aloud, and suddenly asked an unexpected question. In the evening she had a habit of yawning nervously and asking short, abrupt questions, not always relevant.

"Volodya," she asked, "what is the meaning of non-resistance to evil?"

"Non-resistance to evil!" repeated her brother, opening his eyes.

"Yes. What do you understand by it?"

"You see, my dear, imagine that thieves or brigands attack you, and you, instead of . . ."

"No, give me a logical definition."

"A logical definition? Um! Well." Vladimir Semyonitch pondered. "Non-resistance to evil means an attitude of non-interference with regard to all that in the sphere of mortality is called evil."

Saying this, Vladimir Semyonitch bent over the table and took up a novel. This novel, written by a woman, dealt with ·the painfulness of the irregular position of a society lady who was living under the same roof with her lover and her illegitimate child. Vladimir Semyonitch was pleased with the excellent tendency of the story, the plot and the presentation of it. Making a brief summary of the novel, he selected the best passages and added to them in his account: "How true to reality, how living, how picturesque! The author is not merely an artist; he is also a subtle psychologist who can see into the hearts of his characters. Take, for example, this vivid description of the emotions of the heroine on meeting her husband," and so on.

"Volodya," Vera Semyonovna interrupted his critical effusions, "I've been haunted by a strange idea since yesterday. I keep wondering where we should all be if human life were ordered on the basis of non-resistance to evil?"

"In all probability, nowhere. Nonresistance to evil would give the full rein to the criminal will, and, to say nothing of civilization, this would leave not one stone standing upon another anywhere on earth."

"What would be left?"

"Bashi-Bazouke and brothels. In my next article I'll talk about that perhaps. Thank you for reminding me."

And a week later my friend kept his promise. That was just at the period —in the eighties—when people were beginning to talk and write of non-re-

sistance, of the right to judge, to punish, to make war; when some people in our set were beginning to do without servants, to retire into the country, to work on the land, and to renounce animal food and carnal love.

After reading her brother's article, Vera Semyonóvna pondered and hardly perceptibly shrugged her shoulders.

"Very nice!" she said. "But still there's a great deal I don't understand. For instance, in Leskov's story 'Belonging to the Cathedral' there is a queer gardener who sows for the benefit of all—for customers, for beggars, and any who care to steal. Did he behave sensibly?"

From his sister's tone and expression Vladimir Semyonitch saw that she did not like his article, and, almost for the first time in his life, his vanity as an author sustained a shock. With a shade of irritation he answered:

"Theft is immoral! To sow for thieves is to recognize the right of thieves to existence. What would you think if I were to establish a newspaper and, dividing it into sections, provide for blackmailing as well as for liberal ideas? Following the example of that gardener, I ought, logically, to provide a section for blackmailers, the intellectual scoundrels? Yes."

Vera Semyonovna made no answer. She got up from the table, moved languidly to the sofa and lay down.

"I don't know, I know nothing about it," she said musingly. "You are probably right, but it seems to me, I feel something false in our resistance to evil, as though there were something concealed or unsaid. God knows, perhaps our methods of resisting evil belong to the category of prejudices which have become so deeply rooted in us, that we are incapable of parting with them, and therefore cannot form a correct judgment of them."

"How do you mean?"

"I don't know how to explain to you. Perhaps man is mistaken in thinking that he is obliged to resist evil and has a right to do so, just as he is mistaken in thinking, for instance that the heart looks like an ace of hearts. It is very possible in resisting evil we ought not to use force, but to use what is the very opposite of force—if you, for instance, don't want this picture stolen from you, you ought to give it away rather than lock it up. . . ."

"That's clever, very clever! If I want to marry a rich, vulgar woman, she ought to prevent me from such a shabby action by hastening to make me an offer herself!"

The brother and sister talked till midnight without understanding each other. If any outsider had overheard them he would hardly have been able to make out what either of them was driving at.

They usually spent the evening at home. There were no friends' houses to which they could go, and they felt no need for friends; they only went to the theater when there was a new play —such was the custom in literary circles—they did not go to concerts, for they did not care for music.

"You may think what you like," Vera Semyonoyna began again the next day, "but for me the question is to a great extent settled. I am firmly convinced that I have no grounds for resisting evil directed against me personally. If they want to kill me, let them. My defending myself will not make the murderer better. All I have now to decide is the second half of the question: how I ought to behave to evil directed against my neighbors?"

"Vera, mind you don't become rabid!" said Vladimir Semyonitch, laughing. "I see non-resistance is becoming your *idée fixe!*"

He wanted to turn off these tedious conversations with a jest, but somehow it was beyond a jest; his smile was artificial and sour. His sister gave up sitting beside his table and gazing reverently at his writing hand, and he felt every evening that behind him on the sofa lay a person who did not agree with him. And his back grew stiff and numb, and there was a chill in his soul. An author's vanity is vindictive, implacable, incapable of forgiveness, and his sister was the first and only person who had laid bare and disturbed that uneasy feeling, which is like a big box of crockery, easy to unpack but impossible to pack up again as it was before.

Weeks and months passed by, and his sister clung to her ideas, and did not sit down by the table. One spring evening Vladimir Semyonitch was sitting at his table writing an article. He was reviewing a novel which described how a village schoolmistress refused the man whom she loved and who loved her, a man both wealthy and intellectual simply because marriage made her work as a schoolmistress impossible. Vera Semyonovna lay on the sofa and brooded.

"My God, how slow it is!" she said, stretching. "How insipid and empty life is! I don't know what to do with myself, and you are wasting your best years in goodness knows what. Like some alchemist, you are rummaging in old rubbish that nobody wants. My God!"

Vladimir Semyonitch dropped his pen and slowly looked round at his sister.

"It's depressing to look at you!" said his sister. "Wagner in 'Faust' dug up worms, but he was looking for a treasure, anyway, and you are looking for worms for the sake of the worms."

"That's vague!"

"Yes, Volodya; all these days I've been thinking, I've been thinking painfully for a long time, and I have come to the conclusion that you are hopelessly reactionary and conventional. Come, ask yourself what is the object of your zealous, conscientious work? Tell me, what is it? Why, everything has long ago been extracted that can be extracted from that rubbish in which you are always rummaging. You may pound water in a mortar and analyse it as long as you like, you'll make nothing more of it than the chemists have made already. . . ."

"Indeed!" drawled Vladimir Semyonitch, getting up. "Yes, all this is old rubbish because these ideas are eternal; but what do you consider new, then?"

"You undertake to work in the domain of thought; it is for you to think of something new. It's not for me to teach you."

"Me—an alchemist!" the critic cried in wonder and indignation, screwing up his eyes ironically. "Art, progress— all that is alchemy?"

"You see, Volodya, it seems to me that if all you thinking people had set yourselves to solving great problems, all these little questions that you fuss about now would solve themselves by

the way. If you go up in a balloon to see a town, you will incidentally, without any effort, see the fields and the villages and the rivers as well. When stearine is manufactured, you get glycerine as a by-product. It seems to me that contemporary thought has settled on one spot and stuck to it. It is prejudiced, apathetic, timid, afraid to take a wide titanic flight, just as you and I are afraid to climb on a high mountain; it is conservative."

Such conversations could not but leave traces. The relations of the brother and sister grew more and more strained every day. The brother became unable to work in his sister's presence, and grew irritable when he knew his sister was lying on the sofa, looking at his back; while the sister frowned nervously and stretched when, trying to bring back the past, he attempted to share his enthusiasms with her. Every evening she complained of being bored, and talked about independence of mind and those who are in the rut of tradition. Carried away by her new ideas, Vera Semyonovna proved that the work that her brother was so engrossed in was conventional, that it was a vain effort of conservative minds to preserve what had already served its turn and was vanishing from the scene of action. She made no end of comparisons. She compared her brother at one time to an alchemist, then to a musty old Believer who would sooner die than listen to reason. By degrees there was a perceptible change in her manner of life, too. She was capable of lying on the sofa all day long doing nothing but thinking, while her face wore a cold, dry expression such as one sees in one-sided people of strong faith. She began to refuse the attentions of the servants, swept and tidied her own room, cleaned her own boots and brushed her own clothes. Her brother could not help looking with irritation and even hatred at her cold face when she went about her menial work. In that work, which was always performed with a certain solemnity, he saw something strained and false, he saw something pharisaical and affected. And knowing he could not touch her by persuasion, he carped at her and teased her like a schoolboy.

"You won't resist evil, but you resist my having servants!" he taunted her. "If servants are an evil, why do you oppose it? That's inconsistent!"

He suffered, was indignant and even ashamed. He felt ashamed when his sister begun doing odd things before strangers.

"It's awful, my dear fellow," he said to me in private, waving his hands in despair. "It seems that our *ingénue* has remained to play a part in the farce, too. She's become morbid to the marrow of her bones! I've washed my hands of her, let her think as she likes; but why does she talk, why does she excite me? She ought to think what it means for me to listen to her. What I feel when in my presence she has the effrontery to support her errors by blasphemously quoting the teaching of Christ! It chokes me! It makes me hot all over to hear my sister propounding her doctrines and trying to distort the Gospel to suit her, when she purposely refrains from mentioning how the money-changers were driven out of the Temple. That's, my dear fellow, what comes of being half educated, undeveloped! That's what comes of medical studies which provide no general culture!"

One day on coming home from the office, Vladimir Semyonitch found his sister crying. She was sitting on the sofa with her head bowed, wringing her hands, and tears were flowing freely down her cheeks. The critic's good heart throbbed with pain. Tears fell from his eyes, too, and he longed to pet his sister, to forgive her, to beg her forgiveness, and to live as they used to before. . . . He knelt down and kissed her head, her hands, her shoulders. . . . She smiled, smiled bitterly, unaccountably, while he with a cry of joy jumped up, seized the magazine from the table and said warmly:

"Hurrah! We'll live as we used to, Verotchka! With God's blessing! And I've such a surprise for you here! Instead of celebrating the occasion with champagne, let us read it together! A splendid, wonderful thing!"

"Oh, no, no!" cried Vera Semyonovna, pushing away the book in alarm. "I've read it already! I don't want it, I don't want it!"

"When did you read it?"

"A year . . . two years ago. . . . I read it long ago, and I know it, I know it!"

"H'm! . . . You're a fanatic!" her brother said coldly, flinging the magazine on to the table.

"No, you are a fanatic, not I! You!" And Vera Semyonovna dissolved into tears again. Her brother stood before her, looked at her quivering shoulders, and thought. He thought, not of the agonies of loneliness endured by any one who begins to think in a new way of his own, not of the inevitable sufferings of a genuine spiritual revolution, but of the outrage of his programme. the outrage of his author's vanity.

From this time he treated his sister

coldly, with careless irony, and he endured her presence in the room as one endures the presence of old women that are dependent on one. For her part, she left off disputing with him and met all of his arguments, jeers, and attacks with a condescending silence which irritated him more than ever.

One summer morning Vera Semyonovna, dressed for traveling with a satchel over her shoulder, went in to her brother and coldly kissed him on the forehead.

"Where are you going?" he asked with surprise.

"To the province of N. to do vaccination work." Her brother went out into the street with her.

"So that's what you've decided upon, you queer girl," he muttered. "Don't you want some money?"

"No, thank you. Good-bye."

The sister shook her brother's hand and set off.

"Why, don't you have a cab?" cried Vladimir Semyonitch.

She did not answer. Her brother gazed after her, watched her rusty-looking waterproof, the swaying of her figure as she slouched along, forced himself to sigh, but did not succeed in rousing a feeling of regret. His sister had become a stranger to him. And he was a stranger to her. Anyway, she did not once look round.

Going back to his room, Vladimir Semyonitch at once sat down to the table and began to work at his article.

I never saw Vera Semyonovna again. Where she is now I do not know. And Vladimir Semyonitch went on writing his articles, laying wreaths on coffins, singing *Gaudeamus,* busying himself over the Mutual Aid Society of Moscow Journalists.

He fell ill with inflammation of the lungs; he was ill in bed for three months —at first at home, and afterwards in the Golitsyn Hospital. An abscess developed in his knee. People said he ought to be sent to the Crimea, and began getting up a collection for him. But he did not go to the Crimea—he died. We buried him in the Vagankovsky Cemetery, on the left side, where artists and literary men are buried.

One day we writers were sitting in the Tatars' restaurant. I mentioned that I had lately been in the Vagankovsky Cemetery and had seen Vladimir Semyonitch's grave there. It was utterly neglected and almost indistinguishable from the rest of the ground, the cross had fallen; it was necessary to collect a few roubles to put it in order.

But they listened to what I said unconcernedly, made no answer, and I could not collect a farthing. No one remembered Vladimir Semyonitch. He was utterly forgotten.

VOLUME II

The Black Monk

CHAPTER I

NERVES

ANDREY VASIL'ICH KOVRIN, Master of Arts, was overworked and nervous. He was not being treated, but one day while sitting with a doctor at wine he happened casually to speak about his health. The physician advised him to pass the spring and summer in the country. Opportunely he received then a long letter from Tanya Pesotski, inviting him to visit Borisovka. He decided that he really required a change.

It was April. He went to his family estate of Kovrinka for three weeks; then, the roads being clear, he started on wheels to see his former guardian and tutor, Pesotski, the great horticulturist. From Kovrinka to Borisovka, where the Pesotskis lived, it was only seventy versts, and it was a pleasure to take the drive.

Egor Semenyeh Pesotski's house was huge, with columns and lions, but the plaster was cracking. The old park, severe and gloomy, laid out in the English style, extended for nearly a verst from the house to the river, and finished in abruptly precipitous clayey banks, on which there grew old pines with bare roots that looked like shaggy paws; down below the water glittered unsociably, and snipe flitted along its surface with plaintive cries. When there you always had the feeling that you must sit down and write a ballad. However, near the house, in the court-

yard and in the fruit orchard, which together with the nurseries covered about thirty acres, it was gay and cheerful even in bad weather. Such wonderful roses, lilies and camellias, such tulips of all imaginable hues, beginning with brilliant white and finishing with tints as black as soot, such a wealth of flowers as Pesotski possessed Kovrin had never seen in any other place. It was only the beginning of spring, and the real luxuriance of the flower-beds was still hidden in the hot-houses; but even those which blossomed in the borders along the walks and here and there on the flower-beds were sufficient to make you feel, when you passed through the garden, that you were in the kingdom of delicate tints, especially in the early morning, when a dewdrop glistened brightly on each petal.

The decorative part of the garden, which Pesotski called contemptuously a mere trifle, had greatly impressed Kovrin in his childhood. What wonderful whimsicalities were to be found there, what far-fetched monstrosities and mockeries of nature! There were espaliers of fruit trees, pear trees that had the form of pyramidal poplars, oaks and limes shaped like balls, an umbrella made of an apple tree, arches, monograms, candelabra and even 1862 formed by a plum tree; this date denoted the year when Pesotski first began to occupy himself with horticulture. There you also found pretty graceful trees with straight strong stems like palms, and only when you examined them closely you saw that they were gooseberries and currants. But what chiefly made the garden pay and produced an animated appearance was the constant movement in it. From early morning till evening people with wheelbarrows, shovels and watering-pots swarmed like ants round the trees, bushes, avenues and flower-beds.

Kovrin arrived at the Pesotskis' in the evening, at past nine o'clock. He found Tania and her father in a very anxious mood. The clear starlit sky and the falling thermometer foretold a morning frost; the head gardener, Ivan Karlych, had gone to town, and there was nobody who could be relied on. During supper nothing but morning frost was talked of, and they settled that Tania was not to go to bed, but walk through the gardens and see if all was in order after midnight, and that her father would get up at three or probably earlier.

Kovrin sat up with Tania, and after midnight he went with her into the orchard. It was very cold. In the yard there was a strong smell of burning. In the large orchard, which was called the commercial orchard and brought Egor Semenych a clear yearly profit of several thousand roubles, a thick, black, biting smoke spread along the earth, and by enveloping the trees saved those thousands from the frost. The trees were planted here in regular rows like the squares of a chess-board, and they looked like ranks of soldiers, this strictly pedentical regularity together with the exact size and similarity of the stems and crowns of the trees made the picture monotonous and dull. Kovrin and Tania passed along the rows, where bonfires of manure, straw and all sorts of refuse were smouldering, and occasionally they met workmen, who were wandering about in the smoke like shadows Only plums, cherries and some sorts of apple trees were in full blossom, but the whole orchard was smothered in smoke, and it was only when they reached the nurseries that Kovrin could draw a long breath.

"From my childhood the smoke here has made me sneeze," he said, shrugging his shoulders; "but I still do not understand how this smoke can protect the trees from frost."

"The smoke takes the place of clouds, when they are absent . . ." Tania answered.

"Why are clouds necessary?"

"In dull and cloudy weather there is never night frost."

"Really?"

He laughed and took her hand. Her broad, serious, cold face, with its finely marked black eyebrows, the high turned-up collar of her coat, which prevented her from moving her head with ease, her whole thin, *svelte* figure, with skirts well tucked up to protect them from the dew, affected him.

"Good Lord, she's already grown up!" he said. "When I last drove away from here, five years ago, you were still quite a child. You were a thin, long-legged, bare-headed girl in short petticoats, and I teased you and called you the heron. . . . What time does!"

"Yes, five years!" Tania sighed. "Much water has flowed away since then. Tell me, Andryusha, quite candidly," she said rapidly, looking into his face, "have we become strangers to you? But, why should I ask? You're a man, you are now living your own interesting life, you are great. . . . Estrangement is so natural! But, however it may be, Andryusha, I want you to consider us as your own people. We have that right."

"Of course you have, Tania!"

"Honour bright?"

"Yes, honour bright."

"You were surprised to-day to see we had so many of your portraits. You know my father adores you. Sometimes I think that he loves you more than he does me. He is proud of you. You are a scholar, an extraordinary man, you have made a brilliant career, and he is convinced that you have become all that because he brought you up. I do not prevent him from thinking this. Let him."

The day began to break; this was chiefly to be noticed by the distinctness with which the clouds of smoke were perceptible in the air, and the bark of the trees became visible. Nightingales were singing and the cry of the quail was borne from the fields.

"It's time to go to bed now," Tania said. "How cold it is!" She took his arm. "Thank you, Andryusha, for coming. We have but few acquaintances here, and they are not interesting. We have nothing but the garden, the garden, the garden—nothing but that. Standard, half-standard." she laughed. "pippins, rennets, codlins, grafting, budding. . . . All, all our life has gone into the garden—I never dream of anything but apples and pears. Of course, all this is good and useful, but some-

times I wish for something else for variety. I remember when you used to come for the holidays or simply on a visit the house seemed to grow fresher and lighter; it was as if the covers had been taken off the lustres and the chairs. I was a child then, still I understood."

She talked for a long time and with great feeling. Suddenly the idea entered his head that in the course of the summer he might become attached to this little, weak, loquacious creature, he might be carried away and fall in love —in their position it was so possible and so natural! This thought amused and moved him; he bent over her charming troubled face and began to sing in a low voice:

"Onegin, I'll not hide from you
I love Tatiana madly . . ."

When they reached the house, Egor Semenych was already up. Kovrin did not want to sleep; he began to talk with the old man and he returned with him to the garden. Egor Semenych was a tall, broad-shouldered man with a large stomach; he suffered from breathlessness, but he always walked so fast that it was difficult to keep up with him. He always had an extremely worried look, and he was always hurrying somewhere, with an expression that seemed to say if he were too late by one minute even, all would be lost!

"Here's a strange thing, my dear fellow," he said, stopping to take breath. "It's freezing on the ground, as you see, but if you raise the thermometer on a stick about fourteen feet above earth it's warm there. . . . Why is it?"

"I really don't know," Kovrin said, laughing.

"Hm. . . . Of course, one can't know everything. . . . However vast a man's understanding may be it can't comprehend everything. You've chiefly gone in for philosophy?"

"Yes. I lecture on psychology, but I study philosophy in general."

"And it does not bore you?"

"On the contrary, it's my very existence."

"Well, may God prosper your work . . ." Egor Semenych exclaimed, and he stroked his grey whiskers reflectively. "God prosper you! . . . I'm very glad for you. . . . Very glad, indeed, my boy. . . ."

Suddenly he seemed to listen, an expression of anger passed over his face and he ran off to one side and was soon lost to sight among the trees in the clouds of smoke.

"Who has tethered a horse to an apple tree?" his despairing, heartrending cry could be heard. "What villain and scoundrel has dared to tie a horse to an apple-tree? Good God, good God! They have dirtied, spoilt, damaged, ruined it. The orchard is lost! The orchard is destroyed! My God!"

When he returned to Kovrin he looked worn out and insulted.

"What can you do with this accursed people?" he said in a plaintive voice, clasping his hands. "Stepka was carting manure during the night and has tied his horse to an apple tree! The villain tied the reins so tight round it that the bark has been rubbed in three places. What do you think of that! I spoke to him, and he only stood openmouthed, blinking his eyes! He ought to be hanged."

When he was somewhat calmer he embraced Kovrin and kissed him on the cheek.

"Well, God help you. . . . God help you . . ." he mumbled. "I'm very glad you've come. Delighted beyond words. . . . Thank you."

Then he went round the whole garden at the same rapid pace and with the same troubled expression, and showed his former ward all the hothouses, conservatories and fruit-sheds, also his two apiaries, which he called the wonder of the century.

While they were walking round the sun rose and shed its brilliant rays over the garden. It became warm. Foreseeing a bright, joyous and long day, Kovrin remembered it was only the beginning of May, and that the whole summer lay before them, also bright, joyous and long, and suddenly a gladsome, youthful feeling was aroused in his breast, like he used to have when running about that garden in his childhood. He embraced the old man and kissed him tenderly. They were both much affected as they went into the house, where they drank tea with cream out of old china cups, and ate rich satisfying cracknels—these trifles again reminded Kovrin of his childhood and youth. The beautiful present and the memories that were aroused in him of the past were blended together; his soul was full and rejoiced.

He waited for Tania to get up and had coffee with her and then a walk, after which he went into his own room and sat down to work. He read with attention, made notes, only raising his eyes from time to time to look out of the open window, or at the fresh flowers, still wet with dew that were in a vase on his table, and then he again lowered his eyes to his book, and it appeared to him that every nerve in his system vibrated with satisfaction.

CHAPTER II

A PALE FACE!

IN the country he continued to lead the same nervous and restless life as in town. He read and wrote very much, he learned Italian, and when he was walking he thought all the time of the pleasure he would have in sitting down to work again. Everybody was astonished how little he slept; if he happened to doze for half an hour during the day he would afterwards not sleep all night, and after a sleepless night he felt himself active and gay, as if nothing had happened.

He talked much, drank wine and smoked expensive cigars. Often, indeed almost every day, some young girls from a neighbouring estate, friends of Tania's, came to the Pesotskis'. They played on the piano and sang together. Sometimes another neighbour, a young man, who played the violin very well, came too. Kovrin listened to the music and singing with avidity, and he was quite overcome by it, which was evidenced by his eyes closing and his head sinking on one side.

One day after the evening tea he was sitting on the balcony reading. At that time Tania—a soprano, one of her friends—a contralto and the young man playing on his violin were practicing Braga's celebrated serenade. Kovrin tried to make out the words—they were Russian—and he was quite unable to understand their meaning. At last laying his book aside and listening attentively he understood: A girl with a diseased imagination heard one night mysterious sounds in the garden, which were so wonderfully beautiful and strange that she thought they were holy harmonies, but so incomprehensible for us mortals that they ascended again to heaven. Once more Kovrin's eyes began to close. He rose, and feeling quite exhausted he began to walk about the drawing-room and then about the dancing hall. When they stopped singing he took Tania's arm and led her on to the balcony.

"Ever since the morning an old legend has been running in my head," he said. "I don't remember if I read it, or whether it was told me, but the legend is a strange one, and not like any other. To begin with it is not very clear. A thousand years ago a certain monk, clad in black, was walking in the desert somewhere in Syria or Arabia. . . . A few miles from the place where he was walking some fishermen saw another black monk moving slowly across the surface of a lake. This other monk was a mirage. Now you must forget all the laws of optics, which the legend evidently does not admit, and listen to the continuation. From the mirage another mirage was obtained, and from that one a third, so that the image of the black monk was reproduced without end in one sphere of the atmosphere after another. He was seen sometimes in Africa, sometimes in Spain, sometimes in India, then again in the far North. . . . At last he went beyond the bounds of the earth's atmosphere and is now wandering over the whole universe, always unable to enter into the conditions where he would be able to disappear. Perhaps at present he may be seen somewhere on Mars or on some star of the Southern Cross. But, my dear, the main point, the very essence of the whole legend, consists in this, that exactly a thousand years from the time the monk was walking in the desert the mirage will again be present in the atmosphere of the world, and it will show itself to men. It appears that those thousand years are nearly accomplished. . . Accordingly to the legend we can expect the Black Monk either to-day or to-morrow."

"A strange mirage," Tiana said. She did not like the legend.

"But the strangest thing is that I can't remember from where this legend has got into my head," Kovrin said, laughing. "Have I read it? Was it told me? Or perhaps I have dreamed about the Black Monk? By God, I can't remember. But the legend interests me. I think of it all day long."

Allowing Tania to return to her guests he left the house, and plunged in meditation he passed along the flower-beds. The sun was already setting. The flowers, perhaps because they had just been watered, exhaled a moist irritating odour. In the house they had again begun to sing, and at that distance the fiddle sounded like a human voice. Kovrin, straining his memory to remember where he had heard or read the legend, bent his steps towards the park, walking slowly, and imperceptibly he arrived at the river.

Running down the steep footpath that passed by the bare roots he came to the water, disturbing some snipe and frightening a pair of ducks. Some of the tops of the gloomy pines were still illuminated by the rays of the setting sun, but on the surface of the river evening had already settled down. Kovrin crossed the footbridge to the other bank. Before him lay a wide field of young rye not yet in flower. Neither a human habitation nor a living soul was to be seen near or far, and it seemed as if this footpath, if only you went far enough along it, would lead to that unknown, mysterious place into which the sun had just descended, and where the glorious blaze of the evening brightness was still widespread.

"What space, what freedom, what quiet is here!" Kovrin thought as he went along the footpath. "It seems as if the whole world was looking at me dissembling and waiting, that I should understand it. . ."

But just then waves passed over the rye and a light wind touched his bare head. A minute later there was again a gust of wind, but a stronger one. The rye began to rustle, and behind it the dull murmur of the pines was heard. Kovrin stopped in amazement. On the horizon something like a whirlwind or a water-spout—a high black column. stretched from the earth to the sky. Its outlines were indistinct; from the first minute it was evident that it did not remain on one spot, but was moving with terrible rapidity—moving straight towards Kovrin, and the nearer it came the smaller and clearer it became. Kovrin rushed to one side into the rye to make room for it, and he had scarcely time to do so. . . .

A monk clad in black, with a grey head and black eyebrows, his arms crossed on his breast, was borne past him. . . . His bare feet did not touch the earth. He had already passed Kovrin for a distance of about twelve feet, when he looked back at him, nodded his head and smiled affably, but at the same time cunningly. What a pale—a terribly pale—and thin face! Again beginning to grow larger, he flew across the river, struck noiselessly against the clayey bank and the pines and, passing through them, disappeared like smoke.

"Well, you see?" Kovrin mumbled. "So the legend is true."

Without trying to explain to himself this strange apparition, but feeling pleased that he had chanced to be so close, and had seen so distinctly not only the black garb, but even the monk's face and eyes, he returned home in pleasant agitation.

In the park and the gardens people were quietly moving about; in the house they were playing—that meant he alone had seen the monk. He was very anxious to tell Tania and Egor Semenych all he had seen, but he thought that they would certainly consider his words mere nonsense, and it would frighten them—it was best to remain silent. He laughed loudly, he sang and danced the mazurka, he was gay and everybody—the guests and Tania—thought that his face had never looked so radiant and inspired, and that he certainly was a most interesting man.

CHAPTER III

SHE LOVES

AFTER supper, when their guests had departed, he went to his room and lay down on the sofa: he wanted to think about the monk. But a minute later Tania entered the room.

"Here, Andryusha, are some of father's articles; read them," she said, giving him a parcel of pamphlets and proofs. "They are splendid articles. He writes very well."

"Well, indeed," said Egor Semenych, with a forced laugh, following her into the room; he was confused. "Don't listen to her, please, and don't read them. However, if you want to go to sleep you may as well read them: they are excellent soporifics."

"I think them excellent articles," Tania said, with deep conviction. "Read them, Andryusha, and persuade papa to write oftener. He might write a whole course of horticulture."

Egor Semenych forced a laugh, blushed and began to say such phrases as confused authors are wont to say. At last he gave in.

"If you must, then first read this article by Gaucher and these Russian notices," he murmured, turning the pamphlets over with trembling hands, "or else you won't understand it. Before reading my refutation you must know what I refute. However, it's all nonsense . . . and very dull. Besides, I should say it's time to go to bed."

Tania left the room. Egor Semenych sat down on the sofa next to Kovrin and sighed deeply.

"Yes, my dear fellow . . ." he began after a short silence. "So it is, my most amiable Master of Arts. Here am I writing articles, taking part in exhibitions, receiving medals. . . . People say Pesotski has apples the size of a man's head, people say Pesotski has made a fortune by his orchards and gardens. In a word, 'Kochubey is rich and famous.' Query: To what does all this lead? The garden is really beautiful— a model garden. . . . It is not simply a garden, it is an institution, possessing great importance for the empire, because it is, so to speak, a step in a new era of Russian economy—of Russian industry. But what for? For what object?"

"The business speaks for itself."

"That is not what I mean. I ask: What will become of the gardens when I die? In the condition you see it now, it will not exist for a single month without me. The whole secret of its success is not because the garden is large and there are many labourers, but because I love the work—you understand? I love it, perhaps more than my own self. Look at me. I do everything myself. I work from morning to night. I do all the grafting myself. I do all the pruning myself— all the planting—everything. When I am assisted I am jealous and irritable to rudeness. The whole secret lies in love, that is, in the vigilant master's eye, in the master's hand too, in the feeling that when you go anywhere, to pay a visit of an hour, you sit there and your heart is not easy; you're not quite yourself, you're afraid something may happen in the garden. When I die who will look after it all? Who will work? A gardener? Workmen? Yes? I tell you, my good friend, the chief enemy in our business is not the hare, not the cockchafer, not the frost, but the stranger."

"But Tania?" Kovrin asked, laughing. "She can't be more injurious than the hare. She loves and understands the business."

"Yes, she loves and understands it. If after my death she gets the garden, and becomes the mistress, I could wish for nothing better. But if, God forbid it, she should get married?" Egor Semenych whispered and looked at Kovrin with alarm. "That's just what

I fear! She gets married, children arrive, and then there's no time to think of the garden. What I chiefly fear is that she'll get married to some young fellow, who'll be stingy and will let the garden to some tradesman, and the whole place will go to the devil in the first year! In our business women are the scourge of God!"

Egor Semenych sighed and was silent for a few moments.

"Perhaps it is egoism, but, to speak frankly, I don't want Tania to marry. I'm afraid. There's a young fop with a fiddle, who comes here and scrapes at it; I know very well Tania will not marry him. I know it very well, but I can't bear him! In general, dear boy, I'm a great oddity. I confess it."

Egor Semenych rose and paced about the room for some time, much agitated; it was evident that he wanted to say something very important, but could not make up his mind to do so.

"I love you very much, and will speak to you quite frankly," he said at last, and thrust his hands into his pockets. "There are certain ticklish subjects I regard quite simply, and I say quite openly what I think of them. I cannot bear so-called hidden thoughts. I say to you plainly: You are the only man I would not be afraid to give my daughter to. You are a clever man, you have a good heart, and you would not allow my cherished work to perish. But the chief reason is—I love you as if you were my son—and I am proud of you. If you and Tania could settle a little romance between yourselves, why—what then? I would be very glad—very happy! As an honest man I say this quite openly, without mincing matters."

Kovrin laughed. Egor Semenych

opened the door to leave the room, but he stopped on the threshold.

"If a son were to be born to you and Tania I'd make a gardener of him," he said reflectively. "However, these are empty thoughts. . . . Sleep well!"

Left alone, Kovrin lay down more comfortably on the sofa and began to look through the articles. One was entitled: "Of Intermediate Culture," another was called: "A few words concerning Mr. Z——'s remarks on the digging up of ground for a new garden," a third was: "More about the budding of dormant eyes"; they were all of a similar nature. But what an uneasy, uneven tone, what nervous almost unhealthy passion! Here was an article one would suppose of the most peaceful nature, and on the most indifferent subject: it was about the Russian Antonov apple. However, Egor Semenych began with, *"audiatur altera pars,"* and finished, *"sapienti sat,"* and between these two quotations there was quite a fountain of various poisonous words addressed to the "learned ignorance of our qualified gardeners who observe nature from the height of their cathedras," or else M. Gaucher, "whose success has been created by the unlearned and the dilettante." Here again, quite out of place, was an insincere regret that it was now no longer possible to flog the peasants who stole fruit and broke the trees.

"The work is pretty, charming, healthy, but even here are passions and war," Kovrin thought. "It must be that everywhere and in all arenas of human activity intellectual people are nervous and remarkable for their heightened sensitiveness. Apparently this is necessary."

He thought of Tania, who was so delighted with her father's articles. She was small, pale and so thin that her collar-bones were visible; she had dark, wide-open clever eyes that were always looking into something, searching for something; her gait was short-stepped and hurried like her father's; she spoke much, she liked to argue, and then even the most unimportant phrase was accompanied by expressive looks and gestures. She certainly was nervous to the highest degree.

Kovrin continued to read, but he could understand nothing, so he threw the book away. The same pleasant excitement he had felt when he danced the mazurka and listened to the music now overcame him again, and aroused in him numberless thoughts. He rose and began to walk about the room, thinking of the black monk. It entered his head that if he alone had seen this strange supernatural monk it must be because he was ill and had hallucinations. This reflection alarmed him, but not for long.

"But I feel very well, and I do nobody any harm; therefore there is nothing bad in my hallucinations," he thought, and he again felt quite contented.

He sat down on the sofa and seized his head in both hands, trying to restrain the incomprehensible joy that filled his whole being, then he went to the table and began to work. But the thoughts he read in the books did not satisfy him. He wanted something gigantic, immense, astounding. Towards morning he undressed and reluctantly lay down in bed: he ought to sleep!

When he heard Egor Semenych's footsteps going down to the garden, Kovrin rang the bell and ordered the man-servant to bring him some wine. He drank several glasses of Château-Laffitte with pleasure, and then covered himself up to the head; his senses became dim and he went to sleep.

CHAPTER IV

TEARS OF TANIA

EGOR SEMENYCH and Tania often quarreled and said unpleasant things to each other.

One morning they had a quarrel. Tania began to cry and went to her room. She did not appear at dinner nor at tea. At first Egor Semenych went about looking very important and sulky, as if he wished everybody to know that for him the interests of justice and order stood above everything in the world, but soon he was unable to maintain that character and became depressed. He wandered sadly about the park and constantly sighed: "Oh, good God, good God!" At dinner he would not eat a crumb. At last feeling guilty and having qualms of conscience he knocked at his daughter's locked door and called to her timidly:

"Tania, Tania!"

And in answer he heard on the other side of the door a weak voice exhausted with crying, but still very positive, reply:

"Leave me alone, I beg you!"

The master's trouble affected the whole house, even the people working in the garden were under its influence. Kovrin was immersed in his own interesting work, but at last he too became sad and felt awkward. In order in some measure to dissipate the general gloomy mood he decided to intervene, and early in the evening he knocked at Tania's door. He was admitted.

"Oh, oh, what a shame!" he began jokingly, looking with astonishment at tania's tear-stained, sad little face that was all covered with red blotches. "Is it possible it is so serious? Oh, oh!"

"If you only knew how he tortures me!" she said, and tears—bitter, plentiful tears—welled up in her large eyes. "He has worn me quite out!" she continued, wringing her hands. "I said nothing to him . . . nothing at all. . . . I only said there is no need to keep . . . extra workmen if . . . if it is possible to get day labourers whenever they are wanted. Why, why the workmen have been doing nothing for a whole week. . . . I . . . I only said this and he shouted at me and he told me . . . many offensive, many deeply insulting things. Why, why?"

"Enough! Enough!" Kovrin said as he arranged a lock of her hair. "You have abused each other, you have wept, and that's enough. One must not be angry for long, that's wrong . . . all the more because he loves you tenderly."

"He . . . he has spoilt my whole life," Tania continued. "I am only insulted and . . . wounded here. He considers me superfluous in his house. What am I to do? He is right. I'll go away from here to-morrow and become a telegraph girl. . . . Let him . . ."

"Well, well, well. . . . Tania, don't cry. You, mustn't, my dear. . . . You are both hot-headed, irritable, and you are both in fault. Come along, I'll make peace between you."

Kovrin spoke affectionately and persuasively, but she continued to cry, her shoulders shaking and her hands clenched, as if a terrible misfortune had befallen her. He was all the more sorry for her because her grief was not serious, yet she suffered deeply. What trifles were sufficient to make this poor creature unhappy for a whole day, yes, perhaps even for her whole life! While comforting Tania, Kovrin thought that besides this girl and her father he might search the whole world without being able to find any other people who loved him as one of their family. If it had not been for these two people perhaps he, who had lost both his parents in his early childhood, would not have known to his very death what sincere affection was, nor that naïve, uncritical love that only exists between very near blood relatives. And he felt that his half-diseased, overtaxed nerves were drawn towards the nerves of this weeping, shuddering girl as iron is drawn to the magnet. He could never love a healthy, strong, red-cheeked woman, but pale, fragile, unhappy Tania attracted him.

He was pleased to stroke her hair, pat her shoulders, press her hands and wipe away her tears. At last she stopped crying; but for a long time she continued to complain about her father, and of her difficult, unbearable life in that house, begging Kovrin to enter into her position; then she gradually began to smile and to sigh that God had given her such a bad character. and at last she laughed aloud, called herself a fool and ran out of the room.

Shortly after, when Kovrin went into the garden, Egor Semenych and Tania were walking together in the avenue eating black bread and salt (they were both hungry), as if nothing had happened.

CHAPTER V

RED SPOTS

DELIGHTED that the part of peacemaker had been successful, Kovrin went into the park. While sitting on a bench thinking he heard the sound of wheels and of girls' laughter—visitors had arrived. When the shades of evening had begun to settle down on the gardens faint sounds of a violin and of voices singing reached his ear, and this reminded him of the black monk. Where, in what land or on what planet was that optical incongruity now being borne?

He had scarcely remembered the legend, and recalled to his memory the dark vision he had seen in the rye field, when just before him a middle-sized man with a bare grey head and bare feet, who looked like a beggar, came silently out of the pine wood, walking with small, unheard steps. On his pale, deathlike face the black eyebrows stood out sharply. Nodding affably this beggar or pilgrim came noiselessly and sat down on the bench. Kovrin recognized in him the black monk. For a minute they looked at each other—Kovrin with astonishment; the monk in a kindly and, as on the previous occasion, in a somewhat cunning manner, and with a self-complacent expression.

"But you are a mirage," Kovrin exclaimed; "why are you here and sitting on one place too? That is not in accordance with the legend."

"That's all the same," the monk replied after a pause, in a low quiet voice, turning his face towards Kovrin. "The mirage, the legend and I are all the products of your excited imagination. I am a phantom."

"Then, you do not exist?" Kovrin asked.

"Think what you like," the monk answered with a faint smile. "I exist in your imagination, and your imagination is part of nature, consequently I exist in nature too."

"You have a very old, clever and expressive face; just as if you had really existed for more than a thousand years," Kovrin said. "I did not know that my imagination was capable of creating such phenomena. But why are you looking at me with such rapture? Do I please you?"

"Yes. You are one of the few who are justly called the chosen of God. You serve the eternal truth. Your thoughts. your intentions. your extraordinary science and you whole life bear the godlike, the heavenly stamp, as they are devoted to the reasonable and the beautiful, that is to say, to that which is eternal."

"You said the eternal truth. . . . But can people attain to the eternal truth, and is it necessary for them if there is no eternal life?"

"There is eternal life," the monk answered.

"Do you believe in the immortality of man?"

"Yes, of course. A great brilliant future awaits you men. And the more men like you there are on earth, the sooner this future will be realized. Without you, the servants of the first cause, you who live with discernment and in freedom, the human race would, indeed, be insignificant. Developing in a natural way it would long have waited for the end of its earthly history. You are leading it to the kingdom of eternal truth several thousand years sooner—and in this lies your great service. . . . You incarnate in yourselves the blessing with which God has honoured mankind."

"But what is the object of eternal life?" Kovrin asked.

"The same as of all life—enjoyment. True enjoyment is knowledge, and

eternal life offers numberless and inexhaustible sources of knowledge; this is the meaning of: 'in my Father's House are many mansions.'"

"If you only knew how pleasant it is to listen to you," Kovrin said, rubbing his hands with satisfaction.

"I'm very pleased."

"But I know that when you go away I will be troubled about your reality. You are a vision, a hallucination. Consequently I am physically ill, I am not normal."

"And what of that! Why are you troubled? You are ill because you have worked beyond your strength and you are exhausted, which means that you have sacrificed your health to an idea, and the time is near when you will sacrifice your life to it too. What could be better? It is the object to which all noble natures, gifted from above, constantly aspire."

"If I know that I am mentally diseased. can I believe in myself?"

"How do you know that the men of genius, who are believed in by the whole world, have not also seen visions? Scholars say now that genius is allied to insanity. My friend, only the ordinary people—the herd—are quite well and normal. All this consideration about the nervous century, overwork, degeneration, etc., can only seriously alarm those whose object in life is the present—that is the people of the herd."

"The Romans said: 'mens sana in corpore sano.'"

"Not all that the Romans and Greeks said is true. Overstrain, excitement, ecstacy, all that distinguishes the prophets, the poets, the martyrs for ideas, from ordinary people, is opposed to the animal side of man's nature, that is, to his physical health. I repeat, if you wish to be healthy and normal go to the herd."

"It is strange, you say what often comes into my mind," Kovrin said. "You appear to have looked into my soul and listened to my most secret thoughts. But let us not speak of me. What do you mean by the eternal truth?"

The monk did not reply. Kovrin glanced at him and could not distinguish his face. The features became misty and melted away. The monk's head and hands gradually disappeared, his body seemed to be blended with the bench and with the evening twilight and then he vanished entirely.

"The hallucination is over," Kovrin said, and he laughed. "What a pity!"

He returned towards the house gay and happy. What little the black monk had said to him flattered not only his self-love, but his whole soul, his whole being. To be one of the chosen, to serve the eternal truth, to stand in the ranks of those who will render mankind worthy of the Kingdom of God a few thousand years sooner than it would otherwise have been, that is, will save mankind from an extra thousand years of struggle, sin and suffering, to sacrifice everything—youth, strength, health, to the idea—to be ready to die for the general good—what a high, what a happy fate! His clean, chaste life, so full of work passed through his memory; he remembered what he himself had learned, what he had taught others, and he arrived at the conclusion that there was no exaggeration in the words the monk had spoken.

Tania came to meet him through the park. She was dressed in another frock.

"Here you are at last!" she said.

"We are looking for you everywhere. But what has happened to you?" she said with astonishment, gazing at his enraptured, beaming countenance and his eyes that were brimming over with tears. "How strange you look, Andryusha."

"I am satisfied, Tania," Kovrin said, putting his hands on her shoulders. "I am more than satisfied, I am happy! Tania, dear Tania, you are a most congenial creature! Dear Tania, I am so glad, so glad!"

He kissed both her hands passionately and continued:

"I have just passed through bright, beautiful, unearthly moments. But I cannot tell you all because you would call me mad, or you would not believe me. Let us talk of you. Dear, charming Tania! I love you, and I have become used to love you. Your nearness, our meetings, ten times daily have become a necessity for my soul. I don't know how I shall be able to exist without you, when I go home."

"Well!" and Tania laughed, "you will forget us in two days. We are little people, and you are a great man."

"No, let us talk seriously," he said. "I will take you with me. Yes? Won't you come with me? You want to be mine?"

"Well, well!" Tania said and again she wanted to laugh, but laughter would not come, and red spots came out on her face.

She began to breathe fast, and she walked on very quickly, not towards the house, but deeper into the park.

"I never thought of this . . . never!" she said, clasping her hands as if in despair.

Kovrin followed her and continued to

speak with the same brilliant, excited face.

"I want love that would conquer me entirely, and that love, Tania, you alone can give me. 1 am happy, happy!"

She was stupefied, she bent, she shrivelled, she seemed suddenly to grow ten years older, and he thought her beautiful and he expressed his thoughts aloud:

"How beautiful she is!"

CHAPTER VI

THE BLACK GUEST

WHEN Egor Semenych heard from Kovrin that the romance had not only begun, but that there was to be a wedding, he walked about the rooms for a long time trying to hide his agitation. His hands began to tremble, his neck seemed to grow thicker and became purple; he ordered his racing droshky to be put to and drove off somewhere. Tania, seeing how he whipped the horse and how low down, almost over his ears, he had pressed his cap, understood his mood, shut herself up in her room and cried all day.

The peaches and plums were already ripening in the hot-houses; the packing and sending off to Moscow of these delicate and tender goods required much attention, trouble and work. Owing to the summer having been very hot and dry, it was necessary to water every tree; this took up much time and labour, besides multitudes of caterpillars appeared on the trees, which the workpeople, as well as Egor Semenych and Tania, crushed with their fingers, to Kovrin's great disgust. Besides all this work it was necessary to accept orders for fruit and trees for the autumn de-

liveries, and to carry on a large correspondence. While at the busiest time, when it seemed that nobody had a moment to spare, the season for field work came on and took away more than half the hands from the garden. Egor Semenych, very much sunburnt, exhausted and irritated, rushed about now in the gardens, now in the fields, crying that he was torn to pieces, and that he would send a bullet through his head.

There was also all the bustle caused by the preparation of the trousseau, on which the Pesotskis set great store; everybody in the house was made quite dizzy by the click of scissors, the noise of sewing machines, the fumes of hot irons and the caprices of the milliner, a nervous lady, who was easily offended. And, as if on purpose, every day saw the arrival of guests, who had to be entertained and fed, and who often even stayed the night. However, all this drudgery passed by almost unperceived as if in a mist. Tania felt that love and happiness had come upon her unawares, although for some reason from the age of fourteen she had been convinced that Kovrin would be sure to marry her. She was amazed, she was perplexed, she could not believe it herself. . . . At times she was suddenly everpowered by such joy, that she wanted to fly above the clouds, and pray to God there; at others, equally suddenly, she would remember that in August she would have to take leave of her paternal home and her father, or—God knows from where the thought would come—that she was insignificant, small and unworthy of such a great man as Kovrin—then she went to her own room, locked herself in and wept bitterly during several hours. When they had company it would suddenly appear to her that Kovrin was uncommonly handsome, and that all the women were in love with him, and were envious of her, then her soul was filled with pride and delight as if she had conquered the whole world, but he had only to smile affably at one of the girls to cause her to tremble with jealousy and retire to her own room; then there were tears again. These new sensations quite took possession of her; she helped her father mechanically, and never noticed the peaches nor the caterpillars, nor the labourers, nor even how quickly the time flew.

Much the same happened to Egor Semenych. He worked from morning to night, he was always hurrying somewhere, he constantly lost his temper, he was irritable, but all this took place in a sort of enchanted state of semi-sleep. It was as if there were two men in him: one was the real Egor Semenych who, listening to his gardener, Ivan Karlych, making his report about the disorders in the gardens, would be indignant, and put his hands to his head in despair; and the other, not the real one who, as if in a half-tipsy state, would suddenly break into the business report in the middle of a word and placing his hand on the gardener's shoulder would begin to murmur:

"Whatever one may say there is much in blood. His mother was a wonderful, a most noble, a most clever woman. It was a delight to look at her good, bright, pure face, like an angel's. She painted beautifully, she wrote verses. she could speak five foreign languages, she sang. . . . Poor thing, may the heavenly kingdom be hers, she died of consumption."

The unreal Egor Semenych sighed, and after a pause continued:

"When he was a boy growing up in my house, he had the same angelic, bright and good face. He has the same look, the same movements and the same soft, elegant manner of speaking that his mother had. And his intellect! He always astonished us by his intellect. By the way, it is not for nothing that he is a Master of Arts! . . . No, not for nothing! But wait a little, Ivan Karlych, you'll see what he'll be in ten years! He'll be quite unapproachable!"

But here the real Egor Semenych, checking himself, made a serious face, caught hold of his head and shouted:

"Devils! They've dirtied, destroyed, devastated everything! The garden is lost! The garden is ruined!"

Kovrin worked with the same zeal as before, and did not notice the hurly-burly around him. Love only added oil to the fire. After each meeting with Tania he returned to his room happy, enraptured, and with the same passion with which he had just kissed Tania and had told her of his love, he seized a book or set to work at his manuscript. All that the black monk had said about the chosen of God, eternal truth, the brilliant future of the human race, etc., only gave his work a special, an uncommon meaning and filled his soul with pride, and the consciousness of his own eminence. Once or twice a week either in the park or in the house he met the black monk and conversed with him for a long time; but this did not frighten him; on the contrary, it delighted him, as he was firmly convinced that such an apparition only visited the chosen, the eminent people, who had devoted themselves to the service of the idea.

One day the monk appeared during dinner and sat down in the dining-room near the window. Kovrin was delighted, and he very adroitly turned the conversation with Egor Semenych and Tania upon subjects that might interest the monk. The black guest listened and nodded his head affably; Egor Semenych and Tania also listened and smiled gaily, never suspecting that Kovrin was not talking to them, but to his vision.

Unperceived the fast of the Assumption was there, and soon after it the wedding-day arrived. The marriage was celebrated according to Egor Semenych's persistent desire "with racket," that is, with senseless festivities that lasted two days. They ate and drank far more than three thousand roubles, but owing to the bad hired band, the shrill toasts, the hurrying to and fro of the lackeys, the noise and the overcrowding, nobody could appreciate the bouquet of the expensive wines nor the taste of the wonderful delicacies that had been ordered from Moscow.

CHAPTER VII

DON'T BE AFRAID!

It happened on one of the long winter nights that Kovrin was lying in bed reading a French novel. Poor little Tania, who was not yet accustomed to live in a town, had a bad headache, as she often had by the evening, and was long since asleep, but from time to time she was uttering disconnected phrases in her sleep.

It had struck three. Kovrin blew out his candle and lay down. He lay long with closed eyes, but could not get to sleep, because (so it seemed to him) it was very hot in the bedroom and Tania was talking in her sleep. At half-past four he again lit the candle, and at that moment he saw the black monk sitting on the arm-chair that stood near the bed.

"How do you do?" the monk said, and after a short pause he asked: "Of what are you thinking now?"

"Of fame," Kovrin answered. "In the French novel I have just been reading there is a man, a young scientist who did stupid things, and who pined away from longing for fame. These longings are incomprehensible to me."

"Because you are wise. You look upon fame with indifference, like a plaything that does not interest you."

"Yes, that is true."

"Fame has no attraction for you. What is there flattering, interesting or instructive in the fact that your name will be carved on your gravestone, and then time will efface this inscription together with its gilding? Besides, happily you are too many for man's weak memory to be able to remember all your names."

"Naturally," Kovrin agreed. "Why should they be remembered? But let us speak of something else. For example, of happiness. What is happiness?"

When the clock struck five he was sitting on his bed with his feet resting on the rug and turning to the monk he was saying:

"In ancient times one happy man was at last frightened at his own happiness—it was so great! And in order to propitiate the gods he sacrificed to them his most precious ring. You know that story? Like Polycrates, I am beginning to be alarmed at my own happiness. It appears to me strange that from morning to night I only experience joy; I am filled with joy and it smothers all other feelings. I do not know what sadness, grief or dullness is. Here am I not asleep. I suffer from sleeplessness, but I am not dull. Quite seriously, I'm beginning to be perplexed."

"Why?" the monk asked in astonishment. "Is joy a superhuman feeling? Ought it not to be the normal condition of man? The higher a man is in his intellectual and moral development, the more free he is, the greater are the pleasures that life offers him. Socrates, Diogenes and Marcus Aurelius knew joy, and not grief. The apostle says: 'Rejoice always.' Therefore rejoice and be happy."

"What if suddenly the gods were angered?" Kovrin said jokingly, and he laughed. "What if they take from me my comfort and make me suffer cold and hunger, it will scarcely be to my taste."

In the meantime Tania had awaked and looked at her husband with amazement and terror. He was talking, addressing himself to the arm-chair, gesticulating and laughing; his eyes glistened and there was something strange in his laughter.

"Andryusha, with whom are you talking?" she asked, catching hold of the hand he was stretching out to the monk. "Andryusha, with whom? . . ."

"Eh? With whom?" Kovrin became confused. "With him. There he sits," he answered, pointing to the black monk.

"There's nobody here . . . nobody! Andryusha, you're ill!"

Tania put her arms round her husband and pressed close to him, and as if to protect him from visions she put her hand over his eyes. "You are ill!" She sobbed and her whole body trembled "Forgive me, darling, my dear one; I have long noticed that your soul is troubled about something. You are mentally ill, Andryusha. . . ."

Her shivering fit was communicated to him. He looked again at the arm-chair, which was now empty; he suddenly felt a weakness in the arms and legs, he was alarmed and began to dress.

"It's nothing, Tania, nothing . . ." he mumbled, shivering. "1 really feel a little out of sorts . . . it's time to admit it."

"I have long noticed it—and papa has noticed it too," she said, trying to restrain her sobs. "You talk to yourself, you smile in a strange way . . . you don't sleep. Oh, my God, my God, save us!" she said in terror. "But you must not be afraid, Andryusha, don't be afraid, for God's sake, don't be afraid. . . ."

She also began to dress. Only now, when he looked at her, Kovrin understood all the danger of his position, he understood what the black monk and his talks with him meant. It was now quite clear to him that he was a madman.

They both dressed, without knowing why, and went into the drawing-room. She went first, he followed her. Here Egor Semenych, who was staying with them, was already standing in his dressing-gown with a candle in his hand.

"Don't be afraid, Andryusha," Tania said again, trembling like one with a fever. "Don't be afraid. Papa, it will soon pass, it will soon pass."

Kovrin was too excited to be able to speak. He wanted to say to his father-in-law in a playful tone:

"Congratulate me, I think I'm out of my mind." but his lips only moved, and he smiled bitterly.

At nine o'clock in the morning he was wrapped up in a fur coat and a shawl and driven in a carriage to the doctor's. He began a cure.

CHAPTER VIII

TORTURE

SUMMER had come back again, and the doctor ordered Kovrin to go to the country. Kovrin was already cured, he had ceased seeing the black monk, and it only was necessary to restore his physical strength. While living on his father-in-law's estate he drank much milk, he worked only two hours a day, he did not drink wine, nor did he smoke.

On the eve of St. Elias's day vespers were celebrated in the house. When the deacon handed the censer to the priest there was an odour of the churchyard in the whole of the huge old hall, and it made Kovrin feel dull. He went into the garden. He walked about there without noticing the magnificent flowers; he sat on one of the benches and then wandered into the park; when he came to the river he went down to the water's edge and stood there for some time plunged in thought looking at the water. The gloomy pines, with their rough roots that but a year ago had seen him so young, joyful and hale, now did not whisper together, but stood motionless and dumb, just as if they did not recognize him. And, really, he was changed since last year; his head was closely cropped, his long beautiful hair was gone, his gait was languid, his face had grown stouter and paler.

He crossed over the foot-bridge to the other bank. Where the year before there had been rye, now mowed-down oats lay in long rows. The sun had already disappeared, and on the horizon the red glow of sunset was still widespread, foretelling wind for the next day. It was quiet. Looking in the direction where a year before the black monk had made his first appearance, Kovrin stood for about twenty minutes till the brightness of the sunset had faded away.

When he returned to the house languid and dissatisfied, vespers were over. Egor Semenych and Tania were sitting on the steps of the terrace drinking tea. They were talking about something, but when they saw Kovrin coming they suddenly were silent, and he concluded, judging by their faces, that the conversation had been about him.

"I think it's time for you to have your milk," Tania said to her husband.

"No, it's not time . . ." he answered as he sat down on the very lowest step. "Drink it yourself. I don't want it."

Tania exchanged an anxious glance with her father and said in a guilty tone:

"You yourself have noticed that milk does you good."

"Oh yes, very much good," Kovrin said, smiling. "I congratulate you; since Friday I have added another pound to my weight." He squeezed his head tightly between his hands and said sadly: "Why, why do you make me have this cure? All sorts of bromatic preparations, idleness, warm baths, watching, poor-spirited, alarm for every mouthful, for every step—all this in the end will make a perfect idiot of me. I went mad, I had the mania of greatness, but for all that I was gay, healthy and even happy; I was interesting and original. Now I have become more sober-minded and matter-of-fact, but in consequence I am now like everybody else. I am mediocre, life is tiresome to me. . . . Oh, how cruelly you have acted towards me! I saw hallucinations; in what way did that interfere with anybody? I ask you, with whom did that interfere?"

"God knows what you are saying!" Egor Semenych said with a sigh. "It's tiresome to listen to you!"

"Then don't listen."

The presence of people, especially of Egor Semenych, irritated Kovrin. He answered him drily, coldly, even rudely, and when he looked at him it was always with derision and with hatred. Egor Semenych was confused and coughed guiltily, although he could feel no blame. Unable to understand this sudden and sharp change in their friendly and kind-hearted relations, Tania pressed close to her father, and looked into his eyes with troubled glances; she wanted to understand the cause, but could not; all that was clear to her was that their relations became with every day worse and worse, that latterly her father had aged very much, and that her husband had become irritable, capricious, quarrelsome and uninteresting. She could no longer laugh and sing, she ate nothing at dinner, she often had sleepless nights, expecting something dreadful, and she was so worn out that once she lay in a faint from dinner-time until evening. During vespers it had appeared to her that her father was crying, and now when they were all three sitting together on the terrace she had to make an effort not to think of this.

"How happy were Buddha, Mohammed and Shakespeare, that their kind relations and doctors did not try to cure them of their ecstasies and inspirations!" Kovrin said. "If Mohammed had taken bromide to calm his nerves, had worked only two hours a day and had drunk milk, as little would have remained of this remarkable man as of his dog. The doctors and the kind relations will in the end so blunt the capacities of mankind that at last mediocrity will be considered genius and civilization will perish. If you only knew how thankful I am to you!" Kovrin said with vexation.

He felt greatly irritated and to prevent himself from saying too much he rose quickly and went into the house. The night was calm, and the scent of tobacco and jalap was borne through the open window. In the large dark ballroom the moonlight lay in green patches on the floor and on the piano. Kovrin remembered his raptures of the previous summer, when the jalaps smelt in the same way and the moon looked in at the windows. In order to renew last year's frame of mind he hurried into his study, lit a strong cigar and ordered the butler to bring him some wine. But the cigar only left an unpleasantly bitter taste in his mouth, and the wine had not the same flavour it had had the year before. What loss of habit does! He got giddy from the cigar, and after two sips of wine he had palpitations of the heart, so he had to take a dose of bromide.

When she was going to bed Tania said to him:

"My father adores you. You are angry with him for some reason and it is killing him. Only look at him: he is ageing not by days, but by hours. I implore you. Andryusha. for God's sake, for the sake of your late father, for the sake of my peace, be more affectionate with him."

"I can't, and I won't."

"But why?" Tania asked, beginning to tremble all over. "Tell me why?"

"Because I don't like him, that's all," Kovrin said carelessly, and shrugged his shoulders; "but let us not talk of him, he is your father."

"I can't, I really can't understand," Tania said, pressing her hands to her temples and looking at a point in front of her. "Something incomprehensible, something terrible is happening in our house You are changed, you are not like yourself. You are clever, you are no ordinary man and you get irritated with trifles; you meddle in all sort of tittle-tattle. Such trifles agitate you, that sometimes one is astonished and cannot believe it, and asks oneself: Is it you? Well, well, don't be angry, don't be angry," she continued, alarmed by her own words and kissing his hands. "You are clever, kind, noble. You will be towards with my father. He is so good."

"He's not good, but good-natured. The good-natured uncles in farces, who are somewhat like your father—well-fed and with good-natured faces, extremely hospitable and a little comical—appeared touching and amusing to me in novels and farces and also in real life at one time—now they are repugnant to me. They are all egoists to the marrow of their bones. What's most repugnant to me is their being overfed and their abdominal, their entirely oxlike or swine-like optimism."

Tania sat down on the bed and laid her head on the pillow.

"This is torture," she said, and her voice showed she was quite exhausted, and that it was difficult for her to speak. "Ever since the winter there has not been a single quiet moment. Good God, it is terrible! I suffer . . ."

"Yes, of course, I am Herod, and you and your little papa are the Egyptian infants. Oh, of course!"

His face appeared to Tania to be ugly and disagreeable; hatred and an expression of derision did not become him. For some time she had noticed there was something wanting in his face; it was as if a change had taken place in his countenance ever since the time his hair had been cut. She wanted to say something insulting to him, but at the moment she caught herself having such inimical feelings that she became alarmed and left the bedroom.

CHAPTER IX

BLOOD OF KOVRIN

KOVRIN was appointed to a professor's chair. His inaugural address was announced for the second of December, and the notice of this lecture was hung up in the corridor of the University. But on the appointed day he sent a telegram to inform the provost that owing to illness he was unable to give the lecture.

He had had a severe hæmorrhage from the throat. For some time he had spat blood, but about twice a month the hæmorrhage was considerable, and after these attacks he experienced great weakness and feel into a somnolent condition. This illness did not cause him any special anxiety, as he knew that his mother had lived for ten years and even longer with exactly the same malady, and the doctors assured him that there was no danger; they advised him only to be calm, to live a regular life and to talk as little as possible.

In January he was again unable to give the lecture owing to the same cause, and in February it was already too late to begin the course, and it had to be postponed until the next year.

At that time he no longer lived with Tania, but with another woman. who was two years older than he was, and who looked after him as if he were a child. His frame of mind was peaceful and tranquil: he obeyed willingly, and when Varvara Nikolaevna decided to take him to the Crimea he consented, although he had a foreboding that nothing good would come of this journey.

They arrived in Sevastopol towards evening and stayed the night at an hotel to rest before proceeding the next day to Yalta. They were both exhausted from the long journey. Varvara Nikolaevna had some tea, went to bed and was soon sound asleep. But Kovrin remained up. An hour before leaving home he had received a letter from Tania, and he had not been able to make up his mind to open it; it was still lying in his side pocket, and the thought of its being there agitated him unpleasantly. In the depths of his soul he now quite sincerely considered his marriage to have been a mistake; he was glad that he had definitely separated from her, and the remembrance of that woman, who at last had turned into a live walking skeleton and in whom all appeared to be dead with the exception of the large clever eyes that looked steadily at you—aroused in him nothing but pity and sorrow for himself, and the handwriting on the envelope reminded him how unjust and cruel he had been two years ago, how he had

vented his own voidness of soul, dullness, solitude and dissatisfaction with life on quite innocent people. This also reminded him of how one day he had torn into small pieces his dissertation and all the articles he had written during his illness and how he had thrown them out of the window, and the scraps of paper, blown about by the wind, had fluttered on to the flowers and the trees: in each line he saw strange pretensions that were founded on nothing, harebrained passions, insolence, the mania of greatness, and this had produced on him the effect of reading a description of his own vices; but when the last copy-book had been torn up and had flown out of the window for some reason he had suddenly become sorry and embittered, and he had gone to his wife and had told her all sorts of unpleasant things. Good God, how he had pestered her! One day wanting to cause her pain he had told her that her father had played an uneviable part in their romance as he had asked him to marry her. Egor Semenych, who had accidentally overheard this, rushed into the room and in his despair was unable to utter a word: he only stood there shifting from one foot to another and uttering a strange lowing sound as if he had been deprived of the power of speech, and Tania, gazing at her father, gave a piercing shriek and fell down in a swoon. It was disgraceful!

All this recurred to his memory at the sight of the familiar handwriting. Kovrin went out on to the balcony; it was a calm warm evening, and there was a scent of the sea. The moon and lights were reflected in the beautiful bay, which was of a colour for which it was difficult to find a name. It was a delicate and soft blending of blue and green; in places the water assumed the colour of green copperas, and in other places it seemed as if the moonlight had solidified, and instead of water had filled the bay, and in general what harmony of colour there was all around, what a peaceful, calm and lofty enjoyment!

In the floor below, just under the balcony, the window was probably open, because one could distinctly hear women's voices and laughter. It was evident an evening party was going on there.

Kovrin made an effort, unsealed the letter and reentering his room he read:

"My father has just died. I owe this to you as you have killed him. Our garden is ruined; strangers are now masters there; that is to say, what my poor father so feared is happening. I owe this to you too. I hate you with my whole soul, and I hope you will soon perish. Oh, how I suffer. My soul is consumed by unbearable pain. May you be accursed. I mistook you for an extraordinary man, for a genius. I loved you, but you proved to be a madman. . . ."

Kovrin could read no farther, he tore up the letter and threw it away. He was overpowered by a feeling of uneasiness that was almost like fear. Varvara Nikolaevna was sleeping behind the screen, and he could hear her breathing; from the story below the sound of women's voices and laughter were borne to him, but he had a sort of feeling that in the whole of the hotel there was not a living soul besides himself. Because unhappy, sorrowing Tania had cursed him in her letter, and had wished him to perish, a feeling of dread came over

him, and he looked furtively at the door as if he feared that the unknown power, which in the space of some two years had caused such ruin in his life and in the lives of those dearest to him, would enter the room and again take possession of him.

By experience he knew that when his nerves were unstrung the best remedy was work. He must sit down to the table and force himself to concentrate his mind on some special subject. He took out of his portfolio a copy-book in which he had jotted down the synopsis of a small compilatory work he had thought of writing if the weather proved to be bad in the Crimea, as it was dull to be without occupation. He sat down to the table and began to work at this synopsis, and it appeared to him that his old peaceful, submissive, equitable frame of mind was coming back. The copy-book with the synopsis aroused in him thoughts of wordly vanities. He thought how much life takes for the insignificant or very ordinary blessings that it is able to give man in exchange. For example, in order to receive before forty an ordinary professorial chair, and to expound in a languid, tiresome, heavy style very ordinary thoughts, which besides are the thoughts of other people— in a word, to attain the position of a moderately good scholar, he, Kovrin, had to study for fifteen years, to work day and night, pass through a serious mental disease, to survive an unsuccessful marriage and commit all sorts of follies and injustices, which it would be pleasant to forget. Kovrin realized now quite plainly that he was an ordinary mediocrity and he was quite satisfied with this, as he considered every man must be contented with what he was.

His synopsis would have been able to calm him if the white scraps of the torn-up letter that lay on the floor had not prevented him from concentrating his thoughts. He rose from the table, collected the fragments of the letter and threw them out of the window; but a light wind was blowing from the sea and the scraps of paper were scattered on the window-sill. He again was seized by a feeling of uneasiness that was almost like fear, and it seemed to him that in the whole of the hotel with the exception of himself there was not a single living soul . . . He went on to the balcony. The bay, as if alive, looked at him with numberless azure, dark blue, turquoise-blue and fiery eyes and enticed him towards itself. It was really hot and sultry, and it would be pleasant to have a bath.

Suddenly in the lower story just under the balcony there was the sound of a violin and two delicate women's voices began to sing. They were singing something very familiar. The song that was being sung below told of a girl who had a sick imagination, who heard mysterious sounds at night in the garden. and made up her mind that they were sacred harmonies that were incomprehensible to us mortals. . . . Kovrin had catchings of his breath and his heart grew heavy with sadness, and a beautiful sweet joy, such as he had long forgotten, throbbed in his breast.

A high black column that looked like a whirlwind or a waterspout appeared on the opposite shores of the bay. With terrible rapidity it moved across the bay in the direction of the hotel, becoming smaller and darker, and Kovrin had scarcely time to stand to one side to make room for it. . . . A monk with a bare head and black eyebrows, barefooted, with hands crossed on his breast, was borne past him and stopped in the middle of the room.

"Why did you not believe me?" he asked reproachfully, and looked kindly at Kovrin. "If you had believed me then, when I told you that you were a genius, you would not have passed these two years so sadly and so miserably."

Kovrin believed that he was the chosen of God and a genius, he instantly remembered all his former conversations with the black monk, and he wanted to speak but blood began to flow from his throat straight on to his breast, and he, not knowing what to do, passed his hands over his chest and his cuffs became saturated with blood. He wanted to call Varvara Nikolaevna, who was sleeping behind the screen; he made an effort and said:

"Tania!"

He fell on the floor and raising himself on his arm again called:

"Tania!"

He called to Tania, he called to the great gardens with their lovely flowers sprinkled with dew, he called to the park, to the pines with their rugged roots, to the fields of rye, to his wonderful science. to his youth, courage, joy, he called to life that was so beautiful. He saw on the floor close to his face a large pool of blood, and from weakness he could not utter another word, but an inexpressible, a boundless happiness filled his whole being. Below, just under the balcony. they were playing the serenade, and the black monk whispered to him that he was a genius and that he was only dying because his weak human body had lost its balance and could no longer serve as the garb for a genius.

When Varvara Nikolaevna awoke and came from behind the screen Kovrin was already dead and his face had stiffened in a blissful smile.

A Family Council

To keep the family skeleton of the Uskoffs off the street, the most rigorous measures were taken. Half of the servants were sent to the theatre and circus, and half stayed in the kitchen. Orders were given to admit no one. The wife of the culprit's uncle, her sister, and the governess, although aware of the mystery, pretended that they knew nothing about it. They sat silently in the dining-room, and never left it.

Sasha Uskoff, aged twenty-five, the cause of all this consternation, arrived some time ago; and on the advice of kind-hearted Ivan Markovitch, his maternal uncle, sat in the corridor outside the study and prepared to confess all and openly.

On the other side of the door the family council was being held. The discussion ran on a ticklish and very disagreeable subject. The facts of the matter were as follows. Sasha Uskoff had discounted at a bankers a forged bill of exchange, the term of which expired three days before; and now his two paternal uncles, and Ivan Markovitch, an uncle on his mother's side, were discussing the solemn problem: should the money be paid and the family honour saved, or should they wash their hands of the whole matter, and leave the law to take its course?

To people unconcerned and un-interested such questions seem very trivial, but for those with whom the solution lies they are extraordinarily complex. The three uncles had already had their say, yet the matter had not advanced a step.

"Heavens!" cried the Colonel, a paternal uncle, in a voice betraying both weariness and irritation. "Heavens! who said that family honour was a prejudice? I never said anything of the kind. I only wanted to save you from looking at the matter from a false stand-point—to point out how easily you may make an irremediable mistake. Yet you don't seem to understand me! I sup-pose I am speaking Russian, not Chinese!"

"My dear fellow, we understand you perfectly," interposed Ivan Markovitch soothingly.

"Then why do you say that I deny family honour? I repeat what I have said! Fam—ily hon—our false—ly under—stood is a pre—ju—dice! Falsely under—stood. mind you! That is my point of view. From any convic-tion whatever, to screen and leave un-punished a rascal. no matter who he is, both contrary to law and unworthy of an honourable man. It is not the saving of the family honour, but civic cowar-dice. Take the Army, for example! The honour of the Army is dearer to a soldier than any other honour. But we do not screen our guilty members . . . we judge them! Do you imagine that the honour of the Army suffers thereby? On the contrary!"

The other paternal uncle, an official of the Crown Council, a rheumatic, taciturn, and not very intelligent man, held his peace all the time, or spoke only of the fact that if the matter came into court the name of the Uskoffs would appear in the newspapers; in his opinion, therefore, to avoid publicity it would be better to hush up the matter while there was still time. But with the exception of this reference to the newspapers, he gave no reason for his opinion.

But kind-hearted Ivan Markovitch, the maternal uncle, spoke fluently and softly with a tremula in his voice. He began with the argument that youth has its claims and its peculiar temptations. Which of us was not once young, and which of us did not sometimes go a step too far? Even leaving aside ordinary mortals, did not history teach that the greatest minds in youth were not always able to avoid infatuations and mistakes. Take for instance the biographies of great writers. What one of them did not gamble and drink, and draw upon himself the condemnation of all right-minded men? While on the one hand we remembered that Sasha's errors had overstepped the boundary into crime, on the other we must take into account that Sasha hardly received any education; he was expelled from the gymnasium when in the fifth form; he lost his parents in early childhood, and thus at the most susceptible age was deprived of control and all beneficent influences. He was a nervous boy, easily excited, without any naturally strong

moral convictions, and he had been spoiled by happiness. Even if he were guilty, still he deserved the sympathy and concern of all sympathetic souls. Punished, of course, he must be; but then, had he not already been punished by his conscience, and the tortures which he must now be feeling as he awaited the decision of his relatives. The comparison with the Army which the Colonel had made was very flattering, and did great honour to his generous mind; the appeal to social feelings showed the nobility of his heart. But it must not be forgotten that the member of society in every individual was closely bound up with the Christian. "And how should we violate our social duty," asked Ivan Markovitch, "if instead of punishing a guilty boy we stretch out to him the hand of mercy?"

Then Ivan Markovitch reverted to the question of the family honour. He himself had not the honour to belong to the distinguished family of Uskoff, but he knew very well that that illustrious race dated its origin from the thirteenth century, and he could not forget for a moment that his beloved, unforgotten sister was the wife of a scion of the race. In one word—the Uskoff family was dear to him for many reasons, and he could not for a moment entertain the thought that for a paltry fifteen hundred roubles a shadow should be cast for ever upon the ancestral tree. And if all the argument already adduced were insufficiently convincing then he, in conclusion, asked his brothers-in-law to explain the problem: What is a crime? A crime was an immoral action, having its impulse in an evil will. So most people thought. But could we affirm that the human will was free to decide? To this important question science could give no conclusive answer. Metaphysicians maintained various divergent theories. For instance, the new school of Lombroso refused to recognize free-will, and held that every crime was the product of purely anatomical peculiarities in the individual.

"Ivan Markovitch!" interrupted the Colonel imploringly. "Do, for Heaven's sake, talk sense. We are speaking seriously about a serious matter . . . and you, about Lombroso! You are a clever man, but think for a moment—how can all this rattle-box rhetoric help us to decide the question?"

Sasha Uskoff sat outside the door and listened. He felt neither fear nor shame nor tedium—only weariness and spiritual vacuity. He felt that it did not matter a kopeck whether he was forgiven or not; he had come here to await his sentence and to offer a frank explanation, only because he was begged to do so by kindly Ivan Markovitch. He was not afraid of the future. It was all the same to him, here in the corridor, in prison, or in Siberia.

"Sibera is only Sibera—the devil take it!"

Life has wearied Sasha, and has become insufferably tedious. He is inextricably in debt, he has not a kopeck in his pocket, his relatives have become odious to him; with his friends and with women he must part sooner or later, for they are already beginning to look at him contemptuously as a parasite. The future is dark.

Sasha, in fact, is indifferent, and only one thing affects him. That is, that through the door he can hear himself being spoken of as a scoundrel and a criminal. All the time he is itching

to jump up, burst into the room, and, in answer to the destestable metallic voice of the Colonel, to cry:

"You are a liar!"

A criminal—it is a horrid word. It is applied as a rule to murderers, thieves, robbers, and people incorrigibly wicked and morally hopeless. But Sasha is far from this. . . . True, he is up to his neck in debts, and never attempts to pay them. But then indebtedness is not a crime, and there are very few men who are not in debt. The Colonel and Ivan Markovitch are both in debt.

"What on earth am I guilty of?" asked Sasha.

He had obtained money by presenting a forged bill. But this was done by every young man he knew. Khandrikoff and Von Burst, for instance, whenever they wanted money, discounted bills with forged acceptances of their parents and friends, and when their own money came in met them. Sasha did exactly the same thing, and only failed to meet his bill owing to Khandrikoff's failure to lend the money which he had promised. It was not he, but circumstance which was at fault. . . . It was true that imitating another man's signature was considered wrong, but that did not make it a crime but merely an ugly formality, a manœuvre constantly adopted which injured nobody; and Sasha when he forged the Colonel's name had no intention of causing loss to anyone.

"It is absurd to pretend that I have been guilty of a crime." thought Sasha. "I have not the character of men who commit crimes. On the contrary, I am easy-going and sensitive . . . when I have money I help the poor. . . ."

While Sasha reasoned thus, the discussion continued on the other side of the door.

"But, gentlemen, this is only the beginning!" cried the Colonel. "Suppose, for the sake of argument, that we let him off and pay the money! He will go on still in the same way and continue to lead his unprincipled life. He will indulge in dissipation, run into debt, go to our tailors and order clothes in our names. What guarantee have we that this scandal will be the last? As far as I am concerned, I tell you frankly that I do not believe in his reformation for one moment."

The official of the Crown Council muttered something in reply. Then Ivan Markovitch began to speak softly and fluently. The Colonel impatiently shifted his chair, and smothered Ivan Markovitch's argument with his detestable, metallic voice. At last the door opened, and out of the study came Ivan Markovitch with red spots on his meagre, clean-shaven face.

"Come!" he said, taking Sasha by the arm. "Come in and make an openhearted confession. Without pride, like a good boy . . . humbly and from the heart."

Sasha went into the study. The official of the Crown Council continued to sit, but the Colonel, hands in pockets, and with one knee resting on his chair, stood before the table. The room was full of smoke and stiflingly hot. Sasha did not look at either the Colonel or his brother, but suddenly feeling ashamed and hurt, glanced anxiously at Ivan Markovitch and muttered:

"I will pay . . . I will give . . ."

"May I ask you on what you relied when you obtained the money on this bill?" rang out the metallic voice.

"I . . . Khandrikoff promised to lend me the money in time."

Sasha said nothing more. He went out of the study and again sat on the chair outside the door. He would have gone away at once had he not been stifled with hatred and with a desire to tear the Colonel to pieces or at least to insult him to his face. But at this moment in the dim twilight around the dining-room appeared a woman's figure. It was the Colonel's wife. She beckoned Sasha, and, wringing her hands, said with tears in her voice:

"*Alexandre,* I know that you do not love me, but . . listen for a moment! My poor boy, how can this have happened? It is awful, awful! For Heaven's sake beg their forgiveness . . justify yourself, implore them!"

Sasha looked at her twitching shoulders, and at the big tears which flowed down her cheeks; he heard behind him the dull, nervous voices of his exhausted uncles, and shrugged his shoulders. He had never expected that his aristocratic relatives would raise such a storm over a paltry fifteen hundred roubles. And he could understand neither the tears nor the trembling voices.

An hour later he heard indications that the Colonel was gaining the day. The other uncles were being won over to his determination to leave the matter to the law.

"It is decided!" said the Colonel stiffly. "*Basta!*"

But having decided thus, the three uncles, even the inexorable Colonel, perceptibly lost heart.

"Heavens!" sighed Ivan Markovitch. "My poor sister!"

And he began in a soft voice to

announce his conviction that his sister, Sasha's mother, was invisibly present in the room. He felt in his heart that this unhappy, sainted woman was weeping, anguishing, interceding for her boy. For the sake of her repose in the other world it would have been better to spare Sasha.

Sasha heard someone whimpering. It was Ivan Markovitch. He wept and muttered something inaudible through the door. The Colonel rose and walked from corner to corner. The discussion began anew. . . .

The clock in the drawing-room struck two. The council was over at last. The Colonel, to avoid meeting a man who had caused him so much shame, left the room through the antechamber. Ivan Markovitch came into the corridor. He was plainly agitated, but rubbed his hands cheerfully. His tear-stained eyes glanced happily around him, and his mouth was twisted into a smile.

"It is all right, my boy!" he said to Sasha. "Heaven be praised! You may go home, child, and sleep quietly. We have decided to pay the money, but only on the condition that you repent sincerely, and agree to come with me to the country to-morrow, and set to work."

A minute afterwards, Ivan Markovitch and Sasha, having put on their overcoats and hats, went down-stairs together. Uncle Ivan muttered something edifying. But Sasha didn't listen; he felt only that something heavy and painful had fallen from his shoulders. He was forgiven—he was free! Joy like a breeze burst into his breast and wrapped his heart with refreshing coolness. He wished to breathe, to move, to live. And looking at the street lamps and at the black sky he remembered that to-day at "The Bear," Von Burst would celebrate his name-day. A new joy seized his soul.

"I will go!" he decided.

But suddenly he remembered that he had not a kopeck, and that his friends already despised him for his penuriousness. He must get money at all cost.

"Uncle, lend me a hundred roubles!" he said to Ivan Markovitch.

Ivan Markovitch looked at him in amazement, and staggered back against a lamp-post."

"Lend me a hundred roubles!" cried Sasha, impatiently shifting from foot to foot, and beginning to lose his temper. "Uncle, I beg of you . . . lend me a hundred roubles!"

His face trembled with excitement. and he nearly rushed at his uncle.

"You won't give them?" he cried, seeing that his uncle was too dumfounded to understand. "Listen, if you refuse to lend them, I'll inform on myself to-morrow. I'll refuse to let you pay the money. I'll forge another to-morrow!"

Thunderstruck, terror-stricken, Ivan Markovitch muttered something incoherent, took from his pocket a hundred-rouble note, and handed it silently to Sasha. And Sasha took it and hurriedly walked away.

And sitting in a droschky, Sasha grew cool again, and felt his heart expand with renewed joy. The claims of youth of which kind-hearted uncle Ivan had spoken at the council-table had inspired and taken possession of him again. He painted in imagination the coming feast, and in his mind, among visions of bottles, women, and boon companions, twinkled a little thought:

"Now I begin to see that I was in the wrong."

Woe

GRIGORI PETROFF, long reputed the cleverest turner and most shiftless muzhik in all Galtchink canton, drove to Zemstvo hospital with his old spouse. It was a good thirty versts, on a road too bad for a driver of experience, much more for lazy Grigori. In the turner's face beat a sharp, icy wind, and it was hard to say whether the snow came from heaven or from earth. Fields, telegraph posts, trees and even the horses were scarcely seen. The mare was worn out and dragged its hoofs out of the deep snow, shaking its head. The turner was in a hurry, and whipped her up.

"Don't cry, Matrena!" he stammered. "Bear it a little longer! We'll soon, God grant, be at the hospital, and then you'll . . . Pavl Ivanuitch'll give you a powder, or let your blood; perhaps he'll rub some sort of spirit into you. Pavl Ivanuitch will do his best. . . . He'll shout, and stamp his feet, but he'll do his best. . . . He's a first-rate doctor, he knows his business, may God be good to him! . . . The minute we arrive he'll run out of his lodgings and look at you. 'What!' he'll shout at me. 'Why didn't you come before? Do you think I am a dog to waste all day with you devils? Why didn't you come in the morning? Begone! Come back to-morrow!' And I will answer, 'Mister doctor! Pavl Ivanuitch! Your honour! . . .'"

The turner whipped his horse, and without looking at his old woman, continued to mutter—

" 'Your honour! Truly before God! . . . on my oath, I started at daybreak.

. . . How could I get here sooner when God . . . the Mother of God was angry and sent such a storm? You can see for yourself! Even with a good horse I couldn't get here in time, and, as you can see for yourself, mine is not a horse, but a disgrace!' And Pavl Inanuitch will frown and shout, 'I know you! Always the same excuse! You, in particular, Grisha! I've known you for years. You stopped five times at a drink-shop!' And I shall answer him, 'Your honour! Don't think me a ruffian! My old woman is giving her soul to God; she's dying! Do you think I'd go near a drink-shop? May they be cursed, these drink-shops!' Then Pavl Ivanuitch will tell them to take you into the hospital. And I shall bow to the ground. 'Pavl Ivanuitch! Your honour! I thank you humbly! Forgive us fools, anathemas; don't condemn us, poor muzhiks! You ought to kick us out of the hall! Yet you come out to meet us, and wet your legs in the snow!'

"And Pavl Ivanuitch will look as if he wanted to hit me, and say, 'Don't throw yourself at my feet, fool! You'd do better to drink less vodka and have pity on your wife. You ought to be flogged!' 'That's God's truth, Pavl Ivanuitch, may I be flogged; may God flog me! But why not throw myself at your feet? You are our benefactor, our own father! Your honour! It is the truth, before God; spit in my face if I lie: as soon as my Matrena, this same Matrena. gets well, I will make anything your honour wants. A cigarcase, if you wish it, of yellow birch . . .

a set of croquet balls, nine-pins—I can make them like the best foreign ones. . . . I will make them all for you. I won't charge a kopeck. In Moscow such cigar-cases cost four roubles. I won't take a kopeck.' And the doctor will laugh and say to me, 'Well, well . . . agreed! I'm sorry for you. Only it's a pity you're such a drunkard!' I know how to manage with these gentlemen! There's no man on earth I can't stand up to. Only may God keep us from losing the road! *Akh,* my eyes are full of snow."

And the turner muttered without cease. As if to dull the pain of his own feelings, he babbled on mechanically. But many as the words on his lips, there were still more thoughts and problems in his head. Woe had come upon the turner suddenly, unexpectedly; and now he could not recover his self-possession. Till now he had lived peacefully in drunken apathy, insensible to sorrow and to joy; and now he had been struck an intolerable blow. The shiftless, drunken lie-abed suddenly found himself busy, tormented, and, it seemed, in conflict with Nature herself.

The turner remembered that his sorrows began only yesterday. When, drunk as usual, he had returned to his home the night before, and, by virtue of old custom, abused his wife and shook his fists at her, the old woman looked at him as she had never looked before. Formerly her old eyes expressed martyrdom, and the affection of a much-beaten, badly-fed dog; this night she looked at him morosely, steadfastly, as only saints and dying women look. With these unaccustomed eyes, all the trouble began. The frightened turner borrowed a neigh-bour's horse, and was driving the old woman to hospital in the hope that Pavl Ivanuitch with powders and ointments would restore to his wife her old expression.

"And listen, Matrena," he stammered. "If Pavl Ivanuitch asks do I ever beat you, say no, never! For I will never beat you again! I swear it. I never did beat you out of anger. I beat you only casually! I am sorry for you now. Another man would pay no attention to you, but I take you to hospital. . . I do my best. But the storm, the storm, Lord God, Thy will! May God keep us from losing the road! Does your side hurt? Matrena, why don't you answer? I ask, does your side hurt?

"Why is it the snow doesn't melt on her face?" he asked himself, feeling a cold wind on his back and frozen legs. "My snow thaws, but hers. . . . It's strange!"

He could not understand why the snow on his wife's face did not thaw, why her face was drawn-out, severe, and serious, and had turned the colour of dirty wax.

"You are a fool!" muttered the turner. "I spoke to you from my conscience, before God!. . . . and you haven't the manners to answer. . . . Fool! If you're not more careful, I won't take you to Pavl Ivanuitch!"

The turner dropped the reins, and thought. He could not make up his mind to look at his wife. He was nervous; and soon his wife's unmannerly silence frightened him. At last, to end his uncertainty, without looking at his wife, he felt her icy hand. The unlifted hand fell, as a whip.

"She's dead, I suppose. An adventure!"

And the turner wept. He wept less from grief than vexation. He reflected how quickly everything happens in this world; how he had hardly entered into his woe ere the woe was past. He hardly seemed to have had time to live with his wife, speak to her, feel for her, and now she was dead. True, they had lived together forty years, but the forty years had fled away like a mist. What with drink, poverty, and quarrels, life had passed away unlived. And, what was bitterest of all, the old woman died at a moment when he felt that he pitied her, could not live without her, and was guilty before her.

"And she even went out and begged," he remembered. "I sent her myself to beg bread. An adventure! She ought to have lived another ten years. She thought, I suppose, that I'm really a bad lot. Mother in heaven, where am I driving to? It's no more a case of cure, but of funerals. Turn back."

The turned turned back and flogged his horse with all his might. The road grew worse and worse. He could no longer see even the yoke. Sometimes the sledge drove into fir-trees, sometimes something dark scratched the turner's hands and flashed past his eyes. But he saw nothing except a whirling field of white.

"To live over again!" he said to himself. He remembered that forty years ago Matrena was young, pretty, and gay, and that she came from a prosperous home. It was his reputation as craftsman that won her. And, indeed, he had every qualification for living well. But soon after marriage he began to drink, he sprawled all day on the stove, and, it seemed to him, he slept ever since. He remembered his wedding-day. but of

what followed he could recall nothing save that he drank, sprawled, fought. And so passed forty years.

The white snow-clouds turned slowly grey. Evening was near.

"Where am I going? asked the turner. "I ought to be taking her home, and here I am still going to hospital! I am going crazy!"

The turner again pulled round his horse and again flogged it. The mare strained all her strength, snorted. and broke into a trot. Behind the turner something tapped, tapped, tapped; and though he dared not look around, he knew that it was his wife's head banging against the back of the sledge. As the air darkened the wind blew colder and sharper.

"To live over again!" thought the turner. "To get new tools, to take orders, to give money to the old woman. . . . Yes!"

He dropped the reins. A moment later he tried to find them, but failed. His hands no longer obeyed him.

"It is all the same," he thought. "She will go on herself. She knows the road. To sleep a bit now. . . . Then the funeral, a mass. . . ."

He closed his eyes and slumbered. A moment later, as it seemed to him, the horse stopped. He opened his eyes and saw before something dark, a cabin or hay rick.

He tried to get out of the seldge to find out where he was, but his body was numbed with such pleasant indolence that he felt he would sooner freeze than move. And he fell restfully asleep.

He awoke in a big room with red walls. Through the window came bright sun-rays. The turner saw men before him, and he obeyed his first instinct to show himself off as a serious man, a man with ideas.

"Have a mass served, brothers!" he begun. "Tell the priest . . ."

"That is all right!" came back voices. "Lie down!"

"*Batiushka!* Pavl Ivanuitch!" said the turner in amazement. He saw the doctor before him. "Your honour! Benefactor!"

He wished to jump up and throw himself at the doctor's feet. But his hands and feet no longer obeyed him.

"Your honour, where are my legs? Where are my hands?"

"Good-bye to your legs and hands! They're frozen off, that's all. Well, well . . . there's no use crying. You are old . . . glory be to God . . . sixty years' life is enough!"

"Forgive me, your honour! If you could give me five or six years!"

"Why do you want them?"

"The horse isn't mine. I must return it! . . . The old woman must be buried. . . . *Akh*, how quickly things happen in this world! Your honour! Pavl Ivanuitch! A cigar-case of birchwood of the first quality? I will make you croquet-balls . . ."

The doctor waved his hand and went out of the room.

The turner was dead.

Women

In the village of Riabuzhka, opposite the church, stands a house with stone foundations, an iron roof two stories high. In the lower story, with the owner, Philip Ivanoff Kamin, nicknamed "Diudya" keeps his family overhead, in rooms hot in summer and cold in winter, lodge passing officials, merchants, and country gentlemen. Diudya rents land, sells a drink of tar honey and magpies; and is worth a good eight thousand roubles as bank records could show.

Feodor, his elder son, is foreman mechanic at a factory; and, as the peasants say, he is so far up the hill that you can't get near him. Homely and sickly Sophia, Feodor's wife, lives at home with her father-in-law, cries half the day, and every Sunday drives to hospital for treatment. Hunchbacked Aliosha, Diudya's second son, also lives at home. He lately married Varvara, who is young, pretty, healthy, poor and fond of dress. The passing officials and traders let no one serve them in room or shop but Varvara.

One evening in July as the sun set, and the air reeked of hay, hot manure, and new milk, into Diudya's yard came a cart with three men. One, aged about thirty, wore a canvas suit; the boy of seven or eight beside him wore a long black coat with big buttons; the third, a young lad in a red shirt, was the driver.

The driver unhitched the horses and walked them up and down the street; and the man of thirty washed, prayed towards the church, and spreading a fur rug beside the cart, sat down with the boy to supper. He ate slowly and gravely; and Diudya, who had studied many a traveller in his day, found him a capable, serious man, who knew his own worth.

Diudya, capless, and in shirt-sleeves, sat on the steps and waited for the traveller to speak. His patrons usually spent the evening story-telling, and their stories gave him pleasure. His old wife Afanasievna and his daughter-in-law Sophia milked cows in a shed; Varvara, wife of his younger son, sat upstairs at an open window and ate sunflower seeds.

"I suppose this boy is your son?" asked Diudya.

"My adopted son," answered the traveller. "I took him, orphan, for the saving of my soul."

The pair soon gossiped at ease. The traveller seemed a takative, eloquent man; and Diudya learned that he was a petty burgher from town, a house-owner, by name Matvei Savvitch, that he was on his way to inspect some gardens which he rented from German colonists, and that the boy's name was Kuzka. It was hot and stifling; no one wished to sleep. When it grew dark, and the sky was dotted with pale stars, Matvei Savvitch began to tell the story of Kuzka. Afanasievna and Sophia stood some way off, and Kuzka loitered at the gate.

"I may say, grandfather, that this story is involved in the extreme," began Matvei Savvitch. "If I were to tell you everything that happened it would last all night. Well! About ten years ago in our street, exactly in a line with us, where now stands the candle factory and oil mill, lived Marya Semionovna Kapluntseff, an old widow with two sons. One of these sons was a tram-conductor; the other, Vasya, a lad of my own age, lived at home with his mother. Old Kapluntseff had kept horses—five pairs of them—and sent his draymen all over town; and his widow continued the business, and, as she managed the draymen no worse than her husband, on some days she made a clear five roubles profit.

"And Vasya, too, had his earnings. He kept prize tumblers and sold them to fanciers; I remember him standing on the roof, throwing up a broom and whistling. and the pigeons would fly right into the sky. He trapped goldfinches and starlings, and made good cages. A trifling business, you think, but you can easily make your ten roubles a month out of trifles. Well . . as time passed the old woman lost the use of her legs, and lay all day in bed. The house remained without mistress, and what is that but a man without eyes? The old woman resolved to marry her Vasya. She hired a match-maker, did everything quickly . . . woman's talk . . . and Vasya went to have a look at his bride. She was the widow Samokvalika's Mashenka. Vasya didn't waste time over it; in one week the whole business was finished. She was a young girl, little, shortish, with a white, pleasant face—all the qualities of a young lady; and a portion too, not bad—five hundred roubles, a cow, a bed! And the old woman—she felt it coming—two days after the wedding set out for Jerusalem of the hills, where there is neither sickness nor sighs. The young ones said mass for her soul and began to live. Six months they lived together happily; and then, suddenly, a new misfortune! Vasya was summoned to draw lots as a conscript. They took him, poor fellow, as a soldier, and remitted nothing. They shaved his head, and packed him off to the kingdom of Poland. It was God's will, and there was no appeal. When he said good-bye to his wife in the yard

he was cool enough, but, looking upwards at the hayloft with the pigeons, he
cried as if his heart would break. It
hurt me to see him. For company's sake
Mashenka took her mother to live with
her; and the mother stayed till child was
born, that is, this same Kuzka; and then
went away to another married daughter
who lived at Oboyan. So Mashenka was
left with her child. And there were five
draymen, all drunken and impudent;
horses and carts; broken fences and soot
catching fire in the chimneys—no affair
at all for a woman. And as I was a
neighbour, she would come to me on all
sorts of business; and I did my best for
her, arranged more than one affair, gave
her advice. And sometimes I would go
to her house, have a drink, and a bit
of a chat. I was a young man, clever,
and I loved to talk about things; and
she, too, was educated and had good
manners. She dressed neatly and carried
a parasol in summer. I remember; I
would start upon theology or politics,
and she felt flattered by this, and would
treat me to tea and jam. . . In short,
grandfather, I will waste no more words
on it, a year had not passed when the
unclean spirit seized me, the enemy of
all mankind! I noticed that when a day
passed without meeting Mashenka I
felt out of sorts, and was bored. And
all my time was spent in finding excuses
to call on her. 'It's time,' I'd say to
myself, 'to put in the double window-
frames'; and I would spend the whole
day in her house putting in the frames,
and carefully leaving the work unfinished, so as to return next day. 'We
ought to count Vasya's pigeons, and
make sure none are lost.' And so on
always. I spent hours talking to her
across the fence; and at last, to avoid

going round to the door, I made a little
gate in the fence. Woman's sex is the
cause of much evil and offence in this
world! Not only we, sinners, but even
holy men are seduced. Mashenka did
not repulse me. When she ought to
have thought of her husband, and kept
guard on her conduct, she fell in love
with me. I noticed soon that she also
was tired of it, and that she spent all
day walking along the fence and looking
through the crevices into my yard.

"My head whirled round. On Thursday in Holy Week I was up early, before
daybreak; I had to go to market. I
had to pass the gate; and the devil
was there! The grating of the gate was
raised, and there stood Mashenka in the
middle of the yard, already up, and
busy feeding the ducks. I lost control
of myself. I called her by name. She
came up and looked at me through the
grating. Her face was white, her eyes
were sleepy and caressing. I liked her
very much! And I began to pay her
compliments as if we were not at the
gate, but as if it were a birthday visit.
And Mashenka blushed, laughed, and
looked at me with the same eyes, never
taking them off me. I went quite mad,
and told her straight that I loved her.
She opened the gate, let me in, and
from that day forward we lived as man
and wife."

Matvei paused. Into the yard, breathless, came hunchback Aliosha, and,
without looking at the group, ran into
the house; a minute later he rushed out
with a concertina, and jingling the cop-
pers in his pocket and chewing a sunflower seed, disappeared behind the gate.

"Who is that man?" asked Matvei
Savvitch.

"My son Alexei," answered Diudya.

"He's gone off to amuse himself, rascal! God cursed him with a hump, so we're not hard on him!"

"He does nothing but play with the children," sighed Afansievna. "Before Shrovetide we married him, and thought he'd improve, but he's got worse than ever."

"It was no use," said Diudya. "We only made a strange girl happy, without profit."

From behind the church came the sound of a mournful but pleasant song. The words were indistinguishable, but the voices, two tenors and a bass, could easily be made out. All listened. Suddenly two of the singers, with a loud laugh, ceased to sing, but the third, the tenor, continued, and sang so high that all mechanically looked upward as if they thought the voice had reached the sky. Varvara came out of the house, and, shading her eyes with her hand as if the sun dazzled her, looked at the church.

"It's the priest's sons and the schoolmaster," she said. Again all three voices sang together. Matvei Savvitch sighed and continued:—

"So it happened, grandfather! . . . Well, in two years a letter came from Vasya. He wrote from Warsaw and told us that he had been discharged for ill-health. He was invalided. But by that time I had driven my madness out of my head, and, what's more, I was thinking of making a good match, and was only waiting an excuse to get rid of my lovebird Every day I resolved to speak to Mashenka, but I never knew how to begin, and I can't abide a woman's howl. The letter gave me my chance. As Mashenka read it aloud to me she turned white as snow, and I said

to her, 'Glory be to God,' I said. 'Thou wilt again be an honest woman.' She answered. 'I never loved him, and I married him against my will. My mother forced me to.' But that doesn't get round the question, fool,' I said. 'Were you married to him in church or not?' 'I was married in church,' she answered me, 'but I love only thee, and I will be thy wife till thy very death. Let people jeer at me! I care nothing for them!' 'You are a believing woman,' I said to her. 'You read the Bible; what is there written there?'"

"Once given to her husband with her husband she must live," said Diudya.

"Husband and wife are of one flesh and blood," resumed Matvei Savvitch. "'Thou and I have sinned,' I said. 'We must listen to our consciences and have the fear of God. We will ask forgiveness of Vasya. He is a peaceful, timid man—he won't murder you. But better,' I added, 'far better in this world to tolerate torture from thy lawful husband than gnash thy teeth when the Day of Judgment is nigh!' The silly wouldn't listen to me. Not a word would she say but 'I love thee!' and nothing more. Vasya came home on the Saturday before Trinity early in the morning. I watched the whole business through the fence. In ran Vasya into the house, and a minute later out he came with Kuzka in his arms, laughing and crying at the same time. He kissed Kuzka and looked up at the hayloft; he wanted to go to his pigeons, but he wouldn't let hold of Kuzka. He was a soft sort of man— sentimental! The day passed quietly enough. They rang the bells for the vesper service, and I kept thinking to myself, 'Why don't they decorate the gates and the yard with birches? Something is wrong,' I thought. I went into their house and looked. Vasya sat on the floor in the middle of the room, twitching his eyes as if in drink; the tears flowed down his cheeks, his hands shook; he took out of his handkerchief cracknels, necklaces, gingerbread—all sorts of gifts—and threw them on the floor. Kuzka—he was then aged three—crept on the floor and chewed the gingerbreads; and Mashenka stood by the stove, pale and trembling, and muttered, 'I am not thy wife; I will not live with thee,' and a lot more nonsense of that kind. I threw myself on the boards at Vasya's feet and said, 'We two are guilty before thee, Vassili Maksimuitch; forgive us for the love of Christ!' and then I rose and said to Mashenka, 'It is your duty, Marya Semionovna, to wash Vassili Maksimuitch's feet, and be to him an obedient wife, and pray for me to God that He, the All-Merciful, may forgive me my sin.' I was inspired by a heavenly angel! I spoke edification; spoke with such feeling that I began to cry. And two days later up to me comes Vasya. 'I forgive you,' says he; 'I forgive you, Matiusha, and I forgive my wife; God be with you both. She is a soldier's wife after all, and women are queer things; she is young, it was hard for her to guard herself. She is not the first, and she will not be the last. There is only one thing,' he added. 'I beg you henceforth to live as if there was nothing between us; let nothing be seen. and I,' he says, 'will try to please her in everything so that she may love me again.' He gave me his hand on it, drank some tea, and went away contented. 'Glory be to God!' I said to myself; and I felt happy that all had been settled so well. But hardly

had Vasya got outside the yard when Mashenka appears. I had no peace, you see! She hung on my neck, howled, and implored me 'For the love of God do not forsake me! I cannot live without thee! I cannot, I cannot!' "

"The shameless trull!" sighed Diudya.

"But I bawled at her, stamped my feet, dragged her into the hall, and locked the door. 'Go back!' I shouted, 'to thy husband. Do not shame me before the people! Have the fear of God in thy heart.' And every day this history was repeated. I stood one morning in the yard near the stable and mended a bridle. Suddenly up I looked, and saw her running through the gate, bare-footed, with nothing on but a petticoat. Straight up to me she ran, seized the bridle, and got covered with tar, and trembling all over, howled, ' I cannot live with that brute! It is beyond my strength. If thou no longer lovest me, then kill me!' It was too much for my patience. I struck her twice with the bridle. But at that moment in runs Vasya and cries despairingly, 'Don't strike her, don't strike her.' But he himself seemed to have gone out of his mind, for, flourishing his arms, he began to beat her with his clenched fists with all his might, then flung her down in the dust, and trampled her into it. I tried to defend her, but he seized hold of the reins, and beat her without mercy. Beat her as he'd beat a horse, gee, gee, gee!"

"A good thing if they did it to you," growled Varvara, walking away. "You murdered our sister between you, accursed!"

"Hold your tongue!" shouted Diudya. "Mare!"

"Gee, gee, gee!" continued Matvei

Savvitch. "One of the draymen ran in from his yard; I called up some of my workmen, and between us we rescued Mashenka and carried her home. It was a shame! She lay there in bed, all bandaged, all in compresses—only her eyes and nose could be seen—and looked up at the ceiling.

" 'Good day, Marya Semionovna,' I would say to her. But she spoke not a word.

"And Vasya sat in another room, tore his hair, and cried, 'I am a ruffian! I have murdered my wife! Send me in Thy mercy, Lord, death.'

"I sat half an hour with Mashenka, and spoke edification. I frightened her.

" 'The righteous,' I said. 'The righteous of this world are rewarded in Paradise, but thy place is fiery Gehenna with all adulteresses . . . . Do not dare resist thy husband, go down on thy knees to him!' But she hadn't a word for me; even her eyes were still; I might as well have preached to a pillar.

"A day later Vasya was taken ill—something, it was, like cholera; and that same evening I heard he was dead. They buried him. Mashenka was not at the funeral; she wouldn't let people see her shameless face and her blue marks. But soon they began to say in town that Vasya's death was not natural, that he was murdered by Mashenka. The police soon heard it. They dug up Vasya, cut him open, and found his stomach full of arsenic. It was a simple case. Of course, the police took away Mashenka, and with her innocent Kuzka. They put her in gaol. . . . About eight months later she was tried. She sat, I remember, in the dock in a grey gown with a white handkerchief on her head—thin, pale, sharp-eyed, the picture of misery. And behind her a soldier with a rifle! Of course she denied it. Some said she'd poisoned her husband; others argued that he had poisoned himself from grief. Anyway, I was a witness. When they questioned me I told them the honest truth. 'She was a sinful woman,' I told them. 'She did not love her husband—it's no use hiding it. She was an obstinate woman. . . .' The trial began in the morning and didn't end till night. It was penal servitude in Sibera, thirteen years of it.

"Mashenka remained in our local gaol three months after trial. I used to go and see her. I was sorry for her, and would bring her tea and sugar. . . . And she—I remember—when she caught sight of me, would wring her hands, and mutter, 'Go away! Go away.' And Kuzka would press himself to her dress, as if he feared I might take him. 'Look!' I would say to Mashenka. 'See what you've brought yourself to! *Akh,* Masha, Masha, perishing soul! When I tried to teach you reason, you wouldn't listen; so weep now! It is you yourself,' I would say, 'who are guilty; accuse yourself!' And I spoke edification to her; but the only words she answered were, 'Go away! Go away!' Then she'd press little Kuzka to the wall, and tremble all over. Well! When she was taken out of our province, I went to see her off at the railway station, and put into her hand a rouble, for Christ's sake. She didn't reach Sibera. Before she had crossed the government frontier she was down with gaol-fever, and in gaol she died."

"To a dog a dog's death!" said Diuyda.

"Kuzka was sent back. I thought the

matter out, and took him to live with me. What else could I do? He's a sprig of a gaol-bird, that's true, but all the same he's a Christian, a living soul. I was sorry for him. I will make him a clerk, and if I have no children of mine, a trader. Nowadays, wherever I go I take him with me; he is learning business."

While Matvei Savvitch told his story, Kuzka sat on a stone at the gate, and, resting his head on his hands, looked at the sky; when it grew dusk he looked like a stump of a tree.

"Kuzka, go to bed!" cried Matvei Savvitch.

"It's time," said Diudya, rising. He yawned audibly, and added, "They think themselves clever and disobey their elders—that's the cause of their troubles."

The moon already shone in the sky overhead; it seemed to speed swiftly to one side and the clouds beneath it to the other; the clouds drifted away and the moon was soon clear of them. Matvei Savvitch prayed towards the church, bade the others good night, and lay on the ground near his cart. Kuzka also prayed, lay down in the cart, and covered himself with a coat; to increase his comfort he made a hollow in the hay, and bent in two until his elbows touched his knees. From the yard could be seen Diudya, lighting a candle in the lower story; after which he took his spectacles, stood in the corner with a book, bowed before the ikon, and read.

The travellers slept. Afanasievna and Sophia crept up to the cart, and looked at Kuzka.

"The orphan's asleep," said the old woman. "All skin and bone, poor lad!

No mother on earth, and no one to feed him on his journey."

"My Grishutka, I think, is about two years older," said Sophia. "He lives in that factory like a slave, and has no mother either. . . . His master beats him. When I first looked at this lad he reminded me of my Grishutka; the blood in my heart froze up."

Five minutes passed in silence.

"I wonder does he remember his mother," said the old woman.

"How should he remember?"

And from Sophia's eyes fell big tears.

"He's twisted himself into a roll," she said, sobbing and laughing from pity and emotion. "Poor little orphan!"

Kuzka started and opened his eyes. He saw above him an ugly, wrinkled, tear-stained face; and near it another face, old and toothless, with a sharp chin and a humped nose; and above the faces was the unfathomable sky with its flying clouds and moon. He cried out with terror. Sophia also cried out; an echo answered both; and the heavy air seemed to tremble with restlessness. A watchman not far off signalled: a dog barked. Matvei Savvitch muttered in his sleep, and turned on the other side.

Late at night when the others—Diudya, his wife, and the watchman—were asleep, Sophia came out to the gate and sat on a bench. The heat was still stifling, and her head ached from crying. The street was wide and long; it stretched two versts to the right, and two more to the left—there was no end to it. One side only was lighted by the moon; the other lay in deep gloom; the long shadows from poplars and starling-cotes stretched across it, and the black and menacing shadow of the church spread far, embracing Diudya's gate and half his house. No one moved or spoke. But from the end of the street came faint sounds of music. Aliosha played on his concertina.

Something moved in the shadow of the church fence; but no one could say whether it was man or cow, or neither— perhaps the sound came from some big bird rustling in the trees. But suddenly out of this shadow came a figure, and this figure stopped, said something in a man's voice, and disappeared down a lane near the church. A minute later, two fathoms from the gate emerged a woman, who, seeing Sophia on the bench, stood still.

"Varvara, is it you?" asked Sophia.

"I."

It was Varvara. She stood still a moment longer, then came up to the bench and sat down.

"Where have you been" asked Sophia.

Varvara was silent.

"You will bring the same end on yourself, young one," said Sophia. "You heard about Mashenka, and the trampling underfoot . . . and the reins. Take care that something of that sort doesn't happen to you."

"I don't care if it does."

Varvara laughed in her handkerchief, and said in a whisper—

"I have been with the priest's son."

"Nonsense?"

"I swear."

"It's a sin!" whispered Sophia.

"I don't care. It's nothing to regret. A sin is a sin, and better the lightning strike me than lead such a life. I am young . . . and healthy, and my husband is a hunchback, miserable, surly, worse than Diudya accursed! Before I was married I had not enough to eat and walked barefoot; but for the sake of Aliosha's money I became a slave, like a fish in a net, and I would sooner sleep with a serpent than with this scabby Aliosha. And your life? Can you bear it? Your Feodor sent you home to his father from the factory, and lives there with another woman; he took your boy away from you and sold you into slavery. You work like a horse, and never hear a decent word. Better never marry, better take half-roubles from the son of the priest, better beg for bread. drown yourself in a well . . ."

"It's a sin!" sighed Sophia.

"I don't care."

From the church again came the mournful song of the three voices, the two tenors and the bass. And again the words were indistinguishable.

And Varvara began to whisper that she went out at night with the priest's son, and told what he said to her, and what his friends were like; and that she carried on also with passing officials and traders. And Sophia began to laugh; she felt it was sinful and awful and sweet to listen; and she envied Varvara, and felt sorry that she had not been a sinner when she was young and handsome.

The church bells struck midnight.

"It's time for bed," said Sophia, rising. "Diudya may catch us."

Both went cautiously into the yard.

"I went away and didn't hear what happened to Mashenka afterwards," said Varvara, spreading her bed under the window.

"She died, he said, in prison. She poisoned her husband."

Varvara lay down beside Sophia, thought, and said softly—

"I could murder my Aliosha without a qualm."

"You talk nonsense, God be with you."

When Sophia was almost asleep Varvara pressed against her and whispered in her ear—

"Let us murder Diudya and Aliosha!"

Sophia shuddered and said nothing at first. After a moment she opened her eyes and looked steadfastly at the sky.

"People would find out," she said.

"Nobody'll find out. Diudya is old; his time, in any case, has come; and Aliosha, they'll say, killed himself with drink."

Neither of the women slept. Both thought, silently.

"It's cold," said Sophia, beginning to shudder. "I expect it will soon be light, Are you asleep?"

"No. . . . Pay no attention to what I said to you," whispered Varvara. "I lose my temper with them, accursed, and sometimes don't myself know what I say. . . . Go to sleep!"

The two women were silent, and gradually calmed down and went to sleep.

Old Afanasievna awoke first of all. She called Sophia, and both went to the shed to milk the cows. Next appeared hunchback Aliosha, hopelessly drunk, and without his concertina. His chest and knees were covered with dust and straw; it was plain he had fallen on the road. Rolling tipsily from side to side, he went into the shed and, without undressing, threw himself on a sledge and at once began to snore. When the rising sun burnt with a fierce glow the crosses on the church, when later the windows imaged it, when across the yard through the dewy grass stretched shadows from the trees, only then did Matvei Savvitch rise and begin to bustle about.

"Kuzka, get up!" he shouted. "It's time to yoke the horses. Look sharp!"

The morning's work began. A young Jewess in a brown, flounced dress led a horse to water. The windlass creaked plaintively, the bucket rattled. Kuzka, sleepy, unrested, covered with dew, sat on the cart and drew on his coat lazily and, listening to the water splashing in the well, shuddered from the cold.

"Auntie!" cried Matvei Savvitch. "Sing out to my lad to come and yoke the horses!"

And at the same minute Diudya called out of the window—

"Sophia, make the Jewess pay a kopeck for the water. They take it always, the scabbies!"

Up and down the street ran bleating sheep; women bawled at the shepherd; and the shepherd played his reed, flourished his whip, and answered in a rough, hoarse bass. Three sheep ran into the yard and crowded together at the fence. The noise awoke Varvara, who took her bed in her arms and went towards the house.

"You might at least drive out the sheep!" cried the old woman. "My fine lady!"

"What more? You think I'll work for a pack of Herods like you," growled Varvara, entering the house.

The axles were soon oiled and the horses harnessed. From the house came Diudya with an abacus, and sitting on the steps, made up his account against the travellers for lodging, oats, and water.

"You charge high, grandfather, for the oats," said Matvei Savvitch.

"If they're too dear, don't take them. We won't force you to."

When the travellers were ready to

climb into the cart an accident delayed them. Kuzka had lost his cap.

"What have you done with it, swine?" bawled Matvei Savvitch angrily. "Where is it gone to?"

Kuzka's face was contorted with terror. He searched about the cart and, finding no cap there, went to the gates. The old woman and Sophia also searched.

"I'll cut off your ears," roared Matvei Savvitch. "Accursed pup!"

The cap was found at the bottom of the cart. Kuzka brushed the hay from it, put it on timidly as if he expected a blow from behind, and took his seat. Matvei Savvitch crossed himself, the driver pulled the reins, and the cart rolled slowly out of the yard.

A Husk

IN a shed belonging to the Starost, Procofi, on the outskirts of the village of Mironocitsk, some belated sportsmen had disposed themselves to spend the night. There were two, the veterinary-surgeon, Ivan Ivanitch, and the schoolmaster, Burkin. Ivan Ivanitch bore a somewhat strange family name— Tchimsha Himalayski—which seemed in no wise to fit him; so in the whole district he was simply known by his name and patronymic. He lived near the town on a stud-farm, and had come to do a little shooting so as to get a breath of fresh air. The schoolmaster, Burkin, spent every summer on the property of Count N——, and for some time had felt quite at home there.

They were not yet asleep. Ivan Ivanitch, a tall, spare old man, with long moustaches, was sitting in the moonlight outside the door, smoking his pipe. Burkin was lying inside on the hay, and could not be seen in the darkness.

They were telling each other stories. Among other things, they spoke about the Starost's wife, Mavra, a healthy and not stupid woman, who in all her life had never been outside her native village, had never seen any town nor railway, and for the last ten years had sat by her stove all day, and taken her walks abroad at nights.

"There is nothing wonderful in that," said Burkin. "People who are solitary by nature, who, like the anchorite crab or snail, seek to retire into their shell, are not so scarce in this world. It may be a manifestation of atavism, a return to that epoch when the predecessors of man were not yet gregarious animals, but lived alone in their holes; and it may also be simply one of the human character's diversities—who knows? I am not a naturalist, and it is not my concern to solve such questions. I only wish to say that people like Mavra are not of such rare occurrence. Why, not to seek further, two months ago a teacher of Greek, a friend of mine, a certain Bielikov, died in our town. You must assuredly have heard of him? His peculiarity was, that even in the very finest weather he would go out in galoshes, carry an umbrella, and wear a wadded coat. His umbrella was always in its sheath, his watch always in a chamois-leather case, and when he pulled out his pocket-knife to sharpen a pencil, that also was in its little case. He wore black eye-glasses, a waist-coat, stuffed cotton wool in his ears, and when he got into a cab he had the hood put up. In fact, one noticed in this individual a fixed and irresistible longing to withdraw into a cover, to make, as it were, a husk around himself, which would isolate him and protect him from outside influences. Actuality annoyed him, alarmed him, kept him in a constant state of suspense, and it may have been to justify this timidity of his, this repugnance to the present, that he always lauded the past and things which had never existed; and the dead tongues which he taught were, in reality, those same galoshes and umbrella behind which he sought protection in actual life.

" 'Oh, how sonorous, how beautiful is the Greek language!' he exclaimed, with a fond expression, and as a proof of his assertion he blinked his eyes, raised a finger, and pronounced the word: 'Anthropos!'

"Bielikov strove, too, to wrap up his thoughts in a sheath. For him the only clear things were circulars and newspaper articles in which something was forbidden. When a circular was published forbidding teachers to be out in the streets after nine o'clock in the evening, or some newspaper article censured carnality, that was definite and obvious to him—and so *basta*. In a decision or a concession always lay an element of doubt, something undefined and disquieting. If the town decided to allow a dramatic circle or a reading-club, or a tea-shop, he would shake his head, and say gently: 'They are quite right; of course, it's most excellent, but what will come of it?'

"Any kind of infraction, deviation, or violation of rules plunged him in despair, although, as it might happen, it had nothing to do with him. If any of his companions were late for the Te Deum, or there were rumors of some students' pranks, or an instructress had been seen late in the evening in the company of some officer, he would get very much agitated, and continually repeat: 'What will come of it?' And at our Teachers' Meetings he simply trampled on us with his precaution, his mistrust, and his sheath-bound statements with respect to things, such as: in mixed schools the young people always behave badly, always make a noise in class. 'Ah; may the heads not hear of it. Ah! What will come of it?' That if Peter were expelled from the second class, and George from the fourth, it would be a very good thing. Well, what with his sighs, his complaints, his black eye-glasses, his small white face—you know he was like a polecat—he so oppressed us that we yielded, lessened Peter's and George's good conduct marks, had them punished, and finally expelled Peter and George.

"He had a peculiar habit of walking unbidden into our rooms. He would come into the class-room, and sit down in silence and as if in contemplation of something. There he would sit, hour after hour, without uttering a word, then go away. This was called 'keeping on good terms with his colleagues.' Apparently, coming thus to our rooms was irksome to him, and he only did it because he considered it a friendly obligation. We teachers were afraid of him. And the director, too, was afraid of him. Just think, we teachers are all a thinking folk, thoroughly orderly, brought up on Turgeniev and Chtche-drine. Yet this specimen of a man, always going about in galoshes and carrying an umbrella, kept in hand the whole school for fully fifteen years! Nay, the whole school?—the whole town! Our womenkind did not organize private theatricals on Saturdays for fear lest he should hear of it; our priests were embarrassed in his presence if they were not fasting, or if they played cards. Under the influence of such a person as was Bielikov, the whole town for the last ten to fifteen years was afraid of everything. They were afraid to speak too loud, to send letters, to make acquaintances, to read books; they were afraid to help the poor, to teach. . . ."

Ivan Ivanitch wished to say something, and coughed, but first took a puff at his pipe, looked at the moon, and then said very deliberately:

"Yes. Thinking, orderly people read Chtchedrine and Turgeniev, there are several Bokels there, and others who submitted and endured. And that's just what it is."

"Bielikov lived where I did," continued Burkin, "on the same floor, next door to me; we saw a lot of each other, and I knew him very intimately. At home it was the same story, dressing-gown, night-cap, shutters, locks, a whole array of protective limitations, and ever, 'What will come of it?' Fasting was injurious, and the reverse useless, so. if you please, they say Bielikov did not keep the fasts, but ate pike-perch with butter. which is not fasting, neither can it be called full fare. He did not keep a woman-servant, for fear of evil suspicions, so he kept a man-cook, Athanasius. a man of sixty, a drunkard and half wit, who had been a soldier-servant,

and had some idea of cooking. Athan-asius generally stood about the door with his arms crossed, and muttering, with a deep sigh, always the same thing: 'They have discharged a lot of *them* now.'

"Bielikov's bedroom was small, about the size of a box, and his bed had curtains. He also lay with his head under the bed-clothes. His room was hot and stuffy; the wind rattled at the door, thrummed in the stove; there were sounds of deep sighing in the kitchen, sighs of ill-omen. . . . And he lay trembling under his bed-clothing. He was afraid something was about to happen, that Athanasius would murder him, that thieves would steal in; all night he would have terrifying dreams, and in the morning, when we went to the school together, he was downcast and pale, and it was quite evident that the thronged school, towards which he was walking, was awful and antagonistic to his whole being, and that to walk alongside of me was irksome to him, who by nature was such a solitary-disposed man.

" 'They make a great deal of noise in our classes,' he said, as if striving to find an explanation for his feeling of depression. 'It's like nothing on earth.'

"Now, would you believe it, this teacher of Greek, this man in the husk, almost got married!"

Ivan Ivanitch glanced quickly round into the shed, and said:

"You're joking!"

"Yes. however strange it may seem, he almost got married. They appointed, as a new teacher of history and geography, a certain Kovalenko. Michael Savitch, a Little Russian. He did not arrive alone, but came with his sister.

Varinka. He was young, tall, sun-burnt, had enormous hands; by his face you could see he had a bass voice, and in face it was so—it seemed to come out of a barrel. She was not quite young—about thirty—but was also tall, well-built, black-browed, red-cheeked, in a word, not a maid but marmalade! She was jolly, noisy, always singing Little Russian songs and roaring with laughter; about nothing she would break out into her loud 'Ha—ha—ha!' Our first real acquaintance with the Kovalenkos took place, I remember, on the director's namesday. Among those austere, deadly-bored pedagogues, who attend the namesday out of necessity, suddenly we see a new Aphrodite born out of the foam: she walked with her hands on her hips, laughed loudly, sang, danced. . . . She sang, with great feeling, 'Blew the whirlwinds,' then another song, and yet another, till she captivated us all, even Bielikov. He sat by her side and said, smiling sweetly:

" 'The Little Russian accents, by their tenderness and soft harmonies, remind one of the ancient Greek.'

"This flattered her, and she began telling him, touchingly and convincingly, of a farm she owned in the district of Gadiatchsko; that on the farm resided her old nurse, and that such pears grew there, such melons, such watermelons! The Little Russians call pumpkins, watermelons, and watermelons, gourds, and they make their borshtcht with little red and bluey ones, 'which are so tasty, so *awfully* tasty.'

"We listened and listened, then, all at once, the very same thought flashed upon us all:

" 'It would be such a good thing to marry them,' whispered the director's wife to me.

"For some reason or other, we all remembered that our Bielikov was unmarried, and it now seemed to us odd that up to this time we had not noticed, had driven from view, such an important detail of his life. How does he usually behave with women, how does he solve for himself this quotidian question? Previously it had had no interest whatever for us; it may be that we never entertained the thought that a man who, in no matter what weather, walked about in galoshes, and slept under a curtain, could love.

" 'He is well over forty, and she is thirty,' putting words to her thought, said the director's wife. 'It's likely she would do very well for him.'

"How much that is useless and absurd do we not do in the provinces out of boredom! And that, because we entirely neglect what ought to be done. For instance, now, why should we all at once find it necessary to marry Bielikov, whom it was impossible even to imagine married to oneself? The director's wife, the inspector's wife, and all the lady-teachers of our school resuscitated, looked better, as if they had suddenly discovered the aim of life. The director's wife takes a box at the theater, and behold! in it sits the radiantly happy Varinka fanning herself, and by her side little Bielikov, sitting doubled up and looking as if he had been dragged there with forceps. I gave a small evening party, and the ladies insisted on my inviting both Bielikov and Varinka. In a word, they were all working the wheels. It seemed also as if Varinka was not averse to getting married. Her life with her brother was not so very cheerful; we knew that they fought and abused each other for days together. Here is an instance: Kovalenko, a tall, strong, clumsy-looking figure, wearing a peasant's shirt, and with a lock of hair falling below his cap on his forehead, strides down the street; he has a packet of books in one hand, and a thick knobbly stick in the other. His sister walks just behind him, also with a packet of books.

" 'All the same, Michael, you did not read it!' she loudly disputes. 'I tell you, I swear you never read it at all!'

" 'And I tell you I did read it!' shouts Kovalenko, thumping his stick on the pavement.

" 'Ah, good God, Mintchick! What do you get so angry for, seeing the essential thing for us is conversation?'

" 'And I tell you, I did read it!' yet louder shouts Kovalenko.

"And if an outsider came to the house, a fusillade began at once. Such a life assuredly bored her, she wanted her own nook; and one must also take her age into consideration. There was not much time to pick and choose; it was better to marry him who offered himself even if he were a teacher of Greek. And one must allow that, so long as they married it did not much matter to our young ladies who the man was. However this may be, Varinka began to show a very decided inclination for Bielikov.

"And what about Bielikov? He visited Kovalenko just as he did us. He would go and see him, and remain seated in silence. He remained silent, and Varinka would sing to him 'Blew the whirlwind,' or gaze at him with her dark pensive eyes, or suddenly burst into a loud 'Ha, ha, ha!'

"In love affairs, and especially with marriage, suggestion plays a great part. Everyone—his companions and the ladies—began to assure Bielikov that he ought to marry, that nothing remained to him in life but to marry. We all congratulated him, uttered divers platitudes with serious faces, such as, Marriage was a serious step. Besides, Varinka was not ugly; she was interesting, she was the daughter of a Councillor, and owned a farm; and, most important of all, she was the first woman who had shown favor and fondness for him. His head began to swim, and he decided that in very deed he ought to get married."

"But then he ought to have thrown aside his galoshes and umbrella," interposed Ivan Ivanitch.

"Imagine, though, this evidently was impossible. He placed Varinka's photograph on his table, was always coming to me and talking about Varinka, about family life, that marriage was a serious step, often visited the Kovalenkos, but his manner of life he changed not a tittle. On the contrary, even his resolve to marry had an almost harmful effect on him; he grew thinner, paler, and seemed to retire further into his husk.

" 'I like Varvara Savischna,' he said to me with a feeble, forced smile, 'and I know marriage is indispensable for everyone, but . . . all this, do you know, has happened so suddenly. . . . I must think it over.'

" 'What is there to think over?' I asked him. 'Marry, and that's all about it.'

" 'No, marriage is a serious matter, and one must first duly consider the actual obligations and responsibilities, so that nothing unforeseen should happen.

It all disturbs me, so that I lie awake every night. And, I confess, it frightens me. She and her brother have a rather strange trend of thought; their reasonings, you know, are somewhat odd, and in character they are intrepid. One might get married, and later, in spite of everything, get into some trouble.'

"So he did not propose, always procrastinated, to the great annoyance of the director's wife and all our womenkind. He was all the time weighing his actual obligations and responsibilities, and, meanwhile, went out walking nearly every day with Varinka, thinking, no doubt, that this was necessary under the circumstances, and came to me to talk over family life. And most likely, in the end he would have proposed, and consummated one of those useless, stupid marriages of which from boredom, and having nothing to do, there are thousands, if, all of a sudden, there had not arisen a *Kolossalische Scandal*. It is incumbent to say that Varinka's brother, Kovalenko, loathed Bielikov, and could not stand him from the first day of their acquaintance.

" 'I cannot understand,' he said to us, shrugging his shoulders, 'how you put up with such a spy, such an abominable rascal. Oh, how you can live here! Your whole atmosphere is stifling and infected. Are all your teachers pedagogues? You are functionary-ridden; yours is not a seat of learning, but an ecclesiastical tribunal, and it has a nauseous stink like a police court. No, mates, I shall stay here a little longer, and then shall go to my farm, and there catch crabs, and teach the Little Russians. I shall go away, and you will remain with your little Judas.'

"Or else, he would laugh till he cried

in deep and high tones, and ask me, waving his hands:

" 'Why does he sit with me? What does he want? He sits there looking at nothing.'

"He also nick-named Bielikov, 'A Chinese Spider.' So, of course, we lost no time in informing him that his sister Varinka was thinking of marrying the 'Chinese Spider.' One day, the director's wife remarked to him, that it would be a very good thing to see his sister married to such a staid and so universally esteemed man as Bielikov was. He frowned, and muttered:

" 'It's not my business. She can marry a reptile if she likes; I don't like interfering with other people.'

"Now, listen what happened next. Some wretch drew a caricature of Bielikov in galoshes, home-spun trousers, holding up his umbrella, and arm-in-arm with Varinka; beneath was the inscription, 'the enamored *anthropos*.' The resemblance was remarkable and exact. It was not the work either of a single night, for all the teachers in the school, male and female, the teachers in the seminary, the functionaries, each received a copy. Bielikov, too, received one. The caricature made a most painful impression on him.

"We left the house together—it happened to be the first of May, a Sunday, and all of us, teachers and pupils, had agreed to meet at the school, and then all go together on foot, out of the town, into the woods. We started out; he greener, gloomier than any cloud.

" 'How bad and wicked some people are!' he began, with quivering lips.

"I at once felt sorry for him. We walked on, when suddenly, imagine, Kovalenko rides by on a bicycle, and behind him Varinka, red and perspiring, but cheerful and happy, also on a bicycle!

" 'We are going ahead,' she called out. 'Oh, such glorious weather—so awfully glorious!' And they were both soon out of sight. Poor Bielikov from green turned white, and seemed turned to stone, he stood still and looked at me.

" 'But I ask you, what is this?' he asked. 'Did my eyesight deceive me, or is it proper for school-teachers and women to ride bicycles?'

" 'What is there improper in that?' I asked. It's very good for their health.'

" 'But it is impossible,' he cried, horrified at my calm. 'What are you saying?'

"He was so upset that he could not go any farther, and went back home.

"The next day, he was all the time nervously rubbing his hands together, having shivers, and looked very far from well. He shirked part of his work, a thing which happened for the first time in his life. He had no supper. Towards evening he put on warmer clothes than ever, although it was quite summer weather outside, and directed his steps towards the Kovalenkos' house. Varinka was not at home, he only found her brother.

" 'Pray, take a seat,' Kovalenko said coldly, and with a frown. He was still half asleep; he had just rested after his dinner, and felt in a very bad temper.

"Bielikov sat down, remained silent for ten minutes, then began:

" 'I have come to you so as to relieve my mind. I am very, very much upset. Some lampooner, with intent to ridicule, has drawn myself and another person in very close proximity. I consider it my duty to assure you that I

am in no way responsible for it. I gave no occasion for such pleasantry; on the contrary, I have behaved all the time like a perfectly respectable man.'

"Kovalenko sat sulking in silence. Bielikov waited a little, then continued quietly in a pained voice:

" 'And I have something else to tell you. I am nearing the end of my work, whereas you are only just at the beginning of yours, and I consider it my duty, as an elder colleague, to give you a warning. You ride a bicycle, and that is a recreation quite unsuitable to an instructor of youth.'

" 'And why?' in a deep voice, inquired Kovalenko.

" 'Is there anything to explain, Michael Savitch? Is it not quite clear? If the teachers ride bicycles, what is there left for the pupils? Nothing is left for them except to walk on their heads! It must be forbidden at once by a circular. I was horrified yesterday! When I saw your sister, my head seemed to swim. A woman or a girl on a bicycle—it's awful!'

" 'What is it you want?'

" 'I want only one thing—that is to warn you, Michael Savitch. You are a young man, and the future is before you; you must be very, very careful, you are in default so often—oh, so very often! You go about in a peasant shirt, walk about the streets with bundles of books, and now, in addition, you ride a bicycle. The director will know that you and your sister ride a bicycle, then it will reach the ears of the curator. . . . That will be nice, won't it?'

" 'That my sister and I ride a bicycle is nobody's business,' said Kovalenko, crimson with rage, 'and whoever interferes with my family or private affairs I will send to the devil!'

"Bielikov turned pale, and rose from his chair.

" 'If you speak to me in that tone, I cannot continue,' said he, 'and I beg you never to express yourself thus about our superiors in my presence. You must be respectful to the authorities.'

" 'And did I say anything against the authorities?" asked Kovalenko, looking angrily at him. 'You will please leave me alone. I am a respectable man, and I do not wish to have any conversation with such a fellow as you. I do not care about spies!'

"Bielikov began to fuss nervously, and put on his things quickly, with an expression of horror on his face, for this was the first time in his life he had been subjected to such rudeness.

" 'You may say what you like,' he said, going out of the door on to the little landing of the staircase, 'but I must warn you that perhaps our conversation has been overheard, so to prevent any misunderstanding and anything happening, I shall have to report the outstanding features of it to the director. That I must do!'

" 'Report it? Get out with you, informer!'

"Kovalenko seized him behind by the collar and gave him a shove, and Bielikov slid down the stairs with a sound of rubbing galoshes. The staircase was long and steep, but he arrived safely at the bottom, stood up, and felt his nose to see if his eye-glasses were unbroken. But just as he was sliding down the stairs, Varinka appeared, with two ladies, and they stood there watching him; this was more dreadful than anything for Bielikov. He felt it would have been better to have broken his neck and both legs than to be ridiculous, for now the whole town would hear of it, it would reach the director's ears, and the curator's. Ah! whatever would come of it? There would be another caricature drawn, and it would end by an order for him to retire.

"When he stood up, Varinka recognized him, and as she looked at his funny face, crumpled coat, and his galoshes, not grasping the situation, but inferring that he himself had fallen unintentionally, could not restrain her laughter, which went ringing through the whole house:

" 'Ha, ha, ha!'

"And this loud rippling 'Ha, ha, ha' put an end to everything: Bielikov's marriage and his terrestrial existence. He no longer heard what Varinka was saying, nor did he see anything further. He returned to his rooms, first of all removed the photograph from his table, then lay down on his bed, not to rise again.

"At the end of three days Athanasius came to me, and asked if it were necessary to send for the doctor, as there was something very wrong with his master. I went to see Bielikov. He lay behind the bed curtains, all covered up, and spoke not a word. If he was asked a question he merely answered Yes or No, and nothing further. He lay there while Athanasius hovered around, frowning, looking gloomy, heaving deep sighs, and smelling of vodka, like a tavern.

"At the end of a month Bielikov died. We all, that is, both schools and the seminary, went to his funeral. And now that he lay in his coffin, his expression was peaceful, contented, even cheerful, just as if he were pleased that, at last, he lay in a sheath out of which he would never more be taken. Yes, he had attained his ideal! And as if in honor of him during his funeral the weather was overcast and rainy, so we all wore galoshes, and held up our umbrellas. Varinka was also at the funeral, and when they lowered the coffin into the grave, she cried a little.

"I have noticed that the Little Russians only cry or laugh—there is no middle mood with them. I confess, that to bury such people as Bielikov gives one the greatest satisfaction. As we returned from the cemetery our faces wore discreet, penitential expressions, no one wished to manifest that feeling of satisfaction, a feeling akin to that which we experienced long, long ago as children, when the elders left the house, and we ran about the garden hour after hour, rejoicing in our untrammeled freedom. Ah, freedom! freedom! Even an illusion of it, even the faintest hope of its possibility gives wings to the soul. Isn't it so?

"We returned from the cemetery in good humor. But hardly more than a week had elapsed before our life was stagnating as before—just as austere, depressing, unintelligible: a life not restricted by circulars, but not solved in any way. And how many more of such people in husks remained, how many others there will be!"

"That's just it," said Ivan Ivanitch, smoking his pipe.

"How many others there will be!" repeated Burkin.

The school-teacher came out of the shed. He was a man of middle height, stout, quite bald, with a black beard almost to his waist; and two dogs followed him out.

"A moon, what a moon!" he said, looking up. It was midnight. On the right was seen the whole village, a long street stretching far away, about five versts. It lay plunged in a soft deep sleep; no movement, no sound, it hardly seemed credible that nature could lie so still. When, on a moonlit night, one sees the wide street of a village, its cottages, haystacks, slumbering willows, one's soul is quieted; for, in this its peace, in this withdrawing from labor, anxiety and sorrow in the shades of the night, it is placid, beautiful, sad. It seems as if the stars were looking at it fondly and tenderly, and that there is no more evil on earth, and all is well. To the left, where the village ended, the field began. It could be seen as far as the horizon, and in the whole length and breadth of this field, bathed in moonlight, there was no movement nor sound either.

"That's just it," repeated Ivan Ivanitch. "But do we not live in towns, are we not stifled and crowded, read useless papers, play vint—is not that a husk? And since we spend all our lives among good-for-nothings, squabblers, fools, idle women, talk and listen to all sorts of nonsense, is not that a husk? Now, if you like, I will tell you a most instructive story."

"No, it's time to go to sleep," answered Burkin. "Tell it tomorrow."

They both went into the shed and lay down on the hay. They had both covered themselves over and were dozing off, when of a sudden were heard some light footsteps, tup, tup . . . someone was walking close to the shed;

they came nearer, then stopped; in a moment, again, tup, tup. . . . The dogs barked.

"That is Mavra," said Burkin.

The sound of steps ceased.

"To see and hear them tell lies," slowly said Ivan Ivanitch, turning over on his other side. "while they call you a fool because you suffer them to lie; to endure offenses and humiliations; not to have the courage openly to declare that you are on the side of honest, free men, but to lie yourself, and smile, and all that for a crust of bread, a warm little nook, some little decoration or other, the value of which is no more than a groat—no. to live on like that is not possible!"

"Come now, that is another subject, Ivan Ivanitch," said the teacher. "Let's sleep."

And in ten minutes Burkin was asleep. But Ivan Ivanitch turned over from one side to the other, and sighed; then he got up, went outside, and, seating himself by the door, smoked his pipe.

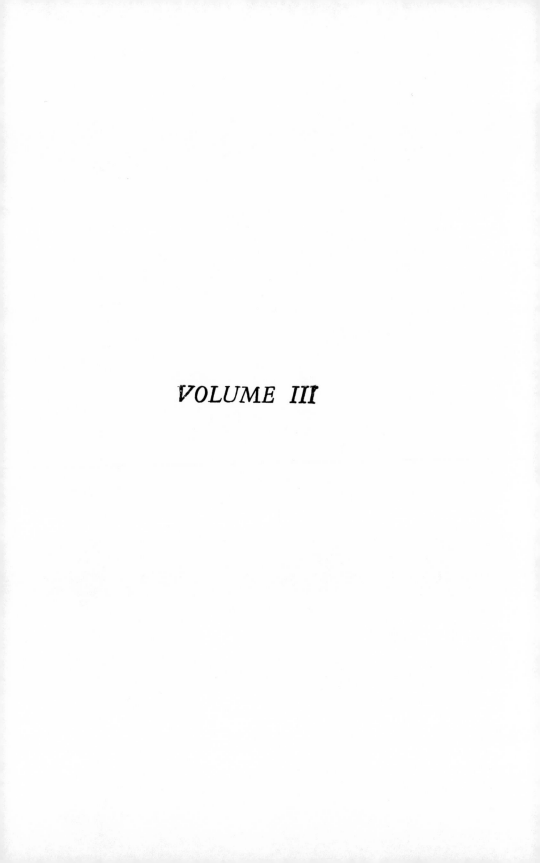

VOLUME III

Anna Round the Neck

CHAPTER I

THE YOUNG COUPLE

AFTER the wedding no refreshments were served. The young couple had each a glass of wine, dressed and drove to the station. Instead of music and dancing—a journey of two hundred versts to pray at a sacred shrine. Many people approved saying, that for Modestus Alekseich, an official of high rank and aged, a noisy wedding might appear out of place; it was tiresome to listen to music when a bureaucrat of fifty-two got married to a girl of just eighteen years. It was also said that Modestus Alekseich, a man of principles, had really arranged this journey to a monastery in order to make his young wife understand that, even in matrimony, he desired religion and morality.

The young couple were escorted to the station by a crowd of colleagues and relations with champagne glasses in their hands, waiting for the train to start in order to shout: "Hurrah!" and Pëtr Leontich, the bride's father, in a top-hat and a schoolmaster's dress-coat, already drunk and very pale, stretched towards the window, his glass in his hand, and said in a beseeching voice:

"Anuta! Anya! Anya, just one word!"

Anya bent out of the window towards him, and he whispered something to her, pouring out on her a strong smell of brandy, and blowing into her ear—but nothing could be understood—he made the sign of the cross over her face, breast and hands; his breathing shook and tears shone in his eyes. Anya's brothers, Petya and Andryusha, gymnasium boys, pulled him from behind by his coat-tails and whispered shamefacedly:

"Papochka, enough! . . . Papochka, don't! . . ."

When the train started, Anya saw her father run a few steps after the coach, with unsteady gait and spilling his wine. What a pitiful, kind and guilty face he had!

"Hur-rah!—ah!" he shouted.

The young couple remained alone. Modestus Alekseich looked round the compartment, arranged their things in the racks and then sat down opposite his young wife, smiling. He was an official of middle height, somewhat stout, puffy and very well-fed, with long whiskers, but no moustache, and his round shaven, sharply outlined chin resembled a heel. The most characteristic trait of his face was the absence of a moustache, and this freshly shaven, bare place gradually merged into fat cheeks that trembled like jellies. His demeanour was sedate, his movements slow, his manner suave.

"At this moment I can't help remembering a certain circumstance," he said, smiling. "Five years ago when Kosorotov received the order of Saint Anna of the second class and came to

115

thank for it His Excellency expressed himself thus: 'Consequently you now have three annas: one in your button-hole and two round your neck.' And I must tell you that just at that time Kosorotov's wife, a very quarrelsome and giddy woman, who was celled Anna, had just returned to him. I trust, when I receive Anna of the second class, His Excellency will have no cause to say the same thing to me."

He smiled with his small eyes. And she also smiled, being troubled at the thought that at any moment this man might kiss her with his full, moist lips, and that now she had not the right to refuse to be kissed. The sleek movements of his bloated body frightened her, she felt terrified and disgusted. He rose, slowly took off his orders, his dress-coat and waistcoat and put on his dressing-gown.

"That's all right," he said, sitting down next to Anya.

She remembered how painful the marriage ceremony had been, when it had appeared to her that the priest, the guests and all the people who were in the church looked at her sadly; why, why had she, such a pretty, nice girl, married this elderly, uninteresting gentleman? That morning she had still been in raptures that everything had been settled so well; but during the marriage ceremony and now, while sitting in the railway coach, she felt culpable, deceived and ridiculous. Now she was married to a rich man, and still she had no money, her bridal dress had been made on credit, and to-day, when her father and brothers had seen her off, she had perceived by their faces that they had not a kopeck in their pockets. Would they have any supper to-day? And to-morrow? And now for some reason she seemed to see her father and the boys sitting hungry and experiencing the same sadness as they felt the first evening after her mother's funeral.

"Oh, how unhappy I am!" she thought. "Why am I so unhappy?"

With the awkwardness of a sedate man who is unaccustomed to the treatment of women, Modestus Alekseich put his arm round her waist and patted her on the shoulders, and she thought of money, of her mother and of her death. When her mother died, her father, Pëtr Leontich, a teacher of calligraphy and drawing in the gymnasium, took to drinking, and they began to feel want; the boys had no boots or galoshes, their father was summoned before the magistrate, there was an execution in their flat and an inventory was made of their furniture. . . . What shame! Anya had to look after her drunken father, darn her brothers' stockings, go to market, and when her beauty, youth and elegant manners were admired, it appeared to her that the whole world saw her cheap hat and the hole in her shoes that was smeared with ink. At night there were tears and troublesome thoughts that she could not get rid of, the dread that very soon, owing to his weakness, her father would be dismissed from the gymnasium, and that he would not be able to endure this and would die like her mother. But then some ladies of their acquaintance had begun to take an interest in her and to look out for a good husband for her. Very soon Modestus Alekseich had been found; he was neither young nor handsome, but he had money. He had about a hundred thousand roubles in the bank and he owned a patrimonial estate which he had leased to somebody. He was a man of principles, and he was in His Excellency's good books; it would be quite easy for him, Anya was told, to get a note from His Excellency to the director of the gymnasium, or even to the curator, with instructions that Pëtr Leontich was not to be dismissed. . . .

While she was thinking of all these details the sound of music and the noise of voices suddenly burst through the window. The train had stopped at a small wayside station. Beyond the platform somebody in the crowd who was playing gaily on an accordion, accompanied by a cheap squeaking fiddle, and from the other side of the tall birches and poplars, from the country houses which were flooded with moonlight came the sounds of a military band: there was a ball in one of them. Crowds of the inhabitants and people from town, who had come down to breathe the pure air, were walking about the platform. Among others was Artynov, the owner of this country resort and a very rich man. He was tall, stout and dark-haired, with the face of an Armenian and goggle eyes, and he was dressed in a strange costume. He wore a Russian shirt which was unbuttoned on the chest, top-boots with spurs, and a long mantle that hung from his shoulders and trailed on the ground like a train. Following him were two large greyhounds, with their sharp muzzles hanging low.

Tears still glistened in Anya's eyes, but she no longer remembered her mother, nor money, nor her wedding; she was pressing the hands of some gymnasium boys and officers, old acquaintances of hers, laughing gaily and saying quickly:

"How do you do! How are you?"

She went out on to the platform, into the moonlight, and stood there in such a way that everybody could see her in her magnificent new dress and hat.

"Why are we standing here?" she asked.

"This is a siding," she was answered. "The post train is expected."

Noticing that Artynov was looking at her, she half closed her eyes coquettishly and began to speak French in a loud voice, and because her own voice sounded so well, because music was heard and the moon was reflected in the pond, because Artynov, that well-known Don Juan and rake, was looking at her covetously, and because all were gay she suddenly felt happy. When the train started again and her friends the officers had saluted her as she left, she began to hum the polka, the sounds of which played by the military band somewhere behind the trees was wafted after her; she returned to her compartment with a feeling as if she had been convinced at this wayside station that she certainly would be happy despite everything.

The young couple remained in the monastery two days, and then they returned to town. Their flat was in a house belonging to the Crown. When Modestus Alekseich went to his office Anya played on the piano, or cried because she was dull, or lay down on the couch and read novels or looked through fashion magazines. At dinner Modestus Alekseich ate very much and talked about politics, about new appointments, promotions and gratuities, about its being necessary to work hard; about family life not being a pleasure, but a duty; he said that if you took care of the kopecks the roubles would take care of themselves, and that he placed religion and morality above everything else on earth. And holding his knife in his fist like a sword, he said:

"Every man must have his duties!"

Anya listened to him, was afraid and could not eat, and she usually rose from table hungry. After dinner her husband rested and snored loudly, and she went over to see her people. Her father and the boys looked at her in quite a strange manner; exactly as if just before she had come they had been blaming her for having married for money an unloved, unpleasant and tiresome man; her rustling dress, bracelets and, in general, her ladylike appearance embarrassed and offended them; in her presence they were a little confused and did not know what to say to her. She sat down and ate with them their cabbage soup, stiff gruel and potatoes fried in mutton dripping that smelt of tallow candles. With a trembling hand Pëtr Leontich took up a decanter and filled his glass, which he drank off quickly, with greediness, with repulsion, then he drank another and a third. . . . Petya and Andryusha. thin, pale little boys, with large eyes, took the decanter away, and said in an abashed voice:

"Don't, Papochka. . . . Enough, Papochka. . . ."

Anya, too, was troubled and implored him not to drink any more; but he suddenly flew out at them and thumped the table with his fist.

"I won't allow anybody to look after me!" he shouted. "Youngsters, girl, I will turn you all out."

But in his voice there could be heard weakness and goodness, and nobody was afraid of him. After dinner he usually made himself smart; with a pale face and a chin that had been cut when shaving; stretching out his thin neck he would stand for half an hour before the mirror, trying to improve his appearance, now by combing his hair, or by twisting his black moustache, or by sprinkling himself with scents and carefully tying his cravat in a bow; and then he put on his gloves, took his silk hat and went out to give private lessons. But if it was a holiday he remained at home and either painted or played on a hormonium, which hissed and wheezed: he tried to draw from it harmonious and melodious tones, and sang in a low voice, or he was angry with the boys.

"Young scamps! Villains, they have spoilt the instrument!"

Of an evening Anya's husband played cards with those of his colleagues, who lived under the same roof in the house belonging to the Crown. During these card parties the wives of the officials also met; they were ugly, tastelessly dressed and as coarse as cooks, and then in their flats there began gossip and scandal that was as ugly and tasteless as they were themselves. It also happened that Modestus Alekseich took Anya to the theatre.

During the intervals he did not let her go from his side for a moment, but walked about the passages and the foyer arm in arm with her. When he bowed to anybody he whispered to Anya: "A councillor of State . . . received by His Excellency," or: "With a fortune . . . he has his own house. . . ."

When they passed through the refreshment-room Anya wanted very much something sweet; she was very fond of chocolates and apple tarts, but she had no money, and she was afraid to ask her husband. He would take up a pear and press it with his fingers in an un-decided way and ask:

"What is the price?"

"Twenty-five kopecks."

"Indeed!" he exclaimed, putting the pear in its place; but as it was awkward to go away from the buffet without buy-ing something he ordered a bottle of soda water and finished the whole bottle himself, while tears appeared in his eyes and Anya hated him at that moment.

Or suddenly he would get quite red and say to her hurriedly:

"Bow to that old lady!"

"But I am not acquainted with her."

"All the same. She is the wife of the Director of the Court of Exchequer! Don't you hear, I tell you to bow!" he grumbled insistently. "Your head won't fall off."

Anya bowed, and her head really did not fall off, but it was painful. She did everything her husband required, and was angry with herself that he had duped her like the veriest little fool. She had married him only for money, and now she had even less than before her mar-riage. Formerly her father would give her from time to time a twenty-kopeck piece, but now she never had a grosh. She could not take it by stealth, nor ask for money; she was afraid of her husband and trembled before him. It appeared to her that she had borne the fear of this man in her soul for very long. At one time in her childhood the power that appeared to her the most terrible and inspired the greatest fear was the director of the gymnasium, who seemed to approach like a cloud or a steam engine ready to crush her; another similar power about which they often talked in the family, and which for some reason they feared, was His Excellency;

there were besides some dozen other powers, though smaller ones, and among them were the teachers of the gym-nasium, with their shaven moustaches, strict, inexorable, and now at last there was Modestus Alekseich, a man with principles, who even in face resembled the director. In Anya's imagination all these powers were blended in one, in the form of a terrible, huge, white bear that moved towards the weak and guilty people, like her father, and she feared to say anything in contradiction to him; but with a forced smile and expression of feigned pleasure she suffered his coarse caresses and defiling embraces that only caused her horror.

Only once Pëtr Leontich had ven-tured to ask him for a loan of fifty roubles in order to settle a very un-pleasant debt, but what suffering it had caused!

"Very well, I will give it," Modestus Alekseich had said after reflection, "but I warn you that I will never again help you until you leave off drinking. Such a weakness is shameful for a man who is in government employ. I cannot refrain from reminding you of the uni-versally known fact that many very capable men have been ruined by this vice, while by temperance they might, perhaps, in time have attained high rank."

This was followed by long periods: "according as . . ." "in consequence of this state . . ." "in consideration of what has been said." Poor Pëtr Leontich suffered from the humiliation, and felt a strong desire to drink.

The boys, too, who came to see Anya usually in torn boots and threadbare trousers, had also to listen to precepts.

"Every man must have his duties!" Modestus Alekseich told them.

But he gave them no money. At the same time he gave Anya rings, bracelets, and brooches, saying it was as well to have these things for a black day. And he often opened her chest of drawers to verify if all these things were safe.

CHAPTER II

THE BALL

MEANWHILE winter had begun. Long before Christmas the local newspapers announced that the usual winter ball would "be given" on the 29th of December in the Hall of the Nobility Club. Every evening when the card-playing was over Modestus Alekseich whispered excitedly with the wives of the officials, looking anxiously at Anya, and afterwards he paced the room from corner to corner for a long time immersed in thought. At last, late at night, he stopped before Anya and said:

"You must have a ball dress made for yourself. Do you understand? But, please, consult Marya Grigorevna and Natalya Kuzminishna."

And he gave her a hundred roubles. She took the money; but when she ordered her dress she did not consult anybody; she only spoke to her father about it, and tried to imagine how her mother would have dressed for the ball. Her late mother had always been dressed in the last fashion, and had always taken great pains with Anya and had dressed her very elegantly—like a doll—and she had taught her to speak French and to dance the mazurka admirably (before she had got married she had been a governess for five years). Like her

mother Anya could make a new dress out of an old one, clean her gloves with benzene, hire jewellery for the evening, and, like her mother, she also knew how to screw up her eyes, burr, get into pretty poses, become enraptured when necessary, or look sad and enigmatic. And from her father she had inherited her dark hair and eyes, her nervousness and her habit of always dressing very carefully.

When Modestus Alekseich, without his coat, came into her room half an hour before they had to start for the ball, in order to fix his order round his neck in front of her pier-glass, he was so enchanted with her beauty and the elegance of her fresh and airy toilette that he combed his whiskers with self-satisfaction, saying:

"So that's how my wife is . . . that's how you are! Anyuta!" he continued, suddenly falling into a solemn tone. "I have made you happy, and to-day you can make me happy. I beg you to get introduced to His Excellency's wife! For God's sake do! Through her I can get the post of first secretary!"

They drove to the ball. Here they were at the Hall of the Nobility at the entrance door with its doorkeeper. The antechamber was full of clothes-pegs, fur coats, sleeping lackeys and bare-necked women, covering themselves with their fans as a protection from the draught; there was a smell of gas and soldiers. When going up the staircase on her husband's arm, Anya heard the sounds of music and saw the reflection of the whole of herself in the huge mirror illuminated by numberless lights, a feeling of joy, and the same presentiment of happiness that she had felt on the moonlit night at the wayside station, awoke in her soul. She walked proudly, with self-confidence, for the first time she felt herself no longer a girl but a married lady, and involuntarily she imitated her late mother in her gait and manner. And for the first time in her life she felt herself rich and free. Even the presence of her husband did not embarrass her, as from the moment she crossed the threshold of the Club she guessed instinctively that the vicinity of her old husband would in no way depreciate her; but, on the contrary, it would stamp her with the piquant mysteriousness that is very attractive to men. The band already resounded in the large hall, and dancing had begun. After their apartments in the government house Anya was bewildered by the impressions of light, of many colours, of music and of noise. She cast a glance over the hall, thinking: "Oh, how delightful!" and she instantly spotted all her friends amid the crowd, all those people she had met formerly at parties or on her promenades, all those officers, teachers, lawyers, officials, landowners, His Excellency,, Artynov and the society ladies smartly decked out and very décolletée, both the pretty and the ugly, who were already taking their places in the kiosks and pavilions of the Charity Bazaar, to begin the sale for the poor. A huge officer in epaulettes—she had made his acquaintance in the Old Kiev Street when she was still a gymnasium girl and now she could not even recall his name—appeared before her as if he had sprung out of the earth and invited her for a waltz, and she flew away from her husband. It seemed to her as if she were sailing in a boat in a severe storm, and her husband had remained far away on the bank. . . . She was a passionate dancer, she danced with enthusiasm waltzes, polkas, quadrilles, passing from hand to hand, becoming dizzy from the music and the noise, mixing up French and Russian words, burring, laughing, not thinking of her husband nor of anybody nor of anything. She had success with the men; that was quite evident—it could not have been otherwise—she was breathless with excitement, she pressed her fan convulsively in her hand and wanted to drink. Her father, in a crumpled dresscoat which exhaled an odour of benzene, came up, offering her a plate with a red ice in his outstretched hand.

"You are bewitching to-day," he said, looking at her enraptured; "never before have I regretted so much that you married with so much haste. . . . Why? I know you did it for our sake, but . . ." with trembling hands he took a packet of rouble notes out of his pocket and said: "To-day I received my fee for lessons, I can repay your husband my debt."

She thrust her plate into his hand and, seized by somebody, she was carried off, and he had a glimpse of her far away, while she, looking over her partner's shoulder, saw her father gliding over the floor with his arm round a lady's waist and twirling with her through the room.

"How charming he is when he is sober!" she thought.

She danced the mazurka with the same huge officer. Walking along in an important and heavy manner, looking like a carcass in uniform, slightly leading with raised shoulders and expanded breast, and hardly stamping with his feet, he appeared very unwilling to dance, while she fluttered beside him exciting him with her beauty and bare neck; her eyes shone provokingly, her movements were passionate, while he became more and more indifferent and stretched out his hand to her graciously like a king.

"Bravo! Bravo!" the public shouted.

Little by little the huge officer was also carried away; he became animated, excited; he succumbed to the enchantment, he was carried away and moved lightly, youthfully, while she only shrugged her shoulders and looked slyly at him, as if now she were the queen and he her slave, and at that moment it seemed to her that the whole hall was looking at them, that all the people were spellbound and envied them. The huge officer had scarcely had time to thank her, when the people around suddenly made way and the men held themselves up stiffly in a strange manner and let their arms fall to their sides. It was His Excellency, in a dress-coat, with two stars on his breast, who was coming towards her. Yes, His Excellency was really coming to her, because he looked straight at her and smiled sweetly, at the same time chewing his lips, as he always did when he saw a pretty woman.

"Very pleased, very pleased . . ." he began. "I shall order your husband to be put under arrest in the guard-house for having hidden away such a treasure from us for so long. I have come to you with a commission from my wife," he continued, giving her his hand. "You must help us. H'm-m, yes, we must award you the prize of beauty . . . as they do in America. . . . H'm-m. . . . The Americans. . . . My wife is waiting for you with impatience."

He led her to one of the huts, to an elderly lady who had a face in which the lower part was disproportionately large, so that it looked as if she had a big stone in her mouth.

"Help us," she said through the nose in a drawling voice. "All the pretty women are working for the Charity Bazaar, but for some reason you alone are amusing yourself. Why don't you want to help us?"

She went away and Anya took her place near the silver samovar and the teacups. Brisk trade began at once. Anya took not less than a rouble for a cup of tea, and she made the huge officer drink three cups. Artynov, the rich man with the goggle eyes, came up to her stall. He was suffering from breathlessness, but he no longer wore the strange costume in which Anya had seen him in the summer; he was now in evening dress, like all the other men. Without removing his eyes from Anya he drank a glass of champagne and paid a hundred roubles for it, then he had a cup of tea and gave another hundred, and all this was done in silence, as he was suffering from asthma. Anya invited purchasers to come in, and she took their money from them, being firmly convinced that her smiles and glances could afford these men nothing but great pleasure. She already understood that she was created solely for this noisy, brilliant, laughing life with music, dancing, admirers, and her former fear, of the power that was approaching and threatened to crush her, appeared to her absurd; she feared nobody any longer, and she only regretted that her mother was not there to rejoice with her at her success.

Pëtr Leontich, already pale, but still firm on his legs, came to the hut and asked for a glass of cognac. Anya blushed, fearing he would say something unsuitable (she was already ashamed that she had such a poor, such an ordinary father); but he emptied his glass, threw a ten-rouble note, which he took from his pocket, on to the counter and went away in an important manner, without having said a word. A little later she saw him with his partner dancing in the *grand rond,* and now he was rather tottery and was calling out something, to the great confusion of his partner, and Anya remembered at a ball, that had taken place three years before, he had also tottered and had called out in the same way; it had finished by the policeman having to take him home to bed, and the next day the Director had threatened to dismiss him. How untimely were these recollections!

When the fires of the samovars had gone out in the huts, and the weary benefactresses had handed over their receipts to the elderly lady with the stone in her mouth, Artynov gave his arm to Anya and led her into the hall, where supper was served for all who had taken part in the Charity Bazaar. There were about twenty people at the supper, hardly more, but it was very noisy. His Excellency proposed the toast: "This luxurious dining-room is the right place to drink to the prosperity of the cheap dining-rooms that are the object of to-day's Bazaar." The Brigadier-General proposed that they should drink "to the power before which even the artillery is powerless," and everybody rose to click glasses with the ladies. It was very, very gay! . . .

The sky was already getting light when Anya was escorted home, and the cooks were going to market. Joyous,

intoxicated, full of new impressions and tired out she undressed, fell on her bed and was instantly fast asleep. . . .

It was past one next day when her maid woke her and announced that Mr. Artynox had come to pay her a visit. She dressed quickly and went into the drawing-room. Soon after Artynov left, His Excellency arrived to thank her for having taken part in the Charity Bazaar. He looked at her sweetly, chewing his lips, kissed her little hand, asked permission to come again and departed, and she stood in the middle of the drawing-room amazed and enchanted, unable to believe in this change in her life, this wonderful change had taken place so quickly; at that very moment her husband, Modestus Alekseich, came into the room. . . . And he, too, stood before her now with that ingratiating, slavishly respectful expression, which she was accustomed to see on his face in the presence of the strong and the illustrious; and with rapture, with indignation, with contempt, already confident that she would not have to suffer for it, she said, pronouncing each word distinctly:

"Go away, blockhead!"

After that Anya never had a single free day, as she took part in picnics, drives and plays. Every day she only returned home towards morning, and lay down in the drawing-room on the floor, and then she told everybody touchingly that she slept under flowers. She required very much money now, but she was no longer afraid of Modestus Alekseich, and she spent his money as if it were her own; she did not ask, or demand, she simply sent him her bills or little notes: "pay the bearer two hundred roubles" or "pay immediately a hundred roubles."

At Easter Modestus Alekseich received the order of St. Anna of the second class. When he went to thank for it, His Excellency put his newspaper aside and sit down deeper into his armchair.

"Consequently, you have now three Annas," he said as he looked at his white hands and pink nails, "one in your buttonhole and two round your neck."

Out of caution Modestus Alekseich put two fingers to his lips, in order not to laugh aloud, and said:

"Now it only remains to await the appearance of a little Vladimir in the world. May I venture to ask Your Excellency to be godfather."

He hinted at a Vladimir of the fourth class, and he already imagined how he would relate everywhere to his friends this joke that was so successful by its ready wit and boldness, and he was preparing to say something equally good, but His Excellency was again entirely absorbed in his newspaper and only nodded his head.

And Anya was always driving about with three horses, she went with Artynov to his shooting-box, she took part in one-act plays, she was at supper-parties; but she went more and more seldom to her own people. They always dined alone now. Pëtr Leontich drank more than formerly; he had no money, and long since the harmonium had been sold for debt. Now the boys never allowed him to go alone into the street, and always followed him, to save him from falling. When it happened that Anya flew past them in the Old Kiev Street, driving with a pair of horses and a side-horse and Artynov on the coach-box instead of a coachman, Pëtr Leontich would take off his top-hat and when about to call to her, Petya and Andryusha would seize him by the arms, and say:

"Don't, Papochka! Enough, Papochka!"

The Incubus

No sooner had Kunin, a young man of thirty, and life-member of the Peasant's Government Board, returned from Petersburg to his estate of Borissov, than he sent a horseman in all haste to Father Jacob Smirnov, the then Priest of Sinkino.

About five hours later Father Jacob appeared.

"Very pleased to make your acquaintance," said Kunin, coming out to greet him in the vestibule. "As I have been living and working here a year, it is time we came to know each other. Welcome. But how young you look!" said Kunin in surprise; "how old are you?"

"Twenty-eight . . ." answered Father Jacob, giving a very slight pressure to the hand held out to him, and blushing, he knew not why. Kunin led his guest into his sitting-room, and took a look at him.

"What a coarse, womanish face," he thought.

Father Jacob's face was certainly of

a very womanish type, with its snub-nose, fat, bright red cheeks, gray-blue eyes, and his scant, faintly marked eye-brows. His hair was long, red, smooth, and dry, and hung down to his shoulders like strands of grass. His moustache was just sprouting into the resemblance of a man's moustache, whereas his beard belonged to that class of good-for-nothing beard, which the Seminarists for some reason call "demivolte." It was scarce and transparent; it would be impossible to smooth or comb such a beard, but it might be snipped now and again. All this scanty vegetation grew in very uneven clumps, just as if Father Jacob, having thought he would disguise himself as a priest, had begun to glue on a beard and had been interrupted halfway through. He wore a cassock the color of coffee diluted with chicory, and it had two large patches at the elbows.

"What a strange being," thought Kunin, looking at the very mud-stained cassock. "He comes into the house for the first time in his life, and can't even dress himself tidily."

"Take a seat, batushka," he began, familiarly rather than affably, and drawing a chair up to the table. "Take a seat, pray!"

Father Jacob coughed into his hand, seated himself awkwardly on the edge of the armchair, and rested both his hands on his knees. He was small, narrow-shouldered, with a perspiring red face; Kunin had never imagined before that such a wanting, pitiable-looking priest could exist in Russia. As Father Jacob sat there on the arm of the chair, his whole attitude, with his palms resting on his knees, seemed to reveal a complete absence of dignity, and even something

equivocal, and from the first produced on Kunin the very worst impression.

"I invited you, batushka, on business." Kunin began, leaning back in his chair. "To my lot has fallen the pleasant obligation of helping you in one of your useful enterprises. The fact is, on my return from Petersburg, I found a letter from the Mareschal on my table. Egor Dmitritch proposes that I should take over the guardianship of the parish church school which is just being opened at Sinkino. I am delighted, batushka, whole-heartedly so—nay more, I seize this opportunity with enthusiasm."

Kunin got up, and walked about the room.

"Of course, Egor Dmitrich, and probably you, know I have not much money at my disposal. My estate is mortgaged, and I live entirely on my pay as life-member of the Board, so that you cannot reckon on great help, but whatever is in my power I will do. What do you think of opening the school, batushka?"

"When there is the money," answered Father Jacob.

"What means are at present at your disposal?"

"Hardly any. The moujiks decided at their meeting that thirty kopeks should be paid yearly for every male; but that is only promised. To provide the bare necessities we want to start with at least two hundred roubles."

"M—yes. Unfortunately I have not that amount at present," sighed Kunin. "I spent it all on the journey. I even owe a little. Let us give all our attention to finding some way."

Kunin began to think aloud. As he gave rein to his reflections, he followed the expression on Father Jacob's face.

seeking for approval or consent, but the face remained impassive and immovable, and expressed nothing but shamefaced timidity and uneasiness. You might think, looking at him, that Kunin was speaking such words of wisdom that Father Jacob could not understand them, was only listening out of politeness, and besides, was afraid lest he should be convicted later of not comprehending.

"The little fellow is obviously not of the brightest," thought Kunin. "Timid and dull beyond measure."

Father Jacob only showed a little animation and broke into a smile when the servant came into the room with a tray, two glasses of tea, and a plate full of cracknels. He took his glass, and at once began to drink his tea.

"Why should not we write to his Eminence?" said Kunin, continuing his reflections aloud. "For properly speaking, it is not the zemstvo, nor us, but the superior spiritual authorities who raised the question of parish church schools. They ought, in reality, to find the money. I remember, I read somewhere that there was a sum of money allotted for that purpose. Do you know anything of it?"

Father Jacob was so busy drinking his tea that he was unable to answer this question at once. He raised his gray-blue eyes on Kunin, thought a moment, then, as if just remembering he had been asked something, made a negative sign of the head. An expression of satisfaction and of the most ordinary and prosaic hunger appeared on his ugly face, and spread from ear to ear. He drank, and gulped, and smacked his lips. When he had finished the very last drop, he put down his glass on the table, took it up again, looked in the bottom, and re-placed it on the table; the expression of satisfaction faded from his face. Then Kunin saw his guest take a cracknel from the biscuit plate, bit it, turn it round in his hand, then swiftly slip it into his pocket.

"This is not very sacerdotal," thought Kunin, contemptuously shrugging his shoulders. "What is it? priestly greed or puerility?"

Having given his guest another glass of tea, and having seen him off from the vestibule, Kunin stretched himself on the sofa, and yielded to the unpleasant feeling with which Father Jacob's visit had affected him.

"What a strange uncivilized man," he thought. "Dirty, slovenly, rude, stupid, and a drunkard undoubtedly. My God, and he is a priest, a spiritual father! An instructor of the people! Just imagine the irony in the deacon's voice as he intones to him at every Mass: 'Give us thy blessing.' A fine superior! Without one drop of dignity, uneducated, secreting biscuits in his pockets like a school-boy—Phew! Good Lord, where were the eyes of the Prelate when he ordained such a man? What do they expect of the people when they give them such instructors? One wants men who. . . ."

Here Kunin thought a little what the Russian priest ought to be like.

"Say, for instance, I was pope. An educated man, liking his duties of pope, could do a great deal; I should have had the school opened long before this. And the sermons? If the pope is only sincere and inspired with love for his work, what wonderful rousing sermons he can deliver!"

Kunin closed his eyes, and mentally composed a sermon.

A little later he was sitting at the table quickly writing it down:

"I will give it to carroty-hair, he can read it in church," he thought.

The following Sunday, Kunin went over in the morning to Sinkino to settle the question of the school, and at the same time to get to know the church of which he was considered a parishioner. It was a beautiful morning, although it was the season of bad roads; the sun was shining and darting its rays into the white layers of lingering snow; the snow, as it took its leave of the earth, glistened with such bright jewels that it dazzled one to look at it; and the winter-corn was growing green through it all. The rooks were sedately hovering over the earth, then one descended, and before settling himself on his feet took a few little jumps.

The wooden church where Kunin now arrived was old and gray; the columns of the porch had once been decorated with white paint, which had entirely peeled off, so they resembled two plain shafts. The picture over the door looked like one continuous black blot. This poverty-stricken appearance touched and moved Kunin; humbly lowering his eyes, he stepped into the church and stood by the door. The service had only just begun—the old Cantor, bent like a bow, was reading the "hours" in a dull monotonous tenor voice; Father Jacob, officiating without a deacon, was incensing the church. Had it not been humility which had induced Kunin to enter this poor little church, he must have smiled at the sight of Father Jacob. This under-sized priest wore a crumpled chasuble, of some frayed yellow material, and it was so much too long for him that it trailed on the ground.

The church was not at all full, and in the first glance Kunin was struck by one extraordinary fact—he could only see old people and children. Where were the adult workers? Where were youth and manhood? But after a while he examined the old people's faces more carefully and discovered that he had mistaken the young for the old. However, he did not attach any particular importance to this little optical illusion. The interior of the church was as old and gray as the exterior. There was not one little space, on the ikonostase or the fawn-colored walls, which was not bespotted and scratched by time. There were plenty of windows, but, the predominating color being gray, the church looked gloomy.

"He who is pure of heart can pray here," thought Kunin. "Just as at St. Peter's in Rome, one is impressed by the grandeur, here one is touched by the modesty and simplicity."

But this prayerful disposition vanished like smoke when Father Jacob went to the altar and began the Mass. Although at a very early age ordained a priest, from the very benches of the seminary, Father Jacob had not yet adopted any regular way of conducting the service. When he read he seemed to be choosing which was the most suitable voice, a high tenor or mezzo-bass. He bowed awkwardly, walked rapidly, closed and opened the holy gates with violence. The old Cantor was evidently ailing and deaf, and frequently did not hear the terminations of prayers, which consequently led to a few little misunderstandings. Father Jacob would not have finished his part before the Cantor would already be intoning his, or else Father Jacob had finished some time, and the old man was still straining his ear towards the altar, listening, and remaining silent till someone pulled at his vestment. The old Cantor had a monotonous asthmatic voice with a quaver in it, and he also lisped. To complete the list of misfortunes, he was accompanied by a very small boy, whose head hardly appeared above the railing of the choir. The boy sang in a shrill treble, and seemed to make every effort not to drop upon the right note. Kunin stopped a little to listen, then went out and smoked; he was completely disenchanted, and looked almost with hatred at the gray church.

"They complain of the loss of religious feeling among the people," he sighed "I should think so; they had better fix us up with a few more of such popes!"

Kunin went back into the church three times, but each time he was forcibly compelled to return to the fresher air outside. He waited for the end of the Mass, then went over to Father Jacob's house. From its exterior the priest's house was in no way distinguishable from a peasant's cottage, although the straw on the roof lay a trifle more evenly, and there were some little white curtains in the windows. Father Jacob led Kunin into a small light room, the floor of which was of clay and the walls pasted over with cheap paper. Apart from some efforts towards luxuriousness in the shape of photographs in frames, and a clock, on the pendulum of which was hung a pair of scissors, the surroundings struck one as very beggarly. Looking at the furniture, one might think Father Jacob had collected them separately on his visits; in one place they had given him a round-three-legged table, in another a stool, in the third a chair with its back curved very far backwards, in a fourth a chair with a very straight back but with a very low sunk seat, in the fifth they must have felt very liberal, and had given him something in the shape of a sofa, with a flat back and a cane seat. This similitude of a sofa was colored in dark red, and smelt strongly of paint. Kunin at first thought of sitting on one of the chairs, then he decided to sit on the stool.

"Is it the first time you have been to our church?" Father Jacob asked, hanging his hat on a large misshapen nail.

"Yes, it's the first time. I'll tell you what, batushka, before we get to business, let's have some tea. I am quite parched."

Father Jacob blinked, gave a croak, and went behind a partition. There was a sound of whispering.

"He must be talking to his wife," thought Kunin. "It will be interesting to see Carroty's popess."

A little while after, Father Jacob came from behind the partition, very red, perspiring, and with an attempt at a smile, sat opposite Kunin on the edge of the sofa.

"They'll prepare the samovar directly," he said, not looking at his guest.

"Good Lord, they have not got the samovar ready," Kunin thought with horror. "Well, we shall have to wait."

"I have brought the rough draft of a letter I have written to the Prelate," he said. "We will read it after our tea; perhaps you will find something to add."

"Very well."

There was silence. Father Jacob glanced uneasily at the partition, smoothed his hair, and blew his nose.

"It's wonderful weather," he said.

"Yes. By the way, I read a very interesting thing last night: the Communal Zemstvo have decided to give back their schools to the clergy. It's very characteristic."

Kunin got up and began walking about the room, at the same time expressing his opinions.

"That is nothing," he said, "if only the clergy were on a level with their calling and clearly understood their task. To my misfortune, I know priests who in intellectual developments, and by their moral qualities, are not fit to be army scribes, much less priests. And you must allow that a bad teacher does less harm to a school than a bad priest."

Kunin glanced at Father Jacob, who was sitting doubled up, thinking intently about something, and obviously not listening to his guest.

"Iasha, just come here a minute," a woman's voice was heard to say behind the partition. Father Jacob gave a start, and went behind the partition; again there was a sound of whispering.

Kunin felt oppressed with despair about the tea.

"No, I won't wait here for some tea," he thought, looking at the clock. "I don't seem exactly a welcome guest. My host has hardly deigned to speak a word; he just sits there blinking his eyes."

Kunin reached for his hat, waited for Father Jacob, then took his departure.

"The morning has been wasted," he thought angrily, on his way back. "Dolt, blockhead, he takes as much interest in the school as I do in last year's snow! No, I won't cook kasha with him! We shall do nothing with that fellow. If the Mareschal knew the kind of pope we had here, he would not be in such a hurry to chatter about a school. We must first look about for a good pope, and then think of the school."

Kunin almost hated Father Jacob now. That pitiable little caricature of a creature in the long crumpled chasuble, with his womanish face, his way of officiating, his manner of life, his servile and timid deference, snuffed out that small particle of religious feeling which had kept till then a place in Kunin's breast, gently simmering along with the other cradle-songs of his childhood. The coldness and inattention, which his sincere and fervid interests in the other one's affairs had encountered, were too much for Kunin's *amour-propre* to bear.

That same evening Kunin walked about his room for a long time, then sat down resolutely at the table, and began a letter to the Prelate. Having requested money and blessings for the school, he, among other things, humbly, and as a son to his father, expressed his opinion on the priest of Sinkino. "He is young, he wrote, "not sufficiently developed, seems somewhat intemperate, and altogether does not answer to those requirements which the centuries have laid upon the Russian people with regard to their pastors."

When he had finished the letter Kunin gave a little sigh of relief, and lay down to sleep with the consciousness of having done a good work.

On the Monday morning, while he was still in bed, they came to announce that Father Jacob wanted to see him. He did not feel inclined to get up, so he told them to say he was not at home. He went away on the Tuesday to an assembly, and, returning on the Saturday, heard from the servants that Father Jacob had called every day during his absence.

"It looks as if he liked my cracknels!" thought Kunin.

On Sunday, towards evening, Father Jacob arrived. This time not only the folds of his cassock but also his hat was bespattered with mud. As on his first visit, he was red in the face and perspiring, and, as then, he sat on the arm of the chair.

Kunin decided not to start the conversation about the school, not to throw away pearls.

"I have brought you a list of the school-books, Paul Michaelitch," Father Jacob began.

"Thank you."

But it was too evident that Father Jacob had not come on account of the list. His whole manner expressed great uneasiness, at the same time decision was clearly written on his face, like someone suddenly illuminated by an idea. He had something important, or at the very least necessary to say, and was endeavoring to overcome his shyness.

"What is he silent for?" angrily thought Kunin. "He has sat himself here—shall I never get rid of him?"

So as somewhat to pass off the awkwardness of his silence, and to conceal the struggle going on within, the priest began to smile constrainedly. What with the perspiration, and the redness of his face, and the incompatibility of the fixed look of his gray-blue eyes with this lengthy tortured smile, Kunin turned away with loathing.

"Excuse me, batushka, I must leave you."

Father Jacob gave a start like someone who had been struck while asleep, then, without ceasing to smile, began in some agitation to arrange the folds of his cassock. Notwithstanding his aversion to this man, Kunin suddenly felt sorry for him, and wished to make amends for his harshness.

"Till next time, batushka," he said, "and before you leave I have a request to make. I have just been inspired, and have written two sermons. I will give them to you to look over. Read them at your leisure."

"Very good," said Father Jacob, covering with his hand Kunin's sermons lying on the table. "I'll take them. . . ."

He stood for a moment, hesitated, and, still arranging the folds of his cassock, suddenly ceased to smile constrainedly, and resolutely raised his head.

"Paul Michaelitch," he said, apparently with an attempt to speak loudly and distinctly.

"What do you want?"

"I heard that you had . . . paid off your secretary, and . . . and . . . were now looking for another. . . ."

"Yes. Have you someone to recommend?"

"I, do you see . . . I . . . Could not you give this place . . . to me?"

"But are you giving up the priesthood?" said Kunin in surprise.

"No, no," quickly answered Father Jacob, turning pale and trembling in all his limbs. "The Lord preserve me! It is not at all necessary—don't fear—I could do it between whiles . . . to increase my income. . . . It would not be necessary—don't worry."

"Hm . . . income. But I only give my secretary twenty roubles a month."

"Ghospodi! but I would take ten," whispered Father Jacob looking round. "I would be content with ten! You . . . you are astonished, and everyone is astonished. The greedy covetous pope, what does he do with his money? I myself feel that it is greedy . . . and condemn, blame myself, and look at people in the face with shame. To you, Paul Michaelitch, I confess, I call the Truth of God to witness. . . ."

Father Jacob took breath, and continued:

"I prepared the whole confession on the way here; but I have forgotten it, and now I can't find the words. I get a yearly income of one hundred and fifty roubles, and everyone wonders what I do with this money. I will clear my conscience: I send forty roubles a year to my brother Peter at the clerical school. I can write it all down, only my paper and pen. . . ."

"Ah, I believe you, I believe you. But what about it?" said Kunin, waving a hand, and feeling a fearful burden imposed on him in this great confidence of his guest, and not knowing how to get out of the way of the fearful glint of his eyes.

"Then, I have not entirely paid off my account at the Consistory; they reckoned two hundred roubles for my time there, to be paid in monthly installments of ten roubles. Consider how much remains to me! And then, besides that, I have to give Father Abraham at least three roubles a month."

"Who is Father Abraham?"

"Father Abraham was priest before me at Sinkino. They dismissed him because . . . of a failing, and he now is living in Sinkino. Where could he go? How was he to get food? He may be old, but he wants a fire, and bread, and clothing. I cannot admit that he in his position should have to beg. If it were so, I should be sinning. It would be to my shame. He owes everyone money, and it would be my sin if I did not pay for him."

Father Jacob jumped up, and, fixing the door with a senseless stare, began to walk from end to end of the room.

"My God! My God!" he muttered, raising and lowering his hands. "Save us Lord, and have mercy! Wherefore take upon oneself such a position if one had so little faith and no strength? There is no end to my despair! Save us, Mother of God!"

"Calm yourself, batushka!" said Kunin.

"I am famished, Paul Michaelitch," continued Father Jacob; "graciously forgive me, for I have not strength left. I know I have only to humble myself to ask, and everyone would help me, but . . . I cannot. It is against my conscience; how can I beg of moujiks? You work here and see for yourself. Who would dare raise a hand to ask the poor? And to beg of the rich, the local landowners, I cannot! It's pride—shame." Father Jacob gesticulated, and nervously combed back his hair with his hands. "It's a disgrace. God! how ashamed I am; I am too proud to let people see my poverty. When you came to see me there was no tea in the house, Paul Michaelitch, not a scrap, and you see, pride prevented my telling you so. I am ashamed of my clothes—just look at these patches; I am ashamed of my chasuble, my hunger. Is it right for a priest to have pride?"

Father Jacob stood still in the middle of the room, as if he did not notice the presence of Kunin, and began to reason with himself.

"Now, suppose I bear hunger and shame? But then, good Lord, I have my wife, and I have taken her from comfortable surroundings; her hands are white and soft, she is accustomed to tea, and white bread, and sheets. When she was with her parents she played the piano; she is still young, not twenty—she would no doubt like to dress up, amuse herself, go and pay visits. But she lives with me less well than any cook, and does not like to show herself in the street. My God! My God! Her only treat is when I bring her an apple, or a cracknel, from one of my visits."

Father Jacob again combed his hair back with his fingers.

"And the result is, not love, but pity. I can't see her without a feeling of pain. And these are the things which happen on earth, ghospodi! Things happen which, if they were in the newspapers, people wouldn't believe them. And when will all this end?"

"That'll do, batushka!" Kunin cried, frightened by his tone. "Why look so gloomily on life?"

"Graciously forgive me, Paul Michaelitch," Father Jacob mumbled as if he were drunk. "Forgive all this—it's nothing, don't notice it. . . . I only blame myself, and will always do so . . . always."

Father Jacob looked around, then whispered:

"One morning, early, I was going from Sinkino to Lutchkovo, when I noticed a woman standing by the river. I went nearer, and couldn't believe my eyes. Mercy! it was the doctor's wife rinsing her linen. . . . The doctor's wife had done her course at the Institute, therefore . . . in order not to be discovered washing, waited her opoprtunity, got up before anyone else, and went a verst away from the village. There's pride! When she saw that I was quite close to her and had discovered her poverty, she grew quite red. I lost my wits, I was scared, I rushed up to her, I wanted to help her, but she hid her linen from me, afraid lest I should see her torn chemises."

"It all seems incredible," said Kunin sitting down, and looking almost with horror at Father Jacob's white face.

"That's just it—incredible. It has never before happened, Paul Michaelitch, never, that the doctor's wife has to go to the river to rinse her linen! Never in any country has it happened! I, as pastor and spiritual father, should not allow this, but what am I to do? What? I myself am just waiting to be attended to for nothing by her husband. You remarked just now: 'It all seemed incredible.' One can't believe one's eyes. During Mass, for instance, I look from the altar, I see my congregation, the hungry Abraham, his wife, and I think of the doctor's wife, with her hands blue from the ice-cold water; believe me, one's senses leave one, and one stands there like a fool, insensible, till the sacristan calls. It's awful!"

Father Jacob again began to walk about.

"Oh, Jesus!" he said, with a gesture of his hands. "Holy Saints! I can't even officiate; you talk to me of a school, while I stand like a wooden figure, understanding nothing, and thinking only of food, even at the altar. But what am I doing?" he suddenly recollected. "You want to go—excuse me, it is just me! . . . forgive me. . . ."

Kunin silently gave his hand to Father Jacob, and accompanied him to the vestibule; then, returning to his room, stood at the window. He saw Father Jacob leave the house, pull his wide-brimmed rusty-colored hat over his eyes, and, hanging his head as if ashamed of his disclosures, slowly walk away.

"I don't see his horse," thought Kunin.

Kunin dared not think that the priest had come to see him day after day on foot: it was seven or eight versts to Sinkino, and mud up to one's neck. A moment after, Kunin saw Andrew, the coachman, and the boy, Paramon, running towards Father Jacob for his blessing, and splashing him with mud as they jumped over the puddles.

Father Jacob slowly took off his hat, blessed Andrew, then blessed the boy and stroked his head.

Kunin passed his hand over his eyes, and it seemed to him there was moisture on it. He left the window, and with a chagrined expression surveyed the room, in which he still seemed to hear the timid choking voice of the priest. He glanced at the table—fortunately, Father Jacob, in his hurry, had forgotten to take the sermons with him; Kunin seized them, tore them into little bits, and flung them with loathing under the table.

"And I did not know!" he moaned, sinking into the sofa. "I, who have been working here for over a year as life-member of the Council, Honorary Justice of the Peace, Member of the School Committee! Blind puppet! Popinjay! We must help him quickly. We must, indeed!"

He tossed uneasily, applied his hand to his forehead, and exerted his brain.

"On the 20th day of this month I shall get my pay of 200 roubles. With some plausible excuse I will slip some into his hand, and some to the doctor's wife. I'll order a thanksgiving service from the one, and I'll feign illness for the doctor, in that way I shall not offend their pride. And I'll help Abraham. . . ." He counted his money on his fingers, and did not like to allow to himself that these 200 roubles were scarcely sufficient to pay the steward, the servants, and the moujik who brought the meat. Involuntarily, he remembered the recent past, in which he had senselessly run through his father's patrimony; when as a twenty-year-old novice he had made presents of expensive fans to courtesans, had paid the cab-driver Kuzma ten roubles a day, and out of vanity had offered presents to actresses. Ah, how useful all those squandered three-rouble, ten-rouble notes would be now!

"Father Abraham lives on three roubles a month," thought Kunin. "For a rouble, the popess could make herself a skirt, and the doctor's wife could have a washer-woman. I will help them all the same. It's a duty!"

And here . . . suddenly . . . Kunin remembered the information he had written to the Prelate, and he shriveled up as if seized by a sudden attack of cold. The recollection of this overwhelmed him with a feeling of crushing shame towards himself and the Invisible Truth. . . .

And so began and ended the sincere efforts towards useful activity of a well-intentioned but thoroughly overfed and inconsiderate being.

Miss N. N.'s Story

About nine years go, during hay-making time, I and Peter Sergéich, assistant magistrate, rode over to the station to fetch the letters, one summer night.

The weather was clear, but when returning we heard thunder and saw an angry black cloud speeding towards us. On its dark background our house and the church looked white and the tall poplars seemed turned to silver. There was a scent of rain and new-mown hay in the air. My companion was gay, laughed and talked all sorts of nonsense. He said if on our way we could come across some mediæval castle, a shelter from the storm, and where in the end we would be killed by the lightning, he would rejoice.

Suddenly the first wave passed over the rye and oat fields, and a violent gust of wind raised a cloud of dust on the road. Peter Sergéich laughed and spurred his horse on.

"Great!" he shouted. "This is ideal!"

Infected by his gaiety and by the thought that I would soon be wet to the skin, and might be killed by the lightning, I also began to laugh.

This whirlwind and the rapid riding against the storm took the breath away, making one feel like a bird; it agitated and tickled the breast. When we rode into our yard the wind had subsided, but large drops of rain rattled on the grass and on the roofs. There was not a soul near the stables.

Peter Sergéich unbridled the horses and led them to the stalls. While waiting for him to finish, I stood at the door and looked at the slanting rain. The luscious and exciting odour of the hay was more perceptible here than in the fields; the clouds and rain made it dusk.

"What a peal!" Peter Sergéich said, coming up to me after a terribly prolonged peal of thunder, when it appeared as if the sky had been rent asunder. "Wasn't that a peal?"

He stood beside me in the doorway, still breathing heavily from the rapid riding, and he looked at me. I noticed that he was admiring me.

"Natalia Vladimirovna," he said, "I would give everything I possess if I could only remain thus and look at you for ever. You are beautiful to-day."

He gazed at me enraptured, and with entreaty in his eyes; his face was pale, and on his beard and moustache raindrops glistened, and they, too, seemed to look at me with love.

"I love you!" he said. "I love you and am happy when I see you. I know you cannot be my wife: I want nothing, I require nothing, but that you should know I love you. Be silent, do not answer me, do not pay any attention to me, only know that you are dear to me, and permit me to look at you."

His enthusiasm was communicated to me. I looked at his inspired face; I heard his voice which was blended with the noise of the rain, and as if enchanted I was unable to move.

I wished to look at his brilliant eyes and listen to him without end.

"You are silent—excellent!" Peter Sergéich said. "Continue to be silent."

I was happy. I laughed with pleasure and ran under the pelting rain into the

134

house; he also laughed, and with a skip and a jump he ran after me.

Making a noise like two children we both rushed, wet and breathless, up the stairs and bounced into the room. My father and brother, who were unaccustomed to see me laughing and gay, looked at me with surprise, and they also began to laugh.

The storm clouds passed away, the thunder became silent, but still the raindrops glistened in Peter Sergéich's beard. The whole of that evening until supper he sang, whistled, played noisily with the dog, chased it round the rooms and just missed knocking the manservant, who was bringing in the samovar, off his legs. At supper he ate very much, talked very loud, and asserted that when you ate fresh cucumbers in the winter you had a taste of spring in the mouth.

When I went to bed I lit my candle, opened the window wide and gave myself up to the undefined feelings that possessed my breast. I remembered that I was free, healthy, distinguished, rich, that I was loved, but chiefly that I was distinguished and rich—distinguished, and rich—how nice that was, my God! . . . Then feeling the cold that was borne to me together with the dew from the garden, I cuddled up in bed and tried to understand if I loved or did not love Peter Sergéich . . . and not being able to understand anything I fell asleep.

In the morning when I saw a trembling spot of sunshine and the shadow of lime branches on my bed, all that had happened the day before arose vividly in my mind. Life appeared to me rich, varied, full of attractions. I

dressed quickly, singing, and ran into the garden. . . .

And what was afterwards? Afterwards—was nothing. In the winter, when we were living in town, Peter Sergéich came to us but seldom. The acquaintances of the country are only charming in the country and in summer —in town, and in winter they lose half their attraction. When in town you offer them tea, they seem to be in other people's coats, and stir their tea too long with the spoons. Sometimes in town Peter Sergéich also spoke of love, but how different it sounded when spoken in the village. In town we felt more strongly the wall that separated us! I was distinguished and rich; and he was poor, he was not even noble, only the son of a deacon, he was only an assistant magistrate; we both—I from youth, and he, God knows why—considered this wall very high and thick, and he, when he came to us in town, smiled affectedly and criticized the higher society, or remained gloomily silent when anybody else was in the drawing-room. There is never a wall that cannot be broken through; but the heroes of present-day fiction, as far as I know them, are too timid, too slow, too lazy and fearsome, and they are too apt to be satisfied with the thought that they are failures, and that their own life has duped them; instead of struggling, they only criticize and call the world mean, and they forget that their own criticism gradually degenerates into meanness.

I was loved; happiness was near, and it appeared to be living shoulder to shoulder with me. I sang as I lived, not trying to understand myself, not knowing for what I waited, or what I wanted from life—and time sped on and on. People passed me with their love, bright days and warm nights flitted by; nightingales sang—there was the scent of hay—and all this so charming and wonderful in recollection passed quickly by me unvalued, as with everybody, leaving no trace and vanished like a mist. . . . Where is it all?

My father died. I have grown old. All that pleased me, that caressed me, that gave me hope—the noise of rain, the rolling of thunder, the thoughts of happiness, the words of love—all this has become a mere recollection, and I see before me a flat, empty plain; there is not a single living soul on the plain, and there on the distant horizon it is dark and terrible . . .

There was a bell. Peter Sergéich had come to see me. When I see the country in winter and remember how green it became for me in summer, I whisper: "Oh, my darlings!"

And when I see the people with whom I passed my spring, I grow sad and warm, and I whisper the same words.

Long since, by my father's influence, he had been transferred to town. He has grown somewhat older, somewhat thinner. Long ago he ceased to talk to me of love, he no longer talked nonsense, he did not like his work; he had some sort of ailment, he was disappointed with something; he had given up expecting anything from life and he had no zest in existence. He sat down near the fire and looked silently into the flames. And I, not knowing what to say, asked:

"Well, what is it?"

"Nothing," he replied.

Then there was silence again. The red glow of the fire skipped about his sad face.

I remembered the past, and suddenly my shoulders began shaking, and I burst into bitter tears. I became unbearably sorry for myself, and for this man, and I passionately longed for that which was passed, and for that which life now refused us. And now I no longer thought that I was distinguished and rich.

I sobbed aloud, pressing my temples and murmured:

"My God, my God, life is ruined . . ."

And he sat there in silence and did not say: "Do not cry." He understood that it was necessary to cry, and that the time had come for that. I saw in his eyes that he was sorry for me, and I, too, was sorry for him, and I was vexed for that poor timid wretch who had not been able to arrange either my life or his own.

When I conducted him to the door it appeared to me that he was purposely very long in the ante-room in putting on his fur coat. He kissed my hand a couple of times, and he looked long into my tear-stained eyes. I think at that moment he remembered the thunderstorm, the streams of rain, our laughter and my face as it was then. He wanted to say something to me, and he would have been glad to have said it; but he said nothing, he only shook his head and pressed my hand hard. God bless him!

When he had gone I returned into my boudoir and sat down again on the carpet in front of the fire. The red coals had changed into ashes and were going out. The frost knocked more fiercely at the windows, and the wind began singing a song about something in the chimney.

My maid came into the room, and thinking I had fallen asleep, called to me. . . .

The Young Wife

THE little town of B——, consisting of two or three crooked streets, was sound asleep. There was a complete stillness in the motionless air. Nothing could be heard but far away, outside the town no doubt, the barking of a dog in a thin, hoarse tenor. It was close upon daybreak.

Everything had long been asleep. The only person not asleep was the young wife of Tchernomordik, a qualified dispenser who kept a chemist's shop at B——. She had gone to bed and got up again three times, but could not sleep, she did not know why. She sat at the open window in her nightdress and looked into the street. She felt bored, depressed, vexed . . . so vexed that she felt quite inclined to cry—again she did not know why. There seemed to be a lump in her chest that kept rising into her throat. . . . A few paces behind her Tchernomordik lay curled up close to the wall, snoring sweetly. A greedy flea was stabbing the bridge of his nose, but he did not feel it, and was positively smiling, for he was dreaming that everyone in the town had a cough, and was buying from him the King of Denmark's cough-drops. He could not have been wakened now by pinpricks or by cannon or by caresses.

The chemist's shop was almost at the extreme end of the town, so that the chemist's wife could see far into the fields. She could see the eastern horizon growing pale by degrees, then turning crimson as though from a great fire. A big broad-faced moon peeped out unexpectedly from behind bushes in the distance. It was red (as a rule when the moon emerges from behind bushes it appears to be blushing).

Suddenly in the stillness of the night there came the sound of footsteps and a jingle of spurs. She could hear voices.

"That must be the officers going home to the camp from the Police Captain's," thought the chemist's wife.

Soon afterwards two figures wearing officers' white tunics came into sight: one big and tall, the other thinner and shorter. . . . They slouched along by the fence, dragging one leg after the other and talking loudly together. As they passed the chemist's shop, they walked more slowly than ever, and glanced up at the windows.

"It smells like a chemist's," said the thin one. "And so it is! Ah, I remember. . . . I came here last week to buy some castor-oil. There's a chemist here with a sour face and the jawbone of an ass! Such a jawbone, my dear fellow! It must have been a jawbone like that Samson killed the Philistines with."

"M'yes," said the big one in a bass voice. "The pharmacist is asleep. And his wife is asleep too. She is a pretty woman, Obtyosov."

"I saw her. I liked her very much. . . . Tell me, doctor, can she possibly love that jawbone of an ass? Can she?"

"No, most likely she does not love him," sighed the doctor, speaking as though he were sorry for the chemist. "The little woman is asleep behind the window, Obtyosov, what? Tossing with the heat, her little mouth half open . . . and one little foot hanging out of bed. I bet that fool the chemist

137

doesn't realize what a lucky fellow he is. . . . No doubt he sees no difference between a woman and a bottle of carbolic!"

"I say, doctor," said the officer, stopping. "Let us go into the shop and buy something. Perhaps we shall see her."

"What an idea—in the night!"

"What of it! They are obliged to serve one even at night. My dear fellow, let us go in!"

"If you like. . . ."

The chemist's wife, hiding behind the curtain, heard a muffled ring. Looking round at her husband, who was smiling and snoring sweetly as before, she threw on her dress, slid her bare feet into her slippers, and ran to the shop.

On the other side of the glass door she could see two shadows. The chemist's wife turned up the lamp and hurried to the door to open it, and now she felt neither vexed nor bored nor inclined to cry, though her heart was thumping. The big doctor and the slender Obtyosov walked in. Now she could get a view of them. The doctor was corpulent and swarthy; he wore a beard and was slow in his movements. At the slightest motion his tunic seemed as though it would crack, and perspiration came on to his face. The officer was rosy, clean-shaven, feminine-looking, and as supple as an English whip.

"What may I give you?" asked the chemist's wife, holding her dress across her bosom.

"Give us . . . er-er . . . four pennyworth of peppermint lozenges!"

Without haste the chemist's wife took down a jar from a shelf and began weighing out lozenges. The customers stared fixedly at her back; the doctor screwed up his eyes like a well-fed cat, while the lieutenant was very grave.

"It's the first time I've seen a lady serving in a chemist's shop," observed the doctor.

"There's nothing out of the way in it," replied the chemist's wife, looking out of the corner of her eye at the rosy-cheeked officer. "My husband has no assistant, and I always help him."

"To be sure. . . . You have a charming little shop! What a number of different . . . jars! And you are not afraid of moving about among the poisons? Brrr!"

The chemist's wife sealed up the parcel and handed it to the doctor. Obtyosov gave her the money. Half a minute of silence followed. . . . The men exchanged glances, took a step towards the door, then looked at one another again.

"Will you give me two pennyworth of soda?" said the doctor.

Again the chemist's wife slowly and languidly raised her hand to the shelf.

"Haven't you in the shop anything . . . such as . . ." muttered Obtyosov, moving his fingers, "something, so to say, allegorical . . . revivifying . . . seltzer-water, for instance. Have you any seltzer-water?"

"Yes," answered the chemist's wife.

"Bravo! You're a fairy, not a woman! Give us three bottles!"

The chemist's wife hurriedly sealed up the soda and vanished through the door into the darkness.

"A peach!" said the doctor, with a wink. "You wouldn't find a pineapple like that in the island of Madeira! Eh? What do you say? Do you hear the snoring, though? That's his worship the chemist enjoying sweet repose."

A minute later the chemist's wife came back and set five bottles on the counter. She had just been in the cellar, and so was flushed and rather excited.

"Sh-sh! . . . quietly!" said Obtyosov when, after uncorking the bottles, she dropped the corkscrew. "Don't make such a noise; you'll wake your husband."

"Well, what if I do wake him?"

"He is sleeping so sweetly . . . he must be dreaming of you. . . . To your health!"

"Besides," boomed the doctor, hiccupping after the seltzer-water, "husbands are such a dull business that it would be very nice of them to be always asleep. How good a drop of red wine would be in this water!"

"What an idea!" laughed the chemist's wife.

"That would be splendid. What a pity they don't sell spirits in chemist's shops. Though you ought to sell wine as a medicine. Have you any *vinum gallicum rubrum?*"

"Yes."

"Well, then, give us some! Bring it here, damn it!"

"How much do you want?"

"*Quantum satis.* . . . Give us an ounce each in the water, and afterwards we'll see. . Obtyosov, what do you say? First with water and afterwards *per se.* . . ."

The doctor and Obtyosov sat down to the counter, took off their caps, and began drinking the wine.

"The wine, one must admit, is wretched stuff! *Vinum nastissimum!* Though in the presence of . . . er . . . it tastes like nectar. You are enchanting, madam! In imagination I kiss your hand."

"I would give a great deal to do so not in imagination," said Obtyosov. "On my honor, I'd give my life."

"That's enough," said Madame Tchernomordik, flushing and assuming a serious expression.

"What a flirt you are, though!" the doctor laughed softly, looking slyly at her from under his brows. "Your eyes seem to be firing shot: piff-paff! I congratulate you: you've conquered! We are vanquished!"

The chemist's wife looked at their ruddy faces, listened to their chatter, and soon she, too, grew quite lively. Oh, she felt so gay! She entered into the conversation, she laughed, flirted, and even, after repeated requests from the customers, drank two ounces of wine.

"You officers ought to come in oftener from the camp," she said; "it's awful how dreary it is here. I'm simply dying of it."

"I should think so!" said the doctor indignantly. "Such a peach, a miracle of nature, thrown away in the wilds! How well Griboyedov said, 'Into the wilds, to Saratov!' It's time for us to be off, though. Delighted to have made your acquaintance . . . very. How much do we owe you?"

The chemist's wife raised her eyes to the ceiling and her lips moved for some time.

"Twelve roubles forty-eight kopecks," she said.

Obtyosov took out of his pocket a fat pocketbook, and after fumbling for some time among the notes, paid.

"Your husband's sleeping sweetly . . . he must be dreaming," he muttered, pressing her hand at parting.

"I don't like to hear silly remarks. . . ."

"What silly remarks? On the contrary, it's not silly at all . . . even Shakespeare said: 'Happy is he who in his youth is young.' "

"Let go my hand."

At last after much talk and after kissing the lady's hand at parting, the customers went out of the shop irresolutely, as though they were wondering whether they had not forgotten something.

She ran quickly into the bedroom and sat down in the same place. She saw the doctor and the officer, on coming out of the shop, walk lazily away a distance of twenty paces; then they stopped and began whispering together. What about? Her heart throbbed, there was a pulsing in her temples, and why she did not know. . . . Her hear beat violently as though those two whispering outside were deciding her fate.

Five minutes later the doctor parted from Obtyosov and walked on, while Obtyosov came back. He walked past the shop once and a second time. . . . He would stop near the door and then take a few steps again. At last the bell tinkled discreetly.

"What? Who is there?" the chemist's wife heard her husband's voice suddenly. "There's a ring at the bell, and you don't hear it," he said, severely. "Is that the way to do things?"

He got up, put on his dressing-gown, and staggering, half asleep, flopped in his slippers to the shop.

"What . . . is it?" he asked Obtyosov.

"Give me . . . give me four pennyworth of peppermint lozenges."

Sniffing continually, yawning, dropping asleep as he moved, and knocking his knees against the counter, the chemist went to the shelf and reached down the jar.

Two minutes later the chemist's wife saw Obtyosov go out of the shop, and, after he had gone some steps, she saw him throw the packet of peppermints on the dusty road. The doctor came from behind a corner to meet him. . . . They met and, gesticulating, vanished in the morning mist.

"How unhappy I am!" said the chemist's wife, looking angrily at her husband, who was undressing quickly to get into bed again. "Oh, how unhappy I am!" she repeated, suddenly melting into bitter tears. "And nobody knows, nobody knows. . . ."

"I forgot fourpence on the counter." muttered the chemist, pulling the quilt over him. "Put it away in the till, please. . . ."

And at once he fell asleep again.

The Peasants

CHAPTER I

BLOWS

Nikolai Tchikildeyeff, waiter, of the Slaviansky Bazaar Hotel at Moscow, became ill. Once in a corridor he stumbled and fell with a tray of ham and peas and had to resign. What money he had, his own and his wife's, soon went on treatment. He was tired of idleness and had to return to his native village. It was cheaper to live at home, after all, and the best place for invalids; and there is some truth in the proverb, "At home the walls feel good."

He arrived at Zhukovo towards evening. He pictured his birthplace as cosy, and comfortable as a child, but now when he entered the hut he knew it was close, and dirty inside. And his wife Olga and little daughter Sasha looked questioningly at the big, sooty stove, black from smoke, which took up half the hut and was covered with flies. The stove was crooked, the logs in the walls sloped, and it seemed that every minute the hut would tumble to pieces. The ikon-corner, instead of pictures, was hung with bottle-labels and newspaper-cuttings. Poverty, poverty! Of the grown-ups no one was at home—they reaped in the fields; and alone on the stove sat an eight-year-old girl, fair-haired, unwashed, and so indifferent that she did not even look at the strangers. Beneath, a white cat rubbed herself against the pot-hanger.

"Puss, puss!" cried Sasha. "Pussy!"

"She can't hear," said the girl on the stove. "She's deaf!"

"How deaf?"

"Deaf. . . . From beating."

The first glance told Nikolai and Olga the life awaiting them; but they said nothing, silently laid down their bundles, and went into the street. The hut was the third from the corner, and the oldest and poorest in sight; its next-door neighbour, indeed, was little better; but the corner cabin boasted an iron roof and curtains in the windows. This cabin had no fence, and stood alone; it was the village inn. In one continuous row stretched other huts; and, as a whole, the village, peaceful and meditative, with the willows, elders, and mountain-ash peeping out of the gardens, was pleasing to see.

Behind the cabins the ground sloped steeply towards the river; and here and there in the clay stuck denuded stones. On the slope, around these stones and the potters' pits, lay heaps of potsherds, some brown, some red; and below stretched a broad, flat, and bright green meadow, already mown, and now given over to the peasants' herds. A verst from the village ran the winding river with its pretty tufted banks; and beyond the river another field, a herd, long strings of white geese; then, as on the village side, a steep ascent. On the crest of the hill rose another village with a five-cupolaed church, and a little beyond it the local noble's house.

"It's a fine place, your village," said Olga, crossing herself towards the church. "What freedom, Lord!"

At that moment (it was Saturday

night) the church bells rang for vesper service. In the valley beneath, two little girls with a water-pail turned their heads towards the church and listened to the bells.

"At the Slaviansky Bazaar they're sitting down to dinner," said Nikolai thoughtfully.

Seated on the brink of the ravine, Nikolai and Olga watched the setting sun and the image of the gold and purple sky in the river and in the church windows, and inhaled the soft, restful, inexpressibly pure air, unknown to them in Moscow. When the sun had set came lowing cattle and bleating sheep; geese flew towards them; and all was silent. The soft light faded from the air and evening shadows swept across the land.

Meantime the absent family returned to the hut. First came Nikolai's father and mother, dry, bent, and toothless, and of equal height. Later, their sons' wives, Marya and Fekla, employed on the noble's farm across the river. Marya, wife of Nikolai's brother Kiriak, had six children; Fekla, wife of Denis, then a soldier, two; and when Nikolai, entering the hut, saw the whole family, all these big and little bodies, which moved in the loft, in cradles, in corners; when he saw the greed with which the old man and women ate black bread soaked in water, he felt that he had made a mistake in coming home, sick, penniless, and—what was worse—with his family.

"And where is brother Kiriak?" he asked, greeting his parents.

"He's watchman at the trader's," answered the old man. "In the wood. He's a good lad, but drinks heavily."

"He's no profit," said the old woman in a lachrymose voice. "Our men are not much use, they bring nothing home with them, and only take things. Our Kiriak drinks; and the old man, there's no use hiding it, himself knows the way to the drink-shop. They've angered our Mother in Heaven!"

In honor of the guests the samovar was brought out. The tea smelt of fish, the sugar was damp and looked as if it had been gnawed, the bread and vessels were covered with cockroaches; it was painful to drink, and painful to hear the talk—of nothing but poverty and sickness. Before they had emptied their first glasses, from the yard came a loud drawling, drunken cry—

"Ma-arya!"

"That sounds like Kiriak," said the old man. "Talk of the devil and he appears!"

The peasants were silent. A moment later came the same cry, rough and drawling, and this time it seemed to come from underground.

"Ma-arya!"

The elder daughter-in-law, Marya, turned deadly pale and pressed her body to the stove; and it was strange to see the expression of terror on the face of this strong, broad-shouldered, ugly woman. Her daughter, the little, indifferent girl who had sat on the stove, suddenly began to cry loudly.

"Stop howling, cholera!" cried angrily Fekla, a good-looking woman, also strong and broad-shouldered. "He won't kill you!"

From the old man Nikolai soon learned that Marya was afraid to live with her husband in the forest; and that when he had drunk too much Kiriak came for her, and made scenes and beat her mercilessly.

"Ma-arya!" came the cry, this time from outside the door.

"Help me, for the love of heaven, help me!" chattered Marya, breathing as if she had been thrown into icy water. "Help me, kinsmen——"

The houseful of children suddenly began to cry, and, seeing them, Sasha did the same. A drunken cough echoed without, and into the hut came a tall, black-bearded muzhik wearing a winter cap. In the dim lamp-light his face was barely visible, and all the more terrible. It was Kiriak. He went straight to his wife, flourished his arm, and struck her with his clenched fist in the face. Marya did not utter a sound, the blow seemed to have stunned her, but she seemed to dwindle; a stream of blood flowed out of her nose.

"It's a shame, a shame," muttered the old man, climbing on the stove. "And before our visitors! It's a sin!"

The old woman kept silence, and, bent in two, seemed lost in thought. Fekla rocked the cradle. Kiriak seized Marya's hand, dragged her to the door, and, to increase her terror, roared like a beast. But at that moment he saw the visitors, and stopped.

"So you've come!" he began, releasing his wife. "My own brother and his family. . . ."

He prayed a moment before the image, staggered, opened his red, drunken eyes, and continued—

"My brother and family have come to their parents' house . . . from Moscow, that means . . . .The old capital, that means, the city of Moscow, mother of cities. . . . Excuse . . ."

Amid the silence of all, he dropped on the bench near the samovar, and began to drink loudly from a saucer. When he had drunk ten cupfuls he leaned back on the bench and began to snore.

Bed-time came. Nikolai, as an invalid, was given a place on the stove beside the old man; Sasha slept on the floor; and Olga went with the young women to the shed.

"Never mind, my heart!" she said, lying on the hay beside Marya. "Crying is no help. You must bear it. In the Bible it is written, 'Whosoever shall smite thee on thy right cheek, turn to him the other also.' Don't cry, my heart!"

And then, in a whisper, she began to tell of Moscow, of her life there, how she had served as housemaid in furnished lodgings.

"In Moscow the houses are big and built of brick," said Olga. "There is no end of churches—forty forties of them—my heart; and the houses are all full of gentlemen, so good-looking, so smart!"

And Marya answered that she had never been in the district town, much less in Moscow; she was illiterate, and knew no prayers, not even "Our Father." Both she and her sister-in-law Fekla, who sat some way off and listened, were ignorant in the extreme, and understood nothing. Both disliked their husbands; Marya dreaded Kiriak, shook with terror when he stayed with her, and after his departure her head ached from the smell of vodka and tobacco. And Fekla, in answer to the question did she want her husband, answered angrily—

"What? . . . Him?"

For a time the women spoke, and then lay down.

It was cold, and a cock crew loudly, hindering sleep. When the blue morning light began to break through the chinks, Fekla rose stealthily and went out, and her movements could be heard, as she ran down the street in her bare feet.

CHAPTER II

MARYA

WHEN Olga went to church she took with her Marya. As they descended the path to the meadow, both were in good humour. Olga liked the freedom of the country; and Marya found in her sister-in-law a kindred spirit. The sun was rising. Close to the meadow flew a sleepy hawk; the river was dull, for there was a slight mist, but the hill beyond it was bathed in light; the church glittered, and rooks cawed in the garden of the big house beyond.

"The old man is not bad," said Marya. "But my mother-in-law is cross and quarrelsome. Our own corn lasted till Shrovetide; now we have to buy at the inn; and the old woman is angry, and says, 'You eat too much.'"

"Never mind, my heart! You must bear that too. It is written in the Bible, 'Come unto Me all ye that are weary and heavy laden.'"

Olga spoke gravely and slowly; and walked, like a pilgrim, quickly and briskly. Every day she read the Gospel, aloud, like a clerk; and though there was much that she did not understand, the sacred words touched her to tears, and words like *astche, dondezhe* she pronounced with beating heart. She believed in God, in the Virgin, in the saints; and her faith was that it was wrong to do evil to any man, even to Germans, gipsies, and Jews. When she read aloud the

Gospel, even when she stopped at words she did not understand, her face grew compassionate, kindly, and bright.

"What part are you from?" asked Marya.

"Vladimir. I have been long in Moscow, since I was eight years old."

They approached the river. On the other bank stood a woman, undressing herself.

"That is our Fekla!" said Marya. "She's been across the river at the squire's house. With the stewards! She's impudent and ill-spoken—awful!"

Black-browed Fekla, with loosened hair, jumped into the river, and, young and firm as a girl, splashed in the water, making big waves.

"She's impudent—awful!" repeated Marya.

Across the river was a shaky bridge of beams, and at that moment beneath it in the clear, transparent water swam carp. On the green bushes, imaged in the water, glistened dew. It was warm and pleasant. What a wonderful morning! And indeed, how splendid would be life in this world were it not for poverty, hideous, hopeless poverty, from which there is no escape! But look back to the village, and memory awakens all the events of yesterday; and the intoxication of joy vanishes in a wink.

The women reached the church. Marya stopped near the door, afraid to go inside. She feared, too, to sit down, though the service would not begin till nine o'clock, and stood all the time.

As the Gospel was being read the worshippers suddenly moved, and made way for the squire's family. In came two girls in white dresses with wide-brimmed hats, and behind them a stout, rosy boy dressed as a sailor. Their coming pleased Olga; she felt that here at last were well-taught, orderly, good-looking people. But Marya looked at them furtively and gloomily. as if they were not human beings but monsters who would crush her if she failed to make way.

And when the deacon sang out in a bass voice, she fancied she heard the cry "Ma-arya!" and shuddered.

CHAPTER III

SONGS

THE village quickly heard of the visitors' arrival, and when church was over the hut was crowded. The Leonuitcheffs, Matveitcheffs, and Ilitchoffs came for news of their kinsmen in Moscow. Every man in Zhukovo who could read and write was taken to Moscow as waiter or boots; and, similarly, the village across the river supplied only bakers; and this custom obtained since before the Emancipation. when a certain legendary Luka Ivanuitch, of Zhukovo, was lord of the buffet in a Moscow club, and hired none but fellow-villagers. These, in turn attaining power, sent for their kinsmen and found them posts in inns and restaurants; so that from that time Zhukovo was called by the local population Khamskaya or Kholuefka. Nikolai was taken to Moscow at the age of eleven, and given a post by Ivan Makaruitch, one of the Matveitcheffs, then porter at the Hermitage Gardens. And, now, turning to the Matveitcheffs, Nikolai said gravely—

"Ivan Makaruitch was my benefactor; it is my duty to pray God for him day and night, for it was through him I became a good man."

"*Batiushka* mine!" said tearfully a tall, old woman, Ivan Makaruitch's sister. "And have you no news of him?"

"He was at Omon's last winter; and this season, I heard, he's in some gardens outside town. . . . He's grown old. Once in the summer he'd bring home ten roubles a day, but now everywhere business is dull—the old man's in a bad way."

The women, old and young, looked at the high felt boots on Nikolai's legs. and at his pale face, and said sadly—

"You're no money-maker, Nikolai Osipuitch, no money-bringer!"

And all caressed Sasha. Sasha was past her tenth birthday. but. small and very thin, she looked not more than seven. Among the sunburnt, untidy village girls, in their long cotton shirts, pale-faced, big-eyed Sasha, with the red ribbon in her hair, seemed a toy, a little strange animal caught in the fields, and brought back to the hut.

"And she knows how to read!" boasted Olga, looking tenderly at her daughter. "Read something, child!" she said, taking a New Testament from the corner. "Read something aloud and let the orthodox listen!"

The old, heavy, leather-bound, bent-edged Bible smelt like a monk. Sasha raised her eyebrows, and began in a loud drawl—

". . . And when they were departed, behold the angel of the Lord appeareth to Joseph in a dream, saying, Arise and take the young child and his mother . . ."

" 'The young child and his mother,' " repeated Olga. She reddened with joy.

". . . and flee into Egypt . . . and

be thou there until I bring thee word. . . ."

At the word "until" Olga could not longer restrain her emotion and began to cry. Marya followed her example, and Ivan Makaruitch's sister cried also. The old man coughed and fussed about, seeking a present for his grandchild, but he found nothing, and waved his hand. When the reading ended, the visitors dispersed to their homes, deeply touched, and pleased with Olga and Sasha.

As the day was Sunday the family remained in the hut. The old woman, whom husband, daughters-in-law, and grandchildren alike addressed as "grandmother," did everything with her own hands: she lighted the stove, set the samovar; she even worked in the fields; and at the same time growled that she was tortured with work. She tortured herself with dread that the family might eat too much, and took care that her husband and daughters-in-law did not sit with idle hands. Once when she found that the innkeeper's geese had got into her kitchen-garden, she rushed at once out of the house armed with a long stick; and for half an hour screamed piercingly over her cabbages, which were as weak and thin as their owner. Later she imagined that a hawk had swooped on her chickens, and with loud curses she flew to meet the hawk. She lost her temper and growled from morning to night, and often screamed so loudly that passers-by stopped to listen.

Her husband she treated badly, denouncing him sometimes as a lie-abed, sometimes as "cholera." The old man was a hopeless, unsubstantial muzhik, and perhaps, indeed, if she had not spurred him on, he would have done no work at all, but sat all day on the stove and talked. He complained to his son at great length of certain enemies in the village and of the wrongs he suffered day by day; and it was tiresome to hear him.

"Yes." he said, putting his arms to his waist. "Yes. A week after Elevation I sold my hay for thirty kopeks a pood. Yes. Good! . . . and this means that one morning I drive my hay cart and interfere with nobody; and suddenly, in an evil moment, I look round, and out of the inn comes the headman, Antip Siedelnikoff. 'Where are you driving, old So-and-so?' and bangs me in the ear!"

Kiriak's head ached badly from drink, and he was ashamed before his brother.

"It's drink that does it. *Akh,* my Lord God!" he stammered, shaking his big head. "You, brother and you, sister, forgive me, for the love of Christ; I feel bad myself."

To celebrate Sunday, they bought herrings at the inn, and made soup of the heads. At midday all sat down to tea and drank until they sweated and, it seemed, swelled up; and when they had drunk the tea they set to on the soup, all eating from the same bowl. The old woman hid away the herrings.

At night a potter baked his pots in the ravine. In the meadow below, the village girls sang in chorus; and some one played a concertina. Beyond the river also glowed a potter's oven, and village girls sang; and from afar the music sounded soft and harmonious. The muzhiks gathered in the inn; they sang tipsily, each a different song; and the language they used made Olga shudder and exclaim—

"Akh, batiushki!"

She was astonished by the incessant blasphemy, and by the fact that the older men, whose time had nearly come, blasphemed worst of all. And the children and girls listened to this language, and seemed in no way uncomfortable; it was plain they were used to it, and had heard it from the cradle.

Midnight came; the potters' fires on both river-banks went out, but on the meadow below and in the inn the merrymaking continued. The old man and Kiriak, both drunk, holding hands, and rolling against one another, came to the shed where Olga lay with Marya.

"Leave her alone!" reasoned the old man. "Leave her. She's not a bad sort. . . . It's a sin. . . ."

"Ma-arya!" roared Kiriak.

"Stop! It's sinful. . . . She's not a bad sort."

The two men stood a moment by the shed and went away.

"I love wild flowers . . ." sang the old man in a high, piercing tenor. "I love to pull them in the fields!"

After this he spat, blasphemed, and went into the hut.

CHAPTER IV

DREAMS!

GRANDMOTHER stationed Sasha in the kitchen garden, and ordered her to keep off the geese. It was a hot August day. The innkeeper's geese could get into the kitchen garden by the back way, but at present they were busy picking up oats near the inn and quietly conversing, though the old gander stood aloof, his head raised as if to make sure that grandmother was not coming with her stick. The other geese could also get into the garden; but these were feeding far across the river, and, like a big white garland, stretched across the meadow. Sasha watched a short time, and then got tired, and, seeing no geese in sight, went down to the ravine.

There she saw Motka, Marya's eldest daughter, standing motionless on a big stone, and looking at the church. Marya had borne thirteen children; but only six remained, all girls, and the eldest was eight years old. Barefooted Motka, in her long shirt, stood in the sun; the sun burnt the top of her head, but she took no notice of this, and seemed turned to stone. Sasha stood beside her, and looking at the church, began—

"God lives in the church. People burn lamps and candles, but God has red lamps, green and blue lamps, like eyes. At night God walks about the church, and with him the Holy Virgin, and holy Nicholas . . . toup, toup, toup! . . . The watchman is frightened, terribly! Yes, my heart," she said, imitating her mother. "When the Day of Judgment comes all the churches will be carried to heaven."

"With the bells?" asked Motka in a bass voice, drawling every word.

"With the bells. And on the Day of Judgment good people will go to paradise, and wicked people will burn in fire eternal and unextinguishable, my heart! To mother and Marya God will say, 'You have offended no one, so go to the right, to paradise'; but He'll say to Kiriak and grandmother, 'You go to the left, into the fire!' And people who eat meat on fast-days will go to the fire too."

She looked up at the sky, opened wide her eyes, and continued—

"Look up at the sky, don't wink . . . and you'll see angels."

Motka looked at the sky, and a minute passed in silence.

"Do you see them?" asked Sasha.

"No," answered Motka in her bass voice.

"But I can. Little angels fly about the sky, with wings . . . little, little, like gnats."

Motka thought, looked at the ground, and asked—

"Will grandmother burn really?"

"She'll burn, my heart."

From the stone to the bottom of the hill was a gentle, even slope covered with green grass so soft that it invited repose. Sasha lay down and slid to the bottom. Motka with a serious, severe face, puffed out her cheeks, lay down, and slid, and as she slid her shirt came up to her shoulders.

"How funny I felt!" said Sasha in delight.

The two children climbed to the top intending to slide down again, but at that moment they heard a familiar, squeaky voice. Terror seized them. Toothless, bony, stooping grandmother, with her short grey hair floating in the wind, armed with the long stick, drove the geese from the kitchen garden, and screamed—

"You've spoiled all the cabbage, accursed; may you choke; threefold anathemas; plagues, there is no peace with you!"

She saw the two girls, threw down her stick, took up a bundle of brush-wood, and seizing Sasha's shoulders with fingers dry and hard as tree-forks, began to beat her. Sasha cried from pain and terror; and at that moment a gander, swinging from foot to foot and stretching out its neck, came up and hissed at the old woman; and when he returned to the geese, all welcomed him approvingly: go-go-go! Thereafter grandmother seized and whipped Motka, and again Motka's shirt went over her shoulders. Trembling with terror, crying loudly, Sasha went back to the hut to complain, and after her went Motka, also crying in her bass voice. Her tears were unwiped away, and her face was wet as if she had been in the river.

"Lord in heaven!" cried Olga as they entered the hut. "Mother of God, what's this?"

Sasha began her story, and at that moment, screaming and swearing, in came grandmother. Fekla lost her temper, and the whole hut was given over to noise.

"Never mind, never mind!" consoled Olga, pale and unnerved, stroking Sasha's head. "She's your grandmother; you've no right to be angry. Never mind, child!"

Nikolai, already tortured by the constant shouting, hunger, smell, and smoke, hating and despising poverty, and ashamed of his parents before his wife and child, swung his legs over the stove and said to his mother with an irritable whine—

"You mustn't touch her! You have no right whatever to beat her!"

"*Nu*, you'll choke there on the stove, corpse!" cried Fekla angrily. "The devil sent you to us, parasite!"

And Sasha and Motka, and all the

little girls, hid on the stove behind Nikolai's back, and the throbbing of their little hearts was almost heard. In every family with an invalid, long sick and hopeless, there are moments when all, timidly, secretly, at the bottom of their hearts, wish for his death; alone, children always dread the death of any one kin to them, and feel terror at the thought. And now the little girls, with bated breath and mournful faces, looked at Nikolai, and thinking that he would soon die, wanted to cry and say something kindly and compassionate.

Nikolai pressed close to Olga, as if seeking a defender, and said in a soft, trembling voice—

"Olga, my dear, I can stand this no longer. It is beyond my strength. For the love of God, for the love of Christ in heaven, write to your sister, Claudia Abramovna; let her sell or pledge everything, and send us the money to get out of this. O Lord," he cried, with longing, "to look at Moscow again, even with one eye! Even to see it in dreams!"

When evening came and the hut grew dark, all felt such tedium that it was hard to speak. Angry grandmother soaked rye crusts in a bowl, and took an hour to eat them. Marya milked the cow, carried in the milkpail, and set it down on a bench; and grandmother slowly poured the milk into jugs, pleased at the thought that now at Assumption fast no one would drink milk, and that it would remain whole. But she poured a little, very little, into a saucer for Fekla's youngest. When she and Marya carried the milk to the cellar Motka suddenly started up, climbed down from the stove, and going to the bench poured the saucer of milk into the wooden bowl of crusts.

Grandmother, back in the hut, sat down again to the crusts, and Sasha and Motka, perched on the stove, looked at her, and saw with joy that she was drinking milk during fast time, and therefore would go to hell. Consoled by this, they lay down to sleep; and Sasha, going off to sleep, imagined the terrible chastisement: a big stove, like the potter's, and a black unclean spirit horned like a cow drove grandmother into the stove with a long stick, as she herself had lately driven the geese.

CHAPTER V

FIRE!

ON the night of Assumption, at eleven o'clock, the young men and girls playing below in the meadow suddenly cried and shrieked and ran back towards the village. The boys and girls who sat above, on the brink of the ravine, at first could not understand the cause of their cries.

"Fire! Fire!" came from beneath in a despairing scream. "The hut's on fire!"

The boys and girls on the ravine turned their heads and saw a picture terrible and rare. Over one of the farthest thatched huts rose a fathom-high pillar of fire which curled and scattered fountain-wise on all sides showers of bright sparks. And immediately afterwards the whole roof caught fire, and the crackling of burning beams was heard by all.

The moonlight faded, and soon the whole village was bathed in a red, trembling glare; black shadows moved across the ground, and there was a smell of burning. The merry-makers from below, all panting, speechless, shuddering, jostled one another and fell: dazzled by the bright light, they saw nothing, and could not even tell who was who. The sight was terrible; and most terrible of all was that in the smoke above the conflagration fluttered doves, and that the men in the inn, knowing nothing of the fire, continued to sing and play the concertina as if nothing had happened.

"Uncle Semion is burning!" cried a loud, hoarse voice.

Marya with chattering teeth wandered about her hut weeping and wringing her hands, although the fire was far away at the other end of the village; Nikolai came out in his felt boots, and after him the children in their shirts. At the village policeman's hut they beat the alarm. Bem, bem, bem! echoed through the air; and this tireless, repeated sound made the heart sink and the listeners turn cold. The old women stood about with images. From the yards were driven sheep, calves, and cows; and the villagers carried into the street their boxes, sheepskins, and pails. A black stallion, kept apart from the herd because he kicked and injured the horses, found himself in freedom, and neighing loudly, he tore up and down the village, and at last stopped beside a cart and kicked it violently.

In the church beyond the river the fire-alarm was rung.

It was hot all around the burning hut, and in the bright glare even the blades of grass were visible. On a box which the peasants had managed to save sat Semion, a big-nosed, red-headed muzhik, in short coat, with a forage-cap pressed down to his ears; his wife lay on her face on the earth and groaned. A little, big-bearded capless, gnome-like stranger of eighty, evidently partial to fires, wandered around, carrying a white bundle; his bald head reflected the glare. The *starosta*, Antip Siedelnikoff, swarthy and black-haired as a gipsy, went up to the hut with his axe, and for no apparent reason beat in all the windows and began to hack at the steps.

"Women, water!" he roared. "Bring the engine! Look sharp!"

The peasants, fresh from merry-making in the inn, dragged up the fire-engine. All were drunk; they staggered and fell; their expressions were helpless, and tears stood in their eyes.

"Bring water, girls!" cried the *starosta*, also drunk. "Look sharp!"

The young women and girls ran down the slope to the well, returned with pails and pitchers of water, and, having emptied them into the engine, ran back for more. Olga, and Marya, and Sasha, and Motka, all helped. The water was pumped up by women and small boys; the hose-nozzle hissed: and the *starosta*, aiming it now at the door, now at the windows, held his finger on the stream of water, so that it hissed still more fiercely.

"Good man, Antip!" came approving cries. "Keep it up!"

And Antip went into the hall and cried thence—

"Bring more water! Do your best, Orthodox men and women, on this unfortunate occasion!"

The muzhiks stood in a crowd with

idle hands and gaped at the fire. No one knew what to start on, not one was capable of help; although around were stacks of grain, hay, outhouses, and heaps of dry brushwood. Kiriak and his father Osip, both tipsy, stood in the crowd. As if to excuse his idleness, the old man turned to the woman who lay on the ground and said—

"Don't worry yourself, gossip! The hut's insured—it's all the same to you!"

And Semion, addressing each muzhik in turn, explained how the hut caught fire.

"That old man there with the bundle is General Zhukoff's servant. . . . He was with our general, heaven kingdom to him! as cook. He comes up to us in the evening and begins, 'Let me sleep here tonight.' . . . We had a drink each, of course. . . . The woman prepared the samovar to get the old man tea, when in an unlucky moment she put it in the hall; and the fire from the chimney, of course, went up to the roof, the straw and all! We were nearly burnt ourselves. And the old man lost his cap; it's a pity."

The fire-alarm boomed without cease; and the bells of the church across the river rang again and again. Olga, panting, bathed in the glare, looked with terror at the red sheep and the red pigeons flying about in the smoke; and it seemed to her that the boom of the fire-alarm pierced into her soul, that the fire would last for ever, and that Sasha was lost. . . . And when the roof crashed in she grew so weak with fear lest the whole village burn that she could no longer carry water;

and she sat on the brink of the ravine with her pail beside her; beside her sat other women, and spoke as if they were speaking of a corpse.

At last from the manor-house came two cartloads of factors and workmen. They brought with them a fire-engine. A very youthful student in white, unbuttoned tunic rode into the village on horseback. Axes crashed, a ladder was placed against the burning log-walls; and up it promptly climbed five men led by the student, who was very red, and shouted sharply and hoarsely, and in a tone which implied that he was well accustomed to extinguishing fires. They took the hut to pieces, beam by beam; and dragged apart stall, the wattle fence, and the nearest hayrick.

"Don't let them break it!" came angry voices from the crowd. "Don't let them!"

Kiriak with a resolute face went into the hut as if to prevent the new-comers breaking, but one of the workmen turned him back with a blow on the neck. Kiriak tumbled, and on all fours crept back to the crowd.

From across the river came two pretty girls in hats; the student's sisters, no doubt. They stood some way off and watched the conflagration. The scattered logs no longer burned, but smoked fiercely; and the student, handling the hose, sent the water sometimes on the logs, sometimes into the crowd, sometimes at the women who were carrying pails.

"George!" cried the frightened girls reproachfully. "George!"

The fire ended. Before the crowd dispersed the dawn had begun; and all faces were pale and a little dark—or so it always seems in early morning when the last stars fade away. As they went to their homes the muzhiks laughed and joked at the expense of General Zhukoff's cook and his burnt cap: they reenacted the fire as a joke, and, it seemed, were sorry it had come so quickly to an end.

"You put out the fire beautifully, sir," said Olga to the student. "Quite in the Moscow way; there we have fires every day."

"Are you really from Moscow?" asked one of the girls.

"Yes. My husband served in the Slaviansky Bazaar. And this is my little girl." She pointed to Sasha, who pressed close to her from the cold. "Also from Moscow, miss."

The girls spoke to the student in French, and handed Sasha a twenty-kopeck piece. When old Osip saw this his face grew bright with hope.

"Thank God, your honour, there was no wind," he said, turning to the student. "We'd have been all burnt up in an hour. Your honour, good gentleman," he added shamefacedly. "It's a cold morning; we want warming badly . . . a half a bottle from your kindness . . ."

Osip's hint proved vain; and, grunting, he staggered home. Olga stood at the end of the village and watched as the two carts forded the stream, and the pretty girls walked through the meadow towards the carriage waiting on the other side. She turned to the hut in ecstasies—

"And such nice people! So good-looking. The young ladies, just like little cherubs!"

"May they burst asunder!" growled sleepy Fekla angrily.

CHAPTER VI

THE HUT

MARYA was unhappy, and said that she wanted to die. But life as she found it was quite to Fekla's taste: she liked the poverty, and the dirt, and the never-ceasing bad language. She ate what she was given without picking and choosing, and could sleep comfortably anywhere; she emptied the slops in front of the steps: threw them, in fact, from the threshold, though in her own naked feet she had to walk through the puddle. And from the first day she hated Olga and Nikolai for no reason save that they loathed this life.

"We'll see what you're going to eat here, my nobles from Moscow!" she said maliciously. "We'll see!"

Once on an early September morning, Fekla, rosy from the cold, healthy, and good-looking, carried up the hill two pails of water; when she entered the hut Marya and Alga sat at the table and drank tea.

"Tea . . . and sugar!" began Fekla ironically. "Fine ladies you are!" she added, setting down the pails. "A nice fashion you've got of drinking tea every day! See that you don't swell up with tea!" she continued, looking with hatred at Olga. "You got a thick snout already in Moscow, fatbeef!"

She swung round the yoke and struck Olga on the shoulder. The two women clapped their hands and exclaimed—

"Akh, batiushki!"

After which Fekla returned to the river to wash clothes, and all the time cursed so loudly that she was heard in the hut.

The day passed, and behind it came the long autumn evening. All sat winding silk, except Fekla, who went down to the river. The silk was given out by a neighbouring factory; and at this work the whole family earned not more than twenty kopecks a week.

"We were better off as serfs," said the old man, winding away busily. "In those days you'd work, and eat, and sleep . . each in its turn. For dinner you'd have *schtchi* and porridge, and for supper again *schtchi* and porridge. Gherkins and cabbage as much as you liked; and you'd eat freely, as much as you liked. And there was more order. Each man knew his place."

The one lamp in the hut burned dimly and smoked. When any worker rose and passed the lamp a black shadow fell on the window, and the bright moonlight shone in. Old Osip related slowly how the peasants lived before the Emancipation; how in these same villages where all to-day lived penuriously there were great shooting parties, and on such days the muzhiks were treated to vodka without end; how whole trains of carts with game for the young squire were hurried off to Moscow; how the wicked were punished with rods or exiled to the estate in Tver, and the good were rewarded. And grandmother also spoke. She remembered everything. She told of her old mistress, a good, God-fearing woman with a wicked, dissolute husband; and of the queer marriages made by all the daughters; one, it appeared, married a drunkard; another a petty tradesman; and the third was carried off clandestinely (she, grandmother, then unmarried, helped in the adventure): and all soon afterwards died of grief as died, indeed, their mother. And, re-

membering these events, grandmother began to cry.

When a knock was heard at the door all started.

"Uncle Osip, let me stay the night!"

Into the hut came the little, bald old man, General Zhukoff's cook, whose cap was burnt in the fire. He sat and listened, and, like his hosts, related many strange happenings. Nikolai, his legs hanging over the stove, listened; and asked what sort of food was eaten at the manor-house. They spoke of *bitki*, cutlets, soups of various kinds, and sauces; and the cook, who, too, had an excellent memory, named certain dishes which no one eats nowadays; there was a dish, for instance, made of ox-eyes, and called "Awake in the morning."

"And did you cook cutlets *maréchal?*" asked Nikolai.

"No."

Nikolai shook his head reproachfully, and said—

"Then you are a queer sort of cook."

The little girls sat and lay on the stove, and looked down with widely opened eyes; there seemed to be no end to them—like cherubs in the sky. The stories delighted them; they sighed, shuddered, and turned pale sometimes from rapture, sometimes from fear; and, breathless, afraid to move, they listened to the stories of their grandmother, which were the most interesting of all.

They went to bed in silence; and the old men, agitated by their stories, thought how glorious was youth, which —however meagre it might be—left behind it only joyful, living, touching recollections; and how terribly cold was this death, which was now so near. Better not think of it! The lamp went out. And the darkness, the two windows, bright with moonshine, the silence, the cradle's creak somehow reminded them that life was now past, and that it would never return. They slumbered, lost consciousness; then suddenly some one jostled their shoulders, or breathed into their cheeks—and there was no real sleep; through their heads crept thoughts of death; they turned round and forgot about death; but their heads were full of old, mean, tedious thoughts, thoughts of need, of forage, of the rise in the price of flour; and again they remembered that life had now passed by, and that it would never return.

"O Lord!" sighed the cook.

Some one tapped cautiously at the window. That must be Fekla. Olga rose, yawned, muttered a prayer, opened the inner door, then drew the bolt in the hall. But no one entered. A draught blew and the moon shone brightly. Through the open door, Olga saw the quiet and deserted street, and the moon itself, swimming high in the sky.

"Who's there?" she cried.

"I!" came a voice. "It's I."

Near the door, pressing close to the wall, stood Fekla, naked as she was born. She shuddered from the cold, her teeth chattered; and in the bright moonlight she was pale, pretty, and strange. The patches of shade and the moonlight on her skin stood out sharply; and plainest of all stood out her dark eyebrows and her young, firm breast.

"Some impudent fellows across the river undressed me and sent me off in this way—as my mother bore me! Bring me something to put on."

"Go into the hut yourself!" whispered Olga, with a shudder.

"The old ones will see me."

And as a fact grandmother got restless, and growled; and the old man asked, "Who is there?" Olga brought out her shirt and petticoat and dressed Fekla; and the two women softly, and doing their best to close the doors without noise, went into the hut.

"So that's you, devil?" came an angry growl from grandmother, who guessed it was Fekla. "May you be . . . night walker . . . there's no peace with you!"

"Don't mind, don't mind," whispered Olga, wrapping Fekla up. "Don't mind, my heart!"

Again silence. The whole family always slept badly; each was troubled by something aggressive and insistent; the old man by a pain in the back; grandmother by worry and ill-temper; Marya by fright; the children by itching and hunger. And to-night the sleep of all was troubled; they rolled from side to side, wandered, and rose constantly to drink.

Fekla suddenly cried out in a loud, rough voice; but soon mastered herself, and merely sobbed quietly until at last she ceased. Now and then from beyond the river were heard the church chimes; but the clock struck strangely; and at first beat struck five, and later three.

"O Lord!" sighed the cook.

From the light in the windows it was hard to judge whether the moon still shone or whether dawn had come. Marya rose and went out; and she was heard milking the cows and shouting "Stand!" Grandmother also went out. It was still dark in the hut, but everything could be seen.

Nikolai, who had spent a sleepless night, climbed down from the stove. He took from a green box his evening dress-coat, put it on, and going over to the window, smoothed the sleeves and the folds, and smiled. Then he took off the coat, returned it to the box, and lay down.

Marya returned, and began to light the stove. Apparently she was not yet quite awake. Probably she still dreamed of something, or recalled the stories of last night, for she stretched herself lazily before the stove and said—

"No, we're better in freedom."

CHAPTER VII

WHO ELSE?

IN the village arrived "the gentleman," as the peasants called the superintendent of police. Every one knew a week ahead the day and cause of his arrival. For though Zhukovo had only forty houses, it owed in arrears to the Imperial Treasury and the Zemstvo more than two thousand roubles.

The superintendent stopped at the inn, drank two glasses of tea, and then walked to the *starosta's* hut, where already waited a crowd of peasants in arrears. The *starosta*, Antip Siedelnikoff, despite his youth—he was little over thirty—was a stern man who always took the side of the authorities, although he himself was poor and paid his taxes irregularly. It was clear to all that he was flattered by his position and revelled in the sense of power, which he had no other way of displaying save by sternness. The *mir* feared and listened to him; when in the street or at the inn he met a drunken man he would seize him, tie his hands behind his back, and put him in the village goal; once, indeed, he even imprisoned grandmother for several days, because, appearing at

the *mir* instead of her husband, she used abusive language. The *starosta* had never lived in town and read no books; but he had a copious collection of learned words and used them so liberally that people respected him, even when they did not understand.

When Osip with his tax book entered the *starosta's* hut, the superintendent, a thin, old, grey-whiskered man in a grey coat, sat at a table in the near corner and made notes in a book. The hut was clean, the walls were decorated with pictures from magazines, and in a prominent place near the ikon hung a portrait of Alexander of Battenberg, ex-Prince of Bulgaria. At the table, with crossed arms, stood Antip Siedelnikoff.

"This man, your honour, owes 119 roubles," he said when it came to Osip's turn. "Before Holy Week, he paid a rouble, since then, nothing."

The superintendent turned his eyes on Osip, and asked—

"What's the reason of that, brother?"

"Your honour, be merciful to me . . ." began Osip in agitation. "Let me explain . . . this summer . . . Squire Liutoretzky . . . 'Osip,' he says, 'sell me your hay. . . . Sell it,' he says. . . . I had a hundred poods for sale, which the women mowed. . . . Well, we bargained. . . . All went well, without friction. . . .'"

He complained of the *starosta*, and now and again turned to the muzhiks as if asking for support; his flushed face sweated, and his eyes turned bright and vicious.

"I don't understand why you tell me all that," said the superintendent. "I ask *you* . . . it's *you* I ask. why you don't pay your arrears? None of you pay, and I am held responsible."

"I'm not able to."

"These expressions are without consequence, your honour," said the *starosta* magniloquently. "In realty, the Tchikildeyeffs belong to the impoverished class, but be so good as to ask the others what is the reason. Vodka and impudence . . . without any comprehension."

The superintendent made a note, and said to Osip in a quiet, even voice, as if he were asking for water—

"Begone!"

Soon afterwards he drove away; and as he sat in his cheap tarantass and coughed, it was plain, even from the appearance of his long, thin back, that he had forgotten Osip, and the *starosta*, and the arrears of Zhukovo, and was thinking of his own domestic affairs. He had hardly covered a verst before Antip Siedelnikoff was carrying off the Tchikildeyeff samovar; and after him ran gradmother, and whined like a dog.

"I won't give it! I won't give it to you, accursed!"

The *starosta* walked quickly, taking big steps; and grandmother, stooping and fierce and breathless, tottered after him; and her green-grey hair floated in the wind. At last she stopped, beat her breast with her fists, and exclaimed, with a whine and a sob—

"Orthodox men who believe in God! *Batiushki*, they're wronging me! Kinsmen, they've robbed me. Oi, oi, will no one help me!"

"Grandmother, grandmother!" said the *starosta* severely, "have some reason in your head!"

With the loss of the samovar, things in the Tchikildeyeffs' hut grew even worse. There was something humiliating and shameful in this last privation, and it seemed that the hut had suddenly lost its honour. The table itself, the chairs, and all the pots, had the *starosta* seized them, would have been less missed. Grandmother screamed, Marya cried, and the children, listening, began to cry also. The old man, with a feeling of guilt, sat gloomily in the corner and held his tongue. And Nikolai was silent. As a rule grandmother liked him and pitied him; but at this crisis her pity evaporated, and she cursed and reproached him, and thrust her fists under his nose. She screamed that he was guilty of the family's misfortunes and asked why he had sent so little home, though he boasted in his letters that he earned fifty roubles a month at the Slaviansky Bazaar. Why did he come home, and still worse, bring his family? If he died whence would the money come for his funeral? . . . And it was painful to look at Nikolai, Olga and Sasha.

The old man grunted, took his cap, and went to the *starosta's*. It was getting dark. Antip Siedelnikoff, with cheeks puffed out, stood at the stove and soldered. It was stifling. His children, skinny and unwashed—not better than the Tchikildeyeffs'—sprawled on the floor; his ugly, freckled wife wound silk. This, too, was an unhappy, Godforsaken family; alone Antip was smart and good-looking. On a bench in a row stood five samovars. The old man prayed towards the Battenberg prince, and began—

"Antip, show the mercy of God: give me the samovar! For the love of God!"

"Bring me three roubles, and then you'll get it."

"I haven't got them."

Antip puffed out his cheeks, the fire hummed and hissed, and the samovars shone. The old man fumbled with his cap, thought a moment, and repeated—

"Give it to me!"

The swarthy *starosta* seemed quite black and resembled a wizard; he turned to Osip and said roughly and quickly—

"All depends from the Rural Chief. In the administrative session of the twenty-sixth of this month you can expose the causes of your dissatisfaction verbally or in writing."

Not one of these learned words was understood by Osip, but he felt contented, and returned to his hut.

Ten days later the superintendent returned, stayed about an hour, and drove away. It had turned windy and cold. but though the river was frozen, there was no snow, and the state of the roads was a torture to every one. On Sunday evening the neighbours looked in to see and talk with Osip. They spoke in the darkness; to work was a sin. and no one lighted the lamp. News was exchanged, chiefly disagreeable. Three houses away the hens had been taken in payment of arrears and sent to the cantonal office. and there they died of starvation; sheep had also been taken, and while they were being driven away tied with ropes and transferred to fresh carts at each village one had died. And now they discussed the question, Who was responsible?

"The Zemstvo!" said Osip. "Who else?"

"Of course, the Zemstvo!"

They accused the Zemstvo of everything—of arrears, of oppression, of famines, although not one of them knew exactly what the Zemstvo was. And that rule had been observed since wealthy peasants with factories, shops, and houses were elected as Zemstvo

members, and being discontented with the institution, thenceforth in their factories and inns abused the Zemstvo.

They complained of the fact that God had sent no snow, and that though it was time to lay in firewood. you could neither drive nor walk upon the frozen roads. Fifteen years before, and earlier, the small-talk of Zhukovo was infinitely more entertaining. In those days every old man pretended he held some secret, knew something, and waited for something; they talked of rescripts with gold seals, redistribution of lands, and hidden treasures, and hinted of things mysterious; to-day the people of Zhukovo had no secrets; their life was open to all; and they had no themes for conversation save need, and forage, and the absence of snow. . . .

For a moment they were silent. But soon they remembered the hens and dead sheep, and returned to the problem, Who was responsible?

"The Zemstvo!" said Osip gloomily. "Who else?"

CHAPTER VIII

DIED

THE parish church was Kosogorovo, six versts away, but the peasants went there only to christen, marry. or bury; they worshipped at the church across the river. On Sundays, when the weather was fine, the village girls dressed in their best and went in a crowd to the service; and the red, yellow, and green dresses fluttering across the meadow were pleasant to see. In bad weather all stayed at home. They fasted. prayed, and prepared for the sacrament. From those who had failed in this duty during the Great Fast, the priest, when he went round the huts with his crucifix, took fifteen kopecks fine.

The old man did not believe in God, because he had hardly ever thought of Him; he admitted the supernatural, but held that that was an affair for women; and when others spoke of religion, or of miracles, and asked him questions on the subject, he scratched himself and said reluctantly—

"Who knows anything about it?"

Grandmother believed vaguely; in her mind all things were confused, and when she began to meditate on death and salvation, hunger and poverty took the upper hand, and she forgot her meditations. She remembered no prayers, but at night before lying down she stood before the ikons and muttered—

"Mother of God of Kazan, Mother of God of Smolensk, Three-Handed Mother of God! . . ."

Marya and Fekla crossed themselves and fasted, but knew nothing of religion. They neither taught their children to pray nor spoke to them of God; and they taught them no principles save that they must not eat meat during fasts. With the other villagers it was the same; few believed and few understood. Nevertheless, all loved the Scriptures, loved them dearly and piously; the misfortune was that there were no books and no one to read and explain, so that when Olga read aloud the Gospel she was treated with respect, and all addressed her and her daughter Sasha as "You."

At Church festivals Olga often walked to neighbouring villages, and even to the district town, where there were two monasteries and twenty-seven churches. She was abstracted, and as she walked on her pilgrimage forgot her family.

When she returned home it seemed that she had only just discovered her husband and daughter, and she smiled and said radiantly—

"God has sent us His mercy!"

Everything that happened in the village repelled and tormented her. On Elijah's Day they drank, at Assumption they drank, at Elevation they drank. At Intercession Zhukovo had its parish festival; and this the muzhiks observed by drinking for three days; they drank fifty roubles from the communal funds; and then went round the huts and collected money for more vodka. On the first days the Tchikildeyeffs killed a ram, and ate mutton in the morning, at dinner, and for supper; and in the night all the children got out of bed to eat more. Kiriak was drunk all three days; he drank away his cap and boots, and beat Marya so badly that she had to be soused with water. And then all were sick with shame.

Despite this, even this Zhukovo, this Kholuefka, had once a real religious festival. That was in August, when through every village in the district was borne the Life-giving Ikon. The day it was due at Zhukovo was windless and dull. Early in the morning the village girls, in their bright, holiday dress, set out to met the ikon, which arrived at evening with a procession and singing; and at that moment the church bells rang loudly. A vast crowd from Zhukovo and neighbouring villages filled the street; there were noise, dust, and crushing. And the old man, grandmother, and Kiriak—all stretched out their hands to the ikon, looked at it greedily, and cried with tears—

"Intercessor, Mother! Intercessor!"

All at once, it seemed, realised that

there is no void between earth and heaven, that the great and strong of this world have not seized upon everything, that there is intercession against injury, against slavish subjection, against heavy, intolerable need, against the terrible vodka.

"Intercessor, Mother!" sobbed Marya. "Mother!"

When the service was said and the ikon carried away, all things were as of old, and noisy, drunken voices echoed from the inn.

Death was dreaded only by the wealthy muzhiks; the richer they grew the less their faith in God and in salvation; and only out of fear of the end of the world, to make certain, so to speak, they lighted candles in the church and said mass. The poorer muzhiks knew no fear of death. They told the old man and grandmother to their faces that they had lived their day, that it was high time to die, and the old man and grandmother listened indifferently. They did not scruple to tell Fekla in Nikolai's presence that when he, Nikolai, died, her husband, Denis, would get his discharge from the army and be sent home. And Marya not only had no fear of death, but was even sorry that it lingered; and she rejoiced when her own children died.

But though they knew no dread of death, they looked on sickness with exaggerated dread. The most trifling ailment, a disordered stomach, a slight chill, sent grandmother on to the stove, where she rolled herself up, and groaned loudly without cease, "I'm dying!" And the old man would send for the priest to confess her and administer the last sacrament. They talked eternally of colds, of worms, of tumours which begin in the stomach and slowly creep towards the heart. Most of all they dreaded colds, and even in summer dressed warmly, and cowered over the stove. Grandmother loved medical treatment, and constantly drove to hospital, where she said she was fifty-eight instead of seventy, for she feared that if the doctor knew her age, he would refuse to treat her, and would tell her it was time to die. She usually started for the hospital at early morning, taking a couple of the little girls, and returned at night, hungry and ill-tempered, with a mixture for herself and ointments for the girls. Once she took with her Nikolai, who for the next two weeks dosed himself with a mixture and said that he felt better.

Grandmother knew every doctor, *feldscher*, and wise-woman within thirty versts and disapproved of all. At Intercession, when the priest made his round of the huts with a crucifix, the clerk told her that near the town prison there was an old man, formerly an army *feldscher*, who doctored cleverly, and he advised grandmother to see him. She took the advice. When the first snow fell she drove into town, and brought back an old, bearded Jew in a long caftan, whose whole face was covered with blue veins. At that time journeymen worked in the hut: an old tailor in terrifying spectacles made a waistcoat out of rags; and two young lads made felt for top-boots. Kiriak, dismissed for drunkenness, and now living at home, sat beside the tailor and mended a horse-collar. The hut was close and smoky The Jew looked at Nikolai, and said that he must be bled.

He applied leeches, and the old tailor, Kiriak, and the little girls looked on, and imagined they saw the disease coming out of Nikolai. And Nikolai also watched the leeches sucking his chest, and saw them fill with dark blood; and feeling that, indeed, something was coming out of him, he smiled contentedly.

"It's a good way!" said the tailor. "God grant that it does him good!"

The Jew applied twelve leeches to Nikolai, then twelve more; drank tea, and drove away. Nikolai began to tremble; his face turned haggard, and—as the women put it—dwindled into a fist; his fingers turned blue. He wrapped himself up in the counterpane and then in a sheepskin coat; but felt colder and colder. Towards evening he was peevish; asked them to lay him on the floor, asked the tailor not to smoke, then lay still under the sheepskin; and towards morning died.

CHAPTER IX

GIVE ALMS!

IT was a rough, a long winter.

Since Christmas there had been no grain, and flour was bought outside. Kiriak, who still lived at home, made scenes at night, causing terror to all; and next morning his head ached, and he was ashamed, so that it was painful to see him. Night and day in the stall a hungry cow lowed, and rent the hearts of grandmother and Marya. And to make things worse the frost grew severer, and the snow heaped itself high in the street, and the winter stretched out. Annunciation was marked by a genuine winter snowstorm, and snow fell in Holy Week.

But even this ended. The beginning of April brought warm days and frosty nights. Winter gave way reluctantly, but the hot sunshine foiled him, and at last the brooks melted and the birds began to sing. The fields and shrubs by the river-side were hidden in spring floods, and from Zhukovo to the village beyond stretched a big lake, given over to wild duck. The spring sunsets, fiery and with splendid clouds, yielded each day sights new and incredible, sights which are often laughed at when they appear on canvas.

The cranes cried mournfully, as if they called on men to follow them. Standing on the brink of the ravine, Olga looked at the flood, at the sun, at the bright, it seemed rejuvenated, church; and her tears flowed and she panted with passionate longing to go away, though it might be to the end of the earth. And indeed, it was decided that she should return to Moscow and seek a place as housemaid; and with her would go Kiriak to earn his living as dvornik, or somehow else. *Akh*, to get away soon!

When the roads dried and the weather turned hot they prepared for the journey. Olga and Sasha with wallets on their backs, both in bast-shoes, left at dawn; and Marya came to see them off. Kiriak, ill, remained for a week more. For the last time Olga prayed towards the church, and thought of her husband, and though she did not cry, her face wrinkled, and seemed ugly, as an old woman's. During the winter she had grown thinner, uglier, and a little grey; instead of the old charm and pleasant smile her face expressed submissiveness and sorrow outlived; and her look was dull and fixed as if she were deaf. She was sorry to leave the village and the muzhiks. She remembered how they carried away Nikolai; how mass was said at nearly every hut; and how all wept, feeling her grief their own. Summer and winter there were hours and days when it seemed to her that these men lived worse than beasts, and to look at them was terrible: they were coarse, dishonest, dirty, drunken; they lived in discord; they fought eternally, because they despised, feared, and suspected one another. Who kept the drink shop and dosed the muzhik with drink? The muzhik. Who squandered and spent on drink the money of the commune, of the school, of the Church? The muzhik. Who stole from his neighbour, burnt his house, perjured himself in court for a bottle of vodka? The muzhik. Who first spoke at the Zemstvo and on other boards against the muzhik? The muzhik. Yes; to live with them was torture! But despite all this, they were men, they suffered and wept as men: and in their whole lives there was not one act for which an excuse might not be found. Labour unbearable, from which the whole body ached at night, fierce winters, scanty harvests, crowding; help from nowhere, and no hope of help! The richer and the stronger gave no help because they themselves were rude, dishonest, intemperate, and foul-tongued; the pettiest official or clerk treated the muzhiks as vagabonds; even the cantonal chiefs and Church elders addressed them as "Thou," and believed they had a right thereto. Yes! And could there be help or good example from the selfish, the greedy, the dissolute, the idle, who came to these villages with but one intent: to insult, terrify, and rob? Olga remembered the piteous, humiliated faces of the old men when in winter Kiriak was brought out to be flogged! And now she was sorry for all these men and women; and on her last walk through the village she looked at every hut.

When she had accompanied them three versts Marya said good-bye; then fell upon her knees, and with her face touching the ground, cried loudly—

"Again I am left alone; alas, poor me, poor, poor, unfortunate! . . ."

And she continued to keen, so that long afterwards Olga and Sasha could see her on her knees, bent on one side, holding her head with her hands. And above her head flew rooks.

The sun rose higher: the day grew warm. Zhukovo was left far behind. The travellers followed many circuitous paths, and Olga and Sasha soon forgot the village and Marya. They were in good humour, and everything amused them. First a mound; then a line of telegraph posts, with mysterious humming wires, which vanished on the horizon, and sped to some unknown destination; then a farm, buried in green, which sent from afar a smell of dampness and hemp, and seemed to say that it was the home of happy people; then a horse's skeleton lying white in a field. And larks sang untiredly; quails cried to one another; and the landrail cried with a sound like the drawing of an old bolt.

At midday Olga and Sasha reached a big village, and, in the broad street, came upon General Zhukoff's old cook. He was hot, and his red, sweating bald patch shone in the sun. At first he did not recognise Olga; then he looked and recognised her, but both, without exchanging a word, continued their paths. Olga stopped and bowed low before the open windows of a hut which seemed richer and newer than its neighbours, and cried in a loud, thin, and singing voice—

"Orthodox Christians. give alms for the love of Christ; Kingdom of Heaven to your father and mother, eternal rest."

"Orthodox Christians," echoed little Sasha. "Give for the love of Christ, Heavenly Kingdom. . . ."

VOLUME IV

The Shooting Party

PRESCRIPT

In the year 1880 during April the doorman Andrey came to my private room and in a mysterious whisper said that a gentleman was demanding insistently to see the editor.

"He appears to be a chinovnik," Andrey added. "He has a cockade. . . ."

"Tell him to come another time," I said, "I am busy now. Tell him the editor only talks on Saturdays."

"He was here the day before yesterday and asked for you. He says his business is urgent. He begs, almost with tears in his eyes, to see you and says he is not free on Saturday. . . ."

I sighed, laid down my pen, and settled myself in my chair to receive the gentleman with the cockade. Young authors, and in general everybody who is new to the profession, are generally so awed by the words "editorial office" that they delay a considerable time. After the editor's "Show him in," they cough and blow their noses a long time, open the door very slowly, come into the room still more slowly, and thus waste your time. The gentleman with the cockade was different. The door had scarcely had time to close after Andrey before I saw a tall, broad-shouldered man, a paper in one hand and a cap with a cockade in the other, facing me.

This man of the interview plays a very important part in my story. I shall describe him.

First, he was as vigorous as a fine cart horse. His face was rosy, his hands strong, his chest deep. Over forty, dressed according to the last fashion, in tweed. A thick gold watch-chain with breloques decorated his chest, and on his little finger a diamond ring shone. But, what is most important, and so essential to the hero of a novel or story of any repute, he was extraordinarily handsome. I am neither a woman nor an artist and have but little understanding of manly beauty, but the appearance of the gentleman with the cockade with his large muscular face remained for ever impressed on me. A real Greek nose with a slight hook, thin lips and blue eyes of virtue and something else of mystery. That "something" can be seen in the eyes of little animals when they are sad or ill. Something imploring, childish, resignedly suffering. . . . Clever people never have such eyes.

His whole face seemed to breathe candour and sincerity. If it be true that the face is the mirror of the soul, I could have taken an oath from the very first day of my acquaintance with the gentleman with the cockade that he was unable to lie. I might even have gambled upon it. Whether I should have lost or not, the reader will see later.

His chestnut hair and beard were thick and soft as silk, and soft hair is the sign of a sweet, sensitive soul. Criminals and abandoned characters have, in most cases, harsh hair. If this be true or not the reader will also see further on. Neither the expression of his face, nor the softness of his beard was as soft and delicate in this gentleman with the cockade as the movements of his huge form. These movements seemed to denote education, lightness, grace, and if you will forgive the expression, something womanly. It would cause my hero but a slight effort to bend a horseshoe or to flatten out a tin sardine box, with his first and at the same time not one of his movements showed his physical strength. He took hold of the door handle or of his hat, as if they were butterflies—delicately, carefully, hardly touching them with his fingers. He walked noiselessly, he pressed my hand feebly. When looking at him you forgot that he was as strong as Goliath, and that he could lift with one hand weights that five men like our office servant Andrey could not have moved. Looking at his light movements. it was impossible to believe that he was strong and heavy. Spencer might have called him a model of grace.

When he entered my office he became confused. His delicate, sensitive nature was probably shocked by my frowning, dissatisfied face.

"For God's sake forgive me!" he began in a soft, mellow baritone voice. "I have broken in upon you not at the appointed time, and I have forced you to make an exception for me. You are very busy! But, Mr. Editor, you see, this is how the case stands. To-morrow I must start for Odessa on very important business. . . . If I had been able to put off this journey till Saturday, I can assure you I would not have asked you to make this exception for me. I submit to rules because I love order. . . ."

"How much he talks!" I thought as I stretched out my hand towards the pen, showing by this movement I was pressed for time. (I was terribly bored by visitors just then.)

"I will only take up a moment of your time," my hero continued in an apologetic tone. "But first allow me to introduce myself. . . . Ivan Petrovich Kamyshev, Bachelor of Law and former examining magistrate. I have not the honour of belonging to the fellowship of authors, nevertheless I appear before you from motives that are purely those of a writer. Notwithstanding his forty years, you have before you a man who wishes to be a beginner. . . . Better late than never!"

"Very pleased. . . . What can I do for you?"

The man wishing to be a beginner sat down and continued, looking at the floor with his imploring eyes:

"I have brought you a short story which I would like to see published in your journal. Mr. Editor, I will tell you quite candidly I have not written this story to attain an author's celebrity, nor for the sake of sweet-sounding words. I am too old for these good things. I venture on the writer's path from purely commercial motives. . . I want to earn something. . . . At the present moment I have absolutely no occupation. I was a magistrate in the S—— district for more than five years, but I did not make a fortune, nor did I keep my innocence either. . . ."

Kamyshev glanced at me with his kind eyes and laughed gently.

"Service is tiresome. . . . I served and served till I was quite fed up, and chucked it. I have no occupation now, sometimes I have nothing to eat. . . .

If, despite its unworthiness, you will publish my story, you will do me more than a great favour. . . . You will help me. . . . A journal is not an alms-house, nor an old-age asylum. . . . I know that, but . . . won't you be so kind. . . ."

"He is lying," I thought.

The breloques and the diamond ring on his little finger belied his having written for the sake of a piece of bread. Besides, a slight cloud passed over Kamyshev's face such as only an experienced eye can trace on the faces of people who seldom lie.

"What is the subject of your story?" I asked.

"The subject? What can I tell you? The subject is not new. . . . Love and murder. . . . But read it, you will see. . . . 'From the Notes of an Examining Magistrate.' . . ."

I probably frowned, for Kamyshev looked confused, his eyes began to blink, he started and continued speaking rapidly:

"My story is written in the conventional style of former examining magistrates, but . . . you will find in it facts, the truth. . . . All that is written, from beginning to end, happened before my eyes. . . . Indeed, I was not only a witness but one of the actors."

"The truth does not matter. . . . It is not absolutely necessary to see a thing to describe it. That is unimportant. The fact is our poor readers have long been fed up with Gaboriau and Shklyarevsky. They are tired of all those mysterious murders, those artful devices of the detectives, and the extraordinary resourcefulness of the examining magistrate. The reading public, of course, varies. but I am talking of

the public that reads our newspaper. What is the title of your story?"

"The Shooting Party."

"Hm! . . That's not serious, you know. . . . And, to be quite frank with you, I have such an amount of copy on hand that it is quite impossible to accept new things, even if they are of undoubted merit."

"Pray accept my work, . . . You say it is not serious, but . . . it is difficult to give a title to a thing before you have seen it. . . . Besides, is it possible you cannot admit that an examining magistrate can write serious works?"

All this Kamyshev said stammeringly, twisting a pencil about between his fingers and looking at his feet. He finished by blinking his eyes and becoming exceedingly confused. I was sorry for him.

"All right, leave it," I said. "But I can't promise that your story will be read very soon. You will have to wait. . . ."

"How long?"

"I don't know. Look in . . . in about two to three months. . . ."

"That's pretty long. . . . But I dare not insist. . . . Let it be as you say. . . ."

Kamyshev rose and took up his cap.

"Thank you for the audience," he said. "I will now go home and dwell in hope. Three months of hope! However, I am boring you. I have the honour to bid you good-bye!"

"One word more, please," I said as I turned over the pages of his thick copy-book, which were written in a very small handwriting. "You write here in the first person. . . You therefore mean the examining magistrate to be yourself?"

"Yes. but under another name. The

part I play in this story is somewhat scandalous. . . . It would have been awkward to give my own name. . . . In three months, then?"

"Yes, not earlier, please. . . . Goodbye!"

The former examining magistrate bowed gallantly, turned the door handle gingerly, and disappeared, leaving his work on my writing table. I took up the copy-book and put it away in the table drawer.

Handsome Kamyshev's story reposed in my table drawer for two months. One day, when leaving my office to go to the country, I remembered it and took it with me.

When I was seated in the railway coach I opened the copy-book and began to read from the middle. The middle interested me. That same evening, notwithstanding my want of leisure, I read the whole story from the beginning to the words "The End." which were written with a great flourish. That night I read the whole story through again, and at sunrise I was walking about the terrace from corner to corner, rubbing my temples as if I wanted to rub out of my head some new and painful thoughts that had suddenly entered my mind. . . . The thoughts were really painful, unbearably sharp. It appeared to me that I, neither an examining magistrate nor even a psychological juryman, had discovered the terrible secret of a man, a secret that did not concern me in the slightest degree. I paced the terrace and tried to persuade myself not to believe in my discovery. . . .

Kamyshev's story did not appear in my newspaper for reasons that I will explain at the end of my talk with the reader. I shall meet the reader once

again. Now, when I am leaving him for a long time, I offer Kamyshev's story for his perusal.

This story is not remarkable in any way. It has many lengthy passages and many inequalities. . . . The author is too fond of effects and strong expressions. . . . It is evident that he is writing for the first time, his hand is unaccustomed, uneducated. Nevertheless, his narrative reads easily. There is a plot, a meaning, too, and what is most important, it is original, very characteristic and what may be called *sui generis.* It also possesses certain literary qualities. It is worth reading. Here it is.

THE NARRATIVE

(From the Notebook of an Examining Magistrate)

CHAPTER I

CRIES!

"THE husband killed his wife! Oh, how stupid you are! Give me some sugar!"

These cries awoke me. I stretched myself, feeling indisposition and heaviness in every limb. One can lie upon one's legs or arms until they are numb, but now it seemed to me that my whole body, from the crown of my head to the soles of my feet, was benumbed. An afternoon snooze in a sultry, dry atmosphere amid the buzzing and humming of flies and mosquitoes does not act in an invigorating manner but has an enervating effect. Broken and bathed in perspiration, I rose and went to the window. The sun was still high and baked with the same ardour it had done three hours before. Many hours still!

remained until sunset and the coolness of the evening.

"The husband killed his wife!"

"Stop lying, Ivan Dem'yanych!" I said as I gave a slight tap to Ivan Dem'yanych's nose. "Husbands kill their wives only in novels and in the tropics, where African passions boil over, my dear. For us such horrors as thefts and burglaries or people living on false passports are quite enough."

"Thefts and burglaries!" Ivan Dem'yanych murmured through his hooked nose. "Oh, how stupid you are!"

"What's to be done, my dear? In what way are we mortals to blame for our brain having its limits? Besides, Ivan Dem'yanych, it is no sin to be a fool in such a temperature. You're my clever darling, but doubtless your brain, too, gets addled and stupid in such heat."

My parrot is not called Polly or by any other of the names given to birds. but he is called Ivan Dem'yanych. He got this name quite by chance. One day, when my man Polycarp was cleaning the cage, he suddenly made a discovery without which my noble bird would still have been called Polly. My lazy servant was suddenly blessed with the idea that my parrot's beak was very like the nose of our village shopkeeper, Ivan Dem'yanych, and from that time the name and patronymic of our long-nosed shopkeeper stuck to my parrot. From that day Polycarp and the whole village christened my extraordinary bird "Ivan Dem'yanych." By Polycarp's will the bird became a personage, and the shopkeeper lost his own name, and to the end of his days he will be known among the villagers under the nickname of the "magistrate's parrot."

I had bought Ivan Dem'yanych from the mother of my predecessor, the examining magistrate, Pospelov, who had died shortly before my appointment. I bought him together with some old oak furniture, various rubbishy kitchen utensils, and in general the whole of the household gods that remained after the deceased. My walls are still decorated with photographs of his relatives, and the portrait of the former occupant is still hanging above my bed. The departed, a lean, muscular man with a red moustache and a thick under-lip, sits looking at me with staring eyes from his faded nutwood frame all the time I am lying on his bed. . . . I had not taken down a single photograph, I had left the house just as I found it. I am too lazy to think of my own comfort, and I don't prevent either corpses or living men from hanging on my walls if the latter wish to do so.*

Ivan Dem'yanych found it as sultry as I did. He fluffed out his feathers, spread his wings, and shrieked out the phrases he had been taught by my predecessor, Pospelov, and by Polycarp. To occupy in some way my after-dinner leisure, I sat down in front of the cage and began to watch the movements of my parrot, who was industriously trying, but without success, to escape from the torments he suffered from the suffocating heat and the insects that dwelt among his feathers.

---

* I beg the reader to excuse such expressions. Kamyshev's story is rich in them, and if I do not omit them it is only because I thought it necessary in the interest of the characterization of the author to print his story *in toto*.
—A. Ch.

. . The poor thing seemed very unhappy. . . .

"At what time does he awake?" was borne to me in a bass voice from the lobby.

"That depends!" Polycarp's voice answered. "Sometimes he wakes at five o'clock, and sometimes he sleeps like a log till morning. . . . Everybody knows he has nothing to do."

"You're his valet, I suppose?"

"His servant. Now don't bother me; hold your tongue. Don't you see I'm reading?"

I peeped into the lobby. My Polycarp was there, lolling on the large red trunk, and, as usual, reading a book. With his sleepy, unblinking eyes fixed attentively on his book, he was moving his lips and frowning. He was evidently irritated by the presence of the stranger, a tall, beared muzhik, who was standing near the trunk persistently trying to inveigle him into conversation. At my appearance the muzhik took a step away from the trunk and drew himself up at attention. Polycarp looked dissatisfied, and without removing his eyes from the book he rose slightly.

"What do you want?" I asked the muzhik.

"I have come from the Count, your honour. The Count sends you his greetings, and begs you to come to him at once. . . ."

"Has the Count arrived?" I asked, much astonished.

"Just so, your honour. . . . He arrived last night. . . . Here's a letter, sir. . . ."

"What the devil has brought him back!" my Polycarp grumbled. "Two summers we've lived peacefully without him, and this year he'll again make a pigsty of the district. We'll again not escape without shame."

"Hold your tongue, your opinion is not asked!"

"I need not be asked. . . . I'll speak unasked. You'll again come home from him in drunken disorder and bathe in the lake just as you are, in all your clothes. . . . I've to clean them afterwards! They cannot be cleaned in three days!"

"What's the Count doing now?" I asked the muzhik.

"He was just sitting down to dinner when he sent me to you. . . . Before dinner he fished from the bathing house, sir. . . . What answer is there?"

I opened the letter and read the following:

"My Dear Lecoq,—If you are still alive, well, and have not forgotten your ever-drunken friend, do not delay a moment. Array yourself in your clothing and fly to me. I only arrived last night and am already dying from ennui. The impatience I feel to see you knows no bounds. I myself wanted to drive over to see you and carry you off to my den, but the heat has fettered all my limbs. I am sitting on one spot fanning myself. Well, how are you? How is your clever Ivan Dem'yanych? Are you still at war with your pedant, Polycarp? Come quickly and tell me everything.
—"Your A. K."

It was not necessary to look at the signature to recognize the drunken, sprawling, ugly handwriting of my friend, Count Alexey Karnéev. The shortness of the letter, its pretension to a certain playfulness and vivacity proved that my friend, with his limited capacities, must have torn up much notepaper before he was able to compose this epistle.

The pronoun "which" was absent from this letter, and adverbs were carefully avoided—both being grammatical forms that were seldom achieved by the Count at a single sitting.

"What answer is there, sir?" the muzhik repeated.

At first I did not reply to this question, and every clean-minded man in my place would have hesitated too. The Count was fond of me, and quite sincerely obtruded his friendship on me. I, on my part, felt nothing like friendship for the Count; I even disliked him. It would therefore have been more honest to reject his friendship once for all than to go to him and dissimulate. Besides, to go to the Count's meant to plunge once more into the life my Polycarp had characterized as a "pigsty," which two years before during the Count's residence on his estate and until he left for Petersburg had injured my good health and had dried up my brain. That loose, unaccustomed life so full of show and drunken madness, had not had time to shatter my constitution, but it had made me notorious in the whole Government. . . . I was popular. . . .

My reason told me the whole truth, a blush of shame for the not distant past suffused my face, my heart sank with fear that I would not possess sufficient manliness to refuse to go to the Count's, but I did not hesitate long. The struggle lasted not more than a minute.

"Give my compliments to the Count," I said to his messenger, "and thank him for thinking of me. . . . Tell him I

am busy, and that. . . . Tell him that I . . ."

And at the very moment my tongue was about to pronounce a decisive "No," I was suddenly overpowered by a feeling of dullness. . . . The young man, full of life, strength and desires, who by the decrees of fate had been cast into this forest village, was seized by a sensation of ennui, of loneliness. . . .

I remembered the Count's gardens with the exuberant vegetation of their cool conservatories, and the semi-darkness of the narrow, neglected avenues. . . . Those avenues protected from the sun by arches of the entwined branches of old limes know me well; they also know the women who sought my love and semi-darkness. . . . I remembered the luxurious drawing-room with the sweet indolence of its velvet 'sofas, heavy curtains and thick carpets, soft as down, with the laziness so loved by young healthy animals. . . . There recurred to my mind my drunken audacity that knew no limits to its boundless satanic pride, and contempt of life. My large body wearied by sleep again longed for movement. . . .

"Tell him I'll come!"

The muzhik bowed and retired.

"If I'd known, I wouldn't have let that devil in!" Polycarp grumbled, quickly turning over the pages of his book in an objectless manner.

"Put that book away and go and saddle Zorka," I said. "Look sharp!"

"Look sharp! Oh, of course, certainly. . . . I'm just going to rush off. . . . It would be all right to go on business, but he'll go to break the devil's horns!"

This was said in an undertone, but

loud enough for me to hear it. Having whispered this impertinence, my servant drew himself up before me and waited for me to flare up in reply, but I pretended not to have heard his words. My silence was the best and sharpest arms I could use in my contests with Polycarp. This contemptuous manner of allowing his venomous words to pass unheeded disarmed him and cut the ground away from under his feet. As a punishment it acted better than a box on the ear or a flood of vituperation. . . . When Polycarp had gone into the yard to saddle Zorka, I peeped into the book which he had been prevented from reading. It was *The Count of Monte Cristo,* Dumas' terrible romance. . . . My civilized fool read everything, beginning with the signboards of the public houses and finishing with Auguste Comte, which was lying in my trunk together with other neglected books that I did not read; but of the whole mass of written and printed matter he only approved of terrible, strongly exciting novels with "celebrated personages," poison and subterranean passages; all the rest he dubbed "nonsense." I shall have again to recur to his reading, now I had to ride off. A quarter of an hour later the hoofs of my Zorka were raising the dust on the road from the village to the Count's estate. The sun was near setting, but the heat and the sultriness were still felt. The hot air was dry and motionless, although my road led along the banks of an enormous lake. . . . On my right I saw the great expanse of water, on the left my sight was caressed by the young vernal foliage of an oak forest; nevertheless, my cheeks suffered the dryness of Sahara. "If there could

only be a storm!" I thought, dreaming of a good cool downpour.

The lake slept peacefully. It did not greet with a single sound the flight of my Zorka, and it was only the piping of a young snipe that broke the grave-like silence of the motionless giant. The sun looked at itself in it as in a huge mirror, and shed a blinding light on the whole of its breadth that extended from my road to the opposite distant banks. And it seemed to my blinded eyes that nature received light from the lake and not from the sun.

The sultriness impelled to slumber the whole of that life in which the lake and its green banks so richly abounded. The birds had hidden themselves, and fish did not splash in the water, the field crickets and the grasshoppers waited in silence for coolness to set in. All around was a waste. From time to time my Zorka bore me into a thick cloud of littoral mosquitoes, and far away on the lake, scarcely moving, I could see the three black boats belonging to old Mikhey, our fisherman, who leased the fishing rights of the whole lake.

CHAPTER II

VODKA

I DID not ride in a straight line as I had to make a circuit along the road that skirted the round lake. It was only possible to go in a straight line by boat, while those who went by the road had to make a large round and the distance was almost eight versts farther. All the way, when looking at the lake, I could see beyond it the opposite clayey banks, on which the bright strip of a blossoming cherry orchard gleamed white, while farther still I could see the roofs of the

Count's barns dotted all over with many coloured pigeons, and rising still higher the small white belfry of the Count's chapel. At the foot of the clayey banks was the bathing house with sailcloth nailed on the sides and sheets hanging to dry on its railings. I saw all this, and it appeared to me as if only a verst separated me from my friend, the Count, while in order to reach his estate I had to ride about sixteen versts.

On the way, I thought of my strange relations to the Count. It was interesting for me to give myself an account of how we stood and try to settle it, but, alas! that account was a task beyond my strength. However much I thought, I could come to no satisfactory decision, and at last I arrived at the conclusion that I was but a bad judge of myself and of man in general. The people who knew both the Count and me explained our mutual connexion. The narrow-browed, who see nothing beyond the tip of their nose, were fond of asserting that the illustrious Count found in the "poor and undistinguished" magistrate a congenial hanger-on and boon companion. To their understanding, I, the writer of these lines, fawned and cringed before the Count for the sake of the crumbs and scraps that fell from his table. In their opinion the illustrious millionaire, who was both the bugbear and the envy of the whole of the S—— district, was very clever and liberal; otherwise his gracious condescension that went as far as friendship for an indigent magistrate and the genuine liberalism that made the Count tolerate my familiarity in addressing him as "thou," would be quite incomprehensible. Cleverer people explained our intimacy by our common "spiritual

interests." The Count and I were of the same age. We had finished our studies in the same university, we were both jurists, and we both knew very little: I knew a little, but the Count had forgotten and drowned in alcohol the little he had ever known. We were both proud, and by virtue of some reason which was only known to ourselves, we shunned the world like misanthropes. We were both indifferent to the opinion of the world—that is of the S—— district—we were both immoral, and would certainly both end badly. These were the "spiritual interests" that united us. This was all that the people who knew us could say about our relations.

They would, of course, have spoken differently had they known how weak, soft and yielding was the nature of my friend, the Count, and how strong and hard was mine. They would have had much to say had they known how fond this infirm man was of me, and how I disliked him! He was the first to offer his friendship and I was the first to say "thou" to him, but with what a difference in the tone! In a fit of kindly feeling he embraced me, and asked me timidly to be his friend. I, on the other hand, once seized by a feeling of contempt and aversion, said to him:

"Canst thou not cease jabbering nonsense?"

And he accepted this "thou" as an expression of friendship and submitted to it from that time, repaying me with an honest, brotherly "thou."

Yes, it would have been better and more honest had I turned my Zorka's head homewards and ridden back to Polycarp and my Ivan Dem'yanych.

Afterwards I often thought: "How much misfortune I would have avoided bearing on my shoulders, how much good I would have brought to my neighbours, if on that night I had had the resolution to turn back, if only my Zorka had gone mad and had carried me far away from that terribly large lake! What numbers of tormenting recollections which now cause my hand to quit the pen and seize my head would not have pressed so heavily on my mind!" But I must not anticipate, all the more as farther on I shall often have to pause on misfortunes. Now for gaiety. . . .

My Zorka bore me into the gates of the Count's yard. At the very gates she stumbled, and I, losing the stirrup, almost fell to the ground.

"An ill omen, sir!" a muzhik, who was standing at one of the doors of the Count's long line of stables, called to me.

I believe that a man falling from a horse may break his neck, but I do not believe in prognostications. Having given the bridle to the muzhik, I beat the dust off my top-boots with my riding-whip and ran into the house. Nobody met me. All the doors and windows of the rooms were wide open, nevertheless the air in the house was heavy, and had a strange smell. It was a mixture of the odour of ancient, deserted apartments with the tart narcotic scent of hothouse plants that have but recently been brought from the conservatories into the rooms. . . . In the drawing-room, two tumbled cushions were lying on one of the sofas that was covered with a light blue silk material, and on a round table before the sofa I saw a glass containing a few drops of a liquid that exhaled an odour of strong Riga balsam. All this denoted that the house was inhabited, but I did not meet a

living soul in any of the eleven rooms that I traversed. The same desertion that was round the lake reigned in the house. . . .

A glass door led into the garden from the so-called "mosaic" drawing-room. I opened it with noise and went down the marble stairs into the garden. I had gone but a few steps through the avenue when I met Nastasia, an old woman of ninety, who had formerly been the Count's nurse. This little wrinkled old creature, forgotten by death, had a bald head and piercing eyes. When you looked at her face you involuntarily remembered the nickname "Scops-Owl" that had been given her in the village. . . When she saw me she trembled and almost dropped a glass of milk she was carrying in both hands.

"How do you do, Scops?" I said to her.

She gave me a sidelong glance and silently went on her way. . . . I seized her by the shoulder.

"Don't be afraid, fool. . . Where's the Count?"

The old woman pointed to her ear.

"Are you deaf? How long have you been deaf?"

Despite her great age, the old woman heard and saw very well, but she found it useful to calumniate her senses. I shook my finger at her and let her go.

Having gone on a few steps farther, I heard voices, and soon after saw people. At the spot where the avenue widened out and formed an open space surrounded by iron benches and shaded by tall white acacias, stood a table on which a samovar shone brightly. People were seated at the table, talking. I went quietly across the grass to the open space and, hiding behind a lilac bush, searched for the Count with my eyes.

My friend, Count Karnéev, was seated at the table on a folding cane-bottomed chair, drinking tea. He was dressed in the same many-coloured dressing-gown in which I had seen him two years before, and he wore a straw hat. His face had a troubled, concentrated expression, and it was very wrinkled, so that a man not acquainted with him might have imagined he was troubled at that moment by some serious thought or anxiety. . . . The Count had not changed at all in appearance during the two years since last we met. He had the same thin body, as frail and wizened as the body of a corn-cake. He had the same narrow, consumptive shoulders, surmounted by a small red-haired head His small nose was as red as formerly, and his cheeks were flabby and hanging like rags, as they had been two years before. On his face there was nothing of boldness, strength or manliness. . . . All were weak, apathetic and languid. The only imposing thing about him was his long, drooping moustache. Somebody had told my friend that a long moustache was very becoming to him. He believed it, and every morning since then he had measured how much longer the growth on his pale lips had become. With this moustache he reminded you of a moustached but very young and puny kitten.

Sitting next to the Count at the table was a stout man with a large closely-cropped head and very dark eyebrows, who was unknown to me. His face was fat and shone like a ripe melon. His moustache was longer than the Count's, his forehead was low, his lips were compressed, and his eyes gazed lazily into the sky. . . . The features of his face were bloated, but nevertheless they were as hard as dried-up skin. The type was not Russian. . . . The stout man was without his coat or waistcoat, and on his shirt there were dark spots caused by perspiration. He was not drinking tea but Seltzer water.

At a respectful distance from the table a short, thick-set man with a stout red neck and sticking out ears was standing. This man was Urbenin, the Count's bailiff. In honour of the Count's arrival he was dressed in a new black suit and was now suffering torments. The perspiration was pouring in streams from his red, sunburnt face. Next to the bailiff stood the muzhik, who had come to me with the letter. It was only here I noticed that this muzhik had only one eye. Standing at attention, not allowing himself the slightest movement, he was like a statue, and waited to be questioned.

"Kusma, you deserve to be thrashed black and blue with your own whip," the bailiff said to him in his reproachful soft bass voice, pausing between each word. "Is it possible to execute the master's orders in such a careless way. You ought to have requested him to come here at once and to have found out when he could be expected."

"Yes, yes, yes. . ." the Count exclaimed nervously. "You ought to have found out everything! He said: 'I'll come!' But that's not enough! I want him at once! Pos-i-tively at once! You asked him to come, but he did not understand!"

"Why do you require him?" the fat man asked the Count.

"I want to see him!"

"Only that? To my mind, Alexey,

that magistrate would do far better if he remained at home to-day. I have no wish for guests."

I opened my eyes. What was the meaning of that masterful, authoritative "I."

"But he's not a guest!" my friend said in an imploring tone. "He won't prevent you from resting after the journey. I beg you not to stand on ceremonies with him. . . . You'll like him at once, my dear boy, and you'll soon be friends with him!"

I came out of my hiding place behind the lilac bushes and went up to the tables. The Count saw and recognized me, and his face brightened with a pleased smile.

"Here he is! Here he is!" he exclaimed, getting red with pleasure, and he jumped up from the table. "How good of you to come!"

He ran towards me, seized me in his arms, embraced and scratched my cheeks several times with his bristly moustache. These kisses were followed by lengthy shaking of my hand and long looks into my eyes.

"You, Sergey, have not changed at all! You're still the same! The same handsome and strong fellow! Thank you for accepting my invitation and coming at once!"

When released from the Count's embrace, I greeted the bailiff, who was an old friend of mine, and sat down at the table.

"Oh, Golubchek!" the Count continued in an excitedly anxious tone. "If you only knew how delighted I am to see your serious countenance again. You are not acquainted? Allow me to introduce you—my good friend, Kaetan Kazimirovich Pshekhotsky. And this,"

he continued, introducing me to the fat man, "is my good old friend, Sergey Petrovich Zinov'ev! Our magistrate."

The stout, dark-browed man rose slightly from his seat and offered me his fat, and terribly sweaty hand.

"Very pleased," he mumbled, examining me from head to foot. "Very glad!"

Having given vent to his feelings and become calm again, the Count filled a glass with cold, dark brown tea for me and moved a box of biscuits towards my hand.

"Eat. . . . When passing through Moscow I bought them at Einem's. I'm very angry with you, Serezha, so angry that I wanted to quarrel with you! . . . Not only have you not written me a line during the whole of the past two years, but you did not even think a single one of my letters worth answering! That's not friendly!"

"I do not know how to write letters," I said. "Besides, I have no time for letter writing. Can you tell me what could I have written to you about?"

"There must have been many things!"

"Indeed, there was nothing. I admit of only three sorts of letters: love, congratulatory, and business letters. The first I did not write to you because you are not a woman, and I am not in love with you; the second you don't require; and from the third category we are relieved as from our birth we have never had any business connexion together."

"That's about true," the Count said, agreeing readily and quickly with everything; "but all the same, you might have written, if only a line. . . . And what's more, as Pëtr Egorych tells me, all these two years you've not set foot here, as though you were living a thousand versts away or disdained my property. You might have lived here, shot over my grounds. Many things might have happened here while I was away."

The Count spoke much and long. When once he began talking about anything, his tongue chattered on without ceasing and without end, quite regardless of the triviality or insignificance of his subject.

In the utterance of sounds he was as untiring as my Ivan Dem'yanych. I could hardly stand him for that facility. This time he was stopped by his butler, Il'ya, a tall, thin man in a well-worn, much-stained livery, who brought the Count a wineglass of vodka and half a tumbler of water on a silver tray. The Count swallowed the vodka, washed it down with some water. making a grimace with a shake of the head.

"So it seems you have not yet stopped tippling vodka!" I said.

"No, Serezha, I have not."

"Well, you might at least drop that drunken habit of making faces and shaking your head! It's disgusting!"

"My dear boy, I'm going to drop everything. . . . The doctors have forbidden me to drink. I drink now only because it's unhealthy to drop habits all at once. . . . It must be done gradually. . . ."

I looked at the Count's unhealthy, worn face, at the wineglass, at the butler in yellow shoes. I looked at the dark-browed Pole, who from the very first moment for some reason had appeared to me to be a scoundrel and a blackguard. I looked at the one-eyed muzhik, who stood there at attention, and a feeling of dread and of oppression came over me. . . . I suddenly wanted to

leave this dirty atmosphere, having first opened the Count's eyes to all the unlimited antipathy I felt for him. . . . There was a moment when I was ready to rise and depart. . . . But I did not go away. . . . I was prevented (I'm ashamed to confess it!) by physical laziness. . . .

"Give me a glass of vodka, too!" I said to Il'ya.

Long shadows began to be cast on the avenue and on the open space where we were sitting. . . .

The distant croaking of frogs, the cawing of crows and the singing of orioles greeted the setting of the sun. A gay evening was just beginning. . . .

"Tell Urbenin to sit down," I whispered to the Count. "He's standing before you like a boy."

"Oh, I never thought of that! Pëtr Egorych," the Count addressed his bailiff, "sit down, please! Why are you standing there?"

Urbenin sat down, casting a grateful glance at me. He who was always healthy and gay appeared to me now to be ill and dull. His face seemed wrinkled and sleepy, his eyes looked at us lazily and as if unwillingly.

"Well, Pëtr Egorych, what's new here? Any pretty girls, eh?" Karnéev asked him. "Isn't there something special . . . something out of the common?"

"It's always the same, your Excellency. . . ."

"Are there no new . . . nice little girls, Pëtr Egorych?"

Moral Pëtr Egorych blushed.

"I don't know, your Excellency. . . . I don't occupy myself with that. . . ."

"There are, your Excellency," broke in the deep bass voice of one-eyed

Kuz'ma, who had been silent all the time. "And quite worth notice, too."

"Are they pretty?"

"There are all sorts, your Excellency, for all tastes. . . . There are dark ones and fair ones—all sorts. . . ."

"O, ho! . . . Stop a minute, stop a minute. . . . I remember you now. . . . My former Leporello, a sort of secretary. . . . Your name's Kuz'ma, I think?"

"Yes, your Excellency. . . ."

"I remember, I remember. . . . Well, and what have you now in view? Something new, all peasant girls?"

"Mostly peasants, of course, but there are finer ones, too. . . ."

"Where have you found finer ones . . ." Il'ya asked, winking at Kuz'ma.

"At Easter the postman's sister-in-law came to stay with him . . . Nastasia Ivanovna. . . . A girl all on springs. I myself would like to eat her, but money is wanted. . . . Cheeks like peaches, and all the rest as good. . . . There's something finer than that, too. It's only waiting for you, your Excellency. Young, plump, jolly . . . a beauty! Such a beauty, your Excellency, as you've scarcely found in Petersburg. . . ."

"Who is it?"

"Olenka, the forester Skvortsov's daughter."

Urbenin's chair cracked under him. Supporting himself with his hands on the table, purple in the face, the bailiff rose slowly and turned towards one-eyed Kuz'ma. The expression on his face of dullness and fatigue had given place to one of great anger.

"Hold your tongue, serf!" he grumbled. "One-eyed vermin! Say what you please, but don't dare to touch respectable people!"

"I'm not touching you, Pëtr Egorych," Kuz'ma said imperturbably.

"I'm not talking about myself, blockhead! Besides. . . . Forgive me, your Excellency," the bailiff turned to the Count, "forgive me for making a scene, but I would beg your Excellency to forbid your Leporello, as you were pleased to call him, to extend his zeal to persons who are worthy of all respect!"

"I don't understand . . ." the Count lisped naively. "He has said nothing very offensive."

Insulted and excited to a degree, Urbenin went away from the table and stood with his side towards us. With his arms crossed on his breast and his eyes blinking, hiding his purple face from us behind the branches of the bushes, he stood plunged in thought.

Had not this man a presentiment that in the near future his moral feelings would have to suffer offences a thousand times more bitter?

"I don't understand what has offended him!" the Count whispered in my ear. "What a caution! There was nothing offensive in what was said."

After two years of sober life, the glass of vodka acted on me in a slightly intoxicating manner. A feeling of lightness, of pleasure, was diffused in my brain and through my whole body. Added to this, I began to feel the coolness of evening, which little by little was supplanting the sultriness of the day. I proposed to take a stroll. The Count and his new Polish friend had their coats brought from the house, and we set off. Urbenin followed us.

CHAPTER III

HER SINS

THE Count's gardens in which we were walking are worthy of special description owing to their striking luxuriousness. From a botanical or an economical point of view, and in many other ways, they are richer and grander than any other gardens I have ever seen. Besides the above-mentioned avenue with its green vaults, you found in them everything that capricious indulgence can demand from pleasure gardens. You found here every variety of indigenous and foreign fruit tree, beginning with the wild cherry and plum and finishing with apricots that were the size of a goose's egg. You came across mulberry trees, barberry bushes, and even olive trees at every step. . . . Here there were half-ruined, moss-grown grottoes, fountains, little ponds destined for goldfish and tame carp. hillocks, pavilions and costly conservatories. . . . And all this rare luxury which had been collected by the hands of grandfathers and fathers, all this wealth of large, full roses, poetical grottoes and endless avenues, was barbarously abandoned to neglect, and given over to the power of weeds, the thievish hatchet and the rooks who unceremoniously built their ugly nests on the branches of rare trees! The lawful possessor of all this wealth walked beside me, and the muscles of his lean, satiated face were no more moved by the sight of this neglect, this crying human slovenliness, than if he had not been the owner of these gardens. Once only, by way of making some remark, he said to his bailiff that it would not be a bad thing if the paths were sanded. He noticed the absence of the sand that was not wanted by anybody, but he did not notice the bare trees that had been frozen in the hard winters, or the cows that were walking about in the garden. In reply to his remark, Urbenin said it would require ten men to keep the garden in order, and as his Excellency was not pleased to reside on his estate, the outlay on the garden would be a useless and unproductive luxury. The Count, of course, agreed with this argument.

"Besides, I must confess I have no time for it!" Urbenin said with a wave of the hand. "All the summer in the fields, and in winter selling the corn in town. . . . There's no time for gardens here!"

The charm of the principal, the so-called "main avenue," consisted in its old broad-spreading limes, and in the masses of tulips that stretched out in two variegated borders at each side of its whole length and finished at the end in a yellow spot. This was a yellow stone pavilion, which at one time had contained a refreshment room, billiards, skittles and other games. We wandered, without any object, towards this pavilion. At its door we were met by a live creature which somewhat unsettled the nerves of my companion, who was never very courageous.

"A snake!" the Count shrieked, seizing me by the hand and turning pale. "Look!"

The Pole stepped back, and then stood stock still with his arms outstretched as if he wanted to bar the way for the apparition. On the upper step of the half-crumbled stone stair there lay a young snake of our ordinary Russian species. When it saw us it raised its head and moved. The Count shrieked again and hid behind me.

"Don't be afraid, your Excellency. . . ." Urbenin said lazily as he placed his foot on the first step.

"But if it bites?"

"It won't bite. Besides, the danger from the bite of these snakes is much exaggerated. I was once bitten by an old snake, and as you see, I didn't die. The sting of a man is worse than a snake's!" Urbenin said with a sigh, wishing to point a moral.

Indeed, the bailiff had not had time to mount two or three steps before the snake stretched out to its full length, and with the rapidity of lightning vanished into a crevice between two stones. When we entered the pavilion we saw another living creature. Lying on the torn and faded cloth of the old billiard table there was an elderly man of middle height in a blue jacket, striped trousers, and a jockey cap. He was sleeping sweetly and quietly. Around his toothless gaping mouth and on his pointed nose flies were making themselves at home. Thin as a skeleton, with an open mouth, lying there immovable, he looked like a corpse that had only just been brought in from the mortuary to be dissected.

"Franz!" said Urbenin, poking him. "Franz!"

After being poked five or six times, Franz shut his mouth, sat up, looked round at us, and lay down again. A minute later his mouth was again open and the flies that were walking about his nose were again disturbed by the slight vibration of his snores.

"He's asleep, the lewd swine!" Urbenin sighed.

"Is he not our gardener, Tricher?" the Count asked.

"No other. . . . That's how he is every day . . . He sleeps like a dead man all day and plays cards all night. I was told he gambled last night till six in the morning."

"What do they play?"

"Games of hazard. . . . Chiefly stukolka."

"Well, such gentlemen work badly. They draw their wages for nothing!"

"It was not to complain, your Excellency," Urbenin hastened to say, "that I told you this, or to express my dissatisfaction; it was only. . . . I am only sorry that so capable a man is a slave to his passions. He really is a hard-working man, capable too. . . . He does not receive wages for nothing."

We glanced again at the gambler Franz and left the pavilion. We then turned towards the garden gate and went into the fields.

There are but few novels in which the garden gate does not play an important part. If you have not noticed this, you have only to inquire of my man Polycarp, who in his lifetime has swallowed multitudes of terrible and not terrible novels, and he will doubtless confirm this insignificant but characteristic fact.

My novel has also not escaped the inevitable garden gate. But my gate is different from others in this, that my pen will have to lead through it many unfortunate and scarcely any happy people; and even this in a direction contrary to the one found in other novels. And what is worse, I had once to describe this gate not as a novel-writer but as an examining magistrate. In my novel more criminals than lovers will pass through it.

A quarter of an hour later, supporting ourselves on our walking sticks, we
wound our way up the hill to what is
known as the "Stone Grave." In the
surrounding villages there is a legend
that under this heap of stones there re-
poses the body of a Tartar Khan, who,
fearing that after his death the enemy
would desecrate his ashes, had ordered
that a mound of stones was to be made
above his body. This legend, however,
is scarcely correct. The layers of stone,
their size and relative position, exclude
the possibility of man's hand having had
a part in the formation of this mound.
It stands solitary in the midst of fields
and has the aspect of an overturned
dome.

From the top of this mound we could
see the lake to the whole of its captivat-
ing extent and indescribable beauty. The
sun, no longer reflected in it, had set,
leaving behind a broad purple stripe that
illuminated the surroundings with a
pleasing rosy-yellow tint. The Count's
manor and homestead with their houses,
church and gardens, lay at our feet, and
on the other side of the lake the little
village where it was my fate to live
looked grey in the distance. As before,
the surface of the lake was without a
ripple. Old Mikhey's little boats, separated from one another, were hurrying
towards the shore.

To the left of my little village the
buildings of the railway station stood
out dark beneath the smoke from the
engines, and behind us at the foot of
the Stone Grave the road was bordered
on either side by towering old poplars.
This road leads to the Count's forest
that extends to the very horizon

The Count and I stood on the top of
the hill. Urbenin and the Pole being

heavy men preferred to wait for us on
the road below.

"Who's that cove?" I asked the
Count, nodding towards the Pole.
"Where did you pick him up?"

"He's a very nice fellow, Serezha;
very nice!" the Count said in an agitated voice. "You'll soon be the best
of friends."

"Oh, that's not likely! Why does he
never speak?"

"He is silent by nature! But he's
very clever!"

"But what sort of a man is he?"

"I became acquainted with him in
Moscow. He is very nice. You'll hear
all about it afterwards, Serezha; don't
ask now. Let's go down."

We descended the hill and went along
the road towards the forest. It began
to be perceptibly darker. The cry of
the cuckoo, and the tired vocal warbles
of a possibly youthful nightingale were
heard in the forest.

"Hollo! Hollo! Catch me!" we
heard a high-pitched voice of a child
shout as we approached the forest.

A little girl of about five with hair as
white as flax, dressed in a sky-blue
frock, ran out of the wood. When she
saw us she laughed aloud, and with a
skip and a jump put her arms round
Urbenin's knee. Urbenin lifted her up
and kissed her cheek.

"My daughter Sasha!" he said. "Let
me introduce her!"

Sasha was pursued out of the wood by
a schoolboy of about fifteen, Urbenin's
son. When he saw us he pulled off his
cap hesitatingly, put it on, and pulled it
off again. He was followed quietly by
a red spot. This red spot attracted our
attention at once. "What a beautiful
apparition!" the Count exclaimed, catch-

ing hold of my hand. "Look! How charming! What girl is this? I did not know that my forests were inhabited by such naiads!"

I looked round at Urbenin in order to ask him who this girl was, and, strange to say, it was only at that moment I noticed that he was terribly drunk. He was as red as a crawfish, he tottered and, seizing my elbow, he whispered into my ear, exhaling the fumes of spirit on me:

"Sergey Petrovich, I implore you prevent the Count from making any further remarks about this girl! He may, from habit say too much; she is a most worthy person!"

This "most worthy person" was represented by a girl of about nineteen, with beautiful fair hair, kind blue eyes and long curls. She was dressed in a bright red frock, made in a fashion that was neither that of a child nor of a young girl. Her legs, straight as needles, in red stockings, were shod with tiny shoes that were small as a child's. All the time I was admiring her she moved about her well-rounded shoulders coquettishly, as if they were cold or as if my gaze bit her.

"Such a young face, and such developed contours!" whispered the Count, who from his earliest youth had lost the capacity of respecting women, and never looked at them otherwise than from the point of view of a spoilt animal.

I remember that a good feeling was ignited in my breast. I was still a poet, and in the company of the woods, of a May night, and the first twinkling of the evening stars, I could only look at a woman as a poet does. . . . I looked at "the girl in red" with the same

veneration I was accustomed to look upon the forests, the hills and the blue sky. I still had a certain amount of the sentimentality I had inherited from my German mother.

"Who is she?" the Count asked.

"She is the daughter of our forester Skvortsov, your Excellency!" Urbenin replied.

"Is she the Olenka. the one-eyed muzhik spoke of?"

"Yes, he mentioned her name," the bailiff answered, looking at me with large, imploring eyes.

The girl in red let us go past her, turning away without taking any notice of us. Her eyes were looking at something at the side, but I, a man who knows women, felt her pupils resting on my face.

"Which of them is the Count?" I heard her whisper behind us.

"That one with the long moustache," the schoolboy answered.

And we heard silvery laughter behind us. It was the laughter of disenchantment. She had thought that the Count, the owner of these immense forests and the broad lake, was I, and not that pigmy with the worn face and long moustache.

I heard a deep sigh issue from Urbenin's powerful breast. That iron man could scarcely move.

"Dismiss the bailiff," I whispered to the Count. "He is ill or—drunk."

"Pëtr Egorych, you seem to be unwell," the Count said, turning to Urbenin. "I do not require you just now, so I will not detain you any longer."

"Your Excellency need not trouble about me. Thank you for your attention, but I am not ill."

I looked back. The red spot had not moved, but was looking after us.

Poor, fair little head! Did I think on that quiet, peaceful May evening that she would afterwards become the heroine of my troubled romance?

Now, while I write these lines, the autumn rain beats fiercely against my warm windows, and the wind howls above me. I gaze at the dark window and on the dark background of night beyond, trying by the strength of my imagination to conjure up again the charming image of my heroine. . . . . I see her with her innocent, childish, naive, kind little face and loving eyes, and I wish to throw down my pen and tear up and burn all that I have already written.

But here, next to my inkstand, is her photograph. Here, the fair little head is represented in all the vain majesty of a beautiful but deeply-fallen woman. Her weary eyes, proud of their depravity, are motionless. Here she is just the serpent, the harm of whose bite Urbenin would scarcely have called exaggerated.

She gave a kiss to the storm, and the storm broke the flower at the very roots. Much was taken, but too dearly was it paid for. The reader will forgive her her sins!

CHAPTER IV

THE WOODS

WE walked through the woods.

The pines were dull in their silent monotony. They all grow in the same way, one like the others, and at every season of the year they retain the same appearance, knowing neither death nor the renewal of spring. Still, they are attractive in their moroseness: immovable, soundless they seem to think mournful thoughts.

"Hadn't we better turn back?" the Count suggested.

This question received no reply. It was all the same to the Pole where he was. Urbenin did not consider his voice decisive, and I was too much delighted with the coolness of the forest and its resinous air to wish to turn back. Besides, it was necessary to kill time till night, even by a simple walk. The thoughts of the approaching wild night were accompanied by a sweet sinking of the heart. I am afraid to confess that I thought of it, and had already mentally a foretaste of its enjoyments. Judging by the impatience with which the Count constantly looked at his watch, it was evident that he, too, was tormented by expectations. We felt that we understood each other.

Near the forester's house, which nestled between pines on a small square open space, we were met by the loud-sounding bark of two small fiery-yellow dogs, of a breed that was unknown to me; they were as glossy and supple as eels. Recognizing Urbenin, they joyfully wagged their tails and ran towards him, from which one could deduce that the bailiff often visted the forester's house. Here, too, near the house, we were met by a lad without boots or cap, with large freckles on his astonished face. For a moment he looked at us in silence with staring eyes, then, evidently recognizing the Count, he gave an exclamation and rushed headlong into the house.

"I know what he's gone for." the Count said, laughing. "I remember him. . . . It's Mit'ka."

The Count was not mistaken. In less

than a minute Mit'ka came out of the house carrying a tray with a glass of vodka and a tumbler half full of water.

"For your good health, your Excellency!" he said, a broad grin suffusing the whole of his stupid, astonished face.

The Count drank off the vodka, washed it down with water in lieu of a snack, but this time he made no wry face. A hundred paces from the house there was an iron seat, as old as the pines above it. We sat down on it and contemplated the May evening in all its tranquil beauty. . . . The frightened crows flew cawing above our heads, the song of nightingales was borne towards us from all sides; these were the only sounds that broke the pervading stillness.

The Count does not know how to be silent, even on such a calm spring evening, when the voice of man is the least agreeable sound.

"1 don't know if you will be satisfied?" he said to me. "I have ordered a fish-soup and game for supper. With the vodka we shall have cold sturgeon and sucking-pig with horse-radish."

As if angered at this prosaic observation, the poetical pines suddenly shook their tops and a gentle rustle passed through the wood. A fresh breeze swept over the glade and played with the grass.

"Down, down!" Urbenin cried to the flame-coloured dogs, who were preventing him from lighting his cigarette with their caresses. "I think we shall have rain before night. I feel it in the air. It was so terribly hot today that it does prophesy rain. It will be a good thing for the corn."

"What's the use of corn to you," I thought, "if the Count will spend it all on drink? The rain need not trouble about it."

Once more a light breeze passed over the forest, but this time it was stronger. The pines and the grass rustled louder.

"Let us go home."

We rose and strolled lazily back towards the little house.

"It is better to be this fair-haired Olenka," I said, addressing myself to Urbenin, "and to live here with the beasts than to be a magistrate and live among men. . . . It's more peaceful. Is it not so, Pëtr Egorych?"

"It's all the same what one is, Sergey Petrovich, if only the soul is at peace."

"Is pretty Olenka's soul at peace?"

"God alone knows the secrets of other people's souls, but I think she has nothing to trouble her. She has not much to worry her, and no more sins than an infant. . . . She's a very good girl! Ah, now the sky is at last beginning to talk of rain. . . ."

A rumble was heard, somewhat like the sound of a distant vehicle or the rattle of a game of skittles. Somewhere, far beyond the forest. there was a peal of thunder. Mit'ka, who had been watching us the whole time, shuddered and crossed himself.

"A thunderstorm!" the Count exclaimed with a start. "What a surprise! The rain will overtake us on our way home. . . . How dark it is! I said we ought to have turned back! And you wouldn't. and went on and on."

"We might wait in the cottage till the storm is over," I suggested.

"Why in the cottage?" Urbenin said hastily, and his eyes blinked in a strange manner. "It will rain all night, so you'll have to remain all night in the cottage! Please, don't trouble. . . . Go quietly on, and Mit'ka shall run on and order your carriage to come to meet you."

"Never mind, perhaps it won't rain all night. . . . Storm clouds usually pass by quickly. . . . Besides, I don't know the new forester as yet, and I'd also like to have a chat with this Olenka . . . and find out what sort of a dickey bird she is. . . ."

"I've no objections!" the Count agreed.

"How can you go there, if—if the place is not—not in order?" Urbenin mumbled anxiously. "Why should your Excellency sit there in a stuffy room when you could be at home? I don't understand what pleasure that can be! . . . How can you get to know the forester if he is ill? . . ."

It was very evident that the bailiff strongly objected to our going into the forester's house. He even spread his arms as if he wanted to bar the way. . . . I understood by his face that he had reasons for preventing us from going in. I respect other people's reasons and secrets, but on this occasion my curiosity was greatly excited. I persisted, and we entered the house.

"Walk into the drawing-room, please," bare-footed Mit'ka spluttered almost choking with delight.

Try to imagine the very smallest drawing-room in the world, with un-painted deal walls. These walls are hung all over with oleographs from the "Niva," photographs in frames made of shells, and testimonials. One testimonial is from a certain baron, expressing his gratitude for many years of service; all the others are for horses. Here and there ivy climbs up the wall. . . . In a corner a small lamp, whose tiny blue flame is faintly reflected on the sil-ver mounting, burns peacefully before a little icon. Chairs that have evidently been only recently bought are pressed close together round the walls. Too many had been purchased, and they had been squeezed together. as there was nowhere else to put them. . . . Here, also, there are armchairs and a sofa in snow-white covers with flounces and laces, crowded up with a polished round table. A tame hare dozes on the sofa. . . . The room is cosy, clean and warm. . . . The presence of a woman can be noticed everywhere. Even the whatnot with books has a look of innocence and womanliness; it appears to be anxious to say that there is nothing on its shelves but wishy-washy novels and mawkish verse. . . . The charm of such warm, cosy rooms is not so much felt in spring as in autumn, when you look for a refuge from the cold and damp-ness.

After much loud snivelling, blowing, and noisy striking of matches, Mit'ka lit two candles and placed them on the table as carefully as if they had been milk. We sat down in the arm-chairs, looked at each other, and laughed.

"Nikolai Efimych is ill in bed," Urbenin said, to explain the absence of the master, "and Olga Nikolaevna has probably gone to accompany my children. . . ."

"Mit'ka, are the doors shut?" we heard a weak tenor voice asking from the next room.

"They're all shut, Nikolai Efimych!" Mit'ka shouted hoarsely, and he rushed headlong into the next room.

"That's right! See that they are all shut," the same weak voice said again. "And locked—firmly locked. . . . If thieves break in, you must tell me. . . .

I'll shoot the villains with my gun . . . the scoundrels!"

"Certainly, Nikolai Efimych!"

We laughed and looked inquiringly at Urbenin. He grew very red, and in order to hide his confusion he began to arrange the curtains of the windows. . . . What does this dream mean? We again looked at each other.

We had no time for perplexity. Hasty steps were heard outside, then a noise in the porch and the slamming of doors. And the "girl in red" rushed into the room.

"I love the thunder in early May," she sang in a loud, shrill soprano voice, and she cut short her song with a burst of laughter, but when she saw us she suddenly stood still and was silent,— she became embarrassed, and went as quietly as a lamb into the room in which the voice of Nikolai Efimych, her father, had been heard.

"She did not expect to see you," Urbenin said, laughing.

A few minutes later she again came quietly into the room, sat down on the chair nearest the door and began to examine us. She stared at us boldly, not as if we were new people for her, but as if we were animals in the Zoological Gardens. For a minute we too looked at her in silence without moving. . . . I would have agreed to sit still and look at her for a whole hour in this way— she was so lovely that evening. As fresh as the air, rosy, breathing rapidly, her bosom rising and falling, her curls scattered wildly on her forehead, on her shoulders, and on her right hand that was raised to arrange her collar; with large, sparkling eyes. . . . And all this was found on one little body that a single glance could envelop. If you glanced for a moment at this small object you saw more than you would if you looked for a whole century at the endless horizon. . . She looked at me seriously, from my feet upwards, inquiringly; when her eyes left me and passed to the Court or to the Pole I began to read in them the contrary: a glance that passed from the head to the feet, and laughter. . . .

I was the first to speak.

"Allow me to introduce myself," I said, rising and going up to her. "Zinov'ev. . . . And let me introduce my friend, Count Karnéev. . . . We beg you to pardon us for breaking into your nice little house without an invitation. . . . We would, of course, never have done so if the storm had not driven us in. . . ."

"But that won't cause our little house to tumble down!" she said, laughing and giving me her hand.

She displayed her splendid white teeth. I sat down on a chair next to her, and told her how quite unexpectedly the storm had overtaken us on our walk. Our conversation began with the weather —the beginning of all beginnings. While we were talking, Mit'ka had had time to offer the Count two glasses of vodka with the inseparable tumbler of water. Thinking that I was not looking at him, the Count made a sweet grimace and shook his head after each glass.

"Perhaps you would like some refreshments?" Olenka asked me, and, not waiting for an answer, she left the room.

The first drops of rain rattled against the panes. . . . I went up to the windows. . . . It was now quite dark, and through the glass I could see nothing but the raindrops creeping down

and the reflection of my own nose.
There was a flash of lightning, which
illuminated some of the nearest pines.

"Are the doors shut?" I heard the
same tenor voice ask again. "Mit'ka,
come here, you vile-spirited scoundrel!
Shut the doors! Oh, Lord, what torments!"

A peasant woman with an enormous,
tightly tied-in stomach and a stupid,
troubled face came into the room, and,
having bowed low to the Count, she
spread a white table-cloth on the table.
Mit'ka followed her carefully carrying
a tray with various *hors d'œuvres*. A
minute later, we had vodka, rum, cheese,
and a dish of some sort of roasted bird
on the table before us. The Count
drank a glass of vodka, but he would
not eat anything. The Pole smelt the
bird mistrustfully, and then began to
carve it.

"The rain has begun! Look!" I said
to Olenka, who had re-entered the room.

"The girl in red" came up to the window where I was standing, and at that
very moment we were illuminated by a
white flash of light. . . . There was a
fearful crash above us, and it appeared
to me that something large and heavy
had been torn from the sky and had
fallen to earth with a terrible racket.
. . . The window panes and the wineglasses that were standing before the
Count jingled and emitted their tinkling
sound. . . . The thunderclap was a
loud one.

"Are you afraid of thunder-storms?"
I asked Olenka.

She only pressed her cheek to her
round shoulders and looked at me with
childish confidence.

"I'm afraid," she whispered after a
moment's reflection. "My mother was

killed by a storm. . . . The newspapers
even wrote about it. . . . My mother
was going through the fields, crying.
. . She had a very bitter life in this
world. God had compassion on her and
killed her with His heavenly electricity."

"How do you know that there is electricity there?"

"I have learned. . . . Do you know?
People who have been killed by a storm
or in war, or who have died after a difficult confinement go to paradise. . . .
This is not written anywhere in books,
but it is true. My mother is now in
paradise! I think the thunder will also
kill me some day, and I shall go to paradise too. . . . Are you a cultivated
man?"

"Yes."

"Then you will not laugh. . . . This
is how I should like to die: to dress in
the most costly fashionable frock, like
the one I saw the other day on our rich
lady, the land-owner Sheffer; to put
bracelets on my arms. . . . Then to
go to the very summit of the 'Stone
Grave' and allow myself to be killed
by the lightning, so that all the people
could see it. . . . A terrible peal of
thunder, and then, you know, the end!"

"What an odd fancy!" I said, laughing and looking into her eyes that were
full of holy horror at this terrible but
effective death. "Then you don't want
to die in an ordinary dress?"

"No! . . . Olenka shook her head
"And so that everybody should see me."

"The frock you are in is far better
than any fashionable and expensive
dress. . . . It suits you. In it you look
like the red flower of the green woods."

"No, that is not true!" And Olenka
sighed ingenuously. "This frock is a
cheap one; it can't be pretty."

The Count came up to our window with the evident intention of talking to pretty Olenka. My friend could speak three European languages, but he did not know how to talk to women. He stood near us awkwardly, smiling in an inane manner; then he lowed,—inarticulately, "Er—yes,"—and retraced his steps to the decanter of vodka.

"You were singing 'I love the thunder in early May,'" I said to Olenka. "Have those verses been set to music?"

"No, I sing all the verses I know to my own melodies."

I happened by chance to glance back. Urbenin was looking at us. In his eyes I read hatred and animosity: passions that were not at all in keeping with his kind, meek face.

"Can he be jealous?" I thought.

The poor fellow caught my inquiring glance, rose from his chair and went into the lobby to look for something. . . . Even by his gait one could see that he was agitated. The peals of thunder became louder and louder, more prolonged, and oftener repeated. . . . The lightning unceasingly illuminated the sky, the pines and the wet earth with its pleasant but blinding light. . . . The rain was not likely to end soon. I left the window and went up to the bookshelves and began to examine Olenka's library. "Tell me what you read, and I will tell you what you are," I said. But out of the goods that were so symmetrically ranged on the shelves it was difficult to arrive at any estimate of Olenka's mental capacities or "educational standard." There was a strange medley on those shelves. Three anthologies, one book of Börne's, Evtushevsky's arithmetic, the second volume of Lermontov's works, Shklyarevsky, a

number of the magazine *Work*, a cookery book, *Skladchina* . . . I might enumerate other books for you but at the moment I took *Skladchina* from the shelf and began to turn over the pages. The door leading into the next room opened, and a person entered the drawing-room, who at once diverted my attention from Olenka's standard of culture. This person was a tall, muscular man in a print dressing-gown and torn slippers, with an original countenance. His face, covered all over with blue veins, was ornamented with a pair of sergeant's moustaches and whiskers, and had in general a strong resemblance to a bird. His whole face seemed to be drawn forwards, as if trying to concentrate itself in the tip of the nose. Such faces are like the spout of a pitcher. This person's small head was set on a long thin throat, with a large Adam's-apple, and shook about like the nesting-box of a starling in the wind. . . . This strange man looked round on us all with his dim green eyes, and then let them rest on the Count.

"Are the doors shut?" he asked in an imploring voice.

The Count looked at me and shrugged his shoulders.

"Don't trouble, papasha!" Olenka answered. "They are all shut. . . Go back to your room!"

"Is the barn door shut?"

"He's a little queer. . . . It takes him sometimes," Urbenin whispered to me as he came in from the lobby. "He's afraid of thieves, and always troubling about the doors, as you see."

"Nikolai Efimych," he continued, addressing this strange apparition, "go back to your room and go to bed! Don't trouble, everything is shut up!"

"And are the windows shut?"

Nikolai Efimych hastily looked to see if the windows were properly bolted, and then without taking any notice of us he shuffled off into his own room.

"The poor fellow has these attacks sometimes," Urbenin began to explain as soon as he had left the room. "He's a good, capable man; he has a family, too—such a misfortune! Almost every summer he is a little out of his mind. . . ."

I looked at Olenka. She became confused and hiding her face from us began to put in order again her books that I had disarranged. She was evidently ashamed of her mad father.

"The carriage is there, your Excellency! Now you can drive home, if you wish!"

"Where has that carriage come from?" I asked.

"I sent for it. . . ."

A minute later I was sitting with the Count in the carriage, listening to the peals of thunder and feeling very angry.

"We've been nicely turned out of the little house by that Pëtr Egorych, the devil take him!" I grumbled, getting really angry. "So he's prevented us from examining Olenka properly! I would not have eaten her! . . . The old fool! The whole time he was bursting with jealousy. . . . He's in love with that girl. . . ."

"Yes, yes, yes. . . . Would you believe it, I noticed that, too! He would not let us go into the house from jealousy. And he sent for the carriage only from jealousy. . . . Ha, ha, ha!"

"The later love comes the more it burns. . . . Besides, brother, it's difficult not to fall in love with this girl in red, if one sees her every day as we saw

her to-day! She's devilish pretty! But she's not for his net. . . He ought to understand it and not be jealous of others so egoistically. . . . Why can't he love and not stand in the way of others, all the more as he must know she's not destined for him? . . . What an old blockhead!"

"Do you remember how enraged he was when Kuz'ma mentioned her name at tea-time?" the Count sniggered. "I thought he was going to thrash us all. . . . A man does not defend the good fame of a woman so hotly if he's indifferent to her. . . ."

"Some men will, brother. . . . But this is not the question. . . . What's important is this. . . . If he can command us in the way he has done to-day, what does he do with the small people, with those who are at his disposal? Doubtless, the stewards, the butlers, the huntsmen and the rest of the small fry are prevented by him from even approaching her! Love and jealousy make a man unjust, heartless, misanthropical. . . . I don't mind betting that for the sake of this Olenka he has worried more than one of the people under his control. It will, therefore, be wise on your part if you put less trust in his complaints of the people in your service and his demands for the dismissal of this or that one. In general, to limit his power for a time. . . . Love will pass —well, and then there will be nothing to fear. He's a kind and honest fellow. . . ."

"And what do you think of her papa?" the Count asked, laughing.

"A madman. . . . He ought to be in a madhouse and not looking after forests. In general you won't be far from the truth if you put up a signboard:

'Madhouse' over the gate of your estate. . . . You have a real Bedlam here! This forester, the Scops-Owl, Franz, who is mad on cards, this old man in love, an excitable girl, a drunken Count. . . . What do you want more?"

"Why, this forester receives a salary! How can he do his work if he is mad?"

"Urbenin evidently only keeps him for his daughter's sake. . . . Urbenin says that Nikolai Efimych has these attacks every summer. . . . That's not likely. . . . This forester is ill, not every summer, but always. . . . By good luck, your Pëtr Egorych seldom lies, and he gives himself away when he does lie about anything. . . ."

"Last year Urbenin informed me that our old forester Akhmet'ev was going to become a monk on Mount Athos, and he recommended me to take the 'experienced, honest and worthy Skvortsov' . . . I, of course, agreed as I always do. Letters are not faces: they do not give themselves away when they lie.

The carriage drove into the courtyard and stopped at the front door. We alighted. The rain had stopped. The thunder cloud, scintillating with lightning and emitting angry grumbles, was hurrying towards the north-east and uncovering more and more the dark blue star-spangled sky. It was like a heavily armed power which having ravaged the country and imposed a terrible tribute, was rushing on to new conquests. . . . The small clouds that remained behind were chasing after it as if fearing to be unable to catch it up. . . . Nature had its peace restored to it.

And that peace seemed astonished at the calm, aromatic air, so full of softness, of the melodies of nightingales, at the silence of the sleeping gardens and the caressing light of the rising moon. The lake awoke after the day's sleep, and by gentle murmurs brought memories of itself to man's hearing. . . .

At such a time it is good to drive through the fields in a comfortable calash or to be rowing on the lake. . . . But we went into the house. . . . There another sort of poetry was awaiting us.

CHAPTER V

TELEGRAM

A MAN who under the influence of mental pain or unbearably oppressive suffering sends a bullet through his own head is called a suicide; but for those who give freedom to their pitiful, soul-debasing passions in the holy days of spring and youth there is no name in man's vocabulary. After the bullet follows the peace of the grave: ruined youth is followed by years of grief and painful recollections. He who has profaned his spring will understand the present condition of my soul. I am not yet old, or grey, but I no longer live. Psychiaters tell us that a soldier, who was wounded at Waterloo, went mad, and afterwards assured everybody—and believed it himself—that he had died at Waterloo, and that what was now considered to be him was only his shadow, a reflection of the past. I am now experiencing something resembling this semi-death. . . .

"I am very glad that you ate nothing at the forester's and haven't spoilt your appetite," the Count said to me as we entered the house. "We shall have an excellent supper. . . . Like old times. . . . Serve supper!" He gave the order to Il'ya who was helping him to take off his coat and put on a dressing gown.

We went into the dining-room. Here on the side-table life was already bubbling over. Bottles of every colour and of every imaginable size were standing in rows as on the shelves of a theatre refreshment-room, reflecting on their sides the light of the lamps while awaiting our attention. All sorts of salted and pickled viands and various *hors d'œuvres* stood on another table with a decanter of vodka and another of English bitters. Near the wine bottles there were two dishes, one of sucking pig and the other of cold sturgeon.

"Well, gentlemen," the Count began as he poured out three glasses of vodka and shivered as if from cold. "To our good health! Kaetan Kazimirovich, take your glass!"

I drank mine off, the Pole only shook his head negatively. He moved the dish of sturgeon towards himself, smelt it, and began to eat.

I must apologize to the reader. I have now to describe something not at all "romantic."

"Well, come on . . . they drank another," the Count said, and filled the glasses again. "Fire away, Lecoq!"

I took up my wineglass, looked at it and put it down again.

"The devil take it, it's long since I drank," I said. "Shouldn't we remember old times?"

Without further reflection, I filled five glasses and emptied them one after another into my mouth. That was the only way I knew how to drink. Small schoolboys learn how to smoke cigarettes from big ones: the Count looked at me, poured out five glasses for himself, and, bending forwards in the form of an arch, frowning and shaking his head, he drank them off. My five glasses appeared to him to be bravado, but I drank them not at all to display my talent for drinking. . . . I wanted to get drunk, to get properly, thoroughly drunk. . . . Drunk as I had not been for a long time while living in my village. Having drunk them, I sat down to table and began to discuss the sucking pig.

Intoxication was not long in succeeding. I soon felt a slight giddiness. There was a pleasant feeling of coolness in my chest—and a happy, expansive condition set in. Without any visible transition I suddenly became very gay. The feeling of emptiness and dullness gave place to a sensation of thorough joy and gaiety. I smiled. I suddenly wanted chatter, laughter, people around me. As I chewed the sucking pig I began to feel the fullness of life, almost the self-sufficiency of life, almost happiness.

"Why don't you drink anything?" I asked the Pole.

"He never drinks," the Count said. "Don't force him to."

"But surely you can drink something!"

The Pole put a large bit of sturgeon into his mouth and shook his head negatively. His silence incensed me.

"I say, Kaeton . . . what's your patronymic? . . . why are you always silent?" I asked him. "I have not had the pleasure of hearing your voice as yet."

His two eyebrows that resembled the outstretched wings of a swallow were raised and he gazed at me.

"Do you wish me to speak?" he asked with a strong Polish accent.

"Very much."

"Why do you wish it?"

"Why, indeed! On board steamers at dinner strangers and people who are not acquainted converse together, and here are we, who have known one another for several hours, looking at each other and not exchanging a single word! What does that look like?"

The Pole remained silent.

"Why are you silent?" I asked again after waiting a moment. "Answer something, can't you?"

"I do not wish to answer you. I hear laughter in your voice, and I do not like derision."

"He's not laughing at all," the Count interposed in alarm. "Where did you fish up that notion, Kaetan? He's quite friendly. . . ."

"Counts and Princes have never spoken to me in such a tone!" Kaetan said, frowning. "I don't like that tone."

"Consequently, you will not honour me with your conversation?" I continued to worry him as I emptied another glass and laughed.

"Do you know my real reason for coming here?" the Count broke in, desirous of changing the conversation. "I haven't told you as yet? In Petersburg I went to the doctor who has always treated me, to consult him about my health. He auscultated, knocked and pressed me everywhere, and said: 'You're not a coward!' Well, you know, though I'm no coward, I grew pale. 'I'm not a coward,' I replied."

"Cut it short, brother. . . . That's tiresome."

"He told me I should soon die if I did not go away from Petersburg! My liver is quite diseased from too much drink. . . . So I decided to come here. It would have been silly to remain there. This estate is so fine—so rich. . . .

The climate alone is worth a fortune! . . . Here, at least, I can occupy myself with my own affairs. Work is the best, the most efficacious medicine. Kaetan, is that not true? I shall look after the estate and chuck drink. . . . The doctor did not allow me a single glass . . . not one!"

"Well, then, don't drink."

"I don't drink. . . . To-day is the last time, in honour of meeting you again"—the Count stretched towards me and gave me a smacking kiss on the cheek—"my dear, good friend. To-morrow—not a drop! To-day, Bacchus takes leave of me for ever. . . . Serezha, let us have a farewell glass of cognac together?"

We drank a glass of cognac.

"I shall get well, Serezha, golabchik, and I shall look after the estate. . . . Rational agriculture! Urbenin—is good, kind . . . he understands everything, but is he the master? He's a routinist! We must send for magazines, read, look into everything, take part in the agricultural and dairy exhibitions, but he is not educated for that! Is it possible he can be in love with Olenka? Ha-ha! I shall look into everything and help him as my assistant. . . . I shall take part in the elections; I shall entertain society. . . . Eh? Even here one can live happily! What do you think? Now there you are, laughing again! Already laughing! One really can't talk with you about anything!"

I was gay, I was amused. The Count amused me; the candles, the bottles amused me; the stucco hares and ducks that ornamented the walls of the dining-room amused me. . . . The only thing that did not amuse me was the sober face of Kaetan Kazimirovich. The presence of this man irritated me.

"Can't you send that Polish nobleman to the devil?" I whispered to the Count.

"What? For God's sake! . . ." the Count murmured, seizing both my hands as if I had been about to beat his Pole. "Let him sit there!"

"I can't look at him! I say," I continued, addressing Pshekhotsky, "you refused to talk to me; but forgive me. I have not yet given up hope of being more closely acquainted with your conversational capacities."

"Leave him alone!" the Count said, pulling me by the sleeve. "I implore you!"

"I shall not stop worrying you until you answer me," I continued. "Why are you frowning? Is it possible that you still hear laughter in my voice?"

"If I had drunk as much as you have, I would talk to you; but as it is we are not a proper pair," the Pole replied.

"That we are not a pair is what was to be proved. . . . That is exactly what I wanted to say. A goose and a swine are no comrades; the drunkard and the sober man are no kin; the drunkard disturbs the sober man, the sober man the drunkard. In the adjoining drawing-room there is a soft and excellent sofa. It's a good thing to lie upon it after sturgeon with horseradish. My voice will not be heard there. Do you not wish to retire to that room?"

The Count clasped his hands and walked about the dining-room with blinking eyes.

He is a coward and is always afraid of "big" talk. I, on the contrary, when drunk, am amused by cross-purposes and discontentedness.

"I don't understand! I don't un-der-stand!" the Count groaned, not knowing what to say or what to do.

He knew it was difficult to stop me.

"I am only slightly acquainted with you," I continued. "Perhaps you are an excellent man, and therefore I don't wish to quarrel with you too soon. . . . I won't quarrel with you. I only invite you to understand that there is no place for a sober man among drunken ones. . . . The presence of a sober man has an irritating effect on the drunken organism! . . . Take that to heart!"

"Say whatever you like!" Pshekhotsky sighed. "Nothing that you can say will provoke me, young man."

"So nothing will provoke you? Will you also not be offended if I call you an obstinate swine?"

The Pole grew red in the face—but only that. The Count became pale, he came up to me, looked imploringly at me, and spread his arms.

"Well, I beg you! Restrain your tongue!"

I had now quite entered into my drunken part, and wanted to go on, but fortunately at that moment the Count and the Pole heard footsteps and Urbenin entered the dining-room.

"I wish you all a good appetite!" he began. "I have come, your Excellency, to find out if you have any orders for me?"

"I have no orders so far, but a request," the Count replied. "I am very glad you have come, Pëtr Egorych. . . . Sit down and have supper with us, and let us talk about the business of the estate. . . ."

Urbenin sat down. The Count drank off a glass of cognac and began to explain his plans for the future rational management of the estate. He spoke very long and wearisomely, often repeating himself and changing the subject. Urbenin listened to him lazily and attentively as serious people listen to the prattle of children and women. He ate his fish-soup, and looked sadly at his plate.

"I have brought some remarkable plans with me!" the Count said among other things. "Remarkable plans! I will show them to you if you wish it?"

Karnéev jumped up and ran into his study for the plans. Urbenin took advantage of his absence to pour out half a tumbler of vodka, gulped it down, and did not even take anything to eat after it.

"Disgusting stuff this vodka is!" he said, looking with abhorrence at the decanter.

"Why didn't you drink while the Count was here, Pëtr Egorych?" I asked him. "Is it possible that you were afraid to?"

"It is better to dissimulate, Sergei Petrovich, and drink in secret than to drink before the Count. You know what a strange character the Count has. . . . If I stole twenty thousand from him and he knew it, he would say nothing owing to his carelessness; but if I forgot to give him an account of ten kopecks that I had spent or drank vodka in his presence, he would begin to lament that his bailiff was a robber. You know him well."

Urbenin half-filled the tumbler again and swigged it off.

"I think you did not drink formerly, Pëtr Egorych," I said.

"Yes, but now I drink . . . I drink terribly!" he whispered. "Terribly, day and night, not giving myself a moment's respite! Even the Count never drank to such an extent as I do now. . It is dreadfully hard, Sergei Petrovich! God alone knows what a weight I have on my heart! It's just grief that makes me drink. . . . I always liked and honoured you, Sergei Petrovich, and I can tell you quite candidly. . . . I'd often be glad to hang myself!"

"For what reason?"

"My own stupidity. . . . Not only children are stupid. . . . There are also fools at fifty. Don't ask the cause."

The Count re-entered the room and put a stop to his effusions.

"A most excellent liqueur," he said, placing a pot-bellied bottle with the seal of the Benedictine monks on the table instead of "the remarkable plans." "When I passed through Moscow I got it at Depré's. Have a glass, Sergei?"

"I thought you had gone to fetch the plans," I said.

"I? What plans? Oh, yes! But, brother, the devil himself couldn't find anything in my portmanteaux. . . . I rummaged and rummaged and gave it up as a bad job. . . . The liqueur is very nice. Won't you have some, Serezha?"

Urbenin remained a little longer, then he took leave and went away. When he left we began to drink claret. This wine quite finished me. I became intoxicated in the way I had wished while riding to the Count's. I became very bold, active and unusually gay. I wanted to do some extraordinary deed, something ludicrous, something that would astonish people. In such moments I thought

I could swim across the lake, unravel the most entangled case, conquer any woman. . . . The world and its life made me enthusiastic; I loved it, but at the same time I wanted to pick a quarrel with somebody, to consume him with venomous jests and ridicule. . . . It was necessary to scoff at the comical, black-browed Pole and the Count, to attack them with biting sarcasm, to turn them to dust.

"Why are you silent?" I began again. "Speak! I am listening to you! Ha-ha! I am awfully fond of hearing people with serious, sedate faces talk childish drivel! . . . It is such mockery, such mockery of the brains of man! . . . The face does not correspond to the brains! In order not to lie, you ought to have the faces of idiots, and you have the countenances of Greek sages!"

I had not finished. . . . My tongue was entangled by the thought that I was talking to people who were nullities, who were unworthy of even half a word! I required a hall filled with people, brilliant women, thousands of lights. . . I rose, took my glass and began walking about the rooms. When we indulge in debauchery, we do not limits ourselves to space. We do not restrict ourselves only to the dining-room, but take the whole house and sometimes even the whole estate.

I chose a Turkish divan in the "Mosaic hall," lay down on it and gave myself up to the power of my fantasy and to castles in the air. Drunken thoughts, one more grandiose, more limitless than the other, took possession of my young brain. A new world arose before me, full of stupefying delights and indescribable beauty.

It only remained for me to talk in rhyme and to see visions.

The Count came to me and sat down on a corner of the divan. . . . He wanted to say something to me. I had begun to read in his eyes the desire to communicate something special to me shortly after the five glasses of vodka described above. I knew of what he wanted to speak.

"What a lot I have drunk today!" he said to me. "This is more harmful to me than any sort of poison . . . But to-day it is for the last time. . . . Upon my honour, the very last time. . . . I have strength of will. . . ."

"All right, all right. . . ."

"For the last . . . Serezha, my dear friend, for the last time. . . . Shouldn't we send a telegram to town for the last time?"

"Why not? Send it. . . ."

"Let's have one last spree in the proper way. . . . Well, get up and write it."

The Count himself did not know how to write telegrams. They always came out too long and insufficient with him. I rose and wrote:

"S—— Restaurant London. Karpov, manager of the chorus. Leave everything and come instantly by the two o'clock train.—The Count."

"It is now a quarter to eleven," the Count said. "The man will take three-quarters of an hour to ride to the station, maximum an hour. . . . Karpov will receive the telegram before one. . . . Consequently they'll have time to catch the train. . . . If they don't catch it, they can come by the goods train. Yes!"

CHAPTER VI

NIGHTS MAD

THE telegram was dispatched with one-eyed Kuz'ma. Il'ya was ordered to send carriages to the station in about an hour. In order to kill time, I began leisurely to light the lamps and candles in all the rooms, then I opened the piano and passed my fingers over the keys.

After that, I remember, I lay down on the same divan and thought of nothing, only waving away with my hand the Count, who came and pestered me with his chatter. I was in a state of drowsiness, half-asleep, conscious only of the brilliant light of the lamps and feeling in a gay and quiet mood. . . The image of the "girl in red," with her head bent towards her shoulder, and her eyes filled with horror at the thought of that effective death, stood before me and quietly shook its little finger at me. . . . The image of another girl, with a pale, proud face, in a black dress, flitted past. She looked at me half-entreatingly, half-reproachfully.

Later on I heard noise, laughter, running about. . . . Deep, dark eyes obscured the light. I saw their brilliancy, their laughter. . . A joyful smile played about the luscious lips. . . . That was how my gipsy Tina smiled.

"Is it you?" her voice asked. "You're asleep? Get up, darling. . . . How long is it since I saw you last!"

I silently pressed her hand and drew her towards me. . . .

"Let us go there. . . . We have all come. . . ."

"Stay! . . . I'm all right here, Tina. . . ."

"But . . . there's too much light. . . . You're mad! . . . They can come. . . ."

"I'll wring the neck of whoever comes! . . . I'm so happy, Tina. . . . Two years have passed since last we met. . . ."

Somebody began to play the piano in the ballroom.

"Akh! Moskva, Moskva, Moskva, white-stoned Moskva!" . . . several voices sang in chorus.

"You see, they are all singing there. . . . Nobody will come in. . . ."

"Yes, yes. . . ."

The meeting with Tina took away my drowsiness. . . . Ten minutes later she led me into the ballroom, where the chorus was standing in a semi-circle. . . . The Count, sitting astride on a chair, was beating time with his hands. . . . Pshekhotsky stood behind his chair, looking with astonished eyes at these singing birds. I tore the balalaika out of Karpov's hands, struck the chords, and—

"Down the Volga. . . . Down the mother Volga."

"Down the Vo-o-o-lga!" the chorus chimed in.

"Ay, burn, speak . . . speak . . ."

I waved my hand, and in an instant with the rapidity of lightning there was another transition. . . .

"Nights of madness, nights of gladness. . . ."

Nothing acts more irritatingly, more titillatingly on my nerves than such rapid transitions. I trembled with rapture, and embracing Tina with one arm and waving the balalaika in the air with the other hand, I sang "Nights of madness" to the end. . . . The balalaika fell noisily on the floor and was shivered into tiny fragments. . . .

"Wine!"

After that my recollections are confused and chaotic. . . . Everything is mixed, confused, entangled; everything is dim, obscure. . . . I remember the grey sky of early morning. . . . We are in a boat. . . . The lake is slightly agitated, and seems to grumble at our debauchery. . . . I am standing up in the middle of the boat, shaking it. . . . Tina tries to convince me I may fall into the water, and implores me to sit down. . . . I deplore loudly that there are no waves on the lake as high as the "Stone Grave," and frighten the martins that flit like white spots over the blue surface of the lake with my shouts. . . . Then follows a long, sultry day, with its endless lunches, its ten-year-old liqueurs, its punches, . . . its debauches. . . . There are only a few moments I can remember of that day. . . . I remember swinging with Tina in the garden. I stand on one end of the board, she on the other. I work energetically, with my whole body as much as my strength permits, and I don't exactly know what I want: that Tina should fall from the swing and be killed, or that she should fly to the very clouds! Tina stands there, pale as death, but proud and self-loving; she has pressed her lips tightly together so as not to betray by a single sound the fear she feels. We fly ever higher and higher, and . . . I can't remember how it ended. Then there follows a walk with Tina in a distant avenue of the park, with green vaults above that protect it from the sun. A poetical twilight, black tresses, luscious lips, whispers. . . . Then the little contralto is

walking beside me, a fair-haired girl with a sharp little nose, childlike eyes and a small waist. I walk about with her until Tina, having followed us, makes a scene. . . . The gipsy is pale and maddened. . . . She calls me "accursed," and, being offended, prepares to return to town. The Count, also pale and with trembling hands, runs along beside us, and, as usual, can't find the proper words to persuade Tina to remain. . . . In the end she boxes my ears. . . . Strange! I, who fly into a rage at the slightest offensive words said by a man, am quite indifferent to a box on the ear given me by a woman. . . . There is again a long "after dinner," again a snake on the steps, again sleeping Franz with flies round his mouth, again the gate. . . . "The girl in red" is standing on the "Stone Grave," but perceiving us from afar, she disappears like a lizard.

By evening we had made it up with Tina and were again friends. The evening was succeeded by the same sort of stormy night, with music, daring singing, with nerve exciting transitions . . . and not a moment's sleep!

"This is self-destruction!" Urbenin whispered to me. He had come in for a moment to listen to our singing.

He was certainly right. Further, I remember: the Count and I are standing in the garden face to face, and quarrelling. Black-browed Kaetan is walking about near us all the time, taking no part in our jollifications, nevertheless he had also not slept, but had followed us about like a shadow. . . . The sky is already brightening, and on the very summits of the highest trees the golden rays of the rising sun are beginning to shine. Around us is the chatter of sparrows, the songs of the starlings, and the rustle and flapping of wings that had become heavy during the night. .   The lowing of the herds and the cries of the shepherds can be heard. A table with a marble slab stands before us. On the table are candles that give out a faint light. Ends of cigarettes, papers from sweets, broken wineglasses, orange peel. . . .

"You must take it!" I say, pressing on the Count a parcel of rouble notes. "I will force you to take it!"

"But it was I who sent for them and not you!" the Count insisted, trying to catch hold of one of my buttons. "I am the master here. . . . I treated you. Why should you pay? Can't you understand you even insult me by offering to do so?"

"I also engaged them, so I pay half. You won't take it? I don't understand such favours! Surely you don't think because you are as rich as the devil that you have the right to confer such favours on me? The devil take it! I engaged Karpov, and I will pay him! I want none of your halves! I wrote the telegram!"

"In a restaurant, Serezha, you may pay as much as you like, but my house is not a restaurant. . . . Besides, I really don't understand why you are making all this fuss. I can't understand your insistent prodigality. You have but little money, while I am rolling in wealth. . . . Justice itself is on my side!"

"Then you will not take it? No? Well, then, you needn't! . . ."

I go up to the faintly burning candles and applying the banknotes to the flame set them on fire and fling them on the ground. Suddenly a groan is torn from Kaetan's breast. He opens his eyes wide, he grows pale, and falling with the whole weight of his heavy body on the ground tries to extinguish the money with the palms of his hands. . . . In this he succeeds.

"I don't understand!" he says, placing the slightly burnt notes in his pocket. "To burn money? As if it were last year's chaff or love letters! . . . It's better that I should give it to the poor than let it be consumed by the flames."

I go into the house. . . . There in every room on the sofas and the carpets the weary gipsies are lying, overcome by fatigue. My Tina is sleeping on the divan in the "mosaic drawing room." She lies stretched out and breathing heavily. Her teeth clenched, her face pale. . . . She is evidently dreaming of the swing. . . . The Scops-Owl is going through all the rooms, looking with her sharp eyes sardonically at the people who had so suddenly broken into the deadly quiet of this forgotten estate. . . . She is not going about and giving her old limbs so much trouble without an object.

That is all that my memory retained after two wild nights; all the rest had escaped my drunken brain, or is not appropriate for description. . . . But this is enough!

At no other time had Zorka borne me with so much zest as on the morning after the burning of the banknotes. . . . She also wanted to go home. . . . The lake quietly rippled its sparkling waves in which the rising sun was reflected and prepared for its daily sleep. The woods and the willows that border the lake stood motionless as if in morning prayer. It is difficult to describe the feelings that filled my soul at the time. . . . Without entering into details, I will only say that I was unspeakably glad and at the same time almost consumed by shame when, turning out of the Count's homestead, I saw on the bank of the lake the holy old face, all wrinkled by honest work and illness, of venerable Mikhey. In appearance Mikhey resembles the fishermen of the Bible. His hair and beard are white as snow, and he gazes contemplatively at the sky. . . . When he stands motionless on the bank and his eyes follow the chasing clouds, you can imagine that he sees angels in the sky. . . . I like such faces! . . .

When I saw him I reined in Zorka and gave him my hand as if I wanted to cleanse myself by the touch of his honest, horny palm. . . . He raised his small sagacious eyes on me and smiled.

"How do you do, good master!" he said, giving me his hand awkwardly. "So you've ridden over again? Or has that old rake come back?"

"Yes, he's back."

"I thought so. . . . I can see it by your face. . . . Here I stand and look. . . . The world's the world. Vanity of vanities. . . . Look there! That German ought to die, and he only thinks of vanities. . . . Do you see?"

The old man pointed with a stick at the Count's bathing-house. A boat was being rowed away quickly from the bathing-house. A man in a jockey cap and a blue jacket was sitting in the boat. It was Franz, the gardener.

"Every morning he takes money to the island and hides it there. The stupid fellow can't understand that for him

sand and money have much the same value. When he dies he can't take it with him. Barin, give me a cigar!"

I offered him my cigar case. He took three cigarettes and put them into his breast pocket. . . .

"That's for my nephew. . . . He can smoke them."

Zorka moved impatiently, and galloped off. I bowed to the old man in gratitude for having been allowed to rest my eyes on his face. For a long time he stood looking after me.

At home I was met by Polycarp. With a contemptuous, a crushing glance, he measured my noble body as if he wanted to know whether this time I had bathed again in all my clothes, or not.

"Congratulations!" he grumbled. "You've enjoyed yourself."

"Hold your tongue, fool!" I said.

His stupid face angered me. I undressed quickly, covered myself with the bedclothes and closed my eyes.

My head became giddy and the world was enveloped in mist. Familiar figures flitted throught the mist. . . . The Count, snakes, Franz, flamé-coloured dogs, "the girl in red," mad Nikolai Efimych.

"The husband killed his wife! Oh, how stupid you are!"

"The girl in red" shook her finger at me, Tina obscured the light with her black eyes, and . . . I fell asleep.

CHAPTER VII

THIEVES SWARMING

"How sweetly and tranquilly he sleeps! When one gazes on this pale, tired face, on this childishly innocent smile, and listens to this regular breathing, one might think that it is not a magistrate who is lying here, but the personification of a quiet conscience! One might think that Count Karnéev had not yet arrived, that there had been neither drunkenness nor gipsies, nor rows on the lake. . . . Get up, you pernicious man! You are unworthy of enjoying such a blessing as peaceful sleep! Arise!"

I opened my eyes and stretched myself voluptuously. . . . A broad sunbeam, in which countless white dust atoms were agitated and chased each other, streamed from the window on to my bed, causing the sunray itself to appear as if tinged with some dull whiteness. . . . The ray disappeared and reappeared before my eyes, as Pavel Ivanovich Voznesensky, our charming district doctor, who was walking about my bedroom, came into or went out of the stream of light. In the long, unbuttoned frockcoat that flapped around him, as if hanging on a clothes rack, with his hands thrust deep into the pockets of his unusually long trousers, the doctor went from corner to corner of my room, from chair to chair, from portrait to portrait, screwing up his short-sighted eyes as he examined whatever came in his way. In accordance with his habit of sticking his nose and letting his eyes peer into everything, he either stooped down or stretched out, peeped into the washstand, into the folds of the closed blinds, into the chinks of the door, into the lamp . . . he seemed to be looking for something or wishing to assure himself that everything was in order. . . . When he looked attentively through his spectacles into a chink, or at a spot on the wallpaper, he frowned, assumed an anxious expression, and smelt it with his long nose. . . . All this he did quite mechanically, involuntarily, and from habit; but at the same time, as his eyes passed rapidly from one object to another, he had the appearance of a connoisseur making an evaluation.

"Get up, don't you hear!" he called to me in his melodious tenor voice, as he looked into the soap-dish and removed a hair from the soap with his nail.

"Ah, ah, ah! How do you do, Mr. Screw!" I yawned, when I saw him bending over the washstand. "What an age we haven't met!"

The whole district knew the doctor by the name of "Screw" from the habit he had of constantly screwing up his eyes. I, too, called him by that nickname. Seeing that I was awake, Voznesensky came and sat down on a corner of my bed and at once took up a box of matches and lifted it close to his screwed-up eyes.

"Only lazy people and those with clear consciences sleep in that way," he said, "and as you are neither the one nor the other, it would be more seemly for you, my friend, to get up somewhat earlier. . . ."

"What o'clock is it?"

"Almost eleven."

"The devil take you, Screwy! Nobody asked you to wake me so early. Do you know, I only got to sleep at past five to-day. and if not for you I would have slept on till evening."

"Indeed!" I heard Polycarp's bass voice say in the next room. "He hasn't slept long enough yet! It's the second day he's sleeping, and it's still too little for him. Do you know what day it is?" Polycarp asked, coming into the bedroom and looking at me in the way clever people look at fools.

"Wednesday," I said.

"Of course, certainly! It's been specially arranged for you that the week shall have two Wednesdays. . . ."

"To-day's Thursday!" the doctor said. "So, my good fellow, you've been pleased to sleep through the whole of Wednesday. Fine! Very fine! Allow me to ask you how much you drank?"

"For twice twenty-four hours I had not slept, and I drank . . . I don't know how much I drank."

Having sent Polycarp away, I began to dress and describe to the doctor what I had lately experienced of "Nights of madness, nights of gladness" which are so delightful and sentimental in the songs and so unsightly in reality. In my description I tried not to go beyond the bounds of "light genre," to keep to facts and not to deviate into moralizing, although all this was contrary to the nature of a man who entertained a passion for inferences and results. . . . I spoke with an air as if I was speaking about trifles that did not trouble me in the slightest degree. In order to spare the chaste ears of Pavel Ivanovich, and knowing his dislike of the Count, I suppressed much, touched lightly on a great deal but nevertheless, despite the playfulness of my tone and the style of caricature I gave to my narrative during the whole course of it, the doctor looked into my face seriously, shaking his head and shrugging his shoulders impatiently from time to time. He never once smiled. It was evident that my "light genre" produced on him far from a light effect.

"Why don't you laugh, Screwy?" I asked when I had finished my description.

"If it had not been you who had told me all this, and if there had not been a certain circumstance, I would not have believed a word of it. It's all too abnormal, my friend!"

"Of what circumstance are you speaking?"

"Last evening the muzhik whom you had belaboured in such an indelicate way with an oar, came to me. . . . Ivan Osipov. . . ."

"Ivan Osipov? . . ." I shrugged my shoulders. "It's the first time I hear his name!"

"A tall, red-haired man . . . with a freckled face. . . . Try to remember! You struck him on the head with an oar."

"I can't remember anything! I don't know an Osipov. . . . I struck nobody with an oar. . . . You've dreamed it all, uncle!"

"God grant that I dreamed it. . . . He came to me with a report from the Karnéev district administration and asked me for a medical certificate. . . . In the report it was stated that the wound was given him by you, and he does not lie. . . . Can you remember now? The wound he had received was above the forehead, just where the hair begins. . . . You got to the bone, my dear sir!"

"I can't remember!" I murmured. . . . "Who is he? What's his occupation?"

"He's an ordinary muzhik from the Karnéev village. He rowed the boat when you were having your spree on the lake."

"Hm! Perhaps! I can't remember.

. . . I was probably drunk, and somehow by chance. . . ."

"No, sir, not by chance. . . . He said you got angry with him about something, you swore at him for a long time, and then getting furious you rushed at him and struck him before witnesses. . . . Besides, you shouted at him: 'I'll kill you, you rascal!'"

"I got very red, and began walking about from corner to corner of the room.

"For the life of me, I can't remember!" I said, trying with all my might to recall what had happened. "I can't remember! You say I 'got furious. . . .' When drunk I become unpardonably nasty!"

"What can you want more!"

"The muzhik evidently wants to make a case of it, but that's not the most important. . . . The most important is the fact itself, the blows. . . . Is it possible that I'm capable of fighting? And why should I strike a poor muzhik?"

"Yes, sir! Of course, I could not give him a certificate, but I told him to apply to you. . . . You'll manage to arrange the matter with him somehow. . . . The wound is a slight one, but considering the case unofficially a wound in the head that goes as far as the skull is a serious affair. . . . There are often cases when an apparently trifling wound in the head which had been considered a slight one has ended with mortification of the bone of the skull and consequently with a journey *ad patres*."

And, carried away by his subject, "Screw" rose from his seat and, walking about the room along the walls and waving his hands, he began to unload all his knowledge of surgical pathology for my benefit. . . . Mortification of the bones of the skull, inflammation of the brain, death, and other horrors poured from his lips with endless explanations, macroscopic and microscopic processes, that accompany this misty and, for me, quite uninteresting *terra incognita*.

"Stop that effusion!" I cried, trying to stop his medical chatter. "Can't you understand how tiresome all this stuff is?"

"No matter that it's tiresome. . . . Listen, and punish yourself. . . Perhaps another time you will be more careful. It may teach you not to do such stupidities. If you don't arrange matters with this scabby Osipov, it may cost you your position! The priest of Themis to be tried for thrashing a man! . . . What a scandal!"

Pavel Ivanovich is the only man whose judgments I listen to with a light heart, without frowning, whom I allow to gaze inquiringly into my eyes and to thrust his investigating hand into the depths of my soul. . . . We two are friends in the very best sense of the word; we respect each other, although we have between us accounts of the most unpleasant, the most delicate nature. . . . Like a black cat, a woman had passed between us. This eternal *casus belli* had been the cause of reckonings between us, but did not make us quarrel, and we continued to be at peace. "Screw" is a very nice fellow. I like his simple and far from plastic face, with its large nose, screwed-up eyes and thin, reddish beard. I like his tall, thin, narrow-shouldered figure, on which his frock-coat and paletot hung as on a clothes-horse.

His badly made trousers formed ugly creases at the knees; and his boots were terribly trodden down at the heels; his white tie was always in the wrong place. But do not think that he was slovenly. . . . You had but to look once at his kind, concentrated face to understand that he had no time to trouble about his own appearance; besides, he did not know how to. . . . He was young, honest, not vain, and loved his medicine, and he was always moving about— this in itself is sufficient to explain to his advantage all the defects of his inelegant toilet. He, like an artist, did not know the value of money, and imperturbably sacrificed his own comfort and the blessings of life to one of his passions, and thus he gave the impression of being a man without means, who could scarcely make both ends meet. . . . He neither smoked nor drank, he spent no money on women, but nevertheless the two thousand roubles he earned by his appointment at the hospital and by private practice passed through his hands as quickly as my money does when I am out on the spree. Two passions drained him: the passion of lending money, and the passion of ordering things he saw advertised in the newspapers. . . . He lent money to whoever asked for it, without any demur not uttering a single word about when it was to be returned. It was not possible either by hook or by crook to eradicate in him his heedless trust in people's conscientiousness, and this confidence was even more apparent in his constantly ordering things that were lauded in newspaper advertisements. . . . He wrote for everything, the necessary and the unnecessary. He wrote for books, telescopes, humorous

magazines, dinner services "composed of 100 articles," chronometers. . . And it was not surprising that the patients who came to Pavel Ivanovich mistook his room for an arsenal or for a museum. He had always been cheated, but his trust was as strong and unshakable as ever. He was a capital fellow, and we shall meet him more than once on the pages of this novel.

"Good gracious! What a time I have been sitting here!" he exclaimed suddenly, looking at the cheap watch with one lid he had ordered from Moscow, and which was "guaranteed for five years," but had already been repaired twice. "I must be off, friend! Goodbye! And mark my words, these sprees of the Count's will lead to no good! To say nothing about your health. . . . Oh, by-the-by! Shall you go to Tenevo to-morrow?"

"What's up there to-morrow?"

"The fête of the Church! Everybody will be there, so come too! You must positively come! I have promised that you will come. Don't make me a liar!"

It was not necessary to ask to whom he had given his word. We understood each other. The doctor then took leave, put on his well-worn overcoat, and went away.

I remained alone. . . . In order to drown the unpleasant thoughts that began to swarm in my head, I went to my writing-table and trying not to think nor to call myself to account, I began to open my post. The first envelope that caught my eye contained the following letter:

"My Darling Serezha,

"Forgive me for troubling you, but I am so surprised that I don't know to

whom to apply. . . . It is shameful!
Of course, now it will be impossible to
get it back, and I'm not sorry, but
judge for yourself: if thieves are to
enjoy indulgence, a respectable woman
cannot feel safe anywhere. After you
left I awoke on the divan and found
many of my things were missing. Somebody had stolen my bracelet, my gold
studs, ten pearls out of my necklace,
and had taken about a hundred roubles
out of my purse. I wanted to complain
to the Count, but he was asleep, so I
went away without doing so. This is
very wrong! The Count's house—and
they steal as in a tavern! Tell the
Count. I send you much love and
kisses.   "Your loving,
                        "TINA."

That his Excellency's house was
swarming with thieves was nothing new
to me; and I added Tina's letter to the
information I had already in my memory on this count. Sooner or later I
would be obliged to use this intelligence
in a case. . . . I knew who the thieves
were.

CHAPTER VIII

THE CHURCH

BLACK-EYED Tina's letter, her large
sprawling handwriting, reminded me of
the mosaic room and aroused in me
desires such as a drunkard has for more
drink; but I overcame them, and by
the strength of my will I forced myself
to work. At first I found it unspeakably
dull to decipher the bold handwriting
of the various commissaries, but gradually my attention became fixed on a
burglary, and I began to work with
delight. All day long I sat working at

my table, and Polycarp passed behind
me from time to time and looked suspiciously at my work. He had no confidence in my sobriety, and at any moment he expected to see me rise from
the table and order Zorka to be saddled; but towards evening, seeing my
persistence, he began to give credence
to my good intentions, and the expression of moroseness on his face gave
place to one of satisfaction. . . . He
began to walk about on tiptoe and to
speak in whispers. . . . When some
young fellows passed my house, playing
on the accordion, he went into the street
and shouted:
"What do you young devils mean by
making such a row here? Can't you go
another way? Don't you know, you
Mahommedans, that the master is working?"
In the evening when he served the
samovar in the dining-room, he quietly
opened my door and called me graciously to come to tea.
"Will you please come to tea?" he
said, sighing gently and smiling respectfully.
And while I was drinking my tea he
came up behind me and kissed me on
the shoulder.
"Now that's better, Sergei Petrovich,"
he mumbled. "Why don't you let that
white-eyebrowed devil be hanged, may
he be. . . . Is it possible with your
high understanding and your education
to occupy yourself with pusillanimous-
ness? Your work is noble. . . . Everybody must glorify you, be afraid of
you; if you break people's heads with
that devil and bathe in the lake in all
your clothes, everyone will say: 'He
has no sense! He's an empty-headed
fellow!' And so that reputation will be

noised about the whole world! Fool-hardiness is suitable for merchants, but not for noblemen. . . . Noblemen require science and office. . . ."

"All right! Enough, enough. . . ."

"Sergey Petrovich, don't keep company with that Count. If you want to have a friend, who could be better than Doctor Pavel Ivanovich? He goes about shabbily dressed, but how clever he is!"

I was melted by Polycarp's sincerity. . . . I wanted to say an affectionate word to him. . . .

"What novel are you reading now?" I asked.

" 'The Count of Monte Cristo.' That's a Count for you! That's a real Count! Not like your smut-Count!"

After tea I again sat down to work and worked until my eyelids began to droop and close my tired eyes. . . . When I went to bed I ordered Polycarp to wake me at five o'clock.

The next morning, before six o'clock, whistling gaily and knocking off the heads of the field flowers. I was walking towards Tenevo, where the fête of the church to which my friend "Screw" had invited me to come was being celebrated that day. It was a glorious morning. Happiness itself appeared to be hanging above the earth, and reflected in every dewdrop, enticed the soul of the passer-by to itself. The woods enwrapped in morning light, were quiet and motionless as if listening to my footsteps, and the chirping brotherhood of birds met me with expressions of mistrust and alarm. . . . The air, impregnated with the evaporation of the fresh green, caressed my healthy lungs with its softness. I breathed it in, and casting my enraptured eyes over the whole distant prospect, I felt the spring and youth, and it seemed to me that the young birches, the grass at the roadside, and the ceaselessly humming cockchafers shared these feelings with me.

"Why is it that there in the world men crowd together in their miserable hovels, in their narrow and limited ideas," I thought, "while they have here so much space for life and thought? Why do they not come here?"

And my poetic imagination refused to be disturbed by thoughts of winter and of bread, those two sorrows that drive poets into cold, prosaic Petersburg and uncleanly Moscow, where fees are paid for verse, but no inspiration can be found.

Peasants' carts and landowners' britzkas hurrying to the liturgy or to market passed me constantly as I trudged along. All the time I had to take off my cap in answer to the courteous bows of the muzhiks and the landowners of my acquaintance. They all offered to give me a lift, but to walk was pleasanter than to drive, and I refused all their offers. Among others the Count's gardener, Franz, in a blue jacket and a jockey cap, passed me on a racing droshky. . . . He looked lazily at me with his sleepy, sour eyes and touched his cap in a still more lazy fashion. Behind him a twelve-gallon barrel with iron hoops, evidently for vodka, was tied to the droshky. . . . Franz's disagreeable phiz and his barrel somewhat disturbed my poetical mood, but very soon poetry triumphed again when I heard the sound of wheels behind me, and looking round I saw a heavy wagonette drawn by a pair of bays, and in the heavy wagonette, on a leathern cushion on a sort of box seat, was my new acquaintance, "the girl in red," who two days before had spoken to me about the "electricity that had killed her mother." Olenka's pretty, freshly washed and somewhat sleepy face beamed and blushed slightly when she saw me striding along the footpath that separated the wood from the road. She nodded merrily to me and smiled in the affable manner of an old acquaintance.

"Good morning!" I shouted to her.

She kissed her hand to me and disappeared from my sight, together with her heavy wagonette, without giving me enough time to admire her fresh, pretty face. This day she was not dressed in red. She wore a sort of dark green costume with large buttons and a broad-brimmed straw hat, but even in this garb she pleased me no less than she had done before. I would have talked to her with pleasure, and I would gladly have heard her voice. I wanted to gaze into her deep eyes in the brilliancy of the sun, as I had gazed into them that night by the flashes of lightning. I wanted to take her down from the ugly wagonette and propose that she should walk beside me for the rest of the way, and I certainly would have done so if it had not been for the "rules of society." For some reason it appeared to me that she would have gladly agreed to this proposal. It was not without some cause that she had twice looked back at me as the wagonette disappeared behind some old alders! . . .

It was about six versts from the place of my abode to Tenevo—nothing of a distance for a young man on a fine morning. Shortly after six I was already making my way between loaded carts and the booths of the fair towards the Tenevo church. Notwithstanding the early hour and the fact that the liturgy in the church was not over as yet, the noise of trade was already in the air. The squeaking of cart wheels, the neighing of horses, the lowing of cattle, and the sounds of toy trumpets were intermixed with the cries of gipsy horse-dealers and the songs of muzhiks, who had already found time to get drunk. What numbers of gay, idle faces! What types! What beauty there was in the movements of these masses, bright with brilliant coloured dresses, on which the morning sun poured its light! All this many-thousand-headed crowd swarmed, moved, made a noise in order to finish the business they had to do in a few hours, and to disperse by the evening, leaving after them, on the market place as a sort of remembrance, refuse of hay, oats spilt here and there, and nutshells. . . . The people, in dense crowds, were going to and coming from the church.

The cross that surmounts the church emitted golden rays, bright as those of the sun. It glittered and seemed to be aflame with golden fire. Beneath it the cupola of the church was burning with the same fire, and the freshly painted green dome shone in the sun, and beyond the sparkling cross the clear blue sky stretched out in the far distance. I passed through the crowds in the churchyard and entered the church. The liturgy had only just begun and the Gospel was being read. The silence of the church was only broken by the voice of the reader and the footsteps of the incensing deacon. The people stood silent and immovable, gazing with reverence through the wide-open holy gates of the altar and listening to the drawling voice of the reader. Village decorum, or, to speak more correctly, village propriety, strictly represses every inclination to violate the reverend quiet of the church. I always felt ashamed when in a church anything caused me to smile or speak. Unfortunately it is but seldom that I do not meet some of my acquaintances who, I regret to say, are only too numerous, and it generally happens that I have hardly entered the church before I am accosted by one of the "intelligentsia," who, after a long introduction about the weather, begins a conversation on his own trivial affairs. I answer "yes" and "no," but I am too considerate to refuse to give him any attention. My consideration often costs me dear. While I talk I glance bashfully at my neighbours who are praying, fearing that my idle chatter may wound them.

This time, as usual, I did not escape from acquaintances. When I entered the church I saw my heroine standing close to the door—that same "girl in red" whom I had met on the way to Tenevo.

Poor little thing! There she stood, red as a crawfish, and perspiring in the midst of the crowd, casting imploring glances on all those faces in the search for a deliverer. She had stuck fast in the densest crowd and, unable to move either forward or backward, looked like a bird who was being tightly squeezed in a fist. When she saw me she smiled bitterly and began nodding her pretty chin.

"For God's sake, escort me to the front!" she said, seizing hold of my sleeve. "It is terribly stuffy here—and so crowded. . . . I beg you!"

"In front it will be as crowded," I replied.

"But there, all the people are well dressed and respectable. . . . Here are only common people. A place is reserved for us in front. . . . You, too, ought to be there. . . ."

Consequently she was red not because it was stuffy and crowded in the church. Her little head was troubled by the question of precedence. I granted the vain girl's prayer, and by carefully pressing aside the people I was able to conduct her to the very dais near the altar on which the flower of our district *beau-monde* was collected. Having placed Olenka in a position that was in accordance with her aristocratic desires, I took up a post at the back of the *beau-monde* and began an inspection.

As usual, the men and women were whispering and giggling. The Justice of the Peace, Kalinin, gesticulating with his hands and shaking his head, was telling the landowner, Deryaev, in an undertone all about his ailments. Deryaev was abusing the doctors almost aloud and advising the justice of the peace to be treated by a certain Evstrat Ivanych. The ladies, perceiving Olenka, pounced upon her as a good subject for their criticism and began whispering. There was only one girl who evidently was praying. . . . She was kneeling, with her black eyes fixed in front of her; she was moving her lips. She did not notice a curl of hair that had got loose under her hat and was hanging in disorder over her temple. . . . She did not notice that Olenka and I had stopped beside her.

She was Nadezhda Nikolaevna, Justice Kalinin's daughter. When I spoke above of the woman, who, like a black cat, had run between the doctor and me, I was speaking of her. . . . The doctor loved her as only such noble natures as my dear "Screw's" are able to love. Now he was standing beside her, as stiff as a pikestaff, with his hands at his sides and his neck stretched out. From time to time his loving eyes glanced inquiringly at her concentrated face. He seemed to be watching her prayer and in his eyes there shone a melancholy, passionate longing to be the object of her prayers. But, to his grief, he knew for whom she was praying. . . . It was not for him. . . .

I made a sign to Pavel Ivanovich when he looked round at me, and we both left the church.

"Let's stroll about the market," I proposed.

We lighted our cigarettes and went towards the booths.

CHAPTER IX

WHY?

"How is Nadezhda Nikolaevna?" I asked the doctor as we entered a tent where playthings were sold.

"Pretty well. . . . I think she's all right. . . ." the doctor replied, frowning at a little soldier with a lilac face and a crimson uniform. "She asked about you. . . ."

"What did she ask about me?"

"Things in general. . . . She is angry that you have not been to see them for so long . . . she wants to see you and to inquire the cause of your sudden coldness towards their house. . . . You used to go there nearly every day and then—dropped them! As if cut off. . . . You don't even bow."

"That's not true, Screw. . . . Want of leisure is really the cause of my ceasing to go to the Kalinins. What's true is true! My connexion with that family is as excellent as formerly. . . .

I always bow if I happen to meet any one of them."

"However, last Thursday, when you met her father, for some reason you did not return his bow."

"I don't like that old blockhead of a Justice," I said, "and I can't look with equanimity at his phiz; but I still have the strength to bow to him and to press the hand he stretches out to me. Perhaps I did not notice him on Thursday, or I did not recognize him. You're not in a good humour to-day, Screwy, and are trying to pick a quarrel."

"I love you. my dear boy," Pavel Ivanovich sighed; "but I don't believe you. . . . 'Did not notice, did not recognize!' . . . I don't require your justifications nor your evasions. . . . What's the use of them when there's so little truth in them? You're an excellent, a good man, but there's a little bit of a screw sticking in your sick brain that—forgive me for saying it—is capable of any offence."

"I'm humbly obliged."

"Don't be offended, golubchek. . . . God grant that I may be mistaken, but you appear to me to be somewhat of a psychopath. Sometimes, quite in spite of your will and the dictates of your excellent nature, you have attacks of such desires and commit such acts that all who know you as a respectable man are quite nonplussed. You make one marvel how your highly moral principles, which I have the honour of knowing, can exist together with your sudden impulses, which, in the end, produce the most screaming abominations! . . . What animal is this?" Pavel Ivanovich asked the salesman abruptly in quite another tone, lifting close to his eyes a wooden animal with a man's nose, a mane, and a grey stripe down its back.

"A lion," the salesman answered, yawning. "Or perhaps some other sort of creature. The deuce only knows!"

From the toy booths we went to the shops where textiles were sold and trade was already very brisk.

"These toys only mislead children," the doctor said. "They give the falsest ideas of flora and fauna. For example, this lion . . . striped, purple, and squeaking. . . . Whoever heard of a lion that squeaks?"

"I say, Screwy," I began, "you evidently want to say something to me and you seem not to be able. . . . Go ahead! . . . I like to hear you, even when you tell me unpleasant things. . . ."

"Whether pleasant or unpleasant, friend, you must listen to me. There is much I want to talk to you about."

"Begin. . . . I am transformed into one very large ear."

"I have already mentioned to you my supposition that you are a psychopath. Now have the goodness to listen to the proofs. . . . I will speak quite frankly, perhaps sometimes sharply. . . . My words may jar on you, but don't be angry, friend. . . . You know my feelings for you. I like you better than anybody else in the district. . . . I speak not to reprove, nor to blame, nor to slay you. Let us both be objective, friend. . . . Let us examine your psyche with an unprejudiced eye, as if it were a liver or a stomach. . . ."

"All right, let's be objective," I agreed.

"Excellent! . . . Then let us begin with your connexion with Kalinin. . . . If you consult your memory it will tell you that you began to visit the Kalinins immediately after your arrival in our God-protected district. Your acquaintance was not sought by them. At first you did not please the Justice of the Peace, owing to your arrogant manner, your sarcastic tone, and your friendship with the dissolute Count, and you would never have been in the Justice's house, if you yourself had not paid him a visit. You remember? You became acquainted with Nadezhda Nikolaevna, and you began to frequent the Justice's house almost every day. . . . Whenever one came to the house you were sure to be there. . . . You were welcomed in the most cordial manner. You were shown all possible marks of friendship—by the father, the mother, and the little sister. . . . They became as much attached to you as if you were a relative. . . . They were enraptured by you . . . you were made much of, they were in fits of laughter over your slightest witticism. . . . You were for them the acme of wisdom, nobility, gentle manners. You appeared to understand all this, and you reciprocated their attachment with attachment—you went there every day, even on the eve of holidays—the days of cleaning and bustle. Lastly, the unhappy love that you aroused in Nadezhda's heart is no secret to you. . . . Is that not so? Well, then, you, knowing she was over head and ears in love with you, continued to go there day after day. . . And what happened then, friend? A year ago, for no apparent reason, you suddenly ceased visiting the house. You were awaited for a week . . . a month. . . . They are still waiting for you, and you still don't appear . . . they write to you . . . you do not reply. . . . You end by not even bowing.

, . . To you, who set so much store by decorum, such conduct must appear as the height of rudeness! Why did you break off your connexion with the Kalinins in such a sharp and off-hand manner? Did they offend you? No. . . . Did they bore you? In that case you might have broken off gradually, and not in such a sharp and insulting manner, for which there was no cause. . . ."

"I stopped visiting a house and therefore have become a psychopath!" I laughed. "How naive you are, Screwy! What difference is there if you suddenly cease an acquaintance or do so gradually? It's even more honest to do so suddenly—there's less hypocrisy in it. But what trifles all these are!"

"Let us admit that all this is trifling, or that the cause of your sharp action is a secret that does not concern other people. But how can you explain your further conduct?"

"For instance?"

"For instance, you appeared one day at a meeting of our Zemstvo Board—I don't know what your business was there—and in reply to the president, who asked you how it came that you were no longer to be met at Kalinin's, you said. . . . Try to remember what you said! 'I'm afraid they want to marry me!' That's what fell from your lips! And this you said during the meeting in a loud and distinct voice, so that all the hundred men who were present could hear you! Pretty? In reply to your words laughter and various offensive witticisms about fishing for husbands could be heard on all sides. Your words were caught up by a certain scamp, who went to Kalinin's and repeated them to Nadenka during dinner.

. . . Why such an insult, Sergei Petrovich?"

Pavel Ivanovich barred the way. He stood before me and continued looking at me with imploring, almost tearful eyes.

"Why such an insult? Why? Because this charming girl loves you? Let us admit that her father, like all fathers, had intentions on your person. . . . He is like all fathers, they all have an eye on you, on me, on Markuzin. . . . All parents are alike! . . . There's not the slightest doubt that she is over head and ears in love; perhaps she had hoped she would become your wife. . . . Is that a reason to give her such a sounding box on the ear? Dyadinka, dyadinka! Was it not you yourself who encouraged these intentions on your person? You went there every day; ordinary guests never go so often. In the daytime you went out fishing with her, in the evening you walked about the garden with her, jealously guarding your tête-à-tête. . . . You learned that she loved you, and you made not the slightest change in your conduct. . . . Was it possible after that not to suspect you of having good intentions? I was convinced, you would marry her! And you—you complained—you laughed! Why! What had she done to you?"

"Don't shout, Screwy, the people are staring at us," I said, getting round Pavel Ivanovich. "Let us change this conversation. It's old women's chatter. I'll explain in a few words, and that must be enough for you. I went to the Kalinins' house because I was dull and also because Nadenka interested me. She's a very interesting girl. . . . Perhaps I might even have married her.

But, finding out that you had preceded me as a candidate for her heart, that you were not indifferent to her, I decided to disappear. . . . It would have been cruel on my part to stand in the way of such a good fellow as yourself. . ."

"Thanks for the favour! I never asked you for this gracious gift, and, as far as I can judge by the expression of your face, you are now not speaking the truth; you are talking nonsense not reflecting on what you say. . . . And besides, the fact of my being a good fellow did not hinder you on one of your last meetings with Nadenka to make her some proposals in the summer-house, which would have brought no good to the excellent young fellow if he had married her."

"O-ho! Screwy, where did you find out about this proposal? It seems that your affairs are not going on badly, if such secrets are confided to you! . . . However, you've grown white with rage and almost look as if you were going to strike me. . . . And just now we agreed to be objective! Screwy, what a funny fellow you are! Well, we've had about enough of all this nonsense. . . . Let's go to the post office. . . ."

CHAPTER X

THE DARK FIGURE

WE went to the post office, which looked out gaily with its three little windows on to the market place. Through the grey paling gleamed the many coloured flower garden of our post-master, Maxim Federovich, who was known in the whole district as a great connoisseur of all that concerned gardening and the art of laying out beds, borders, lawns, etc.

We found Maxim Fedorovich very pleasantly occupied. Smiling, and red with pleasure, he was seated at his green table, turning over hundred-rouble notes as if they were a book. Evidently even the sight of another man's money had a pleasing effect on his frame of mind.

"How do you do, Maxim Fedorovich?" I said to him. "Where have you got such a pile of money?"

"It's to be sent to St. Petersburg," the postmaster replied, smiling sweetly, and he pointed his chin at the corner of the room where a dark figure was sitting on the only chair in the post office.

This dark figure rose when he saw me and came towards us. I recognized my new acquaintance, my new enemy, whom I had so grievously insulted when I had got drunk at the Count's.

"My best greetings!" he said.

"How are you, Kaetan Kazimirovich?" I answered, pretending not to notice his outstretched hand. "How's the Count?"

"Thank God, he's quite well. . . . He's only a little dull. . . . He's expecting you to come every minute."

I read on Pshekhotsky's face the desire to converse with me. How could that desire have arisen after the "swine" with which I had treated him on that evening, and what caused this change of tone?"

"What a lot of money you have!" I said, gazing at the packet of hundred-rouble notes he was sending away.

It seemed as if somebody had given a fillip to my brain! I noticed that one of the hundred-rouble notes had charred edges, and one corner had been quite burnt off. . . . It was the hundred-rouble note which I had wanted to burn in the flame of a Chandor candle, when the Count refused to accept it from me as my share of the payment for the gipsies, and which Pshekhotsky had picked up when I flung it on the ground.

"It's better that I should give it to the poor, than let it be consumed by the flames," he had said then.

To what "poor" was he sending it now?

"Seven thousand five hundred roubles," Maxim Fedorovich counted in a drawling voice. "Quite right!"

It is ill to pry into the secrets of other people, but I wanted terribly to find out whose this money was and to whom this black-browed Pole was sending it to Petersburg. This money was certainly not his, and the Count had nobody to whom he would send it.

"He has plundered the drunken Count," I thought. "If deaf and silly Scops-Owl knows how to plunder the Count, what difficulty will this goose have in thrusting his paw into his pockets?"

"Oh, by-the-by, I'll also take this opportunity of sending some money," Pavel Ivanovich said hastily. "Do you know, gentlemen, it's quite incredible! For fifteen roubles you can get five things, carriage free! A telescope, a chronometer, a calendar, and something more. . . . Maxim Fedorovich, kindly let me have a sheet of paper and an envelope!"

Screw sent off his fifteen roubles, I received my newspaper and a letter, and we left the post office.

We went towards the church. Screwy paced after me, as pale and dismal as an autumn day. The conversation in which he had tried to show himself to be "objective" had excited him quite beyond all expectation.

All the church bells were being rung. An apparently endless crowd was slowly descending the steps that led from the church porch.

Ancient banners and a dark cross were held high above the crowd, at the head of the procession. The sun played gaily on the vestments of the priests, and the icon of the Holy Virgin emitted blinding rays. . . .

"Ah, there are our people!" the doctor said, pointing to the *beau-monde* of our district which had separated itself from the crowd and was standing aside.

"Your people, but not mine," I said.

"That's all the same. . . . Let us join them. . . ."

I approached my acquaintances and bowed. The Justice of the Peace, Kalinin, a tall, broad-shouldered man with a grey beard and crawfish-like eyes, was standing in front of all the others, whispering something in his daughter's ear. Trying to appear as if he had not noticed me, he made not the slightest movement in answer to my general salute that had been made in his direction.

"Good-bye, my angel," he said in a lachrymose voice as he kissed his daughter on the forehead. "Drive home alone. I shall be back by evening. My visits will take but little time."

Having kissed his daughter again and smiled sweetly on the *beau-monde,* he frowned fiercely, and turning sharply round on one heel, towards a muzhik wearing the disc of a foreman, he said hoarsely to him:

"When will they allow my carriage to drive up?"

The muzhik became excited and waved his arms.

"Look out!"

The crowd that was following the procession made way and the carriage of the Justice of the Peace drove up with chic and the sound of bells to where Kalinin was standing. He sat down, bowed majestically, and alarming the crowd by his "Look out!" he disappeared from sight without casting a single glance at me.

"What a majestic swine!" I whispered in the doctor's ear. "Come along!"

"Don't you want to say a word to Nadezhda Nicolaevna?" Pavel Ivanovich asked:

"It's time for me to go home. I'm in a hurry."

The doctor looked at me angrily, sighed, and turned away. I made a general bow and went towards the booths. As I was making my way through the dense crowd, I turned to look back at the Justice's daughter. She was looking after me and appeared to be trying whether I could bear her pure, searching gaze, so full of bitter injury and reproach.

Her eyes said: "Why?"

Something stirred in my breast, and I felt remorse and shame for my silly conduct. I suddenly felt a wish to return and caress and fondle with all the strength of my soft, and not yet quite corrupt, soul this girl who loved me passionately, and who had been so grievously wronged by me; and to tell her that it was not I who was in fault, but my accursed pride that prevented me from living, breathing or advancing a step. Silly, conceited, foppish pride, full of vanity. Could I, a frivolous man, stretch out the hand of reconciliation, when I knew and saw that every one of my movements was watched by the eyes of the district gossips and the "ill-omened old women"? Sooner let them laugh her to scorn and cover her with derisive glances and smiles, than undeceive them of the "inflexibility" of my character and the pride, which silly women admired so much in me.

Just before, when I had spoken with Pavel Ivanovich about the reasons that had caused me suddenly to cease my visits to the Kalinins, I had not been candid and quite inaccurate. . . . I had held back the real reason; I had concealed it because I was ashamed of its triviality. . . . The cause was as tiny as a grain of dust. . . . It was this. On the occasion of my last visit, after I had given up Zorka to the coachman and was entering the Kalinin's house, the following phrase reached my ears:

"Nadenka, where are you? . . . Your betrothed has come!"

These words were spoken by her father, the Justice of the Peace, who probably did not think that I might hear him. But I heard him, and my self-love was aroused.

"I her betrothed?" I thought. "Who allowed you to call me her betrothed? On what basis?"

And something snapped in my breast. Pride rebelled within me, and I forgot all I had remembered when riding to Kalinin's. . . . I forgot that I had allured the young girl, and I myself was being attracted by her to such a degree that I was unable to pass a single evening without her company. . . . I forgot her lovely eyes that never left my memory either by night or day, her kind smile, her melodious voice. . . . I forgot the quiet summer evenings that will never return either for her or me. . . .

Everything had crumbled away before the pressure of the devilish pride that had been aroused by the silly phrase of her simple-minded father. . . . I left the house in a rage, mounted Zorka, and galloped off, vowing to snub Kalinin, who without my permission had dared to consider me as his daughter's betrothed.

"Besides, Voznesensky is in love with her," I thought, trying to justify my sudden departure. as I rode home. "He began to twirl around her before I did, and they were considered to be engaged when I made her acquaintance. I won't interfere with him!"

From that day I never put a foot in Kalinin's house, though there were moments when I suffered from longing to see Nadia, and my soul yearned for the renewal of the past. . . . But the whole district knew of the rupture, knew that I had "bolted" from marriage. . . . How could my pride make concessions?

Who can tell? If Kalinin had not said those words, and if I had not been so stupidly proud and touchy, perhaps I would not have had to look back, nor she to gaze at me with such eyes. . . . But even those eyes were better, even the feeling of being wronged and of reproach was better, than what I saw in those eyes a few months after our meeting in the Tenevo church! The grief that shone in the depths of those black eyes now was only the beginning of the terrible misfortune that, like the sudden onrush of a train, swept that girl from the earth. They were like little flowers compared to those berries that were then already ripening in order to pour terrible poison into her frail body and anguished heart.

CHAPTER XI

MUCH LINEN

WHEN I left Tenevo I took the same road by which I had come. The sun showed it was already midday. As in the morning, peasants' carts and landowners' britzkas beguiled my hearing by their squeaking and the metallic rumble of their bells. Again, the gardener, Franz, drove past me with his vodka barrel, but this time it was probably full. Again his eyes gave me a sour look, and he touched his cap. His nasty face jarred on me, but this time again the disagreeable impression that the meeting with him had made on me was entirely wiped away by the forester's daughter, Olenka, whose heavy wagonette caught me up.

"Give me a lift!" I called to her.

She nodded gaily to me and stopped her vehicle. I sat down beside her, and the wagonette rattled on along the road, which like a light stripe cut through the three versts of the Tenevo forest. For about two minutes we looked at each other in silence.

"What a pretty girl she really is!" I thought as I looked at her throat and chubby chin. "If I were told to choose between Nadenka and her, I would choose her. . . . She's more natural, fresher, her nature is broader, bolder. . . . If she fell into good hands, much could be made of her! . . . The other is morose, visionary . . . clever."

Lying at Olenka's feet there were two pieces of linen and several parcels.

"What a number of purchases you have made!" I said. "For what can you want so much linen?"

"That's not all I need!" Olenka replied. "I only bought these among all the rest. To-day I was a whole hour buying things in the market; to-morrow I must go to make purchases in the town. . . . And then all this must be made up. . . . I say, don't you know any woman who would go out to sew?"

"No, I think not. . . . But why have you to buy so many things? Why have they to be sewn? God knows your family is not large. . . . One, two . . . there, I've counted you all. . . ."

"How queer all you men are! You don't understand anything! Wait till you get married, you yourself will be angry then if after the wedding your wife comes to you all slovenly. I know Pëtr Egorych is not in want of anything. Still, it seems a bit awkward not to appear as a good housewife from the first. . . ."

"What has Pëtr Egorych to do with it?"

"Hm! . . . You are laughing at me, as if you don't know!" Olenka said and blushed slightly.

"Young lady, you are talking in riddles."

"Have you really not heard? Why, I am going to marry Pëtr Egorych!"

"Marry?" I said in astonishment, making big eyes. "What Pëtr Egorych?"

"Oh, good Lord! Urbenin, of course!"

I stared at her blushing and smiling face.

"You? Going to marry . . . Urbenin? What a joke!"

"It's not a joke at all. . . . I really can't understand where you see the joke. . . ."

"You to marry . . . Urbenin . . . ." I repeated, getting pale, I really don't know why. "If this is not a joke, what is it?"

"What joke! I can't understand what

is there extraordinary—what is there strange in it?" Olenka said, pouting.

A minute passed in silence. . . . I gazed at the pretty girl, at her young, almost childish face, and was astonished that she could make such terrible jokes! I instantly pictured to myself Urbenin, elderly, fat, red-faced with his standing-out ears and hard hands, whose very touch could only scratch that young female body which had scarcely begun to live. . . . Surely the thought of such a picture must frighten this pretty wood fay, who knew how to look poetically at the sky when it is reft by lightning and thunder growls angrily! I, even I, was frightened!

"It's true he's a little old," Olenka sighed, "but he loves me. . . . His love is trustworthy."

"It's not a matter of trustworthy love, but of happiness. . . ."

"I shall be happy with him. . . . He has means, thank God, and he's no pauper, no beggar, but a nobleman. Of course, I'm not in love with him, but are only those who marry for love happy? Oh, I know those marriages for love!"

"My child, when have you had time to stuff your brain with this terrible worldly wisdom?" I asked. "Admitted that you are joking with me, but where have you learned to joke in such a coarse, old way? . . . Where? When?"

Olenka looked at me with astonishment and shrugged her shoulders.

"I don't understand what you are saying," she said. "You don't like to see a young girl marry an old man? Is that so?"

Olenka suddenly blushed all over, her chin moved nervously, and without waiting for my answer she rattled on rapidly.

"This does not please you? Then have the goodness to go into the wood . . . into that dullness, where there is nothing except merlins and a mad father . . . and wait there until a young suitor comes along! It pleased you the other evening, but if you saw it in winter, when one only wishes . . . that death might come——"

"Oh, all this is absurd, Olenka, all this is unripe, silly! If you are not joking. . . . I don't even know what to say! You had better be silent and not offend the air with your tongue. I, in your place, would have hanged myself on seven aspens, and you buy linen . . . and smile. Akh!"

"In any case, he with his means will have father cured," she whispered.

"How much do you require for your father's cure?" I cried. "Take it from me—a hundred? Two hundred? . . . A thousand? Olenka, it's not your father's cure that you want!

The news Olenka had communicated to me had excited me so much, that I had not even noticed that the wagonette had driven past my village, or how it had turned into the Count's yard and stopped at the bailiff's porch. When I saw the children run out, and the smile ⌒ Urbenin's face, who also had rushed out to help Olenka down, I jumped out of the wagonette and ran into the Count's house without even taking leave. Here further news awaited me.

CHAPTER XII

MY GLANCE!

"How opportune! How opportune!" the Count cried as he greeted me and scratched my cheek with his long, pointed moustache. "You could not have chosen a happier time! We have only just sat down to luncheon. . . . Of course you are acquainted. . . . You have doubtless often had collisions in your legal department. . . . Ha, ha!"

With both hands the Count pointed to two men who, seated in soft armchairs, were partaking of cold tongue. In one I had the vexation of recognizing the Justice of the Peace, Kalinin; the other, a little grey-haired man with a large moonlike bald pate, was my good friend, Babaev, a rich landowner who occupied the post of perpetual member of our district council. Having exchanged bows, I looked with astonishment at Kalinin. I knew how much he disliked the Count and what reports he had set in circulation in the district about the man at whose table he was now eating tongue and green peas with such appetite and drinking ten-year-old liqueur. How could a respectable man explain such a visit? The Justice of the Peace caught my glance and evidently understood it.

"I have devoted this day to visits," he said to me. "I am driving round the whole district. . . And, as you see, I have also called upon his Excellency. . . ."

Il'ya brought a fourth cover. I sat down, drank a glass of vodka, and began to lunch.

"It's wrong, your Excellency, very wrong!" Kalinin said, continuing the conversation my entrance had interrupted. "It's no sin for us little people, but you are an illustrious man, a rich man, a brilliant man. . . . It's a sin for you to fail."

"That's quite true; it's a sin," Babaev acquiesced.

"What's it all about?" I asked.

"Nikolai Ignat'ich has given me a good idea!" the Count said, nodding to the justice of the peace. "He came to me. . . . We sat down to lunch, and I began complaining of being dull. . . ."

"And he complained to me of being dull," Kalinin interrupted the Count. "Dullness, melancholy . . . this and that. . . . In a word, disillusionment. A sort of Onegin. 'Your Excellency,' I said, 'you're yourself to blame. . . .' 'How so?' 'Quite simply. . . . In order not to be dull,' I said, 'accept some office . . . occupy yourself with the management of your estate. . . . Farming is excellent, wonderful. . . .' He tells me he intends to occupy himself with farming, but still he is dull. . . . What fails him is, so to speak, the entertaining, the stimulating element. There is not the—how am I to express myself? —er—strong sensations. . . ."

"Well, and what idea did you give him?"

"I really suggested no idea, I only reproached his Excellency. 'How is it your Excellency,' I said, 'that you, a young, cultivated, brilliant man, can live in such seclusion? Is it not a sin?' I asked. 'You go nowhere, you receive nobody, you are seen nowhere. . . . You live like an old man, or a hermit. . . What would it cost you to arrange parties . . . so to speak, at homes?'"

"Why should he have at homes?" I asked.

"How can you ask? First. if his Excellency gave evening parties, he would become acquainted with society—study it, so to speak. . . . Secondly, society would have the honour of becoming more closely acquainted with one of the richest of our landowners. . . There would be, so to speak, a mutual exchange of thoughts, conversation, gaiety. . . . And when one comes to think of it, how many cultivated young ladies and men we have among us! . . . What musical evenings, dances, picnics could be arranged! Only think! The reception rooms are huge, there are pavilions in the gardens, and so on, and so on. Nobody in the government ever dreamed of the private theatricals or the concerts that could be got up. . . . Yes, by God! Only imagine them! Now all this is lost, is buried in the earth; but then . . . one must only know how to! If I had his Excellency's means, I would show them how to live! And he says: 'Dull'! By God! it's laughable to listen to it. . . . It makes one feel ashamed. . . ."

And Kalinin began to blink with his eyes, wishing to appear to be really ashamed. . . .

"All this is quite just," the Count said, rising from his seat and thrusting his hands into his pockets. "I could give excellent evening parties. . . . Concerts, private theatricals . . . all this could be arranged charmingly. Besides, these parties would not only entertain society, they would have an educational influence too! . . . Don't you think so?"

"Well, yes," I acquiesced. "As soon as our young ladies see your moustachioed physiognomy they will at once be penetrated by the spirit of civilization. . . ."

"Serezha, you're always joking," the Count said, somewhat offended, "and you never give me any friendly advice! Everything is laughable for you! My friend, it is about time to drop these student habits!"

The Count began to pace about the room from corner to corner, and to explain to me in long and tiresome suppositions the benefits that his evening parties might bring to humanity. Music, literature, the drama, riding, shooting. The shooting alone might unite all the best forces of the district! . . .

"We shall revert to the subject," the Count said to Kalinin in taking leave of him after lunch.

"Then, if I understand your Excellency, the district may hope?" the Justice of the Peace inquired.

"Certainly, certainly. . . . I will develop this idea and see what I can do. . . . I am happy . . . delighted. You can tell everybody. . . ."

It was a sight to note the look of beatitude that was imprinted on the face of the Justice of the Peace as he took his seat in his carriage and said to the coachman: "Go!" He was so delighted that he even forgot our differences and in taking leave he called me "golubchék" and pressed my hand warmly.

After the visitors had left, the Count and I sat down to table again and continued our lunch. We lunched till seven o'clock in the evening, when the crockery was removed from the table and dinner was served. Young drunkards know how to shorten the time between meals. The whole time we drank and ate small pieces, by which means we sustained the appetite which would have failed us if we had entirely ceased to eat.

"Did you send money to anybody today?" I asked the Count, remembering the packets of hundred-rouble notes I had seen in the morning in the Tenevo post office.

"I sent no money."

"Tell me, please, is your—what's his name?—new friend, Kazimir Kaetanych, or Kaetan Kazimirovich, a wealthy man?"

"No, Serezha. He's a poor beggar! But what a soul he has—what a heart! You are wrong in speaking so disdainfully of him . . . and you bully him. Brother, you must learn to discriminate between people. Let's have another glass?"

Pshekhotsky returned for dinner. When he saw me sitting at table and drinking, he frowned, and after turning about round our table for a time he seemed to think it best to retire to his own room. He refused to have any dinner, pleading a bad headache, but he expressed no objection when the Count advised him to go to bed and have his dinner there.

During the second course, Urbenin came in. I hardly recognized him. His broad red face beamed all over with pleasure. A happy smile seemed to be playing on his sticking-out ears and on the thick fingers with which he was arranging his smart new necktie all the time.

"One of the cows is ill, your Excellency," he reported. "I sent for the vet., but it appears he had gone away somewhere. Wouldn't it be a good thing to send to town for the veterinary surgeon? If I send to him he will not listen and will not come, but if you write to him it will be quite a different matter. Perhaps it is a mere trifle, but it may be something serious."

"All right, I will write . . ." the Count grumbled.

"I congratulate you, Pëtr Egorych,"

I said, rising and stretching out my hand to the bailiff.

"On what occasion?" he murmured.

"Why, you are about to get married!"

"Yes, yes, just fancy! He's going to get married!" the Count began, winking at blushing Urbenin. "What do you think of him? Ha, ha, ha! He was silent, never said a word, and then suddenly—this bombshell. And do you know whom he is going to marry? We guessed it that evening! Pëtr Egorych, we settled then that in your scamp of a heart something improper was going on. When he looked at you and Olenka he said: 'That fellow's bitten!' Ha, ha! Sit down and have dinner with us, Pëtr Egorych!"

Urbenin sat down carefully and respectfully and made a sign with his eyes to Il'ya to bring him a plate of soup. I poured him out a glass of vodka.

"I don't drink, sir," he said.

"Nonsense, you drink more than we do."

"I used to drink, but now I don't," the bailiff said, smiling. "Now, I mustn't drink. . . . There's no cause. Thank God, everything is settled, satisfactorily everything is arranged, all exactly as my heart had desired, even better than I could have expected."

"Well, then, to your happiness you can drink this," I said, pouring him out a glass of sherry.

"This—why not? I really did drink hard. Now I can confess it to his Excellency. Sometimes from morning to night. When I rose in the morning I remembered it . . . well, naturally, I went to the cupboard at once. Now, thank God, I have nothing to drown in vodka."

Urbenin drank the glass of sherry. I poured out a second. He drank this one too, and imperceptibly got drunk. . . .

"I can scarcely believe it," he said, laughing a happy childish laugh. "I look at this ring and remember her words when she gave her consent—I can still scarcely believe it. . . . It seems laughable. . . . How could I, at my age, with my appearance, hope that this deserving girl would not disdain to become mine . . . the mother of my orphan children? Why, she's a beauty, as you have been pleased to notice; an angel incorporate! Wonders without end! You have filled my glass again? Why not, for the last time. . . . I drank to drown care, I will now drink to happiness. How I suffered, gentlemen! What grief I endured! I saw her first a year ago, and would you believe it—from that time I have not slept quietly a single night; there was not a single day on which I did not drown this—silly weakness with vodka . . . and scolded myself for this folly. . . . I sometimes looked at her through the window and admired her and . . . tore out the hair of my head. . . . At times I could have hanged myself . . . But, thank God, I ventured and proposed, and, do you know, it took me quite by surprise. Ha, ha! I heard, but I could not believe mine own ears. She said: 'I agree,' and it appeared to me like: 'Go to the devil, you old dotard!' . . . Afterward, when she kissed me, I was convinced. . . ."

At the recollection of that first kiss received from poetical Olenka, Urbenin closed his eyes and, despite his fifty years, he blushed like a boy. . . . this appeared disgusting to me.

"Gentlemen," he said, looking at us with happy, kind eyes, "why don't you get married? Why are you wasting your lives, throwing them out of the window? Why do you shun that which is the greatest blessing of all who live upon the earth? The delight that debauchery gives is not a hundredth part of what a quiet family life would give you! Young men, your Excellency and you, Sergei Petrovich . . . I am happy now, and . . . God knows how I love you both! Forgive me for giving stupid advice but . . . I want you both to be happy! Why don't you get married? Family life is a blessing. . . . It's every man's duty! . . ."

The happy and fond look on the face of the old man, who was about to marry a young girl and was advising us to alter our dissolute existence for a quiet family life, became unbearable to me.

"Yes," I said, "family life is a duty. I agree with you. And therefore you are acquitting yourself of this duty for the second time?"

"Yes, for the second time. I am fond of family life in general. To be a bachelor or a widower is only half a life for me. Whatever you may say, gentlemen, wedlock is a great thing!"

"Certainly . . . even when the husband is almost three times as old as his wife?"

Urbenin blushed. The hand that was lifting a spoonful of soup to his mouth trembled, and the soup was pouring again into the plate.

"I understand what you want to say, Sergei Petrovich," he mumbled. "I thank you for your frankness. I ask myself: Is it not mean? I suffer! But where has one time to question oneself, to settle various questions when every moment one feels happy, when one forget one's age, ugliness . . . the whole

homo sum, Sergei Petrovich! And when for a second, thoughts run through my pate of the inequality of years, I don't break my head for an answer, but calm myself as well as I can. I think I have made Olga happy. I have given her a father and my children a mother. Besides, all this is like a novel, and . . . my head feels giddy. It was wrong to make me drink sherry."

Urbenin rose, wiped his face with his napkin, and sat down again. A minute later he gulped down another glass of sherry and looked at me for a long time with an imploring glance as if he were begging me for mercy, and suddenly his shoulders began to shake, and quite unexpectedly he burst into sobs like a boy.

"It's nothing . . . nothing!" he mumbled, trying to master his sobs. "Don't be uneasy. After your words my heart grew sick with a strange foreboding. But it is nothing."

Urbenin's foreboding was realized, realized so soon that I have not time to change my pen and begin a new page. From the next chapter my calm muse will change the expression of calmness on her face for one of passion and affliction. The introduction is finished and the drama begins.

The criminal will of man enters upon its rights.

CHAPTER XIII

THE LITTLE DEVIL

I REMEMBER a fine Sunday morning. Through the windows of the Count's church the diaphanous blue sky could be seen and the whole of the church, from its painted cupola to its floor, was flooded by soft sunrays in which little clouds of incense played about gaily.

. . . The songs of swallows and starlings were borne in through the open
doors and windows. . . . One sparrow,
evidently a very bold little fellow, flew
in at the door, and having circled, chirping, several times round and round above
our heads, flew out again through one
of the windows. . . . In the church
itself there was also singing. . . . They
sang sweetly, with feeling, and with the
enthusiasm for which our Little Russian
singers are so celebrated when they feel
themselves the heroes of the moment,
and that all eyes are bent upon them.
. . . The melodies were all gay and
playful, like the soft, bright sunspots
that played upon the walls and the
clothes of the congregation. . . . In
the unschooled but soft and fresh notes
of the tenor my ear seemed to catch,
despite the gay wedding melodies, deep,
melancholy, chest chords. It appeared
as if this tenor was sorry to see that next
to young, pretty and poetical Olenka
there stood Urbenin, heavy, bear-like,
and getting on in years. . . '. And it
was not only the tenor who was sorry to
see this ill-assorted pair. . . . On many
of the faces that lay within the field of
my vision, notwithstanding all their efforts to appear gay and unconcerned,
even an idiot could have read an expression of compassion.

Arrayed in a new dress suit, I stood
behind Olenka, holding the crown over
her head. I was pale and felt unwell.
. . . I had a racking headache, the result of the previous night's carouse and
a pleasure party on the lake and the
whole time I was looking to see if the
hand that held the crown did not tremble. . . . My soul felt the disagreeable
presentiment of dread that is felt in a
forest on a rainy autumn night. I was

vexed, disgusted, sorry. . . . Cats
seemed to be scratching at my heart,
somewhat resembling qualms of conscience. . . . There in the depths of the
very bottom of my heart, a little devil
was seated who obstinately, persistently
whispered to me that if Olenka's marriage with clumsy Urbenin was a sin, I
was the cause of that sin. . . . Where
did such thoughts come from? How
could I have saved this little fool from
the unknown risks of her indubitable
mistake? . . .

"Who knows?" whispered the little
devil. "Who should know better than
you?"

In my time I have known many ill-
assorted marriages. I have often stood
before Pukirev's picture. I have read
numberless novels based on disagree-
ments between husband and wife; besides, I have known the physiology that
irrevocably punishes ill-assorted marriages, but never once in my whole life
had I experienced that terrible spiritual
condition from which I was unable to
escape all the time I was standing behind Olenka, executing the functions of
best man.

"If my soul is agitated only by commiseration, how is it that I never felt
that compassion before when I assisted
at other weddings? . . ."

"There is no commiseration here,"
the little devil whispered, "but jealousy. . . ."

One can only be jealous of those one
loves, but do I love the girl in red? If I
loved all the girls I have met while living under the moon, my heart would not
suffice; besides, it would be too much of
a good thing. . . .

My friend Count Karnéev was standing quite at the back near the door be-

hind the churchwarden's counter, selling wax tapers. He was well groomed, with well smoothed hair, and exhaled a narcotic, suffocating odour of scents. That day he looked such a darling that when I greeted him in the morning I could not refrain from saying:

"Alexey, to-day you are looking like an ideal quadrille dancer!"

He greeted everybody who entered or left with the sweetest of smiles, and I heard the ponderous compliments with which he rewarded each lady who bought a candle from him. He, the spoilt child of Fortune, who never had copper coins, did not know how to handle them, and was constantly dropping on the floor five and three-kopeck pieces. Near him, leaning against the counter, Kalinin stood majestically with a Stanislav decoration on a ribbon round his neck. His countenance shone and beamed. He was pleased that his idea of "at homes" had fallen on good soil, and was already beginning to bear fruit. In the depths of his soul he was showering on Urbenin a thousand thanks; his marriage was an absurdity, but it was a good opportunity to get the first "at home" arranged.

Vain Olenka must have rejoiced. . . . From the nuptial lectern to the doors of the high altar stretched out two rows of the most representative ladies of our district flower garden. The guests were decked out as smartly as they would have been if the Count himself was being married: more elegant toilets could not have been desired. . . . The assembly consisted almost exclusively of aristocrats . . . Not a single priest's wife, not a single tradesman's wife. . . . There were even among them ladies to whom Olenka would formerly never have considered herself entitled to bow. . . .

And Olenka's bridegroom—a bailiff, a privileged retainer; but from this her vanity could not suffer. He was a nobleman and the possessor of a mortgaged estate in the neighbouring district. . . . His father had been marshal of the district and he himself had for more than nine years been a magistrate in his own native district. . . . What more could have been desired by the ambitious daughter of a personal nobleman? Even the fact that her best man was known in the whole province as a *bon vivant* and a Don Juan could tickle her pride. . . . . All the women were looking at him. . . . He was as showy as forty thousand best men thrown into one, and what was not the least important, he had not refused to be her best man, she, a simple little girl, when, as everybody knew, he had even refused aristocrats when they had asked him to be their best man. . . .

But vain Olenka did not rejoice. . . . She was as pale as the linen she had but lately brought home from the Tenevo market. The hand in which she held the candle shook slightly and her chin trembled from time to time. In her eyes there was a certain dullness, as if something had suddenly astonished or frightened her. . . . There was not a sign of that gaiety which had shone in her eyes even the day before when she was running about the garden talking with enthusiasm of the sort of wallpaper she would have in her drawing-room, and saying on what days she would receive guests, and so on. Her face was now too serious, more serious than the solemn occasion demanded. . . .

Urbenin was in a new dress-suit. He was respectably dressed, but his hair was arranged as the orthodox Russians wore their hair in the year 'twelve. As usual, he was red in the face, and serious. His eyes prayed and the signs of the cross he made after every "Lord have mercy upon us" were not made in a mechanical manner.

Urbenin's children by his first marriage—the schoolboy Grisha and the little fair-haired girl Sasha,—were standing just behind me. They gazed at the back of their father's red head and at his standing-out ears, and their faces seemed to represent notes of interrogation. They could not understand why Aunt Olia had given herself to their father, and why he was taking her into his house. Sasha was only surprised, but the fourteen-year-old Grisha frowned and looked scowlingly at him. He would certainly have replied in the negative if his father had asked his permission to marry. . . .

The marriage service was performed with special solemnity. Three priests and two deacons officiated. The service lasted long, so long, indeed, that my arm was quite tired of holding the crown, and the ladies who love to see a wedding ceased looking at the bridal pair. The chief priest read the prayers, with pauses, without leaving out a single one. The choir sang something very long and complicated; the cantor took advantage of the occasion to display the compass of his voice, reading the Gospels with extra slowness. But at last the chief priest took the crown out of my hands . . . the young couple kissed each other. . . . The guests got excited, the straight lines were broken, congratulations, kisses and exclamations were heard. Urbenin, beaming and smiling, took his young wife on his arm, and we all went out into the air.

If anybody who was in the church with me finds this description incomplete and not quite accurate, let him set down these oversights to the headache from which I was suffering and the abovementioned spiritual depression which prevented me from observing and noting. . . . Certainly, if I had known at the time that I would have to write a novel, I would not have looked at the floor as I did on that day, and I would not have paid attention to my headache!

Fate sometimes allows itself bitter and malignant jokes! The young couple had scarcely had time to leave the church when they were met by an unexpected and unwished for surprise. When the wedding procession, bright with many tints and colours in the sunlight, was proceeding from the church to the Count's house, Olenka suddenly made a backward step, stopped, and gave her husband's elbow such a violent pull that he staggered.

"He's been let out!" she said aloud, looking at me with terror.

Poor little thing! Her insane father, the forester Skvortsov, was running down the avenue to meet the procession. Waving his hands and stumbling along with rolling, insane eyes, he presented a most unattractive picture. However, all this would possibly have been decent if he had not been in his print dressing-gown and downtrodden slippers, the raggedness of which was of ill accord with the elegant wedding finery of his daughter. His face looked sleepy, his dishevelled hair was blown about by the wind, his nightshirt was unbuttoned.

"Olenka!" he mumbled when he had

come up to them. "Why have you left me?"

Olenka blushed scarlet and looked askance at the smiling ladies. The poor little thing was consumed by shame.

"Mit'ka did not lock the door!" the forester continued, turning to us. "It would not be difficult for robbers to get in! . . . The samovar was stolen out of the kitchen last summer, and now she wants us to be robbed again."

"I don't know who can have let him out!" Urbenin whispered to me. "I ordered him to be locked up. . . . Golubchik, Sergei Petrovich, have pity on us; get us out of this awkward position somehow! Anyhow!"

"I know who stole your samovar," I said to the forester. "Come along, I'll show you where it is."

Taking Skvortsov round the waist, I led him towards the church. I took him into the churchyard and talked to him until, by my calculation, I thought the wedding procession ought to be in the house, then I left him without having told him where his stolen samovar was to be found.

Although this meeting with the madman was quite unexpected and extraordinary, it was soon forgotten. . . . A new surprise that Fate had prepared for the young couple was still more unusual.

CHAPTER XIV

A COLD KISS

An hour later we were all seated at long tables, dining.

To anybody who was accustomed to cobwebs, mildew and wild gipsy whoops in the Count's apartments it must have seemed strange to look on the workaday, prosaical crowd that now, by their habitual chatter, broke the usual silence of the ancient and deserted halls. This many coloured noisy throng looked like a flight of starlings which in flying past had alighted to rest in a neglected churchyard or—may the noble bird forgive me such a comparison!— a flight of storks that in the twilight of one of their migratory days had settled down on the ruins of a deserted castle.

I sat there hating that crowd which frivolously examined the decaying wealth of the Counts Karnéev. The mosaic walls, the carved ceilings, the rich Persian carpets and the rococo furniture excited enthusiasm and astonishment. A self-satisfied smile never left the Count's moustachioed face. He received the enthusiastic flattery of his guests as something that he deserved, though in reality all the riches and luxuries of his deserted mansion were not acquired in any way thanks to him, but on the contrary, he merited the bitterest reproaches and contempt for the barbarously dull indifference with which he treated all the wealth, that had been collected by his fathers and grandfathers, collected not in days, but in scores of years! It was only the mentally blind or the poor of spirit who could not see in every slab of damp marble, in every picture, in each dark corner of the Count's garden, the sweat, the tears and the callosities on the hands of the people whose children now swarmed in the little log huts of the Count's miserable villages. . . . Among all those people seated at the wedding feast, rich, independent people, people who might easily have told him the plainest truths, there was not one who would have told the Count that his self-satisfied grin was stupid and out of place. . . . Everybody found it necessary to smile flatteringly and to burn paltry incense before him. If this was ordinary politeness (with us, many love to throw everything on politeness and propriety), I would prefer the churl who eats with his hands, who takes the bread from his neighbour's plate, and blows his nose between two fingers, to these dandies.

Urbenin smiled, but he had his own reasons for this. He smiled flatteringly, respectfully, and in a childlike, happy manner. His broad smiles were the result of a sort of dog's happiness. A devoted and loving dog, who had been fondled and petted, and now in sign of gratitude wagged its tail gaily and with sincerity.

Like Risler Senior in Alphonse Daudet's novel, beaming and rubbing his hands with delight, he gazed at his young wife, and from the superabundance of his feelings could not refrain from asking question after question:

"Who could have thought that this young beauty would fall in love with an old man like myself? Is it possible she could not find anybody younger and more elegant? Women's hearts are incomprehensible!"

He even had the courage to turn to me and blurt out:

"When one looks around, what an age this is we live in! He, he! When an old man can carry off such a fairy from under the nose of youth! Where have you all had your eyes? He, he. . . . Young men are not what they used to be!"

Not knowing what to do or how to express the feelings of gratitude that were overflowing in this broad breast, he was constantly jumping up, stretching out his glass towards the Count's glass and saying in a voice that trembled with emotion:

"Your Excellency, my feelings toward you are well known. This day you have done so much for me that my affection for you appears like nothing. How have I merited such a great favour, your Excellency, or that you should take such an interest in my joy? It is only Counts and bankers who celebrate their weddings in such a way! What luxury, what an assembly of notable guests! . . . Oh, what can I say! . . . Believe me, your Excellency, I shall never forget you, as I shall never forget this best and happiest day of my life."

And so on. . . . Olenka was evidently not pleased with her husband's florid respectfulness. One could see she was annoyed at his speeches, that raised smiles on the faces of the guests and even caused them to feel ashamed for him. Notwithstanding the glass of champagne she had drunk, she was still not gay, and morose as before. . . . She was as pale as she had been in church, and the same look of dread was in her eyes. . . . She was silent, she answered lazily to all the questions that were asked, scarcely smiled at the Count's witticisms, and she hardly touched the expensive dishes. . . . In proportion as Urbenin became slightly intoxicated and thought himself the happiest of mortals, her pretty face appeared more and more unhappy. It made me sorrowful to look at her, and in order not to look at her face I tried not to lift my eyes off my plate.

How could her sadness be explained? Was not regret beginning to gnaw at the poor girl's heart? Or perhaps her vanity had expected even greater pomp?

During the second course when I lifted my eyes and looked at her, I was painfully struck by her expression. The poor girl in trying to answer some of the Count's silly remarks, was making strenuous efforts to swallow something; sobs were welling in her throat. She did not remove her handkerchief from her mouth, and looked at us timidly, like a frightened little animal, to see if we did not notice that she wanted to cry.

"Why are you looking so glum today?" the Count asked. "Oh, ho! Pëtr Egorych, it's your fault! Have the goodness to cheer your wife up! Ladies and gentlemen, I demand a kiss! Ha, ha! . . . The kiss I demand is, of course, not for me, but only . . . that they should kiss each other! Bitter!"

"Bitter!" echoed Kalinin.

Urbenin, smiling all over his red face, rose and began to blink. Olenka forced by the calls and the demands of the guests, rose slightly and offered her motionless, lifeless lips to Urbenin. He kissed her. . . Olenka pressed her lips together as if she feared they would be kissed another time, and glanced at me. . . . Probably my look was an evil one. Catching my eye, she suddenly blushed, and taking up her handkerchief, she began to blow her nose, trying in that way to hide her terrible confusion. . . . The thought entered my mind that she was ashamed before me, ashamed of that kiss, ashamed of her marriage.

"What have 1 to do with you?" I thought, but at the same time I did not remove my eyes from her face, trying to discover the cause of her confusion.

The poor little thing could not stand my gaze. It is true the blush of shame soon left her face, but in place of it tears began to rise up in her eyes, real tears such as I had never before seen on her face. Pressing her handkerchief to her face. she rose and rushed out of the dining-room.

"Olga Nikolaevna has a bad headache," I hastened to say in order to explain her departure. "Already this morning she complained of her head. . . ."

"Not at all, brother," the Count said jokingly. "A headache has nothing to do with it. It's all caused by the kiss, it has confused her. Ladies and gentlemen, I announce a severe reprimand for the bridegroom! He has not taught his bride how to kiss! Ha, ha, ha!"

The guests, delighted with the Count's wit, began to laugh. . . . But they ought not to have laughed. . . .

Five minutes passed, ten minutes passed, and the bride did not return. . . . A silence fell on the party. . . . Even the Count ceased joking. Olenka's absence was all the more striking as she had left suddenly without saying a word. . . . To say nothing about etiquette, which had received a shock first of all, Olenka had left the table immediately after the kiss, so it was evident she was cross at having been forced to kiss her husband. . . . It was impossible to suppose she had gone away because she was confused. . . . One can be confused for a minute, for two, but not for an eternity as the first ten minutes of her absence appeared to us all. What a number of evil thoughts entered into the half tipsy minds of the men, what scandals were being prepared by the charming ladies! The bride had risen and left the table! What an effective and scenic point for a drama in the provincial "fashionable world"!

Urbenin began to be uneasy and looked round.

"Nerves. . ." he muttered. "Or perhaps something has gone wrong with her toilet. . . . Who can account for anything with these women? She'll come back directly—this very minute."

But when another ten minutes had passed and she had not appeared, he looked at me with such unhappy, imploring eyes that I was sorry for him.

"Would it matter if I went to look for her?" his eyes asked. "Won't you help me, golubchik, to get out of this horrible position? Of all here you are the cleverest, the boldest, the most ready-witted man. Do help me!"

I saw the entreaty in his unhappy eyes and decided to help him. How I helped him the reader will see farther on. . . . I will only say that the bear who assisted the hermit in Krylov's fable loses all its animal majesty, becomes pale, and turns into an innocent infusoria when I think of myself in the part of the "obliging fool." . . . The resemblance between me and the bear consists only in this that we both went to help quite sincerely without foreseeing any bad consequences from our help, but the difference between us is enormous. . . . The stone with which I struck Urbenin's forehead was many times more weighty.

"Where is Olga Nikolaevna?" I asked the lackey who had brought round the salad.

"She went into the garden, sir," he replied.

"This is becoming quite impossible, mesdames!" I said in a jocular tone, addressing myself to the ladies. "The bride has gone away and my wine has become quite sour! . . . I must go to look for her and bring her back, even if all her teeth were aching! The best man is an official personage, and he is going to show his authority!"

I rose, amid the loud applause of my friend the Count, left the dining-room and went into the garden. The hot rays of the midday sun poured straight upon my head, which was already excited by wine. Suffocating heat and sultriness seemed to strike me in the face. I went along one of the side avenues at a venture, and, whistling some sort of melody, I gave full scope to my capacities as an ordinary detective. I examined all the bushes, summerhouses and caves, and when I began to be tormented by the regret that I had turned to the right instead of to the left, I suddenly heard a strange sound. Somebody was laughing or crying. The sounds issued from one of the grottoes that I had left to examine last of all. Quickly entering it, I found the object of my search enveloped in dampness, the smell of mildew, mushrooms, and lime.

She stood there leaning against a wooden column that was covered with black moss, and lifting her eyes full of horror and despair on me, she tore at her hair. Tears poured from her eyes as from a sponge that is pressed.

"What have I done? What have I done?" she muttered.

"Yes, Olia, what have you done?" I said, standing before her with folded arms.

"Why did I marry him? Where were my eyes? Where was my sense?"

"Yes, Olia. . . . It is difficult to explain your action. To explain it by inexperience is too indulgent; to explain it by depravity—I would rather not. . . ."

"I only understood it to-day . . . only to-day! Why did I not understand it yesterday? Now all is irrevocable, all is lost! All, all! I might have married the man I love, the man who loves me!"

"Who is that, Olia?" I asked.

"You!" she said, looking me straight and openly in the eyes. "But I was too hasty! I was foolish! You are clever, noble, young. . . . You are rich! You appeared to me unattainable!"

"Well, that's enough, Olia," I said, taking her by the hand. "Wipe your little eyes and come along. . . . They are waiting for you there. . . . Well, don't cry any more, don't cry. . . ." I kissed her hand. . . . "That's enough, little girl! You have done a foolish thing and are now paying for it. . . . It was your fault. . . . Well, that's enough, be calm. . . ."

"But you love me? Yes? You are so big, so handsome! Don't you love me?"

"It's time to go, my darling. . . ." I said, noticing to my great horror that I was kissing her forehead, taking her round the waist, that she was scorching me with her hot breath and that she was hanging round my neck.

"Enough!" I mumbled. "That must satisfy you!"

Five minutes later, when I carried her out of the grotto in my arms and troubled by new impressions put her on her feet, I saw Pshekhotsky standing almost at the entrance. . . . He stood there, looking at me maliciously and applauding silently. . . . I measured him with my glance, and giving Olga my arm, walked off towards the house.

"We'll see the last of you here to-day," I said, looking back at Pshekhotsky. "You will have to pay for this spying!"

My kisses had probably been ardent because Olga's face was burning as if ablaze. There were no traces of the recently shed tears to be seen on it.

"Now, as the saying is, the ocean is but knee-deep for me," she murmured as we went together towards the house and she pressed my elbow convulsively. "This morning I did not know where to hide myself from terror, and now . . . now, my good giant, I don't know what to do from happiness! My husband is sitting and waiting for me there. . . . Ha, ha! . . . What's that to me? If he were even a crocodile, a terrible serpent . . . I'm afraid of nothing! I love you, and that's all I want to know!"

I looked at her face, radiant with happiness, at her eyes, brim full of joyful, satisfied love, and my heart sank with fear for the future of this pretty and happy creature: her love for me was but an extra impulse towards the abyss. . . . How will this laughing woman with no thought for the future end? . . . My heart misgave me and sank with a feeling that cannot be called either pity or sympathy, because it was stronger than these feelings. I stopped and laid my hand on Olga's shoulder. . . . I had never before seen anything more beautiful, graceful and at the same time more pitiful. . . . There was no time for reasoning, deliberation or thought, and, carried away by my feeling, I exclaimed:

"Olga, come home with me at once! This instant!"

"How? What did you say?" she asked, unable to understand my somewhat solemn tone.

"Let us drive to my house immediately!"

Olga smiled and pointed to the house. . . .

"Well, and what of that?" I said. "Isn't it all the same if I take you tomorrow or to-day? But the sooner the better. . . . Come!"

"But . . . that's somehow strange——"

"Girl, you're afraid of the scandal? Yes, there'll be an unusual, a grandiose scandal, but a thousand scandals are better than that you should remain here! I won't leave you here! I can't leave you here! Olga, do you understand? Cast aside your faint-heartedness, your womanly logic, and obey me! Obey me if you do not desire your own ruin!"

Olga's eyes said that she did not understand me. . . . Meanwhile time did not stop but went its course, and it was impossible for us to remain standing in the avenue while they were expecting us *there*. We had to decide. . . . I pressed to my heart "the girl in red," who actually was my wife now, and at that moment it appeared to me that I really loved her. . . .

loved her with a husband's love, that she was mine, and that her fate rested on my conscience. . . . I saw that I was united with this creature for ever, irrevocably.

"Listen, my darling, my treasure!" I said. "It's a bold step. . . . It will separate us from our nearest friends; it will call down upon our heads a thousand reproaches and tearful lamentations. Perhaps it will even spoil my career; it will cause me a thousand unsurmountable unpleasantnesses, but, my darling, it is settled! You will be my wife! . . . I want no better wife. God preserve me from all other women! I will make you happy; I will take care of you like the apple of my eye, as long as I live; I will educate you—make a woman of you! I promise you this, and here is my honest hand on it!"

I spoke with sincere passion, with feeling, like a stage lover acting the most pathetic scene of his part. I spoke very well, I seemed to be inspired by the touch of an eagle's wing that was soaring over our heads. My Olia took my outstretched hand, held it in her own small hands, and kissed it tenderly. But this was not a sign of assent. On the silly little face of an inexperienced woman who had never before heard such speech, there appeared a look of perplexity. . . . She still could not understand me.

"You say I am to go to you?" she said reflectively. "I don't quite understand you. . . . Don't you know what *he* would say?"

"What have you to do with what he would say?"

"How so? No, Serezha! Better say no more. . . Please leave that alone. . . . You love me, and I want nothing more. With your love I'm ready to go to hell."

"But, little fool, how will you manage it?"

"I shall live here, and you—why you will come every day. . . . I will come to meet you."

"But I can't imagine such a life for you without a shudder! At night—he; in the day—1. . . . No, that is impossible! Olia, I love you so much at the present moment that . . . I am madly jealous. . . . I never suspected I had the capacity for such feelings."

But what imprudence! I had my arm round her waist, and she was stroking my hand tenderly at the time when at any moment one could expect somebody would be passing down the avenue and might see us.

"Come," I said, removing my arm. "Put on your cloak and let us be off!"

"How quickly you want to do things," she murmured in a tearful voice. "You hurry as if to a fire. And God only knows what you have invented! To run away immediately after the marriage! What will people say?"

And Olenka shrugged her shoulders. Her face wore such a look of perplexity, astonishment and incomprehension that I only waved my hand and postponed settling her "life questions" to another moment. Besides, there was no time to continue our conversation: we were going up the stone stairs that led to the terrace and heard the sound of voices. At the dining-room door Olia arranged her hair, saw that her dress was in order, and went into the room.

No signs of confusion could be noticed on her face. She entered the room much more boldly than I had expected.

"Ladies and gentlemen, I have brought back the fugitive," I said as I sat down in my place. "I found her with difficulty. . . . I'm quite tired out by this search. I went into the garden, I looked around, and there she was walking about in the avenue. . . . 'Why are you here?' I asked her. 'Just so,' she answered. 'It's so stuffy.'"

Olia looked at me, at the guests, at her husband, and began to laugh. Something amused her, and she became gay. I read on her face the wish to share with all that crowd of diners the sudden happiness that she had experienced; and not being able to give expression to it in words, she poured it out in her laughter.

"What a funny person I am!" she said. "I am laughing, and I don't know why I am laughing. . . . Count, laugh!"

"Bitter," cried Balinin.

Urbenin coughed and looked inquiringly at Olia.

"Well?" she said, with a momentary frown.

"They are calling out 'bitter,'" Urbenin smiled, and rising, he wiped his lips with his napkin.

Olga rose too and allowed him to kiss her immovable lips. . . . The kiss was a cold one, but it served to increase the fire that was smouldering in my breast and threatened every moment to burst into flame. . . . I turned away and with compressed lips awaited the end of the dinner. . . . Fortunately the end was soon reached, otherwise I would not have been able to endure it.

CHAPTER XV

HER QUESTION

"COME here!" I said to the Count rudely, going up to him after dinner.

The Count looked at me with astonishment and followed me into the empty room to which I led him.

"What do you want, my dear friend?" he asked as he unbuttoned his waistcoat and hiccuped.

"Choose one of us. . . ." I said, scarcely able to stand on my feet from the rage that mastered me. "Either me or Pshekhotsky! If you don't promise me that in an hour that scoundrel shall leave your estate, I will never set my foot here again! . . . I give you half a minute to make your choice!"

The Count dropped the cigar out of his mouth and spread his arms. . . .

"What's the matter with you, Serezha?" he asked, opening his eyes wide. "You look quite wild!"

"No useless words, if you please! I cannot endure that spy, scoundrel, rogue, your friend Pshekhotsky, and in the name of our close friendship I demand that he shall no longer be here, and instantly, too!"

"But what has he done to you?" the Count asked, much agitated. "Why are you attacking him?"

"I ask you again: me or him?"

"But, golubchik, you are placing me in a horribly awkward position. . . . Stop! There's a feather on your dress coat! . . . You are demanding the impossible from me!"

"Good-bye!" I said. "I am no longer acquainted with you."

And turning sharply on my heel, I went into the ante-room, put on my overcoat and hastened out of the house. When crossing the garden towards the servants' department, where I wanted to give the order to have my horse put to, I was stopped. Coming towards me with a small cup of coffee in her hand, I was met by Nadia Kalinin. She was also at Urbenin's wedding, but a sort of undefined fear had forced me to avoid speaking to her, and during the whole day I had not gone up to her, nor said a word to her.

"Sergey Petrovich!" she said in an unnaturally deep voice when in passing her I slightly raised my hat. "Stop!"

"What may your commands be?" I asked, as I came up to her.

"I have nothing to command. . . . Besides, you are no lackey," she said, gazing straight into my eyes and becoming terribly pale. "You are hurrying somewhere, but if you have time might I detain you for a moment?"

"Certainly! . . . I can't understand why you ask it? . . ."

"In that case let us sit down. . . . Sergey Petrovich," she continued, after we had seated ourselves. "All this day you have tried to avoid seeing me, and have gone round me, as if you were afraid of meeting me and as if on purpose, I had decided to speak to you. . . . I am proud and egoistical. . . . I do not know how to obtrude myself. . . . but once in a lifetime one can sacrifice pride."

"To what do you refer?"

"I had decided to ask you. . . . The question is humiliating, it is difficult for me. . . . I don't know how I shall stand it. . . . Answer me without looking at me. . . . Sergey Petrovich, is it possible you are not sorry for me?"

Nadia looked at me and slightly shook her head. Her face became paler. Her upper lip trembled and was drawn to one side.

"Sergey Petrovich! I always think that . . . you have been separated from me by some misunderstanding, some caprice. . . . I think if we had an explanation, all would go on as formerly. If I did not think it, I would not have strength to put you the question you are about to hear. Sergey Petrovich, I am unhappy. . . . You must see it. . . . My life is no life. . . . All is dried up. . . . And chiefly . . . this uncertainty . . . one does not know, whether to hope or not. . . . Your conduct towards me is so incomprehensible that it is impossible to arrive at any certain conclusion. . . . Tell me, and I shall know what to do. . . . My life will then have an aim. . . . I shall then decide on something.

"Nadezhda Nikolaevna, you wish to ask me about something?" I said, preparing in my mind an answer to the question I had a presentiment was coming.

"Yes, I want to ask. . . . The question is humiliating. . . . If anybody were listening to us they might think I was obtruding myself, in a word,—was a sort of Pushkin's Tatiana. . . . But this question has been tortured from me. . . ."

The question was really forced from her by torture. When Nadia turned her face towards me to put that question, I became frightened: Nadia trembled, pressed her fingers together convulsively, and pressed from her lips with melancholy sadness the fatal words. Her pallor was terrible.

"May I hope?" she whispered at last. "Do not be afraid to tell me candidly. . . . Whatever the answer may be, it will be better than uncertainty. What is it? May I hope?"

She waited for an answer, meanwhile the state of my soul was such that I was incapable of making a sensible answer. Drunk, excited by the occurrence in the grotto, enraged by Pshekhotsky's spying, and Olga's indecision, and the stupid conversation I had had with the Count, I scarcely heard Nadia.

"May I hope?" she repeated. "Answer me!"

"Ach, I can't answer now, Nadezhda Nikolaevna!" I said with a wave of the hand as I rose. "I am incapable at the present moment of giving you any sort of answer. Forgive me, I neither heard nor understood you. I am stupid and excited. . . . It's really a pity you took the trouble."

I again waved my hand and left Nadia. It was only afterwards when I became calm again, that I understood how stupid and cruel I had been in not giving the girl an answer to her simple and ingenuous question. Why did I not answer her?

Now when I can look back dispassionately at the past, I do not explain my cruelty by the condition of my soul. It appears to me that in not giving a straightforward answer I was coquetting and playing the fool. It is difficult to understand the human soul, but it is still more difficult to understand one's own soul. If I really was playing the fool, may God forgive me. Although to make game of another's suffering ought not to be forgiven.

CHAPTER XVI

A MISTAKE IN MARRYING

FOR three days I wandered about my rooms from corner to corner like a wolf in a cage, trying with all the strength of my unstable will to prevent myself from leaving the house. I did not touch the pile of papers that were lying on the table patiently awaiting my attention; I received nobody; I quarrelled with Polycarp; I was irritable. . . . I did not allow myself to go to the Count's estate, and this obstinacy cost me great nervous labour. A thousand times I took up my hat and as often threw it down again. . . . Sometimes I decided to defy the whole world and go to Olga, whatever it might cost; at others I drenched myself with the cold decision to remain at home. . . .

My reason told me not to go to the Count's estate. Since I had sworn to the Count never to set foot in his house again, could I sacrifice my self-love and pride? What would that moustachioed coxcomb think if, after our stupid conversation, I went to him as if nothing had happened? Would it not be a confession of my own injustice?

Besides, as an honest man I ought to break off all connexion with Olga. All further intercourse with her could only lead to her ruin. She had made a mistake in marrying Urbenin; in falling in love with me she had made another mistake. If she had a secret lover while living with her old husband, would she not be like a depraved doll? To say nothing about how abominable in principle, such a life is, it was necessary also to think of the consequences.

What a coward I am! I was afraid of the consequences, of the present, of

the past. . . . An ordinary man will laugh at my reasoning. He would not have paced from corner to corner, he would not have seized his head in both hands, he would not have made all sorts of plans, but he would have left all to life which grinds into flour even millstones. Life would have digested everything without asking for his aid or permission. . . . But I am fearsome almost to cowardice. Pacing from corner to corner, I suffered from compassion for Olga, and at the same time I feared she would understand the proposal I had made her in a moment of passion, and would appear in my house to stay as I had promised her, *for ever*. What would have happened if she had listened to me and had come home with me? How long would that *for ever* have lasted, and what would life with me have given poor Olga? I would not have given her family life and would consequently not have given her happiness. No, I ought not to go to Olga!

At the same time my soul was drawn frantically towards her. I was as melancholy as a boy, in love for the first time, who is refused a rendezvous. Tempted by what had occurred in the grotto, I yearned for another meeting, and the alluring vision of Olga, who, as I well knew, was also expecting me, and was pining away from longing, never left my mind for a moment.

The Count sent me letter after letter, each one more rueful and humiliating than the last. . . . He implored me to "forget everything" and come to him; he apologized for Pshekhotsky, he begged me to forgive that "kind, simple, but somewhat shallow man," he was surprised that owing to trifles I had decided to break off old and friendly connexions. In one of his last letters he promised to come to me and, if I wished it, to bring Pshekhotsky with him, who would ask my pardon, "although he did not feel that he was at all in fault." I read the letters and in answer begged each messenger to leave me in peace. I knew well how to be capricious!

At the very height of my nervous agitation, when I, standing at the window, was deciding to go away somewhere—anywhere except to the Count's estate —when I was tormenting myself with arguments, self-reproaches, and visions of love that awaited me with Olga, my door opened quietly, I heard light footsteps behind me, and soon my neck was encircled by two pretty little arms.

"Olga, is that you?" I asked and looked round.

I recognized her by her hot breath, by the manner in which she hung on my neck, and even by her scent. Pressing her head to my cheek, she appeared to me extraordinarily happy. . . . From happiness she could not say a word. . . . I pressed her to my breast and— where had the melancholy, and all the questions with which I had been tormenting myself during the whole of three days, disappeared? I laughed and jumped about with joy like the veriest schoolboy.

Olga was in a blue silk dress, which suited her pale face and splendid flaxen hair very well. The dress was in the latest fashion and must have been very expensive. It probably cost Urbenin a quarter of his yearly salary.

"How lovely you are to-day!" I said, lifting Olga up in my arms and kissing her neck. "Well, what? How are you? Quite well?"

"Why, you haven't much of a place here!" she said, casting her eyes round my study. "You're a rich man, you receive a high salary, and yet . . . you live quite poorly.'

"Not everybody can live as luxuriously as the Count, my darling," I said. "But let us leave my wealth in peace. What good genius has brought you into my den?"

"Stop, Serezha! You'll tumble my frock. . . . Put me down. . . . I've only come to you for a moment, darling! I told everybody at home I was going to Akat'ikha, the Count's washerwoman, who lives here only three doors off. Let me go, darling! . . . It's awkward. Why haven't you been to see me for so long?"

I answered something, placed her on a chair opposite me, and began to contemplate her beauty. For a minute we looked at each other in silence.

"You are very pretty, Olia!" I sighed. "It's a pity and an insult that you're so pretty!"

"Why is it a pity?"

"The devil only knows who's got you."

"But what do you want more? Am not I yours? Here I am. . . . Listen, Serezha! . . . Will you tell me the truth if I ask you?"

"Of course, only the truth."

"Would you have married me if I had not married Pëtr Egorych?"

"Probably not," I wanted to say, but why should I probe the painful wound in poor Olia's heart that was already so troubled?

"Certainly," I said in the tone of a man speaking the truth.

Olia sighed and cast her eyes down.

"What a mistake I've made! What a mistake! And what's worst of all it can't be rectified! I suppose I can't get divorced from him?"

"You can't."

"I can't understand why I was in such a hurry! We girls are so silly and giddy. . . . There's nobody to whip us! However, one can't undo the past, and to reason about it is useless. . . . Neither reasoning nor tears are of any good. Serezha, I cried all last night! He was there . . . lying next to me, and I was thinking of you. . . . I couldn't sleep. . . . I wanted to run away in the night, even into the wood to father. . . . It is better to live with a mad father than with this—what's his name."

"Reasoning won't help. . . . Olia, you ought to have reasoned when you drove home with me from Tenevo, and were so happy at getting married to a rich man. . . . It's too late to practice eloquence now. . . ."

"Too late. . . . Then let it be so!" Olga said with a decisive wave of the hand. It will be possible to live, if it is no worse. . . . Good-bye, I must be off. . . ."

"No, not good-bye. . . ."

I drew Olia towards me and covered her face with kisses, as if I were trying to reward myself for the lost three days. She pressed close against me like a cold lamb and warmed my face with her hot breath. . . . There was stillness in the room. . . .

"The husband killed his wife!" bawled my parrot.

Olia shivered, released herself from my embraces, and looked inquiringly at me.

"It's only the parrot, my soul," I said. "Calm yourself."

"The husband killed his wife!" Ivan Dem'yanych repeated again.

Olia rose, put on her hat in silence, and gave me her hand. Dread was written on her face.

"What if Urbenin gets to know?" she asked, looking at me with wide-open eyes. "He is capable of killing me."

"What nonsense!" I said, laughing. "What sort of a fellow would I be if I allowed him to kill you? He's hardly capable of such an unusual act as a murder. . . . Are you going? Well, then, good-bye, my child! . . . I will wait. . . . To-morrow, in the wood, near the house where you lived. . . . Shall we meet there?" . . .

After seeing Olia off, I returned to my study, where I found Polycarp. He was standing in the middle of the room, he looked sternly at me and shook his head contemptuously.

"Sergei Petrovich, see that this sort of thing does not happen here again; I won't have it," he said in the tone of a severe parent. "I don't wish it. . . ."

"What's 'it'?"

"That thing. . . . You think I did not see? I saw everything. . . . See that she doesn't dare to come here again. This is no house for that sort of philandering. There are other places for that. . . ."

I was in the best of humours, so Polycarp's spying and mentorial tone did not make me angry. I only laughed and sent him to the kitchen.

I had hardly had time to collect my thoughts after Olga's visit when another guest arrived. A carriage rattled up to my door and Polycarp, spitting to each side and with mumbled abuse announced the arrival of "that there fellow, may he be . . . !" etc., etc. It was the Count, whom he hated with the whole strength of his soul. The Count entered, looked tearfully at me, and shook his head.

"You turn away. . . . You don't want to speak . . ."

"I don't turn away," I said.

"I am so fond of you, Serezha, and you . . for a trifle! Why do you wound me? Why?"

The Count sat down, sighed, and shook his head.

"Well, you've played the fool long enough!" I said. "All right!"

I had a strong influence upon this weak, puny little man; it was as strong as my contempt for him. . . . My contemptuous tone never offended him; on the contrary. . . . When he heard my "All right!" he jumped up and embraced me.

"I have brought him with me. . . . He is sitting in the carriage. . . . Do you wish him to apologize?"

"Do you know his fault?"

"No. . . ."

"So much the better. He needn't apologize, but you had better warn him that if ever a similar thing occurs, I'll not get excited, but I will take my own measures."

"Then, Serezha, it's peace? Excellent! That ought to have been long ago; the deuce only knows what you quarrelled about! Like two schoolgirls! Oh, by-the-by, golubchek, haven't you got half a glass of vodka? My throat is terribly dry!"

I ordered vodka to be served. The Count drank two glasses, sprawled himself out on the sofa, and began to chatter.

"I say, brother, I just met Olia. . . . A fine girl! I must tell you, I'm beginning to detest Urbenin. . . . That means that Olenka is beginning to please

me . . . She's devilish pretty! I think of making up to her."

"One ought not to touch the married ones!" I said with a sigh.

"Come now, he's an old man. . . . It's no sin to juggle Pëtr Egorych out of his wife. . . . She's no mate for him. . . . He's like a dog; he can't eat it himself, and won't let others have it. . . . I'm going to begin my siege to-day; I'll begin systematically. . . . She's such a ducky—h'm!—quite chic, brother! One licks one's chops!"

The Count drank a third glass and continued:

"Of the girls here, do you know who pleases me too? Nadenka, that fool Kalinin's daughter. . . . A burning brunette, you know the sort, pale, with wonderful eyes. . . . I must also cast my line there . . . I'm giving a party at Whitsuntide, a musical, vocal, literary evening on purpose to invite her . . . As it turns out, it's not so bad here; quite jolly! There's society, and women . . . and . . . May I have five winks here . . . only a moment?"

"You may . . . But how about Pshekhotsky in the carriage?"

"He may wait, the devil take him! . . . Brother, I myself don't like him."

The Count raised himself on his elbow and said mysteriously:

"I keep him only from necessity . . . because I must. . . . May the devil take him!"

The Count's elbow gave way, his head sank on the cushion. A minute later snores were heard.

In the evening after the Count had left, I had another visitor; the doctor, Pavel Ivanovich. He came to inform me of Nadezhda Nikolaevna's illness and also that she had definitely refused him her hand. The poor fellow was down-hearted and went about like a drenched hen.

CHAPTER XVII

ALL-POWERFUL

THE poetical month of May had passed.

The lilacs and tulips were over, and fate decreed that with them the ecstasies of love, which, notwithstanding their guiltiness and painfulness, had yet occasionally afforded us sweet moments that can never be effaced from our memory, should likewise wither. There are moments for which one would give months, yea, even years!

On a June evening when the sun was already set, but its broad track in purple and gold still glowed in the distant West, fortelling a calm and clear day for the morrow, I rode on Zorka up to the house where Urbenin lived. On that evening the Count was giving a musical party. The guests were already arriving, but the Count was not at home; he had gone for a ride and had left word he would return soon.

A little later I was standing at the porch, holding my horse by the bridle and chatting with Urbenin's little daughter, Sasha. Urbenin himself was sitting on the steps with his head supported on his fists, looking into the distance, which could be seen through the open gates. He was gloomy and answered my questions reluctantly. I left him in peace and occupied myself with Sasha.

"Where is your new máma?" I asked her.

"She has gone out riding with the Count. She rides with him every day."

"Every day!" Urbenin grumbled with a sigh.

Much could be heard in that sigh. The same feelings could be heard in it that were agitating my soul and that I was trying to explain to myself, but was unable to do so, and therefore became lost in conjecture.

Every day Olga went out for rides with the Count. But that was a trifle. Olga could not fall in love with the Count, and Urbenin's jealousy was groundless. We ought not to have been jealous of the Count, but of something else which, however, I could not understand for a long time. This "something else" built up a whole wall between Olga and me. She continued to love me, but after the visit which has been described in the last chapter, she had not been to my house more than twice, and when we met in other places she flared up in a strange way and obstinately refused to answer my questions. She returned my caresses with passion, but her movements were sudden and startled, so that our short rendezvous only left a feeling of painful perplexity in my mind. Her conscience was not clean; this was clear, but what was the real cause? Nothing could be read on Olga's guilty face.

"I hope your new máma is well?" I asked Sasha.

"She's quite well. Only in the night she had toothache. She cried."

"She cried." Urbenin repeated, looking at Sasha. "Did you see it? My darling, you only dreamed it."

Olga had not had toothache. If she had cried it was not with pain, but for something else. . . . I wanted to continue talking to Sasha, but I did not succeed in this, as at that moment the noise of horses' hoofs was heard and

we soon saw the riders—a man in-
elegantly jumping about in his saddle,
and a graceful lady rider. In order to
hide my joy from Olga, I took Sasha
into my arms and, smothing her fair
hair with my hand, I kissed her on the
forehead.

"Sasha, how pretty you are!" I said.
"And what nice curls you have!"

Olga cast a rapid glance at me, returned my bow in silence, and leaning
on the Count's arm, entered the house.
Urbenin rose and followed her.

Five minutes later the Count came out
of the house. He was gay. I had
never seen him so gay before. Even
his face had a fresher look.

"Congratulate me," he said, giggling,
as he took my arm.

"What on?"

"On my conquest. . . . One more
ride like this, and I swear by the ashes
of my noble ancestors I shall tear the
petals from this flower."

"You have not torn them off yet?"

"As yet? . . . Almost! During
ten minutes, 'Thy hand in my hand,'"
the Count sang, "and . . . not once
did she draw it away. . . . I kissed
it! Wait for tomorrow. Now let us
go. They are expecting me. Oh, by-
the-by, golubchek, I want to talk to you
about something. Tell me, old man,
is it true what people say—that you
are . . . that you entertain evil intentions with regard to Nadenka
Kalinin?"

"Why?"

"If that were true, I won't come in
your way. It's not in my principles to
put a spoke in another's wheels. If,
however, you have no sort of intentions,
then of course——"

"I have none."

"*Merci*, my soul!"

The Count thought of killing two
hares at the same time, and was firmly
convinced that he would succeed. On
the evening I am describing I watched
the chase of these two hares. The chase
was stupid and as comical as a good
caricature. When watching it one could
only laugh or be revolted at the Count's
vulgarity, but nobody could have thought
that this schoolboy chase would end with
the moral fall of some. the ruin and
the crimes of others!

The Count not only killed two hares,
but more! He killed them, but he did
not get their skins and their flesh.

I saw him secretly press Olga's hand,
who received him each time with a
friendly smile and looked after him with
a contemptuous grimace. Once, evidently wishing to show that there were
no secrets between us, he even kissed
her hand in my presence.

"What a blockhead!" she whispered
into my ear, and wiped her hand.

"I say, Olga," I asked, when the Count
had gone away. "I think there is something you want to tell me. What is
it?"

I looked searchingly into her face. She
blushed scarlet and began to blink in a
frightened manner, like a cat who has
been caught stealing.

"Olga," I said sternly, "you must tell
me! I demand it!"

"Yes, there is something I want to
tell you," she whispered. "I love you—
I can't live without you—but . . .
my darling, don't come to see me any
more. Don't love me any more, and
don't call me Olia. It can't go on . . .
It's impossible. . . . And don't let
anybody see that you love me."

"But why is this?"

"I want it. The reasons you need not know, and I won't tell you. Go. . . . Leave me!"

I did not leave her, and she herself was obliged to bring our conversation to an end. Taking the arm of her husband, who was passing us at that moment, she nodded to me with a hypocritical smile, and went away.

The Count's other hare—Nadenka Kalinin—was honoured that evening by the Count's special attention. The whole evening he hovered around her, he told her anecdotes, he was witty, he flirted with her, and she, pale and exhausted, drew her lips to one side in a forced smile. The justice of the peace, Kalinin, watched them all the time, stroking his beard and coughing importantly. That the Count was paying court to his daughter was agreeable to him. "He has a Count as son-in-law!" What thought could be sweeter for a provincial *bon-vivant?* From the moment that the Count began to pay court to his daughter he had grown at least three feet in height in his own estimation. And with what stately glances he measured me, how maliciously he coughed when he talked to me! "So you stood on ceremonies and went away—it was all one to us! . Now we have a Count!"

The day after the party I was again at the Count's estate. This time I did not talk with Sasha but with her brother, the schoolboy. The boy led me into the garden and poured out his whole soul to me. These confidences were the result of my questions as to how he got on with his "new mother."

"She's your good acquaintance," he began, nervously unbuttoning his uniform. "You will repeat it to her; but I don't care. You may tell her whatever you like! She's spiteful, she's base!"

He told me that Olga had taken his room from him, she had sent away their old nurse who had served at Urbenin's for ten years, she was always screaming about something and always angry.

"Yesterday you admired sister Sasha's hair. . . . Hadn't she pretty hair? Just like flax! This morning she cut it all off!"

"That was jealousy," I thus explained to myself Olga's invasion into the hairdresser's domain.

"She was evidently envious that you had praised Sasha's hair and not her own," the boy said in confirmation of my thought. "She worries papasha, too. Papasha is spending a terrible lot of money on her, and is neglecting his work. . . . He has again begun to drink! Again! She's a little fool. . . . She cries all day that she has to live in poverty in such a small house. Is it papasha's fault that he has little money?"

The boy told me many sad things. He saw that which his blinded father did not see or did not want to see. In the poor boy's opinion his father was wronged, his sister was wronged, his old nurse had been wronged. He had been deprived of his little den where he had been used to occupy himself with his books, and feed the goldfinches he had caught. Everybody had been wronged, everybody was laughed at by his stupid and all-powerful stepmother! But the poor boy could not have imagined the terrible wrong that his young stepmother would inflict on his family, and of which I was witness that very evening after my talk with him. Everything else grew dim before that wrong, the cropping of Sasha's hair appeared as a mere trifle in comparison with it.

CHAPTER XVIII

WRATH!

LATE at night I was sitting with the Count. As usual, we were drinking. The Count was quite drunk, I only slightly.

"To-day I was allowed accidentally to touch her waist," he mumbled. "To-morrow, therefore, we can begin to go further."

"Well, and Nadia? How do things stand with Nadia?"

"We are progressing! I've only begun with her as yet. So far, we are passing through the period of conversations with the eyes. I love to read in her sad black eyes, brother. Something is written there that words are unable to express, that only the soul can understand. Let's have another drink!"

"It seems that you please her since she has the patince to listen to you for hours at a time. You also please her papa!"

"Her papa? Are you talking about that blockhead? Ha, ha! The simpleton suspects me of honourable intentions."

The Count coughed and drank.

"He thinks I'll marry her! To say nothing of my not being able to marry, when one considers the question honestly it would be more honest in me to seduce a girl than to marry her. . . . An eternal life with a drunken, coughing, semi-old man . . . br-r-r! My wife would pine away, or she would run away the next day. . . . What noise is that?"

The Count and I jumped up. . . . Several doors were slammed to, and almost at the same moment Olga rushed into the room. She was as white as snow, and trembled like a chord that had been struck violently. Her hair was falling loose around her. The pupils of her eyes were dilated. She was out of breath and was crumpling in her hand the front pleats of her dressing-gown.

"Olga, what is the matter with you?" I asked, seizing her by the hand and turning pale.

The Count ought to have been surprised at this familiar form of address, but he did not hear it. His whole person was turned into one large note of interrogation, and with open mouth and staring eyes he stood looking at Olga as if she were an apparition.

"What has happened?" I asked.

"He beats me!" Olga said, and fell sobbing on to an armchair. "He beats me!"

"Who is he?"

"My husband! I can't live with him! I have left him!"

"This is revolting!" the Count exclaimed, and he struck the table with his fist. "What right has he? This is tyranny! This . . . the devil only knows what it is! To beat his wife? To beat! What did he do it for?"

"For nothing, for nothing at all," Olga said, wiping away her tears. "I pulled my handkerchief out of my pocket, and the letter you sent me yesterday fell on the floor. . . . He seized it and read it . . . and began to beat me. . . . He clutched my hand and crushed it—look, there are still red spots on it—and demanded an explanation. . . . Instead of explaining, I ran here. . . . Can't you defend me? He has not the right to treat his wife so roughly! I'm no cook! I'm a noblewoman!"

The Count paced about the room and jabbered with his drunken, muddling tongue some sort of nonsense which when rendered into sober language was intended to mean "of the status of women in Russia."

"This is barbarous! This is New Zealand! Does this muzhik also think that at his funeral his wife will have her throat cut? Savages when they go into the next world take their wives with them!"

I could not recover from my surprise. How was this sudden visit of Olga's in a nightdress to be understood? What was I to think—what to decide? If she had been beaten, if her dignity had been wounded, why had she not run away to her father or to the housekeeper? . . . Lastly why not to me, who was certainly near to her? And had she really been insulted? My heart told me of the innocence of simple-minded Urbenin, and understanding the truth, it sank with the pain that the stupefied husband must have been feeling at that time. Without asking any questions, not knowing where to commence, I began to soothe Olga and offered her wine.

"What a mistake I made! What a mistake!" she sighed between her tears, lifting the wineglass to her lips. "What sanctimoniousness he feigned when he was courting me! I thought he was an angel and not a man!"

"So you wanted him to be pleased with the letter that fell out of your pocket?" I asked. "You wanted him to burst out laughing?"

"Don't let us talk about it!" the Count interrupted. "Whatever might

have been, his action was dastardly all the same. Women are not treated in that way. I'll challenge him. I'll teach him. Olga Nikolaevna, believe me he'll have to suffer for this!"

The Count gobbled like a young turkey cock, although he had no authority to come between husband and wife. I kept silent and did not contradict him, because I knew that to take vengeance for another man's wife was limited to drunken ebullitions of words between four walls, and that everything about the duel would be forgottten the next day. But why was Olga silent? . . . I did not wish to think that she was not loth to have the proposed service rendered her by the Count. I did not wish to think that this silly, beautiful cat had so little dignity, that she would willingly consent to the drunken Count being judge between man and wife.

"I'll mix him with the dirt!" piped this newly-fledged knight-errant. "I'll end by boxing his ears! I'll do it to-morrow!"

And she did not stop the mouth of that blackguard, who in his drunken mood was insulting a man whose only blame was that he had made a mistake and was now being duped. Urbenin had seized and pressed her hand very roughly, and this had caused her scandalous flight to the Count's house, and now, when before her eyes this drunken and morally degenerate creature was defaming the honest name and pouring filthy slops on a man, who at that time must have been languishing in melancholy and uncertainty, knowing that he was deceived, she did not even move a hair of her eyebrows!

While the Count was pouring out his wrath and Olga was wiping her eyes, the manservant brought in some roast partridges. . . . The Count put half a partridge on his guest's plate. She shook her head negatively and then mechanically took up her knife and fork and began to eat. The partridge was followed by a large glass of wine, and soon there were no more signs of tears with the exception of red spots near the eyes and occasional deep sighs.

Soon we heard laughter. . . . Olga laughed like a consoled child who had forgotten its injury. And the Count looking at her laughed too.

"Do you know what I have thought of?" he began, sitting down next to her. "I want to arrange private theatricals. We shall act plays in which there are good women's parts. Eh? What do you say to that?"

They began to talk about the private theatricals. How ill this silly chatter accorded with the terror that had but lately been depicted on Olga's face, when only an hour before she had rushed into the room, pale and weeping, with flowing hair! How cheap were those terrors, those tears!

Meanwhile time went on. The clock struck twelve. Respectable women go to bed at that time. Olga ought to have gone away long since. But the clock struck half-past twelve; it struck one, and she was still sitting there chatting with the Count.

"It's time to go to bed," I said, looking at my watch. "I'm off! . . Olga Nikolaevna, will you permit me to escort you?"

Olga looked at me and then at the Count.

"Where am I to go?" she murmured. "I can't go to him!"

"Yes, yes; of course, you can't go to him," the Count said. "Who can answer for his not beating you again? No, no!"

I walked about the room. All was quiet. I paced from corner to corner and my friend and my mistress followed my steps with their eyes. I seemed to understand this quiet and these glances. There was something expectant and impatient in them. I put my hat on the table and sat down on the sofa.

"So, sir," the Count mumbled and rubbed his hands impatiently. "So, sir. . . . Things are like this. . . ."

The clock struck half-past one. The Count looked quickly at the clock, frowned and began to walk about the room. I could see by the glances he cast on me that he wanted to say something, something important but ticklish and unpleasant.

"I say, Serezha!" he at last picked up courage, sat down next to me, and whispered in my ear. "Golubchek, don't be offended. . . . Of course, you will understand my position, and you won't find my request strange or rude."

"Tell me quickly. No need to mince matters!"

"You see how things stand . . . how . . . Go away, golubchek! You are interfering with *us*. . . She will remain with me. . . . Forgive me for sending you away, but . . . you will understand my impatience!"

"All right!"

My friend was loathsome. If I had not been fastidious, perhaps I would have crushed him like a beetle, when he, shivering as if with fever, asked me to leave him alone with Urbenin's wife. He, the debilitated anchorite, steeped through and through with spirits and disease, wanted to take the poetic "girl in red" who dreamed of an effective death and had been nurtured by the forests and the angry lake! No, she must be miles away from him!

I went up to her.

"I am going," I said.

She nodded her head.

"Am I to go away? Yes?" I asked, trying to read the truth in her lovely, blushing little face. "Yes?"

With the very slightest movement of her long black eyelashes she answered "Yes."

"You have considered well?"

She turned away from me, as one turns away from an annoying wind. She did not want to speak. Why should she speak? It is impossible to answer a long subject briefly, and there was neither time nor place for long speeches.

I took up my hat and left the room without taking leave. Afterwards, Olga told me that immediately after my departure, as soon as the sound of my steps became mingled with the noise of the wind in the garden, the drunken Count was pressing her in his embrace. And she, closing her eyes and stopping up her mouth and nostrils, was scarcely able to keep her feet from a feeling of disgust. There was even a moment when she had almost torn herself away from his embraces and rushed into the lake. There were moments when she tore her hair and wept. It is not easy to sell oneself.

When I left the house and went towards the stables, I had to pass the bailiff's house. I looked in at the window. Pëtr Egorych was seated at a table by the dim light of a smoking oil lamp that had been turned up too high. I did not see his face. It was covered by his hands. But the whole of his robust, awkward figure displayed so much sorrow, anguish and despair that it was not necessary to see the face to understand the condition of his soul. Two bottles stood before him; one was empty, the other only just begun. They were both vodka bottles. The poor devil was seeking peace not in himself, nor in other people, but in alcohol.

Five minutes later I was riding home. The darkness was terrible. The lake blustered wrathfully and seemed to be angry that I, such a sinner, who had just been the witness of a sinful deed, should dare to infringe its austere peace. I could not see the lake for the darkness. It seemed as if an unseen monster was roaring, that the very darkness which enveloped me was roaring too.

I pulled up Zorka, closed my eyes, and meditated to the roaring of the monster.

"What if I returned at once and destroyed them?"

Terrible wrath raged in my soul. All the little of goodness and honesty that remained in me after long years of a depraved life, all that corruption had left, all that I guarded and cherished, that I was proud of, was insulted, spat upon, splashed with filth!

I had known venal women before, I had bought them, studied them, but they had not had the innocent rosy cheeks and sincere blue eyes that I had seen on the May morning when I walked through the wood to the Tenevo fair. . . . I myself, corrupt to the marrow of my bones, had forgiven, had preached tolerance of everything vicious, and I was indulgent to weakness. . . . I was convinced that it was impossible to demand of dirt that it should not be dirt, and that one cannot blame those ducats which from the force of circumstances have fallen into the mire. But I had not known before that ducats could melt in the mire and be blended with it into a single mass. Consequently gold could also dissolve!

A strong gust of wind blew off my hat and bore it into the surrounding darkness. In its flight my hat touched Zorka's head. She took fright, reared on her hind legs and galloped off along the familiar road.

When I reached home I threw myself on the bed. Polycarp suggested that I should undress, and he got sworn at and called a "devil" for no earthly reason.

"Devil yourself!" Polycarp grumbled as he went away from my bed.

"What did you say. What did you say?" I shouted.

"None so deaf as those who will not hear!"

"Oh, ho! . . . You dare to be impudent!" I thundered and poured out all my bile on my poor lackey. "Get out! That no trace of you be left, scoundrel! Out with you!"

And without waiting for my man to leave the room, I fell on the bed and began to sob like a boy. My overstrained nerves could bear no more. Powerless wrath, wounded feelings, jealousy—all had to have vent in one way or another.

"The husband killed his wife!" squalled my parrot, raising his yellow feathers.

Under the influence of this cry the thought entered my head that Urbenin might really kill his wife.

Falling asleep, I dreamed of murders.

My nightmare was suffocating and painful. . . . It appeared to me that my hands were stroking something cold, and I had only to open my eyes to see a corpse. I dreamed that Urbenin was standing at the head of my bed, looking at me with imploring eyes.

CHAPTER XIX

SOURCES

AFTER the night that is described above a calm set in.

I remained at home, only allowing myself to leave the house or ride about on business. Heaps of work had accumulated, therefore it was impossible for me to be dull. From morning till night I sat at my writing-table scribbling, or examining people who had fallen into my magisterial claws. I was no longer drawn to Karnéevka, the Count's estate.

I thought no more of Olga. That which falls from the load is lost; and she was just what had fallen from my load and was, as I thought, irrecoverably lost. I thought no more about her and did not want to think about her.

"Silly, vicious trash!" I said to myself whenever her memory arose in my mind in the midst of my strenuous work.

Occasionally, however, when I lay down to sleep or when I awoke in the morning, I remembered various moments of our acquaintance, and the short connexion I had had with Olga. I remembered the "Stone Grave," the little house in the wood in which "the girl in red" lived, the road to Tenevo, the meeting in the grotto . . . and my heart began to beat faster. . . . I experienced bitter heartache. . . . But it was not for long. The bright memories were soon obliterated under the weight of the gloomy ones. What poetry of the past could withstand the filth of the present? And now, when I had finished with Olga, I looked upon this "poetry" quite differently to formerly. . . . Now I looked upon it as an optical illusion, a lie, hypocrisy . . . and it lost half its charm in my eyes.

The Count had become quite repugnant to me. I was glad not to see him, and I was always angry when his moustachioed face rose timidly to my mind. Every day he sent me letters in which he implored me not to sulk but to come to see the no longer "solitary hermit." Had I listened to his letters, I would have been doing a displeasure to myself.

"It's finished!" I thought. "Thank God! . . . It bored me. . . ."

I decided to break off all connexion with the Count, and this decision did not cost me the slightest struggle. Now I was not at all the same man that I had been three weeks before, when after the quarrel about Pshekhotsky I could scarcely bring myself to sit at home. There was no attraction now.

Sitting always at home bored me at last, and I wrote to Doctor Pavel Ivanovich, asking him to come and have a chat. For some reason I received no reply to this letter, so I wrote another. But the second received the same answer as the first. Evidently dear "Screw" pretended to be angry. . . . The poor fellow having received a refusal from Nadenka Kalinin, looked upon me as the cause of his misfortune. He had the right to be angry, and if he had ever been angry before it was merely because he did not know how to.

"When had he time to learn?" I thought, being perplexed at not receiving answers to my letters.

In the third week of obstinate seclusion in my own house the Count paid me a visit. Having scolded me for not riding over to see him nor sending him answers to his letters, he stretched himself out on the sofa and before he began to snore he spoke on his favourite theme—on women.

"I understand," he began languidly, screwing up his eyes and placing his hands under his head, "that you are delicate and susceptible. You don't come to me from fear of breaking into our duet . . . interfering. . . . An unwelcome guest is worse than a Tartar, a guest during the honeymoon is worse than a horned devil. I understand you. But, my dear friend, you forget that you are a friend and not a guest, that you are loved, esteemed. By your presence you would only complete the harmony. . . . And what harmony, my dear brother! A harmony that I am unable to describe to you!"

The Count pulled his hands out from under his head and began to wave them about.

"I myself am unable to understand if I am living happily or not. The devil himself would not be able to understand it. There are certainly moments when one would give half one's life for a 'bis,' but on the other hand there are days when one paces the rooms from corner to corner, as if beside oneself and ready to cry. . . ."

"For what reason?"

"Brother, I can't understand that Olga. She's a sort of ague and not a woman. In ague one has either fever or shivering fits. That's how she is; five changes every day. She is either gay or so dull that she swallows her tears and prays. . . . Sometimes she loves me, sometimes she doesn't. There are moments when she caresses me as no woman has ever caressed me in my whole life. But sometimes it is like this: You awake unexpectedly, you open your eyes, and you see a face turned on you . . . such a terrible, such a savage face . . . a face that is all distorted with malignancy and aversion. . . . When one sees such a thing all the enchantment vanishes. . . . And she often looks at me in that way. . . ."

"With aversion?"

"Well, yes! . . . I can't understand it. . . . She swears that she came to me only for love, and still hardly a night passes that I do not see that face. How is it to be explained? I begin to think, though of course I don't want to believe it, that she can't bear me and has given herself to me for those rags which I buy for her now. She's terribly fond of rags! She's capable of standing before the mirror from morning to evening in a new frock; she is capable of crying for days and nights about a spoilt flounce. . . . She's terribly vain. What chiefly pleases her in me is that I'm a Count. She would never have loved me had I not been a Count. Never a dinner or supper passes that she does not reproach me with tears in her eyes, for not surrounding myself with aristocratic society. You see, she would like to reign in that society. . . . A strange girl!"

The Count fixed his dim eyes on the ceiling and became pensive. I noticed, to my great astonishment, that this time, as an exception, he was sober. This struck and even touched me.

"You are quite normal to-day," I said. "You are not drunk, and you don't ask for vodka. What's the meaning of this dream?"

"Yes, so it is! I had no time to drink, I've been thinking. . . . I must tell you, Serezha, I'm seriously in love; it's no joke. I am terribly fond of her. It's quite natural, too. . . . She's a rare woman, not of the ordinary sort, to say nothing of her appearance. Not much intellect, to be sure, but what feeling, elegance, freshness! She can't be compared with my former Amalias, Angelicas, and Grushas, whose love I have enjoyed till now. She's something from another world, a world I do not know."

"Philosophizing!" I laughed.

"I'm captivated, I've almost fallen in love! But now I see it is useless to try to square a naught. It was only a mask that raised false expectations in me. The pink cheeks of innocence proved to be rouge, the kiss of love—the request to buy a new frock. . . . I took her into my house like a wife, and she behaves like a mistress who is paid with money. But it's enough now. I am restraining my soul's expectations, and am beginning to see in Olga a mistress. . . . Enough!"

"Well, why not? How about the husband?"

"The husband? Hm! . . . What do you think he's about?"

"I think it is impossible to imagine a more unhappy man."

"You think that? Quite uselessly. . . . He's such a scoundrel, such a rascal, that I am not at all sorry for him. . . . A rascal can never be unhappy, he'll always find his way out."

"Why do you abuse him in that way?"

"Because he's a rogue. You know that I esteemed him, that I trusted him as a friend . . . I and you too—in general everybody considered him an honest, respectable man who was incapable of cheating. Meanwhile he has been robbing, plundering me! Taking advantage of his position of bailiff, he disposed of my property as he liked. The only things he did not take were those that could not be moved from their places."

I, who knew Urbenin to be a man in the highest degree honest and disinterested, jumped up as if I had been stung when I heard these words spoken by the Count, and went up to him.

"Have you caught him in the act of stealing?" I asked.

"No, but I know of his thievish tricks from trustworthy sources."

"May I ask from what sources?"

"You needn't be uneasy. I would not accuse a man without cause. Olga has told me all about him. Even before she became his wife she saw with her own eyes what loads of slaughtered fowls and geese he sent to town. She saw how my geese and fowls were sent as presents to a certain benefactor where his son, the schoolboy, lodged. More than that, she saw flour, millet and lard being dispatched there. Admitted that all these are trifles, but did these trifles belong to him? Here we have not a question of value but of principle. Principles were trespassed against. There's more, sir! She saw in his cupboard packets of money. In answer to her question whose money it was and where he had got it, he begged her not to mention to anybody that he had money. My dear fellow, you know he's as poor as a church mouse! His salary is scarcely sufficient for his board. Can you explain to me where this money came from?"

"And you, stupid fool, believe this little vermin?" I cried, stirred to the depths of my soul. "She is not satisfied with having run away from him and disgraced him in the eyes of the whole district. She must now betray him! What an amount of meanness is contained in that small and fragile body! Fowls, geese, millet. . . . Master, master! Your political economistic feelings, your agricultural stupidity are offended that at holiday time he sent a present of a slaughtered bird which the foxes or polecats would have eaten, if it had not been killed, and given away, but have you even once checked the huge accounts that Urbenin has handed in? Have you ever counted up the thousands and the tens of thousands? No? Then what is the use of talking to you? You are stupid and a beast. You would be glad to incriminate the husband of your mistress, but you don't know how!"

"My connexion with Olga has nothing to do with the matter. If he's her husband or not her husband is all one, but since he has robbed me, I must plainly call him a thief. But let us leave this roguery alone. Tell me, is it honest or dishonest to receive a salary and for whole days to lie about dead drunk? He is drunk every day. There wasn't a single day that I did not see him reeling about! Low and disgusting! Decent people don't act in that way."

"It's just because he's decent that he gets drunk," I said.

"You have a kind of passion for taking the part of such gentlemen. But I have decided to be unmerciful. I paid him off to-day and told him to clear out and make room for another. My patience is exhausted!"

I considered it unnecessary to try to convince the Count that he was unjust, unpractical and stupid. It was not for me to defend Urbenin against the Count.

Five days later I heard that Urbenin with his schoolboy son and his little daughter had gone to live in the town. I was told that he drove to town drunk, half dead, and that he had twice fallen out of the cart. The schoolboy and Sasha had cried all the way.

CHAPTER XX

THEY ARE VENAL!

SHORTLY after Urbenin had left, I was obliged to go to the Count's estate, quite against my will. One of the Count's stables had been broken into at night and several valuable saddles had been carried off by the thieves. The examining magistrate, that is I, had been informed and *nolens-volens,* I was obliged to go there.

I found the Count drunk and angry. He was wandering about the rooms seeking a refuge from his melancholy but could not find one.

"I am worried by that Olga!" he said waving his hand. "She got angry with me this morning and she left the house threatening to drown herself! And, as you see, there are no signs of her yet. I know she won't drown herself. Still, it is nasty of her. Yesterday, all day long, she was rubbing her eyes and breaking crockery; the day before she over-ate herself with chocolate. The devil only knows what such natures are!"

I comforted the Count as well as I could and sat down to dinner with him.

"No, it's time to give up such child-ishness," he kept mumbling during dinner. "It's high time, for it is all stupid and ridiculous. Besides, I must also confess she is beginning to bore me with her sudden changes. I want something quiet, orderly, modest, you know—something like Nadenka Kalinin . . . a splendid girl!"

After dinner when I was walking in the garden I met the "drowned girl." When she saw me she became very red and (a strange woman) she began to laugh with joy. The shame on her face was mingled with pleasure, sorrow with happiness. For a moment she looked at me askance, then she rushed towards me and hung on my neck without saying a word.

"I love you!" she whispered, clinging to my neck. "I have been so sad without you. I should have died if you had not come."

I embraced her and silently led her to one of the summer-houses. Ten minutes later when parting from her, I took out of my pocket a twenty-five-rouble note and handed it to her. She opened her eyes wide.

"What is that for?"

"I am paying you for to-day's love."

Olga did not understand and continued to look at me with astonishment.

"You see, there are women who love for money," I explained. "They are venal. They must be paid for with money. Take it! If you take money from others why don't you want to take anything from he? I wish for no favours!"

Olga did not understand my cynicism in insulting her in this way. She did not know life as yet, and she did not understand the meaning of "venal women."

CHAPTER XXI

THAT LOUD LAUGH

It was a fine August day.

The sun warmed us in summer, and the blue sky fondly enticed you to wander far afield, but the air already bore presages of autumn. In the green foliage of the pensive forest the worn-out leaves were already assuming golden tints and the darkening fields looked melancholy and sad.

A dull presentiment of inevitable autumn weighed heavily on us all. It was not difficult to foresee the nearness of a catastrophe. The roll of thunder and the rain must soon come to refresh the sultry atmosphere. It is sultry before a thunderstorm when dark leaden clouds approach in the sky, and moral sultriness was oppressing us all. It was apparent in everything—in our movements, in our smiles, in our speech.

I was driving in a light wagonette. The daughter of the Justice of the Peace, Nadinka, was sitting beside me. She was white as snow, her chin and lips trembled as they do before tears, her deep eyes were full of sorrow, while all the time she laughed and tried to appear very gay.

In front and behind us a number of vehicles of all sorts, of all times, of all sizes were moving in the same direction. Ladies and men on horseback were riding on either side. Count Karnéev, clad in a green shooting costume that looked more like a buffoon's than a sportsman's, bending slightly forward and to one side, galloped about unmercifully on his black horse. Looking at his bent body and at the expression of pain that constantly appeared on his lean face, one could have thought that he was riding for the first time. A new double-barrelled gun was slung across his back, and at his side he had a game-bag in which a wounded woodcock tossed about.

Olga Urbenin was the ornament of the cavalcade. Seated on a black horse, which the Count had given her, dressed in a black riding-habit, with a white feather in her hat, she no longer resembled that "girl in red" who had met us in the wood only a few months before. Now there was something majestic, something of the *grande dame* in her figure. Each flourish of her whip, each smile was calculated to look aristocratic and majestic. In her movements, in her smiles there was something provocative, something incendiary. She held her head high in a foppishly arrogant manner, and from the height of her mount poured contempt on the whole company, as if in disdain of the loud remarks that were sent after her by our virtuous ladies. Coquetting with her impudence and her position "at the Count's," she seemed to defy everybody, just as if she did not know that the Count was already tired of her, and was only awaiting the moment when he could disentangle himself from her.

"The Count wants to send me away!" she said to me with a loud laugh when the cavalcade rode out of the yard. Therefore she knew her position and she understood it.

But why that loud laugh? I looked at her and was perplexed. Where could this dweller in the forests have found so much push? Where had she found time to sit her horse with so much grace, to move her nostrils proudly, and to show off with commanding gestures?

"A depraved woman is like a swine,"

Doctor Pavel Ivanovich said to me. "If you set her down to table she puts her legs on it."

But his explanation was too simple. Nobody could be more infatuated with Olga than I was, and I was the first to be ready to throw stones at her; still, the uneasy voice of truth whispered to me that this was not push nor the swagger of a prosperous and satisfied woman, but the despairing presentiment of the near and inevitable catastrophe.

We were returning from the shoot to which we had gone early in the morning. The sport had been bad. Near the marshes, on which we had set great hopes, we met a party of sportsmen, who told us the game was wild. Three woodcocks and one duckling was all the game we were able to send to the other world as the whole result of ten guns. At last one of the lady riders had an attack of toothache and we were obliged to hurry back. We returned along a good road that passed through the fields on which the sheaves of newly reaped rye were looking yellow against the background of the dark, gloomy forests. . . . Near the horizon the church and houses of the Count's estate gleamed white. To their right the mirror-like surface of the lake stretched out wide, and to the left the "Stone Grave" rose darkly. . .

"What a terrible woman!" Nadinka whispered to me every time Olga came up to our wagonette. "What a terrible woman! She's as bad as she's pretty! . . How long ago is it since you were best man at her wedding? She has not had time to wear out her wedding shoes, and she is already wearing another man's silk and is flaunting in another man's diamonds. If she has such instincts it

would have been more tactful had she waited a year or two. . . ."

"She's in a hurry to live! She has no time to wait!" I sighed.

"Do you know what has become of her husband?"

"I hear he is drinking. . . ."

"Yes. . . . The day before yesterday father was in town and saw him driving in a droshky. His head was hanging to one side, he was without a hat, and his face was dirty. . . . He's a lost man! He's terribly poor, I hear: they have nothing to eat, the flat is not paid for. Poor little Sasha is for days without food. Father described all this to the Count. . . . You know the Count! He is honest, kind, but he is not fond of thinking about anything, or reasoning. 'I'll send him a hundred roubles,' he said. And he did it at once. I don't think he could have insulted Urbenin more than by sending this money. . . . He'll feel insulted by the Count's gift and will drink all the more."

"Yes, the Count is stupid," I said. "He might have sent him the money through me, and in my name."

"He had no right to send him money! Have I the right to feed you if I am strangling you, and you hate me?"

"That is quite true. . . ."

We were silent and pensive. . . . The thought of Urbenin's fate was always very painful to me; now when his ruined wife was caracoling before my eyes, this thought aroused in me a whole train of sad reflections. . . . What would become of him and of his children? In what way would she end? In what moral puddle would this pitiful, puny Count end his days?

The creature seated next to me was the only one who was respectable and worthy of esteem. There were only two people in our district whom I was capable of liking and respecting, and who alone had the right of turning from me because they stood higher than I did. . . . These were Nadezhda Kalinin and Doctor Pavel Ivanovich. . . . what awaited them?

"Nadezhda Nikolaevna," I said to her, "quite without wishing it, I have caused you no little sorrow, and less than anybody else have I the right to expect your confidence. But I swear to you nobody will understand you as well as I can. Your sorrow is my sorrow, your joy is my joy. If I ask you a question, don't suspect it is from idle curiosity. Tell me, my dear, why do you allow this pigmy Count to approach you? What prevents you from sending him away and not listening to his abominable amiabilities? His courting is no honour to a respectable woman! Why do you give these scandalmongers the right to couple your name with his?"

Nadinka looked at me with her bright eyes, and evidently reading sincerity in my face, she smiled gaily.

"What do they say?" she asked.

"They say your papa and you are trying to catch the Count, and that in the end you'll find the Count is only pulling your leg."

"They speak so because they don't know the Count!" Nadinka flared up. "The shameless slanderers! They are used to seeing only the bad side of people. . . . The good is inaccessible for their understanding."

"And have you found the good in him?"

"Yes, I have found it! You are the first who ought to know. I would not have let him approach me if I had not been certain of his honourable intentions!"

"Consequently your affairs have already reached 'honourable intentions,' " I said with astonishment. "Soon! . . . And on what are they based—these honourable intentions?"

"Do you wish to know?" she asked, and her eyes sparkled. "Those scandalmongers do not lie: I wish to marry him! Don't look so surprised, and don't laugh! You will say that to get married without love is dishonest and so on. It has already been said a thousand times, but . . . what am I to do? To feel that one is a useless bit of furniture in this world is very hard. . . . It's hard to live without an object. . . . When this man, whom you dislike so much, will have made me his wife, I shall have an object in life. . . . I will improve him, I will teach him to leave off drinking. I will teach him to work. . . . Look at him! He does not look like a man now, and I will make a man of him."

"Et cetera, et cetera," I said. "You will take care of his enormous fortune, you will do acts of charity. . . . The whole of the district will bless you, and will look upon you as a good angel sent down to comfort the miserable. . . . You will be the mother and the educator of his children. . . . Yes, a great work indeed! You are a clever girl, but you reason like a schoolgirl!"

"My idea may be worthless, it may be ludicrous and naïve, but I live by it. . . . Under its influence I have become well and gay. . . . Do not disenchant me! Let me disenchant myself, but not now, at some other time . . . afterwards, in the distant future. . . . Let us change the subject!"

"Just one more indiscreet question! Do you expect him to propose?"

"Yes. . . . To judge by the note I received from him to-day, my fate will be decided this evening . . . to-day. . . . He writes that he has something very important to say to me. . . . The happiness of the whole of his life depends upon my answer."

"Thank you for your frankness," I said.

The meaning of the note that Nadia had received was quite clear to me. A base proposal awaited the poor girl. I decided to save her from that ordeal.

"We have already arrived at our wood," the Count said, coming up to our wagonette. "Nadezhda Nikolaevna, would you not wish to make a halt here?"

And without waiting for an answer he clapped his hands and ordered in a loud, shaky voice:

"Ha-a-lt!"

We settled ourselves down in the skirts of the wood. The sun had sunk behind the trees, illuminating with purple and gold only the summits of the very highest alders and playing on the golden cross of the Count's church that could be seen in the distance. Flocks of frightened orioles and sparrow hawks soared over our heads. One of the men fired into them, alarming this feathered kingdom, still more, which aroused an indefatigable bird concert. This sort of concert has its charms in the spring and summer, but when you feel the approach of the cold autumn, in the air, it only irritates the nerves and reminds one of their near migration.

The coolness of evening spread from the dense forest. The ladies' noses became blue and the chilly Count began rubbing his hands. Nothing at that moment could be more appropriate than the odour of charcoal in the samovars and the clatter of the tea service. One-eyed Kuz'ma, puffing and panting and stumbling about in the long grass, dragged forward a case of cognac. We began to warm ourselves.

A long outing in the fresh cool air acts on the appetite better than any appetizing drops, and after it the balyk, the caviar, the roast partridge and the other viands were as caressing to the sight as roses are on an early spring morning.

"You are wise to-day," I said to the Count as I helped myself to a slice of balyk. "Wise as you have never been before. It would have been difficult to arrange things better. . . ."

"We have arranged it together, the Count and I," Kalinin said with a giggle as he winked towards the coachmen, who were getting the hampers and baskets of provisions, wines and crockery out of the vehicles. "The little picnic will be a great success. . . . Towards the end there will be champagne!"

On this occasion the face of the Justice of the Peace shone with satisfaction as it had never shone before. Did he not expect that in the evening his Nadinka would have a proposal made to her? Did he not have the champagne prepared in order to drink the health of the young couple? I looked attentively at his face and, as usual, I could read nothing there but careless satisfaction, satiety, and the stupid self-importance that was suffused over the whole of his portly figure.

We fell upon the *hors d'œuvres* gaily.

Only two of the guests looked with indifference on the luxurious viands that were spread out on carpets before us: these two were Olga and Nadezhda Kalinin. The first was standing to one side leaning against the back of a wagonette, motionless and silently gazing at the game-bag that the Count had thrown on the ground. In the game-bag a wounded woodcock was moving about. Olga watched the movements of the unfortunate bird and seemed to be expecting its death.

Nadia was sitting next to me and looked with indifference on the gaily chewing mouths.

"When will all this be over?" her tired eyes said.

I offered her a sandwich with caviar. She thanked me and put it to one side. She evidently did not wish to eat.

"Olga Nikolaevna, why don't you sit down?" the Count called to Olga.

Olga did not answer but continued to stare as immovable as a statue, looking at the bird.

"What heartless people there are," I said, going up to Olga. "Is it possible that you, a woman, are capable of watching with indifference the suffering of this woodcock? Instead of looking at his contortions, it would be better if you ordered it to be dispatched."

"Others suffer; let him suffer too," Olga answered, frowning, without looking at me.

"Who else is suffering?"

"Leave me in peace!" she said hoarsely. "I am not disposed to speak to you to-day . . . nor with your friend, that fool the Count! Go away from me!"

She glanced at me with eyes that were full of wrath and tears. Her face was pale, her lips trembled.

"What a change!" I said as I lifted up the game-bag and wrung the woodcock's neck. "What a tone! I am astounded! Quite astounded!"

"Leave me in peace, I tell you! I'm not in the humour for jokes!"

"What's the matter with you, my enchantress?"

Olga looked at me from head to foot and turned her back on me.

"Only depraved and venal women are spoken to in that tone," she continued. "You consider me such an one . . . well, then, go to those saints! . . . I am worse and baser than any other here. . . . When you were driving with that virtuous Nadinka you were afraid to look at me. . . . Well, then, go to her! What are you waiting for? Go!"

"Yes, you are worse and baser than any other here," I said, feeling that I was gradually being mastered by rage. "Yes, you are depraved and venal."

"Yes, I remember how you offered me damned money. . . . Then I did not know its meaning; now I understand. . . ."

Rage mastered me completely. And this rage was as strong as the love had been that at one time was beginning to be born in me for "the girl in red." . . . And who could—what stone could have remained indifferent? I saw before me beauty that had been cast by merciless fate into the mire. No mercy was shown to either youth, beauty or grace. . . . Now, when this woman appeared to me more beautiful than ever, I felt what a loss nature had sustained in her person, and my soul was filled with painful anger at the injustice of fate and the order of things. . . .

In moments of anger I am unable to control myself. I do not know what more Olga would have had to hear from me if she had not turned her back upon me and gone away. She walked slowly towards the trees and soon disappeared behind them. . . . It appeared to me that she was crying. . . .

"Ladies and gentlemen," I heard Kalinin making a speech. "On this day when we all have met for . . . for . . . in order to unite . . . we are assembled here, we are all acquainted with each other, we are all enjoying ourselves and this long desired union we owe to nobody else but to our luminary, to the star of our province. . . . Count, don't get confused. . . . The ladies understand of whom I am speaking. . . . He, he he! Well, ladies and gentlemen, let us continue. As we owe all this to our enlightened, to our youthful . . . youthful . . . Count Karnéev, I propose that we drink this glass to . . . But who is driving this way? Who is it?"

A calash was driving from the direction of the Count's house towards the clearing where we were seated.

"Who can it be?" the Count said in astonishment, turning his field glass on the calash. "Hm! . . . strange! . . . It must be someone passing by. . . . Oh, no! I see Kaetan Kazimirovich's face. . . . With whom is he?"

Suddenly the Count sprang up as if he had been stung. His face became deadly pale, and the field glass fell from his hand. His eyes strayed around like the eyes of an entrapped mouse, and they rested sometimes on me, sometimes on Nadia, as if looking for aid. Not

everybody noticed his confusion as the attention of most was directed on the approaching calash.

"Serezha, come here for a minute!" he whispered to me, seizing hold of my arm and leading me to one side. "Golubchek, I implore you as a friend, as the best of men! . . . No questions, no interrogating glances, no astonishment! I will tell you all afterwards! I swear that not an iota will remain a secret from you! . . . It is such a misfortune in my life, such a misfortune, that I am unable to find words to express it! You will know all, but no questions now! Help me!"

Meanwhile the calash came nearer and nearer. . . . At last it stopped, and the Count's stupid secret became the property of the whole district. Pshekhotsky, clad in a new unbleached silk suit, panting and smiling, crawled out of the calash. After him a young lady of about three-and-twenty sprang out adroitly. She was a tall, graceful, fair woman with regular but not sympathetic features, and with dark blue eyes. I only remember those dark blue expressionless eyes, a powdered nose, a heavy, luxurious dress and several massive bracelets on each arm. . . . I remember that the scent of the evening dampness and the spilt cognac had to give way before the penetrating odour of some sort of perfume.

"What a numerous party!" the stranger said in broken Russian. "It must be very gay! How do you do, Alexis?"

She went up to Alexis and offered him her cheek, which the Count smacked hastily and glanced uneasily at his guests.

"My wife, let me introduce her!" he

mumbled. "And these, Zosia, are my good friends. . . . Hm, hm! . . . I've a cough!"

"And I have only just arrived! Kaetan advised me to rest! But I said: 'Why should I rest sinçe I slept the whole way here! I would sooner go to the shooting party!' I dressed and here I am. . . . Kaetan, where are my cigarettes?"

Pshekhotsky sprang forward and handed the fair lady her golden cigarette case.

"And this is my wife's brother . . ." the Count continued to mumble, pointing at Pshekhotsky. "Why don't you help me?" and he gave me a poke in the ribs. "Help me out, for God's sake!"

I have been told that Kalinin fainted, and that Nadia, who wished to help him, could not rise from her seat. I have been told many got into their vehicles and drove away. All this I did not see. I remember that I went into the wood, and searching for a footpath, without looking in front, I went where my feet led me.*

When I came out of the wood, bits of clay were hanging to my feet, and I was covered with dirt. I had probably been obliged to jump over brooks, but I could not remember this fact. It seemed to me as though I had been severely beaten with sticks; I felt so weary and exhausted. I ought to have gone to the Count's stable yard, mounted my Zorka and ridden away. But I did not do so, and went home on foot. I could not bring myself to see the Count or his accursed estate.*

.   .   .   .   .

My road led along the banks of the lake. That watery monster was already beginning to roar out its evening song. High waves with white crests covered the whole of its vast extent. In the air there was noise and rumbling. A cold, damp wind penetrated to my very bones. To the left lay the angry lake; from the right came the monotonous noise of the austere forest. I felt myself alone with nature as if I had been confronted with it. It appeared as if the whole of its wrath, the whole of these noises and roars, was directed only on my head. In other circumstances I might have felt timidity, but now I scarcely noticed the giants that surrounded me. What was the wrath of nature compared with the storm that was raging within me? †

CHAPTER XXII

WHY DID I KILL IT?

WHEN I reached home I fell upon my bed without undressing.

"Shameless eyes, again he has bathed in the lake in all his clothes!" grumbled Polycarp as he pulled off my wet and

---

* At this point of Kamyshev's manuscript a hundred lines have been effaced.—A. Ch.

* At this place of the manuscript, a pretty girl's face, with an expression of horror on it, is drawn in pen and ink. All that is written below it has been carefully blotted out. The upper half of the next page is also scratched out and only one word: "temple," can be deciphered through the dense ink blots.—A. Ch.

† Here again there are erasures.

—A. Ch.

dirty garments. "Again a punishment for me! Again we have the noble, the educated, worse than any chimney-sweep. . . . I don't know what they taught you in the 'versity!"

I, who could not bear the human voice or man's face, wanted to shout at Polycarp that he should leave me in peace, but the words died away on my lips. My tongue was as enfeebled and powerless as the rest of my body. Though it was painful for me, still I was obliged to let Polycarp pull off all my clothes, even to my wet underlinen.

"He might turn round at least," my servant grumbled as he rolled me over from side to side like a small doll. "To-morrow I'll give warning! Never again . . . for no amount of money! I, old fool, have had enough of this! May the devil take me if I remain any longer!"

The fresh warm linen did not warm or calm me. I trembled so much with rage and fear, that my very teeth chattered. My fear was inexplicable. I was not frightened by apparitions or by spectres risen from the grave, not even by the portrait of Pospelov, my predecessor, which was hanging just above my head. He never took his lifeless eyes off my face, and seemed to wink at me. But I was quite unaffected when I looked at him. My future was not brilliant, but all the same I could say with great probability that there was nothing that threatened me, that there were no black clouds near. Death was not to be expected soon; I had no terrible diseases, and I took no heed of personal misfortunes. . . . What did I fear, then, and why did my teeth chatter?

I could not even understand my wrath . .

The Count's "secret" could not have enraged me so greatly. I had nothing to do with the Count, nor with the marriage, which he had concealed from me.

It only remains to explain the condition of my soul at that time by fatigue and nervous derangement. That is the only explanation I can find.

When Polycarp left the room I covered myself up to the head and wanted to sleep. It was dark and quiet. The parrot moved about restlessly in its cage, and the regular ticking of the hanging clock in Polycarp's room could be heard through the wall. Peace and quiet reigned everywhere else. Physical and moral exhaustion overpowered me, and I began to doze. . . . I felt that a certain weight gradually fell from me, and hateful images melted into mist. . . . I remember I even began to dream. I dreamed that on a bright winter morning I was walking in the Nevsky of Petersburg, and, having nothing to do, looked into the shop windows. My heart was light and gay. . . . I had not to hurry anywhere. I had nothing to do, I was absolutely free. The consciousness that I was far from my village, from the Count's estate and from the cold and sullen lake, made me feel all the more peaceful and gay. I stopped before one of the largest windows and began to examine ladies' hats. The hats were familiar to me. . . . I had seen Olga in one of them, Nadia in another; a third I had seen on the day of the shooting party on the fair-haired head of that Zosia, who had arrived so unexpectedly. . . . Familiar faces smiled at me under the hats. . . . When I wanted to say something to them they all three blended together into one large red face. This face moved its eyes angrily and stuck out its tongue. . . . Somebody pressed my neck from behind. . . .

"The husband killed his wife!" the red face shouted.

I shuddered, cried out, and jumped out of my bed as if I had been stung. I had terrible palpitations of the heart, a cold sweat came out on my brow.

"The husband killed his wife!" the parrot repeated again. "Give me some sugar! How stupid you are! Fool!"

"It was only the parrot!" I said to calm myself as I got into bed again. "Thank God!"

I heard a monotonous murmur. . . . It was the rain pattering on the roof. . . . The clouds I had seen when walking on the banks of the lake had now covered the whole sky. There were slight flashes of lightning that lighted up the portrait of the late Pospelov. . . . The thunder rumbled just over my bed. . . ."

"The last thunderstorm of this summer," I thought.

I remembered one of the first storms. . . . Just the same sort of thunder had rumbled overhead in the forest the first time I was in the forester's house. . . . The "girl in red" and I were standing at the window then, looking out at the pine trees that were illuminated by the lightning. Dread shone in the eyes of that beautiful creature. She told me her mother had been killed by lightning, and that she herself was thirsting for an effective death. . . . She wanted to be dressed like the richest lady of the district. She understood that luxurious dress

suited her beauty. And, conscious of her vain majesty, she wanted to mount to the top of the "Stone Grave" and there meet an effective death.

Her wish had . . . though not on the sto . . .*

Losing all hope of falling asleep, I rose and sat down on the bed. The quiet murmur of the rain gradually changed into the angry roar I was so fond of hearing when my soul was free from dread and wrath. . . . Now this roar appeared to me to be ominous. One clap of thunder succeeded the other without intermission.

"The husband killed his wife!" croaked the parrot.

Those were its last words. . . . Closing my eyes in pusillanimous fear, I groped my way in the dark to the cage and hurled it into a corner. . . .

"May the devil take you!" I cried, when I heard the clatter of the falling cage and the squeak of the parrot.

Poor, noble bird! That flight into the corner cost it dear. The next day the cage contained only a cold corpse. Why did I kill it? If its favourite phrase about a husband who kills his wife remin . . .†

My predecessor's mother when she gave up the lodging to me made me pay

---

* Here, unfortunately, there are again erasures. It is evident Kamyshev blotted out not at the time of writing but afterwards. At the end of the novel I will draw *special* attention to these erasures.—A. Ch.

† Here nearly a whole page is carelessly blotted out. Only a few words are spared, which give no clue to the meaning of what is obliterated.—A. Ch.

for the whole of the furniture, not excepting the photographs of people I did not know. But she did not take a kopeck from me for the expensive parrot. On the eve of her departure for Finland she passed the whole night taking leave of her noble bird. I remember the sobs and the lamentations that accompanied this leave-taking. I remember the tears she shed when asking me to take care of her friend until her return. I gave her my word of honour that her parrot would not regret having made my acquaintance. And I had not kept that word! I had killed the bird. I can imagine what the old woman would say if she knew of the fate of her screamer!

CHAPTER XXIII

A LETTER

SOMEBODY tapped gently at my window. The little house in which I lived stood on the high road, and was one of the first houses in the village, and I often heard a tap at my window, especially in bad weather when a wayfarer sought a night's lodging. This time it was no wayfarer who knocked at my window. I went up to the window and waited there for a flash of lightning, when I saw the dark silhouette of a tall thin man. He was standing before the window and seemed to be shivering with cold. I opened the window.

"Who is there? What do you want?" I asked.

"Sergey Petrovich, it's I" I heard a plaintive voice, such as people who are starved with cold and fright. "It's I! I've come to you, dear friend!"

To my great astonishment, I recognized in the plaintive voice of the dark silhouette the voice of my friend Doctor Pavel Ivanovitch. This visit of "Screw's," who led a regular life and went to bed before twelve, was quite incomprehensible. What could have caused him to change his rules and appear at my house at two o'clock in the night, and in such weather too?"

"What do you want?" I asked, at the same time in the bottom of my heart sending this unexpected guest to the devil.

"Forgive me, golubchik. . . . I wanted to knock at the door, but your Polycarp is sure to be sleeping like a dead man now, so I decided to tap at the window."

"But what do you want?"

Pavel Ivanovich came close up to my window and mumbled something incomprehensible. He was trembling, and looked like a drunken man.

"I am listening!" I said, losing my patience.

"You . . . you are angry, I see; but . . . if you only knew all that has happened you would cease to be angry at your sleep being disturbed by visitors at an unseemly hour. It's no time for sleep now. Oh, my God, my God! I have lived in the world for thirty years, and to-day is the first time I am terribly unhappy! I am unhappy, Sergey Petrovich!"

"Ach! but what has happened? And what have I to do with it? I myself can scarcely stand on my legs. . . . I can't be bothered about others!"

"Sergey Petrovich!" Screw said in a plaintive voice, stretching out towards my head his hand wet with rain, "Honest man! My friend!"

And then I heard a man crying. The doctor wept.

"Pavel Ivanovich, go home!" I said after a short silence. "1 can't talk with you now. . . . I am afraid of my own mood, and of yours. We won't understand each other. . . ."

"My dear friend!" the doctor said in an imploring voice, "Marry her."

"You've gone mad!" I said, and banged the window to. . . .

First the parrot, then the doctor suffered from my mood. I did not ask him to come in, and I slammed the window in his face. Two rude and indecorous sallies for which I would have challenged anybody, even a woman, to a duel.* But meek and good-natured "Screw" had no idea about duels. He did not know what it is to be angry.

About two minutes later there was a flash of lightning, and glancing out of the window I saw the bent figure of my guest. His pose this time was one of supplication, of expectancy, the pose of a beggar watching for alms. He was probably waiting for me to pardon him. and to allow him to say what he had to communicate.

Fortunately my conscience was moved; I was sorry for myself, sorry that nature had implanted in me so much violence and meanness. My base

---

* The last sentence is written above some erased lines in which, however, one can decipher: "would have torn his head from his shoulders and broken all the windows."—A. Ch.

soul as well as my healthy body were as hard as flint.*

I went to the window and opened it. "Come into the room!" I said.

"Never! . . . Every minute is precious! Poor Nadia has poisoned herself, and the doctor cannot leave her side. . . . With difficulty we saved the poor thing. . . . Such a misfortune! And you don't want to hear it and slam the window to!"

"Still she is alive?"

"'Still'! . . . My good friend, that is not the way to speak about misfortunes! Who could have supposed that such a clever, honest nature would want to depart this life on account of such a creature as that Count? No, my friend, it is a misfortune for men that women cannot be perfect! However clever a woman may be, with whatever perfections she may be endowed. she has still a screw in her that prevents her and other people from living. . . . For instance, let us take Nadia. . . . Why did she do it? Self-love, nothing but self-love! Unhealthy self-love! In order to wound you she conceived the idea of marrying this Count. . . . She neither wanted his money nor his title . . . she only wanted to satisfy her monstrous self-

---

* Here follows a pretentiously-plastic explanation of the spiritual endurance of the author. The sight of human affliction, blood, post-mortem examinations, etc., etc., he maintains, produce no effect on him. The whole of this passage bears the imprint of boastful *naïveté* and insincerity. It astonishes by its coarseness, and I have deleted it. As a characterization of Kamyshev it has no importance.—A. Ch.

love. . . . Suddenly a failure! You know that *his* wife has arrived. . . . It appears that this debauchee is married. . . . And people say that women are more enduring, that they know how to suffer better than men! Where is there endurance here, when such a miserable cause makes them snatch up sulphur matches? This is not endurance, it is vanity!"

"You will catch cold. . . ."

"What I have just seen is worse than any cold.   Those eyes, that pallor. . . . Oh! To unsuccessful love, to the unsuccessful attempt to mortify you is now added unsuccessful suicide. . . . It is difficult to imagine greater misfortunes! .   . My dear fellow, if you have but a drop of compassion, if . . . if you would see her . . . Well, why should you not go to her? You love her! Even if you do not love her, why should you not sacrifice your leisure to her? Human life is precious, and for it one can give . . . all! Save her life!"

Somebody knocked loudly at my door. I shuddered   . . My heart bled. . . . I do not believe in presentiments, but this time my alarm was not without cause. . . . Somebody was knocking at my door from without. . . .

"Who is there?" I cried out of the window.

"I come to beg your favour!"

"What do you want?"

"A letter from the Count, your Honour! There has been a murder!"

A dark figure muffled up in a sheepskin coat came to the window and, swearing at the weather, handed me a letter. . . . I hurried away from the window, lit a candle, and read the following: "For God's sake forget everything in the world and come at once! Olga has been murdered. I have lost my head and am going mad.—Yours, A. K."

Olga murdered! My head grew dizzy, and it was black before my eyes, from this short phrase. . . . I sat down on the bed and my hands fell at my sides. I was unable to reason!

"Is that you, Pavel Ivanovich?" I heard the voice of the muzhik who had been sent to me ask. "I was just going to drive to you. . . . I have a letter for you, too."

Five minutes later "Screw" and I were driving in a closed carriage toward's the Count's estate. The rain rattled on the roof of the carriage, and the whole time there were blinding flashes of lightning in front of us.

CHAPTER XXIV

ACCURSED

WE heard the roar of the lake. . . . The last act of the drama was just beginning, and two of the actors were driving to see a harrowing sight.

"Well, and what do you think awaits us?" I asked dear Pavel Ivanovich.

"I can't imagine. . . . I don't know. . . ."

"I also don't know. . . ."

"Hamlet once regretted that the Lord of heaven and earth had forbidden the sin of suicide; in like manner I regret that fate has made me a doctor. . . . I regret it deeply!"

"I fear that, in my turn, I must regret that I am an examining magistrate." I said. "If the Count has not made a mistake and confounded murder with suicide, and if Olga has really been murdered, my poor nerves will have much to suffer!"

"You can refuse this affair!"

I looked inquiringly at Pavel Ivanovich, but, of course, owing to the darkness, I could see nothing. . . . How could he know that I could refuse this affair? I was Olga's lover, but who knew it, with the exception of Olga herself and perhaps also Pshekhotsky, who had favoured me once with applause?

"Why do you think I can refuse?" I asked "Screw."

"You could fall ill, or tender your resignation. All this is not dishonourable, because there is somebody to take your place. A doctor is placed in quite other conditions."

"Only that?" I thought.

Our carriage, after a long, wearisome drive over the clayey roads, stopped at last before the porch. Two windows just above the porch were brightly illuminated. Through the one on the right side, which was in Olga's room, a dim light issued. All the other windows looked like black spots. On the stairs we met the Scops-Owl. She looked at me with her piercing little eyes, and her wrinkled face became more wrinkled in an evil, mocking smile.

Her eyes seemed to say "You have a great surprise!"

She probably thought we had come to carouse, and we did not know there was grief in the house.

"Let me draw your attention to this," I said to Pavel Ivanovich, as I pulled the cap off the old woman's head and exposed her completely bare pate. "This old witch is ninety years old, my good soul. If some day you and I had to make a post-mortem examination of her, we should arrive at very different conclusions. You would find senile atrophy of the brain, and I would assure you that she was the cleverest and the most cunning creature in the whole district. . . . The devil in petticoats!"

I was astounded when I entered the ballroom. The picture I saw there was quite unexpected. All the chairs and sofas were occupied by people. . . . Groups of people were standing about in the corners and near the windows. . . . Where had they all come from? If anybody had told me I would meet these people there, I would have laughed at him. Their presence was so improbable and out of place in the Count's house at that time, when in one of the rooms Olga was either dying or already lying dead. They were the gipsy chorus of the chief gipsy Karpov from the restaurant "London"; the same chorus which is known to the reader from one of the first chapters of this book.

When I entered the room my old friend Tina, having recognized me, left one of the groups and came towards me with a cry of joy. A smile spread over her pale and dark complexioned cheeks when I gave her my hand, and tears rose to her eyes when she wanted to tell me something. . . . Tears prevented her from speaking, and I was not able to obtain a single word from her. I turned to the other gipsies, and they explained their presence in the house in this way. In the morning the Count had sent them a telegram demanding that the whole chorus should be at the Count's estate without fail by nine o'clock that evening. In execution of this order they had taken the train and had been in this hall by eight o'clock.

"We had thought to afford pleasure

to his Excellency and his guests. . . . We know so many new songs! . . .And suddenly. . . ."

"And suddenly a muzhik arrived on horseback, with the news that a brutal murder had been committed at the shooting party and with the order to prepare a bed for Olga Nikolaevna. The muzhik was not believed, because he was as drunk as a swine, but when a noise was heard on the stairs and a black figure was borne through the dancing hall, there was no more possibility to doubt. . . ."

"And now we don't know what to do! We can't remain here. . . . When the priest comes it is time for gay people to depart. . . . Besides, all the chorus girls are alarmed and crying. . . . They can't be in the same house with a corpse. . . . We must go away, but they won't give us horses! His Excellency the Count is lying ill in bed and will not see anybody, and the servants only laugh at us when we ask for horses. . . . How can we go on foot in such weather and on such a dark night? The servants are in general terribly rude! When we asked for a samovar for our ladies they sent us to the devil. . . ."

All these complaints ended in tearful requests to my magnanimity. Could I not obtain vehicles to enable them to depart from this "accursed" house?

"If the horses are not in the paddocks, and the coachmen have not been sent somewhere, you shall get away," I said. "I'll give the order. . . ."

The poor people, dressed out in their burlesque costumes, and accustomed to coquet with their swaggering manners, looked very awkward with their sober countenances and undecided poses. My promise to get them sent to the station somewhat encouraged them. The whispers of the men turned into loud talk, and the women ceased crying.

CHAPTER XXV

STARING WILDLY

THEN I went to the Count's study, and as I passed through a whole suite of dark, unlighted rooms, I looked into one of the numerous doors. I saw a touching picture. At a table near a boiling samovar Zosia and her brother Pshekhotsky were seated. . . . Zosia, dressed in a light blouse but still wearing the same bracelets and rings, was smelling at a scent bottle and sipping tea from her cup with fastidious languor. Her eyes were red with weeping. . . . Probably the occurrences at the shooting party had shaken her nerves very much, and had spoilt her frame of mind for a long time to come. Pshekhotsky, with his usual wooden face, was lapping up his tea in large gulps from the saucer and saying something to his sister. To judge from the mentor-like expression of his face, he was trying to calm her and persuade her not to cry.

I naturally found the Count with entirely shattered nerves. This puny and flabby man looked thinner and more fallen in than ever. . . . He was pale, and his lips trembled as if with ague. His head was tied up in a white pocket-handkerchief, which exhaled a strong odour of vinegar that filled the whole room. When I entered the room he jumped up from the sofa, on which he was lying, and rushed towards me wrapped up in the folds of his dressing-gown.

"Oh! oh!" he began, trembling and in a choking voice. "Well?"

And uttering some inarticulate sounds, he pulled me by the sleeve to the sofa and, waiting till I was seated, he pressed against me like a frightened dog and began to pour out all his grievances.

"Who could have expected it? Eh? Wait a moment, golubchik, I'll cover myself up with the plaid. . . . I have fever. . . . Murdered, poor thing! And how brutally murdered! She's still alive, but the village doctor says she'll die this night. . . . A terrible day! . . . She arrived without rhyme or reason, that . . . wife of mine . . . may the devil take her! . . . That was my most unfortunate mistake, Serezha; I was married in Petersburg when drunk. I hid it from you. I was ashamed of it, but there—she has arrived, and you can see her for yourself. . . . Look and be punished. . . . Oh, the accursed weakness! Under the influence of the moment and vodka, I'm capable of doing anything you like! The arrival of my wife is the first present, the scandal with Olga the second. . . . I'm expecting a third. . . . I know what will happen next. . . . I know! I'll go mad! . . ."

Having drunk three glasses of vodka and called himself an ass, a scoundrel and a drunkard, the Count began in a whimpering voice and a confused manner to describe the drama that had taken place at the shooting party. . . . What he told me was approximately the following: About twenty or thirty minutes after I had left, when the astonishment at Zosia's arrival had somewhat subsided, and when Zosia herself, having made acquaintance with the guests, began to play the part of host-

ess, the company suddenly heard a piercing, heartrending shriek. This shriek came from the forest and was repeated four times. It was so extraordinary that the people who heard it sprang to their feet, the dogs began to bark, and the horses pricked up their ears. The shriek was unnatural, but the Count was able to recognize in it a woman's voice. . . . There were notes of despair and terror in it. . . .

Women must shriek in that way when they see a ghost, or at the sudden death of a child. . . . The alarmed guests looked at the Count; the Count looked at them. . . . For about three minutes there was the silence of the grave.

While the ladies and gentlemen looked at each other, the coachmen and lackeys rushed towards the place from which the cry had come. The first messenger of grief was the old manservant, Il'ya. He ran back to the clearing from the forest, with a pale face, dilated pupils, and wanted to say something, but breathlessness and excitement prevented him from speaking. At last, overcoming his agitation, he crossed himself and said:

"The missis has been murdered!"

"What missis? Who had murdered her?"

But Il'ya made no reply to these questions. . . . The part of the second messenger fell to the lot of a man who was not expected and whose appearance caused general surprise. Both the sudden appearance and the look of this man were astonishing. . . . When the Count saw him, and remembered that Olga was walking about in the forest, his heart sank, and from a terrible presentiment his legs gave way under him.

It was Pëtr Egorych Urbenin, the

Count's former bailiff and Olga's husband. At first the company heard heavy footsteps and the cracking of brushwood. . . . It seemed as if a bear was making his way from the forest to the clearing. Then the heavy form of unfortunate Pëtr Egorych came in sight. When he came out of the forest and saw the company assembled on the clearing, he stepped back and stopped as if he were rooted to the ground. For about two minutes he remained silent and motionless, and in this way gave the people time to examine him properly. He had his usual grey jacket on and trousers that were already well worn. He was without a hat, and his matted hair stuck to his sweaty brow and temples. . . . His face, which was usually purple and often almost blue, was now quite pale. . . . His eyes looked around senselessly, staring wildly. . . . His hands and lips trembled. . . .

But what was the most astonishing and what instantly attracted the attention of the stupefied spectators were his blood-stained hands. . . . Both his hands and shirt cuffs were thickly covered with blood, as if they had been washed in a bath of blood.

Three minutes Urbenin remained dumbfounded. and then, as if awakening from a dream, he sat down on the grass cross-legged and groaned. The dogs, scenting something unwonted, surrounded him and raised a bark. . . . Having glanced round the assembled company with dim eyes, Urbenin covered his face with both hands and again there was silence. . . .

"Olga, Olga, what have you done!" he groaned.

Heartrending sobs were torn from his breast and shook his broad shoulders.

. . . When he removed the hands from his face the whole company saw the marks of blood that they had left on his cheeks and forehead.

When he got to this place the Count waved his hands convulsively, seized a glass of vodka, drank it off, and continued:

"From that point my recollections become mixed. You can well understand all these events had so stunned me that I had lost the power of thinking. . . . I can remember nothing that happened afterwards! I only remember that the men brought some sort of a body in a torn, blood-stained dress out of the wood. . . . I could not look at it! They put it into a calash and drove off. . . . I did not hear either groans or weeping. . . . They say that the small dagger which she always carried about with her had been thrust into her side. . . . You remember it? I had given it to her. It was a blunt dagger—blunter than the edge of this glass. . . . What strength was necessary to plunge it in! Brother, I like Caucasian arms. but now may the deuce take all those arms! Tomorrow 1 will order them all to be thrown away."

The Count drank another glass of vodka and continued:

"But what a shame! What an abomination! We brought her to the house. . . . You can understand our despair, our horror, when suddenly, may the devil take all the gipsies, we heard gay singing! . . . They were all ranged in a row, singing at the top of their voices! . . . You see, they wanted to receive us with chic, but it turned out quite misplaced. . . . It was like Ivanushka-the-fool, who, meeting a funeral, became excited and shouted: "Pull away, you can't pull it over!' Yes, brother! I wanted to entertain my guests and had ordered the gipsies, and what a muddle came of it! Not gipsies ought to have been sent for but doctors and priests. And now I don't know what to do! What am I to do? I don't know any of these formalities and customs. I don't know whom to call in, for whom to send. . . . Perhaps the police ought to come, the Public Prosecutor. . . . How the devil can I know? Thank goodness, Father Jeremiah, having heard about the scandal, came to give her the Communion. I should never have thought of sending for him. I implore you, dear friend, make all the necessary arrangements! By God, I'm going mad! The arrival of my wife, the murder . . . Brr! . . . Where is my wife now? Have you seen her?"

"I've seen her. She's drinking tea with Pshekhotsky."

"With her brother, you say. . . . Pshekhotsky, he's a rogue! When I ran away from Petersburg secretly, he found out about my flight and has stuck to me. What an amount of money he has been able to squeeze out of me during the whole of this time no one can calculate!"

I had not time to talk long to the Count. I rose and went to the door.

"Listen," the Count stopped me. "I say, Serezha . . . that Urbenin won't stab me?"

"Did he stab Olga, then?"

"To be sure, he . . . I can't understand, however, how he came there! What the deuce brought him to the forest? And why just to that forest? Admitting that he hid himself there and waited for us, but how could he know

that I wanted to stop just in that place and not in any other?"

"You don't understand anything," I said. "By-the-by, once for all I must beg you. . . . If I undertake this case, please don't tell me your opinions. Have the goodness to answer my questions and nothing more."

CHAPTER XXVI

OLGA REFUSES

WHEN I left the Count I went to the room where Olga was lying. . . .*

A little blue lamp was burning in the room and faintly lighted up her face. . . . It was impossible either to read or write by its light. Olga was lying on her bed, her head bandaged up. One could only see her pale sharp nose and the eyelids that closed her eyes. At the moment I entered the room her bosom was bared and the doctors were placing a bag of ice on it.† Olga was therefore still alive. Two doctors were attending on her. When I entered, Pavel Ivanovich, screwing up his eyes, was auscultating her heart with much panting and puffing.

The district doctor, who looked a worn-out and sickly man, was sitting pensively near the bed in an arm-chair and seemed to be feeling her pulse.

---

* Here two lines are blotted out.
—A. Ch.

† I draw the reader's attention to a certain circumstance. Kamyshev, who loved on every occasion, even in his disputes with Polycarp, to descant on the condition of his soul, says not a word of the impression made on him by the sight of the dying Olga. I think this omission was intentional.—A. Ch.

Father Jeremiah, who had just finished his work, was wrapping up the cross in his stole and preparing to depart.

"Pëtr Egorych, do not grieve!" he said with a sigh and looked towards the corner of the room. "Everything is God's will. Turn for protection to God."

Urbenin was seated on a stool in a corner of the room. He was so much changed that I hardly recognized him. Want of work and drink during the last month had told as much on his clothes as on his appearance; his clothes were worn out, his face too.

The poor fellow sat there motionless, supporting his head on his fists and never taking his eyes off the bed. . . . His hands and face were still stained with blood. . . . He had forgotten to wash them. . . .

Oh, the prediction of my soul and of my poor bird!

Whenever the noble bird which I had killed screamed out his phrase about the husband who killed his wife, Urbenin's figure always arose before my mind's eye. Why? . . . I knew that jealous husbands often kill their unfaithful wives; at the same time I knew that such men as Urbenin do not kill people. . . . And I drove away the thought of the possibility of Olga being killed by her husband as something absurd.

"Was it he or not he?" I asked myself as I looked at his unhappy face.

And to speak candidly I did not give myself an affirmative answer, despite the Count's story and the blood I saw on his hands and face.

"If he had killed her he would have washed off that blood long ago," I said to myself, remembering the following proposition of a magistrate of my ac-

quaintance: "A murderer cannot bear the blood of his victim."

If I had wished to tax my memory I could have remembered many aphorisms of a similar nature, but I must not anticipate or fill my mind with premature conclusions.

"My respects!" the district doctor said to me. "I am very glad you have come. . . . Please can you tell me who is master here?"

"There is no master. . . . Chaos reigns here," I answered.

"A very good apophthegm, but it does not assist me," the district doctor answered with bitterness. "For the last three hours I have been asking, imploring to have a bottle of port or champagne sent here and not a soul has deigned to listen to my prayer! They are all as deaf as posts! They have only just brought the ice I ordered three hours ago. What does it mean? A woman is dying here, and they only seem to laugh! The Count is pleased to sit in his study drinking liqueurs, and they can't bring even a wineglass here! I wanted to send to the chemist in the town, and I was told all the horses are worn out, and there's nobody who can go as they are all drunk. . . . I wanted to send to my hospital for medicines and bandages and they favoured me with a fellow who could hardly stand on his legs. I sent him two hours ago, and what do you think? They tell me he has only just started! Is that not disgusting? They're all drunk, rude, ill-bred! . . They all seem idiots! By God, it is the first time in my life I've come across such heartless people!"

The doctor's indignation was justifiable. He had not exaggerated, rather the contrary. . . . A whole night would have been too short a time for pouring out one's gall on all the disorders and malpractices that could be found on the Count's estate. The servants were all abominable, having been demoralized by the want of work and supervision. Among them there was not a single man-servant who could not have served as a type of a servant who had lived long and feathered his nest in the Count's service.

I went off to get some wine. Having distributed three or four cuffs, I succeeded in obtaining both champagne and Valerian drops, to the unspeakable delight of the doctors. An hour later* the doctor's assistant came from the hospital bringing with him all that was necessary.

Pavel Ivanovich succeeded in pouring into Olga's mouth a tablespoon of champagne. She made an effort to swallow and groaned. Then they injected some sort of drops under the skin.

------

* I must draw the reader's attention to a very important circumstance. During from two to three hours M. Kamyshev only walks about from room to room, shares the doctor's indignation about the servants, boxes their ears to right and left, and so on. Can you recognize in him an examining magistrate? He evidently was in no hurry, and was only trying to kill time. Evidently he knew who the murderer was. Besides, there are the quite unnecessary searches made in the Scops-Owl's room and the examination of the gipsies, that appear more like banter than cross-questioning, and could only have been undertaken to pass the time.—A. Ch.

"Olga Nikolaevna!" the district doctor shouted into her ear. "Olga Ni-ko-la-evna!"

"It is difficult to expect her to regain consciousness!" Pavel Ivanovich said with a sigh. "The loss of blood has been great, besides the blow she received on the head with some blunt instrument must have caused concussion of the brain."

It is not my business to decide if there had been concussion of the brain or not, but Olga opened her eyes and asked for something to drink. . . . The stimulants had had effect.

"Now you can ask her whatever you require . . ." Pavel Ivanovich said, nudging my elbow. "Ask."

I went up to the bed. Olga's eyes were turned on me.

"Where am I?" she asked.

"Olga Nikolaevna!" I began, "do you know me?"

During several seconds Olga looked at me and then closed her eyes.

"Yes!" she groaned. "Yes!"

"I am Zinov'ev, the examining magistrate. I had the honour of being acquainted with you, and if you remember, I was best man at your wedding. . . ."

"Is it thou?" Olga whispered, stretching out her left arm. "Sit down. . . ."

"She is delirious!" Screw sighed.

"I am Zinov'ev, the magistrate," I continued. "If you remember, I was at the shooting party. How do you feel?"

"Ask essential questions!" the district doctor whispered to me. "I cannot answer for the consciousness being lasting. . . ."

"I beg you not to teach me!" I said

in an offended tone. "I know what I have to say. . . . Olga Nikolaevna," I continued, turning to her, "I beg you to remember the events of the past day. I will help you. . . . At one o'clock you mounted your horse and rode out with a large party to a shoot. . . . The shoot lasted for about four hours. . . . Then there was a halt on a clearing in the forest. . . . Do you remember?"

"And thou . . . and thou didst . . . kill . . ."

"The woodcock? After I had killed the wounded woodcock you frowned and went away from the rest of the party. . . . You went into the forest. . . .* Now try to collect all your strength and to exert your memory. During your walk in the wood you were assaulted by a person unknown to us. I ask you, as the examining magistrate, who was it?"

Olga opened her eyes and looked at me.

"Tell us the name of that man! There are three other persons in the room besides me. . . ."

Olga shook her head negatively.

"You must name him," I continued. "He will suffer a severe penalty. The law will make him pay dearly for his

brutality! He will be sent to penal servitude.* . . . I am waiting."

Olga smiled and shook her head negatively. The further examination produced no results. I was not able to obtain another word from Olga, not a single movement. At a quarter to five she passed away.

CHAPTER XXVII

WHO WAS THE MURDERER?

ABOUT seven o'clock in the morning the village elder and his assistants, whom I had sent for, arrived from the village. It was impossible to drive to the scene of the crime: the rain that had begun in the night was still pouring down in buckets. Little puddles had become lakes. The grey sky looked gloomy, and there was no promise of sunlight. The soaked trees appeared dejected with their drooping branches, and sprinkled a whole shower of large drops at every gust of wind. It was impossible to go there. Besides, it might have been useless. The trace of the crime, such as bloodstains, human footprints, etc., had probably been washed away during the night. But the formalities demanded that the scene of the crime should be examined, and I deferred this visit until after the arrival of the police, and in the meantime I made out a draft of the official report of the case, and occupied myself with the examination

---

* This avoidance of questions of the first importance could only have had one object, to gain time and to await a loss of consciousness, when Olga would be unable to name the murderer. It is a characteristic process and it is astonishing that the doctors did not set the right value on it.—A. Ch.

*At the first glance all this appears naïve. It is evident Kamyshev wanted to make Olga understand what serious consequences her declaration would have for the murderer. If the murderer was dear to her, *ergo*, she must remain silent.
—A. Ch.

of witnesses. First of all I examined the gipsies. The poor singers had passed the whole night sitting up in the ball-rooms expecting to have horses given them to convey them to the station. But horses were not provided; the servants, when asked, only sent them to the devil, warning them at the same time that his Excellency had forbidden anybody to be admitted to him. They were also not given the samovar they asked for in the morning. The more than singular and indefinite position in which they found themselves in a strange house in which a corpse was lying, the uncertainty as to when they could get away, and the damp melancholy weather had driven the gipsies, both men and women, into such a state of distress that in one night they had become thin and pale. They wandered about from room to room, evidently much alarmed and expecting some serious issue. By my examination I only increased their anxiety. First because my lengthy examination delayed their departure from the accursed house indefinitely, and secondly it alarmed them. The simple people, imagining that they were seriously suspected of the murder, began to assure me with tears in their eyes, that they were not guilty and knew nothing about the matter. Tina, seeing me as an official personage, quite forgot our former connexion, and while speaking to me trembled and almost fainted with fright like a whipped little girl. In reply to my request not to be excited, and my assurance that I saw in them nothing but witnesses, the assistants of justice, they informed me in one voice that they had never been witnesses, that they knew nothing, and that they trusted that in future God

would deliver them from all close acquaintance with judicial people.

I asked them by what road they had driven from the station, had they not passed through that part of the forest where the murder had been committed, had any member of their party quitted it for even a short time, and had they not heard Olga's heartrending shriek.* This examination led to nothing. The gipsies, alarmed by it, only sent two members of the chorus to the village to hire vehicles. The poor people wanted terribly to get away. For their misfortune there was already much talk in the village about the murder in the forest, and these swarthy messengers were looked at with suspicion; they were arrested and brought to me. It was only towards evening that the harassed chorus was able to get free from this nightmare and breathe freely, as having hired five peasants' carts at three times the proper fare, they drove away from the Count's house. Afterwards they were paid for their visit, but nobody paid them for the moral suffering that they had endured in the Count's apartments. . . .

Having examined them, I made a search in the Scops-Owl's room.† In her trunks I found quantities of all

---

* If all this was necessary for M. Kamyshev, would it not have been easier to question the coachmen who had driven the gipsies?—A. Ch.

† Why? We can admit that all this was done by the examining magistrate in a drunken or sleepy condition, but why write about it? Would it not have been better to hide from the reader these gross mistakes?—A. Ch.

sorts of old woman's rubbish, but although I looked through all the old caps and darned stockings, I found neither money nor valuables that the old woman had stolen from the Count or his guests. . . . Nor did I find the things that had been stolen from Tina some time before. . . . Evidently the old witch had another hiding-place only known to herself.

I will not give here the preliminary report I drafted about the information I had obtained or the searches I had made. . . . It was long; besides, I have forgotten most of it. I will only give a general idea of it. First of all I described the condition in which I found Olga, and I gave an account of every detail of my examination of her. By this examination it was evident that Olga was quite conscious when she answered me and purposely concealed the name of the murderer. She did not *want* that the murderer should suffer the penalty, and this inevitably led to the supposition that the criminal was near and dear to her.

The examination of her clothes, which I made together with the commissary of the rural police who arrived very soon, produced very much. . . . The jacket of her riding habit, made of velvet with a silk lining, was still moist. The right side in which there was the hole made by the dagger was saturated with blood and in places bore marks of clotted blood. . . . The loss of blood had been very great, and it was astonishing that Olga had not died on the spot. The left side was also bloodstained. The left sleeve was torn at the shoulder and at the wrist. . . . The two upper buttons were torn off, and at our examination we did not find

them. The skirt of the riding habit, made of black cashmere, was found to be terribly crumpled; it had been crumpled when they had carried Olga out of the wood to the vehicle and from the vehicle to her bed. Then it had been pulled off, rolled into a disorderly heap, and flung under the bed. It was torn at the waistband. This tear was about ten inches long and in the length, and had probably been made while she was being carried or when it was pulled off; it might also have been made during her lifetime. Olga, who did not like mending, and not knowing to whom to give the habit to be mended, might have hidden away the tear under her bodice. I don't think any signs could be seen in this of the savage rage of the criminal, on which the assistant public prosecutor laid such special emphasis in his speech at the trial. The right side of the belt and the right-hand pocket were saturated with blood. The pocket-handkerchief and the gloves, that were in this pocket, were like two formless lumps of a rusty colour. The whole of the riding-habit, to the very end of the skirt, was bespattered with spots of blood of various forms and sizes. . . . Most of them, as it was afterwards explained, were the impressions of the blood-stained fingers and palms belonging to the coachmen and lackeys who had carried Olga. . . . The chemise was bloody, especially on the right side of which there was a hole produced by the cut of an instrument. There, as also on the left shoulder of the bodice, and near the wrists there were rents, and the wristband was almost torn off.

The things that Olga had worn, such as her gold watch, a long gold chain, a diamond brooch, ear-rings, rings and a purse containing silver coins, were found with the clothes. It was clear the crime had not been committed with the intent of robbery.

The results of the post-mortem examination, made by "Screw" and the district doctor in my presence on the day after Olga's death, were set down in a very long report, of which I give here only a general outline. The doctors found that the external injuries were as follows: on the left side of the head, at the juncture of the temporal and the parietal bones, there was a wound of about one and a half inches in length that went as far as the bone. The edges of the wound were not smooth nor rectilinear. . . . It had been inflicted by a blunt instrument, probably as we subsequently decided by the haft of the dagger. On the neck at the level of the lower cervical vertebræ a red line was visible that had the form of a semicircle and extended across the back half of the neck. On the whole length of this line there were injuries to the skin and slight bruises. On the left arm, an inch and a half above the wrist, four blue spots were found. One was on the back of the hand and the three others on the lower side. They were caused by pressure, probably of fingers. . . . This was confirmed by the little scratch made by a nail that was visible on one spot. The reader will remember that the place where these spots were found corresponds with the place where the left sleeve and the left cuff of the bodice of the riding habit were torn. . . . Between the fourth and fifth ribs on an imaginary vertical line drawn from the centre of the armpit there was a large gaping wound of an inch in length. The edges were smooth, as if

cut and steeped with liquid and clotted blood. . . . The wound was deep. . . . It was made by a sharp instrument, and as it appeared from the preliminary information, by the dagger which exactly corresponded in width with the size of the wound.

The interior examination gave as result a wound in the right lung and the pleura, inflammation of the lung and hæmmorrhage in the cavity of the pleura.

As far as I can remember, the doctors arrived approximately at the following conclusion: (a) death was caused by anæmia consequent on a great loss of blood; the loss of blood was explained by the presence of a gaping wound on the right side of the breast. (b) the wound on the head must be considered a serious injury, and the wound in the breast as undoubtedly mortal; the latter must be reckoned as the immediate cause of death. (c) the wound on the head was given with a blunt instrument; the wound in the breast by a sharp and probably a double-edged one. (d) the deceased could not have inflicted all the above-mentioned injuries upon herself with her own hand; and (e) there probably had been no offence against feminine honour.

In order not to put it off till Doomsday and then repeat myself, I will give the reader at once the picture of the murder I sketched while under the impression of the first inspections, two or three examinations, and the perusal of the report of the post-mortem examination.

Olga, having left the rest of the party, walked about the wood. Lost in a reverie or plunged in her own sad thoughts—the reader will remember her mood on that ill-fated evening—she wandered deep into the forest. There she was met by the murderer. When she was standing under a tree, occupied with her own thoughts, the man came up and spoke to her. . . . This man did not awaken suspicions in her, otherwise she would have called for help, but that cry would not have been heart-rending. While talking to her the murderer seized hold of her left arm with such strength that he tore the sleeve of her bodice and her chemise and left a mark in the form of four spots. It was at that moment probably that she shrieked, and this was the shriek heard by the party. . . . She shrieked from pain and evidently because she read in the face and movements of the murderer what his intentions were. Either wishing that she should not shriek again, or perhaps acting under the influence of wrathful feelings, he seized the breast of her dress near the collar, which is proved by the two upper buttons that were torn off and the red line the doctors found on her body. The murderer in clutching at her breast and shaking her, had tightened the gold watch-chain she wore round her neck. . . . The friction and the pressure of the chain produced the red line. Then the murderer dealt her a blow on the head with some blunt weapon, for example, a stick or even the scabbard of the dagger that hung from Olga's girdle. Then flying into a passion, or finding that one wound was insufficient, he drew the dagger and plunged it into her right side with force—I say with force, because the dagger was blunt.

This was the gloomy aspect of the picture that I had the right to draw on the strength of the above-mentioned data. The question who was the murderer was evidently not difficult to determine and seemed to resolve itself. First the murderer was not guided by covetous motives but something else. . . . Therefore it was impossible to suspect some wandering vagabond or ragamuffin, who might be fishing in the lake. The shriek of his victim could not have disarmed a robber: to take off the brooch and the watch was the work of a second.

Secondly, Olga had purposely not told me the name of the murderer, which she would not have done if the murderer had been a common robber. Evidently the murderer was dear to her, and she did not wish that he should suffer severe punishment on her account. . . . Such people could only have been her mad father; her husband, whom she did not love, but before whom she felt herself guilty; or the Count, to whom perhaps in her soul she felt under obligations. . . . Her mad father was sitting at home in his little house in the forest on the evening of the murder, as his servant affirmed afterwards, composing a letter to the chief of the district police, requesting him to overcome the imaginary robbers who surrounded his house day and night. . . . The Count had never left his guests before and at the moment the murder was committed. Therefore, the whole weight of suspicion fell on unfortunate Urbenin. His unexpected appearance, his mien, and all the rest could only serve as good evidence.

Thirdly, during the last months Olga's life had been one continuous romance. And this romance was of the sort that usually ends with crime and capital punishment. An old, doting husband, unfaithfulness, jealousy, blows, flight to the lover-Count, two months after the marriage. . . . If the beautiful heroine of such a romance is killed, do not look for robbers or rascals, but search for the heroes of the romance. On this third count the most suitable hero-murderer was again Urbenin.

CHAPTER XXVIII

WHY HANDS BLOOD-STAINED?

I MADE the preliminary examinations in the mosaic room in which I had loved at one time to loll on the soft divan and pay court to gipsies.

The first person I examined was Urbenin. He was brought to me from Olga's room, where he continued to sit on a stool in a corner and never removed his eyes from the empty bed. . . . For a moment he stood before me in silence, looking at me with indifference, then probably thinking that I wanted to speak to him in my character of examining magistrate, he said in the tired voice of a man who was broken by grief and anguish:

"Sergei Petrovich, examine the other witnesses first, please, and me afterwards. . . . I can't . . ."

Urbenin considered himself a witness, or thought that he would be considered one. . . .

"No, I require to examine you just now," I said. "Be seated, please. . . ."

Urbenin sat down opposite to me and bent his head. He was weary and ill, he answered reluctantly, and it was only with difficulty I was able to squeeze his deposition out of him.

He deposed that he was Pëtr Egorych Urbenin, nobleman, fifty years of age, belonging to the Orthodox Faith. That

he owned an estate in the neighbouring K—— district where he belonged to the electorate, and had served for the last triennials as honorary magistrate. Being ruined, he had mortgaged his estate and had considered it necessary to go into service. He had entered the Count's service as bailiff six years ago. Liking agriculture, he was not ashamed of being in the service of a private individual, and considered that it was only the foolish who were ashamed of work. He received his salary from the Count regularly, and he had nothing to complain of. He had a son and daughter from his first marriage, etc., etc., etc.

He had married Olga because he was passionately in love with her. He had struggled long and painfully with his feelings, but neither common sense nor the logic of a practical elderly mind— in fact, nothing had effect: he was obliged to succumb to his feelings and he got married. He knew that Olga did not marry him for love, but considering her to be moral in the highest degree, he decided to content himself with her faithfulness and friendship which he had hoped to merit.

When he had come to the place where his disenchantment and the wrongs done to his grey hairs began, Urbenin asked permission not to speak of "the past which God will forgive her" or at least to defer the conversation about that to a future time.

"I can't. . . . It's hard. . . . Besides, you yourself saw it."

"Very well, let us leave it for another time. . . . Only tell me now, did you beat your wife? It is reported that one day, finding a note from the Count in her possession, you struck her. . . ."

"That is not true. . . . I only seized

her by the arm, she began to cry, and that same evening she went to complain. . . ."

"Did you know of her connexion with the Count?"

"I have begged that this subject should be deferred. . . . And what is the use of it?"

"Answer me only this one question, which is of great importance. . . . Was your wife's connexion with the Count known to you?"

"Undoubtedly. . . ."

"I shall write that down, and all the rest concerning your wife's unfaithfulness can be left for the next time. . . . Now we shall revert to another question. Will you explain to me how it came that you were in the forest where Olga Nikolaevna was murdered? . . . You were as you say, in the town. . . . How did you appear in the forest?"

"Yes, sir, 1 had been living in town with a cousin ever since I lost my place. . . . I passed my time in looking for a place and in drinking to forget my sorrows. . . . I had been drinking specially hard this last month. For example, I can't remember what happened last week as I was always drunk. . . . The day before yesterday I got drunk too. . . . In a word I am lost. . . . Irremediably lost! . . ."

"You wanted to tell me how it was that you appeared yesterday in the forest?"

"Yes, sir. . . . I awoke yesterday morning early, about four o'clock. . . . My head was aching from the previous day's drink, I had pains in all my limbs as if 1 had fever. . . . I lay on my bed and saw through the window the sun rise, and I remembered . . . many things. . . . A weight was on my heart.

. . . Suddenly I wanted to see her . . . to see her once more, perhaps for the last time. I was seized by wrath and melancholy. . . . I drew from my pocket the hundred-rouble note the Count had sent me. I looked at it, and then trampled it underfoot. . . . I trampled on it till I decided to go and fling this charity into his face. However hungry and ragged I may be, I cannot sell my honour, and every attempt to buy it I consider a personal insult. So you see, sir, I wanted to have a look at Olga and fling the money into the ugly mug of that seducer. And this longing overpowered me to such an extent that I almost went out of my mind. I had no money to drive here; I could not spend *his* hundred roubles on myself. I started on foot. By good luck a muzhik I know overtook me, and drove me eighteen versts for ten kopecks, otherwise I might still have been trudging along. The muzhik set me down in Tenevo. From there 1 came here on foot and arrived about four o'clock.

"Did anybody see you here at that time?"

"Yes, sir. The watchman, Nikolai, was sitting at the gate and told me the masters were not at home, they had all gone out shooting. I was almost worn out with fatigue, but the desire to see my wife was stronger than my pains. I had to go on foot without a moment's rest to the place where they were shooting. I did not go by the road, but started through the forest. I know every tree, and it would be as difficult for me to lose myself in the Count's forests as it would be in my own house."

"But going through the forest and not by the road you might have missed the shooting party."

"No, sir, I kept so close to the road all the time that I could not only hear the shots but the conversations too."

"Consequently you did not expect to meet your wife in the forest?"

Urbenin looked at me with astonishment, and, after thinking for a short time, he replied:

"Pardon me, but that is a strange question. One can't expect to meet a wolf, and to expect a terrible misfortune is equally impossible. God sends them unexpectedly. For example, this dreadful occurrence. . . . I was walking through the Ol'khovsky wood, not expecting any grief because I have grief enough as it is, when suddenly I heard a strange shriek. That shriek was so piercing that it appeared to me as if somebody had cut into my ear. . . . I ran towards the cry. . . ."

Urbenin's mouth was drawn to one side, his chin trembled, his eyes blinked, and he began to sob.

"I ran towards the cry, and suddenly I saw . . . Olga lying on the ground. Her hair and forehead were bloody, her face terrible. I began to shout, to call her by her name. . . . She did not move. . . . I kissed her, I raised her up. . . ."

Urbenin choked and covered his face with his hands. After a minute he continued:

"I did not see the scoundrel . . . When I was running towards her I heard somebody's hasty footsteps. He was probably running away."

"All this is an excellent invention, Pëtr Egorych," I said. "But do you know magistrates have little belief in such rare occurrences as the coincidence of the murder with your accidental walk, etc. It's not badly invented, but it explains very little."

"What do you mean by invented?" Urbenin asked, opening his eyes wide. "I have invented nothing, sir. . . ."

Suddenly Urbenin got very red and rose.

"It appears that you suspect me. . . ." he mumbled. "Of course, anybody can suspect, but you, Sergei Petrovich, have known me long. . . . It's a sin for you to brand me with such a suspicion. . . . But you know me."

"I know you, certainly . . . but my private opinion is here of no avail. . . . The law reserves the right of private opinion for the jurymen, the examining magistrate has only to deal with evidence. There is much evidence, Pëtr Egorych."

Urbenin cast an alarmed look at me and shrugged his shoulders.

"Whatever the evidence may be," he said, "you must understand. . . . Now, could I? . . . I! Besides whom?! I might be able to kill a quail or a woodcock, but a human being . . . a woman who was dearer to me than life, my salvation . . . the very thought of whom illuminates my gloomy nature like the sun. . . . And suddenly you suspect me!"

Urbenin waved his hand resignedly and sat down again.

"As it is, I long for death, and you wrong me besides! If an unknown functionary wronged me, I'd say nothing; but you, Sergei Petrovich! . . . May I go away, sir?"

"You may. . . . I shall examine you again to-morrow, and in the meantime, Pëtr Egorych, I must put you under arrest. . . . I hope that before to-morrow's examination you will have had time to appreciate the importance of all the evidence there is against you, and you will not waste time uselessly, but confess. I am convinced that Olka Nikolaevna was murdered by you. . . . I have nothing more to say to you to-day. . . . You may go."

Having said this I bent over my papers. . . . Urbenin looked at me in perplexity, rose, and stretched out his arms in a strange way.

"Are you joking . . . or serious?" he asked.

"This is no time for joking," I said. "You may go."

Urbenin remained standing before me. I looked up at him. He was pale and looked with perplexity at my papers.

"Why are your hands blood-stained, Pëtr Egorych?" I asked.

He looked down at his hands on which there still were marks of blood, and he moved his fingers.

"Why there is blood? . . . Hm . . . If this is part of the evidence, it is but poor evidence. . . . When I lifted up blood-stained Olga I could not help dirtying my hands with blood. I was not wearing gloves."

"You just told me that when you found your wife all bloody, you called for help. . . . How is it that nobody heard your cries?"

"I don't know, I was so stunned by the sight of Olia, that I was unable to cry aloud. . . . Besides, I know nothing. . . It is useless for me to try to exculpate myself, and it's not in my principles to do so."

"You would hardly have shouted. . . . Having killed your wife, you ran away, and were terribly astonished when you saw people on the clearing."

"I never noticed your people. I paid no heed to people."

With this my examination for that day was concluded. After that Urbenin was confined in one of the outhouses on the Count's estate and watched.

CHAPTER XXIX

THE SCENE OF THE CRIME

On the second or third day the Assistant Public Prosecutor, Polugradov, arrived post-haste from the town; he is a man I cannot think of without spoiling my frame of mind. Imagine a tall, lean man, of about thirty, clean shaven, smartly dressed, and with hair curled like a sheep's; his features were thin, but so dry and unexpressive that it was not difficult to guess the emptiness and foppishness of the individual to whom they belonged; his voice was low, sugary, and mawkishly polite.

He arrived early in the morning, with two portmanteaux in a hired calash. First of all he inquired with a very concerned face, complaining affectedly of fatigue, if a room had been prepared for him in the Count's house. By my orders a small but very cosy and light room had been assigned to him, where everything he might need, beginning with a marble washstand, and ending with matches, had been arranged.

"I—I say, my good fellow! Bring me some hot water!" he began while settling down in his room, and fastidiously sniffing the air; "Some hot water, please, I say, young man!"

Before beginning work he washed, dressed, and arranged his hair for a long time; he even brushed his teeth with some sort of red powder, and occupied about three minutes in trimming his sharp, pink nails.

"Well, sir," he said at last, settling down to work, and turning over the leaves of our report. "What's it all about?"

I told him what was the matter, not leaving out a single detail. . . .

"Have you been to the scene of the crime?"

"No, I have not been there yet."

The Assistant Public Prosecutor frowned, passed his white womanish hand over his freshly washed brow, and began walking about the room.

"I can't understand your reason for not having been there," he mumbled. "I should suppose that was the first thing that ought to have been done. Did you forget or thought it unnecessary?"

"Neither the one nor the other: yesterday I waited for the police, and intend to go to-day."

"Now nothing remains there: it has rained all these days, and you have given the criminal time to obliterate his traces. Of course you placed a guard at the spot? No? I don't understand!"

And the dandy shrugged his shoulders authoritatively.

"You'd better drink your tea, it's getting cold," I said, in a tone of indifference.

"I like it cold." .

The Assistant of the Public Prosecutor bent over the papers, and with a loud sniff he began to read aloud in an undertone, occasionally jotting down his remarks and corrections. Two or three times his mouth was drawn to one side in a sarcastic smile: for some reason neither my official report nor the doctors'

pleased this cunning rogue.* In this sleek, well-brushed, and cleanly-washed government official, stuffed full of conceit and a high opinion of his own worth, the pedant was clearly apparent.

By midday we were on the scene of the crime. It was raining hard. Of course we neither found spots nor traces; all had been washed away by the rain. By some chance I found one of the buttons that were missing on Olga's riding habit, and the Assistant Prosecutor picked up a sort of reddish pulp, that subsequently proved to be a red wrapper from a packet of tobacco. At first we stumbled upon a bush which had two twigs broken at one side. The Assistant Prosecutor was delighted at finding these twigs. They might have been broken by the criminal and would therefore indicate the way he had gone after killing Olga. But the joy of the Prosecutor was unfounded: we soon found a number of bushes with twigs and nibbled leaves; it turned out that a herd of cattle had passed over the scene of the murder.

After making a plan of the place and questioning the coachmen we had taken with us as to the position in which they had found Olga we returned to the house with long faces. An onlooker might have noticed a certain laziness and apathy in our movements while we were examining the scene of the crime. . . . Perhaps our move-

---

* Kamyshev abuses the Assistant Public Prosecutor quite without cause. The only thing in which this prosecutor can be blamed is that his face did not please M. Kamyshev. It would have been more honest to admit inexperience or intentional mistakes.—A. Ch.

ments were paralysed to a certain extent by the conviction that the criminal was already in our hands, and therefore it was unnecessary to enter on any Lecoq-like analysis.

On his return from the forest Polugradov again passed a long time in washing and dressing, and he again called for hot water. Having finished his toilet he expressed a wish to examine Urbenin once more. Poor Pëtr Egorych had nothing new to tell us at this examination; as before he denied his guilt, and thought nothing of our evidence.

"I am astonished that I can be suspected," he said, shrugging his shoulders: "Strange!"

"My good fellow, don't play the *naïf*," Polugradov said to him. "Nobody is suspected without cause, and if somebody is suspected there is good cause for it!"

"Whatever the causes may be, however strong the evidence may be, one must reason in a humane manner! Don't you understand, I can't murder? I can't . . . Consequently what is your evidence worth?"

"Well!" and the Assistant Prosecutor waved his hand: "what a trouble these educated criminals are; one can make a muzhik understand, but try to talk to one of these! 'I can't' . . . 'in a humane manner' . . . there they go strumming on psychology!"

"I am no criminal," Urbenin said quite offended, "I beg you to be more careful in your expressions. . . ."

"Hold your tongue, my good fellow! We have no time to apologize nor to listen to your dissatisfaction. . . If you don't wish to confess, you need

not confess, but allow us to consider you a liar. . . ."

"As you like," Urbenin grumbled. "You can do with me what you like now. . . . You have the power. . . ."

Urbenin made a gesture of indifference, and continued to look out of the window.

"Besides, it's all the same to me: my life is lost."

"Listen to me, Pëtr Egorych," I said, "yesterday and the day before you were so overcome by grief, that you were scarcely able to keep on your legs, and you were hardly able to give more than laconic answers; to-day, on the contrary, you have such a blooming, of course, only comparatively blooming, and gay appearance, and even strike out into idle talk. Usually sorrowful people have no wish to talk, while you not only launch out into long conversations, but even make all sorts of trivial complaints. In what way can such a sudden change be explained?"

"And how do you explain it?" Urbenin asked, screwing up his eyes at me in a derisive manner.

"I explain it in this way: that you have forgotten your part. It is difficult to act for any length of time; one either forgets one's part, or it bores one. . . ."

"Consequently, that was all an invention," said Urbenin, smiling; "and it does honour to your perspicacity. . . . Yes, you are right; a great change has taken place in me. . . ."

"Can you explain it to us?"

"Certainly, I see no cause for hiding it. Yesterday I was so entirely broken and oppressed by my grief, that I thought of taking my life . . . of going mad . . . but this night I thought better of it . . . the thought entered my mind that death had saved Olia from a life of depravity, that it had torn her out of the dirty hands of that good-for-nothing who has ruined me; I am not jealous of death; it is better for Olga to belong to death, than to the Count. This thought cheered and strengthened me: now there is no longer the same weight on my soul."

"Cleverly invented," Polugradov murmured under his breath, as he sat swinging his leg, "he is never at a loss for an answer!"

"I feel that I am speaking the truth, and I can't understand that you cultivated men cannot see the difference between truth and dissimulation! However, prejudice is too strong a feeling; under its influence it is difficult not to err; I can understand your position, I can imagine what will be, when trusting in your evidence, I am brought up for trial. . . . I can imagine how, taking into consideration my brutal physiognomy, my drunkenness . . . My physiognomy is not brutal, but prejudice will have its own. . . ."

"Very well, very well, enough," Polugradov said, bending over his papers, "Go!" . . ."

After Urbenin had left, we proceeded to examine the Count. His Excellency was pleased to come to the examination in his dressing-gown, with a vinegar bandage on his head; having been introduced to Polugradov he sank into an armchair, and began to give his evidence:

"I shall tell you everything from the very beginning. . . . Well, and how is your President Lionsky, getting on? Has he still not divorced his wife? I made his acquaintance in Petersburg, quite by chance. . . . Gentlemen,

why don't you order something to be brought? Somehow it's jollier to talk with a glass of cognac before you. . . . I have not the slightest doubt that Urbenin committed this murder."

And the Count told us all that the reader already knows. At the request of the prosecutor he told us all the details of his life with Olga, and described the delights of living with a beautiful woman, and was so carried away by his subject, that he smacked his lips, and winked several times. From his evidence I learned a very important detail that is unknown to the reader. I learned that Urbenin while living in the town had constantly bombarded the Count with letters; in some letters he cursed him, in others he implored him to return his wife to him, promising to forget all wrongs, and dishonour; the poor devil caught at these letters like a drowning man catches at straws.

The Assistant Prosecutor examined two or three of the coachmen and then, having had a very good dinner, he gave me a long list of instructions, and drove away. Before leaving he went into the adjoining house where Urbenin was confined, and told him that our suspicions of his guilt had become certainties. Urbenin only shrugged his shoulders, and asked permission to be present at his wife's funeral; this permission was granted him.

Polugradov did not lie to Urbenin: yes, our suspicions had become convictions, we were convinced that we knew who the criminal was, and that he was already in our hands; but this conviction did not abide with us for long! . . .

CHAPTER XXX

THEY LIE!

ONE fine morning, just as I was sealing up a parcel which I was about to send by the guard, who was to take Urbenin to the town, where he was to be imprisoned in the castle-prison, I heard a terrible noise. Looking out of the window I saw an amusing sight: some dozen strong young fellows were dragging one-eyed Kuz'ma out of the servants' kitchen.

Kuz'ma pale and dishevelled had his feet firmly planted on the ground, and being deprived of the use of his arms, butted at his adversaries with his large head.

"Your Honour, please go there!" Il'ya said to me, in great alarm, "he . . . does not want to some!"

"Who does not want to come?"

"The murderer."

"What murderer?"

"Kuz'ma. . . . He committed the murder, your Honour . . . Pëtr Egorych is suffering unjustly. . . . By God, sir."

I went into the yard and walked towards the servants' kitchen, where Kuz'ma, who had torn himself out of the strong arms of his opponents, was administering cuffs to right and left.

"What's the matter?" I asked, when I came up to the crowd.

And I was told something very strange and unexpected.

"Your Honour, Kuz'ma killed her!"

"They lie!" Kuz'ma shouted. "May God kill me if they don't lie!"

"But why did you, son of a devil, wash off the blood, if your conscience is clear? Stop a moment, his Honour will examine all this!"

The breaker-in, Trifon. riding past the river, saw Kuz'ma washing something carefully in the water. At first Trifon thought he was washing linen, but looking more attentively he saw it was a poddevka and a waistcoat. He thought this strange: garments of cloth are not washed.

"What are you doing?" Trifon called to him.

Kuz'ma became confused. Looking more attentively Trifon noticed brown spots on the poddevka.

"I guessed at once that it must be blood . . . I went into the kitchen and told our people; they watched, and saw him at night hanging out the poddevka to dry. Of course they took fright. Why should he wash it, if he is not guilty? He must have something on his soul, he is trying to hide. . . . We thought and thought, and decided to bring him to your Honour. . . . We pull him along, and he backs and spits into our eyes. Why should he back if he is not guilty?"

From further examination it appeared that just before the murder, at the time when the Count and his guests were sitting in the clearing, drinking tea, Kuz'ma had gone into the forest. He had not aided in carrying Olga, and therefore could not have got dirtied with blood at that time.

When he was brought to my room Kuz'ma was so excited that at first he could not utter a word; turning up the white of his single eye he crossed himself and mumbled oaths.

"Be calm; tell me what you know and I will let you go," I said to him.

Kuz'ma fell at my feet, stammered and called on God.

"May I perish if it's I. . . . May

neither my father nor my mother. . . .
Your Honour! May God destroy my
soul. . . ."

"You went into the forest?"

"That's quite true, sir, I went. . . .
I had served cognac to the guests and,
forgive me, I had tippled a little; it
went to my head, and I wanted to lie
down; I went, lay down, and fell asleep.
. . . But who killed her, or how I don't
know, so help me God. . . . It's the
truth I'm telling you!"

"But why did you wash off the
blood?"

"I was afraid that people might
imagine . . . that I might be taken as
a witness. . . ."

"How did the blood come on to
your poddevka?"

"I don't know, your Honour."

"How is is possible you can't know?
Isn't the poddevka yours?"

"Yes, certainly it's mine, but I don't
know: I saw the blood when I woke up
again."

"So, then, I suppose you dirtied the
poddevka with blood in your sleep?"

"Just so. . . ."

"Well, my man, go and think it
over. . . . You're talking nonsense;
think well and tell me to-morrow. . . .
Go!"

The following morning, when I awoke,
I was informed that Kuz'ma wanted to
speak to me. I ordered him to be
brought in.

"Have you bethought yourself?" I
asked him.

"Just so, I've bethought myself. . . ."

"How did the blood get on your poddevka?"

"Your Honour, I remember as if in
a dream: I remember something, as

in a fog, but if it is true or not I
can't say."

"What do you remember?"

Kuz'ma turned up his eye, thought,
and said:

"Extraordinary . . . it's like in a
dream or a fog. . . . I lay upon the
grass drunk and dozing. I was not
quite asleep. . . . I only heard somebody was passing, trampling heavily
with his feet. . . . I opened my eyes
and saw, as if I was unconscious, or in
a dream; a gentleman came up to me,
he bends over me and wiped his hands
in my skirts. . . . he wiped them in my
poddevka, and then rubbed his hand
on my waistcoat. . . . so."

"What gentleman was it?"

"I don't know; I only remember it
was not a muzhik, but a gentleman. . . .
in gentleman's clothes; but what gentleman it was, what sort of face he had I
can't remember at all."

"What was the colour of his clothes?"

"Who can say! Perhaps it was white,
perhaps black. . . . I only remember
it was a gentleman, and that's all I can
remember. . . . Akh, yes, I can remember! When he bent down and
wiped his hands he said: 'Drunken
swine!'"

"You dreamt this?"

"I don't know . . . perhaps I dreamt
it. . . . But then where did the blood
come from?"

"Was the gentleman you saw like
Pëtr Egorych?"

"It appears to me he wasn't . . .
but perhaps it was. . . . but he would
not swear and call people swine."

"Try to remember. . . . Go, sit
down and think. . . .Perhaps you may
succeed in remembering."

"I'll try."

CHAPTER XXXI

SOLITARY CONFINEMENT

THIS unexpected eruption of one-eyed Kuz'ma into the almost finished romance produced an entanglement that it was scarcely possible to unravel. I was quite bewildered, and did not know how I was to understand Kuz'ma. He denied positively any guilt; besides, the preliminary investigations were against his guilt. Olga had been murdered not from motives of greed, according to the doctors "it was probable" that no attempt against her honour had been made; it was only possible to admit that Kuz'ma had killed her and had not availed himself of one of these reasons because he was very drunk and had lost his reasoning powers. All this did not tally with the setting of the murder.

But if Kuz'ma was not guilty, why had he not explained the presence of blood on his poddevka, and why had he invented dreams and hallucinations? Why had he implicated this gentleman, whom he had seen and heard, but had forgotten so entirely that he could not even remember the colour of his clothes?

Polugradov hurried back post haste. "Now you see, sir!" he said, "if you had examined the scene of the crime at once, believe me all would have been plain now, as plain as a pikestaff! If you had examined all the servants at once, we could then have known who had carried Olga Nikolaevna and who had not. And now we can't even find out at what distance from the scene of the crime this drunkard was lying!"

He cross-questioned Kuz'ma for about two hours, but could get nothing

new out of him; he only said that while half asleep he had seen a gentleman, that the gentleman had wiped his hands on the skirts of his poddevka and had sworn at him as a "drunken swine," but he could not say who this gentleman was, nor what his face and clothes were like.

"How much cognac did you drink?"

"I finished half a bottle."

"Perhaps it was not cognac?"

"No, sir, it was real fine champagne."

"So you even know the names of wines!" the Assistant Prosecutor said, laughing.

"How should I not know them? I've served these masters for more than thirty years, thank God? I've had time to learn. . . ."

For some reason the Assistant Prosecutor required that Kuz'ma should be confronted with Urbenin. . . . Kuz'ma looked for a long time at Urbenin, shook his head and said

"No, I can't remember . . . perhaps it was Pëtr Egorych, perhaps it was not. . . . Who can say?"

Polugradov shrugged his shoulders and drove away, leaving me to choose which was the right one of the two murderers.

The investigations were protracted. . . . Urbenin and Kuz'ma were imprisoned in the guard-house of the village in which I lived. Poor Pëtr Egorych lost courage very much; he grew thin and grey and fell into a religious mood; two or three times he sent to beg me to let him see the laws about punishments; it was evident he was interested in the extent of the punishment that awaited him.

"What will become of my children?" he asked me at one of the examinations.

"If I were alone your mistake would not grieve me very much; but I must live . . . live for the children! They will perish without me. Besides, I . . . I am not able to part from them! What are you doing with me?"

When the guards said "thou" to him, and when he had to go a couple of times, from my village to the town and back on foot under escort, in the sight of all the people who knew him, he became despondent and nervous.

"These are not jurists," he cried so that he was heard in the whole of the guard-house. "They are nothing but cruel, heartless boys, without mercy either for people or truth! I know why I am confined here, I know it! By casting the blame on me they want to hide the real culprit! The Count killed her; and if it was not the Count, it was his hireling!"

When he heard that Kuz'ma had been arrested, he was at first very pleased.

"Now the hireling has been found!" he said to me. "Now he's been found!"

But soon, when he saw he was not released and when he was informed of Kuz'ma's testimony, he again became depressed.

"Now I'm lost," he said, "definitely lost. In order to get out of prison this one-eyed devil will be sure sooner or later to name me and say it was I who wiped my hands in his skirts. But you yourself saw that my hands had not been wiped!"

Sooner or later our suspicions would have to be elucidated.

About the end of November of that year, when snow began to drift before my windows and the lake looked like an endless white desert, Kuz'ma wanted to see me; he sent the guard to me to say he had "bethought himself." I ordered him to be brought to me.

"I am very pleased that you have at last bethought yourself," I greeted him. "It is high time to finish with this dissembling and this leading us all by the nose like little children. Well, of what have you bethought yourself?"

Kuz'ma did not answer; he stood in the middle of my room in silence, staring at me without winking. . . . Fright shone in his eyes; his whole person showed signs of great fright; he was pale and trembling, and a cold perspiration poured down his face.

"Well, speak! What have you remembered?" I asked again.

"Something, so extraordinary, that nothing can be more wonderful," he said. "Yesterday I remembered what sort of a tie that gentleman was wearing, and this night I was thinking and remembered his face."

"Then who was it?"

"I'm afraid to say, your Honour; allow me not to speak: it's too strange and wonderful; I think I must have dreamt it or imagined it. . . ."

"Well, what have you imagined?"

"No, allow me not to speak. If I tell you, you'll condemn me. . . . Allow me to think, and I'll tell you to-morrow. Fearful!"

"Pshaw!" I began to get angry. "Why did you trouble me if you can't speak? Why did you come here?"

"I thought I would tell you, but now I'm afraid. No, your Honour, please let me go. . . . I'd better tell you to-morrow. . . . If I tell you you'll get so angry that I'd sooner go to Siberia—you'll condemn me. . . ."

I got angry and ordered Kuz'ma * to be taken away. In the evening of that very day, in order not to lose time and to put an end to this tiresome "case about the murder," I went to the guard-house and cheated Urbenin by telling him that Kuz'ma had named him as the murderer.

"I expected it," Urbenin said with a wave of his hand. "It's all one to me. . . ."

Solitary confinement had greatly affected Urbenin's health; he had grown yellow and had lost almost half his weight. I promised him to order the guards to allow him to walk about the corridors in the day and even in the night.

"There's no fear of your trying to escape." I said.

Urbenin thanked me, and after my departure he walked about the corridor; his door was no longer kept locked.

On leaving him I knocked at the door behind which Kuz'ma was seated.

"Well, have you bethought yourself yet?" I asked.

"No, sir," a weak voice answered. "Let the Prosecutor come; I will tell him, but I won't tell you."

"As you like!"

The next morning all was settled. The watchman Egor came running

---

* A fine examining magistrate! Instead of continuing the examination and extorting the necessary evidence, he gets angry—an occupation that does not enter into the duties of an official. Besides, I put little trust in all this. . . . Even if M. Kamyshev cared so little about his duties, simple, human curiosity ought to have obliged him to continue the examination.—A. Ch.

---

to me and informed me that one-eyed Kuz'ma had been found in his bed dead. I hastened to the guard-house to assure myself of the fact. The strong, big muzhik, who but the day before was full of health and in order to get free had invented all sorts of tales, was as stark and cold as a stone. . . . I will not stop to describe the horror the guards and I felt; it will be understood by the reader. Kuz'ma was precious for me both as accuser and as witness, for the warders he was a prisoner for whose death or flight they would be severely punished. . . . Our horror was only increased when at the post-mortem examination it was discovered that he had died a violent death. . . . Kuz'ma had died from suffocation. . . . Once convinced that he had been suffocated, I began to search for the culprit, and I had not to search long. . . . He was near. . . .

"You scoundrel! It was not enough for you to kill your wife," I said, "but you must take the life of the man who convicted you! And you continue to act your dirty, roguish comedy!"

Urbenin grew deadly pale and began to shake. . . .

"You lie!" he cried, striking himself on the breast with his fist.

"I do not lie! You shed crocodile tears at our evidence and made game of it. . . . There were moments when I almost wished to believe you more than our evidence. . . . Oh, you are a good actor! . . . But now I won't believe you, even should blood flow from your eyes instead of these play-actor's false tears! Say that you killed Kuz'ma!"

"You are either drunk or are laughing at me! Sergei Petrovich, all pa-

tience and submissiveness has its limits;
I can bear this no longer!"

And Urbenin, with flashing eyes,
struck the table with his clenched fist.

"Yesterday I had the imprudence to
give you more liberty," I continued,
"by allowing you that which no other
prisoner is allowed, to walk about the
corridors. And now it appears, out of
gratitude you went to the door of that
unfortunate Kuz'ma and suffocated a
sleeping man! Do you know that you
have destroyed not only Kuz'ma; the
warders will also be ruined on your
account."

"What have I done, good God?"
Urbenin said, seizing hold of his head.

"Do you want the proofs? I will give
them. . . . By my orders your door
was left open. . . . The foolish
warders opened the door and forgot to
hide the lock. . . . All the cells are
opened with the same key. . . . In
the night you took your key and going
into the corridor, you opened your
neighbour's door with it. . . . Having
smothered him, you locked the door
and put the key into your own lock."

"Why should I smother him? Why?"

"Because he denounced you. . . . If
yesterday I had not given you this
news, he would have been alive now.
. . . It is sinful and shameful, Pëtr
Egorych!"

"Sergei Petrovich, young man," the
murderer suddenly said in a soft, tender
voice, seizing me by the hand, "you are
an honest and respectable man! Do
not ruin and stain yourself with false
suspicions and over-hasty accusations!
You cannot understand how cruelly and
painfully you have wounded me by
casting upon my soul, which is in no
way guilty, a new accusation. . . . I

am a martyr, Sergei Petrovich! Fear
to wrong a martyr! The time will come
when you will have to beg my pardon,
and that time will be soon. . . . You
can't really want to accuse me! But
this pardon will not satisfy you. . . .
Instead of assailing me so terribly with
insults, it would have been better if in
a humane—I will not say a friendly—
way (you have already renounced all
friendly relations) you had questioned
me. . . . As a witness and your assistant, I would have brought more
profit to justice than in the role of the
accused. If we even take this new
accusation . . . I could tell you much.
I did not sleep last night, and heard
everything."

"What did you hear?"

"Last night, at about two o'clock
. . . all was dark. . . . I heard somebody walking about the corridor very
gently, and constantly touching my
door . . . he walked and walked, and
then opened my door and came in."

"Who was it?"

"I don't know; it was dark—I did
not see. . . . He stood for about a
minute and went away again . . .
exactly as you said. . . . He took the
key out of my door and opened the
next cell. Two minutes later I heard
a guttural sound and then a bustle. I
thought it was the warder walking
about and bustling, and the sounds I
took for snores, otherwise I would have
made a noise."

"Fables," I said. "There was nobody
here but you who could have killed
Kuz'ma. The warders were all asleep.
The wife of one of them, who could
not sleep the whole night, has given
evidence that all three warders slept
like dead men all the night and never

left their beds for a minute; the poor fellows did not know that such brutes could be found in this miserable guard-house. They have been serving here for more than twenty years, and during all that time they have never had a single case of a prisoner having escaped, to say nothing of such an abomination as a murder. Now, thanks to you, their life has been turned upside down; I, too, will have to suffer on your account because I did not send you to the town prison, and even gave you the liberty of walking about the corridors. Thank you!"

This was my last conversation with Urbenin. I never spoke to him again, if I do not count the two or three answers I gave to the questions he put to me when he was seated in the dock.

CHAPTER XXXII

THE RAINBOW

I HAVE said that my novel is a story of crime, and now, when the case of the murder of Olga Urbenin is complicated by another murder, in many ways mysterious and incomprehensible, the reader is entitled to expect that the novel will enter upon its most interesting and exciting phase. The discovery of the criminal, and the reasons for his crime, offer a wide field for the display of ingenuity and sharp-wittedness. Here evil will and cunning are at war with knowledge and skill, a war that is interesting in all its manifestations. . . .

I led the war and the reader has the right to expect me to describe the means that led to my victory, and he is doubtless expecting all sorts of detective finesses such as shine in the novels of Gaboriau and our Shklya-revsky; and I am ready to satisfy the reader's expectations, but . . . one of the chief characters leaves the field of battle without waiting for the end of the combat—he is not made a participator in the victory; all that he had done so far was lost for him—and he goes over into the crowd of spectators. That character in the drama is your humble servant. On the day following the above conversation with Urbenin I received an invitation, or, more correctly speaking, an order to hand in my resignation. The tittle-tattle and talk of our district gossips had done its work. . . . The murder in the guard-house, the evidence that the Assistant Prosecutor had collected, unknown to me, from the servants, and, if the reader still remembers it, the blow I had dealt a muzhik on the head with an oar on the occasion of one of our former revels, had all greatly contributed to my dismissal. The muzhik started the case. All sorts of alterations took place. In the course of two days I had to hand over the case of the murder to the magistrate for specially important affairs.

Thanks to the talk and the newspaper reports, the entire attention of the Prosecutor was aroused. The Prosecutor himself came to the Count's estate every other day and assisted at the examinations. The official reports of our doctors were sent to the medical board and higher. There was even a question of having the bodies exhumed and having a fresh post-mortem examination, which, by the way, would have led to nothing.

Urbenin was taken a couple of times to the chief town of the government to have his mental capacities tested, and both times he was found quite normal. I was given the part of witness.* The new examining magistrates were so carried away by their zeal that even my Polycarp was called up as witness.

A year after my resignation, when I was living in Moscow, I received a summons to appear at the trial of the Urbenin case. I was glad of the opportunity of seeing again the places to which I was drawn by habit, and I went. The Count, who was residing in Petersburg, did not go there, but sent a medical certificate instead.

The case was tried in our district town in a division of the Court of Justice. Polugradov—that same Polugradov who cleaned his teeth four times a day with red powder—conducted the prosecution; a certain Smirnyaev, a tall, lean, fair-haired man with a sentimental face and long straight hair, acted for the defence The jury was exclusively composed of shopkeepers and peasants, of whom only four could read and write; the others, when they were given to read Urbenin's letters to his wife, sweated and got confused. The chief juryman was Ivan Dem'yanych, the shopkeeper from my village, after whom my late parrot had been named.

When I came into the court I did not recognize Urbenin; he had become quite grey, and his body had grown twenty years older. I had expected to read on his face indifference for his fate and apathy, but I was mistaken. Urbenin was deeply interested in the

---

* A part that was certainly better suited to M. Kamyshev than the part of examining magistrate; in the Urbenin case he could not be examining magistrate.—A. Ch.

trial; he brought in an exception against three of the jurymen, gave long explanations, and questioned the witnesses; he absolutely denied any guilt, and he questioned all the witnesses. who did not give evidence in his favour, very minutely.

The witness Pshekhotsky deposed that I had had a connexion with the late Olga.

"That's a lie!" Urbenin shouted. "He lies! I don't trust my wife, but I trust him!"

When I gave my evidence the counsel for the defence asked me in what relations I stood to Olga, and informed me of the evidence that Pshekhotsky, who had on one occasion applauded me, had given. To have spoken the truth would have been to give evidence in favour of the accused. The more depraved the wife, the more lenient the jury is towards the Othello-husband. I understood this. . . . On the other hand, if I spoke the truth I would have wounded Urbenin. . . . In hearing it he would have felt an incurable pain. . . . I thought it better to lie.

I said "No."

In his speech the Public Prosecutor described Olga's murder in vivid colours and drew especial attention to the brutality of the murderer, to his malignancy. . . . "An old, worn-out voluptuary saw a girl, young and pretty. Knowing the whole horror of her position in the house of her mad father, he enticed her to come to him by a bit of bread, a dwelling, and some bright-coloured rags. . . . She agreed. An old, well-to-do husband is easier to be borne than a mad father and poverty. But she was young, and youth, gentlemen of the jury, possesses its own inalienable rights. . . . A girl brought up on novels, in the midst of nature, sooner or later was bound to fall in love. . . ." And so on in the same style. It finished up with "He who had not given her anything more than his age and bright coloured rags, seeing his prize slipping away from him, falls into the fury of a brute, to whose nose a red-hot iron had been applied. He had loved in a brutish way and he must hate in a brutish way," etc., etc.

In charging Urbenin with Kuz'ma's murder, Polugradov drew special attention to those thief-like processes, well thought out and weighed, that accomplished the murder of a "sleeping man who the day before had had the imprudence to give testimony against him." "I suppose you cannot doubt that Kuz'ma wanted to tell the Public Prosecutor something specially concerning him."

The counsel for the defence, Smirnyaev, did not deny Urbenin's guilt; he only begged them to admit that Urbenin had acted under the influence of a state of temporary insanity, and to have indulgence for him. When describing how painfully the feelings of jealousy are, he cited as an example Shakespeare's "Othello." He looked at that all-human type from every side, giving extracts from various critics, and got into such a maze that the presiding judge had to stop him with the remark that "a knowledge of foreign literature was not obligatory for the jurymen."

Taking advantage of having the last word, Urbenin called God to witness that he was not guilty either in deed or thought.

"It is all the same to me where I am—in this district where everything reminds me of my unmerited shame and of my wife, or in penal servitude; but it is the fate of my children that is troubling me."

And, turning to the public, Urbenin began to cry, and begged that his children might be cared for.

"Take them. The Count will not lose the opportunity of vaunting his generosity, but I have already warned the children; they will not accept a crumb from him."

Then, noticing me among the public, he looked at me with suppliant eyes and said:

"Defend my children from the Count's favours!"

He apparently had quite forgotten the impending verdict, and his thoughts were only centred on his children. He talked about them until he was stopped by the presiding judge.

The jury were not long in consultation. Urbenin was found guilty, without extenuating circumstances on any count.

He was condemned to the loss of all civil rights, transportation and hard labour for fifteen years.

So dearly had he to pay for his having met on a fine May morning the poetical "girl in red."

More than eight years have passed since the events described above happened. Some of the actors in the drama are dead and decomposed, others are bearing the punishment of their sins, others are wearily dragging on life, struggling with dullness and awaiting death from day to day.

Much is changed during these eight years. . . . Count Karnéev, who has never ceased to entertain the sincerest friendship for me, has sunk into utter drunkenness. His estate which was the scene of the drama has passed from him into the hands of his wife and Pshekhotsky. He is now poor, and is supported by me. Sometimes of an evening, lying on the sofa in my room in the boarding-house, he likes to remember the good old times.

"It would be fine to listen to the gipsies now!" he murmurs. "Serezha, send for some cognac!"

I am also changed. My strength is gradually deserting me, and I feel youth and health leaving my body. I no longer possess the same physical strength, I have not the same alertness, the same endurance which I was proud of displaying formerly, when I could carouse night after night and could drink quantities which now I could hardly lift.

Wrinkles are appearing on my face one after the other; my hair is getting thin, my voice is becoming coarse and less strong. . . . Life is finished.

I remember the past as if it were yesterday. I see places and people's faces as if in a mist. I have not the power to regard them impartially; I love and hate them with the former intensity, and never a day passes that I, being filled with feelings of indignation or hatred, do not seize hold of my head. As formerly, I consider the Count odious. Olga infamous, Kalinin ludicrous owing to his stupid presumption. Evil I hold to be evil, sin to be sin.

But not infrequently there are moments when, looking intently at a portrait that is standing on my writing-table, I feel an irresistible desire to walk with the "girl in red" through the forest, under the sounds of the tall pines, and to press her to my breast regardless of everything. In such moments I forgive the lies, the fall into the dirty abyss, I am ready to forgive everything, if only a small part of the past could be repeated once more. . . . Wearied of the dullness of town, I want to hear once again the roar of the giant lake and gallop along its banks on my Zorka. . . . I would forgive and forget everything if I could once again go along the road to Tenevo and meet the gardener Franz with his vodka barrel and jockey-cap. . . . There are moments when I am even ready to press the blood-stained hand of good-natured Pëtr Egorych, and talk with him about religion, the harvest and the enlightenment of the people. . . . I would like to meet "Screw" and his Nadenka again. . . .

Life is mad, licentious, turbulent— like a lake on an August night. . . . Many victims have disappeared for ever beneath its dark waves. . . . Heavy dregs lie at the bottom.

But why, at certain moments, do I love it? Why do I forgive it, and in my soul hurry towards it like an affectionate son, like a bird released from a cage?

At this moment the life I see from the window of my room in these chambers reminds me of a grey circle; it is grey in colour without any light or shade. . . .

But, if I close my eyes and remember the past, I see a rainbow formed by the sun's spectrum. . . . Yes, it is stormy there, but it is lighter too. . . .

—S. ZINOV'EV.

POSTSCRIPT

At the bottom of the manuscript there is written:

DEAR SIR, MR. EDITOR! I beg you to publish the novel (or story, if you prefer it) which I submit to you herewith, as far as possible, in its entirety, without abridgment, cuts or additions. However, changes can be made with the consent of the author. In case you find it unsuitable I beg you to keep the MSS. to be returned. My address (temporary) is Moscow in the Anglia Chambers, on the Tverskoy Ivan Petrovich Kamyshev P.S.—The fee is at the discretion of the Editor.

Year and date.

Now that the reader has become acquainted with Kamyshev's novel, I will continue my interrupted talk with him. First of all, I must inform the reader that the promise I made to him in the beginning of this novel has not been kept: Kamyshev's novel has not been printed without omissions, not *in toto*, as I promised, but it is considerably shortened. The fact is, that the "Shooting Party" could not be printed in the newspaper which was mentioned in the first chapter of this work, the newspaper ceased to exist when the manuscript was sent to press. The present editorial board, in accepting Kamyshev's novel, found it impossible to publish it without cuts. During the time it was appearing, every chapter that was sent to me in proof was accompanied by the request to "make changes." However, not wishing to take on my soul the sin of changing another man's work, I found it better and more profitable to leave out whole passages rather than to make changes of unsuitable places. With my assent the editor left out many places that shocked by their cynicism, length, or the carelessness of their literary style. These omissions and cuts demanded both care and time, which is the cause that many chapters were late. Among other passages we left out two descriptions of nocturnal orgies. One of these orgies took place in the Count's house, the other on the lake. We also left out a description of Polycarp's library and of the original manner in which he read; this passage was found too much drawn out and exaggerated.

The chapter I stood up for most of all and which the editor chiefly disliked was one in which the desperate card gambling that was the rage among the Count's servants was minutely described. The most passionate gamblers were the gardener Franz and the old woman nicknamed the Scops-Owl. While Kamyshev was conducting the investigations he passed by one of the summerhouses, and looking in he saw mad play going on; the players were the Scops-Owl, Franz and—Pshekhotsky. They were playing "Stukolka," at twenty kopeck points and a fine that reached thirty roubles. Kamyshev joined the players and "cleared them out" as if they had been partridges. Franz, who had lost everything but wished to continue, went to the island where he had hidden his money. Kamyshev followed him, marked where he had concealed his money, and afterwards robbed the gardener, not leaving a kopeck in his hoard. The money he had taken he gave to the fisherman Mikhey. This strange charity admirably characterizes this hare-brained magistrate, but it is written so carelessly and the conversation of the gamblers glitters with such pearls of obscenity that the editor would not even consent to have alterations made.

The description of certain meetings of Olga and Kamyshev are omitted; an explanation between him and Nadenka Kalinin, etc., etc., are also left out. But I think what is printed is sufficient to characterize my hero. *Sapienti sat.* . . .

Exactly three months later the door-keeper Andrey announced the arrival of the gentleman "with the cockade."

"Ask him in!" I said.

Kamyshev entered, the same rosy-cheeked. handsome and healthy man he had been three months before. His steps, as formerly, were noiseless. . . . He put down his hat on the window with so much care that one might have imagined that he had deposited something heavy. . . . Out of his eyes there shone, as before, something childlike and infinitely good-natured.

"I am again troubling you!" he began smiling, and he sat down carefully. "For God's sake, forgive me! Well, what? What sentence has been passed on my manuscript?"

"Guilty, but deserving of indulgence," I replied.

Kamyshev laughed and blew his nose in a scented handkerchief.

"Consequently, banishment into the flames of the fireplace?" he asked.

"No, why such strictness? It does not merit punitive measures; we will employ a corrective treatment."

"Must it be corrected?"

"Yes, certain things. . . . by mutual consent. . . ."

We were silent for a quarter of a minute. I had terrible palpitations of the heart and my temples throbbed, but to show that I was agitated did not enter into my plans.

"By mutual consent," I repeated. "Last time you told me that you had taken the subject of your novel from real occurrences."

"Yes, and I am ready to confirm it now. If you have read my novel, may I have the honour of introducing myself as Zinov'ef."

"Consequently, you were best-man at Olga Nikolaevna's wedding."

"Both best-man and friend of the house. Am I not sympathetic in this manuscript?" Kamyshev laughed, stroked his knees and got very red. "A fine fellow, eh? I ought to have been flogged, but there was nobody to do it."

"So, sir. . . . I liked your novel: it is better and more interesting than most novels of crimes. Only by mutual consent you and I must make some essential changes in it."

"That's possible. For example, what do you consider requires change?"

"The very *habitus* of the novel, its character It has, as in all novels treating of crimes, everything: crime. evidence, an inquest, even fifteen years' penal servitude as a dessert, but the most essential thing is lacking."

"What is that?"

"The real culprit is not in it. . . ."

Kamyshev made large eyes and rose.

"Candidly speaking, I don't understand you," he said after a short pause. "If you do not consider the man who commits murder and strangles a real culprit, then. . . . I don't know who ought to be considered culpable. Criminals are, of course, the product of society, and society is guilty, but . . . if one is to devote oneself to the higher considerations one must cease writing novels and write reports."

"Akh, what sort of higher considerations are there here! It was not Urbenin who committed the murder!"

"How so?" Kamyshev asked, approaching nearer to me.

"Not Urbenin!"

"Perhaps. *Errare humanum est*—and magistrates are not perfect: there are often errors of justice under the moon. You consider that we were mistaken?"

No, you did not make a mistake; you wished to make a mistake."

"Forgive me, I again do not understand," and Kamyshev smiled: "If you find that the inquest led to a mistake, and even, if I understand you right, to a premeditated mistake, it would be interesting to know your point of view. Who was the murderer in your opinion?"

"You!"

Kamyshev looked at me with astonishment, almost with terror, grew very red and stepped back. Then turning away, he went to the window and began to laugh.

"Here's a nice go!" he muttered, breathing on the glass and nervously drawing figures on it.

I watched his hand as he drew, and it appeared to me that I recognized in it the only iron, muscular hand that, with a single effort, would have been able to strangle sleeping Kuz'ma, or mangle Olga's frail body. The thought that I saw before me a murderer filled my soul with unwonted feelings of horror and fear . . . not for myself—

no!—but for him, for this handsome and graceful giant . . . in general for man. . .

"You murdered them!" I repeated.

"If you are not joking, allow me to congratulate you on the discovery," Kamyshev said laughing, but still not looking at me: "However, judging by your trembling voice, and your paleness, it is difficult to suppose that you are joking. What a nervous man you are!"

Kamyshev turned his flushed face towards me and, forcing himself to smile, he continued:

"It is interesting how such an idea could have come into your head! Have I written something like that in my novel? By God, that's interesting. Tell me, please! It really is interesting once in a lifetime to try what it feels like to be looked upon as a murderer."

"You are a murderer," I said, "and you are not able to hide it. In the novel you lied, and now you are proving yourself but a poor actor."

"This is really quite interesting; upon my word, it would be curious to hear. . . ."

"If you are curious, then listen."

I jumped up and began walking about the room in great agitation. Kamyshev looked out of the door and closed it tight. By this precaution he gave himself away.

"What are you afraid of?" I asked.

Kamyshev became confused, coughed and shrugged his shoulders.

"I'm not afraid of anything, I only . . . only looked—looked out of the door. So you wanted this too! Well, now tell me!"

"May I put you some questions?"

"As many as you like."

"I warn you that I am no magistrate, and I am no master in cross-examination; do not expect order or system, and therefore please do not disconcert or puzzle me. First tell me where you disappeared after you had left the clearing on which the shooting party was feasting?"

"In the novel it is mentioned: I went home."

"In the novel the description of the way you went is carefully effaced. Did you not go through the forest?"

"Yes."

"Consequently, you could have met Olga?"

"Yes, I could," Kamyshev said smiling.

"And you met her."

"No, I did not meet her."

"In your investigations you forgot to question one very important witness, and that was yourself. . . . Did you hear the shriek of the victim?"

"No. . . . Well, baten'ka, you don't know how to cross-examine at all."

This familiar baten'ka jarred on me; it accorded but ill with the apologies and the disconcertion with which our conversation had begun. Soon I noticed that Kamyshev looked upon me with condescension,—from above—and almost with admiration of my inexperience in extricating myself from the number of questions that were troubling me.

"Let us admit that you did not meet Olga in the forest," I continued, "though it was more difficult for Urbenin to meet Olga than for you, as Urbenin did not know she was in the forest, and, therefore, did not look for her, while you, being drunk and maddened, would probably have looked for her. You certainly did look for her, otherwise what would be your object in going home through the forest instead of by the road? . . . But let us admit that you did not meet her. . . . How is your gloomy, your almost mad frame of mind, in the evening of the ill-fated day, to be explained? What induced you to kill the parrot, who cried out about the husband who killed his wife? I think he reminded you of your own evil deed. That night you were summoned to the Count's house, and instead of beginning your investigations at once, you delayed until the police arrived almost four and twenty hours later, and you yourself probably never noticed it. . . . Only those magistrates who already know who the criminal is can delay in that way. . . . The criminal was known to you. . . . Further,—Olga did not mention the name of the murderer because he was dear to her. . . . If her husband had been the murderer she would have named him. If she had been capable of informing against him to her lover the Count, it would not have cost her anything to accuse him of murder: she did not love him, and he was not dear to her. . . . She loved you, and it was just you, who were dear to her . . . she wanted to spare you. . . . Allow me to ask why did you delay asking her a straight question when she regained consciousness for a moment? Why did you ask her all sorts of questions that had nothing to do with the matter? Allow me to think you did this only to mark time, in order to prevent her from naming you. Then Olga dies. . . . In your novel you do not say a word about the impression that her death made on you. . . . In this I see caution: you do not forget to write about the number of glasses you emptied, but such an important event as the death of 'the girl in red' passes in the novel without leaving any traces. . . . Why?"

"Go on, go on. . . ."

"You made all your investigations in a most slovenly way. . . . It is hard to admit, that you, a clever and very cunning man, did not do so purposely. All your investigations remind one of a letter that is purposely written with grammatical errors. The exaggeration gives you away. . . . Why did you not examine the scene of the crime? Not because you forgot to do so, or considered it unimportant, but because you waited for the rain to wash away your traces. You write little about the examination of the servants. Consequently, Kuz'ma was not examined by you until he was caught washing his poddevka. . . . You evidently had no cause to mix him up in the affair. Why did you not question any of the guests, who had been feasting with you on the clearing? They had seen the blood stains on Urbenin, and had heard Olga's shriek,—they ought to have been examined. But you did not do it, because one of them might have remembered at his examination, that shortly before the murder you had suddenly gone into the forest and been lost. Afterwards they probably were questioned, but this circumstance had already been forgotten by them. . . ."

"Cute!" Kamyshev said, rubbing his hands; go on, go on!"

"Is it possible that what has already been said is not enough for you? To prove conclusively that Olga was murdered by you, and no other, I must remind you that you were her lover, whom she had jilted for a man you despised! A husband can kill from jealously. I presume a lover can do so, too. . . . Now let us advert to Kuz'ma. . . . To judge by his last interrogation, that took place on the eve of his death, he had you in his mind; you had wiped your hands on his poddevka, and you had called him a swine. . . . If it had not been you, why did you interrupt your examination at the most interesting point? Why did you not ask about the colour of the murderer's necktie, when Kuz'ma had informed you he had remembered what the colour of his necktie was? Why did you give Urbenin liberty just when Kuz'ma remembered the name of the murderer? Why not before or after? It was evident you required a man who might walk about the corridors at night. . . . And so you killed Kuz'ma, fearing that he would denounce you."

"Well, enough!" Kamyshev said laughing. "That will do! You are in such a passion, and have grown so pale that it seems as if at any moment you might faint. Do not continue. You are right. I really did kill them."

This was followed by a silence. I paced the room from corner to corner. Kamyshev did the same.

"I killed them!" Kamyshev continued. "You have caught the secret by the tail,—it's your good luck. Not many will have that success. Most of your readers will abuse Urbenin, and be amazed at my magisterial cleverness and acumen."

At that moment my assistant came into my office and interrupted our conversation. Noticing that I was occupied and excited he hovered for a moment around my writing-table, looked at Kamyshev, and left the room. When he had gone Kamyshev went to the window and began to breathe on the glass.

"Eight years have passed since then," he began again, after a short silence, "and for eight years I have borne this secret with me. But such a secret and live blood are incompatible in the same organism; it is impossible to know without punishment what the rest of mankind does not know. For all these eight years I have felt myself a martyr. It was not my conscience that tormented me, no! Conscience is a thing apart . . . and I don't pay much attention to it. It can easily be stifled by reasoning about its expansibility. When reason does not work, I smother it with wine and women. With women I have my former success,—this I only mention by the way. But I was tormented by something else. The whole time I thought it strange that people should look upon me as an ordinary man. During all these eight years not a single living soul has looked at me searchingly; it appeared strange to me that I had not to hide. A terrible secret is concealed in me, and still I walk about the streets. I go to dinner-parties. I flirt with women! For a criminal man such a position is unnatural and painful. I would not be tormented if I had to hide and dissemble. Psychosis, baten'ka! At last I was seized by a kind of passion. . . . I suddenly wanted to pour myself out in some way on everybody, to shout my secret at them all, though nobody is worth a sneeze . . . to do something like that . . . something extraordinary. And so I wrote this novel—indictment, in which only the witness will have any difficulty

in recognizing me as a man with a secret. . . . There is not a page that does not give the key to the puzzle. Is that not true? You doubtless understand it at once. When I wrote it I took into consideration the standard of the average reader. . . ."

We were again disturbed. Andrey entered the room bringing two glasses of tea on a tray. . . . I hastened to send him away.

"Now it appears to be easier for me," Kamyshev said smiling, "now you look upon me not as an ordinary man, but as a man with a secret,—and I feel myself in a natural position. . . . But. . . . However, it is already three o'clock, and somebody is waiting for me in the cab. . . ."

"Stay, put down your hat. . . . You have told me what made you take up authorship, now tell me how you murdered."

"Do you want to know that as a supplement of what you have read? Very well. I killed in a state of aberration. Nowadays people even smoke and drink tea under the influence of aberration. In your excitement you have taken up my glass instead of your own, and you smoke more than usual. . . . Life is all aberration . . . so it appears to me. . . . When I went into the wood my thoughts were far away from murder; I went there with only one object: to find Olga and to continue to sting her. . . . When I am drunk I always feel the necessity to sting. . . . I met her about two hundred paces from the clearing. . . . She was standing under a tree and looking pensively at the sky. . . . I called to her. . . . When she saw me she smiled and stretched out her arms to me. . . .

" 'Don't scold me, I'm so unhappy!' she said.

"That evening she looked so beautiful, that I, drunk as I was, forgot everything in the world and pressed her in my arms. . . . She swore to me that she had never loved anybody but me . . . and that was true . . . she really loved me . . . and in the very midst of her assurance she suddenly took it into her head to say a horrible phrase: 'How unhappy I am! If I had not got married to Urbenin, I might now have married the Count!' This phrase was like a pail of cold water for me. . . . All that was boiling in my breast bubbled over. I seized the vile little creature by the shoulder and threw her to the ground as you throw a ball. My rage reached its maximum. . . . Well. . . . I finished her. . . . I just finished her. . . . Kuz'ma's case, you understand. . . ."

I glanced at Kamyshev. On his face I could neither read repentance nor regret. "I just finished her" was said as easily as "I just had a smoke." In my turn I also experienced a feeling of wrath and loathing. . . . I turned away.

"And Urbenin is in penal servitude?" I asked quietly.

"Yes. . . . I heard he had died on the way, but that is not certain. . . . What then?"

"What then? An innocent man is suffering and you ask 'What then?' "

"But what am I to do? To go and confess?"

"I should think so."

"Well, let us suppose it! . . . I have nothing against taking Urbenin's place, but I won't yield without a fight. . . . Let them take me if they want, but I won't go to them. Why did they not take me when I was in their hands? At Olga's funeral I squalled so long, and had such hysterics that even the blind must have seen the truth. . . . It is not my fault that they are stupid."

"You are odious to me," I said.

"That is natural. . . . I am odious to myself. . . ."

There was silence again. . . . I opened the cash-book and began mechanically to count up the numbers. . . . Kamyshev took up his hat.

"I see you are stifled while I am here," he said. "By-the-by, don't you want to see Count Karnéev? There he is sitting in the cab!"

I went up to the window and glanced at him. . . . Sitting in the cab with his back towards us sat a small stooping figure, in a shabby hat and a faded collar. It was difficult to recognize in him one of the actors of the drama!

"I heard that Urbenin's son is living here in Moscow in the Andréev Chambers," Kamyshev said. "I want to arrange that the Count should receive alms from him. . . . Let at least one be punished! However, I must say adieu!"

Kamyshev nodded and hastened out of the room. I sat down at the table and gave myself up to bitter thoughts. I felt stifled.

VOLUME V

A Terrible Night

IVAN PETROVITCH REQUIEMOV became pallid, put out the lamp and began in an agitated voice:

"Not a glimmer of light pierced the thick darkness that hung over the earth on Christmas Eve, 1883. I was returning home from the house of a friend, who is now dead, where we had all remained late holding a spiritistic séance. For some reason the small by-streets, through which I had to go, were dark, and I had to make my way by groping. I was living at the time in Moscow, near the church of the Assumption on the Tombtsa, in a house belonging to the government official Cadaverov, one of the most obscure parts of the Arbat. My thoughts as I walked home were sad and depressing.

" 'Your life is drawing to an end. . . . Repent. . . .'

"These were the words Spinoza, whose spirit we had been able to call up, had addressed to me at the séance. I had asked for them again, and the saucer had not only repeated them, but had added 'to-night.' I am no believer in spiritism, but the thoughts of death, makes me gloomy. Ladies and gentlemen, death is unavoidable, is a daily occurrence, but nevertheless to man's nature it is a subject abhorrent. Now, when I was surrounded by cold, impenetrable darkness, when before my eyes I could only see torrents of raindrops, when the wind howled plaintively above my head, and there was not a single living soul anywhere near me, nor was a human sound to be heard, my soul became filled with an un-

defined, unaccountable dread. I, a man free from prejudices, hastened along, fearing to look back, or to the side. It seemed to me if I looked back I would inevitably see death like a spectre behind me."

Requiemov breathed heavily, he gulped down a glass of water, and continued:

"This undefined dread, you will understand, did not leave me even when having mounted to the fourth story of Cadaverov's house I opened the door and entered my room. It was dark in my modest dwelling. The wind moaned in the stove as if begging to be let into the warmth, and knocked at the door of the ventilator.

" 'If Spinoza is to be believed,' I said to myself, smiling, 'I am to die to-night amid this lamentation. It certainly is eerie!'

"I lit a match. . . . A furious gust of wind passed over the roof of the house. The gentle wailing changed into wrathful roars. Somewhere below a half-detached shutter clattered and the door of my ventilator squeaked plaintively for help. . . .

" 'It's bad for the houseless on a night like this,' I thought.

"But it was no time to give oneself up to such reflections. When the sulphur on the match I had lighted gave out a blue flame, and I cast my eyes round the room, I saw an unexpected and terrible sight. . . . What a pity the gust of wind had not reached my match! Then, perhaps I would have seen nothing and my hair would not have stood on end. I shrieked, I made a step towards the door, and filled with horror, despair and amazement I closed my eyes.

"There was a coffin in the middle of the room.

"The blue light burnt but a short time; still I had been able to discern the outlines of the coffin. . . . I saw the pink glimmer and sparkle of the brocade, I saw the gold galloon cross on the lid. There are things, ladies and gentlemen, that stamp themselves on your memory, though you have seen them only for an instant. So it was with this coffin. I only saw it for a second, but I can remember it in all its smallest details. It was a coffin for a person of middle height, and judging by its pink colour it was for a young girl. The rich brocade, the feet, the bronze handles—all denoted that the corpse was rich.

"I rushed headlong out of my room and without reasoning, without thinking, only feeling an inexpressible dread, I tore down the stairs. The corridors and the staircase were dark, my legs got entangled in the skirts of my long fur coat, and it was a marvel that I did not fall down and break my neck. When I found myself in the street I leaned against a wet lamp-post and began to get calm. My heart palpitated, my breathing was heavy . . ."

One of the listeners turned up the lamp and moved closer to the narrator, who continued:

"I would not have been surprised if I had found my room on fire, if a robber or a mad dog had been there. . . . I would not have been surprised if the ceiling had fallen down, if the floor had collapsed, if the walls had

fallen in. . . . All that is natural and comprehensible. But how could a coffin have got into my room? Where did it come from? An expensive, a woman's coffin, evidently made for some young aristocrat—how could it have found its way into the wretched room of a small government official? Was it empty, or did it contain a corpse? . . . Who was she, this rich girl who had died so inopportunely, and was now paying me this strange and terrible visit? A painful secret!

" 'If this is no miracle it must be a crime,' shot through my head.

"I was lost in conjectures. During my absence the door had been locked and the place where I hid the key was known only to my most intimate friends. My friends could not have placed the coffin there! . . . It might also be supposed that the coffin had been brought to me by the undertakers owing to some error. They might have mistaken the house or gone to the wrong story or the wrong door, and had carried the coffin into the wrong flat. But who does not know that our coffin-makers will never leave a room until they have been paid for their work, or at least have received a good tip?

" 'The spirits have foretold my death.' I thought. 'Can it be they who have taken the trouble to provide me with a coffin in due time?'

"Ladies and gentlemen, I do not believe nor have I ever believed in spiritism, but such a coincidence might even plunge a philosopher into a mystical frame of mind.

" 'All this is stupid, and I am as cowardly as a school-boy,' I decided at last. 'It was only an optical illusion —nothing more! While walking home my frame of mind had been so gloomy that it is not surprising that my unstrung nerves made me see a coffin. . . . Of course, it was only an optical illusion! What else could it be?'

"The rain beat in my face, and the wind tore fiercely at my coat and cap. . . . I was cold and wet through and through. I had to go somewhere—but where? To return to my own room would expose me to the risk of again seeing the coffin, and it would be beyond my strength to bear that sight. Without a single living soul near me, not hearing a single human sound, left alone face to face with that coffin in which perhaps a corpse was lying, I might lose my senses. On the other hand, to remain in the street under the torrents of rain and in the cold was impossible.

"I decided to go and pass the night at my friend Restov's room, who, as you all know, afterwards shot himself. At the time he was living in furnished rooms in the house belonging to the merchant Skullov, situated in the Dead Lane."

Requiemov wiped away the cold sweat that had appeared on his pale face, and, heaving a deep sigh, continued:

"I did not find my friend in. I knocked at his door, and at last being convinced that he was out, I felt about on the transom for the key, opened the door and went in. I threw my wet fur-coat on the floor, groped about in the darkness for the sofa and sat down to rest. It was dark. . . . The wind hummed sadly in the window ventilator. The cricket was singing its monotonous song in the stove. The bells in the Kremlin were ringing for the Christmas matins. I hastened to strike a match. But the light did not relieve me of my gloomy mood; on the contrary, a terrible, an inexpressible horror mastered me once more. I shrieked, staggered and rushed out of the room almost beside myself.

"In my friend's room, as in my own, I also saw a coffin!

"My friend's coffin was nearly twice the size of mine, and the brown material with which it was covered gave it an especially gloomy appearance. How had it got there? It could only be an optical illusion—how was it possible to doubt it. . . . There could not be coffins in every room! My nerves were evidently diseased. . . . I had hallucinations. Wherever I might go now I would always see before me the terrible dwelling of the dead. Consequently I was mad, I was infected with something like 'coffin-mania' and the cause of my mental derangement was not far to seek: it was only necessary to remember the spiritistic séance and Spinoza's words. . . .

" 'I am going mad!' I thought in terror, seizing my head in my hands. 'My God! My God! What am I to do?'

"My head was ready to burst, my legs failed me. . . . The rain poured down as if out of buckets, the wind pierced me through and through, and I had neither a fur-coat nor a cap. I could not go back to fetch them from the room . . . that was beyond my strength. . . . Dread clasped me firmly in its cold embrace. My hair stood on end, cold perspiration streamed down my face, although I believed that it was only hallucinations.

"What was I to do?" Requiemov continued. "I was out of my mind, and

I risked catching a severe cold. Fortunately, I remembered that my good friend Godsacreov, who had but lately received his doctor's degree, was living not far from the Dead Lane. He had also been with us at the spiritistic séance. I hastened to him. . . . At that time he had not yet married the rich merchant's daughter, and was living in the fifth story of the house belonging to the State Councillor Graveyardin.

"At Godsacreov's my nerves were destined to be subjected to further torture. As I was mounting to the fifth story I heard a terrible noise. Somebody was running about upstairs, stamping heavily with his feet and slamming doors.

" 'Help!' I heard somebody cry in a voice that pierced the very soul. 'Help! Porter!'

"A moment later a dark figure in a fur-coat and a crushed silk hat rushed down the stairs towards me.

" 'Godsacreov,' I cried, recognizing my friend. 'Is it you? What is the matter?'

"When Godsacreov reached the landing on which I was standing he stopped and seized me convulsively by the hand. He was pale, he breathed heavily and trembled. His eyes wandered restlessly around, his chest heaved. . . .

" 'Is that you, Requiemov?' he asked in a hoarse voice. 'Is it really you? You are pale, like one risen from the grave. . . . But no, are you not a hallucination? My God. . . . You look terrible! . . .'

" 'But what's the matter with you? You look like a ghost!'

" 'Och! wait, my dear fellow, let me recover my breath. . . . I am glad to have met you, if it really is you and not an optical illusion. That damned spiritistic séance. . . . It has so upset my nerves that, would you believe it, just now, when I came home, I saw in my room . . . a coffin!'

"I could not believe my own ears, and asked him to repeat what he had said.

" 'A coffin, a real coffin!' the doctor repeated, sitting down on the steps quite exhausted. 'I am no coward, but the devil himself would be frightened if, after a spiritistic séance, he ran up against a coffin.'

"Stammering and confusedly I told the doctor about the coffins I had seen. . . .

"For a minute we looked at each other with staring eyes, and open-mouthed with astonishment. Then to convince ourselves that we were not dreaming we began pinching each other.

" 'We both feel pain,' the doctor said, 'so at the present moment we are not asleep, and we are not dreaming of each other. Therefore, my coffin and both your coffins were not optical illusions, but something that exists. What are we to do now, old man?'

"We stood for a whole hour on the cold staircase, lost in guesses and conjectures; we got terribly cold and at last decided to conquer our cowardly fear, arouse the man-servant on duty and go with him to the doctor's room. So we went. We entered the room, lit a candle and we really saw a coffin covered with white silver brocade with gold fringe and tassels. The man-servant piously crossed himself.

" 'Now we can find out,' the doctor said, still trembling in every limb, 'if the coffin is empty or if it is . . . inhabited!'

"After long and quite comprehensible hesitation the doctor bent over the coffin and, pressing his lips together from fright and expectation, he tore off the lid of the coffin.

"We looked into the coffin and . . .

"The coffin was empty. . . .

"There was no corpse in it, but instead we found the following letter:

" 'DEAR GODSACREOV,

" 'You know that my father-in-law's business has got into a terrible mess. He is over head and ears in debt. To-morrow or the day after there will be an execution in his house, and this would entirely ruin his family and mine, and would ruin our honour too, which is more precious than anything else for me. At a family council we held yesterday we decided to hide everything valuable or of worth. As the whole of my father-in-law's property consists of coffins (he is, as you doubtless know, the best undertaker in town), we decided to hide away all the best coffins. I entreat you, as a friend, to save our property and our honour!

Hoping that you will help us to save our goods, I send you, dear old fellow, one coffin, with the request that you will hide it in your rooms, and keep it till called for. Without the assistance of our friends and acquaintances we are ruined. I hope that you will not refuse me this assistance, all the more as the coffin will not remain with you for more than a week. To everyone whom I consider as our sincere friend I have sent a coffin, trusting in their magnanimity and nobility.

" 'Your affectionate,
" 'IVAN JAWIN.'

"For three months after that I had to undergo a cure for my shattered nerves, while our friend, the undertaker's son-in-law, saved both his honour and his property, and is now the owner of an undertaker's business; he arranges funeral processions, sells monuments and gravestones. His business, however, is not getting on very well, and every evening when I come home I always expect to find next to my bed a white marble monument or a catafalque."

In Exile

OLD Semión, nicknamed Wiseacre, and a young unknown Tartar, sat by the bonfire near the river. The other three ferrymen lay in the hut. Semión, sixty years old, and toothless, but broad-shouldered and strong, was drunk; he would have been asleep long ago if it had not been for vodka and a dread that his companions in the hut might want his. The Tartar was sick and weary; and sat there, wrapped up in his rags, holding forth on the glories of life in Simbirsk, and of the fair and smart wife he had left behind him. He was about twenty-five years old, but now in the light of the camp fire his pale, sad and sickly face seemed boyish.

"Yes, you can hardly call it paradise," said Wiseacre. Water, banks, and clay and that's all. Holy Week is gone, but there is still ice floating down the river, and now snow."

"Misery, misery!" moaned the Tartar, looking round him in terror.

Ten paces below them lay the river, dark and cold, grumbling, it seemed, at itself, as it clove a path through the steep clay banks, and bore itself swiftly to the sea. Up against the bank lay one of the great barges which the ferrymen call *karbases*. On the opposite side, far away, rising and falling, and mingling with one another, crept little serpents of fire. It was the burning of last year's grass. And behind the serpents of fire darkness again. From the river came the noise of little ice floes crashing against the barge. Darkness only, and cold!

The Tartar looked at the sky. There were as many stars there as in his own country, just the same blackness above him. But something was lacking. At home in Simbirsk government there were no such stars and no such heaven.

"Misery, misery!" he repeated.

"You'll get used to it," said Wiseacre, grinning. "You're young and foolish now—your mother's milk is still wet on your lips, only youth and folly could make you imagine there's no one more miserable than you. But the time'll come when you'll say, 'God grant every one such a life as this!' Look at me, for instance. In a week's time the water will have fallen, we'll launch the small boat, you'll be off to Siberia to amuse yourselves, and I'll remain here and row from one side to another. Twenty years now I've been ferrying. Day and night! Salmon and pike beneath the water and I above it! And

God be thanked! I don't want for anything! God grant everyone such a life!"

The Tartar thrust some brushwood into the fire, lay closer to it, and said:

"My father is ill. When he dies my mother and wife are coming. They promised me."

"What do you want with a mother and wife?" asked Wiseacre, "put that out of your head, it's all nonsense, brother! It's the devil's doing to make you think such thoughts. Don't listen to him, accursed! If he begins about women, answer him back, 'Don't want them.' If he comes about freedom, answer him back, 'Don't want it.' You don't want anything. Neither father, nor mother, nor wife, nor freedom, nor house, nor home. You don't want anything, d——n them!"

Wiseacre took a drink from his flask and continued:

"I, brother, am no simple mujik, but a sexton's son, and when I lived in freedom in Kursk wore a frockcoat, yet now I have brought myself to such a point that I can sleep naked on the earth and eat grass. And God grant everyone such a life! I don't want anything, and I don't fear anyone, and I know there is no one richer and freer than I in the world. The first day I came here from Russia I persisted, 'I don't want anything.' The devil took me on also about wife, and home, and freedom, but I answered him back 'I don't want anything.' I tired him out, and now, as you see, I live well, and don't complain. If any one bates an inch to the devil, or listens to him even once, he's lost—there's no salvation for him—he sinks in the bog to the crown of his head, and never gets out.

"Don't think it's only our brother, the stupid mujik, that gets lost. The well-born and educated lose themselves also. Fifteen years ago they sent a gentleman here from Russia. He wouldn't share something with his brothers, and did something dishonest with a will. Belonged, they said, to a prince's or a baron's family—maybe he was an official, who can tell? Well, anyway he came, and the first thing he did was to buy himself a house and land in Mukhortinsk. 'I want,' he says, 'to live by my work, by the sweat of my brow, because,' he says, 'I am no longer a gentleman, but a convict.' 'Well,' I said, 'may God help him, he can do nothing better.' He was a young man, fussy, and fond of talking; mowed his own grass, caught fish, and rode on horseback sixty versts a day. That was the cause of the misfortune. From the first year he used to ride to Guirino, to the post office. He would stand with me in the boat and sigh: 'Akh, Semión, how long they are sending me money from home.' 'You don't want it, Vassili Sergeyitch,' I answered, 'what good is money to you? Give up the old ways, forget them as if they never were, as if you had dreamt them, and begin to live anew. Pay no attention,' I said, 'to the devil, he'll bring you nothing but ill. At present, you want only money, but in a little time you'll want something more. If you want to be happy, don't wish for anything at all. Yes. . . . Already.' I used to say to him, 'fortune has done you and me a bad turn—there's no good begging charity from her, and bowing down to her—you must despise and laugh at her. Then she'll begin to laugh herself.' So I used to talk to him.

"Well, two years after he came, he drove down to the ferry in good spirits. He was rubbing his hands and laughing. 'I am going to Guirino,' he says, 'to meet my wife. She has taken pity on me, and is coming. She is a good wife.' He was out of breath from joy.

"The next day he came back with his wife. She was a young woman, a good-looking one, in a hat, with a little girl in her arms. And my Vassili Sergeyitch bustles about her, feasts his eyes on her, and praises her up to the skies, 'Yes, brother Semión, even in Siberia people live.' 'Well,' I thought, 'he won't always think so.' From that time out, every week, he rode to Guirino to inquire whether money had been sent to him from Russia. Money he wanted without end. 'For my sake,' he used to say, 'she is burying her youth and beauty in Siberia, and sharing my miserable life. For this reason I must procure her every enjoyment.' And to make things gayer for her, he makes acquaintance with officials and all kinds of people. All this company, of course, had to be fed and kept in drink, a piano must be got, and a shaggy dog for the sofa—in one word, extravagance, luxury. . . . She didn't live with him long. How could she? Mud, water, cold, neither vegetable nor fruit, bears and drunkards around her, and she a woman from Petersburg, petted and spoiled. . . . Of course, she got sick of it. . . . Yes, and a husband, too, no longer a man, but a convict. . . . Well, after three years, I remember, on Assumption Eve, I heard shouting from the opposite bank. When I rowed across I saw the lady all wrapped up, and with her a young man, one of the officials. A troïka! I rowed them across, they got into the troïka and drove off. Towards morning Vassili Sergeyoitch drives up in hot haste. 'Did my wife go by,' he asked, 'with a man in spectacles?' 'Yes,' I said, 'seek the wind in the field.' He drove after them, and chased them for five days. When I ferried him back, he threw himself into the bottom of the boat, beat his head against the planks, and howled. I laughed and reminded him, 'even in Siberia people live!' But that only made him worse.

"After this he tried to regain his freedom. His wife had gone back to Russia, and he thought only of seeing her, and getting her to return to him. Every day he galloped off to one place or another, one day to the post office, the next to town to see the authorities. He sent in petitions asking for pardon and permission to return to Russia—on telegrams alone, he used to say, he spent two hundred roubles. He sold his land and mortgaged his house to a Jew. He got grey-haired and bent, and his face turned yellow like a consumptive's. He could not speak without tears coming into his eyes. Eight years he spent sending in petitions. Then he came to life again; he had got a new consolation. The daughter, you see, was growing up. He doted on her. And to tell the truth, she wasn't bad-looking—pretty, black-browed, and high-spirited. Every Sunday he rode with her to the church at Guirino. They would stand side by side in the boat, she laughing, and he never lifting his eyes from her. 'Yes,' he said, 'Semión, even in Siberia people live, and are happy. See what a daughter I've got! you might go a thousand versts and never see another like her.' The daugh-

ter, as I said, was really good-looking. 'But wait a little,' I used to say to myself, 'the girl is young, the blood flows in her veins, she wants to live; and what is life here?' Anyway, brother, she began to grieve. Pined and declined, dwindled away, got ill, and now can't stand on her legs. Consumption! There's your Siberian happiness! That's the way people live in Siberia! . . . And my Vassili Sergeyitch spends his time driving about to doctors and bringing them home. Once let him hear there's a doctor or a magic curer within two or three hundred versts, and after him he must go. . . . It's terrible to think of the amount of money he spends, he might as well drink it. . . She'll die all the same, nothing'll save her, and then he'll be altogether lost. Whether he hangs himself from grief or runs off to Russia it's all the same. If he runs away they'll catch him, then we'll have a trial and penal servitude, and the rest of it. . . ."

"It was very well for him," said the Tartar, shuddering with the cold.

"What was well?"

"Wife and daughter. . . . Whatever he suffers, whatever punishment he'll have, at any rate he saw them. . . . *You* say you don't want anything. But to have nothing is bad. His wife lived with him three years, God granted him that. To have nothing is bad, but three years is good. You don't understand."

Trembling with cold, finding only with painful difficulty the proper Russian words, the Tartar began to beg that God might save him from dying in a strange land, and being buried in the cold earth. If his wife were to come to him, even for one day, even for one hour, for such happiness he would consent to undergo the most frightful tortures, and thank God for them. Better one day's happiness than nothing!

And he again told the story of how he had left at home a handsome and clever wife. Then, putting both his hands to his head, he began to cry, and to assure Semión that he was guilty of nothing, and was suffering unjustly. His two brothers and his uncle had stolen a peasant's horses, and beaten the old man half to death. But society had treated him unfairly, and sent the three brothers to Siberia, while the uncle, a rich man, remained at home.

"You'll get used to it!" said Semión.

The Tartar said nothing, and only turned his wet eyes on the fire; his face expressed doubt and alarm, as if he did not yet understand why he lay there in darkness and in cold among strangers, and not at Simbirsk. Wiseacre lay beside the fire, laughed silently at something, and hummed a tune.

"What happiness can she have with her father?" he began after a few minutes' silence. "He loves her, and finds her a consolation, that's true. But you can't put your finger in his eyes; he's a cross old man, a stern old man. And with young girls you don't want sternness. What they want is caresses, and ha! ha! ha! and ho! ho! ho!—perfume and pomade. Yes . . . Akh, business, business!" He sighed, lifting himself clumsily. "Vodka all gone—means it's time to go to bed. Well, I'm off, brother."

The Tartar added some more brushwood to the fire, lay down again, and began to think of his native village and of his wife; if his wife would only come for a week, for a day, let her go back if she liked! Better a few days, even a day, than nothing! But if his wife kept her promise and came, what would he feed her with? Where would she live?

"How can you live without anything to eat?" he asked aloud.

For working day and night at an oar they paid him only ten kopecks a day. True, passengers sometimes gave money for tea and vodka, but the others shared this among themselves, gave nothing to the Tartar, and only laughed at him. From poverty he was hungry, cold, and frightened. His whole body ached and trembled. If he went into the hut there would be nothing for him to cover himself with. Here, too, he had nothing to cover himself with, but he might keep up the fire.

In a week the waters would have fallen, and the ferrymen, with the exception of Semión, would no longer be wanted. The Tartar must begin his tramp from village to village asking for bread and work. His wife was only seventeen years old; she was pretty, modest, and spoiled. How could she tramp with uncovered face through the villages and ask for bread? It was too horrible to think of.

When next the Tartar looked up it was dawn. The barge, the willows, and the ripples stood out plainly. You might turn round and see the clayey slope, with its brown thatched hut at the bottom, and above it the huts of the village. In the village the cocks already crowed.

The clayey slope, the barge, the river, the strange wicked people, hunger, cold, sickness—in reality there was none of this at all. It was only a dream, thought the Tartar. He felt that he was sleeping, and heard himself snore. Of course, he was at home in Simbirsk, he had only to call his wife by name and she would call back; in the next room lay his old mother. . . . What terrible things are dreams! . . . Where do they come from? . . . The Tartar smiled and opened his eyes. What river was this? The Volga?

It began to snow.

"Ahoy!" came a voice from the other side, "boatman!"

The Tartar shook himself, and went to awaken his companions. Dragging on their sheepskin coats on the way, swearing in voices hoarse from sleep, the ferrymen appeared on the bank. After sleep, the river, with its piercing breeze, evidently seemed to them a nightmare. They tumbled lazily into the boat. The Tartar and three ferrymen took up the long, wide-bladed oars which looked in the darkness like the claws of a crab. Semión threw himself on his stomach across the helm. On the opposite bank the shouting continued, and twice revolver shots were heard. The stranger evidently thought that the ferrymen were asleep or had gone into the village to the kabak.

"You'll get across in time," said Wiseacre in the tone of a man who is convinced that in this world there is no need for hurry. "It's all the same in the end; you'll gain nothing by making a noise."

The heavy, awkward barge parted from the bank, cleaving a path through the willows, and only the slow movement of the willows backward showed that it was moving at all. The ferrymen slowly raised their oars in time. Wiseacre lay on his stomach across the helm, and, describing a bow in the air, swung slowly from one side to the other. In the dim light it seemed as if the men were sitting on some long-clawed antediluvian animal, floating with it into the cold desolate land that is sometimes seen in nightmares.

The willows soon were passed and the open water reached. On the other bank the creak and measured dipping of the oars were already audible, and cries of "Quicker, quicker!" came back across the water. Ten minutes more and the barge struck heavily against the landing-stage.

"It keeps on falling, it keeps on falling," grumbled Semión, rubbing the snow from his face. "Where it all comes from God only knows!"

On the bank stood a frail old man of low stature in a short foxskin coat and white lambskin cap. He stood immovable at some distance from the horses; his face had a gloomy concentrated expression, as if he were trying to remember something, and were angry with his disobedient memory. When Semión approached him, and, smiling, took off his cap, he began:

"I am going in great haste to Anastasevka. My daughter is worse. In Anastasevka, I am told, a new doctor has been appointed."

The ferrymen dragged the cart on to the barge, and started back. The man, whom Semión called Vassili Sergeyitch, stood all the time immovable, tightly compressing his thick fingers, and when the driver asked for permission to smoke in his presence, answered nothing, as if he had not heard. Semión, lying on his stomach across the helm, looked at him maliciously, and said:

"Even in Siberia people live! Even in Siberia!"

Wiseacre's face bore a triumphant expression, as if he had demonstrated something, and rejoiced that things had justified his prediction. The miserable, helpless expression of the man in the foxskin coat evidently only increased his delight.

"It's muddy travelling at this time, Vassili Sergeyitch," he said, as they harnessed the horses on the river bank. "You might have waited another week or two till it got drier. For the matter of that, you might just as well not go at all. . . . If there was any sense in going it would be another matter, but you yourself know that you might go on for ever and nothing would come of it. . . . Well?"

Vassili Sergeyitch silently handed the men some money, climbed into the cart, and drove off.

"After that doctor again," said Semión, shuddering from the cold. "Yes, look for a real doctor—chase the wind in the field, seize the devil by the tail, damn him. Akh, what characters these people are! Lord forgive me, a sinner!"

The Tartar walked up to Semión, and looked at him with hatred and repulsion. Then, trembling, and mixing Tartar words with his broken Russian, he said:

"He is a good man, a good man, and you are bad. You are bad. He is a good soul, a great one, but you are a beast. . . . He is living, but you are dead. . . . God made men that they might have joys and sorrows, but you ask for nothing. . . . You are a stone, —earth! A stone wants nothing, and you want nothing. . . . You are a stone, and God has no love for you. But him He loves!"

All laughed; the Tartar alone frowned disgustedly, shook his hand, and, pulling his rags more closely round him, walked back to the fire. Semión and the ferrymen returned to the hut.

"Cold!" said one ferryman in a hoarse voice, stretching himself on the straw with which the floor was covered.

"Yes, it's not warm," said another. "A galley-slave's life!"

All lay down. The door opened before the wind, and snowflakes whirled through the hut. But no one rose to shut it, all were too cold and lazy.

"I, for one, am all right," said Semión. "God grant everyone such a life."

"You, it is known, were born a galley-slave—the devil himself wouldn't take you."

From the yard came strange sounds like the whining of a dog.

"What's that? Who's there?"

"It's the Tartar crying."

"Well . . what a character!"

"He'll get used to it," said Semión, and went off to sleep.

Soon all the others followed his example. But the door remained unshut.

The Proposal

VALANTIN PETROVICH PEREDERKIN, a handsome young man, put on his evening suit, patent leather shoes, and his opera hat and drove to the house of Princess Vera Zapiskina, bursting for joy.

It is a thousand pities, reader, that you do not know the Princess Vera, that sweet, enchanting creature, with blue eyes and silken curls of fascinating waves.

The waves of the sea break on the rocks, but the waves of her hair, on the contrary, would break and scatter in fragments the hardest stone. One would have to be wooden to resist her smile, or the charm that her small but graceful figure spread round her, or when she laughs, or shows her flashing white teeth in fair speech.

Perederkin was received.

He sat down opposite the Princess and, feeling helpless with emotion, began:

"Princess, can you listen to me?"

"Oh, yes."

"Princess—forgive me—I don't know where to begin. It is so unexpected for you . . . so sudden. . . . You will not take it ill?"

He pulled his pocket-handkerchief out of his pocket and mopped his face, while the Princess smiled sweetly and looked inquiringly at him.

"Princess," he continued, "from the moment I saw you for the first time my soul was filled with an unconquerable desire. . . . This desire gives me no peace by night, or day . . . and if it is not satisfied I . . . I shall be miserable."

The Princess lowered her eyes meditatively.

Perederkin hesitated, and then continued:

"You, of course, will be surprised . . . you are above everything earthly, but . . . for me you are the most suitable . . ."

Silence.

"More especially as my estate touches yours. . . . I am rich. . . ."

"But what is it all about?" the Princess asked quietly.

"What it is all about, Princess, Perederkin exclaimed with emotion, rising from his seat, "I entreat you, do not refuse. . . . Do not ruin my plans by your refusal. My dear, let me propose. . . ."

Valantin Petrovich sat down again hastily, and bending towards the Princess, whispered:

"The proposal is a most profitable one. In one year we shall sell a million poods of tallow. Let us start on our adjoining estates a limited liability company for tallow-boiling. . . ."

The Princess reflected for a moment and then answered:

"With pleasure."

The reader who expected a melodramatic ending will be disappointed.

Who to Blame?

As my uncle Pyotr Demyanitch, a lean, bilious collegiate councillor, exceedingly like a stale smoked fish with a stick through it, was getting ready to go to the high school, where he taught Latin, he noticed that the corner of his grammar was nibbled by mice.

"I say, Praskovya," he said, going into the kitchen and addressing the cook, "how it is we have got mice here? Upon my word! yesterday my top hat was nibbled, today they have disfigured my Latin grammar. . . . At this rate they will soon begin eating my clothes!"

"What can I do? I did not bring them in!" answered Praskovya.

"We must do something! You had better get a cat, hadn't you?" . . .

"I've got a cat, but what good is it?"

And Praskovya pointed to the corner where a white kitten, thin as a match, lay curled up asleep beside a broom.

"Why it is no good?" asked Pyotr Demyanitch.

"It's young yet, and foolish. It's not two months old yet."

"H'm. . . . Then it must be trained. It had much better be learning instead of lying there."

"Saying this, Pyotr Demyanitch sighed with a careworn air and went out of the kitchen. The kitten raised his head, looked lazily after him, and shut his eyes again.

The kitten lay awake thinking. Of what? Unacquainted with real life, having no store of accumulated impressions, his mental processes could only be instinctive, and he could but picture life in accordance with the conceptions that he had inherited, together with his flesh and blood, from his ancestors, the tigers (*vide* Darwin). His thoughts were of the nature of day-dreams. His feline imagination pictured something like the Arabian desert, over which flitted shadows closely resembling Praskovya, the stove, the broom. In the midst of the shadows there suddenly appeared a saucer of milk; the saucer began to grow paws, it began moving and displayed a tendency to run; the kitten made a bound, and with a thrill of blood-thirsty sensuality thrust his claws into it. . . . When the saucer had vanished into obscurity a piece of meat appeared, dropped by Praskovya; the meat ran away with a cowardly squeak, but the kitten made a bound and got his claws into it. . . . Everything that rose before the imagination of the young dreamer had for its starting point leaps, claws and teeth. . . . The soul of another is darkness, and a cat's soul more than most, but how near the visions just described are to the truth may be seen from the following fact: under the influence of his day-dreams the kitten suddenly leaped up, looked with flashing eyes at Praskovya, ruffled up his coat, and making one bound, thrust his claws into the cook's skirt. Obviously he was born a mouse catcher, a worthy son of his blood-thirsty ancestors. Fate had destined him to be the terror of cellars, store rooms and corn bins, and had it not been for education . . . we will not anticipate, however.

307

On his way home from the high school, Pyotr Demyanitch went into a general shop and bought a mouse trap for fifteen kopecks. At dinner he fixed a little bit of his rissole on the hook, and set the trap under the sofa, where there were heaps of the pupils' old exercise books, which Praskovya used for various domestic purposes. At six o'clock in the evening, when the worthy Latin master was sitting at the table correcting his pupils' exercises, there was a sudden "klop!" so loud that my uncle started and dropped his pen. He went at once to the sofa and took out the trap. A neat little mouse, the size of a thimble, was sniffing the wires and trembling with fear.

"Aha," muttered Pyotr Demyanitch, and he looked at the mouse malignantly. as though he were about to give him a bad mark. "You are caught, wretch! Wait a bit! I'll teach you to eat my grammar!"

Having gloated over his victim, Pyotr Demyanitch put the mouse trap on the floor and called:

"Praskovya, there's a mouse caught! Bring the kitten here!"

"I'm coming," responded Praskovya, and a minute later she came in with the descendant of tigers in her arms.

"Capital!" said Pyotr Demyanitch, rubbing his hands. "We will give him a lesson. . . . Put him down opposite the mouse trap . . . that's it. . . . Let him sniff it and look at it. . . . That's it. . . ."

The kitten looked wonderingly at my uncle, at his arm chair, sniffed the mouse trap in bewilderment, then, frightened probably by the glaring lamplight and the attention directed to him, made a dash and ran in terror to the door.

"Stop!" shouted my uncle, seizing him by the tail, "stop, you rascal! He's afraid of a mouse, the idiot! Look! It's a mouse! Look! Well? Look, I tell you!"

Pyotr Demyanitch took the kitten by the scruff of the neck and pushed him with his nose against the mouse trap.

"Look, you carrion! Take him and hold him, Praskovya. . . . Hold him opposite the door of the trap. . . . When I let the mouse out, you let him go instantly. . . . Do you hear? . . . Instantly let go! Now!"

My uncle assumed a mysterious expression and lifted the door of the trap. . . . The mouse came out irresolutely, sniffed the air, and flew like an arrow under the sofa. . . . The kitten on being released darted under the table with his tail in the air.

"It has got away! got away!" cried Pyotr Demyanitch, looking ferocious. "Where is he, the scoundrel? Under the table? You wait. . . ."

My uncle dragged the kitten from under the table and shook him in the air.

"Wretched little beast." he muttered, smacking him on the ear. "Take that, take that! Will you shirk it next time? Wr-r-r-etch. . . ."

Next day Praskovya heard again the summons.

"Praskovya, there is a mouse caught! Bring the kitten here!"

After the outrage of the previous day the kitten had taken refuge under the stove and had not come out all night. When Praskovya pulled him out and, carrying him by the scruff of the neck into the study, set him down before the mouse trap, he trembled all over and mewed piteously.

"Come, let him feel at home first," Pyotr Demyanitch commanded. "Let him look and sniff. Look and learn! Stop, plague take you!" he shouted, noticing that the kitten was backing away from the mouse trap. "I'll thrash you! Hold him by the ear! That's it. . . . Well now, set him down before the trap. . . ."

My uncle slowly lifted the door of the trap . . . the mouse whisked under the very nose of the kitten, flung itself against Praskovya's hand and fled under the cupboard; the kitten, feeling himself free, took a desperate bound and retreated under the sofa.

"He's let another mouse go!" bawled Pyotr Demyanitch. "Do you call that a cat? Nasty little beast! Thrash him! thrash him by the mouse trap!"

When the third mouse had been caught, the kitten shivered all over at the sight of the mouse trap and its inmate, and scratched Praskovya's hand. . . . After the fourth mouse my uncle flew into a rage, kicked the kitten, and said:

"Take the nasty thing away! Get rid of it! Chuck it away! It's no earthly use!"

A year passed, the thin, frail kitten had turned into a solid and sagacious tom cat. One day he was on his way by the back yards to an amatory interview. He had just reached his destination when he suddenly heard a rustle, and thereupon caught sight of a mouse which ran from a water trough towards a stable; my hero's hair stood on end, he arched his back, hissed, and trembling all over, took to ignominious flight.

Alas! sometimes I feel myself in the ludicrous position of the flying cat. Like the kitten, I had in my day the honor of being taught Latin by my uncle. Now, whenever I chance to see some work of classical antiquity, instead of being moved to eager enthusiasm, I begin recalling, *ut consecutivum,* the irregular verbs, the sallow grey face of my uncle, the ablative absolute. . . . I turn pale, my hair stands up on my head. and, like the cat, I take to ignominious flight.

Rothschild's Fiddle

THE town was no larger than a village and was so inhabited almost entirely by old people of long life that it was positively calamitous. In the hospital, and even in the prison, coffins were seldom needed. In one word, business was bad. If Yacob Ivanof had been coffin-maker in the government town, he would have owned his

own house, and called himself Yakob Matvieitch; but, as it was, he was only Yakob, with a street nickname of "Bronza"; and lived like a peasant in a little, old, one room cabin; and in this room lived he, Marfa, the stove, a double bed, the coffins, a joiner's bench, and all the household articles.

Yet Yakob made coffins, durable and

fine. For peasants and petty trades-people he made them all of one size (his own); and this method was perfect. for though seventy years of age, there was not a taller or stouter man in the town or prison. For women and for men of good birth he made his coffins to measure, using for this purpose an iron yardwand. Orders for children's coffins he accepted very unwillingly, made them without measurement, as if in contempt, and every time when paid for his work exclaimed: "Thanks. But I confess I don't care much for wasting time on trifles."

In addition to coffin-making Yakob drew a small income from his skill with the fiddle. At weddings in the town there usually played a Jewish orchestra, the conductor of which was the tin-smith Moses Ilitch Shakhkes, who kept more than half the takings for himself. As Yakob played very well upon the fiddle, being particularly skilful with Russian songs, Shakhkes sometimes employed him in the orchestra, paying him fifty kopecks a day, exclusive of gifts from the guests. When Bronza sat in the orchestra he perspired and his face grew purple; it was always hot, the smell of garlic was suffocating; the fiddle whined, at his right ear snored the double-bass, at his left wept the flute, played by a lanky, red-haired Jew with a whole network of red and blue veins upon his face, who bore the same surname as the famous millionaire Rothschild. And even the merriest tunes this accursed Jew managed to play sadly. Without any tangible cause Yakob had become slowly penetrated with hatred and contempt for Jews, and especially for Rothschild; he began with irritation, then swore at him, and

once even was about to hit him; but Rothschild flared up, and, looking at him furiously, said:

"If it were not that I respect you for your talents, I should send you flying out of the window."

Then he began to cry. So Bronza was employed in the orchestra very seldom, and only in cases of extreme need when one of the Jews was absent. Yakob had never been in a good humour. He was always overwhelmed by the sense of the losses which he suffered. For instance, on Sundays and saints' days it was a sin to work, Monday was a tiresome day—and so on; so that in one way or another, there were about two hundred days in the year when he was compelled to sit with his hands idle. That was one loss! If anyone in the town got married without music, or if Shakhkes did not employ Yakob, that was another loss. The Inspector of Police was ill for two years, and Yakob waited with impatience for his death, yet in the end the Inspector transferred himself to the government town for the purpose of treatment, where he got worse and died. There was another loss, a loss at the very least of ten roubles, as the Inspector's coffin would have been an expensive one lined with brocade. Regrets for his losses generally overtook Yakob at night; he lay in bed with the fiddle beside him, and, with his head full of such speculations, would take the bow, the fiddle giving out through the darkness a melancholy sound which made Yakob feel better.

On the sixth of May last year Marfa was suddenly taken ill. She breathed heavily, drank much water and staggered. Yet next morning she lighted the stove, and even went for water. Towards evening she lay down. All day Yakob had played on the fiddle, and when it grew dark he took the book in which every day he inscribed his losses, and from want of something better to do, began to add them up. The total amounted to more than a thousand roubles. The thought of such losses so horrified him that he threw the book on the floor and stamped his feet. Then he took up the book, snapped his fingers, and sighed heavily. His face was purple, and wet with perspiration. He reflected that if this thousand roubles had been lodged in the bank the interest per annum would have amounted to at least forty roubles. That meant that the forty roubles were also a loss. In one word, wherever you turn, everywhere you meet with loss, and profits none.

"Yakob," cried Marfa unexpectedly, "I am dying."

He glanced at his wife. Her face was red from fever and unusually clear and joyful: and Bronza, who was accustomed to see her pale, timid, and unhappy-looking, felt confused. It seemed as if she were indeed dying, and were happy in the knowledge that she was leaving for ever the cabin, the coffins, and Yakob. And now she looked at the ceiling and twitched her lips. as if she had seen Death her deliverer, and were whispering with him.

Morning came; through the window might be seen the rising of the sun. Looking at his old wife, Yakob somehow remembered that all his life he had never treated her kindly, never caressed her, never pitied her, never thought of buying her a kerchief for her head, never carried away from the weddings a piece of tasty food, but only roared at her, abused her for his losses, and rushed at her with shut fists. True, he had never beaten her, but he had often frightened her out of her life and left her rooted to the ground with terror. Yes, and he had forbidden her to drink tea, as the losses without that were great enough; so she drank always hot water. And now, beginning to understand why she had such a strange, enraptured face, he felt uncomfortable.

When the sun had risen high he borrowed a cart from a neighbour, and brought Marfa to the hospital. There were not many patients there, and he had to wait only three hours. To his joy he was received not by the doctor but by the feldscher, Maxim Nikolaitch. an old man of whom it was said that, although he was drunken and quarrelsome, he knew more than the doctor.

"May your health be good!" said Yakob, leading the old woman into the dispensary. "Forgive me, Maxim Nikolaitch, for troubling you with my empty affairs. But there, you can see for yourself my object is ill. The companion of my life, as they say, excuse the expression . . ."

Contracting his grey brows and smoothing his whiskers, the feldscher began to examine the old woman, who sat on the tabouret, bent, skinny, sharp-nosed, and with open mouth so that she resembled a bird that is about to drink.

"So . . ." said the feldscher slowly, and then sighed. "Influenza and may be a bit of a fever. There is typhus now in the town . . what can I do? She is an old woman, glory be to God. . . . How old?"

"Sixty-nine years, Maxim Nikolaitch."

"An old woman. It's high time for her."

"Of course! Your remark is very just," said Yakob, smiling out of politeness; but allow me to make one remark; every insect is fond of life."

The feldscher replied in a tone which implied that upon him alone depended her life or death. "I will tell you what you'll do, friend; put on her head a cold compress, and give her these powders twice a day. And good-bye to you."

By the expression of the feldscher's face, Yacob saw that it was a bad business, and that no powders would make it any better; it was quite plain to him that Marfa was beyond repair, and would assuredly die, if not to-day then to-morrow. He touched the feldscher on the arm, blinked his eyes, and said in a whisper:

"Yes, Maxim Nikolaitch, but you will let her blood."

"I have no time, no time, friend. Take your old woman, and God be with you!"

"Do me this one kindness!" implored Yakob. "You yourself know that if she merely had her stomach out of order, or some internal organ wrong, then powders and mixtures would cure; but she has caught cold. In cases of cold the first thing is to bleed the patient."

But the feldscher had already called for the next patient, and into the dispensary came a peasant woman with a little boy.

"Be off!" he said to Yakob, with a frown.

"At least try the effect of leeches. I will pray God eternally for you."

The feldscher lost his temper, and roared:

"Not another word."

Yakob also lost his temper, and grew purple in the face; but he said nothing more and took Marfa under his arm and led her out of the room. As soon as he had got her into the cart, he looked angrily and contemptuously at the hospital and said:

"What an artist! He will let the blood of a rich man, but for a poor man grudges even a leech. Herod!"

When they arrived home, and entered the cabin, Marfa stood for a moment holding on to the stove. She was afraid that if she were to lie down Yakob would begin to complain about his losses, and abuse her for lying in bed and doing no work. And Yakob looked at her with tedium in his soul and remembered that to-morrow was John the Baptist, and the day after Nikolai the Miracle-worker, and then came Sunday, and after that Monday—another idle day. For four days no work could be done, and Marfa would be sure to die on one of these days. Her coffin must be made to-day. He took the iron yardwand, went up to the old woman and took her measure. After that she lay down, and Yakob crossed himself, and began to make a coffin.

When the work was finished, Bronza put on his spectacles and wrote in his book of losses:

"Marfa Ivanova's coffin—2 roubles, 40 kopecks."

And he sighed. All the time Marfa had lain silently with her eyes closed. Towards evening, when it was growing dark, she called her husband:

"Rememberest, Yakob?" she said, looking at him joyfully. "Rememberest, fifty years ago God gave us a baby with yellow hair. Thou and I then sat every day by the river . . . under the willow . . . and sang songs." And laughing bitterly she added: "The child died."

"That is all imagination," said Yakob.

Later on came the priest, administered to Mafa the Sacrament and extreme unction. Marfa began to mutter something incomprehensible, and towards morning, died.

The old-women neighbours washed her, wrapped her in her winding sheet, and laid her out. To avoid having to pay the deacon's fee, Yakob himself read the psalms; and escaped a fee also at the graveyard, as the watchman there was his godfather. Four peasants carried the coffin free, out of respect for the deceased. After the coffin walked a procession of old women, beggars, and two cripples. The peasants on the road crossed themselves piously. And Yakob was very satisfied that everything passed off in honour, order, and cheapness, without offence to anyone. When saying good-bye for the last time to Marfa, he tapped the coffin with his fingers, and thought "An excellent piece of work."

But while he was returning from the graveyard he was overcome with extreme weariness. He felt unwell. he breathed feverishly and heavily, he could hardly stand on his feet. His brain was full of unaccustomed thoughts. He remembered again that he had never taken pity on Marfa and never caressed her. The fifty-two years during which they had lived in the same cabin stretched back to eternity, yet in the whole of that eternity he had never thought of her, never paid any attention

to her, but treated her as if she were a cat or a dog. Yet every day she had lighted the stove, boiled and baked, fetched water, chopped wood, slept with him on the same bed; and when he returned drunk from weddings, she had taken his fiddle respectfully, and hung it on the wall, and put him to bed—all this silently with a timid, worried expression on her face. And now he felt that he could take pity on her, and would like to buy her a present, but it was too late. . . .

Towards Yakob smiling and bowing came Rothschild.

"I was looking for you, uncle," he said. "Moses Ilitch sends his compliments, and asks you to come across to him at once."

Yakob felt inclined to cry.

"Begone!" he shouted, and continued his path.

"You can't mean that," cried Rothschild in alarm, running after him. "Moses Ilitch will take offence! He wants you at once."

The way in which the Jew puffed and blinked, and the multitude of his red freckles awoke in Yakob disgust. He felt disgust, too, for his green frockcoat. with its black patches, and his whole fragile, delicate figure.

"What do you mean by coming after me, garlic?" he shouted. "Keep off!"

The Jew also grew angry, and cried:

"If you don't take care to be a little politer I will send you flying over the fence."

"Out of my sight!" roared Yakob, rushing on him with clenched fists. "Out of my sight, abortion, or I will beat the soul out of your cursed body! I have no peace with Jews."

Rothschild was frozen with terror; he

squatted down and waved his arms above his head. as if warding off blows, and then jumped up and ran for his life. While running he hopped, and flourished his hands; and the twitching of his long, fleshless spine could plainly be seen. The boys in the street were delighted with the incident, and rushed after him, crying, "Jew! Jew!" The dogs pursued him with loud barks. Someone laughed, then someone whistled, and the dogs barked louder and louder. Then, it must have been. a dog bit Rothschild, for there rang out a sickly, despairing cry.

Yakob walked past the common, and then along the outskirts of the town; and the street boys cried, "Bronza! Bronza!" With a piping note snipe flew around him, and ducks quacked. The sun baked everything, and from the water came scintillations so bright that it was painful to look at. Yakob walked along the path by the side of the river, and watched a stout, red-cheeked lady come out of the bathing-place. Not far from the bathing-place sat a group of boys catching crabs with meat; and seeing him they cried maliciously, "Bronza! Bronza!" And at this moment before him rose a thick old willow with an immense hollow in it, and on it a raven's nest. . . . And suddenly in Yakob's mind awoke the memory of the child with the yellow hair of whom Marfa had spoken. . . Yes, it was the same yellow, green, silent, sad. . . . How it had aged, poor thing!

He sat underneath it, and began to remember. On the other bank, where was now a flooded meadow, there then stood a great birch forest, and farther away, where the now bare hill glim-

mered on the horizon, was an old pine wood. Up and down the river went barges. But now everything was flat and smooth; on the opposite bank stood only a single birch, young and shapely, like a girl; and on the river were only ducks and geese where once had floated barges. It seemed that since those days even the geese had become smaller. Yakob closed his eyes, and in imagination saw flying towards him an immense flock of white geese.

He began to wonder how it was that in the last forty or fifty years of his life he had never been near the river, or if he had, had never noticed it. Yet it was a respectable river, and by no means contemptible; it would have been possible to fish in it, and the fish might have been sold to tradesmen, officials, and the attendant at the railway station buffet, and the money could have been lodged in the bank; he might have used it for rowing from country-house to country-house and playing on the fiddle, and everyone would have paid him money; he might even have tried to act as bargee—it would have been better than making coffins; he might have kept geese, killed them and sent them to Moscow in the winter-time—from the feathers alone he would have made as much as ten roubles a year. But he had yawned away his life, and done nothing. What losses! Akh, what losses! and if he had done all together —caught fish, played on the fiddle, acted as bargee, and kept geese—what a sum he would have amassed! But he had never even dreamed of this; life had passed without profits, without any satisfaction; everything had passed away unnoticed; before him nothing remained. But look backward—nothing but losses, such losses that to think of them it makes the blood run cold. And why cannot a man live without these losses? Why had the birch wood and the pine forest both been cut down? Why is the common pasture unused? Why do people do exactly what they ought not to do? Why did he all his life scream, roar, clench his fists, insult his wife? For what imaginable purpose did he frighten and insult the Jew? Why, indeed, do people prevent one another living in peace? All these are also losses! Terrible losses! If it were not for hatred and malice people would draw from one another incalculable profits.

Evening and night, twinkled in Yakob's brain the willow, the fish, the dead geese, Marfa with her profile like that of a bird about to drink, the pale, pitiable face of Rothschild, and an army of snouts thrusting themselves out of the darkness and muttering about losses. He shifted from side to side, and five times in the night rose from his bed and played on the fiddle.

In the morning he rose with an effort and went to the hospital. The same Maxim Nikolaitch ordered him to bind his head with a cold compress, and gave him powders; and by the expression of his face and by his tone Yakob saw that it was a bad business, and that no powders would make it any better. But upon his way home he reflected that from death at least there would be one profit; it would no longer be necessary to eat, to drink, to pay taxes, or to injure others; and as a man lies in his grave not one year, but hundreds and thousands of years, the profit was enormous. The life of man was, in short, a loss, and only his death a profit. Yet this consideration, though entirely just, was offensive and bitter; for why in this world is it so ordered that life, which is given to a man only once, passes by without profit?

He did not regret dying, but as soon as he arrived home and saw his fiddle, his heart fell, and he felt sorry. The fiddle could not be taken to the grave; it must remain an orphan, and the same thing would happen with it as had happened with the birchwood and the pine-forest. Everything in this world decayed, and would decay! Yakob went to the door of the hut and sat upon the threshold stone, pressing his fiddle to his shoulder. Still thinking of life, full of decay and full of losses, he began to play, and as the tune poured out plaintively and touchingly, the tears flowed down his cheeks. And the harder he thought, the sadder was the song of the fiddle.

The latch creaked twice, and in the wicket door appeared Rothschild. The first half of the yard he crossed boldly, but seeing Yakob, he stopped short, shrivelled up, and apparently from fright began to make signs as if he wished to tell the time with his fingers.

"Come on, don't be afraid," said Yakob kindly, beckoning him. "Come!"

With a look of distrust and terror Rothschild drew near and stopped about two yards away.

"Don't beat me, Yakob, it is not my fault!" he said, with a bow. "Moses Ilitch has sent me again. 'Don't be afraid!' he said, 'go to Yakob again and tell him that without him we cannot possibly get on.' The wedding is on Wednesday. Shapovaloff's daughter is marrying a wealthy man. . . . It will be a first-class wedding," added the Jew, blinking one eye.

"I cannot go," answered Yakob, breathing heavily. "I am ill, brother."

And again he took his bow, and the tears burst from his eyes and fell upon the fiddle. Rothschild listened attentively, standing by his side with arms folded upon his chest. The distrustful, terrified expression upon his face little by little changed into a look of suffering and grief. he rolled his eyes as if in an ecstacy of torment, and ejaculated "Wachchch!" And the tears slowly rolled down his cheeks and made little black patches on his green frock-coat.

All day long Yakob lay in bed and worried. With evening came the priest, and, confessing him, asked whether he had any particular sin which he would like to confess; and Yakob exerted his fading memory, and remembering Marfa's unhappy face, and the Jew's des-pairing cry when he was bitten by the dog, said in a hardly audible voice: "Give the fiddle to Rothschild."

And now in the town everyone asks: Where did Rothschild get such an excellent fiddle? Did he buy it or steal it . . . or did he get it in pledge? Long ago he abandoned his flute, and now plays on the fiddle only. From beneath his bow issue the same mournful sounds as formerly came from the flute; but when he tries to repeat the tune that Yakob played when he sat on the threshold stone, the fiddle emits sounds so passionately sad and full of grief that the listeners weep; and he himself rolls his eyes and ejaculates "Wach-chch!" . . . But this new song so pleases everyone in the town that wealthy traders and officials never fail to engage Rothschild for their social gatherings, and even force him to play it as many as ten times,

---

Sleepyhead

NIGHT. Nursemaid Varka, aged thirteen, rocks the cradle and sings softly to the baby:

"Bayu, bayushki, bayú!
Nurse will sing a song to you! . . ."

Before the ikon a green lamp burns; across the room from wall to wall is a cord holding baby-clothes and a great pair of black trousers. Above the lamp shines a great green spot on the ceiling and the baby-clothes and trousers cast long shadows on the stove. on the cradle, on Varka. . . . When the lamp flickers, the spot and shadows flicker weirdly in unison. There is a stifling smell of soup and boots.

The child is hoarse from crying but never ceases. And Varka wants to sleep. Her head hurts, her eyelids droop, her neck twists. She can hardly move, and it seems to her that her face is petrified, and that her head has shrivelled up to the size of a pinhead. *"Bayu, bayushki, bayú!"* she murmurs, "Nurse is making pap for you. . . ."

In the stove chirrups a cricket. In the next room behind that door snore

Varka's master and the journeyman Athanasius. The cradle creaks plaintively, Varka murmurs—and the two sounds mingle soothingly in a lullaby sweet to the ears of those who lie in bed. But now the music is only irritating and oppressive, for it inclines to sleep, and sleep is impossible. If Varka, which God forbid, were to go to sleep, her master and mistress would beat her.

The lamp flickers. The green spot and the shadows move about, they pass Into the half-open, motionless eyes of Varka, and in her half-awakened brain blend in misty images. She sees dark clouds chasing one another across the sky'and crying like the child. And then a wind blows; the clouds vanish; and Varka sees a wide road covered with liquid mud; along the road stretch waggons, men with satchels on their backs crawl along, and shadows move backwards and forwards; on either side through the chilly, thick mist are visible hills. And suddenly the men with the satchels, and the shadows collapse in the liquid mud. "Why is this?" asks Varka. "To sleep, to sleep!" comes the answer. And they sleep soundly, sleep sweetly; and on the telegraph wires perch crows, and cry like children, and try to awaken them.

"*Bayu, bayushki, bayú.* Nurse will sing a song to you," murmurs Varka; and now she sees herself in a dark and stifling cabin.

On the floor lies her dead father, Yéfim Stépanoff. She cannot see him, but she hears him rolling from side to side, and groaning. In his own words he "has had a rupture." The pain is so intense that he cannot utter a single word, and only inhales air and emits through his lips a drumming sound.

"Bu, bu, bu, bu, bu. . . ."

Mother Pelageya has run to the manor-hour to tell the squire that Yéfim is dying. She has been gone a long time . . . will she ever return? Varka lies on the stove, and listens to her father's "Bu, bu, bu, bu." And then someone drives up to the cabin door. It is the doctor, sent from the manor-house where he is staying as a guest. The doctor comes into the hut; in the darkness he is invisible, but Varka can hear him coughing and hear the creaking of the door.

"Bring a light!" he says.

"Bu. bu. bu." answers Yéfim.

Pelageya runs to the stove and searches for a jar of matches. A minute passes in silence. The doctor dives into his pockets and lights a match himself.

"Immediately *batiushka*, immediately!" cries Pelageya, running out of the cabin. In a minute she returns with a candle end.

Yéfim's cheeks are flushed, his eyes sparkle, and his look is piercing, as if he could see through the doctor and the cabin wall.

"Well. what's the matter with you?" asks the doctor, bending over him. "Ah! You have been like this long?"

"What's the matter? The time has come, your honour, to die. . . . I shall not live any longer. . . ."

"Nonsense. . . . We'll soon cure you!"

"As you will, your honour. Thank you humbly . . . only we understand. . . . If we must die, we must die. . . ."

Half an hour the doctor spends with Yéfim; then he rises and says:

"I can do nothing. . . . You must go to the hospital; there they will operate on you. You must go at once . . .

without fail! It is late, and they will all be asleep at the hospital . . . but never mind, I will give you a note. . . . Do you hear?"

"*Batiushka,* how can he go to the hospital?" asks Pelageya. "We have no horse."

"Never mind, I will speak to the squire, he will lend you one."

The doctor leaves, the light goes out, and again Varka hears: "Bu, bu, bu." In half an hour someone drives up to the cabin. . . . This is the cart for Yéfim to go to hospital in. . . . Yéfim gets ready and goes. . . .

And now comes a clear and fine morning. Pelageya is not at home; she has gone to the hospital to find out how Yéfim is. . . . There is a child crying, and Varka hears someone singing with her own voice:

"*Bayu, bayushki, bayú,* Nurse will sing a song to you. . . ."

Pelageya returns, she crosses herself and whispers:

"Last night he was better, towards morning he gave his soul to God. . . . Heavenly kingdom, eternal rest! . . . They say we brought him too late. . . . We should have done it sooner. . . ."

Varka goes into the wood, and cries, and suddenly someone slaps her on the nape of the neck with such force that her forehead bangs against a birch tree. She lifts her head, and sees before her her master, the shoemaker.

"What are you doing, scabby?" he asks. "The child is crying and you are asleep."

He gives her a slap on the ear; and she shakes her head, rocks the cradle, and murmurs her lullaby. The green spot, the shadows from the trousers and the baby-clothes, tremble, wink at her,

and soon again possess her brain. Again she sees a road covered with liquid mud. Men with satchels on their backs, and shadows lie down and sleep soundly. When she looks at them Karka passionately desires to sleep; she would lie down with joy; but mother Pelageya comes along and hurries her. They are going to town to seek situations.

"Give me a kopeck for the love of Christ," says her mother to everyone she meets. "Show the pity of God, merciful gentleman!"

"Give me here the child," cries a well-known voice. "Give me the child," repeats the same voice, but this time angrily and sharply. "You are asleep, beast!"

Varka jumps up, and looking around her remembers where she is; there is neither road, nor Pelageya, nor people, but only, standing in the middle of the room, her mistress who has come to feed the child. While the stout, broad-shouldered woman feeds and soothes the baby, Varka stands still, looks at her, and waits till she has finished.

And outside the window the air grows blue, the shadows fade and the green spot on the ceiling pales. It will soon be morning.

"Take it," says her mistress, buttoning her nightdress. "It is crying. The evil eye is upon it!"

Varka takes the child, lays it in the cradle, and again begins rocking. The shadows and the green spot fade away, and there is nothing now to set her brain going. But, as before, she wants to sleep, wants passionately to sleep. Varka lays her head on the edge of the cradle and rocks it with her whole body so as to drive away sleep; but her eyelids droop again, and her head is heavy.

"Varka, light the stove!" rings the voice of her master from behind the door.

That is to say: it is at last time to get up and begin the day's work. Varka leaves the cradle, and runs to the shed for wood. She is delighted. When she runs or walks she does not feel the want of sleep as badly as when she is sitting down. She brings in wood, lights the stove, and feels how her petrified face is waking up, and how her thoughts are clearing.

"Varka, get ready the samovar!" cries her mistress.

Varka cuts splinters of wood, and has hardly lighted them and laid them in the samovar when another order comes:

"Varka, clean your master's goloshes!"

Varka sits on the floor, cleans the goloshes, and thinks how delightful it would be to thrust her head into the big, deep golosh, and slumber in it awhile. . . . And suddenly the golosh grows, swells, and fills the whole room. Varka drops the brush, but immediately shakes her head, distends her eyes, and tries to look at things as if they had not grown and did not move in her eyes.

"Varka, wash the steps outside . . . the customers will be scandalised!"

Varka cleans the steps, tidies the room, and then lights another stove and runs into the shop. There is much work to be done, and not a moment free.

But nothing is so tiresome as to stand at the kitchen-table and peel potatoes. Varka's head falls on the table, the potatoes glimmer in her eyes, the knife drops from her hand, and

around her bustles her stout, angry mistress with sleeves tucked up, and talks so loudly that her voice rings in Varka's ears. It is torture, too, to wait at table, to wash up, and to sew. There are moments when she wishes, notwithstanding everything around her, to throw herself on the floor and sleep.

The day passes. And watching how the windows darken, Varka presses her petrified temples. and smiles, herself not knowing why. The darkness caresses her drooping eyelids, and promises a sound sleep soon. But towards evening the bootmaker's rooms are full of visitors.

"Varka, prepare the samovar!" cries her mistress.

It is a small samovar, and before the guests are tired of drinking tea, it has to be filled and heated five times. After tea Varka stands a whole hour on one spot, looks at the guests, and waits for orders.

"Varka, run and buy three bottles of beer!"

Varka jumps from her place, and tries to run as quickly as possible so as to drive away sleep.

"Varka, go for vodka! Varka, where is the corkscrew? Varka, clean the herrings!"

At last the guests are gone; the fires are extinguished; master and mistress go to bed.

"Varka, rock the cradle!" echoes the last order.

In the stove chirrups a cricket; the green spot on the ceiling, and the shadows from the trousers and baby-clothes again twinkle before Varka's half-opened eyes, they wink at her, and obscure her brain.

"Bayu, bayushki, bayú," she mur-

murs, "Nurse will sing a song to you. . . ."

But the child cries and wearies itself with crying. Varka sees again the muddy road, the men with satchels, Pelageya, and father Yéfim. She remembers, she recognises them all, but in her semi-slumber she cannot understand the force which binds her, hand and foot, and crushes her, and ruins her life. She looks around her, and seeks that force that she may rid herself of it. But she cannot find it. And at last, tortured, she strains all her strength and sight; she looks upward at the winking green spot, and as she hears the cry of the baby, she finds the enemy who is crushing her heart.

The enemy is the child.

Varka laughs. She is astonished. How was it that never before could she understand such a simple thing? The green spot, the shadows, and the cricket, it seems, all smile and are surprised at it.

An idea takes possession of Varka. She rises from the stool, and, smiling broadly with unwinking eyes, walks up and down the room. She is delighted and touched by the thought that she will soon be delivered from the child who has bound her, hand and foot. To kill the child, and then to sleep, sleep, sleep. . . .

And smiling and blinking and threatening the green spot with her fingers, Varka steals to the cradle and bends over the child. . . . And having smothered the child she drops to the floor, and, laughing with joy at the thought that she can sleep, in a moment sleeps as soundly as the dead child.

The Princess

THROUGH the wide, so-called "Red" gates of the monastery of N. came a calash drawn by four well-fed, blooded horses. While still far away the senior monks and lay brethren, grouped near the nobles' half of the monastery inn, from the coachman and horses surmised that the visitor was their princess, Vera Gavriilovna.

An aged footman jumped down from the box and helped the princess to alight. She raised her dark veil, came up to the senior monks, accepted their blessing, nodded kindly to the lay brethren, and went to her rooms.

"Well, were you longing to see your princess?" she said to the monks who carried her luggage. "It's a whole month since my last visit. . . . And where is the Father Archimandrite? Heavens, I burn with impatience! Wonderful, wonderful old man! You should be proud of him."

When the Archimandrite appeared, the princess became exuberant, crossed her arms on her breast, and inclined her brow for his blessing.

"No, no! Let me kiss it!" she cried, seizing his hand and kissing it greedily thrice. "How glad, how glad I am, holy father, to see you at last! You, of course, have forgotten your princess; but I have all along been living my real life in this delightful monastery. How charming everything! Do you know, in this life for God, far from the world's vanities, there is a peculiar charm, holy father, a charm which I feel with my whole soul, but cannot express in words!"

The princess's cheeks grew red and tears came into her eyes. She spoke with passion and without pausing, and the seventy-year-old Archimandrite, serious, ugly and bashful, kept silence, or interjected abruptly, as a soldier—

"Exactly so, your Excellency . . . I hear . . . I understand. . . ."

"How long will you honour us by staying?" he asked at last.

"Only to-night. In the morning I must drive over to Claudia Nikolaievna —we haven't met for ages. But after to-morrow I shall return, and stay three or four days. I want to rest my soul with you, holy father."

The princess liked to stay in the monastery of N. Within the last two years she had come to love it so dearly that she drove over nearly every summer month, staying sometimes two days, sometimes three, sometimes all the week. The timid lay brethren, the silence, the low ceilings, the smell of cypress, the modest food, the cheap window curtains—all these touched her, awakened joyful emotions, and inclined her to meditation and kindly thoughts. Hardly had she been in her rooms half an hour before it seemed that she, too, had grown timid and modest, and that she smelt of cypress; the past dwindled away and lost its meaning; and the princess began to feel that despite her twenty-nine years, she was very like the old Archimandrite, and had been born, as he, not for wealth and worldly greatness, but for a silent life, veiled from the world outside, a life of twilight, twilight as the rooms. . . .

So it is. Into the dark cell of an ascetic lost in prayer breaks some unexpected sun-ray; a bird perches near the window and sings its song: the grim ascetic cannot but smile, and in his heart, under the heavy burden of remorse, as from under a stone, springs a fountain of quiet, sinless joy. The princess felt that she brought hither some such consolation as the sun-ray, or the bird. Her happy, affable smile, her kindly looks, her voice, her humour, her figure—little, graceful, dressed in simple black—these must indeed awaken in these simple, severe people feelings of emotion and charm. "God has sent us an angel!" must be the thought of the monks. And, feeling that this must indeed be the thought of all, she smiled still more kindly, and tried to look like a bird.

Having taken tea and rested, the princess went for a walk. The sun had set. The monastery garden breathed to the princess moist odours of newly watered mignonette; the even chanting of the monks borne from the chapel was pleasant, yet sad. The vesper service had begun. The dark windows with little hospitable lamps, the shadows, the old monk with the mug seated in the porch near the image—all expressed such deep, unrebelling restfulness that the princess, somehow, felt that she wanted to cry.

And outside the gates, on the path between wall and birches, evening had already fallen. The air darkened swiftly, swiftly. The princess walked down the path, sat on a bench, and thought.

She thought how good it would be to settle for life in this monastery, where all was silent and resigned as the summer night; to forget for ever her ingrate, dissolute prince, her great estates, the creditors who troubled her every day, her misfortunes, her maid Dasha, on whose face she had only that morning seen an impudent grin. How good it would be to sit out life on this bench and peer between birch-trunks into the valley where the evening mist wandered in patches about; and far, far overhead, in a black, veil-like cloud, rooks flew home to their nests; to watch the two lay brethren, one on a piebald horse, the other on foot, who drove in the horses for the night, both enjoying freedom and playing like little children —their young voices rang loudly through the motionless air, and she could hear every word. How good to sit alone and lend ear to the stillness; now a breeze blew and shook the tree-tops; now a frog rustled in last year's grass; now, beyond the wall, a clock struck the quarters. To sit here, motionless; to listen; to think, to think, to think.

An old woman with a wallet passed down the path. The princess thought that she would stop this old woman and say something kindly, something helpful, and from the heart. But the woman did not look round, and disappeared at a turn in the path.

A little later a tall, grey-bearded man, in a straw hat, came down the path. When he reached the princess he took off his hat and bowed, and from the bald forehead and sharp, humped nose the princess saw that it was Doctor Mikhail Ivanovitch, five years ago her employé at Dubovki. She remembered hearing that this doctor's wife had died a year before, and she wished to show her sympathy and to console him.

"Doctor, you did not recognise me, I think?" she said smiling kindly.

"Yes, princess, I did," he answered. He raised his hat again.

"Thanks; I thought you had forgotten your princess. People remember only their enemies; they forget their friends. You came to pray!"

"I stay here every Saturday night—professionally. I am the monastery doctor."

"And how are you?" asked the princess, with a sigh. "I heard that you lost your wife. How sad!"

"Yes, princess; it was very sad for me."

"What can we do? We must bear our sufferings meekly. Without God's will not one hair falls from a man's head."

"Yes, princess."

The princess's sighs and kindly, affable smile were met by the doctor coldly and drily. And his expression was cold and dry.

"What shall I say to him?" thought the princess.

"What ages since we last met!" she said at last. "Five whole years! How much has happened, what changes have taken place—it frightens me to think of them! You know that I'm married . . . from a countess become a princess. And that I've already managed to part from my husband . . ."

"Yes, I heard."

"God sent me many trials. You have no doubt heard, too, that I am nearly ruined. To pay my unhappy husband's debts they sold Dubovki and Kiriakovo and Sophino. I have kept only Baranovo and Mikhailtsevo. It frightens me to look back: how many changes; how many misfortunes; how many mistakes!"

"Yes, princess, the mistakes were many."

The princess reddened. She knew her mistakes; they were so intimate that she only could think and speak of them. But, unable to restrain herself she asked—

"Of what mistakes do you speak?"

"You mentioned them yourself, therefore you must know." The doctor spoke with a laugh. "Why dwell on them?"

"No; tell me, doctor. I shall be grateful. And, please, no ceremony; I love to hear the truth."

"I am not your judge, princess."

"Not my judge? But from your tone it's certain you know something. What is it?"

"If you insist, I'll tell you. But I am a bad hand at explaining myself, and may be misunderstood. . . ."

The doctor thought a moment, and began—

"There were many mistakes, but the greatest, in my opinion, was the general spirit which . . . reigned on all your estates. You see, I cannot express myself. What I want to say is that it was not love, but aversion to men which showed itself in everything. On this aversion was built your whole life system—aversion to human voices, to faces, to heads, to steps . . . in one word, to all that constitutes a man. At your doors and staircases stood overfed, insolent, idle lackeys whose business it was to keep out any one badly dressed; in your hall were high-backed chairs so that the footmen at your balls and receptions should not stain the walls with the backs of their heads; the rooms

had thick carpets to deaden human footsteps; every one who entered was warned to speak as softly and as little as possible, and that he should say nothing which might affect unpleasantly the imagination or nerves. And in your own room you gave no man your hand or asked him to sit, just as now you have neither given me your hand nor asked me to sit . . ."

"Please sit down if you will," said the princess, extending her hand, with a smile. "You should not be angry over such trifles."

"But am I angry?" laughed the doctor. He took off his hat, waved it, and continued hotly. "I tell you frankly I have long been waiting a chance to tell you everything—everything. . . . That is I want to say that you look on your fellow-creatures much as Napoleon, who regarded them as food for cannon, with this difference: that Napoleon at least had ideas, but you—except aversion—have nothing."

"I have aversion to men?" smiled the princess, shrugging her shoulders in surprise. "I?"

"Yes; you! You want facts? Listen! In Mikhailtsevo living on alms are three of your former cooks, who lost their sight in your kitchens from the heat. Every one healthy, strong, and handsome on your tens of thousands of acres is taken by you or your friends as footman, lackey, coachman. All these two-legged creatures are brought up in . . . lackeyism, overfed, coarsened, robbed of the image of God . . . Young doctors, agriculturists, teachers, intelligent workmen of all kinds, my God, are torn from work, from honest toil, and bribed with a bit of bread to play in various dolls' comedies which would make any decent man blush! No young man can serve with you three years without turning into a hypocrite, a flatterer, an informer. . . . Is that right? Your Polish stewards, those base spies, all these Gaetans and Casimirs who gallop from morning to night over your tens of thousands of acres, and for your benefit alone suck blood out of every stone! . . Excuse me for speaking incoherently, but that doesn't matter. The common people, in your opinion, are not human beings. Yes. and the princes, counts, and bishops who visit you, you look on as decorations and not as living men. But the chief thing . . . the thing that angers me most of all, is that you have property worth a million, yet do for your fellow-creatures nothing!"

Surprised, frightened, offended, the princess sat still. She was at a loss what to say or do. Never before had she been spoken to in that tone. The doctor's unpleasant, angry voice, his awkward, stammering words, hammered in her ears; and it seemed from his gesticulations that he would strike her in the face with his hat.

"That is untrue!" she said gently and appealingly. "I have done much good to people, and you yourself know it."

"Delightful!" cried the doctor. "So you mean to say you regard your charitable work seriously, as something useful, not as a dolls' comedy? It was a comedy from beginning to end, a farce of love-my-neighbor, a farce so transparent that even children and stupid muzhik-women saw through it. Take your—what do you call it?—your hospital for homeless old women, in which you forced me to play the rôle of chief physician while you yourself played the rôle of patroness! O Lord our God, what a comical institution! You built a house with parquet floors, set a weathercock on the roof, and collected ten old village women, and set them to sleep under frieze counterpanes, between sheets of Dutch linen, and eat sugar-candy!"

The doctor laughed loudly into his hat, and stammered quickly—

"A comedy! The servants kept the sheets and counterpanes under lock and key to prevent the old women soiling them—let them sleep, old devil's pepper-castors, on the floor! And the old women daren't sit on their beds, or wear their jackets, or walk on the polished floor! All was kept for show, and hidden away as if the women were thieves; and the old women were fed and clothed secretly by charity, and day and night prayed to God to save them from prison, from the soul-saving exhortations of the well-fed rascals whom you commissioned to look after them. And the higher authorities, what did they do? It's too delightful for words. On two evenings a week up there galloped thirty-five thousand couriers to announce that to-morrow the princess—that is you—would visit the home. Which meant that to-morrow I must neglect my patients, dress myself up, and go on parade. Very well! I would arrive. The old women would sit in a row in clean, new dresses and wait. Near them would walk that retired garrison rat—the inspector—with his sugary, informer's grin. The old women would yawn and look at one another, afraid even to grumble! And we would all wait. Then up gallops the under-steward, half an hour later the senior steward, then the factor, then some one else, and yet another . . . gallopers without end! And all with the same severe, ceremonial faces! We would wait and wait, stand on one leg, then on the other, look at our watches —all this, of course, in dead silence, for we all hated one another. A whole hour would pass, then another hour, at last a *calèche* would appear far off and . . . and . . ."

The doctor laughed dryly, and continued in a thin tenor—

"Down you'd get from your carriage; and the old witches, at a signal from the garrison rat, would sing, 'How glorious is our Lord in Zion, The tongue cannot express . . .' It was too delightful!"

The doctor laughed in a bass note, and waved his arm to imply that amusement forbade him to continue. His laugh was hard and heavy as the laugh of a bad man, and his teeth ground together. His voice, his face, his glittering, somewhat impudent eyes, showed how deeply he despised the princess, her home, and the old women. In what he had said so awkwardly and rudely, there was nothing really laughable, but he laughed with content, even with pleasure.

"And the school?" he resumed, out of breath with laughter. "Do you remember your attempt to teach the muzhik's children? You must have taught them nicely, for soon all the boys ran away, and had to be flogged and bribed to go back to your school. And remember how you tried to feed unweaned children out of bottles—with your own hands!—while their mothers worked in the fields! You wandered about the village weeping that there were no children to be had—their

mothers had taken them with them to the fields. And then the headman ordered them to leave their children behind for your amusement! Too delightful for words! All fled your benefactions as mice flee cats! And why? Not because people are ignorant and thankless as you imagined, but because in all your undertakings—forgive my frankness—there was not one spark of love or mercy. Only a wish to amuse yourself with living dolls! Nothing more! . . . A woman who doesn't know a man from a lapdog should not busy herself with charity. There is a great difference, I assure you, between men and lapdogs!"

The princess's heart beat quickly; the hammering rang in her ears; and again it seemed that the doctor would strike her with his hat. He spoke quickly, passionately, and without impressiveness; he stammered and gesticulated too much; and all she realised was that she listened to a rude, ill-tempered, ill-bred man; what he wanted to say and what he said, she failed to understand.

"Go away!" she said in a tearful voice, lifting her hands as if to ward off the doctor's hat. "Go away!"

"And how did you behave to your employés?" continued the doctor excitedly. "You treated them not as human beings, but worse than outcasts are treated. Allow me, for instance, to ask you why you got rid of me? I served faithfully ten years, first your father, then yourself, and I served honestly, without holiday or rest. I earned the love of all for a hundred versts around; and then . . . suddenly, one fine day, I am told I am wanted no more. And why? To this day I don't know. I, a doctor of medicine, a noble, a graduate of Moscow. the father of a family, I, it appears, am such an insignificant underling that I can be thrown out by the scruff of the neck without a word of explanation! Why make ceremony with me? I heard later that my wife, without my knowledge, went to you three times to petition for me, and that you did not receive her once. And she cried, I was told, in the hall. And for that I will never forgive her, never! . . . never!"

The doctor stopped, and, grinding his teeth, tried to find something more vindictive and painful. The moment he succeeded, his cold, frowning face shone with pleasure.

"Take your relations with this monastery!" he began eagerly. "You spare no one, and the holier the place the more certain it is to suffer from your charity and angel ways. Why do you come here? What do you want with these monks, let me ask? What is Hecuba to you, and you to Hecuba? Again the same broad farce, the same pose, the same scoffing at human souls, and nothing more! You do not believe in these monks' God; your heart has a god of its own discovered at spiritualist *séances;* on the Church's mysteries you look condescendingly, you ignore the services, you sleep till midday. . . . Why do you come here? . . . Why to a strange monastery with your own private god, imagining the monastery thinks it a great honour? Ask yourself, if nothing else, what your visits cost these monks! It pleased you to come here to-day, so two days ago a horseman had to be sent ahead to warn the monks. They spent all yesterday preparing your rooms, and waiting. To-day comes your advance-guard, an impudent serving-maid who fusses about the yard, asks questions, orders people about. . . I cannot tolerate it. The monks wasted all to-day looking out for you. If you're received without proper ceremony, woe to every one! You would complain to the Bishop. 'Your holiness, the monks don't love me! True, I am a great sinner; but I am so unhappy!' Already one monastery got a reprimand on your account. The Archimandrite here is a busy, studious man; he has not a moment free; yet you send for him to your rooms! No respect even for age and rank! . . . If you did a lot for this monastery, there might be some excuse. But all this time the monks have not had a hundred roubles from you!"

When the princess was troubled, puzzled, or offended; when she was at a loss what to do, she usually wept. And here at last she covered her face, and cried a thin, childish cry. The doctor held his peace, and looked at her. His face darkened.

"Forgive me, princess," he said in a restrained voice. "I forgot myself, and gave way to wicked feelings. That was not right."

And with a confused cough, and his hat still in his hand, he walked quickly away.

The sky was already strewn with stars. The moon, it seemed, rose behind the monastery, for the sky above the roof was pale, transparent, and tender. Bats flew noiselessly past the white monastery walls.

The clock slowly struck three-quarters. It was a quarter to eight. The princess rose, and walked slowly to the gate. She was offended, and cried; and it seemed that trees and stars and bats felt pity for her, and that the clock, chiming musically. showed its compassion. She wept; and thought how good it would be to enter the monastery for life; on still summer evenings she would walk alone the garden paths, offended, insulted, uncomprehended on earth, with only God and the stars in heaven to see the sufferer's tears. In the chapel the vesper service continued. The princess stopped and listened to the chanting; how fine these voices sounded in the motionless, dark air! How sweet to weep and suffer, and listen to these hymns!

When she returned to her rooms she looked at her tear-stained face in a mirror, powdered it, and sat down to supper. The monks knew how she loved pickled sterlet, little mushrooms, Malaga, and simple honey gingerbread which smelt of cypress in the mouth; and each time she came they laid before her these. As she ate the mushrooms and drank the Malaga, the princess thought that she would soon be ruined and forsaken; that the stewards, agents, clerks, and maids for whom she had done so much would betray her, and speak to her insolently; that the whole world would fall upon her, condemn her, turn her to scorn; and that she would give up her title, luxury, society, and retire to this monastery, uttering to no one a word of reproach; that she would pray for her enemies; that suddenly all would understand her, and beg for forgiveness, but it would be too late. . . .

After supper she fell upon her knees in the ikon-corner and read two chapters of the Gospel. Her maid got ready her room, and she went to bed. The princess stretched herself under the white counterpane, sighed sweetly and

deeply, as people sigh after tears, then closed her eyes and went to sleep.

She awoke next morning, and looked at her watch: it was half-past eight. Across the carpet fell a narrow, bright belt of light, which came from the window but barely lighted the room. Behind the black curtains buzzed flies.

"It is early," she said to herself, and closed her eyes.

She stretched herself, surrendered herself to the feeling of comfort and cosiness; and recalled last night's meeting with the doctor and the thoughts which had lulled her to sleep; and she remembered that she was unhappy. Her husband in St. Petersburg, her stewards, doctors, neighbours, official friends, all returned to her. A long line of faces swept through her imagination. She smiled softly, and thought that if all these men could read her heart and understand her, she would have them at her feet.

A quarter of an hour before midday she called her maid.

"Come, dress me, Dasha!" she said lazily. "No . . . first tell them to harness the horses. I am going to Claudia Nikolaievna's."

Once outside her rooms the bright daylight made her blink; and she smiled with pleasure—the day was wonderfully fine. She looked through her blinking eyes at the monks who crowded on the steps to see her off; she nodded her head kindly and said—

"Good-bye, my friends! For two days only!"

It was a pleasant surprise also that the doctor came to see her off. His face was pale and severe.

"Princess!" he began, with a guilty smile, taking off his hat. "I have been waiting for you . . . Forgive me. . . . An evil, revengeful feeling carried me away last night, and I talked . . . nonsense to you. . . . I ask your pardon!"

The princess again smiled kindly, and offered her hand. The doctor kissed it, and reddened.

Doing her best to look like a bird, the princess swept into the carriage, and nodded her head to all. In her heart again reigned joy, warmth, and brightness; and she felt that her smile was more than ever caressing and tender. As the carriage rolled through the yard, then by the dusty road past huts and gardens, past long carters' teams, past strings of pilgrims on their way to prayer, she continued to blink and smile. What greater joy, she reflected, than to bring with oneself warmth and light and comfort, to forgive offences, to smile kindly to foes. The roadside peasants bowed, the *calèche* rocked easily; its wheels raised whirls of dust borne by the wind upon the golden rye; and the princess felt that she rocked not on the carriage cushions but on the clouds above, and that she herself was a light, transparent cloud.

"How happy I am!" she whispered, closing her eyes. "How happy I am!"

Fish

A SUMMER morning. The air is still; there is no sound but the churring of a grasshopper on the river bank, and somewhere the timid cooing of a turtle-dove. Feathery clouds stand motionless in the sky, looking like snow scattered about . . . Gerassim, the carpenter, a tall gaunt peasant, with a curly red head and a face overgrown with hair, is laboring near an unfinished bathing shed. . . . He puffs and pants and, blinking furiously, is trying to get hold of something under the roots of the willows in the water. His face is covered with perspiration. A couple of yards from him Lubim, the carpenter, a young hunchback with a triangular face and narrow Chinese-looking eyes, is standing up to his neck in water. Both Gerassim and Lubim are in shirts and linen breeches. Both are blue with cold, for they have been more than an hour already in the water.

"But why do you keep poking with your hand?" cries the hunchback Lubim, shivering as though in a fever. "You blockhead! Hold him, hold him, or else he'll get away, the anathema! Hold him, I tell you!"

"He won't get away. . . . Where can he get to? He's under a root," says Gerassim in a hoarse, hollow bass, which seems to come not from his throat, but from the depths of his stomach. "He's slippery, the beggar, and there's nothing to catch hold of."

"Get him by the gills, by the gills!"

"There's no seeing his gills . . . Stay, I've got hold of something. . . . I've got him by the lip. . . . He's biting, the brute!"

"Don't pull him out by the lip, don't —or you'll let him go! Take him by the gills, take him by the gills. . . . You've begun poking with your hand again! You are a senseless man, the

Queen of Heaven forgive me! Catch hold!"

"Catch hold!" Gerassim mimics him. "You're a fine one to give orders . . . . You'd better come and catch hold of him yourself, you hunchback devil . . . . What are you standing there for?"

"I would catch hold of him if it were possible. But can I stand by the bank, and me as short as I am? It's deep there."

"It doesn't matter if it is deep. . . . You must swim."

The hunchback waves his arms, swims up to Gerassim, and catches hold of the twigs. At the first attempt to stand up, he goes into the water over his head and begins blowing up bubbles.

"I told you it was deep," he says, rolling his eyes angrily. "Am I to sit on your neck or what?"

"Stand on a root . . . there are a lot of roots like a ladder." The hunchback gropes for a root with his heel, and tightly gripping several twigs, stands on it. . . . Having got his balance, and established himself in his new position, he bends down, and trying not to get the water into his mouth, begins fumbling with his right hand among the roots. Getting entangled among the weeds and slipping on the mossy roots he finds his hand in contact with the sharp pinchers of a crawfish.

"As though we wanted to see you, you demon!" says Lubim, and he angrily flings the crawfish on the bank.

At last his hand feels Gerassim's arm, and groping its way along it comes to something cold and slimy.

"Here he is!" says Lubim with a grin. "A fine fellow! Move your fingers, I'll get him directly . . . by the gills. Stop, don't prod me with your elbow. . . I'll

have him in a minute, in a minute, only let me get hold of him. . . . The beggar has got a long way under the roots, there is nothing to get hold of. . . . One can't get to the head . . . one can only feel its belly. . . . Kill that gnat on my neck—it's stinging! I'll get him by the gills, directly. . . . Come to one side and give him a push! Poke him with your finger!"

The hunchback puffs out his cheeks, holds his breath, opens his eyes wide, and apparently has already got his fingers in the gills, but at that moment the twigs to which he is holding on with his left hand break, and losing his balance he plops into the water! Eddies race away from the bank as though frightened, and little bubbles come up from the spot where he has fallen in. The hunchback swims out and, snorting, clutches at the twigs.

"You'll be drowned next, you stupid, and I shall have to answer for you," wheezes Gerassim. "Clamber out, the devil take you! I'll get him out myself."

High words follow. . . . The sun is baking hot. The shadows begin to grow shorter and to draw in on themselves, like the horns of a snail. . . . The high grass warmed by the sun begins to give out a strong, heavy smell of honey. It will soon be mid-day, and Gerassim and Lubim are still floundering under the willow tree. The husky bass and the shrill, frozen tenor persistently disturb the stillness of the summer day.

"Pull him out by the gills, pull him out! Stay, I'll push him out! Where are you shoving your great ugly fist? Poke him with your finger—you pig's face! Get round by the side! get to the left, to the left, there's a big hole on the right! You'll be a supper for the water devil! Pull it by the lip!"

There is the sound of the flick of a whip. . . . A herd of cattle. driven by Yefim, the shepherd, saunter lazily down the sloping bank to drink. The shepherd. a decrepit old man. with one eye and crooked mouth, walks with his head bowed, looking at his feet. The first to reach the water are the sheep, then come the horses, and last of all the cows.

"Push him from below!" he hears Lubim's voice. "Stick your finger in! Are you deaf, fellow. or what? Tfoo!"

"What are you after, lads?" shouts Yefim.

"An eel-pout! We can't get him out! He's hidden under the roots. Get round to the side! To the side!"

For a minute Yefim screws up his eye at the fishermen, then he takes off his bark shoes, throws his sack off his shoulders, and takes off his shirt. He has not the patience to take off his breeches, but. making the sign of the cross, he steps into the water, holding out his thin dark arms to balance himself. . . . For fifty paces he walks along the slimy bottom, then he takes to swimming.

"Wait a minute, lads!" he shouts. "Wait! Don't be in a hurry to pull him out, you'll lose him. You must do it properly!"

Yefim joins the carpenters and all three. shoving each other with their knees and their elbows, puffing and swearing at one another, bustle about the same spot. Lubim. the hunchback, gets a mouthful of water, and the air rings with his hard spasmodic coughing.

"Where's the shepherd?" comes a shout from the bank. "Yefim! Shep-

herd! Where are you? The cattle are in the garden! Drive them out, drive them out of the garden! Where is he, the old brigand?"

First men's voices are heard, then a woman's. The master himself, Andrey Andreitch, wearing a dressing-gown made of a Persian shawl and carrying a newspaper in his hand, appears from behind the garden fence. He looks inquiringly towards the shouts which come from the river, and then trips rapidly towards the bathing shed.

"What's this? Who's shouting?" he asks sternly, seeing through the branches of the willow the three wet heads of the fishermen. "What are you so busy about there?"

"Catching a fish," mutters Yefim, without raising his head.

"I'll give it to you! The beasts are in the garden and he is fishing! . . . When will that bathing shed be done, you devils? You've been at work two days, and what is there to show for it?"

"It . . . will soon be done," grunts Gerassim; "summer is long, you'll have plenty of time to wash. your honor. . . . Pfrrr! . . . We can't manage this eel-pout here anyhow. . . He's got under a root and sits there as if he were in a hole and won't budge one way or another. . . ."

"An eel-pout?" says the master, and his eyes begin to glisten. "Get him out quickly then."

"You'll give us half a rouble for it presently . . . if we oblige you. . . . A huge eel-pout, as fat as a merchant's wife. . . . It's worth half a rouble, your honor, for the trouble. . . . Don't squeeze him, Lubim, don't squeeze him, you'll spoil him! Push him up from below! Pull the root upwards, my good man . . . what's your name? Upwards, not downwards, you brute! Don't swing your legs!"

Five minutes pass, ten. . . . The master loses all patience.

"Vassily!" he shouts, turning towards the garden. "Vaska! Call Vassily to me!"

The coachman Vassily runs up. He is chewing something and breathing hard.

"Go into the water," the master orders him. "Help them to pull out that eel-pout. They can't get him out."

Vassily rapidly undresses and gets into the water.

"In a minute. . . . I'll get him in a minute," he mutters. "Where's the eel-pout? We'll have him out in a trice! You'd better go, Yefim. An old man like you ought to be minding his own business instead of being here. Where's that eel-pout? I'll have him in a minute. . . . Here he is! Let go."

"What's the good of saying that? We know all about that! You get it out!"

"But there is no getting it out like this! One must get hold of it by the head."

"And the head is under the root! We know that, you fool!"

"Now then, don't talk or you'll catch it! You dirty cur!"

"Before the master to use such language," mutters Yefim. "You won't get him out, lads! He's fixed himself much too cleverly!"

"Wait a minute, I'll come directly," says the master, and he begins hurriedly undressing. "Four fools, and can't get an eel-pout!"

When he is undressed, Andrey Andreitch gives himself time to cool and gets into the water. But even his interference leads to nothing.

"We must chop the root off," Lubim decided at last. "Gerassim, go and get an axe! Give me an axe!"

"Don't chop your fingers off," says the master, when the blows of the axe on the root under water are heard. "Yefim, get out of this! Stay, I'll get the eel-pout. . . . You'll never do it."

The root is hacked a little. They partly break it off, and Andrey Andreitch, to his immense satisfaction, feels his fingers under the gills of the fish.

"I'm pulling him out, lads! Don't crowd round . . . stand still. . . . I am pulling him out!"

The head of a big eel-pout, and behind it its long black body, nearly a yard long, appears on the surface of the water. The fish flaps its tail heavily and tries to tear itself away.

"None of your nonsense, my boy! Fiddlesticks! I've got you! Aha!"

A honied smile overspreads all the faces. A minute passes in silent contemplation.

"A famous eel-pout," mutters Yefim, scratching under his shoulder-blades. "I'll be bound it weighs ten pounds."

"Mm! . . . Yes," the master assents. "The liver is fairly swollen! It seems to stand out! A-ach!"

The fish makes a sudden, unexpected upward movement with its tail and the fishermen hear a loud splash . . . they all put out their hands, but it is too late; they have seen the last of the eel-pout.

Mass for the Sinner

AT the church of the Odigitrieff Virgin in Verchnive Zaprudni village the service had just ended. The worshippers moved from their places and left the church; and soon no one remained save the shopkeeper, Andrei Andreitch, one of the oldest residents, and a member of the local "Intelligentsia." Andrei Andreitch leaned on his elbow on the rail of the choir and waited. On his face, well shaven, fat, and marked with traces of old pimples, were two inimical expressions; resignation to inscrutable destiny, and unlimited, dull contempt for his fellow-worshippers in their cheap overcoats and gaudy handkerchiefs. As it was Sunday, he was dressed in his best. He wore a cloth overcoat with yellow bone buttons, blue trousers outside his top-boots, and solid goloshes, such big, awkward goloshes as are worn only by people positive, deliberate, and convinced in their faith.

His greasy, idle eyes were bent on the iconostasis. Familiar to him were the lengthy faces of the saints, the watchman Matvei, who puffed out his cheeks and blew out the candles, the tarnished candelabra, the threadbare carpet, the clerk Lopukhoff, who ran anxiously from the altar carrying the host to the sexton. All these things he had seen long ago, and again and again, as often as his five fingers. But one thing was unfamiliar. At the north door stood Father Grigori, still in priestly vestments, and angrily twitching his bushy eyebrows.

"What is he frowning at, God be with him?" thought the shopkeeper.

"Yes, and he shakes his hand! And stamps his foot! Tell me what that means, please. What does it all mean, Heavenly Mother? Whom is he glaring at?"

Andrei Andreitch looked around, and saw that the church was already deserted. At the door thronged a dozen men, but their backs were turned to the altar.

"Come at once when you are called! Why do you stand there, looking like a statue?" came Father Grigori's angry voice. "I am calling *you!*"

The shopkeeper looked at Father Grigori's red, wrathful face, and for the first time realised that the frowning eyebrows and twitching fingers were directed at himself. He started, walked away from the choir, and resolutely, in his creaking goloshes, went up to the altar.

"Andrei Andreitch, was it you who handed this in during oblation, for the repose of Marya?" asked the priest, looking furiously at the shopkeeper's fat, perspiring face.

"Yes."

"So . . . and that means that you wrote it too? You?"

And Father Grigori wrathfully pushed a slip of paper under the shopkeeper's eyes. On this paper, given in by Andrei Andreitch during oblation, in a big, wandering hand, was written—

"Pray for the soul of God's slave, the Adulteress Marya."

"Exactly; I wrote it . . ." answered the shopkeeper.

"How dare you write such a thing?" whispered the priest slowly, and his

332

hoarse whisper expressed indignation and horror.

The shopkeeper looked at him with dull amazement and doubt, and felt frightened; from the day of his birth, Father Grigori had never spoken so angrily to a member of the Verchniye Zaprudni "Intelligentsia." For a moment the two men faced each other in silence. The tradesman's surprise was so great that his fat face seemed to melt on all sides, as wet dough.

"How dare you?" repeated the priest.

"I don't understand," said Andrei Andreitch doubtfully.

"So you don't understand," whispered Father Grigori, receding in amazement, and flourishing his arms. "What have you got on your shoulders? A head, is it, or some other object? You hand a paper across the altar with a word which even in the street is regarded as improper! Why do you stick out your eyes? Is it possible you do not know the meaning of this word?"

"This, I suppose, is all about the word 'adulteress,'" stammered the shopkeeper, reddening and blinking his eyes. "I see nothing wrong. Our Lord, in His mercy, this same thing . . . forgave an adulteress . . . prepared a place for her; yes, and the life of the blessed Mary of Egypt shows in what sense this word, excuse . . ."

The shopkeeper was about to adduce some other defence, but he lost the thread, and rubbed his lips with his cuff.

"So that's how you understand it!" The priest again flourished his hand impatiently. "You forget that our Lord forgave her—understand that—but you condemn her, you call her an improper name! And who is it? Your own daughter! Not merely in the sacred Scriptures, even in the profane, you will never read of such an act! I repeat to you, Andrei, don't try to be clever! Don't play the philosopher, brother! If God gave you a speculative head, and you don't know how to manage it, then better not speculate. . . . Don't try and be too clever—be silent!"

"Yes. but, you know, she . . . excuse my using the word, she was an actress," protested the shopkeeper.

"An actress! No matter what her career, it is your duty, once she's dead, to forget it, and not to write it on paper!"

"I understand . . ." consented the shopkeeper.

"You should be forced to do penance," growled the deacon from behind the altar, looking derisively at Andrei Andreitch's guilty face. "Then you'd soon drop your clever words. Your daughter was a well-known actress. Even in the newspapers they mentioned her death. . . . Philosopher!"

"I understand, of course . . . really," stammered the shopkeeper. "It was an unsuitable word, but I used it not in condemnation, Father Grigori; I wished to express myself scripturally . . . in short, to make you understand who it was you were to pray for. People always hand in some description, for instance: the infant John, the drowned woman Pelageya, the soldier Pegor, murdered Paul, and so on. . . . That is all I wanted."

"You are wrong, Andrei! God will forgive you, but take care the next time! And the chief thing is this; don't be too clever, and think like others. Abase yourself ten times and begone!"

"Yes," said the shopkeeper, rejoiced that the ordeal was over. His face again resumed its expression of dignified self-importance. "Ten adorations! I understand. But now, *batiushka*, allow me to make a request. Because I, after all, was her father . . . you yourself know; in spite of everything she was my daughter. I should like to ask you to say the mass for her soul to-day. And I venture to ask you also, father deacon!"

"That is right!" said Father Grigori, taking off his surplice. "I praise you for that. I can approve of it. . . . Now begone! We will come out at once."

Andrei Andreitch walked heavily from the altar, and, red-faced, with a solemn memorial-service expression, stood in the middle of the church. The watchman Matvei set before him a table with a crucifixion; and after a brief delay the mass began.

The church was still. Audible only were the censer's metallic ring and the droning voices. Near Andrei Andreitch stood the watchman Matvei, the midwife Makarievna, and her little son Mitka, with the paralysed hand. No one else attended. The clerk sang badly in an ugly, dull bass, but his words were so mournful that the shopkeeper gradually lost his pompous expression, and felt real grief. He remembered his little Mashutka. . . . He remembered the day she was born, when he served as footman at Verchniye Zaprudni Hall; remembered how in the rush of his footman's existence, he never noticed that his little girl was growing up. Those long years during

which she changed into a graceful girl, fair-haired, with eyes as big as copecks, sped away unobserved. He remembered that she was brought up, as the children of all the favoured servants, with the young ladies of the house; how the squire's family, merely from lack of other work, taught her to read, to write, and to dance; and how he, Andrei, took no part in her training. Only when at long intervals he met her at the gate, or on the landing, he would remember that she was his daughter and begin, as far as time allowed, to teach her her prayers and read from the Bible. Yes, and what fame he gained for knowledge of the rubric and the Holy Scriptures! And the little girl, however rigid and pompous her father's face, listened with delight. She yawned, it is true, as she repeated the prayers; but when, stammering and doing his best to speak magniloquently, he told her Bible stories she was all ears. And at Esau's lentils, the doom of Sodom, and the woes of little Joseph she turned pale, and opened wide her big blue eyes.

And then, when he retired from his post as footman, and with his savings opened a shop in the village, the family took Mashutka away to Moscow.

He remembered how three years before her death she came to him on a visit. She was already a young woman, graceful and well built, with the dress and manners of a gentlewoman. And she spoke so cleverly, as if out of a book, smoked cigarettes, and slept till midday. Andrei Andreitch asked her what was her business; and she, looking him straight in the face, said boldly, "I am an actress!" And this frank avowal seemed to the retired footman the height of immodesty. Mashutka began to tell her father of her stage triumphs and of her stage life; but seeing her father's purple face, she stopped suddenly. In silence, without exchanging a glance, they had spent three weeks together until it was time for Mashutka to go. Before leaving, she begged her father to walk with her along the river bank. And, shameful as it was to appear in daylight before honest people with a daughter who was a vagrant play-actress, he conceded her prayer.

"What glorious country you have!" she said ecstatically as they walked. "What ravines, what marshes! Heavens, how beautiful is my native land!"

And she began to cry.

"Such things only take up space," thought Andrei Andreitch, with a dull look at the ravines. He understood nothing of his child's delight. "There is as much use from them as milk from a goat!"

And she continued to cry, inhaling the air greedily, as if she knew that her breaths were already numbered. . . .

Andrei Andreitch shook his head as a bitten horse, and to quench these painful memories, began to cross himself vigorously.

"Remember, Lord," he muttered, "thy dead slave, the Adulteress Marya, and forgive her all her sins!"

Again the improper word burst from his lips; but he did not notice it; what was set so deeply in his mind was not to be uprooted with a spade, much less by the admonitions of Father Grigori. Makarievna sighed, and whispered something, and paralysed Mitka seemed lost in thought.

". . . where there is neither sorrow, nor sickness, nor sighing!" droned the clerk, covering his face with his right hand.

From the censer rose a pillar of blue smoke and swam in the broad, oblique sun-ray which cut the obscure emptiness of the church. And it seemed that with the smoke there floated in the sun-ray the soul of the dead girl. Eddies of smoke, like infants' curls, were swept upwards to the window; and the grief and affliction with which this poor soul was full, seemed to pass away.

The Lament

It was twilight. A thick wet snow is slowly twirling around the newly lighted street-lamps, and lying in soft thin layers on the roofs, the horses' backs, people's shoulders and hats. The cab-driver, Iona Potapov, is quite white, and looks like a phantom; he is bent double as far as a human body can bend double; he is seated on his box, and never makes a move. If a whole snowdrift fell on him, it seems as if he would not find it necessary to shake it off. His little horse is also quite white, and remains motionless; its immobility, its angularity, and its straight wooden-looking legs. even close by, give it the appearance of a gingerbread horse worth a kopek. It is, no doubt, plunged in deep thought. If you were snatched from the plow, from your usual gray surroundings, and were thrown into this slough full of monstrous lights, unceasing noise and hurrying people, you too would find it difficult not to think.

Iona and his little horse have not moved from their place for a long while. They left their yard before dinner, and up to now, not a "fare." The evening mist is descending over the town, the white lights of the lamps are replacing brighter rays, and the hubbub of the street is getting louder. "Cabby, for Viborg way!" suddenly hears Iona. "Cabby!"

Iona jumps, and through his snow-covered eye-lashes, sees an officer in a greatcoat. with his hood over his head.

"Viborg way!" the officer repeats. "Are you asleep, eh? Viborg way!"

With a nod of assent Iona picks up the reins, in consequence of which layers of snow slip off the horse's back and neck. The officer seats himself in the sleigh, the cab-driver smacks his lips to encourage his horse, stretches out his neck like a swan, sits up, and, more from habit than necessity, brandishes his whip. The little horse also stretches his neck, bends his wooden-looking legs, and makes a move undecidedly.

"What are you doing, were-wolf!" is the exclamation Iona hears, from the dark mass moving to and fro as soon as they started.

"Where the devil are you going? To the r-r-right!"

"You do not know how to drive. Keep to the right!" calls the officer angrily.

A coachman from a private carriage swears at him; a passer-by, who has run across the road and rubbed his shoulder against the horse's nose, looks at him furiously as he sweeps the snow from his sleeve. Iona shifts about on his seat as if he were on needles, moves his elbows as if he were trying to keep his equilibrium, and gapes about like someone suffocating, and who does not understand why and wherefore he is there.

"What scoundrels they all are!" jokes the officer; "one would think they had all entered into an agreement to jostle you or fall under your horse."

Iona looks round at the officer, and moves his lips. He evidently wants to say something, but the only sound that issues is a snuffle.

"What?" asks the officer.

Iona twists his mouth into a smile, and with an effort says hoarsely:

"My son, barin, died this week."

"Hm! What did he die of?"

Iona turns with his whole body towards his fare, and says:

"And who knows! They say high fever. He was three days in hospital, and then died. . . . God's will be done."

"Turn round! The devil!" sounded from the darkness. "Have you popped off, old doggie, eh? Use your eyes!"

"Go on, go on," said the officer, "otherwise we shall not get there by tomorrow. Hurry up a bit!"

The cab-driver again stretches his neck, sits up, and, with a bad grace, brandishes his whip. Several times again he turns to look at his fare, but the latter had closed his eyes, and apparently is not disposed to listen. Having deposited the officer in the Viborg, he stops by the tavern, doubles himself up on his seat, and again remains motionless, while the snow once more begins to cover him and his horse. An hour, and another. . . . Then, along the footpath, with a squeak of goloshes, and quarrelling, came three young men, two of them tall and lanky, the third one short and hump-backed.

"Cabby, to the Police Bridge!" in a cracked voice calls the hump-back. "The three of us for two griveniks!" (20 kopeks.)

Iona picks up his reins, and smacks his lips. Two griveniks is not a fair price, but he does not mind if it is a rouble or five kopeks—to him it is all the same now, so long as they are wayfarers. The young men, jostling each other and using bad language, approach the sleigh, and all three at once try to get onto the seat; then begins a discussion which two shall sit and who shall be the one to stand. After wrangling, abusing each other, and much petulance, it was at last decided that the hump-back should stand, as he was the smallest.

"Now then, hurry up!" says the hump-back in a twanging voice, as he takes his place, and breathes in Iona's neck. "Old furry! Here, mate, what a cap you have got, there is not a worse one to be found in all Petersburg! . . ."

"Hi—hi,—hi—hi," giggles I o n a. "Such a. . . ."

"Now you, 'such a,' hurry up, are you going the whole way at this pace? Are you? . . . Do you want it in the neck?"

"My head feels like bursting," says one of the lanky ones. "Last night at the Donkmasovs, Vaska and I drank the whole of four bottles of cognac."

"I don't understand what you lie for," said the other lanky one angrily; "you lie like a brute."

"God strike me, it's the truth!"

"It's as much a truth as that a louse coughs!"

"Hi, hi." grins Iona, "what gay young gentlemen!"

"Pshaw, go to the devil!" indignantly says the hump-back.

"Are you going to get on or not, you old pest? Is that the way to drive? Use the whip a bit! Go on, devil, go on, give it him well!"

Iona feels at his back the little man wriggling, and the tremble in his voice. He listens to the insults hurled at him, sees the people, and little by little the feeling of loneliness leaves him. The hump-back goes on swearing until he gets mixed up in some elaborate six-foot oath, or chokes with coughing. The lankies begin to talk about a certain Nadejda Petrovna. Iona looks round at them several times; he waits for a temporary silence, then, turning round again, he murmurs:

"My son . . . died this week."

"We must all die," sighed the hump-back, wiping his lips after an attack of coughing. "Now, hurry up, hurry up! Gentlemen, I really cannot go any farther like this! When will he get us there?"

"Well, just you stimulate him a little in the neck!"

"You old pest, do you hear, I'll bone your neck for you! If one treated the like of you with ceremony one would have to go on foot! Do you hear, old serpent Gorinytch! Or do you not care a spit?"

Iona hears rather than feels the blows they deal him.

"Hi, hi," he laughs. "They are gay young gentlemen, God bless 'em!"

"Cabby, are you married?" asks a lanky one.

"I? Hi, hi, gay young gentlemen! Now 1 have only a wife and the moist ground. . . . Hi, ho, ho . . that is to say, the grave. My son has died, and I am alive. . . . A wonderful thing, death mistook the door . . . instead of coming to me, it went to my son. . . ."

Iona turns round to tell them how his son died, but at this moment the hump-back, giving a little sigh, announces, "Thank God, they have at last reached their destination," and Iona watches them disappear through the dark entrance. Once more he is alone, and again surrounded by silence. . . . His grief, which had abated for a short while, returns and rends his heart with greater force. With an anxious and a hurried look, he searches among the crowds passing on either side of the street to find if there is just one person who will listen to him. But the crowds hurry by without noticing him or his trouble. Yet it is such an immense, illimitable grief. Should his heart break and the grief pour out, it would flow over the whole earth it seems, and yet, no one sees it. It has managed to conceal itself in such an insignificant shell that no one can see it even by day and with a light.

Iona sees a hall-porter with some sacking, and decides to talk to him.

"Friend, what sort of time is it?" he asks.

"Past nine. What are you standing here for? Move on."

Iona moves on a few steps, doubles himself up, and abandons himself to his grief. He sees it is useless to turn to people for help. In less than five minutes he straightens himself, holds up his head as if he felt some sharp pain, and gives a tug at the reins: he can bear it no longer. "The stables," he thinks, and the little horse, as if he understood, starts off at a trot.

About an hour and a half later Iona is seated by a large dirty stove. Around the stove, on the floor, on the benches, people are snoring; the air is thick and suffocatingly hot. Iona looks at the sleepers, scratches himself, and regrets having returned so early.

"I have not even earned my fodder," he thinks. "That's what's my trouble. A man who knows his job, who has had enough to eat, and his horse too, can always sleep peacefully."

A young cab-driver in one of the corners half gets up, grunts sleepily, and stretches towards a bucket of water.

"Do you want a drink?" Iona asks him.

"Don't I want a drink!"

"That's so? Your good health! But listen, mate—you know, my son is dead. . . . Did you hear? This week, in hospital. . . . It's a long story."

Iona looks to see what effect his words have, but sees none—the young man has hidden his face, and is fast asleep again. The old man sighs, and scratches his head. Just as much as the young one wanted to drink, the old man wanted to talk. It will soon be a week since his son died, and he has not been able to speak about it properly to anyone. One must tell it slowly and carefully; how his son fell ill, how he suffered, what he said before he died, how he died. One must describe every detail of the funeral, and the journey to the hospital to fetch the defunct's clothes. His daughter Anissia remained in the village—one must talk about her too. Was it nothing he had to tell? Surely the listener would gasp and sigh, and sympathize with him? It is better, too, to talk to women; although they are stupid, two words are enough to make them sob.

"I'll go and look at my horse," thinks Iona; "there's always time to sleep No fear of that!"

He puts on his coat, and goes to the stables to his horse; he thinks of the corn, the hay, the weather. When he is alone, he dare not think of his son; he could speak about him to anyone, but to think of him, and picture him to himself, is unbearably painful.

"Are you tucking in?" Iona asks his horse, looking at his bright eyes; "go on. tuck in, though we've not earned our corn, we can eat hay. Yes! I am too old to drive—my son could have, not I. He was a first-rate cab-driver. If only he had lived!"

Iona is silent for a moment, then continues:

"That's how it is, my old horse. There's no more Kuzma Ionitch. He has left us to live, and he went off pop. Now let's say, you had a foal, you were the foal's mother, and suddenly, let's say, that foal went and left you to live after him. It would be sad, wouldn't it?"

The little horse munches, listens, and breathes over his master's hand. . . .

Iona's feelings are too much for him, and he tells the little horse the whole story.

Oysters

I CAN easily recall the rainy twilight autumn evening when I stood with my father in a crowded Moscow street and fell ill, strangely. I suffered no pain, but my legs gave way, my head hung on one side, and my speech failed. I felt that I should soon fall.

Had I been taken to hospital at the moment, the doctor would have written: "Fames"—a complaint uncommon in medical text-books.

Beside me on the pavement stood my father in a ragged summer overcoat and a check cap. On his feet were big, clumsy goloshes. Fearing that people might see he had neither boots nor stockings. he wrapped his legs in old gaiters.

The more tattered and dirty became that once smart summer overcoat, the greater became my love. He had come to the capital five months before to seek work as a clerk. Five months he had tramped the city, seeking employment; only to-day for the first time he had screwed up his courage to beg for alms in the street.

In front of us rose a big, three-storied house with a blue signboard "Restaurant." My head hung helplessly back, and on one side. Involuntarily I looked upward at the bright restaurant windows. Behind them glimmered human figures. To the right were an orchestrion, two oleographs, and hanging lamps. While trying to pierce the obscurity my eyes fell on a white patch. The patch was motionless; its rectangular contour stood out sharply against the universal background of dark brown. When I strained my eyes I could see that the patch was a notice on the wall, and it was plain that something was printed upon it, but what that something was I could not see.

I must have kept my eyes on the notice at least half an hour. Its whiteness beckoned to me, and, it seemed, almost hypnotised my brain. I tried to read it, and my attempts were fruitless.

But at last the strange sickness entered into its rights.

The roar of the traffic rose to thunder; in the smell of the street I could distinguish a thousand smells; and the restaurant lights and street lamps seemed to flash like lightning. And I began to make out things that I could not make out before.

"Oysters," I read on the notice.

A strange word. I had lived in the world already eight years and three months, and had never heard this word. What did it mean? Was it the proprietor's surname? No, for signboards with innkeepers' names hang outside the doors, and not on the walls inside.

"Father, what are oysters?" I asked hoarsely, trying to turn my face towards his.

My father did not hear me. He was looking at the flow of the crowd, and following every passer-by with his eyes. From his face I judged that he dearly longed to speak to the passers, but the fatal, leaden words hung on his trembling lips, and would not tear themselves off. One passer-by he even stopped and touched on the sleeve, but when the man turned to him my father stammered, "I beg your pardon," and fell back in confusion.

"Papa, what does 'oysters' mean?" I repeated.

"It is a kind of animal. . . . It lives in the sea. . . ."

And in a wink I visualised this mysterious animal. Something between a fish and a crab, it must be, I concluded; and as it came from the sea, of course it made up into delightful dishes, hot *bouillabaisse* with fragrant peppercorns and bay leaves, or sour *solianka* with gristle, crab-sauce, or cold with horseradish. . . . I vividly pictured to myself how this fish is brought from the market, cleaned, and thrust quickly into a pot . . . quickly, quickly, because every one is hungry . . . frightfully hungry. From the restaurant kitchen came the smell of boiled fish and crab soup.

This smell began to tickle my palate and nostrils; I felt it permeating my whole body. The restaurant, my father, the white notice, my sleeve, all exhaled it so strongly that I began to chew. I chewed and swallowed as if my mouth were really full of the strange animal that lives in the sea. . . .

The pleasure was too much for my strength, and to prevent myself falling I caught my father's cuff, and leaned against his wet summer overcoat. My father shuddered. He was cold. . . .

"Father, can you eat oysters on fast days?" I asked.

"You eat them alive . . ." he answered. "They are in shells . . . like tortoises, only in double shells."

The seductive smell suddenly ceased

to tickle my nostrils, and the illusion faded. Now I understood!

"How horrible!" I exclaimed. "How hideous!"

So that was the meaning of oysters! However, hideous as they were, my imagination could paint them. I imagined an animal like a frog. The frog sat in the shell, looked out with big, bright eyes, and moved its disgusting jaws. What on earth could be more horrible to a boy who had lived in the world just eight years and three months? Frenchmen, they said, ate frogs. But children—never! And I saw this fish being carried from market in its shell, with claws, bright eyes, and shiny tail. . . . The children all hide themselves, and the cook, blinking squeamishly, takes the animal by the claws, puts it on a dish, and carries it to the dining-room. The grown-ups take it, and eat . . . eat it alive, eyes, teeth, claws. And it hisses, and tries to bite their lips.

I frowned disgustedly. But why did my teeth begin to chew? An animal, disgusting, detestable, frightful, but still I ate it, ate it greedily, fearing to notice its taste and smell. I ate in imagination, and my nerves seemed braced, and my heart beat stronger. . . . One animal was finished, already I saw the bright eyes of a second, a third. . . . I ate these also. At last I ate the table-napkin, the plate, my father's goloshes, the white notice. . . . I ate everything before me, because I felt that only eating would cure my complaint. The oysters glared frightfully from their bright eyes, they made me sick, I shuddered at the thought of them, but I wanted to eat. To eat!

"Give me some oysters! Give me some oysters." The cry burst from my lips, and I stretched out my hands.

"Give me a kopeck, gentlemen!" I heard suddenly my father's dulled, choked voice. "I am ashamed to ask, but, my God, I can bear it no longer!"

"Give me some oysters!" I cried, seizing my father's coat-tails.

"And so you eat oysters! Such a little whipper-snapper!" I heard a voice beside me.

Before me stood two men in silk hats, and looked at me with a laugh.

"Do you mean to say that this little manikin eats oysters? Really! This is too delightful! How does he eat them?"

I remember a strong hand dragged me into the glaring restaurant. In a minute a crowd had gathered, and looked at me with curiosity and amusement. I sat at a table, and ate something slippy, damp, and mouldy. I ate greedily, not chewing, not daring to look, not even knowing what I ate. It seemed to me that if I opened my eyes. I should see at once the bright eyes, the claws, the sharp teeth.

I began to chew something hard. There was a crunching sound.

"Good heavens, he's eating the shells!" laughed the crowd. "Donkey, who ever heard of eating oyster shells?"

After this, I remember only my terrible thirst. I lay on my bed, kept awake by repletion. and by a strange taste in my hot mouth. My father walked up and down the room and gesticulated.

"I have caught cold, I think!" he said. "I feel something queer in my head. . . . As if there is something inside it. . . . But perhaps it is only . . . because I had no food to-day. I have been strange altogether . . . stupid. I saw those gentlemen paying ten roubles for oysters; why didn't I go and ask them for something . . . in loan? I am sure they would have given it."

Towards morning I fell asleep, and dreamed of a frog sitting in a shell and twitching its eyes. At midday thirst awoke me. I sought my father; he still walked up and down the room and gesticulated.

Vanka

NINE-YEAR-OLD Vanka Zhukov. who had been apprentice to the shoemaker Aliakhin for three months, did not go to bed the night before Christmas. He waited till the master and mistress and the assistants had gone out to an early church-service, to procure from his employer's cupboard a small phial of ink and a penholder with a rusty nib; then, spreading a crumpled sheet of paper in front of him, he began to write.

Before, however, deciding to make the first letter, he looked furtively at the door and at the window, glanced several times at the sombre ikon, on either side of which stretched shelves full of lasts, and heaved a heart-rending sigh. The sheet of paper was spread on a bench, and he himself was on his knees in front of it.

"Dear Grandfather Konstantin Makarych," he wrote, "I am writing you a letter. I wish you a Happy Christmas and all God's holy best. I have no mamma or papa, you are all I have."

Vanka gave a look towards the window in which shone the reflection of his candle, and vividly pictured to himself his grandfather, Konstantin Makarych, who was night-watchman, at Messrs. Zhivarev. He was a small, lean, unusually lively and active old man of sixty-five, always smiling and bleareyed. All day he slept in the servants' kitchen or trifled with the cooks. At night, enveloped in an ample sheepskin coat, he strayed round the domain tapping with his cudgel. Behind him each hanging its head, walked the old bitch Kashtanka, and the dog Viun, so named because of his black coat and long body and his resemblance to a loach. Viun was an unusually civil and friendly dog, looking as kindly at a stranger as at his masters, but he was not to be trusted. Beneath his deference and humbleness was hid the most inquisitorial maliciousness. No one knew better than he how to sneak up and take a bite at a leg, or slip into the larder or steal a muzhik's chicken. More than once they had nearly broken his hind-legs, twice he had been hung up, every week he was nearly flogged to death, but he always recovered.

At this moment, for certain, Vanka's grandfather must be standing at the gate, blinking his eyes at the bright red windows of the village church, stamping his feet in their high felt boots, and jesting with the people in the yard; his cudgel will be hanging from his belt, he will be hugging himself with cold, giving a little dry, old man's cough, and at times pinching a servant-girl or a cook.

"Won't we take some snuff?" he asks, holding out his snuff-box to the women. The women take a pinch of snuff, and sneeze.

The old man goes into indescribable ecstasies, breaks into loud laughter, and cries:

"Off with it, it will freeze to your nose!"

He gives his snuff to the dogs, too. Kashtanka sneezes, twitches her nose, and walks away offended. Viun deferentially refuses to sniff and wags his tail. It is glorious weather, not a breath of wind, clear, and frosty; it is a dark night, but the whole village, its white roofs and streaks of smoke from the chimneys, the trees silvered with hoarfrost, and the snowdrifts, you can see it all. The sky scintillates with bright twinkling stars, and the Milky Way stands out so clearly that it looks as if it had been polished and rubbed over with snow for the holidays. . . .

Vanka sighs, dips his pen in the ink, and continues to write:

"Last night I got a thrashing, my master dragged me by my hair into the yard, and belaboured me with a shoemaker's stirrup, because, while I was rocking his brat in its cradle, I unfortunately fell asleep. And during the week, my mistress told me to clean a herring, and I began by its tail, so she took the herring and stuck its snout into my face. The assistants tease me, send me to the tavern for vodka, make me steal the master's cucumbers, and the master beats me with whatever is handy. Food there is none: in the morning it's bread, at dinner gruel, and in the evening bread again. As for tea or sour-cabbage soup, the master and the mistress themselves guzzle that. They make me sleep in the vestibule, and when their brat cries, I don't sleep at all, but have to rock the cradle. Dear Grandpapa, for Heaven's sake, take me away from here, home to our village, I can't bear this any more. . . . I bow to the ground to you, and will pray to God for ever and ever, take me from here or I shall die. . . ."

The corners of Vanka's mouth went down, he rubbed his eyes with his dirty fist, and sobbed.

"I'll grate your tobacco for you," he continued, "I'll pray to God for you, and if there is anything wrong, then flog me like the grey goat. And if you really think I shan't find work, then I'll ask the manager, for Christ's sake, to let me clean the boots, or I'll go instead of Fedya as underherdsman. Dear Grandpapa, I can't bear this any more, it'll kill me. . . . I wanted to run away to our village, but I have no boots, and I was afraid of the frost, and when I grow up I'll look after you, no one shall harm you, and when you die I'll pray for the repose of your soul, just like I do for mamma Pelagueva.

"As for Moscow, it is a large town, there are all gentlemen's houses, lots of horses, no sheep, and the dogs are not vicious. The children don't come round at Christmas with a star, no one is allowed to sing in the choir, and once I saw in a shop window hooks on a line and fishing rods, all for sale, and for every kind of fish, awfully convenient. And there was one hook which would catch a sheat-fish weighing a pound. And there are shops with guns, like the master's, and I am sure they must cost 100 rubles each. And in the meat-shops there are woodcocks, partridges, and hares, but who shot them or where they come from, the shopman won't say.

"Dear Grandpapa, and when the masters give a Christmas tree, take a golden walnut and hide it in my green box. Ask the young lady, Olga Ignatyevna, for it, say it's for Vanka."

Vanka sighed convulsively, and again stared at the window. He remembered that his grandfather always went to the forest for the Christmas tree, and took his grandson with him. What happy times! The frost crackled, his grandfather crackled, and as they both did, Vanka did the same. Then before cutting down the Christmas tree his grandfather smoked his pipe, took a long pinch of snuff, and made fun of poor frozen little Vanka. . . . The young fir trees, wrapt in hoar-frost, stood motionless, waiting for which of them would die. Suddenly a hare springing from somewhere would dart over the snowdrift. . . . His grandfather could not help shouting:

"Catch it, catch it, catch it! Ah, short-tailed devil!"

When the tree was down, his grandfather dragged it to the master's house, and there they set about decorating it. The young lady, Olga Ignatyevna, Vanka's great friend, busied herself most about it. When little Vanka's mother, Pelagueya, was still alive, and was servant-woman in the house, Olga Ignatyevna used to stuff him with sugar-candy, and, having nothing to do, taught him to read, write, count up to one hundred, and even to dance the quadrille. When Pelagueya died, they placed the orphan Vanka in the kitchen with his grandfather, and from the kitchen he was sent to Moscow to Aliakhin, the shoemaker.

"Come quick, dear Grandpapa," continued Vanka, "I beseech you for Christ's sake take me from here. Have pity on a poor orphan, for here they beat me, and I am frightfully hungry, and so sad that I can't tell you, I cry all the time. The other day the master hit me on the head with a last; 1 fell to the ground, and only just returned to life. My life is a misfortune, worse than any dog's. . . . I send greetings to Aliona, to one-eyed Tegor, and the coachman, and don't let any one have my mouth-organ. I remain, your grandson, Ivan Zhukov, dear Grandpapa, do come."

Vanka folded his sheet of paper in four, and put it into an envelope purchased the night before for a kopek. He thought a little, dipped the pen into the ink, and wrote the address:

"The village, to my grandfather." He then scratched his head, thought again, and added: "Konstantin Makarych." Pleased at not having been interfered with in his writing, he put on his cap, and, without putting on his sheep-skin coat, ran out in his shirt-sleeves into the street.

The shopman at the poulterer's, from whom he had inquired the night before, had told him that letters were to be put into post-boxes, and from there they were conveyed over the whole earth in mail troikas by drunken post-boys and to the sound of bells. Vanka ran to the first post-box and slipped his precious letter into the slit.

An hour afterwards, lulled by hope.

he was sleeping soundly. In his dreams he saw a stove, by the stove his grandfather sitting with his legs dangling down, barefooted, and reading a letter to the cooks, and Viun walking round the stove wagging his tail.

Zinotchka

ON beds of new-mown hay in a peasant's cabin a party of sportsmen were spending the night. Outside, a concertina moaned plaintively in the moonlight. The hay exhaled a heavy, irritating smell. The sportsmen spoke of dogs, of women, of love, of game. When they had ruined all the women they knew and told a hundred wild stories, the stoutest of the party, who looked in the darkness like a haycock and spoke like a staff-officer, yawned loudly and said:

"Women exist only for that—to love our brother only. But tell me, can any of you brag about being really hated—hated with fury, hated as devils hate? Can you?"

Silence.

"I fancy not," resumed the staff-officer's bass. "I alone have had that experience. I have been hated by a girl, and a pretty girl; and, in my own person, studied all the symptoms of first hate. I say 'first,' gentlemen, because it was the converse of first love. But, as a fact, I gained my queer experience at an age when I had no definite ideas about either love or hatred. I was only eight years old. But that is not the point; the girl herself is the centre of the story. However. . . . Listen!

"One fine summer evening before sunset, with my governess Zinotchka, an entrancing, romantic creature just out of school, I sat in the nursery at lessons. Zinotchka looked abstractedly out of the window and said to me—

" 'Yes, we inhale oxygen. Now tell me, Petya, what do we exhale?'

" 'Carbonic acid gas,' I answered, also looking out of the window.

" 'Quite right,' said Zinotchka. 'The plants, on the other hand, inhale carbonic acid and exhale oxygen. Carbonic acid gas is contained in seltzer water and in samovar smoke. . . . It is a very dangerous gas. Near Naples there is a so-called Dog's Cavern full of it; if you put a dog in this cavern it is quickly suffocated.'

"This unhappy cavern near Naples was a physical phenomenon which no governess ever forgot. Zinotchka always impressed on me strongly the value of natural science, though she knew nothing about chemistry save the fate of these dogs.

"She told me to repeat the facts. I repeated them; whereupon she asked me, 'What is the horizon?' I answered. While we were busy with the horizon my father was in the yard preparing a shooting excursion. The dogs whined, the horses paced impatiently; the servants filled the tarantass with bags of food—all sorts of good things! Alongside the tarantass waited our two-seated droschky, which was to take my mother and sisters on a birthday visit to Ivanitsky's. All were going somewhere, except myself, and my elder brother, who complained of a bad toothache. You can imagine my envy and boredom.

" 'So . . . what is it we inhale?' asked Zinotchka, looking out of the window.

" 'Oxygen.'

" 'Yes; and the horizon is the place where, as it seems to us, the earth is joined to the sky.'

"But at this point the tarantass drove away, and after it the droschky. I looked at Zinotchka and saw that she took from her pocket a piece of paper, crushed it nervously, and pressed it to her forehead. When she had done this she started and looked at the clock.

" 'So . . . remember,' she resumed. 'Near Naples there is a so-called Dog's Cavern . . .'—here she again looked at the clock and continued—'where, as it seems to us, the earth is joined to the sky.'

"Poor Zinotchka walked up and down the room in intense agitation and continued to look at the clock. But my lessons were due to last another half-hour.

" 'Take your arithmetic,' she said, breathing heavily, and turning over the pages with a trembling hand. 'Try and solve Problem No. 325. I shall be back immediately.'

"Zinotchka left the room. I heard her fluttering down the stairs, and soon saw through the window her blue dress flashing through the yard and vanishing at the garden gate. Her feverish movements, the redness of her cheeks, her intense agitation aroused my curiosity. Where had she run to, and why? Being intelligent beyond my years, I reasoned it out and understood everything. Taking advantage of my rigid parents' absence, she had gone to plunder the raspberry bushes or, perhaps, to pick wild cherries. If that was so, then I, too, devil take me! would go and pick wild cherries. I threw my lesson-book away and ran into the garden. At the cherry-trees, which I made for first, Zinotchka was not to be seen. Having ignored the raspberries, the gooseberries, and passed our watchman's hut, she was making her way to the pond, pale as death, and starting at every sound. I stole after her, undiscovered, and saw, gentlemen, a most amazing sight! Near the pond, between the trunks of two old willows, stood my elder brother Sasha without the least sign of toothache about him. He looked at approaching Zinotchka, and his whole face, like the sun, was lighted with rapturous delight. And Zinotchka, as if she were being driven into the Dog's Cavern to inhale carbonic acid gas, walked towards him slowly, breathing with difficulty, and hanging back her head. Everything showed that this was the first such meeting of her life. In a moment she stood before my brother, and for a few seconds they looked silently at one another as if they could not credit their own eyes. . . . And then some inexplicable force seemed to push Zinotchka from behind; she laid her hand on Sasha's shoulder and pressed her head against his waistcoat. My brave Sasha smiled, muttered something inaudible, and with the awkwardness of a man very much in love put both his hands to Zinotchka's face. And then, gentlemen, wonders! . . . The hill behind which the sun was sinking, the two willow-trees, the green banks, the sky—all of these were imaged in the pond. Silence . . . you can imagine it! Over the sedges swept a million gold butterflies with long whiskers, beyond the garden a shepherd drove his flock! It was a picture for the gods!

"But of all that I saw, I understood only one thing. Sasha was kissing Zinotchka! It was improper! If mother knew. They would hear more of it. With a feeling of shame I returned to the nursery, and witnessed no more of the tryst. Being intelligent beyond my years, I bent over my lesson-books, thought, and reasoned it out. And my face grew radiant with a smile of victory. On the one hand, it was profitable to possess another's secret; on the other, it was flattering that persons in authority, like Sasha and Zinotchka, had been detected in ignorance of the social properties. Now they had fallen into my power; and their peace henceforth depended only on my generosity. They would know that soon!

"When bedtime came, Zinotchka as usual came to the nursery to make sure that I had said my prayers and had not got into bed in my clothes. I looked at her pretty, radiant face, and grinned. The secret rent me asunder, and demanded an outlet. I began with hints, and revelled in the effect.

" 'Aha, I know!' I began. 'Aha!'

" 'What do you know?'

" 'Aha! I saw you kissing Sasha behind the willows. I went after you, and watched!'

"Zinotchka started and turned a fiery red. Struck dumb by my words, she dropped into a chair on which were a glass of water and a candlestick.

" 'I saw you and Sasha . . . kiss-

ing . . .' I repeated, hopping, and enjoying her confusion. 'Aha! Wait till I tell mother.'

"At first Zinotchka looked at me earnestly and in terror. Then, convinced that I really did know everything, she seized my hand despairingly, and whispered tremulously—

" 'Petya, that is mean. . . . I implore you! For the love of God! be a man . . . don't say anything. . . . Honest boys do not spy. It is mean. I implore you!'

"Poor Zinotchka feared my mother as fire; my mother was a virtuous and high-principled lady. That was one reason for her fright. The second, no doubt, was that my grinning snout seemed a profanation of her first, pure, romantic love. You can imagine her feelings! Through my fault, she must have lain awake all night, for she appeared at breakfast next morning with dark blue circles round her eyes. . . . When after breakfast I came across Sasha I could not curb the temptation to grin and boast.

" 'Aha! I know. I saw you kissing Mademoiselle Zina!'

"Sasha looked at me and said—

" 'You are an idiot!'

"He was harder to frighten than Zinotchka, and the blow failed. That disappointed me. That Sasha was so bold was proof that he didn't believe I had seen the kiss. But, wait, I consoled myself; I could prove it. At lessons that morning Zinotchka kept her eyes turned away, and stammered constantly.

"She showed no fear; but tried to placate me, gave me full marks for everything, and never once complained to my father of my tricks. Being intelligent beyond my years, I exploited her secret to my profit; I learned no lessons, entered the class-room walking on my hands, and was grossly impertinent—in short, if I had continued in the same spirit to this day, I should be an expert black-mailer. But only a week passed. The secret irritated and tormented me—it was a splinter in my soul. Heedless of results, I could no longer combat the impulse to let it out, and enjoy the effect. One day at dinner when there were many visitors I grinned sheepishly, looked cunningly at Zinotchka, and began—

" 'Aha! I know. . . . I saw . . .'

" 'What did you see?' asked my mother.

"Again I looked cunningly at Zinotchka, and then Sasha. You should have seen how Zinotchka flared up, and Sasha's ferocious eyes! I bit my tongue and said no more. Zinotchka turned slowly pale, ground her teeth, and ate nothing. During preparation, that evening, I noticed that a sudden change had come over Zinotchka. Her face was severer, colder, marble-like; and her eyes had a strange expression. I give you my word that even in dogs when they tear to pieces a wolf I have never seen such devouring, annihilating eyes. I was soon to learn what the expression meant. In the midst of a lesson Zinotchka ground her teeth and hissed in my face—

" 'I detest you! If you only knew, wretch, disgusting animal, how I hate you; how I hate your cropped head, your infamous ass's ears!'

"But she took fright immediately and continued—

" 'I did not mean that for you. I was only repeating a part from a play. . . .'

"After that, gentlemen, she came to my bed every night and looked me steadfastly in the face. She hated me passionately. Yet she could not live without me. It somehow seemed a need for her to watch my detestable face. And then I remember one delightful summer evening. There was a smell of hay, stillness, and so on. The moon shone. I was walking down a garden path, thinking of cherry jam. Suddenly up to me came pale and pretty Zinotchka, seized my arm, and, panting, avowed her feelings.

" 'Oh, how I hate you! I have never wished any one such evil as I wish you! I want you to understand that!'

"You can imagine it! The moon, the pale face exhaling passion, the stillness! And, little pig that I was, I revelled in it. I listened to Zinotchka, looked at her eyes. . . . At first it was delightful, because it was new. But in a moment I was overtaken by terror; I screamed loudly, and ran into the house.

"I decided that the only thing was to complain to my mother. And I complained, and told her how I had seen Sasha and Zinotchka kissing. I was an idiot, and did not foresee the result; otherwise I should have held my tongue. . . . When my mother heard me she flamed with indignation, and said—

" 'It is not your business to talk of such things. . . . You are too young. But what an example to children!'

"My mother was not only virtuous, she was tactful too. She did her best to avoid a scandal; and rid herself of Zinotchka not at once, but gradually, systematically, as people rid themselves of respectable but tiresome visitors. I remember that when Zinotchka drove away her last glance was directed to the window at which I sat, and I assure you that to this day I remember that look.

"Not long afterwards Zinotchka was my brother's wife. That is the Zinaida Nikolaievna whom you all know. I never met her again until I was a junker. It was hard for her to recognize in the moustached officer the detested Petya—still, her manner to me was not quite that of a relative. . . . And even to-day, despite my good-humoured bald head, my peaceful figure, and meek looks, Zinotchka always looks at me a little askance, and seems out of sorts when I visit my brother. . . . It is plain that first hate is not as quickly forgotten as first love. . . . By Jove! The cocks are crowing already. Good night!"

The Privy Councillor

In the beginning of April, 1870, my mother, Clavdïa Arkhipovna, the widow of a first lieutenant, received a letter from her brother, Ivan, the Privy Councillor, of St. Petersburg, in which, besides other pieces of news, he wrote: "The liver complaint from which I suffer has forced me hitherto to live abroad every summer; but as my cash is very small, it is probable, dear sister, I may come to Kochuevka this summer on a visit."

My mother grew pale when she read this letter, but soon a curious look both sad and gay appeared on her countenance. This struggle between tears and laughter always reminded me of the twinkling and spluttering of a brightly burning candle sprayed with water. Having read the letter a second time, my mother called her household together, and with a voice trembling with emotion she began to explain to us that there had been four brothers Gundasov: one died a baby, another went to the wars and died, the third and no disgrace—was an actor, and the fourth . . .

"The fourth—he is far above us," my mother sobbed; "my own brother . . . we grew up together. . . . Ah, how I tremble . . . Why, he is a Privy Councillor—a general! . . . How shall I greet him . . . my angel? How shall I, a silly, uneducated old woman, be able to converse with him . . . I have not seen him for fifteen years! Andryushenka," my mother continued, turning to me, "be happy, you little goose! It is for your good luck that God sends him to us!"

As soon as we had heard a very minute history of the whole Gundasov family, a running about and a bustle began in the whole estate, such as I had never seen except before Christmas and Easter. The only things that had pity shown them were the vault of heaven and the water in the river, everything else was unmercifully cleaned, washed and painted. If the sky had been smaller and not so high, and the water of the river had not run so swiftly, even they would have been scrubbed with sand and rubbed with bast. The walls, that were already white as snow, were white-washed all over, the floors always bright and shining were polished every day. The tom-cat, Dock (one day during my childhood I had cut off a good quarter of his tail with the chopper used for breaking sugar, and that is how he came by the name of Dock), was banished from the dwelling-rooms and given into the charge of Anisya; and Fedka was told that if the dogs came anywhere near the porch God would punish him. But nobody suffered more than the poor sofas, chairs and carpets. At no previous time had they been beaten with sticks so unmercifully as they were beaten now, in the expectation of our guest. My pigeons, hearing the noise of beating, were so excited that they almost flew away to heaven.

The tailor, Spiridon, came from Novostroevka. He was the only tailor in the whole district who dared to work for the gentry. He was a good, capable, hard-working man, who did not drink and who had certain ideals of style and elegance; but, nevertheless, he worked abominably. The thought that he did not make his things sufficiently fashionable caused him to alter each article five or six times. He often went to the nearest town, trudging along on foot, to study the fashions worn by the local dandies, with the result that in the end he made our clothes in a way that even a caricaturist would have thought exaggerated and overdone. To be fashionable we strutted about in trousers, which were so narrow, and jackets, which were so short, that when we found ourselves in the company of young ladies we felt ashamed.

Spiridon took my measure carefully and slowly. He measured me from every point, up and down, round and round, as if I were a barrel for which he had to make hoops; he made careful notes with a thick pencil on a piece of paper and covered his measure with three-cornered marks. When he had finished with me it was the turn of my tutor, Egor Alexeevich Pobedimsky. My never-to-be-forgotten tutor was just at the age when young men are much occupied with the cultivation of their moustache, and think a great deal about their personal appearance and the fit of their clothes, so you may imagine with what trepidation Spiridon turned to him. Egor Alexeevich had to throw his head back, stretch out his legs in the form of a reversed letter V; first he had to raise his arms, then to lower them again. Spiridon measured him several times circling round and round like an enamoured pigeon round his mate, now and again sinking on one knee and bending his body into a hook. . . . My mother, faint and weary from all her exertions and troubles, flushed from constant ironing, looked on during this lengthy process and kept repeating:

"Now mind, Spiridon, God will punish you if you spoil the cloth. You will have no more luck if you fail to get a good fit."

My mother's words only made Spiridon become hot and cold, because he was sure he would not get the right fit. He took one rouble and twenty kopecks for making my suit, and for Pobedimsky's two roubles; the cloth, lining and buttons were provided by us. This cannot be called exorbitant, as Novostroevka was about ten versts distant from our place, and the tailor came to try on about four times. Each time we tried on the narrow trousers, drawing them on with difficulty, and got into the exceedingly tight jackets, which were tacked together with white threads, my prudish mother frowned and seemed astonished.

"Good Lord, what vulgar new fashions! One's ashamed to look at you. If my brother were not a man about town, I would certainly never think of having such fashionable clothes made for you."

Spiridon, glad that she blamed the fashions and not his work, shrugged his shoulders and drew a long breath as much as to say: "What can you do? 'Tis the spirit of the age!"

The excitement with which we awaited the arrival of our guest could only be compared with the tension of spiritists at a séance, when expecting the apparition of the spirit. My mother suffered from sick-headaches and she was constantly in tears. I lost my appetite, slept badly and did not learn my lessons. The longing speedily to see the general did not desert me even in my dreams. I constantly dreamed of him, that is to say, of a man with epaulets, a high gold-embroidered collar that reached to his ears, with a drawn sword in his hand, just like the man whose portrait hung in our drawing-room, above the sofa, and stared with terrible black eyes on all who dared to look at him. Only Pobedimsky remained quite composed. He was not afraid, nor delighted: only from time to time, when my mother related the history of the Gundasov family, he would remark:

"Yes, it will be pleasant to converse with a man of the world."

Everybody on our estate looked upon my tutor as a person possessing an exceptional nature. He was a pimply young man of twenty, with a low forehead and unusually long disorderly hair. His nose was so long that, when he wanted to examine anything closely, my tutor had to bend his head on one side like a bird. In our eyes there was no man as learned, wise and gallant in the whole district. He had passed through six classes of the gymnasium, and had then entered a veterinary college, from which, in less than six months, he had been expelled. The cause of his expulsion he kept a profound secret, which enabled anybody, wishing to do so, to look upon my tutor as a man who had been victimized, and they surrounded him with an atmosphere of mystery. He spoke little, and on serious subjects only; he did not fast during Lent; and he looked upon life from a contemptuous height, which, however, did not prevent him from accepting presents from my mother, in the shape of suits of clothes, or of painting grinning faces with red teeth on my paper kites. My mother did not like his "pride," but she bowed before his learning.

We had not long to wait for our guest. In the beginning of May two loads of trunks and portmanteaus arrived from the nearest station. These trunks looked so majestic that the coachmen, quite automatically, took off their caps as they got them down from the carts.

"There must be uniforms and gunpowder in these trunks," I thought.

Why gunpowder? Probably the dignity of a general was closely connected in my mind with cannon and gunpowder.

The next day, May 10th, when I awoke, my nurse told me in a whisper that my uncle had arrived. I got up quickly, washed anyhow and rushed out of the room without saying my prayers. In the passage I butted into a tall, square-built gentleman, with fashionable whiskers, dressed in a smart overcoat. Almost dying of fright, and scarcely remembering the instructions my mother had given me as to how I should greet my uncle, I approached this formidable personage, bowed low, knocking my heels together, and stooped to kiss his hand; but the gentleman would not allow me to do so and informed me that he was not my uncle, but only my uncle's valet Peter. The sight of this Peter, who was dressed in a much richer style than either I or Pobedimsky, astonished me greatly, and I must confess I can't get over it to this very day. Who could have thought that such sedate, serious people, with such strict and clever eyes could, by any possibility, be servants? And for what reason?

Peter told me that my uncle was with my mother in the garden, so I scampered after them.

Nature, not knowing the history of the Gundasov family, nor my uncle's rank, felt much more free and less shy than I did. The noise that went on in the garden was like the row of a country fair. Numberless starlings cutting through the air chased the gnats and flies over the paths and the flower-beds with noise and chatter. Flocks of chirping sparrows hid in the lilac bushes, which were covered with delicate fragrant blossoms, that seemed to stretch out straight into your face. The songs of thrushes, the twittering of innumerable small birds, and the humming of bees and gnats were heard on all sides. At another time I would have started to chase the grasshoppers, or to throw stones at a crow that was sitting on a mound of earth beneath the aspen trees, and turned his long beak from side to side, but now I dared not think of any mischief. My heart throbbed and there was a cold feeling in my stomach. I was preparing myself to meet the man with the epaulets, the drawn sword and the fierce eyes.

But imagine my disenchantment! Walking by my mother's side in the garden I saw a thin, little dandy in a white silk suit and a white cap. He had his hands in his pockets and his head well thrown back, and he kept constantly running in advance of my mother; he looked quite a young man. There was so much life and movement in his whole figure that the treacherous signs of age could only be noticed when you got near him from behind, and saw beneath his cap the silver gleam of his closely cropped hair. Instead of the dignity and stiffness of a general, I saw almost boyish agility; instead of the embroidered high collar that reached to the ears, an ordinary blue silk cravat. My mother and my uncle were walking slowly in the avenue and talking together. I approached quietly from behind and waited until one of them should turn round.

"What a paradise you have here, Kladya!" my uncle said. "How charming, how nice everything is! If I had only known what a beautiful place you have, I would never have gone abroad during all these years."

My uncle bent down quickly and smelled a tulip. All he saw charmed and interested him. It seemed almost as if it were the first time in his life that he had seen a garden or a sunny day. This strange man moved as if worked by wires and never ceased speaking, not allowing my mother time to put in a word. Suddenly, at the turn of the road, Pobedimsky appeared from behind a group of elders. His apparition was so unexpected that my uncle started and stepped back. In honour of the occasion my tutor wore his Inverness coat with large cape-like sleeves, which made him look like a windmill, especially when you saw him from behind. His mien was majestic and solemn. Pressing his hat to his breast, in the Spanish fashion, as the marquises do in melodrama, he took a step forward and made my uncle a profound bow, bending his body with a slight inclination to one side.

"I have the honour of introducing myself to Your Excellency," he said in a loud voice. "I am the pedagogue and instructor of your nephew, a former student of the Veterinary Institution, the nobleman Pobedimsky."

This politeness on the part of my tutor pleased my mother very much. She smiled and waited, hoping to hear some further clever remarks; but my tutor, expecting that in reply to his majestic greeting he would receive an equally majestic answer (that is to say, a general-like H'm! and two fingers of an outstretched hand), was very much confused and taken aback when the general laughed affably and shook his hand in a friendly and hearty manner.

He mumbled something incoherent, coughed and retired.

"Is that not splendid!" laughed my uncle; "just look at him, he has put on his large flapping coat and thinks he is a very clever fellow. That pleases me, I swear, by God! What an amount of youthful assurance and life there is in that stupid flapping coat. . . . Ah! and who is this boy?" he said suddenly, turning round and seeing me.

"That is my Andryushenka," said my mother, flushing. "My consolation!"

I scraped my foot in the sand and bowed low.

"A fine boy, a fine boy," my uncle mumbled, removing his hand from my lips and stroking my hair. "Your name is Andryusha? So, so, h'm! Yes, I swear, by God! . . . . H'm! You have lessons?"

With fond exaggeration my mother began to describe the progress I had made in science and religion, while I, according to the prearranged programme, walked at my uncle's side and continued to make low obeisances. We had just got to the point when my mother began to throw out hints, that owing to my quite exceptional capacities it would be a good thing if I could get into a military school at the expense of the Crown, and when I, also according to programme, began to cry and to beg my uncle to use his influence, when he suddenly stopped, and spreading his arms in astonishment exclaimed:

"Good gracious! What is this?"

Coming along the path towards us was Tatiana Ivanovna, the wife of Fedor Petrovich, our bailiff. She was carrying a white starched petticoat and a long ironing-board. In passing she looked up timidly at our guest from beneath her long eyelashes and blushed.

"It gets better and better every hour," my uncle murmured between his teeth, looking after her with admiration. "You have a surprise at every step, sister; I swear, by God!"

"She's our beauty," my mother answered. "Fedor brought her from an estate a hundred versts from here."

Not everybody would have called Tatiana Ivanovna a beauty. She was a plump, graceful little woman of about twenty, with dark brown hair and brown eyes, almost rosy and nice-looking, but neither in her face nor in her figure was there a single decided line, no bold stroke on which the eye could rest; it seemed as if nature, when she created her, had been without any inspiration, or boldness. Tatiana Ivanovna was timid, easily confused and good-tempered; she went about smoothing and noiselessly, she spoke little and seldom smiled; her whole life was even and placid as her own unwrinkled face and smoothly brushed hair. My uncle screwed up his eyes and looking after her smiled. My mother looked fixedly at his smiling face, and became very grave.

"And so, brother, you have never married," she said with a little sigh.

"No, I never married."

"Why?" my mother asked quietly.

"How am I to tell you? It just happened so. In my youth I worked so hard that I had no time to live, and when I wanted to begin living I looked round and found I had already fifty years behind me. . . . I had had no time. However, it's dull to talk about it now . . ."

My mother and my uncle both sighed at the same time and went on. I lagged behind and ran away to find my tutor, with whom I wanted to talk about our impressions. I found Pobedimsky standing in the middle of the yard, looking majestically at the sky.

"One sees that he is a cultivated man," he said twisting his head. "I hope we shall get on together."

In about an hour my mother joined us.

"Now, my dears, here's another trouble," she commenced panting for breath. "My brother has brought his valet with him; and this valet is such a fine gentleman that we can't put him to sleep in the kitchen, or give him a bed in the passage; he must, forsooth, have his own room. I can't think where I am to lodge him. What would you say, children, to going for a time into the farm-house, to Fedor, 1 could then give the valet your room? Eh?"

We agreed at once, because we should be much freer if we lived in the farm-house than we were in the house, always under mother's eyes.

"There's nothing but one trouble after another," my poor mother continued. "Now my brother says that he cannot dine at twelve o'clock, but must have his dinner at seven, as they do in the capital. All this bother will drive me mad. By seven o'clock the dinner will be quite spoilt if it's left in the oven. . . . It's certain men never understand domestic affairs, even when they are very clever. . . . I shall have to make two dinners. . . . . You, children, will dine as usual at midday, while I, poor old woman, will have to hold out until seven, on my brother's account."

Then with a deep sigh my mother ordered me to do all I could to please my uncle, whom God had sent to me as a blessing and for my good fortune, and then she ran away to the kitchen. That very day Pobedimsky and I removed to the farm-house where Fedor lived. We were lodged in a passage room that lay between the lobby and the room occupied by our bailiff.

Notwithstanding the arrival of my uncle and our new quarters, life went on much in the usual way, and contrary to our expectations, it was dull and monotonous. In honour of our guest we were given holidays. Pobedimsky, who never read anything, nor occupied himself in any way, sat most of the time on his bed, looking over his long nose into vacancy, and he seemed to be thinking. From time to time he would get up, try on his new suit and then sit down again to meditate in silence. Only one thing bothered him—and that was the flies, which he mercilessly tried to kill by slapping his hands together. After dinner he usually rested, and the sound of his snores made the whole place melancholy. I either ran about the garden all day long, or sat in our room in the farm-house and made paper kites.

During the first two or three weeks we seldom saw my uncle. For whole days together he sat in his room and worked regardless of the heat or the flies. His unusual capacity for sitting still, as if glued to his chair, astonished us very much, and we considered it a great feat. For us lazy boys, who knew nothing of systematic work, his industry seemed to be quite a marvel. He got up at about nine o'clock, and would sit at his table without moving until dinner; then having had his dinner he would return to his work and sit on until late at night. Whenever I peeped at

him through the keyhole, I always saw the same sight; my uncle sitting at his table and working. The work he did seemed to consist of writing with one hand and turning over the leaves of a book with the other, and strange to say, it made him move all over. He swung his legs like a pendulum, whistled softly and kept time by nodding his head. His appearance all the while was quite absent-minded and light-hearted, not as if he were working, but rather as if he were having a game of noughts and crosses with himself. He was always dressed in a short silk jacket and wore a very bright-coloured tie, and every time I peeped throught the keyhole I seemed to smell the odour of effeminate scents. He only left his room to come to dinner, but he always ate very little.

"I can't understand my brother," mother complained. "Every day I kill turkeys and pigeons for him, I even prepare fruit salads with my own hands, but he only eats a plate of soup and a tiny bit of meat as big as your finger, and then retires to his room again. When I beg him to eat a little more he returns to the table and takes a glass of milk. Now what's there in a glass of milk? . . . Only slops. . . . You can die from such diet. If you try to persuade him he only laughs and jokes. No, my darling does not like our food!"

The evenings were much gayer than the days. Usually when the sun was setting and the long shadows appeared in the yard we, that is to say, Tatiana Ivanovna, Pobedimsky and I, could be found sitting on the little perron of our house. We sat there in silence until it became dark. Yes, what can you talk about when every subject has already been discussed? We had had our subject of conversation—the arrival of my uncle, but that had been exhausted too. My tutor never took his eyes off Tatiana Ivanovna, and sighed deeply at intervals. . . . At the time I did not understand these sighs and never tried to fathom their meaning, but now—they explain to me very much.

When the shadows joined together and formed one uniform darkness our bailiff, Fedor, returned from shooting or from the fields. Fedor always produced on me the impression of a wild and terrible man. He was the son of a Russionized gipsy. He had a dark complexion, large black eyes, curly black locks and a dark dishevelled beard. Our farm labourers had given him the nickname of "the deuce." Besides the appearance he had also much of the gipsy nature. He could not sit at home and often disappeared for whole days in the fields or out shooting. He was sullen, bilious and silent, and neither feared anyone nor admitted any authority. He was rude to my mother; he said "thou" to me, and looked upon the learning of Pobedimsky with disdain. All this was excused him, because we considered him a passionate, hot-tempered man who was in ill-health. My mother valued him because, notwithstanding his gipsy origin, he was ideally honest and industrious. He loved his wife, Tatiana Ivanovna, passionately, as gipsies love, but with a love that was gloomy and seemed to cause suffering. In our presence he never fondled his wife, but only gazed at her with staring eyes and his mouth drawn to one side.

When he returned home from the fields he would go into the house, deposit his gun angrily and noisily in a corner, come to us on the perron and sit down next to his wife. After resting he would ask her some questions about the housekeeping, and then sink into silence.

"Let us sing," I suggested.

My tutor tuned his guitar and began to sing with the deep bass voice of a deacon: "In the midst of outstretched valleys." We all joined in. My tutor took the bass, Fedor sang a scarcely audible tenor, while Tatiana and I sang treble in unison.

When the whole sky began to twinkle with stars and the frogs ceased to croak, our supper was brought us from the kitchen. We went into the house and sat down to eat. My tutor and the gipsy ate ravenously, and with so much noise that it was difficult to know if they were cracking bones, or if it was the crunching of their own jaws, while Tatiana Ivanovna and I had hardly time to eat our share. After supper the farmhouse sank into profound slumber

One evening, about the end of May, we were sitting in this way on the perron waiting for supper, when suddenly a shadow appeared as if it had sprung up out of the earth and Gundasov stood before us. He looked at us for a long time, and at last clasping his hand and laughing merrily he exclaimed:

"An idyll! They sing and dream of the moon. Beautiful, I swear, by God! May I sit down near you and dream?

We said nothing but looked at each other. My uncle sat down on the lower step, yawned and looked at the sky. There was silence. Pobedimsky, who had long been wanting to converse with a new man, was delighted to have this opportunity, and was the first to break silence. For intellectual conversation he had only one subject and that was about epizoa. It often happens when one finds oneself in a thousand-headed crowd, for some reason it is only the features of a single face that impress themselves on the memory, and you remember them long after. So it was with Pobedimsky; of all that he had heard during the half-year he had been at the Veterinary College he could remember only one thing.

"Epizoa cause enormous losses to the national husbandry. In the conflict with them the community must go hand in hand with the government."

Before saying this to Gundasov my tutor coughed three times, and in his excitement he flapped the wings of his Inverness coat repeatedly. Hearing this remark about epizoa my uncle looked at him attentively and gave an amused sniff.

"I swear, by God, this is lovely," he murmured, looking at us as if we had been wax figures. "This is really life! That's how it ought to be in reality! And why are you silent, Pelagea Ivanovna?" he asked, turning to Tatiana Ivanovna.

She became confused and began to cough.

"Talk, good people, sing . . . play! Do not lose time. That rascal time has a way of running on, he does not wait! I swear, by God, you have not time to look round before old age is there. . . . Then it is too late to begin living. What do you say, Pelagea Ivanovna? One must not sit silent and immovable."

At that moment our supper was brought from the kitchen. My uncle came into the house with us, and for company sake he ate five curd cakes and the wing of a duck. He ate and

looked at us. We all aroused raptures in him, and seemed to affect him. No matter what nonsense my unforgetable tutor talked or whatever Tatiana Ivanovna did, he found charming—admirable. After supper Tatiana Ivanovna sat down quietly in a corner to knit, and he did not take his eyes off her little fingers and chatted unceasingly.

"You, my friends, must hasten to live," he said. "God forbid that you should sacrifice the present for the future! In the present is youth, health, flame—the future is deception . . . smoke! As soon as you attain twenty years, begin to live."

Here Tatiana Ivanovna dropped a knitting-needle, and my uncle springing from his chair picked it up and handed it to her with a bow. It was then, I perceived for the first time, that there were more refined people in the world than Pobedimsky.

"Yes," my uncle continued, "love, marry, commit follies. . . . Follies are much more vital and healthy than our efforts and strivings after a rational life."

My uncle talked much and long; so long, indeed, that he bored us, and I sat in a corner of the room on a trunk, and as I listened I began to doze. I was annoyed that he never once took any notice of me. He only left our house at two o'clock in the morning long after I, being unable to wrestle any longer with my drowsiness, was fast asleep.

From that day my uncle began to come to the farmhouse every evening to see us. He sang with us, he had supper with us and remained every night until two o'clock, chatting incessantly and always on the same subject. His evening and night occupations were quite given up, and at the end of June, when the Privy Councillor had learned to eat my mother's turkeys and fruit salads, the day work was also abandoned. My uncle tore himself away from his table and was drawn into "life." During the day he walked about the garden whistling, and bothered the workmen by making them talk to him and tell him all sorts of tales. Whenever he saw Tatiana Ivanovna he always ran after her, and if she was carrying anything would offer to help her, which confused her horribly.

As the summer advanced my uncle became more and more giddy, brisk and distracted. Pobedimsky was quite disappointed in him.

"He is much too one-sided," he said. "There's not a single sign that he has stood on the highest steps of the hierarchy. He does not even understand how to talk. After every word you have: 'I swear, by God!' No, he does not please me!"

From the moment that my uncle began to visit us in the farm-house, a marked change took place in Fedor, and in my tutor. Fedor ceased to go out shooting; he returned home earlier and became more gloomy, and his eyes seemed to flash angrily on his wife in quite an unaccountable manner. My tutor never mentioned epizoa in my uncle's presence; he grew morose and often smiled ironically.

"There he comes, our mouse-coloured goat," he would grumble when he saw my uncle approaching our house.

I attributed the change that had taken place in both of them to his having offended them. My thoughtless uncle was always mixing up their names, and to the very last day of his stay he was unable to distinguish which was my tutor and which was Tatiana Ivanovna's husband. and Tatiana Ivanovna he called sometimes Nastasia, or Pelagea, or Eudoxia. All the time he declared he was charmed with us, and said endearing things to us all, laughing and behaving just like a little boy. All this might have given offense to young men; but I now understand it was not a question of offence, but of deeper feelings.

I remember one night I sat dozing in the corner on a trunk. My eyes seemed glued together with a sticky glue, and my body, tired out with running about all day, swayed from side to side. I struggled with sleep, and tried to see what was going on around me. It was about midnight, Tatiana Ivanovna, rosy and quiet as usual, was sitting at a small table sewing a shirt for her husband. Fedor glowered at her with gloomy and jealous eyes from one corner of the room, and Pobedimsky sat in another disappearing into the high collar of his shirt and sniffing angrily. My uncle walked from one end of the room to the other and was thinking of something. Silence reigned, and you could only hear the rustle of the linen in Tatiana Ivanovna's hands.

My uncle stopped suddenly before Tatiana Ivanovna and said:

"You are all so young, fresh and good; you live so tranquilly in this quiet place that I envy you. I have become attached to your kind of life, and my heart sinks when I think I must soon go away from here. Believe me when I say so! Believe me, I am quite sincere!"

Sleep closed my eyes, and I forgot where I was. When a sharp knock awoke me, my uncle was standing before Tatiana Ivanovna, looking at her with admiration. His cheeks were burning.

"My life is lost," he said. "I have never lived. Your young face reminds me of my lost youth; I would be glad to sit here for the rest of my days, looking at you. I would be happy if I could take you with me to Petersburg."

"Why?" Fedor asked in a hoarse voice.

"I would put you on my writing-table under a glass case, admire you and show you to others. Do you know, Tatiana Ivanovna, we have none like you there? We have wealth, distinction, sometimes beauty, but we have not this vital truth, this healthy tranquility."

My uncle sat down next to Tatiana Ivanovna and took her hand.

"So, you don't want to go with me to Petersburg?" he said, laughing. "In that case let me only have your hand to take with me? . . A lovely hand! . . . . What, not even that? Ah, well, you're a miser, then let me only kiss it?"

At that moment the cracking of a chair was heard. Fedor jumped up, and with measured heavy strides came to his wife. His face was a deadly grey and quivering. He struck the table with his clenched fist with all his might and said in a hollow voice:

"I won't allow it!"

At the same moment Pobedimsky also sprang from his chair. He looked pale, too, and vicious as he approached Tatiana Ivanovna, and he also struck the table with his fist.

"I . . . I won't allow it!"

"What? What is the matter?" asked my astonished uncle.

"I won't allow it!" Fedor repeated, striking the table again.

My uncle jumped up, blinking in a frightened manner; he wanted to speak, but astonishment and fear prevented him from saying a word, and looking confused he hobbled away with the tottering gait of an old man, leaving his hat in our house. Shortly after, when my mother, all of a flutter, came running into the room to see what was the matter, she found Fedor and Pobedimsky still standing like two blacksmiths, hammering on the table with their fists and repeating: "I won't allow it!"

"What has happened here?" my mother asked. "What has caused my brother to fall ill? What is the matter?"

Seeing Tatiana Ivanovna's pale and frightened face and her enraged husband, my mother evidently guessed what was the matter; she sighed and shook her head.

"Now, that's enough! Enough hammering on the table!" she said. "Fedor, stop! And why are you thumping too, Egor Alexeevich? What have you got to do with the matter?"

Pobedimsky suddenly seemed to collect himself, and became very confused. Fedor looked at him fiercely, then at his wife, and began to walk about the room. After my mother had left us I witnessed a scene that haunted me like a bad dream for long after. I saw Fedor catch hold of my tutor, lift him into the air and hurl him out of the door. . . .

When I awoke in the morning my tutor was not in his bed. In answer to my questions, nurse told me in a whisper that early that morning my tutor had been taken to the hospital to have his broken arm set. This news made me sad, and thinking of last night's row I went into the yard.

The weather was dull. The sky was covered with low clouds, a sharp breeze swept along the ground and raised dust, papers and feathers from the earth. You felt the approach of rain. Both people and animals were affected by a feeling of melancholy. When I went into the house I was asked not to make a noise and to walk about quietly, as my mother had a bad headache and was in bed. What was I to do? I went out of the gate, sat down on a bench and began to try to understand the meaning of what I had heard and seen the previous day. From our gate a road led past the smithy, and past a pool of water that never dried up, to the high road, I looked at the telegraph posts encircled by clouds of dust, I looked at the sleepy birds sitting on the wires, and I became so melancholy that at last I began to cry.

A dusty wagonette crammed full of people from the town, probably going on a pilgrimage, passed along the high road. The wagonette had scarcely had time to get out of sight when a light droshky and pair of fine horses came along the road. Standing up in the droshky, holding on to the coachman's belt, was the district police master, Akim Nikitich. To my great amazement the droshky turned up our road, and drove rapidly past me into the yard. I had not recovered from my surprise at this visit of the police master, when I heard the sound of bells and a calash with three horses came in sight. The district judge was standing in this calash and directing the coachman towards our gate.

"What is the meaning of this?" I thought as the dust-covered judge passed by. "It is probably Pobedimsky, who has accused Fedor of assault, and they have come to take him to prison."

The mystery was not so easily solved. The police master and judge were only the forerunners. In less than five minutes a carriage drove into the yard, passing me so rapidly that I was only able to distinguish a red beard through the window.

Lost in conjectures and having a presentiment of something unpleasant, I went into the house. In the lobby the first person I met was my mother. She was very pale and looked with anxiety at the door behind which men's voices were heard talking. The guests had arrived so suddenly that they had found her in the midst of her bad headache.

"Mama, who has come?" I asked.

"Sister," my uncle's voice called to her. "send in some refreshments for the Governor and me, please."

"It is easy to ask for refreshments," my mother murmured, almost fainting with alarm, "what can I prepare at a moment's notice? I shall be disgraced in my old age."

Putting her hands to her head, my mother rushed into the kitchen. The unexpected arrival of the Governor aroused all the inhabitants of the manor, and hurried them on to their legs. Then there began terrible slaughter. The throats were cut of about six fowls, five turkeys, eight ducks, and in the hurry the old gander was also beheaded. He was the progenitor of our flock of geese and my mother's great favourite. The coachman and the man-cook seemed to have gone out of their minds and slaughtered without regard to race or age. For the sake of some sort of sauce, two of my valuable tumbler pigeons were sacrificed, and they were as dear to me as the old gander was to my mother. For a long time I could not forgive the Governor for having been the cause of their death.

In the evening when the Governor and his suite, after partaking of a copious meal, got into their carriages and drove away, I went into the house to see the remains of the feast. Looking into the sitting-room I saw that both my mother and my uncle were there. My uncle, with hands behind his back, paced nervously backward and forward near the walls of the room, shrugging his shoulders. My mother, looking thin and weary, sat helplessly on the sofa, and followed each of my uncle's movements with heavy eyes.

"Pardon me, sister, but that is not the way to do things," my uncle grumbled, frowning. "I introduced the Governor to you, and you did not even give him your hand! You made him feel quite uncomfortable, poor man! No, this will never do. . . . Simplicity is a good thing, but it must have its bounds. . . . I swear, by God! . . . And then that dinner! . . . Is it possible to offer such dinners? What sort of rags did you serve for the fourth course?"

"That was duck with a sweet sauce," my mother answered quietly.

"A duck! . . . Excuse me, sister, but, but, . . . I have a heartburn. . . . I am ill!"

My uncle made a wry face, and looking as if he wanted to cry, he continued:

"Why the deuce did that Governor come! What did I want with his visit? Phew! . . . What a heartburn! I shan't be able to sleep, or to work. I am quite unstrung. . . I don't understand how you can live here without work, in this dullness. . . . Ah! . . . Now the pain begins again . . . here at the pit of the stomach."

My uncle frowned and walked about quicker.

"Brother," my mother asked quietly, "what does your journey abroad cost you?"

"At the very least three thousand," my uncle replied in a tearful voice. "I would gladly go; but where am I to find the money? I haven't got a kopeck. . . . Phew! this heartburn!"

My uncle stopped at the window and looked out sadly on the grey dull landscape, and then he began to walk about again.

There was a short silence, my mother looked long at the icon as if meditating on something and beginning to cry she said:

"Brother, I will give you these three thousand . . ."

.   .   .   .   .

Three days later the majestic trunks were sent to the station and the Privy Councillor soon followed them. When he took leave of my mother he began to cry, and for a long time he could not tear his lips away from her hand, but as soon as he was seated in the calash his face lighted up with a childlike joy. Beaming and happy he settled himself comfortably in his seat and kissed his hand in farewell to my weeping mother.

when suddenly his eyes alighted on me. An expression of the greatest surprise appeared on his face and he asked:

"Who is this boy?"

My mother, who had assured me that God had sent my uncle as a blessing for me, was greatly distressed by the question. There were no questions that troubled me. I looked at the happy face of my uncle and for some reason I felt sorry for him. I couldn't help it; I sprang into the calash and embraced that giddy, light-hearted man, so weak and yet so human. Looking into his eyes and wishing to say something agreeable, I asked:

"Uncle, have you ever been in a battle?"

"Ah, you dear boy!" laughed my uncle, kissing me. "A dear boy! I swear, by God! How natural all this is, how living! I swear, by God!"

The calash drove off. I stood looking after it, and for a long time this parting: "I swear, by God!" rang in my ears.

The Wager

CHAPTER I

THE PLAN

It was a dark autumn night. The old banker paced up and down his study, thinking of the party he had given in the autumn fifteen years before. Many clever men had been at that party, and the conversation had been interesting. One of the subjects they had talked of was the death penalty. The guests, among whom were many learned men and several journalists, were mostly against capital punishment. They considered this form of penalty out of date, not justifiable in a Christian State and immoral. In the opinion of many, capital punishment ought to be replaced everywhere by solitary confinement for life.

"I do not agree with you there," the host said. "I have neither tried the death penalty nor solitary confinement, but if one may judge à priori, in my opinion to condemn a man to death is more moral and more humane than solitary confinement. An executioner kills at once, solitary confinement kills gradually. Which executioner is more humane, he who kills with one stroke or he who takes away your life, little by little, during long years?"

"Both the one and the other are immoral," said one of the guests, "for both have the same object—to take away life. The State is not God. The State has no right to take away that which it cannot give back, even if it wanted to."

One of the guests, a jurist, a young man of twenty-five years of age, when asked his opinion on the subject replied:

"Both capital punishment and solitary imprisonment for life are equally immoral, but if I were told to choose between death and solitary confinement for life I would certainly choose the latter. To live under any conditions is better than not to live at all."

The discussion became very animated. The banker, who was younger then and more impulsive, suddenly lost control of himself, and striking the table, he turned to the young jurist and exclaimed:

"That is not true! I bet you two million roubles that you would not be able to stand solitary confinement in a cell for even five years."

"If you are serious," the jurist answered, "I accept your wager. I bet that I will remain in solitary confinement not only five, but fifteen years."

"Fifteen! I accept it," the banker cried. "Gentlemen, bear witness, I stake two millions."

"Done," said the jurist; "you stake millions and I stake my liberty."

So this cruel and senseless wager was made. The banker, who at that time scarcely knew how many millions he possessed—spoilt as he was by success in his hazardous speculations—was delighted with this wager. During supper he joked and chaffed the jurist about it.

"Think better of it, young man, while yet there is time. Two millions are as nothing to me, I can easily risk losing them, but you, remember you are risking three or four of the best years of your life. I say three or four years, because you will not stand it longer. Besides, don't forget that a voluntary imprisonment is much harder to bear than one you are forced to undergo. The knowledge that at any moment you have the right to go free will poison your whole existence in the prisoner's solitary cell. . . . I am sorry for you!"

Now the banker, thinking of all this as he paced up and down, asked himself:

"What was the use of this bet? What profit is it to anyone, that this jurist has sacrificed fifteen of the best years of his life; and that 1 throw away two millions? Can it prove to mankind that capital punishment is better or worse than lifelong imprisonment? No . . . a thousand times no. . . . It was senseless . . . madness. . . . On my part it was the caprice of a man with super-abundance, and on his the common greed for wealth."

He also remembered what had taken place after that party. It had been arranged that the jurist should serve his time of solitary confinement in a detached building that stood in the banker's grounds, and be strictly watched. It had also been decided that during the fifteen years he should be deprived of the right to cross the threshold of the building in which he was confined; of seeing any human being; of hearing the voice of any man; or of receiving letters or newspapers. He was allowed to have musical instruments, to read books, to write letters, to drink wine and to smoke tobacco. It was settled that his only communications with the outer world were to be effected in silence through a small window made specially for the purpose. All that he required, books, notes, food, wine and anything else he might want, he was to get in any quantity he desired by passing out a note through the window. The terms of the wager were settled with regard to all possible contingencies, and they entered into the most minute details, so as to make the confinement strictly solitary, and binding the jurist to remain in prison exactly fifteen years from twelve o'clock on the 14th of November, 1870, until twelve o'clock on the 14th of November, 1885.

The slightest attempt on the part of the jurist to evade any of the conditions of the wager, or to leave his confinement even two minutes before the settled time, would release the banker from his obligations to pay the two millions.

Judging by his short letters, the prisoner suffered greatly during the first year from solitude and ennui. At every hour of the day, and even at night, the sounds of the piano could be heard in his room. He did not ask for wine or tobacco. "Wine," he wrote, "arouses desire, the worst enemy of a prisoner, besides there is nothing more dull than to drink good wine in solitude; and tobacco spoils the air of my room." During the first year the jurist asked for books, mostly of a light character: novels with complicated love plots, detective stories, fantastic tales, comedies and the like.

During the second year the sounds of music ceased, and the jurist asked for the works of various classical authors. In the fifth year the sounds of music were heard again, and the prisoner asked for wine. His guards reported that this year, whenever they looked through the window, they noticed that he only ate, drank, lay on his bed, often yawned and spoke angrily to himself. He read no books. Sometimes at night he sat down to write, and wrote for hours, but in the morning he tore into small scraps all that he had written. More than once he was heard weeping.

In the second half of the sixth year the prisoner began diligently to study languages and to read philosophy and history. He was so industrious in the study of these sciences that the banker had scarcely time to supply him with all the books he required. In the course of four years he demanded no less than six hundred volumes. Once during this time of mental activity the banker received from the prisoner, among other letters, the following:

"My Dear Gaoler,

I write this letter in six languages. Show it to people who know them. Let them read it, and if they do not find a single error in it, I entreat you to order a shot to be fired in your garden. This shot will tell me that my application has not been in vain. The genius of all centuries and lands speaks in different tongues, but the same flame burns in them all. Oh, if you could only know what a sublime joy fills my soul now that I can understand them!"

The request of the prisoner was gratified. The banker ordered that two shots should be fired in the garden.

After the tenth year of his confinement the prisoner constantly sat motionless at the table and read the New Testament. It seemed strange to the banker that a man who, in the course of four years, had been able to master six hundred volumes, written by the wisest of mankind, should employ more than a year in the reading of a comparatively short and easily comprehensible book. After the Bible, he began to study the history of religion and works on theology.

During the last two years of his imprisonment the captive read very much, but without confining himself to any branch of literature. sometimes he occupied himself with natural history, sometimes he asked for Byron and Shakespeare. Often on the same note he would ask for works on chemistry and medicine, novels and some books on philosophy or a theological treatise. His reading was so varied that he seemed like a drowning man swimming in the sea surrounded by fragments of wreckage, and eagerly trying to save himself by clinging first to one fragment and then to another.

CHAPTER II

THE PAPER

THE old banker remembered all that had happened during the past years, and he thought:

"To-morrow at twelve o'clock he will be free. In fulfilment of our wager I shall have to pay him two millions. What will remain for me? If I pay this money all will be lost. I shall be a ruined man."

Fifteen years ago he could hardly count his millions, but now he was afraid to ask himself whether he had more money or debts. Hazardous gambling on 'change, risky speculations and the impetuosity, which even in his old age often mastered his prudence, had little by little undermined his business, and the fearless self-confident proud millionaire had become a second-rate banker, who trembled at every rise or fall of the market.

"A damned wager," the old man murmured, raising his hands to his head in despair; "why didn't this man die? He is now only forty years of age. He will take from me all I possess—marry, enjoy his life and speculate on 'change. While day after day I, like a beggar, envious of his prosperity, shall hear him say the same words. . . . 'I owe you all the happiness I enjoy in life, let me help you?' No, this is more than I can bear."

The only escape from bankruptcy and shame is the death of this man."

Three o'clock struck. The banker listened. All was quiet in the house; the only sound that could be heard was the rustle of the frozen leaves in the night wind. Trying to make no noise he took from his safe the key to the door that had not been opened for fifteen years, and putting on his great-coat he went into the garden.

The night was cold and dark. It was raining. A sharp, damp wind blew over the garden and moaned through the trees, giving no rest to the dry autumn leaves that had not yet fallen. The banker strained his eyes, but he could see neither the ground under his feet, nor the white statues which decorated the garden, nor the trees, nor the garden house. Carefully going towards the house he called twice to the watchman. There was no answer. The watchman had evidently taken shelter from the weather, and was sleeping soundly either in the kitchen, or the conservatory.

"If only I have the courage to execute my plan," the old man thought, "suspicion will fall first on the watchman."

Groping his way in the darkness he at last found the steps and the door and he entered the lobby of the little house, then he made his way into the small passage, where he struck a match. Not a soul was to be seen. Somebody's bedstead without a mattress stood in the passage, and in a far corner an iron stove loomed in the darkness. The seals on the door of the room, where the prisoner was confined, were in perfect order.

When the match went out, the old

man, trembling with excitement, looked through a small peep-hole in the door.

In the room a candle burned dimly. The prisoner was seated at the table. All that could be seen of him was his back, his hair and his hands, that were resting on the table. On two arm-chairs and scattered on the floor were numerous open books.

Five minutes passed, and the prisoner did not move. Fifteen years of imprisonment had taught him to sit motionless. The banker tapped gently on the glass of the peephole, but the prisoner did not answer this sound by the slightest movement. Then the banker carefully removed the seals from the door and inserted the key to the keyhole. The rusty lock gave out a hoarse sound, and the door squeaked on its hinges. The banker expected to hear an exclamation of surprise or the sound of feet, but three minutes passed and all remained silent as before on the other side of the door. . . . He decided to enter the room.

Sitting at the table was a man, hardly human in appearance. He resembled a skeleton covered with skin, with long womanlike hair and a shaggy beard. His face was yellow, with earthy tints and hollow cheeks. His back was long and narrow, and the hand, on which his unkempt head was resting, was so thin that it was frightful to look at. His hair was turning white, and looking at his old and sunken face, none would have believed that he was a man of only forty years of age. He was sleeping. Lying on the table before his sunken head was a sheet of paper, on which something was written in very small characters.

"Wretched man," thought the banker,

he is sleeping and probably dreaming of millions. I could easily take this half-dead creature, throw his on the bed and smother the last sparks of life with the pillow in such a way that even the most skilled examination would not be able to reveal the traces of violence. However, let me first see what he has written here."

The banker took up a paper from the table and read the following:

"To-morrow at twelve o'clock I shall be free, and the right to have intercourse with my fellow-men will be mine; but before leaving this room, and again looking on the sun, I find it necessary to say a few words to you. With a clear conscience, and before God, who sees me, I declare to you that I despise freedom and life and health and all that your books call the joys of this world.

"For fifteen years I have studied attentively the life of this world. It is true I neither saw the earth nor its peoples, but in your books I lived. . . . I drank luscious wines, I sang songs, I hunted the deer and the wild boar in the forests. . . . I loved women. Like clouds airy beauties, created by the genius of your great poets, visited me in the night and whispered wonderful tales which intoxicated me. In your books I climbed to the summit of Elburz and Mont Blanc, and I saw from those heights the sun rise in the morning, and at night it shed its purple glow over the sky and the ocean and the mountain-tops. I saw beneath me the flashing lightning cut through the clouds. I saw green fields, forests, rivers, lakes and towns. I heard the song of the sirens and the music of the shepherd's reed-pipes. I felt the touch of the wings of beautiful demons, who had flown to me to talk about God. In your books I cast myself down into bottomless abysses, performed wonders, committed murder, set towns on fire, preached new religions, conquered whole kingdoms. . . .

"Your books gave me wisdom. All that had been achieved by the untiring brain of man during long centuries is stored in my brain in a small compressed mass. . . . I know I am wiser than you all. . . .

"And I despise all your books, I despise all earthly blessings and wisdom. All is worthless and false, hollow and deceiving like the mirage. You may be proud, wise and beautiful, but death will wipe you away from the face of the earth, as it does the mice that live beneath your floor; and your heirs, your history, your immortal geniuses will freeze or burn with the destruction of your earth.

"You have gone mad and are not following the right path. You take falsehood for truth. and deformity for beauty. You would be surprised if instead of fruit there appeared on your apple and orange trees frogs and lizards, or if your roses exhaled the smell of sweating horses; so I am surprised that you barter heaven for earth. . . I do not want to understand you.

"To prove to you how I despise all that you value I renounce the two millions on which I looked, at one time, as the opening of paradise for me, and which I now scorn. To deprive myself of the right to receive them, I will leave my prison five hours before the appointed time, and by so doing break the terms of our compact. . . ."

The banker read these lines, replaced the paper on the table, kissed the strange man, who had written them, on the head and with tears in his eyes quietly left the house. Never before, not even after sustaining serious losses on 'change, had he despised himself as he did at that moment. When he reached his own house he went to bed, but the emotion he had just experienced, and tears that he could not repress. kept him long awake. . . .

. . . . .

The next morning the trembling and pale watchman came to imform him that they had seen the man, who lived in the small house, crawl through the window into the garden, go to the gate and then disappear. On hearing this the banker followed by his servants went to make sure that his prisoner had really run away. . . .

Not to arouse idle talk, he took from the table the paper containing the prisoner's renunciation, and on returning home he locked it up in his safe.

VOLUME VI

The Cossack

MAXIM TORCHAKOV, citizen of Berdiansk and the tenant of the Lower Farm, was returning from church with his wife. The Easter cake, the Kulich, that had been blessed at the midnight service, was guarded between them. The sun had not yet risen, but the east, pink and gold, was dissipating away the mists of the early morning. All was quiet. A quail called: "pit-poidem, pit-poidem," and far over the plain, flapping its heavy wings, a sleepy kite flew afar. The steppes held nothing else of life.

Torchakov drove along, thinking that in the whole year there was no better or gayer holiday than Easter. It was the first Easter he was celebrating since his recent marriage. Whatever he looked upon, whatever he thought of seemed to him lovely and happy. He thought of his homestead, his house, his wife, and all appeared to him gay, bountiful and happy. Everything made him feel happy: the glow of the eastern sunrise, the young grass, even his squeaking britska, and the kite soaring in the sky. And when he stopped on the way to run into a tavern, to light his cigarette and have a drink, he became even more jolly.

"It is called a great day," he said, "and it is a great day, sure enough. Wait a moment, Liza, the sun will soon begin to dance. He dances every Easter! So he must be happy too."

"He is not alive," his wife remarked.

"There are people on him," Torchakov exclaimed, "by God, there are! Ivan Stepanich told he that there are people on all the planets, on the sun and the moon too. . . . That's true. . . . But perhaps the learned talk nonsense; the evil one tempts them! . . . Stop! Is that a horse? So it is."

Half-way to their home, at the Crooked Valley, Torchakov and his wife saw a saddled horse standing quietly on the road, smelling last year's steppe grass. By the roadside, on a mound of grass, a red-haired Cossack was seated, almost bent double, looking at his feet.

"Christ is risen!" Maxim called to him. "Woah!"

"Verily He is," the Cossack answered, without looking up.

"Where are you going?"

"Home, on leave."

"Then why are you sitting here?"

"Just so. . . . I'm ill. . . . I can't go further."

"What's wrong with you?"

"Everything."

"M'm! . . . What a misfortune! People are keeping holiday, and you are ill. You'd better go on to the village, or to the inn. What's the good of sitting here?"

The Cossack raised his head, looked at Maxim, his wife, and at the horse with the weary eyes of an invalid.

"Are you coming from church?" he asked.

"Yes, we're coming from church."

"I have been caught on the highway this holiday. God did not allow me to

369

get home. I want to mount and get on, but I have no strength. You orthodox Christians might give me, a poor traveler, some of your consecrated Kulich with which to break my fast.

"Some Kulich?" Torchakov repeated. "So I can. . . . Wait a moment. . . . directly. . . ."

Maxim began hastily to search in his pockets, and looking at his wife he said:

"I have no knife. There is nothing to cut it with, and to break it would spoil the whole Kulich. There's a fix! Just look if you haven't a knife."

The Cossack got up, groaned and going to his saddle found a knife.

"What's this nonsense?" Torchakov's wife said crossly. "I won't allow you to spoil the Kulich. And what should I look like if I brought it home already cut? Ride on to the village where the muzhiks live, there you will be able to break your fast," and she took the napkin, with the Kulich, from her husband saying: "I won't give it. One must keep the rules. This is no ordinary cake, but a Kulich that has been blessed; it's a sin to crumble it uselessly."

"Well, well! Cossack, don't be angry," Torchakov laughed. "The wife won't allow it! Good-bye, a pleasant journey to you!"

Maxim took up the reins, smacked his lips and the britska continued its journey with much squeaking. His wife grumbled for a long time, and tried to prove that to cut into a Kulich before you got home was a sin and against all rules. In the east, piercing through thick clouds, the first rays of the rising sun shone forth; the song of a lark was heard in the sky. Now not only

one, but three kites, keeping at a respectful distance from each other, soared over the steppes. The grasshoppers began to chirp in the young grass.

After driving about a verst from the Crooked Valley, Torchakov turned round and looked back.

"No signs of the Cossack," he said. "It's heartrending to fall ill on the road. . . . Nothing could be worse . . . he must go on . . . and he can't . . . he has no strength. . . . He might even die on the road. . . . We did not give him any Kulich, Liza, and we ought to have given him a bit. . . . He wanted to break his fast too."

The sun rose, but Torchakov could not see if he were dancing or not. For the rest of the way he said nothing, but sat thinking and looking at his horse's black tail. He did not know why he had become dull, and why nothing of the holiday happiness remained in his heart. When he got home and had exchanged Easter greetings with his labourers, he felt gayer and began to chat. He sat down to break his fast, and after eating a slice of the consecrated Kulich, he looked at his wife sadly and said:

"It was wrong, Liza, that we did not give the Cossack something with which to break his fast."

"By God, you're a crank," Liza exclaimed, surprised, and she shrugged her shoulders. "Where did you fish up this new-fangled idea? Who ever heard of distributing the blessed Kulich on the highways? Is it a cake? Now, that it is on the table and has been cut into, everybody may eat of it, even your Cossack. Do you think I'd care?"

"That's all very well, but we ought to have given some to the Cossack. He was worse off than a beggar, or an orphan. On the high road, far from home and ill."

Torchakov drank half a glass of tea, and then he could not eat or drink any more. He did not want to eat, the tea would not go down his throat and he became sad again. After breaking their fast he and his wife retired to bed. About two hours later, when Liza awoke, he was standing at the window looking into the yard.

"Have you got up already?" his wife asked.

"I don't know why it is, but I can't sleep. . . Liza," he sighed, "we wronged that Cossack."

"There you are again with your Cossack," yawned his wife. "Can't you get him out of your head?"

"He has served his Tsar, perhaps shed his blood, and we treated him like a swine. We ought to have brought him home with us, the poor invalid, to feed him; but we did not even give him a piece of bread."

"Do you think I would allow you to spoil the Kulich for no purpose? And a consecrated one too! You would have cut it up on the way, and I would have been shamed at home. That's what you wanted!"

Maxim said nothing, but went quietly into the kitchen; he cut a slice of Kulich, wrapped it up, with five eggs, in a napkin, and took it into the barn to find his workmen.

"Kus'ma, drop that accordion," he said to one of them; "saddle the bay, or Ivanchik, and ride quickly to the Crooked Valley. There you will find a sick Cossack, with his horse; give him this. Perhaps he has not ridden away yet."

Maxim again became more cheerful; but after waiting several hours for Kus'ma he lost patience and could wait no longer, so he saddled a horse and rode out to meet him.

He met him almost at the Crooked Valley.

"Well, have you seen the Cossack?"

"No, he is nowhere. He must have ridden away."

"H'm! What a misfortune!"

Torchakov took the bundle from Kus'ma and rode on. When he got to Shustrova he asked the peasants:

"Brothers, have you seen a sick Cossack with a horse? Hasn't he passed this way? A red-haired man on a bay horse?"

The peasants looked at each other, and said they had seen no Cossack.

"A returning post-chaise went by, that's true. But no Cossack or anything else passed this way—no, there was nothing."

Maxim returned home in time for dinner.

"That Cossack is sticking in my head, do what I will," he said to his wife. "He gives me no peace! I am always thinking of him. What if God wanted to test us, and sent an angel or a saint in the guise of a Cossack, to meet up on our path? Things like that do happen. It was not right, Liza, to wrong a man so."

"Why are you always bothering me about your Cossack." Liza lost patience. "He sticks to us like pitch."

"You know you are not kind," Maxim said, looking into his wife's face.

And for the first time since he was married he noticed that his wife was not kind.

"And what if I am not kind?" Liza cried angrily, thumping the table with a spoon. "I won't have the consecrated

Kulich distributed to every drunkard on the roadside."

"But was the Cossack drunk?"

"He was drunk."

"Na, you fool!"

Maxim rose from the table and began to accuse his young wife of being uncharitable and silly. She also got cross, and answering reproaches with reproaches she began to cry, and went into her bedroom, declaring that she would go back to her father. Since their marriage this was the first domestic scene the Torchakov's had had. Until evening he went about his farmyard thinking of his wife's face, and now it appeared to him to be wicked and ugly. The Cossack, as if on purpose, would not get out of his thoughts, and Maxim was pursued all the time either by his sick eyes or their wrong deed.

"Ah! We have wronged a man!" he kept on mumbling to himself.

In the evening when it got dark he was seized with an irresistible melancholy, such as he had never known before. This fit of melancholy, and because he was angry with his wife, made him drink, and he got drunk—drunk as he had never been since his marriage. When drunk he used all sorts of bad language, and abused his wife, telling her that she had a wicked, ugly face, and that he would turn her out next day and send her back to her father. The day after the holidays he wanted to get over his drunken fit by taking another glass, but he only got drunk again.

.   .   .   .   .

From that day the trouble began.

The horses, the cows, the sheep and the beehives began little by little to disappear from the yard. Maxim got drunk oftener and oftener, debt grew, his aversion for his wife increased. All his misfortunes Maxim explained to himself as being caused by his unkind wife; but chiefly because God was angry with him on account of the sick Cossack.

Liza saw the ruin around them, but she could not understand who was the cause of it.

At the Manor

PAVEL ILITCH RASHEVITCH paced the room, stepping softly on the Little Russian parquet, and casting a long shadow on the walls and ceiling; his visitor, Monsieur Meyer, Examining Magistrate, sat smoking on a Turkish divan, with one leg bent under him. It was eleven o'clock, and from the next room could be heard the supper bustle.

"I don't dispute it for a moment!" said Rashevitch. "As far as fraternity and equality go the swineherd Mitka is as good a man as Goethe or Frederick the Great. But look at it from the point of view of science, and you cannot possibly deny that the white bone is not a prejudice, not a silly feminine creation. The white bone, my friend, has a natural-historical foundation, and to deny it, in my mind, is as foolish as to deny the antlers of a stag. Look at it as a question of fact! You are a jurist, and never studied anything else, so you may well deceive yourself with illusions as to equality, fraternity, and that sort of thing. But, on my side, I am incorrigible Darwinian, and for me such words as race, aristocracy, noble blood are no empty sounds."

Rashevitch was aroused, and spoke with feeling. His eyes glittered, his pince-nez jumped off his nose, he twitched his shoulders nervously, and at the word "Darwinian" glanced defiantly at the mirror, and with his two hands divided his grey beard. He wore a short, well-worn jacket, and narrow trousers; but the rapidity of his movements and the smartness of the short jacket did not suit him at all, and his big, long-haired, handsome head, which reminded one of a bishop or a venerable poet, seemed to be set on the body of a tall, thin, and affected youth. When he opened his legs widely, his long shadow resembled a pair of scissors.

As a rule he loved the sound of his own voice; and it always seemed to him that he was saying something new and original. In the presence of Meyer he felt an unusual elevation of spirits and flow of thought. He liked the magistrate, who enlivened him by his youthful ways, his health, his fine manners, his solidity, and, even more, by the kindly relations which he had established with the family. Speaking generally, Rashevitch was not a favorite with his acquaintances. They avoided him, and he knew it. They declared that he had driven his wife into the grave with his perpetual talk, and called him, almost to his face, a beast and a toad. Meyer alone, being an unprejudiced new-comer, visited him often and willingly, and had even been heard to say that Rashevitch and his daughters were the only persons in the district

with whom he felt at home. And Rashevitch reciprocated his esteem—all the more sincerely because Meyer was a young man, and an excellent match for his elder daughter, Zhenya.

And now, enjoying his thoughts and the sound of his own voice, and looking with satisfaction at the stout, well-groomed, respectable figure of his visitor, Rashevitch reflected how he would settle Zhenya for life as the wife of a good man, and, in addition, transfer all the work of managing the estate to his son-in-law's shoulders. It was not particularly agreeable work. The interest had not been paid into the bank for more than two terms, and the various arrears and penalties amounted to over twenty thousand roubles.

"There can hardly be a shadow of doubt," continued Rashevitch, becoming more and more possessed by his subject, "that if some Richard the Lionhearted or Frederick Barbarossa, for instance, a man courageous and magnanimous, has a son, his good qualities will be inherited by the son, together with his bumps; and if this courage and magnanimity are fostered in the son by education and exercise, and he marries a princess also courageous and magnanimous, then these qualities will be transmitted to the grandson, and so on, until they become peculiarities of the species, and descend organically, so to speak, in flesh and blood. Thanks to severe sexual selection, thanks to the fact that noble families instinctively preserve themselves from base alliances, and that young people of position do not marry the devil knows whom, their high spiritual qualities have reproduced themselves from generation to generation, they have been perpetuated, and in the course of ages have become even more perfect and loftier. For all that is good in humanity we are indebted to Nature, to the regular, natural-historical, expedient course of things, strenuously in the course of centuries separating the white bone from the black. Yes, my friend! It is not the potboy's child, the cookmaid's brat who has given us literature, science, art, justice, the ideas of honour and of duty. . . . For all these, humanity is indebted exclusively to the white bone; and in this sense, from the point of view of natural history, worthless Sabakevitch, merely because he is a white bone, is a million times higher and more useful than the best tradesman, let him endow fifty museums! You may say what you like, but if I refuse to give my hand to the potboy's or the cookmaid's son, by that refusal I preserve from stain the best that is on the earth, and subserve one of the highest destinies of mother Nature, leading us to perfection. . . ."

Rashevitch stood still, and smoothed down his beard with both hands. His scissors-like shadow stood still also.

"Take our dear Mother Russia!" he continued, thrusting his hands into his pockets, and balancing himself alternately on toes and heels. "Who are our best people? Take our first-class artists, authors, composers. . . . Who are they? All these, my dear sir, are representatives of the white bone. Pushkin, Gogol, Lermontoff, Turgenieff, Tolstoy. . . . Were these cookmaid's children?"

"Gontcharoff was a tradesman," said Meyer.

"What does that prove? The exception, my friend, proves the rule. And as to the genius of Gontcharoff there can be two opinions. But let us leave names and return to facts. Tell me how you can reply, sir, to the eloquent fact that when the potboy climbs to a higher place than he was born in—when he reaches eminence in literature, in science, in local government, in law— what have you to say to the fact that Nature herself intervenes on behalf of the most sacred human rights, and declares war against him? As a matter of fact, hardly has the potboy succeeded in stepping into other people's shoes when he begins to languish, wither, go out of his mind, and degenerate; and nowhere will you meet so many dwarfs, physical cripples, consumptives, and starvelings as among these gentry. They die away like flies in autumn. And it is a good thing. If it were not for this salutary degeneration, not one stone of our civilization would remain upon another—the potboy would destroy it all. . . . Be so good as to tell me, please, what this invasion has given us up to the present time? What has the potboy brought with him?"

Rashevitch made a mysterious, frightened face, and continued:

"Never before did our science and literature find themselves at such a low ebb as now. The present generation, sir, has neither ideas nor ideals, and all its activity is restricted to an attempt to tear the last shirt off someone else's back. All your present-day men who give themselves out as progressive and incorruptible may be bought for a silver rouble; and modern intelligent society is distinguished by only one thing, that is, that if you mix in it you must keep your hand on your pocket, else it will steal your purse." Rashevitch blinked and smiled. "Steal your purse!" he repeated, with a happy laugh. "And morals? What morals have we?" Rashevitch glanced at the door. "You can no longer be surprised if your wife robs you and abandons you—that is a mere trifle. At the present day, my friend, every twelve-year-old girl looks out for a lover; and all these amateur theatricals and literary evenings are invented only for the purpose of catching rich *parvenus* as sweethearts. Mothers sell their daughters, husbands are asked openly at what price they will sell their wives, and you may even trade, my friend, . . ."

Up to this Meyer had said nothing, and sat motionless. Now he rose from the sofa, and looked at the clock.

"Excuse me, Pavel Ilitch," he said, "but it's time for me to go."

But Rashevitch, who had not finished, took him by the arm, set him down forcibly upon the sofa, and swore he should not leave the house without supper. Meyer again sat motionless and listened; but soon began to look at Rashevitch with an expression of doubt and alarm, as if he were only just beginning to understand his character. When at last the maid entered, saying that the young ladies had sent her to say that supper was ready, he sighed faintly, and went out of the study first.

In the dining-room, already at the table, sat Rashevitch's daughters, Zhenya and Iraida, respectively aged twenty-four and twenty-two. They were of equal stature, and both black-eyed and very pale. Zhenya had her hair down, but Iraida's was twisted into a high top-knot. Before eating anything each drank a glass of spirits, with an expression meant to imply that they were drinking accidentally, and for the first

time in their lives. After this they looked confused, and tittered.

"Don't be silly, girls!" said Rashevitch.

Zhenya and Iraida spoke French to one another and Russian to their father and the visitor. . . . Interrupting one another, and mixing French and Russian, they began to remark that just at this time of the year, that is in August, they used to leave home for the Institute. How jolly that was! But now there was no place to go for a change, and they lived at the manor-house winter and summer. How tiresome!

"Don't be silly, girls!" repeated Rashevitch.

"In short, that is exactly how things stand," he said, looking affectionately at the magistrate. "We, in the goodness and simplicity of our hearts, and from fear of being suspected of retrograde tendencies, fraternise—excuse the expression — with all kinds of human trash, and preach equality and fraternity with upstarts and *nouveaux riches!* Yet if we paused to reflect for a single minute we should see how criminal is our kindness. For all that our ancestors attained to in the course of centuries will be derided and destroyed in a single day by these modern Huns.'

After supper all went into the drawing-room. Zhenya and Iraida lighted the piano candles and got ready their music. . . But their parent continued to hold forth, and there was no knowing when he would end. Bored and irritated, they looked at their egoist father for whom, they concluded, the satisfaction of chattering and showing off his brains, was dearer than the future happiness of his daughters. Here was Meyer, the only young man who frequented the house—for the sake, they knew, of tender feminine society—yet the unwearying old man kept possession of him, and never let him escape for a moment.

"Just as western chivalry repelled the onslaught of the Mongols, so must we, before it is too late, combine and strike together at the enemy." Rashevitch spoke apostolically, and lifted his right hand on high. "Let me appear before the potboy no longer as plain Pavel Ilitch, but as a strong and menacing Richard the Lion-Heart! Fling your scruples behind you—enough! Let us swear a sacred compact that when the potboy approaches we will fling him words of contempt straight in the face! Hands off! Back to your pots! Straight in the face!" In ecstacy, Rashevitch thrust out a bent forefinger, and repeated: "Straight in the face! In the face! In the face!"

Meyer averted his eyes. "I cannot tolerate this any longer!" he said.

"And may I ask why?" asked Rashevitch, scenting the beginnings of a prolonged and interesting argument.

"Because I myself am the son of an artisan."

And having so spoken, Meyer reddened, his neck seemed to swell, and tears sparkled in his eyes.

"My father was a plain working man," he said in an abrupt, broken voice. "But I can see nothing bad in that."

Rashevitch was thunderstruck. In his confusion he looked as if he had been detected in a serious crime; he looked at Meyer with a dumbfounded face, and said not a word. Zhenya and Iraida blushed, and bent over their music. They were thoroughly ashamed of their tactless father. A minute passed in silence, and the situation was becoming unbearable when suddenly a sickly, strained voice—it seemed utterly *mal à propos*—stammered forth the words:

"Yes, I am a tradesman's son, and I am proud of it."

And Meyer, awkwardly stumbling over the furniture, said good-bye, and walked quickly into the hall, although the trap had not been ordered.

"You will have a dark drive," stammered Rashevitch, going after him. "The moon rises late to-night."

They stood on the steps in the darkness and waited for the horses. It was cold.

"Did you see the falling star?" asked Meyer, buttoning his overcoat.

"In August falling stars are very plentiful."

When at last the trap drove round to the door, Rashevitch looked attentively at the heavens, and said, with a sigh:

"A phenomenon worthy of the pen of Flammarion. . . "

Having parted from his guest, he walked up and down the garden, and tried to persuade himself that such a stupid misunderstanding had not really taken place. He was angry, and ashamed of himself. In the first place, he knew that it was extremely tactless and incautious to raise this accursed conversation about the white bone without knowing anything of the origin of his guest He told himself, with perfect justice, that for him there was no excuse, for he had had a lesson before, having once in a railway carriage set about abusing Germans to fellow-passengers who, it turned out, were themselves Germans. . . . And in the second place he was convinced that Meyer would come no more. These *intellectuals* who have sprung from the people are sensitive, vain, obstinate, and revengeful.

"It is a bad business . . . bad . . . bad!" he muttered, spitting; he felt awkward and disgusted, as if he had just eaten soap. "It is a bad business!"

Through the open window he could see into the drawing-room where Zhenya with her hair down, pale and frightened, spoke excitedly to her sister. . . . Iraida walked from corner to corner, apparently lost in thought; and then began to speak, also excitedly and with an indignant face. Then both spoke together. Rashevitch could not distinguish a word, but he knew too well the subject of their conversation. Zhenya was grumbling that her father with his eternal chattering drove every decent man from the house, and had to-day robbed them of their last acquaintance, it might have been husband; and now the poor young man could not find a place in the whole district wherein to rest his soul. And Iraida, if judged correctly from the despairing way in which she raised her arms, lamented bitterly their wearisome life at home and their ruined youth.

Going up to his bedroom, Rashevitch sat on the bed and undressed himself slowly. He felt that he was a persecuted man, and was tormented by the same feeling as though he had eaten soap. He was thoroughly ashamed of himself. When he had undressed he gazed sadly at his long, veined, old-man's legs, and remembered that in the country round he was nicknamed "the toad," and that never a conversation passed without making him

ashamed of himself. By some extraordinary fatality every discussion ended badly. He began softly, kindly, with good intentions, and called himself genially an "old student," an "idealist," a "Don Quixote." But gradually, and unnoticed by himself, he passed on to abuse and calumny, and, what is more surprising, delivered himself of sincere criticisms of science, art, and morals, although it was twenty years since he had read a book, been farther than the government town, or had any channel for learning what was going on in the world around him. Even when he sat down to write a congratulatory letter he invariably ended by abusing something or somebody. And as he reflected upon this, it seemed all the more strange, since he knew himself in reality to be a sensitive, lachrymose old man. It seemed almost as if he were possessed by an unclean spirit which filled him against his will with hatred and grumbling.

"A bad business!" he sighed, getting into bed. "A bad business!"

His daughters also could not sleep. Laughter and lamentation resounded through the house. Zhenya was in hysterics. Shortly afterwards Iraida also began to cry. More than once the barefooted housemaid ran up and down the corridor.

"What a scandal!" muttered Rashevitch, sighing, and turning uneasily from side to side. "A bad business!"

He slept, but nightmare gave him no peace. He thought that he was standing in the middle of the room, naked, and tall as a giraffe, thrusting out his forefinger, and saying:

"In the face! In the face! In the face!"

He awoke in terror, and the first thing he remembered was, that last evening a serious misunderstanding had occurred, and that Meyer would never visit him again. He remembered then that the interest had to be lodged in the bank, that he must find husbands for his daughters, and that he must eat and drink. He remembered sickness, old age, and unpleasantness; that winter would soon be upon him, and that there was no wood. . . .

At nine o'clock he dressed slowly, then drank some tea and ate two large slices of bread and butter. . . . His daughters did not come down to breakfast, they did not wish to see his face; and this offended him. For a time he lay upon the study sofa, and then sat at his writing-table and began to write a letter to his daughters. His hand trembled and his eyes itched. He wrote that he was now old, that nobody wanted him, and nobody loved him; so he begged his children to forget him, and when he died, to bury him in a plain, deal coffin, without ceremony, or to send his body to Kharkoff for dissection in the Anatomical Theatre. He felt that every line breathed malice and affectation . . . but he could not stop himself, and wrote on and on and on . . .

"The toad!" rang a voice from the next room; it was the voice of his elder daughter, an indignant, hissing voice. "The toad!"

"The toad!" repeated the younger in echo. "The toad!"

An Event

MORN. Through the frost of the window-panes bright sun-rays filled the nursery. Vanya, a boy of six, with a nose like a button, and his sister Nina, aged four, curly-headed, stout, and small for her age, awoke, and glared angrily at one another through the bars of their cribs.

Nurse cried, "For shame, children! Everyone has finished breakfast, and you can't keep your eyes open . . ."

The sun-rays played on the carpet, the walls, nurse's skirt, and the children. But the children cared not. They had awakened on the wrong side of their beds. Nina pouted, made a face, and yelled:

"Te-ea! Nurse, te-ea!"

Vanya frowned, and looked about for trouble. He had just blinked his eyes and opened his mouth, when mother's voice came from the dining-room:

"Don't forget to give the cat milk; she has got kittens."

Vanya and Nina lengthened their faces and looked questioningly at one another. Then both screamed, jumped out of bed, and, making the air ring with deafening yells, ran barefooted in their nightdresses into the kitchen.

"The cat's got kittens! The cat's got kittens!" they screamed.

In the kitchen under a bench stood a small box, a box which Stepan used for coke when he lighted the stove. Out· of this box gazed the cat. Her grey face expressed extreme exhaustion, her green eyes with their little black pupils looked languishing and sentimental. . . . From her face it was plain that to complete her happiness only one thing was lacking, and that was the presence of the father of her children, to whom she had given herself heart and soul. She attempted to mew, and opened her mouth wide, but only succeeded in making a hissing sound. . . . The kittens squealed.

The children squatted on the ground in front of the box, and, without moving, but holding their breath, looked at the cat. . . . They were astonished and thunderstruck, and did not hear the grumbling of the pursuing nurse. In the eyes of both shone sincere felicity.

In the up-bringing of children, domestic animals play an unnoticed but unquestionably beneficent part. Which of us cannot remember strong but magnanimous dogs, lazy lapdogs, birds who died in captivity, dull-witted but haughty turkey-cocks, kindly old-lady-cats who forgave us when we stood on their tails for a joke and caused them intense pain? It might even be argued that the patience, faithfulness, all-forgivingness and sincerity of our domestic animals act on the childish brain much more powerfully than the long lectures of dry and pale Karl Karlovitch, or the obscure explanations of the governess who tries to prove to children that water is composed of hydrogen and oxygen.

"What duckies!" cried Nina, overflowing with gay laughter. "They're exactly like mice!"

"One, two, three!" counted Vanya. "Three kittens. That's one for me, one for you, and one for somebody else."

"Murrrm . . . murrrm," purred the mother, flattered by so much attention. "Murrrm!"

When they had looked for a while at the kittens, the children took them from under the cat and began to smooth them down, and afterwards, not satisfied with this, laid them in the skirts of their nightdresses and ran from one room to another.

"Mamma, the cat's got kittens!" they cried.

Mother sat in the dining-room, talking to a stranger. When she saw her children unwashed, undressed, with their nightdresses on high, she got red, and looked at them severely.

"Drop your nightdresses, shameless!" she said. "Run away at once, or you'll be punished."

But the children paid no attention either to their mother's threats or to the presence of the stranger. They put the kittens down on the carpet and raised a deafening howl. Beside them walked the old cat, and mewed imploringly. When in a few minutes the children were dragged off to the nursery to dress, say their prayers, and have their breakfast, they were full of a passionate wish to escape from these prosaic duties and return to the kitchen.

Ordinary occupations and games were quite forgotten From the moment of their appearance in the world the kittens obscured everything, and took their place as the living novelty and heart-swelling of the day. If you had offered Vanya or Nina a bushel of sweets for each kitten, or a thousand threepenny-bits, they would have rejected the offer without a moment's hesitation. Till dinner-time, in spite of the warm protests of nurse and the cook, they sat in the kitchen and played with the kittens. Their faces were serious, concentrated, and expressive of anxiety. They had to provide not only for the present condition, but also for the future of the kittens. So they decided that one kitten would remain at home with the old cat, so as to console its mother, that the other would be sent to the country-house, and that the third would live in the cellar and eat the rats.

"But why can't they see?" asked Nina. "They have blind eyes, like beggars."

The question troubled Vanya. He did his best to open one of the kitten's eyes, for a long time puffed and snuffled, but the operation was fruitless. But another circumstance worried the children extremely—the kittens obstinately refused the proffered meat and milk. Everything that was laid before their little snouts was eaten up by their grey mother.

"Let's build houses for the kittens," proposed Vanya. "We will make them live in different houses, and the cat will pay them visits. . . ." In three corners of the kitchen they set up old hat-boxes. But the separation of the family seemed premature; the old cat, preserving on her face her former plaintive and sentimental expression, paid visits to all the boxes and took her children home again.

"The cat is their mother," said Vanya, "but who is their father?"

"Yes, who is their father?" repeated Nina.

"They can't live without a father."

For a long time Vanya and Nina discussed the problem, who should be father of the kittens. In the end their choice fell on a big dark-red horse whose tail had been torn off. He had been cast away in the store-room under the staircase, together with the remnants of other toys that had outlived their generation. They took the horse from the store-room and stood it beside the box.

"Look out!" they warned him. "Stand there and see that they behave themselves."

All this was said and done in a serious manner, and with an expression of solicitude. Outside the box and the kittens, Vanya and Nina would recognise no other world. Their happiness had no bounds. But they were destined to endure moments of unutterable torture.

Just before dinner Vanya sat in his father's study, and looked thoughtfully at the table. Near the lamp, across a packet of stamped paper, crawled a kitten. Vanya watched its movements attentively, and occasionally poked it in the snout with a pencil. . . . Suddenly, as if springing out of the floor, appeared his father.

"What is this?" cried an angry voice.

"It is . . . it is a kitten, papa."

"I'll teach you to bring your kittens here, wretched child! Look what you've done! Ruined a whole package of paper!"

To Vanya's astonishment, his father did not share his sympathy with kittens, and, instead of going into raptures and rejoicing, pulled Vanya's ear, and cried:

"Stepan, take away this abomination!"

At dinner the scandal was repeated. . . . During the second course the diners suddenly heard a faint squeal. They began to search for the cause, and

found a kitten under Nina's pinafore.
"Ninka! Go out of the room!" said
her father angrily. "The kittens must
be thrown into the sink this minute!
I won't tolerate these abominations in
the house!"

Vanya and Nina were terror-stricken.
Death in the sink, apart from its cruelty, threatened to deprive the cat and
the wooden horse of their children, to
desolate the box, to destroy all their
plans for the future—that beautiful
future when one kitten would console
its old mother, the second live in the
country, and the third catch rats in the
cellar. . . . They began to cry, and
implored mercy for the kittens. Their
father consented to spare them, but
only on the condition that the children
should not dare to go into the kitchen
or touch the kittens again.

After dinner, Vanya and Nina wandered from one room to another and
languished. The prohibition on going
to the kitchen drove them to despair.
They refused sweets; and were naughty,
and rude to their mother. In the evening when Uncle Petrusha came they
took him aside and complained of their
father for threatening to throw the
kittens into the sink.

"Uncle Petrusha," they implored,
"tell mamma to put the kittens in the
nursery. . . . Do!"

"Well . . . all right!" said their
uncle, tearing himself away. "Agreed!"

Uncle Petrusha seldom came alone.
Along with him came Nero, a big black
dog, of Danish origin, with hanging
ears and a tail as hard as a stick. Nero
was silent, morose, and altogether taken
up with his own dignity. To the children he paid not the slightest attention; and, when he marched past them,
knocked his tail against them as if they
were chairs. Vanya and Nina detested
him from the bottom of their hearts.
But on this occasion practical considerations gained the upper hand over
mere sentiment.

"Do you know what, Nina?" said
Vanya, opening wide his eyes. "Let
us make Nero the father instead of
the horse! The horse is dead, but
Nero's alive."

The whole evening they waited impatiently for their father to sit down
to his game of *vint*, when they might
take Nero to the kitchen without being
observed. . . . At last father sat
down to his cards, mother bustled
around the samovar, and did not see
the children. . . . The happy moment
had come!

"Come!" whispered Vanya to his
sister.

But at that very moment Stepan
came into their room, and said with a
grin:

"I beg your pardon, ma'am. Nero
has eaten the kittens."

Nina and Vanya turned pale, and
looked with horror at Stepan.

"Yes, ma'am . . ." grinned the
servant. "He went straight to the box
and gobbled them up."

The children expected everyone in
the house to rise in alarm and fly at
the guilty Nero. But their parents sat
calmly in their chairs, and only expressed surprise at the appetite of the
big dog. Father and mother laughed.
. . . Nero marched up to the table,
flourished his tail, and licked himself
complacently. . . . Only the cat
seemed disturbed; she stretched out
her tail, and walked about the room

looking suspiciously at everyone and mewing plaintively.

"Now, children, time for bed! Ten o'clock!" cried mother.

And Vanya and Nina were put to bed, where they wept over the injured cat, whose life had been desolated by cruel, nasty, unpunished Nero.

Art

A GLOOMY winter morning.

On the smooth and glittering surface of the river Bystryanka, sprinkled here and there with snow, stand two peasants, scrubby little Seryozhka and the church beadle, Matvey. Seryozhka, a short-legged, ragged, mangy-looking fellow of thirty, stares angrily at the ice. Tufts of wool hang from his shaggy sheepskin like a mangy dog. In his hands he holds a compass made of two pointed sticks. Matvey, a fine-looking old man in a new sheepskin and high felt boots, looks with mild blue eyes upwards where on the high sloping bank a village nestles picturesquely. In his hands there is a heavy crowbar.

"Well, are we going to stand like this till evening with our arms folded?" says Seryozhka, breaking the silence and turning his angry eyes on Matvey. "Have you come here to stand about, old fool, or to work?"

"Well you . . . er . . . show me . . ." Matvey mutters, blinking mildly.

"Show you. . . . It's always me; me to show you, and me to do it. They have no sense of their own! Mark it out with the compasses, that's what's wanted! You can't break the ice without marking it out. Mark it out! Take the compass."

Matvey takes the compasses from Seryozhka's hands, and, shuffling heavily on the same spot and jerking with his elbows in all directions, he begins awkwardly trying to describe a circle on the ice. Seryozhka screws up his eyes contemptuously and obviously enjoys his awkwardness and incompetence.

"Eh-eh-eh!" he mutters angrily. "Even that you can't do! The fact is you are a stupid peasant, a woodenhead! You ought to be grazing geese and not making a Jordan! Give the compasses here! Give them here, I say!"

Seryozhka snatches the compasses out of the hands of the perspiring Matvey, and in an instant, jauntily twirling round on one heel, he describes a circle on the ice. The outline of the new Jordan is ready now, all that is left to do is to break the ice. . . .

But before proceeding to the work Seryozhka spends a long time in airs and graces, whims and reproaches. . . .

"I am not obliged to work for you! You are employed in the church, you do it!"

He obviously enjoys the peculiar position in which he has been placed by the fate that has bestowed on him the rare talent of surprising the whole parish once a year by his art. Poor mild Matvey has to listen to many venomous and contemptuous words from him

Seryozhka sets to work with vexation, with anger. He is lazy. He has hardly described the circle when he is already itching to go up to the village to drink tea, lounge about, and babble. . . .

"I'll be back directly," he says, lighting his cigarette, "and meanwhile you had better bring something to sit on and sweep up, instead of standing there counting the crows."

Matvey is left alone. The air is gray and harsh but still. The white church peeps out genially from behind the huts scattered on the river bank. Jackdaws are incessantly circling round its golden crosses. On one side of the village where the river bank breaks off and is steep a hobbled horse is standing at the very edge, motionless as a stone, probably asleep or deep in thought.

Matvey, too, stands motionless as a statue, waiting patiently. The dreamily brooding look of the river, the circling of the jackdaws, and the sight of the horse make him drowsy. One hour passes, a second, and still Seryozhka does not come. The river has long been swept and a box brought to sit on, but the drunken fellow does not appear. Matvey waits and merely yawns. The feeling of boredom is one of which he knows nothing. If he were told to stand on the river for a day, a month, or a year he would stand there.

At last Seryozhka comes into sight from behind the huts. He walks with a lurching gait, scarcely moving. He is too lazy to go the long way round, and he comes not by the road, but prefers a short cut in a straight line down the bank, and sticks in the snow, hangs on to the bushes, slides on his back as he comes—and all this slowly, with pauses.

"What are you about?" he cries, falling on Matvey at once. "Why are you standing there doing nothing? When are you going to break the ice?"

Matvey crosses himself, takes the crowbar in both hands, and begins breaking the ice, carefully keeping to the circle that has been drawn. Seryozhka sits down on the box and watches the heavy clumsy movements of his assistant.

"Easy at the edges! Easy there!" he commands. "If you can't do it properly, you shouldn't undertake it; once you have undertaken it you should do it. You!"

A crowd collects on the top of the bank. At the sight of the spectators Seryozhka becomes even more excited.

"I declare I am not going to do it . . ." he says, lighting a stinking cigarette and spitting on the ground. "I should like to see how you get on without me. Last year at Kostyukovo, Styopka Gulkov undertook to make a Jordan as I do. And what did it amount to—it was a laughing-stock. The Kostyukovo folks came to ours—crowds and crowds of them! The people flocked from all the villages."

"Because except for ours there is nowhere a proper Jordan . . ."

"Work, there is no time for talking. . . . Yes, old man . . . you won't find another Jordan like it in the whole province. The soldiers say you would look in vain, they are not so good even in the towns. Easy, easy!"

Matvey puffs and groans. The work is not easy. The ice is firm and thick; and he has to break it and at once take the pieces away that the open space may not be blocked up.

But, hard as the work is and senseless as Seryozhka's commands are, by three o'clock there is a large circle of dark water in the Bystryanka.

"It was better last year," says Seryozhka angrily. "You can't do even that! Ah! dummy! To keep such fools in the temple of God! Go and bring a board to make the pegs! Bring the ring, you crow! And—er . . . get some bread somewhere . . . and some cucumbers, or something."

Matvey goes off and soon afterwards comes back, carrying on his shoulders an immense wooden ring which had been painted in previous years in patterns of various colors. In the center of the ring is a red cross, at the circumference holes for the pegs. Seryozhka takes the ring and covers the hole in the ice with it.

"Just right . . . it fits. . . . We have only to renew the paint and it will be first-rate. . . . Come, why are you standing still? Make the lectern. Or—er—go and get some logs to make the cross. . . ."

Matvey, who has not tasted food or drink all day, trudges up the hill again. Lazy as Seryozhka is, he makes the pegs with his own hands. He knows that those pegs have a miraculous power: whoever gets hold of a peg after the blessing of the water will be lucky for the whole year. Such work is really worth doing.

But the real work begins the following day. Then Seryozhka displays himself before the ignorant Matvey in all the greatness of his talent. There is no end to his babble, his fault-finding, his whims and fancies. If Matvey nails

two big pieces of wood to make a cross, he is dissatisfied and tells him to do it again. If Matvey stands still, Seryozhka asks him angrily why he does not go; if he moves, Seryozhka shouts to him not to go away but to do his work. He is not satisfied with his tools, with the weather, or with his own talent; nothing pleases him.

Matvey saws out a great big piece of ice for a lectern.

"Why have you broken off the corner?" cries Seryozhka, and glares at him furiously. "Why have you broken off the corner? I ask you."

"Forgive me, for Christ's sake."

"Do it over again!"

Matvey saws again . . . and there is no end to his sufferings. A lectern is to stand by the hole in the ice that is covered by the painted ring; on the lectern is to be carved the cross and the open gospel. But that is not all. Behind the lectern there is to be a high cross to be seen by all the crowd and to glitter in the sun as though sprinkled with diamonds and rubies. On the cross is to be a dove carved out of ice. The path from the church to the Jordan is to be strewn with branches of fir and juniper. All this is their task.

First of all Seryozhka sets to work on the lectern. He works with a file, a chisel, and an awl. He is perfectly successful in the cross on the lectern, the gospel, and the drapery that hangs down the lectern. Then he begins on the dove. While he is trying to carve an expression of meekness and humility on the face of the dove, Matvey, lumbering about like a bear, is coating with ice the cross he has made of wood. He takes the cross and dips it in the hole. Waiting till the water has frozen on the cross he dips it in a second time, and so on till the cross is covered with a thick layer of ice. . . . It is a difficult job, calling for a great deal of strength and patience.

But now the delicate work is finished. Seryozhka races about the village like one possessed. He swears and vows he will go at once to the river and smash all his work. He is looking for suitable paints.

His pockets are full of ochre, dark blue, red lead, and verdigris; without paying a farthing he rushes headlong from one shop to another. The shop is next door to the tavern. Here he has a drink; with a wave of his hand he darts off without paying. At one hut he gets beetroot leaves, at another an onion skin, out of which he makes a yellow color. He swears, shoves, threatens, and . . . not a soul murmurs! They all smile at him, they sympathize with him, call him Sergey Nikititch; they all feel that his art is not a personal affair but something that concerns them all, the whole people. One creates, the others help him. Seryozhka in himself is a nonentity, a sluggard, a drunkard, and a wastrel, but when he has red lead or compasses in his hand he is at once something higher, a servant of God.

Epiphany morning comes. The precincts of the church and both banks of the river for a long distance are swarming with people. Everything that makes up the Jordan is scrupulously concealed under new mats. Seryozhka is meekly moving about near the mats, trying to conceal his emotion. He sees thousands of people. There are many here from other par-

ishes; these people have come many a mile on foot through the frost and the snow merely to see his celebrated Jordan. Matvey, who had finished his coarse, rough work, is by now back in the church, there is no sight, no sound of him; he is already forgotten. . . . The weather is lovely. . . There is not a cloud in the sky. The sunshine is dazzling.

The church bells ring out on the hill. . . . Thousands of heads are bared, thousands of hands are moving, there are thousands of signs of the cross!

And Seryozhka does not know what to do with himself for impatience. But now they are ringing the bells for the Sacrament; then half an hour later a certain agitation is perceptible in the belfry and among the people. Banners are borne out of the church one after the other, while the bells peal in joyous haste. . . . Seryozhka, trembling, pulls away the mat . . . and the people behold something extraordinary. The lectern, the wooden ring, the pegs, and the cross in the ice are iridescent with thousands of colors. The cross and the dove glitter so dazzlingly that it hurts the eyes to look at them. Merciful God, how fine it is! A murmur of wonder and delight runs through the crowd; the bells peal more loudly still, the day grows brighter; the banners oscillate and move over the crowd as over the waves. The procession, glittering with the settings of the ikons and the vestments of the clergy, comes slowly down the road and turns towards the Jordan. Hands are waved to the belfry for the ringing to cease, and the blessing of the water begins. The priests conduct the service slowly, deliberately, evidently trying to prolong the ceremony and the joy of praying all gathered together. There is perfect stillness.

But now they plunge the cross in, and the air echoes with an extraordinary din. Guns are fired, the bells peal furiously, loud exclamations of delight, shouts, and a rush to get the pegs. Seryozhka listens to this uproar, sees thousands of eyes fixed upon him, and the lazy fellow's soul is filled with a sense of glory and triumph.

The Birds

THERE is a small square near the monastery of the Holy Birth which is called Trubnoy, or simply Truboy; there is a market there on Sundays. Hundreds of sheepskins, wadded coats, fur caps, and chimneypot hats swarm there, like crabs in a sieve. There is the sound of the twitter of birds in all sorts of keys, recalling the spring. If the sun is shining, and there are no clouds in the sky, the singing of the birds and the smell of hay make a more vivid impression, and this reminder of spring sets one thinking and carries one's fancy far, far away. Along one side of the square there stands a string of waggons. The waggons are loaded, not with hay, not with cabbages, nor with beans, but with goldfinches, siskins, larks, blackbirds and thrushes, bluetits, bullfinches. All of them are hopping about in rough, homemade cages, twittering and looking with envy at the free sparrows. The goldfinches cost five kopeks, the siskins are rather more expensive, while the value of the other birds is quite indeterminate.

"How much is a lark?"

The seller himself does not know the value of a lark. He scratches his head and asks whatever comes into it, a rouble, or three kopeks, according to the purchaser. There are expensive birds too. A faded old blackbird, with most of its feathers plucked out of its tail, sits on a dirty perch. He is dignified, grave, and motionless as a retired general. He has waved his claw in resignation to his captivity long ago, and looks at the blue sky with indifference. Probably, owing to this indifference, he is considered a sagacious bird. He is not to be bought for less than forty kopeks. Schoolboys, workmen, young men in stylish greatcoats, and bird-fanciers in incredibly shabby caps, in ragged trousers that are turned up at the ankles, and look as though they had been gnawed by mice, crowd round the birds, splashing through the mud. The young people and the workmen are sold hens for cocks, young birds for old ones. . . . They know very little about birds. But there is no deceiving the bird-fancier. He sees and understands his bird from a distance.

"There is no relying on that bird," a fancier will say, looking into a siskin's beak, and counting the feathers on its tail. "He sings now, it's true, but what of it? I sing in company too. No, my boy, shout, sing to me without company; sing in solitude, if you can. . . . You give me that one yonder that sits and holds its tongue! Give me the quiet one! That one says nothing, so he thinks the more. . . ."

Among the waggons of birds there are some full of other live creatures. Here you see hares, rabbits, hedgehogs, guinea-pigs, pole-cats. A hare sits sorrowfully nibbling the straw. The guinea-pigs shiver with cold, while the hedgehogs look out with curiosity from under their prickles at the public.

"I have read somewhere," says a post-official in a faded overcoat, looking lovingly at the hare, and addressing no one in particular, "I have read that some learned man had a cat and a mouse and a falcon and a sparrow, who all ate out of one bowl!"

"That's very possible, sir. The cat must have been beaten, and the falcon, I dare say, had all its tail pulled out. There's no great cleverness in that, sir. A friend of mine had a cat who, saving your presence, used to eat his cucumbers. He thrashed her with a big whip for a fortnight, till he taught her not to. A hare can learn to light matches if you beat it. Does that surprise you? It's very simple! It takes the match in its mouth and strikes it. An animal is like a man. A man's made wiser by beating, and it's the same with a beast!"

Men in long, full-skirted coats move backwards and forwards in the crowd with cocks and ducks under their arms. The fowls are all lean and hungry. Chickens poke their ugly, mangy-looking heads out of their cages and peck at something in the mud. Boys with pigeons stare into your face and try to detect in you a pigeon-fancier.

"Yes, indeed! It's no use talking to you," someone shouts angrily. "You should look before you speak! Do you call this a pigeon? It is an eagle, not a pigeon!"

A tall thin man, with a shaven upper lip and side whiskers, who looks like a sick and drunken footman, is selling a snow-white lap-dog. The old lap-dog whines.

"She told me to sell the nasty thing," says the footman, with a contemptuous snigger. "She is bankrupt in her old age, has nothing to eat,. and here now is selling her dogs and cats. She cries, and kisses them on their filthy snouts. And then she is so hard up that she sells them. 'Pon my soul, it is a fact! Buy it, gentlemen! The money is wanted for coffee."

But no one laughs. A boy who is standing by screws up one eye and looks at him gravely with compassion.

The most interesting of all is the fish section. Some dozen peasants are sitting in a row. Before each of them is a pail, and in each pail there is a veritable little hell. There, in the thick, greenish water are swarms of little carp, eels, small fry, water-snails, frogs, and newts. Big water-beetles with broken legs scurry over the small surface, clambering on the carp, and jumping over the frogs. The creatures have a strong hold on life. The frogs climb on the beetles, the newts on the frogs. The dark green tench, as more expensive fish, enjoy an exceptional position; they are kept in a special jar where they can't swim, but still they are not so cramped. . . .

"The carp is a grand fish! The carp's the fish to keep, your honor, plague take him! You can keep him for a year in a pail and he'll live! It's a week since I caught these very fish. I caught them, sir, in Pereva, and have come from there on foot. The carp are two kopeks each, the eels are three, and the minnows are ten kopeks the dozen, plague take them! Five kopeks' worth of minnows, sir? Won't you take some worms?"

The seller thrusts his coarse rough fingers into the pail and pulls out of it a soft minnow, or a little carp, the size of a nail. Fishing lines, hooks, and tackle are laid out near the pails, and pond-worms glow with a crimson light in the sun.

An old fancier in a fur cap, iron-rimmed spectacles, and goloshes that look like two dreadnoughts, walks about by the waggons of birds and pails of fish. He is, as they call him here, "a type." He hasn't a farthing to bless himself with, but in spite of that he haggles, gets excited, and pesters purchasers with advice. He has thoroughly examined all the hares, pigeons, and fish; examined them in every detail, fixed the kind, the age, and the price of each one of them a good hour ago. He is as interested as a child in the goldfinches, the carp, and the minnows. Talk to him, for instance, about thrushes, and the queer old fellow will tell you things you could not find in any book. He will tell you them with enthusiasm, with passion, and will scold you too for your ignorance. Of goldfinches and bullfinches he is ready to talk endlessly, opening his eyes wide and gesticulating violently with his hands. He is only to be met here at the market in the cold weather; in the summer he is somewhere in the country, catching quails with a bird-call and angling for fish.

And here is another "type," a very tall, very thin, close-shaven gentleman in dark spectacles, wearing a cap with a cockade, and looking like a scrivener of by-gone days. He is a fancier; he is a man of decent position, a teacher in a high school, and that is well known to the *habitués* of the market, and they treat him with respect, greet him with bows, and have even invented for him a special title: "Your Scholarship." At Suharev market he rummages among the books, and at Trubnoy looks out for good pigeons.

"Please, sir!" the pigeon-sellers shout to him, "Mr. Schoolmaster, your Scholarship, take notice of my tumblers! your Scholarship!"

"Your Scholarship!" is shouted at him from every side.

"Your Scholarship!" an urchin repeats somewhere on the boulevard.

And his "Scholarship," apparently quite accustomed to his title, grave and severe, takes a pigeon in both hands, and lifting it above his head, begins examining it, and as he does so frowns and looks graver than ever, like a conspirator.

And Trubnoy Square, that little bit of Moscow where animals are so tenderly loved, and where they are so tortured, lives its little life, grows noisy and excited, and the business-like or pious people who pass by along the boulevard cannot make out what has brought this crowd of people, this medley of caps, fur hats, and chimney-pots together; what they are talking about there, what they are buying and selling.

Ward No. 6

CHAPTER I

PATIENTS

AT the side of the hospital yard stands a large wing, nearly surrounded by a forest of burdocks, nettles, and wild hemp. The roof is red, the chimney is breaking, the steps are rotten and grass-filled and the plaster is almost gone. The front gazes at the hospital, the back at the fields, by a grey, spiked fence. The spikes with their sharp points, the fence, the wing itself, have that dismal look which is seen only in hospitals and prisons.

Come along the narrow path, open the hall-door, enter the hall, and view piles of rubbish. Mattresses, tattered dressing-gowns, trousers, shirts, shoes and boots lie in tangled and crushed heaps, that befoul the air.

On the top of this rubbish heap, pipe eternally in mouth, lies the watchman Nikita, an old soldier. His face is coarse and drink-sodden, his hanging eye-brows give him the appearance of a sheep-dog, he is small and sinewy, but his carriage is impressive and his fists are strong. He belongs to that class of simple, expeditious, positive, and dull persons, who above all things in the world worship order, and find in this a justification of their existence. He beats his charges in the face, in the chest, in the back, in short, wherever his fists chance to strike; and he is convinced that without this beating there would be no order in the universe.

After you pass through Nikita's hall, you enter the large, roomy dormitory which takes up the rest of the wing. In this room the walls are painted a dirty blue, the ceiling is black with soot like the ceiling of a chimneyless hut; it is plain that in winter the stove smokes, and the air is suffocating. The windows are disfigured with iron bars, the floor is damp and splintered, there is a smell of sour cabbage, a smell of unsnuffed wicks, a smell of bugs and ammonia. And at the moment of entry all these smells produce upon you the impression that you have entered a cage of wild beasts.

Around the room stand beds, screwed to the floor. Sitting or lying on them, dressed in blue dressing-gowns, and wearing nightcaps after the manner of our forefathers, are men. It is the lunatic asylum, and these are the lunatics.

There are only five patients. One is of noble birth, the others are men of lower origin. The nearest to the door, a tall, thin man of the petty trading class, looks fixedly at one point. He has a red moustache and tear-stained eyes, and supports his head on one hand. In the books of the asylum his complaint is described as hypochondria; in reality, he is suffering from progressive paralysis. · Day and night he mourns, shakes his head, sighs, and smiles bitterly. In conversation he seldom joins, and usually refuses to answer questions. He eats and drinks mechanically. Judged by his emaciation, his flushed cheeks, and his painful, hacking cough, he is wasting away from consumption.

Beside him is a little, active old man

with a pointed beard, and the black, fuzzy hair of a negro. He spends all day in walking from window to window, or sitting on his bed, with legs doubled underneath him as if he were a Turk. He is as tireless as a bullfinch, and all day chirrups, titters, and sings in a low voice. His childish gaiety and lively character are shown also at night when he rises to "pray to God," that is, to beat his breast with his clenched fists, and pick at the doors. This is Moséika, a Jew and an idiot. He went out of his mind twenty years ago when his cap factory was destroyed by fire.

Of all the captives in Ward No. 6, he alone has permission to leave the asylum, and he is even allowed to wander about the yard and the streets. This privilege, which he has enjoyed for many years, was probably accorded to him as the oldest inmate of the asylum, and as a quiet, harmless fool, the jester of the town, who may be seen in the streets surrounded by dogs and little boys. Wrapped in his old dressing-gown, with a ridiculous nightcap and slippers, sometimes barefooted, and generally without his trousers, he walks the streets, stopping at doorways and entering small shops to beg for kopecks. Sometimes he is given *kvas*, sometimes bread, sometimes a kopeck, so that he returns to the ward wealthy and sated. But all that he brings home is taken by Nikita for his own particular benefit. The old soldier does this roughly and angrily, turning out the Jew's pockets, calling God to witness that he will never allow him outside the asylum again, and swearing that to him disorder is the most detestable thing in the world.

Moséika loves to make himself useful to others. He fetches water for his companions, tucks them in when they go to bed, promises to bring each a kopeck when he next returns from the town, and to make them new caps. He feeds with a spoon his paralytic neighbour on the left; and all this he does, not out of sympathy for others or for considerations of humanity, but from a love of imitation, and in a sort of involuntary subjection to his neighbour on the right, Iván Gromof.

Iván Dmítritch Gromof is a man of thirty-three years of age. He is a noble by birth. and has been an usher in the law courts, and a government secretary; but now he suffers from the mania of persecution. He lies upon his bed twisted into a lump resembling a roll of bread, or marches from corner to corner for the sake of motion. He is always in a state of excitement and agitation; and seems strained by some dull, indefinable expectation. It needs but the slightest rustle in the hall, the slightest noise in the yard, to make him raise his head and listen intently. Is it for him they are coming? Are they searching for him? And his face immediately takes on an expression of restlessness and repulsion.

There is something attractive about his broad, high cheek-boned face, which reflects, as a mirror, the tortured wrestlings and eternal terror of his mind. His grimaces are strange and sickly; but the delicate lines engraven on his face by sincere suffering express reason and intelligence, and his eyes burn with a healthy and passionate glow. There is something attractive also in his character, in his politeness, his attentiveness, and in the singular delicacy of his bearing towards everyone except Nikita. If his neighbour drops a spoon or a button he jumps immediately out of bed and picks it up. When he wakes he invariably says, "Good morning!" to his companions; and every evening on going to bed wishes them "good night!"

But madness shows itself in other things besides his grimaces and continual mental tension. In the evening he wraps himself in his dressing-gown, and, trembling all over, and chattering his teeth, he walks from corner to corner, and in between the beds. He seems to be in a state of fever. From his sudden stoppages and strange looks at his fellow-prisoners it is plain that he has something very serious to say; but, no doubt, remembering that they will neither listen nor understand, he says nothing, shakes his head impatiently, and continues his walk. But at last the desire to speak conquers all other considerations, and he gives way, and speaks passionately. His words are incoherent, gusty, and delirious; he cannot always be understood; but the sound of his voice expresses some exceptional goodness. In every word you hear the madman and the man. He speaks of human baseness, of violence trampling over truth, of the beautiful life on earth that is to come, and of the barred windows which remind him every moment of the folly and cruelty of the strong. And he hums medleys of old but forgotten songs.

CHAPTER II

NEVER IN LOVE

FIFTEEN years before, in his own house, in the best street in the town, lived an official named Gromof—a solid and prosperous man. Gromof had two sons, Sergéi and Iván. Sergéi, when a student in the fourth class, was seized with consumption and died; and his death was the first of a series of misfortunes which overtook the Gromofs. A week after Sergéi's death his old father was tried for forgery and misappropriation of public moneys, and soon afterwards died of typhus in the prison infirmary. His house and all his belongings were sold by auction, and Iván Dmítritch and his mother remained without a penny.

When his father was alive, Iván Dmítritch studied at St. Petersburg University, received an allowance of sixty or seventy roubles a month, and had no idea of the meaning of poverty. Now he had to change his whole life. From early morning till late at night he gave cheap lessons to students and copied documents, yet starved, for all his earnings went to support his mother. The life was impossible, and Iván Dmítritch ruined his health and spirits, threw up his university studies, and returned home. Through interest he obtained an appointment as usher in the district school; but he was disliked by his colleagues, failed to get on with the pupils, and gave up the post. His mother died. For six months he lived without resources, eating black bread and drinking water, until at last he obtained an appointment as Usher of the Court. This duty he fulfilled until he was discharged owing to illness.

Never, even in his student days, had he had the appearance of a strong man. He was pale, thin, and sensitive to cold; he ate little and slept badly. A single glass of wine made him giddy and sent him into hysterics. His disposition impelled him to seek companionship, but thanks to his irritable and suspicious character he never became intimate with anyone, and had no friends. Of his fellow-citizens he always spoke with contempt, condemning as disgusting and repulsive their gross ignorance and torpid, animal life. He spoke in a tenor voice, loudly and passionately, and always seemed to be in a sincere state of indignation, excitement, or rapture. However he began a conversation, it ended always in one way—in a lament that the town was stifling and tiresome, that its people had no high interests, but led a dull, unmeaning life, varied only by violence, coarse debauchery and hypocrisy; that scoundrels were fed and clothed while honest men ate crusts; that the town was crying out for schools, honest newspapers, a theatre, public lectures, an union of intellectual forces; and that the time had come for the townspeople to awaken to, and be shocked at, the state of affairs. In his judgments of men he laid on his colours thickly, using only white and black, and recognising no gradations; for him humanity was divided into two sections, honest men and rogues—there was nothing between. Of woman and woman's love he spoke passionately and with rapture. But he had never been in love.

In the town, notwithstanding his nervous character and censorious temper, he was loved, and called caressingly "Vanya." His innate delicacy, his attentiveness, his neatness, his moral purity, his worn coat, his sickly appearance, the misfortunes of his family, inspired in all feelings of warmth and compassion. Besides, he was educated and well-read; in the opinion of the townsmen he knew everything; and occupied among them the place of a walking reference-book. He read much. He

would sit for hours at the club, pluck nervously at his beard, and turn over the pages of books and magazines—by his face it might be seen that he was not reading but devouring. Yet reading was apparently merely one of his nervous habits, for with equal avidity he read everything that fell into his hands, even old newspapers and calendars. At home he always read, lying down.

CHAPTER III

IVAN'S CAPTURE

ONE autumn morning, Iván Dmítritch, with the collar of his coat turned up, trudged through the mud to the house of a certain tradesman to receive money due on a writ of execution. As always in the morning, he was in a gloomy mood. Passing through a lane, he met two convicts in chains and with them four warders armed with rifles. Iván Dmítritch had often met convicts before, and they had awakened in him a feeling of sympathy and confusion. But this meeting produced upon him an unusual impression. It suddenly occurred to him that he too might be shackled and driven through the mud to prison. Having finished his work, he was returning home when he met a police-inspector, an acquaintance, who greeted him and walked with him a few yards down the street. This seemed to him for some reason suspicious. At home visions of convicts and of soldiers armed with rifles haunted him all day, and an inexplicable spiritual dread prevented him from reading or concentrating his mind. In the evening he sat without a fire, and lay awake all night thinking how he also might be arrested, manacled, and flung into prison. He knew that he had committed no crime, and was quite confident that he would never commit murder, arson, or robbery; but then, he remembered, how easy it was to commit a crime by accident or involuntarily, and how common were convictions on false evidence and owing to judicial errors! And in the present state of human affairs how probable, how little to be wondered at, were judicial errors! Men who witness the sufferings of others only from a professional standpoint; for instance, judges, policemen, doctors, became hardened to such a degree that even if they wished otherwise they could not resist the habit of treating accused persons formally; they got to resemble those peasants who kill sheep and calves in their back-yards without even noticing the blood. In view of the soulless relationship to human personality which everywhere obtains, all that a judge thinks of is the observance of certain formalities, and then all is over, and an innocent man perhaps deprived of his civil rights or sent to the gallows. Who indeed would expect justice or intercession in this dirty, sleepy little town, two hundred versts from the nearest railway? And indeed was it not ridiculous to expect justice when society regards every form of violence as rational, expedient, and necessary; and when an act of common mercy such as the acquittal of an accused man calls for an explosion of unsatisfied vindictiveness!

Next morning Iván Dmítritch awoke in terror with drops of cold sweat on his forehead. He felt convinced that he might be arrested at any moment. That the evening's gloomy thoughts had haunted him so persistently, he concluded, must mean that there was some ground for his apprehensions. Could such thoughts come into his head without cause?

A policeman walked slowly past the window; that must mean something. Two men in plain clothes stopped outside the gate, and stood without saying a word. Why were they silent?

For a time, Iván Dmítritch spent his days and nights in torture. Every man who passed the window or entered the yard was a spy or detective. Every day at twelve o'clock the Chief Constable drove through the street on his way from his suburban house to the Department of Police, and every day it seemed to Iván Dmítritch that the Constable was driving with unaccustomed haste, and that there was a peculiar expression on his face; he was going, in short, to announce that a great criminal had appeared in the town. Iván Dmítritch shuddered at every sound, trembled at every knock at the yard-gate, and was in torment when any strange man visited his landlady. When he met a gendarme in the street, he smiled, whistled, and tried to assume an indifferent air. For whole nights, expecting arrest, he never closed his eyes, but snored carefully so that his landlady might think he was asleep; for if a man did not sleep at night it meant that he was tormented by the gnawings of conscience, and that might be taken as a clue. Reality and healthy reasoning convinced him that his fears were absurd and psychopathic, and that, regarded from a broad standpoint, there was nothing very terrible in arrest and imprisonment for a man whose conscience was clean. But the more consistently and logically he reasoned the stronger grew his spiritual torture; his efforts reminded him of the efforts of a pioneer to hack a path through virgin forest, the harder he worked with the hatchet the thicker and stronger became the undergrowth. So in the end, seeing that his efforts were useless, he ceased to struggle, and gave himself up to terror and despair.

He avoided others and became more and more solitary in his habits. His duties had always been detestable, now they became intolerable. He imagined that someone would hide money in his pockets and then denounce him for taking bribes, that he would make mistakes in official documents which were equivalent to forgery, or that he would lose the money entrusted to him. Never was his mind so supple and ingenious as when he was engaged in inventing various reasons for fearing for his freedom and honour. On the other hand, his interest in the outside world decreased correspondingly, he lost his passion for books, and his memory daily betrayed him.

Next spring when the snow had melted, the semi-decomposed corpses of an old woman and a boy, marked with indications of violence, were found in a ravine beside the graveyard. The townspeople talked of nothing but the discovery and the problem: who were the unknown murderers? In order to avert suspicion, Iván Dmítritch walked about the streets and smiled; and when he met his acquaintances, first grew pale and then blushed, and declared vehemently that there was no more detestable crime than the killing of the weak and defenceless. But this pretence soon exhausted him, and after consideration he decided that the best thing he could do was to hide in his landlady's cellar In the cellar therefore, chilled to the bone, he remained all day, all next night, and yet another day, after which, waiting until it was dark, he crept secretly back to his room. Till daylight he stood motionless in the middle of the room, and listened. At sunrise a number of artisans rang at the gate. Iván Dmítritch knew very well that they had come to put up a new stove in the kitchen; but his terror suggested that they were constables in disguise. He crept quietly out of his room, and overcome by panic, without cap or coat, fled down the street. Behind him ran barking dogs, a woman called after him, in his ears the wind whistled, and it seemed to him that the scattered violences of the whole world had united and were chasing him through the town.

He was captured and brought home. His landlady sent for a doctor. Doctor Andréi Yéfimitch Rágin, of whom we shall hear again, prescribed cold compresses for his head, ordered him to take drops of bay rum, and went away saying that he would come no more, as it was not right to prevent people going out of their minds. So, as there were no means of treating him at home, Iván Dmítritch was sent to hospital, and put into the ward for sick men. He did not sleep at night, was unruly, and disturbed his neighbours, so that soon, by arrangement with Doctor Andréi Yéfimitch, he was transferred to Ward No. 6.

Before a year had passed, the townspeople had quite forgotten Iván Dmítritch; and his books, piled up in a sledge by his landlady and covered with a curtain, were torn to pieces by children.

CHAPTER IV

THE FIFTH

IVAN DMITRITCH'S neighbour on the left, I have already said, was the Jew Moséika; his neighbour on the right was a fat, almost globular muzhik with a dull, meaningless face. This torpid, gluttonous, and uncleanly animal had long lost all capacity for thought and feeling. He exhaled a sharp, suffocating smell. When Nikita was obliged to attend on him he used to beat him terribly, beat him with all his strength and without regard for his own fists; and it was not this violence which was so frightful— the terror of that was mitigated by custom—but the fact that the stupefied animal made no answer to the blows either by sound or movement or even by expression in his eyes, but merely rocked from side to side like a heavy cask.

The fifth and last occupant of Ward No. 6 was a townsman who had served once as a sorter in the Post Office. He was a little, thin, fair-headed man, with a kindly, but somewhat cunning face. Judged by his clever, tranquil eyes, which looked out on the world frankly and merrily, he was the possessor of some valuable and pleasant secret. Under his pillow and mattress he had something hidden which he refused to show to anyone, not out of fear of losing it, but out of shame. Occasionally he walked to the window, and turning his back upon his fellow-prisoners, held something to his breast and looked earnestly at it; but if anyone approached he became confused and hid it away. But it was not hard to guess his secret.

"Congratulate me!" he used to say to Iván Dmítritch. "I have been deco-rated with the Stanislas of the second degree with a star. As a rule the second degree with a star is given only to foreigners, but for some reason they have made an exception in my case." And then, shrugging his shoulders as if in doubt, he would add: "That is something you never expected, you must admit."

"I understand nothing about it," answered Iván Dmítritch, gloomily.

"Do you know what I shall get sooner or later?" continued the ex-sorter, winking slyly. "I shall certainly receive the Swedish Pole Star. An order of that kind is worth trying for. A white cross and a black ribbon. It is very handsome."

In no other place in the world, probably, is life so monotonous as in the wing. In the morning the patients, with the exception of the paralytic and the fat muzhik, wash themselves in a great bucket which is placed in the hall, and dry themselves in the skirts of their dressing-gowns. After this they drink tea out of tin mugs brought by Nikita from the hospital. At midday they dine on *shtchi* made with sour cabbage, and porridge, and in the evening they sup on the porridge left over from dinner. Between meals they lie down, sleep, look out of the windows, and walk from corner to corner.

And so on every day. Even the ex-sorter talks always of the same decorations.

Fresh faces are seldom seen in Ward No. 6. Years ago the doctor gave orders that no fresh patients should be admitted, and in this world people rarely visit lunatic asylums for pleasure.

But once every two months comes Semión Lazaritch the barber. With

Nikita's assistance, he cuts the patients' hair; and on the consternation of the victims every time they see his drunken, grinning face, there is no need to dwell.

With this exception no one ever enters the ward. From day to day the patients are condemned to see only Nikita. But at last a strange rumour obtained circulation in the hospital. It was rumoured the doctor had begun to pay visits to Ward No. 6.

CHAPTER V

THE DOCTOR

It was indeed a strange rumour!

Doctor Andréi Yéfimitch Rágin was a remarkable man in his way. In early youth, so they said, he was very pious, and intended to make a career in the Church. But when in the year 1863 he finished his studies in the gymnasium and prepared to enter the Ecclesiastical Academy, his father, a surgeon and a doctor of medicine, poured ridicule on these intentions, and declared categorically that if Andréi became a priest he would disown him for ever. Whether this story is true or not it is impossible to say, but it is certain that Andréi Yéfimitch more than once admitted that he had never felt any vocation for medicine or, indeed, for specialised sciences at all.

Certain it is, also, that he never became a priest, but completed a course of study in the medical faculty of his university. He showed no particular trace of godliness, and at the beginning of his medical career was as little like a priest as at the end.

In appearance he was as heavy and rudely built as a peasant. His bearded face, his straight hair, and his strong, awkward build recalled some innkeeper on a main road—incontinent and stubborn. He was tall and broad-shouldered, and had enormous feet, and hands with which, it seemed, he could easily crush the life out of a man's body. Yet his walk was noiseless, cautious, and insinuating; and when he met anyone in a narrow passage he was always the first to step aside, and to say—not as might be expected in a bass voice—in a soft, piping tenor: "Excuse me!"

On his neck, Andréi Yéfimitch had a small tumour which forbade his wearing starched collars; he always wore a soft linen or print shirt. Indeed, in no respect did he dress like a doctor; he wore the same suit for ten years, and when he did buy new clothing—at a Jew's store—it always looked as worn and crumpled as his old clothes. In one and the same frock-coat he received his patients, dined, and attended entertainments; and this not from penuriousness but from a genuine contempt for appearances.

When Andréi Yéfimitch first came to the town to take up his duties as physician to the hospital, that "charitable institution" was in a state of inconceivable disorder. In the wards, in the corridors, and even in the open air of the yard it was impossible to breathe owing to the stench. The male attendants, the nurses and their children, slept in the dormitories together with the patients. It was complained that the hospitable was becoming uninhabitable owing to the invasion of beetles, bugs, and mice. In the surgical department there were only two scalpels, nowhere was there a thermometer, and the baths were used for storing potatoes in. The superintendent, the housekeeper, and the feldscher robbed the sick, and of the former doctor, Andréi Yéfimitch's predecessor, it was said that he sold the hospital spirits secretly, and kept up a whole harem recruited from among the nurses and female patients. In the town these scandals were well-known and even exaggerated; but the townspeople were indifferent, and even excused the abuses on the ground that the patients were all either petty tradespeople or peasants who lived at home among conditions so much worse that they had no right to complain; such gentry, they added, must not expect to be fed on grouse! Others argued that as no small town had sufficient resources to support a good hospital without subsidies from the Zemstvo, they might thank God they had a bad one; and the Zemstvo refused to open a hospital in the town on the ground that there was already one.

When he inspected the hospital for the first time, Andréi Yéfimitch saw at once that the whole institution was hopelessly bad, and in the highest degree dangerous to the health of the inmates. He concluded that the best thing to do was to discharge the patients and to close the hospital. But he knew that to effect this his wish alone was not enough; and he reasoned that if the physical and moral uncleanliness were driven from one place it would merely be transplanted to another; it was necessary, in fact, to wait until it cleaned itself out. To these considerations he added that if people opened a hospital and tolerated its abuses they must have need of it; and, no doubt, such abominations were necessary, and in the course of time would evolve something useful, as good soil results

from manuring. And, indeed, on this earth there is nothing good that has not had evil germs in its beginning.

Having taken up his duties, therefore, Andréi Yéfimitch looked upon the abuses with apparent indifference. He merely asked the servants and nurses not to sleep in the wards, and bought two cases of instruments; but he allowed the superintendent. the housekeeper. and the feldscher to remain in their positions.

Andréi Yéfimitch was passionately enamoured of intellect and honesty, but he had neither the character nor the confidence in his own powers necessary to establish around himself an intelligent and honest life. To command, to prohibit, to insist, he had never learned. It seemed almost that he had sworn an oath never to raise his voice or to use the imperative mood. . . . Even to use the words "give" or "bring" was difficult for him. When he felt hungry, he coughed irresolutely and said to his cook, "Suppose I were to have a cup of tea," or "I was thinking about dining." To tell the superintendent that he must cease his robberies, to dismiss him, or to abolish altogether his parasitical office he had not the strength. When he was deceived or flattered, or handed accounts for signature which he knew to have been falsified, he would redden all over and feel guilty, yet sign the accounts; and when the patients complained that they were hungry or had been ill-treated by the nurses, he merely got confused, and stammered guiltily:

"Very well, very well, I will investigate the matter. . . . No doubt there is some misunderstanding. . . ."

At first Andréi Yéfimitch worked very

zealously. He attended to patients from morning until dinner-time, performed operations, and even occupied himself with obstetrics. He gained a reputation for exceptional skill in the treatment of women and children. But he soon began visibly to weary of the monotony and uselessness of his work. One day he would receive thirty patients, the next day the number had grown to thirty-five, the next day to forty, and so on from day to day, and year to year. Yet the death-rate in the town did not decrease, and the number of patients never grew less. To give any real assistance to forty patients in the few hours between morning and dinner-time was physically impossible; in other words, he became an involuntary deceiver. The twelve thousand persons received every year, he reasoned, were therefore twelve thousand dupes. To place the serious cases in the wards and treat them according to the rules of medical science was impossible, because there were no rules and no science; whereas if he left philosophy and followed the regulations pedantically as other doctors did, he would still be in difficulty, for in the first place were needed cleanliness and fresh air, and not filth; wholesome food, and not *shtchi* made of stinking sour cabbage; and honest assistants, not thieves.

And, indeed, why hinder people dying, if death is the normal and lawful end of us all? What does it matter whether some tradesman or petty official lives, or does not live, an extra five years? We pretend to see the object of medical science in its mitigation of suffering, but we cannot but ask ourselves the question: Why should suffering be mitigated? In the first place, we are told

that suffering leads men to perfection; and in the second, it is plain that if men were really able to alleviate their sufferings with pills and potions, they would abandon that religion and philosophy in which until now they had found not only consolation, but even happiness. Pushkin suffered agonising torment before his death; Heine lay for years in a state of paralysis. Why, then, interfere with the suffering of some mere Andréi Yéfimitch or Matrena Savishin, whose lives are meaningless, and would be as vacuous as the life of the amœba if it were not for suffering?

Defeated by such arguments, Andréi Yéfimitch dropped his hands upon his knees, and ceased his daily attendances at the hospital.

CHAPTER VI

FATE

His life passed thus. At eight in the morning he rose and took his breakfast. After that he either sat in his study and read, or visited the hospital. In the hospital in a narrow, dark corridor waited the out-patients. With heavy boots clattering on the brick floor, servants and nurses ran past them; emaciated patients in dressing-gowns staggered by; and vessels of filth, and corpses were carried out. And among them children cried and draughts blew. Andréi Yéfimitch knew well that to the fevered, the consumptive, and the impressionable such surroundings were torment; but what could he do? In the reception-room he was met by the feldscher, Sergéi Sergéyitch, a little fat man, with a beardless, well-washed, puffy face, and easy manners. Sergéi Sergéyitch always wore clothes which resembled a senator's more than a surgeon's; in the town he had a large practice, and believed that he knew more than the doctor, who had no practice at all. In the corner of the room hung a case of ikons with a heavy lamp in front; on the walls were portraits of bishops, a view of Sviatogorsk Monastery, and garlands of withered corn-flowers. Sergéi Sergéyitch was religious, and the images had been placed in the room at his expense; every Sunday by his command one of the patients read the acathistus, and when the reading was concluded, Sergéi Sergéyitch went around the wards with a censer and sprinkled them piously.

There were many patients and little time. The examination was therefore limited to a few short questions, and to the distribution of such simple remedies as castor-oil and ointments. Andréi Yéfimitch sat with his head resting on his hands, lost in thought, and asked questions mechanically; and Sergéi Sergéyitch sat beside him, and sometimes interjected a word.

"We become ill and suffer deprivation," he would sometimes say, "only because we pray too little to God."

In these hours Andréi Yéfimitch performed no operations; he had got out of practice, and the sight of blood affected him unpleasantly. When he had to open a child's mouth, to examine its throat for instance, if the child cried and defended itself with its hands, the doctor's head went round and tears came into his eyes. He made haste to prescribe a remedy, and motioned to the mother to take it away as quickly as possible.

He quickly wearied of the timidity of the patients, of their shiftless ways, of the proximity of the pompous Sergéi

Sergéyitch, of the portraits on the walls, and of his own questions—questions which he had asked without change for more than twenty years. And he would sometimes leave the hospital after having examined five or six patients, the remainder in his absence being treated by the feldscher.

With the pleasant reflection that thank God he had no private practice and no one to interfere with him, Andréi Yéfimitch on returning home would sit at his study-table and begin to read. He read much, and always with pleasure. Half his salary went on the purchase of books, and of the six rooms in his flat three were crowded with books and old newspapers. Above all things he loved history and philosophy; but of medical publications he subscribed only to *The Doctor*, which he always began to read at the end. Every day he read uninterruptedly for several hours, and it never wearied him. He read, not quickly and eagerly as Iván Dmítritch had read, but slowly, often stopping at passages which pleased him or which he did not understand. Beside his books stood a decanter of vodka, and a salted cucumber or soaked apple; and every half-hour he poured himself out a glass of vodka, and drank it without lifting his eyes from his book, and then—again without lifting his eyes—took the cucumber and bit a piece off.

At three o'clock he would walk cautiously to the kitchen door, cough, and say:

"Dáryushka, I was thinking of dining. . . ."

After a bad and ill-served dinner, Andréi Yéfimitch walked about his rooms, with his arms crossed on his chest, and thought. Sometimes the kitchen door creaked, and the red, sleepy face of Dáryushka appeared.

"Andréi Yéfimitch, is it time for your beer?" she would ask solicitously.

"No, not yet," he would answer. "I'll wait a little longer. . . ."

In the evening came the postmaster, Mikhail Averyanitch, the only man in the town whose society did not weary Andréi Yéfimitch. Mikhail Averyanitch had once been a rich country gentleman and had served in a cavalry regiment, but having ruined himself he took a position in the Post Office to save himself from beggary in his old age. He had a brisk, wholesome appearance, magnificent grey whiskers, well-bred manners, and a loud but pleasant voice. When visitors at the Post Office protested, refused to agree with him, or began to argue, Mikhail Averyanitch became purple, shook all over, and roared at the top of his voice: "Silence!" so that the Post Office had the reputation of a place of terror. Mikhail Averyanitch was fond of Andréi Yéfimitch and respected his attainments and the nobility of his heart. But the other townspeople he treated haughtily as inferiors.

"Well, here I am!" he would begin. "How are you, my dear? . . . But perhaps I bore you? Eh?"

"On the contrary. I am delighted," answered the doctor. "I am always glad to see you."

The friends would sit on the study sofa and smoke for a time silently.

"Dáryushka, suppose I were to have a little beer . . ." said Andréi Yéfimitch.

The first bottle was drunk in silence. The doctor was lost in thought, while Mikhail Averyanitch had the gay and active expression of a man who has something very interesting to relate. The conversation was always begun by the doctor.

"What a pity!" he would say, slowly and quietly, looking away from his friend—he never looked anyone in the face. "What a pity, my dear Mikhail Averyanitch, what a pity it is that there is not a soul in this town who cares to engage in an intellectual or interesting conversation! It is a great deprivation for us. Even the so-called intelligent classes never rise above commonplaces; the level of their development, I assure you, is no higher than that of the lower order."

"Entirely true. I agree with you."

"As you yourself know very well," continued the doctor, pausing intermittently, "as you know, everything in this world is insignificant and uninteresting except the higher phenomena of the human intellect. Intellect creates a sharp distinction between the animal and the man, it reminds the latter of his divinity, and to a certain extent compensates him for the immortality which he has not. As the result of this, intellect serves as the only fountain of enjoyment. When we say we see and hear around us no evidence of intellect, we mean thereby that we are deprived of true happiness. True, we have our books, but that is a very different thing from living converse and communication. If I may use a not very apt simile, books are the accompaniment, but conversation is the singing."

"That is entirely true."

A silence followed. From the kitchen came Dáryushka, and, with her head resting on her hands and an expression of stupid vexation on her face, stood at the door and listened.

"Akh!" sighed Mikhail Averyanitch, "why seek intellect among the men of the present day?"

And he began to relate how in the old days life was wholesome, gay, and interesting, how the intellect of Russia was really enlightened, and how high a place was given to the ideas of honour and friendship. Money was lent without I.O.U.s, and it was regarded as shameful not to stretch out the hand of aid to a needy friend What marches there were. what adventures, what fights, what companions-in-arms, what women! The Caucasus, what a marvellous country! And the wife of the commander of his battalion—what a strange woman! —who put on an officer's uniform and drove into the mountains at night without an escort. They said she had a romance with a prince in one of the villages.

"Heavenly mother! Lord preserve us!" sighed Dáryushka.

"And how we drank! How we used to eat! What desperate Liberals we were!"

Andréi Yéfimitch listened, but heard nothing; he was thinking of something else and drinking his beer.

"I often dream of clever people and have imaginary conversations with them," he said, suddenly, interrupting Mikhail Averyanitch. "My father gave me a splendid education, but, under the influence of the ideas current in the sixties, forced me to become a doctor. It seems to me that if I had disobeyed him I might now be living in the very centre of the intellectual movement— probably a member of some faculty. Of course intellect itself is not eternal but transitory—but you already know why I worship it so. Life is a vexatious snare. When a reflecting man attains manhood and ripe consciousness, he cannot but feel himself in a trap from which there is no escape. . . . By an accident, without consulting his own will, he is called from non-existence into life. . . . Why? He wishes to know the aim and significance of his existence; he is answered with silence or absurdities; he knocks but it is not opened to him; and death itself comes against his will. And so, as prisoners united by common misfortune are relieved when they meet, men inclined to analysis and generalisation do not notice the snare in which they live when they spend their days in the exchange of free ideas. In this sense intellect is an irreplaceable enjoyment."

"Entirely true!"

And still with his face averted from his companion, Andréi Yéfimitch, in a soft voice, with constant pauses, continues to speak of clever men and of the joy of communion with them, and Mikhail Averyanitch listens attentively and says: "It is entirely true."

"Then you do not believe in the immortality of the soul?" asked the post-master.

"No, my dear Mikhail Averyanitch. 1 do not believe, and 1 have no reason for believing."

"I admit that I also doubt it. Still I have a feeling that I can never die. 'Come,' I say to myself, "Come, old man, it's time for you to die.' But in my heart a voice answers: 'Don't believe it, you will never die.' "

At nine o'clock Mikhail Averyanitch takes leave. As he puts on his overcoat in the hall, he says with a sigh:

"Yes, what a desert fate has planted us in! And what is worst of all, we shall have to die here. *Akh!*"

CHAPTER VII

THOUGHTS

WHEN he has parted from his friend, Andréi Yéfimitch sits at his table and again begins to read. The stillness of evening, the stillness of night is unbroken by a single sound; time, it seems, stands still and perishes, and the doctor perishes also, till it seems that nothing exists but a book and a green lamp-shade. Then the rude, peasant face of the doctor, as he thinks of the achievements of the human intellect, becomes gradually illumined by a smile of emotion and rapture. Oh, why is man not immortal? he asks. For what end exist brain-centres and convolutions, to what end vision, speech, consciousness, genius, if all are condemned to pass into the earth, to grow cold with it, and for countless millions of years, without aim or object, to be borne with it around the sun? In order that the human frame may decay and be whirled around the sun, is it necessary to drag man with his high, his divine mind, out of non-existence, as if in mockery, and to turn him again into earth?

Immortality of matter! What cowardice to console ourselves with this fictitious immortality! Unconscious processes working themselves out in nature—processes lower even than folly, for in folly there is at least consciousness and volition, while in these processes there is neither! Yet they say to men, "Be at rest, thy substance, rotting in the earth, will give life to other organisms"—in other words, thou wilt be more foolish than folly! Only the coward, who has more fear of death than sense of dignity, can console himself with the knowledge that his body in the course of time will live again in grass, in stones, in the toad. To seek immortality in the indestructibility of matter is, indeed, as strange as to prophesy a brilliant future for the case when the costly violin is broken and worthless.

When the clock strikes, Andréi Yéfimitch leans back in his chair, shuts his eyes, and thinks. Under the influence of the lofty thoughts which he has just been reading, he throws a glance over the present and the past. The past is repellent, better not think of it! And the present is but as the past. He knows that in this very moment, while his thoughts are sweeping round the sun with the cooling earth, in the hospital building in a line with his lodgings, lie men tortured by pain and tormented by uncleanliness; one cannot sleep owing to the insects, and howls in his pain; another is catching erysipelas, and groaning at the tightness of his bandages; others are playing cards with the nurses, and drinking vodka. In this very year no less than twelve thousand persons were duped; the whole work of the hospital, as twenty years before, is based on robbery, scandal, intrigue, nepotism, and gross charlatanry; altogether, the hospital is an immoral institution, and a source of danger to the health of its inmates. And Andréi Yéfimitch knows that inside the iron bars of Ward No. 6, Nikita beats the patients with his fists, and that, outside, Moséika wanders about the streets begging for kopecks.

Yet he knows very well that in the last twenty-five years a fabulous revolution has taken place in the doctor's art. When he studied at the university it had seemed to him that medicine would soon be overtaken by the lot of alchemy and metaphysics, but now the records of its feats which he reads at night touch him, astonish him, and even send him into raptures. What a revolution! what unexpected brilliance! Thanks to antiseptics, operations are every day performed which the great Pigoroff regarded as impossible. Ordinary Zemstvo doctors perform such operations as the resection of the knee articulations, of a hundred operations on the stomach only one results in death, and the stone is now such a trifle that it has ceased to be written about. Complaints which were once only alleviated are now entirely cured. And hypnotism, the theory of heredity, the discoveries of Pasteur and Koch, statistics of hygiene, even Russian Zemstvo medicine! Psychiatry, with its classification of diseases, its methods of diagnosis, its methods of cure—what a transformation of the methods of the past! No longer are lunatics drenched with cold water and confined in strait waistcoats; they are treated as human beings, and even—as Andréi Yéfimitch read in the newspapers—have their own special dramatic entertainments and dances. Andréi Yéfimitch is well aware that in the modern world such an abomination as Ward No. 6 is possible only in a town situated two hundred versts from a railway, where the Mayor and Councillors are half-educated tradesmen, who regard a doctor as a priest to whom everything must be entrusted without criticism, even though he were to dose his patients with molten tin. In any other town the public and the Press would long ago have torn this little Bastille to pieces.

"But in the end?" asks Andréi Yéfimitch, opening his eyes. "What is the difference? In spite of antiseptics and Koch and Pasteur, the essence of the matter has no way changed. Disease and death still exist. Lunatics are amused with dances and theatricals, but they are still kept prisoners. . . . In other words, all these things are vanity and folly, and between the best hospital in Vienna and the hospital here there is in reality no difference at all."

But vexation and a feeling akin to envy forbid indifference. It all arises out of weariness. Andréi Yéfimitch's head falls upon his book, he rests his head comfortably on his hands and thinks:

"I am engaged in a bad work, and I receive a salary from the men whom I deceive. I am not an honest man. . . . But then by myself I am nothing; I am only part of a necessary social evil; all the officials in the district are bad, and draw their salaries without doing their work. . . . In other words, it is not I who am guilty of dishonesty, but Time. . . . If I were born two hundred years hence I should be a different man."

When the clock strikes three, he puts out his lamp and goes up to his bedroom. But he has no wish to sleep.

CHAPTER VIII

THE ASSISTANT

Two years ago, in a fit of liberality, the Zemstvo determined to appropriate three hundred roubles a year to the increase of the *personnel* of the hospital, until such time as they should open one of their own. They sent, therefore, as assistant to Andréi Yéfimitch, the district physician Yevgéniï Feódoritch Khobótoff. Khobótoff was a very young man, under thirty, tall and dark, with small eyes and high cheek-bones; evidently of Asiatic origin. He arrived in the town without a kopeck, with a small portmanteau as his only luggage, and was accompanied by a young, unattractive woman, whom he called his cook. This woman's child completed the party. Khobótoff wore a peaked cap and high boots, and—in winter—a short fur coat. He was soon on intimate terms with the feldscher, Sergéi Sergéyitch, and with the bursar, but the rest of the officials he avoided and denounced as aristocrats. He possessed only one book, "Prescriptions of the Vienna Hospital in 1881," and when he visited the hospital he always brought it with him. He did not care for cards, and in the evenings spent his time playing billiards at the club.

Khobótoff visited the hospital twice a week, inspected the wards, and received out-patients. The strange absence of antiseptics, cupping-glasses, and other necessaries seemed to trouble him, but he made no attempt to introduce a new order, fearing to offend Andréi Yéfimitch, whom he regarded as an old rogue, suspected of having large means, and secretly envied. He would willingly have occupied his position.

CHAPTER IX

RELEASE ME!

ONE spring evening towards the end of March, when the snow had disappeared and starlings sang in the hospital garden, the doctor was standing at his gate saying good-bye to his friend the postmaster. At that moment the Jew Moséika, returning with his booty, entered the yard. He was capless, wore a pair of goloshes on his stockingless feet, and held in his hand a small bag of coins.

"Give me a kopeck?" he said to the doctor, shuddering from the cold and grinning.

Andréi Yéfimitch, who could refuse no one, gave him a ten-kopeck piece.

"How wrong this is!" he thought, as he looked at the Jew's bare legs and thin ankles. "Wet, I suppose?"

And impelled by a feeling of pity and squeamishness he entered the wing after Moséika, looking all the time now at the Jew's bald head, now at his ankles. When the doctor entered, Nikita jumped off his rubbish-heap and stretched himself.

"Good evening, Nikita!" said the doctor softly. "Suppose you give this man a pair of boots . . . that is . . . he might catch cold."

"Yes, your Honour. I will ask the superintendent."

"Please. Ask him in my name. Say that I spoke about it."

The door of the ward was open. Iván Dmítritch, who was lying on his bed, and listening with alarm to the unknown voice, suddenly recognised the doctor. He shook with anger, jumped off his bed, and with a flushed, malicious face, and staring eyeballs, ran into the middle of the room.

"It is the doctor!" he cried, with a loud laugh. "At last! Lord, I congratulate you, the doctor honours us with a visit! Accused monster!" he squealed, and in an ecstacy of rage never before seen in the hospital, stamped his feet. "Kill this monster! No, killing is not enough for him! Drown him in the closet!"

Andréi Yéfimitch heard him. He looked into the ward and asked mildly: "For what?"

"For what!" screamed Iván Dmítritch, approaching with a threatening face, and convulsively clutching his dressing-gown. "For what! Thief!" He spoke in a tone of disgust, and twisted his lips as if about to spit.

"Charlatan! Hangman!"

"Be quiet!" said Andréi Yéfimitch, smiling guiltily. "I assure you I have never stolen anything. . . . I see that you are angry with me. Be calm, I implore you, if you can, and tell me why you want to kill me."

"For keeping me here."

"I do that because you are ill."

"Yes! Ill! But surely tens, hundreds, thousands of madmen live unmolested merely because you in your ignorance cannot distinguish them from the sane. You, the feldscher, the superintendent, all the rascals employed in the hospital are immeasurably lower in morals than the worst of us; why, then, are we here instead of you? Where is the logic?"

"It is not a question of morality or logic. It depends on circumstances. The man who is put here, here he stays, and the man who is not here lives in freedom, that is all. For the fact that I am a doctor and you a lunatic neither morals nor logic is responsible, but only empty circumstance."

"This nonsense I do not understand!" answered Iván Dmítritch, sitting down on his bed.

Moséika, whom Nikita was afraid to search in the doctor's presence, spread out on his bed his booty—pieces of bread, papers, and bones; and trembling with the cold, talked Yiddish in a sing-song voice. Apparently he imagined that he was opening a shop.

"Release me!" said Iván Dmítritch. His voice trembled.

"I cannot."

"Why not?"

"Because it is not in my power. Judge for yourself! What good would it do you if I released you? Suppose I do! The townspeople or the police will capture you and send you back."

"Yes, that is true, it is true . . ." said Iván Dmítritch, rubbing his forehead. "It is terrible! But what can I do? What?"

His voice, his intelligent, youthful face pleased Andréi Yéfimitch. He wished to caress him and quiet him. He sat beside him on the bed, thought for a moment, and said:

"You ask what is to be done. The best thing in your position would be to run away. But unfortunately that is useless. You would be captured. When society resolves to protect itself from criminals, lunatics, and inconvenient people, it is irresistible. One thing alone remains to you, to console yourself with the thought that your stay here is necessary."

"It is necessary to no one."

"Once prisons and asylums exist, someone must inhabit them. If it is not you it will be I, if not I then someone else. But wait! In the far future there will be neither prisons nor madhouses, nor barred windows, nor dressing-gowns. . . . Such a time will come sooner or later."

Iván Dmítritch smiled contemptuously.

"You are laughing at me," he said, winking. "Such gentry as you and your assistant Nikita has no business with the future. But you may be assured, sir, that better times are in store for us. What if I do express myself vulgarly— laugh at me!—but the dawn of a new life will shine, and truth will triumph . . . and it will be on our side the holiday will be. I shall not see it, but our posterity shall. . . . I congratulate them with my whole soul, and rejoice—rejoice for them! Forward! God help you, friends!"

Iván Dmítritch's eyes glittered; he rose, stretched out his eyes to the window, and said in an agitated voice:

"For these barred windows I bless you. Hail to the truth! I rejoice!"

"I see no cause for rejoicing," said Andréi Yéfimitch, whom Iván Dmítritch's movements, though they seemed theatrical, pleased. "Prisons and asylums will no longer be, and justice, as you put it, will triumph. But the essence of things will never change, the laws of Nature will remain the same. Men will be diseased, grow old, and die, just as now. However glorious the dawn which enlightens your life, in the end of ends you will be nailed down in a coffin and flung into a pit."

"But immortality?"

"Nonsense!"

"You do not believe, but I believe. Dostoyeffsky or Voltaire or someone said that if there were no God men would have invented one. And I am deeply convinced that if there were no immortality it would sooner or later have been invented by the great human intellect."

"You speak well," said Andréi Yéfimitch, smiling with pleasure. "It is

well that you believe. With such faith as yours you would live happily though entombed in a wall. May I ask where you were educated?"

"I was at college, but never graduated."

"You are a thoughtful and penetrating man. You would find tranquillity in any environment. The free and profound thought which aspires to the comprehension of life; and high contempt for the vanity of the world—these are two blessings higher than which no man can know. And these you will enjoy though you live behind a dozen barred windows. Diogenes lived in a tub, yet he was happier than all the kings of the earth."

"Your Diogenes was a blockhead!" cried Iván Dmítritch gloomily. "What do you tell me about Diogenes and the understanding of life?" He spoke angrily, and sprang up. "I love life, love it passionately. I have the mania of persecution, a ceaseless, tormenting terror, but there are moments when I am seized by the thirst of life, and in those moments I fear to go out of my mind. I long to live . . . terribly!"

He walked up and down the ward in agitation, and continued in a lower voice:

"When I meditate I am visited by visions. Men come to me, I hear voices and music, and it seems to me that I am walking through woods, on the shores of the sea; and I long passionately for the vanities and worries of life. . . . Tell me! What is the news?"

"You ask about the town, or generally?"

"First tell me about the town, and then generally."

"What is there? The town is tiresome to the point of torment. There is no one to talk to, no one to listen to. There are no new people. But lately we got a new doctor, Khobótoff, a young man."

"He has been here. A fool?"

"Yes, an uneducated man. It is strange, do you know. If you judge by metropolitan life there is no intellectual stagnation in Russia, but genuine activity; in other words, there are real men. But for some reason or other they always send such fellows here. It is an unfortunate town."

"An unfortunate town," sighed Iván Dmítritch. "And what news is there generally? What have you in the newspapers and reviews?"

In the ward it was already dark. The doctor rose, and told his patient what was being written in Russia and abroad, and what were the current tendencies of the world. Iván Dmítritch listened attentively, and asked questions. But suddenly, as if he had just remembered something terrible, he seized his head and threw himself on the bed, with his back turned to the doctor.

"What is the matter?" asked Andréi Yéfimitch.

"You will not hear another word from me," said Iván Dmítritch rudely. "Go away!"

"Why?"

"I tell you, go away! Go to the devil!"

Andréi Yéfimitch shrugged his shoulders, sighed, and left the ward. As he passed through the hall, he said:

"Suppose you were to clear some of this away, Nikita. . . . The smell is frightful."

"Yes, your Honour!"

"What a delightful young man!"

thought Andréi Yéfimitch, as he walked home. "He is the first man worth talking to whom I have met all the time I have lived in this town. He can reason and interests himself only with what is essential."

As he read in his study, as he went to bed, all the time, he thought of Iván Dmítritch. When he awoke next morning, he remembered that he had made the acquaintance of a clever and interesting man. And he decided to pay him another visit at the first opportunity.

CHAPTER X

CONVERSATION

IVAN DMITRITCH lay in the same position as on the day before, holding his head in his hands, his legs being doubled up underneath him.

"Good morning, my friend," said Andréi Yéfimitch. "You are not asleep?"

"In the first place I am not your friend," said Iván Dmítritch, keeping his face turned towards the pillow; "and in the second, you are troubling yourself in vain; you will not get from me a single word."

"That is strange," said Andréi Yéfimitch. "Yesterday we were speaking as friends, but suddenly you took offence and stopped short. . . . Perhaps I spoke awkwardly, or expressed opinions differing widely from your own."

"You won't catch me!" said Iván Dmítritch, rising from the bed and looking at the doctor ironically and suspiciously. "You may go and spy and cross-examine somewhere else; here there is nothing for you to do. I know very well why you came yesterday."

"That is a strange idea," laughed the

doctor. "But why do you assume that I am spying?"

"I assume it. . . . Whether spy or doctor it is all the same."

"Yes, but . . . excuse me. . . ."

The doctor sat on a stool beside the bed, and shook his head reproachfully. "Even suppose you are right, suppose I am following your words only in order to betray you to the police, what would happen? They would arrest you and try you. But then, in the dock or in prison would you be worse off than here? In exile or penal servitude, you would not suffer any more than now. . . . What, then, do you fear?"

Apparently these words affected Iván Dmítritch. He sat down quietly.

It was five o'clock, the hour when Andréi Yéfimitch usually walked up and down his room and Dáryushka asked him whether it was time for his beer. The weather was calm and clear.

"After dinner I went out for a walk, and you see where I've come," said the doctor. "It is almost spring."

"What month is it?" asked Iván Dmítritch. "March?"

"Yes, we are at the end of March."

"Is it very muddy?"

"Not very. The paths in the garden are clear."

"How glorious it would be to drive somewhere outside the town!" said Iván Dmítritch, rubbing his red eyes as if they were sleepy, "and then to return to a warm comfortable study . . . and to be cured of headache by a decent doctor. . . . For years past I have not lived like a human being. . . . Things are abominable here,—intolerable, disgusting!"

After last evening's excitement he was tired and weak, and he spoke unwillingly. His fingers twitched, and from his face it was plain that his head ached badly.

"Between a warm, comfortable study and this ward there is no difference," said Andréi Yéfimitch. "The rest and tranquillity of a man are not outside but within him."

"What do you mean by that?"

"Ordinary men find good and evil outside, that is, in their carriages and comfortable rooms; but the thinking man finds them within himself."

"Go and preach that philosophy in Greece, where it is warm and smells of oranges—it doesn't suit this climate. With whom was it I spoke of Diogenes? With you?"

"Yes, yesterday with me."

"Diogenes had no need of a study and a warm house, he was comfortable without them. . . . Lie in a tub and eat oranges and olives! Set him down in Russia—not in December, but even in May. He would freeze even in May with the cold."

"No. Cold, like every other feeling, may be disregarded. As Marcus Aurelius said, pain is the living conception of pain; make an effort of the will to change this conception, cease to complain, and the pain disappears. The wise man, the man of thought and penetration, is distinguished by his contempt for suffering; he is always content and he is surprised by nothing."

"That means that I am an idiot because I suffer, because I am discontented, and marvel at the baseness of men."

"Your discontent is in vain. Think more, and you will realise how trifling are all the things which now excite you.

. . . Try to understand life—in this is true beatitude."

"Understand!" frowned Iván Dmítritch. "External, internal. . . . Excuse me, but I cannot understand you. I know only one thing," he continued, rising and looking angrily at the doctor. "I know only that God created me of warm blood and nerves; yes! and organic tissue, if it be capable of life, must respond to irritation. And I respond to it! Pain I answer with tears and cries, baseness with indignation, meanness with repulsion. In my mind, that is right, and it is that which is called life. The lower the organism the less susceptible is it, and the more feebly it responds to irritation; the higher it is the more sensitively it responds. How is it you do not know that? A doctor—yet you do not know such truisms! If you would despise suffering, be always contented, and marvel at nothing, you must lower yourself to the condition of that . . ." Iván Dmítritch pointed to the fat, greasy muzhik, "or inure yourself to suffering until you lose all susceptibility—in other words, cease to live. Excuse me, but I am not a wise man and not a philosopher," continued Iván Dmítritch irritably, "and I do not understand these things. I am not in a condition to reason."

"But you reason admirably."

"The Stoics whom you travesty were remarkable men, but their teaching died two thousand years ago, and since then it has not advanced, nor will it advance, an inch, for it is not a practical or a living creed. It was successful only with a minority who spent their lives in study and trifled with gospels of all sorts; the majority never understood it.

. . A creed which teaches indifference to wealth, indifference to the conveniences of life, and contempt for suffering, is quite incomprehensible to the great majority who never knew either wealth or the conveniences of life, and to whom contempt for suffering would mean contempt for their own lives, which are made up of feelings of hunger, cold, loss, insult, and a Hamlet-like terror of death. All life lies in these feelings, and life may be hated or wearied of, but never despised. Yes, I repeat it, the teaching of the Stoics can never have a future; from the beginning of time life has consisted in sensibility to pain and response to irritation."

Iván Dmítrich suddenly lost the thread of his thoughts, ceased speaking, and rubbed his forehead irritably.

"I had something important to say, but have gone off the track," he continued. "What was I saying? Yes, this is it. One of these Stoics sold himself into slavery to redeem a friend. Now what does that mean but that even a Stoic responded to irritation, for to perform such a magnanimous deed as the ruin of one's self for the sake of a friend demands a disturbed and sympathetic heart. I have forgotten here in prison all that I learnt, otherwise I should have other illustrations. But think of Christ! Christ rebelled against actuality by weeping, by smiling, by grieving, by anger, even by weariness. Not with a smile did He go forth to meet suffering, nor did He despise death, but prayed in the garden of Gethsemane that this cup might pass from Him."

Iván Dmítritch laughed and sat down.

"Suppose that contentment and tranquillity are not outside but within a man," he continued. "Suppose that we must despise suffering and marvel at nothing. But you do not say on what foundation you base this theory. You are a wise man? A philosopher?"

"I am not a philosopher, but everyone must preach this because it is rational."

But I wish to know why in this matter of understanding life, despising suffering, and the rest of it, you consider yourself competent to judge? Have you ever suffered? What is your idea of suffering? Were you ever flogged when you were a child?"

"No, my parents were averse to corporal punishment."

"But my father flogged me cruelly. He was a stern hemorrhoidal official with a long nose and a yellow neck. But what of you? In your whole life no one has ever laid a finger on you, and you are as healthy as a bull. You grew up under your father's wing, studied at his expense, and then dropped at once into a fat sinecure. More than twenty years you have lived in free lodgings, with free fire and free lights, with servants, with the right to work how, and as much as, you like, or to do nothing. By character you were an idle and a feeble man, and you strove to build up your life so as to avoid trouble. You left your work to feldschers and other scoundrels, and sat at home in warmth and quiet, heaped up money, read books, and enjoyed your own reflections about all kinds of exalted nonsense, and"—Iván Dmítritch looked at the doctor's nose—"drank beer. In one word, you have not seen life, you know nothing about it, and of realities you have only a theoretical knowledge. Yes, you despise suffering and marvel at nothing for very good reasons; because your theory of the vanity of things, external and internal happiness, contempt for life, for suffering and for death, and so on—this is the philosophy best suited to a Russian lie-abed. You see, for instance, a muzhik beating his wife. Why interfere? let him beat her! It is all the same, both will be dead sooner or later, and then, does not the wife-beater injure himself and not his victim? To get drunk is stupid and wrong, but the man who drinks dies, and the woman who drinks dies also! A woman comes to you with a toothache. Well, what of that? Pain is the conception of pain, without sickness you cannot live, all must die, and therefore take yourself off, my good woman, and don't interfere with my thoughts and my vodka! A young man comes to you for advice: what should he do, how ought he to live? Before answering, most men would think, but your answer is always ready: Aspire to understand life and to real goodness? And what is this fantastic real goodness? No answer! We are imprisoned behind iron bars, we rot and we are tortured, but this, in reality, is reasonable and beautiful because between this ward and a comfortable warm study there is no real difference! A convenient philosophy; your conscience is clean, and you feel yourself to be a wise man. No, sir, this is not philosophy, not breadth of view, but idleness, charlatanism, somnolent folly . . . Yes," repeated Iván Dmítritch angrily. "You despise suffering, but squeeze your finger in the door and you will howl for your life!"

"But suppose I do not howl." said Andréi Yéfimitch, smiling indulgently.

"What! Well, if you had a stroke of paralysis, or if some impudent fellow, taking advantage of his position in the world, insulted you publicly, and you had no redress—then you would know what it meant to tell others to understand life and aspire to real good."

"This is original," said Andréi Yéfimitch, beaming with satisfaction and rubbing his hands. "I am delighted with your love of generalisation; and the character which you have just drawn is simply brilliant. I confess that conversation with you gives me great pleasure. But now, as I have heard you out, will you listen to me . . ."

CHAPTER XI

ON THE BED

THIS conversation, which lasted for an hour longer. apparently made a great impression on Andréi Yéfimitch. He took to visiting the ward every day. He went there in the morning, and again after dinner, and often darkness found him in conversation with Iván Dmítritch. At first Iván Dmítritch was shy with him, suspected him of some evil intention, and openly expressed his suspicions. But at last he got used to him; and his rude bearing softened into indulgent irony.

A report soon spread through the hospital that Doctor Andréi Yéfimitch paid daily visits to Ward No. 6. Neither the feldscher, nor Nikita, nor the nurses could understand his object; why he spent whole hours in the ward, what he was talking about, or why he did not write prescriptions. His conduct appeared strange to everyone. Mikhail Averyanitch sometimes failed to find him at home, and Dáryushka was very

alarmed, for the doctor no longer drank his beer at the usual hour, and sometimes even came home late for dinner.

One day—it was at the end of June —Doctor Khobótoff went to Andréi Yéfimitch's house to see him on a business matter. Not finding him at home, he looked for him in the yard, where he was told that the old doctor was in the asylum. Khobótoff entered the hall of the ward, and standing there listened to the following conversation:

"We will never agree, and you will never succeed in converting me to your faith," said Iván Dmítritch irritably. "You are altogether ignorant of realities, you have never suffered, but only, like a leech, fed on the sufferings of others. But I have suffered without cease from the day of my birth until now. Therefore I tell you frankly I consider myself much higher than you, and more competent in all respects. It is not for you to teach me."

"I certainly have no wish to convert you to my faith," said Andréi Yéfimitch softly, and evidently with regret that he was misunderstood. "That is not the question, my friend. Suffering and joy are transitory—leave them, God be with them! The essence of the matter is that you and I recognise in one another men of thought. and this makes us solid however different our views. If you knew, my friend, how I am weary of the general idiocy around me, the lack of talent, the dullness—if you knew the joy with which I speak to you! You are a clever man, and it is a pleasure to be with you."

Khobótoff opened the door and looked into the room. Iván Dmítritch with a nightcap on his head and Doctor Andréi Yéfimitch sat side by side on the bed. The lunatic shuddered, made strange laces, and convulsively clutched his dressing-gown; and the doctor sat motionless, inclining his head, and his face was red and helpless and sad. Khobótoff shrugged his shoulders, laughed, and looked at Nikita. Nikita also shrugged his shoulders.

Next day Khobótoff again came to the wing, this time together with the feldscher. They stood in the hall and listened:

"Our grandfather, it seems, is quite gone," said Khobótoff going out of the wing.

"Lord, have mercy upon us—sinners!" sighed the pompous Sergéi Sergéyitch, going round the pools in order to keep his shiny boots clear of the mud. "I confess, my dear Yevgénii Feódoritch, I have long expected this."

CHAPTER XII

MYSTERY!

AFTER this incident, Andréi Yéfimitch began to notice that he was surrounded by a strange atmosphere of mystery. . . . The servants, the nurses, and the patients whom he met looked questioningly at one another, and whispered among themselves. When he met little Masha, the superintendent's daughter, in the hospital garden, and smilingly went over to her, as usual, to stroke her hair, for some inexplicable reason she ran away. When the postmaster, Mikhail Averyanitch, sat listening to him he no longer said: "Entirely true!" but got red in the face and stammered, "Yes yes . . . yes . . ." and sometimes, looking at his friend thoughtfully and sorrowfully, advised him to give up vodka and beer. But when doing this, as became a man of delicacy, he did not speak openly, but dropped gentle hints, telling stories, now of a certain battalion commander, an excellent man, now of the regimental chaplain, a first-rate little fellow, who drank a good deal and was taken ill, yet having given up drink got quite well. Twice or thrice Andréi Yéfimitch was visited by his colleague Khobótoff, who also asked him to give up spirits, and, without giving him any reason, advised him to try bromide of potassium.

In August Andréi Yéfimitch received a letter from the Mayor asking him to come and see him on very important business. On arriving at the Town Hall at the appointed time he found awaiting him the head of the recruiting department, the superintendent of the district school, a member of the Town Council, Khobótoff, and a stout, fair-haired man, who was introduced as a doctor. This doctor, who bore an unpronounceable Polish name, lived on a stud-farm some thirty versts away, and was passing through the town on his way home.

"Here is a communication about your department," said the Town Councillor, turning to Andréi Yéfimitch. "You see, Yevgénii Feódoritch says that there is no room for the dispensing room in the main building, and that it must be transferred to one of the wings. That of course, is easy, it can be transferred any day, but the chief thing is that the wing is in want of repair."

"Yes, we can hardly get on without that," answered Andréi Yéfimitch after a moment's thought. "But if the corner wing is to be fitted up as a dispensary you will have to spend at least five hundred roubles on it. It is unproductive expenditure."

For a few minutes all were silent.

"I had the honour to announce to you, ten years ago," continued Andréi Yéfimitch in a soft voice, "that this hospital, under present conditions, is a luxury altogether beyond the means of the town. It was built in the forties, when the means for its support were greater. The town wastes too much money on unnecessary buildings and sinecure offices. I think that with the money we spend we could keep up two model hospitals; that is, of course, with a different order of things."

"Well, then, let us reform the present order," said the Town Councillor.

"I have already had the honour to advise you to transfer the medical department to the Zemstvo."

"Yes, and hand over to the Zemstvo funds which it will pocket," laughed the fair-haired doctor.

"That is just what happens," said the Town Councillor, laughing also.

Andréi Yéfimitch looked feebly at the fair-haired doctor, and said:

"We must be just in our judgments."

Again all were silent. Tea was brought in. The chief of the recruiting department, apparently in a state of confusion, touched Andréi Yéfimitch's hand across the table, and said:

"You have quite forgotten us, doctor. But then you were always a monk; you don't play cards, and you don't care for women. We bore you, I'm afraid."

And all agreed that it was tiresome for any decent man to live in such a town. Neither theatres, nor concerts, and at the last club-dance about twenty women present and only two men. Young men no longer danced, but crowded round the supper-table or played cards together. And Andréi Yéfimitch, in a slow and soft voice, without looking at those around him, began to lament that the citizens wasted their vital energy, their intellects, and their feelings over cards and scandal, and neither cared nor knew how to pass the time in interesting conversation, in reading, or in taking advantage of the pleasures which intellect alone yields. Intellect is the only interesting and distinguished thing in the world; all the rest is petty and base. Khobótoff listened attentively to his colleague, and suddenly asked:

"Andréi Yéfimitch, what is the day of the month?"

Having received an answer, he and the fair-haired doctor, both in the tone of examiners convinced of their own incapacity, asked Andréi Yéfimitch a number of other questions: what was the day of the week, how many days were there in the year, and was it true that in Ward No. 6 there was a remarkable prophet?

In answer to this last question Andréi Yéfimitch got red in the face, and said:

"Yes, he is insane. . . . But he is a most interesting young man."

No other questions were asked.

As Andréi Yéfimitch put on his coat, the chief of the recruiting department put his hand on his shoulder and said, with a sigh:

"For us—old men—it is time to take a rest."

As he left the Town Hall, Andréi Yéfimitch understood that he had been before a commission appointed to test his mental sanity. He remembered the questions put to him, reddened, and for the first time in his life felt pity for the medical art.

"My God!" he thought. "Those men have only just been studying psychiatry and passing examinations! Where does their monstrous ignorance come from? They have no ideas about psychiatry."

For the first time in his life he felt insulted and angry.

Towards evening Mikhail Averyanitch came to see him. Without a word of greeting, the postmaster went up to him took him by both hands, and said in an agitated voice:

"My dear friend, my dear friend, let me see that you believe in my sincere affection for you. Reward me as your friend!" And preventing Andréi Yéfimitch saying a word, he continued in extreme agitation: "You know that I love you for the culture and nobility of your mind. Listen to me, like a good man! The rules of their profession compel the doctors to hide the truth from you, but I, in soldier style, will tell it to you flatly. You are unwell! Excuse me, old friend, but that is the plain truth, and it has been noticed by everyone around you. Only this moment Doctor Yevgénii Feódoritch said that for the benefit of your health you needed rest and recreation. It is entirely true! And things fit in admirably. In a few days I will take my leave, and go off for change of air. Prove to me that you are my friend, and come with me. Come!"

"I feel very well," said Andréi Yéfimitch, after a moment's thought; "and I cannot go. Allow me to prove my friendship in some other way."

To go away without any good reason, without his books, without Dáryushka, without beer—suddenly to destroy the order of life observed for twenty years —when he first thought of it, the project seemed wild and fantastic. But he remembered the talk in the Town Hall, and the torments which he had suffered on the way home; and the idea of leaving for a short time a town where stupid men considered him mad, delighted him.

"But where do you intend to go?" he asked.

"To Moscow, to Petersburg, to Warsaw. . . . In Warsaw I spent some of the happiest days of my life. An astonishing city! Come!"

CHAPTER XIII

WHICH MAD?

A WEEK after this conversation, Andréi Yéfimitch received a formal proposal to take a rest, that is, to retire from his post, and he received the proposal with indifference. Still a week later, he and Mikhail Averyanitch were sitting in the post tarantass and driving to the railway station. The weather was cool and clear, the sky blue and transparent. The two hundred versts were traversed in two days and two nights. When they stopped at the post-houses and were given dirty glasses for tea, or were delayed over the horses, Mikhail Averyanitch grew purple, shook all over, and roared "Silence! Don't argue!" . . . And as they sat in the tarantass he talked incessantly of his travels in the Caucasus and in Poland. What adventures he had, what meetings! He spoke in a loud voice, and all the time made such astonished eyes that it might have been thought he was lying. As he told his stories he breathed in the doctor's face and laughed in his ear. All this incommoded the doctor and hindered his thinking and concentrating his mind.

For reasons of economy they travelled as third-class, in a non-smoking carriage. Half of the passengers were clean. Mikhail Averyanitch struck up acquaintance with all, and as he shifted from seat to seat, announced in a loud voice that it was a mistake to travel on these tormenting r a i l w a y s. Nothing but rascals around! What a different thing to ride on horseback; in a single day you cover a hundred versts, and at the end feel wholesome and fresh. Yes, and we had been cursed with famines as the result of the draining of the Pinsky marshes! Everywhere nothing but disorder! Mikhail Averyanitch lost his temper, spoke loudly, and allowed no one else to say a word. His incessant chatter, broken only by loud laughter and expressive gesticulations, bored Andréi Yéfimitch.

"Which of us is the more mad?" he asked himself. "I who do my best not to disturb my fellow-travellers, or this egoist who thinks he is cleverer and more interesting than anyone else, and gives no one a moment's rest?"

In Moscow, Mikhail Averyanitch donned his military tunic without shoulder-straps, and trousers with red piping. Out of doors he wore an army forage-cap and cloak, and was saluted by the soldiers. To Andréi Yéfimitch he began to seem a man who had lost all the good points of the upper classes and retained only the bad. He loved people to dance attendance on him even when it was quite unnecessary. Matches lay before him on the table and he saw them, yet he roared to the waiter to hand them to him; he marched about in his underclothing before the chambermaid; he addressed the waitresses— even the elderly ones—indiscriminately as "thou," and when he was irritated called them blockheads and fools. This, thought Andréi Yéfimitch, is no doubt gentlemanly, but it is detestable.

First of all, Mikhail Averyanitch brought his friend to the Iverskaya. He prayed piously, bowed to the ground, shed tears, and when he had finished, sighed deeply and said:

"Even an unbeliever feels himself at peace after he has prayed. Kiss the image, dear!"

Andréi Yéfimitch got red in the face and kissed the image; and Mikhail Averyanitch puffed out his lips, shook his head, prayed in a whisper; and again into his eyes came tears. After this they visited the Kremlin and inspected the Tsar-Cannon and the Tsar-Bell, touched them with their fingers, admired the view across the Moscow River, and spent some time in the Temple of the Saviour and afterwards in the Rumiantseff Museum.

They dined at Testoff's. Mikhail Averyanitch stroked his whiskers, gazed long at the *menu*, and said to the waiter in the tone of a gourmet who feels at home in restaurants:

"We'll see what you'll feed us with to-day, angel!"

CHAPTER XIV
HONOUR BEFORE EVERYTHING

THE doctor walked and drank and ate and inspected, but his feelings remained unchanged; he was vexed with Mikhail Averyanitch. He longed to get a rest from his companion, to escape from him, but the postmaster considered it his duty not to let him out of his sight, and to see that he tasted every possible form of recreation. For two days Andréi Yéfimitch endured it, but on the third declared that he was unwell, and would remain all day at home.

Mikhail Averyanitch said that in that case he also would remain at home. And indeed, he added, a rest was necessary, otherwise they would have no strength left. Andréi Yéfimitch lay on the sofa with his face to the wall, and with clenched teeth listened to his friend, who assured him that France would sooner or later inevitably destroy Germany, that in Moscow there are a great many swindlers, and that you cannot judge of the merits of a horse by its appearance. The doctor's heart throbbed, his ears hummed, but from motives of delicacy he could not ask his friend to leave him alone or be silent. But happily Mikhail Averyanitch grew tired of sitting in the room, and after dinner went for a walk.

Left alone, Andréi Yéfimitch surrendered himself to the feeling of rest. How delightful it was to lie motionless on the sofa and know that he was alone in the room! Without solitude true happiness was impossible. The fallen angel was faithless to God probably only because he longed for solitude, which angels knew not. Andréi Yéfimitch wished to reflect upon what he had seen and heard in the last few days. But he could not drive Mikhail Averyanitch out of his mind.

"But then he obtained leave and came with me purely out of friendship and generosity," he thought with vexation. "Yet there is nothing more detestable than his maternal care. He is good and generous and a gay companion—but tiresome! Intolerably tiresome! He is one of those men who say only clever things, yet you cannot help feeling that they are stupid at bottom."

Next day Andréi Yéfimitch said he was still ill, and remained in his room.

He lay with his face to the back of the sofa, was bored when he was listening to conversation, and happy only when he was left alone. He was angry with himself for leaving home, he was angry with Mikhail Averyanitch, who every day became more garrulous and free-making; to concentrate his thoughts on a serious, elevated plane he failed utterly.

"I am now being tested by the realities of which Iván Dmítritch spoke," he thought, angered at his own pettiness. "But this is nothing . . . I will go home, and things will be as before."

In St. Petersburg the incidents of Moscow were repeated; whole days he never left his room, but lay on the sofa, and rose only when he wanted to drink beer.

All the time, Mikhail Averyanitch was in a great hurry to get to Warsaw

"My dear friend, why must I go there?" asked Andréi Yéfimitch imploringly. "Go yourself, and let me go home. I beg you!"

"Not for a million!" protested Mikhail Averyanitch. "It is an astonishing city! In Warsaw I spent the happiest days of my life."

Andréi Yéfimitch had not the character to persist, and with a twinge of pain accompanied his friend to Warsaw. When he got there he stayed all day in the hotel, lay on the sofa, and was angry with himself, and with the waiters who stubbornly refused to understand Russian. Mikhail Averyanitch, healthy, gay, and active as ever, drove from morning to night about the city and sought out his old acquaintances. Several nights he stayed out altogether. After one of these nights, spent it is uncertain where, he returned early in the morning, dishevelled and excited. For a long time he walked up and down the room, and at last stopped and exclaimed:

"Honour before everything!"

Again he walked up and down the room, seized his head in his hands, and declaimed tragically:

"Yes! Honour before everything! Cursed be the hour when it entered my head to come near this Babylon! . . . My dear friend," he turned to Andréi Yéfimitch, "I have lost heavily at cards. Lend me five hundred roubles!"

Andréi Yéfimitch counted the money, and gave it silently to his friend. Mikhail Averyanitch, purple from shame and indignation, cursed incoherently and needlessly, put on his cap, and went out. After two hours' absence he returned, threw himself into an armchair, sighed loudly, and said:

"Honour is saved! Let us go away, my friend! Not another minute will I rest in this accursed city! They are all scoundrels! . . . Austrian spies!"

When the travellers returned it was the beginning of November, and the streets were covered with snow. Doctor Khobótoff occupied Andréi Yéfimitch's position at the hospital, but lived at his own rooms, waiting until Andréi Yéfimitch returned and gave up the official quarters. The ugly woman whom he called his cook already lived in one of the wings.

Fresh scandals in connection with the hospital were being circulated in the town. It was said that the ugly woman had quarrelled with the superintendent, who had gone down before her on his knees and begged forgiveness. On the day of his return Andréi Yéfimitch had to look for new lodgings.

"My friend," began the postmaster timidly, "forgive the indelicate question, what money have you got?"

Andréi Yéfimitch silently counted his money, and said:

"Eighty-six roubles."

"You don't understand me," said Mikhail Averyanitch in confusion. "I ask what means have you—generally?"

"I have told you already—eighty-six roubles. . . . Beyond that I have nothing."

Mikhail Averyanitch was well aware that the doctor was an honest and straightforward man. But he believed that he had at least twenty thousand roubles in capital. Now learning that his friend was a beggar and had nothing to live on, he began to cry, and embraced him.

CHAPTER XV

PENNILESS

ANDREI YEFIMITCH migrated to the three-windowed house of Madame Byelof, a woman belonging to the petty trading class. In this house were only three rooms and a kitchen. Of these rooms two, with windows opening on the street, were occupied by the doctor, while in the third and in the kitchen lived Dáryushka, the landlady, and three children. Occasionally the number was added to by a drunken workman, Madame Byelof's lover, who made scenes at night and terrified Dáryushka and the children. When he came, sat in the kitchen, and demanded vodka, the others were crowded out, and the doctor in compassion took the crying children to his own room, and put them to sleep on the floor. This always gave him great satisfaction.

As before, he rose at eight o'clock,

took his breakfast, and sat down and read his old books and reviews. For new books he had no money. But whether it was because the books were old or because the surroundings were changed, reading no longer interested him, and even tired him. So to pass the time he compiled a detailed catalogue of his books, and pasted labels on the backs; and this mechanical work seemed to him much more interesting than reading. The more monotonous and trifling the occupation the more it calmed his mind, he thought of nothing, and time passed quickly. Even to sit in the kitchen and peel potatoes with Dáryushka or to pick the dirt out of buckwheat meal interested him. On Saturdays and Sundays he went to church. Standing at the wall, he blinked his eyes, listened to the singing, and thought of his father, his mother, the university, religion; he felt calm and melancholy, and when leaving the church, regretted that the service had not lasted longer.

Twice he visited the hospital for the purpose of seeing Iván Dmítritch. But on both occasions Gromof was unusually angry and excited; he asked to be left in peace, declared that he had long ago wearied of empty chatter, and that he would regard solitary confinement as a deliverance from these accursed, base people. Was it possible they would refuse him that? When Andréi Yéfimitch took leave of him and wished him good night, he snapped and said: "Take yourself to the devil!"

And Andréi Yéfimitch felt undecided as to whether he should go a third time or not. But he wished to go.

In the old times Andréi Yéfimitch had been in the habit of spending the time after dinner in walking about his rooms and thinking. But now from dinner to tea-time he lay on the sofa with his face to the wall and surrendered himself to trivial thoughts, which he found himself unable to conquer. He considered himself injured by the fact that after twenty years' service he had been given neither a pension nor a grant. True he had not done his duties honestly, but then were not pensions given to all old servants indiscriminately, without regard to their honesty or otherwise? Modern ideas did not regard rank, orders, and pensions as the reward of moral perfection or capacity, and why must he alone be the exception? He was absolutely penniless. He was ashamed to pass the shop where he dealt or to meet the proprietor. For beer alone he was in debt thirty-two roubles. He was in debt also to his landlady. Dáryushka secretly sold old clothing and books, and lied to the landlady, declaring that her master was about to come into a lot of money.

Andréi Yéfimitch was angry with himself for having wasted on his journey the thousand roubles which he had saved. What could he not do with a thousand roubles now? He was annoyed, also, because others would not leave him alone. Khobótoff considered it his duty to pay periodical visits to his sick colleague; and everything about him was repulsive to Andréi Yéfimitch —his sated face, his condescending bad manners, the word "colleague," and the high boots. But the greatest annoyance of all was that he considered it his duty to cure Andréi Yéfimitch, and even imagined he was curing him. On every occasion he brought a phial of bromide of potassium and a rhubarb pill.

Mikhail Averyanitch also considered it his duty to visit his sick friend and amuse him. He entered the room with affected freeness, laughed unnaturally, and assured Andréi Yéfimitch that to-day he looked splendid, and that, glory be to God! he was getting all right. From this alone it might be concluded that he regarded the case as hopeless. He had not yet paid off the Warsaw debt, and being ashamed of himself and constrained, he laughed all the louder, and told ridiculous anecdotes. His stories now seemed endless, and were a source of torment both to Andréi Yéfimitch and to himself.

When the postmaster was present, Andréi Yéfimitch usually lay on the sofa, his face turned to the wall, with clenched teeth, listening. It seemed to him that a crust was forming about his heart, and after every visit he felt the crust becoming thicker, and threatening to extend to his throat. To exorcise these trivial afflictions he reflected that he. and Khobótoff, and Mikhail Averyanitch would, sooner or later, perish, leaving behind themselves not a trace. When a million years had passed by, a spirit flying through space would see only a frozen globe and naked stones. All — culture and morals — everything would pass away; even the burdock would not grow. Why, then, should he trouble himself with feelings of shame on account of a shopkeeper, of insignificant Khobótoff, of the terrible friendship of Mikhail Averyanitch. It was all folly and vanity.

But such reasoning did not console him. He had hardly succeeded in painting a vivid picture of the frozen globe after a million years of decay, when from behind a naked rock appeared Khobótoff in his top-boots, and beside him stood Mikhail Averyanitch, with an affected laugh, and a shamefaced whisper on his lips: "And the Warsaw debt, old man, I will repay in a few days . . . without fail!"

CHAPTER XVI

AN INTERESTING CASE

MIKHAIL AVERYANITCH arrived after dinner one evening when Andréi Yéfimitch was lying on the sofa. At the same time came Khobótoff with his bromide of potassium. Andréi Yéfimitch rose slowly, sat down again, and supported himself by resting his hands upon the sofa edge.

"To-day, my dear," began Mikhail Averyanitch, "to-day your complexion is much healthier than yesterday. You are a hero! I swear to God, a hero!"

"It's time, indeed it's time for you to recover, colleague," said Khobótoff. yawning. "You must be tired of the delay yourself."

"Never mind, we'll soon be all right," said Mikhail Averyanitch gaily. "Why, we'll live for another hundred years! Eh?"

"Perhaps not a hundred, but a safe twenty," said Khobótoff consolingly. "Don't worry, colleague, don't worry!"

"We'll let them see!" laughed Mikhail Averyanitch, slapping his friend on the knee. "We'll show how the trick is done! Next summer, with God's will, we'll fly away to the Caucasus, and gallop all over the country—trot, trot, trot! And when we come back from the Caucasus we'll dance at your wedding!" Mikhail Averyanitch winked slyly. "We'll marry you, my friend, we'll find the bride!"

Andréi Yéfimitch felt that the crust had risen to his throat. His heart beat painfully.

"This is absurd," he said, rising suddenly and going over to the window. "Is it possible you don't understand that you are talking nonsense?"

He wished to speak to his visitors softly and politely, but could not restrain himself, and, against his own will, clenched his fists, and raised them threateningly above his head.

"Leave me!" he cried, in a voice which was not his own. His face was purple and he trembled all over. "Begone! Both of you! Go!"

Mikhail Averyanitch and Khobótoff rose, and looked at him, at first in astonishment, then in terror.

"Begone both of you!" continued Andréi Yéfimitch. "Stupid idiots! Fools! I want neither your friendship nor your medicines, idiots! This is base, it is abominable!"

Khobótoff and the postmaster exchanged confused glances, staggered to the door, and went into the hall. Andréi Yéfimitch seized the phial of bromide of potassium, and flung it after them, breaking it upon the threshold.

"Take yourselves to the devil!" he cried, running after them into the hall. "To the devil!"

After his visitors had gone he lay on the sofa, trembling as if in fever, and repeated—

"Stupid idiots! Dull fools!"

When he calmed down, the first thought that entered his head was that poor Mikhail Averyanitch must now be terribly ashamed and wretched, and that the scene that had passed was something very terrible. Nothing of the kind had ever happened before. What had become of his intellect and tact? Where were now his understanding of the world and his philosophical indifference?

All night the doctor was kept awake by feelings of shame and vexation. At nine o'clock next morning, he went to the post office and apologized to the postmaster.

"Do not refer to what happened!" said the postmaster, with a sigh. Touched by Andréi Yéfimitch's conduct, he pressed his hands warmly. "No man should trouble over such trifles. . . . Lubiakin!" he roared so loudly that the clerks and visitors trembled. "Bring a chair! . . . And you just wait!" he cried to a peasant woman, who held a registered letter through the grating. "Don't you see that I am engaged? . . . We will forget all that," he continued tenderly, turning to Andréi Yéfimitch. "Sit down, my old friend!"

He stroked his eyebrows silently for a minute, and continued:

"It never entered my head to take offence. Illness is a very strange thing, I understand that. Yesterday your fit frightened both the doctor and myself, and we talked of you for a long time. My dear friend, why will you not pay more attention to your complaint? Do you think you can go on living in this way? Forgive the plain speaking of a friend." He dropped his voice to a whisper. "But you live among hopeless surroundings—closeness, uncleanliness, no one to look after you, nothing to take for your ailment. . . . My dear friend, both I and the doctor implore you with all our hearts—listen to our advice—go into the hospital. There you will get wholesome food, care and treatment. Yevgénïi Feódoritch—although, between ourselves, *de mauvais ton*—is a capable man, and you can fully rely upon him. He gave me his word that he would take care of you."

Andréi Yéfimitch was touched by the sincere concern of his friend, and the tears that trickled down the postmaster's cheeks.

"My dear friend, don't believe them! he whispered, laying his hand upon his heart. "It is all a delusion. My complaint lies merely in this, that in twenty years I found in this town only one intelligent man, and he was a lunatic. I suffer from no disease whatever; my misfortune is that I have fallen into a magic circle from which there is no escape. It is all the same to me—I am ready for anything."

"Then you will go into some hospital?"

"It is all the same—even into the pit."

"Give me your word, friend, that you will obey Yevgénïi Feódoritch in everything."

"I give you my word. But I repeat that I have fallen into a magic circle. Everything now, even the sincere concern of my friends, tends only to the same thing—to my destruction. 1 am perishing, and I have the courage to acknowledge it."

"Nonsense, you will get all right!"

"What is the use of talking like hat?" said Andréi Yéfimitch irritably. "There are few men who at the close of their lives do not experience what I am experiencing now. When people tell you that you have disease of the kidneys or a dilated heart, and set about to cure you; when they tell you that you are a madman or a criminal—in one word, when they begin to turn their attention on to you—you may recognize that you are in a magic circle from which there is no escape. You may try to escape, but that makes things worse. Give in, for no human efforts will save you. So it seems to me."

All this time, people were gathering at the grating. Andréi Yéfimitch disliked interrupting the postmaster's work, and took his leave. Mikhail Averyanitch once more made him give his word of honour, and escorted him to the door.

The same day towards evening Khobótoff, in his short fur coat and high boots, arrived unexpectedly, and, as if nothing had happened the day before, said:

"I have come to you on a matter of business, colleague. I want you to come with me to a consultation. Eh?"

Thinking that Khobótoff wanted to amuse him with a walk, or give him some opportunity of earning money, Andréi Yéfimitch dressed, and went with him into the street. He was glad of the chance to redeem his rudeness of the day before, thankful for the apparent reconciliation, and grateful of Khobótoff for not hinting at the incident. From this uncultured man who would have expected such delicacy?

"And where is your patient?" asked Andréi Yéfimitch.

"At the hospital. For a long time past I have wanted you to see him. . . . A most interesting case."

They entered the hospital yard, and passing through the main building, went to the wing where the lunatics were confined. When they entered the hall, Nikita as usual jumped up and stretched himself.

"One of them has such strange complications in the lungs," whispered Khobótoff as he entered the ward with Andréi Yéfimitch. "But wait here. I shall be back immediately. I must get my stethoscope."

And he left the room.

CHAPTER XVII

COLD SWEAT

It was already twilight. Iván Dmítritch lay on his bed with his face buried in the pillow; the paralytic sat motionless, and wept softly and twitched his lips; the fat muzhik and the ex-sorter slept. It was very quiet.

Andréi Yéfimitch sat on Iván Dmítritch's bed and listened. Half an hour passed by, but Khobótoff did not come. Instead of Khobótoff came Nikita carrying in his arm a dressing-gown, some linen, and a pair of slippers.

"Please to put on these, your honour," he said calmly. "There is your bed, this way, please," he added, pointing at a vacant bed, evidently only just set up. "And don't take on; with God's will you will soon be well!"

Andréi Yéfimitch understood. Without a word he walked over to the bed indicated by Nikita and sat upon it. Then, seeing that Nikita was waiting, he stripped himself and felt ashamed. He put on the hospital clothing; the flannels were too small, the shirt was too long, and the dressing-gown smelt of smoked fish.

"You will soon be all right, God grant it!" repeated Nikita.

He took up Andréi Yéfimitch's clothes, went out, and locked the door.

"It is all the same," thought Andréi Yéfimitch, shamefacedly gathering the dressing-gown around him, and feeling like a convict in his new garments. "It is all the same. In dress clothes, in uniform . . . or in this dressing-gown."

But his watch? And the memorandum book in his side pocket? And the cigarettes? Where had Nikita taken his clothes? To the day of his death he would never again wear trousers, a waistcoat, or boots. It was strange and incredible at first. Andréi Yéfimitch was firmly convinced that there was no difference whatever between Madame Byeloff's house and Ward No. 6, and that all in this world is folly and vanity; but he could not prevent his hands trembling, and his feet were cold. He was hurt, too, by the thought that Iván Dmítritch would rise and see him in the dressing-gown. He rose, walked up and down the room, and again sat down.

He remained sitting for half an hour, weary to the point of grief. Would it be possible to live here a day, a week, even years, as these others had done? He must sit down, and walk about and again sit down; and then he might look out of the window, and again walk from end to end of the room. And afterwards? Just to sit all day still as an idol, and think! No, it was impossible.

Andréi Yéfimitch lay down on his bed, but almost immediately rose, rubbed with his cuff the cold sweat from his forehead, and felt that his whole face smelt of dried fish. He walked up and down the ward.

"This is some misunderstanding . . ." he said, opening his arms. "It only needs an explanation, it is a misunderstanding. . . ."

At this moment Iván Dmítritch awoke. He sat up in bed, rested his head and his hands, and spat. Then he looked idly at the doctor, apparently at first understanding nothing. But soon his sleepy face grew contemptuous and malícious.

"So they have brought you here, my friend," he began in a voice hoarse from sleep. He blinked one eye. "I am very glad! You drank other men's blood, and now they will drink yours! Admirable!"

"It is some misunderstanding . . ." began Andréi Yéfimitch, frightened by the lunatic's words. He shrugged his shoulders and repeated. "It is a misunderstanding . . . of some kind."

Iván Dmítritch again spat, and lay down on his bed.

"Accursed life!" he growled. "But what is most bitter, most abominable of all, is that this life ends not with rewards for suffering, not with apotheoses as in operas, but in death; men come and drag the corpse by its arms and legs into the cellar. Brrrrrr! . . . Well, never mind! . . . For all that we have suffered in this, in the other world we will be repaid with a holiday! From the other world I shall return hither as a shadow, and terrify these monsters! . . . I will turn their heads grey!"

Moséika entered the ward, and seeing the doctor, stretched out his hand, and said:

"Give me a kopeck!"

CHAPTER XVIII

OPEN! I DEMAND IT!

ANDREI YEFIMITCH went across to the window, and looked out into the fields. It was getting dark, and on the horizon rose a cold, livid moon. Near the hospital railings, a hundred fathoms away, not more, rose a lofty, white building, surrounded by a stone wall. It was the prison.

"That is actuality," thought Andréi Yéfimitch, and he felt terrified.

Everything was terrible: the moon, the prison, the spikes in the fence, and the blaze in the distant bonemill. Andréi Yéfimitch turned away from the window, and saw before him a man with glittering stars and orders upon his breast. The man smiled and winked cunningly. And this, too, seemed terrible.

He tried to assure himself that in the moon and in the prison there was nothing peculiar at all, that even sane men wear orders, and that the best of things in their turn rot and turn into dust. But despair suddenly seized him, he took hold of the grating with both hands, and jerked it with all his strength. But the bars stood firm.

That it might be less terrible, he went to Iván Dmítritch's bed, and sat upon it.

"I have lost my spirits, friend," he said, stammering, trembling, and rubbing the cold sweat from his face. "My spirits have fallen."

"But why don't you philosophise?" asked Iván Dmítritch ironically.

"My God, my God! . . . Yes, yes! . . . Once you said that in Russia there is no philosophy; but all philosophise, even triflers. But the philosophising of triflers does no harm to anyone," said Andréi Yéfimitch as if he wanted to cry. "But why, my dear friend, why this malicious laughter? Why should not triflers philosophise if they are not satisfied? For a clever, cultivated, proud, freedom-loving man, built in the image of God, there is no course left but to come as doctor to a dirty, stupid town, and lead a life of jars, leeches, and gallipots. Charlatanry, narrowness, baseness! Oh, my God!"

"You chatter nonsense! If you didn't want to be a doctor, why weren't you a minister of state?"

"I could not. We are weak, my friend. I was indifferent to things, I reasoned actively and wholesomely, but it needed but the first touch of actuality to make me lose heart, and surrender. . . . We are weak, we are worthless! . . . And you also, my friend. You are able, you are noble, with your mother's milk you drank in draughts of happiness, yet hardly had you entered upon life when you wearied of it. . . . We are weak, weak!"

In addition to terror and the feeling of insult, Andréi Yéfimitch had been tortured by some importunate craving ever since the approach of evening. Finally he came to the conclusion that he wanted to smoke and drink beer.

"I am going out, my friend," he said. "I will tell them to bring lights. . . . I cannot in this way. . . . I am not in a state. . . ."

He went to the door and opened it, but immediately Nikita jumped up and barred the way.

"Where are you going to? You can't, you can't!" he cried. "It's time for bed!"

"But only for a minute. . . . I want to go into the yard. . . . I want to have a walk in the yard," said Andréi Yéfimitch.

"You can't. I have orders against it. . . . You know yourself."

Nikita banged the door and set his back against it.

"But if I go out what harm will it do?" asked Andréi Yéfimitch. "I don't understand! Nikita, I must go out!" he cried in a trembling voice. "I must go!"

"Don't create disorder; it is not right!" said Nitkita in an edifying tone.

"The devil knows what is the meaning of this!" suddenly screamed Iván Dmítritch, jumping from his bed. "What right has he to refuse to let us go? How dare they keep us here? The law allows no man to be deprived of freedom without a trial! This is violence . . . tyranny!"

"Of course it is tyranny," said Andréi Yéfimitch, encouraging Gromof. "I must go! I have to go out! He has no right! Let me out, I tell you!"

"Do you hear, stupid dog!" screamed Iván Dmítritch, thumping the door with his fists. "Open, or I will smash the door! Blood-sucker!"

"Open!" cried Andréi Yéfimitch, trembling all over. "I demand it!"

"Talk away!" answered Nikita through the door. "Talk away!"

"Go, then, for Yevgénii Feódoritch! Say that I ask him to come . . . For a minute!"

"To-morrow he will come all right."

"They will never let us go!" cried Iván Dmítritch. "We will all die here! Oh, God is it possible that in the other world there is no hell, that these villains will be forgiven? Where is there justice? Open, scoundrel, I am choking!" Gromof cried out in a hoarse voice, and flung himself against the door. "I will dash my brains out! Assassins!"

Nikita flung open the door, and with both hands and his knees roughly pushed Andréi Yéfimitch back into the room, and struck him with his clenched fist full in the face. It seemed to Andréi Yéfimitch that a great salt wave had suddenly dashed upon his head and flung him upon his bed; in his mouth was a taste of salt, and the blood seemed to burst from his gums. As if trying to swim away from the wave, he flourished his arms and seized the bedstead. But at this moment Nikita struck him again and again in the back.

Iván Dmítritch screamed loudly. He also had evidently been beaten.

Then all was quiet. Liquid moonlight poured through between the iron bars, and on the floor lay a network shadow. All were terrified. Andréi Yéfimitch lay on the bed and held his breath in terror, awaiting another blow.

It seemed as if someone had taken a sickle, thrust it into his chest and turned it around. In his agony he bit his pillow and ground his teeth, and suddenly into his head amid the chaos flashed the intolerable thought that such misery had been borne year after year by these helpless men who now lay in the moonlight like black shadows about him. In twenty years he had never known of it, and never wanted to know. He did not know, he had no idea of their wretchedness, therefore he was not guilty; but conscience, as rude and unaccommodating as Nikita's fists, sent an icy·thrill through him from head to foot. He jumped from his bed and tried to scream with all his might, to fly from the ward and kill Nikita, and Khobótoff, and the superintendent, and the feldscher, and himself. But not a sound came from his throat, his feet rebelled against him, he panted, he tore his gown and shirt, and fell insensible on the bed.

CHAPTER XIX

A GREEN FILM

NEXT morning his head ached, his ears hummed, and he was weak. The memory of his weakness on the day before made him feel ashamed. Yesterday he had shown a petty spirit, he had feared even the moon, and honestly expressed feelings and thoughts which he had never suspected could exist in himself. For instance, the thought about the discontent of philosophic triflers. But now he was quite indifferent.

He neither ate nor drank, but lay motionless and silent.

"It is all the same to me," he thought when he was questioned. "I shall not answer . . . It is all the same. . . ."

After dinner Mikhail Averyanitch brought him a quarter of a pound of tea and a pound of marmalade. Dáryushka also came, and for a whole hour stood beside the bed with a dull expression of uncomprehending affliction. Doctor Khobótoff also paid him a visit. He brought a phial of bromide of potassium, and ordered Nikita to fumigate the ward.

Towards evening Andréi Yéfimitch died from an apoplectic stroke. At first he felt chill, and sickness; something loathsome like rotting sour cabbage or bad eggs seemed to permeate his whole body even to his fingers, to extend from his stomach to his head, and to flow in his eyes and ears. A green film appeared before his eyes. Andréi Yéfimitch realised that his hour had come; and remembered that Iván Dmítritch, Mikhail Averyanitch, and millions of others believed in immortality. But immortality he did not desire, and thought of it only for a moment. A herd of antelopes, extraordinarily beautiful and graceful, of which he had been reading the day before, rushed past him; then a woman stretched out to him a hand holding a registered letter. . . . Mikhail Averyanitch said something. Then all vanished and Andréi Yéfimitch died.

The servants came in, took him by the shoulders and legs, and carried him to the chapel. There he lay on a table with open eyes, and at night the moon shown down upon him. In the morning came Sergéi Sergéyitch, piously prayed before a crucifix, and closed the eyes of his former chief.

Next day Andréi Yéfimitch was buried. Only Mikhail Averyanitch and Dáryushka were present at the funeral.

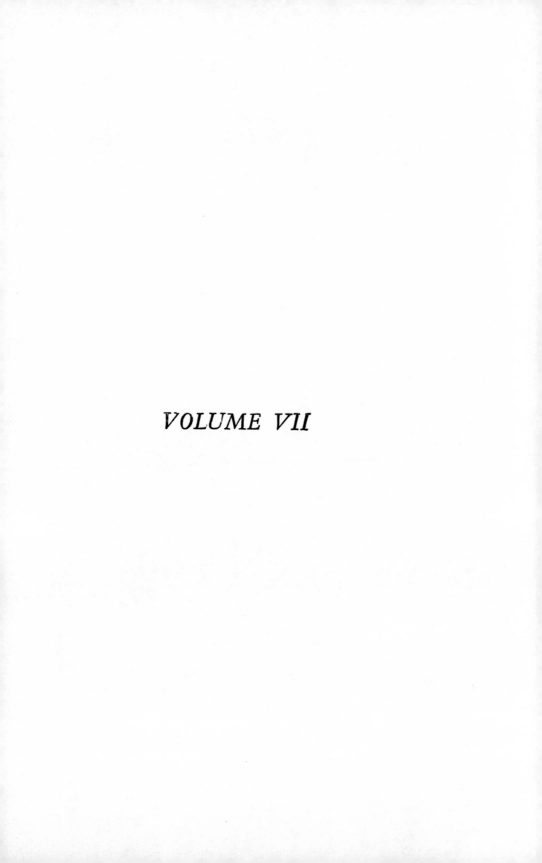

VOLUME VII

At Home

"GRIGORIEVITCH sent over for some book, but I said that you were out. The postman has brought the newspapers and two letters. And, Yevgénii Petróvitch, I must ask you to do something about Serózha. I caught him smoking the day before yesterday, and to-day. When I began to scold him, in his usual way he covered his ears, and roared so as to drown my voice."

Yevgénii Petróvitch Buikovsky, Procuror of the District Court, who had just returned from the Session House, looked for a moment at the governess and laughed:

"Serózha smoking! I can imagine that twig with a cigarette! How old is he?"

"Seven. Of course you may not take it seriously, but at his age smoking is a ruinous habit, and should be rooted out now."

"Very true. But where does he get the tobacco?"

"On your table."

"On my table! Ask him to come here."

When the governess left the room, Buikovsky sat in his armchair in front of his desk, shut his eyes, and began to think. He pictured in imagination his Serózha with a gigantic cigarette a yard long, surrounded by clouds of tobacco smoke. The caricature made him laugh in spite of himself; but at the same time the serious, worried face of his governess reminded him of a time, now long passed by, a half-forgotten time, when smoking in the schoolroom or nursery inspired in teachers and parents a strange and not quite comprehensible horror. No other word but horror would describe it. The culprits were mercilessly flogged, expelled from school, their lives marred, and this, although not one of the schoolmasters or parents could say what precisely constitutes the danger and guilt of smoking. Even very intelligent men did not hesitate to fight a vice which they did not understand. Yevgénii Petróvitch remembered the director of his own school, a benevolent and highly educated old man who was struck with such terror when he caught a boy with a cigarette that he became pale, immediately convoked an extraordinary council of masters, and condemned the offender to expulsion. Such indeed appears to be the law of life; the more intangible the evil the more fiercely and mercilessly is it combated.

The Procuror remembered two or three cases of expulsion, and recalling the subsequent lives of the victims, he could not but conclude that such punishment was often a much greater evil than the vice itself. . . . But the animal organism is gifted with capacity to adapt itself rapidly, to accustom itself to changes, to different atmospheres, otherwise every man would feel that his rational actions were based upon an irrational foundation, and that there was little reasoned truth and conviction even in such responsibilities — responsibilities terrible in their results—as those of the schoolmaster, and lawyer, the writer. . . .

427

And such thoughts, light and inconsequential, which enter only a tired and resting brain, wandered about in Yevgénïi Petróvitch's head; they spring no one knows where or why, vanish soon, and, it would seem, wander only on the outskirts of the brain without penetrating far. For men who are obliged for whole hours, even for whole days, to think official thoughts all in the same direction, such free, domestic speculations are an agreeable comfort.

It was nine o'clock. Overhead from the second story came the footfalls of someone walking from corner to corner; and still higher, on the third story, someone was playing scales. The footsteps of the man who, judging by his walk, was thinking tensely or suffering from toothache, and the monotonous scales in the evening stillness, combined to create a drowsy atmosphere favourable to idle thoughts. From the nursery came the voices of Serózha and his governess.

"Papa has come?" cried the boy. "Papa has co-o-me! Papa! papa!"

"*Votre père vous appelle, allez vite,*" cried the governess, piping like a frightened bird. . . . "Do you hear?"

"What shall I say to him?" thought Yevgénïi Petróvitch.

And before he had decided what to say, in came his son Serózha, a boy of seven years old. He was one of those little boys whose sex can be distinguished only by their clothes—weakly, pale-faced, delicate. . . . Everything about him seemed tender and soft; his movements, his curly hair, his looks, his velvet jacket.

"Good evening, papa," he began in a soft voice, climbing on his father's knee, and kissing his neck. "You wanted me?"

"Wait a minute, wait a minute, Sergéi Yevgénitch," answered the Procuror, pushing him off. "Before I allow you to kiss me I want to talk to you, and to talk seriously. . . . I am very angry with you, and do not love you any more . . . understand that, brother; I do not love you, and you are not my son. . . . No!"

Serózha looked earnestly at his father, turned his eyes on to the chair, and shrugged his shoulders.

"What have I done?" he asked in doubt, twitching his eyes. "I have not been in your study all day and touched nothing."

"Natálya Semiónovna has just been complaining to me that she caught you smoking. . . . Is it true? Do you smoke?"

"Yes, I smoked once, father. . . . It is true."

"There, you see, you tell lies also," said the Procuror, frowning, and trying at the same time to smother a smile. "Natálya Semiónovna saw you smoking twice. That is to say, you are found out in three acts of misconduct—you smoke, you take another person's tobacco, and you lie. Three faults!"

"Akh, yes," remembered Serózha, with smiling eyes. "It is true. I smoked twice—to-day and once before."

"That is to say you smoked not once but twice. I am very, very displeased with you! You used to be a good boy, but now I see you are spoiled and have become naughty."

Yevgénïi Petróvitch straightened Serózha's collar, and thought: "What else shall I say to him?"

"It is very bad," he continued. "I

did not expect this from you. In the first place you have no right to go to another person's table and take tobacco which does not belong to you. A man has a right to enjoy only his own property, and if he takes another's then . . . he is a wicked man." (This is not the way to go about it, thought the Procuror.) "For instance, Natálya Semiónovna has a boxful of dresses. That is her box, and we have not, that is neither you nor I have, any right to touch it, as it is not ours. . . . Isn't that plain? You have your horses and pictures . . . I do not take them. Perhaps I have often felt that I wanted to take them . . . but they are yours, not mine!"

"Please, father, take them if you like," said Serózha, raising his eyebrows. "Always take anything of mine, father. This yellow dog which is on your table is mine, but I don't mind. . . ."

"You don't understand me." said Buikovsky. "The dog you gave me, it is now mine, and I can do with it what I like; but the tobacco I did not give to you. The tobacco is mine." (How can I make him understand? thought the Procuror. Not in this way.) "If I feel that I want to smoke someone else's tobacco I first of all ask for permission. . . ."

And idly joining phrase to phrase, and imitating the language of children, Buikovsky began to explain what is meant by property. Serózha looked at his chest, and listened attentively (he loved to talk to his father in the evenings), then set his elbows on the table edge and began to concentrate his short-sighted eyes upon the papers and inkstand. His glance wandered around the table, and paused on a bottle of gum-arabic.

"Papa, what is gum made of?" he asked, suddenly lifting the bottle to his eyes.

Buikovsky took the bottle, put it back on the table, and continued:

"In the second place, you smoke. . . . That is very bad! If I smoke, then . . . it does not follow that everyone may. I smoke, and know . . . that it is not clever, and I scold myself, and do not love myself on account of it. . . ." (I am a nice teacher, thought the Procuror.) "Tobacco seriously injures the health, and people who smoke die sooner than they ought to. It is particularly injurious to little boys like you. You have a weak chest, you have not yet got strong, and in weak people tobacco smoke produces consumption and other complaints. Uncle Ignatius died of consumption. If he had not smoked perhaps he would have been alive to-day."

Serózha looked thoughtfully at the lamp, touched the shade with his fingers, and sighed.

"Uncle Ignatius played splendidly on the fiddle!" he said. "His fiddle is now at Grigorievitch's."

Serózha again set his elbows on the table and lost himself in thought. On his pale face was the expression of one who is listening intently or following the course of his own thoughts; sorrow and something like fright showed themselves in his big, staring eyes. Probably he was thinking of death, which had so lately carried away his mother and Uncle Ignatius. Death is a thing which carries away mothers and uncles and leaves on the earth only children and fiddles. Dead people live in the sky somewhere, near the stars, and thence look down upon the earth. How do they bear the separation?

"What shall I say to him?" asked the Procuror. "He is not listening. Apparently he thinks there is nothing serious either in his faults or in my arguments. How can I explain it to him?"

The Procuror rose and walked up and down the room.

"In my time these questions were decided very simply," he thought. "Every boy caught smoking was flogged. The cowards and babies, therefore, gave up smoking, but the brave and cunning bore their floggings, carried the tobacco in their boots and smoked in the stable. When they were caught in the stable and again flogged, they smoked on the river-bank . . . and so on until they were grown up. My own mother in order to keep me from smoking used to give me money and sweets. Nowadays all these methods are regarded as petty or immoral. Taking logic as his standpoint, the modern teacher tries to inspire in the child good principles not out of fear, not out of wish for distinction or reward, but consciously."

While he walked and talked, Serózha climbed on the chair next the table and began to draw. To prevent the destruction of business papers and the splashing of ink, his father had provided a packet of paper, cut especially for him, and a blue pencil.

"To-day the cook was chopping cabbage and cut her finger," he said, meantime sketching a house and twitching his eyebrows. "She cried so loud that we were all frightened and ran into the kitchen. Such a stupid! Natálya Semiónovna ordered her to bathe her finger in cold water, but she sucked it. . . . How could she put her dirty finger in her mouth! Papa, that is bad manners!"

He further told how during dinnertime an organ-grinder came into the yard with a little girl who sang and danced to his music.

"He has his own current of thoughts," thought the Procuror. "In his head he has a world of his own, and he knows better than anyone else what is serious and what is not. To gain his attention and conscience it is no use imitating his language . . . what is wanted is to understand and reason also in his manner. He would understand me perfectly if I really disliked tobacco, if I were angry, or cried. . . . For that reason mothers are irreplacable in bringing up children, for they alone can feel and cry and laugh like children. . . . With logic and morals nothing can be done. What shall I say to him?"

And Yevgénii Petróvitch found it strange and absurd that he, an experienced jurist, half his life struggling with all kinds of interruptions, prejudices, and punishments, was absolutely at a loss for something to say to his son.

"Listen, give me your word of honour that you will not smoke!" he said.

"Word of honour!" drawled Serózha, pressing hard on his pencil and bending down to the sketch. "Word of honour!"

"But has he any idea what 'word of honour' means?" Buikovsky asked himself. "No, I am a bad teacher! If a schoolmaster or any of our lawyers were to see me now, he would call me a rag, and suspect me of super-subtlety. . . . But in school and in court all these stupid problems are decided much more simply than at home when you are dealing with those whom you love. Love is exacting and complicates the business. If this boy were not my son, but a pupil or a prisoner at the bar, I should not be such a coward and scatter-brains. . . ."

Yevgénii Petróvitch sat at the table and took up one of Serózha's sketches. It depicted a house with a crooked roof, and smoke which, like lightning, zig-zagged from the chimney to the edge of the paper; beside the house stood a soldier with dots for eyes, and a bay-onet shaped like a figure four.

"A man cannot be taller than a house," said the Procuror. "Look! the roof of your house only goes up to the soldier's shoulder."

Serózha climbed on his father's knee, and wriggled for a long time before he felt comfortable.

"No, papa," he said, looking at the drawing. "If you drew the soldier smaller you wouldn't be able to see his eyes."

Was it necessary to argue? From daily observation the Procuror had be-come convinced that children, like savages, have their own artistic outlook, and their own requirments, inaccessible to the understanding of adults. Under close observation Serózha to an adult seemed abnormal. He found it possible and reasonable to draw men taller than houses, and to express with the pencil not only objects but also his own senti-ments. Thus, the sound of an orchestra he drew as a round, smoky spot; whistling as a spiral thread. . . . Ac-cording to his ideas, sounds were closely allied with forms and colour, and when painting letters he always coloured L yellow, M red, A black, and so on.

Throwing away his sketch, Serózha again wriggled, settled himself more comfortably, and occupied himself with his father's beard. First he carefully smoothed it down, then divided it in two, and arranged it to look like whiskers.

"Now you are like Iván Stepáno-vitch," he muttered; "but wait, in a minute you will be like . . . like the porter. Papa, why do porters stand in doorways? Is it to keep out robbers?"

The Procuror felt on his face the child's breath, touched with his cheek the child's hair. In his heart rose a sudden feeling of warmth and softness, a softness that made it seem that not only his hands but all his soul lay upon the velvet of Serózha's coat. He looked into the great, dark eyes of his child, and it seemed to him that out of their big pupils looked at him his mother, and his wife, and all whom he had ever loved.

"What is the good of thrashing him?" he asked. "Punishment is . . . and why turn myself into a schoolmaster? . . . Formerly men were simple; they thought less, and solved problems bravely. . . . Now, we think too much; logic has eaten us up. . . . The more cultivated a man, the more he thinks, the more he surrenders himself to sub-tleties, the less firm is his will, the greater his timidity in the face of affairs. And, indeed, if you look into it, what a lot of courage and faith in one's self does it need to teach a child, to judge a criminal, to write a big book. . . ."

The clock struck ten.

"Now, child, time for bed," said the Procuror. "Say good night, and go."

"No, papa," frowned Serózha. "I may stay a little longer. Talk to me about something. Tell me a story."

"I will, only after the story you must go straight to bed."

Yevgénii Petróvitch sometimes spent his free evenings telling Serózha stories. Like most men of affairs he could not repeat by heart a single verse or remember a single fairy tale; and every time was obliged to improvise. As a rule he began with the jingle, "Once upon a time, and a very good time it was," and followed this up with all kinds of innocent nonsense, at the beginning having not the slightest idea of what would be the middle and the end. Scenery, characters, situations all came at hazard, and fable and moral flowed out by themselves without regard to the teller's will. Serózha dearly loved these improvisations, and the Procuror noticed that the simpler and less pretentious the plots, the more they affected the child.

"Listen," he began, raising his eyes to the ceiling. "Once upon a time, and a very good time it was, there lived an old, a very, very old tsar, with a long grey beard, and . . . this kind of mustaches. Well! He lived in a glass palace which shone and sparkled in the sun like a big lump of clean ice. . . . The palace . . . brother mine . . . the palace stood in a great garden where, you know, grew oranges . . . pears, cherry trees . . . and blossomed tulips, roses, water lilies . . . and birds of different colours sang. . . . Yes. . . . On the trees hung glass bells which, when the breeze blew, sounded so musically that it was a joy to listen. Glass gives out a softer and more tender sound than metal. . . . Well? Where was I? In the garden were fountains. . . . You remember you saw a fountain in the country, at Aunt Sonia's. Just the same kind

of fountains stood in the king's garden, only they were much bigger, and the jets of water rose as high as the tops of the tallest poplars."

Yevgénii Petróvitch thought for a moment and continued:

"The old tsar had an only son, the heir to his throne—a little boy about your size. He was a good boy. He was never peevish, went to bed early, never touched anything on the table . . . and in all ways was a model. But he had one fault—he smoked."

Serózha listened intently, and without blinking looked straight in his father's eyes. The Procuror continued, and thought: "What next?" He hesitated for a moment, and ended his story thus:

"From too much smoking, the tsarevitch got ill with consumption, and died . . . when he was twenty years old. His sick and feeble old father was left without any help. There was no one to govern the kingdom and defend the palace. His enemies came and killed the old man, and destroyed the palace, and now in the garden are neither cherry trees nor birds nor bells. . . . So it was, brother."

The end of the plot seemed to Yevgénii Petróvitch naïve and ridiculous. But on Serózha the whole story produced a strong impression. Again his eyes took on an expression of sorrow and something like fright; he looked thoughtfully at the dark window, shuddered, and said in a weak voice:

"I will not smoke any more."

"They will tell me that this parable acted by means of beauty and artistic form," he speculated. "That may be so, but that is no consolation. . . . That does not make it an honest method. . . . Why is it morals and truth cannot be presented in a raw form, but only with mixtures, always sugared and gilded like a pill. This is not normal. . . . It is falsification, deception . . . a trick."

And he thought of those assessors who find it absolutely necessary to make a "speech;" of the public which understands history only through epics and historical novels; and of himself drawing a philosophy of life not from sermons and laws, but from fables, romances, poetry. . . .

"Medicine must be sweetened, truth made beautiful. . . . And this good fortune man has taken advantage of from the time of Adam. . . . And after all maybe it is natural thus, and cannot be otherwise . . there are in nature many useful and expedient deceits and illusions. . . ."

He sat down to his work, but idle, domestic thoughts long wondered in his brain. From the third story no longer came the sound of scales. But the occupant of the second story long continued to walk up and down. . . .

An Adventure

IT was in that wood yonder, behind the creek, that it happened, sir. My father, the kingdom of Heaven be his, was taking five hundred rubles to the master; in those days our fellows and the Shepelevsky peasants used to rent land from the master, so father was taking money for the half-year. He was a God-fearing man, he used to read the scriptures, and as for cheating or wronging anyone, or defrauding—God forbid, and the peasants honored him greatly, and when someone had to be sent to the town about taxes or suchlike, or with money, they used to send him. He was a man above the ordinary, but, not that I'd speak ill of him, he had a weakness. He was fond of a drop. There was no getting him past a tavern; he would go in, drink a glass, and be completely done for! He was aware of this weakness in himself, and when he was carrying public money, that he might not fall asleep or lose it by some

chance, he always took me or my sister Anyutka with him.

To tell the truth, all our family have a great taste for vodka. I can read and write, I served for six years at a tobacconist's in the town, and I can talk to any educated gentleman, and can use very fine language, but, it is perfectly true, sir, as I read in a book, that vodka is the blood of Satan. Through vodka my face has darkened. And there is nothing seemly about me, and here, as you may see, sir, I am a cab-driver like an ignorant, uneducated peasant.

And so, as I was telling you, father was taking the money to the master, Anyutka was going with him, and at that time Anyutka was seven or maybe eight—a silly chit, not that high. He got as far as Kalantchiko successfully; he was sober, but when he reached Kalantchiko and went into Moiseika's tavern, this same weakness of his came upon him. He drank three glasses and set to bragging before people:

"I am a plain humble man," he says, "but I have five hundred rubles in my pocket; if I like," says he, "I could buy up the tavern and all the crockery and Moiseika and his Jewess and his little Jews. I can buy it all out and out," he said. That was his way of joking, to be sure, but then he began complaining: "It's a worry, good Christian people," said he, "to be a rich man, a merchant, or anything of that kind. If you have no money you have no care, if you have money you must watch over your pocket the whole time that wicked men may not rob you. It's a terror to live in the world for a man who has a lot of money."

The drunken people listened of course, took it in, and made a note of it. And in those days they were making a railway line at Kalantchiko, and there were swarms and swarms of tramps and vagabonds of all sorts like locusts. Father pulled himself up afterwards, but it was too late. A word is not a sparrow, if it flies out you can't catch it. They drove, sir, by the wood, and all at once there was someone galloping on horseback behind them. Father was not of the chicken-hearted brigade— that I couldn't say—but he felt uneasy; there was no regular road through the wood, nothing went that way but hay and timber, and there was no cause for anyone to be galloping there, particularly in working hours. One wouldn't be galloping after any good.

"It seems as though they are after someone," said father to Anyutka, "they are galloping so furiously. I ought to have kept quiet in the tavern, a plague on my tongue. Oh, little daughter, my heart misgives me, there is something wrong!"

He did not spend long in hesitation about his dangerous position, and he said to my sister Anyutka:

"Things don't look very bright, they really are in pursuit. Anyway, Anyutka dear, you take the money, put it away in your skirts, and go hide behind a bush. If by ill-luck they attack me, you run back to mother, and give her the money. Let her take it to the village elder. Only mind you don't let anyone see you; keep to the wood and by the creek, that no one may see you. Run your best and call on the merciful God. Christ be with you!"

Father thrust the parcel of notes on Anyutka, and she looked out the thickest of the bushes and hid herself. Soon after, three men on horseback galloped up to father. One a stalwart, big-jawed fellow, in crimson shirt and high boots, and the other two, ragged, shabby fellows, navvies from the line. As my father feared, so it really turned out, sir. The one in the crimson shirt, the sturdy strong fellow, a man above the ordinary, left his horse, and all three made for father.

"Halt you, so-and-so! Where's the money!"

"What money? Go to the devil!"

"Oh, the money you are taking the master for the rent. Hand it over, you bald devil, or we will throttle you, and you'll die in your sins."

And they began to practice their villainy on father, and, instead of beseeching them, weeping, or anything of the sort, father got angry and began to reprove them with the greatest severity.

"What are you pestering me for?" said he. "You are a dirty lot. There is no fear of God in you, plague take you! It's not money you want, but a beating, to make your backs smart for three years after. Be off, blockheads, or I shall defend myself. I have a revolver that takes six bullets, it's in my bosom!"

But his words did not deter the robbers, and they began beating him with anything they could lay their hands on.

They looked through everything in the cart, searched my father thoroughly, even taking off his boots; when they found that beating father only made him swear at them more, they began torturing him in all sorts of ways. All the time Anyutka was sitting behind the bush, and saw it all, poor dear. When she saw father lying on the ground and gasping, she started off and ran her hardest through the thicket and the creek towards home. She was only a little girl, with no understanding; she did not know the way, just ran on not knowing where she was going. It was some six miles to our home. Anyone else might have run there in an hour, but a little child, as we all know, takes two steps back to one forward, and indeed it is not everyone who can run barefoot through the prickly bushes; you want to be used to it, too, and our girls used always to be crowding together on the stove or in the yard, and were afraid to run in the forest.

Towards evening Anyutka somehow reached a habitation; she looked, it was a hut. It was the forester's hut, in the Crown forest; some merchants were renting it at the time and burning charcoal. She knocked. A woman, the forester's wife, came out to her. Anyutka, first of all, burst out crying, and told her everything just as it was, and even told her about the money. The forester's wife was full of pity for her.

"My poor little dear! Poor mite, God has preserved you, poor little one! My precious! Come into the hut, and I will give you something to eat."

She began to make up to Anyutka, gave her food and drink, and even wept with her, and was so attentive to her that the girl, only think, gave her the parcel of notes.

, "I will put it away, darling, and to-morrow morning I will give it back and take you home, dearie."

The woman took the money, and put Anyutka to sleep on the stove where at the time the brooms were drying. And on the same stove, on the brooms, the forester's daughter, a girl as small as our Anyutka, was asleep. And Any-utka used to tell us afterwards that there was such a scent from the brooms, they smelt of honey! Anyutka lay down, but she could not get to sleep, she kept crying quietly; she was sorry for father, and terrified. But, sir, an hour or two passed, and she saw those very three robbers who had tortured father walk into the hut; and the one in the crimson shirt, with big jaws, their leader, went up to the woman and said:

"Well, wife, we have simply murdered a man for nothing. Today we killed a man at dinner time. We killed him all right, but not a farthing did we find."

So this fellow in the crimson shirt turned out to be the forester, the woman's husband.

"The man's dead for nothing," said his ragged companions. "In vain we have taken a sin on our souls."

The forester's wife looked at all three and laughed.

"What are you laughing at, silly?"

"I am laughing because I haven't

murdered anyone, and I have not taken any sin on my soul, but I have found the money."

"What money? What nonsense are you talking!"

"Here, look whether I am talking nonsense."

The forester's wife untied the parcel and, wicked woman, showed them the money. Then she described how Anyutka had come, what she had said, and so on. The murderers were delighted and began to divide the money between them; they almost quarreled, then they sat down on the table, you know, to drink. And Anyutka lay there, poor child, hearing every word and shaking like a Jew in a frying pan. What was she to do? And from their words she learned that father was dead and lying across the road, and she fancied, in her foolishness, that the wolves and the dogs would eat father, and that our horse had gone far away into the forest, and would be eaten by wolves, too, and that she, Anyutka herself, would be put in prison and beaten, because she had not taken care of the money. The robbers got drunk and sent the woman for vodka. They gave her five roubles for vodka and sweet wine. They set to singing and drinking on other people's money. They drank and drank, the dogs, and sent the woman off again that they might drink beyond all bounds.

"We will keep it up till morning," they cried. "We have plenty of money now, there is no need to spare! Drink, and don't drink away your wits."

And so at midnight, when they were all fairly fuddled, the woman ran off for vodka the third time, and the forester strode twice up and down the cottage, and he was staggering.

"Look here, lads," he said, "we must make away with the girl, too! If we leave her, she will be the first to bear witness against us."

They talked it over and discussed it, and decided that Anyutka must not be left alive, that she must be killed. Of course, to murder an innocent child is a fearful thing, even a man drunken or crazy would not take such a job on himself. They were quarreling for maybe an hour which was to kill her, one tried to put it on the other, they almost fought again, and no one would agree to do it; then they cast lots. It fell to the forester. He drank another full glass, cleared his throat, and went to the other room for an axe.

But Anyutka was a sharp wench. For all she was so simple, she thought of something that, I must say, not many an educated man would have thought of. Maybe the Lord had compassion on her, and gave her sense for the moment, or perhaps it was that fright sharpened her wits. Anyway when it came to the test it turned out that she was cleverer than anyone. She got up stealthily, prayed to God, took the little sheepskin, the one the forester's wife had put over her, and, you understand, the forester's little daughter, a girl of the same age as herself, was lying on the stove beside her. She covered this girl with the sheepskin, and took the woman's jacket off her and threw it over herself. Disguised herself, in fact. She put it over her head, and so walked across the hut by the drunken men, and they thought it was the forester's daughter, and did not even look at her. Luckily for her the woman was not in the hut; she had gone for vodka, or maybe she would not have escaped the axe, for a woman's eyes are as far-seeing as a buzzard's. A woman's eyes are sharp.

Anyutka came out of the hut, and ran as fast as her legs could carry her. All night she was lost in the forest, but towards morning she came out to the edge and ran along the road. By the mercy of God she met the clerk, Yegor Danlitch, the kingdom of Heaven be his. He was going along with his hooks to catch fish. Anyutka told him all about it. He went back quicker than he came—thought no more of the fish—gathered the peasants together in the village, and off they went to the forester's.

They got there, and all the murderers were lying side by side, dead drunk, each where he had fallen; the woman, too. was drunk. First thing they searched them; they took the money and then looked on the stove—the Holy Cross be with us! The forester's child was lying on the brooms, under the sheep skin, and her head was in a pool of blood, chopped off by the axe. They roused the peasants and the woman, tied their hands behind them, and took them to the district court; the woman howled, but the forester only shook his head and asked:

"You might give me a drop, lads! My head aches!"

Afterwards they were tried in the town in due course, and punished with the utmost rigor of the law.

So that's what happened, sir, beyond the forest there, that lies behind the creek. Now you can scarcely see it, the sun is setting red behind it. I have been talking to you, and the horses have stopped, as though they were listening, too. Hey there, my beauties! Move more briskly, the good gentleman will give us something extra. Hey, you darlings.

A Father

"I DON'T deny it: I have drunk too much. . . . Forgive me; I happened to pass by the public, and, it's hot, brother! so I drank.

Old Musátoff took a rag from his pocket, and wiped the sweat from his clean-shaven face.

"I have come to you, Bórenka, angel mine, just for a minute," he continued, looking at his son, "on very important business. Forgive me for bothering you. Tell me, my life . . . do you happen to have ten roubles to spare till Tuesday? . . . Yesterday my room rent was due, but you understand. Not a kopeck!"

Young Musátoff went out silently, and behind the door whispered his housekeeper and colleagues in the Civil Service with whom he shared the villa. In a minute he returned, and handed his father a ten-rouble note without a word. The old gentleman took it without even looking at it, put it in his pocket, and said:

"*Merci!* And how is the world using you? We haven't met for ages."

"Yes, it is a long time—since All Saints' Day."

"Five times I did my best to get over to you, but never could get time. First one matter, then another . . . simply ruination! But, Boris, I may confess it, I am not telling the truth. . . . I lie. . . . I always lie. Don't believe me, Bórenka. I promised to let you have the ten roubles back on Tuesday; don't believe that either! Don't believe a single word I say! I have no business matters at all, simply idleness, drink, and shame to show myself in the street in this get-up. But you, Bórenka, will forgive me. Three times I sent the girl for money, and wrote you piteous letters. For the money, thanks! But don't believe the letters. . . . I lied. It hurts me to plunder you in this way, angel mine; I know that you can hardly make both ends meet, and live—so to say—on locusts. But with impudence like mine you can do nothing. A rascal who only shows his face when he wants money! . . . Forgive me, Bórenka, I tell you the plain truth, because I cannot look with indifference upon your angel face. . . ."

A minute passed in silence. The old man sighed deeply, and began:

"Let us make the supposition, brother, that you were to treat me to a glass of beer."

Without a word, Boris again went out and whispered outside the door. The beer was brought in. At the sight of the bottle Musátoff enlivened, and suddenly changed his tone.

"The other day I was at the races," he began, making frightened faces. "There were three of us, and together we put in the totalisator a three-rouble note on Shustri. And good luck to Shustri! With the risk of one rouble we each got back thirty-two. It is a noble sport. The old woman always pitches into me about the races, but I go. I love it!"

Boris, a young fair-haired man, with a sad, apathetic face, walked from corner to corner, and listened silently. When Musátoff interrupted his story in order to cough, he went up to him and said:

"The other day, papa, I bought myself a new pair of boots, but they turned out too small. I wish you would take them off my hands. I will let you have them cheap!"

"I shall be charmed!" said the old man, with a grimace. "Only for the same price—without any reduction."

"Very well. . . . We will regard that as a loan also."

Boris stretched his arm under the bed, and pulled out the new boots. Old Musátoff removed his own awkward brown shoes—plainly someone else's—and tried the new boots on.

"Like a shot!" he exclaimed. "Your hand on it. . . . I'll take them. On Tuesday, when I get my pension, I'll send the money. . . . But I may as well confess, 1 lie." He resumed his former piteous tone. "About the races I lied, and about the pension I lie. You are deceiving me, Bórenka. . . . I see very well through your magnanimous pretext. I can see through you! The boots are too small for you because your heart is too large! Akh, Borya, Borya, I understand it . . . and I feel it!"

"You have gone to your new rooms?" asked Boris, with the object of changing the subject.

"Yes, brother, into the new rooms. . . . Every month we shift. With a character like the old woman's we cannot stay anywhere."

"I have been at the old rooms. But now I want to ask you to come to the

country. In your state of health it will
do you good to be in the fresh air."

Musátoff waved his hand. "The old
woman wouldn't let me go, and myself
I don't care to. A hundred times you
have tried to drag me out of the pit.
. . . I have tried to drag myself . . .
but the devil an improvement! Give it
up! In the pit I'll die as I have lived.
At this moment I sit in front of you
and look at your angel face . . . yet I
am being dragged down into the pit.
It's destiny, brother! You can't get
flies from a dunghill to a rose bush. No.
. . . Well, I'm off . . . it's getting
dark."

"If you wait a minute, we'll go together. I have business in town myself."

Musátoff and his son put on their
coats, and went out. By the time they
had found a droschky it was quite
dark, and the windows were lighted up.

"I know I'm ruining you, Bórenka,"
stammered the father. "My poor, poor
children! What an affliction to be
cursed with such a father! Bórenka,
angel mine, I cannot lie when I see your
face. Forgive me! . . . To what a
pass, my God, has impudence brought
me! This very minute I have taken
your money, and shamed you with my
drunken face; your brothers also I
spunge on and put to shame. If you
had seen me yesterday! I won't hide
anything, Bórenka. Yesterday our
neighbours—all the rascality, in short—
came in to see the old woman. I drank
with them, and actually abused you behind your back, and complained that
you had neglected me. I tried, you understand, to get the drunken old women
to pity me, and played the part of an
unhappy father. That's my besetting

sin; when I want to hide my faults, I
heap them on the heads of my innocent children. . . . But I cannot lie to
you, Bórenka, or hide things. I came
to you in pride, but when I had felt
your kindness and all-mercifulness, my
tongue clove to the roof of my mouth,
and all my conscience turned upside
down."

"Yes, father, but let us talk about
something else."

"Mother of God, what children I
have!" continued the old man, paying
no attention to his son. "What a glory
the Lord has sent me! Such children
should be sent not to me, a good-for-
nothing, but to a real man with a soul
and a heart. I am not worthy of it!"

Musátoff took off his cap and crossed
himself piously thrice.

"Glory be to Thee, O God!" he
sighed, looking around as if seeking an
ikon. "Astonishing, priceless children!
Three sons I have, and all of them the
same! Sober, serious, diligent—and
what intellects! Cabman, what intellects! Gregory alone has as much
brains as ten ordinary men. French
. . . and German . . . he speaks both
. . . and you never get tired of listening. Children, children mine, I cannot
believe that you are mine at all! I
don't believe it! You, Bórenka, are a
very martyr! I am ruining you . . .
before long I shall have ruined you.
You give me money without end, although you know very well that not a
kopeck goes on necessaries. Only the
other day I sent you a piteous letter
about my illness. . . . But I lied; the
money was wanted to buy rum. Yet
you gave it to me sooner than offend
your old father with a refusal. All this
I know . . . and feel . . . Grisha also

is a martyr. On Thursday, angel mine, I went to his office, drunk, dirty, ragged . . . smelling of vodka like a cellar. I went straight up to him and began in my usual vulgar slang, although he was with the other clerks, the head of the department—and petitioners all around! Disgraced him for his whole life! . . Yet he never got the least confused, only a little pale; he smiled, and got up from his desk as if nothing were wrong—even introduced me to his colleagues. And he brought me the whole way home, without a word of reproach! I spunge on him even worse than on you!

"Then take your brother, Sasha! There's another martyr! Married to a colonel's daughter, moving in a circle of aristocrats, with a dot . . . and everything else. . . . He, at any rate, you would think would have nothing to do with me. Well, brother, what does he do? When he gets married the very first thing after the wedding he comes to me with his young wife, and pays me the first visit . . . to my lair, to the lair . . . I swear to God!"

The old man began to sob, but soon laughed again.

"At the very moment, as the fates would have it, when we were eating scraped radishes and kvas, and frying fish, with a stench in the room enough to stink out the devil. I was lying drunk as usual, and the old woman jumps up and greets them with a face the colour of beefsteak . . . in one word, a scandal. But Sasha bore it all."

"Yes, our Sasha is a good man," said Boris.

"Incomparable! You are all of you gold, both you and Grisha, and Sasha and Sonia. I torture, pester, disgrace, and spunge on you, yet in my whole life I have never heard a word of reproach, or seen a single sidelong look. If you had a decent father it would be different, but . . . You have never had anything from me but evil. I am a wicked, dissolute man. . . . Now, thank God, I have quieted down, and have no character left in me, but formerly, when you were little children, I had a character and no mistake. Whatever I said or did seemed to me gospel! I remember! I used to come back late from the club, drunk and irritated, and begin to abuse your poor mother about the household expenses. I would keep on at her all night, and imagine that she was in the wrong; in the morning you would get up and go to school, but all the time I would keep on showing her that I had a character. Heaven rest her soul, how I tortured the poor martyr! And when you came back from school and found me asleep you weren't allowed your dinner until I got up. And after dinner the same music! P'rhaps you remember. May God forbid that anyone else should be cursed with such a father! He sent you to me as a blessing. A blessing! Continue in this way, children, to the end. Honour thy father that thy days may be long in the land! For your goodness Heaven will reward you with long life! Cabman, stop!"

Musátoff alighted and ran into a beerhouse. After a delay of half an hour he returned, grunted tipsily, and took his seat.

And where is Sonia now?" he asked. "Still at the boarding-school?"

"No, she finished last May. She lives now with Sasha's aunt."

"What?" exclaimed the old man.

"Left school? And a glorious girl, God bless her—went with her brothers. *Akh,* Bórenka, no mother, no one to console her! Tell me, Bórenka, does she know . . . does she know that I am alive? Eh?"

Boris did not answer. Five minutes passed in deep silence. The old man sobbed, wiped his face with a rag, and said:

"I love her, Bórenka! She was the only daughter, and in old age there is no consolation like a daughter. If I could only see her for a moment. Tell me, Bórenka, may I?"

"Of course, whenever you like."

"And she won't object?"

"Of course not; she herself went to look for you."

"I swear to God! There is a nest of angels! Cabman, eh? Arrange it, Bórenka, angel! Of course she is a young lady now, *délicatesse . . . consommé,* and all that sort of thing in the noble style. So I can't see her in this get-up. But all this, Bórenka, we can arrange. For three days I won't taste a drop—that'll bring my accursed drunken snout into shape. Then I will go to your place and put on a suit of your clothes, and get a shave and have my hair cut. Then you will drive over and take me with you? Is it agreed?"

"All right."

"Cabman, stop!"

The old man jumped out of the carriage and ran into another beershop. Before they reached his lodgings he visited two more; and every time his son waited silently and patiently. When, having dismissed the cabman, they crossed the broad, muddy yard to the rooms of the "old woman," Musátoff

looked confused and guilty, grunted timidly, and smacked his lips.

"Bórenka," he began, in an imploring voice, "if the old woman says anything of that kind to you—you understand—don't pay any attention to her. And be polite to her. She is very ignorant and impertinent, but not a bad sort at bottom. She has a good, warm heart."

They crossed the yard and entered a dark hall. The door squeaked, the kitchen smelt, the samovar smoked, and shrill voices were heard. . . . While they passed through the kitchen Boris noticed only the black smoke, a rope with washing spread out, and the chimney of a samovar, through the chinks of which burst golden sparks.

"This is my cell," said Musátoff, bowing his head, and showing his son into a little, low-ceilinged room, filled with atmosphere unbearable from proximity to the kitchen. At a table sat three women, helping one another to food. Seeing the guest, they looked at one another and stopped eating.

"Well, did you get it?" asked one, apparently "the old woman," roughly.

"Got it, got it," stammered the old man. "Now, Boris, do us the honour! Sit down! With us, brother—young man—everything is simple. . . . We live in a simple way."

Musátoff fussed about without any visible reason. He was ashamed before his son, and at the same time apparently wished to bear himself before the women as a man of importance and a forsaken, unhappy father.

"Yes, brother mine—young man—we live simply, without show-off," he stammered. "We are plain folk, young man. . . . We are not like you . . . we do not trouble to throw dust in other people's eyes. No! . . . A drop of vodka, eh?"

One of the women, ashamed of drinking before a stranger, sighed and said:

"I must have another glass after these mushrooms. After mushrooms, whether you like it or not, you have to drink. . . . Ivan Gerasiuitch, ask him . . . perhaps he'll have a drink."

"Drink, young man!" said Musátoff, without looking at his son. "Wines and liqueurs we don't keep, brother, we live plainly."

"I'm afraid our arrangements don't suit him," sighed the old woman.

"Leave him alone, leave him alone, he'll drink all right."

To avoid giving offence to his father, Boris took a glass, and drained it in silence. When the samovar was brought in he, silently and with a melancholy air—again to please his father—drank two cups of atrocious tea. And without a word he listened while the "old woman" lamented the fact that in this world you will sometimes find cruel and godless children who forsake their parents in their old age.

"I know what you are thinking," said the drunken old man, falling into his customary state of excitement. "You are thinking that I have fallen in the world, that I have dirtied myself, that I am an object of pity! But in my mind this simple life is far more natural than yours, young man. I do not need for anything . . . and I have no intention of humiliating myself . . . I can stand a lot . . . but tolerance is at an end when a brat of a boy looks at me with pity."

When he had drunk his tea, he cleaned a herring, and squeezed onion on it with such vigour that tears of emotion sprang into his eyes. He spoke again of the totalisator, of his winnings, and of a hat of Panama straw for which he had paid sixteen roubles the day before. He lied with the same appetite with which he had drunk and devoured the herring. His son sat silently for more than an hour, and then rose to take leave.

"I wouldn't think of detaining you," said Musátoff stiffly. "I ask your pardon, young man, for not living in the way to which you are accustomed."

He bristled up, sniffed with dignity, and winked to the women.

"Good-bye, young man!" he said, escorting his son into the hall. *"Attendez!"*

But in the hall, where it was quite dark, he suddenly pressed his face to his son's arm, and sobbed.

"If I could only see Sóniushka!" he whispered. "Arrange it, Bórenka, angel mine! I will have a shave, and put on one of your suits . . . and make a severe face. I won't open my mouth while she's present. I won't say a word. I swear to God!"

He glanced timidly at the door, from behind which came the shrill voices of the women, smothered his sobs, and said in a loud voice:

"Well, good-bye, young man! *"Attendez!"*

Two Tragedies

SIX-YEAR-OLD Andreï, the only son of Dr. Kiríloff, a Zemstvo physician, died from diphtheria one September morn at ten o'clock. The doctor's wife had just thrown herself upon her knees at the bedside of her dead child, in despair, when the hall-door bell rang violently.

All the servants had been sent out of the house that morning to avoid infection; and Kiríloff, in his shirtsleeves, with sweating face, and hands burned with carbolic acid, opened the door himself. The hall was dark, and the stranger appeared dimly to Kiríloff of middle height, with a white muffler, and a big, pale face—so pale that at first it seemed to shine.

"Is the doctor at home?" he asked quickly.

"I am the doctor," answered Kiríloff, "what do you want?"

"I am glad!" said the stranger. He stretched out through the darkness for the doctor's hand, found it, and pressed it tightly. I am very . . . very glad. We are acquaintances. My name is Abógin. . . . I had the pleasure of meeting you last summer at Gnutcheff's. I am very glad that you are in. . . For the love of Christ do not refuse to come with me at once. . . . My wife is dangerously ill. . . . I have brought a trap."

From Abógin's voice and movements it was plain that he was greatly agitated. Like a man frightened by a fire or by a mad dog, he could not contain his breath. He spoke rapidly in a trembling voice, and something inexpressibly sincere and childishly imploring sounded in his speech. But, like all men frightened and thunder-struck, he spoke in short abrupt phrases, and used many superfluous and inconsequential words.

"I was afraid I should not find you at home," he continued. "While I was driving here I was in a state of torture. . . . Dress and come at once, for the love of God. . . . It happened thus. Paptchinski—Alexander Simiónevitch—whom you know, had driven over. . . . We talked for awhile . . . then we had tea; suddenly my wife screamed, laid her hand upon her heart, and fell against the back of the chair. We put her on the bed. . . . I bathed her forehead with ammonia, and sprinkled her with water . . . she lies like a corpse. . . . It is aneurism. . . . Come. . . . Her father died from aneurism. . . ."

Kiríloff listened and said nothing. It seemed he had forgotten his own language. But when Abógin repeated what he had said about Paptchinski and about his wife's father, the doctor shook his head, and said apathetically, drawling every word:

"Excuse me, I cannot go . . . . Five minutes ago . . . . my child died."

"Is it possible?" cried Abógin, taking a step back. "Good God, at what an unlucky time I have come! An amazingly unhappy day . . . amazing! What a coincidence . . . as if on purpose."

Abógin put his hand upon the door-handle, and inclined his head as if in doubt. He was plainly undecided as to what to do; whether to go, or again to ask the doctor to come.

"Listen to me," he said passionately, seizing Kiríloff by the arm; "I thoroughly understand your position.

God is my witness that I feel shame in trying to distract your attention at such a moment, but . . . what can I do? Judge yourself—whom can I apply to? Except you, there is no doctor in the neighbourhood. Come! For the love of God! It is not for myself I ask. . . . It is not I who am ill."

A silence followed. Kiríloff turned his back to Abógin, for a moment stood still, and went slowly from the ante-room into the hall. Judging by his uncertain, mechanical gait, by the care with which he straightened the shade upon the unlit lamp, and looked into a thick book which lay upon the table— in this moment he had no intentions, no wishes, thought of nothing; and probably had even forgotten that in the anteroom a stranger was waiting. The twilight and silence of the hall apparently intensified his stupor. Walking from the hall into his study, he raised his right leg high, and sought with his hands the doorpost. All his figure showed a strange uncertainty, as if he were in another's house, or for the first time in life were intoxicated, and were surrendering himself questioningly to the new sensation. Along the wall of the study and across the bookshelves ran a long zone of light. Together with a heavy, close smell carbolic and ether, this light came from a slightly opened door which led from the study into the bedroom. The doctor threw himself into an armchair before the table. A minute he looked drowsily at the illumined books, and then rose, and went into the bedroom.

In the bedroom reigned the silence of the grave. All, to the smallest trifle, spoke eloquently of a struggle just lived through, of exhaustion, and of final rest.

A candle standing on the stool among phials, boxes, and jars, and a large lamp upon the dressing-table lighted the room. On the bed beside the window lay a boy with open eyes and an expression of surprise upon his face. He did not move, but his eyes, it seemed, every second grew darker and darker, and vanished into his skull. With her hands upon his body, and her face hidden in the folds of the bedclothes, knelt the mother. Like the child, she made no movement; life showed itself alone in the bend of her back and in the position of her hands. She pressed against the bed with all her being, with force and eagerness, as if she feared to destroy the tranquil and convenient pose which she had found for her weary body. Counterpane, dressings, jars, pools on the floor, brushes and spoons scattered here and there, the white bottle of lime-water, the very air, heavy and stifling—all were dead and seemed immersed in rest.

The doctor stopped near his wife, thrust his hands into his trouser pockets, and turning his head, bent his gaze upon his son. His face expressed indifference; only by the drops upon his beard could it be seen that he had just been crying.

The repellant terror which we conceive when we speak of death was absent from the room. The general stupefaction, the mother's pose, the father's indifferent face, exhaled something attractive and touching; exhaled that subtle, intangible beauty of human sorrow which cannot be analysed or described, and which music alone can express. Beauty breathed even in the grim tranquility of the mourners. Kiríloff and his wife were silent; they did not weep, as if in addition to the weight of their sorrow they were conscious also of the poetry of their position. It seemed that they were thinking how in its time their youth had passed, how now with this child had passed even their right to have children at all. The doctor was forty-four years old, already grey, with the face of an old man; his faded and sickly wife, thirty-five. Andreï was not only their only son, but also their last.

In contrast with his wife, Kiríloff belonged to those natures which in time of spiritual pain feel a need for movement. After standing five minutes beside his wife, he, again lifting high his right leg, went from the bedroom into a little room half taken up by a long, broad sofa, and thence into the kitchen. After wandering about the stove and the cook's bed he bowed his head and went through a little door back to the ante-room.

Here again he saw the white muffler and the pale face.

"At last!" sighed Abógin, taking hold of the door-handle. "Come, please!"

The doctor shuddered, looked at him, and remembered.

"Listen to me; have I not already told you I cannot come?" he said, waking up. "How extraordinary!"

"Doctor, I am not made of stone. . . . I thoroughly understand your position. . . . I symapthize with you!" said Abógin, with an imploring voice, laying one hand upon his muffler. "But I am not asking this for myself. . . My wife is dying! If you had heard her cry, if you had seen her face, then you would understand my persistence! My God! and I thought that you had gone to get ready! Dr. Kiríloff, time is precious. Come, I implore you!"

"I cannot go," said Kiríloff with a pause between each word. Then he returned to the hall.

Abógin went after him, and seized him by the arm.

"You are overcome by your sorrow—that I understand. But remember . . . I am not asking you to come and cure a toothache . . . not as an adviser . . . but to save a human life," he continued, in the voice of a beggar. "A human life should be supreme over every personal sorrow. . . . I beg of you manliness, an exploit! . . . In the name of humanity!"

"Humanity is a stick with two ends," said Kiríloff with irritation. "In the name of the same humanity I beg of you not to drag me away. How strange this seems! Here I am hardly standing on my legs, yet you worry me with your humanity! At the present moment I am good for nothing. . . . I will not go on any consideration! And for whom should I leave my wife? No. . . . No."

Kiríloff waved his hands and staggered back.

"Do not . . . do not ask me," he continued in a frightened voice. "Excuse me. . . . By the Thirteenth Volume of the Code I am bound to go, and you have the right to drag me by the arm. . . . If you will have it, drag me . . . but I am useless. . . . Even for conversation I am not in a fit state. . . . Excuse me."

"It is useless, doctor, for you to speak to me in that tone." said Abógin, again taking Kiríloff's arm. "The devil take your Thirteenth Volume! . . . To do violence to your will I have no right. If you will, come; if you don't, then God be with you; but it is not to your will that I appeal, but to your heart! . . . A young woman is at the point of death! This moment your own son has died, and who if not you should understand my terror!"

Abógin's voice trembled with agitation; in tremble and in tone was something more persuasive than in the words. He was certainly sincere; but it was remarkable that no matter how well chosen his phrases, they seemed to come from him stilted, soulless, inappropriately ornate, to such an extent that they seemed an insult to the atmosphere of the doctor's house and to his own dying wife. He felt this himself, and therefore, fearing to be misunderstood, he tried with all his force to make his voice sound soft and tender, so as to win if not with words at least by sincerity of tone. In general, phrases, however beautiful and profound, act only on those who are indifferent, and seldom satisfy the happy or unhappy; it is for this reason that the most touching expression of joy or sorrow is always silence; sweethearts understand one another best when they are silent; and a burning passionate eulogy spoken above a grave touches only the strangers present, and seems to widow and child inexpressive and cold.

Kiríloff stood still and said nothing. When Abógin used some more phrases about the high vocation of a physician, self-sacrifice, and so on, the doctor asked gloomily:

"Is it far?"

"Something between thirteen and fourteen versts. I have excellent horses. I give you my word of honour to bring you there and back in an hour. In a single hour!"

The last words acted on the doctor more powerfully than the references to humanity and the vocation of a doctor. He thought for a moment and said, with a sigh:

"All right. . . . I will go."

With a rapid, steady gait he went into his study, and after a moment's delay returned with a long overcoat. Moving nervously beside him, shuffling his feet, and overjoyed, Abógin helped him into his coat. Together they left the house.

It was dark outside, but not so dark as in the ante-room. In the darkness was clearly defined the outline of the tall, stooping doctor, with his long, narrow beard and eagle nose. As for Abógin, in addition to his pale face the doctor could now distinguish a big head, and a little student's cap barely covering the crown. The white muffler gleamed only in front; behind, it was hidden under long hair.

"Believe me, I appreciate your generosity," he muttered, seating the doctor in the calèche. "We will get there in no time. Listen, Luka, old man, drive as hard as you can! Quick!"

The coachman drove rapidly. First they flew past a row of ugly buildings, with a great open yard; everywhere around it was dark, but from a window a bright light glimmered through the palisade, and three windows in the upper story of the great block seemed paler than the air. After that they drove through intense darkness. There was a smell of mushroom dampness, and a lisping of trees; ravens awakened by the noise of the calèche stirred in the foliage, and raised a frightened, complaining cry, as if they knew that Kiríloff's son was dead, and that Abógin's wife was dying. They flashed past single trees, past a coppice: a pond, crossed with great black shadows, scintillated— and the calèche rolled across a level plain. The cry of the ravens was heard indistinctly far behind, and then ceased entirely.

For nearly the whole way Abógin and Kiríloff were silent. Only once, Abógin sighed and exclaimed:

"A frightful business! A man never so loves those who are near to him as when he is in danger of losing them."

And when the calèche slowly crossed the river, Kiríloff started suddenly as if he were frightened by the plash of the water, and moved.

"Listen! Let me go for a moment," he said wearily. "I will come again. I must send a feldscher to my wife. She is alone!"

Abógin did not answer. The calèche, swaying and banging over the stones, crossed a sandy bank and rolled onward. Kiríloff, wrapped in weariness, looked around him. Behind, in the scanty starlight, gleamed the road; and the willows by the river bank vanished in the darkness. To the right stretched a plain, flat and interminable as heaven; and far in the distance, no doubt on some sodden marsh, gleamed will-of-the-wisps. On the left, running parallel to the road, stretched a hillock, shaggy with a small shrubbery, and over the hill hung immovably a great half-moon, rosy, half muffled in the mist and fringed with light clouds, which, it seemed, watched it on every side, that it might not escape.

On all sides Nature exhaled something hopeless and sickly; the earth, like a fallen woman sitting in her dark chamber and trying to forget the past, seemed tormented with remembrances of spring and summer, and waited in apathy the inevitable winter. Everywhere the world seemed a dark, unfathomable deep, an icy pit from which there was no escape either for Kiríloff or for Abógin or for the red half-moon. . . .

The nearer to its goal whirled the calèche, the more impatient seemed Abógin. He shifted, jumped up, and looked over the coachman's shoulder. And when at last the carriage stopped before steps handsomely covered with striped drugget, he looked up at the lighted windows of the second story, and panted audibly.

"If anything happens . . . I will never survive it," he said, entering the hall with Kiríloff, and rubbing his hands in agitation. But after listening a moment, he added, "There is no confusion . . . things must be going well."

In the hall were neither voices nor footsteps, and the whole house, notwithstanding its brilliant lights, seemed asleep. Only now, for the first time, the doctor and Abógin, after their sojourn in darkness, could see one another plainly. Kiríloff was tall, round-shouldered, and ugly, and was carelessly dressed. His thick, almost negro, lips, his eagle nose, and his withered, indifferent glance, expressed something cutting, unkindly, and rude. His uncombed hair, his sunken temples, the premature grey in the long, narrow beard, through which appeared his chin, the pale grey of his skin, and his careless, angular manners, all reflected a career of need endured, of misfortune, of weariness with life and with men. Judging by his dry figure, no one would ever believe that this man had a wife, and that he had wept over his child.

Abógin was a contrast. He was a thick-set, solid blond, with a big head, with heavy but soft features; and he was dressed elegantly and fashionably. From his carriage, from his closely-buttoned frock-coat, from his mane of hair, and from his face, flowed something noble and leonine; he walked with his head erect and his chest expanded, he spoke in an agreeable baritone, and the way in which he took off his muffler and smoothed his hair breathed a delicate, feminine elegance. Even his pallor, and the childish terror with which, while taking off his coat, he looked up the staircase, did not detract from his dignity, or diminish the satiety, health, and aplomb which his whole figure breathed.

"There is no one about . . . I can hear nothing," he said, going upstairs. "There is no confusion. . . . God is merciful!"

He led the doctor through the hall into a great drawing-room. with a black piano, and lustres in white covers. From this they went into a small, cosy, and well-furnished dining-room, full of a pleasant, rosy twilight.

"Wait a moment," said Abógin, "I shall be back immediately. I will look around and tell them you are here. . . ."

Kiríloff remained alone. The luxury of the room, the pleasant twilight, and even his presence in the unknown house of a stranger, which had the character of an adventure, apparently did not affect him. He lay back in the armchair and examined his hands burnt with carbolic acid. Only faintly could he see the bright red lamp shade and a violoncello case. But looking at the other side of the room, where ticked a clock, he noticed a stuffed wolf, as solid and sated as Abógin himself.

Not a sound. . . . Then in a distant room someone loudly ejaculated "Ah!"; a glass door. probably the door of a wardrobe, closed . . . and again all was silent. After waiting a moment Kiríloff ceased to examine his hands, and raised his eyes upon the door through which Abógin had gone.

On the threshold stood Abógin. But it was not the Abógin who had left the room. The expression of satiety, the delicate elegance had vanished; his face, his figure, his pose were contorted by a repulsive expression not quite of terror, not quite of physical pain. His nose, his lips, his moustaches, all his features twitched; it seemed they wished to tear themselves off his face; and his eyes were transfigured as if from torture.

Abógin walked heavily into the middle of the room, bent himself in two, groaned, and shook his fists.

"Deceived!" he shouted, with a strong hissing accentuation of the second syllable. "Cheated! Gone! Got ill, and sent for a doctor, only to fly with that buffoon Paptchinski! My God!"

Abógin walked heavily up to the doctor, stretched up to his face his white, soft fists, and, shaking them, continued in a howl:

"Gone! Deceived! But why this extra lie? My God! My God! But why this filthy swindler's trick, this devilish reptile play? What have I ever done? Gone!"

The tears burst from his eyes. He turned on one foot and walked up and down the room. And now in his short coat, in the narrow, fashionable trousers, which made his legs seem too thin for his body, with his great head and mane, he still more closely resembled a lion. On the doctor's indifferent face appeared curiosity. He rose and looked at Abógin.

"Be so good as to tell me . . . where is the patient?"

"Patient! Patient!" cried Abógin.

with a laugh, a sob, and a shaking of his fists. "This is no sick woman, but a woman accursed! Meanness, baseness, lower than Satan himself could have conceived! Sent for a doctor, to fly with him—to fly with that buffoon, that clown, that Alphonse. Oh, God, better a thousand times that she had died! I cannot bear it. . . . I cannot bear it!"

The doctor drew himself up. His eyes blinked and filled with tears, his narrow beard moved to the right and to the left in accord with the movement of his jaws.

"Be so good as to inform me what is the meaning of this?" he asked, looking around him in curiosity. "My child lies dead, my wife in despair is left alone in a great house. I myself can hardly stand on my feet, for three nights I have not slept and what is this? Am I brought here to play in some trivial comedy, to take the part of a property-man. . . . I don't understand it!"

Abógin opened one of his fists, flung upon the floor a crumpled paper, and trod on it as upon an insect which he wished to crush.

"And I never saw it! I never understood!" he said through his clenched teeth, shaking one of his fists beside his face, with an expression as if someone had trod upon a corn. "I never noticed that he rode here every day, never noticed that to-day he came in a carriage! Why in a carriage? And I never noticed! Fool!"

"I don't understand . . . I really don't understand," stammered Kiríloff. "What is the meaning of this? This is practical joking at the expense of another . . . it is mocking at human suffering. It is impossible. . . . I have never heard of such a thing!"

With the dull astonishment depicted on his face of a man who is only beginning to understand that he has been badly insulted, the doctor shrugged his shoulders, and not knowing what to say, threw himself in exhaustion into the chair.

"Got tired of me, loved another! Well, God be with them! But why this deception, why this base, this traitorous trick?" cried Abógin in a whining voice. "Why? For what? What have I done to her? Listen, doctor," he said passionately, coming nearer to Kiríloff. "You are the involuntary witness of my misfortune, and I will not conceal from you the truth. I swear to you that I loved that woman, that I loved her to adoration, that I was her slave. For her I gave up everything; I quarrelled with my parents, I threw up my career and my music, I forgave her what I could not have forgiven in my own mother or sister. . . . I have never said an unkind word to her. . . . I gave her no cause! But why this lie? I do not ask for love, but why this shameless deception? If a woman doesn't love, then let her say so openly, honestly, all the more since she knew my views on that subject. . . ."

With tears in his eyes, and with his body trembling all over, Abógin sincerely poured forth to the doctor his whole soul. He spoke passionately, with both hands pressed to his heart, he revealed family secrets without a moment's hesitation; and, it seemed, was even relieved when these secrets escaped him. Had he spoken thus for an hour, for two hours, and poured out his soul, he would certainly have felt better. Who knows whether the doctor might not have listened to him, sympathised with him as a friend, and, even without protest, become reconciled to his own unhappiness. . . . But it happened otherwise. While Abógin spoke, the insulted doctor changed. The indifference and surprise on his face gave way little by little to an expression of bitter offence, indignation, and wrath. His features became sharper, harder, and more disagreeable. And finally when Abógin held before his eyes the photograph of a young woman with a face handsome but dry and inexpressive as a nun's, and asked him could he, looking at this photograph, imagine that she was capable of telling a lie, the doctor suddenly leaped up, averted his eyes, and said, rudely ringing out every word:

"What do you mean by talking to me like this? I don't want to hear you! I will not listen!" He shouted and banged his fist upon the table. "What have I to do with your stupid secrets, devil take them! You dare to communicate to me these base trifles! Do you not see that I have already been insulted enough? Am I a lackey who will bear insults without retaliation?"

Abógin staggered backwards, and looked at Kiríloff in amazement.

"Why did you bring me here?" continued the doctor, shaking his beard. . . . "If you marry filth, then storm with your filth, and play your melodramas; but what affair is that of mine? What have I to do with your romances? Leave me alone! Display your well-born meanness, show off your humane ideas, (the doctor pointed to the violoncello case) play on your double basses and trombones, get as fat as a capon, but do not dare to mock the personality of another. If you cannot respect it, then rid it of your detestable attention!"

Abógin reddened. "What does all this mean?" he asked.

"It means this: that it is base and infamous to play practical jokes on other men. I am a doctor; you regard doctors and all other working men who do not smell of scent and prostitution as your lackeys and your servants. But reflect, reflect—no one has given you the right to make a property man of a suffering human being!"

"You dare to speak this to me?" said Abógin; and his face again twitched, this time plainly from anger.

"Yes . . . and you, knowing of the misery in my home, have dared to drag me here to witness this insanity," cried the doctor, again banging his fist upon the table. "Who gave you the right to mock at human misfortune?"

"You are out of your mind," said Abógin. "You are not generous. I also am deeply unhappy, and . . ."

"Unhappy!" cried Kiríloff, with a contemptuous laugh. "Do not touch that word; it ill becomes you. Oafs who have no money to meet their bills also call themselves unfortunate. Geese that are stuffed with too much fat are also unhappy. Insignificant curs!"

"You forget yourself, you forget yourself!" screamed Abógin. "For words like those . . . people are horsewhipped. Do you hear me?"

He suddenly thrust his hand into his side pocket, took out a pocket-book, and taking two bank-notes, flung them on the table.

"There you have the money for your visit!" he said, dilating his nostrils "You are paid!"

"Do not dare to offer money to me," cried Kiríloff, sweeping the notes on to the floor. "For insults money is not the payment."

The two men stood face to face, and in their anger flung insults at one another. It is certain that never in their lives had they uttered so many unjust, inhuman, and ridiculous words. In each was fully expressed the egoism of the unfortunate. And men who are unfortunate, egoistical, angry, unjust, and heartless are even less than stupid men capable of understanding one another. For misfortune does not unite, but severs; and those who should be bound by community of sorrow are much more unjust and heartless than the happy and contented.

"Be so good as to send me home!" cried the doctor at last.

Abógin rang sharply. Receiving no answer he rang again, and angrily flung the bell upon the floor; it fell heavily on the carpet and emitted a plaintive and ominous sound. . . . A footman appeared.

"Where have you been hiding yourself? May Satan take you!" roared Abógin, rushing at him with clenched fists. "Where have you been? Go, tell them at once to give this gentleman the calèche, and get the carriage ready for me! . . . Stop!" he cried, when the servant turned to go. "To-morrow let none of you traitors remain in this house! The whole pack of you! I will get others! Curs!"

Awaiting their carriages, Abógin and Kiríloff were silent. The first had already regained his expression of satiety and his delicate elegance. He walked up and down the room, shook his head

gracefully, and apparently thought something out. His anger had not yet evaporated, but he tried to look as if he did not notice his enemy. . . . The doctor stood, with one hand on the edge of the table, and looked at Abógin with deep, somewhat cynical and ugly contempt—with the eyes of sorrow and misfortune when they see before them satiety and elegance.

When, after a short delay, the doctor took his seat in the calèche, his eyes retained their contemptuous look. It was dark, much darker than an hour before. The red half-moon had fallen below the hill, and the clouds that had guarded it lay in black spots among the stars. A carriage with red lamps rattled along the road, and overtook Kiríloff. It was Abógin, driving away to protest . . . and make a fool of himself. . . .

And all the way home Kiríloff thought, not of his wife or of dead Andreï, but of Abógin and of the people who lived in the house which he had just left. His thoughts were unjust, heartless, inhuman. He condemned Abógin and his wife, and Paptchinski, and all that class of persons who live in a rosy twilight and smell of perfumes; all the way he hated and despised them to the point of torture; and his mind was full of unshakeable convictions as to the worthlessness of such people.

Time will pass; the sorrow of Kiríloff will pass away also, but this conviction—unjust, unworthy of a human heart—will never pass away, and will remain with the doctor to the day of his death.

The Rook

THE rooks had arrived and swarmed in great circles around the Russian cornfields. I singled out the most important-looking I could find, and began to talk to him. Unfortunately I hit upon a rook who was a moralist and a great reasoner; consequently our conversation was a dull one.

This is what we talked about:

I. "It's said that you rooks live to a great age. The naturalists cite you and the pike as the chief examples of longevity. How old are you?"

The Rook. "I am three hundred and seventy-six years old."

I. "Well, I never! You've lived precious long! In your place, old bird, the devil only knows how many articles I could have written for the *Russian Antiquarian* and the *Historical Journal.* If I had lived three hundred and seventy-six years I can't imagine how many novels, stories, plays, scenes and other trifles I should have written. What numbers of fees I should have pocketed! Now, what have you, old rook, done during all these years?"

The Rook. "Nothing, Mr. man. I have only eaten, drunk, slept and multiplied."

I. "Shame! I really feel shame for you, silly old bird. You have lived in the world three hundred and seventy-six years, and you are as stupid to-day as you were three hundred years ago. Not a ha'p'orth of progress."

The Rook. "Wisdom, Mr. Man, comes not from age, but from education and learning. Look at China—she has existed much longer than I have, and she is still as great a simpleton to-day as she was a thousand years ago."

I (with astonishment). "Three hundred and seventy-six years! What do you call that? An eternity! During that time I should have been able to attend lectures in every faculty; I could have been married twenty times; tried every profession and employment; attained the devil only knows what high rank, and, no doubt, have died a Rothschild. Just think of it, you fool, one rouble placed in a bank at five per cent compound interest becomes in two hundred and eighty-three years a million. Just calculate. That means, if you had placed one rouble on interest two hundred and eighty-three years ago, you would have had a million roubles to-day. Ah, you fool, you fool! Are you not ashamed, don't you feel a fool to be so stupid?"

The Rook. "Not at all. We are stupid; but we can comfort ourselves with the thought that during the four hundred years of our life we do fewer foolish things than man does during his forty years. Yes, Mr. Man, I have lived three hundred and seventy-six years, and I have never once seen rooks make war on one another, or kill one another, and you can't remember a single year without war. We do not rob one another, or open savings banks or schools for modern languages; we do not bear false witness or blackmail; we do not write bad novels and bad verse, or edit blasphemous newspapers. . . . I have

452

lived three hundred and seventy-six years and I have never seen that our mates have been unfaithful to, or have injured their husbands . . . and with you, Mr. Man. how is it? We have no flunkeys, no back-biters, no sycophants, no swindlers, no panderers, no hypocrites . . ."

At that moment this talker was called by his companions, and flew away over the fields before he had time to finish his sentence.

On the Way

In the room which the innkeeper, the Cossack Semión Tchistoplui, called "The Traveller,"—meaning thereby, "reserved for travellers,"—a tall and heavy shouldered man of about forty years of age sat at a large table asleep. A fragment of a tallow candle, stuck in a jar, illumined his fair hair, his broad nose, his sunburnt cheeks, and the big brows. . . . Taken one by one, all his features—his nose, his cheeks, his eyebrows—were as rude and heavy as the furniture. Taken together they produced an effect of singularly united proportion. Such, indeed, is often the character of the Russian face; the bigger, the sharper the features, the softer and more gentle the whole. The sleeper was dressed well, in a threadbare jacket bound with new wide braid, a plush waistcoat. and loose black trousers, with large boots.

On a bench which stretched the whole way round the room slept a girl some eight years of age. She lay upon a foxskin overcoat, and wore a brown dress and long black stockings. Her face was pale, her hair fair, her shoulders narrow, her body slight and frail; but her nose ended in just such an ugly lump as the man's. She slept soundly, and did not seem to feel that the crescent comb which had fallen from her hair was cutting into her cheek.

"The Traveller" had a holiday air. The atmosphere smelt of newly-washed floors; there were no rags on the line which stretched diagonally across the room; and in the ikon corner, casting a red reflection upon the image of St. George the Victory-Bringer, burned a lamp. With a severe and cautious gradation from the divine to the earthly, there stretched from each side of the image a row of gaudily-painted pictures. In the dim light thrown from the lamp and candle-end these pictures seemed to form a continuous belt covered with black patches; but when the tiled stove, wishing to sing in accord with the weather, drew in the blast with a howl, and the logs, as if angered, burst into ruddy flames and roared with rage, rosy patches quivered along the walls; and above the head of the sleeping man might be seen first the faces of seraphim, then the Shah Nasr Edin, and finally a greasy, sunburnt boy, with staring eyes, whispering something into the ear of a girl with a singularly blunt and indifferent face.

The storm howled outside. Something wild and angry, but deeply miserable, whirled round the inn with the fury of a beast, and strove to burst its way in. It banged against the doors, it beat on the windows and roof, it tore the walls, it threatened, it implored, it quieted down, and then with the joyous howl of triumphant treachery it rushed up the stove pipe; but here the logs burst into flame, and the fire, like a chained hound, rose up in rage to meet its enemy. There was a sobbing, a hissing, and an angry roar. In all this might be distinguished both irritated weariness and unsatisfied hate, and the angered impotence of one accustomed to victory.

Enchanted by the wild, inhuman music, "The Traveller" seemed numbed into immobility for ever. But the door creaked on its hinges, and into the inn came the potboy in a new calico shirt. He walked with a limp, twitched his sleepy eyes, snuffed the candle with his fingers, and went out. The bells of the village church of Rogatchi, three hundred yards away, began to strike twelve. It was midnight. The storm played with the sounds as with snowflakes. it chased them to infinite distances, it cut some short and stretched some into long undulating notes; and it smothered others altogether in the universal tumult. But suddenly a chime resounded so loudly through the room that it might have been rung under the window. The girl on the foxskin overcoat started and raised her head. For a moment she gazed vacantly at the black window, then turned her eyes upon Nasr Edin, on whose face the firelight gleamed, and finally looked at the sleeping man.

"Papa!" she cried.

But her father did not move. The girl peevishly twitched her eyebrows, and lay down again with her legs bent under her. A loud yawn sounded outside the door. Again the hinges squeaked, and indistinct voices were heard. Someone entered, shook the snow from his coat, and stamped his feet heavily.

"Who is it?" drawled a female voice.

"Mademoiselle Ilováisky," answered a bass.

Again the door creaked. The storm tore into the cabin and howled. Someone, no doubt the limping boy, went to the door of "The Traveller," coughed respectfully, and raised the latch.

"Come in, please," said the female voice. "It is all quite clean, honey!"

The door flew open. On the threshold appeared a bearded muzhik, dressed in a coachman's caftan, covered with snow from head to foot. He stooped under the weight of a heavy portmanteau. Behind him entered a little female figure, not half his height, faceless and handless. rolled into a shapeless bundle, and covered also with snow. Both coachman and bundle smelt of damp. The candle-flame trembled.

"What nonsense!" cried the bundle angrily. "Of course we can go on! It is only twelve versts more. chiefly wood. There is no fear of our losing the way."

"Lose our way or not, it's all the same . . . the horses won't go an inch farther," answered the coachman. "Lord bless you, miss. . . . As if I had done it on purpose!"

"Heaven knows where you've landed me! . . Hush! there's someone asleep. You may go!"

The coachman shook the caked snow from his shoulders, set down the portmanteau, snuffled, and went out. And the little girl, watching, saw two tiny hands creeping out of the middle of the bundle, stretching upward, and undoing the network of shawls, handkerchiefs, and scarfs. First on the floor fell a heavy shawl, then a hood, and after it a white knitted muffler. Having freed its head, the bundle removed its cloak, and shrivelled suddenly into half its former size. Now it appeared in a long, grey ulster, with immense buttons and yawning pockets. From one pocket it drew a paper parcel. From the other came a bunch of keys, which the bundle put down so incautiously that the sleeping man started and opened his eyes. For a moment he looked around him vacantly, as if not realising where he was, then shook his head, walked to the corner of the room, and sat down. The bundle took off its ulster, again reduced itself by half, drew off its shoes, and also sat down.

It no longer resembled a bundle. It was a woman, a tiny, fragile brunette of some twenty years of age, thin as a serpent, with a long pale face, and curly hair. Her nose was long and sharp, her chin long and sharp, her eyelashes long; and thanks to a general sharpness the expression of her face was stinging. Dressed in a tight-fitting black gown, with lace on the neck and sleeves, with sharp elbows and long, rosy fingers, she called to mind portraits of English ladies of the middle of the century. The serious, self-centered expression of her face served only to increase the resemblance.

The brunette looked around the room, glanced side-long at the man and girl, and, shrugging her shoulders, went over and sat at the window. The dark windows trembled in the damp west wind. Outside great flakes of snow, flashing white, darted against the glass, clung to it for a second, and were whirled away by the storm. The wild music grew louder.

There was a long silence. At last the little girl rose suddenly, and, angrily ringing out every word, exclaimed:

"Lord! Lord! How unhappy I am! The most miserable being in the world!"

The man rose, and with a guilty air, ill-suited to his gigantic stature and long beard, went to the bench.

"You're not sleeping, dearie? What do you want?" He spoke in the voice of a man who is excusing himself.

"I don't want anything! My shoulder hurts! You are a wicked man, father, and God will punish you! Wait! "You'll see how he'll punish you!"

"I know it's painful, darling . . . but what can I do?" He spoke in the tone employed by husbands when they make excuses to their angry wives. "If your shoulder hurts it is the long journey that is guilty. To-morrow it will be over, then we shall rest and the pain will stop. . . ."

"To-morrow! To-morrow! . . . Every day you say to-morrow! We shall go on for another twenty days!"

"Listen, friend, I give you my word of honour that this is the last day. I never tell you untruths. If the storm delayed us, that is not my fault."

"I can bear it no longer! I cannot! I cannot!"

Sasha pulled in her leg sharply, and filled the room with a disagreeable whining cry. Her father waved his arm, and looked absent-mindedly at the brunette. The brunette shrugged her shoulders, and walked irresolutely towards Sasha.

"Tell me, dear," she said, "why are you crying? It is very nasty to have a sore shoulder . . . but what can be done?"

"The fact is, mademoiselle," said the man apologetically, "we have had no sleep for two nights, and drove here in a villainous cart. No wonder she is ill and unhappy. A drunken driver . . . the luggage stolen . . . all the time in a snowstorm . . . but what's the good of crying? . . . I, too, am tired out with sleeping in a sitting position, so tired that I feel almost drunk. Listen, Sasha . . . even as they are things are bad enough . . . yet you must cry!"

He turned his head away, waved his arm, and sat down.

"Of course, you mustn't cry!" said the brunette. "Only babies cry. If you are ill, dearie, you must undress and go to sleep. . . . Come, let me undress you!"

With the girl undressed and comforted, silence again took possession of the room. The brunette sat at the window, and looked questioningly at the wall, the ikon, and the stove. Apparently things around seemed very strange to her, the room, the girl with her fat nose and boy's short nightgown, and the girl's father. That strange man sat in the corner, looking vacantly about him like a drunken man, and rubbing his face with his hands. He kept silence, blinked his eyes; and judging from his guilty figure no one would expect that he would be the first to break the silence. Yet it was he who began. He smoothed his trousers, coughed, laughed, and said:

"A comedy, I swear to God! . . . I look around, and can't believe my eyes. Why did destiny bring us to this accursed inn? What did she mean to express by it? But life sometimes makes such a *salto mortale*, that you look and can't believe your eyes. Are you going far, miss?"

"Not very far," answered the brunette. "I was going from home, about twenty versts away, to a farm of ours where my father and brother are staying. I am Mademoiselle Ilováisky, and the farm is Ilováisk. It is twelve versts from this. What disagreeable weather!"

"It could hardly be worse."

The lame pot-boy entered the room, and stuck a fresh candle end in the pomade jar.

"Get the samovar!" said the man.

"Nobody drinks tea at this hour," grinned the boy. "It is a sin before Mass."

"Don't you mind . . . it is not you that'll burn in hell, but we. . . ."

While they drank their tea the conversation continued. Mdlle. Ilováisky learned that the stranger's name was Grigóri Petróvitch Likharyóff, that he was a brother of Likharyóff, the Marshal of the Nobility in the neighbouring district, that he had himself once been a landed proprietor, but had gone through everything. And in turn Likharyóff learned that his companion was Márya Mikháilovna Ilováisky, that her father had a large estate, and that all the management fell upon her shoulders, as both father and brother were improvident, looked at life through their fingers, and thought of little but greyhounds. . . .

"My father and brother are quite alone on the farm," said Mdlle. Ilováisky, moving her fingers (she had a habit in conversation of moving her fingers before her stinging face, and after every phrase, licking her lips with a pointed tongue); "they are the most helpless creatures on the face of the earth, and can't lift a finger to help themselves. My father is muddle-headed, and my brother every evening tired off his feet. Imagine! . . . who is to get them food after the Fast? Mother is dead, and our servants cannot lay a cloth without my supervision. They will be without proper food, while I spend all night here. It is very funny!"

Mdlle. Ilováisky shrugged her shoulders, sipped her tea, and said:

"There are certain holidays which have a peculiar smell. Easter, Trinity, and Christmas each has its own smell. Even atheists love these holidays. My brother, for instance, says there is no God, but at Easter he is the first to run off to the morning service."

Likharyóff lifted his eyes, turned them on his companion and laughed.

"They say that there is no God," continued Mdlle. Ilováisky, also laughing, "but why then, be so good as to tell me, do all celebrated writers, scholars, and clever men generally, believe at the close of their lives?"

"The man who in youth has not learnt to believe does not believe in old age, be he a thousand times a writer."

Judged by his cough, Likharyóff had a bass voice, but now either from fear of speaking too loud, or from a needless bashfulness, he spoke in a tenor. After a moment's silence, he sighed and continued:

"This is how I understand it. Faith is a quality of the soul. It is the same as talent . . . It is congenital. As far as I can judge from my own case, from those whom I have met in life, from all that I see around me, this congenital faith is inherent in all Russians to an astonishing degree. . . . May I have another cup? . . . Russian life presents itself as a continuous series of faiths and infatuations, but unbelief or negation it has not—if I may so express it—even smelt. That a Russian does not believe in God is merely a way of

saying that he believes in something else."

Likharyóff took from Mdlle. Ilováisky another cup of tea, gulped down half of it at once, and continued:

"Let me tell you about myself. In my soul Nature planted exceptional capacity for belief. Half my life have I lived an atheist and a Nihilist, yet never was there a single moment when I did not believe. Natural gifts display themselves generally in early childhood, and my capacity for faith showed itself at a time when I could walk upright underneath the table. My mother used to make us children eat a lot, and when she gave us our meals, she had a habit of saying, 'Eat, children; there's nothing on earth like soup!' I believed this: I ate soup ten times a day, swallowed it like a shark to the point of vomiting and disgust. My nurse used to tell me fairy tales, and I believed in ghosts, in fairies, in wood-demons, in every kind of monster. I remember well! I used to steal corrosive sublimate from father's room, sprinkle it on gingerbread, and leave it in the attic, so that the ghosts might eat it and die. But when I learned to read and to understand what I read, my beliefs got beyond description. I even ran away to America, I joined a gang of robbers, I tried to enter a monastery, I hired boys to torture me for Christ's sake. When I ran away to America I did not go alone, but took with me just such another fool, and I was glad when we froze nearly to death, and when I was flogged. When I ran away to join the robbers, I returned every time with a broken skin. Most untranquil childhood! But when I was sent to school, and learned that the earth goes round the sun, and that white light so far from being white is composed of seven primary colours, my head went round entirely. At home everything seemed hideous, my mother, in the name of Elijah, denying lightning conductors, my father indifferent to the truths I preached. My new enlightenment inspired me! Like a madman I rushed about the house; I preached my truths to the stable boys, I was driven to despair by ignorance, I flamed with hatred against all who saw in the white light only white. . . . But this is nonsense. . . . Serious, so to speak, manly infatuations began with me only at college. . . . Have you completed a university course?"

"At Novotcherkask—in the Don Institute."

"But that is not a university course. You can hardly know what this science is. All sciences, whatever they may be, have only one and the same passport, without which they are meaningless—an aspiration to truth! Every one of them—even your wretched pharmacology—has its end, not in profit, not in convenience and advantage to life, but in truth. It is astonishing! When you begin the study of any science you are captivated from the first. I tell you, there is nothing more seductive and gracious, nothing so seizes and overwhelms the human soul, as the beginning of a science. In the first five or six lectures you are exalted by the very brightest hopes—you seem already the master of eternal truth. . . . Well, I gave myself to science passionately, as to a woman loved. I was its slave, and, except it, would recognise no other sun. Day and night, night and day, without unbending my back, I studied. I learnt off formulas by heart; I ruined myself

on books; I wept when I saw with my own eyes others exploiting science for personal aims. . . . But I got over my infatuation soon. The fact is, every science has a beginning, but it has no end—it is like a recurring decimal. Zoology discovered thirty-five thousand species of insects; chemistry counts sixty elementary substances. If, as time goes by, you add to these figures ten ciphers, you will be just as far from the end as now, for all contemporary scientific research consists in the multiplication of figures. . . . This I began to understand when I myself discovered the thirty-five-thousand-and-first species, and gained no satisfaction. But I had no disillusion to outlive, for a new faith immediately appeared. I thrust myself into Nihilism with its proclamations, its hideous deeds, its tricks of all sorts. I went down to the people; I served as factory-hand; I greased the axles of railway carriages; I turned myself into a bargee. It was while thus wandering all over the face of Russia that I first saw Russian life. I became an impassioned admirer of that life. I loved the Russian people to distraction; I loved and trusted in its God, in its language, in its creations. . . . And so on eternally. . . . In my time I have been a Slavophile, and bored Aksakoff with my letters; and an Ukrainophile, and an archæologist, and a collector of specimens of popular creative art. . . . I have been carried away by ideas, by men, by events, by places. . . . I have been carried away unceasingly. . . . Five years ago I embodied as the negation of property; my latest faith was non-resistance to evil."

Sasha sighed gustily and moved. Likharyóff rose and went over to her.

"Will you have some tea, darling?"
he asked tenderly.

"Drink it yourself!" answered Sasha.

"You have lived a varied life," said
Márya Mikháilovna. "You have something to remember."

"Yes, yes; it is all very genial when
you sit at the tea-table and gossip with
a good companion; but you do not ask
me what has all this gaiety cost me.
With what have I paid for the diversity
of my life? You must remember, in
the first place, that I did not believe
like a German Doctor of Philosophy.
I did not live as a hermit, but my every
faith bent me as a bow, and tore my
body to pieces. Judge for yourself!
Once I was as rich as my brother: now
I am a beggar. Into this whirlpool of
infatuation I cast my own estate, the
property of my wife, the money of
many others. I am forty-two to-day,
with old age staring me in the face, and
I am homeless as a dog that has lost
his master by night. In my whole life
I have never known repose. My soul
was in constant torment; I suffered even
from my hopes. . . . I have worn
myself out with heavy unregulated work;
I have suffered deprivation; five times
I have been in prison. I have wandered through Archangel and Tobolsk
. . . the very memory sickens me. I
lived, but in the vortex never felt the
process of life. Will you believe it, I
never noticed how my wife loved me—
when my children were born. What
more can I tell you? To all who loved
me I brought misfortune. . . . My
mother has mourned for me now fifteen
years, and my own brothers, who through
me have been made to blush, who have
been made to bend their backs, whose
hearts have been sickened, whose money

has been wasted, have grown at last to
hate me like poison."

Likharyóff rose and again sat down.

"If I were only unhappy I should
be thankful to God," he continued,
looking at Mdlle. Ilováisky. "But my
personal unhappiness fades away when
I remember how often in my infatuations I was ridiculous, far from the
truth, unjust, cruel, dangerous! How
often with my whole soul have I hated
and despised those whom I ought to
have loved, and loved those whom I
ought to have hated! To-day, I believe;
I fall down on my face and worship: to-
morrow, like a coward, I flee from the
gods and friends of yesterday, and
silently swallow some scoundrel! God
alone knows how many times I have
wept with shame for my infatuations!
Never in my life have I consciously lied
or committed a wrong, yet my conscience is unclean! I cannot even boast
that my hands are unstained with blood,
for before my own eyes my wife faded
to death—worn out by my improvidence. My own wife! . . . Listen;
there are now in fashion two opposing
opinions of woman. One class measures
her skull to prove that she is lower than
man, to determine her defects, to justify their own animality. The other
would employ all their strength in lifting woman to their own level—that is
to say, force her to learn by heart
thirty-five thousand species of insects,
to talk and write the same nonsense as
they themselves talk and write."

Likharyóff's face darkened.

"But I tell you that woman always
was and always will be the slave of
man!" he said in a bass voice, thumping his fist on the table. "She is wax—
tender, plastic wax—from which man

can mould what he will. Lord in heaven! Yet of some trumpery infatuation for manhood she cuts her hair, forsakes her family, dies in a foreign land. . . . Of all the ideas to which she sacrifices herself not one is feminine! . . . Devoted, unthinking slave! Skulls I have never measured; but this I say from bitter, grievous experience: The proudest, the most independent women—once I had succeeded in communicating to them my inspiration, came after me, unreasoning, asking no questions, obeying my every wish. Of a nun I made a Nihilist, who, as I afterwards learned, killed a gendarme. My wife never forsook me in all my wanderings, and like a weathercock changed her faith as I changed my infatuations."

With excitement Likharóff jumped up, and walked up and down the room.

"Noble, exalted slavery!" he exclaimed, gesticulating. "In this, in this alone, is hidden the true significance of woman's life. . . . Out of all the vile nonsense which accumulated in my head during my relations with women, one thing, as water from a filter, has come out pure, and that is neither ideas, nor philosophy, nor clever phrases, but this extraordinary submissiveness of fate, this uncommon benevolence, this all-merciful kindness."

Likharyóff clenched his fists, concentrated his eyes upon a single point, and, as if tasting every word, filtered through his clenched teeth:

"This magnanimous endurance, faith to the grave, the poetry of the heart. It is in this . . . yes, it is in this that the meaning of life is found, in this unmurmuring martyrdom, in the tears that soften stone, in the infinite all-forgiving love, which sweeps into the chaos of life in lightness and warmth. . . ."

Márya Mikháilovna rose slowly, took a step towards Likharyóff, and set her eyes piercingly upon his face. By the tears which sparkled on his eyelashes, by the trembling, passionate voice, by the flushed cheeks, she saw at a glance that women were not the accidental theme of his conversation. No, they were the object of his new infatuation, or, as he put it, of his new belief. For the first time in her life she saw before her a man in the ecstacy of a burning, prophetic faith. Gesticulating—rolling his eyes, he seemed insane and ecstatical; but in the fire in his eyes, in the torrent of his words, in all the movements of his gigantic body, she saw only such beauty, that, herself, not knowing what she did, she stood silently before him as if rooted to the ground, and looked with rapture into his face.

"Take my mother, for example!" he said, with an imploring look, stretching out his arms to her. "I poisoned her life, I disgraced in her eyes the race of Likharyóff, I brought her only such evil as is brought by the bitterest foe, and . . . what? My brothers give her odd kopecks for wafers and collections, and she, violating her religious feeling, hoards up those kopecks, and sends them secretly to me! Such deeds as this educate and ennoble the soul more than all your theories, subtle phrases, thirty-five thousand species! . . . But I might give you a thousand instances! Take your own case! Outside storm and darkness, yet through storm and darkness and cold, you drive, fearless, to your father and brother, that their holidays may be warmed by your caresses, although they, it may well be, have forgotten your existence. But wait! The day will come when you will learn to love a man, and you will go after him to the North Pole. . . . You would go!"

"Yes . . . if I loved him."

"You see!" rejoiced Likharyóff, stamping his feet. "Oh, God, how happy I am to have met you here! . . . Such has always been my good fortune . . . everywhere I meet with kind acquaintances. Not a day passes that I do not meet some man for whom I would give my own soul! In this world there are many more good people than evil! Already you and I have spoken frankly and out of heart, as if we had known one another a thousand years. It is possible for a man to live his own life, to keep silent for ten years, to be reticent with his own wife and friends, and then some day suddenly he meets a cadet in a railway carriage, and reveals to him his whole soul. . . . You . . . I have the honour to see you for the first time, but I have confessed myself as I never did before. Why?"

Likharyóff rubbed his hands and smiled gaily. Then he walked up and down the room and talked again of women. The church bell chimed for the morning service.

"Heavens!" wept Sasha. "He won't let me sleep with his talk!"

"*Akh,* yes!" stammered Likharyóff. "Forgive me, darling. Sleep, sleep. . . . In addition to her, I have two boys," he whispered. "They live with their uncle, but she cannot bear to be a day without her father. . . . Suffers, grumbles, but sticks to me as a fly to honey. . . . But I have been talking nonsense, mademoiselle, and have pre-vented you also from sleeping. Shall I make your bed?"

Without waiting for an answer, he shook out the wet cloak, and stretched it on the bench with the fur on top, picked up the scattered mufflers and shawls, and rolled the ulster into a pillow—all this silently, with an expression of servile adoration, as though he were dealing not with women's rags, but with fragments of holy vessels. His whole figure seemed to express guilt and confusion, as if in the presence of such a tiny being he were ashamed of his height and strength. . . .

When Mdlle. Ilováisky had lain down he extinguished the candle, and sat on a stool near the stove. . . .

"Yes," he whispered, smoking a thick cigarette, and puffing the smoke into the stove. "Nature has set in every Russian an enquiring mind, a tendency to speculation, and extraordinary capacity for belief; but all these are broken into dust against our improvidence, indolence, and fantastic triviality. . . ."

Márya Mikháilovna looked in astonishment into the darkness, but she could see only the red spot on the ikon, and the quivering glare from the stove on Likharyóff's face. The darkness, the clang of the church bells, the roar of the storm, the limping boy. peevish Sasha and unhappy Likharyóff—all these mingled, fused in one great impression, and the whole of God's world seemed to her fantastic, full of mystery and magical forces. The words of Likharyóff resounded in her ears, and human life seemed to her a lovely, poetical fairy-tale, to which there was no end.

The great impression grew and grew,

until it absorbed all consciousness and was transformed into a sweet sleep. Mdlle. Ilováisky slept. But in sleep she continued to see the lamp, and the thick nose with the red light dancing upon it. She was awakened by a cry.

"Papa, dear," tenderly implored a child's voice. "Let us go back to uncle's! There is a Christmas tree. Stepa and Kolya are there!"

"What can I do, darling?" reasoned a soft, male bass. "Try and understand me. . . ."

And to the child's crying was added the man's. The cry of this double misery breaking through the howl of the storm, touched upon the ears of the girl with such soft, human music, that she could not withstand the emotion, and wept also. And she listened as the great black shadow walked across the room, lifted up the fallen shawl and wrapped it round her feet.

Awakened again by a strange roar, she sprang up and looked around her. Through the windows, covered halfway up in snow, gleamed the blue dawn. The room itself was full of a grey twilight, through which she could see the stove, the sleeping girl, and Nasr Edin. The lamp and stove had both gone out. Through the wide-open door of the room could be seen the public hall of the inn with its tables and benches. A man with a blunt, gypsy face and staring eyes stood in the middle of the room in a pool of melted snow, and held up a stick with a red star on the top. Around him was a throng of boys, immovable as statues, and covered with snow. The light of the star, piercing through its red paper covering, flushed their wet faces. The crowd roared in discord,

and out of their roar Mdlle. Ilováisky understood only one quatrain:—

"Hey, boy, bold and fearless,
Take a knife sharp and shiny,
Come, kill and kill the Jew,
The sorrowing son . . ."

At the counter stood Likharyóff, looking with emotion at the singers, and tramping his feet in time. Seeing Márya Mikháilovna he smiled broadly, and entered the room. She also smiled.

"Congratulations!" he said. " see you have slept well."

Mdlle. Ilováisky looked at him silently, and continued to smile.

After last night's conversation he seemed to her no longer tall and broad-shouldered, but a little man. A big steamer seems small to those who have crossed the ocean.

"It is time for me to go," she said. "I must get ready. Tell me, where are you going to?"

"I? First to Klinushka station, thence to Siergievo, and from Sergievo a drive of forty versts to the coal mines of a certain General Shashkovsky. My brothers have got me a place as manager. . . . I will dig coal."

"Allow me . . . I know these mines. Shashkovsky is my uncle. But . . . why are you going there?" asked Márya Mikháilovna in surprise.

"As manager. I am to manage the mines."

"I don't understand." She shrugged her shoulders. "You say you are going to these mines. Do you know what that means? Do you know that it is all bare steppe, that there is not a soul near . . . that the tedium is such that you could not live there a single day? The coal is bad, nobody buys it, and my uncle is a maniac, a despot, a bankrupt. . . . He will not even pay your salary."

"It is the same,' said Likharyóff indifferently. "Even for the mines, thanks!"

Mdlle. Ilováisky again shrugged her shoulders, and walked up and down the room in agitation.

"I cannot understand, I cannot understand," she said, moving her fingers before her face. "This is inconceivable . . . it is madness. Surely you must realise that this . . . it is worse than exile. It is a grave for a living man. Ahk, heavens!" she said passionately, approaching Likharyóff and moving her fingers before his smiling face. Her upper lip trembled and her stinging face grew pale. "Imagine it . . . a bare steppe . . . and solitude. Not a soul to say a word to . . . and you . . . infatuated with women! Mines and women!"

Mdlle. Ilováisky seemed ashamed of her warmth, and, turning away from Likharyóff, went over to the window.

"No . . . no . . . you cannot go there!" she said, rubbing her finger down the window-pane.

Not only through her head, but through her whole body ran a feeling that here behind her stood an unhappy, forsaken, perishing man. But he, as if unconscious of his misery, as if he had not wept the night before, looked at her and smiled good-humouredly. It would have been better if he had continued to cry. For a few minutes in agitation she walked up and down the room, and then stopped in the corner and began to think. Likharyóff said something, but she did not hear him. Turning her back to him, she took

a credit note from her purse, smoothed it in her hand, and then, looking at him, blushed and thrust it into her pocket.

Outside the inn resounded the coachman's voice. Silently, with a severe, concentrated expression, Mdlle. Ilováisky began to put on her wraps. Likharyóff rolled her up in them, and chatted gaily. But every word caused her intolerable pain. It is not pleasant to listen to the jests of the wretched or dying.

When the transformation of a living woman into a formless bundle was complete, Mdlle. Ilováisky looked for the last time around "The Traveller," stood silent a moment, and then went out slowly. Likharyóff escorted her.

Outside, God alone knows why, the storm still raged. Great clouds of big, soft snowflakes restlessly whirled over the ground, finding no abiding place. Horses, sledge, trees, the bull tethered to the post—all were white, and seemed made of down.

"Well, God bless you!" stammered Likharyóff, as he helped Márya Mikhálilovna into the sledge. "Don't think ill of me!"

Mdlle. Ilováisky said nothing. When the sledge started and began to circle round a great snowdrift, she looked at Likharyóff as if she wished to say something. Likharyóff ran up to the sledge, but she said not a word, and only gazed at him through her long eyelashes to which the snowflakes already clung.

Whether it be that his sensitive mind read this glance aright, or whether, as it may have been, that his imagination led him astray, it suddenly struck him that but a little more and this girl would have forgiven him his age, his failures, his misfortunes, and followed him, neither questioning nor reasoning, to the ends of the earth. For a long time he stood as if rooted to the spot, and gazed at the track left by the sledge-runners. The snowflakes settled swiftly on his hair, his beard, his shoulders. But soon the traces of the sledge-runners vanished. and he, covered with snow, began to resemble a white boulder, his eyes all the time continuing to search for something through the clouds of snow.

Children

PAPA and mamma and Aunt Nayda are not at home. They have gone to a christening party at the house of that old officer who rides on a little gray horse. While waiting for them to come home, Grisha, Anya, Alyosha, Sonya, and the cook's son, Andrey, are sitting at the table in the dining-room, playing at loto. To tell the truth, it is bedtime, but how can one go to sleep without hearing from mamma what the baby was like at the christening, and what they had for supper? The table, lighted by a hanging lamp. is dotted with numbers, nut-shells, scraps of paper, and little bits of glass   Two cards lie in front of each player, and a heap of bits of glass for covering the numbers. In the middle of the table is a white saucer with five kopecks in it. Beside the saucer are a half-eaten apple, a pair of scissors, and a plate on which they have been told to put their nut-shells. The children are playing for money. The stake is a kopeck. The rule is: if any-one cheats, he is turned out at once. There is no one in the dinning-room but the players. and nurse Agafya Ivanovna, is in the kitchen. showing the cook how to cut a pattern, while their elder brother, Vasya, a schoolboy in the fifth class, is lying on the sofa in the draw-ing-room, feeling bored.

They are playing with zest. The greatest excitement is expressed on the face of Grisha. He is a small boy of nine, with a head cropped so that the bare skin shows through, chubby cheeks, and thick lips like a Negro's. He is already in the preparatory class, and so is regarded as grown up, and the clever-est. He is playing entirely for the sake of the money. If there had been no kopecks in the saucer, he would have been asleep long ago. His brown eyes stray uneasily and jealously over the other players' cards. The fear that he may not win, envy, and the financial combi-nations of which his cropped head is full, will not let him sit still and concentrate his mind. He fidgets as though he were sitting on thorns. When he wins, he snatches up the money greedily, and in-stantly puts it in his pocket. His sister. Anya, a girl of eight, with a sharp chin and clever shining eyes, is also afraid that someone else may win. She flushes and turns pale, and watches the players keenly. The kopecks do not interest her. Success in the game is for her a question of vanity. The other sister, Sonya, a child of six with a curly head, and a complexion such as is seen only in very healthy children, expensive dolls, and the faces on bonbon boxes, is playing loto for the process of the game itself. There is bliss all over her face. Whoever wins, she laughs and claps her hands. Alyosha, a chubby, spherical little figure, gasps, breathes hard through his nose, and stares open-eyed at the cards. He is moved neither by covetousness nor vanity. So long as he is not driven out of the room, or sent to bed, he is thankful. He looks phlegmatic, but at heart he is rather a little beast. He is not there so much for the sake of the loto, as for the sake of the misunderstandings which are inevitable in the game. He is greatly delighted if one hits another, or calls him names. He ought to have run off somewhere long ago, but he won't leave the table for a minute, for fear they should steal his counters or his kopecks. As he can only count the units and numbers which end in nought, Anya covers his numbers for him. The fifth player, the cook's son, Andrey, a dark-skinned and sickly looking boy in a cotton shirt, with a copper cross on his breast, stands motionless, looking dreamily at the numbers. He takes no interest in winning, or in the success of the others, because he is entirely engrossed by the arithmetic of the game, and its far from complex theory; "How many numbers there are in the world," he is thinking, "and how is it they don't get mixed up?"

They all shout out the numbers in turn, except Sonya and Alyosha. To vary the monotony, they have invented in the course of time a number of synonyms and comic nicknames. Seven for instance, is called the "ovenrake," eleven the "sticks," seventy-seven "Semyon

Semyonitch," ninety "grandfather," and so on. The game is going merrily.

"Thirty-two" cries Grisha, drawing the little red cylinders out of his father's cap. "Seventeen! Ovenrake! Twenty-eight! Lay them straight. . . ."

Anya sees that Andrey has let twenty-eight slip. At any other time she would have pointed it out to him, but now when her vanity lies in the saucer with the kopecks, she is triumphant.

"Twenty-three!" Grisha goes on, "Semyon Semyonitch! Nine!"

"A beetle, a beetle," cries Sonya, pointing to a beetle running across the table. "Aie!"

"Don't kill it," says Alyosha, in his deep bass, "perhaps it's got children. . . ."

Sonya follows the black beetle with her eyes and wonders about its children: what tiny little beetles they must be!

"Forty-three! One!" Grisha goes on, unhappy at the thought that Anya has already made two fours. "Six!"

"Game! I have got the game!" cries Sonya, rolling her eyes coquettishly and giggling.

The players' countenances lengthen.

"Must make sure!" says Grisha, looking with hatred at Sonya.

Exercising his rights as a big boy, and the cleverest, Grisha takes upon himself to decide. What he wants, that they do. Sonya's reckoning is slowly and carefully verified, and to the great regret of her fellow players, it appears that she has not cheated. Another game is begun.

"I did see something yesterday!" says Anya, as though to herself. "Filipp Filippitch turned his eyelids inside out somehow and his eyes looked red and dreadful, like an evil spirit's."

"I saw it too," says Grisha. "Eight! And a boy at our school can move his ears. Twenty-seven!"

Andrey looks up at Grisha, meditates, and says:

"I can move my ears too. . . ."

"Well then, move them."

Andrey moves his eyes, his lips, and his fingers, and fancies that his ears are moving too. Everyone laughs.

"He is a horrid man, that Filipp Filippitch," sighs Sonya. "He came into our nursery yesterday, and I had nothing on but my chemise. . . . And I felt so improper!"

"Game!" Grisha c r i e s suddenly, snatching the money from the saucer. "I've got the game! You can look and see if you like."

The cook's son looks up and turns pale.

"Then I can't go on playing any more," he whispers.

"Because . . . because I have got no more money."

"You can't play without money," says Grisha.

Andrey ransacks his pockets once more to make sure. Finding nothing in them but crumbs and a bitten pencil, he drops the corners of his mouth and begins blinking miserably. He is on the point of crying. . . .

"I'll put it down for you!" says Sonya, unable to endure his look of agony. "Only mind you must pay me back afterwards."

The money is brought and the game goes on.

"I believe they are ringing somewhere," says Anya, opening her eyes wide.

They all leave off playing and gaze open-mouthed at the dark window. The reflection of the lamp glimmers in the darkness.

"It was your fancy."

"At night they only ring in the cemetery," says Andrey. . . .

"And what do they ring there for?"

"To prevent robbers from breaking into the church. They are afraid of the bells."

"And what do robbers break into the church for?" asks Sonya.

"Everyone knows what for: to kill the watchmen."

A minute passes in silence. They all look at one another, shudder, and go on playing. This time Andrey wins.

"He has cheated," Alyosha booms out, apropos of nothing.

"What a lie, I haven't cheated."

Andrey turns pale, his mouth works, and he gives Alyosha a slap on the head! Alyosha glares angrily, jumps up, and with one knee on the table, slaps Andrey on the cheek! Each gives the other a second blow, and both howl. Sonya, feeling such horrors too much for her, begins crying too, and the dining room resounds with lamentations on various notes. But do not imagine that that is the end of the game. Before five minutes are over, the children are laughing and talking peaceably again. Their faces are tear-stained, but that does not prevent them from smiling; Alyosha is positively blissful, there has been a squabble.

Vasya, the fifth form schoolboy, walks into the dining-room. He looks sleepy and disillusioned.

"This is revolting!" he thinks, seeing Grisha feel in his pockets in which the kopecks are jingling. "How can they give children money? And how can they let them play games of chance? A

nice way to bring them up, I must say!
It's revolting!"

But the children's play is so tempting
that he feels an inclination to join them
and to try his luck.

"Wait a minute and I'll sit down to
a game," he says.

"Put down a kopeck!"

"In a minute," he says, fumbling in
his pockets. "I haven't a kopeck, but
here is a rouble. I'll stake a rouble."

"No, no, no. . . . You must put down
a kopeck."

"You stupids. A rouble is worth
more than a kopeck anyway," the
schoolboy explains. "Whoever wins
can give me change."

"No, please! Go away!"

The fifth form schoolboy shrugs his
shoulders, and goes into the kitchen to
get change from the servants. It appears there is not a single kopeck in the
kitchen.

"In that case, you give me change,"
he urges Grisha, coming back from the
kitchen. "I'll pay you for the change.
Won't you? Come, give me ten kopecks
for a rouble."

Grisha looks suspiciously at Vasya,
wondering whether it isn't some trick, a
swindle.

"I won't," he says, holding his
pockets.

Vasya begins to get cross, and abuses
them, calling them idiots and blockheads.

"I'll put down a stake for you,
Vasya!" says Sonya. "Sit down." He
sits down and lays two cards before him.
Anya begins counting the numbers.

"I've dropped a kopeck!" Grisha announces suddenly, in an agitated voice.
"Wait!"

He takes the lamp, and creeps under
the table to look for the kopeck. They
clutch at nutshells and all sorts of nasti-
ness, knock their heads together, but do
not find the kopeck. They begin looking again, and look till Vasya takes the
lamp out of Grisha's hands and puts it
in its place. Grisha goes on looking in
the dark. But at last the kopeck is
found. The players sit down at the
table and mean to go on playing.

"Sonya is asleep!" Alyosha announces.

Sonya, with her curly head lying on
her arms, is in a sweet, tranquil sleep, as
though she had been asleep for an hour.
She has fallen asleep by accident, while
the others were looking for the kopeck.

"Come along, lie on mamma's bed!"
says Anya, leading her away from the
table. "Come along!"

They all troop out with her, and five
minutes later mamma's bed presents a
curious spectacle. Sonya is asleep.
Alyosha is snoring beside her. With
their heads to the others' feet, sleep
Grisha and Anya. The cook's son, Andrey too, has managed to snuggle in beside them. Near them lie the kopecks,
that have lost their power till the next
game. Good-night!

Head Gardener's Tale

THE sale of flowers on ·Count N.'s estate was attended by few; I, a neighboring country gentleman, and a young lumber-dealer. While the workmen carried out our purchases to the carts, we sat at the greenhouse door, and talked away on every conceivable topic. On that warm April morning, to sit in the garden, hear the birds, and see the flowers was free and healthful.

The packing was superintended by the gardener, Mikhail Karlovitch, a worthy old man, with a fat, clean-shaven face, in a waist-coat of fur. He kept silence severely, and listened intently to our conversation, waiting to hear something new. We all considered him a German, though as a fact his father was a Swede and his mother Russian, and he was orthodox. He spoke Russian and read Swedish, and German, and knew no greater pleasure than to be lent some new book, or talked to, for instance, about Ibsen.

He had his weaknesses, innocent, most of them, enough: he called himself head gardener, though he had no juniors; his expression was always needlessly elated and grave; he tolerated no contradiction, and expected others to listen seriously and attentively.

"That young fellow, there, I may tell you, is a pretty rascal," said my neighbour, pointing to a swarthy, gipsy-like workman who drove a water-cart past. "Only last week he was tried for robbery and acquitted. The jury found him insane, though you can see from his snout he's as healthy as a bull. It seems to have become the fashion in Russia lately to acquit criminals, and explain their crimes by mental abnormality. These acquittals, this general weakness and condonation, will have a bad effect. They demoralise the masses; they blunt the sense of justice. People get used to seeing crime go unpunished. Shakespeare put it aptly when he wrote that 'Virtue itself turns vice, being misapplied.'"

"That's true," consented the timber-merchant. "Murder and incendiarism have increased since these acquittals began. Ask the muzhiks."

The gardener Mikhail Karlovitch turned to us and said—

"Do you know, gentlemen, that I always welcome these acquittals? I feel no fear for the cause of morals and justice when I hear the verdict: Not Guilty. On the contrary, I am delighted. Even when reason tells me that the jurymen have made a mistake, even then I rejoice. I put it to you, gentlemen; if judges and jurymen put more faith in *men*—than in clues, speeches, and articles put in evidence, is not this faith in men a higher thing than all practical considerations? Such faith is accessible only to the few—to those who understand and feel Christ."

"It's a good thought," I said.

"And now a new thought. I remember some time long ago hearing a legend on this theme. And a very fine legend," said the gardener, smiling. "I was told it by my late grandmother, my father's mother, a wonderful old woman! She told it in Swedish: in Russian it's less effective, less classical, so to speak."

We asked him to tell us the story, and forget the rudeness of the Russian

468

language. Flattered and content, he lighted a cigarette, looked angrily at the workmen, and began:—

"To a little town, somewhere, there came an old, solitary, ugly man, by name Thompson — or Wilson — the name doesn't count. His profession was a good one: he cured the sick. He was morose a n d uncommunicative, and spoke only when his work required it. He paid no visits, confined his intercourse to silent bows, and lived as modestly as a hermit. The explanation was that he was a scholar; and in those days scholars were different from ordinary men. They spent their days and nights in meditation, in reading books, and in curing the sick; they looked on everything else as worthless, and had no time to speak needless words. The townspeople understood this thoroughly, and did their best not to waste his time with visits and empty gossip. They rejoiced that God at last had sent them a man who could cure their complaints, and were proud to have among them such a remarkable man.

" 'He knows everything,' they said.

"But that was not enough. They might' have added, 'He loves every one.' For in this man's breast beat a good, an angel's heart. He forgot that the townspeople were no kin of his, that they were strangers to him; and he loved them as his children, and for their sake was ready to lay down his own life. He suffered, indeed, from consumption; he coughed; yet when they summoned him to some ailing townsman he forgot his own complaints, sacrificed himself, and, panting, hurried up steep hills. He ignored heat and cold; he despised hunger and thirst. He took no fees, and —stranger than all—when his patients

died, he followed their coffins to the grave and wept with their kinsmen.

"Soon he became such a needed part of the town's life that people wondered how they had lived before he came. They were grateful beyond words. Old and young, good and bad, honest and thieves—in one word, all—respected him and knew his worth. The town and neighbourhood had not one man who would do this benefactor a wrong, or even think of such. When he left his house his doors and windows lay open, for he knew that the most abandoned thief would not offend him. Sometimes, following his work of mercy, he crossed hills and forests full of hungry vagabonds. But he felt at ease. Once indeed by night when he returned from a sick-bed he was attacked by robbers in a wood. But when they saw his face they took off their caps respectfully and offered him food. When he said that he was not hungry they gave him a warm cloak and led him safe to town, happy that Fate had sent them a chance to show their gratitude to their benefactor. And, further—you can imagine it—my grandmother added that even horses, cows, and dogs knew him, and showed their joy when they saw him.

"But one fine day this man, whose holiness, it seemed, guarded him from all evil, whom even robbers respected— one fine day this man was found murdered. Bloody, with battered skull, he lay in a ravine, and his pale face expressed amazement. Yes; not fear, but merely surprise was his feeling when he saw his executioner before him. You can imagine the grief of the people of the town and neighbourhood! 'What man,' they asked themselves in despair, 'what man could possibly kill our friend?'

The magistrates who held the inquest and saw the good man's body came to this conclusion. 'Here,' they said, 'we have all the signs of murder. But as there exists not on earth a man who would kill our doctor, this can be no case of murder; and the marks on his body are a mere accident. It is plain that the doctor fell into the ravine in the darkness and dashed himself to death.'

"And this opinion was shared by all the town. They buried their doctor, and no one thenceforth spoke of his death as a crime. That a man should exist so infamous as to kill their friend they refused to believe. Even infamy has its limits? Is it not so?

"But not long afterwards—you may imagine it—chance pointed to the murderer. A notorious ne'er-do-well and evil-liver, who had been more than once in gaol, was caught in a drink-shop selling for liquor the doctor's snuff-box and watch. When taxed with the crime he lost his head and told transparent lies. They searched his house and found in his bed a blood-stained shirt and the doctor's lancet, which was set with gold. What further clues were wanted? He was put in gaol. The townspeople were horrified, but they continued to say—

"'Incredible! It is impossible. Be sure there is no mistake; circumstantial evidence like this often leads to injustice!'

"On trial the murderer obstinately denied his guilt. Everything told against him, and to find him innocent was as hard as to find this earth black. But the judges seemed to have gone out of their minds; they weighed every item of evidence a dozen times; they looked incredulously at the witnesses, they turned red, and drank water. . . The trial began at early morning and ended only at night.

"'Prisoner!' began the presiding judge, turning to the murderer. 'The court has found you guilty of the murder of Doctor N., and condemns you . . .'

"He intended to say 'to be hanged till you are dead,' but the paper on which the verdict was written dropped from his hand, he rubbed the sweat from his forehead, and cried out—

"'No! May God visit it on me if I judge unjustly, but I swear that this man is innocent! I will not admit the thought that there is a man on earth who would kill our friend the doctor! There is no man alive who would fall so low!'

"'There is no such man alive!' cried the other judges.

"'There is none!' echoed the crowd in court. 'Release him.'

"So the murderer was dismissed in peace, and not one man censured the judges for injustice. And God, added my grandmother, for such faith in his creatures forgave the townspeople all their sins. For He rejoices to think that man is indeed His image, and grieves when, forgetting their human worth, men judge men as dogs. It may be, the verdict of acquittal caused the townspeople harm; but, on the other hand reflect on the beneficent influence of his faith in men, this faith which never lies dead, which fosters our most generous feelings, and inspires us to love and respect our fellow-men. And that is a great thing."

Mikhail Karlovitch said no more. My neighbour was about to reply, but the old gardener with a gesture indicating that he disliked contradiction returned to the carts, and, with his old grave expression, resumed his work.

The Runaway

THERE was no end. Pashka and his mother, drenched with rain, mile after mile, across fields, then by woodland paths trudged on and on till morn. After that he stood two hours waiting in a dark entrance-hall. In the hall, of course, it was warmer and drier than outside; but even there raindrops entered, and as the hall slowly filled with patients, Pashka, pushing through, pressed his face against a sheepskin coat savoring of salted fish, and slumbered.

At last the bolt slipped, the door opened, and Pashka and his mother found themselves in the waiting-room. Yet another long delay! The patients sat on benches motionless and silent. Pashka stared at the crowd, and likewise held his tongue, though he witnessed many ludicrous, inexplicable things. But once when a boy hopped into the room on one leg, he nudged his mother's side, grinned in his sleeve, and exclaimed—

"Look, mother—a sparrow!"

"Don't talk, child, don't talk!"

At a little window appeared the *feldscher's* sleepy face. "Come and give your names."

The waiting patients, among them the funny, hopping boy, crowded round the window. Of each the *feldscher* asked name and patronymic, age, village, dates of illness, and other questions. From his mother's answer, Pashka learnt that his name was Pavl Galaktionoff, that he was seven years old, and that he had been ill since Easter.

When the names were entered there was another short delay; and then through the waiting-room walked the doctor, in white apron, with a towel on his shoulder. As he passed the hopping boy, he shrugged his shoulders, and said in a sing-song voice—

"You're a donkey! Now aren't you a donkey? I told you Monday, and you come on Friday! Don't worry yourself so far as I'm concerned, but if you're not careful, fool, you'll lose your leg!"

The hopping boy blinked, grimaced piteously as if asking for alms, and began—

"Ivan Nikolaitch, be so kind . . ."

"None of your Ivan Nikolaitch!" said the doctor teasingly. "I told you Monday—you should obey! You're a donkey, that's all."

The reception began. The doctor sat in his room, and called for the patients in turn. Now and then from the room came shrill exclamations, the sobs of children, and the doctor's angry exclamations—

"Don't howl. I won't murder you! Sit quiet!"

At last came Pashka's turn. "Pavl Galaktionoff!" cried the doctor. Pashka's mother at first seemed dazed, as if the summons were unexpected; but she recovered herself, took Pashka's hand, and led him into the doctor's room. The doctor sat on a table, and tapped mechanically with a mallet a thick book.

"What is the matter?" he asked, without looking at his visitors.

"My boy has a boil, *batiushka,* on his elbow," answered Pashka's mother; and her expression implied that she herself was suffering from Pashka's boil.

471

"Take off his clothes!"

Pashka, panting, untied his necker-chief, rubbed his nose on his sleeve, and began to unbutton his coat.

"Woman! have you come to pay me a visit?" said the doctor irritably. "Why don't you hurry? Are you the only one waiting?"

Pashka hurriedly threw his coat on the floor, and, with his mother's help, took off his shirt. The doctor looked at him absent-mindedly, and slapped him on the bare stomach.

"Serious, brother Pashka," he exclaimed. "You have outgrown your corporation!" When he had said this, he sighed, and added, "Show me your elbow!"

Pashka took fright at a bowl of blood-tinged water, looked at the doctor's apron, and began to cry.

"For shame!" said the doctor mockingly. "He's big enough to get married, yet he begins to howl. For shame!"

Pashka tried to stop his tears. He looked at his mother, and his expression said, "Don't tell them at home that I cried at the hospital."

The doctor examined the elbow, pinched it, sighed, smacked his lips, and again felt the elbow.

"You ought to be whipped, woman!" he said. "Why didn't you bring him sooner? His arm is nearly gone! Look at him, idiot, can't you see that the joint is diseased?"

"It is you who know best, *batiushka!*" said Pashka's mother.

"*Batiushka!* the lad's arm is rotting off, and you with your *batiushka!* What sort of a workman will he make without arms? You'll have to nurse him all his life! If you've got a pimple on your nose you run off here for treatment, but you let your own child rot for six months! You people are all the same!"

He lighted a cigarette. While it burned away he scolded Pashka's mother, hummed a tune, shook his head rhythmically, and thought something out. Naked Pashka stood before him, listened to the tune, and watched the smoke. When the cigarette went out the doctor started, and said in a low voice—

Listen, woman! Ointments and mixtures are no use in this case; you must leave him here."

"If it must be so, *batiushka,* so be it."

"We must have an operation. . . . And you, Pashka, you must stay," said the doctor, patting his shoulder. "We will let mother go, but you, brother, you will stay with me. It is not bad here, brother! I have raspberry bushes. You and I, Pashka, as soon as we get better, will go and catch thrushes, and I will show you a fox. We shall pay visits together. Eh? Will you stay? And mother will come for you to-morrow."

Pashka looked questioningly at his mother.

"You must stay, child," she said.

"Of course he'll stay," said the doctor merrily. "There is nothing to argue about! I'll show him a live fox. We'll drive to the fair and buy sugar-candy. Marya Denisovna, take him upstairs!"

The doctor was certainly a merry, talkative man; and Pashka was attracted, all the more because he had never been at a fair, and wanted to see a live fox. But his mother? He thought the problem out, and decided to ask the doctor to let his mother remain with him; but before he could open his mouth the nurse was leading him upstairs. With mouth wide open, he looked around. The stairs, the floors, the door-posts, all were painted a beautiful yellow; and everywhere there was a tempting smell of fast-butter. Everywhere hung lamps, everywhere lay carpets; and brass water-taps projected from every wall. But most of all Pashka was pleased by his bed with its grey, shaggy counterpane. He felt the pillows and the counterpane, and came to the conclusion that the doctor had a very nice house.

It was a little ward with only three cots. The first was vacant, the second Pashka's; and on the third sat a very old man with sour eyes, who coughed without cease, and spat into a bowl. From his bed Pashka could see through the open door part of another ward with two beds; on one lay a thin, very pallid man with a caoutchouc bladder on his head. A peasant, arms apart, with bandaged head, looking very like an old woman, sat on the other.

Having set Pashka on his bed, the nurse left him. She returned immediately with an armful of clothes. "These are for you," she said to him. "Put them on."

Pashka took off his old clothes, and, not without pleasure, arrayed himself in his new garments. After donning a shirt, a pair of trousers, and a grey dressing-gown, he looked at himself complacently, and thought how he would like to walk down the village street in his new clothes. Imagination painted his mother sending him to the kitchen garden by the river, to pluck cabbage leaves for the pig, while the village boys

and girls stood round him and gaped enviously at his dressing-gown.

When next the nurse returned she brought two tin bowls, two spoons, and two slices of bread. She gave one bowl to the old man, and the other to Pashka. "Eat!" she said.

When Pashka examined the bowl he found it full of greasy soup with a piece of meat at the bottom; and again he reasoned that the doctor lived very comfortably, and was not half as angry as he seemed. He dallied over the soup, licked the spoon after each mouthful, and when nothing remained but the meat, cast a sidelong glance at the old man, and felt envy. With a sigh, he began the meat, trying to make it last as long as possible. But his efforts were in vain; the meat vanished speedily. There remained only the bread. Bread without condiment is tasteless food, but there was no remedy; after weighing the problem, he ate the bread also. And just as he had finished it the nurse arrived with two more bowls. This time the bowls contained roast beef and potatoes.

"Where is your bread?" she asked. Pashka did not answer, but distended his cheeks and puffed out the air.

"You've gobbled it up?" said the nurse reproachfully. "What will you eat your meat with?" She left him, and returned with more bread. Never in his life had Pashka eaten roast beef, and, trying it now, he found it very tasty. But it disappeared in a few seconds; and again only the bread was left, a bigger slice than the first. The old man, having finished his dinner, hid his bread in a drawer; and Pashka resolved to do the same, but after a moment's hesitation, he ate it up.

After dinner he set out to explore. In the next ward he found four men, in addition to those he had seen from his bed. Only one drew his attention. This was a tall, skeleton peasant, morose and hairy-faced, who sat on his bed, shook his head incessantly, and waved his arms pendulum-wise. Pashka could not tear his eyes away. At first the peasant's measured pendulum movements seemed droll, and made for the amusement of onlookers; but when Pashka looked at the peasant's face, he understood that this meant intolerable pain, and he felt sorry. In the third ward were two men with dark-red faces —red as if plastered with clay. They sat up motionless in bed, and, with their strange faces and nearly hidden features, resembled heathen gods.

"Auntie, why are they like that?" he asked the nurse.

"They are small-pox patients, laddie."

When Pashka returned to his own room he sat on his bed, and waited for the doctor to come and catch thrushes or drive to the fair. But the doctor tarried. At the door of the next ward the *feldscher* stood for a moment. He bent over the patient with the ice-bag, and cried—

"Mikhailo!"

But sleeping Mikhailo did not hear. The *feldscher* waved his hand, and went away. While waiting for the doctor, Pashka looked at his neighbour. The old man continued to cough, and spit into the bowl, and his cough was drawn-out and wheezy. But one thing pleased Pashka intensely. When the old man, having coughed, inhaled a breath, something whistled in his chest, and sang in different notes.

"Grandfather, what is that whistling in your inside?" asked Pashka.

The old man did not answer. Pashka waited a minute, and began again.

"Grandfather, where is the fox?"

"What fox?"

"The live one."

"Where should it be? In the wood, of course."

The hours slipped by, but no doctor came. At last the nurse brought Pashka's tea, and scolded him for having eaten the bread; the *feldscher* returned and tried to waken Mikhailo; the lamps were lighted; but still no doctor. It was already too late to drive to the fair or catch thrushes. Pashka stretched himself on his bed and began to think. He thought of the doctor's promised sugar-candy, of his mother's face and voice, of the darkness in the cabin at home, of querulous Yegorovna. And he suddenly felt tedium and grief. But remembering that his mother would come in the morning, he smiled, and fell asleep.

He was awakened by a noise. Men walked in the adjoining ward and spoke in whispers. The dim gleam of night-lights and lamps showed three figures moving near Mikhailo's bed.

"Shall we take him on the mattress, or as he is?" asked one.

"As he is. There's no room for the mattress. *Akh,* he's dead at a bad hour, heaven rest his soul!"

Then—one of the figures taking Mikhailo's shoulders, another his feet—they lifted him, and the folds of his dressing-gown hung limply in the air. The third— it was the woman-like peasant—crossed himself; and all three, shuffling their feet, tripping in the folds of the dressing-gown, went out of the ward.

The sleeping man's chest whistled, and sang in different notes. Pashka heard it, looked in fright at the black windows, and jumped out of bed in panic.

"Mother!" he screamed.

And, without awaiting an answer, he rushed into the adjoining ward. The lamps and nightlights barely banished the gloom; the patients, agitated by Mikhailo's death, were sitting up in their beds. Grim, dishevelled, haunted by shades, they looked like giants; they seemed to increase in size; and far away in a dark corner sat a peasant nodding his head and swinging his pendulous hands. Without seeing the door, Pashka tore through the smallpox ward into the corridor, thence into an endless chamber full of long-haired monsters with ancient faces. He flew through the women's ward, again reached the corridor, recognised the balustrade, and rushed downstairs. And there, finding himself in the waiting-room where he had sat that morning, he looked wildly for the door.

The latch rattled, a cold wind blew, and Pashka, stumbling, sped into the yard, in his head a single thought: to flee, to flee! He did not know the road, but felt that it was enough to run without cease and that he would soon be at home with his mother. The moon shone through the clouds of an overcast sky. Pashka ran straight ahead, dashed round a shed into the shrubbery, stood a second in doubt, then rushed back to the hospital and ran around it. But there he stopped in indecision, for suddenly before his eyes rose the white crosses of a graveyard.

"Mother!" he screamed, and turned back again.

And at last, as he dashed past the black menacing building, he saw a lighted window.

In the darkness, the bright red patch breathed terror. But Pashka, mad with panic, unknowing whither to flee, turned towards it with relief. Beside the window were steps and a hall door with a white notice-board. Pashka rushed up the steps, and looked through the window. A sharp, breathless joy suddenly seized him. For there in the window at a table sat the merry, talkative doctor with a book in his hands. Pashka laughed with joy; he tried to cry out; but some irresistible force suppressed his breath, and struck him on the legs, and he staggered and fell senseless on the steps.

When he came to himself it was quite light; and the sing-song voice that had promised the fair, the thrushes, and the fox whispered in his ear—

"You're a donkey, Pashka! Now aren't you a donkey? You ought to be whipped. . . ."

The Reed

COMING from the thick fir-wood, Meliton Shishkoff, steward at Dementieff's farm, walked by the margin of the wood, his gun shouldered. Damka, his half hunting and house dog, pregnant but thin, dragged herself after her master. Cloudy the morning was. The mist-shrouded trees scattered big drops, and decay was smelling ubiquitously.

Ahead, where the wood ended, rose birches. Some one behind the birches played a home-made shepherd's reed, only half a dozen notes, with no attempt at melody, and his music sounded coarse and monotonous.

Where the forest thinned and fir-trees mingled with young birches Meliton saw a herd. Hamshackled horses, cows, and sheep wandered between the bushes, and, making the branches crackle, snuffed at the forest grass. Near the edge of the wood, leaning against a wet birch-trunk, stood an old, thin shepherd, capless, in a tattered frieze caftan. Lost in thought, he looked at the ground and piped his reed mechanically.

"Morning, grandfather! God be good!" Meliton greeted him in a thin, hoarse voice, in no way suited to his great height and big, fleshy face. "You play your reed well! Whose are the animals?"

"Artamonoff's," answered the shepherd reluctantly. He thrust his reed into the bosom of his caftan.

"And the wood also is Artamonoff's?" asked Meliton, looking around. "Of course, Artamonoff's . . . I don't know where I am I scratched my face to pieces in the briers."

He sat down on the wet ground and rolled a cigarette in a piece of newspaper.

Like his liquid voice, everything about Meliton was petty and clashed with his stature, breadth, and fleshy face—his smile, his eyes, his buttons, the cap which barely kept on his solid, close-clipped head. As he spoke and smiled, his clean-shaven, puffy face and his whole figure expressed childishness, timidity, and meekness.

"It's bad weather, God better it!" he said, turning away his head. "The oats are not yet in, and the rain is on us, Lord help us!"

The shepherd looked at the drizzling· sky, at the wood, at the steward's soaked clothing, thought, and made no reply.

"The whole summer's been the same . . ." sighed Meliton. "Bad for the muzhiks, and for the quality no consolation. . . ."

Again the shepherd looked at the sky, again he thought, and then began, with pauses, as if chewing each word.

"The whole world goes the same way. . . . You can expect no good."

"But how are things with you?" asked Meliton. He lighted his cigarette. "Have you seen any woodcock broods in Artamonoff's clearing?"

The shepherd was silent. Again he looked at the sky and about him, thought, and blinked his eyes. . . . It was plain that he ascribed no small weight to his own words, and to increase their value delayed them with a certain solemnity. His glance was keen, with the keenness of the old and grave; and the upturned nostrils and saddle-shaped depression in his nose expressed cunning and contempt.

"No, it seems, I saw none," he answered. "Our gamekeeper, Artemka, says that he saw one brood near Pustoshka on Elijah's Day. I expect he lied. Birds are scarce."

"Yes, brother, scarce! . . . Everywhere scarce. Shooting's hardly worth while. . . . There's no game at all, and what there is isn't worth shooting. Little bits of things; it's painful to see them."

Meliton laughed and waved his hand.

"What's happening all over this world makes me laugh. The birds have gone off the rails; they sit so late that some haven't hatched out by Peter's Day."

"All things go the same way," said the shepherd, lifting his face. "Last year game birds were scarce, this year they're scarcer still, and in five years to come—mark my words—there won't be one left! Not only no game, but no birds of any kind."

"That's true," said Meliton thoughtfully. "That's true!"

The shepherd laughed bitterly and shook his head.

"It's a miracle!" he said. "What has become of them all? Twenty years gone by, I remember, there were geese and cranes, ducks and grouse—flocks upon flocks of them! I remember: the squire and his friends would come down and shoot, and all you could hear all day was pu, pu, pu, pu, pu! Plover and snipe without end of them, and little teals and woodcock as common as starlings—or sparrows, if you will. No end of them! Where are they gone? Even the birds of prey are gone! Gone are the eagles and the hawks and the owls. . . .

Beasts of all sorts are few. The wolf and the fox are rare sights to-day, not to mention bears and otters. And in those days there were elks. Forty years I watch the works of God from day to day, and all, I can see it plainly, is going in one way!"

"What way?"

"To the worse, lad. To ruin's the only conclusion. . . . The time is nigh for God's world to perish."

The old man put on his cap and looked up.

"It's a pity!" he sighed after a short silence. "Lord, what a pity! It's God's will, of course—not we made the world, but it's a pity, brother! When a tree is withered, or a cow dies, we're sorry to see it. But what do you say, good man, to the whole world perishing? What good, Lord Jesus? And the sun . . . and the sky, and the woods . . . and the rivers . . . and the beasts— surely all these were made, adapted, fitted to one another. Each for its own work, each in its own place. . . . And all this will perish!"

A mournful smile passed over the shepherd's face, and he blinked his eyes.

"You think the whole world perishes?" said Meliton thoughtfully. "It may be; perhaps we are really near the end. But I don't believe that birds alone prove anything."

"Not birds only," replied the shepherd. "But beasts also . . . and cattle and bees and fish. . . . If you don't believe what I say, ask the old men. They'll tell you that fish are not what they used to be. In the sea, in the lakes, in the rivers, the fish grow less and less. In our Pestchanka, I remember, we caught pike a full yard long. Burbot were everywhere, and roach and bream —every fish on earth showed himself sometimes; but now if you catch a nine-inch pike or perch you may thank the Lord. There isn't even a carp left. Every year things get worse and worse, and soon you'll see there'll be no fish at all. . . . And take the rivers of the present day! The rivers are drying up."

"That's true."

"It is. They're shallower and shallower every year; and already, brother, there are no deep pools as there used to be. Do you see those bushes?" The old man pointed aside. "Behind them there's an old channel; in my father's time, the Pestchanka flowed there; but look now, and see where the devil has taken it! It changes its course and will change it till it dries up altogether. And what's become of the smaller streams? In this very wood there was a brook so big that the muzhiks laid nets in it and caught pike; wild ducks wintered there; and now even in flood-time you can't float a boat in it. Yes, brother. Look where you will, everything is bad. Everything!"

The pair were silent. Meliton, lost in thought, stared at one point. He sought but one place in Nature untouched by the all-embracing ruin. On the mist and oblique rain-belts, as on muffed glass, slipped bright spots and at once vanished—the rising sun strove to pierce the clouds and look upon the earth.

"And the forests?" stammered Meliton.

"And the forests," repeated the shepherd. "The forests are cut down, burnt, and dried up, and no new trees grow. What does grow is soon cut down; today it is up—to-morrow—look over

your shoulder!—and down it's cut. . . . And so on without end until none remain! I, good man, have been watching the village flock ever since the Emancipation, and before that I was shepherd to the squire, shepherd in this very place; and I can't recall a summer day in all my life when I wasn't here. And all those years I observe the world of God. I have seen with my own eyes, brother; and I can tell you that all things that grow are on the way to ruin. Take rye, or oats, or even any flower; they're all on their way to the same end."

"The people, perhaps, are better?" said the steward.

"How better?"

"Cleverer."

"Cleverer maybe. Yes, that's true, but what good is cleverness? What use are brains to people on the brink of ruin? You don't want your brains to die. What good are brains to the sportsman if there is no game? That's just how I reason it: God's given us men brains, and taken away our strength. The people have grown weak, too weak to talk about. Look at me! I have not a kopeck of money; in all the village, I am the last muzhik. But all the same, lad, I have strength. I am a strong man. Look at me! Seventy years I've lived; and I watch these flocks day after day, yes, and by night—I watch them for twenty kopecks and never sleep and never catch cold! My son is a cleverer man; but put him in my place, and next day he'll come and ask for higher wages, or go into the hospital. So it is! Beyond bread I ask for nothing; it's written, give us this day our daily bread; but your muzhik nowadays must have tea and vodka, and white bread, and he sleeps from sundown to dawn, and drinks medicines, and is spoilt all round. And why? Because he's weak, he has no strength to endure. He would like to do without sleep, but his eyes shut— he's no good for anything!"

"That's true," said Meliton. "The muzhik nowadays is good for nothing."

"There's no use hiding it; we get worse every year. And as for the gentry, they're weaker still than the muzhiks. Your gentleman of to-day learns everything that's no good for him to know. And what use is it? . . . Skinny, weak, like some Hungarian or Frenchman; no dignity, nothing to look at; only one thing to boast of—he knows he's a gentleman. He sits with a rod and catches fish, or lies on his back reading books, or goes among the muzhiks and talks to them, and when he sees some one hungry hires him as a clerk. He lives among triflers, and has no real business in him. The old gentry were generals—the new ones are trash!"

"They're impoverished—badly," said Meliton.

"Because God's taken their strength, that's why. You've no chance against God."

Again Meliton stared fixedly at one point. After thinking a moment, he sighed, as sigh grave, sagacious men, shook his head, and said—

"What is the cause? We sin much. . . . We have forgotten God. . . . And now see the result. The time draws nigh for the end of everything. The world can't last for ever . . . it, too, must have a rest."

The shepherd sighed. He wished, it seemed, to drop a painful subject. He returned to the birches, and began to count the cattle.

"Gei, gei, gei!" he cried. "Gei, gei, gei! I can't abide you. The devil seems to drive you the wrong way."

He glared angrily and went among the bushes to collect his herd. Meliton rose, and walked slowly by the edge of the wood. He looked at the ground, and thought and tried to remember a single thing that was not yet tainted by death. Again on the slant rain-belts slipped bright spots; they quivered in the tree-tops, and were extinguished in the wet leaves. Damka found a hedgehog under a brush, and to call her master's attention, whined.

"You had an eclipse, or not?" cried the shepherd from behind the bushes.

"Yes," cried Meliton.

"You had? . . . Everywhere the people complain of it. That means, brother, there's disorder in heaven too. An eclipse isn't sent for nothing. Gei, gei, gei!"

Having got his flock together, the shepherd leaned against a birch-tree, and, looking at the sky, drew the reed idly from his bosom and began to play. He played mechanically as before, keeping half a dozen notes, as if he handled the reed for the first time; and the notes came forth irresolutely, without order, with no melody imaginable; so that Meliton, deep in thought on the world's coming destruction, found the music painful and unpleasant and wished it would cease. The high, piping notes, which trembled and died away, seemed to weep disconsolately, as if the reed itself were pained and frightened; and the lower notes seemed to speak of the mist, the grey heavens, the melancholy trees. The music, in truth, seemed made for the weather, the old man, and his words.

Meliton felt impelled to complain. He went up to the shepherd, looked at his sad, ironical face and at the reed, and muttered—

"And life has grown worse, grandfather! There's no living nowadays. Famines . . . and poverty . . . murrain, sickness! We are crushed by need."

The steward's puffy face turned purple, and his expression was feminine and plaintive. He twitched his fingers, as if seeking words to clothe inexpressible affliction, and continued—

"Eight children, a wife . . . a mother still alive, and ten roubles a month for wages, to board myself! My wife a devil from poverty . . . and I a drunkard! I am a deliberate, grave man. I want to sit at home in peace; but all day long, like a dog, I wander about with my gun . . because it is more than I can bear. I hate my home!"

Afraid that his tongue had carried him away, and that he had said what should be concealed, the steward waved his hand, and continued bitterly—

"If the world must perish, then let it—the sooner the better! There's no use delaying it, no use in suffering without cause. . . ."

The old man took the reed from his lips, and, closing one eye, looked along it. His face was sad, and covered with drops as with tears. He smiled and answered—

"It's a pity, brother! Lord, what a pity! The earth, the woods, the sky . . . the beasts and birds! . . . all these were made, adapted to their uses, each has its mind! And all will perish. . . . But most luckless of all are we men!"

In the forest rustled heavy rain. Meliton looked towards the sound, buttoned his coat to the neck, and said—

"I must go back to the village. Goodbye, grandfather! What is your name?"

"Poor Luka."

"Well, good-bye, Luka. Thanks for your good words. Damka! Come!"

Having taken leave of the shepherd, Meliton walked along the wood, and thence through a meadow that gradually merged in a marsh. The water rose in his foot-prints, and the rusty reed-grass bent, as if afraid of his tread. Beyond the marsh, on the banks of the Pestchanka of which grandfather Luka had spoken, rose willows; and behind the willows, in blue patches, stood the squire's barns. The world around presaged the coming of that sad, inevitable time when fields turn dark, when earth grows muddy and cold, when the weeping willow is sadder and down its trunk creep tears, when the crane alone evades the universal wretchedness; and even he, afraid to anger grieved Nature by boasting his delight, fills the air with a tedious, melancholy song.

Meliton walked to the river, and heard the sounds of the reed fading slowly away. He still wished to complain. He looked about him sadly, filled with intolerable pity for the sky, the earth, the sun, the woods, his Damka; and as a high note from the reed whined and trembled past his ears, he felt intense bitterness and offence at the chaos reigning throughout the world.

The high note quivered, and ceased, and the reed was still.

In the Ravine

CHAPTER I

THE VILLAGE

THE village of Ukleevo lay in a ravine. Only the belfry and the tall chimneys were visible from the high road or the railway. When a stranger came he was told:

"That's the village where the precenter ate all the caviar at the funeral."

In the house of the manufacturer Kostyukov the old precentor, noticing a jar of large-grained caviar, had begun eating it greedily during a funeral. His sleeve was pulled, but he had lost all feeling. He ate up all the four pounds of caviar. The caviar was remembered even after his death. That had occured ten years before, but somehow this was all they could tell you about the Ukleevo village, such was the people.

The village was never free from fever, and the mud there was thick even in summer, especially near the fences, which were overhung by old willows that cast their shade far around. Here there was always a smell of refuse from the factory and of acetic acid that was used in the manufacture of the prints. The factories—three print-works and one tannery—were not in the village, but some distance from it. They were only small works, and not more than four hundred hands were employed in them. The water in the river often had a bad smell from the tannery; the refuse infected the meadow and the peasants' cattle suffered from anthrax, so the factory was ordered to be closed down. It was considered to be closed; but it really worked secretly, as was well known to the commissary of the rural police and to the district doctor, who each received ten roubles a month from the manufacturer. There were only two passably good houses built of brick and covered with sheet iron in the whole village; one was occupied by the district administration and the other, a two-story house that stood just opposite the church, belonged to Grigory Petrovich Zybukin, a burgher of Epifan.

Grigory kept a grocer's shop, but this was only to save appearances; he really sold vodka, cattle, hides, corn, pigs—in fact he traded in anything that came to hand, and once, when there was a demand from abroad for magpies, as it was the fashion to trim ladies' hats with them, he made thirty kopecks on every pair he sold. He also bought timber for felling, lent money out at interest, and was, in general, an enterprising old man.

He had two sons. The eldest, Anisim, served in the police, in the detective department, and was but seldom at home. The youngest, Stepan, helped his father in his business, but much assistance was not expected from him, as he had bad health and was deaf; his wife, Aksinia, however, a pretty well-built woman, who walked about on holidays in a hat and with a parasol, rose early, went to bed late and all day long ran about with her skirts well tucked up, rattling her keys from barn to cellar or served in the shop, and old Zybukin, looking at her gaily with sparkling eyes, would feel

481

sorry that his eldest son was not married to her, but that she was the wife of the younger, the deaf one, who evidently had not much appreciation for womanly beauty.

The old man always had a disposition for domestic life, and he loved his family above everything in the world, especially his eldest son, the detective, and his daughter-in-law. Hardly had Aksinia got married to his deaf son before she showed quite unusual capacities for business; she soon knew to whom credit could be given, and who could be trusted; she always kept the keys beside her, and never gave them up, not even to her husband; she rattled at the abacus as she made up the accounts; she looked at the horses' teeth like the muzhiks, and she was always laughing or scolding. The old man only smiled at whatever she did or said, and he would mumble contentedly:

"Ah! That's a daughter-in-law! Ah, you're a real beauty, *matushka*. . . ."

He was a widower, but a year after his son's wedding he could endure it no longer and got married too. A girl was found for him in a village thirty versts from Ukleevo. Varvara Nikolaevna came from a good family; she was not quite young, but good-looking and showy. She had scarcely had time to settle town in her room in the upper story before everything became bright in the house; it seemed as if new panes had been put into the windows. The icon lamps burnt brightly, the tables were covered with snow-white cloths; on the window-sills and in the little garden flowers with red centres appeared; and at dinner they no longer ate out of one bowl, but a plate stood before each. Varvara Nikolaevna had a kind, pleasant smile, and it seemed as if everything in the house smiled around her. And, what never had been before, beggars, pilgrims and wanderers began to come into the yard; beneath the windows the plaintive sing-song voices of the Ukleevo old women and the apologetic coughs of the feeble, lean old men, who had been discharged from the factories for drunkenness, were to be heard. Varvara helped them all with money, bread, old clothes and, later on, when she had become more used to the place, she began to take things from the shop. Once the deaf man saw her take two packets of an eighth of a pound of tea and, as he was troubled about it, he told his father.

"Mama has taken two eighths of tea. How am I to book it?"

The old man did not answer him, but stood for some time in silence, thinking and moving his eyebrows; then he went upstairs to his wife.

"Varcarushka, *matushka*," he said affectionately, "if you require anything out of the shop, take it. Take whatever you want, you're welcome to it. Don't hesitate."

And the next day the deaf man called to her as he ran across the yard:

"Mama, if you need anything, take it!"

There was something new, something gay and bright, in the fact that she gave alms, as there was in the icon lamps and the red flowers. On the last days before a fast, on the fête of their village which lasted three days, when they sold to the muzhiks rotten, salt beef with such a heavy odour about it that it was difficult to stand near the barrel, and they received as pledges from the drunkards scythes, caps and their wives' dresses;

when the workmen from the factories, grown dizzy from the bad vodka, wallowed in the dirt; and sin, that was as thick as fog, appeared to hang around in the air, then it seemed to grow lighter from the thought that there was a quiet, tidy woman in the house who had nothing to do with the salt beef nor the vodka; and her charity acted in those painful foggy days like the safety-valve of an engine.

The days in Zubukin's house were all busy. The sun had not yet risen when Aksinia could be heard spluttering as she washed in the passage; the samovar boiling in the kitchen hummed ominously, foretelling something evil. Old Grigory Petrovich, small and clean, clad in a long black frock-coat, print trousers and shiny high boots, went about the rooms tapping with his heels like the father-in-law in the old song. The shop was opened. When it became light a racing droshky was brought to the door and the fine old man, who nobody would have guessed was already fifty-six years old, took his seat in it, pressing his large cap well over his ears. His wife and daughter-in-law were there to see him off. At such times when he was dressed in a good clean coat, and a fine black horse that had cost three hundred roubles was harnessed to the droshky, the old man did not like that any muzhiks should approach him, or come with their petitions or complaints; he could not bear the muzhiks, but disdained them, and if he saw that one of them was waiting near the gate he would shout angrily:

"Why are you standing there? Move on!"

Or if it was a beggar he would cry out:

"God will provide."

He drove off on business; his wife, in a dark dress and a black apron, did out the rooms or helped in the kitchen. Aksinia carried on the trade in the shop, and in the whole yard the tinkle of bottles or money, the sound of her laughter, or her shouts, and also the angry voices of the customers, whom she tried to overreach, could be heard; at the same time it was evident that a secret trade in vodka was going on there. The deaf man also sat in the shop; or he walked about the street without a cap and his hands in his pockets looking absent-mindedly either at the village huts or at the sky. About six times a day they had tea, and four times they sat down to the table to eat. In the evening they counted the day's receipts and wrote up the books and then they slept soundly.

All three print-works in Ukleevo were connected by telephone with the houses of the manufacturers, Khrymin senior, Khrymin junior, and Kostyukov. A telephone had also been installed in the office of the district administration, but it soon ceased to act there, as bugs and cockroaches made it their abode. The district head-clerk was almost illiterate, and wrote every word in the official documents with capital letters, but when the telephone was spoiled he said:

"Yes, now we shall indeed find it difficult to get on without a telephone."

The senior Khrymins were always at law with the junior Khrymins; sometimes the junior Khrymins quarrelled among themselves and went to law too, and then their print-works were closed down for a month or two, until they had made up their differences. This greatly diverted the inhabitants of

Ukleevo, as each new quarrel provided them with subjects for much gossip and scandal. On holidays Kostyukov and the junior Khrymins used to drive about through Ukleevo at such speed that they overran the calves. Aksinia, dressed up in her Sunday best and a rustling starched petticoat, walked about in front of her shop. The junior Khrymins would catch her up and carry her off as if by force. It was then, too, that old Zybukin, taking Varvara with him, would drive out to display his new horse.

In the evening after these drives, when people had gone to bed, the sounds of a costly accordion could be heard in the junior Khrymin's yard, and if there was a moon these notes acted on the soul in a disquieting and joyful manner, and Ukleevo did not appear quite such a hole.

CHAPTER II

THE DATE

THE eldest son, Anisim, came home very seldom, and only for the great Holy Days; but he often sent presents and letters by fellow-villagers, who were returning home. The letters were written by somebody else in a beautiful handwriting, each one on a sheet of paper that looked like a petition, and they were full of expressions that Anisim never used in speaking, such as: "Dear papa and mama, I send you a pound of flower of tea to be used for the satisfaction of your physical requirements."

At the foot of each letter there was scrawled, as if with a spoiled pen: "Anisim Zybukin," and beneath this again in the same beautiful handwriting: "Agent."

These letters were read aloud several times, and the old man, who was quite affected by them and red in the face from excitement, would say:

"Well, well, he did not want to live at home, but went on a learned career. What then, let him have his own way! Each one has his destiny."

It happened just before the Carnival that there was a heavy fall of rain and sleet; the old man and Varvara went to the window to look at it, and they saw Anisim coming in a sledge from the station. He had not been expected. When he entered the room he seemed troubled and alarmed, and the whole time he stayed this look did not leave him, but his manner was free. He was in no haste to leave, and it almost appeared that he had been discharged from the service. Varvara was pleased to see him; she looked at him in a sly manner, sighed and shook her head.

"How is it, *batushka*," she said. "this young fellow is already twenty-eight, and he still lives the life of a bachelor, O-ho-ho! . . ."

From the next room her quiet even speech could be heard; "O-ho-ho," she began to whisper with the old man and with Aksinia, and their faces assumed the cunning and mysterious expression of plotters.

They decided to find Anisim a wife.

"O-ho-ho! . . . Your younger brother has long been married," Varvara said, "and you're still without a mate, like a cock in the market. What sort of life is this? This one and that one has got married; God willing, why don't you get married too. then you can do as you like, you'll go back to work and your wife will remain at home to help. You young fellows live without order, and, I see, you forget all rules. O-ho-ho! you're all sinners, you townfolk."

As they were rich when one of the Zybukins got married, only the prettiest girl was chosen for him. For Anisim they also looked for a pretty girl. He himself had an uninteresting insignificant appearance; he was frail, unhealthy, small of stature and he had stout round cheeks that looked as if they had been blown out; his eyes never twinkled, but his gaze was sharp; he had a small, thin red beard, and when thinking he always stuck it into his mouth and bit the ends of the hairs; besides he often drank too much, and this could be noticed in his face and his gait. But when he was informed that a wife, and a very pretty one too, had been found for him he only said:

"Well, I am not a fright either. I must confess that in our family we Zybukins are all handsome."

Close to the town lay the village of Torguevo. Quite recently one half of it had been joined to the town, the other half remained a village. In the first part a widow lived in her own house; she had a sister, who was very poor, and went out to char; this sister had a daughter called Lipa, who also went out to do day work. In Torguevo much was talked about this girl's beauty, but all the young men were held back by her terrible poverty: people said it would only be a man well on in years, or a widower, who would wed her despite her poverty, or he might simply take her to live with him, and in that way her mother would also not be in want. Varvara heard about Lipa from the matchmakers, and she drove over to Torguevo.

After that a proper *smotriny* with refreshments and wine was arranged in her aunt's house, and Lipa was in a new pink dress made for the occasion and a crimson ribbon shone like flame in her hair. She was thin, weak and pale, with fine delicate features that were tanned by her exposure to the air as a day labourer: a sad, timid smile never left her face, and she had a childlike, trustful and inquiring gaze.

She looked very young, almost a child, with a scarcely perceptible bosom, but in years she was old enough to marry. She really was very pretty, and there was only one thing in her that might displease—this was her hands, large as a man's, that now hung idly down like two big claws.

"She has no dowry—we don't mind that," the old man said to her aunt; "for our son, Stepan, we also took a girl from a poor family, and now we can't praise her enough. In the house and in the business she has golden hands."

Lipa stood at the door and seemed to wish to say: "Do with me what you like; I trust you," and her mother, Praskovya, the charwoman, hid herself in the kitchen, and almost fainted from timidity. Once in her youth it had happened that a tradesman in whose house she washed the floors had flown into a passion and had trampled her underfoot; she had been very much alarmed, almost stupefied, and from that time fear had always dwelt in her soul; and from fear her legs, arms and cheeks had trembled ever since. Sitting in the kitchen she tried to hear what the guests were saying, and the whole time she crossed herself, pressing her fingers to her forehead and looking towards the icon. Anisim, who was slightly tipsy, opened the kitchen door and said jocularly:

"Why are you sitting there, mama dear? We are quite dull without you."

And Praskovya, pressing her hands to her thin withered bosom, said timidly:

"For goodness sake, why, sir . . . I am very much obliged to you, sir."

After the *smotriny* the day for the wedding was fixed. Then Anisim went about the house whistling, or suddenly remembering something he would stop and stand motionless thinking, with his eyes fixed on the floor, looking so intently as if he wished to pierce the depths of the earth with his glance. He neither expressed his satisfaction at getting married, and so soon, too—the wedding was to be on Low Sunday—nor even the wish to see his betrothed; he only went about whistling. It was very evident he was getting married because his father and stepmother wished him to, and because it was the custom in the village that the sons should marry, so that there might be another assistant in the house. When he went away he seemed in no haste, and he behaved quite differently than he had done on former visits—he was more free-and-easy, and he talked all sorts of nonsense.

CHAPTER III

STOP!

Two dressmakers lived in the village of Shikalova; they were sisters and belonged to the religious sect of the Khlystovtsy. New dresses for the wedding were ordered of them, and they often came to try them on and stayed

long drinking tea. For Varvara they were making a brown dress trimmed with black lace and jet, and for Aksinia a light green dress with a yellow front and a train. When the dressmakers had finished their work, Zybukin paid them, not in money however, but in goods from his shop, and they went away sadly, carrying various parcels containing stearin candles and sardines, which were quite unnecessary for them, and when they had got clear of the village they sat down on a mound and wept.

Anisim arrived three days before the wedding, smartly dressed in quite new clothes. He wore shining new india-rubber galoshes, and instead of a cravat a red cord with little balls at the end, and thrown over his shoulders was an overcoat—also quite new.

After having gravely prayed to God he greeted his father, and gave him ten silver roubles and ten half-rouble coins; he gave Varvara as many and he gave Aksinia twenty quarter-rouble pieces. The chief charm of this present was that all these coins were quite new, as if specially chosen, and glistened in the sun. Anisim made great efforts to look sedate and serious, and he puffed out his cheeks, but he smelled of brandy; he had probably gone to the refreshment bar at each station. And again there was the same free-and-easy manner that did not accord with the man at all. Then Anisim and the old man sat down to eat and to drink tea, and Varvara played with the new coins and inquired about the people from their village who were living in town.

"Thank God, they are all getting on and living well," Anisim answered. "There has only been an event in Ivan

Egorov's life: his old woman, Sophia Nikiforovna, is dead. She died of consumption. The memorial dinner for the repose of her soul was ordered at a confectioner's for two-and-a-half roubles for each person. There was also grape wines. There were some muzhiks .—from our village among the guests— and for them also two-and-a-half roubles was paid. They ate nothing. As if muzhiks understand sauces!"

"Two-and-a-half roubles!" the old man said, and he shook his head.

"Well, you see, it's not like the village there! You go to a restaurant to have a snack, you order this and that, you meet friends, you have drinks; before you know where you are it's dawn, and then you're in for three or four roubles each. When Samorodov is there he likes to finish up with coffee and cognac—and cognac is sixty kopecks a wineglass."

"He always lies," the old man mumbled, delighted; "he always lies."

"Now I'm always with Samorodov. He's the Samorodov who writes my letters to you. He writes beautifully. And, mama, if I were to tell you," Anisim continued addressing Varvara, "what sort of a man this Samorodov is, you would not believe it. We all call him Mukhtar; he's like an Armenian—quite black. But I see through him; I know all his affairs, just like my own five fingers, mama, and he feels it, and is always coming after me; there's no shaking him off, fire and water won't separate us now. It seems a bit uncanny for him, but he can't live without me. Wherever I go, he goes too. I have a good eye, mama, a true eye. I walk about the market; a muzhik is selling a shirt. 'Stop, that shirt has

been stolen!' And it turns out to be true—the shirt had been stolen."

"How did you know it?" Varvara asked.

"It's just my eye. I don't know what sort of a shirt it is. I'm somehow drawn towards it: it's stolen, that's why. With us in the detective service they say: 'Ah, Anisim has gone to shoot snipe!' That means, to look for stolen goods. Yes. . . . Everyone can steal, but how is it to be hidden! The world is large, but there's nowhere to hide stolen goods."

"Last week in our village the Guntorevs were robbed of a ram and two ewes," Varvara said and sighed. "There's nobody to look for them. . . . O-ho-ho! . . .

"Why not? I don't mind trying. It's easy to find them."

.   .   .   .   .   .

The wedding-day arrived. It was a cold, clear and gay April day. From the early morning carts and droshkies, harnessed with two and three horses, decorated with many-coloured ribbons and with tinkling bells, drove about the village of Ukleevo. The rooks, who were disturbed by this driving, made a noise in the willows and the starlings sang, without stopping, enough to crack their voices, as if they, too, were delighted that there was a wedding in Zybukin's house.

In the house the tables were already arranged with long fish, hams, stuffed poultry, boxes of sprats, all sorts of salted and pickled delicacies and a whole army of bottles of vodka and wine; there was a scent of smoked sausage and tinned lobster that had turned sour. Old Zybukin, tapping with his heels, went round the tables, stopping here and there to sharpen one knife against another. Varvara was constantly calling for something, or with a troubled look and very much out of breath she was running to the kitchen, where ever since dawn Kostyukov's man-cook and Khrymin junior's cook had been hard at work. Aksinia, in curl papers, without a dress, in her stays and squeaky new shoes, rushed about the yard like a whirlwind, and only gleams of her bare knees and bosom could be seen. There was noise, scolding, swearing; t h e passers-by stopped at the wide-open gate, and everywhere it was felt that something unusual was being prepared.

"They've gone for the bride!"

The tinkle of bells could be heard, and it gradually died away in the distance far beyond the village. . . . Soon after two o'clock the people began to assemble; the bells could again be heard. "The bride is coming!" The church was packed. the church lustre was lighted, the choir was singing and they sang, as old Zybukin had wished, from notes. The brilliancy of the lights and of the bright coloured dresses blinded Lipa; it appeared to her that the choristers, with their loud voices, were knocking with hammers at her head; the stays she wore for the first time in her life, and her shoes squeezed her, and she looked as if she had just recovered from a faint—she gazed around and could not understand anything. Anisim, dressed in a black frock-coat with a red cord instead of a cravat, stood meditative, staring at one point, and when the choristers sang very loud he crossed himself rapidly. He felt agitated and wanted to cry. He had known this church from his early child-hood; here his late mother had brought him to the communion; here at one time he had sung with the boys in the choir; how well he knew every corner, every icon. Now he was being married; he must get married for the sake of order, but he did not think about it any more, he seemed to have forgotten it, and he thought no more about his wedding. Tears prevented him from seeing the icons, he had a load on his heart; he prayed and asked God to avert the inevitable misfortune that was ready to overwhelm him. if not to-day then to-morrow, and that it might pass by like a thunder cloud goes past a village in time of drought, without giving a drop of rain. What numbers of sins he had piled up in the past, what numbers of sins, not to be escaped from, not to be repaired, so that it was absurd to ask for pardon. Still he asked for pardon and even sobbed quite loud, but nobody took any notice of it as they thought he was drunk.

A child's alarmed cry was heard.

"Dear mama, take me away; darling mammy, take me away!"

"Quiet there!" the priest shouted.

When the young couple drove back from church the crowd ran after them; near the shop, near the gate and in the yard a crowd had collected. The village women came to cheer. The bride and bridegroom had scarcely crossed the threshold when the choir, who were standing ready in the passage with notes in their hands, welcomed them by the loud singing of a wedding hymn, and a band, that had been ordered from town. struck up playing. Sparkling wine from the Don was handed round in high wineglasses, and the carpenter-contractor Elizarov, a tall,

spare old man with such thick eyebrows
that his eyes were hardly to be seen,
turning towards them, addressed the
newly married pair:

"Anisim and you, dear child, love one
another; live according to God's ordi-
nance, children, and the Queen of
Heaven will not desert you." He fell
on the old man's shoulder, sobbing.
"Grigory Petrovich, let us weep, let us
weep for joy!" he said in a shrill, high
voice, but instantly burst out laughing,
and continued in a loud, deep bass:
"Ha-ha-ha! Here you have a fair
daughter-in-law. All with her is in
order, all smooth, nothing rattles, the
whole mechanism is in order, there are
many screws."

He came from the Egorevsky district,
but since quite a young man he had
worked in Ukleevo, both in the factories and in the district, and had become accustomed to the place. For
long he had been known as an old man,
spare and tall as he was now, and he
had long since received the nickname
of the "Crutch." Perhaps it had been
given him because for more than forty
years he had only been occupied with
repairs in the factories—he judged
every person and everything by their
solidity—wondering if they required
repair. Before he sat down to table he
tried several chairs to see if they were
sound, he even touched the fish.

After the sparkling wine had been
drunk they all sat down to table. The
guests talked and moved their chairs,
the choir sang in the passage, the band
played and the women in the yard
cheered in unison. All these noises,
produced at the same time, formed a
terribly wild combination of sounds,
which made one feel quite dizzy.

Crutch fidgeted about on his chair,
he jostled his neighbours with his
elbows, preventing them from talking,
and he was either weeping or laughing.

"Children, children, children," he
mumbled rapidly. "Aksinia, *matushka,*
Varvarushka, let us all live in peace
and unity—my dear little axes. . . ."

He never drank much and now he
had got tipsy from one glass of English
bitters. This horrible bitters, concocted
of God only knows what, made all those
who had drunk it feel dizzy, it seemed
to stun them. Their tongues refused
to obey.

The clergy was there, the clerks from
the factories, with their wives, the shopkeepers and the innkeepers from other
villages. The head of the district administration and his secretary, who had
served together for fourteen years and
who, during the whole of that time,
had never made out or signed a single
document, nor let a single man leave
the office without having cheated or
wronged him in some way, were now
sitting side by side. They were both
stout, well-fed men, and it seemed that
their very system was so thoroughly
impregnated with falsehood that even
the skin of their faces was of a specially rascally nature. The secretary's
wife, a skinny, squinting woman, had
brought all her children with her, and
like a bird of prey she was constantly
looking askance at the various dishes
and pouncing upon everything that
came to hand, which she hid away in
her own or her children's pockets.

Lipa sat like a statue of stone, with
the same impassible expression on her
face that it had worn in church.
Anisim had never spoken to her from
the time he had made her acquaintance,

so that he did not even know what her voice sounded like, and now sitting next to her he still remained silent and drank English bitters; but when he had become intoxicated he began to talk, addressing himself to Lipa's aunt, who was sitting opposite:

"I have a friend, whose name is Samorodov. Quite an exceptional man. He's a personal notable citizen, and he can talk! But, Auntie, I see through him, and he feels it too. Permit me to drink a glass to Samorodov's health with you!"

Varvara, weary and worried, went round the table pressing her guests to eat, and she was evidently pleased that there were so many good things to offer, and that everything was in abundance; nobody would criticize them now. The sun set, but the feast still continued; the people could no longer understand what they ate; it was impossible to hear what was said, and only from time to time, when the music ceased, a woman in the yard was distinctly heard shouting:

"They have sucked our blood, the Herods, is there no ruin for them?"

In the evening there was dancing. The junior Khrymins arrived, bringing their own wine with them, and one of them, when he took part in a quadrille, danced, holding a bottle in each hand and a wineglass between his teeth, which caused great amusement. In the midst of the quadrille some of the men began dancing the Russian dance. Aksinia, in her green dress, flitted about and wind seemed to blow from her train. Somebody trod upon it and tore off the flounce, at which Crutch shouted:

"Hullo! The base-board has been torn off! Children, children!"

Aksinia had naïve grey eyes that seldom blinked, and a naïve smile constantly played on her face. In these unblinking eyes, in her small head on her long neck and in her graceful movements there was something serpentine. All in green with a yellow breast and with her smile she looked like a snake that gazes on the passers-by in spring from among the young rye, stretching out its neck and raising its head. The Khrymins were very free with her, and it was quite evident that she was on the most intimate terms with the eldest of them. But the deaf man did not understand anything, and did not look at her: he sat with his legs crossed, eating nuts and cracking them between his teeth with so much noise that it appeared as if he were shooting out of a pistol.

Now Zybukin himself went into the middle of the room and began to wave his handkerchief, making a sign that he too wanted to dance a Russian dance, and in the whole house and in the yard there was a murmur of approbation.

"He's going to dance. He himself's going to dance."

Varvara danced, but the old man only waved his handkerchief and beat time with his heels. Those who watched him there and in the yard hanging on to each other as they looked through the window were in raptures, and for a moment forgave him everything—both his wealth and his injuries.

"Grigory Petrovich's a trump," could be heard in the crowd. "Go it! There's go in you still! Ha-ha!"

All this finished late at night, at past one o'clock. Anisim, very shaky on his legs, went the round of the choristers and musicians, giving to each as a parting gift a new half-rouble. The old man, not at all shaky but treading more heavily on one leg, conducted his guests to the door, saying to each:

"The wedding has cost two thousand roubles."

When the guests were departing it was discovered that somebody had exchanged an old overcoat for a very good one belonging to an elegant inn-keeper, and Anisim suddenly became excited, and shouted:

"Stop! I will find it at once! I know who stole it! Stop!"

He rushed into the street in pursuit of someone; he was caught however, and brought home, led arm-in-arm; when there he was pushed, tipsy, red with anger and wet, into the room where her aunt had already undressed Lipa, and the door was locked from without.

CHAPTER IV

TREASURES

FIVE days passed. Anisim was preparing to go back to town, and he went upstairs to take leave of Varvara. All the icon lamps were burning in her room, and there was a smell of incense. She was seated near the window knitting a stocking of red worsted.

"You've stayed with us a short time," she said. "You find it dull, I expect? O-ho-ho! . . . We live well, we have everything in plenty and your wedding was celebrated worthily in the proper way; the old man says: it cost two thousand. In a word we live like merchants, but it's dull here. We wrong the people too much. My heart aches, dear friend, to see how we wrong them. Oh, good Lord! It's either a

horse that is exchanged, or we buy something, or we hire a labourer—in everything there is cheating. Cheating and cheating. The fast oil in the shop is bitter and rancid, worse than other people's tar. Now tell me, honestly, can't one trade in good oil?"

"Each knows his own business best, mama."

"Must we not all die? Oh-oh! You ought really to speak to father! . . ."

"Why don't you speak to him yourself?"

"Well—well! I give him my opinion, and he says the very words you do: 'Each knows his own business best.' God's judgment is righteous."

"Of course, nobody will look into it," Anisim said and sighed. "There's no God after all, mama. Who's to look into it!"

Varvara gazed at him with astonishment, laughed and clasped her hands. He became confused because she believed his words so sincerely and looked upon him as an oddity.

"Perhaps God exists, but there is no faith," he said. "When I was being married I was not quite myself. It was as though you take an egg from under a hen and a chick pipes in it, so my conscience suddenly piped and while I was being married I thought the whole time: there is a God! But when I left the church it was as nothing. Besides, how am I to know if there is a God or not? In childhood we were not taught that, and the infant at his mother's breast is already taught to know his own business. Papa also does not believe in God. The other day you said that Guntorov's sheep had been stolen. . . . I have found them; a Shikalov peasant stole them; he stole them, but their hides are in papa's hands . . . That's faith for you!"

Anisim winked and shook his head.

"The chief of the district does not believe in God," he continued, "nor the secretary either. And if they go to church, and keep the fasts, it's only that people might not speak badly of them, and in case there should really be a Last Judgment. Now they say that the end of the world has come, because people have grown weak, and don't honour their parents and so on. That's all nonsense. I understand it in this way, mama, that the whole trouble comes because people have no conscience. I see through them, mama, and understand. I see when a man has on a stolen shirt. You see a man sitting in a tavern, and you think he's only drinking tea; I see the tea too, but I see besides that he has no conscience. I go about all day, and there's no man with a conscience. And the whole reason is because they do not know if there is a God or not. . . . Well. *mamasha*, good-bye. Be well and happy, and bear me no ill-will."

Anisim bowed to the ground before Varvara.

"We thank you for everything, *mamasha*," he said. "You have brought our family much profit. You are a very superior woman, and I am much obliged to you."

Anisim left the room much agitated, but returned and said:

"Samorodov has inveigled me in a certain business: I shall become rich or perish. If anything happens, *mamasha*, comfort my father."

"Come now, what is this? O-ho-ho. . . . God is merciful! But Anisim, you ought to be more caressing with your wife, you only look at each other and pout; you might at least smile."

"But she's so queer . . ." Anisim said, and he sighed. "She understands nothing; she never speaks. She's very young, let her grow up."

A large well-fed white horse, harnessed to a light cart, was already standing at the door.

Old Zybukin, with a little run, jumped into it like a young man and took the reins. Anisim kissed Varvara, Aksinia and his brother. Lipa was also standing motionless at the door and looking in another direction, as if she had not come out to see her husband off, but by accident and for no special reason. Anisim went up to her and just touched her cheek with his lips.

"Good-bye," he said.

And without looking round at him she smiled in a strange way, her face seemed to quiver, and for some reason everybody was sorry for her. Anisim also jumped in and put his arms a-kimbo, for he thought himself handsome.

As they drove up out of the ravine Anisim looked back at the village. It was a warm, clear day. For the first time the cattle had been driven out, and the girls and old women dressed in their holiday finery were going about near the herd. The brown bull bellowed, rejoicing at his liberty, and pawed the ground with his fore legs. Everywhere, above, below, the larks were singing. Anisim looked back at the church, so well proportioned and white—it had recently been whitewashed—and he remembered that only five days before he had prayed in it; he looked back at the school with its green roof, at the river where, as a boy, he had bathed and fished, and gladness throbbed in his breast, and he wished that suddenly a wall might grow up before him and prevent him from going any farther, and that he might remain only with the past.

When they got to the station they went to the bar and had a glass of sherry. The old man put his hand in his pocket for his purse in order to pay.

"I stand this," Anisim said.

The old man slapped him on the shoulder with emotion and winked at the bar-keeper, as much as to say: "See what a son I have."

"Anisim, why don't you remain at home in the business?" he said. "You would be priceless! I'd cover you with gold from head to foot, my son."

"I can't, *papasha!*"

The sherry was sour and it smelled of sealing-wax, still they each had another glass.

When the old man returned from the station at the first moment he could not recognize his youngest daughter-in-law. Lipa changed as soon as her husband had driven out of the yard, and had suddenly become gay. Barefooted, in an old worn petticoat, with her sleeves tucked up to the shoulders, she was washing the floor in the passage and the stairs, singing in a small silvery voice, and when she carried out the large tub with slops and looked at the sun with her childish smile, it appeared as if she, too, were a lark.

An old labourer, who was passing the porch, shook his head and quacked:

"Yes, Grigory Petrovich, God has sent you good daughters-in-law! They're not women, but real treasures."

CHAPTER V

MY GOD!

ON Friday, the eighth of July, Elizarov, who went by the nickname of Crutch, was returning with Lipa from the village of Kazansky, where they had been to the service in the church in honour of its Patron saint, the Holy Virgin of Kazan. Far in the rear they were followed by Lipa's mother, Praskovya, who constantly lagged behind, being ill and breathless. It was almost evening.

"Ah, ah!" . . . Crutch exclaimed with astonishment as he listened to Lipa. "Ah, ah! . . . Well!"

"I am very fond of jam, Il'ya Makarich," Lipa said. "I like to sit down in a quiet corner and drink tea with jam. Or, Varvara Nikolaevna and I drink tea together, and she tells me something touching. She has a lot of jam—four jars. 'Have some more, Lipa,' she says, 'don't be afraid.'"

"Ah, ah! Four jars!"

"They live well. They have tea with white rolls; and there's as much meat as you can eat, too. They live well, but it's terrible in their house, Il'ya Makarich. Oh, how terrible!"

"What is so terrible, my child?" Crutch asked, and he looked back to see how far behind Praskovya was.

"At first after the wedding I was afraid of Anisim Grigorich. He was all right, he did not ill-treat me; but only when he came near me it made my flesh creep, all my bones were frozen. I did not sleep a single night; all the time I shivered and prayed to God. And now, Il'ya Makarich, I'm afraid of Aksinia. She's all right, always smiling; but sometimes she looks in at the window and her eyes are such angry ones, and they look green as a sheep-pen. The junior Khrymins are leading her astray. 'Your old man has some land at Butekino,' they say to her, 'about forty acres; this soil is sandy and there's water too,' so they say: 'Aksinia, build a brick-kiln there on your own account, and we will take a share in the business! Bricks are at twenty roubles the thousand. It's a profitable business.' Yesterday at dinner Aksinia said to the old man: 'I want to start brick works at Butekino; I'll be a merchant on my own.' That's what she said and smiled. But Grigory Petrovich's face became dark; it was evident he was not pleased. 'As long as I live,' he said, 'we can't separate, we must all go together.' She cast up her eyes and ground her teeth. . . . Fritters were served—but she would not eat!"

"Ah, ah!" Crutch exclaimed in aston-ishment. "She would not eat!"

"Just have the goodness to tell me when does she sleep?" Lipa continued. "She sleeps half an hour and then jumps up again and walks about; she's always walking and poking about; look-ing if the muzhiks have not set some-thing on fire, or stolen something. . . I'm afraid to be with her, Il'ya Maka-rich! And after the wedding the junior Khrymins never went to bed at all, but went straight to town for their lawsuit, and people say Aksinia is the cause of it. Two of the brothers promised to build her brick works, and the third is offended at this, and their factory has been closed down for more than a month, and my Uncle Prokhor is with-out work and begs for crusts from door to door. I tell him to go out to plough or to saw wood, why shame oneself!

'I'm unused to peasant's work, I don't know how to do it, Lipinka,' he says."

Near a small aspen wood they sat down to rest and to wait for Praskovya. Elizarov had been a contractor for a very long time; but he kept no horse and went everywhere in the district on foot, with a bag in which he carried bread and onions, taking long strides and swung his arms. It was difficult to walk alongside of him.

At the beginning of the wood there was a boundary post. Elizarov touched it, to see if it was solid. Praskovia, quite breathless, caught them up there. Her wrinkled face, that always looked alarmed, was now beaming with happi-ness; that day she had been to church like other people, and afterwards had gone to the market, and had drunk pear *kvass!* This happened seldom, and it seemed to her that this was the first day of pleasure she had had in her whole life. Having rested they all three went on together. The sun was setting, and its rays, penetrating through the wood, lighted up the stems of the trees. In front of them loud voices could be heard. The Ukleevo girls had long since passed them, but they had evidently stayed in this wood, probably to look for mushrooms.

"Heigh! girls!" Elizarov shouted. "Heigh, beauties!"

In answer there was only laughter.

"Crutch is coming! Crutch! Old crank!"

And the echo laughed too. They had now left the wood behind them. The tops of the factory chimneys could be seen, the cross on the belfry glittered; it was the village, "that same village where the precentor ate all the caviar at the funeral." They had now almost reached home; they had only to go down into this deep ravine. Lipa and Praskovya, who had been walking barefoot, sat down on the grass to put on their stockings and boots; the contractor sat down too. Looking down from above, Ukleevo, nestling among its willows with its white church and swift river, seemed beautiful and peaceful; only the roofs of the factories that were painted from economy a dull greyish colour seemed disturbing. On the opposite slopes rye could be seen, in cocks, in sheaves, here, there and everywhere, as if it had been scattered by a gale; some was only just reaped and lay in rows; and there were oat fields also getting ripe that glittered in the sun's rays like mother-of-pearl. It was harvest time. That day was a holiday, the next Saturday the rye had to be brought in, the hay carted, and then Sunday, again a holiday; every day there were rumbles of distant thunder; it was sultry, it looked like rain, and gazing at his fields everyone wondered if God would give him time to get in his corn; and his soul was gay and joyful, though at the same time troubled.

"Mowers are dear just now," Praskovya said. "A rouble and forty a day."

The people from the market at Kazanskay continued to flow past: women, hands from the factories in new caps, beggars, children. . . . Now the dust was raised by a passing cart with a horse that had not been sold, and seemed to be glad of it, running behind; then somebody passed leading an obstinate cow by the horns; again a cart jogged along, full of drunken muzhiks, with their legs hanging over the sides. One old woman came dragging along a boy in a large hat and high boots; the boy was overcome by the heat and his heavy boots which prevented him from bending his knees, but he never ceased blowing vigorously at a toy trumpet; they had gone down into the ravine and had turned into the street, and still the sound of the trumpet could be heard.

"Our manufacturers are somehow not quite themselves . . ." Elizarov said. "Bad luck! Kostyukov got angry with me. 'Too many boards have been used for the cornice.' 'Too many? As many as were needed, Vasili Danilich,' I said, 'have been used. I don't eat boards with my porridge.' 'How dare you use such words to me? Blockhead . . . this, that and the other! Don't forget yourself. I made you a contractor!' he shouted. 'A wonder, indeed! When I was no contractor,' I said, 'I drank tea every day all the same.' 'You're all rascals,' he said. I held my tongue. 'We're rascals in this world,' I thought. 'You'll all be rascals in the next.' Ha-ha-ha! The next day he was softer. 'Don't be angry with me for my words, Makarich,' he said. 'If I spoke a word too much, you can't help admitting I'm a first guild merchant, and your superior. You ought to hold your tongue.' 'You're a first guild merchant and I'm a carpenter,' said I; 'that's quite true. Saint Joseph was a carpenter too,' said I. 'Our work is righteous and pleasing in God's sight. If you wish to be my superior, why then pray have the goodness, Vasili Danilich.' After this conversation I thought: 'Who is superior, a first guild merchant or a carpenter? Surely the carpenter, children.' "

Crutch reflected and then added:

"It's so, children. He who works and suffers is surely superior."

The sun had set. Above the river, in the church close and on the meadows near the factories, a thick mist, white as milk, was rising. The darkness was coming on quickly, here and there a light gleamed below, and it seemed as if the mist was hiding a bottomless abyss beneath it. Lipa and her mother —who had been born beggars, and were quite ready to remain so to the end, giving to others everything except their frightened and meek souls—may perhaps have had now for a moment an indistinct glimmer that in this vast, mysterious world, in the endless lines of life, even they were powers, and they were superior to somebody else. It was pleasant for them to sit up there; they smiled happily, and quite forgot that they must also return to the ravine.

At last they reached home. At the gates, and near the shop, the mowers were sitting on the grass. Usually the Ukleevo peasants would not work for Zybukin, and he was obliged to hire strangers, and now it appeared in the gloom that the people who were seated there were men with long black beards. The shop was still open, and through the open door the deaf man could be seen playing draughts with a boy. The mowers were either singing in a low, hardly audible voice, or were loudly demanding payment for the previous day's work; but they were not paid, to prevent them from going away before the morrow. Old Zybukin, without either coat or waistcoat, was seated near the porch with Aksinia, drinking tea under the shade of the birch trees; a lighted lamp stood on the table.

"Eh, granddad," a mower called out from the other side of the gate, in a mocking tone. "Pay us at least the half! Eh, granddad!"

Laughter was heard, and they again began to sing in a low, scarcely audible voice. . . . Crutch sat down to drink tea.

"Well, and so we went to the fair," he began to relate. "We amused ourselves very well, children, thank God. But an unpleasant thing happened. Sashka, the smith, bought some tobacco and gave the shopkeeper a silver half-rouble. The half-rouble was a false one," Crutch continued, looking round; he wished to speak in a whisper, but he spoke in a hoarse, choking voice that was heard by everyobdy. "And the half-rouble was false. He was asked where he had received it? 'Anisim Zybukin gave it to me!' ne said, 'when we were at his wedding.' . . . The policeman was called, and he was led away. Take care, Petrovich, that trouble does not come of it—people may talk . . ."

"Granddad, eh granddad," the same voice called again from behind the gates. "Granddad, eh!"

There was a long silence.

"Ah, children, children, children . . ." Crutch muttered rapidly as he rose from his seat; he was getting very drowsy. "Well, thank you for your tea and sugar, my child. It's time to go to bed. I'm getting rotten, all my beams are rotting away. Ha-ha-ha!"

And in going away he added:

"It's probably time to die."

He sobbed. Old Zybukin did not finish his tea, but sat there for some time, thinking; and the expression on his face seemed to be one of listening to Crutch's receding footsteps, though he was long since in the street.

"Sashka, the smith, probably lied," Aksinia said, guessing his thoughts.

He went into the house, but soon returned with a roll; he undid it and the silver roubles glittered; they were all quite new. He took one up, tested it with his teeth and threw it on the table, then he threw down another. . . .

"The roubles are really false . . ." he said, and he looked at Aksinia as if in perplexity. "They are the ones Anisim brought—his present. Take them, daughter," he whispered, and pressed the roll into her hand; "take them and throw them into the well. . . . The devil take them. And see there is no talk. Whatever happens. . . . Take the samovar away, put out the lights. . . ."

Lipa and Praskovya, who were sitting in the coach-house, saw the lights go out one after another; it was only upstairs in Varvara's room that the red and blue icon lamps shone dimly, and a breath of peace, ease and ignorance seemed to come thence. Praskovya could not get accustomed to the idea that her daughter had married a rich man, and when she came there she pressed timidly against the walls and smiled suppliantly, and they sent her out tea and sugar. And Lipa was also unable to become accustomed to her new position, and after her husband had left she did not sleep in her own bed, but anywhere—in the kitchen, in the coach-house—and every day she washed the floors or the linen, and it appeared to her that she was out to char. And now when they got back from their

pilgrimage they had drunk tea in the kitchen with the cook, and then they had gone into the coach-house and lay down on the floor in a corner between the sledge and the wall. It was dark there and it smelled of harness. The lights were extinguished in the whole house and they heard the deaf man shutting up the shop, and the mowers settling down for the night in the yard. Far away at the junior Khrymins somebody was playing on a costly accordion. . . . Praskovya and Lipa were beginning to doze.

When they were roused by somebody's footsteps the moon was shining brightly. Aksinia was standing at the door of the coach-house holding her bedding in her hands.

"It's probably cooler here . . ." she said, and coming in she lay down almost at the threshold, so that the whole of her figure was in the moonlight.

She did not sleep but breathed heavily, and tossing about from the heat she threw off almost everything she had on her—and in the magic of the moonlight what a beautiful, what a proud animal she was! After a little time footsteps were heard again, and the old man dressed all in white, appeared in the doorway.

"Aksinia," he called, "are you here?"

"Well!" she said angrily.

"I told you to throw the money into the well. Did you do it?"

"What next! Why throw property into the water? I gave them to the mowers."

"Oh, my God!" the old man exclaimed in amazement and alarm. "You mischief-making woman! Oh, my God!"

He clasped his hands and went away, mumbling something. Shortly after

Aksinia sat up, sighed heavily from vexation and then, rising, took up her bedding and went away.

"Why did you let me marry into this house, mother darling!" Lipa exclaimed.

"A girl must marry, daughter. That is ordained not by us."

A feeling of inconsolable grief was about to overcome them, but it appeared to them that somebody was looking down from the high heavens, from the blue sky, whence the stars saw everything that happened in Ukleevo and kept guard over them. And however much the evil might be, still the night was calm and lovely, and there was truth in God's world and always would be, the same calm and lovely truth, and everything on the earth waits till it is able to blend with truth, as the moonlight blends with the night.

Both of them were soothed, and pressing close together they fell asleep.

CHAPTER VI

TEARS

LONG since the news had arrived that Anisim had been sent to prison for the coining and the circulation of false money. Months passed, more than half a year passed, the long winter was over, spring had come and the people in the house and in the village had become accustomed to the fact that Anisim was in prison. When anybody passed the house or the shop at night he would remember that Anisim was lying in prison. Or when the churchyard bell tolled for some reason, people remembered that he was lying in prison awaiting his trial.

It appeared as if a shadow had fallen on the house. The building had grown darker, the roof had become rusty, the door of the shop, which was covered with sheet iron and painted green, had faded, and even old Zybukin seemed to have grown darker. It was long since he had had his hair and beard cut, and they were much overgrown; he no longer sat down in his cart with a run, and he did not shout to the beggars, "God will give." His strength was beginning to fail him, and this could be noticed in everything. People feared him less; the local police officer had drawn up a protocol in the shop, although he received as heretofore what was due, and three times he had been cited to town to be tried for the secret sale of spirits, but the case was always adjourned, owing to the non-appearance of the witnesses; and the old man was tired out.

He often went to see his son; he hired somebody, he presented a petition to somebody. he presented a banner to some institution. He gave a silver holder for a teaglass, with an inscription in, enamel, "The soul knows moderation," and a long spoon to the chief warden of the prison where his son was confined.

"Solicit, petition, leave no stone unturned," Varvara said. "O-ho-ho! You ought to ask some of the gentry, they might write to the chief judge. . . . They might let him be free till the trial! Why oppress the lad!"

She too grieved; she grew stouter and her hair became whiter, but she continued to light the icon lamps in her room, and saw that everything should be clean and in order in the house, and she treated her guests to jam and apple-jelly. The deaf man and Aksinia carried on the trade of the shop. They began a new business—the brick works in Butekino—and Aksinia drove there almost every day. She drove herself, and when she met acquaintances she would stretch out her neck, like a snake in the young rye, and smile naïvely and enigmatically. Lipa played all the time with her child, which had been born just before Lent. It was a small baby, lean and yellow, and it was strange that he could cry and look around, and that he was considered a person, and was even called Nikifor. He lay in his cradle, and Lipa, going to the door and bowing, would say:

"How do you do, Nikifor Anisimich?"

Then she rushed towards him and covered him with kisses. And again she went to the door and again she said:

"How do you do, Nikifor Anisimich?"

And he kicked about his red little legs, and his tears were mixed with laughter as it was with the carpenter Elizarov.

At last the day of the trial was appointed. The old man went to town five days before. Then they heard that several muzhiks from the village were taken there as witnesses; their old labourer also went, as he had received a summons too.

The trial was on a Thursday. But Sunday passed and the old man had not returned, and there was no news from him. On Tuesday towards evening Varvara was sitting near the open window to listen if there were no sounds of the old man's returning. In the next room Lipa was playing with her baby.

She was rocking it in her arms, and was saying to it with delight:

"You will grow up big, very big! You will be a muzhik, and we'll go out together to day work. We'll go together to day work!"

"Come now!" Varvara said, offended. "What sort of day work have you, silly girl, invented? He'll be a merchant with us! . ."

Lipa began to sing in a low voice, but soon after she forgot and again said:

"You'll grow big, very big; you'll be a muzhik, we'll go together to day work!"

"Come now! You're repeating it again!"

Lipa with Nikifor in her arms stopped in the doorway and asked:

"Maminka, why do I love him so much? Why do I pity him so much?" she continued with a shaky voice, and her eyes glittered with tears. "Who is he? What is there of him? He's light as a feather, as a crumb, yet I love him, I love him like a real man. He can't do anything, he can't speak, yet I understand all that he wants by his little eyes."

Varvara sat listening; she heard the noise of the evening train coming into the station. Had the old man arrived by it? She did not hear or understand what Lipa was saying, she did not notice how time passed, she only trembled all over, and it was not from fear, but from curiosity. She saw a cart full of muzhiks drive past quickly and noisily. They were the witnesses who were returning from the station. The old labourer jumped off his cart as it passed the shop and he went into the yard. She heard how he was greeted in the yard, and he was asked about something. . . .

"Deprived of all rights and property," he said in a loud voice, "and six years of Siberia with hard labour."

She saw Aksinia come out of the shop by the back door; she had just been delivering some kerosene, and had a bottle in one hand and a watering-pot in the other and she was holding a silver coin in her mouth.

"Where is *papasha?*" she asked hissingly.

"At the station," the workman answered. "'I'll come home when it gets darker,' he said."

When it became known in the yard that Anisim had been condemned to hard labour, the cook in the kitchen began wailing vociferously in the way they do for a dead man, as she thought this was demanded by propriety:

"And why have you deserted us, Anisim Grigorievich, our bright falcon? . . ."

The alarmed dogs began to bark. Varvara ran to the window, stunned by her grief, and called out to the cook at the top of her voice:

"Enough, Stepanida, enough; Don't overpower us, for Christ's sake!"

They forgot to put on the samovar, they could think of nothing. It was only Lipa who could not understand what had happened, and continued to carry her child about.

When the old man arrived from the station, nobody asked him any questions. He greeted everybody, and then went through all the rooms in silence; he would not have any supper.

"There was nobody with influence . . ." Varvara began, when they remained alone. "I told you to ask the gentry. . . . You did not listen to me then. . . . A petition might . . ."

"I did what I could!" the old man said, and he seemed to wipe the past away with a gesture of his hand. "When Anisim was condemned I went to the gentleman who had defended him. 'Nothing can be done now, it's too late.' And Anisim himself said: 'Too late.' Still, when I left the court I spoke to an advocate; I gave him an advance. . . . I shall wait a week and then go again. It's God's will . . . ."

The old man again went through all the rooms in silence, and when he returned to Varvara he said:

"I think I'm ill. My head is misty. . . . My thoughts get mixed."

He shut the door so that Lipa should not hear him, and continued in a whisper:

"I'm not in luck with money. Do you remember the week after Easter, just before his wedding, Anisim gave me some new silver roubles and half-roubles? One roll I put away at once, and the others I mixed with my own money. . . . Formerly when my uncle, Dmitry Filatych, was still alive, God rest his soul, he used to go to Moscow to buy goods and sometimes to the Crimea too. Well, he had a wife, and while he was away on business this wife amused herself with other men. There were six children, and it often happened when uncle got tipsy he would laugh: 'I can't for the life of me make out which are my children and which are "others."' He was easygoing. That's just how it is with me now: I can't make out which money is real and which counterfeit. And they appear to me all false."

"Well I never! God preserve you!"

"I took my ticket at the station and gave three roubles, and it appeared to me they were all false. I became frightened. I must be ill."

"You don't say so. We are all in God's hands. . . . O-ho-ho . . ." Varvara continued and she shook her head. "One must think about it, Petrovich. Who knows what may happen; you're not a young man. Should you die, see that your grandson is not wronged when you're no more. Oh, I'm afraid they'll wrong Nikifor, they'll wrong him; His father can be counted as no more; his mother is young and silly. . . . You could make over some land to the boy. Why not Butekino, Petrovich; it really would be a good thing! . . . Think of it . . ." Varvara continued to persuade him. "He's a nice boy, it would be a pity. Why not go to-morrow and have the deed made out? Why wait?"

"I'd quite forgotten the grandson . . ." Zybukin said. "I must go and see him. So you say the boy is a fine one? Well, let him grow up; God bless him!"

He opened the door and beckoned with his finger for Lipa to come to him. She approached with her baby in her arms.

"Lipinka, if you want anything, ask for it," he said. "Eat whatever you like, we wont grudge it, if you're only well . . ." He made the sign of the cross over the infant. "And take care of my grandson. My son is no more, but my grandson has remained."

Tears flowed down his cheeks; he sobbed and turned away. Shortly after he went to bed, and fell into a deep sleep after seven sleepless nights.

CHAPTER VII

OVER NIKIFOR

THE old man went to town for a short time. Somebody told Aksinia that he had been at a notary's. in order to make his will, and that he had left Butekino, where she was baking bricks, to his grandson Nikifor. She was informed of this in the morning, when the old man and Varvara were sitting under a birch tree near the door, drinking tea. She shut up the shop, both from the street and from the yard she collected all the keys that were in her keeping and flung them down at the old man's feet.

"I'm not going to work for you any more!" she shouted in a loud voice, and then suddenly began to sob. "It appears I'm not your daughter-in-law, but your servant! All the people are laughing at me and saying: 'See what a servant Zybukin has hired!' I've never hired myself to you! I'm no beggar, I'm no slave, I have a father and a mother."

She did not wipe away her tears, but stared at the old man with tear-stained, wicked eyes, that squinted with rage; her face and neck were red and stained, for she was shouting with her whole might.

"I won't serve you any more!" she continued. "I'm tired out! When it's a case of work, or to sit in the shop all day long, and at night to slip out for vodka, that's good enough for me; but when land is to be given away then it's the convict's wife and her little devil! She's mistress here, a fine lady, and I'm to be her servant! Give her everything —the galley-slave—may it choke her; I'm going home! Find another fool to serve you, you damned Herods!"

The old man had never once in his

life scolded or punished his children, and he had never admitted, even in thought, that a member of his family could use abusive language to him, or act towards him with want of respect; now he was greatly alarmed; he ran into the house and hid behind a cupboard, while Varvara was so panic-stricken that she could not rise from her seat, but only waved her arms about as if she was defending herself from a swarm of bees.

"Good gracious! What's the meaning of this?" she muttered in terror. "Why is she shouting? O-ho-ho! . . . The people will hear her! Be quiet. . . . Oh, be quiet!"

"You've given the galley-slave Butekino," Aksinia continued to shout. "Now you can give her all the rest—I want nothing from you! The devil take you all! You're all one gang! I've seen enough of you! You plundered those who came on foot and those who drove here, robbers, you plundered the old and the young! Who sold vodka without a license? and the false money? You stuffed your trunks with false money—and now I've become unnecessary!"

Near the widely opened gate a crowd had collected, and were looking into the yard.

"Let the people look," Aksinia cried. "I'll shame you! You'll be consumed with shame! You'll fall at my feet! Eh, Stepan!" she shouted to the deaf man. "Let's drive home this very minute. Let's go to my father and mother. I don't want to live with prisoners! Buck up!"

Linen was hanging out to dry on cords drawn across the yard; she tore down her own petticoats and bodices, which were still quite wet, and threw them over the deaf man's arm. Then still more enraged she rushed about the yard between the rows of linen, tearing it all down and trampling what was not hers in the dust.

"Oh, my good sirs, silence her!" Varvara groaned. "What does she want? Give her Butekino, give it her for the sake of Christ in heaven."

"Well, what a woman!" the people at the gate said. "There's a woman for you! She's in a terrible rage!"

Aksinia rushed into the kitchen, where a wash was going on at that time. Lipa alone was washing, and the cook had gone to the river to rinse the linen. Steam was rising from the wash tub and from the boiler that stood on the stove, and the kitchen was thick and heavy with mist. There was a heap of still unwashed linen lying on the floor and Nikifor was lying kicking his legs about on a bench near this heap, so that if he fell he would not hurt himself. At the moment Aksinia entered the kitchen Lipa had just taken one of Aksinia's shifts from that heap, had put it into the wash tub and was stretching out her hand to take the large ladle with boiling water that was standing on the table.

"Give it here!" Aksinia said, looking at her with hatred, and she snatched the shift out of the wash tub. It's not your business to touch my linen! You're a convict's wife and must know your place, and what you are!"

Lipa looked at her panic-stricken, not understanding what had happened; but she caught the look that Aksinia cast on the child, and suddenly understood and became deadly pale. . . .

"You have taken my land, that's also for you!"

Saying this, Aksinia snatched up the ladle of boiling water and poured it over Nikifor.

Then a scream was heard, such as never before had been heard in Ukleevo, and it was hardly credible that a small feeble creature like Lipa could have uttered such a cry. Suddenly it became quiet in the yard. Aksinia went silently into the house with her usual naïve smile. . . . The deaf man continued to roam about the yard carrying his armful of wet linen and then he began to hang it up again, silently and without hurrying. Till the cook returned from the river nobody had the courage to enter the kitchen and see what had happened there.

CHAPTER VIII

CONVICT'S WIFE

NIKIFOR was taken to the district hospital, but towards evening he died. Lipa would not wait to be fetched, but wrapped the dead child in a blanket and carried it home.

The hospital, but recently built, stood high up on a hill, and its large windows shone brightly in the setting sun, and it seemed to be on fire inside. Below it lay a little village. Lipa went along the road, and before reaching the village she sat down near a small pond. A woman brought a horse to the water, but it would not drink.

"What do you want then?" the woman said, perplexed. "What do you want?"

A boy in a red shirt was sitting close to the water, washing his father's boots. Not another soul was to be seen either in the village or on the hill.

"It does not drink . . ." Lipa said, looking at the horse.

Then the woman and the boy with the boots went away and nobody was to be seen. The sun went to bed and covered itself up with purple and gold brocade, and long red and purple clouds watched over its repose, stretching themselves out across the sky. Somewhere far away the call of a bittern could be heard that sounded doleful and cow-house. The cry of this mysterious dull like a cow that was shut up in the bird was heard every spring, but they did not know what it was nor where it lived. The hill near the hospital, the bushes by the pond behind the village and all around the fields trilled with the songs of nightingales. The cuckoo was numbering the years of somebody's life. and always got wrong and began over again. In the pond angrily straining to outcry each other the frogs croaked, and one could even distinguish the words, "You're like that, you're like that!" what a noise there was! It appeared as if all these creatures cried and sang on purpose, to prevent everybody from sleeping during this spring night, but that all, even the angry frogs, valued and enjoyed every minute: why, life is given only once!

The crescent moon shone silvery in the sky, and there were many stars. Lipa could not remember how long she sat near the pond, but when she rose and went on, everything was sleeping in the village, and not a single light was to be seen. There were about twelve versts to her home, and her strength failed her: she did not know how to go on. The moon shone sometimes in front, sometimes to the right, and the same cuckoo kept calling; but now with a hoarse voice and laughter as if mocking her: "Oh, look out. you'll miss your way!"

Lipa walked fast, and lost the handkerchief she had on her head. . . . She looked at the sky and wondered where her boy was now: was he following her or flying up there on high near the stars and did not think any more about his mother? Oh, how solitary it is in the fields at night, in the midst of all this singing, when you yourself cannot sing, in the midst of all these incessant cries of joy when you cannot rejoice, when the moon, also solitary and for whom it is all the same; whether it is spring now or winter, whether people are alive or dead, looks down from the sky. . . . When the soul is sad it is hard to be without people around you. If only her mother, Praskovya, were with her, r Crutch, or the cook, or one of the muzhiks!

"Boo!" called the bittern. "Boo-oo!"

Then suddenly human speech was distinctly heard.

"Vavila. harness the horses."

In front of her, at the roadside, a fire was burning; there were no flames; only glowing embers were still to be seen. The chewing of horses could be heard. Through the darkness the outlines of two carts. one with a cask; the other, a lower one, was loaded with sacks, and the figures of two men could be seen; one of the men was leading a horse to harness it to the cart, the other man stood motionless near the fire. with his arms behind his back. A dog growled near the carts. The man who was leading the horse stopped and said:

"Somebody must be coming along the road."

"Sharik, be quiet!" the other man called to the dog.

By the voice one could know that the last speaker was an old man. Lipa stopped and said:

"God help you!"

The old man came up to her, but did not answer at once.

"How do you do?"

"Your dog won't bite, grandfather?"

"Don't fear, come on. He won't touch you. . . ."

"I was in the hospital," Lipa said after a short silence. "My little son died there. I'm carrying him home."

It was evidently unpleasant for the old man to hear this, for he went away and said hurriedly:

"That does not matter, my dear. It's God's will. Don't dawdle, boy!" he said turning to his companion. "Look sharp!"

"I can't find your yoke!" the lad said. "It's not here!"

"You're obstinate, Vavila."

The old man took a brand from the fire, blew upon it, lighting up only his own eyes and nose, then when they had found the yoke he came up to Lipa with his light and looked upon her; there was a look of sympathy and softness in his eyes.

"You're a mother," he said. "Every mother is grieved at the loss of her child."

He sighed and shook his head. Vavila threw something into the fire and trampled upon it; it became very dark at once. The vision disappeared, and as before there was only the field, the starlit sky, the noise of the birds who prevented each other from sleeping. A corn-crake uttered its sharp cry, apparently just at the place where the fire had been burning.

But a moment after the carts could again be seen, and the old man and long-legged Vavila. The carts squeaked as they drove on to the road.

"Are you saints?" Lipa asked the old man.

"No. We come from Firsanov."

"You looked at me just now, and my heart grew soft. The lad is quiet too. So I thought: they must be saints."

"Have you far to go?"

"To Ukleevo."

"Sit down, we can take you to Kuz'-menok. Then you go straight, we turn to the left."

Vavila sat down in the cart with the cask, the old man and Lipa got into the other. They went on at a foot-pace, Vavila in front.

"My little son suffered all day," Lipa said. "He looked with his little eyes and was silent, he wanted to say something, but could not. Lord God! Queen of Heaven! From grief I kept falling on the floor all the time. I stood there, and fell down near the bed. Tell me, grandfather, why the little ones have to suffer before death. When a grown man suffers, a muzhik or a woman, then their sins are forgiven them; but why should a little one, who has no sins, suffer? Why?"

"Who can say!" the old man answered.

They drove on for about half an hour in silence.

"One can't know everything, the why and the wherefore." the old man said. "Birds have been given not four wings, but two, because they can fly with two wings; so also man has been given to know not everything, but only half or a quarter. As much as he ought to know to be able to live, so much he knows."

"Grandfather, it will be easier for me to go on foot. Now my heart shakes."

"Never mind. Sit still."

The old man yawned and made the sign of the cross over his mouth.

"Never mind," he repeated. "Your grief is only half a grief. Life is long—there will still be good things and bad things, there'll be all sorts of things in it. Mother Russia is great!" he said, and looked all around him. "I've been all over Russia, and have seen everything in her, and, my dear, you can believe my words. There'll be good and bad. I've walked on foot over the whole of Siberia. I've been on the Amour, on the Altai; I emigrated to Siberia and have ploughed the land there; then I became home-sick. I longed for Mother Russia, and returned to my native village. We returned to Russia on foot; I remember we were floating on a ferry-boat, I was thin and lean, all tattered and torn, barefoot and shivering, sucking a crust, when a gentleman who was also crossing in the ferry-boat—if he's dead may the Heavenly Kingdom be his—looked at me with pity and tears flowed from his eyes. 'Oh,' he said, 'your bread is black—your days are black too. . . .' I got back to my village, as one says, without house or home. I'd had a wife; she remained in Siberia, buried. So, I live as a workman. And what of that? I'll tell you more. I've known good and bad since then. And I don't want to die yet, my dear, I'd like to live another twenty years; so, you see, there's been more good than bad. Yes, and Mother Russia is great!" he said and he again looked round on all sides and he looked back.

"Grandfather," Lipa asked, "after a man dies, for how many days does his soul remain on earth?"

"Who can tell! Let's ask Vavila—he's been to school. Now all sorts of things are taught. Vavila!" the old man called to him.

"Eh?"

"Vavila, after a man dies, for how many days does his soul remain on earth?"

Vavila stopped his horse and only then he answered:

"For nine days. My Uncle Kiril died, but his soul remained in our *isba* for thirteen days."

"How do you know that?"

"For thirteen days there was crackling in our stove."

"Well, all right. Go on," the old man said, and it was quite clear he did not believe anything of the sort.

Near Kuz'menok the carts turned on to the high road and Lipa went on. The dawn was beginning. When she went down into the ravine the Ukleevo huts and the church hid themselves in the fog. It was cold and it seemed to her that the same cuckoo was still calling.

When Lipa arrived at home the cattle had not as yet been sent out to pasture; everybody slept. She sat down on the doorstep and waited. The first to come out was the old man; at the first glance he understood what had happened. and for a long time he was unable to utter a word, but could only smack his lips.

"Oh, Lipa." he said at last. "you were not able to protect my grandson . . ."

He went to wake Varvara. She clasped her hands and began to sob; but she commenced at once laying out the child.

"He was a fine boy . . ." she said. "O-ho-ho! . . . She had but one boy, and could not even take care of him, the stupid girl . . ."

Prayers for the dead were said morning and evening. On the second day he was buried, and after the burial the guests and the clergy ate very much and greedily as though they had not eaten for a long time. Lipa served at table, and the priest, raising his fork on which there was a salted mushroom, said to her:

"Do not grieve for the infant, for of such is the kingdom of heaven."

It was only after all had left that Lipa really understood that Nikifor was no more and would never be again, she understood this and burst into sobs. She did not know into which room she ought to go, in order to cry and sob, as she felt that in this house, after the death of the boy, there was no place for her, that she had nothing more to do there, that she was superfluous; and the others felt it too.

"Well, why are you making such a row here?" Aksinia shouted, suddenly appearing in the doorway; in honour of the funeral she was dressed in quite new clothes and powdered. "Shut up!"

Lipa wanted to cease crying but could not, and only sobbed the louder.

"Do you hear?" Aksinia shouted, and stamped her foot with rage. "Whom am I speaking to? Get out of the house, and see that no trace remains of you, convict's wife. Out with you!"

"Well, well, well!" the old man exclaimed. "Aksinia, *matushka,* be calm. She's crying . . . it's quite natural . . . she has lost her child. . . ."

"It's quite natural . . ." Aksinia mimicked. "She may pass the night here, but tomorrow there must be no trace of her! It's quite natural!" she repeated, and laughing she turned to go to the shop.

Early the next morning Lipa went away to Torguevo to her mother.

CHAPTER IX

NOTHING TO EAT

Now the roof of the shop and the door have been painted and shine like new; on the window-sill bright coloured geraniums blossom as formerly, and that which had happened three years ago in Zybukin's house and yard has almost been forgotten.

Old Grigory Petrovich is still considered the master but really the whole business is now in Aksinia's hands; it is she who sells and buys and without her consent nothing can be done. The brick-field was working well; as bricks were required on the railway line the price had risen to twenty-four roubles the thousand. The women and the girls carted the bricks to the station and loaded the waggons, and they received for this work twenty-five kopecks per day.

Aksinia had entered into partnership with the Khrymin juniors, and their factory went by the name of Khrymin Juniors and Co. They had opened a tavern near the station; they did not play any longer on the expensive accordion in their factory yard, but now they play on it in this tavern: the chief of the post department, who had also started some sort of commerce, and the stationmaster, who had done the same, often came here. The Khrymin juniors had given deaf Stepan a gold watch, and he constantly took it out of his pocket and held it to his ear.

People in the village said that Aksinia had become very powerful; and really, when in the morning she drove over to her brick works, with her naïve smile. looking pretty and happy, or when afterwards she gave orders at the works, one felt that she had great power. Everybody in the house was afraid of her, and in the village and at the works too. If she went to the post office the postmaster would jump from his chair and say to her:

"Have the goodness to be seated, Xenia Abramovna."

One day a landowner, a dandy in a *poddevka*, made of fine cloth and in patent leather top-boots, who was already getting on in years, when selling her a horse was so captivated that he gave her the horse for the price she wanted. He held her hand long in his, and looking into her gay, artful and naïve eyes, he said:

"For a woman like you, Xenia Abramovna, I am ready to do whatever she desires. Only tell me when we can meet, so that nobody should disturb us?"

"Whenever you like!"

After that this aged dandy began coming to the shop in order to drink beer. The beer was abominable and as bitter as wormwood. The landowner shook his head. but drank it.

Old Zybukin no longer interfered in the business. He never kept any money in his own possession, as he was quite unable to distinguish a real coin from a false one, but he kept silent and never told anybody about this weakness. He also became forgetful, and if he was not given food he never asked for it; they had become used to have their meals without him, and Varvara often said:

"Yesterday again he went to bed without eating."

She said it with indifference as she had become accustomed to it. For some reason, both in summer and winter he went about in his fur coat, and it was only on very hot days that he did not leave the house. Usually dressed in his fur coat, with the collar turned up and the coat well wrapped round him, he walked about the village, on the road to the station, or he would sit from morning to night on the bench near the church gate. He would sit there motionless. The passers-by bowed to him, but he did not return their salutes, for he did not like the muzhiks any more than he had done. If he was asked about anything he answered quite sensibly and politely but briefly.

In the village reports went about that his daughter-in-law had turned him out of his own house and gave him nothing to eat, and that he was supported by charity; some people rejoiced, others were sorry for him.

Varvara had grown still stouter and more grey, and as formerly she did good deeds, and Aksinia did not prevent her. There was so much jam now that they were unable to finish it before the new season came on; it became candied and Varvara almost cried, not knowing what to do with it.

Anisim was almost forgotten. One day a letter from him arrived. It was written in verse on a large sheet of paper like a petition, in the same beautiful handwriting as formerly. Evidently his friend Samorodov was sharing his punishment. Beneath the verses one line was written in an ugly scarcely legible handwriting: "I am always ill here, I am sad, help for Christ's sake."

Once—it was on a bright autumn day, towards evening—old Zybukin was sitting near the church gate, with the collar of his fur coat turned up, so that nothing but his nose and the peak of his cap could be seen. At the other end of the long bench Elizarov was seated, and next to him sat Yakov, the watchman from the school-house, a toothless old man of seventy. Crutch and the watchman were conversing

"Children must feed and look after the old people—honour thy father and thy mother," Yakov said with irascibility; "and she, the daughter-in-law, has turned the old man out of his own house. The old man has nothing to eat or to drink—where is he to go? It's the third day he's eaten nothing."

"The third day," Crutch repeated with astonishment.

"He sits in this way, and says nothing. He has grown weak. Why is he silent? He ought to go to law—the court would not praise her."

"Who has been praised by the court?" Crutch asked, not having heard correctly.

"What for?"

"The woman's not a bad one—painstaking. In their business it's impossible without it . . . that is, without sin. . . ."

"Out of his own house," Yakov continued irritably.

"Get your own house first—then turn people out of it. Eh! well, they've found a fine one, don't you think! A perfect plague!"

Zybukin heard, but did not move.

"It's all one if it's your own house or another's if it's only warm, and the women don't scold . . ." Crutch said, and laughed. "When I was younger I regretted my Nastasia very much. She was a quiet woman. But she was always saying: 'Makarich, buy a house! Buy a house, Makarich! Buy a horse, Makarich!' She was dying, and still she said: 'Makarich, buy a racing droshky, so as not to go on foot.' And I only bought her ginger-bread; nothing else."

"The husband is deaf and stupid," Yakov continued, paying no attention to Crutch. "A fool's no better than a goose. How can he understand anything? You may beat a goose on the head and with a stick—even then it won't understand."

Crutch got up from his seat to go home to the factory. Yakov also rose and they went away together, continuing their talk. When they had gone about fifty paces old Zybukin also rose and went slowly after them, taking unsteady steps as if he were walking on ice.

The village was already sinking into the twilight of evening, and the sun shone only on the upper part of the road that curled about like a snake from the bottom to the top. The old women were returning from the wood, with the children; they were carrying baskets of mushrooms. The women and the girls were coming in a crowd from the station, where they had been loading waggons with bricks, and their noses and their cheeks just under the eyes were covered with red brick dust. They were singing. Lipa walked in front, singing in a small thin voice and looking up at the sky, as if in triumph and gladness that the day, thank God, was over and she might rest. Her mother, the charwoman, Praskovya, was also in the crowd of women, walking with a bundle in her hand and, as always, breathing heavily.

"Good evening, Makarich," Lipa said when she saw Crutch. "Good evening, dear!"

"Good evening, Lipynka!" Crutch answered, delighted to see her. "Butterflies, little girls love the rich carpenter! Ho-ho-ho! My children, my dear children" (Crutch sobbed). "My dear little hatchets."

Crutch and Yakov went on, and the girls could hear them talking. A little farther on the girls met old Zybukin, and they became instantly silent. Lipa and Praskovya stayed behind, and when the old man came up to them Lipa bowed low and said:

"How do you do, Grigory Petrovich!"

Her mother also bowed. The old man stopped and looked at them without saying a word; his lips trembled, and his eyes filled with tears. Lipa took out of the bundle her mother was carrying a piece of pie and handed it to him. He took it and began to eat.

The sun had quite set now, its brilliancy had faded away from the heights and the road. It was becoming dark and cold. Lipa and Praskovya went on, and for a long time they continued to cross themselves.

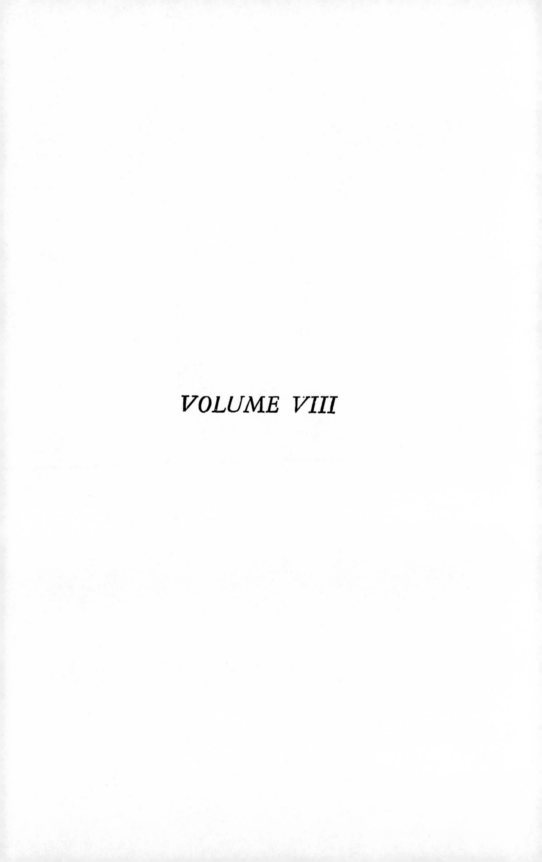

VOLUME VIII

The Cherry Orchard

DRAMATIS PERSONAE

MADAME RANEVSKY, *a landowner.*

ANYA, *her daughter, aged 17.*

BARBARA, *her adopted daughter, aged 27.*

LEONID GAYEF, *brother of Madame Ranévsky.*

LOPAKHIN, *a merchant.*

PETER TROPHIMOF, *a student.*

SIMEONOF-PISHTCHIK, *a landowner.*

CHARLOTTE, *a governess.*

EPHIKHODOF, *a clerk.*

DUNYASHA. *a housemaid.*

FIRS, *a man-servant, aged 87.*

YASHA, *a young man-servant.*

TRAMP.

STATIONMASTER, POST OFFICE OFFICIALS, GUESTS, SERVANTS, ETC.

The action takes place on Madame Ranévsky's property.

ACT I

A room which is still called the nursery. One door leads to ANYA'S *room. Dawn, the sun will soon rise. It is already May, the cherry-trees are in blossom, but it is cold in the garden and there is a morning frost. The windows are closed.*

Enter DUNYASHA *with a candle, and* LOPAKHIN *with a book in his hand.*

LOPAKHIN. Here's the train, thank heaven. What is the time?

DUNYASHA. Near two. [*Putting the candle out.*] It is light already.

LOPAKHIN. How late is the train? Two hours at least. [*Yawning and stretching.*] A fine mess I have made of it. I came to meet them at the station and then I went and fell asleep, as I sat in my chair. What trouble! Why did you not rouse me?

DUNYASHA. I thought that you had gone. [*She listens.*] I think they are coming.

LOPAKHIN. [*Listening*] No; they have got to get the baggage and the rest. [*A pause.*] Madame Ranévsky has been five years abroad. I wonder what she is like now. What a fine character she is! So easy and simple. I remember when I was only fifteen my old father (he used to keep a shop here in the village then) struck me in the face with his fist and my nose bled. We were out in the courtyard, and he had been drinking. Madame Ranévsky, I remember it like yesterday, still a slender young girl, brought me to the wash-hand stand, here, in this very room, in the nursery. 'Don't cry, little peasant,' she said, 'it'll be alright for your wedding.' [*A pause.*] 'Little peasant!' . . . My father, it is true, was a peasant, and here am I in a white waistcoat and brown boots; a silk purse out of a sow's ear; just turned rich, with plenty of money, but still a peasant of the peasants. [*Turning over the pages of the book.*] Here's this book that I was reading without any attention and fell asleep.

DUNYASHA. The dogs never slept all night, they knew that their master and mistress were coming.

511

LOPAKHIN. What's the matter with you, Dunyásha? You're all . . .

DUNYASHA. My hands are trembling, I feel quite faint.

LOPAKHIN. You are too refined, Dunyásha, that's what it is. You dress yourself like a young lady, and look at your hair! You ought not to do it; you ought to remember your place.

Enter EPHIKHODOF *with a nosegay. He is dressed in a short jacket and brightly polished boots which squeak noisily. As he comes in he drops the nosegay.*

EPHIKHODOF [*picking it up*]. The gardener has sent this; he says it is to go in the dining-room. [*Handing it to* DUNYASHA.]

LOPAKHIN. And bring me some quass.

DUNYASHA. Yes, sir.

[*Exit* DUNYASHA.]

EPHIKHODOF. There's a frost this morning, three degrees, and the cherry-trees all in blossom. I can't say I think much of our climate; [*sighing*] that is impossible. Our climate is not adapted to contribute; and I should like to add, with your permission, that only two days ago I bought myself a new pair of boots, and I venture to assure you they do squeak beyond all bearing. What am I to grease them with?

LOPAKHIN. Get out; I'm tired of you.

EPHIKHODOF. Every day some misfortune happens to me; but do I grumble? No; I am used to it; I can afford to smile. [*Enter* DUNYASHA, *and hands a glass of quass to* LOPAKHIN.] I must be going. [*He knocks against a chair, which falls to the ground.*] There you are! [*In a voice*

of triumph.] You see, if I may venture on the expression, the sort of incidents *inter alia*. It really is astonishing!

[*Exit* EPHIKHODOF.]

DUNYASHA. To tell you the truth, Yermoláĭ Alexéyitch, Ephikhódof has made me a proposal.

LOPAKHIN. Hmph!

DUNYASHA. I hardly know what to do. He is such a well-behaved young man, only so often when he talks one doesn't know what he means. It is all so nice and full of good feeling, but you can't make out what it means. I fancy I am rather fond of him. He adores me passionately. He is a most unfortunate man; every day something seems to happen to him. They call him 'Twenty-two misfortunes,' that's his nickname.

LOPAKHIN [*listening*]. There, surely that is them coming!

DUNYASHA. They're coming! Oh, what is the matter with me? I am all turning cold.

LOPAKHIN. Yes, there they are, and no mistake. Let's go and meet them. Will she know me again, I wonder? It is five years since we met.

DUNYASHA. I am going to faint! . . . I am going to faint!

[*Two carriages are heard driving up to the house.* LOPAKHIN *and* DUNYASHA *exeunt quickly. The stage remains empty. A hubbub begins in the neighbouring rooms.* FIRS *walks hastily across the stage, leaning on a walking-stick. He has been to meet them at the station. He is wearing an old-fashioned livery and a tall hat; he mumbles something to himself but not a word is audible. The noise behind the scenes grows louder and louder. A voice says: 'Let's go this way.'*

[*Enter* MADAME RANEVSKY, ANYA, CHARLOTTE, *leading a little dog on a chain, all dressed in travelling dresses;* BARBARA *in greatcoat with a kerchief over her head,* GAYEF, SIMEONOF-PISHTCHIK, LOPAKHIN, DUNYASHA, *carrying parcel and umbrella, servants with luggage, all cross the stage.*]

ANYA. Come through this way. Do you remember what room this is, mamma?

MADAME RANEVSKY [*joyfully through her tears*]. The nursery.

BARBARA. How cold it is. My hands are simply frozen. [*To* MADAME RANEVSKY.] Your two rooms, the white room and the violet room, are just the same as they were, mamma.

MADAME RANEVSKY. My nursery, my dear, beautiful nursery! This is where I used to sleep when I was a little girl. [*Crying.*] I am like a little girl still. [*Kissing* GAYEF *and* BARBARA *and then* GAYEF *again.*] Barbara has not altered a bit, she is just like a num, and I knew Dunyásha at once. [*Kissing* DUNYASHA.]

GAYEF. Your train was two hours late. What do you think of that? There's punctuality for you!

CHARLOTTE [*to* SIMEONOF-PISHT-CHIK]. My little dog eats nuts.

PISHTCHIK [*astonished*]. You don't say so! well I never!

[*Exeunt all but* ANYA *and* DUNYASHA.]

DUNYASHA. At last you've come!

[*She takes off* ANYA's *overcoat and hat.*]

ANYA. I have not slept for four nights on the journey. I am frozen to death.

DUNYASHA. It was Lent when you went away. There was snow on the ground, it was freezing; but now! Oh, my dear! [*Laughing and kissing her.*] How I have waited for you, my joy, my light! Oh, I must tell you something at once, I cannot wait another minute.

ANYA [*without interest*]. What, again?

DUNYASHA. Ephikhódof, the clerk, proposed to me in Easter week.

ANYA. Same old story. . . . [*Putting her hair straight.*] All my hairpins have dropped out. [*She is very tired, staggering with fatigue.*]

DUNYASHA. I hardly know what to think of it. He loves me! oh, how he loves me!

ANYA [*looking into her bedroom, affectionately*]. My room, my windows, just as if I had never gone away! I am at home again! When I wake up in the morning I shall run out into the garden. . . . Oh, if only I could get to sleep! I have not slept the whole journey from Paris, I was so nervous and anxious.

DUNYASHA. Monsieur Trophímof arrived the day before yesterday.

ANYA [*joyfully*]. Peter?

DUNYASHA. He is sleeping outside in the bath-house; he is living there. He was afraid he might be in the way. [*Looking at her watch.*] I'd like to go and wake him, only Mamzelle Barbara told me not to. 'Mind you don't wake him,' she said.

[*Enter* BARBARA *with bunch of keys hanging from her girdle.*]

BARBARA. Dunyásha, go and get some coffee, quick. Mamma wants some coffee.

DUNYASHA. In a minute.

[*Exit* DUNYASHA.]

BARBARA. Well, thank heaven, you have come. Here you are at home again. [*Caressing her.*] My little darling is back! My pretty one is back!

ANYA. What I've had to go through!

BARBARA. I can believe you.

ANYA. I left here in Holy Week. How cold it was! Charlotte would talk the whole way and keep doing conjuring tricks. What on earth made you tie Charlotte round my neck?

BARBARA. Well, you couldn't travel alone, my pet. At seventeen!

ANYA. When we got to Paris, it was so cold! there was snow on the ground. I can't talk French a bit. Mamma was on the fifth floor of a big house. When I arrived there were a lot of Frenchmen with her, and ladies, and an old Catholic priest with a book, and it was very uncomfortable and full of tobacco smoke. I suddenly felt so sorry for mamma, oh, so sorry! I took her head in my arms and squeezed it and could not let it go, and then mamma kept kissing me and crying.

BARBARA [*crying*]. Don't go on, don't go on!

ANYA. She's sold her villa near Mentone already. She's nothing left, absolutely nothing; and I hadn't a farthing either. We only just managed to get home. And mamma won't understand! We get out at a station to have some dinner, and she asks for all the most expensive things and gives the waiters a florin each for a tip; and Charlotte does the same. And Yásha wanted his portion too. It was too awful! Yásha is mamma's new man-servant. We have brought him back with us.

BARBARA. I've seen the rascal.

ANYA. Come, tell me all about everything! Has the interest on the mortgage been paid?

BARBARA. How could it be?

ANYA. Oh dear! Oh dear!

BARBARA. The property will be sold in August.

ANYA. Oh dear! Oh dear!

LOPAKHIN [*looking in at the door and mooing like a cow*]. Moo-o.

[*He goes away again.*]

BARBARA [*laughing through her tears, and shaking her fist at the door*]. Oh, I should like to give him one!

ANYA [*embracing* BARBARA *softly*]. Barbara, has he proposed to you? [BARBARA *shakes her head.*] And yet I am sure he loves you. Why don't you come to an understanding? What are you waiting for?

BARBARA. I don't think anything will come of it. He has so much to do; he can't be bothered with me; he hardly takes any notice. Confound the man, I can't bear to see him! Everyone talks about our marriage; everyone congratulates me, but, as a matter of fact, there is nothing in it; it's all a dream. [*Changing her tone.*] You've got on a brooch like a bee.

ANYA [*sadly*]. Mamma bought it me. [*Going into her room, talking gaily, like a child.*] When I was in Paris, I went up in a balloon!

BARBARA. How glad I am you are back, my little pet! my pretty one! [DUNYASHA *has already returned with a coffee-pot and begins to prepare the coffee.*] [*Standing by the door.*] I trudge about all day looking after things, and I think and think. What are we to do? If only we could marry you to some rich man it would be a load off my mind. I would go into a retreat, and then to Kief, to Moscow;

I would tramp about from one holy place to another, always tramping and tramping. What bliss!

ANYA. The birds are singing in the garden. What time is it now?

BARBARA. It must be past two. It is time to go to bed, my darling. [*Following* ANYA *into her room.*] What bliss!

[*Enter* YASHA *with a shawl and a travelling bag.*]

YASHA [*crossing the stage, delicately*]. May I pass this way, mademoiselle?

DUNYASHA. One would hardly know you, Yásha. How you've changed abroad!

YASHA. Ahem! and who may you be?

DUNYASHA. When you left here I was a little thing like that. [*Indicating with her hand.*] My name is Dunyásha, Theodore Kozoyédoi's daughter. Don't you remember me?

YASHA. Ahem! You little cucumber!

[*He looks round cautiously, then embraces her. She screams and drops a saucer. Exit* YASHA, *hastily.*]

BARBARA [*in the doorway, crossly*]. What's all this?

DUNYASHA [*crying*]. I've broken a saucer.

BARBARA. Well, it brings luck.

[*Enter* ANYA *from her room.*]

ANYA. We must tell mamma that Peter's here.

BARBARA. I've told them not to wake him.

ANYA [*thoughtfully*]. It's just six years since papa died. And only a month afterwards poor little Grisha was drowned in the river; my pretty little brother, only seven years old! It was too much for mamma; she ran away,

ran away without looking back. [*Shuddering.*] How well I can understand her, if only she knew! [*A pause.*] Peter Trophímof was Grisha's tutor; he might remind her.

[*Enter* FIRS *in long coat and white waistcoat.*]

FIRS [*going over to the coffee-pot, anxiously*]. My mistress is going to take coffee here. [*Putting on white gloves.*] Is the coffee ready? [*Sternly, to* DUNYASHA.] Here, girl, where's the cream?

DUNYASHA. Oh, dear! Oh dear!

[*Exit* DUNYASHA *hastily.*]

FIRS [*bustling about the coffee-pot*]. Ah, you . . . job-lot! [*Mumbling to himself.*] She's come back from Paris. The master went to Paris once in a post-chaise. [*Laughing.*]

BARBARA. What is it, Firs?

FIRS. I beg your pardon? [*Joyfully.*] My mistress has come home; at last I've seen her. Now I'm ready to die.

[*He cries with joy. Enter* MADAME RANEVSKY, LOPAKHIN, GAYEF *and* PISHTCHIK; PISHTCHIK *in Russian breeches and coat of fine cloth.* GAYEF *as he enters makes gestures as if playing billiards.*]

MADAME RANEVSKY. What was the expression? Let me see. 'I'll put the red in the corner pocket; double into the middle——'

GAYEF. I'll chip the red in the right-hand top. Once upon a time, Lyuba, when we were children, we used to sleep here side by side in two little cots, and now I'm fifty-one, and can't bring myself to believe it.

LOPAKHIN. Yes; time flies.

GAYEF. Who's that?

LOPAKHIN. Time flies, I say.

GAYEF. There's a smell of patchouli!

ANYA. I am going to bed. Good-night, mamma. [*Kissing her mother.*]

MADAME RANEVSKY. My beloved little girl! [*Kissing her hands.*] Are you glad you're home again? I can't come to my right senses.

ANYA. Good-night, uncle.

GAYEF [*kissing her face and hands*]. God bless you, little Anya. How like your mother you are! [*To* MADAME RANEVSKY.] You were just such another girl at her age. Lyuba.

[ANYA *shakes hands with* LOPAKHIN *and* SIMEONOF-PISHTCHIK *and exit, shutting her bedroom door behind her.*]

MADAME RANEVSKY. She's very, very tired.

PISHTCHIK. It must have been a long journey.

BARBARA [*to* LOPAKHIN. *and* PISHTCHIK.] Well, gentlemen, it's past two; time you were off

MADAME RANEVSKY [*laughing*]. You haven't changed a bit, Barbara! [*Drawing her to herself and kissing her.*] I'll just finish my coffee, then we'll all go. [FIRS *puts a footstool under her feet.*] Thank you. friend. I'm used to my coffee. I drink it day and night. Thank you, you dear old man. [*Kissing* FIRS.]

BARBARA. I'll go and see if they've got all the luggage. [*Exit* BARBARA.]

MADAME RANEVSKY. Can it be me that's sitting here? [*Laughing.*] I want to jump and wave my arms about. [*Pausing and covering her face.*] Surely I must be dreaming! God knows I love my country. I love it tenderly. I couldn't see out of the window from the train, I was crying so. [*Crying.*] However, I must drink my coffee.

Thank you Firs; thank you, dear old man. I'm so glad to find you still alive.

FIRS. The day before yesterday.

GAYEF. He's hard of hearing.

LOPAKHIN. I've got to be off for Kharkof by the five o'clock train. Such a nuisance! I wanted to stay and look at you and talk to you. You're as splendid as you always were.

PISHTCHIK [*sighing heavily*]. Handsomer than ever and dressed like a Parisian . . perish my waggon and all its wheels!

LOPAKHIN. Your brother, Leoníd Andréyitch, says I'm a snob, a money-grubber. He can say what he likes. I don't care a hang. Only I want you to believe in me as you used to; I want your wonderful, touching eyes to look at me as they used to. Merciful God in heaven! My father was your father's serf, and your grandfather's serf before him; but you, you did so much for me in the old days that I've forgotten everything, and I love you like a sister—more than a sister.

MADAME RANEVSKY. I can't sit still! I can't do it! [*Jumping up and walking about in great agitation.*] This happiness is more than I can bear. Laugh at me! I am a fool! [*Kissing a cupboard.*] My darling old cupboard! [*Caressing a table.*] My dear little table!

GAYEF. Nurse is dead since you went away.

MADAME RANEVSKY [*sitting down and drinking coffee*]. Yes, Heaven rest her soul. They wrote and told me.

GAYEF. And Anastási is dead. Squint-eyed Peter has left us and works in the town at the Police Inspector's now.

[GAYEF *takes out a box of sugar candy*

from his pocket, and begins to eat it.]

PISHTCHIK. My daughter Dáshenka sent her compliments.

LOPAKHIN. I long to say something charming and delightful to you. [*Looking at his watch.*] I'm just off; there's no time to talk. Well, yes, I'll put it in two or three words. You know that your cherry orchard is going to be sold to pay the mortgage: the sale is fixed for the twenty-second of August; but don't you be uneasy, my dear lady; sleep peacefully; there's a way out of it. This is my plan. Listen to me carefully. Your property is only fifteen miles from the town; the railway runs close beside it; and if only you will cut up the cherry orchard and the land along the river into building lots and let it off on lease for villas, you will get at least two thousand five hundred pounds a year out of it.

GAYEF. Come, come! What rubbish you're talking!

MADAME RANEVSKY. I don't quite understand what you mean, Yermolái Alexéyitch.

LOPAKHIN. You will get a pound a year at least for every acre from the tenants, and if you advertise the thing at once, I am ready to bet whatever you like, by the autumn you won't have a clod of that earth left on your hands. It'll all be snapped up. In two words, I congratulate you; you are saved. It's a first-class site, with a good deep river. Only of course you will have to put it in order and clear the ground; you will have to pull down all the old buildings—this house, for instance, which is no longer fit for anything; you'll have to cut down the cherry orchard. . . .

MADAME RANEVSKY. Cut down the cherry orchard! Excuse me, but you don't know what you're talking about. If there is one thing that's interesting, remarkable in fact, in the whole province, it's our cherry orchard.

LOPAKHIN. There's nothing remarkable about the orchard except that it's a very big one. It only bears once every two years, and then you don't know what to do with the fruit. Nobody wants to buy it.

GAYEF. Our cherry orchard is mentioned in Andréyevsky's Encyclopaedia.

LOPAKHIN [*looking at his watch*]. If we don't make up our minds or think of any way, on the twenty-second of August the cherry orchard and the whole property will be sold by auction. Come, make up your mind! There's no other way out of it, I swear—absolutely none.

FIRS. In the old days, forty or fifty years ago, they used to dry the cherries and soak 'em and pickle 'em, and make jam of 'em; and the dried cherries . . .

GAYEF. Shut up, Firs.

FIRS. The dried cherries used to be sent in waggons to Moscow and Kharkof. A heap of money! The dried cherries were soft and juicy and sweet and sweet-smelling then. They knew some way in those days.

MADAME RANEVSKY. And why don't they do it now?

FIRS. They've forgotten. Nobody remembers how to do it.

PISHTCHIK [*to* MADAME RANEVSKY]. What about Paris? How did you get on? Did you eat frogs?

MADAME RANEVSKY. Crocodiles.

PISHTCHIK. You don't say so! Well, I never!

LOPAKHIN. Until a little while ago there was nothing but gentry and peasants in the villages; but now villa residents have made their appearance. All the towns, even the little ones, are surrounded by villas now. In another twenty years the villa resident will have multiplied like anything. At present he only sits and drinks tea on his verandah, but it is quite likely that he will soon take to cultivating his three acres of land, and then your old cherry orchard will become fruitful, rich and happy. . . .

GAYEF [*angry*]. What gibberish!

[*Enter* BARBARA *and* YASHA.]

BARBARA [*taking out a key and noisily unlocking an old-fashioned cupboard*]. There are two telegrams for you, mamma. Here they are.

MADAME RANEVSKY [*tearing them up without reading them*]. They're from Paris. I've done with Paris.

GAYEF. Do you know how old this cupboard is, Lyuba? A week ago I pulled out the bottom drawer and saw a date burnt in it. That cupboard was made exactly a hundred years ago. What do you think of that, eh? We might celebrate its jubilee It's only an inanimate thing, but for all that it's a historic cupboard.

PISHTCHIK. [*Astonished.*] A hundred years? Well, I never!

GAYEF [*touching the cupboard*]. Yes, it's a wonderful thing. . . . Beloved and venerable cupboard; honour and glory to your existence; which for more than a hundred years has been directed to the noble ideals of justice and virtue. Your silent summons to profitable labour has never weakened in all these hundred years. [*Crying.*] You have upheld the courage of succeeding generations of our human kind; you have upheld faith in a better future

and cherished in us ideals of goodness and social consciousness. [*A pause.*]

LOPAKHIN. Yes. . . .

MADAME RANEVSKY. You haven't changed, Leoníd.

GAYEF [*embarrassed*]. Off the white in the corner, chip the red in the middle pocket!

LOPAKHIN [*looking at his watch*]. Well, I must be off.

YASHA [*handing a box to* MADAME RANEVSKY]. Perhaps you'll take your pills now.

PISHTCHIK. You oughtn't to take medicine, dear lady. It does you neither good nor harm. Give them here, my friend. [*He empties all the pills into the palm of his hand, blows on them, puts them in his mouth and swallows them down with a draught of quass.*] There!

MADAME RANEVSKY [*alarmed*]. Have you gone off your head?

PISHTCHIK. I've taken all the pills.

LOPAKHIN. Greedy fellow! [*Everyone laughs.*]

FIRS [*mumbling*]. They were here in Easter week and finished off a gallon of pickled gherkins.

MADAME RANEVSKY. What's he talking about?

BARBARA. He's been mumbling like that these three years. We've got used to it.

YASHA. Advancing age.

[CHARLOTTE *crosses in a white frock, very thin, tightly laced, with a lorgnette at her waist.*]

LOPAKHIN. Excuse me, Chanotte Ivánovna, I've not paid my respects to you yet. [*He prepares to kiss her hand.*]

CHARLOTTE [*drawing her hand away*]. If one allows you to kiss one's hand, you will want to kiss one's elbow next, and then one's shoulder.

LOPAKHIN, I'm having no luck to-day. [*All laugh.*] Charlotte Ivánovna, do us a conjuring trick.

MADAME RANEVSKY. Charlotte, do do us a conjuring trick.

CHARLOTTE. No, thank you. I'm going to bed.

[*Exit* CHARLOTTE.]

LOPAKHIN. We shall meet again in three weeks. [*Kissing* MADAME RANE-VSKY'S *hand.*] Meanwhile, good-bye. I must be off. [*To* GAYEF.] So-long. [*Kissing* PISHTCHIK.] Ta-ta. [*Shaking hands with* BARBARA, *then with* FIRS *and* YASHA.] I hate having to go. [*To* MADAME RANEVSKY.] If you make up your mind about the villas, let me know, and I'll raise you five thousand pounds at once. Think it over seriously.

BARBARA [*angrily*]. For heaven's sake do go!

LOPAKHIN. I'm going, I'm going.

[*Exit* LOPAKHIN.]

GAYEF. Snob! . . . However, *pardon!* Barbara's going to marry him; he's Barbara's young man.

BARBARA. You talk too much, uncle.

MADAME RANEVSKY. Why, Barbara, I shall be very glad. He's a nice man.

PISHTCHIK. Not a doubt about it. . . . A most worthy individual. My Dáshenka, she says . . . oh, she says . . . lots of things. [*Snoring and waking up again at once.*] By the by, dear lady, can you lend me twenty-five pounds? I've got to pay the interest on my mortgage to-morrow.

BARBARA [*alarmed*]. We can't! we can't!

MADAME RANEVSKY. It really is a fact that I haven't any money.

PISHTCHIK. I'll find it somewhere.

[*Laughing.*] I never lose hope. Last time I thought: 'Now I really am done for, I'm a ruined man,' when behold, they ran a railway over my land and paid me compensation. And so it'll be again; something will happen, if not to-day, then to-morrow. Dáshenka may win the twenty-thousand-pound prize; she's got a ticket in the lottery.

MADAME RANEVSKY. The coffee's finished. Let's go to bed.

FIRS [*brushing* GAYEF'S *clothes, admonishingly*]. You've put on the wrong trousers again. Whatever am I to do with you?

BARBARA [*softly*]. Anya is asleep. [*She opens the window quietly.*] The sun's up already; it isn't cold now. Look, mamma, how lovely the trees are. Heavens! what a sweet air! The starlings are singing!

GAYEF [*opening the other window*]. The orchard is all white. You've not forgotten it, Lyuba? This long avenue going straight on, straight on, like a ribbon between the trees? It shines like silver on moonlight nights. Do you remember? You've not forgotten?

MADAME RANEVSKY [*looking out into the garden*]. Oh, my childhood, my pure and happy childhood! I used to sleep in this nursery. I used to look out from here into the garden. Happiness awoke with me every morning! and the orchard was just the same then as it is now; nothing is altered. [*Laughing with joy.*] It is all white, all white! Oh, my cherry orchard! After the dark and stormy autumn and the frosts of winter you are young again and full of happiness; the angels of heaven have not abandoned you. Oh! if only I could free my neck and shoulders from the stone that weighs them down! If only I could forget my past!

GAYEF Yes; and this orchard will be sold to pay our debts, however impossible it may seem. . . .

MADAME RANEVSKY. Look! There's mamma walking in the orchard . . . in a white frock! [*Laughing with joy.*] There she is!

GAYEF. Where?

BARBARA. Heaven help you!

MADAME RANEVSKY. There's no one there, really. It only looked like it; there on the right where the path turns down to the summer-house; there's a white tree that leans over and looks like a woman. [*Enter* TROPHIMOF *in a shabby student uniform and spectacles.*] What a wonderful orchard, with its white masses of blossom and the blue sky above!

TROPHIMOF. Lyubóf Andréyevna! [*She looks round at him.*] I only want to say, 'How do you do,' and go away at once. [*Kissing her hand eagerly.*] I was told to wait till the morning, but I hadn't the patience.

[MADAME RANEVSKY *looks at him in astonishment.*]

BARBARA [*crying*]. This is Peter Trophímof.

TROPHIMOF. Peter Trophímof; I was Grisha's tutor, you know. Have I really altered so much?

[MADAME RANEVSKY *embraces him and cries softly.*]

GAYEF. Come, come, that's enough, Lyuba!

BARBARA [*crying*]. I told you to wait till to-morrow, you know, Peter.

MADAME RANEVSKY. My little Grisha! My little boy! Grisha . . . my son. . . .

BARBARA. It can't be helped, mamma. It was the will of God.

TROPHIMOF [*gently, crying*]. There, there!

MADAME RANEVSKY [*crying*]. He was drowned. My little boy was drowned. Why? What was the use of that, my dear? [*In a softer voice.*] Anya's asleep in there, and I am speaking so loud, and making a noise. . . . But tell me, Peter, why have you grown so ugly? Why have you grown so old?

TROPHIMOF. An old woman in the train called me a 'mouldy gentleman.'

MADAME RANEVSKY. You were quite a boy then, a dear little student, and now your hair's going and you wear spectacles. Are you really still a student? [*Going towards the door.*]

TROPHIMOF. Yes, I expect I shall be a perpetual student.

MADAME RANEVSKY [*kissing her brother and then* BARBARA]. Well, go to bed. You've grown old too, Leoníd.

PISHTCHIK [*following her*]. Yes, yes; time for bed. Oh, oh, my gout! I'll stay the night here. Don't forget, Lyubóf Andréyevna, my angel, to-morrow morning . . . twenty-five.

GAYEF. He's still on the same string.

PISHTCHIK. Twenty-five . . . to pay the interest on my mortgage.

MADAME RANEVSKY. I haven't any money, my friend.

PISHTCHIK. I'll pay you back, dear lady. It's a trifling sum.

MADAME RANEVSKY. Well, well, Leoníd will give it to you. Let him have it, Leoníd.

GAYEF [*ironical*]. I'll give it him right enough! Hold your pocket wide!

MADAME RANEVSKY. It can't be

helped. . . . He needs it. He'll pay it back.

[*Exeunt* MADAME RANEVSKY, TROPHIMOF, PISHTCHIK *and* FIRS. GAYEF, BARBARA *and* YASHA *remain*.]

GAYEF. My sister hasn't lost her old habit of scattering the money. [*To* YASHA.] Go away, my lad! You smell of chicken.

YASHA [*laughing*]. You're just the same as you always were, Leoníd Andréyevitch!

GAYEF. Who's that? [*To Barbara*.] What does he say?

BARBARA [*to* YASHA]. Your mother's come up from the village. She's been waiting for you since yesterday in the servants' hall. She wants to see you.

YASHA. What a nuisance she is!

BARBARA. You wicked, unnatural son!

YASHA. Well, what do I want with her? She might just as well have waited till to-morrow.

[*Exit* YASHA.]

BARBARA. Mamma is just like she used to be; she hasn't changed a bit. If she had her way, she'd give away everything she has.

GAYEF. Yes. [*A pause.*] If people recommend very many cures for an illness, that means that the illness is incurable. I think and think, I batter my brains; I know of many remedies, very many, and that means really that there is none. How nice it would be to get a fortune left one by somebody! How nice it would be if Anya could marry a very rich man! How nice it would be to go to Yaroslav and try my luck with my aunt the Countess. My aunt is very, very rich, you know.

BARBARA [*crying softly*]. If only God would help us!

GAYEF. Don't howl! My aunt is very rich, but she does not like us. In the first place, my sister married a solicitor, not a nobleman. [ANYA *appears in the doorway.*] She married a man who was not a nobleman, and it's no good pretending that she has led a virtuous life. She's a dear, kind, charming creature, and I love her very much, but whatever mitigating circumstances one may find for her, there's no getting round it that she's a sinful woman. You can see it in her every gesture.

BARBARA [*whispering*]. Anya is standing in the door!

GAYEF. Who's that? [*A pause.*] It's very odd, something's got into my right eye. I can't see properly out of it. Last Thursday when I was down at the District Court . . .

[ANYA *comes down.*]

BARBARA. Why aren't you asleep, Anya?

ANYA. I can't sleep. It's no good trying.

GAYEF. My little pet! [*Kissing* ANYA's *hands and face.*] My little girl! [*Crying.*] You're not my niece; you're my angel; you're my everything. Trust me, trust me. . . .

ANYA. I do trust you, uncle. Everyone loves you, everyone respects you; but dear, dear uncle, you ought to hold your tongue, only to hold your tongue. What were you saying just now about mamma? about your own sister? What was the good of saying that?

GAYEF. Yes, yes. [*Covering his face with her hand.*] You're quite right; it was awful of me! Lord, Lord! save me from myself! And a little while ago I made a speech over a cupboard What a stupid thing to do! As soon as I had done it, I knew it was stupid.

BARBARA. Yes, really, uncle. You ought to hold your tongue. Say nothing; that's all that's wanted.

ANYA. If only you would hold your tongue, you'd be so much happier!

GAYEF. I will! I will! [*Kissing* ANYA'S *and* BARBARA'S *hands.*] I'll hold my tongue. But there's one thing I must say; it's business. Last Thursday, when I was down at the District Court, a lot of us were there together, we began to talk about this and that, one thing and another, and it seems I could arrange a loan on note of hand to pay the interest into the bank.

BARBARA. If only Heaven would help us!

GAYEF. I'll go on Tuesday and talk it over again. [*To* BARBARA.] Don't howl! [*To* ANYA.] Your mamma shall have a talk with Lopákhin. Of course he won't refuse her. And as soon as you are rested you must go to see your grand-mother, the Countess, at Yaroslav. We'll operate from three points, and the trick is done. We'll pay the interest, I'm certain of it. [*Taking sugar candy.*] I swear on my honour, or whatever you will, the property shall not be sold. [*Excitedly.*] I swear by my hope of eternal happiness! There's my hand on it. Call me a base, dishonourable man if I let it go to auction. I swear by my whole being.

ANYA [*calm again and happy*]. What a dear you are, uncle, and how clever! [*Embraces him.*] Now I'm easy again. I'm easy again! I'm happy!

[*Enter* FIRS.]

FIRS [*reproachfully*]. Leonid Andréyevitch, have you no fear of God? When are you going to bed?

GAYEF. I'm just off—just off. You get along, Firs. I'll undress myself all right. Come, children, bye-bye! Details to-morrow, but now let's go to bed. [*Kissing* ANYA *and* BARBARA.] I'm a good Liberal, a man of the eighties. People abuse the eighties, but I think that I may say I've suffered something for my convictions in my time. It's not for nothing that the peasants love me. We ought to know the peasants; we ought to know with what . . .

ANYA. You're at it again, uncle!

BARBARA. Why don't you hold your tongue, uncle?

FIRS [*angrily*]. Leoníd Andréyevitch!

GAYEF. I'm coming; I'm coming. Now go to bed. Off two cushions in the middle pocket! I start another life! . . .

[*Exit, with* FIRS *hobbling after him.*]

ANYA. Now my mind is at rest. I don't want to go to Yaroslav; I don't like grandmamma; but my mind is at rest, thanks to Uncle Leoníd. [*She sits down.*]

BARBARA. Time for bed. I'm off. Whilst you were away there's been a scandal. You know that nobody lives in the old servants' quarters except the old people, Ephim, Pauline, Evstignéy and old Karp. Well, they took to having in all sorts of queer fish to sleep there with them. I didn't say a word. But at last I heard they had spread a report that I had given orders that they were to have nothing but peas to eat; out of stinginess, you understand? It was all Evstignéy's doing. 'Very well,' I said to myself, 'you wait a bit.' So I sent for Evstignéy. [*Yawning.*] He comes. 'Now then, Evstignéy.' I said, 'you old imbecile, how do you dare . . .' [*Looking at* ANYA.] Anya, Anya! [*A *pause.*] She's asleep. [*Taking* ANYA's *arm.*] Let's go to bed. Come along. [*Leading her away.*] Sleep on, my little one! Come alone; come along! [*They go towards* ANYA's *room. In the distance beyond the orchard a shepherd plays his pipe.* TROPHIMOF *crosses the stage and, seeing* BARBARA *and* ANYA, *stops.*] 'Sh! She's asleep, she's asleep! Come along, my love.

ANYA [*drowsily*]. I'm so tired! Listen to the bells! Uncle, dear uncle! Mamma! Uncle!

BARBARA. Come along, my love! Come along.

[*Exeunt* BARBARA *and* ANYA *to the bedroom.*]

TROPHIMOF [*with emotion*]. My sunshine! My spring!

CURTAIN

ACT II

In the open fields; an old crooked half-ruined shrine. Near it a well; big stones, apparently old tombstones; an old bench. Road to the estate beyond. On one side rise dark poplar-trees. Beyond them begins the cherry orchard. In the distance a row of telegraph poles, and, far away on the horizon, the dim outlines of a big town, visible only in fine, clear weather. It is near sunset.

CHARLOTTE, YASHA *and* DUNYASHA *sit on the bench.* EPHIKHODOF *stands by them and plays on a guitar; they meditate.* CHARLOTTE *wears an old peaked cap. She has taken a gun from off her shoulders and is mending the buckle of the strap.*

CHARLOTTE [*thoughtfully*]. I have no proper passport. I don't know how old I am; I always feel I am still young.

When I was a little girl my father and mother used to go about from one country fair to another, giving performances, and very good ones too. I used to do the *salto mortale* and all sorts of tricks. When papa and mamma died an old German lady adopted me and educated me. Good! When I grew up I became a governess. But where I come from and who I am, I haven't a notion. Who my parents were—very likely they weren't married—I don't know. [*Taking a cucumber from her pocket and beginning to eat it.*] I don't know anything about it. [*A pause.*] I long to talk so, and I have no one to talk to, I have no friends or relations.

EPHIKHODOF [*playing on the guitar and singing*].

'What is the noisy world to me?
Oh, what are friends and foes?'

How sweet it is to play upon a mandoline!

DUNYASHA. That's a guitar, not a mandoline. [*She looks at herself in a hand-glass and powders her face.*]

EPHIKHODOF. For the madman who loves, it is a mandoline. [*Singing.*]

'Oh, that my heart were cheered
By the warmth of requited love.'

[YASHA *joins in.*]

CHARLOTTE. How badly these people do sing! Foo! Like jackals howling!

DUNYASHA [*to* YASHA]. What happiness it must be to live abroad!

YASHA. Of course it is; I quite agree with you. [*He yawns and lights a cigar.*]

EPHIKHODOF. It stands to reason. Everything abroad has attained a certain culmination.

YASHA. That's right.

EPHIKHODOF. I am a man of cultivation; I have studied various remarkable books, but I cannot fathom the direction of my preferences; do I want to live or do I want to shoot myself, so to speak? But in order to be ready for all contingencies, I always carry a revolver in my pocket. Here it is. [*Showing revolver.*]

CHARLOTTE. That's done. I'm off. [*Slinging the rifle over her shoulder.*] You're a clever fellow, Ephikhódof, and very alarming. Women must fall madly in love with you. Brrr! [*Going.*] These clever people are all so stupid; I have no one to talk to. I am always alone, always alone; I have no friends or relations, and who I am, or why I exist, is a mystery.

[*Exit slowly.*]

EPHIKHODOF. Strictly speaking, without touching upon other matters, I must protest *inter alia* that destiny treats me with the utmost rigour, as a tempest might treat a small ship. If I labour under a misapprehension, how is it that when I woke up this morning, behold, so to speak, I perceived sitting on my chest a spider of praeternatural dimensions, like that [*indicating with both hands*]? And if I go to take a draught of quass, I am sure to find something of the most indelicate character, in the nature of a cockroach. [*A pause.*] Have you read Buckle? [*A pause.*] [*To* DUNYASHA.] I should like to trouble you, Avdotya Fëdorovna, for a momentary interview.

DUNYASHA. Talk away.

EPHIKHODOF. I should prefer to conduct it *tête-à-tête.* [*Sighing.*]

DUNYASHA [*confused*]. Very well, only first please fetch me my cloak. It's by the cupboard. It's rather damp here.

EPHIKHODOF. Very well, mademoiselle. I will go and fetch it, mademoiselle. Now I know what to do with my revolver.

[*Takes his guitar and exit, playing.*]

YASHA. Twenty-two misfortunes! Between you and me, he's a stupid fellow. [*Yawning.*]

DUNYASHA. Heaven help him, he'll shoot himself! [*A pause.*] I have grown so nervous, I am always in a twitter. I was quite a little girl when they took me into the household, and now I have got quite disused to common life, and my hands are as white as white, like a lady's. I have grown so refined, so delicate and genteel, I am afraid of everything. I'm always frightened. And if you deceive me, Yásha, I don't know what will happen to my nerves.

YASHA [*kissing her*]. You little cucumber! Of course every girl ought to behave herself properly; there's nothing I dislike as much as when girls aren't proper in their behaviour.

DUNYASHA. I've fallen dreadfully in love with you. You're so educated; you can talk about anything! [*A pause.*]

YASHA [*yawning*]. Yes., . . . The way I look at it is this; if a girl falls in love with anybody, then I call her immoral. [*A pause.*] How pleasant it is to smoke one's cigar in the open air. [*Listening.*] There's someone coming. It's the missis and the rest of 'em. . . . [DUNYASHA *embraces him hastily.*] Go towards the house as if you'd just been for a bathe. Go by this path or else they'll meet you and think that I've been walking out with you. I can't stand that sort of thing.

DUNYASHA [coughing softly]. Your cigar has given me a headache.

[Exit DUNYASHA.]

[YASHA remains sitting by the shrine. Enter MADAME RANEVSKY, GAYEF and LOPAKHIN.]

LOPAKHIN. You must make up your minds once and for all. Time waits for no man. The question is perfectly simple. Are you going to let off the land for villas or not? Answer in one word; yes or no. Only one word!

MADAME RANEVSKY. Who's smoking horrible cigars here? [She sits down.]

GAYEF. How handy it is now they've built that railway. [Sitting.] We've been into town for lunch and back again. . . . Red in the middle! I must just go up to the house and have a game.

MADAME RANEVSKY. There's no hurry.

LOPAKHIN. Only one word—yes or no! [Entreatingly.] Come, answer the question!

GAYEF [yawning]. Who's that?

MADAME RANEVSKY [looking into her purse]. I had a lot of money yesterday but there's hardly any left now. Poor Barbara tries to save money by feeding us all on milk soup; the old people in the kitchen get nothing but peas, and yet I go squandering aimlessly. . . . [Dropping her purse and scattering gold coins; vexed.] There, I've dropped it all!

YASHA. Allow me, I'll pick it up. [Collecting the coins.]

MADAME RANEVSKY. Yes, please do, Yásha! Whatever made me go into town for lunch? I hate your horried restaurant with the organ and the table-cloths all smelling of soap. Why do you drink so much, Leoníd? Why do you eat so much? Why do you talk so

much? You talked too much at the restaurant again, and most unsuitably, about the seventies, and the decadents. And to whom? Fancy talking about decedents to the waiters!

LOPAKHIN. Quite true.

GAYEF [with a gesture]. I'm incorrigible, that's plain. [Irritably to YASHA.] What do you keep dodging about in front of me for?

YASHA [laughing]. I can't hear your voice without laughing.

GAYEF [to MADAME RANEVSKY]. Either he or I . . .

MADAME RANEVSKY. Go away, Yásha; run along.

YASHA [handing MADAME RANEVSKY her purse]. I'll go at once. [Restraining his laughter with difficulty.] This very minute.

[Exit YASHA.]

LOPAKHIN. Derigánof, the millionaire, wants to buy your property. They say he'll come to the auction himself.

MADAME RANEVSKY. How did you hear?

LOPAKHIN. I was told so in town.

GAYEF. Our aunt at Yaroslav has promised to send something; but I don't know when, or how much.

LOPAKHIN. How much will she send? Ten thousand pounds? Twenty thousand pounds?

MADAME RANEVSKY. Oh, come . . . A thousand or fifteen hundred at the most.

LOPAKHIN. Excuse me, but in all my life I never met anybody so frivolous as you two, so crazy and unbusiness-like! I tell you in plain Russian your property is going to be sold, and you don't seem to understand what I say.

MADAME RANEVSKY. Well, what are

we to do? Tell us what you want us to do.

LOPAKHIN. Don't I tell you every day? Every day I say the same thing over and over again. You must lease off the cherry orchard and the rest of the estate for villas; you must do it at once, this very moment; the auction will be on you in two twos! Try and understand. Once you make up your mind there are to be villas, you can get all the money you want, and you're saved.

MADAME RANEVSKY. Villas and villa residents, oh, please, . . . it's so vulgar!

GAYEF. I quite agree with you.

LOPAKHIN. I shall either cry, or scream, or faint. I can't stand it! You'll be the death of me. [To GAYEF.] You're an old woman!

GAYEF. Who's that?

LOPAKHIN. You're an old woman! [Going.]

MADAME RANEVSKY [frightened]. No, don't go. Stay here, there's a dear! Perhaps we shall think of some way.

LOPAKHIN. What's the good of thinking!

MADAME RANEVSKY. Please don't go; I want you. At any rate it's gayer when you're here. [A pause.] I keep expecting something to happen, as if the house were going to tumble down about our ears.

GAYEF [in deep abstraction]. Off the cushion on the corner; double into the middle pocket. . . .

MADAME RANEVSKY. We have been very, very sinful!

LOPAKHIN. You! What sins have you committed?

GAYEF [eating candy]. They say I've devoured all my substance in sugar candy. [Laughing.]

MADAME RANEVSKY. Oh, the sins that I have committed . . . I've always squandered money at random like a madwoman; I married a man who made nothing but debts. My husband drank himself to death on champagne; he was a fearful drinker. Then for my sins I fell in love and went off with another man; and immediately—that was my first punishment—a blow full on the head . . . here, in this very river . . . my little boy was drowned; and I went abroad, right, right away, never to come back any more, never to see this river again. . . . I shut my eyes and ran, like a mad thing, and he came after me, pitiless and cruel. I bought a villa at Mentone, because he fell ill there, and for three years I knew no rest day or night; the sick man tormented and wore down my soul. Then, last year, when my villa was sold to pay my debts, I went off to Paris, and he came and robbed me of everything, left me and took up with another woman, and I tried to poison myself. . . . It was all so stupid, so humiliating. . . . Then suddenly I longed to be back in Russia, in my own country, with my little girl. . . . [Wiping away her tears.] Lord, Lord, be merciful to me; forgive my sins! Do not punish me any more! [Taking a telegram from her pocket.] I got this to-day from Paris. . . . He asks to be forgiven, begs me to go back. . . . [Tearing up the telegram.] Isn't that music that I hear? [Listening.]

GAYEF. That's our famous Jewish band. You remember? Four fiddles, a flute and a double bass.

MADAME RANEVSKY. Does it still

exist? We must make them come up some time; we'll have a dance.

LOPAKHIN [*listening*]. I don't hear anything. [*Singing softly.*]

'The Germans for a fee will turn
A Russ into a Frenchman.'

[*Laughing.*] I saw a very funny piece at the theatre last night; awfully funny!

MADAME RANEVSKY. It probably wasn't a bit funny. You people ought to go and see plays; you ought to try to see yourselves; to see what a dull life you lead, and how much too much you talk.

LOPAKHIN. Quite right. To tell the honest truth, our life's an imbecile affair. [*A pause.*] My papa was a peasant, an idiot; he understood nothing; he taught me nothing; all he did was to beat me when he was drunk, with a walking-stick. As a matter of fact I'm just as big a blockhead and idiot as he was. I never did any lessons; my handwriting's abominable; I write so badly I'm ashamed before people; like a pig.

MADAME RANEVSKY. You ought to get married.

LOPAKHIN. Yes, that's true.

MADAME RANEVSKY. Why not marry Barbara? She's a nice girl.

LOPAKHIN. Yes.

MADAME RANEVSKY. She's a nice straightforward creature; works all day; and what's most important, she loves you. You've been fond of her for a long time.

LOPAKHIN. Well, why not? I'm quite willing. She's a very nice girl. [*A pause.*]

GAYEF. I've been offered a place in a bank. Six hundred pounds a year. Do you hear?

MADAME RANEVSKY. You in a bank! Stay where you are.

[*Enter* FIRS *carrying an overcoat.*]

FIRS [*to* GAYEF]. Put this on, please, master; it's getting damp.

GAYEF [*putting on the coat*]. What a plague you are, Firs!

FIRS. What's the use. . . . You went off and never told me. [*Examining his clothes.*]

MADAME RANEVSKY. How old you've got, Firs!

FIRS. I beg your pardon?

LOPAKHIN. She says how old you've got!

FIRS. I've been alive a long time. When they found me a wife, your father wasn't even born yet. [*Laughing.*] And when the Liberation came I was already chief valet. But I wouldn't have any Liberation then; I stayed with the master. [*A pause.*] I remember how happy everybody was, but why they were happy they didn't know themselves.

LOPAKHIN. It was fine before then. Anyway they used to flog 'em.

FIRS [*mishearing him.*] I should think so! The peasants minded the masters, and the masters minded the peasants, but now it's all higgledy-piggledy; you can't make head or tail of it.

GAYEF. Shut up, Firs. I must go into town again to-morrow. I've been promised an introduction to a general who'll lend money on a bill.

LOPAKHIN. You'll do no good. You won't even pay the interest; set your mind at ease about that.

MADAME RANEVSKY [*to* LOPAKHIN]. He's only talking nonsense. There's no such general at all.

[*Enter* TROPHIMOF, ANYA *and* BARBARA.]

GAYEF. Here come the others.

ANYA. Here's the mamma.

MADAME RANEVSKY [*tenderly*]. Come along, come along, . . my little ones. . . . [*Embracing* ANYA *and* BARBARA.] If only you knew how much I love you both! Sit beside me . . . there, like that. [*Everyone sits.*]

LOPAKHIN. The Perpetual Student's always among the girls.

TROPHIMOF. It's no affair of yours.

LOPAKHIN. He's nearly fifty and still a student.

TROPHIMOF. Stop your idiotic jokes!

LOPAKHIN. What are you losing your temper for, silly?

TROPHIMOF. Why can't you leave me alone?

LOPAKHIN [*laughing*]. I should like to know what your opinion is of me?

TROPHIMOF. My opinion of you, Yermolái Alexéyitch, is this. You're a rich man; you'll soon be a millionaire. Just a beast of prey which devours everything that comes in its way is necessary for the conversion of matter, so you are necessary too.

[*All laugh.*]

BARBARA. Tell us something about the planets, Peter, instead.

MADAME RANEVSKY. No. Let's go on with the conversation we were having yesterday.

TROPHIMOF. What about?

GAYEF. About the proud man.

TROPHIMOF. We had a long talk yesterday, but we didn't come to any conclusion. There is something mystical in the proud man in the sense in which you use the words. You may be right from your point of view, but, if we look at it simple-mindedly, what room is there for pride? Is there any sense in it, when man is so poorly constructed from the physiological point of view, when the vast majority of us are so gross and stupid and profoundly unhappy? We must give up admiring ourselves. The only thing to do is to work.

GAYEF. We shall die all the same.

TROPHIMOF. Who knows? And what does it mean, to die? Perhaps man has a hundred senses, and when he dies only the five senses that we know perish with him, and the other ninety-five remain alive.

MADAME RANEVSKY. How clever you are, Peter.

LOPAKHIN [*ironically*]. Oh, extraordinary!

TROPHIMOF. Mankind marches forward, perfecting its strength. Everything that is unattainable for us now will one day be near and clear; but we must work; we must help with all our force those who seek for truth. At present only a few men work in Russia. The vast majority of the educated people that I know seek after nothing, do nothing, and are as yet incapable of work. They call themselves the 'Intelligentsia,' they say 'thou' and 'thee' to the servants, they treat the peasants like animals, learn nothing, read nothing serious, do absolutely nothing, only talk about science, and understand little or nothing about art. They are all serious; they all have solemn faces; they only discuss important subjects; they philosophise; but meanwhile the vast majority of us, ninety-nine per cent., live like savages; at the least thing they curse and punch people's heads; they eat like beasts and sleep in dirt and bad air; there are bugs everywhere, evil smells, damp and moral degradation. . . . It's plain that all our clever conversations are only meant to distract our own attention and other people's. Show me where those crèches are, that they're always talking so much about; or those reading-rooms. They are only things people write about in novels; they don't really exist at all. Nothing exists but dirt, vulgarity and Asiatic ways. I am afraid of solemn faces; I dislike them; I am afraid of solemn conversations. Let us rather hold our tongues.

LOPAKHIN. Do you know, I get up at five every morning. I work from morning till night; I am always handling my own money or other people's, and I see the sort of men there are about me. One only has to begin to do anything to see how few honest and decent people there are. Sometimes, as I lie awake in bed, I think: 'O Lord, you have given us mighty forests, boundless fields and immeasurable horizons, and we, living in their midst, ought really to be giants.'

MADAME RANEVSKY. Oh dear, you want giants! They are all very well in fairy stories; but in real life they are rather alarming. [EPHIKHODOF passes at the back of the scene, playing on his guitar.] [Pensively.] There goes Ephikhódof.

ANYA [pensively]. There goes Ephikhódof.

GAYEF. The sun has set.

TROPHIMOF. Yes.

GAYEF [as if declaiming, but not loud]. O Nature, wonderful Nature, you glow with eternal light; beautiful and indifferent, you whom we call our mother, uniting in yourself both life and death, you animate and you destroy. . . .

BARBARA [entreatingly]. Uncle!

ANYA. You're at it again, uncle!

TROPHIMOF. You'd far better double the red into the middle pocket.

GAYEF. I'll hold my tongue! I'll hold my tongue!

[They all sit pensively. Silence reigns, broken only by the mumbling of old FIRS. Suddenly a distant sound is heard as if from the sky, the sound of a string breaking, dying away, melancholy.]

MADAME RANEVSKY. What's that?

LOPAKHIN. I don't know. It's a lifting-tub given way somewhere away in the mines. It must be a long way off.

GAYEF. Perhaps it's some sort of bird . . . a heron, or something.

TROPHIMOF. Or an owl. . . .

MADAME RANEVSKY [shuddering]. There's something uncanny about it!

FIRS. The same thing happened before the great misfortune: the owl screeched and the samovar kept humming.

GAYEF. What great misfortune?

FIRS. The liberation. [A pause.]

MADAME RANEVSKY. Come, everyone, let's go in; it's getting late. [To ANYA.] You've tears in your eyes. What is it, little one? [Embracing her.]

ANYA. Nothing, mamma. I'm all right.

TROPHIMOF. There's someone coming.

[A Tramp appears in a torn white-peaked cap and overcoat. He is slightly drunk.]

TRAMP. Excuse me, but can I go through this way straight to the station?

GAYEF. Certainly. Follow this path.

TRAMP. I am uncommonly obliged to you, sir. [Coughing.] We're having lovely weather. [Declaiming.] 'Brother, my suffering brother' . . . 'Come forth to the Volga. Who moans?' . . . [To BARBARA.] Mademoiselle, please spare a sixpence for a hungry fellow-countryman.

[BARBARA, frightened, screams.]

LOPAKHIN [angrily]. There's a decency for every indecency to observe!

MADAME RANEVSKY. Take this; here you are. [*Fumbling in her purse.*] I haven't any silver. . . . Never mind, take this sovereign.

TRAMP. I am uncommonly obliged to you, madam.

[*Exit* TRAMP. *Laughter.*]

BARBARA [*frightened*]. I'm going! I'm going! Oh, mamma, there's nothing for the servants to eat at home, and you've gone and given this man a sovereign.

MADAME RANEVSKY. What's to be done with your stupid old mother? I'll give you up everything I have when I get back. Yermolái Alexéyitch, lend me some more money.

LOPAKHIN. Very good.

MADAME RANEVSKY. Come along, everyone; it's time to go in. We've settled all about your marriage between us, Barbara. I wish you joy.

BARBARA [*through her tears*]. You mustn't joke about such things, mamma.

LOPAKHIN. Amelie, get thee to a nunnery, go!

GAYEF. My hands are all trembling; it's ages since I had a game of billiards.

LOPAKHIN. Amelia, nymphlet, in thine orisons remember me.

MADAME RANEVSKY. Come along. It's nearly supper-time.

BARBARA. How he frightened me! My heart is simply throbbing.

LOPAKHIN. Allow me to remind you, the cherry orchard is to be sold on the twenty-second of August. Bear that in mind; bear that in mind!

[*Exeunt omnes except* TROPHIMOF *and* ANYA.]

ANYA [*laughing*]. Many thanks to the Tramp for frightening Barbara; at last we are alone.

TROPHIMOF. Barbara's afraid we shall go and fall in love with each other. Day after day she never leaves us alone. With her narrow mind she cannot understand that we are above love. To avoid everything petty, everything illusory, everything that prevents one from being free and happy, that is the whole meaning and purpose of our life. Forward! We march on irresistibly towards that bright star which burns far, far before us! Forward! Don't tarry, comrades!

ANYA [*clasping her hands*]. What beautiful things you say! [*A pause.*] Isn't it enchanting here to-day!

TROPHIMOF. Yes, it's wonderful weather.

ANYA. What have you done to me, Peter? Why is it that I no longer love the cherry orchard as I did? I used to love it so tenderly; I thought there was no better place on earth than our garden.

TROPHIMOF. All Russia is our garden. The earth is great and beautiful; it is full of wonderful places. [*A pause.*] Think, Anya, your grandfather, your great-grandfather and all your ancestors were serf-owners, owners of living souls. Do not human spirits look out at you from every tree in the orchard, from every leaf and every stem? Do you not hear human voices? . . . Oh! it is terrible. Your orchard frightens me. When I walk through it in the evening or at night, the rugged bark on the trees glows with a dim light, and the cherry-trees seem to see all that happened a hundred and two hundred years ago in painful and oppressive dreams. Well, well, we have fallen at least two hundred years behind the times. We have achieved nothing at all as yet; we have not made up our minds how we stand with the past; we only philosophise, complain of boredom, or drink vodka. It is so plain that, before we can live in the present, we must first redeem the past, and have done with it; and it is only by suffering that we can redeem it, only by strenuous, unremitting toil. Understand that, Anya.

ANYA. The house we live in has long since ceased to be our house; and I shall go away, I give you my word.

TROPHIMOF. If you have the household keys, throw them in the well and go away. Be free, be free as the wind.

ANYA [enthusiastically]. How beautifully you put it!

TROPHIMOF. Believe what I say, Anya; believe what I say. I'm not thirty yet; I am still young, still a student; but what I have been through! I am hungry as the winter; I am sick, anxious, poor as a beggar. Fate has tossed me hither and thither; I have been everywhere, everywhere. But wherever I have been, every minute, day and night, my soul has been full of mysterious anticipations. I feel the approach of happiness; Anya; I see it coming. . . .

ANYA [pensively]. The moon is rising.

[EPHIKHODOF is heard still playing the same sad tune on his guitar. The moon rises. Somewhere beyond the poplar-trees, BARBARA is heard calling for ANYA: 'Anya, where are you?']

TROPHIMOF. Yes, the moon is rising. [A pause.] There it is, there is happiness; it is coming towards us, nearer and nearer; I can hear the sound of its footsteps. . . . And if we do not see it, if we do not know it, what does it matter? Others will see it.

BARBARA [without]. Anya? Where are you?

TROPHIMOF. There's Barbara again! [Angrily.] It really is too bad!

ANYA. Never mind. Let us go down to the river. It's lovely there.

TROPHIMOF. Come on!

[Exeunt ANYA and TROPHIMOF.]

BARBARA [without]. Anya! Anya!

CURTAIN

ACT III

A sitting-room separated by an arch from a big drawing-room behind. Chandelier lighted. The Jewish band mentioned in Act II is heard playing on the landing. Evening. In the drawing-room they are dancing the grand rond. SIMEONOF-PISHTCHIK is heard crying: 'Promenade à une paire!'

[The dancers come down into the sitting-room. The first pair consists of PISHTCHIK and CHARLOTTE; the second of TROPHIMOF and MADAME RANEVSKY; the third of ANYA and the POST OFFICE OFFICIAL; the fourth of BARBARA and the STATION-MASTER, etc., etc. BARBARA is crying softly and wipes away the tears as she dances. In the last pair comes DUNYASHA. They cross the sitting-room.]

PISHTCHIK. Grand rond, balancez . . . Les cavaliers à genou et remerciez vos dames.

[FIRS in evening dress carries seltzer water across on a tray. PISHTCHIK and TROPHIMOF come down into the sitting-room.]

PISHTCHIK. I am a full-blooded man; I've had two strokes already; it's hard work dancing, but, as the saying goes: 'If you run with the pack, bark or no, but anyway wag your tail.' I'm as strong as a horse. My old father, who was fond of his joke, rest his soul, used to say, talking of our pedigree, that the ancient stock of the Simeónof-Píshtchiks was descended from that very horse that Caligula made a senator. . . . [*Sitting.*] But the worst of it is, I've got no money. A hungry dog believes in nothing but meat. [*Snoring and waking up again at once.*] I'm just the same. . . . It's nothing but money, money, with me.

TROPHIMOF. Yes, it's quite true, there is something horselike about your build.

PISHTCHIK. Well, well . . . a horse is a jolly creature . . . you can sell a horse.

[*A sound of billiards being played in the next room.* BARBARA *appears in the drawing-room beyond the arch.*]

TROPHIMOF [*teasing her*]. Madame Lopákhin! Madame Lopákhin!

BARBARA [*angrily*]. Mouldy gentleman!

TROPHIMOF. Yes, I'm a mouldy gentleman, and I'm proud of it.

BARBARA [*bitterly*]. We've hired the band, but where's the money to pay for it?

[*Exit* BARBARA.]

TROPHIMOF [*to* PISHTCHIK]. If the energy which you have spent in the course of your whole life in looking for money to pay the interest on your loans had been diverted to some other purpose, you would have had enough of it, I dare say, to turn the world upside down.

PISHTCHIK. Nietzsche, the philosopher, a very remarkable man, very famous, a man of gigantic intellect, says in his works that it's quite right to forge banknotes.

TROPHIMOF. What, have you read Nietzsche?

PISHTCHIK. Well . . . Dáshenka told me. . . . But I'm in such a hole, I'd forge 'em for two-pence. I've got

to pay thirty-one pounds the day after to-morrow. . . . I've got thirteen pounds already. [*Feeling his pockets; alarmed.*] My money's gone! I've lost my money! [*Crying.*] Where's my money got to? [*Joyfully.*] Here it is, inside the lining. . . . It's thrown me all in a perspiration.

[*Enter* MADAME RANEVSKY *and* CHARLOTTE.]

MADAME RANEVSKY [*humming a lezginka*]. Why is Leoníd so long? What can he be doing in the town? [*To* DUNYASHA.] Dunyásha, ask the musicians if they'll have some tea.

TROPHIMOF. The sale did not come off, in all probability.

MADAME RANEVSKY. It was a stupid day for the musicians to come; it was a stupid day to have this dance. . . . Well, well, it doesn't matter. . . . [*She sits down and sings softly to herself.*]

CHARLOTTE [*giving* PISHTCHIK *a pack of cards*]. Here is a pack of cards. Think of any card you like.

PISHTCHIK. I've thought of one.

CHARLOTTE. Now shuffle the pack. That's all right. Give them here, or, most worthy Mr. Píshtchik. Ein, zwei, drei! Now look and you'll find it in your side pocket.

PISHTCHIK [*taking a card from his side pocket*]. The Eight of Spades. You're perfectly right. [*Astonished.*] Well, I never!

CHARLOTTE [*holding the pack on the palm of her hand, to* TROPHIMOF]. Say quickly, what's the top card?

TROPHIMOF. Well, say the Queen of Spades.

CHARLOTTE. Right! [*To* PISHTCHIK.] Now then, what's the top card?

PISHTCHIK. Ace of Hearts.

CHARLOTTE. Right! [*She claps her*

hands; the pack of cards disappears.]
What a beautiful day we've been having.

[*A mysterious female* VOICE *answers her as if from under the floor:* 'Yes, indeed, a charming day, mademoiselle.*']

CHARLOTTE. You are my beautiful ideal.

THE VOICE. '*I think you also ferry peautiful, mademoiselle.*'

STATION-MASTER [*applauding*]. Bravo. Miss Ventriloquist!

PISHTCHIK [*astonished*]. Well, I never! Bewitching Charlotte Ivánovna, I'm head over ears in love with you.

CHARLOTTE. In love! [*Shrugging her shoulders.*] Are you capable of love? Gater Mensch, aber schlechter Musikant!

TROPHIMOF [*slapping* PISHTCHIK *on the shoulder*]. You old horse!

CHARLOTTE. Now attention, please; one more trick. [*Taking a shawl from a chair.*] Now here's a shawl, and a very pretty shawl; I'm going to sell this very pretty shawl. [*Shaking it.*] Who'll buy? who'll buy?

PISHTCHIK [*astonished*]. Well I never!

CHARLOTTE. Ein, zwei, drei! [*She lifts the shawl quickly; behind it stands* ANYA, *who drops a curtsy, runs to her mother, kisses her, then runs up into the drawing-room amid general applause.*]

MADAME RANEVSKY [*applauding*]. Bravo! bravo!

CHARLOTTE. Once more. Ein, zwei. drei! [*She lifts up the shawl; behind it stands* BARBARA, *bowing.*]

PISHTCHIK [*astonished*]. *Well I* never!

CHARLOTTE. That's all. [*She throws the shawl over* PISHTCHIK, *makes a curtsy and runs up into the drawing-room.*]

PISHTCHIK [*hurrying after her*]. You little rascal . . . there's a girl for you, there's a girl. . . .

[*Exit.*]

MADAME RANEVSKY. And still no sign of Leonid. What he's doing in the town so long, I can't understand. It must be all over by now; the property's sold; or the auction never came off; why does he keep me in suspense so long?

BARBARA [*trying to soothe her*]. Uncle has bought it, I am sure of that.

TROPHIMOF [*mockingly*]. Of course he has!

BARBARA. Grannie sent him a power of attorney to buy it in her name and transfer the mortgage. She's done it for Anya's sake. I'm perfectly sure that Heaven will help us and uncle will buy it.

MADAME RANEVSKY. Your Yaroslav grannie sent fifteen hundred pounds to buy the property in her name—she doesn't trust us—but it wouldn't be enough even to pay the interest. [*Covering her face with her hands.*] My fate is being decided to-day, my fate. . . .

TROPHIMOF [*teasing* BARBARA]. Madame Lopákhin!

BARBARA [*angrily*]. Perpetual Student! He's been sent down twice from the University.

MADAME RANEVSKY. Why do you get angry, Barbara? He calls you Madame Lopákhin for fun. Why not? You can marry Lopákhin if you like; he's a nice, interesting man; you needn't if you don't; nobody wants to force you, my pet.

BARBARA. I take it very seriously,

mamma, I must confess. He's a nice man and I like him.

MADAME RANEVSKY. Then marry him. There's no good putting it off that I can see.

BARBARA. But, mamma, I can't propose to him myself. For two whole years everybody's been talking about him to me, everyone; but he either says nothing or makes a joke of it. I quite understand. He's making money; he's always busy; he can't be bothered with me. If I only had some money, even a little, even ten pounds, I would give everything up and go right away. I would go into a nunnery.

TROPHIMOF [mockingly]. What bliss!

BARBARA [to TROPHIMOF]. A student ought to be intelligent. [In a gentler voice, crying.] How ugly you've grown, Peter; how old you've grown! [She stops crying; to MADAME RANEVSKY.] But I can't live without work, mamma. I must have something to do every minute of the day.

[Enter YASHA.]

YASHA [trying not to laugh]. Ephikhódof has broken a billiard cue.

[Exit YASHA.]

BARBARA. What's Ephikhódof doing here? Who gave him leave to play billiards? I don't understand these people.

[Exit BARBARA.]

MADAME RANEVSKY. Don't tease her, Peter. Don't you see that she's unhappy enough already?

TROPHIMOF. I wish she wouldn't be so fussy, always meddling in other people's affairs. The whole summer she's given me and Anya no peace; she is afraid we'll work up a romance between us. What business is it of hers? I'm sure I never gave her any grounds; I'm not likely to be so commonplace. We are above love!

MADAME RANEVSKY. Then I suppose I must be beneath love. [Deeply agitated.] Why doesn't Leoníd come? Oh, if only I knew whether the property's sold or not! It seems such an impossible disaster, that I don't know what to think. . . . I'm bewildered. . . . I shall burst out screaming, I shall do something idiotic. Save me, Peter; say something to me, say something. . . .

TROPHIMOF. Whether the property is sold to-day or whether it's not sold, surely it's all one? It's all over with it long ago; there's no turning back, the path is overgrown. Be calm, dear Lyubóf Andréyevna. You mustn't deceive yourself any longer; for once you must look the truth straight in the face.

MADAME RANEVSKY. What truth? You can see what's truth, and what's untruth, but I seem to have lost the power of vision; I see nothing. You settle every important question so boldly; but tell me, Peter, isn't that because you're young, because you have never solved any question of your own as yet by suffering? You look boldly ahead; isn't it only that you don't see or divine anything terrible in the future; because life is still hidden from your young eyes? You are bolder, honester, deeper than we are, but reflect, show me just a finger's breadth of consideration, take pity on me. Don't you see? I was born here, my father and mother lived here, and my grandfather; I love this house; without the cherry orchard my life has no meaning for me, and if it must be sold, then for heaven's sake sell me too! [Embracing TROPHIMOF and kissing him on the forehead.] My little boy was drowned here. [Crying.]

Be gentle with me, dear, kind Peter.

TROPHIMOF. You know I sympathise with all my heart.

MADAME RANEVSKY. Yes, yes, but you ought to say it somehow differently. [*Taking out her handkerchief and dropping a telegram.*] I am so wretched to-day, you can't imagine! All this noise jars on me, my heart jumps at every sound. I tremble all over; but I can't shut myself up; I am afraid of the silence when I'm alone. Don't be hard on me, Peter; I love you like a son. I would gladly let Anya marry you, I swear it; but you must work, Peter; you must get your degree. You do nothing; Fate tosses you about from place to place; and that's not right. It's true what I say, isn't it? And you must do something to your beard to make it grow better. [*Laughing.*] I can't help laughing at you.

TROPHIMOF [*picking up the telegram*]. I don't wish to be an Adonis.

MADAME RANEVSKY. It's a telegram from Paris. I get them every day. One came yesterday, another to-day. That savage is ill again; he's in a bad way. . . . He asks me to forgive him, he begs me to come; and I really ought to go to Paris and be with him. You look at me sternly; but what am I to do, Peter? What am I to do? He's ill, he's lonely, he's unhappy. Who is to look after him? Who is to keep him from doing stupid things? Who is to give him his medicine when it's time? After all, why should I be ashamed to say it? I love him, that's plain. I love him, I love him. . . . My love is like a stone tied round my neck; it's dragging me down to the bottom; but I love my stone. I can't live without it. [*Squeezing* TROPHIMOF's *hand.*] Don't think ill

of me, Peter; don't say anything! Don't say anything!

TROPHIMOF [*crying*]. Forgive my bluntness, for heaven's sake; but the man has simply robbed you.

MADAME RANEVSKY. No, no, no! [*Stopping her ears.*] You mustn't say that!

TROPHIMOF. He's a rascal; everybody sees it but yourself; he's a petty rascal, a ne'er-do-well. . .

MADAME RANEVSKY [*angry but restrained*]. You're twenty-six or twenty-seven, and you're still a Lower School boy!

TROPHIMOF. Who cares?

MADAME RANEVSKY. You ought to be a man by now; at your age you ought to understand people who love. You ought to love someone yourself, you ought to be in love! [*Angrily.*] Yes, yes! It's not purity with you; it's simply you're a smug, a figure of fun, a freak. . . .

TROPHIMOF [*horrified*]. What does she say?

MADAME RANEVSKY. 'I am above love!' You're not above love; you're simply what Firs calls a 'job-lot.' At your age you ought to be ashamed not to have a mistress!

TROPHIMOF [*aghast*]. This is awful! What does she say? [*Going quickly up into the drawing-room, clasping his head with his hands.*] This is something awful! I can't stand it; I'm off . . . [*Exit, but returns at once.*] All is over between us!

[*Exit to landing.*]

MADAME RANEVSKY [*calling after him*]. Stop, Peter! Don't be ridiculous; I was only joking! Peter!

[TROPHIMOF *is heard on the landing going quickly down the stairs, and sud-*

denly falling down them with a crash. ANYA and BARBARA scream. A moment later the sound of laughter.]

MADAME RANEVSKY. What has happened?

[ANYA runs in.]

ANYA [laughing]. Peter's tumbled downstairs. [She runs out again.]

MADAME RANEVSKY. What a ridiculous fellow he is!

[The STATION-MASTER stands in the middle of the drawing-room behind the arch and recites Alexey Tolstoy's poem, 'The Sinner.' Everybody stops to listen, but after a few lines the sound of a waltz is heard from the landing and he breaks off. All dance. TROPHIMOF, ANYA, BARBARA and MADAME RANEVSKY enter from the landing.]

MADAME RANEVSKY. Come, Peter. come, you pure spirit. . . . I beg your pardon. Let's have a dance. [She dances with TROPHIMOF. ANYA and BARBARA dance.]

[Enter FIRS, and stands his walking-stick by the side door. Enter YASHA by the drawing-room; he stands looking at the dancers.]

YASHA. Well, grandfather?

FIRS. I'm not feeling well. In the old days it was generals and barons and admirals that danced at our dances, but now we send for the Postmaster and the Station-Master, and even they make a favour of coming. I'm sort of weak all over. The old master, their grandfather, used to give us all sealing wax, when we had anything the matter. I've taken sealing wax every day for twenty years and more. Perhaps that's why I'm still alive.

YASHA. I'm sick of you, grandfather. [Yawning.] I wish you'd die and have done with it.

FIRS. Ah! you . . . job-lot! [He mumbles to himself.]

[TROPHIMOF and MADAME RANEVSKY dance beyond the arch and down into the sitting-room.]

MADAME RANEVSKY. Merci. I'll sit down. [Sitting.] I'm tired.

[Enter ANYA.]

ANYA [agitated]. There was somebody in the kitchen just now saying that the cherry orchard was sold to-day.

MADAME RANEVSKY. Sold? Who to?

ANYA. He didn't say who to. He's gone. [She dances with TROPHIMOF. Both dance up into the drawing-room.]

YASHA. It was some old fellow chattering; a stranger.

FIRS. And still Leoníd Andréyitch doesn't come. He's wearing his light overcoat demi-saison; he'll catch cold as like as not. Ah, young wood, green wood!

MADAME RANEVSKY. This is killing me. Yásha, go and find out who it was sold to.

YASHA. Why, he's gone long ago, the old man. [Laughs.]

MADAME RANEVSKY [vexed]. What are you laughing at? What are you glad about?

YASHA. He's a ridiculous fellow, is Ephikhódof. Nothing in him. Twenty-two misfortunes!

MADAME RANEVSKY. Firs, if the property is sold, where will you go to?

FIRS. Wherever you tell me, there I'll go.

MADAME RANEVSKY. Why do you look like that? Are you ill? You ought to be in bed.

FIRS [ironically]. Oh yes, I'll go to bed, and who'll hand the things around, who'll give orders? I've the whole house on my hands.

YASHA. Lyubóf Andréyevna! Let me ask a favour of you; be so kind; if you go to Paris again, take me with you, I beseech you. It's absolutely impossible for me to stay here. [*Looking about; sotto voce.*] What's the use of talking? You can see for yourself this is a barbarous country; the people have no morals; and the boredom! The food in the kitchen is something shocking, and on the top of it old Firs goes about mumbling irrelevant nonsense. Take me back with you; be so kind!

[*Enter* PISHTCHIK.]

PISHTCHIK. May I have the pleasure . . . a bit of a waltz. charming lady? [MADAME RANEVSKY *takes his arm.*] All the same, enchanting lady, you must let me have eighteen pounds. [*Dancing.*] Let me have . . . eighteen pounds.

[*Exeunt dancing through the arch.*]

YASHA [*singing to himself*].

'Oh, wilt thou understand
The turmoil of my soul?'

[*Beyond the arch appears a figure in grey tall hat and check trousers, jumping and waving its arms. Cries of 'Bravo, Charlotte Ivánovna.'*]

DUNYASHA [*stopping to powder her face*]. Mamselle Anya tells me I'm to dance; there are so many gentlemen and so few ladies. But dancing makes me giddy and makes my heart beat, Firs Nikoláyevitch; and just now the gentleman from the post office said something so nice to me, oh, so nice! It quite took my breath away. [*The music stops.*]

FIRS. What did he say to you?

DUNYASHA. He said, 'You are like a flower.'

YASHA [*yawning*]. Cad!

[*Exit* YASHA.]

DUNYASHA. Like a flower! I am so ladylike and refined, I dote on compliments.

FIRS. You'll come to a bad end.

[*Enter* EPHIKHODOF.]

EPHIKHODOF. You are not pleased to see me, Avdótya Fyódorovna, no more than if I were some sort of insect. [*Sighing.*] Ah! Life! Life!

DUNYASHA. What do you want?

EPHIKHODOF. Undoubtedly perhaps you are right. [*Sighing.*] But of course, if one regards it, so to speak, from the point of view, if I may allow myself the expression, and with apologies for my frankness, you have finally reduced me to a state of mind. I quite appreciate my destiny; every day some misfortune happens to me, and I have long since grown accustomed to it, and face my fortune with a smile. You have passed your word to me, and although I . . .

DUNYASHA. Let us talk of this another time, if you please; but now leave me in peace. I am busy meditating. [*Playing with her fan.*]

EPHIKHODOF. Every day some misfortune befalls me, and yet, if I may venture to say so, I meet them with smiles and even laughter.

[*Enter* BARBARA *from the drawing-room.*]

BARBARA [*to* EPHIKHODOF]. Haven't you gone yet, Simeon? You seem to pay no attention to what you're told. [*To* DUNYASHA.] You get out of here, Dunyásha. [*To* EPHIKHODOF.] First you play billiards and break a cue, and then you march about the drawing-room as if you were a guest!

EPHIKHODOF. Allow me to inform

you that it's not your place to call me to account.

BARBARA. I'm not calling you to account; I'm merely talking to you. All you can do is to walk about from one place to another, without ever doing a stroke of work; and why on earth we keep a clerk at all heaven only knows.

EPHIKHODOF [offended]. Whether I work, or whether I walk, or whether I eat, or whether I play billiards is a question to be decided only by my elders and people who understand.

BARBARA [furious]. How dare you talk to me like that! How dare you! I don't understand things, don't I? You clear out of here this minute! Do you hear me? This minute!

EPHIKHODOF [flinching]. I must beg you to express yourself in genteeler language.

BARBARA [beside herself]. You clear out this instant second! Out you go! [Following him as he retreats towards the door.] Twenty-two misfortunes! Make yourself scarce! Get out of my sight!

[Exit EPHIKHODOF.]

EPHIKHODOF [without]. I shall lodge a complaint against you.

BARBARA. What! You're coming back, are you? [Seizing the walking-stick left at the door by FIRS.] Come on! Come on! Come on! I'll teach you! Are you coming? Are you coming? Then take that. [She slashes with the stick.]

[Enter LOPAKHIN.]

LOPAKHIN. Many thanks; much obliged.

BARBARA [still angry, but ironical]. Sorry!

LOPAKHIN. Don't mention it. I'm very grateful for your warm reception.

BARBARA. It's not worth thanking me

for. [She walks away, then looks round and asks in a gentle voice.] I didn't hurt you?

LOPAKHIN. Oh, no, nothing to matter. I shall have a bump like a goose's egg, that's all.

[Voices from the drawing-room: 'Lopákhin has arrived! Yermolái Alexé-yitch!']

PISHTCHIK. Let my eyes see him, let my ears hear him! [He and LOPAKHIN kiss.] You smell of brandy, old man. We're having a high time, too.

[Enter MADAME RANEVSKY.]

MADAME RANEVSKY. Is it you, Yermolái Alexéyitch? Why have you been so long? Where is Leoníd?

LOPAKHIN. Leoníd Andréyitch came back with me. He's just coming.

MADAME RANEVSKY [agitated]. What happened? Did the sale come off? Tell me, tell me!

LOPAKHIN [embarrassed, afraid of showing his pleasure.] The sale was all over by four o'clock. We missed the train and had to wait till half-past eight. [Sighing heavily.] · Ouf! I'm rather giddy. . . .

[Enter GAYEF. In one hand he carries parcels; with the other he wipes away his tears.]

MADAME RANEVSKY. What happened, Lénya? Come, Lénya! [Impatiently, crying.] Be quick, be quick, for heaven's sake!

GAYEF [answering her only with an up and down gesture of the hand; to FIRS, crying]. Here, take these. . . . Here are some anchovies and Black Sea herrings. I've had nothing to eat all day. Lord, . what I've been through! [Through the open door of the billiard-room comes the click of the billiard balls and YASHA's voice: 'Seven, eight-

ven!' GAYEF'S *expression changes; he stops crying.*] I'm frightfully tired. Come and help me change, Firs. [*He goes up through the drawing-room,* FIRS *following.*]

PISHTCHIK: What about the sale? Come on, tell us all about it.

MADAME RANEVSKY. Was the cherry orchard sold?

LOPAKHIN. Yes.

MADAME RANEVSKY. Who bought it?

LOPAKHIN. I did. [*A pause.* MADAME RANEVSKY *is overwhelmed at the news. She would fall to the ground but for the chair and table by her.* BARBARA *takes the keys from her belt, throws them on the floor in the middle of the sitting-room, and exit.*] I bought it. Wait a bit; don't hurry me; my head's in a whirl; I can't speak. . . . [*Laughing.*] When we got to the sale, Deriganof was there already. Leoníd André-yitch had only fifteen hundred pounds, and Deriganof bid three thousand more than the mortgage right away. When I saw how things stood, I went for him and bid four thousand. He said four thousand five hundred. I said five thousand five hundred. He went up by five hundreds, you see, and I went up by thousands. . . . Well, it was soon over. I bid nine thousand more than the mortgage, and got it; and now the cherry orchard is mine! Mine! [*Laughing.*] Heaven's alive! Just think of it! The cherry orchard is mine! Tell me that I'm drunk; tell me that I'm off my head; tell me that it's all a dream! . . . [*Stamping his feet.*] Don't laugh at me! If only my father and my grandfather could rise from their graves and see the whole affair, how their Yermolái, their flogged and ignorant Yermolái, who used to run about barefooted

in the winter, how this same Yermolái had bought a property that hasn't its equal for beauty anywhere in the whole world! I have bought the property where my father and grandfather were slaves, where they weren't even allowed into the kitchen. I'm asleep, it's only a vision, it isn't real. . . . 'Tis the fruit of imagination, wrapped in the mists of ignorance. [*Picking up the keys and smiling affectionately.*] She's thrown down her keys; she wants to show that she's no longer mistress here. . . . [*Jingling them together.*] Well, well, what's the odds? [*The musicians are heard tuning up.*] Hey, musicians, play! I want to hear you. Come everyone and see Yermolái Lopákhin lay his axe to the cherry orchard, come and see the trees fall down! We'll fill the place with villas; our grandsons and great-grandsons shall see a new life here. . . . Strike up, music! [*The band plays.* MADAME RANEVSKY *sinks into a chair and weeps bitterly.*] [*Reproachfully.*] Oh, why, why didn't you listen to me? You can't put the clock back now, poor dear. [*Crying.*] Oh, that all this were past and over! Oh, that our unhappy topsy-turvy life were changed!

PISHTCHIK [*taking him by the arm, sotto voce*]. She's crying. Let's go into the drawing-room and leave her alone to . . . Come on. [*Taking him by the arm, and going up towards the drawing-room.*]

LOPAKHIN. What's up? Play your best, musicians! Let everything be as I want. [*Ironically.*] Here comes the new squire, the owner of the cherry orchard! [*Knocking up by accident against a table and nearly throwing down the candelabra.*] Never mind, I can pay for everything!

[*Exit with* PISHTCHIK. *Nobody remains in the drawing-room or sitting-room except* MADAME RANEVSKY, *who sits huddled together, weeping bitterly. The band plays softly. Enter* ANYA *and* TROPHIMOF *quickly.* ANYA *goes to her mother and kneels before her.* TROPHIMOF *stands in the entry to the drawing-room.*]

ANYA. Mamma! Are you crying, mamma? My dear, good, sweet mamma! Darling, I love you! I bless you! The cherry orchard is sold; it's gone; it's quite true, it's quite true. But don't cry, mamma, you've still got life before you, you've still got your pure and lovely soul. Come with me, darling; come away from here. We'll plant a new garden, still lovelier than this. You will see it and understand, and happiness, deep, tranquil happiness will sink down on your soul, like the sun at eventide, and you'll smile, mamma. Come, darling, come with me!

CURTAIN

ACT IV

Same scene as Act I. There are no window-curtains, no pictures. The little furniture left is stacked in a corner, as if for sale. A feeling of emptiness. By the door to the hall and at the back of the scene are piled portmanteaux, bundles, etc. The door is open and the voices of BARBARA *and* ANYA *are audible.*

[LOPAKHIN *stands waiting.* YASHA *holds a tray with small tumblers full of champagne.* EPHIKHODOF *is tying up a box in the hall. A distant murmur of voices behind the scene; the* PEASANTS *have come to say good-bye.*]

GAYEF [*without*]. Thank you, my lads, thank you.

YASHA. The common people have come to say good-bye. I'll tell you what I think, Yermolái Alexéyitch; they're good fellows but rather stupid.

[*The murmur of voices dies away. Enter* MADAME RANEVSKY *and* GAYEF *from the hall. She is not crying, but she is pale, her face twitches, she cannot speak.*]

GAYEF. You gave them your purse, Lyuba. That was wrong, very wrong!

MADAME RANEVSKY. I couldn't help it, I couldn't help it!

[*Exeunt both.*]

LOPAKHIN [*calling after them through the doorway*]. Please come here! Won't you come here? Just a glass to say good-bye. I forgot to bring any from town, and could only raise one bottle at the station. Come along. [*A pause.*] What, won't you have any? [*Returning from the door.*] If I'd known, I wouldn't have bought it. I shan't have any either. [YASHA *sets the tray down carefully on a chair.*] Drink it yourself, Yásha.

YASHA. Here's to our departure! Good luck to them that stay! [*Drinking.*] This isn't real champagne, you take my word for it.

LOPAKHIN. Sixteen shillings a bottle. [*A pause.*] It's devilish cold in here.

YASHA. The fires weren't lighted to-day; we're all going away. [*He laughs.*]

LOPAKHIN. What are you laughing for?

YASHA. Just pleasure.

LOPAKHIN. Here we are in October, but it's as calm and sunny as summer. Good building weather. [*Looking at his watch and speaking off.*] Don't forget that there's only forty-seven minutes before the train goes. You must start for the station in twenty minutes. Make haste.

[*Enter* TROPHIMOF *in an overcoat, from out of doors.*]

TROPHIMOF. I think it's time we were off. The carriages are round. What the deuce has become of my goloshes? I've lost 'em. [*Calling off.*] Anya, my goloshes have disappeared. I can't find them anywhere!

LOPAKHIN. I've got to go to Kharkof. I'll start in the same train with you. I'm going to spend the winter in Kharkof. I've been loafing about all this time with you people, eating my head off for want of work. I can't live without work, I don't know what to do with my hands; they dangle about as if they didn't belong to me.

TROPHIMOF. Well, we're going now, and you'll be able to get back to your beneficent labours.

LOPAKHIN. Have a glass.

TROPHIMOF. Not for me.

LOPAKHIN. Well, so you're off to Moscow?

TROPHIMOF. Yes, I'll see them into the town, and go on to Moscow to-morrow.

LOPAKHIN. Well, well. . . . I suppose the professors haven't started their lectures yet; they're waiting till you arrive.

TROPHIMOF. It is no affair of yours.

LOPAKHIN. How many years have you been up at the University?

TROPHIMOF. Try and think of some new joke; this one's getting a bit flat. [*Looking for his goloshes.*] Look here, I dare say we shan't meet again, so let me give you a bit of advice as a keepsake: Don't flap your hands about! Get out of the habit of flapping. Building villas, prophesying that villa residents will turn into small freeholders, all that sort of thing is flapping too. Well, when all's said and done, I like you. You have thin, delicate, artist fingers; you have a delicate artist soul.

LOPAKHIN [*embracing him*]. Goodbye, old chap. Thank you for every·· thing. Take some money off me for the journey if you want it.

TROPHIMOF. What for? I don't want it.

LOPAKHIN. But you haven't got any.

TROPHIMOF. Yes, I have. Many thanks. I got some for a translation. Here it is, in my pocket. [*Anxiously.*] I can't find my goloshes anywhere!

BARBARA [*from the next room*]. Here, take your garbage away! [*She throws a pair of goloshes on the stage.*]

TROPHIMOF. What are you so cross about, Barbara? Humph! . . . But those aren't *my* goloshes!

LOPAKHIN. In the spring I sowed three thousand acres of poppy and I have cleared four thousand pounds net profit. When my poppies were in flower, what a picture they made! So you see, I cleared four thousand pounds; and I wanted to lend you a bit because I've got it to spare. What's the good of being stuck up? I'm a peasant. . . . As man to man. . . .

TROPHIMOF. Your father was a peasant; mine was a chemist; it doesn't prove anything. [LOPAKHIN *takes out his pocket-book with paper money.*] Shut up, shut up. . . . If you offered me twenty thousand pounds I would not take it. I am a free man; nothing that you value so highly, all of you, rich and poor, has the smallest power over me; it's like thistledown floating on the wind. I can do without you; I can go past you; I'm strong and proud. Mankind marches forward to the highest truth, to the highest happiness possible on earth, and I march in the foremost ranks.

LOPAKHIN. Will you get there?

TROPHIMOF. Yes. [*A pause.*] I will get there myself or I will show others the way.

[*The sound of axes hewing is heard in the distance.*]

LOPAKHIN. Well, good-bye, old chap; it is time to start. Here we stand swaggering to each other, and life goes by all the time without heeding us. When I work for hours without getting tired, I get easy in my mind and I seem to know why I exist. But God alone knows what most of the people in Russia were born for. . . . Well, who cares? It doesn't affect the circulation of work. They say Leonid Andréyitch has got a place; he's going to be in a bank and get six hundred pounds a year. . . . He won't sit it out, he's too lazy.

ANYA [*in the doorway*]. Mamma says, will you stop cutting down the orchard till she has gone.

TROPHIMOF. Really, haven't you got tact enough for that?

[*Exit* TROPHIMOF *by the hall.*]

LOPAKHIN. Of course, I'll stop them at once. What fools they are!

[*Exit after* TROPHIMOF.]

ANYA. Has Firs been sent to the hospital?

YASHA. I told 'em this morning. They're sure to have sent him.

ANYA [*to* EPHIKHODOF, *who crosses*]. Simeon Pantelèyitch, please find out if Firs has been sent to the hospital.

YASHA [*offended*]. I told George this morning. What's the good of asking a dozen times?

EPHIKHODOF. Our centenarian friend, in my conclusive opinion, is hardly worth tinkering; it's time he was dispatched to his forefathers. I can only say I envy him. [*Putting down a portmanteau on a bandbox and crushing it flat.*] There you are! I knew how it would be!

[*Exit.*]

YASHA [*jeering*]. Twenty-two misfortunes.

BARBARA [*without*]. Has Firs been sent to the hospital?

ANYA. Yes.

BARBARA. Why didn't they take the note to the doctor?

ANYA. We must send it after them.

[*Exit* ANYA.]

BARBARA [*from the next room*]. Where's Yásha? Tell him his mother is here. She wants to say good-bye to him.

YASHA [*with a gesture of impatience*]. It's enough to try the patience of a saint!

[DUNYASHA *has been busying herself with the luggage. Seeing* YASHA *alone, she approaches him.*]

DUNYASHA. You might just look once at me, Yásha. You are going away, you are leaving me. [*Crying and throwing her arms round his neck.*]

YASHA. What's the good of crying? [*Drinking champagne.*] In six days I shall be back in Paris. To-morrow we take the express, off we go, and that's the last of us! I can hardly believe it's true. Vive la France! This place don't suit me. I can't bear it . . . it can't be helped. I have had enough barbarism; I'm fed up. [*Drinking champagne.*] What's the good of crying? You be a good girl, and you'll have no call to cry.

DUNYASHA [*powdering her face and looking into a glass*]. Write me a letter from Paris. I've been so fond of you,

Yásha, ever so fond! I am a delicate creature, Yásha.

YASHA. Here's somebody coming. [*He busies himself with the luggage, singing under his breath.*]

[*Enter* MADAME RANEVSKY, GAYEF, ANYA *and* CHARLOTTE.]

GAYEF. We'll have to be off; it's nearly time. [*Looking at* YASHA.] Who is it smells of red herring?

MADAME RANEVSKY. We must take our seats in ten minutes. [*Looking round the room.*] Good-bye, dear old house, good-bye, grandpapa! When winter is past and spring comes again, you will be here no more; they will have pulled you down. Oh, think of all these walls have seen! [*Kissing* ANYA *passionately.*] My treasure, you look radiant, your eyes flash like two diamonds. Are you happy? very happy?

ANYA. Very, very happy. We're beginning a new life, mamma.

GAYEF [*gaily*]. She's quite right, everything's all right now. Till the cherry orchard was sold we were all agitated and miserable; but once the thing was settled finally and irrevocably, we all calmed down and got jolly again. I'm a bank clerk now; I'm a financier . . . red in the middle! And you, Lyuba, whatever you may say, you're looking ever so much better, not a doubt about it.

MADAME RANEVSKY. Yes, my nerves are better; it's quite true. [*She is helped on with her hat and coat.*] I sleep well now. Take my things out, Yásha. We must be off. [*To* ANYA.] We shall soon meet again, darling. . . . I'm off to Paris; I shall live on the money your grandmother sent from Yaroslav to buy the property. God

bless your grandmother! I'm afraid it won't last long.

ANYA. You'll come back very, very soon, won't you, mamma? I'm going to work and pass the examination at the Gymnase and get a place and help you. We'll read all sorts of books together, won't we, mamma? [*Kissing her mother's hands.*] We'll read in the long autumn evenings, we'll read heaps of books, and a new, wonderful world will open up before us. [*Meditating.*] . . . Come back, mamma!

MADAME RANEVSKY. I'll come back, my angel. [*Embracing her.*]

[*Enter* LOPAKHIN. CHARLOTTE *sings softly.*]

GAYEF. Happy Charlotte, she's singing.

CHARLOTTE [*taking a bundle of rugs, like a swaddled baby*]. Hush-a-bye, baby, on the tree top . . . [*The baby answers, 'Wah, wah.'*] Hush, my little one, hush, my pretty one! ['*Wah, wah.*'] You'll break your mother's heart. [*She throws the bundle down on the floor again.*] Don't forget to find me a new place, please. I can't do without it.

LOPAKHIN. We'll find you a place, Charlotte Ivánovna, don't be afraid.

GAYEF. Everybody's deserting us. Barbara's going. Nobody seems to want us.

CHARLOTTE. There's nowhere for me to live in the town. I'm obliged to go. [*Hums a tune.*] What's the odds?

[*Enter* PISHTCHIK.]

LOPAKHIN. Nature's masterpiece!

PISHTCHIK [*panting*]. Oy, oy, let me get my breath again! . . . I'm done up! . . . My noble friends! . . . Give me some water.

GAYEF. Wants some money, I suppose. No, thank you: I'll keep out of harm's way.

[*Exit.*]

PISHTCHIK. It's ages since I have been here, fairest lady. [*To* LOPAKHIN.] You here? Glad to see you, you man of gigantic intellect. Take this; it's for you. [*Giving* LOPAKHIN *money.*] Forty pounds! I still owe you eighty-four.

LOPAKHIN [*amazed, shrugging his shoulders*]. Its like a thing in a dream! Where did you get it from?

PISHTCHIK. Wait a bit. . . . I'm hot. . . . A most remarkable thing! Some Englishmen came and found some sort of white clay on my land. [*To* MADAME RANEVSKY.] And here's forty pounds for you, lovely, wonderful lady. [*Giving her money.*] The rest another time. [*Drinking water.*] Only just now a young man in the train was saying that some . . . some great philosopher advises us all to jump off roofs. . . . Jump, he says, and there's an end of it. [*With an astonished air.*] Just think of that! More water!

LOPAKHIN. Who were the Englishmen?

PISHTCHIK. I leased them the plot with the clay on it for twenty-four years. But I haven't any time now . . . I must be getting on. I must go to Znoikof's. to Kardamónof's. . . . I owe everybody money. [*Drinking.*] Good-bye to everyone; I'll look in on Thursday.

MADAME RANEVSKY. We're just moving into town, and to-morrow I go abroad.

PISHTCHIK. What! [*Alarmed.*] What are you going into town for? Why, what's happened to the furniture? . . . Trunks? . . . Oh, it's all right. [*Crying.*] It's all right. People of powerful intellect . . . those Englishmen. It's all right. Be happy . . . God be with you . . . it's all right. Everything in this world has come to an end. [*Kissing* MADAME RANEVSKY's *hand.*] If ever the news reaches you that *I* have come to an end, give a thought to the old . . . horse, and say, 'Once there lived a certain Simeónof-Píshtchik, Heaven rest his soul.' . . . Remarkable weather we're having. . . . Yes. . . . [*Goes out deeply moved. Returns at once and says from the doorway.*] Dáshenka sent her compliments.

[*Exit.*]

MADAME RANEVSKY. Now we can go. I have only two things on my mind. One is poor old Firs. [*Looking at her watch.*] We can still stay five minutes.

ANYA. Firs has been sent to the hospital already, mamma. Yásha sent him off this morning.

MADAME RANEVSKY. My second anxiety is Barbara. She's used to getting up early and working, and now that she has no work to do she's like a fish out of water. She has grown thin and pale and taken to crying, poor dear. . . . [*A pause.*] You know very well, Yermolái Alexéyitch, I always hoped . . . to see her married to you, and as far as I can see, you're looking out for a wife. [*She whispers to* ANYA, *who nods to* CHARLOTTE, *and both exeunt.*] She loves you; you like her; and I can't make out why you seem to fight shy of each other. I don't understand it.

LOPAKHIN. I don't understand it either, to tell you the truth. It all seems so odd. If there's still time, I'll do it this moment. Let's get it over and have done with it; without you there, I feel as if I should never propose to her.

MADAME RANEVSKY. A capital idea!

After all, it doesn't take more than a minute. I'll call her at once.

LOPAKHIN. And here's the champagne all ready. [*Looking at the glasses.*] Empty; someone's drunk it. [YASHA *coughs.*] That's what they call lapping it up and no mistake!

MADAME RANEVSKY [*animated.*] Capital! We'll all go away. . . . *Allez*, Yásha. I'll call her. [*At the door.*] Barbara, leave all that and come here. Come along!

[*Exeunt* MADAME RANEVSKY *and* YASHA.]

LOPAKHIN [*looking at his watch*]. Yes.

[*A pause. A stifled laugh behind the door; whispering; at last enter* BARBARA.]

BARBARA [*examining the luggage*]. Very odd; I can't find it anywhere . . .

LOPAKHIN. What are you looking for?

BARBARA. I packed it myself, and can't remember. [*A pause.*]

LOPAKHIN. Where are you going to-day, Varvára Mikháilovna?

BARBARA. Me? I'm going to the Ragulins'. I'm engaged to go and keep house for them, to be housekeeper or whatever it is.

LOPAKHIN. Oh, at Yáshnevo? That's about fifty miles from here. [*A pause.*] Well, so life in this house is over now.

BARBARA [*looking at the luggage*]. Wherever can it be? Perhaps I put it in the trunk. . . . Yes, life here is over now: there won't be any more . . .

LOPAKHIN. And I'm off to Kharkof at once . . . by the same train. A lot of business to do. I'm leaving Ephikhódof to look after this place. I've taken him on.

BARBARA. Have you?

LOPAKHIN. At this time last year snow was falling already, if you remember; but now it's fine and sunny. Still, it's cold for all that. Three degrees of frost.

BARBARA. Where there? I didn't look. [*A pause.*] Besides, the thermometer's broken. [*A pause.*]

A VOICE [*at the outer door*]. Yermolái Alexéyitch!

LOPAKHIN [*as if he had only been waiting to be called*]. I'm just coming! [*Exit* LOPAKHIN *quickly.*]

[BARBARA *sits on the floor, puts her head on a bundle and sobs softly. The door opens and* MADAME RANEVSKY *comes in cautiously.*]

MADAME RANEVSKY. Well? [*A pause.*] We must be off.

BARBARA [*no longer crying, wiping her eyes*]. Yes, it's time, mamma. I shall get to the Ragulins' all right to-day, so long as I don't miss the train.

MADAME RANEVSKY [*calling off*]. Put on your things, Anya.

[*Enter* ANYA, *then* GAYEF *and* CHARLOTTE. GAYEF *wears a warm overcoat with a hood. The servants and drivers come in.* EPHIKHODOF *busies himself about the luggage.*]

MADAME RANEVSKY. Now we can start on our journey.

ANYA. [*Delighted.*] We can start on our journey!

GAYEF. My friends, my dear, beloved friends!

Now that I am leaving this house for ever, can I keep silence? Can I refrain from expressing those emotions which fill my whole being at such a moment?

ANYA. [*Pleadingly.*] Uncle!

BARBARA. Uncle, what's the good?

GAYEF. [*Sadly.*] Double the red in the middle pocket. I'll hold my tongue.

Enter TROPHIMOF, *then* LOPAKIN.

TROPHIMOF. Come along, it's time to start.

LOPAKHIN. Ephikhódof, my coat.

MADAME RANEVSKY. I must sit here another minute. It's just as if I had never noticed before what the walls and ceilings of the house were like. I look at them hungrily, with such tender love. . . .

GAYEF. I remember, when I was six years old, how I sat in this window on Trinity Sunday, and watched father starting out for church.

MADAME RANEVSKY. Has everything been cleared out?

LOPAKHIN. Apparently everything. [*To* EPHIKHODOF, *putting on his overcoat.*] See that everything's in order, Ephikhódof.

EPHIKHODOF. [*In a hoarse voice.*] You trust me, Yermolái Alexéyitch.

LOPAKHIN. What's up with your voice?

EPHIKHODOF. I was just having a drink of water. I swallowed something.

YASHA. [*Contemptuously.*] Cad!

MADAME RANEVSKY. We're going, and not a soul will be left here.

LOPAKHIN. Until the spring.

[BARBARA *pulls an umbrella out of a bundle of rugs, as if she were brandishing it to strike.* LOPAKHIN *pretends to be frightened.*]

BARBARA. Don't be so silly! I never thought of such a thing.

TROPHIMOF. Come, we'd better go and get in. It's time to start. The train will be in immediately.

BARBARA. There are your goloshes, Peter, by that portmanteau. [*Crying.*] What dirty old things they are!

TROPHIMOF. [*Putting on his goloshes.*] Come along.

GAYEF. [*Much moved, afraid of crying.*] The train . . . the station . . . double the red in the middle; doublette to pot the white in the corner. . . .

MADAME RANEVSKY. Come on!

LOPAKHIN. Is everyone here? No one left in there? [*Locking the door.*] There are things stacked in there; I must lock them up. Come on!

ANYA. Good-bye, house! good-bye, old life!

TROPHIMOF. Welcome, new life!

[*Exit with* ANYA. BARBARA *looks round the room, and exit slowly. Exeunt* YASHA, *and* CHARLOTTE *with her dog.*]

LOPAKHIN. Till the spring, then. Go on, everybody. So-long!

[*Exit.*] [MADAME RANEVSKY *and* GAYEF *remain alone. They seem to have been waiting for this, throw their arms round each other's necks and sob restrainedly and gently, afraid of being overheard.*]

GAYEF. [*In despair.*] My sister! my sister!

MADAME RANEVSKY. Oh, my dear, sweet lovely orchard! My life, my youth, my happiness. farewell! Farewell!

ANYA. [*Calling gaily, without.*] Mamma!

TROPHIMOF. [*Gay and excited.*] Aoo!

MADAME RANEVSKY. One last look at the walls and the windows. . . . Our dear mother used to walk up and down this room.

GAYEF. My sister! my sister!

ANYA. [*Without.*] Aoo!

MADAME RANEVSKY. We're coming. [*Exeunt.*]

[*The stage is empty. One hears all the doors being locked, and the carriages driving away. All is quiet. Amid the* silence the thud of the axes on the trees echoes sad and lonely. The sound of footsteps. FIRS appears in the doorway R. He is dressed, as always, in his long coat and white waistcoat; he wears slippers. He is ill.]

FIRS. [Going to the door L. and trying the handle.] Locked. They've gone. [Sitting on the sofa.]

They've forgotten me. Never mind! I'll sit here. Leoníd Andréyitch is sure to have put on his cloth coat instead of his fur. [He sighs anxiously.] He hadn't me to see. Young wood, green

wood! [He mumbles something incomprehensible.] Life has gone by as if I'd never lived. [Lying down.] I'll lie down. There's no strength left in you; there's nothing, nothing. Ah, you . . . job-lot!

[He lies motionless. A distant sound is heard, as if from the sky, the sound of a string breaking, dying away, melancholy. Silence ensues, broken only by the stroke of the axe on the trees far away in the cherry orchard.]

CURTAIN

The Three Sisters

DRAMATIS PERSONAE

ANDREY SERGEYEVITCH PROSOROV.

NATALIA IVANOVNA [NATASHA], his fiancée, later his wife, 28 years old.

OLGA ⎫
MASHA ⎬ his sisters.
IRINA ⎭

FEODOR ILITCH KULIGIN, high school teacher, married to MASHA, 20 years old.

ALEXANDER IGNATEYEVITCH VERSHININ, lieutenant-colonel in charge of a battery, 42 years old.

NICOLAI LVOVITCH TUZENBACH, baron, lieutenant in the army, 30 years old.

VASSILI VASSILEVITCH SOLENI, captain.

IVAN ROMANOVITCH CHEBUTIKIN, army doctor, 60 years old.

ALEXEY PETROVITCH FEDOTIK, sub-lieutenant.

VLADIMIR CARLOVITCH RODE, sub-lieutenant.

FERAPONT, door-keeper at local council offices, an old man.

ANFISA, nurse, 80 years old.

The action takes place in a provincial town.

ACT I

In PROSOROV'S house. A sitting-room with pillars; behind is seen a large dining-room. It is midday, the sun is shining brightly outside. In the dining-room the table is being laid for lunch.

OLGA, in the regulation blue dress of a teacher at a girl's high school, is walking about correcting exercise books; MASHA, in a black dress, with a hat on her knees, sits and reads a book; IRINA, in white, stands about, with a thoughtful expression.

OLGA. A year since father died last May the fifth, on your name-day, Irina. It was very cold then, and snowing. I thought I would never live, and you were in a dead faint. And now a year has gone by and it does not affect us, and you are wearing a white dress and look happy. [*Clock strikes twelve.*] And the clock struck just the same way then. [*Pause.*] I remember that there was music at the funeral, and they fired a volley in the cemetery. A general in command but few people present. Rain and snow.

IRINA. Why recall it?

BARON TUZENBACH, CHEBUTIKIN *and* SOLENI *appear by the table in the dining-room, behind the pillars.*

OLGA. It's so warm to-day that we can keep the windows open, though the birches are not yet in flower. Father was put in command of a brigade, and he rode out of Moscow with us eleven years ago. I remember perfectly that it was early in May and all Moscow was blooming. It was warm too, everything in sunshine. Eleven years, and I remember everything as if we rode out only yesterday. Oh God! When I awoke this morning and saw all the light and the spring, I was homesick.

CHEBUTIKIN. Will you take a bet on it?

TUZENBACH. Don't be foolish.

MASHA, *lost in a reverie over her book, whistles softly.*

OLGA. Don't whistle, Masha. How can you! [*Pause.*] I'm always having headaches from having to go to the High School every day and then teach till evening. Strange thoughts come to me, as if I were aged. And really, during these four years I have been feeling as if every day had been drained from me. And only one desire grows and gains in strength . . .

IRINA. To go away to Moscow. To sell the house, leave all and go to Moscow. . . .

OLGA. Yes! To Moscow, and as soon as possible.

CHEBUTIKIN *and* TUZENBACH *laugh.*

IRINA. I expect Andrey will become a professor, but still, he won't want to live here. Only poor Masha must go on living here.

OLGA. Masha can come to Moscow every summer.

MASHA *is whistling gently.*

IRINA. Everything will be arranged, please God. [*Looks out of window*] It's nice out to-day. I don't know why I'm so happy: I remembered this morning that it was my name-day, and I suddenly felt glad and remembered my childhood, when mother was still with us. What beautiful thoughts I had, what thoughts!

OLGA. You're all radiance to-day, I've never seen you look so lovely. And Masha is pretty, too. Andrey wouldn't be bad-looking, if he wasn't so stout; it does spoil his appearance. But I've grown old and very thin, I suppose it's because I get angry with the girls at school. To-day I'm free. I'm at home. I haven't got a headache, and I feel younger than I was yesterday. I'm only twenty-eight. . . . All's well, God is everywhere, but it seems to me that if only I were married and could stay at home all day, it would be even better. [*Pause.*] I should love my husband.

TUZENBACH. [*To* SOLENI.] I'm tired of listening to the rot you talk. [*Entering the sitting-room*] I forgot to say that Vershinin, our new lieutenant-colonel of artillery, is coming to see us to-day. [*Sits down to the piano.*]

OLGA. That's good. I'm glad.

IRINA. Is he old?

TUZENBACH. Oh, no. Forty or forty-five, at the very outside. [*Plays softly.*] He seems rather a good sort. He's certainly no fool, only he likes to hear himself speak.

IRINA. Is he interesting?

TUZENBACH. Oh, he's all right, but there's his wife, his mother-in-law, and two daughters. This is his second wife. He pays calls and tells everybody that he's got a wife and two daughters. He'll tell you so here. The wife isn't all there, she does her hair like a flapper and gushes extremely. She talks philosophy and tries to commit suicide every now and again, apparently in order to annoy her husband. I should have left her long ago, but he bears up patiently, and just grumbles.

SOLENI. [*Enters with* CHEBUTIKIN *from the dining-room.*] With one hand I can only lift fifty-four pounds, but with both hands I can lift 180, or even 200 pounds. From this I conclude that two men are not twice as strong as one, but three times, perhaps even more. . .

CHEBUTIKIN. [*Reads a newspaper as he walks.*] If your hair is coming out . . . take an ounce of naphthaline and half a bottle of spirit . . . dissolve and use daily. . . . [*Makes a note in his pocket diary.*] When found make a note of! Not that I want it though. . . . [*Crosses it out.*] It doesn't matter.

IRINA. Ivan Romanovitch, dear Ivan Romanovitch!

CHEBUTIKIN. What does my own little girl want?

IRINA. Ivan Romanovitch, dear Ivan Romanovitch! I feel as if I were sailing under the broad blue sky with great white birds around me. Why is that? Why?

CHEBUTIKIN. [*Kisses her hands, tenderly.*] My white bird. . . .

IRINA. When I woke up to-day and got up and dressed myself, I suddenly began to feel as if everything in this life was open to me, and that I knew how I must live. Dear Ivan Romanovitch, I know everything. A man must work, toil in the sweat of his brow, whoever he may be, for that is the meaning and object of his life, his happiness, his enthusiasm. How fine it is to be a workman who gets up at daybreak and breaks stones in the street, or a shepherd, or a schoolmaster, who teaches children, or an engine-driver on the railway. . . . My God, let alone a man, it's better to be an ox, or just a horse, so long as it can work, than a young woman who wakes up at twelve o'clock, has her coffee in bed, and then spends two hours dressing. . . . Oh it's awful! Sometimes when it's hot, your thirst can be just as tiresome as my need for work. And if I don't get up early in future and work, Ivan Romanovitch, then you may refuse me your friendship.

CHEBUTIKIN. [*Tenderly.*] I'll refuse, I'll refuse. . . .

OLGA. Father used to make us get up at seven. Now Irina wakes at seven and lies and meditates about something till nine at least. And she looks so serious! [*Laughs.*]

IRINA. You're so used to seeing me as a little girl that it seems queer to you when my face is serious. I'm twenty!

TUZENBACH. How well I can understand that craving for work, oh God! I've never worked once in my life. I was born in Petersburg, a chilly, lazy place, in a family which never knew what work or worry meant. I remember that when I used to come home from my regiment, a footman used to have to pull off my boots while I fidgeted and my mother looked on in adoration and wondered why other people didn't see me in the same light. They shielded me from work; but only just in time! A new age is dawning, the people are marching on us all, a powerful, health-giving storm is gathering, it is drawing near, soon it will be upon us and it will drive away laziness, indifference, the prejudice against labour, and rotten dullness from our society. I shall work, and in twenty-five or thirty years, every man will have to work. Every one!

CHEBUTIKIN. I shan't work.

TUZENBACH. You don't matter.

SOLENI. In twenty-five years' time, we shall all be dead, thank the Lord. In two or three years' time apoplexy will carry you off, or else I'll blow your brains out. my pet.

Takes a scent-bottle out of his pocket and sprinkles his chest and hands.

CHEBUTIKIN. [*Laughs.*] It's quite true, I never have worked. After I came down from the university I never stirred a finger or opened a book, I just read the papers. . . . [*Takes another newspaper out of his pocket.*] Here we are. . . I've learnt from the papers that there used to be one, Dobrolubov, for instance, but what he wrote—I don't know . . . God only knows. . . . [*Somebody is heard tapping on the floor from below.*] There. . . They're calling me downstairs, somebody's come to see me. I'll be back in a minute . . . won't be long. . . .

[*Exit hurriedly, scratching his beard.*]

IRINA. He's up to something.

TUZENBACH. Yes, he looked so pleased as he went out that I'm pretty certain he'll bring you a present in a moment.

IRINA. How unpleasant!

OLGA. Yes, it's awful. He's always doing silly things.

MASHA. "There stands a green oak by the sea.
And a chain of bright gold is around it . .
And a chain of bright gold is around it. . . ."

[*Gets up and sings softly.*]

OLGA. You're not very bright to-day, Masha. [MASHA *sings, putting on her hat.*] Where are you off to?

MASHA. Home.

IRINA. That's odd. . . .

TUZENBACH. On a name-day, too!

MASHA. It doesn't matter. I'll come in the evening. Good-bye. dear. [*Kisses* IRINA.] Many happy returns, though I've said it before. In the old days when father was alive, every time we had a name-day, thirty or forty officers used to come, and there was lots of noise and fun, and to-day there's only a man and a half, and it's quiet as a desert . . . I'm off . . . . I've got the hump to-day, and am not at all cheerful. so don't you mind me. [*Laughs through her tears.*] We'll have a talk later on, but good-bye for the present, my dear; I'll go somewhere.

IRINA. [*Displeased.*] You are queer. . . .

OLGA. [*Crying.*] I understand you, Masha.

SOLENI. When a man talks philosophy, well, it is philosophy or at any rate sophistry; but when a woman, or two women talk philosophy—it's all my eye.

MASHA. What do you mean by that, you very awful man?

SOLENI. Oh, nothing. You came down on me before I could say . . . help! [Pause.]

MASHA. [Angrily, to OLGA.] Don't cry!

Enter ANFISA and FERAPONT with a cake.

ANFISA. This way, my dear. Come in, your feet are clean. [To IRINA.] From the District Council, from Mihail Ivanitch Protopopov . . . a cake.

IRINA. Thank you. Please thank him. [Takes the cake.]

FERAPONT. What?

IRINA. [Louder.] Please thank him.

OLGA. Give him a pie, nurse. Ferapont, go, she'll give you a pie.

FERAPONT. What?

ANFISA. Come on, gran'fer, Ferapont Spiridonitch. Come on. [Exeunt.]

MASHA. I don't like this Mihail Potapitch or Ivanitch, Protopopov. We oughtn't to invite him here.

IRINA. I never asked him.

MASHA. That's all right.

Enter CHEBUTIKIN followed by a soldier with a silver samovar; there is a rumble of dissatisfied surprise.

OLGA. [Covers her face with her hands.] A samovar! That's awful! [Exit into the dining-room, to the table.]

IRINA. My dear Ivan Romanovitch, what are you doing!

TUZENBACH. [Laughs.] I told you so!

MASHA. Ivan Romanovitch, you are simply shameless!

CHEBUTIKIN. My dear good girl, you are the only thing, and the dearest thing I have in the world. I'll soon be sixty. I'm an old man, a lonely worthless old man. The only good thing in me is my love for you, and if it hadn't been for that, I would have been dead long ago. . . . [To IRINA.] My dear little girl, I've known you since the day of your birth, I've carried you in my arms . . . I loved your dead mother. . . .

MASHA. But your presents are so expensive!

CHEBUTIKIN. [Angrily, through his tears.] Expensive presents. . . . You really are! . . . [To the orderly.] Take the samovar in there. . . . [Teasing.] Expensive presents!

The orderly goes into the dining-room with the samovar.

ANFISA. [Enters and crosses stage.] My dear, there's a strange Colonel come! He's taken off his coat already. Children, he's coming here. Irina darling, you'll be a nice and polite little girl, won't you. . . . Sh uld have lunched a long time ago. . . . Oh, Lord . . .
[Exit.]

TUZENBACH. It must be Vershinin. [Enter VERSHININ.] Lieutenant-Colonel Vershinin!

VERSHININ. [To MASHA and IRINA.] I have the honour to introduce myself, my name is Vershinin. I am very glad indeed to be able to come at last. How you've grown! Oh! Oh!

IRINA. Please sit down. We're very glad you've come.

VERSHININ. [Gaily.] I am glad, very glad! But there are three sisters, surely. I remember—three little girls. I forget your faces, but your father, Colonel Prosorov, used to have three little girls. I remember that perfectly, I saw them with my own eyes. How time does fly! Oh, dear, how it flies!

TUZENBACH. Alexander Ignateyevitch comes from Moscow.

IRINA. From Moscow? Are you from Moscow?

VERSHININ. Yes, that's so. Your father used to be in charge of a battery there, and I was an officer in the same brigade. [*To* MASHA.] I seem to remember your face a little.

MASHA. I don't remember you.

IRINA. Olga! Olga! [*Shouts into the dining-room.*] Olga! Come along! [OLGA *enters from the dining-room.*] Lieutenant-Colonel Vershinin comes from Moscow, as it happens.

VERSHININ. I take it that you are Olga Sergeyevna, the eldest and that you are Maria . . . and you are Irina, the youngest. . . .

OLGA. So you come from Moscow?

VERSHININ. Yes. I went to school in Moscow and began my service there; I was there for a long time until at last I got my battery and moved over here, as you see. I don't really remember you, I only remember that there used to be three sisters. I remember your father well; I have only to shut my eyes to see him as he was. I used to come to your house in Moscow. . . .

OLGA. I used to think I remembered everybody, but . . .

VERSHININ. My name is Alexander Ignateyevitch.

IRINA. Alexander Ignateyevitch, you've come from Moscow. That is really a surprise!

OLGA. We are going to live there, you see.

IRINA. We think we may be there this autumn. It's our native town, we

were born there. In Old Basmanni Road. . . . [*They both laugh for joy.*]

MASHA. We've unexpectedly met a fellow countryman. [*Briskly.*] I remember: Do you remember, Olga, they used to speak at home of a "lovelorn Major." You were only a Lieutenant then, and in love with somebody, but for some reason they always called you a Major for fun.

VERSHININ. [*Laughs.*] That's it . . . the lovelorn Major, that's got it!

MASHA. You only wore moustaches then. You have grown older! [*Through her tears.*] You have grown older!

VERSHININ. Yes, when they used to call me the lovelorn Major, I was young and in love. I've grown out of both now.

OLGA. But you haven't a single white hair yet. You're older, but you're not yet old.

VERSHININ. I'm forty-two, anyway. Have you been away from Moscow long?

IRINA. Eleven years. What are you crying for, Masha, you little fool. . . . [*Crying.*] And I'm crying too.

MASHA. It's all right. And where did you live?

VERSHININ. Old Basmanni Road.

OLGA. Same as we.

VERSHININ. Once I used to live in German Street. That was when the Red Barracks were my headquarters. There's an ugly bridge in between, where the water rushes underneath. One gets melancholy when one is alone there. [*Pause.*] Here the river is so wide and fine! It's a splendid river!

OLGA. Yes, but it's so cold. It's very cold here, and the midges. . . .

VERSHININ. What are you saying!

Here you've got such a fine healthy Russian climate. You've a forest, a river . . . and birches. Dear, modest birches, I like them more than any other tree. It's good to live here. Only it's odd that the railway station should be thirteen miles way . . . Nobody knows why.

SOLENI. I know why. [*All look at him.*] Because if it was near it wouldn't be far off, and if it's far off, it can't be near. [*An awkward pause.*]

TUZENBACH. Funny man.

OLGA. Now I know who you are. I remember.

VERSHININ. I used to know your mother.

CHEBUTIKIN. She was a good woman, rest her soul.

IRINA. Mother is buried in Moscow.

OLGA. At the Novo-Devichi Cemetery.

MASHA. Do you know, I'm beginning to forget her face. We'll be forgotten in just the same way.

VERSHININ. Yes, they'll forget us. It's our fate, it can't be helped. A time will come when everything that seems serious, significant, or very important to us will be forgotten, or considered trivial. [*Pause.*] And the curious thing is that we can't possibly find out what will come to be regarded as great and important, and what will be feeble, or silly. Didn't the discoveries of Copernicus, or Columbus, say, seem unnecessary and ludicrous at first, while wasn't it thought that some rubbish written by a fool, held all the truth? And it may so happen that our present existence, with which we are so satisfied, will in time appear strange, inconvenient, stupid, unclean, perhaps even sinful. . . .

TUZENBACH. Who knows? But on the other hand, they may call our life noble and honour its memory. We've abolished torture and capital punishment, we live in security, but how much suffering there is still!

SOLENI. [*In a feeble voice.*] There. there. . . . The Baron will go without his dinner if you only let him talk philosophy.

TUZENBACH. Vassili Vassilevitch, kindly leave me alone. [*Changes his chair.*] You're very dull, you know.

SOLENI. [*Feebly.*] There, there, there.

TUZENBACH. [*To* VERSHININ.] The sufferings we see to-day—there are so many of them!—still indicate a certain moral improvement in society.

VERSHININ. Yes, yes, of course.

CHEBUTIKIN. You said just now, Baron, that they may call our life noble; but we are very petty. . . . [*Stands up.*] See how little I am. [*Violin played behind.*]

MASHA. That's Andrey playing—our brother.

IRINA. He's the learned member of the family. I expect he will be a professor some day. Father was a soldier, but his son chose an academic career for himself.

MASHA. That was father's wish.

OLGA. We ragged him to-day. We think he's a little in love.

IRINA. To a local lady. She will probably come here to-day.

MASHA. You should see the way she dresses! Quite prettily, q u i t e fashionably too, but so badly! Some queer bright yellow skirt with a wretched little fringe and a red bodice. And such a complexion! Andrey isn't in love. After all he has taste, he's simply making fun of us. I heard yesterday that she was going to marry Protopopov, the chairman of the Local Council. That would do her nicely. . . [*At the side door.*] Andrey, come here! Just for a minute, dear! [*Enter ANDREY.*]

OLGA. My brother, Andrey Sergeyevitch.

VERSHININ. My name is Vershinin.

ANDREY. Mine is Prosorov. [*Wipes his perspiring hands.*] You've come to take charge of the battery?

OLGA. Just think, Alexander Ignateyevitch comes from Moscow.

ANDREY. That's all right. Now my little sisters won't give you any rest.

VERSHININ. I've already managed to bore your sisters.

IRINA. Just look what a nice little photograph frame Andrey gave me today. [*Shows it.*] He made it himself.

VERSHININ. [*Looks at the frame and does not know what to say.*] Yes. . . . It's a thing that . . .

IRINA. And he made that frame there, on the piano as well. [*Andrey waves his hand and walks away.*]

OLGA. He's got a degree, and plays the violin, and cuts all sorts of things out of wood, and is really a domestic Admirable Crichton. Don't go away, Andrey! He's got into a habit of always going away. Come here!

MASHA *and* IRINA *take his arms and laughingly lead him back.*

MASHA. Come on, come on!

ANDREY. Please leave me alone.

MASHA. You are funny. Alexander Ignateyevitch used to be called the lovelorn Major, but he never minded.

VERSHININ. Not in the least.

MASHA. I'd like to call you a lovelorn fiddler!

IRINA. Or the lovelorn professor!

OLGA. He's in love! little Andrey is in love!

IRINA. [*Applauds.*] Bravo! Bravo! Encore! Little Andrey is in love.

CHEBUTIKIN. [*Goes up behind ANDREY and takes him around the waist with both arms.*] Nature only brought us into the world that we should love!

Roars with laughter, then sits down and reads a newspaper which he takes out of his pocket.

ANDREY. That's enough, quite enough. . . . [*Wipes his face.*] I couldn't sleep all night and now I can't quite find my feet, so to speak. I read until four o'clock, then tried to sleep, but nothing happened. I thought about one thing and another, and then it dawned and the sun crawled into my bedroom. This summer, while I'm here, I want to translate a book from the English. . . .

VERSHININ. Do you read English?

ANDREY. Yes; father, rest his soul, educated us almost violently. It may seem funny and silly, but it's nevertheless true, that after his death I began to fill out and get rounder, as if my body had had some great pressure taken off it. Thanks to father, my sisters and I know French, German, and English, and Irina knows Italian as well. But we paid dearly for it all!

MASHA. A knowledge of three languages is an unnecessary luxury in this town. It isn't even a luxury but a sort of useless extra, like a sixth finger. We know a lot too much.

VERSHININ. Well, I say! [*Laughs.*] You know a lot too much! I don't think there can really be a town so dull and stupid as to have no place for a clever, cultured person. Let us suppose even that among the hundred thousand inhabitants of this backward and uneducated town, there are only three persons like yourself. It stands to reason that you won't be able to conquer that dark mob around you; little by little as you grow older you will be bound to give way and lose yourselves in this crowd of a hundred thousand human beings; their life will suck you up in itself; but still, you won't disappear having influenced nobody; later on, others like you will come, perhaps six of them, then twelve, and so on, until at last your sort will be in the majority. In two or three hundred years' time life on this earth will be unimaginably beautiful and wonderful. Mankind needs such a life, and if it is not ours to-day then we must look ahead for it, wait, think, prepare for it. We must see and know more than our fathers and grandfathers saw and knew. [*Laughs.*] And you complain that you know too much.

MASHA. [*Takes off her hat.*] I'll stay to lunch.

IRINA. [*Sighs.*] Yes, all that ought to be written down.

ANDREY *has gone out quietly.*

TUZENBACH. You say that many years later on, life on this earth will be beautiful and wonderful. That's true. But to share in it now, even though at a distance, we must prepare by work. . . .

VERSHININ. [*Gets up.*] Yes. What a lot of flowers you have. [*Looks round.*] It's a beautiful flat. I envy you! I've spent my whole life in rooms with two chairs, one sofa, and fires which always smoke. I've never had flowers like these in my life. . . . [*Rubs his hands.*] Well, well!

TUZENBACH. Yes, we must work. You are probably thinking to yourself: the

German lets himself go. But I assure you I'm a Russian, I can't even speak German. My father belonged to the Orthodox Church. . . . [*Pause.*]

VERSHININ. [*Walks about the stage.*] I often wonder: suppose we could begin life over again, knowing what we were doing? Suppose we could use one life, already ended, as a sort of rough draft for another? I think that every one of us would try, more than anything else, not to repeat himself, at the very least he would rearrange his manner of life, he would make sure of rooms like these, with flowers and light . . . I have a wife and two daughters, my wife's health is delicate and so on and so on, and if I had to begin life all over again I would not marry . . . No, no!

[*Enter* KULIGIN *in a regulation jacket.*]

KULIGIN. [*Going up to* IRINA.] Dear sister, allow me to congratulate you on the day sacred to your good angel and to wish you, sincerely and from the bottom of my heart, good health and all that one can wish for a girl of your years. And then let me offer you this book as a present. [*Gives it to her.*] It is the history of our High School during the last fifty years, written by myself. The book is worthless, and written because I had nothing to do, but read it all the same. Good day, gentlemen! [*To* VERSHININ.] My name is Kuligin, I am a master of the local High School. [*To* IRINA.] In this book you will find a list of all those who have taken a full course at our High School during these fifty years. *Feci quod potin, faciant meliora potentes.* [*Kisses* MASHA.]

IRINA. But you gave me one of these at Easter.

KULIGIN. [*Laughs.*] I couldn't have, surely! You'd better give it back to me in that case, or else give it to the Colonel. Take it, Colonel. You'll read it some day when you're bored.

VERSHININ. Thank you. [*Prepares to go.*] I am extremely happy to have made the acquaintance of . . .

OLGA. Must you go? No, not yet?

IRINA. You'll stop and have lunch with us. Please do.

OLGA. Yes, please!

VERSHININ. [*Bows.*] I seem to have dropped in on your name-day. Forgive me, I didn't know, and I didn't offer you my congratulations. . . .

[*Goes with* OLGA *into the dining-room.*]

KULIGIN. To-day is Sunday, the day of rest, so let us rest and rejoice, each in a manner compatible with his age and disposition. The carpets will have to be taken up for the summer and put away till winter . . Persian powder or napthaline. . . . The Romans were healthy because they knew both how to work and how to rest, they had *mens sana in corpore sano.* Their life ran along certain recognized patterns. Our director says: "The chief thing about each life is its pattern. Whoever loses his pattern is lost himself"—and it's just the same in our daily life. [*Takes* MASHA *by the waist, laughing.*] Masha loves me. My wife loves me. And you ought to put the window curtains away with the carpets. . . . I'm feeling awfully pleased with life to-day. Masha, we've got to be at the director's at four. They're getting up a walk for the pedagogues and their families.

MASHA. I shan't go.

KULIGIN. [*Hurt.*] My dear Masha, why not?

MASHA. I'll tell you later. . . . [*Angrily.*] All right, I'll go, only please stand back. . . . [*Steps away.*]

KULIGIN. And then we're to spend the evening at the director's. In spite of his ill-health that man tries, above everything else, to be sociable. A splendid, illuminating personality. A wonderful man. After yesterday's committee he said to me: "I'm tired, Feodor Ilitch, I'm tired!" [*Looks at the clock, then at his watch.*] Your clock is seven minutes fast. "Yes," he said, "I'm tired." [*Violin played off.*]

OLGA. Let's go and have lunch! There's to be a master-piece of baking!

KULIGIN. Oh my dear Olga, my dear. Yesterday I was working till eleven o'clock at night, and got awfully tired. To-day I'm quite happy. [*Goes into dining-room.*] My dear . . .

CHEBUTIKIN. [*Puts his paper into his pocket, and combs his beard.*] A pie? Splendid!

MASHA. [*Severely to* CHEBUTIKIN.] Only mind; you're not to drink anything to-day. Do you hear? It's bad for you.

CHEBUTIKIN. Oh, that's all right. I haven't been drunk for two years. And it's all the same, anyway!

MASHA. You're not to dare to drink, all the same. [*Angrily, but so that her husband should not hear.*] Another dull evening at the director's, confound it!

TUZENBACH. I shouldn't go if I were you. . . . It's quite simple.

CHEBUTIKIN. Don't go.

MASHA. Yes, "don't go. . . ." It's a cursed, unbearable life. . . . [*Goes into dining-room.*]

CHEBUTIKIN. [*Follows her.*] It's not so bad.

SOLENI. [*Going into the dining-room.*] There, there, there. . . .

TUZENBACH. Vassili Vassilevitch, that's enough. Be quiet!

SOLENI. There, there, there. . . .

KULIGIN. [*Gaily.*] Your health, Colonel! I'm a pedagogue and not quite at home here. I'm Masha's husband. . . . She's a good sort, a very good sort. . . .

VERSHININ. I'll have some of this black vodka. . . . [*Drinks.*] Your health! [*To* OLGA.] I'm very comfortable here!

Only IRINA *and* TUZENBACH *are now left in the sitting-room.*

IRINA. Masha's out of sorts to-day. She married when she was eighteen, when he seemed to her the wisest of men. And now it's different. He's the kindest man, but not the wisest.

OLGA. [*Impatiently*] Andrey, when are you coming?

ANDREY. [*Off.*] One minute. [*Enters and goes to the table.*]

TUZENBACH. What are you thinking about?

IRINA. I don't like this Soleni of yours and i'm afraid of him. He only says silly things.

TUZENBACH. He's a queer man. I'm sorry for him, though he vexes me. I think he's shy. When there are just two of us he's quite all right and very good company; when other people are about he's rough and hectoring. Don't let's go in, let them have their meal without us. Let me stay with you. What are you thinking of? [*Pause.*] You're twenty. I'm not yet thirty. How many years are there left to us. with their long, long lines of days, filled with my love for you. . . .

IRINA. Nicolai Lvovitch, don't speak to me of love.

TUZENBACH. [*Does not hear.*] I've a great thirst for life, struggle, and work, and this thirst has united with my love for you, Irina, and you're so beautiful, and life seems so beautiful to me! What are you thinking about?

IRINA. You say that life is beautiful. Yes, if only it seems so! The life of us three hasn't been beautiful yet; it has been stifling us as if it was weeds . . . I'm crying. I oughtn't. . . . [*Dries her tears, smiles.*] We must work, work. That is why we are unhappy and look at the world so sadly; we don't know what work is. Our parents despised work. . . .

Enter NATALIA IVANOVNA; *she wears a pink dress and a green sash.*

NATASHA. They're already at lunch . . . I'm late . . . [*Carefully examines herself in a mirror, and puts herself straight.*] I think my hair's done all right. . . . [*Sees* IRINA.] Dear Irina Sergeyevna, I congratulate you! [*Kisses her firmly and at length.*] You've so many visitors, I'm really ashamed. . . . How do you do, Baron!

OLGA. [*Enters from dining-room.*] Here's Natalia Ivanovna. How are you, dear! [*They kiss.*]

NATASHA. Happy returns. I'm awfully shy, you've so many people here.

OLGA. All our friends. [*Frightened, in an undertone.*] You're wearing a green sash! My dear, you shouldn't!

NATASHA. Is it a sign of anything?

OLGA. No, it simply doesn't go well . . . and it looks so queer.

NATASHA. [*In a tearful voice.*] Yes?

But it isn't really green, it's too dull for that.

[*Goes into dining-room with* OLGA.]
They have all sat down to lunch in the dining-room, the sitting-room is empty.

KULIGIN. I wish you a nice *fiancé*, Irina. It's quite time you married.

CHEBUTIKIN. Natalia Ivanovna, I wish you the same.

KULIGIN. Natalia. Ivanovna has a *fiancé* already.

MASHA. [*Raps with her fork on a plate.*] Let's all get drunk and make life purple for once!

KULIGIN. You've lost three good conduct marks.

VERSHININ. This is a nice drink. What's it made of?

SOLENI. Blackbeetles.

IRINA. [*Tearfully.*] Phoo! How disgusting!

OLGA. There is to be roast turkey and a sweet apple pie for dinner. Thank goodness I can spend all day and the evening at home. You'll come in the evening, ladies and gentlemen. . . .

VERSHININ. And please may I come in the evening!

IRINA. Please do.

NATASHA. They don't stand on ceremony here.

CHEBUTIKIN. Nature only brought us into the world that we should love!
[*Laughs.*]

ANDREY. [*Angrily.*] Please don't! Aren't you tired of it?

Enter FEDOTIK *and* RODE *with a large basket of flowers.*

FEDOTIK. They're lunching already.

RODE. [*Loudly and thickly.*] Lunching? Yes, so they are. . . .

FEDOTIK. Wait a minute! [*Takes a photograph.*] That's one. No, just a moment. . . . [*Takes another.*] That's two. Now we're ready!

They take the basket and go into the dining-room, where they have a noisy reception.

RODE. [*Loudly.*] Congratulations and best wishes! Lovely weather to-day, simply perfect. Was out walking with the High School students all the morning. I take their drills.

FEDOTIK. You may move, Irina Sergeyevna! [*Takes a photograph.*] You look well to-day. [*Takes a humming-top out of his pocket.*] Here's a humming-top, by the way. It's got a lovely note!

IRINA. How awfully nice!

MASHA. "There stands a green oak
　　by the sea,
　　And a chain of bright gold
　　　is around it . . .
　　And a chain of bright. gold
　　　is around it . . ."

[*Tearfully.*] What am I saying that for? I've had those words running in my head all day. . . .

KULIGIN. There are thirteen at table!

RODE. [*Aloud.*] Surely you don't believe in that superstition? [*Laughter.*]

KULIGIN. If there are thirteen at table then it means there are lovers present. It isn't you, Ivan Romanovitch, hang it all. . . . [*Laughter.*]

CHEBUTIKIN. I'm a hardened sinner, but I really don't see why Natalia Ivanovna should blush. . . .

Loud laughter; NATASHA *runs out into the sitting-room, followed by* ANDREY.

ANDREY. Don't pay any attention to them! Wait . . . do stop, please. . . .

NATASHA. I'm shy . . . I don't know what's the matter with me and they're all laughing at me. It wasn't nice of me to leave the table like that, but I can't . . . I can't. [*Covers her face with her hands.*]

ANDREY. My dear, I beg you. I implore you not to excite yourself. I assure you they're only joking, they're kind people. My dear, good girl, they're all kind and sincere people, and they like both you and me. Come here to the window, they can't see us here. . . . [*Looks round.*]

NATASHA. I'm so unaccustomed to meeting people!

ANDREY. Oh your youth, your splendid, beautiful youth! My darling, don't be so excited! Believe me, believe me . . . I'm so happy, my soul is full of love, of ecstasy. . . . They don't see us! They can't! Why, why or when did I fall in love with you—Oh, I can't understand anything. My dear, my pure darling, be my wife! I love you, love you . . . as never before. . . . [*They kiss.*]

Two officers come in and, seeing the lovers kiss, stop in astonishment.

CURTAIN

ACT II

Scene as before. It is 8 p. m. Somebody is heard playing a concertina outside in the street. There is no fire. NATALYA IVANOVNA *enters in indoor dress carrying a candle; she stops by the door which leads into* ANDREY'S *room.*

NATASHA. What are you doing, ANDREY? Are you reading? It's nothing, only I. . . . [*She opens another door, and looks in, then closes it.*] Isn't there any fire. . . .

ANDREY. [*Enters with book in hand.*] What are you doing, Natasha?

NATASHA. I was looking to see if there wasn't a fire. It's Shrovetide, and

the servant is simply beside herself; I must look out that something doesn't happen. When I came through the dining-room yesterday midnight, there was a candle burning. I couldn't get her to tell me who had lighted it. [*Puts down her candle.*] What's the time?

ANDREY. [*Looks at his watch.*] A quarter past eight.

NATASHA. And Olga and Irina aren't in yet. The poor things are still at work. Olga at the teacher's council, Irina at the telegraph office. . . . [*Sighs.*] I said to your sister this morning, "Irina, darling, you must take care of yourself." But she pays no attention. Did you say it was a quarter past eight? I am afraid little Bobby is quite ill. Why is he so cold? He was feverish yesterday, but to-day he is quite cold . . . I am so frightened!

ANDREY. It's all right, Natasha. The boy is well.

NATASHA. Still, I think we ought to put him on a diet. I am so afraid. And the entertainers were to be here after nine; they had better not come, Andrey.

ANDREY. I don't know. After all, they were asked.

NATASHA. This morning, when the little boy woke up and saw me he suddenly smiled; that means he knew me. "Good morning, Bobby!" I said, "good morning, darling." And he laughed. Children understand, they understand very well. So I'll tell them, Andrey dear, not to receive the entertainers.

ANDREY. [*Hesitatingly.*] But what about my sisters. This is their flat.

NATASHA. They'll do as I want them. They are so kind. . . [*Going.*] I ordered sour milk for supper. The doctor says you must eat sour milk and nothing else, or you won't get thin.

[*Stops.*] Bobby is so cold. I'm afraid his room is too cold for him. It would be nice to put him into another room till the warm weather comes. Irina's room, for instance, is just right for a child: it's dry and has the sun all day. I must tell her, she can share Olga's room. . . . It isn't as if she was at home in the daytime, she only sleeps here. . . . [*A pause.*] Andrey, darling, why are you so silent?

ANDREY. I was just thinking. . . . There is really nothing to say. . . .

NATASHA. Yes . . . there was something I wanted to tell you . . . Oh, yes. Ferapont has come from the Council offices, he wants to see you.

ANDREY. [*Yawns.*] Call him here.

NATASHA *goes out;* ANDREY *reads his book, stooping over the candle she has left behind.* FERAPONT *enters; he wears a tattered old coat with the collar up. His ears are muffled.*

ANDREY. Good morning, grandfather. What have you to say?

FERAPONT. The Chairman sends a book and some documents or other. Here. . . . [*Hands him a book and a packet.*]

ANDREY. Thank you. It's all right. Why couldn't you come earlier? It's past eight now.

FERAPONT. What?

ANDREY. [*Louder.*] I say you've come late, it's past eight.

FERAPONT. Yes, yes. I came when it was still light, but they wouldn't let me in. They said you were busy. Well, what was I to do. If you're busy, you're busy, and I'm in no hurry. [*He thinks that* ANDREY *is asking him something.*] What?

ANDREY. Nothing. [*Looks through the book.*] To-morrow's Friday. I'm not supposed to go to work, but I'll come—all the same . . . and do some work. It's dull at home. . . . [*Pause.*] Oh, my dear old man, how strangely life changes, and how it deceives! To-day, out of sheer boredom, I took up this book—old university lectures, and I couldn't help laughing. My God, I'm secretary of the local district council, the council which has Protopopov for its chairman, yes, I'm secretary, and the summit of my ambitions is—to become a member of the council! I to be a member of the local district council, I. who dream every night that I'm a professor of Moscow University, a famous scholar of whom all Russia is proud!

FERAPONT. I can't tell . . . I'm hard of hearing. . . .

ANDREY. If you weren't, I don't suppose I should talk to you. I've got to talk to somebody, and my wife doesn't understand me, and I'm a bit afraid of my sisters—I don't know why unless it is that they may make fun of me and make me feel ashamed . . . I don't drink, I don't like public-houses, but how I should like to be sitting just now in Tyestov's place in Moscow, or at the Great Moscow, old fellow!

FERAPONT. Moscow? That's where a contractor was once telling that some merchants or other were eating pancakes; one ate forty pancakes and he went and died, he was saying. Either forty or fifty, I forget which.

ANDREY. In Moscow you can sit in an enormous restaurant where you don't know anybody and where nobody knows you, and you don't feel all the same that you're a stranger. And here you know everybody and everybody knows you, and you, and you're a stranger . . . and a lonely stranger.

FERAPONT. What? And the same contractor was telling—perhaps he was lying—that there was a cable stretching right across Moscow.

ANDREY. What for?

FERAPONT. I can't tell. The contractor said so.

ANDREY. Rubbish. [*He reads.*] Were you ever in Moscow?

FERAPONT. [*After a pause.*] No, God did not lead me there. [*Pause.*] Shall I go?

ANDREY. You may go. Good-bye. [FERAPONT *goes.*] Good-bye. [*Reads.*] You can come to-morrow and fetch these documents. . . . Go along. . . . [*Pause.*] He's gone. [*A ring.*] Yes, yes. . . . [*Stretches himself and slowly goes into his own room.*]

Behind the scene the nurse is singing a lullaby to the child. MASHA *and* VERSHININ *come in. While they talk, a maidservant lights candles and a lamp.*

MASHA. I don't know. [*Pause.*] I don't know. Of course, habit counts for a great deal. After father's death, for instance, it took us a long time to get used to the absence of orderlies. But, apart from habit, it seems to me in all fairness that, however it may be in other towns, the best and most-educated people are army men.

VERSHININ. I'm thirsty. I should like some tea.

MASHA. [*Glancing at her watch.*] They'll bring some soon. I was given in marriage when I was eighteen, and I was afraid of my husband because he was a teacher and I'd only just left school. He then seemed to me frightfully wise and learned and important.

And now, unfortunately, that has changed.

VERSHININ. Yes . . . yes.

MASHA. I don't speak of my husband, I've grown used to him, but civilians in general are so often course, impolite, uneducated. Their rudeness offends me, it angers me. I suffer when I see that a man isn't quite sufficiently refined, or delicate, or polite. I simply suffer agonies when I happen to be among schoolmasters, my husband's colleagues.

VERSHININ. Yes . . . It seems to me that civilians and army men are equally interesting, in this town, at any rate. It's all the same! If you listen to a member of the local intelligentsia, whether to civilian or military. he will tell you that he's sick of his wife, sick of his house, sick of his estate, sick of his horses. . . . We Russians are extremely gifted in the direction of thinking on an exalted plane, but, tell me, why do we aim so low in real life? Why?

MASHA. Why?

VERSHININ. Why is a Russian sick of his children, sick of his wife? And why are his wife and children sick of him?

MASHA. You're a little downhearted to-day.

VERSHININ. Perhaps I am. I haven't had any dinner, I've had nothing since the morning. My daughter is a little unwell, and when my girls are ill, I get very anxious and my conscience tortures me because they have such a mother. Oh, if you had seen her to-day! What a trivial personality! We began quarrelling at seven in the morning and at nine I slammed the door and went out. [*Pause.*] I never speak of her, it's strange that I bear my complaints to you alone. [*Kisses her hand.*] Don't be angry with me. I haven't anybody but you, nobody at all. . . . [*Pause.*

MASHA. What a noise in the oven. Just before father's death there was a noise in the pipe, just like that.

VERSHININ Are you superstitious?

MASHA. Yes.

VERSHININ. That's strange. [*Kisses her hand.*] You are a splendid, wonderful woman. Splendid, wonderful! It is dark here, but I see your sparkling eyes.

MASHA. [*Sits on another chair.*] There is more light here.

VERSHININ. I love you, love you, love you . . . I love your eyes, your movements, I dream of them. . . . Splendid, wonderful woman!

MASHA. [*Laughing.*] When you talk to me like that, I laugh; I don't know why, for I'm afraid. Don't repeat it, please. . . . [*In an undertone.*] No, go on, it's all the same to me. . . . [*Covers her face with her hands.*] Somebody's coming, let's talk about something else. . . .

IRINA *and* TUZENBACH *come in through the dining-room.*

TUZENBACH. My surname is really triple. I am called Baron Tuzenbach-Krone-Altschauer, but I am Russian and Orthodox, the same as you. There is very little German left in me, unless perhaps it is the patience and the obstinacy with which I bore you. I see you home every night.

IRINA. How tired I am!

TUZENBACH. And I'll come to the telegraph office to see you home every day for ten or twenty years, until you drive me away. [*He sees MASHA and VERSHININ; joyfully.*] Is that you? How do you do.

IRINA. Well, I am home at last. [*To

MASHA.*] A lady came to-day to telegraph to her brother in Saratov that her son died to-day, and she couldn't remember the address anyhow. So she sent the telegram without an address, just to Saratov. She was crying. And for some reason or other I was rude to her. "I've no time," I said. It was so stupid. Are the entertainers coming to-night?

MASHA. Yes.

IRINA. [*Sitting down in an armchair.*] I want rest. I am tired.

TUZENBACH. [*Smiling.*] When you come home from your work you seem so young, and so unfortunate. . . . [*Pause.*]

IRINA. I am tired. No, I don't like the telegraph office, I don't like it.

MASHA. You've grown thinner. . . . [*Whistles a little.*] And you look younger, and your face has become like a boy's.

TUZENBACH. That's the way she does her hair.

IRINA. I must find another job, this one won't do for me. What I wanted, what I hoped to get, just that is lacking here. Labour without poetry, without ideas. . . . [*A knock on the door.*] The doctor is knocking. [*To TUZENBACH.*] Will you knock, dear. I can't . . . I'm tired. . . . [*TUZENBACH knocks.*] He'll come in a minute. Something ought to be done. Yesterday the doctor and Andrey played cards at the club and lost money. Andrey seems to have lost 200 roubles.

MASHA. [*With indifference.*] What can we do now?

IRINA. He lost money a fortnight ago, he lost money in December. Perhaps if he lost everything we should go away from this town. Oh, my God, I dream of Moscow every night. I'm just like a lunatic. [*Laughs.*] We go there in June, and before June there's still . . . February, March, April, May . . . nearly half a year!

MASHA. Only Natasha musn't get to know of these losses.

IRINA. I expect it will be all the same to her.

CHEBUTIKIN, *who has only just got out of bed—he was resting after dinner —comes into the dining-room and combs his beard. He then sits by the table and takes a newspaper from his pocket.*

MASHA. Here he is. . . . Has he paid his rent?

IRINA. [*Laughs.*] No. He's been here eight months and hasn't paid a copeck. Seems to have forgotten.

MASHA. [*Laughs.*] What dignity in his pose! [*They all laugh. A pause.*]

IRINA. Why are you so silent, Alexander Ignateyevitch?

VERSHININ. I don't know. I want some tea. Half my life for a tumbler of tea: I haven't had anything since morning.

CHEBUTIKIN. Irina Sergeyevna!

IRINA. What is it?

CHEBUTIKIN. Please come here, *Venez ici.* [IRINA *goes and sits by the table.*] I can't do without you. [IRINA *begins to play patience.*]

VERSHININ. Well, if we can't have any tea, let's philosophize, at any rate.

TUZENBACH. Yes. let's. About what?

VERSHININ. About what? Let us meditate . . about life as it will be after our time; for example, in two or three hundred years.

TUZENBACH. Well? After our time people will fly about in balloons, the cut of one's coat will change, perhaps they'll discover a sixth sense and develop it, but life will remain the same, laborious, mysterious, and happy. And in a thousand years' time, people will still be sighing: "Life is hard!"—and at the same time they'll be just as afraid of death, and unwilling to meet it, as we are.

VERSHININ. [*Thoughtfully.*] How can I put it? It seems to me that everything on earth must change, little by little, and is already changing under our very eyes. After two or three hundred years, after a thousand—the actual time doesn't matter—a new and happy age will begin. We, of course, shall not take part in it, but we live and work and even suffer to-day that it should come. We create it—and in that one object is our destiny, if you like, our happiness.

MASHA *laughs softly.*

TUZENBACH. What is it?

MASHA. I don't know. I've been laughing all day, ever since morning.

VERSHININ. I finished my education at the same point as you, I have not studied at universities; I read a lot, but I cannot choose my books and perhaps what I read is not at all what I should, but the longer I love, the more I want to know. My hair is turning white, I am nearly an old man now, but I know so little, oh, so little! But I think I know the things that matter most, and that are most real. I know them well. And I wish I could make you understand that there is no happiness for us, that there should not and cannot be. . . . We must only work and work, and happiness is only for our distant posterity. [*Pause.*] If not for me, then for the descendants of my descendants.

FEDOTIK *and* RODE *come into the din-*

ing-room; they sit and sing softly, strumming on a guitar.

TUZENBACH. According to you, one should not even think about happiness! But suppose I am happy!

VERSHININ. No.

TUZENBACH. [*Moves his hands and laughs.*] We do not seem to understand each other. How can I convince you? [MASHA *laughs quietly,* TUZENBACH *continues, pointing at her.*] Yes, laugh! [*To* VERSHININ.] Not only after two or three centuries, but in a million years, life will still be as it was; life does not change, it remains for ever, following its own laws which do not concern us, or which, at any rate, you will never find out. Migrant birds, cranes for example, fly and fly, and whatever thoughts, high or low, enter their heads, they will still fly and not know why or where. They fly and will continue to fly, whatever philosophers come to life among them; they may philosophize as much as they like, only they will fly. . .

MASHA. Still, is there a meaning?

TUZENBACH. A meaning. . . . Now the snow is falling. What meaning? [*Pause.*]

MASHA. It seems to me that a man must have faith, or must search for a faith, or his life will be empty, empty. . . . To live and not know why the cranes fly, why babies are born, why are stars in the sky. . . . Either you must know why you live, or everything is trivial, not worth a straw. [*A pause.*]

VERSHININ. Still, I am sorry that my youth has gone.

MASHA. Gogol says: life in this world is a dull matter, my masters!

TUZENBACH. And I say it's difficult to argue with you, my masters! Hang it all.

CHEBUTIKIN. [*Reading.*] Balzac was married at Berdichev. [IRINA *is singing softly.*] That's worth making note of. [*He makes a note.*] Balzac was married at Berdichev. [*Goes on reading.*]

IRINA. [*Laying out cards, thoughtfully.*] Balzac was married at Berdichev.

TUZENBACH. The die is cast. I've handed in my resignation, Maria Serge-yevna.

MASHA. So I heard. I don't see what good it is; I don't like civilians.

TUZENBACH. Never mind. . . . [*Gets up.*] I'm not handsome; what use am I as a soldier? Well, it makes no difference . . . I shall work. If only just once in my life I could work so that I could come home in the evening, fall exhausted on my bed, and go to sleep at once. [*Going into the dining-room.*] Workmen, I suppose, do sleep soundly!

FEDOTIK. [*To* IRINA.] I bought some coloured pencils for you at Pizhikov's in the Moscow Road, just now. And here is a little knife.

IRINA. You have got into the habit of behaving to me as if I am a little girl, but I am grown up. [*Takes the pencils and the knife, then, with joy.*] How lovely!

FEDOTIK. And I bought myself a knife . . . look at it . . . one blade, another, a third, an ear-scoop, scissors, nail-cleaners. . . .

RODE. [*Loudly.*] Doctor, how old are you?

CHEBUTIKIN. I? Thirty-two [*Laughter.*]

FEDOTIK. I'll show you another kind of patience. . . . [*Lays out cards.*]

A samovar is brought in; ANFISA

attends to it; a little later NATASHA *enters and helps by the table;* SOLENI *arrives and, after greetings, sits by the table.*

VERSHININ. What a wind!

MASHA. Yes. I'm tired of winter. I've already forgotten what summer's like.

IRINA. It's coming out I see. We're going to Moscow.

FEDOTIK. No, it won't come out. Look, the eight was on the two of spades. [*Laughs.*] That means you won't go to Moscow.

CHEBUTIKIN. [*Reading paper.*] Tsitsigar. Smallpox is raging here.

ANFISA. [*Coming up to* MASHA.] Masha, have some tea, little mother. [*To* VERSHININ.] Please have some, sir . . . excuse me, but I've forgotten your name. . . .

MASHA. Bring some here, nurse. I shan't go over there.

IRINA. Nurse!

ANFISA. Coming, coming!

NATASHA. [*To* SOLENI.] Children at the breast understand perfectly. I said "Good morning, Bobby; good morning, dear!" And he looked at me in quite an unusual way. You think it's only the mother in me that is speaking; I assure you that isn't so! He's a wonderful child.

SOLENI. If he was my child I'd roast him on a frying-pan and eat him.

Takes his tumbler into the drawing-room and sits in a corner.

NATASHA. [*Covers her face in her hands.*] Vulgar, ill-bred man!

MASHA. He's lucky who doesn't notice whether it's winter now, or summer. I think that if I were in Moscow, I shouldn't mind about the weather.

VERSHININ. A few days ago I was reading the prison diary of a French minister. He had been sentenced on account of the Panama scandal. With what joy, what delight, he speaks of the birds he saw through the prison windows, which he had never noticed while he was a minister. Now, of course, that he is at liberty, he notices birds no more than he did before. When you go to live in Moscow you'll not notice it, in just the same way. There can be no happiness for us, it only exists in our wishes.

TUZENBACH. [*Takes cardboard box from the table.*] Where are the pastries?

IRINA. Soleni has eaten them.

TUZENBACH. All of them?

ANFISA. [*Serving tea.*] There's a letter for you.

VERSHININ. For me? [*Takes the letter.*] From my daughter. [*Reads.*] Yes, of course . . . I will go quietly. Excuse me, Maria Sergeyevna. I shan't have any tea. [*Stands up, excited.*] That eternal story. . . .

MASHA. What is it? Is it a secret?

VERSHININ. [*Quietly.*] My wife has poisoned herself again. I must go. I'll go out quietly. It's all awfully unpleasant. [*Kisses* MASHA'S *hand.*] My dear, my splendid, good woman . . . I'll go this way, quietly. [*Exit.*]

ANFISA. Where has he gone? And I'd served tea . . . . What a man.

MASHA. [*Angrily.*] Be quiet! You bother so one can't have a moment's peace. . . . [*Goes to the table with her cup.*] I'm tired of you, old woman!

ANFISA. My dear! Why are you offended!

ANDREY'S VOICE. Anfisa!

ANFISA. [*Mocking.*] Anfisa! He sits there and . . . [*Exit.*]

MASHA. [*In the dining-room, by*

the table angrily.] Let me sit down! [*Disturbs the cards on the table.*] Here you are, spreading your cards out. Have some tea!

IRINA. You are cross, Masha.

MASHA. If 1 am cross, then don't talk to me. Don't touch me!

CHEBUTIKIN. Don't touch her, don't touch her. . . .

MASHA. You're sixty, but you're like a boy, always up to some beastly nonsense.

NATASHA. [*Sighs.*] Dear Masha, why use such expressions? With your beautiful exterior you would be simply fascinating in good society, I tell you so directly, if it wasn't for your words. *Je vous prie, pardonnez moi, Maria, mais vous avez des manières un peu gossières.*

TUZENBACH. [*R e s t r a i n i n g his laughter.*] Give me . . . give me . . . there's some cognac, I think.

NATASHA. *Il paraît, que mon Bodick déjà ne dort pas,* he has awakened. He isn't well to-day. I'll go to him, excuse me. . . . [*Exit.*]

IRINA. Where has Alexander Ignateyevitch gone?

MASHA. Home. Something extraordinary has happened to his wife again.

TUZENBACH. [*Goes to* SOLENI *with a cognac-flask in his hands.*] You go on sitting by yourself, thinking of something—goodness knows what. Come and let's make peace. Let's have some cognac. [*They drink.*] I expect I'll have to play the piano all night, some rubbish most likely . . . well, so be it!

SOLENI. Why make peace? I haven't quarrelled with you.

TUZENBACH. You always make me feel as if something has taken place between us. You've a strange character, you must admit.

SOLENI. [*Declaims.*] "I am strange. but who is not? Don't be angry, Aleko!"

TUZENBACH. And what has Aleko to to do with it? [*Pause.*]

SOLENI. When I'm with one other man I behave just like everybody else, but in company I'm dull and shy and . . . talk all manner of rubbish. But I'm more honest and more honourable than very, very many people. And I can prove it.

TUZENBACH. I often get angry with you, you always fasten on to me in company, but I like you all the same. I'm going to drink my fill to-night, whatever happens. Drink, now!

SOLENI. Let's drink. [*They drink.*] I never had anything against you, Baron. But my character is like Lermontov's. [*In a low voice.*] I even rather resemble Lermontov, they say. . . .

Takes a scent-bottle from his pocket, and scents his hands.

TUZENBACH. I've sent in my resignation. Basta! I've been thinking about it for five years, and at last made up my mind. I shall work.

SOLENI [*Declaims.*] "Do not be angry, Aleko . . . forget, forget, thy dreams of yore. . . ."

While he is speaking ANDREY *enters quietly with a book, and sits by the table.*

TUZENBACH. I shall work.

CHEBUTIKIN [*Going with* IRINA *into the dining-room.*] And the food was also real Caucasian onion soup, and, for a roast some chehartma.

SOLENI. Cheremsha isn't meat at all, but a plant something like an onion.

CHEBUTIKIN. No, my angel. Chehartma isn't onion, but roast mutton.

SOLENI. And I tell you, cheremsha—is a sort of onion.

CHEBUTIKIN. And I tell you, che-hartma—is mutton.

SOLENI. And I tell you, cheremsha—is a sort of onion.

CHEBUTIKIN. What's the use of arguing! You've never been in the Caucasus, and never ate any chehartma.

SOLENI. I never ate it, because I hate it. It smells like garlic.

ANDREY. [*Imploring.*] Please, please! I ask you!

TUZENBACH. When are the entertainers coming?

IRINA. They promised for about nine; that is, quite soon.

TUZENBACH. [*Embraces* ANDREY.]
"Oh my house, my house, my new-built house."

ANDREY [*Dances and sings.*]
"Newly-built of maple-wood."

CHEBUTIKIN. [*Dances.*]
"Its walls are like a sieve!"
[*Laughter.*]

TUZENBACH. [*Kisses* ANDREY.] Hang it all, let's drink. Andrey, old boy, let's drink with you. And I'll go with you, Andrey, to the University of Moscow.

SOLENI. Which one? There are two universities in Moscow.

ANDREY. There's one university in Moscow.

SOLENI. Two, I tell you.

ANDREY. Don't care if there are three. So much the better.

SOLENI. There are two universities in Moscow! [*There are murmurs and "hushes."*] There are two universities in Moscow, the old one and the new one. And if you don't like to listen, if my words annoy you, then I need not speak. I can even go into another room. . . . [*Exit.*]

TUZENBACH. Bravo, bravo! [*Laughs.*] Come on, now. I'm going to play. Funny man, Soleni. . . . [*Goes to the piano and plays a waltz.*]

MASHA. [*Dancing solo.*] The Baron's drunk, the Baron's drunk, the Baron's drunk!

NATASHA *comes in.*

NATASHA. [*To* CHEBUTIKIN.] Ivan Romanovitch!

Says something to CHEBUTIKIN, *then goes out quietly;* CHEBUTIKIN *touches* TUZENBACH *on the shoulder and whispers something to him.*

IRINA. What is it?

CHEBUTIKIN. Time for us to go. Good-bye.

TUZENBACH. Good-night. It's time we went.

IRINA. But really the entertainers?

ANDREY. [*In confusion.*] There won't be any entertainers. You see, dear, Natasha says that Bobby isn't quite well, and so. . . . In a word, I don't care, and it's absolutely all one to me.

IRINA [*Shrugging her shoulders.*] Bobby ill!

MASHA. What is she thinking of! Well, if they are sent home, I suppose they must go. [*To* IRINA.] Bobby's all right, it's she herself. . . . Here! [*Taps her forehead.*] Little bourgeoise!

ANDREY *goes to his room through the right-hand door,* CHEBUTIKIN *follows him. In the dining-room they are saying good-bye.*

FEDOTIK. What a shame! I was expecting to spend the evening here, but of course, if the little baby is ill . . . I'll bring him some toys to-morrow.

RODE. [*Loudly.*] I slept late after dinner to-day because I thought I was going to dance all night. It's only nine o'clock now!

MASHA. Let's go into the street, we can talk there. Then we can settle things.

Good-byes and good nights are heard. TUZENBACH'S *merry laughter is heard.* [*All go out.*] ANFISA *and the maid clear the table, and put out the lights.* [*The nurse sings.*] ANDREY, *wearing an overcoat and a hat, and* CHEBUTIKIN *enter silently.*

CHEBUTIKIN. I never managed to get married because my life flashed by like lightning, and because I was madly in love with your mother, who was married.

ANDREY. One shouldn't marry. One shouldn't, because it's dull.

CHEBUTIKIN. So there I am, in my loneliness. Say what you will, loneliness is a terrible thing, old fellow. . . . Though really . . . of course, it absolutely doesn't matter!

ANDREY. Let's be quicker.

CHEBUTIKIN. What are you in such a hurry for? We shall be in time.

ANDREY. I'm afraid my wife may stop me.

CHEBUTIKIN. Ah!

ANDREY. I shan't play to-night, I shall only sit and look on. I don't feel very well. . . . What am I to do for my asthma, Ivan Romanovitch?

CHEBUTIKIN. Don't ask me! I don't remember, old fellow, I don't know.

ANDREY. Let's go through the kitchen. [*They go out.*]

A bell rings, then a second time; voices and laughter are heard.

IRINA. [*Enters.*] What's that?

ANFISA [*Whispers.*] The entertainers! [*Bell.*]

IRINA. Tell them there's nobody at home, nurse. They must excuse us.

ANFISA *goes out.* IRINA *walks about the room deep in thought; she is excited.* SOLENI *enters.*

SOLENI. [*In surprise.*] There's nobody here. . . . Where are they all?

IRINA. They've gone home.

SOLENI. How strange. Are you here alone?

IRINA. Yes, alone. [*A pause.*] Good-bye.

SOLENI. Just now I behaved tactlessly, with insufficient reserve. But you are not like all the others, you are noble and pure, you can see the truth. . . . You alone can understand me. I love you deeply, beyond measure. I love you.

IRINA. Good-bye! Go away.

SOLENI. I cannot live without you. [*Follows her.*] Oh, my happiness! [*Through his tears.*] Oh, joy! Wonderful, marvelous, glorious eyes, such as I have never seen before. . . .

IRINA. [*Coldly.*] Stop it, Vassili Vassilevitch!

SOLENI. This is the first time I speak to you of love, and it is as if I am no longer on the earth, but on another planet. [*Wipes his forehead.*] Well never mind. I can't make you love me by force, of course . . but I don't intend to have any more-favoured rivals. . . . . No . . . I swear to you by all the saints, I shall kill my rival. . . . Oh, beautiful one!

NATASHA *enters with a candle; she looks in through one door, then through another, and goes past the door leading to her husband's room.*

NATASHA. Here's Andrey. Let him go on reading. Excuse me, Vassili Vassilevitch, I did not know you were here; I am engaged in domesticities.

SOLENI. It's all the same to me. Good-bye! [*Exit.*]

NATASHA. You're so tired, my poor dear girl! [*Kisses* IRINA.] If you only went to bed earlier.

IRINA. Is Bobby asleep?

NATASHA. Yes, but restlessly. By the way, dear, I wanted to tell you, but either you weren't at home, or I was busy . . . I think Bobby's present nursery is cold and damp. And your room would be so nice for the child. My dear, darling girl, do change over to Olga's for a bit!

IRINA. [*Not understanding.*] Where? *The bells of a troika are heard as it drives up to the house.*

NATASHA. You and Olga can share a room, for the time being, and Bobby can have yours. He's such a darling; to-day I said to him, "Bobby, you're mine! Mine." And he looked at me with his dear little eyes. [*A bell rings.*] It must be Olga. How late she is! [*The maid enters and whispers to* NATASHA.] Protopopov? What a queer man to do such a thing. Protopopov's come and wants me to go for a drive with him in his troika. [*Laughs.*] How funny these men are. . . . [*A bell rings.*] Somebody has come. Suppose I did go and have half an hour's drive. . . . [*To the maid.*] Say I shan't be long. [*Bell rings.*] Somebody's ringing, it must be Olga. [*Exit.*]

The maid runs out; IRINA *sits deep in thought;* KULIGIN *and* OLGA *enter, followed by* VERSHININ.

KULIGIN. Well, there you are. And you said there was going to be a party.

VERSHININ. It's queer; I went away not long ago, half an hour ago, and they were expecting entertainers.

IRINA. They've all gone.

KULIGIN. Has Masha gone too? Where has she gone? And what's Protopopov waiting for downstairs in his troika? Whom is he expecting?

IRINA. Don't ask questions . . . I'm tired.

KULIGIN. Oh, you're all whimsies. . . .

OLGA. My committee meeting is only just over. I'm tired out. Our charwoman is ill, so I had to take her place. My head, my head is aching. . . . [*Sits.*] Andrey lost 200 roubles at cards yesterday . . the whole town is talking about it. . . .

KULIGIN. Yes, my meeting tired me too. [*Sits.*]

VERSHININ. My wife took it into her head to frighten me just now by nearly poisoning herself. It's all right now, and I'm glad; I can rest now. . . . But perhaps we ought to go away? Well, my best wishes, Feodor Ilitch, let's go somewhere together! I can't, I absolutely can't stop at home. . . . Come on!

KULIGIN. I'm tired. I won't go. [*Gets up.*] I'm tired. Has my wife gone home?

IRINA. I suppose so.

KULIGIN. [*Kisses* IRINA'S *hand.*] Good-bye, I'm going to rest all day to-morrow and the day after. Best wishes! [*Going.*] I should like some tea. I was looking forward to spending the whole evening in pleasant company and—*o, fallacem hominum spem!* . . . Accusative case after an interjection. . .

VERSHININ. Then I'll go somewhere by myself. [*Exit with* KULIGIN, *whistling.*]

OLGA. I've such a headache . . . Andrey has been losing money. . . . The whole town is talking. . . . I'll go and lie down. [*Going.*] I'm free to-morrow. . . . Oh, my God, what a mercy! I'm free to-morrow, I'm free the day after. . . . Oh my head, my head. . . . [*Exit.*]

IRINA. [*Alone.*] *They've all gone.* Nobody's left.

A concertina is being played in the street. The nurse sings.

NATASHA. [*In fur coat and cap, steps across the dining-room, followed by the maid.*] I'll be back in half an hour. I'm only going for a little drive. [*Exit.*]

IRINA. [*Alone in her misery.*] To Moscow! Moscow! Moscow!

CURTAIN

ACT III

The room shared by OLGA *and* IRINA. *Beds, screened off, on the right and left. It is past 2 a. m. Behind the stage a fire-alarm is ringing; it has apparently been going for some time. Nobody in the house has gone to bed yet.* MASHA *is lying on a sofa dressed, as usual, in black. Enter* OLGA *and* ANFISA.

ANFISA. Now they are downstairs, sitting under the stairs. I said to them, "Won't you come up," I said, "You can't go on like this," and they simply cried, "We don't know where father is." They said, "He may be burnt up by now." What an idea! And in the yard there are some people . . . also undressed.

OLGA. [*Takes a dress out of the cupboard.*] Take this grey dress. . . . And this . . . and the blouse as well. . . . Take the skirt, too, nurse. . . . My God! How awful it is! The whole of the Kirsanovsky Road seems to have burned down. Take this . . . and this. . . . [*Throws clothes into her hands.*] The poor Vershinins are so frightened

. . . Their house was nearly burnt. They ought to come here for the night. . . . They shouldn't be allowed to go home. . . . Poor Fedotik is completely burnt out, there's nothing left. . . .

ANFISA. Couldn't you call Ferapont, Olga dear. I can hardly manage. . . .

OLGA. [*Rings.*] They'll never answer. [*At the door.*] Come here, whoever there is! [*Through the open door can be seen a window, red with flame: a fire-engine is heard passing the house.*] How awful this is. And how I'm sick of it! [FERAPONT *enters.*] Take these things down. . . . The Kolotilin girls are down below . . . and let them have them. This too. . . .

FERAPONT. Yes'm. In the y e a r twelve Moscow was burning too. Oh, my God! The Frenchmen were surprised.

OLGA. Go on, go on. . . .

FERAPONT. Yes'm. [*Exit.*]

OLGA. Nurse, dear, let them have everything. We don't want anything. Give it all to them, nurse. . . . I'm tired, I can hardly keep on my legs. . . . The Vershinins mustn't be allowed to go home. . . . The girls can sleep in the drawing-room, and Alexander Ignateyevitch can go downstairs to the Baron's flat . . . Fedotik can go there, too, or else into our dining-room. . . . The doctor is drunk, beastly drunk, as if on purpose, so nobody can go to him. Vershinin's wife, too, may go into the drawing-room.

ANFISA. [*Tired.*] Olga, dear girl, don't dismiss me! Don't dismiss me!

OLGA. You're talking nonsense, nurse. Nobody is dismissing you.

ANFISA. [*Puts* OLGA's *head against her bosom.*] My dear, precious girl, I'm working, I'm toiling away . . . I'm growing weak, and they'll all say go away! And where shall I go? Where? I'm eighty. Eighty-one years old. . . .

OLGA. You sit down, nurse dear. . . . You're tired, poor dear. . . . [*Makes her sit down.*] Rest, dear. You're so pale!

NATASHA *comes in.*

NATASHA. They are saying that a committee to assist the sufferers from the fire must be formed at once. What do you think of that? It's a beautiful idea. Of course the poor ought to be helped, it's the duty of the rich. Bobby and little Sophy are sleeping, sleeping as if nothing at all was the matter. There's such a lot of people here, the place is full of them, wherever you go. There's influenza in the town now. I'm afraid the children may catch it.

OLGA. [*Not attending.*] In this room we can't see the fire, it's quiet here. . . .

NATASHA. Yes . . . I suppose I'm all untidy. [*Before the looking-glass.*] They say I'm growing stout . . . it isn't true! Certainly it isn't! Masha's asleep; the poor thing is tired out. . . . [*Coldly, to* ANFISA.] Don't dare to be seated in my presence! Get up! Out of this! [*Exit* ANFISA; *a pause.*] I don't understand what makes you keep on that old woman!

OLGA. [*Confusedly.*] Excuse me, I don't understand either . . .

NATASHA. She's no good here. She comes from the country, she ought to live there. . . . Spoiling her, I call it! I like order in the house! We don't want any unnecessary people here. [*Strokes her cheek.*] You're tired, poor thing! Our head mistress is tired! And when my little Sophie grows up and goes to school I shall be so afraid of you.

OLGA. I shan't be head mistress.

NATASHA. They'll appoint you, Olga. It's settled.

OLGA. I'll refuse the post. I can't . . . I'm not strong enough. . . . [*Drinks water.*] You were so rude to nurse just now . . . I'm sorry. I can't stand it . . . everything seems dark in front of me . . . .

NATASHA. [*Excited.*] Forgive me, Olga, forgive me . . . I didn't want to annoy you.

MASHA *gets up, takes pillow and goes out angrily.*

OLGA. Remember, dear . . . we have been brought up, in an unusual way, perhaps, but I can't bear this. Such behaviour has a bad effect on me, I get ill . . . I simply lose heart!

NATASHA. Forgive me, forgive me. . . . [*Kisses her.*]

OLGA. Even the least bit of rudeness, the slightest impoliteness, upsets me.

NATASHA. I often say too much, it's true, but you must agree, dear, that she could just as well live in the country.

OLGA. She has been with us for thirty years.

NATASHA. But she can't do any work now. Either I don't understand, or you don't want to understand me. She's no good for work, she can only sleep or sit about.

OLGA. And let her sit about.

NATASHA. [*Surprised.*] What do you mean? She's only a servant. [*Crying.*] I don't understand you, Olga. I've got a nurse, a wet-nurse, we've a cook, a housemaid . . . what do we want that old woman for as well? What good is she? [*Fire-alarm behind the stage.*]

OLGA. I've grown ten years older to-night.

NATASHA. We must come to an agreement, Olga. Your place is the school, mine—the home. You devote yourself to teaching, I, to the household. And if I talk about servants, then I do know what I am talking about; I do know what I am talking about. . . . . And to-morrow there's to be no more of that old thief, that old hag . . . [*Stamping*] that witch! And don't you dare to annoy me! Don't you dare! [*Stopping short.*] Really, if you don't move downstairs, we shall always be quarrelling. This is awful.

Enter KULIGIN.

KULIGIN. Where's Masha? It's time we went home. The fire seems to be going down. [*Stretches himself.*] Only one block has burnt down. but there was such a wind that it seemed at first the whole town was going to burn. [*Sits.*] I'm tired out. My dear Olga . . . I often think that if it hadn't been for Masha, I should have married you. You are awfully nice. . . . I am absolutely tired out. [*Listens.*]

OLGA. What is it?

KULIGIN. The doctor, of course, has been drinking hard; he's terribly drunk. He might have done it on purpose! [*Gets up.*] He seems to be coming here. . . . Do you hear him? Yes, here. . . . [*Laughs.*] What a man . . . really . . . I'll hide myself. [*Goes to the cupboard and stands in the corner.*] What a rogue.

OLGA. He hadn't touched a drop for two years, and now he suddenly goes and gets drunk. . . .

[*Retires with* NATASHA *to the back of the room.*]

CHEBUTIKIN *enters; apparently sober, he stops, looks round, then goes to the wash-stand and begins to wash his hands.*

CHEBUTIKIN. [*Angrily.*] Devil take them all . . . take them all. . . . They think I'm a doctor and can cure everything, and I know abolutely nothing, I've forgotten all I ever knew, I remember nothing, absolutely nothing. [OLGA *and* NATASHA *go out, unnoticed by him.*] Devil take it. Last Wednesday I attended a woman in Zasip—and she died, and it's my fault that she died. Yes . . . I used to know a certain amount five-and-twenty years ago, but I don't remember anything now. Nothing. Perhaps I'm not really a man, and am only pretending that I've got arms and legs and a head; perhaps I don't exist at all, and only imagine that I walk, and eat, and sleep. [*Cries.*] Oh, if only I didn't exist! [*Stops crying; angrily.*] The devil only knows. . . . Day before yesterday they were talking in the club; they said, Shakespeare, Voltaire . . I'd never read, never read at all, and I put on an expression as if I had read. And so did the others. Oh, how beastly! How petty! And then I remembered the woman I killed on Wednesday . . . and I couldn't get her out of my mind, and everything in my mind became crooked, nasty, wretched. . . So I went and drank. . . .

IRINA, VERSHININ *and* TUZENBACH *enter;* TUZENBACH *is wearing new and fashionable civilian clothes.*

IRINA. Let's sit down here. Nobody will come in here.

VERSHININ. The whole town would have been destroyed if it hadn't been for the soldiers. Good men! [*Rubs his hands appreciatively.*] Splendid people! Oh, what a fine lot!

KULIGIN. [*Coming up to him.*] What's the time?

TUZENBACH. It's past three now. It's dawning.

IRINA. They are all sitting in the dining-room, nobody is going. And that Soleni of yours is sitting there. . . . [*To* CHEBUTIKIN.] Hadn't you better be going to sleep, doctor?

CHEBUTIKIN. It's all right . . . thank you. . . . [*Combs his beard.*]

KULIGIN. [*Laughs.*] Speaking's a bit difficult, eh, Ivan Romanovitch! [*Pats him on the shoulder.*] Good man! *In vino veritas*, the ancients used to say.

TUZENBACH. They keep on asking me to get up a concert in aid of the sufferers.

IRINA. As if one could do anything. . . .

TUZENBACH. It might be arranged, if necessary. In my opinion Maria Sergeyevna is an excellent pianist.

KULIGIN. Yes, excellent!

IRINA. She's forgotten everything. She hasn't played for three years . . . or four.

TUZENBACH. In this town absolutely nobody understands music, not a soul except myself, but I do understand it, and assure you on my word of honour that Maria Sergeyevna plays excellently, almost with genius.

KULIGIN. You are right, Baron, I'm awfully fond of Masha. She's very fine.

TUZENBACH. To be able to play so admirably and to realize at the same time that nobody, nobody can understand you!

KULIGIN. [*Sighs.*] Yes. . . . But will it be quite all right for her to take part in a concert? [*Pause.*] You see, I don't know anything about it. Perhaps it will even be all to the good. Although I must admit that our Director is a good man, a very good man even, a very clever man, still he has such views . .

Of course it isn't his business but still if you wish it, perhaps I'd better talk to him.

CHEBUTIKIN *takes a porcelain clock into his hands and examines it.*

VERSHININ. I got so dirty while the fire was on, I don't look like anybody on earth. [*Pause.*] Yesterday I happened to hear, casually, that they want to transfer our brigade to some distant place. Some said to Poland, others, to Chita.

TUZENBACH. I heard so, too. Well, if it is so, the town will be quite empty.

IRINA. And we'll go away, too!

CHEBUTIKIN. [*Drops the clock which breaks to pieces.*] To smithereens!

A pause; everybody is pained and confused.

KULIGIN. [*Gathering up the pieces.*] To smash such a valuable object—oh, Ivan Romanovitch, Ivan Romanovitch! A very bad mark for your misbehaviour!

IRINA. That clock used to belong to our mother.

CHEBUTIKIN. Perhaps. . . To your mother, your mother. Perhaps I didn't break it; it only looks as if I broke it. Perhaps we only think that we exist, when really we don't. I don't know anything, nobody knows anything. [*At the door.*] What are you looking at? Natasha has a little romance with Protopopov, and you don't see it. . . . There you sit and see nothing, and Natasha has a little romance with Protopopov. . . . [*Sings.*] Won't you please accept this date. . . . [*Exit.*]

VERSHININ. Yes. [*Laughs*] How strange everything really is! [*Pause.*] When the fire broke out, I hurried off home; when I get there I see the house is whole, uninjured, and in no danger, but my two girls are standing by the door in just their underclothes, their mother isn't there, the crowd is excited, horses and dogs are running about, and the girls' faces are so agitated, terrified, beseeching, and I don't know what else. My heart was pained when I saw those faces. My God, I thought, what these girls will have to put up with if they live long! I caught them up and ran, and still kept on thinking the one thing: what they will have to live through in this world! [*Fire-alarm; a pause.*] I come here and find their mother shouting and angry. [MASHA *enters with a pillow and sits on the sofa.*] And when my girls were standing by the door in just their underclothes, and the street was red from the fire, there was a dreadful noise, and I thought that something of the sort used to happen many years ago when an enemy made a sudden attack, and looted, and burned. . . . And at the same time what a difference there really is between the present and the past! And when a little more time has gone by, in two or three hundred years perhaps, people will look at our present life with just the same fear, and the same contempt, and the whole past will seem clumsy and dull, and very uncomfortable, and strange. Oh, indeed, what a life there will be, what a life! [*Laughs.*] Forgive me, I've dropped into philosophy again. Please let me continue. I do awfully want to philosophize, it's just how I feel at present. [*Pause.*] As if they are all asleep. As I was saying: what a life there will be! Only just imagine. . . . There are only three persons like yourselves in the town just now, but in future generations there will be more and more, and still more. and the time will come when everything will change and become as

you would have it, people will live as you do, and then you too will go out of date; people will be born who are better than you. . . . [*Laughs.*] Yes, to-day I am quite exceptionally in the vein. I am devilishly keen on living. . . . [*Sings.*]

"The power of love all ages know,
    From its assaults great good does
        grow."

[*Laughs.*]

MASHA. Trum-tum-tum . . .

VERSHININ. Tum-tum . .

MASHA. Tra-ra-ra?

VERSHININ. Tra-ta-ta.

[*Enter* FEDOTIK.]

FEDOTIK. [*Dancing.*] I'm burnt out, I'm burnt out! Down to the ground! [*Laughter.*]

IRINA. I don't see anything funny about it. Is everything burnt?

FEDOTIK. [*Laughs.*] Absolutely. Nothing left at all. The guitar's burnt, and the photographs are burnt, and all my correspondence. . . . And I was going to make you a present of a note-book, and that's burnt too.

[SOLENI *comes in.*]

IRINA. No, you can't come here, Vassili Vassilevitch. Please go away.

SOLENI. Why can the Baron come here and I can't?

VERSHININ. We really must go. How's the fire.

SOLENI. They say it's going down. No, I absolutely don't see why the Baron can, and I can't? [*Scents his hands.*]

VERSHININ. Trum-tum-tum.

MASHA. Trum-tum.

VERSHININ. [*Laughs to* SOLINI.] Let's go into the dining-room.

SOLENI. Very well, we'll make a note of it. "If I should try to make this clear, the geese would be annoyed, I fear." [*Looks at* TUZENBACH.] There, there, there. . . .

[*Goes out with* VERSHININ *and* FEDOTIC.]

IRINA. How Soleni smelt of tobacco. . . . [*In surprise.*] The Baron's asleep! Baron! Baron!

TUZENBACH. [*Waking.*] I am tired, I must say. . . . The brickworks. . . . No, I'm not wandering, I mean it; I'm going to start work soon at the brickworks . . . I've already talked it over. [*Tenderly, to* IRINA.] You're so pale, and beautiful, and charming. . . . Your paleness seems to shine through the dark air as if it was a light. . . . You are sad, displeased with life. . . . Oh, come with me, let's go and work together!

MASHA. Nicolai Lvovitch, go away from here.

TUZENBACH. [*Laughs.*] Are you here? I didn't see you. [*Kisses* IRINA's *hand.*] Good-bye, I'll go . . . I look at you now and I remember, as if it was long ago, your name to-day, when you, cheerfully and merrily, were talking about the joys of labour. . . . And how happy life seemed to me, then! What has happened to it now? [*Kisses her hand.*] There are tears in your eyes. Go to bed now; it is already day . . . the morning begins. . . . If only I was allowed to give my life for you!

MASHA. Nicolai Lvovitch, go away! What business . . .

TUZENBACH. I'm off. [*Exit.*]

MASHA. [*Lies down.*] Are you asleep, Feodor?

KULIGIN. Eh?

MASHA. Shouldn't you go home.

KULIGIN. My dear Masha, my darling Masha. . . .

IRINA. She's tired out. You might let her rest, Fedia.

KULIGIN. I'll go at once. My wife's a good, splendid . . . I love you, my only one. . . .

MASHA. [*Angrily.*] Amo, amas. amat, amamus, amatis, amant.

KULIGIN. [*Laughs.*] No, she really is wonderful. I've been your husband seven years, and it seems as if I was only married yesterday. On my word. No, you really are a wonderful woman. I'm satisfied, I'm satisfied, I'm satisfied!

MASHA. I'm bored, I'm bored, I'm bored. . . . [*Sits up.*] But I can't get it out of my head. . . . It's simply disgraceful. It has been gnawing away at me . . . I can't keep silent. I mean about Andrey. . . . He has mortgaged this house with the bank, and his wife has got all the money; but the house doesn't belong to him alone, but to the four of us! He ought to know that, if he's an honorable man.

KULIGIN. What's the use, Masha? Andrey is in debt all round; well, let him do as he pleases.

MASHA. It's disgraceful, anyway. [*Lies down.*]

KULIGIN. You and I are not poor. I work, take my classes, give private lessons . . . I am a plain, honest man . . . Omnia mea mecum porto, as they say.

MASHA. I don't want anything, but the unfairness of it disgusts me. [*Pause.*] You go, Feodor.

KULIGIN. [*Kisses her.*] You're tired, just rest for half an hour, and I'll sit and wait for you. Sleep. . . . [*Going.*] I'm satisfied, I'm satisfied, I'm satisfied. [*Exit.*]

IRINA. Yes, really, our Andrey has grown smaller; how he's snuffed out and aged with that woman! He used to want to be a professor, and yesterday he was boasting that at last he had been made a member of the district council. He is a member, and Protopopov is chairman. . . The whole town talks and laughs about it, and he alone knows and sees nothing. . . . And now everybody's gone to look at the fire, but he sits alone in his room and pays no attention, only just plays on his fiddle. [*Nervily.*] Oh, it's awful, awful, awful. [*Weeps.*] I can't, I can't bear it any longer! . . . I can't, I can't! . . . [OLGA *comes in and clears up at her little table.* IRINA *is sobbing loudly.*] Throw me out, throw me out, I can't bear any more!

OLGA. [*Alarmed.*] What is it, what is it? Dear!

IRENA. [*Sobbing.*] Where? Where has everything gone? Where is it all? Oh my God, my God! I've forgotten everything, everything . . . I don't remember what is the Italian for window or, well, for ceiling . . . I forget everything, every day I forget it, and life passes and will never return, and we'll never go away to Moscow . . . I see that we'll never go. . . .

OLGA. Dear, dear. . . .

IRINA. [*Controlling herself.*] Oh, I am unhappy . . . I can't work, I shan't work. Enough, enough! I used to be a telegraphist, now I work at the town council offices, and I have nothing but hate and contempt for all they give me to do . . . I am already twenty-three, I have already been at work for a long while, and my brain has dried up, and I've grown thinner, plainer, older, and there is no relief of any sort, and time goes and it seems all the while as if I am going away from the real, the beautiful life, further and further away, down some precipice. I'm in despair and I can't understand how it is that I am still alive, that I haven't killed myself.

OLGA. Don't cry, dear girl, don't cry . . . I suffer, too.

IRINA. I'm not crying, not crying. . . . Enough. . . . Look, I'm not crying any more. Enough . . . enough!

OLGA. Dear, I tell you as a sister and a friend, if you want my advice, marry the Baron. [IRINA *cries softly.*] You respect him, you think highly of him. . . . It is true that he is not handsome, but he is so honorable and clean . . . people don't marry from love, but in order to do one's duty. I think so, at any rate, and I'd marry without being in love. Whoever he was, I should marry him, so long as he was a decent man. Even if he was old. . . .

IRINA. I was always waiting until we should be settled in Moscow, there I should meet my true love; I used to think about him, and love him. . . But it's all turned out to be nonsense, all nonsense. . . .

OLGA. [*Embraces her sister.*] My dear, beautiful sister, I understand everything; when Baron Nicolai Lvovitch left the army and came in evening dress, he seemed so bad-looking to me that I even started crying . . He asked, "What are you crying for?" How could I tell him! But if God brought him to marry you, I should be happy. That would be different, quite different.

NATASHA *with a candle walks across the stage from right to left without saying anything.*

MASHA. [*Sitting up.*] She walks as if she's set something on fire.

OLGA. Masha, you're silly, you're the silliest of the family. Please forgive me for saying so. [*Pause.*]

MASHA. I want to make a confession, dear sisters. My soul is in pain. I will confess to you, and never again to anybody . . . I'll tell you this minute. [*Softly.*] It's my secret but you must know everything . . . I can't be silent. . . . [*Pause.*] I love, I love . . . I love that man. . . . You saw him only just now. . . . Why don't I say it . . . in one word. I love Vershinin.

OLGA. [*Goes behind her screen.*] Stop that, I don't hear you in any case.

MASHA. What am I to do? [*Takes her head in her hands.*] First he seemed queer to me, then I was sorry for him . . . then I fell in love with him . . . fell in love with his voice. his words, his misfortunes, his two daughters.

OLGA. [*Behind the screen.*] I'm not listening. You may talk any nonsense you like, it will be all the same. I shan't hear.

MASHA. Oh, Olga, you are foolish. I am in love—that means that is to be my fate. It means that is to be my lot. . . . And he loves me. . . . It is all awful. Yes; it isn't good, is it? [*Takes* IRINA'S *hand and draws her to her.*] Oh, my dear. . . . How are we going to live through our lives, what is to become of us. . . . When you read a novel it all seems so old and easy, but when you fall in love yourself, then you learn that nobody knows anything, and each must decide for himself. . . . My dear ones, my sisters . . . I've confessed, now I shall keep silence. . . . Like the lunatics in Gogol's story, I'm going to be silent . . . silent. . . .

ANDREY *enters, followed by* FERAPONT

ANDREY. [*Angrily.*] What do you want? I don't understand.

FERAPONT. [*At the door, impatiently.*] I've already told you ten times, Andrey Sergeyevitch.

ANDREY. In the first place I'm not Andrey Sergeyevitch, but sir.

FERAPONT. The firemen, sir, ask if they can go across your garden to the river. Else they go right round, right round; it's a nuisance.

ANDREY. All right. Tell them it's all right. [*Exit* FERAPONT.] I'm tired of them. Where is Olga? [*Olga comes out from behind the screen.*] I came to you for the key of the cupboard. I lost my own. You've got a little key. [OLGA *gives him the key;* IRINA *goes behind her screen; pause.*] What a huge fire! It's going down now. Hang it all, that Ferapont made me so angry that I talked nonsense to him. . . . Sir, indeed. . . . [*A pause.*] Why are you so silent, Olga? [*Pause.*] It's time you stopped all that nonsense and behaved as if you were properly alive. . . . You are here, Masha. Irina is here, well, since we're all here, let's come to a complete understanding, once and for all. What have you against me? What is it?

OLGA. Please don't, Andrey dear. We'll talk to-morrow. [*Excited.*] What an awful night!

ANDREY. [*Much confused.*] Don't excite yourself. I ask you in perfect calmness; what have you against me? Tell me straight.

VERSHININ'S VOICE. Trum-tum-tum!

MASHA. [*Stands; loudly.*] Tra-ta-ta! [*To* OLGA.] Good-bye, Olga, God bless you. [*Goes behind screen and kisses* IRENA.] Sleep well. . . . Good-bye, Andrey. Go away now, they're tired

. . you can explain to-morrow. . . . [*Exit.*]

ANDREY. I'll only say this and go. Just now. . . . In the first place, you've got something against Natasha, my wife; I've noticed it since the very day of my marriage. Natasha is a beautiful and honest creature, straight and honourable—that's my opinion. I love and respect my wife; understand it, I respect her, and I insist that others should respect her too. I repeat, she's an honest and honourable person, and all your disapproval is simply silly. . . . [*Pause.*] In the second place, you seem to be annoyed because I am not a professor, and I am not engaged in study. But I work for the zemstvo, I am a member of the district council, and I consider my service as worthy and as high as the service of science. I am a member of the district council, and I am proud of it, if you want to know. . . . [*Pause.*] In the third place, I have still this to say . . . that I have mortgaged the house without obtaining your permission. . . . For that I am to blame, and ask to be forgiven. My debts led me into doing it . . . thirty-five thousand . . . I do not play at cards any more. I stopped long ago, but the chief thing I have to say in my defence is that you girls receive a pension, and I don't . . . my wages, so to speak. . . . [*Pause.*]

KULIGIN. [*At the door.*] Is Masha there? [*Excitedly.*] Where is she? It's queer. . . . [*Exit.*]

ANDREY. They don't hear. Natasha is a splendid, honest person. [*Walks about in silence, then stops.*] When I married I thought we should be happy . . . all of us. . . . But, my God. . . . [*Weeps.*] My dear, dear sisters, don't

believe me, don't believe me. . . . [*Exit.*]

Fire-alarm. The stage is clear.

IRINA. [*Behind her screen.*] Olga, who's knocking on the floor?

OLGA. It's doctor Ivan Romanovitch. He's drunk.

IRINA. What a restless night! [*Pause.*] Olga! [*Looks out.*] Did you hear? They are taking the brigade away from us; it's going to be transferred to some place far away.

OLGA. It's only a rumour.

IRINA. Then we shall be left alone. . . . Olga!

OLGA. Well?

IRINA. My dear, darling sister, I esteem, I highly value the Baron, he's a splendid man; I'll marry him, I'll consent, only let's go to Moscow! I implore you, let's go! There's nothing better than Moscow on earth! Let's go, Olga, let's go!

CURTAIN

ACT IV

The old garden at the house of the PROSOROVS. *There is a long avenue of firs, at the end of which the river can be seen. There is a forest on the far side of the river. On the right is the terrace of the house: bottles and tumblers are on a table here; it is evident that champagne has just been drunk. It is midday. Every now and again passers-by walk across the garden, from the road to the river; five soldiers go past rapidly.* CHEBUTIKIN, *in a comfortable frame of mind which does not desert him throughout the act, sits in an armchair in the garden, waiting to be called. He wears a peaked cap and has a stick.* IRINA, KULIGIN *with a cross hanging from his neck and without his moustaches, and* TUZENBACH *are standing on the terrace seeing off* FEDOTIK *and* RODE, *who are coming down into the garden; both officers are in service uniform.*

TUZENBACH. [*Exchanges kisses with* FEDOTICK.] You're a good sort, we got on so well together. [*Exchanges kisses with* RODE.] Once again. . . . Good-bye, old man!

IRINA. Au revoir!

FEDOTIK. It isn't au revoir, it's good-bye; we'll never meet again!

KULIGIN. Who knows! [*Wipes his eyes; smiles.*] Here I've started crying!

IRINA. We'll meet again sometime.

FEDOTIK. After ten years—or fifteen? We'll hardly know one another then; we'll say, "How do you do?" coldly. . . . [*Takes a snapshot.*] Keep still. . . . Once more, for the last time.

RODE. [*Embracing* TUZENBACH.] We shan't meet again. . . . [*Kisses* IRINA'S *hand.*] Thank you for everything, for everything!

FEDOTIK. [*Grieved.*] Don't be in such a hurry!

TUZENBACH. We shall meet again, if God wills it. Write to us. Be sure to write.

RODE. [*Looking round the garden.*] Good-bye, trees! [*Shouts.*] Yo-ho! [*Pause.*] Good-bye, echo!

KULIGIN. Best wishes. Go and get yourselves wives there in Poland. . . . Your Polish wife will clasp you and call you "kochanku!" [*Laughs.*]

FEDOTIK. [*Looking at the time.*] There's less than an hour left. Soleni is the only one of our battery who is going on the barge; the rest of us are going with the main body. Three batteries are leaving to-day, another three to-morrow and then the town will be quiet and peaceful.

TUZENBACH. And terribly dull.

RODE. And where is Maria Sergeyevna?

KULIGIN. Masha is in the garden.

FEDOTIK. We'd like to say good-bye to her.

RODE. Good-bye, I must go, or else I'll start weeping. . . . [*Quickly embraces* KULIGIN *and* TUZENBACH, *and kisses* IRINA'S *hand.*] We've been so happy here. . . .

FEDOTIK. [*To* KULIGIN.] Here's a keepsake for you . . . a note-book with a pencil. . . . We'll go to the river from here. . . . [*They go aside and both look round.*]

RODE. [*Shouts.*] Yo-ho!

KULIGIN. [*Shouts.*] Good-bye.

At the back of the stage FEDOTIK *and* RODE *meet* MASHA; *they say good-bye and go out with her.*

IRINA. They've gone. . . . [*Sits on the bottom step of the terrace.*]

CHEBUTIKIN. And they forgot to say good-bye to me.

IRINA. But why is that?

CHEBUTIKIN. I just forgot, somehow. Though I'll soon see them again, I'm going to-morrow. Yes . . . just one day left. I shall be retired in a year, then I'll come here again and finish my life near you. I've only one year before I get my pension. . . . [*Puts one newspaper into his pocket and takes another out.*] I'll come here to you and change my life radically . . . I'll be so quiet . . . so agree . . . agreeable, respectable. . . .

IRINA. Yes, you ought to change your life, dear man, somehow or other.

CHEBUTIKIN. Yes, I feel it. [*Sings softly.*]

"Tarara-boom-deay. . . ."

KULIGIN. We won't reform Ivan Romanovitch! We won't reform him!

CHEBUTIKIN. If only I was apprenticed to you! Then I'd reform.

IRINA. Feodor has shaved his moustache! I can't bear to look at him.

KULIGIN. Well, what about it?

CHEBUTIKIN. I could tell you what your face looks like now, but it wouldn't be polite.

KULIGIN. Well! It's the custom, it's *modus vivendi.* Our Director is clean-shaven, and so I too, when I received my inspectorship, had my moustaches removed. Nobody likes it, but it's all one to me. I'm satisfied. Whether I've got moustaches or not, I'm satisfied. . . . [*Sits.*]

At the back of the stage ANDREY *is wheeling a perambulator containing a sleeping infant.*

IRINA. Ivan Romanovitch, be a darling. I'm awfully worried. You were out on the boulevard last night; tell me, what happened?

CHEBUTIKIN. What h a p p e n e d ? Nothing. Q u i t e a trifling matter. [*Reads paper.*] Of no importance!

KULIGIN. They say that Soleni and the Baron met yesterday on the boulevard near the theatre. . . .

TUZENBACH. Stop! What right. . . . [*Waves his hand and goes into the house.*]

KULIGIN. Near the theatre . . . Soleni started behaving offensively to the Baron, who lost his temper and said something nasty. . . .

CHEBUTIKIN. I don't know. It's all bunkum.

KULIGIN. At some seminary or other a master wrote "bunkum" on an essay, and the student couldn't make the letters out—thought it was a Latin word "luckum." [*Laughs.*] Awfully funny, that. They say that Soleni is in love with Irina and hates the Baron. . . . That's quite natural. Irina is a very nice girl. She's even like Masha, she's so thoughtful. . . . Only, Irina, your character is gentler. Though Masha's character, too, is a very good one. I'm very fond of Masha.

[*Shouts of "Yo-ho!" are heard behind the stage.*]

IRINA. [*Shudders.*] Everything seems to frighten me today. [*Pause.*] I've got everything ready, and I send my things off after dinner. The Baron and I will be married to-morrow, and to-morrow we go away to the brickworks, and the next day I go to school, and the new life begins. God will help me! When I took my examination for the teacher's post, I actually wept for joy and gratitude. . . . [*Pause.*] The cart will be here in a minute for my things. . . .

KULIGIN. Somehow or other, all this doesn't seem at all serious. As if it was all ideas, and nothing really serious. Still, with all my soul I wish you happiness.

CHEBUTIKIN. [*With deep feeling.*] My splendid . . . my dear, precious girl. . . . You've gone on far ahead, I won't catch up with you. I'm left behind like a migrant bird grown old, and unable to fly. Fly, my dear, fly, and God be with you! [*Pause.*] It's a pity you shaved your moustaches, Feodor Ilitch.

KULIGIN. Oh, drop it! [*Sighs.*] To-day the soldiers will be gone, and everything will go on as in the old days. Say what you will, Masha is a good, honest woman. I love her very much, and thank my fate for her. People have such different fates. There's a Kosirev who works in the excise department here. He was at school with me; he was expelled from the fifth class of the High School for being entirely unable to understand *ut consecutivum*. He's awfully hard up now and in very poor health, and when I meet him I say to him, "How do you do, *ut consecutivum*." "Yes," he says, "precisely *consecutivum* . . ." and coughs. But I've been successful all my life, I'm happy, and I even have a Stanislaus Cross, of the second class, and now I myself teach others that *ut consecutivum*. Of course, I'm a clever man, much cleverer than many, but happiness doesn't only lie in that. . . .

"The Maiden's Prayer" is being played on the piano in the house.

IRINA. To-morrow night I shan't hear that "Maiden's Prayer" any more, and I shan't be meeting Protopopov. . . . [*Pause.*] Protopopov is sitting there in the drawing-room; and he came to-day. . . .

KULIGIN. Hasn't the head-mistress come yet?

IRINA. No. She has been sent for. If you only knew how difficult it is for me to live alone, without Olga. . . . She lives at the High School; she, a head-mistress, busy all day with her affairs and I'm alone, bored, with nothing to do, and hate the room I live in. . . . I've made up my mind; if I can't live in Moscow, then it must come to this. It's fate. It can't be helped. It's all the will of God, that's the truth. Nicolai Lvovitch made me a proposal. . . . Well? I thought it over and made up my mind. He's a good man . . . it's quite remarkable how good he is. . . . And suddenly my soul put out wings, I became happy, and light-hearted, and once again the desire for work, work, came over me. . . . Only something happened yesterday, some secret dread has been hanging over me. . . .

CHEBUTIKIN. Luckum. Rubbish.

NATASHA. [*At the window.*] The head-mistress.

KULIGIN. The head-mistress has come. Let's go.

[*Exit with* IRINA *into the house.*]

CHEBUTIKIN. "It is my washing day. . . . Tara-ra . . . boom-deay."

MASHA *approaches,* ANDREY *is wheeling a perambulator at the back.*

MASHA. Here you are, sitting here, doing nothing.

CHEBUTIKIN. What then?

MASHA. [*Sits.*] Nothing. . . . [*Pause.*] Did you love my mother?

CHEBUTIKIN. Very much.

MASHA. And did she love you?

CHEBUTIKIN. [*After a pause.*] I don't remember that.

MASHA. Is my man here? When our cook Martha used to ask about her gendarme, she used to say my man. Is he here?

CHEBUTIKIN. Not yet.

MASHA. When you take your happiness in little bits, in snatches, and then lose it, as I have done, you gradually get coarser, more bitter. [*Points to her bosom.*] I'm boiling in here. . . . [*Looks at* ANDREY *with the perambulator.*] There's our brother Andrey. . . . All our hopes in him have gone. There was once a great bell, a thousand persons were hoisting it, much money and labour had been spent on it, when it suddenly fell and was broken. Suddenly, for no particular reason. . . . Andrey is like that. . . .

ANDREY. When are they going to

stop making such a noise in the house? It's awful.

CHEBUTIKIN. They won't be much longer. [*Looks at his watch.*] My watch is very old-fashioned, it strikes the hours. . . . [*Winds the watch and makes it strike.*] The first, second, and fifth batteries are to leave at one o'clock precisely. [*Pause.*] And I go to-morrow.

ANDREY. For good?

CHEBUTIKIN. I don't know. Perhaps I'll return in a year The devil only knows . . . it's all one. . . .

[*Somewhere a harp and violin are being played.*]

ANDREY. The town will grow empty. It will be as if they put a cover over it. [*Pause.*] Something happened yesterday by the theater. The whole town knows of it, but I don't.

CHEBUTIKIN. Nothing. A silly little affair. Soleni started irritating the Baron, who lost his temper and insulted him, and so at last Soleni had to challenge him. [*Looks at his watch.*] It's about time, I think. . . . At half-past twelve. in the public wood, that one you can see from here across the river. . . . Piff-paff. [*Laughs.*] Soleni thinks he's Lermontov, and even writes verses. That's all very well, but this is his third duel.

MASHA. Whose?

CHEBUTIKIN. Soleni's.

MASHA. And the Baron?

CHEBUTIKIN. What about the Baron? [*Pause.*]

MASHA. Everything's all muddled up in my head. . . . But I say it ought not to be allowed. He might wound the Baron or even kill him.

CHEBUTIKIN. The Baron is a good man. but one Baron more or less—what difference does it make? It's all the same! [*Beyond the garden somebody shouts "Co-ee! Hallo!"*] You wait. That's Skvortsov shouting; one of the seconds. He's in a boat. [*Pause.*]

ANDREY. In my opinion it's simply immoral to fight in a duel, or to be present, even in the quality of a doctor.

CHEBUTIKIN. It only seems so. . . . We don't exist, there's nothing on earth, we don't really live, it only seems that we live. Does it matter, anyway!

MASHA. You talk and talk the whole day long. . . . [*Going.*] You live in a climate like this, where it might snow any moment, and there you talk. . . . [*Stops.*] I won't go into the house, I can't go there. . . . Tell me when Vershinin comes. . . [*Goes along the avenue.*] The migrant birds are already on the wing. . . . [*Looks up.*] Swans or geese. My dear, happy things. . . . [*Exit.*]

ANDREY. Our house will be empty. The officers will go away, you are going. my sister is getting married, and I alone will remain in the house.

CHEBUTIKIN. And your wife?

FERAPONT *enters with some documents.*

ANDREY. A wife's a wife. She's honest, well-bred, yes, and kind, but with all that there is still something about her that degenerates her into a petty, blind, even in some respects misshapen animal. In any case. she isn't a man. I tell you as a friend, as the only man to whom I can lay bare my soul. I love Natasha, it's true, but sometimes she seems extraordinarily vulgar, and then I lose myself and can't understand why I love her so much, or, at any rate, used to love her. . . .

CHEBUTIKIN. [*Rises.*] I'm going away to-morrow, old chap, and perhaps we'll never meet again, so here's my advice. Put on your cap, take a stick in your hand, go . . . go on and on, without looking round. And the farther you go, the better.

SOLENI *goes across the back of the stage with two officers; he catches sight of* CHEBUTIKIN, *and turns to him, the officers go on.*

SOLENI. Doctor, it's time. It's half-past twelve already. [*Shakes hands with* ANDREY.]

CHEBUTIKIN. Half a minute. I'm tired of the lot of you. [*To* ANDREY.] If anybody asks for me, say I'll be back soon. . . . [*Sighs.*] Oh, oh, oh!

SOLENI. "He didn't have the time to sigh. The bear sat on him heavily." [*Goes up to him.*] What are you groaning about, old man?

CHEBUTIKIN. Stop it!

SOLENI. How's your health?

CHEBUTIKIN [*angry*]. Mind your own business.

SOLENI. The old man is unnecessarily excited. I won't go far, I'll only just bring him down like a snipe. [*Takes out his scent-bottle and scents his hands.*] I've poured out a whole bottle of scent to-day and they still smell . . . of a dead body. [*Pause.*] Yes. . . . You remember the poem

"But he, the rebel seeks the storm,
As if the storm will bring him rest . . ."?

CHEBUTIKIN. Yes.

"He didn't have the time to sigh,
The bear sat on him heavily."

[*Exit with* SOLENI.]

Shouts are heard. ANDREY *and* FERAPONT *come in.*

FERAPONT. Documents to sign. . . .

ANDREY [*irritated*]. Go away! Leave me! Please! [*Goes away with the perambulator.*]

FERAPONT. That's what documents are for, to be signed. [*Retires to back of stage.*]

Enter IRINA, *with* TUZENBACH *in a straw hat;* KULIGIN *walks across the stage, shouting "Co-ee, Masha, co-ee!"*

TUZENBACH. He seems to be the only man in the town who is glad that the soldiers are going.

IRINA. One can understand that. [*Pause.*] The town will be empty.

TUZENBACH. My dear, I shall return soon.

IRINA. Where are you going?

TUZENBACH. I must go into the town and then . . . see the others off.

IRINA. It's not true . . . Nicolai, why are you so absent-minded to-day? [*Pause.*] What took place by the theatre yesterday?

TUZENBACH [*making a movement of impatience*]. In an hour's time I shall return and be with you again. [*Kisses her hands.*] My darling . . . [*Looking her closely in the face*] it's five years now since I fell in love with you, and still I can't get used to it, and you seem to me to grow more and more beautiful. What lovely, wonderful hair! What eyes! I'm going to take you away to-morrow. We shall work, we shall be rich, my dreams will come true. You will be happy. There's only one thing, one thing only: you don't love me!

IRINA. It isn't in my power! I shall be your wife, I shall be true to you, and obedient to you, but I can't love you. What can I do! [*Cries.*] I have never been in love in my life. Oh, I used to think so much of love, I have been thinking about it for so long by day and by night, but my soul is like an expensive piano which is locked and the key lost. [*Pause.*] You seem so unhappy.

TUZENBACH. I didn't sleep all night. There is nothing in my life so awful as to be able to frighten me, only that lost key torments my soul and does not let me sleep. Say something to me. [*Pause.*] Say something to me. . . .

IRINA. What can I say, what?

TUZENBACH. Anything.

IRINA. Don't! don't! [*Pause.*]

TUZENBACH. It is curious how silly trivial little things, sometimes for no apparent reason, become significant. At first you laugh at these things, you think they are of no importance. you go on and you feel that you haven't got the strength to stop yourself. Ob don't let's talk about it! I am happy. It is as if for the first time in my life I see these firs, maples, beeches, and they all look at me inquisitively and wait. What beautiful trees and how beautiful, when one comes to think of it, life must be near them! [*A shout of Co-ee! in the distance.*] It's time I went. . . . There's a tree which has dried up but it still sways in the breeze with the others. And so it seems to me that if I die, I shall still take part in life in one way or another. Good-bye, dear. . . . [*Kisses her hands.*] The papers which you gave me are on my table under the calendar.

IRINA. I am coming with you.

TUZENBACH [*nervously*]. No, no! [*He goes quickly and stops in the avenue.*] Irina!

IRINA. What is it?

TUZENBACH [*not knowing what to say*]. I haven't had any coffee to-day. Tell them to make me some. . . . [*He goes out quickly.*]

IRINA *stands deep in thought. Then she goes to the back of the stage and sits on a swing.* ANDREY *comes in with the perambulator and* FERAPONT *also appears.*

FERAPONT. Andrey Sergeyevitch, it isn't as if the documents were mine, they are the government's. I didn't make them.

ANDREY. Oh, what has become of my past and where is it? I used to be young, happy, clever, I used to be able to think and frame clever ideas, the present and the future seemed to me full of hope. Why do we, almost before we have begun to live, become dull, grey, uninteresting, lazy, apathetic, useless, unhappy. . . . This town has already been in existence for two hundred years and it has a hundred thousand inhabitants, not one of whom is in any way different from the others. There has never been, now or at any other time, a single leader of men, a single scholar, an artist, a man of even the slightest eminence who might arouse envy or a passionate desire to be imitated. They only eat, drink, sleep, and then they die . . . more people are born and also eat, drink, sleep, and so as not to go silly from boredom, they try to make life many-sided with their beastly backbiting, vodka, cards, and litigation. The wives deceive their husbands, and the husbands lie, and pretend they see nothing and hear nothing, and the evil influence irresistibly oppresses the children and the divine spark in them is extinguished, and they become just as pitiful corpses and just as much like one another as their fathers and mothers. . . [*Angrily to* FERAPONT.] What do you want?

FERAPONT. What? Documents want signing.

ANDREY. I'm tired of you.

FERAPONT [*handing him papers*]. The hall-porter from the law courts was say·

ing just now that in the winter there were two hundred degrees of frost in Petersburg.

ANDREY. The present is beastly, but when I think of the future, how good it is! I feel so light, so free; there is a light in the distance, I see freedom. I see myself and my children freeing ourselves from vanities, from kvass, from goose baked with cabbage, from after-dinner naps, from base idleness. . . .

FERAPONT. He was saying that two thousand people were frozen to death. The people were frightened, he said. In Petersburg or Moscow, I don't remember which.

ANDREY [*overcome by a tender emotion*]. My dear sisters, my beautiful sisters! [*Crying.*] Masha, my sister. . . .

NATASHA [*at the window*]. Who's talking so loudly out here? Is that you, Andrey? You'll wake little Sophie. *Il ne faut pas faire du bruit, la Sophie est dormée deja. Vous êtes un ours.* [*Angrily.*] If you want to talk, then give the perambulator and the baby to somebody else. Ferapont, take the perambulator!

FERAPONT. Yes'm. [*Takes the perambulator.*]

ANDREY [*confused*]. I'm speaking quietly.

NATASHA [*at the window, nursing her boy*.] Bobby! Naughty Bobby! Bad little Bobby!

ANDREY [*looking through the papers*]. All right, I'll look them over and sign if necessary, and you can take them back to the offices. . . .

Goes into house reading papers; FERAPONT *takes the perambulator to the back of the garden.*

NATASHA [*at the window*]. Bobby, what's your mother's name? Dear, dear! And who's this? That's Aunt Olga. Say to your aunt, "How do you do, Olga!"

Two wandering musicians, a man and a girl, are playing on a violin and a harp. VERSHININ, OLGA, *and* ANFISA *come out of the house and listen for a minute in silence;* IRINA *comes up to them.*

OLGA. Our garden might be a public thoroughfare, from the way people walk and ride across it. Nurse, give those musicians something!

ANFISA [*gives money to the musicians*]. Go away with God's blessing on you. [*The musicians bow and go away.*] A bitter sort of people. You don't play on a full stomach. [*To* IRINA.] How do you do, Arisha! [*Kisses her.*] Well, little girl, here I am, still alive! Still alive! In the High School, together with little Olga, in her official apartments . . . so the Lord has appointed for my old age. Sinful woman that I am, I've never lived like that in my life before. . . . A large flat, government property, and I've a whole room and bed to myself. All government property. I wake up at nights and, oh God, and Holy Mother, there isn't a happier person than I!

VERSHININ [*looks at his watch*]. We are going soon, Olga Sergeyevna. It's time for me to go. [*Pause.*] I wish you every . . . every . . . Where's Maria Sergeyevna?

IRINA. She's somewhere in the garden. I'll go and look for her.

VERSHININ. If you'll be so kind. I haven't time.

ANFISA. I'll go and look, too. [*Shouts.*] Little Masha, co'ee! [*Goes out with* IRINA *down into the garden.*] Co-ee, co-ee!

VERSHININ Everything comes to an end. And so we, too, must part. [*Looks at his watch.*] The town gave us a sort of farewell breakfast, we had champagne to drink and the mayor made a speech, and I ate and listened, but my soul was here all the time. . . . [*Looks round the garden.*] I'm so used to you now.

OLGA. Shall we ever meet again?

VERSHININ. Probably not. [*Pause.*] My wife and both my daughters will stay here another two months. If anything happens, or if anything has to be done . . .

OLGA. Yes, yes, of course. You need not worry. [*Pause.*] To-morrow there won't be a single soldier left in the town, it will all be a memory, and, of course, for us a new life will begin. . . . [*Pause.*] None of our plans are coming right. I didn't want to be a headmistress. but they made me one, all the same. It means there's no chance of Moscow. . . .

VERSHININ. Well . . . thank you for everything. Forgive me if I've . . . I've said such an awful lot—forgive me for that too, don't think badly of me.

OLGA [*wipes her eyes*]. Why isn't Masha coming   . .

VERSHININ. What else can I say in parting? Can I philosophize about anything? [*Laughs.*] Life is heavy. To many of us it seems dull and hopeless, but still, it must be acknowledged that it is getting lighter and clearer, and it seems that the time is not far off when it will be quite clear. [*Looks at his watch.*] It's time I went! Mankind used to be absorbed in wars, and all its existence was filled with campaigns, attacks, defeats, now we've outlived all that, leaving after us a great waste place, which there is nothing to fill with at present; but mankind is looking for something, and will certainly find it. Oh, if it only happened more quickly. [*Pause.*] If only education could be added to industry, and industry to education. [*Looks at his watch.*] It's time I went. . . .

OLGA. Here she comes.

Enter MASHA.

VERSHININ. I came to say good-bye. . . .

OLGA *steps aside a little, so as not to be in their way.*

MASHA [*looking him in the face*]. Good-bye. . . . [*Prolonged kiss.*]

OLGA. Don't, don't. [MASHA *is crying bitterly.*]

VERSHININ. White to me. . . . Don't forget! Let me go. . . . It's time. Take her, Olga Sergeyevna . . . it's time . . . I'm late . . . I'm late . . .

He kisses OLGA's *hand in evident emotion, then embraces* MASHA *once more and goes out quickly.*

OLGA. Don't, Masha! Stop, dear. . . . . [KULIGIN *enters.*]

KULIGIN [*confused*]. Never mind, let her cry, let her. . . . My dear Masha, my good Masha. . . . You're my wife, and I'm happy, whatever happens . . . I'm not complaining, I don't reproach you at all. . . . Olga is a witness to it. . . . Let's begin to live again as we used to, and not by a single word, or hint . . .

MASHA [*restraining her sobs*]. "There stands a green oak by the sea, And a chain of bright gold is around it. . . . And a chain of bright gold is around it. . . ."

I'm going off my head. . . . "There

stands . . . a green oak . . . by the sea." . . .

OLGA. Don't, Masha, don't . . . give her some water. . . .

MASHA. I'm not crying any more. . . .

KULIGIN. She's not crying any more . . . she's a good . . . [*A shot is heard from a distance.*]

MASHA. "There stands a green oak by the sea,

And a chain of bright gold is around it . . .

An oak of green gold. . . ." I'm mixing it up. . . . [*Drinks some water.*] Life is dull . . . I don't want anything more now . . . I'll be all right in a moment. . . . It doesn't matter. . . . What do those lines mean? Why do they run in my head? My thoughts are all tangled.

[*IRINA enters.*]

OLGA. Be quiet, Masha. There's a good girl. . . . Let's go in.

MASHA [*angrily*]. I shan't go in there. [*Sobs, but controls herself at once.*] I'm not going to go into the house, I won't go. . . .

IRINA. Let's sit here together and say nothing. I'm going away to-morrow. . . . [*Pause.*]

KULIGIN. Yesterday I took away these whiskers and this beard from a boy in the third class. . . . [*He puts on the whiskers and beard.*] Don't I look like the German master. . . . [*Laughs.*] Don't I? The boys are amusing.

MASHA. You really do look like that German of yours.

OLGA [*laughs*]. Yes. [*MASHA weeps.*]

IRINA. Don't, Masha!

KULIGIN. It's a very good likeness. . . .

Enter NATASHA.

NATASHA [*to the maid*]. What? Mihail Ivanitch Protopopov will sit with little Sophie, and Andrey Sergeyevitch can take little Bobby out. Children are such a bother. . . [*To IRINA.*] Irina, it's such a pity you're going away to-morrow. Do stop just another week. [*Sees KULIGIN and screams; he laughs and takes off his beard and whiskers.*] How you frightened me! [*To IRINA.*] I've grown used to you and do you think it will be easy for me to part from you? I'm going to have Andrey and his violin put into your room—let him fiddle away in there!—and we'll put little Sophie into his room. The beautiful, lovely child! What a little girlie! To-day she looked at me with such pretty eyes and said "Mamma!"

KULIGIN. A beautiful child, it's quite true.

NATASHA. That means I shall have the place to myself to-morrow. [*Sighs.*] In the first place I shall have that avenue of fir-trees cut down, then that maple. It's so ugly at nights. . . . [*To IRINA.*] That belt doesn't suit you at all, dear. . . . It's an error of taste. And I'll give orders to have lots and lots of little flowers planted here, and they'll smell. . . . [*Severely.*] Why is there a fork lying about here on the seat? [*Going towards the house, to the maid.*] Why is there a fork lying about here on the seat, I say? [*Shouts.*] Don't you dare to answer me!

KULIGIN. Temper! temper!

[*A march is played off; they all listen.*]

OLGA. They're going.

CHEBUTIKIN *comes in.*

MASHA. They're going. Well, well. . . . Bon voyage! [*To her husband.*]

We must be going home. . . . Where's my coat and hat?

KULIGIN. I took them in . . . I'll bring them, in a moment.

OLGA. Yes, now we can all go home. It's time.

CHEBUTIKIN. Olga Sergeyevna!

OLGA. What is it? [*Pause.*] What is it?

CHEBUTIKIN. Nothing . . . I don't know how to tell you. . . . [*Whispers to her.*]

OLGA [*frightened*]. It can't be true!

CHEBUTIKIN. Yes . . . such a story . . . I'm tired out, exhausted, I won't say any more. . . . [*Sadly.*] Still, it's all the same!

MASHA. What's happened?

OLGA [*embraces* IRINA]. *This is a terrible day* . . . I don't know how to tell you, dear. . . .

IRINA. What is it? Tell me quickly, what is it? For God's sake! [*Cries.*]

CHEBUTIKIN. The Baron was killed in the duel just now.

IRINA [*cries softly*]. I knew it, I knew it. . . .

CHEBUTIKIN [*sits on a bench at the back of the stage*]. I'm tired. . . . [*Takes a paper from his pocket.*] Let 'em cry. . . [*Sings softly.*] "Tarara-boom-deay, it is my washing day. . . ." Isn't it all the same!

[*The three sisters are standing, pressing against one another.*]

MASHA. Oh, how the music plays! They are leaving us, one has quite left us, quite and for ever. We remain alone, to begin our life over again. We must live . . . we must live. . . .

IRINA [*puts her head on* OLGA's *bosom*]. There will come a time when everybody will know why, for what purpose, there is all this suffering, and there will be no more mysteries. But now we must live . . . we must work, just work! To-morrow, I'll go away alone, and I'll teach and give my whole life to those who, perhaps, need it. It's autumn now, soon it will be winter, the snow will cover everything, and I shall be working, working. . . .

OLGA [*embraces both her sisters*]. The bands are playing so gaily, so bravely, and one does so want to live! Oh, my God! Time will pass on, and we shall depart for ever, we shall be forgotten; they will forget our faces, voices, and even how many there were of us, but our sufferings will turn into joy for those who will live after us, happiness and peace will reign on earth, and people will remember with kindly words, and bless those who are living now. Oh dear sisters, our life is not yet at an end. Let us live. The music is so gay, so joyful, and, it seems that in a little while we shall know why we are living, why we are suffering. . . . If we could only know, if we could only know!

[*The music has been growing softer and softer;* KULIGIN, *smiling happily, brings out the hat and coat;*

ANDREY *wheels out the perambulator in which* BOBBY *is sitting.*]

CHEBUTIKIN [*sings softly*]. "Tara . . . ra-boom-deay. . . . It is my washing-day." . . . [*Reads a paper.*] It's all the same! It's all the same!

OLGA. If only we could know, if only we could know!

CURTAIN

The Sea-Gull

DRAMATIS PERSONAE

MADAME ARCADINA, *an actress.*
CONSTANTINE TREPLEF, *her son.*
SORIN, *her brother.*
NINA, *daughter of a rich land owner.*
SHAMRAYEF, *retired lieutenant, Manager of* SORIN's *estate.*
PAULINE, *his wife.*
MASHA, *their daughter.*
TRIGORIN, *a writer.*
DORN, *a doctor.*
MEDVEDENKO, *a schoolmaster.*
YAKOF.
COOK.

The action takes place on SORIN's *Estate.*

Two years elapse between Acts III and IV.

ACT I

In the park of SORIN's *estate. A broad avenue runs away from the spectators into the depths of the park towards a lake; the avenue is blocked by a rough stage knocked together for amateur theatricals, concealing the lake. Bushes to right and left. A table and chairs.*

The sun has just set. On the stage behind the curtain, which is down, are YAKOF *and other workmen; coughing and hammering.*

Enter MASHA *and* MEDVEDENKO, *returning from a walk.*

MEDVEDENKO. Why always in black?

MASHA. I'm in mourning for my life. I am sad.

MEDVEDENKO. Why? [*Reflectively.*] I don't understand. . . . You're strong and financially fairly comfortable. My life is far heavier to bear than yours. I'm paid only forty-eight shillings a month, minus a deduction for the pension fund; yet I don't wear mourning. [*They sit.*]

MASHA. It isn't a question of money. Even a pauper may be happy.

MEDVEDENKO. In books, yes; but in life, there's me and my mother, two sisters, my brother, and my salary's only forty-eight shillings a month. One must eat and drink, have tea, sugar and tobacco. That is certain.

MASHA. [*Looking round at the stage.*] The play begins very soon.

MEDVEDENKO. Yes. Nina Zarétchnaya is to star and the play is by Constantine Tréplef. They are in love and to-day their spirits will unite to produce a masterpiece. But my spirit and yours have no connection. I love you; I cannot sit at home for longing for you; every day I come four miles on foot and four miles back again and meet only with a "I can't" on your part. Naturally I have no means; we're a big family. Why should anyone want to marry a man who cannot even feed himself.

MASHA. Bosh! [*Taking snuff.*] I am like by your affection, but I cannot return it; that's all. [*Offering him the snuff-box.*] Help yourself.

MEDVEDENKO. Not for me. [*A pause.*]

MASHA. It's getting warm; we shall probably have a storm to-night. You are always either philosophising or talking about money. You think there is no greater trouble that poverty; but

589

I think it is a thousand times easier to wear rags and beg for bread than . . . However, that is beyond you.

[*Enter* SORIN *and* TREPLEF, R.]

SORIN [*leaning on a stick*]. My dear friend, I never *do* feel at home in the country. And naturally, I'm too old to get used to it now. I went to bed at ten last night and woke this morning at nine, feeling as if my brain were full of glue. [*Laughing.*] After dinner I fell asleep again without intending it, and now I'm restless from nightmare, confound it all. . . .

TREPLEF. Yes, you ought to live in town. [*Seeing* MASHA *and* MEDVEDENKO.] Hullo! You'll be called when the play begins; but you musn't sit here now. I must ask you to go away, please.

SORIN [*to* MASHA]. Márya Ilyínitchna, would you kindly ask your father to have that dog unchained, to keep it from howling? My sister had another sleepless night.

MASHA. You must speak to my father yourself. I'm not going to. So please don't ask me. [*To* MEDVEDENKO.] Come on.

MEDVEDENKO [*to* TREPLEF]. Let us know before the play begins, then.

[*Exeunt* MEDVEDENKO *and* MASHA.]

SORIN. That means that the dog will howl all night again. There you are! I've never had my own way in the country. In the old days, whenever I took a month's holiday and came here to recoup and all the rest of it, I was always worried so with every sort of nonsense, that before the first day was out I was wishing myself back again. [*Laughing.*] I always enjoyed the going away most. . . . And now I've retired, I've nowhere to go to, confound it all. Whether one likes it or not one's got to lump it. . . .

YAKOF [*from the stage to* TREPLEF]. We're going to have a bath, Constantine Gavrílitch.

TREPLEF. All right. But you must be back at your places in ten minutes. [*Looking at his watch.*] It begins very soon.

YAKOF. Very good, sir.

[*Exit.*]

TREPLEF [*glancing at the stage*]. What do you think of that for a theatre? Curtain, first wing, second wing, and then empty space. No scenery. You look straight on to the lake and the horizon. The curtain goes up at exactly half-past eight, when the moon rises.

SORIN. Magnificent!

TREPLEF. If Nina is late, of course the whole effect will be spoilt. It's time she arrived. Her father and stepmother are always watching her, and it's as hard for her to escape from the house as it is for a prisoner to escape from jail. [*Puts his uncle's tie straight.*] Your hair and beard are all rumpled. You ought to have them cut, don't you think?

SORIN [*smoothing out his beard*]. It's the tragedy of my life. Even when I was young I always looked as if I had taken to drink and all the rest of it. Women never loved me. [*Sitting.*] Why is your mother in such low spirits?

TREPLEF. Oh, she's bored. [*Sitting by him.*] She's jealous. She's already hostile to me and to the whole performance, because it's Nina Zarétchnaya acting and not she. She hates my play, even before she's seen it.

SORIN [*laughing*]. Well I never Well I never!

TREPLEF. She is vexed at the idea of Nina Zarétchnaya and not herself having a success even in this poor little theatre. [*Looking at his watch.*] She is a psychological curiosity, is my mother. A clever and gifted woman, who can cry over a novel, will reel you off Nekrásof's poems by heart, and is the perfection of a sick nurse; but venture to praise Eleonora Duse before her! Oho! ho! You must praise nobody but her, write about her, shout about her, and go into ecstasies over her wonderful performance in *La Dame aux Camélias*, or *The Fumes of Life;* but as she cannot have these intoxicating pleasures down here in the country, she's bored and gets spiteful; we are her enemies, she thinks; it's all our fault. Then, she's superstitious, is afraid of the number thirteen, or three candles on a table. She's a miser, too. She has seven thousand pounds in the bank at Odessa; I know it for certain. But ask her to lend you anything and she'll cry.

SORIN. You have got it into your head that she doesn't like your play, and you are nervous and all the rest of it. Set your mind at rest, your mother worships you.

TREPLEF [*pulling the petals from a flower.*] She loves me, she loves me not, she loves me, she loves me not, she loves me, she loves me not. [*Laughs.*] You see, my mother doesn't love me. Why should she? She wants to live, to love, to wear pretty frocks; and I, I am twenty-five years old, and a perpetual reminder that she is no longer young. When I'm not there, she is only thirty-two; when I am, she's forty-three, and she hates me for that. She also knows that I don't believe in the

stage. She loves the stage; she thinks that she is advancing the cause of humanity and her sacred art; but I regard the stage of to-day as mere routine and prejudice. When the curtain goes up and the gifted beings, the high priests of the sacred art, appear by electric light, in a room with three sides to it, representing how people eat, drink, love, walk and wear their jackets; when they strive to squeeze out a moral from the flat, vulgar pictures and the flat, vulgar phrases, a little tiny moral, easy to comprehend and handy for home consumption, when in a thousand variations they offer me always the same thing over and over again—then I take to my heels and run, as Maupassant ran from the Eiffel Tower, which crushed his brain by its overwhelming vulgarity.

SORIN. We must get along without the stage.

TREPLEF. We must have new formulae. That's what we want. And if there *are* none, then it's better to have nothing at all. [*Looks at his watch.*] I love my mother, I love her dearly; but it's a tomfool life that she leads with this novelist always at her elbow, and her name for ever in the papers—it disgusts me! Sometimes it is just the egotism of the ordinary man that speaks in me! I am sorry that I have a famous actress for my mother, and I feel that if she had been an ordinary woman I should have been happier. Uncle Peter, what position could be more hopeless and absurd than mine was at home with her? Her drawing-room filled with nothing but celebrities, actors and writers, and among them all the only nobody, myself, tolerated only because I was her son. Who am I? What am I? Sent down from the

University without a degree through circumstances for which the editor cannot hold himself responsible, as they say; with no talents, without a farthing, and according to my passport a Kief artisan; for my father was officially reckoned a Kief artisan, although he was a famous actor. So that when these actors and writers in her drawing-room graciously bestowed their attention on me, it seemed to me that they were merely taking the measure of my insignificance; I guessed their thoughts and felt the humiliation.

SORIN. What sort of man is this novelist, by the by? I can't make him out. He never talks.

TREPLEF. Intelligent, simple, inclined to melancholy. Quite a good chap. Famous already, before he's forty, and sated with everything. . . . As for his writings . . . what shall I say? Charming, talented . . . but . . . you wouldn't want to read Trigórin after Tolstoy or Zola.

SORIN. I love literary people, my boy. There was a time when I passionately desired two things; I wanted to be married, and I wanted to be a literary man, but neither of them came my way. Ah! how pleasant to be even an unknown writer, confound it all.

TREPLEF [listening]. I hear someone coming. [Embracing SORIN.] I cannot live without her. . . . Even the sound of her footsteps is charming. . . . I am insanely happy.

[Enter NINA. TREPLEF goes quickly to meet her.]

TREPLEF. My lovely one, my dream. . . .

NINA [agitated]. I'm not late . . . I'm sure I'm not late. . . .

TREPLEF [kissing her hands]. No. no, no. . . .

NINA. I've been so anxious all day; I was so frightened. I was afraid father would not let me come. . . . But at last he's gone out, just now, with my stepmother. There's a red glow in the sky, the moon is beginning to rise, and I whipped up the horses as fast as I could. [Laughing.] But I am happy now. [Squeezing SORIN's hand heartily.]

SORIN [laughing]. You've been crying, I can see. . . . Hey, hey! You naughty girl!

NINA. It's quite true. You see how out of breath I am. I've got to go in half-an-hour; we must hurry. I must, I must; don't detain me for heaven's sake. Father doesn't know I'm here.

TREPLEF. It's quite true, it's time to begin. I must go and call the others.

SORIN. I'll go, I'll go, confound it all. I won't be a minute. [Goes R., singing.] 'To France were returning two Grenadiers!' [Looks round.] I remember I started singing like that one day, and an Assistant Procureur who was standing by said: 'Your Excellency. you have a very strong voice.' Then he pondered, and added: 'Strong, but ugly!'

[Exit, laughing.]

NINA. My father and his wife won't let me come here. They say that you are all Bohemians. . . . They are afraid of my becoming an actress. But I am drawn towards the lake like a seagull. My heart is full of you. [Looks round.]

TREPLEF. We are alone.

NINA. Isn't there someone over there?

TREPLEF. No, there's no one. [Kissing her.]

NINA. What sort of tree is that?

TREPLEF. It's an elm.

NINA. Why is it so dark?

TREPLEF. It's evening already; everything looks darker. Don't go away early, I entreat you.

NINA. I must.

TREPLEF. Shall I drive over to-night, Nina? I will stand all night in the garden and look up at your window.

NINA. You musn't. The watchman will see you. Trésor is not used to you yet; he'll bark.

TREPLEF. I love you.

NINA. 'Sh!

TREPLEF [hearing footsteps]. Who's there? Is that you, Yákof?

YAKOF [on the stage]. Yes, sir.

TREPLEF. Get to your places. It's time to begin. Is the moon up?

YAKOF. Yes, sir.

TREPLEF. Have you the methylated spirits? And the sulphur? [To NINA.] When the red eyes appear, there has to be a smell of sulphur. You'd better go, you'll find everything there. Are you nervous?

NINA. Yes, very. I don't mind your mother; I'm not afraid of her; but Trigórin will be here. I am frightened at acting before him. Such a famous writer! Is he young?

TREPLEF. Yes.

NINA. What wonderful stories he writes!

TREPLEF [coldly]. Does he? I don't read them.

NINA. Your play is very hard to act. There are no live people in it.

TREPLEF. Live people! why should there be? A writer's business is not to represent life as it is; nor as he thinks it ought to be, but as it appears in reveries.

NINA. There's very little action in your piece; it is all lines. And I think a play ought always to have a love interest in it. . . .

[Exeunt behind the stage.]

[Enter PAULINE and DORN.]

PAULINE. It is getting damp. Go back and put on your goloshes.

DORN. I'm too hot.

PAULINE. You take no care of yourself. It's all obstinacy. You're a doctor, and you know perfectly well that the damp air is bad for you; but you like to give me pain; you sat on the verandah the whole of yesterday evening on purpose.

DORN [singing]. 'Say not that I have spoilt thy youth.'

PAULINE. You were so taken up talking to Madame Arcádina, you did not notice the cold. Confess, that you admire her.

DORN. I am fifty-five.

PAULINE. Nonsense, that's not old for a man. You are well preserved and women still admire you.

DORN. Then what do you want of me?

PAULINE. You men are always ready to fall down and grovel before an actress. Always!

DORN [singing]. 'Once more, once more before thee, love.' If society is fond of actors and actresses and treats them differently, for instance, from shopkeepers, that is very natural. That is idealism.

PAULINE. Women have always fallen in love with you, and thrown themselves at your head. Is that idealism too?

DORN [shrugs his shoulders]. Why, there has always been something charming in the relation of women to me. What they principally liked in me was the skilful doctor. Ten or fifteen years ago, you remember, I was the only decent *accoucheur* in the whole province. Besides, I was always an honest man.

PAULINE [*taking his hand*]. My beloved!

DORN. Hush! There's somebody coming.

[*Enter* ARCADINA, *arm-in-arm with* SORIN, TRIGORIN, SHAMRAYEF, MEDVE-DENKO, MASHA.]

SHAMRAYEF. In 1873 at the Fair at Poltava she acted superbly! A wonderful piece of acting! Do you happen to know too what's become of Chadin, Paul Chadin, the comedian? As Raspluyef he was simply A1; better than Sadovsky, I assure you. What's become of *him?*

ARCADINA. You are always wanting to know about somebody before the flood. How should I know? [*Sits.*]

SHAMRAYEF [*sighing*]. Good old Paul Chadin! We have no one like that now. The stage has gone to the dogs, Irina Nikolayevna. There were mighty oaks in the old days, but now we see nothing but stumps.

DORN. There are not many really brilliant people on the stage now, that is true; but the average actor is far better.

SHAMRAYEF. I can't agree with you. However, it's a matter of taste. De gustibus aut bene, aut nihil.

[TREPLEF *comes out from behind the stage.*]

ARCADINA. My dear child, when does the thing begin?

TREPLEF. In a minute. Please be patient.

ARCADINA: 'My son,
Thou turnst mine eyes into my very soul,
And there I see such blank and grained
       spots
As will not leave their tinct.'

TREPLEF. 'Leave wringing of your hands. Peace, sit you down, and let me wring your heart.' [*A horn is blown from the stage.*] Now then, the play begins. Attention, please! [*A pause.*] I speak first. [*He thumps with a stick; raising his voice.*] Hearken, ye venerable ancient shades, that hover in the night-time over this lake; send sleep upon us and let us dream of what will be in 200,000 years.

SORIN. In 200,000 years there will be nothing at all.

TREPLEF. Then let them represent that nothing to us.

ARCADINA. Come on! We sleep.

The curtain rises; the view opens on the lake; the moon is above the horizon, reflected in the water; NINA *discovered sitting on a rock. dressed in white.*

NINA. Men and lions, eagles and partridges, antlered deer, geese, spiders, the silent fishes dwelling in the water, star-fish and tiny creatures invisible to the eye—these and every form of life, ay, every form of life, have ended their melancholy round and become extinct. . . . Thousands of centuries have passed since this earth bore any living being on its bosom. All in vain does yon pale moon light her lamp. No longer do the cranes wake and cry in the meadows; the hum of the cockchafers is silent in the linden groves. All is cold, cold, cold. Empty, empty, empty. Terrible, terrible, terrible. [*A pause.*] The bodies of living beings have vanished into dust; the Eternal Matter has converted them into stones, into water, into clouds, and all their spirits are merged in one. I am that spirit, the universal spirit of the world. In me is the spirit of Alexander the

Great, of Cæsar, of Shakespeare, of Napoleon, and of the meanest of leeches. In me the consciousness of men is merged with the instinct of animals; I remember everything, everything, everything, and in myself relive each individual life.

Marsh fires appear.

ARCADINA [*in a low voice*] This is going to be something decadent.

TREPLEF [*with reproachful entreaty*]. Mother!

NINA. I am alone. Once in a hundred years I open my lips to speak, and my voice echoes sadly in this emptiness and no one hears. . . . You too, pale fires, you hear me not. . . . The corruption of the marsh engenders you towards morning, and you wander till the dawn, but without thought, without will, without throb of life. Fearing lest life should arise in you, the father of Eternal Matter, the Devil, effects in you, as in stones and water, a perpetual mutation of atoms; you change unceasingly. In all the universe spirit alone remains constant and unchanging. [*A pause.*] Like a captive flung into a deep empty well, I know not where I am nor what awaits me. One thing only is revealed to me, that in the cruel and stubborn struggle with the Devil, the principle of material forces, it is fated that I shall be victorious; and thereafter, spirit and matter are to merge together in exquisite harmony and the reign of Universal Will is to begin. But that cannot be till, little by little, after a long, long series of centuries, the moon, the shining dog-star and the earth are turned to dust. . . . Till then there shall be horror and desolation. . . . [*A pause; against the background of the lake appear two red spots.*]

Behold, my mighty antagonist, the Devil, approaches. I see his awful, blood-red eyes . . .

ARCADINA. There's a smell of sulphur. Is that part of it?

TREPLEF. Yes.

ARCADINA [*laughing*]. I see, a scenic effect.

TREPLEF. Mother!

NINA. He is lonely without man.

PAULINE [*to* DORN]. Why, you've taken your hat off. Put it on again, or you'll catch cold.

ARCADINA. The doctor's taking off his hat to the Devil, the father of Eternal Matter.

TREPLEF [*angry, in a loud voice*]. The play is over! That's enough! Curtain!

ARCADINA. What are you angry about?

TREPLEF. That's enough. Curtain! Lower the curtain! [*Stamping.*] Curtain! [*The curtain is lowered.*] I must apologise. I ought to have remembered that only a few chosen spirits can write plays or act them. I have been infringing the monopoly. You . . . I . . . [*Is about to add something, but makes a gesture of renouncing the idea, and Exit L.*]

ARCADINA. What's the matter with him?

SORIN. Irene, my dear, you oughtn't to treat a young man's *amour propre* like that.

ARCADINA. Why, what have I said?

SORIN. You have hurt his feelings.

ARCADINA. He warned us beforehand that it was all a joke; I've only taken him at his word and treated it as a joke.

SORIN. But still . . .

ARCADINA. And now it appears that

he has written a masterpiece. Mercy on us! So he has got up this performance and stifled us with brimstone not as a joke, but as a demonstration. . . . He wanted to teach us how to write and what we ought to act. Really, this sort of thing gets tedious! These perpetual digs and pin-pricks would wear out the patience of a saint. He's a peevish, conceited boy.

SORIN. He only wanted to give you pleasure.

ARCADINA. Did he? Then why couldn't he choose some ordinary sort of play, instead of making us listen to this decadent nonsense? I don't mind listening to nonsense now and again for fun; but this pretends to show us new forms, a new era in art. I see no new forms in it; I see nothing but an evil disposition.

TRIGORIN. Everyone writes as he wants to, and as he can.

ARCADINA. Let him write as he wants and can, and welcome; only let him leave me in peace.

DORN [singing]. 'Great Jove, art angry yet' . . .

ARCADINA. I'm not Jove, I'm a woman. [Lighting a cigarette.] Besides, I'm not angry; I only think it's a pity that a young man should spend his time so tediously. I had no intention of hurting his feelings.

MEDVEDENKO. No one has any grounds for differentiating spirit and matter; spirit itself is very likely a collection of material atoms. [Eagerly to TRIGORIN.] Ah, if only someone would write a play and put it on the stage. showing the life we schoolmasters lead! It's a hard, hard life!

ARCADINA. Quite true; but don't let us talk about plays or atoms. What a

glorious evening! Do you hear? The peasants are singing. [Listening.] How beautiful!

PAULINE. That's on the farther shore. [A pause.]

ARCADINA. [To TRIGORIN.] Sit by me here. Ten or fifteen years ago there was music and singing to be heard here by the lake almost every evening. There were six big country houses round the shore. It was all laughter, and noise, and the firing of guns . . . and love-making, love-making without end. The Jeune Premier, the idol of all six houses, was our friend here. [Nodding at DORN.] You haven't met? Dr. Dorn, Eugene Sergéitch. He is still charming, but in those days he was irresistible. But my conscience is beginning to prick me. Why did I hurt my poor boy's feelings? I feel uneasy. [Calling.] Constantine! Dear boy! Constantine!

MASHA. I'll go and look for him.

ARCADINA. Do, there's a dear.

MASHA [going L.] A-oo! Constantine Gavrilovitch! A-oo!

[Exit.]

NINA [coming from behind the stage]. Evidently we're not to go on. I can come out. How do you do? [Kisses ARCADINA and PAULINE.]

SORIN. Bravo, bravo.

ARCADINA. Bravo, bravo. We were all enchanted. With such a face and figure, with such a lovely voice, it is wicked to stay hidden in the country. I am sure that you have talent. Mark my words! You must go on the stage.

NINA. Oh, it is the dream of my life! [Sighing.] But it can never be realised.

ARCADINA. Who knows? Let me introduce you: Trigórin, Boris Alexéyevitch.

NINA. Oh, I'm so glad. [*Shyly.*] I read all you write. . . .

ARCADINA [*making* NINA *sit by her*]. Don't be shy, my dear. He has a simple soul, although he's a celebrity. You see, he's just as shy himself.

DORN. I suppose we can have the curtain up again now? It feels rather uncanny like this.

SHAMRAYEF [*Loud*]. Yákof, pull the curtain up, my lad, will you?

Curtain is raised.

NINA [*to* TRIGORIN]. It's a strange play, isn't it?

TRIGORIN. I didn't understand a word. However, I enjoyed looking on. You acted with such sincerity. And the scenery was lovely. [*A pause.*] No doubt there are a great many fish in this lake?

NINA. Yes.

TRIGORIN. I love fishing. I know no greater pleasure than to sit towards evening by the water and watch a float.

NINA. Surely, for one who has tasted the pleasure of creation, all other pleasures cease to exist.

ARCADINA [*laughing*]. You mustn't talk to him like that. If people make him pretty speeches he runs away.

SHAMRAYEF. I remember one day in the opera-house at Moscow, the famous Silva took the low C. As luck would have it, there was one of our Synod choirmen sitting in the gallery; imagine our astonishment when all of a sudden we heard a voice from the gallery, 'Bravo, Silva,' a whole octave lower. Like this. [*In a deep bass voice.*] 'Bravo, Silva.' The audience was dumbfounded. [*A pause.*]

DORN. There's an angel flying over the park.

NINA. I must be off. Good-bye.

ARCADINA. Where are you going? Why so early? We won't let you go.

NINA. Papa's expecting me.

ARCADINA. It's too bad of him. [*They kiss.*] Well, we can't help it. It's very, very sad to part with you.

NINA. If only you knew how unwilling I am to go.

ARCADINA. Somebody must see you home, darling.

NINA [*alarmed*]. Oh no, no!

SORIN [*imploringly*]. Don't go!

NINA. I must, Peter Nikolayevitch.

SORIN. Stay just for an hour, confound it all. It's too bad.

NINA [*hesitating; then crying.*] I can't. [*Shakes hands and exit quickly.*]

ARCADINA. There's a really unfortunate girl! They say that her mother left her husband all her huge fortune when she died, down to the last farthing, and now this child is left with nothing, for he's made a will bequeathing it all to his second wife. It's monstrous.

DORN. Yes, her papa's a pretty mean sort of a sneak, to do him justice.

SORIN [*rubbing his hands to warm them*]. We'd better be going too; it's getting damp. My legs are beginning to ache.

ARCADINA. They're like bits of wood, you can hardly walk on them. Come along, ill-fated patriarch! [*Takes his arm.*]

SHAMRAYEF [*offering his arm to his wife*]. Madame?

SORIN. There's that dog howling again. [*To* SHAMRAYEF.] Please tell them to unchain that dog, Ilyá Afanásyevitch.

SHAMRAYEF. Can't be done, Peter Nikolayevitch; I'm afraid of thieves breaking into the barn. I've got the millet there. [*To* MEDVEDENKO, *who walks beside him.*]   Yes, a whole octave lower: 'Bravo, Silva!' And not a concert singer, mind you, but an ordinary Synod choirman.

MEDVEDENKO.   And what salary does a Synod choirman get?

[*Exeunt Omnes, except* DORN.]

DORN [*alone*].   I don't know. Perhaps I don't understand anything, or I'm going off my head, but the fact is I liked the play. There was something in it. When the girl spoke of her solitude, and then afterwards when the Devil's red eyes appeared, my hands trembled with excitement. It was fresh and naïf. There he comes apparently. I want to say all the nice things I can to him.

[*Enter* TREPLEF.]

TREPLEF.   They're all gone.

DORN.   I'm here.

TREPLEF.   Masha's looking for me all over the park. Repulsive female!

DORN.   Constantine Gavrilovitch, I liked your play extremely. It was a curious kind of thing and I didn't hear the end, but all the same it made a deep impression on me. You are a man of talent and you must go on.

[TREPLEF *squeezes his hands and embraces him eagerly.*]

DORN.   What a nervous creature you are! Tears in his eyes! What did I want to say? You have chosen a subject in the realm of abstract ideas. You were quite right; every artistic production ought to express a great thought. Nothing is beautiful unless it is serious. How pale you are!

TREPLEF.   So you think that I ought to go on?

DORN.   Yes. But represent only what is important and eternal. You know that I have lived my life with

variety and discrimination; I'm quite contented; but if ever I felt the elevation of spirit which comes to artists in the moment of creation, I am sure that I should despise my material envelope and all that belongs to it and be carried away from the earth aloft into the heights.

TREPLEF.   Excuse me, where is Nina Zarétchnaya?

DORN.   And then there's another thing. In every production there must be a clear and well-defined idea. You must know what your object is in writing; otherwise, if you travel this picturesque path without a well-defined aim, you will go astray and your talent will be your ruin.

TREPLEF [*impatiently*].   Where is Nina Zarétchnaya?

DORN.   She's gone home.

TREPLEF [*in despair*].   What am I to do? I want to see her. I *must* see her. I shall drive after her.

[*Enter* MASHA.]

DORN [*to* TREPLEF].   Calm yourself, my friend.

TREPLEF.   All the same I shall go after her. I must go after her.

MASHA.   Please go up to the house, Constantine Gavrilovitch. Your mother's waiting for you. She's anxious about you.

TREPLEF.   Tell her I've gone out. And please, all of you, leave me in peace! Leave me alone! Don't follow me about!

DORN.   Come, come, my dear boy. You mustn't talk like that. . . . It isn't right.

TREPLEF [*with tears in his eyes*]. Good-bye, doctor. Thank you.

[*Exit.*]

DORN [*sighing*].   Ah, youth! youth!

MASHA. When there is nothing else left to say, people say: 'Ah, youth! youth! [*Takes snuff.*]

DORN [*taking* MASHA'S *snuff-box and throwing it into the bushes*]. A filthy habit! [*Pause.*] They seem to be having music up at the house. We must go in.

MASHA. Stop a moment.

DORN. Eh?

MASHA. I want to say something to you again. I want to talk. [*Agitated.*] I don't care for my father, but my heart goes out to you. I somehow feel, with all my soul, that you are near to me. . . . Come, help me. Help me, or I shall commit some folly, I shall make havoc of my life. . . . I can't hold out any longer.

DORN. What is it? How am I to help you?

MASHA. I am in pain. No one knows my sufferings. [*Laying her head on his breast, softly.*] I am in love with Constance.

DORN. What bundles of nerves they all are! And what a lot of love. . . . Oh. magic lake! Oh, magic lake! [*Tenderly.*] What can I do, my child? What can I do?

CURTAIN

ACT II

The croquet lawn. Far up at the back, on the right, the house with big verandah. On the left the lake is visible, with the reflection of the sun twinkling in the waters. Flower-beds. Mid-day; hot. At the side of the croquet lawn, in the shade of an old lime-tree, sit ARCADINA, DORN *and* MASHA *on a bench.* DORN *has a book open on his knees.*

ARCADINA [*to* MASHA]. Come, get up. [*They get up.*] Let us stand side by side. You are twenty-two and I am nearly twice as much. Eugene Sergéitch, which of us looks the youngest?

DORN. You do of course.

ARCADINA. There! And why? Because I work, because I feel, because I am always on the move. While you remain sitting in one place; you don't live. And I make it a rule never to look forward into the future. I never think about old age or death. What will be will be.

MASHA. And I, I have a feeling as if I had been born ages and ages ago. I drag my life, a dead weight, after me, like the train of an endless dress. Often I have no desire to live. [*Sits.*] Of course, this is all rubbish. One must shake one-self and throw it all off.

DORN [*singing softly*]. 'Tell my lady of love, O gentle flowers!'

ARCADINA. Then again, I am always 'correct,' like an Englishman. I keep myself up to the mark, as they say, and am always dressed, and have my hair done *comme il faut*. I should never dream of leaving the house, even to come into the garden like this, in a *négligé*, or with my hair undone. Never. The reason I am so well preserved is that I have never been a dowdy, never let myself go as some do. . . . [*Walks up and down the crocquet lawn with arms akimbo.*] There! you see? as light as a bird: ready to act the part of a girl of fifteen any day.

DORN. Well, I'm going on anyway [*taking up his book*]. We'd got as far as the cornchandler and the rats.

ARCADINA. And the rats. Go on [*Sits.*] No, give it to me. I'll read It's my turn [*taking the book and look·*

ing for the place.] And the rats. Here we are [*reading.*] 'Truly, it is just as dangerous for people of fashion to beguile novelists to their houses as it would be for a cornchandler to rear rats in his granary. And yet they are much sought after. When a woman has chosen the writer that she wishes to take captive, she lays siege to him by means of flattery and delicate attentions. . . .' That may be true in France, but we have nothing of the sort in Russia; we have no programme. As a rule, before a Russian woman takes her writer captive she's head over ears in love with him. No need to look far afield: take me and Trigórin, for instance.

Enter SORIN, *leaning on a stick;* NINA *beside him.* MEDVEDENKO *wheels a chair behind them.*

SORIN [*as if talking to a child*]. Eh? so we're having a treat? We're happy for once, confound it all! [*To* ARCADINA.] Such fun! Papa and stepmamma have gone to Tver, and we're free for three whole days.

NINA [*sitting by* ARCADINA *and embracing her*]. I am so happy! Now I belong to you.

SORIN [*sitting in his chair*]. She's in looks to-day.

ARCADINA. Well dressed and interesting. That's a good girl! [*Kisses her.*] We mustn't praise you too much for fear of bewitching you. Where is Trigórin?

NINA. Down at the bathing-place, fishing.

ARCADINA. I wonder he doesn't get sick of it! [*Prepares to go on reading.*]

NINA. What is the book?

ARCADINA. Maupassant's *On the Water*, my dear. [*Reads a few lines to herself.*] The rest's dull and quite un-

true. [*Shutting the book.*] I am feeling anxious and perturbed. Tell me, what is the matter with my son? Why is he so gloomy and morose? He passes whole days together on the lake and I hardly ever see him.

MASHA. He is troubled at heart. [*To* NINA; *timidly.*] I wish you would recite something from his play.

NINA. [*Shrugging her shoulders.*] Really? It's so dull.

MASHA [*With restrained enthusiasm*]. When *he* reads anything aloud, his eyes glow and his face turns pale. He has a beautiful melancholy voice, and manners like a poet.

[SORIN *snores audibly.*]

DORN. Good-night.

ARCADINA. Peter!

SORIN. Eh?

ARCADINA. Are you sleep?

SORIN. Not I. [*A pause.*]

ARCADINA. It's so foolish of you not to undergo a treatment, Peter.

SORIN. I should be delighted, but Dorn won't let me.

DORN. A treatment at sixty!

SORIN. Even at sixty one wants to live.

DORN [*Testily*]. Eh! Very well then, take Valerian drops.

ARCADINA. I think he ought to go and take the waters somewhere.

DORN. All right. He can go if he likes . . . or he can stop at home if he likes.

ARCADINA. How's one to understand you?

DORN. There's nothing to understand. It's perfectly plain. [*A pause.*]

MEDVEDENKO. Peter Nikolayevitch ought to give up smoking.

SORIN. Rubbish!

DORN. No, it's not rubbish. Wine

and tobacco rob us of our individuality. After a cigar or a glass of vodka you are no longer Peter Nikolayevitch but Peter Nikolayevitch plus somebody else. Your ego evaporates, and you think of yourself in the third person; not as 'me' but as 'him.'

SORIN [*laughing.*] It's all very well for you to talk. You've lived in your time; but what about me? I have spent twenty-eight years in the law courts, but I haven't begun to live yet, haven't had any experiences, confound it all, and isn't it natural that I long to live at last? You are sated and indifferent and therefore you are disposed to philosophise; but I want to live, and that's why I drink sherry at dinner and smoke cigars and all the rest of it. That's all.

DORN. One ought to be serious about life. But to take medicine at sixty and lament that one did not have fun enough when one was young, that, if you'll excuse me, is frivolous.

MASHA [*Rising*]. It must be lunchtime. [*Walking lazily.*] My leg's gone to sleep.

[*Exit.*]

DORN. She's going to get down a couple of glasses of vodka before lunch.

SORIN. The poor thing gets no enjoyment out of life.

DORN. Rot, your Excellency.

SORIN. You talk like a man who has had his fill.

ARCADINA. Oh dear! oh dear! what can be more tedious than this truly rural country tedium! So hot! so quiet! No one does anything; everyone philosophises. You're pleasant company, my friends, and it's very nice to hear you talk, but . . . Oh, to be sitting in one's hotel, studying one's part, how very much nicer!

NINA [*enthusiastically*]. Oh, indeed! How well I can understand you!

SORIN. Of course it's better in town. Sitting in one's study, all visitors have to send their names up by the footman, a telephone handy . . . cabs in the street and all the rest of it. . . .

DORN. [*singing*]. 'Tell my lady of love, O gentle flowers!'

Enter SHAMRAYEF; *after him* PAULINE.

SHAMRAYEF. There they are. Goodday to you. [*Kisses* ARCADINA'*s hand, then* NINA'*s.*] [*To* ARCADINA.] Very glad to see you in such good health. My wife tells me you were thinking of driving into town with her to-day. Is that true?

ARCADINA. Yes, we're going into town.

SHAMRAYEF. Hm! That's all very well, but how do you propose to get there, my dear madam? We're carrying the rye to-day, and all the labourers are busy. What horses are you to have, I should like to know?

ARCADINA. What horses? How should I know what horses?

SORIN. There are the carriage horses.

SHAMRAYEF [*excited.*] The carriage horses? And where am I to get collars from? Where am I to get collars? It really is extraordinary! Incomprehensible! My dear madam, you must excuse me. I have the greatest respect for your talents. I am ready to give ten years of my life for you, but horses I cannot let you have.

ARCADINA. But if I have to go into town? This is really too much.

SHAMRAYEF. My dear lady! You do not know what farming means.

ARCADINA [*angry*]. It is the old story again! If that is the case, I go back to Moscow to-day. Send to the village to hire horses for me, or I shall go to the station on foot.

SHAMRAYEF [*angry*]. In that case I resign my post! You must look for a new agent!

[*Exit.*]

ARCADINA. It is the same thing every summer; every summer I am insulted here. I will never set foot in this place again.

[*Exit L., towards the bathing-place.*]
A minute later she is seen going up to the house.

TRIGORIN *follows her with fishing rods and pail.*

SORIN [*angry*]. This is effrontery! This is beyond all bounds! I'll stand it no more, confound it all! Let *all* the horses be brought here at once!

NINA [*to* PAULINE]. Refuse Madame Arcádina, the famous actress! Is not every lightest wish of hers, or even caprice, of more importance than your farming arrangements? It is absolutely incredible.

PAULINE [*in despair*]. What can I do? Imagine yourself in my position. What can I do?

SORIN [*to* NINA]. Let us follow my sister. We will all entreat her not to go away, eh? [*Looking in the direction where* SHAMRAYEF *went out.*] Hateful fellow! Tyrant!

NINA [*preventing him from rising*]. Sit down, sit down. We will wheel you. [*She and* MEDVEDENKO *wheel the chair.*] What an awful thing to have happened!

SORIN. Perfectly awful. But he shall not get out of it like that. I shall give him a piece of my mind.

[*Exeunt.* DORN *and* PAULINE *remain.*]

DORN. How monotonous people are!

Of course the right thing would have been to fire your husband right out and have done with him, but the end of it will be that this old woman Peter Sorin and his sister will apologise and ask him to forgive them. You'll see.

PAULINE. He has sent the carriage horses to help carry the rye. These misunderstandings happen day after day. If you knew how agitating it all is for me. I shall be ill; see, I am all trembling. . . . His bad manners are more than I can bear. [*Entreating.*] Eugene, my dearest, my darling, let me leave him and come to you. Time is flying over us, we are no longer young; let us have done with concealment and falsehood before our days are ended. [*A pause.*]

DORN. I am fifty-five. It is too late to change my way of life.

PAULINE. I know why you refuse. It is because there are other women besides myself who are dear to you. You cannot let them all come to you. I understand. Forgive me; you are tired of me.

NINA *appears near the house picking flowers.*

DORN. No, no, I'm not tired of you.

PAULINE. I suffer agonies of jealousy. Of course you are a doctor; you cannot avoid women. I understand.

DORN [*to* NINA, *who comes down*]. How are they getting on?

NINA. Madame Arcádina is crying and Monsieur Sorin has got asthma.

DORN [*rising*]. I must go and give them both some Valerian drops.

NINA [*giving him her flowers*]. These are for you.

DORN. Merci bien. [*Goes towards the house.*]

PAULINE [*following him*]. What

pretty flowers! [*Near the house, in a low voice.*] Give me those flowers! Give me those flowers! [*She tears them up and throws them aside.*]

[*Exeunt into the house.*]

NINA [*alone*]. How strange to see an eminent actress in tears, and all about such a trifle! And is it not wonderful that a famous writer, the darling of the public, mentioned daily in the papers, with his photograph in the shop windows, his books translated into foreign languages, should spend his whole day fishing and be delighted because he has caught two chub. I imagined that famous people were proud and inaccessible, that they despised the crowd, and by their fame, by the glamour of their names, as it were, revenged themselves on the world for giving birth and riches the first place. But it seems they cry, fish, play cards, laugh, and get angry like everyone else. . . .

Enter TREPLEF, *hatless, with a gun and a dead seagull.*

TREPLEF [*at the gate*]. Are you alone?

NINA. Yes. [TREPLEF *lays the bird at her feet.*]

NINA. What does that mean?

TREPLEF. I have been brute enough to shoot this seagull. I lay it at your feet.

NINA. What is the matter with you? [*She takes up the gull and looks at it.*]

TREPLEF [*after a pause*]. I shall soon kill myself in the same way.

NINA. You are not yourself.

TREPLEF. No, not since you ceased to be yourself. You have changed towards me: you look coldly at me; you are not at ease when I am by.

NINA. You have grown nervous and irritable of late; you express yourself incomprehensibly in what seems to be symbols. This seagull seems to be another symbol; but, I am afraid I don't understand [*Laying it on the seat.*] I am too simple to understand you.

TREPLEF. It began the night of the idiotic fiasco of my play. Women cannot forgive failure. I have burnt everything, everything to the last scrap. If only you knew how unhappy I am! Your sudden indifference to me is terrible, incredible, as if I woke one morning and behold, this lake had dried up or run away into the earth. You said just now that you are too simple to understand me. Oh, what is there to understand? My play was a failure; you despise my inspiration; you look on me as commonplace and worthless, like hundreds of others. . . . [*Stamping.*] How well I understand it! How well I can understand it! I feel as if there were a nail being driven into my brain. The devil take it. The devil take my vanity too, which sucks out my blood, sucks it out like a snake. [*Seeing* TRIGORIN, *who reads a notebook as he walks.*] There goes the man of real talent; he walks like Hamlet; with a book too. [*Mocking.*] 'Words, words, words!' This sun has not yet risen on you, yet you smile already, your looks are melted in his rays. I will not stand in your way.

[*Exit quickly.*]

TRIGORIN [*writing in his book*]. Takes snuff and drinks vodka. . . . . Always dressed in black. Schoolmaster in love with her.

NINA. Good-morning, Boris Alexéyevitch.

TRIGORIN. Good-morning. It appears

that owing to some unexpected turn of events we are leaving to-day. You and I are hardly likely to meet again. I am sorry. I do not often come across young women, young interesting women; I have already forgotten how one feels at eighteen or nineteen and I cannot imagine it very clearly; so that the young women in my stories and novels are generally untrue to life. How I should like to be in your place, if only for an hour, so as to know what you think and what manner of creature you are altogether.

NINA. And how I should like to be in your place!

TRIGORIN. Why?

NINA. So as to know how it feels to be a gifted and famous writer. What does fame feel like? What sensation does it produce in you?

TRIGORIN. What sensation? Evidently, none. I never thought about it. [*Reflecting.*] One of two things; either you exaggerate my fame, or fame produces no sensation.

NINA. But if you read about yourself in the papers?

TRIGORIN. When they praise me I like it; when they abuse me I feel low-spirited for a day or two.

NINA. What a world to live in! How I envy you, if you but knew it! How different are the lots of different people! Some can hardly drag on their tedious. insignificant existence, they are all alike, all miserable; others, like you for instance—you are one in a million—are blessed with a brilliant, interesting life, all full of meaning. . . . You are happy.

TRIGORIN. Am I? [*Shrugging his shoulders.*] Hm! . . . You talk of fame and happiness, of some brilliant,

interesting life; but for me all these pretty words, if I may say so, are just like marmalade, which I never eat. You are very young and very kind.

NINA. What a delightful life is yours!

TRIGORIN. What is there so very fine about it? [*Looking at his watch.*] I must be off to my writing in a moment. You must excuse me; I can't stop. [Laughs.] You have trodden on my favourite corn, as they say, and you see, I begin to get excited and angry at once. However, let us talk. We'll talk about my delightful, brilliant life. . . . Come on; where shall we begin? [*Meditating.*] You have heard of obsessions, when a man is haunted day and night, say, by the idea of the moon or something? Well, I've got my moon Day and night I am obsessed by the same persistent thought; I must write, I must write, I must write. . . . No sooner have I finished one story than I am somehow compelled to write another, then a third, after the third a fourth. I write without stopping, except to change horses like a post-chaise. I have no choice. What is there brilliant or delightful in that, I should like to know? It's a dog's life! Here I am talking to you, excited and delighted, yet never for one moment do I forget that there is an unfinished story waiting for me indoors. I see a cloud shaped like a grand piano. I think: I must mention somewhere in a story that a cloud went by, shaped like a grand piano. I smell heliotrope. I say to myself: Sickly smell, mourning shade, must be mentioned in describing a summer evening. I lie in wait for each phrase, for each word that falls from my lips or yours and hasten to lock all these words and phrases away in my literary storeroom: They may come in handy some day. When I finish a piece of work, I fly to the theatre or go fishing, in the hope of resting, of forgetting myself, but no, a new subject is already turning, like a heavy iron ball, in my brain, some invisible force drags me to my table and I must make haste to write and write. And so on for ever and ever. I have no rest from myself; I feel that I am devouring my own life, that for the honey which I give to unknown mouths out in the void, I rob my choicest flowers of their pollen,. pluck the flowers themselves and trample on their roots. Surely I must be mad? Surely my friends and acquaintances do not treat me as they would treat a sane man? 'What are you writing at now? What are we going to have next?' So the same thing goes on over and over again, until I feel as if my friends' interest, their praise and admiration, were all a deception; they are deceiving me as one deceives a sick man, and sometimes I'm afraid that at any moment they may steal on me from behind and seize me and carry me off, like Póprishtchin, to a madhouse. In the old days, my young best days, when I was a beginner, my work was a continual torture. An unimportant writer, especially when things are going against him, feels clumsy. awkward and superfluous; his nerves are strained and tormented; he cannot keep from hovering about people who have to do with art and literature, unrecognised, unnoticed, afraid to look men frankly in the eye, like a passionate gambler who has no money to play with. The reader that I never saw presented himself to my imagination as something unfriendly and mistrustful. I was afraid of the public; it terrified me; and when each new play of mine was put on, I felt every time that the dark ones in the audience were hostile and the fair ones coldly indifferent. How frightful it was! What agony I went through!

NINA. But surely inspiration and the process of creation give you sublime and happy moments?

TRIGORIN. Yes. It's a pleasant feeling writing; . . . and looking over proofs is pleasant, too. But as soon as the thing is published my heart sinks, and I see that it is a failure, a mistake, that I ought not to have written it at all; then I am angry with myself and feel horrible. . . . [Laughing.] And the public reads it and says: 'How charming! How clever! . . . How charming, but not a patch on Tolstoy!' or 'It's a delightful story, but not so good as Turgénef's Fathers and Sons.' And so on, to my dying day, my writings will always be clever and charming, clever and charming, nothing more. And when I die, my friends, passing by my grave, will say: 'Here lies Trigórin. He was a charming writer, but not so good as Turgénef.'

NINA. You must excuse me; I refuse to understand you. You are simply spoilt by success.

TRIGORIN. By what success? I've never satisfied myself. I do not care for myself as a writer. The worst of it is that I live in a kind of bewilderment and often do not understand what I write. I love water like this, trees, sky; I have the feeling for nature; it wakes a passion in me, an irresistible desire to write. But I am something more than a landscape-painter; I am a citizen as well; I love my country, I love the people; I feel that if I am a writer I am bound to speak of the people, of its sufferings, of its future, to speak of science, of the rights of man, etcetera, etcetera: and I speak about it all, volubly, and am attacked angrily in return by everyone; I dart from side to side like a fox run down by the hounds; I see that life and science fly farther and farther ahead of me, and I fall farther and farther behind, like the countryman running after the train; and in the end I feel that the only thing I can write of is the landscape, and in everything else I am untrue to life. false to the very marrow of my bones.

NINA. You work too hard; you have no time or wish to realise your own importance. You may be dissatisfied with yourself, but in the eyes of others you are great and wonderful. If I were a writer like you I would sacrifice my whole life to the million, but I would realise that its only happiness was to raise itself up to me; they should pull my chariot along.

TRIGORIN. Chariot, indeed! . . . Am I an Agamemnon then, eh? [*They both smile.*]

NINA. For such happiness as to be a writer or an actress I would endure the hatred of my nearest and dearest. I would endure poverty and disillusionment. I would lodge in a garret and live on black bread. I would suffer dissatisfaction with myself, the consciousness of my own imperfections, but in return I would demand glory . . . real, ringing glory. [*Covering her face with her hands.*] My head swims. Ouf!

ARCADINA [*heard from the house*]. Boris Alexéyevitch!

TRIGORIN. I'm being called. To pack, no doubt. But I don't want to go away. [*Looking at the lake.*] Isn't it heavenly? Just look at it!

NINA. You see that house and garden on the farther shore?

TRIGORIN. Yes.

NINA. They used to belong to my mother. I was born there. I have spent the whole of my life by this lake and I know every little island on it.

TRIGORIN. It's perfectly delicious here! [*Seeing the seagull.*] And what's this?

NINA. A seagull. Constantine Gavrilovitch shot it.

TRIGORIN. It's a lovely bird. I don't want to go away at all. Persuade Madame Arcádina to stay. [*Writes in his notebook.*]

NINA. What are you writing?

TRIGORIN. I was just making a note. A subject occurred to me. [*Putting notebook away.*] A subject for a short story. A girl—like yourself, say—lives from her childhood on the shores of a lake. She loves the lake like a seagull, and is happy and free like a seagull. But a man comes along by chance and sees her and ruins her, like this seagull, just to amuse himself. [*A pause.* AR-CADINA *appears at a window.*]

ARCADINA. Where are you, Boris Alexéyevitch?

TRIGORIN. Coming! [*Looks back at* NINA *as he goes. At the window, to* ARCADINA.] What is it?

ARCADINA. We're staying on.

[*Exit* TRIGORIN *into the house.*]

NINA. [*Coming down to the foot-*

lights. *After a pause and meditation.*]
It's like a dream!

CURTAIN

ACT III

Dining-room in SORIN'S *house. Doors
right and left. Sideboard. Cupboard
with medicaments. Table C. Trunks
and bandboxes; preparations for departure.* TRIGORIN *lunching,* MASHA
standing by the table.

MASHA. I tell you all this because
you're a novelist. You can make use of
it, if you like. I tell you candidly, if
he had wounded himself seriously I
should not have consented to live another
minute. And yet I'm a brave woman.
I've made up my mind; I will tear this
love out of my heart, I will tear it out
by the roots.

TRIGORIN. How are you going to do
that?

MASHA. I am marrying, marrying
Medvédenko.

TRIGORIN. The schoolmaster?

MASHA. Yes.

TRIGORIN. I don't see the necessity.

MASHA. What? to love without hope,
for years and years to be waiting and
waiting. . . . No. Once I am married,
there will be no question of love; new
cares will drown all traces of the old life.
And yet it's a wrench. . . . Shall we
have another go?

TRIGORIN. Won't it be rather a lot?

MASHA. Nonsense. [*Pours out a
glass of vodka for each.*] Don't look at
me like that. More women drink than
you think. Some drink openly like I
do; most of them drink secretly. Yes,
it's always vodka or brandy. [*They
click glasses.*] Here's luck. You're a
simple-minded soul! I am sorry you're
going. [*They drink.*]

TRIGORIN. I don't want to go myself.

MASHA. Ask her to stop on.

TRIGORIN. No, she won't stop now.
Her son has been behaving extremely
tactlessly. First he tried to shoot himself, and now I'm told he wants to challenge me to a duel. And why? He
sulks and sneers and preaches new
forms. . . . Well, there's room for all
of us, both new and old; why should we
jostle one another?

MASHA. He's jealous too. However,
it's no affair of mine. [*A pause.* YAKOF
*crosses R. to L. with a portmanteau.
Enter* NINA, *and stops by the window.*]
My schoolmaster's not particularly
clever, but he's a good fellow, poor
devil, and devoted to me. I'm sorry for
him. I'm sorry for his old mother too.
Well, I wish you the best of everything.
Think no evil of us. [*Shakes him
warmly by the hand.*] Thank you for
all your friendliness. Send me your
books, and mind and put your auto-
graph in them. Only don't write: 'To
my friend So and So, from the author,'
but just: 'To Masha, 22, of no occupation, born into this world for no apparent purpose.' Good-bye. [*Exit.*]

NINA [*holding out her clenched hand
towards* TRIGORIN]. Odd or even?

TRIGORIN. Even.

NINA [*sighing*]. 'No.' I have only
one pea in my hand. The question was,
whether I was to become an actress or
not. If only someone would advise
me!

TRIGORIN. It's a question one can't
advise on. [*A pause.*]

NINA. We are parting to-day and
very likely we shall never meet again.

Please accept this little medallion as a keepsake. I have had your initials engraved on it . . . and on the other side the name of your book, *Days and Nights*.

TRIGORIN. How graceful! [*Kissing the medallion.*] What a charming present!

NINA. Think of me sometimes.

TRIGORIN. I will indeed. I will think of you as you were that sunny day, do you remember? a week ago, when you wore a cotton frock . . . and we talked . . . and there was a seagull lying on the seat.

NINA [*meditatively*]. A seagull, yes. [*A pause.*] We can't talk any more; there's somebody coming. . . Give me two minutes before you go, I entreat you. . . .   [*Exit L.*]

At the same moment enter ARCADINA R., SORIN *in swallowtail coat, with the star of an order; then* YAKOF, *busy with luggage.*

ARCADINA [*to* SORIN]. Stay at home, you old man. You oughtn't to go gadding about with your rheumatism. [*To* TRIGORIN.] Who was it just went out? Nina?

TRIGORIN. Yes.

ARCADINA. *Pardon!* We interrupted you. [*Sitting.*] I think I've packed everything. I'm worn out.

TRIGORIN [*reading the inscription on the medallion*]. 'Days and Nights, page 121, lines 11 and 12.'

YAKOF [*clearing the table*]. Am I to pack the fishing rods too, sir?

TRIGORIN. Yes. I shall want them again. And you can give the books away.

YAKOF. Very good, sir.

TRIGORIN [*to himself*]. 'Page 121, lines 11 and 12.' What can those lines contain? [*To* ARCADINA.] Have you got my books anywhere in the house?

ARCADINA. Yes, in Peter's study; in the corner cupboard.

TRIGORIN. 'Page 121.'   [*Exit.*]

ARCADINA. You'd really better stop at home, Peter.

SORIN. I shall feel dreadfully dull without you when you're gone.

ARCADINA. And will you be any the better for running into town?

SORIN. I don't suppose I shall, but all the same . . . [*Laughing.*] There's the laying the foundation stone of the new Council-house and all the rest of it. . . . I must shake off this stickle-back life if it's only for an hour or two! I've been lying too long on the shelf like an old cigarette-holder. I've ordered my cart at one; we'll start together.

ARCADINA [*after a pause*]. Well, be happy here; don't be bored; don't catch cold. Keep an eye on my boy. Take care of him. Give him good advice. [*A pause.*] I shall go away without having found out why Constantine tried to shoot himself. I expect the chief reason was jealousy; and the sooner I take Trigórin away the better.

SORIN. Well, now, how shall I put it? . . . there were other reasons too: It's very natural; a clever young man, living in the depths of the country, with no money, no position, no future. He has no occupation. He is ashamed and afraid of his indolence. I love him dearly and he is fond of me, but still, confound it all, he feels as if he were in the way here, only a parasite, a hanger-on. It's very natural, a man's vanity . . .

ARCADINA. He's a great trial. [*Meditating.*] He might go into a Government office, perhaps. . . .

SORIN [*whistling; then hesitatingly*]. I fancy the best thing would be if you were to . . . if you were to let him have a little money. In the first place he ought to be dressed like a human being and all the rest of it. He's been wearing the same jacket these three years; he hasn't got an overcoat at all. . . . [*Laughing.*] Then the lad ought to see life a bit. . . . Go abroad and all that. . . . It don't cost much.

ARCADINA. Still. . . . Well, I might manage the clothes, but as for going abroad . . . No, I can't manage the clothes either just at present. [*Resolutely.*] I haven't any money. [SORIN *laughs.*] I haven't.

SORIN [*whistling*]. Well, well! Don't be angry, my dear. I believe you. . . . You're a large-hearted, admirable woman.

ARCADINA [*crying*]. I haven't any money.

SORIN. If I had any myself, of course, I'd let him have it, but I have nothing, not a penny piece. [*Laughing.*] Shamrayef collars all my pension and spends it on the farm, the cattle and the bees, and no one ever sees it again. The bees die, the cows die, I can never have any horses. . . .

ARCADINA. Well, I have got some money; but remember, please, I'm an artiste; my wardrobe alone has simply ruined me.

SORIN. You're a dear good thing. . . . I respect you . . . I . . . But I'm feeling queer again. [*Staggers.*] My head's going round. [*Holding on to the table.*] I feel faint and all the rest of it.

ARCADINA [*frightened*]. Peter! [*Trying to support him.*] Petrusha, my darling! [*Shouting.*] Help! help! [*Enter*

TREPLEF, *with bandage on head, and* MEDVEDENKO.] He's fainting!

SORIN. All right, all right! [*Smiles and drinks some water.*] It's gone and all the rest of it.

TREPLEF. Don't be afraid, mother, there's no danger. Uncle Peter often gets like that nowadays. [*To* SORIN.] You'd better lie down, uncle.

SORIN. Yes, I will for a bit. But I'll go into town all the same. I'll lie down first; of course, of course. [*Goes R., leaning on stick.*]

MEDVEDENKO [*giving him an arm*]. There's a riddle: He walks on four legs in the morning, on two at noon, on three in the evening. . . .

SORIN [*laughing*]. Quite so. And on his back at night. Don't you trouble, I can manage. . . .

MEDVEDENKO. Nonsense! come along! [*Exeunt* MEDVEDENKO *and* SORIN *R.*]

ARCADINA. He quite frightened me.

TREPLEF. It's bad for his health living in the country. He's miserable. Now if, in a sudden burst of generosity, you could lend him a couple of hundred pounds, he would be able to spend the whole year in town.

ARCADINA. I haven't any money. I'm an actress, not a banker. [*A pause.*]

TREPLEF. Please change my bandage, mother. You do it so well.

ARCADINA [*getting iodoform and a drawerful of bandages from the medicine cupboard.*] The doctor's late.

TREPLEF. It's twelve and he promised to be here by ten.

ARCADINA. Sit down. [*Taking off bandage.*] You look as if you had a turban on. A man asked the servants yesterday what nationality you were. It's almost healed up. There's hardly anything left there. [*Kissing his head.*]

You promise not to play at chik-chik again while I'm away?

TREPLEF. I promise, mother. That was in a moment of despair when I had lost all self-control. It won't happen again. [*Kissing her hand.*] You have the hands of an angel. I remember a long time ago, when you were still on the Imperial stage—I was quite little then—there was a fight in the courtyard of the house we lived in; a washerwoman who lodged there got awfully knocked about. You remember? She was picked up senseless. . . . You were always going in to see her, taking her medicine and bathing her children in the washtub. Don't you remember?

ARCADINA. No. [*Putting on a new bandage.*]

TREPLEF. There were two balletgirls lodging in the same place. . . . They used to come in for coffee. . . .

ARCADINA. I remember that.

TREPLEF. They were very pious. [*A pause.*] These last few days I have loved you just as tenderly and trustfully as when I was a child. I have nobody left now but you. But why, oh why, do you submit to this man's influence?

ARCADINA. You don't understand him, Constantine. He has the noblest nature in the world. . . .

TREPLEF. Yet when he was told that I meant to challenge him to fight, his noble nature did not prevent him from playing the coward. He is going away. It's an ignominious flight!

ARCADINA. What rubbish! It was I who asked him to go.

TREPLEF. The noblest nature in the world! Here are you and I almost quarrelling about him, and where is he? In the garden or the drawing-room laughing at us, improving Nina's mind, and trying to persuade her that he's a genius.

ARCADINA. It seems to give you pleasure to try and hurt my feelings. I respect Trigórin and I must ask you not to abuse him to my face.

TREPLEF. And I *don't* respect him. You want *me* to believe him a genius too; but you must excuse me, I can't tell lies; his writings make me sick.

ARCADINA. This is mere envy. Conceited people with no talent have no resource but to jeer at really talented people. It relieves their feelings, no doubt!

TREPLEF [*ironically*]. Really talented people! [*Angry.*] I am more talented than all of you put together if it comes to that! [*Tearing off the bandages.*] You apostles of the commonplace have taken the front seat in all the arts for yourselves and call nothing but what you do yourselves legitimate and real; you persecute and stifle all the rest. I don't believe in any of you; I don't believe in *you* and I don't believe in *him!*

ARCADINA. Decadent!

TREPLEF. Go back to your beloved theatre and act your pitiful stupid plays!

ARCADINA. I never acted in such plays. Leave me! You cannot even write a miserable vaudeville if you try! Kiev artisan! Parasite!

TREPLEF. Skinflint!

ARCADINA. Tatterdemalion! [*TREPLEF sits down and cries quietly.*] You insignificant nobody! [*Walking up and down agitatedly.*] Don't cry. Don't cry, I say. [*Crying.*] Please don't cry. [*Kissing his forehead, cheeks and head.*] My darling child, forgive me. . . . Forgive your wicked mother! Forgive your unhappy mother!

TREPLEF [*embracing her*]. If only you knew! I have lost everything. She doesn't love me and I cannot write any more . . . all my hopes are lost.

ARCADINA. Don't lose heart. It will be all right in the end. He is going away; she will love you again. [*Wiping away his tears.*] Stop crying. We are friends once more.

TREPLEF [*kissing her hands*]. Yes, mother.

ARCADINA [*tenderly*]. Be friends with him too. You mustn't have a duel. You won't have one?

TREPLEF. Very well. But you mustn't let me meet him any more, mother. It hurts me; it is too much for me. [*Enter* TRIGORIN.] There! I will go away. [*Hastily puts the medicaments away in the cupboard.*] The doctor shall bandage me when he comes.

TRIGORIN [*looking for the place in a book*]. Page 121. Lines 11 and 12. Ha! [*Reading.*] 'If ever my life can be of use to you, come and take it.' [TREPLEF *picks up his bandage and goes.*]

ARCADINA [*looking at the time*]. The horses will soon be round.

TRIGORIN [*to himself*]. 'If ever my life can be of use to you, come and take it.'

ARCADINA. You've got your things all packed, I hope?

TRIGORIN [*impatiently*]. Yes, yes. [*Reflectively.*] Why do I hear the sound of anguish in this cry of a pure spirit? Why does my heart sink so painfully? 'If ever my life can be of use to you, come and take it.' [*To* ARCADINA.] Let us stay another day. [*She shakes her head.*] Let us stay.

ARCADINA. Dear friend, I know what makes you want to stay. You should have some self-control. You've lost

your senses a little; come back to reason.

TRIGORIN. And do you too come back to reason; be thoughtful and considerate, I beseech you; look at all this like a real friend. [*Pressing her hand.*] You are capable of a sacrifice. Be kind and set me free!

ARCADINA [*in deep agitation*]. Are you so much in love?

TRIGORIN. Something beckons me towards her. Perhaps this is the very thing that I really need. . . .

ARCADINA. The love of a provincial girl? Oh, how little you know yourself.

TRIGORIN. People sometimes sleep as they walk; and even while I talk to you, it is as if I were asleep and saw her in my dreams. . . . Wonderful sweet visions possess me. . . . Set me free!

ARCADINA [*trembling*]. No. no. I am an ordinary woman; I cannot be talked to so. Don't torment me, Boris. I am frightened.

TRIGORIN. If you will try you can be an extraordinary woman. A sweet poetical young love, wafting me away into the world of reveries, there is nothing on earth can give happiness like that. Such a love I have never yet experienced. As a young man I had no time; I was wearing out editors' thresholds, struggling with poverty . . . and now at last it stands before me beckoning, this love. . . . Should I not be a fool to fly from it?

ARCADINA [*angrily*]. You have gone out of your mind.

TRIGORIN. Who cares?

ARCADINA. You are all banded together to-day to torment me. [*Crying.*]

TRIGORIN [*taking his head between his hands*]. She doesn't understand. She refuses to understand.

ARCADINA. Am I so old and ugly already that men can say what they like about other women to me? [*Embracing and kissing him.*] Oh, you are mad, mad! My darling, wonderful Boris! Last page of my life! [*Kneeling.*] My joy, my pride, my bliss. [*Embracing his knees.*] If you desert me even for an hour, I cannot survive it, I shall go out of my mind, my splendid incomparable friend, my king.

TRIGORIN. Someone might come in. [*Helping her to rise.*]

ARCADINA. Who cares? I am not ashamed of my love for you. [*Kissing his hands.*] You are rash and wild, my treasure; what you want to do is madness; you shall not, I will not let you. [*Laughing.*] You are mine! mine! This forehead is mine, these eyes are mine, this lovely silky hair is mine. . . . You are all mine! You are so clever, so gifted, the best of all the writers of the day, you are the only hope of Russia. . . . You have such a gift of sincerity, simplicity, freshness and bracing humour. . . . In a single stroke you give the essence of a character or a landscape; your people are all alive. Oh, no one can read you without delight! Do you think this is mere incense and flattery? Come, look me in the eyes, right in the eyes. Do I look like a liar? You see, there is nobody but me who knows your true value; nobody; I am the only person who tells you the truth, my precious darling. . . . You'll come? Say you will. You won't desert me?

TRIGORIN. I have no will of my own. I never had a will of my own. Weak-kneed, flabby and submissive; everything that women hate. Take me, carry me away, but never let me stir an inch from your side.

ARCADINA [*to herself*]. He's mine! [*Carelessly.*] Well, stay if you like. I'll go to-day and you follow a week later. After all, why should you hurry?

TRIGORIN. No. We'll go together.

ARCADINA. As you please. We'll go together if you like. [*A pause.* TRIGORIN *writes in his notebook.*] What's that?

TRIGORIN. I heard a good expression this morning: the corn was 'shuckled' by the wind. It may come in some time. [*Stretching.*] So we are off? Railway carriages again, stations, refreshment rooms, mutton chops and conversations.

Enter SHAMRAYEF.

SHAMRAYEF. I have the melancholy honour of announcing that the carriage is round. It's time to start for the station, dear lady; the train comes in at two-five. Now don't forget to inquire, if you'll be so good, Irina Nikolayevna, what has become of Suzdáltsef. Is he alive? Is he well? Many's the drink we had together. He was inimitable in *The Lyons Mail.* He was playing at that time at Elizavétgrad with Izmailov the tragedian, another remarkable man. . . . No hurry, my dear lady, we've still got another five minutes to spare. They played the conspirators once in a melodrama, and when they were suddenly found out, the line was: 'We are caught like rats in a trap'; but Izmailov said, 'like trats in a rap'! instead. [*Laughing.*] 'Trats in a rap'!

[*While he is speaking* YAKOF *is busy with the luggage; a housemaid brings* ARCADINA *her hat, mantle, parasol and gloves; everyone helps* ARCADINA *to dress. A man-cook looks in L. and after a little while enters irresolutely. Enter* PAULINE, *then* SORIN *and* MEDVEDENKO.] PAULINE [*offering a basket*]. Here are some plums for the journey. They're nice and sweet. I thought you might enjoy them.

ARCADINA. How kind of you, Pauline Andréyevna.

PAULINE. Good-bye, my dear. If there was ever anything amiss, forgive it. [*Crying.*]

ARCADINA [*embracing her*]. Everything has been perfect, perfect! Only you mustn't cry.

PAULINE. Our sands are running out.

ARCADINA. It can't be helped.

SORIN [*with cape-coat, hat, stick; entering L. and crossing room*]. Time to be off, Irene; you mustn't be late, confound it all. I'm going to get in.

MEDVEDENKO. I shall go to the station on foot to see you off. I'll be there in no time.   [*Exit.*]

ARCADINA. Good-bye, everyone. If we're alive and well we shall meet again in the summer. [*House-maid, man-cook and YAKOF kiss her hand.*] Don't forget me. [*Giving the cook a rouble.*] There's a rouble to divide among you.

COOK. Our humblest thanks, lady. A good journey to you! We are very content with you!

YAKOF. Heaven send you happy times!

SHAMRAYEF. Make us happy with a little letter. [*To* TRIGORIN.] Good-bye, Boris Alexéyevitch!

ARCADINA. Where's Constantine? Tell him that I am off. We must say good-bye. [*To* YAKOF.] Think no evil of us. I've given the cook a rouble. It's for the three of you.

[*Exeunt all R. Stage empty. Noise of farewells and departure behind the scene. Housemaid comes back for the basket of plums, and exit with it.*]

TRIGORIN [*coming back*]. I've left my stick behind. I think she's out there on the verandah. [*Goes L. and meets* NINA, *entering.*] Ah, it's you. We're off.

NINA. I felt that we should meet again. [*Agitatedly.*] Boris Alexéyevitch, I have made up my mind beyond recall; the die is cast; I am going on the stage. To-morrow I shall be gone from here; I am leaving my father; I am giving up everything and beginning a new life. I am going where you are going . . . to Moscow. We shall meet there.

TRIGORIN [*looking round*]. Stop at the 'Slavyansky Bazaar.' Let me know at once. Molchanóvska, Grokhólsky's house . . . I'm in a hurry. . . . [*A pause.*]

NINA. One minute more.

TRIGORIN [*murmuring*]. How beautiful you are! . . . What joy to think that we shall meet again so soon. [*She lays her head on his bosom.*] I shall see these lovely eyes once more, this inexpressibly tender, charming smile, this sweet face, this expression of angelic purity. . . . My darling! [*A long kiss.*]

CURTAIN

Two years elapse between the third and fourth Acts.

ACT IV

One of the drawing-rooms in SORIN'S *house, converted by* CONSTANTINE *into a study. Door R. and L. A glass door in the back on to the verandah. Besides usual drawing-room furniture, a writing-table stands up R., a Turkish divan by the door L., bookcase, books on window-sills and chairs. Evening. Twilight. One lamp alight, with shade. The wind howls in the trees and chimneys.*

Watchman beats a board outside as he passes.

[*Enter* MEDVEDENKO *and* MASHA.]

MASHA [*calling*]. Constantine Gavrilovitch! Constantine Gavrilovitch! [*Looking about.*] There's no one here. The old man keeps asking every minute 'Where's Constantine? Where's Constantine?' He can't live without him.

MEDVEDENKO. He's afraid of solitude. [*Listening.*] What a fearful storm! It's been like this for two whole days.

MASHA [*turning up the lamp*]. There are waves on the lake, great big ones.

MEDVEDENKO. How dark it is in the garden! They ought to have that stage in the garden pulled down. It stands all bare and ugly like a skeleton, and the curtain flaps in the wind. As I came by yesterday evening I thought I heard someone crying there.

MASHA. Did you? [*A pause.*]

MEDVEDENKO. Let's go home, Masha.

MASHA [*shaking her head*]. I shall stay the night here.

MEDVEDENKO [*imploringly*]. Come home, Masha. Our baby must be starving.

MASHA. Rubbish. Matróna will feed it. [*A pause.*]

MEDVEDENKO. Poor little beggar; three nights away from its mother.

MASHA. What a bore you are! In the old days you used at any rate to philosophise; but now it's always baby, baby, home, home. Can't you find anything new to say?

MEDVEDENKO. Let's go, Masha.

MASHA. Go yourself.

MEDVEDENKO. Your father won't let me have a horse.

MASHA. Yes, he will. You ask him, he'll let you have one fast enough.

MEDVEDENKO. Well, I'll try. Then you'll come to-morrow?

MASHA [*taking snuff*]. All right. Can't you leave me alone? [*Enter* TREPLEF, *carrying pillows and blankets, and* PAULINE *with sheets. They put them on the Turkish divan and* TREPLEF *goes and sits at the writing-table.*] What's this about, mother?

PAULINE. Monsieur Sorin wants his bed made in Constantine's room.

MASHA. I'll help. [*Spreading sheets.*]

PAULINE [*sighing*]. Old folk are just like children. [*Goes to writing-table, leans on her elbow and looks over* CONSTANTINE'S *manuscript. A pause.*]

MEDVEDENKO. Well, I'll be off. Good-bye, Masha. [*Kissing his wife's hand.*] Good-bye, mother. [*Offering to kiss* PAULINE'S *hand.*]

PAULINE [*sourly*]. There, go along, do!

MEDVEDENKO. Good-bye, Constantine Gavrilovitch. [CONSTANTINE *shakes hands silently.*]

[*Exit* MEDVEDENKO.]

PAULINE [*looking at the manuscript*]. Nobody ever imagined that you would become a real writer, Constantine. But now, thank heaven, the magazines send you money for your stories. [*Stroking his hair.*] And you've grown so handsome. Dear, good Constantine, try and be kinder to my Masha.

MASHA [*laying the bed*]. Do leave him alone, mother.

PAULINE [*to* CONSTANTINE]. She's such a dear. [*A pause.*] All that a woman asks, Constantine, is to be looked at kindly. I know it myself. . . . [CONSTANTINE *rises and leaves the room silently.*]

MASHA. Now you've made him

angry. Why couldn't you leave him alone?

PAULINE. I'm so sorry for you, Masha.

MASHA. No need, thank you.

PAULINE. My heart aches again for you. I see it all; I understand it all.

MASHA. Bah! Hopeless love only exists in novels. Rubbish! One only has to keep oneself in hand, and not to sit waiting and waiting for what can never come. If love strikes root in one's heart, one must turn it out. Well, they've promised to transfer Simeon to another district. Once we get there I shall forget everything; I will tear it out by the roots.

A melancholy waltz is played two rooms away.

PAULINE. There's Constantine playing. That means he's unhappy.

MASHA [*silently dancing a few turns to the waltz*]. The chief thing is not to have him always before one's eyes. If only they will transfer my Simeon. Once we're there I shall forget him in a month. This is all fiddlesticks.

[*Enter* DORN *and* MEDVEDENKO L., *wheeling* SORIN *in a chair.*]

MEDVEDENKO. I have six mouths in the house to feed now. And flour's four and sixpence a hundredweight.

DORN. You won't get much change out of that.

MEDVEDENKO. Ah! It's all very well for you to laugh. You're rolling in money.

DORN. Rolling in money? After thirty years of practice, my dear fellow, thirty years of practice, during which I could never call my soul my own day or night, all that I managed to scrape together was two hundred pounds,

and that I spent when I went abroad just lately. I haven't a farthing.

MASHA [*to* MEDVEDENKO]. So you've not gone yet?

MEDVEDENKO [*apologetically*]. How can I, if they won't let me have a horse?

MASHA [*murmuring, bitterly*]. I wish my eyes may never light on you again.

SORIN'S *chair is placed on the* L. *side of the stage.* PAULINE, MASHA *and* DORN *sit by it.* MEDVEDENKO, *downcast, goes apart.*

DORN. Why, what a lot of changes you've been making. You've turned the drawing-room into a study.

MASHA. It's more convenient for Constantine Gavrilovitch to work here. When he feels inclined he can go out into the garden to think.

[*The watchman beats his board outside.*]

SORIN. Where's Irene?

DORN. Gone to the station to meet Trigórin. She'll be back immediately.

SORIN. If you thought it necessary to send for my sister to come, I must be dangerously ill. [*A pause.*] It's too bad, here am I dangerously ill and nobody will give me any medicine!

DORN. Well, what medicine do you want? Valerian drops? Soda? Quinine?

SORIN. Oh! more philosophy, I suppose. It's simply the devil! [*Nodding at the divan.*] Is that laid for me?

PAULINE. Yes, it's for you, Peter Nikolayevitch.

SORIN. Many thanks.

DORN [*singing*]. 'The moon swims by in the clouds of night.'

SORIN. I shall give Constantine a subject for a story. It's to be called 'The Man who wanted to,' *'L'homme qui a voulu.'* When I was a young man I wanted to be a writer, and I didn't become one; I wanted to be a good speaker and was a vile one. [*Mimicking himself.*] 'And, er, so to speak, er, as I was saying . . .' And my perorations that went on and on, till one was bathed in perspiration. . . . I wanted to marry and remained a bachelor; I wanted to live and die in town, and here I am ending my days in the country and all the rest of it.

DORN. You wanted to be made an Actual State Councillor, and you were.

SORIN [*laughing*]. I never tried for that. It came of its own accord.

DORN. To express dissatisfaction with life at sixty-two, you must confess, is ungenerous.

SORIN. What a pig-headed fellow you are! Don't you understand? I want to *live!*

DORN. That's frivolous. By the laws of nature every life must come to an end.

SORIN. You talk as a man who has had his fill. You're sated and therefore indifferent to life; it's all the same to you. But even you will be afraid of death.

DORN. The fear of death is an animal fear. One ought to repress it. The only people who are consciously afraid are those who believe in eternal life; they are frightened by the knowledge of their sins. But you, in the first place, you're an unbeliever, and in the second, what sins can you have on your mind? You've served twenty-five years in the Law Courts, nothing more.

SORIN. [*Laughing.*] Twenty-eight.

Enter TREPLEF, *and sits on a foot-stool at* SORIN's *feet.* MASHA *cannot keep her eyes off him.*

DORN. We are preventing Constantine Gavrilovitch from working.

TREPLEF. No, it's all right. [*Pause.*]

MEDVEDENKO. Allow me to ask you, doctor, what town pleased you most abroad?

DORN. Genoa.

TREPLEF. Why Genoa?

DORN. The crowd in the streets is so charming in Genoa. If you go out from your hotel in the evening you find the whole street overflowing with people. You go about aimlessly in the crowd, zigzagging to and fro, you live with its life, you fuse your individuality with its, and you begin to believe that a Universal Spirit is really possible, like that one that Nina Zarétchnaya once acted in your play. By the by, where *is* Nina Zarétchnaya? How's she getting on?

TREPLEF. She's quite well, I imagine.

DORN. I was told she was living some curious sort of life. What was it?

TREPLEF. It's a long story, doctor.

DORN. Well, make it a short one.
[*A pause.*]

TREPLEF. She ran away from home and went to Trigórin. That you know.

DORN. Yes, I know.

TREPLEF. She had a baby. The baby died. Trigórin got tired of her and went back to his old ties, as one might have expected. Besides, he never gave up his old ties, but, like the backboneless creature he is, managed to carry on with both at the same time. As far as I can make out from what I've heard. Nina's private life has been disastrous.

DORN. And on the stage?

TREPLEF. Still worse, I should say. She came out first at a summer theatre near Moscow, and then went off to the provinces. I kept her in sight for some time and followed her wherever she went. She was always trying to do big parts, but acted crudely and inartistically, mouthing her words and making awkward gestures. There were moments when she showed some talent in screaming and dying, but they were only moments.

DORN. Still, you think she has some gift for it?

TREPLEF. It was hard to make out. I should think so, certainly. I saw her, but she refused to see me, and the servants wouldn't let me into her rooms. I understood her mood and did not insist on an interview. [*A pause.*] What else is there to tell you? Afterwards, when I got back home I used to get letters from her, nice, friendly, interesting letters; she didn't complain, but I could see that she was profoundly unhappy; in every line one felt her strained and tortured nerves. Her imagination was a little discolored. She signed herself 'Seagull.' In *Rusalka* the miller says he is a raven; so she said in her leters that she was a seagull. And now she's here.

DORN. How do you mean, here?

TREPLEF. Down in the town, at an inn. She's been in rooms there five or six days. I drove in in the hope of seeing her. Marya Illyínitchna [*Indicating* MASHA.] went too, but she won't see anyone. Medvédenko declares he saw her crossing the fields yesterday afternoon, a mile and a half from here.

MEDVEDENKO. Yes, I saw her. She was going the other way, towards the town. I took off my hat and asked why she didn't come and stay with us. She said she would.

TREPLEF. She won't. [*A pause.*] Her father and stepmother refuse to know

her. They've put watchmen everywhere to prevent her even getting near the grounds. [TREPLEF *and* DORN *go to the writing-table.*] How easy it is to be a philosopher on paper, doctor, and how hard it is in real life.

SORIN. What a charming girl she was!

DORN. Eh, what?

SORIN. I say what a charming girl she was. His Excellency Councillor Sorin was in love with her for a time.

DORN. Old Don Juan!

[SHAMRAYEF's *laugh is heard without.*]

PAULINE. It sounds as if they were back from the station.

TREPLEF. Yes, I can hear mother.

[*Enter* ARCADINA *and* TRIGORIN, SHAMRAYEF *following.*]

SHAMRAYEF. [*As he enters.*] We all grow old and battered under the influence of the elements, but you, dear lady, are as young as ever, with your lovely frocks, such life, such grace. . . .

ARCADINA. You want to bewitch me with praise again, you tiresome man!

TRIGORIN. [*To* SORIN.] How do you do, Peter Nikolayevitch? What do you mean by being ill? It's very wrong of you. [*Seeing* MASHA, *delighted.*] Marya Ilyínitchna!

MASHA. Not forgotten me? [*Shaking hands.*]

TRIGORIN. Married?

MASHA. Long ago.

TRIGORIN. Happy? [*Salutes* DORN *and* MEDVEDENKO, *then goes irresolutely towards* TREPLEF.] Irina Nikolayevna said that you had overlooked the past and forgiven me.

[TREPLEF *gives him his hand.*]

ARCADINA. [*To her son.*] Trigórin

has brought the magazine with your new story.

TREPLEF. [*Taking the magazine; to* TRIGORIN.] Many thanks. You're very kind. [*They both sit.*]

TRIGORIN. Your admirers send you their respects. . . . People in Moscow and St. Petersburg are interested in you; I am always being asked about you. They want to know what you look like, how old you are, dark or fair. For some reason or other they all imagine that you're no longer young. And nobody knows your real name, of course, as you write under a *nom de plume*. You're a mystery, like the Man in the Iron Mask.

TREPLEF. Have you come for long?

TRIGORIN. No, I mean to go to Moscow to-morrow. I can't stop. I'm trying to get a novel finished, and then I've promised to write something for an annual. In fact, it's the old story.

[*While they are talking* ARCADINA *and* PAULINE *bring a card-table to the middle of the room and open it;* SHAMRAYEF *lights the candles and brings chairs. Things for a game of loto are brought from a cupboard.*]

TRIGORIN. Your weather welcomes me here in the most inhospitable manner. It's a cruel wind. To-morrow morning, if it goes down, I shall go and fish in the lake. And I want to look round the garden and see the place where your play was acted, you remember? I've got a subject ready for writing; I want to refresh my memory as to the scene of action.

MASHA. [*To* SHAMRAYEF.] Papa, will you let Simeon have a horse? He's got to go home.

SHAMRAYEF. [*Ironical.*] A horse! Go home! [*Severely.*] Didn't you see for yourself, the horses have just been to the station? They can't go out again.

MASHA. But they're not the only ones. . . . [*Seeing that her father won't answer, she makes a gesture of breaking off.*] You're all more trouble than you're worth!

MEDVEDENKO. I'll do it on foot, Masha. It's all right. . . .

PAULINE. [*Sighing.*] On foot, in weather like this. . . . [*Seating herself at the card-table.*] Now come along, everyone.

MEDVEDENKO. It's not more than four miles. . . . Good-bye. [*Kissing his wife's hand.*] Good-bye, mother. [PAULINE, *his mother-in-law, unwillingly gives him her hand to kiss.*] I wouldn't have troubled anyone, only the baby . . . [*He bows to the company.*] Good-bye.

[*Exit, with a guilty air.*]

SHAMRAYEF. He'll get there right enough. He's not a general.

PAULINE. [*Rapping on the table.*] Now then, come along. Don't let's waste time; they'll be calling us to supper very soon.

[SHAMRAYEF, MASHA *and* DORN *sit at the card-table.*]

ARCADINA. [*To* TRIGORIN.] When the long autumn evenings begin we always play loto here. Just look; the old loto-set that we used to play with with mother, when we were children. Won't you have a game with us till supper-time? [*She and* TRIGORIN *sit at the card-table.*] It's a tedious game, but it's all right when you're used to it. [*She deals three cards to each.*]

TREPLEF. [*Looking through the magazine.*] He's read his own story and hasn't even cut mine. [*Puts magazine on writing-table, then goes to the door*

L.; *as he passes his mother he kisses her on the head.*]

ARCADINA. Aren't you coming, Constantine?

TREPLEF. No, thanks; I don't feel like it. I'm going for a turn round the house. [*Exit.*]

ARCADINA. The stake's twopence. Put in for me, doctor.

DORN. Very good, mum.

MASHA. Everybody put in? I begin. . . . Twenty-two!

ARCADINA. Yes.

MASHA. Three!

DORN. Here you are.

MASHA. Have you marked three? Eight! Eighty-one! Ten!

SHAMRAYEF. Not so quick.

ARCADINA. Such a reception I had at Kharkof! Saints in heaven! My head still goes round with it.

MASHA. Thirty-four!

[*A melancholy waltz behind the scenes.*]

ARCADINA. The students gave me quite an ovation. Three baskets of flowers, two bouquets and look at that! [*Taking a brooch from her bosom and throwing it on the table.*]

SHAMRAYEF. Why, that's no end of a . . .

MASHA. Fifty!

DORN. Five O.

ARCADINA. I was wearing a charming frock . . . my frocks are one of my strong points.

PAULINE. [*Listening to the music.*] Do you hear Constantine? He's unhappy, poor lamb.

SHAMRAYEF. They abuse him a good deal in the papers.

MASHA. Seventy-seven!

ARCADINA. Who cares for the papers!

TRIGORIN. He has no luck. He can't

somehow get into his natural stride. There's always something queer and vague about it, almost like delirium at times. Never a single living character.

MASHA. Eleven!

ARCADINA. [*Looking round at* SORIN.] Are you bored, Peter? [*A pause,*] He's asleep.

DORN. The Actual State Councillor is asleep.

MASHA. Seven! Ninety!

TRIGORIN. If I lived in a country house like this, by a lake, do you think I would ever write another line? I would conquer the passion and spend my whole time fishing.

MASHA. Twenty-eight!

TRIGORIN. To catch a roach or a perch . . . what bliss!

DORN. For my part, I believe in Constantine. He'll do something. He'll do something! He thinks in pictures, his stories are bright and full of colour; I feel them very deeply. It's a pity only that he has no definite purpose before his eyes. He produces an impression and there he stops; producing impressions won't take you very far. Are you glad you've a son who is a writer, Irina Nikolayevna?

ARCADINA. Fancy, I've never read a line of his. I never have time.

MASHA. Twenty-six!

[*Enter* TREPLEF *quietly: he goes to his table.*]

SHAMRAYEF. [*To* TRIGORIN.] We've still got that thing of yours, Boris Alexéyevitch.

TRIGORIN. What thing?

SHAMRAYEF. Constantine Gavrilovitch shot a seagull one day, and you asked me to have it stuffed for you.

TRIGORIN. Did I? [*Meditating.*] I don't remember.

MASHA. Sixty-six! One!

TREPLEF. [*Opening the window and listening.*] How dark it is! I wonder why I feel so uneasy. . . .

ARCADINA. Shut the window, dear; it makes a draught. [TREPLEF *shuts it.*]

MASHA. Eighty-eight!

TRIGORIN. Ha, ha! I've won.

ARCADINA. [*Gaily.*] Well done! Well done!

SHAMRAYEF. Bravo.

ARCADINA. Trigórin is always lucky wherever he goes. [*Rising.*] And now let's go and get something to eat. The eminent novelist has had no dinner to-day. We'll go on after supper. Constantine, put your writing away and come to supper.

TREPLEF. I don't want anything thanks, mother. I'm not hungry.

ARCADINA. As you please. [*Walking* SORIN.] Supper-time, Peter. [*Taking* SHAMRAYEF'S *arm.*] I will tell you about my reception at Kharkof.

[PAULINE *puts out the candles on the card table; she and* DORN *wheel* SORIN'S *chair. Exeunt omnes L.* TREPLEF *remains alone at his writing-table.*]

TREPLEF. [*Preparing to write; reads through what he has already written.*] I have talked so much about new formulae, and now I feel that I'm slipping back little by little into the old common-places. [*Reading.*] 'The placard on the hoarding informed the public . . .' 'Her pale face framed in masses of dark hair . . .' 'Informed the public.' 'Framed in masses' . . . How cheap! [*Scratching out.*] I'll begin with the hero being woken by the sound of rain, and throw the rest overboard. The description of the moonlight night is tedious and artificial. Tri-

górin has worked himself out a method, it's easy for him. The neck of a broken bottle glimmering on the mill-dam and the black shadow of the water-wheel, and there's your moonlight night complete; but here am I with my tremulous rays and the twinkling stars and the distant sound of a piano fainting on the prefumed air. . . . It's frightful! [*A pause.*] Yes, I'm coming more and more to the conclusion that it doesn't matter whether the formulae are new or old; a man's got to write without thinking of form at all, just because it flows naturally out of his soul. [*Someone knocks at the window by the table.*] What's that? [*Looking out.*] I don't see anything. [*Opens the glass door and looks into the garden.*] Someone ran down the steps. [*Calling.*] Who's there? [*Goes out; walks quickly along the verandah outside, and returns a moment later with* NINA ZARETCHNAYA.] Nina! Nina! [*Nina lays her head on his bosom and sobs restrainedly.*] [*With emotion.*] Nina! Nina! Is it you? is it you? I had a sort of presentiment; all day my heart has been in anguish. [*Takes off her hat and cloak.*] Oh, my dearest, my loveliest! She has come at last! We mustn't cry, we mustn't cry!

NINA. Is there anyone here?

TREPLEF. No one.

NINA. Lock the door; they may come in.

TREPLEF. No one will come in.

NINA. I know that Irina Nikolayevna is here. Lock the door.

TREPLEF. [*Locks the door R. and goes to the door L.*] There's no lock on this one. I'll put a chair against it. [*Puts an arm-chair against the door.*] Don't be afraid, no one will come in.

NINA. [*Looking him hard in the*

face.] Let me look at you. [*Looking round the room.*] How warm and cosy. . . . This used to be the drawing-room. Am I much changed?

TREPLEF. Yes, you're thinner and your eyes are bigger. Nina, how strange it is to see you at last! Why would you not let me in when I visited you? Why have you not come before? I know you have been here nearly a week. I've been to the inn several times every day and stood under your window like a beggar.

NINA. I was afraid you must hate me. I dream every night that you look at me and do not recognise me. If only you knew! Every day since I came I've been walking up here by the lake. I've been so often near the house but did not dare to come in. Let's sit down. [*They sit.*] Let's sit here and talk and talk. How pleasant it is here, how warm and comfortable. . . . Do you hear the wind? There's a passage in Turgénef: 'Blessed is he who sits beneath a roof on such a night, in his own comfortable corner.' I am a seagull. No, that's wrong. [*Rubs her forehead.*] What was I saying? Yes . . . Turgénef. . . . 'And the Lord help all homeless wanderers.' . . . I'm all right. [*Sobbing.*]

TREPLEF. Nina! you're crying again. . . Nina!

NINA. I'm all right. I feel the better for it . . . I haven't cried for two years. Yesterday evening I came into the garden to see if our stage was still standing. It's still there. I cried for the first time in two years, and felt relieved, and easier in my mind. See, I'm not crying any more. [*Taking his hand.*] So you've become a writer. You're a writer and I'm an actress. We're both caught up in the vortex. Once I lived so happily, with a child's happiness; I would wake of a morning and sing with glee; I loved you and dreamed of fame; and now? Early to-morrow morning I must travel to Yeletz, third class, with peasants, and at Yeletz I shall have to put up with the attentions of the educated shopkeepers. . . . How brutal life is!

TREPLEF. Why Yeletz?

NINA. I've accepted an engagement for the whole winter. I must start to-morrow.

TREPLEF. Nina, I cursed you and hated you at first; I tore up your letters and your photographs! but all the time I knew that my heart was bound to you for ever. Try as I may, I cannot cease loving you, Nina. Ever since I lost you and began to get my stories printed, my life has been intolerable. How I have suffered! . . . My youth was snatched from me, as it were. and I feel as if I had lived for ninety years. I call to you; I kiss the ground where you have passed; wherever I look I see your face with that caressing smile which shone upon me in the best years of my life. . . .

NINA. [*Wildly.*] Why does he say that? Why does he say that?

TREPLEF. I am alone in the world, unwarmed by any affection; it chills me like a dungeon, and whatever I write is hollow, dull and gloomy. Stay here, Nina, I beseech you, or let me come away with you! [NINA *puts on her hat and cloak quickly.*] Nina, why are you doing that? For God's sake, Nina . . . [*He watches her putting on her things.*] [*A pause.*]

NINA. My trap is at the garden gate. Don't come and see me out. I'll manage all right. [*Crying.*] Give me some water.

TREPLEF. [*Giving her water.*] Where are you going to?

NINA. Back to the town. [*A pause.*] Is Irina Nikolayevna here?

TREPLEF. Yes . . . Uncle Peter was taken ill on Thursday; we wired for her to come.

NINA. Why do you say you kissed the ground where I had walked? You ought to kill me. [*Leaning against the table.*] Oh. I am so tired! If I could only rest . . . if I could only rest. [*Raising her head.*] I am a seagull . . . no, that's wrong. I am an actress. Yes, yes. [*Hearing* ARCADINA *and* TRIGORIN *laughing, she listens, then runs to the door* R. *and looks through the keyhole.*] So he's here too! . . . [*Coming back to* TREPLEF] Yes, yes. . . . I'm all right. . . . He didn't believe in the stage; he always laughed at my ambitions; little by little I came not to believe in it either; I lost heart. . . . And on the top of that the anxieties of love, jealousy, perpetual fear for the child . . . I became trivial and commonplace; I acted without meaning . . . I did not know what to do with my hands, or how to stand on the stage. I had no control over my voice. You can't imagine how you feel when you know that you are acting atrociously. I am a seagull. No, that's wrong. . . . Do you remember, you shot a seagull? 'A man comes along by chance and sees her, and, just to amuse himself, ruins her. . . . A subject for a short story.' . . . No, that's not it. . . [*Rubbing her forehead.*] What was I talking about? . . . Ah, about acting. I'm not like that now . . I'm a real actress now. When I act I rejoice, I delight in it;

I am intoxicated and feel that I am splendid. Since I got here I have been walking all the time and thinking, thinking and feeling how my inner strength grows day by day . . . and now I see at last, Constantine, that in our sort of work, whether we are actors or writers, the chief thing is not fame or glory, not what I dreamed of, but the gift of patience. One must bear one's cross and have faith. My faith makes me suffer less, and when I think of my vocation I am no longer afraid of life.

TREPLEF. [*Sadly.*] You have found your road, you know where you are going; but I am still adrift in a welter of images and dreams, and cannot tell what use it all is to anyone. I have no faith and I do not know what my vocation is.

NINA. [*Listening.*] 'Sh. . . . I'm going. Good-bye. When I am a great actress, come and see me act. You promise? And now . . . [*Shaking his hand.*] It's late. I can hardly stand up, I'm so tired and hungry. . . .

TREPLEF. Stay here. I'll get you some supper.

NINA. No, no. Don't go see me out; I can find my way. The trap is quite near. . . . So she brought him here with her? Well, well, it's all one. When you see Trigórin don't tell him I've been. . . . I love him; yes. I love him more than ever. . . . 'A subject for a short story.' . . . I love him, love him passionately, desperately. How pleasant it was in the old days, Constantine! You remember? How clear and warm, how joyful and how pure our life was! And our feelings—they were like the sweetest, daintiest flowers. . . . You remember? [*Reciting.*] 'Men and lions, eagles and partridges, antlered deer, geese, spiders, the silent fishes dwelling in the water, star-fish and tiny creatures invisible to the eye—these and every form of life, ay, every form of life, have ended their melancholy round and become extinct. Thousands of centuries have passed since this earth bore any living being on its bosom. All in vain does yon pale moon light her lamp. No longer do the cranes wake and cry in the meadows; the hum of the cockchafers is silent in the linden groves. . . .' [*She embraces* TREPLEF *impulsively and runs out by the glass door.*]

TREPLEF. [*After a pause.*] I hope nobody will meet her in the garden and tell mother. Mother might be annoyed. . . .

[*For two minutes he silently tears up all his manuscripts and throws them under the table, then unlocks the door R. and exit.*]

DORN. [*Trying to open the door L.*] Funny. It seems to be locked. . . . [*Entering and putting back the armchair in its place.*] H'm, obstacle race.

Enter ARCADINA *and* PAULINE; *behind them* YAKOF, *with bottles, and* MASHA; *then* SHAMRAYEF *and* TRIGORIN.

ARCADINA. Put the claret and beer here on the table for Boris Alexéyevitch. We'll drink while we play. Now come along and sit down, all of you.

PAULINE. [*To* YAKOF.] And bring tea at once. [*Lighting the candles and sitting at the card table.*]

SHAMRAYEF. [*Taking* TRIGORIN *to the cupboard.*] There's the thing I was talking of. . . . [*Gets a stuffed seagull out.*] You asked to have it done.

TRIGORIN. [*Looking at the seagull.*] I don't remember. [*After thinking.*] No, I don't remember.

[*Report of a pistol behind the scenes R. Everyone starts.*]

ARCADINA. [*Alarmed.*] What's that?

DORN. It's all right. I expect something's busted in my traveling medicine-chest. Don't be alarmed. [*Exit R., and returns a moment later.*] As I expected. My ether bottle's burst. [*Singing.*] 'Once more, once more before thee, love.'

ARCADINA. [*Sitting at the table.*] Good heavens, I was quite frightened. It reminded me of that time when . . . [*Covering her face with her hands.*] I felt quite faint. . . .

DORN. [*Taking up* TREPLEF'S *magazine and turning over the pages; to* TRIGORIN.] There was an article in this paper about a month or two ago . . a letter from America, and I wanted to ask you, among other things . . . [*Puts his arm round* TRIGORIN'S *waist and brings him to the footlights.*] . . . I'm very much interested in the question . . . [*In a lower tone.*] Get Irina Nikolayevna away from here. The fact is, Constantine has shot himself. . . .

CURTAIN

The Wedding

DRAMATIS PERSONAE

EVDOKIM ZAHAROVITCH ZHIGALOV, *a retired Civil Servant.*

NASTASYA TIMOFEYEVNA, *his wife.*

DASHENKA, *their daughter.*

EPAMINOND MAXIMOVITCH APLOMBOV, *Dashenka's bridegroom.*

FYODOR YAKOVLEVITCH REVUNOV-KARAULOV, *a retired captain.*

ANDREY ANDREYEVITCH NUNIN, *an insurance agent.*

ANNA MARTINOVNA ZMEYUKINA, *a midwife, aged 30, in a brilliantly red dress.*

IVAN MIHAILOVITCH YATS, *a telegraphist.*

HARLAMPI SPIRIDONOVITCH DIMBA, *a Greek confectioner.*

DMITRI STEPANOVITCH MOZGOVOY, *a sailor of the Imperial Navy (Volunteer Fleet).*

GROOMSMEN, GENTLEMEN, WAITERS, ETC.

The scene is laid in one of the rooms of Andronov's Restaurant.

ACT I

A brilliantly illuminated room. A large table, laid for supper. Waiters in dress-jackets are fussing round the table. An orchestra behind the scene is playing the music of the last figure of a quadrille.

ANNA MARTINOVNA ZMEYUKINA, YATS, *and a* GROOMSMAN *cross the stage.*

ZMEYUKINA. No, never!

YATS. [*Following her.*] Have pity on us! Have pity!

ZMEYUKINA. No, never!

GROOMSMAN. [*Chasing them.*] Stop this! Where are you off to? What about the *grand ronde? Grand ronde, s'il vous plaît!* [*They all go off.*]

Enter NASTASYA TIMOFEYEVNA *and* APLOMBOV.

NASTASYA TIMOFEYEVNA. You had better be dancing than troubling me with your speeches.

APLOMBOV. I'm not a Spinosa to go making figures-of-eight with my legs. I am a serious man, and I see no amusement in vain pleasures. But it isn't just a matter of dances. You must excuse me, *maman,* but your behaviour in many ways I am unable to understand. For instance, in addition to domestic affairs, you promised also to give me, with your daughter, two lottery tickets. Where are they?

NASTASYA TIMOFEYEVNA. My head's aching a little . . . probably the weather. . . . If only it thawed!

APLOMBOV. No excuse! I only found out to-day that those tickets are in pawn. You must excuse me, *maman,* but it's only swindlers who behave like that. I'm not doing this for profit—I don't want your tickets—but on principle; and I don't allow myself to be done by anybody. I have made your daughter happy, and if you don't give me the tickets to-day I'll make short work of her. I'm an honourable man!

NASTASYA TIMOFEYEVNA. [*Looks round the table and counts up the covers.*] One, two, three, four, five . . .

A WAITER. Would like the ices served with rum, madeira, or separate?

APLOMBOV. With rum. And tell the

624

manager that there's not enough wine. Tell him to prepare some more Haut Sauterne. [*To* NASTASYA TIMOFE-YEVNA.] You also promised that a general was to be here to supper. Where is he?

NASTASYA TIMOFEYEVNA. That isn't my fault, my dear.

APLOMBOV. Whose then?

NASTASYA TIMOFEYEVNA. It's Andrey Andreyevitch's fault. . . . Yesterday he came to see us and promised to bring a perfectly real general. [*Sighs.*] Perhaps he couldn't find one anywhere. . . You think we don't mind? We'd give our child all. A general, of course . . .

APLOMBOV. But there's more. . . . Everybody, including yourself, *maman*, is aware of the fact that Yats, that telegraphist, wanted Dashenka before I proposed to her. Why did you invite him? Surely you knew I would not like it!

NASTASYA TIMOFEYEVNA. Oh, how can you? Epamimond Maximovitch was married himself only the other day, and you've already tired me and Dashenka out with your talk. What will you be like in a year's time? You are horrid, really horrid.

APLOMBOV. Then you don't like to hear the truth? Aha! Oh, oh! Then behave honourably. I only want you to do one thing, be honourable!

Couples dancing the grand ronde *come in at one door and out at the other end. The first couple are* DASHENKA *with one of the* GROOMSMEN. *The last are* YATS *and* ZMEYUKINA. *These two remain behind.* ZHIGALOV *and* DIMBA *enter and go up to the table.*

GROOMSMAN. [*Shouting.*] *Promenade! Messieurs, promenade!* [*Behind.*] *Promenade!*

[*The dancers have all left the scene.*]

YATS. [*To* ZMEYUKINA.] Have pity! Have pity, adorable Anna Martinovna.

ZMEYUKINA. Oh, what a man! . . . I've already told you that I've no voice to-day.

YATS. I implore you to sing! Just one note! Have pity! Just one note!

ZMEYUKINA. I'm tired of you. . . . [*Sits and fans herself.*]

YATS. No, you're simply heartless! To be so cruel—if I may express myself—and to have such a beautiful, beautiful voice! With such a voice, if you will forgive my using the word, you shouldn't be a midwife, but sing at concerts, at public gatherings! For example, how divinely you do that *fioritura* . . . that . . . [*Sings.*] "I loved you; love was vain then. . . ." Exquisite!

ZMEYUKINA. [*Sings.*] "I loved you, and may love again." Is that it?

YATS. That's it! Beautiful!

ZMEYUKINA. No, I've no voice to-day. . . . There, wave this fan for me . . . it's hot! [*To* APLOMBOV.] Epaminond Maximovitch, why are you so melancholy? A bridegroom shouldn't be! Aren't you ashamed of yourself, you wretch? Well, what are you so thoughtful about?

APLOMBOV. Marriage is a serious step! Everything must be considered from all sides, thoroughly.

ZMEYUKINA. What beastly sceptics you all are! I feel quite suffocated with you all around. . . . Give me atmosphere! Do you hear? Give me atmosphere! [*Sings a few notes.*]

YATS. Beautiful! Beautiful!

ZMEYUKINA. Fan me, fan me, or I feel I shall have a heart attack in a minute. Tell me, please, why do I feel so suffocated?

YATS. It's because you're sweating. . . .

ZMEYUKINA. Foo, how vulgar you are! Don't dare to use such words!

YATS. Beg pardon! Of course, you're used, if I may say so, to aristocratic society and . . .

ZMEYUKINA. Oh, leave me alone. Give me poetry, delight! Fan me, fan me!

ZHIGALOV. [To DIMBA.] Let's have another, what? [Pours out.] One can always drink. So long only, Harlampi Spiridonovitch, as one doesn't forget one's business. Drink and be merry. And if you can drink at somebody else's expense, then why not drink? You can drink. . . . Your health! [They drink.] And do you have tigers in Greece?

DIMBA Yes.

ZHIGALOV. And lions?

DIMBA. And lions too. In Russia zere's nussing, and in Greece zere's everysing—my fazer and uncle and brozeres—and here zere's nussing.

ZHIGALOV. H'm. . . . And are there whales in Greece?

DIMBA. Yes, everysing.

NASTASYA TIMOFEYEVNA. [To her husband.] What are they all eating and drinking like that for? It's time for everybody to sit down to supper. Don't keep on shoving your fork into the lobsters. . . . They're for the general. He may come yet. . . .

ZHIGALOV. And are there lobsters in Greece?

DIMBA. Yes . . . zere is everysing.

ZHIGALOV. H'm. . . . And Civil Servants.

ZMEYUKINA. I can imagine what the atmosphere is like in Greece!

ZHIGALOV. There must be a lot of swindling. The Greeks are just like the Armenians or gipsies. They sell you a sponge or a goldfish and all the time they are looking out for a chance of getting something extra out of you. Let's have another, what?

NASTASYA TIMOFEYEVNA. What do you want to go on having another for? It's time everybody sat down to supper. It's past eleven.

ZHIGALOV. If it's time, then it's time. Ladies and gentlemen, please! [Shouts.] Supper! Young people!

NASTASYA TIMOFEYEVNA. Dear visitors, please be seated!

ZMEYUKINA. [Sitting down at the table.] Give me poetry.

"And he, the rebel, seeks the storm,
As if the storm can give him peace."

Give me the storm! ,

YATS. [Aside.] Wonderful woman! I'm in love! Up to my ears!

Enter DASHENKA, MOZGOVOY, GROOMSMEN, various ladies and gentlemen, etc. They all noisily seat themselves at the table. There is a minute's pause. while the band plays a march.

MOZGOVOY. [Rising.] Ladies and gentlemen! I must tell you this. . . . We are going to have a great many toasts and speeches. Don't let's wait, but begin at once. Ladies and gentlemen, the newly married!

The band plays a flourish. Cheers. Glasses are touched. APLOMBOV and DASHENKA kiss each other.

YATS. Beautiful! Beautiful! I must say, ladies and gentlemen, giving honour where it is due, that this room and the accommodation generally are splendid! Excellent, wonderful! Only you know, there's one thing we haven't got—electric light, if I may say so! Into every country electric light has already been introduced, only Russia lags behind.

ZHIGALOV. [*Meditatively.*] Electricity . . . h'm. . . . In my opinion electric lighting is just a swindle. . . . They put a live coal in and think you don't see them! No, if you want a light, then you don't take a coal, but something real, something special, that you can get hold of! You must have a fire, you understand, which is natural. not just an invention!

YATS. If you'd ever seen an electric battery, and how it's made up, you'd think differently.

ZHIGALOV. Don't want to see one. It's a swindle, a fraud on the public. . . . . They want to squeeze our last breath out of us. . . . We know then, these . . . And, young man, instead of defending a swindle, you would be much better occupied if you had another yourself and poured out some for other people—yes!

APLOMBOV. 1 entirely agree with you, papa. Why start a learned discussion. I myself have no objection to talking about every possible scientific discovery, but this isn't the time for all that! [*To* DASHENKA.] What do you think, *ma chère?*

DASHENKA. They want to show how educated they are, and so they always talk about things we can't understand.

NASTASYA TIMOFEYEVNA. Thank God. we've lived our time without being educated, and here we are marrying off our third daughter to an honest man. And if you think we're uneducated, then what do you want to come here for? Go to your educated friends!

YATS. I, Nastasya Timofeyevna, have always held your family in respect. and if I start talking about electric

lighting it doesn't mean that I'm proud. I'll drink, to show you. I have always sincerely wished Daria Evdokimovna a good husband. In these days, Nastasya Timofeyevna, it is difficult to find a good husband. Nowadays everybody is on the look-out for a marriage where there is profit. money. . . .

APLOMBOV. That's a hint!

YATS. [*His courage failing.*] I wasn't hinting at anything. . . . Present company is always excepted. . . . I was . . . only in general. . . . Please! Everybody knows that you're marrying for love . . . the dowry is quite trifling.

NASTASYA TIMOFEYEVNA. No, it isn't trifling! You be careful what you say. Besides a thousand roubles of good money, we're giving three dresses, the bed, and all the furniture. You won't find another dowry like that in a hurry!

YATS. I didn't mean . . . The furniture's splendid, of course, and . . . and the dresses, but I never hinted at what they are getting offended at.

NASTASYA TIMOFEYEVNA. Don't you go making hints. We respect you on account of your parents, and we've invited you to the wedding, and here you go talking. If you knew that Epaminond Maximovitch was marrying for profit, why didn't you say so before? [*Tearfully.*] I brought her up. I fed her, I nursed her . . . I cared for her more than if she was an emerald jewel, my little girl. . . .

APLOMBOV. And you go and believe him? Thank you so much! I'm very grateful to you! [*To* YATS.] And as for you, Mr. Yats, although you are acquainted with me, I shan't allow you to behave like this in another's house. Please get out of this!

YATS. What do you mean?

APLOMBOV. I want you to be as straightforward as I am! In short, please get out! [*Band plays a flourish.*]

THE GENTLEMAN. Leave him alone! Sit down! Is it worth it! Let him be! Stop it now!

YATS. I never . . . I . . . I don't understand. . . . Please, I'll go. . . . Only you first give me the five roubles which you borrowed from me last year on the strength of a *piqué* waistcoat, if I may say so. Then I'll just have another drink and . . . go, only give me the money first.

VARIOUS GENTLEMEN. Sit down; That's enough! Is it worth it, just for such trifles?

A GROOMSMAN. [*Shouts.*] The health of the bride's parents, Evdokim Zaharitch and Nastasya Timofeyevna! [*Band plays a flourish. Cheers.*]

ZHIGALOV. [*Bows in all directions, in great emotion.*] I thank you! Dear guests! I am very grateful to you for not having forgotten and for having conferred this honour upon us without being standoffish. And you must not think that I'm a rascal, or that I'm trying to swindle anybody. I'm speaking from my heart—from the purity of my soul! I wouldn't deny anything to good people! We thank you very humbly! [*Kisses.*]

DASHENKA. [*To her mother.*] Mama, why are you crying? I'm so happy!

APLOMBOV. *Mamam* is disturbed at your coming separation. But I should advise her rather to remember the last talk we had.

YATS. Don't cry, Nastasya Timofeyevna! Just think what are human tears, anyway? Just petty psychiatry, and nothing more!

ZHIGALOV. And are there any red-haired men in Greece?

DIMBA. Yes, everysing is zere.

ZHIGALOV. But you don't have our kinds of mushroom.

DIMBA. Yes, we've got zem and everysing.

MOZGOVOY. Harlampi Spiridonovitch, it's your turn to speak! Ladies and gentlemen, a speech!

ALL. [*To DIMBA.*] Speech! speech! Your turn!

DIMBA. Why? I don't understand. . . . What is it!

ZMEYUKINA. No, no! You can't refuse! It's your turn! Get up!

DIMBA. [*Gets up, confused.*] I can't say what . . . Zere's Russia and zere's Greece. Zere's people in Russia and people in Greece. . . . And zere's people swimming the sea in karavs, which mean sips, and people on the land in railway trains. I understand. We are Greeks and you are Russians, and I want nussing. . . . I can tell you . . . zere's Russia and zere's Greece . . .

Enter NUNIN.

NUNIN. Wait, ladies and gentlemen, don't eat now! Wait! Just one minute, Nastasya Timofeyevna! Just come here, if you don't mind! [*Takes NASTASYA TIMOFEYEVNA aside, puffing.*] Listen. . . . The General's coming . . . I found one at last. . . . I'm simply worn out. . . . A real General, a solid one—old, you know, aged perhaps eighty, or even ninety.

NATASYA TIMOFEYEVNA. When is he coming?

NUNIN. This minute. You'll be grateful to me all your life.

NASTASYA TIMOFEYEVNA. You're not deceiving me, Andrey darling?

NUNIN. Well, now, am I a swindler? You needn't worry!

NASTASYA TIMOFEYEVNA. [Sighs.] One doesn't like to spend money for nothing, Andrey darling!

NUNIN. Don't worry! He's not a general, he's a dream! [Raises his voice.] I said to him: "You've quite forgotten us, your Excellency! It isn't kind of your Excellency to forget your old friends! Nastasya Timofeyevna," I said to him, "she's very annoyed with you about it!" [Goes and sits at the table.] And he says to me: "But, my friend, how can I go when I don't know the bridegroom?" Oh, nonsense, your excellency, why stand on ceremony? The bridegroom," I said to him, "he's a fine fellow, very free and easy. He's a valuer," I said, "at the Law courts, and don't you think, your excellency, that he's some rascal, some knave of hearts. Nowadays," I said to him, "even decent women are employed at the Law courts." He slapped me on the shoulder, we smoked a Havana cigar each, and now he's coming. . . . Wait a little, ladies and gentlemen, don't eat. . . .

APLOMBOV. When's he coming?

NUNIN. This minute. When I left him he was already putting on his goloshes. Wait a little, ladies and gentlemen, don't eat yet.

APLOMBOV. The band should be told to play a march.

NUNIN. [Shouts.] Musicians; A march!

[The band plays a march for a minute.]

A WAITER. Mr. Revunov-Karaulov!

ZHIGALOV, NASTASYA TIMOFEYEVNA, and NUNIN run to meet him. Enter REVUNOV-KARAULOV.

NASTASYA TIMOFEYEVNA. [Bowing.] Please come in, your excellency! So glad you've come!

REVUNOV. Awfully.

ZHIGALOV. We, your excellency, aren't celebrities, we aren't important, but quite ordinary, but don't think on that account that there's any fraud. We put good people into the best place, we begrudge nothing. Please!

REVUNOV. Awfully glad!

NUNIN. Let me introduce to you, your excellency, the bridegroom, Epaminond Maximovitch Aplombov, with his newly born . . . I mean his newly married wife! Ivan Mihailovitch Yats, employed on the telegraph! A foreigner of Greek nationality, a confectioner by trade, Harlampi Spiridonovitch Dimba! Osip Lukitch Babelmandebsky! And so on, and so on. . . . The rest are just trash. Sit down, your excellency!

REVUNOV. Awfully! Excuse me, ladies and gentlemen, I just want to say two words to Andrey. [Takes NUNIN aside.] I say, old man, I'm a little put out. . . . Why do you call me your excellency? I'm not a general! I don't rank as the equivalent of a colonel, even.

NUNIN. [Whispers.] I know, only, Fyodor Yakovlevitch, be a good man and let us call you your excellency: The family here, you see is patriarchal; it respects the aged, it likes rank.

REVUNOV. Oh, if it's like that, very well. . . . [Goes to the table.] Awfully!

NASTASYA TIMOFEYEVNA. Sit down, your excellency! Be so good as to have some of this, your excellency! Only forgive us for not being used to etiquette; we're plain people!

REVUNOV. [Not hearing.] What? Hm . . . yes. [Pause.] Yes. . . . In the old days everybody used to live simply and was happy. In spite of my rank, I am

630 WORKS OF ANTON CHEKHOV

a man who lives plainly. To-day Andrey comes to me and asks me to come here to the wedding. "How shall I go," I said, "when I don't know them? It's not good manners!" But he says: "They are good, simple, patriarchal people, glad to see anybody." Well, if that's the case . . . why not? Very glad to come. It's very dull for me at home by myself, and if my presence at a wedding can make anybody happy, then I'm delighted to be here. . . .

ZHIGALOV. Then that's sincere, is it, your excellency? I respect that! I'm a plain man myself, without any deception, and I respect others who are like that. Eat, your excellency!

APLOMBOV. Is it long since you retired, your excellency?

REVUNOV. Eh? Yes, yes. . . . Quite true. Yes. . . . But, excuse me, what is this? The fish is sour . . . and the bread is sour. I can't eat this! [APLOMBOV and DASHENKA kiss each other.] He, he, he . . . Your health! [Pause.] Yes. . . . In the old days everything was simple and everybody was glad. . . . I love simplicity. . . . I'm an old man. I retired in 1865. I'm 72. Yes, of course, in my younger days it was different, but—[Sees MOZGOVOY.] You there . . . a sailor, are you?

MOZGOVOY. Yes, just so.

REVUNOV. Aha, so . . . yes. The navy means hard work. There's a lot to think about and get a headache over. Every insignificant word has, so to speak, its special meaning! For instance, "Hoist her top-sheets and main-sail!" What's it mean? A sailor can tell! He, he!—With almost mathematical precision!

NUNIN. The health of his excellency Fyodor Yakovlevitch Revunov-Karau-lov! [Band plays a flourish. Cheers.]

YATS. You, your excellency, have just expressed yourself on the subject of the hard work involved in a naval career. But is telegraphy any easier? Nowadays, your excellency, nobody is appointed to the telegraphs if he cannot read and write French and German. But the transmission of telegrams is the most difficult thing of all. Awfully difficult! Just listen.

Taps with his fork on the table, like a telegraphic transmitter.

REVUNOV. What does that mean?

YATS. It means, "I honour you, your excellency, for your virtues." You think it's easy? Listen now. [Taps.]

REVUNOV. Louder; I can't hear. .

YATS. That means, "Madam, how happy I am to hold you in my embraces!"

REVUNOV. What madam are you talking about? Yes. . . . [To MOZGOVOY.] Yes, if there's a head-wind you must . . . let's see . . . you must hoist your foretop halyards and topsail halyards! The order is: "On the crosstrees to the foretop halyards and topsail halyards" . . . and at the same time, as the sails get loose, you take hold underneath of the foresail and foretopsail halyards, stays and braces.

A GROOMSMAN. [Rising.] Ladies and gentlemen . . .

REVUNOV. [Cutting him short.] Yes . . . there are a great many orders to give. "Furl the fore-topsail and the fore-top-gallant sail!!" Well, what does that mean? It's very simple! It means that if the top and top-gallant sails are lifting the halyards, they must level the foretop and foretop-gallant halyards on the hoist and at the same time the top-gallant braces, as needed, are loosened according to the direction of the wind . . .

NUNIN. [*To* REVUNOV.] Fyodor Yakovlevitch, Mme. Zhigalov asks you to talk about something else. It's very dull for the guests, who can't understand. . . .

REVUNOV. What? Who's dull? [*To* MOZGOVOY.] Young man! Now suppose the ship is lying by the wind, on the starboard tack, under full sail, and you've got to bring her before the wind. What's the order? Well, first you whistle up above! He, he!

NUNIN. Fyodor Yakovlevitch, that's enough. Eat something.

REVUNOV. As soon as the men are on deck you give the order, "To your places!" What a life! You give orders, and at the same time you've got to keep your eyes on the sailors, who run about like flashes of lightning and get the sails and braces right. And at last you can't restrain yourself, and you shout, "Good children!" [*He chokes and coughs.*]

A GROOMSMAN. [*Making haste to use the ensuing pause to advantage.*] On this occasion, so to speak, on the day on which we have met together to honour our dear . . .

REVUNOV. [*Interrupting.*] Yes, you've got to remember all that! For instance, "Hoist the topsail halyards. Lower the topsail gallants!"

THE GROOMSMAN. [*Annoyed.*] Why does he keep on interrupting? We shan't get through a single speech like that!

NASTASYA TIMOFEYEVNA. We are dull people, your excellency, and don't understand a word of all that, but if you were to tell us something appropriate . .

REVUNOV. [*Not hearing.*] I've already had supper, thank you. Did you say there was goose? Thanks . . . yes.

I've remembered the old days. . . . It's pleasant, young man! You sail on the sea, you have no worries, and . . . [*In an excited tone of voice.*] do you remember the joy of tacking? Is there a sailor who doesn't glow at the memory of that manœuvre? As soon as the word is given and the whistle blown and the crew begins to go up—it's as if an electric spark has run through them all. From the captain to the cabin-boy, everybody's' excited.

ZMEYUKINA. How dull! How dull! [*General murmur.*]

REVUNOV. [*Who has not heard it properly.*] Thank you, I've had supper. [*With enthusiasm.*] Everybody's ready, and looks to the senior officer. He gives the command: "Stand by, gallants and topsail braces on the starboard side, main and counter-braces to port!" Everything's done in a twinkling. Topsheets and jib-sheets are pulled . . . taken to starboard. [*Stands up.*] The ship takes the wind and at last the sails fill out. The senior officer orders, "To the braces," and himself keeps his eye on the mainsail, and when at last this sail is filling out and the ship begins to turn, he yells at the top of his voice, "Let go the braces! Loose the main halyards!" Everything flies about, there's a general confusion for a moment —and everything is done without an error. The ship has been tacked!

NASTASYA TIMOFEYEVNA. [*Exploding.*] General, your manners. . . . You ought to be ashamed of yourself, at your age!

REVUNOV. Did you say sausage? No, I haven't had any . . . thank you.

NASTASYA TIMOFEYEVNA. [*Loudly.*] I say you ought to be ashamed of yourself at your age! General, your manners are awful!

NUNIN. [*Confused.*] Ladies and gentlemen, is it worth it? Really . . .

REVUNOV. In the first place, I'm not a general, but a second-class naval captain, which, according to the table of precedence, corresponds to a lieutenant-colonel.

NASTASYA TIMOFEYEVNA. If you're not a general, then what did you go and take our money for? We never paid you money to behave like that!

REVUNOV. [*Upset.*] What money?

NASTASYA TIMOFEYEVNA. You know what money. You know that you got 25 roubles from Andrey Andreyevitch. . . . [*To* NUNIN.] And you look out, Andrey! I never asked you to hire a man like that!

NUNIN. There now . . . let it drop. Is it worth it?

REVUNOV. Paid . . . hired. . . . What is it?

APLOMBOV. Just let me ask you this. Did you receive 25 roubles from Andrey Andreyevitch?

REVUNOV. What 25 roubles? [*Suddenly realizing.*] That's what it is! Now I understand it all. . . . How mean! How mean!

APLOMBOV. Did you take the money?

REVUNOV. I haven't taken any money! Get away from me! [*Leaves the table.*] How mean! How low! To insult an old man, a sailor, an officer who has served long and faithfully! If you were decent people I could call somebody out, but what can I do now? [*Absently.*] Where's the door? Which way do I go? Waiter, show me the way out! Waiter! [*Going.*] How mean! How low! [*Exit.*]

NASTASYA TIMOFEYEVNA. Andrey, where are those 25 roubles?

NUNIN. Is it worth while bothering about such trifles? What does it matter! Everybody's happy here, and here you go. . . . [*Shouts.*] The health of the bride and bridegroom! A march! A march! [*The band plays a march.*] The health of the bride and bridegroom!

ZMEYUKINA. I'm suffocating! Give me atmosphere! I'm suffocating with you all round me!

YATS. [*In a transport of delight.*] My beauty! My beauty! [*Uproar.*]

A GROOMSMAN. [*Trying to shout everybody else down.*] Ladies and gentlemen! On this occasion, if I may say so . . .

CURTAIN

VOLUME IX

The Bear

DRAMATIS PERSONAE

ELENA IVANOVNA POPOVA, *a landowning little widow, with dimples on her cheeks.*
GRIGORY STEPANOVITCH SMIRNOV, *a middle-aged landowner.*
LUKA, *Popova's aged footman.*

ACT I

A drawing-room in POPOVA'S *house.*
POPOVA *is in deep mourning and has her eyes fixed on a photograph.* LUKA *is haranguing her.*

LUKA. It isn't right, madam. . . . You're just ruining yourself. The maid and the cook have gone fruit picking, every one is having a good time, even the cat walks about in the yard, catching midgets; only you sit in this room all day, as if this was a convent. It's a whole year that you have stayed in the house!

POPOVA. I shall never go out. . . . Why should I? My life is over. He is in his grave, and I have buried myself between four walls. . . . We are both dead.

LUKA. Nicolai Mihailovitch is dead, well, it's the will of God, and may his soul rest in peace. . . . You've mourned him—and quite right. But you can't go on weeping and wearing mourning for ever. My old woman died too, when her time came. Well? I grieved over her for a month, and that's enough for her, but if I've got to weep for a whole age, the old woman isn't worth it. [*Sighs.*] You've forgotten all your neighbours

are all neglected. You don't go anywhere, and you see nobody. We live like spiders, and never see light. The mice have eaten my livery. It is not because there are no good people around, for the district's full of them. There's a regiment quartered at Riblov, and the officers are handsome—you can never gaze your fill at them. And, every Friday, there's a ball at the camp, and every day the soldier's band plays. . . . Eh, my lady! You're young and beautiful, with roses in your cheek—if you only took a little pleasure. Beauty fades quick. In ten years' time you'll want to be a pea-hen yourself among the officers, but it will be too late.

POPOVA. [*With determination.*] I must ask you never to talk to me about it! You know that when Nicolai Mihailovitch died, life lost all its meaning for me. I vowed always to wear mourning, never to see the light. . . . You hear? Let his spirit see how well I love him. . . . I know it's no secret to you that he was often cruel, and . . . and even unfaithful, but I shall be true till death, and show him how I love. There, beyond the grave, he will see me as I was before he died.

LUKA. Don't talk that way! Go and have a walk in the garden, or else order Toby or Giant to be harnessed, and then drive out to see some of the neighbors.

POPOVA. Oh! [*Weeps.*]

LUKA. Madam! Dear madam! What is it? Bless you!

POPOVA. He was so fond of Toby!

He always used to ride him to the Korchagins and Vlasovs. How well he could ride! What a figure when he reined in his steed! Do you remember? Toby, Toby! Tell them to give him an extra feed of oats.

LUKA. Yes, madam. [*A bell rings noisily.*]

POPOVA. [*Shaking.*] Who's that? Tell them that I receive nobody.

LUKA. Yes, madam. [*Exit.*]

POPOVA. [*Looks at the photograph.*] You will see, *Nicolas,* how I can love and forgive. . . . My love will die out with me, only when this poor heart will cease to beat. [*Laughs through her tears.*] And aren't you ashamed? I am a good and virtuous little wife. I've locked myself in, and will be true to you till the grave, and you . . . aren't you ashamed, you bad child? You deceived me, had rows with me, left me alone for weeks on end . . . .

LUKA *enters in consternation.*

LUKA. Madam, somebody is asking for you. He wants to see you. . . .

POPOVA. But didn't you tell him that since the death of my husband I've stopped receiving?

LUKA. I did, but he wouldn't even listen; says that it's a very pressing affair.

POPOVA. I do not re-ceive!

LUKA. I told him so, but the . . . devil . . . curses and pushes himself right in. . . . He's in the dining-room now.

POPOVA. [*Annoyed.*] Very well, ask him in. . . . What manners! [*Exit LUKA.*] How these people annoy me! What does he want of me? Why should he disturb my peace? [*Sighs.*] No I see that I shall have to go into a convent after all. [*Thoughfully.*] Yes, into a convent. . . .

[*Enter LUKA with SMIRNOV.*]

SMIRNOV. [*To LUKA.*] You fool, you're too fond of talking. . . . Ass! [*Sees POPOVA and speaks with respect.*] Madam, I have the honour to present myself, I am Grigory Stepanovitch Smirnov, landowner and retired lieutenant of artillery! I am compelled to disturb you on a very pressing affair.

POPOVA. [*Not giving him her hand.*] What do you want?

SMIRNOV. Your late husband, with whom I had the honour of being acquainted, died in my debt for one thousand two hundred roubles, on two bills of exchange. As I've got to pay the interest on a mortgage to-morrow, I've come to ask you, madam, to pay me the money to-day.

POPOVA. One thousand two hundred. . . . And what was my husband in debt to you for?

SMIRNOV. He used to buy oats from me.

POPOVA. [*Sighing, to LUKA.*] So don't you forget, Luka, to give Toby an extra feed of oats. [*Exit LUKA.*] If Nicolai Mihailovitch died in debt to you, then I shall certainly pay you, but you must excuse me to-day, as I haven't any spare cash. The day after to-morrow my steward will be back from town, and I'll give him instructions to settle your account, but at the moment I cannot do as you wish. . . . Moreover, it's exactly seven months to-day since the death of my husband, and I'm in a state of mind which absolutely prevents me from giving money matters my attention.

SMIRNOV. And I'm in a state of mind which, if I don't pay the interest due to-morrow, will force me to make a graceful exit from this life feet first. They'll take my estate!

POPOVA. You'll have your money the day after to-morrow.

SMIRNOV. I don't want the money the day after to-morrow, I want it to-day.

POPOVA. You must excuse me, I can't pay you.

SMIRNOV. And I can't wait till after to-morrow.

POPOVA. Well, what can I do, if I haven't the money now!

SMIRNOV. You mean to say, you can't pay me?

POPOVA. I can't.

SMIRNOV. Hm! It that the last word you've got to say?

POPOVA. Yes, the last word.

SMIRNOV. The last word? Absolutely your last?

POPOVA. Absolutely.

SMIRNOV. Thank you so much. I'll make a note of it. [*Shrugs his shoulders.*] And then people want me to keep calm! I meet a man on the road, and he asks me: "Why are you always so angry, Grigory Stepanovitch?" But how on earth am I not to get angry? I want the money desperately. I rode out yesterday, early in the morning, and called on all my debtors, and not a single one of them paid up! I was just about dead-beat after it all, slept, goodness knows where, in some inn, kept by a Jew, with a vodka-barrel by my head. At last I get here, seventy versts from home, and hope to get something, and I am received by you with a "state of mind"! How shouldn't I get angry.

POPOVA. I thought I distinctly said my steward will pay you when he returns from town.

SMIRNOV. I didn't come to your steward, but to you! What the devil, excuse my saying so, have I to do with your steward!

POPOVA. Excuse me, sir, I am not accustomed to listen to such expressions or to such a tone of voice. I want to hear no more. [*Makes a rapid exit.*]

SMIRNOV. Well, there! "A state of mind." . . . "Husband died seven months ago!" Must I pay the interest, or mustn't I? I ask you: Must I pay, or must I not? Suppose your husband is dead, and you've got a state of mind, and nonsense of that sort. . . . And your steward's gone away somewhere, devil take him, what do you want me to do? Do you think I can fly away from my creditors in a balloon, or what? Or do you expect me to go and run my head into a brick wall? I go to Grusdev and he isn't at home, Yaroshevitch has hidden himself, I had a violent row with Kuritsin and nearly threw him out of the window, Mazugo has something the matter with his bowels, and this woman has "a state of mind." Not one of the swine wants to pay me! Just because I'm too gentle with them, because I'm a rag, just weak wax in their hands! I'm much too gentle with them! Well, just you wait! You'll find out what I'm like! I shan't let you play about with me, confound it! I shall jolly well stay here until she pays! Brr! . . . How angry I am to-day, how angry I am! All my inside is quivering with anger, and I can't even breathe. . . . Foo, my word, I even feel sick! [*Yells.*] Waiter!

Enter LUKA.

LUKA. What is it?

SMIRNOV. Get me some kvass or water! [*Exit* LUKA.] What a way to reason! A man is in desperate need of his money, and she won't pay it because, you see, she is not disposed to attend to money matters! . . . That's real silly feminine logic. That's why I never did like, and don't like now, to have to talk to women. I'd rather sit on a barrel of gunpowder than talk to a woman. Brr! . . . I feel quite chilly—and it's all on account of that little bit of fluff! I can't even see one of these poetic creatures from a distance without breaking out into a cold sweat out of sheer anger. I can't look at them.

Enter LUKA *with water.*

LUKA. Madam is ill and will see nobody.

SMIRNOV. Get out! [*Exit* LUKA.] Ill and will see nobody! No, it's all right, you don't see me. . . . I'm going to stay and will sit here till you give me the money. You can be ill for a week, if you like, and I'll stay here for a week. . . . If you're ill for a year—I'll stay for a year. I'm going to get my own, my dear! You don't get at me with your widow's weeds and your dimpled cheeks! I know those dimples! [*Shouts through the window.*] Simeon, take them out! We aren't going away at once! I'm staying here! Tell them in the stable to give the horses some oats! You fool, you've let the near horse's leg get tied up in the reins again! [*Teasingly.*] "Never mind. . . ." I'll give it you. "Never mind." [*Goes away from the window.*] Oh, it's bad. . . . The heat's frightful, nobody pays up. I slept badly, and on top of everything else here's a bit of fluff in mourning with "a state of mind." . . . My head's aching. . . . Shall I have some vodka, what? Yes, I think I will. [*Yells.*] Waiter!

Enter LUKA.

LUKA. What is it?

SMIRNOV. A glass of vodka! [*Exit* LUKA.] Ouf! [*Sits and inspects himself.*] I must say I look well! Dust all over, boots dirty, unwashed, unkempt, straw on my waistcoat. . . . The dear lady may well have taken me for a brigand. [*Yawns.*] It's rather impolite to come into a drawing-room in this state, but it can't be helped. . . . I am not here as a visitor, but as a creditor, and there's no dress specially prescribed for creditors. . . .

Enter LUKA *with the vodka.*

LUKA. You allow yourself to go very far, sir. . . .

SMIRNOV [*angrily*]. What?

LUKA. I . . . er . . . nothing . . . I really . . .

SMIRNOV. Whom are you talking to? Shut up!

LUKA [*aside*]. The devil's come to stay. . . . Bad luck that brought him. . . . [*Exit.*]

SMIRNOV. Oh, how angry I am! So angry that I think I could grind the whole world to dust. . . . I even feel sick. . . . [*Yells.*] Waiter!

Enter POPOVA.

POPOVA [*her eyes downcast*]. Sir, in my solitude I have grown unaccustomed to the masculine voice, and I can't stand shouting. I must ask you not to disturb my peace.

SMIRNOV. Pay me the money, and I'll go.

POPOVA. I told you perfectly plainly; I haven't any money to spare; wait until the day after to-morrow.

SMIRNOV. And I told you perfectly plainly I don't want the money the day after to-morrow, but to-day. If you don't pay me to-day, I'll have to hang myself to-morrow.

POPOVA. But what can I do if I

haven't got the money? You're so strange!

SMIRNOV. Then you won't pay me now? Eh?

POPOVA. I can't. . . .

SMIRNOV. In that case I stay here and shall wait until I get it. [*Sits down.*] You're going to pay me the day after to-morrow? Very well! I'll stay here until the day after to-morrow. I'll sit here all the time. . . . [*Jumps up.*] I ask you: Have I got to pay the interest to-morrow, or haven't I? Or do you think I'm doing this for a joke?

POPOVA. Please don't shout. This isn't a stable!

SMIRNOV. I wasn't asking you about a stable, but whether I'd got my interest to pay to-morrow or not?

POPOVA. You don't know how to behave before women!

SMIRNOV. No, I do know how to behave before women!

POPOVA. No, you don't! You're a rude, ill-bred man! Decent people don't talk to a woman like that!

SMIRNOV. What a business! How do you want me to talk to you? In French, or what? [*Loses his temper and lisps.*] *Madame, je vous prie.* . . . How happy I am that you don't pay me. . . . Ah, pardon. I have disturbed you! Such lovely weather to-day! And how well you look in mourning! [*Bows.*]

POPOVA. That's silly and rude.

SMIRNOV [*teasing her*]. Silly and rude! I don't know how to behave before women! Madam, in my time I've seen more women than you've seen sparrows! Three times I've fought duels on account of women. I've refused twelve women, and nine have refused me! Yes! There was a time when I played the fool, scented myself, used

honeyed words, wore jewellery, made beautiful bows. . . . I used to love, to suffer, to sight at the moon, to get sour, to thaw, to freeze. . . . I used to love passionately, madly, every blessed way, devil take me; I used to chatter like a magpie about emancipation, and wasted half my wealth on tender feelings, but now—you must excuse me! You won't get round me like that now! I've had enough! Black eyes, passionate eyes, ruby lips, dimpled cheeks, the moon, whispers, timid breathing—I wouldn't give a brass farthing for the lot, madam! Present company always excepted, all women, great or little, are insincere, crooked, backbiters, envious, liars to the marrow of their bones, vain, trivial, merciless, unreasonable, and, as far as this is concerned [*taps his forehead*] excuse my outspokenness, a sparrow can give ten points to any philosopher in petticoats you like to name! You look at one of these poetic creatures; all muslin, an ethereal demigoddess, you have a million transports of joy, and you look into her soul—and see a common crocodile! [*He grips the back of a chair; the chair creaks and breaks.*] But the most disgusting thing of all is that this crocodile for some reason or other imagines that its *chef d'œuvre,* its privilege and monopoly, is its tender feelings. Why, confound it, hang me on that nail feet upwards, if you like, but have you met a woman who can love anybody except a lapdog? When she's in love, can she do anything but snivel and slobber? While a man is suffering and making sacrifices all her love expresses itself in her playing about with her scarf, and trying to hook him more firmly by the nose. You have the misfortune to be a woman, you know from yourself what is the nature of woman. Tell me truthfully, have you ever seen a woman who was sincere, faithful, and constant? You haven't! Only freaks and old women are faithful and constant! You'll meet a cat with a horn or a white woodcock sooner than a constant woman!

POPOVA. Then, according to you, who is faithful and constant in love? Is it the man?

SMIRNOV. Yes, the man!

POPOVA. The man! [*Laughs bitterly.*] Men are faithful and constant in love! What an idea! [*With heat.*] What right have you to talk like that? Men are faithful and constant! Since we are talking about it, I'll tell you that of all the men I knew and know, the best was my late husband. . . . I loved him passionately with all my being, as only a young and imaginative woman can love, I gave him my youth, my happiness, my life, my fortune, I breathed in him, I worshipped him as if I were a heathen, and . . . and what then? This best of men shamelessly deceived me at every step! After his death I found in his desk a whole drawerful of love-letters, and when he was alive—it's an awful thing to remember!—he used to leave me alone for weeks at a time, and make love to other women and betray me before my very eyes; he wasted my money, and made fun of my feelings. . . . And, in spite of all that, I loved him and was true to him. . . . And not only that, but, now that he is dead, I am still true and constant to his memory. I have shut myself for ever within these four walls, and will wear these weeds to the very end. . . .

SMIRNOV [*laughs contemptuously*]. Weeds! . . . I don't understand what

you take me for? As if I don't know why you wear that black domino and bury yourself between four walls! I should say I did! It's so mysterious, so poetic! When some junker or some tame poet goes past your windows he'll think: "There lives the mysterious Tamara who, for the love of her husband, buried herself between four walls." We know these games!

POPOVA [*exploding*]. What? How dare you say all that to me?

SMIRNOV. You may have buried yourself alive, but you haven't forgotten to powder your face!

POPOVA. How dare you speak to me like that?

SMIRNOV. Please don't shout, I'm not your steward! You must allow me to call things by their real names. I'm not a woman, and I'm used to saying what I think straight out! Don't you shout, either!

POPOVA. I'm not shouting, it's you! Please leave me alone!

SMIRNOV. Pay me my money and I'll go.

POPOVA. I shan't give you any money!

SMIRNOV. Oh, no, you will.

POPOVA. I shan't give you a farthing, just to spite you. You leave me alone!

SMIRNOV. I have not the pleasure of being either your husband or your fiancé, so please don't make scenes. [*Sits.*] I don't like it.

POPOVA [*choking with rage*]. So you sit down?

SMIRNOV. I do.

POPOVA. I ask you to go away!

SMIRNOV. Give me my money. . . . [*Aside.*] Oh, how angry I am! How angry I am!

POPOVA. I don't want to talk to impudent scoundrels! Get out of this! [*Pause.*] Aren't you going? No?

SMIRNOV. No.

POPOVA. No?

SMIRNOV. No!

POPOVA. Very well then! [*Rings, enter* LUKA.] Luka, show this gentleman out!

LUKA [*approaches* SMIRNOV]. Would you mind going out, sir, as you're asked to! You needn't . . .

SMIRNOV [*jumps up*]. Shut up! Who are you talking to? I'll chop you into pieces!

LUKA [*clutches at his heart*]. Little fathers! . . . What people! . . . [*Falls into a chair.*] Oh, I'm ill, I'm ill! I can't breathe!

POPOVA. Where's Dasha? Dasha! [*Shouts.*] Dasha! Pelageya! Dasha! [*Rings.*]

LUKA. Oh! They've all gone out to pick fruit. . . . There's nobody at home! I'm ill! Water!

POPOVA. Get out of this, now.

SMIRNOV. Can't you be more polite?

POPOVA [*clenches her fists and stamps her foot*]. You're a boor! A coarse bear! A Bourbon! A monster!

SMIRNOV. What? What did you say?

POPOVA. I said you are a bear, a monster!

SMIRNOV [*approaching her*]. May I ask what right you have to insult me?

POPOVA. And suppose I am insulting you? Do you think I'm afraid of you?

SMIRNOV. And do you think that just because you're a poetic creature you can insult me with impunity? Eh? We'll fight it out!

LUKA. Little fathers! . . . What people! . . . Water!

SMIRNOV. Pistols!

POPOVA. Do you think I'm afraid of you just because you have large fists and a bull's throat? Eh? You Bourbon!

SMIRNOV. We'll fight it out! I'm not going to be insulted by anybody, and I don't care if you are a woman, one of the "softer sex," indeed!

POPOVA [*trying to interrupt him*]. Bear! Bear! Bear!

SMIRNOV. It's about time we got rid of the prejudice that only men need pay for their insults. Devil take it, if you want equality of rights you can have it. We're going to fight it out!

POPOVA. With pistols? Very well!

SMIRNOV. This very minute.

POPOVA. This very minute! My husband had some pistols. . . . I'll bring them here. [*Is going, but turns back.*] What pleasure it will give me to put a bullet into your thick head! Devil take you! [*Exit.*]

SMIRNOV. I'll bring her down like a chicken! I'm not a little boy or a sentimental puppy; I don't care about this "softer sex."

LUKA. Gracious little fathers! . . . [*Kneels.*] Have pity on a poor old man, and go away from here! You've frightened her to death, and now you want to shoot her!

SMIRNOV [*not hearing him*]. If she fights, well that's equality of rights, emancipation, and all that! Here the sexes are equal! I'll shoot her on principle! But what a woman! [*Parodying her.*] "Devil take you! I'll put a bullet into your thick head." Eh? How she reddened, how her cheeks shone! . . . She accepted my challenge! My word, it's the first time in my life that I've seen. . . .

LUKA. Go away, sir, and I'll always pray to God for you!

SMIRNOV. She is a woman! That's the sort I can understand! A real woman! Not a sour-faced jellybag, but fire, gunpowder. a rocket! I'm even sorry to have to kill her!

LUKA [weeps]. Dear . . . dear sir, do go away!

SMIRNOV. I absolutely like her! Absolutely! Even though her cheeks are dimpled, I like her! I'm almost ready to let the debt go . . . and I'm not angry any longer. . . . Wonderful woman!

Enter POPOVA *with pistols.*

POPOVA. Here are the pistols. . . . But before we fight you must show me how to fire. I've never held a pistol in my hands before.

LUKA. Oh, Lord, have mercy and save her. . . . I'll go and find the coachman and the gardener. . . . Why has this infliction come on us. . . . [*Exit.*]

SMIRNOV [*examining the pistols*]. You see, there are several sorts of pistols. . . . There are Mortimer pistols, specially made for duels, they fire a percussion-cap. These are Smith and Wesson revolvers, triple action, with extractors. . . . These are excellent pistols. They can't cost less than ninety roubles the pair. . . You must hold the revolver like this. . . . [*Aside.*] Her eyes, her eyes! What an inspiring woman!

POPOVA. Like this?

SMIRNOV. Yes, like this. . . . Then you cock the trigger, and take aim like this. . . . Put your head back a little! Hold your arm out properly. . . . Like that. . . . Then you press this thing with your finger—and that's all. The great thing is to keep cool and aim steadily. . . . Try not to jerk your arm.

POPOVA. Very well. . . . It's incon-venient to shoot in a room, let's go into the garden.

SMIRNOV. Come along then. But I warn you, I'm going to fire in the air.

POPOVA. That's the last straw! Why?

SMIRNOV. Because . . . because . . . it's my affair.

POPOVA. Are you afraid? Yes? Ah! No, sir, you don't get out of it! You come with me! I shan't have any peace until I've made a hole in your forehead . . . that forehead which I hate so much! Are you afraid?

SMIRNOV. Yes, I am afraid.

POPOVA. You lie! Why won't you fight?

SMIRNOV. Because . . . because you . . . because I like you.

POPOVA [*laughs*]. He likes me! He dares to say that he likes me! [*Points to the door.*] That's the way.

SMIRNOV [*loads the revolver in silence, takes his cap and goes to the door. There he stops for half a minute, while they look at each other in silence, then he hesitatingly approaches* POPOVA]. Listen. . . . Are you still angry? I'm devilishly annoyed, too . . . but, do you understand . . . how can I express myself? . . . The fact is, you see, it's like this, so to speak. . . . [*Shouts.*] Well, is it my fault that I like you? [*He snatches at the back of a chair; the chair creaks and breaks.*] Devil take it, how I'm smashing up your furniture! I like you! Do you understand? I . . . I almost love you!

POPOVA. Get away from me—I hate you!

SMIRNOV. God, what a woman! I've never in my life seen one like her! I'm lost! Done for! Fallen into a mousetrap, like a mouse!

POPOVA. Stand back, or I'll fire!

SMIRNOV. Fire, then! You can't understand what happiness it would be to die before those beautiful eyes, to be shot by a revolver held in that little, velvet hand. . . . I'm out of my senses! Think, and make up your mind at once, because if I go out we shall never see each other again! Decide now. . . . I am a landowner, of respectable character, have an income of ten thousand a year. . . . I can put a bullet through a coin tossed into the air as it comes down. . . . I own some fine horses. . . . Will you be my wife?

POPOVA [*indignantly shakes her revolver*]. Let's fight! Let's go out!

SMIRNOV. I'm mad. . . . I understand nothing. . . . [*Yells.*] Waiter, water!

POPOVA [*yells*]. Let's go out and fight!

SMIRNOV. I'm off my head, I'm in love like a boy, like a fool! [*Snatches her hand, she screams with pain.*] I love you! [*Kneels.*] I love you as I've never loved before! I've refused twelve women, nine have refused me, but I never loved one of them as I love you. . . . I'm weak, I'm wax, I've melted. . . . I'm on my knees like a fool, offering you my hand. . . . Shame, shame! I haven't been in love for five years, I'd taken a vow, and now all of a sudden I'm in love, like a fish out of water! I offer you my hand. Yes or no? You don't want me? Very well! [*Gets up and quickly goes to the door.*]

POPOVA. Stop.

SMIRNOV [*stops*]. Well?

POPOVA. Nothing, go away. . . . No, stop. . . . No, go away, go away! I hate you! Or no. . . . Don't go away! Oh, if you knew how angry I am, how angry I am! [*Throws her revolver on the table.*] My fingers have swollen because of all this. . . . [*Tears her handkerchief in temper.*] What are you waiting for? Get out!

SMIRNOV. Good-bye.

POPOVA. Yes, yes, go away! . . . [*Yells.*] Where are you going? Stop. . . . . No, go away. Oh, how angry I am! Don't come near me, don't come near me!

SMIRNOV [*approaching her*]. How angry I am with myself! I'm in love like a student, I've been on my knees. . . . [*Rudely.*] I love you! What do I want to fall in love with you for? To-morrow I've got to pay the interest, and begin mowing, and here you. . . .. [*Puts his arms around her.*] I shall never forgive myself for this. . . .

POPOVA. Get away from me! Take your hands away! I hate you! Let's go and fight!

A prolonged kiss. Enter LUKA *with an axe, the* GARDENER *with a rake, the* COACHMAN *with a pitchfork, and* WORKMEN *with poles.*

LUKA [*catches sight of the pair kissing*]. Little fathers! [*Pause.*]

POPOVA. [*lowering her eyes*]. Luka, tell them in the stables that Toby isn't to have any oats at all to-day.

CURTAIN

The High-Road

TIHON EVSTIGNEYEV, *the proprietor of an inn.*
SEMYON SERGEYEVITCH BORTSOV, *a ruined landowner.*
MARIA EGOROVNA, *his wife.*
SAVVA, *an aged pilgrim.*
NAZAROVNA ⎱
EFIMOVNA ⎰ *women pilgrims.*
FEDYA, *a labourer.*
EGOR MERIK, *a tramp.*
KUSMA, *a driver.*
POSTMAN.
BORTSOV'S WIFE'S COACHMAN.
PILGRIMS, CATTLE-DEALERS, ETC.

The action takes place in a province of Southern Russia.

ACT I

The scene is laid in TIHON'S *bar. On the right is the bar-counter and shelves with bottles. At the back is a door leading out of the house. Over it, on the outside, hangs a dirty red lantern. The floor and the forms, which stand against the wall, are closely occupied by pilgrims and passers-by. Many of them, for lack of space, are sleeping as they sit. It is late at night. As the curtain rises thunder is heard, and lightning is seen through the door.*
TIHON *is behind the counter.* FEDYA *is half-lying in a heap on one of the forms, and is quietly playing on a concertina. Next to him is* BORTSOV, *wearing a shabby summer overcoat.* SAVVA, NAZAROVNA, *and* EFIMOVNA *are stretched out on the floor by the benches.*

EFIMOVNA. [*To* NAZAROVNA.] Give the old fellow a shove dear! Can't get any answer from him.

NAZAROVNA. [*Lifting the corner of a cloth covering off* SAVVA's *face.*] Are you alive or dead, you pious man?

SAVVA. Why should I be dead? I'm alive, mother! [*Raises himself on his elbow.*] Cover up my feet, mother! That's it. More on the right one. God be good to us.

NAZAROVNA. [*Wrapping up* SAVVA's *feet.*] Sleep, little father.

SAVVA. What sleep can I have? If only I could endure this pain, mother; sleep's quite another matter. A sinner doesn't deserve it. Did you hear a noise, pilgrim-woman?

NAZAROVNA. God is sending a storm. The wind is wailing, and the rain is pouring. All down the roof and into the windows like dried peas.· Do you hear? The windows of heaven are opened . . . [*Thunder.*] Holy, holy, holy. . . .

FEDYA. And it roars and thunders, and rages, and never ceases! Hoooo . . . It's like the noise of a forest. . . . Hoooo. . . . The wind is wailing like a dog. . . . [*Shrinking back.*] It's cold! My clothes are wet, it's all coming in through the open door . . . you might put me through a wringer. . . . [*Plays softly.*] My concertina's damp, and so there's no music for you, my Orthodox brethren, or else I'd give you such a concert, I tell you! Something marvellous! You can have a quadrille, or a polka, if you like, or some Russian dance for two. . . . I can do all. In the town, at the Grand Hotel, I was always without money, but I did wonders on

642

my concertina. And I can play a guitar.

A VOICE FROM THE CORNER. Silly words from a silly fool.

FEDYA. I can hear another of them. [*Pause.*]

NAZAROVNA. [*To* SAVVA.] Lie where it is warm now, old man, and warm your feet. [*Pause.*] Old man! Man of God! [*Shakes* SAVVA.] Do you want to die?

FEDYA. Drink a little vodka, grandfather. Drink, and it'll burn in your stomach, and fire your heart. Drink now!

NAZAROVNA. Don't, young man! Perhaps the old man is rendering his soul to God, or repenting for his sins, and you talk like that, and play your concertina. . . . Put it down! You've no shame!

FEDYA. And what are you sticking to him for? He can't do anything and you . . . with your old women's talk . . . He can't say a word in reply, and you're glad, and happy because he's listening to your nonsense. . . . You go on sleeping, grandfather, never mind her! Let her talk, don't you take any notice of her. A woman's tongue is the devil's broom—it will sweep the good man and the clever man both out of the house. Don't you mind. . . . [*Waves his hands.*] But it's thin you are, brother of mine! Terrible! Like a dead skeleton! No life in you! Are you really dying?

SAVVA. Why should I die? Save me, O Lord, from dying in vain. . . . I'll suffer a little, and then get up with God's help. . . . The Mother of God won't let me die in a strange land . . . I'll die at home.

FEDYA. Are you from far off?

SAVVA. From Vologda. The town itself. . . . I live there.

FEDYA. And where is this Vologda?

TIHON. The other side of Moscow. . . .

FEDYA. Well, well, well. . . . You have come a long way, old man! On foot?

SAVVA. On foot, young man. I've been to Tihon of the Don, and I'm going to the Holy Hills. . . . From there, if God wills it, to Odessa. . . . They say you can get to Jerusalem cheap from there, for twenty-one roubles, they say. . . .

FEDYA. And have you been to Moscow?

SAVVA. Rather! Five times. . . .

FEDYA. Is it a good town? [*Smokes.*] Well-standing?

SAVVA. There are many holy places there, young man. . . . Where there are many holy places it's always a good town. . . .

BORTSOV [*goes up to the counter, to* TIHON]. Once more, please! For the sake of Christ, give it to me!

FEDYA. The chief thing about a town is that it should be clean. If it's dusty, it must be watered; if it's dirty, it must be cleaned. There ought to be big houses . . . a theatre . . . police . . . cabs, which . . . I've lived in a town myself, I understand.

BORTSOV. Just a little glass. I'll pay you for it later.

TIHON. That's enough now.

BORTSOV. I ask you! Do be kind to me!

TIHON. Get away!

BORTSOV. You don't understand me. . . . Understand me, you fool, if there's a drop of brain in your peasant's wooden head, that it isn't I who am asking you, but my inside, using the words you understand, that's what's asking! My illness is what's asking! Understand!

TIHON. We don't understand anything. . . . Get back!

BORTSOV. Because if I don't have a drink at once, just you understand this, if I don't satisfy my needs, I may commit some crime God only knows what I might do! In the time you've kept this place, you rascal, haven't you seen a lot of drunkards, and haven't you yet got to understand what they're like? They're diseased! You can do anything you like to them, but you must give them vodka! Well, now, I implore you! Please! I humbly ask you! God only knows how humbly!

TIHON. You can have the vodka if you pay for it.

BORTSOV. Where am I to get the money? I've drunk it all! Down to the ground! What can I give you? I've only got this coat, but I can't give you that. I've nothing on underneath. . . . Would you like my cap? [Takes it off and gives it to TIHON.]

TIHON [looks it over]. Hm. . . . There are all sorts of caps. . . . It might be a sieve from the holes in it. . . .

FEDYA [laughs]. A gentleman's cap! You've got to take it off in front of the mam'selles. How do you do, good-bye! How are you?

TIHON [returns the cap to BORTSOV]. I wouldn't give anything for it. It's muck.

BORTSOV. If you don't like it, then let me owe you for the drink! I'll bring in your five copecks on my way back from town. You can take it and choke yourself with it then! Choke

yourself! I hope it sticks in your throat! [Coughs.] I hate you!

TIHON [banging the bar-counter with his fist]. Why do you keep on like that? What a man! What are you here for, you swindler?

BORTSOV. I want a drink! It's not I, it's my disease! Understand that!

TIHON. Don't you make me lose my temper, or you'll soon find yourself outside!

BORTSOV. What am I to do? [Retires from the bar-counter.] What am I to do? [Is thoughtful.]

EFIMOVNA. It's the devil tormenting you. Don't you mind him, sir. The damned one keeps whispering, 'Drink! Drink!' And you answer him, 'I shan't drink! I shan't drink!' He'll go then.

FEDYA. It's drumming in his head. . . . His stomach's leading him on! [Laughs.] Your honour's a happy man. Lie down and go to sleep! What's the use of standing like a scarecrow in the middle of the inn! This isn't an orchard!

BORTSOV [angrily]. Shut up! Nobody spoke to you, you donkey.

FEDYA. Go on, go on! We've seen the like of you before! There's a lot like you tramping the high road! As to being a donkey, you wait till I've given you a clout on the ear and you'll howl worse than the wind. Donkey yourself! Fool! [Pause.] Scum!

NAZAROVNA. The old man may be saying a prayer, or giving up his soul to God, and here are these unclean ones wrangling with one another and saying all sorts of . . . Have shame on yourselves!

FEDYA. Here, you cabbage-stalk, you keep quiet, even if you are in a public-house. Just you behave like everybody else.

BORTSOV. What am I to do? What will become of me? How can I make him understand? What else can I say to him? [*To* TIHON.] The blood's boiling in my chest! Uncle Tihon! [*Weeps.*] Uncle Tihon!

SAVVA [*groans*]. I've got shooting-pains in my leg, like bullets of fire. . . . Little mother, pilgrim.

EFIMOVNA. What is it, little father?

SAVVA. Who's that crying?

EFIMOVNA. The gentleman.

SAVVA. Ask him to shed a tear for me, that I might die in Vologda. Tearful prayers are heard.

BORTSOV. I'm not praying, grandfather! These aren't tears! Just juice! My soul is crushed, and the juice is running. [*Sits by* SAVVA.] Juice! But you wouldn't understand! You, with your darkened brain, wouldn't understand. You people are all in the dark!

SAVVA. Where will you find those who live in the light?

BORTSOV. They do exist, grandfather. . . . They would understand!

SAVVA. Yes, yes, dear friend. . . . The saints lived in the light. . . . They understood all our griefs. . . . You needn't even tell them . . . and they'll understand. . . . Just by looking at your eyes. . . . And then you'll have such peace, as if you were never in grief at all—it will all go!

FEDYA. And have you ever seen any saints?

SAVVA. It has happened, young man. . . . There are many of all sorts on this earth. Sinners, and servants of God.

BORTSOV. I don't understand all this. . . . [*Gets up quickly.*] What's the use of talking when you don't understand, and what sort of a brain have I now? I've only an instinct, a thirst! [*Goes quickly to the counter.*] Tihon, take my coat! Understand? [*Tries to take it off.*] My coat . . .

TIHON. And what is there under your coat? [*Looks under it.*] Your naked body? Don't take it off, I shan't have it. . . . I'm not going to burden my soul with a sin.

[*Enter* MERIK.]

BORTSOV. Very well, I'll take the sin on myself! Do you agree?

MERIK. [*In silence takes off his outer cloak and remains in a sleeveless jacket. He carries an axe in his belt.*] A vagrant may sweat where a bear will freeze. I am hot. [*Puts his axe on the floor and takes off his jacket.*] You get rid of a pailful of sweat while you drag one leg out of the mud. And while you are dragging it out, the other one goes farther in.

EFIMOVNA. Yes, that's true . . . is the rain stopping, dear?

MERIK [*glancing at* EFIMOVNA]. I don't talk to old women. [*A pause.*]

BORTSOV [*to* TIHON]. I'll take the sin on myself. Do you hear me or don't you?

TIHON. I don't want to hear you, get away!

MERIK. It's as dark as if the sky was painted with pitch. You can't see your own nose. And the rain beats into your face like a snowstorm! [*Picks up his clothes and axe.*]

FEDYA. It's a good thing for the likes of us thieves. When the cat's away the mice will play.

MERIK. Who says that?

FEDYA. Look and see . . . before you forget.

MERIK. We'll make a note of it. . . . [*Goes up to* TIHON.] How do you do, you with the large face! Don't you remember me?

TIHON. If I'm to remember every one of you drunkards that walks the high road, I reckon I'd need ten holes in my forehead.

MERIK. Just look at me. . . . [*A pause.*]

TIHON. Oh, yes, I remember. I knew you by your eyes! [*Gives him his hand.*] Andrey Polikarpov?

MERIK. I used to be Andrey Polikarpov, but now I am Egor Merik.

TIHON. Why's that?

MERIK. I call myself after whatever passport God gives me. I've been Merik for two months. [*Thunder.*] Rrrr. . . . Go on thundering, I'm not afraid! [*Looks round.*] Any police here?

TIHON. What are you talking about, making mountains out of mole-hills? . . . The people here are all right. . . . The police are fast asleep in their feather beds now. . . . [*Loudly.*] Orthodox brothers, mind your pockets and your clothes. or you'll have cause to regret it. The man's a rascal! He'll rob you!

MERIK. They can look out for their money, but as to their clothes—I shan't touch them. I've nowhere to take them.

TIHON. Where's the devil taking you to?

MERIK. To Kuban.

TIHON. My word!

FEDYA. To Kuban? Really? [*Sitting up.*] It's a fine place. You wouldn't see such a country, brother, if you were to fall asleep and dream for three years. They say the birds there, and the beasts are—my God! The grass grows all the year round, the people are good, and they've so much land they don't know

what to do with it! The authorities, they say . . . a soldier was telling me the other day . . . give a hundred dessiatins a head. There's happiness, God strike me!

MERIK. Happiness. . . . Happiness goes behind you. . . . You don't see it. It's as near as your elbow is, but you can't bite it. It's all silly. . . . [*Looking round at the benches and the people.*] Like a lot of prisoners. . . . A poor lot.

EFIMOVNA [*to* MERIK]. What great, angry eyes! There's an enemy in you, young man. . . . Don't you look at us!

MERIK. Yes, you're a poor lot here.

EFIMOVNA. Turn away! [*Nudges* SAVVA.] Savva, darling, a wicked man is looking at us. He'll do us harm, dear. [*To* MERIK.] Turn away, I tell you, you snake!

SAVVA. He won't touch us, mother, he won't touch us. . . . God won't let him.

MERIK. All right, Orthodox brothers! [*Shrugs his shoulders.*] Be quiet! You aren't asleep, you bandy-legged fools! Why don't you say something?

EFIMOVNA. Take your great eyes away! Take away that devil's own pride!

MERIK. Be quiet, you crooked old woman! I didn't come with the devil's pride, but with kind words, wishing to honour your bitter lot! You're huddled together like flies because of the cold— I'd be sorry for you, speak kindly to you, pity your poverty, and here you go grumbling away! There's no need for that! [*Goes up to* FEDYA.] Where are you from?

FEDYA. I live in these parts. I work at the Khamonyevsky brickworks.

MERIK. Get up.

FEDYA [*raising himself*]. Well?

MERIK. Get up, right up. I'm going to lie down here.

FEDYA. What's that. . . . It isn't your place, is it?

MERIK. Yes, mine. Go and lie on the ground!

FEDYA. You get out of this, you tramp. I'm not afraid of you.

MERIK. You're very quick with your tongue. . . . Get up, and don't talk about it! You'll be sorry for it, you silly.

TIHON [*to* FEDYA]. Don't contradict him, young man. Never mind.

FEDYA. What right have you? You stick out your fishy eyes and think I'm afraid! [*Picks up his belongings and stretches himself out on the ground.*] You devil! [*Lies down and covers himself all over.*]

MERIK [*stretching himself out on the bench*]. I don't expect you've ever seen a devil or you wouldn't call me one. Devils aren't like that. [*Lies down, putting his axe next to him.*] Lie down, little brother axe . . . let me cover you.

TIHON. Where did you get the axe from?

MERIK. Stole it. . . . Stole it, and now I've got to fuss over it like a child with a new toy; I don't like to throw it away, and I've nowhere to put it. Like a beastly wife. . . . Yes. . . . [*Covering himself over.*] Devils aren't like that, brother.

FEDYA [*uncovering his head*]. What are they like?

MERIK. Like steam, like air. . . . Just blow into the air. [*Blows.*] They're like that, you can't see them.

A VOICE FROM THE CORNER. You can see them if you sit under a harrow.

MERIK. I've tried, but I didn't see any. . . . Old women's tales, and silly old men's, too. . . . You won't see a devil or a ghost or a corpse. . . . Our eyes weren't made so that we could see everything. . . . When I was a boy, I used to walk in the woods at night on purpose to see the demon of the woods. . . . I'd shout and shout, and there might be some spirit, I'd call for the demon of the woods and not blink my eyes: I'd see all sorts of little things moving about, but no demon. I used to go and walk about churchyards at night, I wanted to see the ghosts—but the old women lie. I saw all sorts of animals, but anything awful—not a sign. Our eyes weren't . . .

THE VOICE FROM THE CORNER. Never mind, it does happen that you do see. . . . In our village a man was gutting a wild boar . . . he was separating the tripe when . . . something jumped out at him!

SAVVA [*raising himself*]. Little children, don't talk about these unclean things. It's a sin, dears!

MERIK. Aaa . . . greybeard! You skeleton! [*Laughs.*] You needn't go to the churchyard to see ghosts, when they get up from under the floor to give advice to their relations. . . . A sin! . . . Don't you teach people your silly notions! You're an ignorant lot of people, living in darkness. . . . [*Lights his pipe.*] My father was a peasant and used to be fond of teaching people. One night he stole a sack of apples from the village priest, and he brings them along and tells us, 'Look, children, mind you don't eat any apples before Easter. it's a sin.' You're like

that. . . . You don't know what a
devil is, but you go calling people
devils. . . . Take this crooked old
woman, for instance. [*Points to* EFI-
MOVNA.] She sees an enemy in me, but
in her time, for some woman's nonsense
or other, she's given her soul to the
devil five times.

EFIMOVNA. Hoo, hoo, hoo. . . .
Gracious heavens! [*Covers her face.*]
Little Savva!

TIHON. What are you frightening
them for? A great pleasure! [*The
door slams in the wind.*] Lord Jesus.
. . . The wind, the wind!

MERIK [*stretching himself*]. Eh, to
show my strength! [*The door slams
again.*] If I could only measure myself
against the wind! Shall I tear the door
down, or suppose I tear up the inn by
the roots! [*Gets up and lies down
again.*] How dull!

NAZAROVNA. You'd better pray, you
heathen! Why are you so restless?

EFIMOVNA. Don't speak to him, leave
him alone! He's looking at us again.
[*To* MERIK.] Don't look at us, evil
man! Your eyes are like the eyes of
a devil before cock-crow!

SAVVA. Let him look, pilgrims! You
pray, and his eyes won't do you any
harm.

BORTSOV. No, I can't. It's too much
for my strength! [*Goes up to the
counter.*] Listen, Tihon, I ask you for
the last time. . . . Just half a glass!

TIHON [*shakes his head*]. T h e
money!

BORTSOV. My God, haven't I told
you! I've drunk it all! Where am I
to get it? And you won't go broke
even if you do let me have a drop of
vodka on tick. A glass of it only costs
you two copecks, and it will save me

from suffering! I am suffering! Understand! I'm in misery, I'm suffering!

TIHON. Go and tell that to someone
else. not to me. . . . Go and ask the
Orthodox, perhaps they'll give you some
for Christ's sake, if they feel like it,
but I'll only give bread for Christ's
sake.

BORTSOV. You can rob those wretches
yourself, I shan't. . . . 1 won't do it!
I won't! Understand? [*Hits the bar-
counter with his fist.*] I won't! [*A
pause.*] Hm . . . just wait. . . .
[*Turns to the pilgrim women.*] It's an
idea, all the same, Orthodox ones! Spare
five copecks! My inside asks for it.
I'm ill!

FEDYA. Oh, you swindler, with your
'spare five copecks.' Won't you have
some water?

BORTSOV. How I am degrading myself! I don't want it! I don't want
anything! 1 was joking!

MERIK. You won't get it out of him,
sir. . . . He's a famous skinflint. . . .
Wait, I've got a five-copeck piece somewhere. . . . We'll have a glass between
us—half each. [*Searches in his pockets.*]
The devil . . . it's lost somewhere.
. . . Thought I heard it tinkling just
now in my pocket. . . . No, no, it
isn't there, brother, it's your luck! [*A
pause.*]

BORTSOV. But if I can't drink. I'll
commit a crime or I'll kill myself. . . .
What shall I do, my God! [*Looks
through the door.*] Shall I go out,
then? Out into this darkness, wherever
my feet take me. . . .

MERIK. Why don't you give him a
sermon, you pilgrims? And you, Tihon,
why don't you drive him out? He
hasn't paid you for his night's accommodation. Chuck him out! Eh, the

people are cruel nowadays. There's no gentleness or kindness in them. . . . A savage people! A man is drowning and they shout to him: 'Hurry up and drown, we've got no time to look at you, we've got to go to work.' As to throwing him a rope—there's no need to worry about that. . . . A rope would cost money.

SAVVA. Don't talk, kind man!

MERIK. Quiet, old wolf! You're a savage race! Herods! Sellers of your souls! [*To* TIHON.] Come here, take off my boots! Look sharp now!

TIHON. Eh, he's let himself go! [*Laughs.*] Awful, isn't it?

MERIK. Go on, do as you're told! Quick, now! [*Pause.*] Do you hear me, or don't you? Am I talking to you or the wall? [*Stands up.*]

TIHON. Well . . . give over.

MERIK. I want you, you fleecer, to take the boots off me, a poor tramp.

TIHON. Well, well . . . don't get excited. Here, have a glass. . . . Have a drink, now!

MERIK. People, what do I want? Do I want him to stand me vodka, or to take off my boots? Didn't I say it properly? [*To* TIHON.] Didn't you hear me rightly? I'll wait a moment, perhaps you'll hear me then.

There is excitement among the pilgrims and tramps, who half-raise themselves in order to look at TIHON *and* MERIK. *They wait in silence.*

TIHON. The devil brought you here! [*Comes out from behind the bar.*] What a gentleman! Come on, now. [*Takes off* MERIK's *boots.*] You child of Cain . . .

MERIK. That's right. Put them side by side. . . . Like that . . . you can go now!

TIHON [*returns to the bar-counter*]. You're too fond of being clever. You do it again and I'll turn you out of the inn! Yes! [*To* BORTSOV, *who is approaching.*] You, again?

BORTSOV. Look here, suppose I give you something made of gold. . . . I will give it to you.

TIHON. What are you shaking for? Talk sense!

BORTSOV. It may be mean and wicked on my part, but what am I to do? I'm doing this wicked thing, not reckoning on what's to come. . . . If I was tried for it, they'd let me off. Take it, only on condition that you return it later, when I come back from town. I give it to you in front of these witnesses. You will be my witnesses! [*Takes a gold medallion out from the breast of his coat.*] Here it is. . . . I ought to take the portrait out, but I've nowhere to put it; I'm wet all over. . . . Well, take the portrait, too! Only mind this . . . don't let your fingers touch that face. . . . Please . . . I was rude to you, my dear fellow, I was a fool, but forgive me and . . . don't touch it with your fingers. . . . Don't look at that face with your eyes. [*Gives* TIHON *the medallion.*]

TIHON [*examining it*]. Stolen property. . . . All right, then, drink. . . . [*Pours out vodka.*] Confound you.

BORTSOV. Only you don't touch it . . . with your fingers. [*Drinks slowly, with feverish pauses.*]

TIHON [*opens the medallion*]. Hm . . . a lady! . . . Where did you get hold of this?

MERIK. Let's have a look. [*Goes to the bar.*] Let's see.

TIHON [*pushes his hand away*].

Where are you going to? You look somewhere else!

FEDYA [*gets up and comes to* TIHON]. I want to look too!

Several of the tramps, etc., approach the bar and form a group. MERIK *grips* TIHON's *hand firmly with both his, looks at the portrait in the medallion in silence. A pause.*

MERIK. A pretty she-devil. A real lady. . . .

FEDYA. A real lady. . . . Look at her cheeks, her eyes. . . . Open your hand, I can't see. Hair coming down to her waist. . . . It is lifelike! She might be going to say something. . . . [*Pause.*]

MERIK. It's destruction for a weak man. A woman like that gets a hold on one and . . . [*waves his hand*] you're done for!

KUSMA's *voice is heard.* "Trrr. . . . Stop, you brutes!" [*Enter* KUSMA.]

KUSMA. There stands an inn upon my way. Shall I drive or walk past it, say? You can pass your own father and not notice him. but you can see an inn in the dark a hundred versts away. Make way, if you believe in God! Hullo, there! [*Planks a five-copeck piece on the counter.*] A glass of real Madeira! Quick!

FEDYA. Oh, you devil!

TIHON. Don't wave your arms about, or you'll hit somebody.

KUSMA. God gave us arms to wave about. Poor sugary things, you're half-melted. You're frightened of the rain, poor delicate things. [*Drinks.*]

EFIMOVNA. You may well get frightened, good man, if you're caught on your way in a night like this. Now, thank God, it's all right, there are many villages and houses where you can

shelter from the weather. but before that there weren't any. Oh, Lord, it was bad! You walk a hundred versts, and not only isn't there a village, or a house, but you don't even see a dry stick. So you sleep on the ground. . . .

KUSMA. Have you been long on this earth, old woman?

EFIMOVNA. Over seventy years, little father.

KUSMA. Over seventy years! You'll soon come to crows' years. [*Looks at* BORTSOV.] And what sort of a raisin is this? [*Staring at* BORTSOV.] Sir! [BORTSOV *recognizes* KUSMA *and retires in confusion to a corner of the room, where he sits on a bench.*] Semyon Sergeyevitch! Is that you, or isn't it? Eh? What are you doing in this place? It's not the sort of place for you, is it?

BORTSOV. Be quiet!

MERIK [*to* KUSMA] Who is it?

KUSMA. A miserable sufferer. [*Paces irritably by the counter.*] Eh? In an inn, my goodness! Tattered! Drunk! I'm upset, brothers . . . upset. . . . [*To* MERIK, *in an undertone.*] It's my master . . . our landlord. Semyon Sergeyevitch and Mr. Bortsov. . . . Have you ever seen a man in such a state? What does he look like? Just . . . it's the drink that brought him to this. . . . Give me some more! [*Drinks.*] I come from his village, Bortsovka; you may have heard of it, it's 200 versts from here, in the Ergovsky district. We used to be his father's serfs. . . . What a shame!

MERIK. Was he rich?

KUSMA. Very.

MERIK. Did he drink it all?

KUSMA. No, my friend, it was some-- thing else. . . . He used to be great and rich and sober. . . . [*To* TIHON.]

Why you yourself used to see him riding, as he used to, past this inn, on his way to the town. Such bold and noble horses! A carriage on springs, of the best quality! He used to own five troikas, brother. . . . Five years ago, I remember, he came here, driving two horses from Mikishinsky, and he paid with a five-rouble piece. . . . I haven't the time, he says, to wait for the change. . . . There!

MERIK. His brain's gone, I suppose.

KUSMA. His brain's all right. . . . It all happened because of his cowardice! From too much fat. First of all, children, because of a woman. . . . He fell in love with a woman of the town, and it seemed to him that there wasn't any more beautiful thing in the wide world. A fool may love as much as a wise man. The girl's people were all right. . . . But she wasn't exactly loose, but just . . giddy . . . always changing her mind! Always winking at one! Always laughing and laughing. . . . No sense at all. The gentry like that, they think that's nice, but we moujiks would soon chuck her out. . . . Well, he fell in love, and his luck ran out. He began to keep company with her, one thing led to another . . . they used to go out in a boat all night, and play pianos. . . .

BORTSOV. Don't tell them, Kusma! Why should you? What has my life got to do with them?

KUSMA. Forgive me, your honour, I'm only telling them a little . . . what does it matter, anyway. . . . I'm shaking all over. Pour out some more. [Drinks.]

MERIK [in a semitone]. And did she love him?

KUSMA [in a semitone which gradu-ally becomes his ordinary voice]. How shouldn't she? He was a man of means. . . . . Of course you'll fall in love when the man has a thousand dessiatins and money to burn. . . . He was a solid, dignified, sober gentleman . . . always the same, like this . . . give me your hand. [Takes MERIK's hand.] 'How do you do and good-bye, do me the favour.' Well, was going one eve-ning past his garden—and what a gar-den, brother, versts of it—I was going along quietly, and I look and see the two of them sitting on a seat and kissing each other. [Imitates the sound.] He kisses her once, and the snake gives him back two. . . . He was holding her white, little hand, and she was all fiery and kept on getting closer and closer, too. . . . 'I love you,' she says. And he, like one of the damned, walks about from one place to another and brags, the coward, about his happiness. . . . Gives one man a rouble, and two to another. . . . Gives me money for a horse. Let off everybody's debts. . . .

BORTSOV. Oh, why tell them all about it? These people haven't any sympathy. . . . It hurts!

KUSMA. It's nothing, sir! They asked me! Why shouldn't I tell them? But if you are angry I won't . . . I won't. . . . What do I care for them. . . . [Post bells are heard.]

FEDYA. Don't s h o u t ; tell us quietly. . . .

KUSMA. I'll tell you quietly. . . . He doesn't want me to, but it can't be helped. . . . But there's nothing more to tell. They got married, that's all. There was nothing else. Pour out another drop for Kusma the stony! [Drinks.] I don't like people getting drunk! Why the time the wedding took place, when the gentlefolk sat down to supper afterwards, she went off in a carriage . . . [*Whispers.*] To the town, to her lover, a lawyer. . . . Eh? What do you think of her now? Just at the very moment! She would be let off lightly if she were killed for it!

MERIK [*thoughtfully*]. Well . . . what happened then?

KUSMA. He went mad. . . . As you see, he started with a fly, as they say, and now it's grown to a bumble-bee. It was a fly then, and now—it's a bumble-bee. . . . And he still loves her. Look at him, he loves her! I expect he's walking now to the town to get a glimpse of her with one eye. . . . He'll get a glimpse of her, and go back. . .

The post has driven up to the inn. The POSTMAN *enters and has a drink.*

TIHON. The post's late to-day!

The POSTMAN *pays in silence and goes out. The post drives off, the bells ringing*].

A VOICE FROM THE CORNER. One could rob the post in weather like this— easy as spitting.

MERIK. I've been alive thirty-five years and I haven't robbed the post once. . . . [*Pause.*] It's gone now . . . too late, too late. . . .

KUSMA. Do you want to smell the inside of a prison?

MERIK. People rob and don't go to prison. And if I do go! [*Suddenly.*] What else?

KUSMA. Do you mean that unfortunate?

MERIK. Who else?

KUSMA. The second reason, brothers, why he was ruined was because of his brother-in-law, his sister's husband. . . . He took it into his head to stand surety at the bank for 30,000 roubles for his brother-in-law. The brother-in-law's a thief. . . . The swindler knows which side his bread's buttered and won't budge an inch. . . . So he doesn't pay up. . . . So our man had to pay up the whole thirty thousand. [*Sighs.*] The fool is suffering for his folly. His wife's got children now by the lawyer and the brother-in-law has bought an estate near Poltava, and our man goes round inns like a fool, and complains to the likes of us: 'I've lost all faith, brothers! I can't believe in anybody now!' It's cowardly! Every man has his grief, a snake that sucks at his heart, and does that mean that he must drink? Take our village elder, for example. His wife plays about with the schoolmaster in broad daylight, and spends his money on drink, but the elder walks about smiling to himself. He's just a little thinner. . . .

TIHON [*sighs*]. When God gives a man strength. . . .

KUSMA. There's all sorts of strength, that's true. . . . Well? How much does it come to? [*Pays.*] Take your pound of flesh! Good-bye, children! Good-night and pleasant dreams! It's time I hurried off. I'm bringing my lady a midwife from the hospital. . . . She must be getting wet with waiting, poor thing. . . [*Runs out. A pause.*]

TIHON. Oh, you! Unhappy man, come and drink this! [*Pours out.*]

BORTSOV [*comes up to the bar hesitatingly and drinks*]. That means I now owe you for two glasses.

TIHON. You don't owe me anything. Just drink and drown your sorrows!

FEDYA. Drink mine, too, sir! Oh! [*Throws down a five-copeck piece.*] If you drink, you die; if you don't drink, you die. It's good not to drink vodka, but by God you're easier when you've got some! Vodka takes grief away. . . . It is hot!

BORTSOV. Foo! The heat!

MERIK. Give it here! [*Takes the medallion from* TIHON *and examines her portrait.*] Hm. Ran off after the wedding. What a woman!

A VOICE FROM THE CORNER. Pour him out another glass, Tihon. Let him drink mine, too.

MERIK [*dashes the medallion to the ground*]. Curse her! [*Goes quickly to his place and lies down, face to the wall. General excitement.*]

BORTSOV. Here, what's that? [*Picks up the medallion.*] How dare you, you beast? What right have you? [*Tearfully.*] Do you want me to kill you? You moujik! You boor!

TIHON. Don't be angry, sir. . . . It isn't glass, it isn't broken. . . . Have another drink and go to sleep. [*Pours out.*] Here I've been listening to you all, and when I ought to have locked up long ago. [*Goes and locks door leading out.*]

BORTSOV [*drinks*]. How dare he? The fool! [*To* MERIK.] Do you understand? You're a fool, a donkey!

SAVVA. Children! If you please! Stop that talking! What's the good of making a noise? Let people go to sleep.

TIHON. Lie down, lie down . . . be quiet! [*Goes behind the counter and locks the till.*] It's time to sleep.

FEDYA. It's time. [*Lies down.*] Pleasant dreams, brothers!

MERIK [*gets up and spreads his short fur and coat on the bench*]. Come on, lie down, sir.

TIHON. And where will you sleep?

MERIK. Oh, anywhere. . . . The floor will do. . . . [*Spreads a coat on the floor.*] It's all one to me. [*Puts the axe by him.*] It would be torture for him to sleep on the floor. He's used to silk and down. . . .

TIHON [*to* BORTSOV]. Lie down, your honour! You've looked at that portrait long enough. [*Puts out a candle.*] Throw it away!

BORTSOV [*swaying about*]. Where can I lie down?

TIHON. In the tramp's place! Didn't you hear him giving it up to you?

BORTSOV [*going up to the vacant place*]. I'm a bit . . . drunk . . . after all that. . . . Is this it? . . . Do I lie down here? Eh?

TIHON. Yes, yes, lie down, don't be afraid. [*Stretches himself on the counter.*]

BORTSOV [*lying down*]. I'm . . . drunk. . . . Everything's going round. . . . [*Opens the medallion.*] Haven't you a little candle? [*Pause.*] You're a queer little woman Masha. . . . Looking at me out of the frame and laughing. . . . [*Laughs.*] I'm drunk! And should you laugh at a man because he's drunk? You look out, as Schastlivtsev says, and . . . love the drunkard.

FEDYA. How the wind howls. It's dreary!

BORTSOV [*laughs*]. What a woman. . . . Why do you keep on going round? I can't catch you!

MERIK. He's wandering. Looked too long at the portrait. [*Laughs.*] What a business! Educated people go and invent all sorts of machines and medicines, but there hasn't yet been a man wise enough to invent a medicine against the female sex. . . . They try to cure every sort of disease, and it never occurs to them that more people die of women than of disease. . . . Sly, stingy, cruel, brainless. . . . The mother-in-law torments the bride and the bride makes things square by swindling the husband . . . and there's no end to it. . . .

TIHON. The women have ruffled his hair for him, and so he's bristly.

MERIK. It isn't only I. . . . From the beginning of the ages, since the world has been in existence, people have complained. . . . It's not for nothing that in the songs and stories the devil and the woman are put side by side. . . . Not for nothing! It's half true, at any rate. . . . [Pause.] Here's the gentleman playing the fool, but I had more sense, didn't I, when I left my father and mother, and became a tramp?

FEDYA. Because of women?

MERIK. Just like the gentleman . . . I walked about like one of the damned, bewitched, blessing my stars . . . on fire day and night, until at last my eyes were opened. . . . It wasn't love, but just a fraud. . . .

FEDYA. What did you do to her?

MERIK. Never you mind. . . [Pause.] Do you think I killed her? . . . I wouldn't do it. . . . If you kill, you are sorry for it. . . . She can live and be happy! If only I'd never set eyes on you, or if I could only forget you, you viper's brood! [A knocking at the door.]

TIHON. Whom have the devils brought. . . . Who's there? [Knocking.] Who knocks? [Gets up and goes to the door.] Who knocks? Go away, we've locked up!

A VOICE. Please let me in, Tihon. The carriage-spring's broken! Be a father to me and help me! If I only had a little string to tie it round with, we'd get there somehow or other.

TIHON. Who are you?

THE VOICE. My lady is going to Varsonofyev from the town. . . . It's only five versts farther on. . . . Do be a good man and help!

TIHON. Go and tell the lady that if she pays ten roubles she can have her string and we'll mend the spring.

THE VOICE. Have you gone mad, or what? Ten roubles! You mad dog! Profiting by our misfortunes!

TIHON. Just as you like. . . . You needn't if you don't want to.

THE VOICE. Very well, wait a bit. [Pause.] She says, all right.

TIHON. Pleased to hear it! [Opens door. The COACHMAN enters.]

COACHMAN. Good evening, Orthodox people! Well, give me the string! Quick! Who'll go and help us, children? There'll be something left over for your trouble!

TIHON. There won't be anything left over. . . . Let them sleep, the two of us can manage.

COACHMAN. Foo, I am tired! It's cold, and there's not a dry spot in all the mud. . . . Another thing, dear. . . . Have you got a little room in here for the lady to warm herself in? The carriage is all on one side, she can't stay in it. . . .

TIHON. What does she want a room for? She can warm herself in here, if she's cold. . . . We'll find a place. [Clears a space next to BORTSOV.] Get up, get up! Just lie on the floor for an hour, and let the lady get warm. [To BORTSOV.] Get up, your honour! Sit up! [BORTSOV sits up.] Here's a place for you.

[Exit COACHMAN.]

FEDYA. Here's a visitor for you, the devil's brought her! Now there'll be no sleep before daylight.

TIHON. I'm sorry I didn't ask for fifteen. . . . She'd have given them. . . . [*Stands expectantly before the door.*] You're a delicate sort of people, I must say. [*Enter* MARIA EGOROVNA, *followed by the* COACHMAN. TIHON *bows.*] Please, your highness! Our room is very humble, full of black-beetles! But don't disdain it!

MARIA EGOROVNA. I can't see anything. . . . Which way do I go?

TIHON. This way, your highness! [*Leads her to the place next to* BORTSOV.] This way, please. [*Blows on the place.*] I haven't any separate rooms, excuse me, but don't you be afraid, madam, the people here are good and quiet. . . .

MARIA EGOROVNA [*sits next to* BORTSOV]. How awfully stuffy! Open the door, at any rate!

TIHON. Yes, madam. [*Runs and opens the door wide.*]

MERIK. We're freezing, and you open the door! [*Gets up and slams it.*] Who are you to be giving orders? [*Lies down.*]

TIHON. Excuse me, your highness, but we've a little fool here . . . a bit cracked. . . . But don't you be frightened, he won't do you any harm. . . . Only you must excuse me, madam, I can't do this for ten roubles. . . . Make it fifteen.

MARIA EGOROVNA. Very well, only be quick.

TIHON. This minute . . . this very instant. [*Drags some string out from under the counter.*] This minute.

[*A pause.*]

BORTSOV [*looking at* MARIA EGOROVNA]. Marie . . . Masha . . .

MARIA EGOROVNA [*looks at* BORTSOV]. What's this?

BORTSOV. Marie . . . is it you? Where do you come from? [MARIA EGOROVNA *recognizes* BORTSOV, *screams and runs off into the centre of the floor.* BORTSOV *follows.*] Marie, it is I . . . I [*Laughs loudly.*] My wife! Marie! Where am I? People, a light!

MARIA EGOROVNA. Get away from me! You lie, it isn't you! It can't be! [*Covers her face with her hands.*] It's a lie, it's all nonsense!

BORTSOV. Her voice, her movements. . . . Marie, it is I! I'll stop in a moment. . . . I was drunk. . . . My head's going round. . . . My God! Stop, stop. . . . I can't understand anything. [*Yells.*] My wife!

Falls at her feet and sobs. A group collects around the husband and wife.

MARIA EGOROVNA. Stand back. [*To the* COACHMAN.] Denis, let's go! I can't stop here any longer!

MERIK [*jumps up and looks her steadily in the face*]. The portrait! [*Grasps her hand.*] It is she! Eh, people, she's the gentleman's wife!

MARIA EGOROVNA. Get away, fellow! [*Tries to tear her hand away from him.*] Denis, why do you stand there staring? [DENIS *and* TIHON *run up to her and get hold of* MERIK'S *arms.*] This thieves' kitchen! Let go my hand! I'm not afraid! . . . Get away from me!

MERIK. Wait a bit, and I'll let go. . . . Just let me say one word to you. . . . One word, so that you may understand. . . . Just wait. . . . [*Turns to* TIHON *and* DENIS.] Get away, you rogues, let go! I shan't let you go till I've had my say! Stop . . . one moment. [*Strikes his forehead with his fist.*] No, God hasn't given me the wisdom! I can't think of the word for you!

MARIA EGOROVNA [*tears away her hand*]. Get away! Drunkards . . . let's go, Denis!

She tries to go out, but MERIK *blocks the door.*

MERIK. Just throw a glance at him, with only one eye if you like! Or say only just one kind little word to him! For God's own sake!

MARIA EGOROVNA. Take away this . . . fool.

MERIK. Then the devil take you, you accursed woman!

He swings his axe. General confusion. Everybody jumps up noisily and with cries of horror. SAVVA *stands between* MERIK *and* MARIA EGOROVNA.

. . . DENIS *forces* MERIK *to one side and carries out his mistress. After this all stand as if turned to stone. A prolonged pause.* BORTSOV *suddenly waves his hands in the air.*

BORTSOV. Marie . . . where are you, Marie!

NAZAROVNA. My God, my God! You've torn up my soul, you murderers! What an accursed night!

MERIK [*lowering his hand; he still holds the axe*]. Did I kill her or no?

TIHON. Thank God, your head is safe. . . .

MERIK. Then I didn't kill her. . . . [*Totters to his bed.*] Fate hasn't sent me to my death because of a stolen axe. . . . [*Falls down and sobs.*] Woe! Woe is me! Have pity on me, Orthodox people!

CURTAIN

The Anniversary

DRAMATIS PERSONAE

ANDREY ANDREYEVITCH SHIPUCHIN, *Chairman of the N—— Joint Stock Bank, a middle-aged man, with a monocle.*

TATIANA ALEXEYEVNA, *his wife, aged 25.*

KUSMA NICOLAIEVITCH KHIRIN, *the bank's aged book-keeper.*

NASTASYA FYODOROVNA MERCHUTKINA, *an old woman wearing an old-fashioned cloak.*

DIRECTORS OF THE BANK.

EMPLOYEES OF THE BANK.

The action takes place at the bank.

ACT I

The private office of the Chairman of Directors. On the left is a door, leading into the public department. There are two desks. The furniture aims at a deliberately luxurious effect, with armchairs covered in velvet, flowers, statues, carpets, and a telephone. It is mid-day. KHIRIN *is alone; he wears long felt boots, and is shouting through the door.*

KHIRIN. Send out to the chemist for 15 copecks' worth of valerian, and tell them to bring water into the Directors' office! This is the thousanth time I've asked! [*Goes to a desk.*] I'm worn out. This is the fourth day I've been working, without sleep. From morning to evening I work here, from evening to morning at home. [*Coughs.*] And I've got an inflammation all over me. I'm feverish, and I cough, my legs ache, my eyes blink. [*Sits.*] Our scoundrel of a Chairman, the brute, is going to read a report at a general meeting. 'Our Bank, its Present and Future.' You'd think he was a Gambetta. . . . [*At work.*] Two . . . one . . . one . . . six . . . nought . . . seven. . . . Next, six . . . nought . . . one . . . six. . . . He wants to trick people, and so I sit here and work for him like a nigger! This report of his is a story-tale and nothing more, and I've got to sit day after day and add figures, devil take his soul! [*Rattles on his counting-frame.*] I can't stand it! [*Writing.*] That is, one . . . three . . . seven . . . two . . . one . . . nought. . . . He promised to reward me for my work. If everything succeeds and the public is fooled, he's promised me a gold charm and 300 roubles bonus. . . . We'll see. [*Works.*] Yes, but if my work all goes for nothing, that's another matter. . . . I'm excitable. . . . If I lose my temper I'll kill somebody!

Noise and applause behind the scenes. SHIPUCHIN's *voice:* 'Thank you! Thank you! I am extremely grateful.' *Enter* SHIPUCHIN. *He wears a frockcoat and white tie; he carries an album which has been just presented to him.*

SHIPUCHIN [*at the door, addresses the outer office*]. This present, my dear colleagues. will be preserved to the day of my death, as a memory of the happiest days of my life! Yes, gentlemen! Once more, I thank you! [*Throws a kiss into the air and turns to* KHIRIN.] My honorable Kusma Nicolaievitch!

All the time that SHIPUCHIN *is on the stage, clerks intermittently come in with papers for his signature and go out.*

KHIRIN [*standing up*]. I have the honour to congratulate you, Andrey Andreyevitch, on the fiftieth anniversary of our Bank, and hope that . . .

SHIPUCHIN. [*Warmly shakes hands.*] Thank you, my friend! Thank you! I think that in view of the unique character of the day, as it is an anniversary, we may kiss each other! . . . [*They kiss.*] I am very, very glad! Thank you for your service . . . for everything! If, in the course of the time during which I have had the honour to be Chairman of this Bank anything useful has been done, the credit is due, more than to anybody else, to my colleagues. [*Sighs.*] Yes, fifteen years! Fifteen years as my name's Shipuchin! [*Changes his tone.*] Where's my report? Is it getting on?

KHIRIN. Yes; there's only five pages left.

SHIPUCHIN. Excellent. Then it will be ready by three?

KHIRIN. If nothing occurs to disturb me, I'll get it done. Nothing of any importance is now left.

SHIPUCHIN. Splendid. Splendid, as my name's Shipuchin! The general meeting will be at four. If you please, my dear fellow. Give me the first half, I'll peruse it. . . . Quick. . . . [*Takes the report.*] I base enormous hopes on this report. It's my *profession de foi,* or, better still, my firework. My firework, as my name's Shipuchin! [*Sits and reads the report to himself.*] I'm hellishly tired. . . . My gout kept on giving me trouble last night, all the morning I was running about, and then these excitements, ovations, agitations, . . . I'm tired!

KHIRIN. Two . . . nought . . . nought . . three . . nine . . . two

. . . nought. I can't see straight after all these figures. . . . Three. . one . . . six . . . four . . . one . . . five. . . . [*Uses the counting-frame.*]

SHIPUCHIN. Another unpleasantness. . . . This morning your wife came to see me and complained about you once again. Said that last night you threatened her and her sister with a knife. Kusma Nicolaievitch, what do you mean by that? Oh, oh!

KHIRIN. [*Rudely.*] As it's an anniversary, Andrey Andreyevitch, I'll ask for a special favour. Please, even if it's only out of respect for my toil, don't interfere in my family life. Please!

SHIPUCHIN. [*Sighs.*] Yours is an impossible character, Kusma Nicolaievitch! You're an excellent and respected man, but you behave to woman like some scoundrel. Yes, really I don't understand why you hate them so?

KHIRIN. I wish I could understand why you love them so! [*Pause.*]

SHIPUCHIN. The employees have just presented me with an album; and the Directors, as I've heard, are going to give me an address and a silver loving-cup. . . . [*Playing with his monocle.*] Very nice, as my name's Shipuchin! It isn't excessive. A certain pomp is essential to the reputation of the Bank, devil take it! You know everything of course. . . . I composed the address myself, and I bought the cup myself, too. . . . Well, then there was 45 roubles for the cover of the address, but you can't do without that. They'd never have thought of it for themselves. [*Looks round.*] Look at the furniture! Just look at it! They say I'm stingy, that all I want is that the locks on the doors should be polished, that the employees should wear fash-

ionable ties, and that a fat hall-porter should stand by the door. No, no, sire. Polished locks and a fat hall-porter mean a good deal. I can behave as I like at home, eat and sleep like a pig, get drunk. . . .

KHIRIN. Please don't make hints.

SHIPUCHIN. Nobody's making hints! What an impossible character yours is. . . . As I was saying, at home I can live like a tradesman, a *parvenu*, and be up to any games I like, but here everything must be *en grand*. This is a Bank! Here every detail must *imponiren*, so to speak, and have a majestic appearance. [*He picks up a paper from the floor and throws it into the fireplace.*] My service to the Bank has been just this—I've raised its reputation. A thing of immense importance is tone! Immense, as my name's Shipuchin! [*Looks over KHIRIN.*] My dear man, a deputation of shareholders may come here any moment, and there you are in felt boots, wearing a scarf . . . in some absurdly coloured jacket. . . . You might have put on a frock-coat, or at any rate a dark jacket. . . .

KHIRIN. My health matters more to me than your shareholders. I've an inflammation all over me.

SHIPUCHIN. [*Excitedly.*] But you will admit that it's untidy! You spoil the *ensemble!*

KHIRIN. If the deputation comes I can go and hide myself. It won't matter if . . . seven . . . one . . . seven . . . two . . . one . . . five . . . nought. I don't like untidiness myself. . . . Seven . . . two . . . nine . . . [*Uses the counting-frame.*] I can't stand untidiness. It would have been wiser of you not to have invited ladies to today's anniversary dinner. . . .

SHIPUCHIN. Oh, that's nothing.

KHIRIN. I know that you're going to have the hall filled with them to-night to make a good show, but you look out, or they'll spoil everything. They cause all sorts of mischief and disorder.

SHIPUCHIN. On the contrary, feminine society elevates!

KHIRIN. Yes. . . . Your wife seems intelligent, but on the Monday of last week she let something off that upset me for two days. In front of a lot of people she suddenly asks: "Is it true that at our Bank my husband bought up a lot of shares of the Driazhsky-Priazhsky Bank, which have been falling on exchange? My husband is so annoyed about it!" This in front of people. Why do you tell them everything, I don't understand. Do you want them to get you into serious trouble?

SHIPUCHIN. Well, that's enough, enough! All that's too dull for an anniversary. Which reminds me, by the way. [Looks at the time.] My wife ought to be here soon. I really ought to have gone to the station, to meet the poor little thing, but there's no time. . . . and I'm tired. I must say I'm not glad of her! That is to say, I am glad, but I'd be gladder if she only stayed another couple of days with her mother. She'll want me to spend the whole evening with her to-night, whereas we have arranged a little excursion for ourselves. . . . [Shivers.] Oh, my nerves have already started dancing me about. They are so strained that I think the very smallest trifle would be enough to make me break into tears! No, I must be strong, as my name's Shipuchin!

Enter TATIANA ALEXEYEVNA SHIP-UCHIN in a waterproof, with a little travelling sachel slung across her shoulder.

SHIPUCHIN. Ah! In the nick of time!

TATIANA ALEXEYEVNA. Darling!

[Runs to her husband: a prolonged kiss.]

SHIPUCHIN. We were only speaking of you just now! [Looks at his watch.]

TATIANA ALEXEYEVNA. [Panting.] Were you very dull without me? Are you well? I haven't been home yet, I came here straight from the station. I've a lot, a lot to tell you. . . . I couldn't wait. . . . I shan't take off my clothes, I'll only stay a minute. [To KHIRIN.] Good morning, Kusma Nicolaievitch! [To her husband.] Is everything all right at home?

SHIPUCHIN. Yes, quite. And, you know, you've got to look plumper and better this week. . . . Well, what sort of a time did you have?

TATIANA ALEXEYEVNA. Splendid. Mamma and Katya send their regards. Vassili Andreitch sends you a kiss. [Kisses him.] Aunt sends you a jar of jam, and is annoyed because you don't write. Zina sends you a kiss. [Kisses.] Oh, if you knew what's happened. If you only knew! I'm even frightened to tell you! Oh, if you only knew! But I see by your eyes that you're sorry I came!

SHIPUCHIN. On the contrary. . . . Darling. . . [Kisses her.]

KHIRIN coughs angrily.

TATIANA ALEXEYEVNA. Oh, poor Katya, poor Katya! I'm so sorry for her, so sorry for her.

SHIPUCHIN. This is the Bank's anniversary to-day, darling, we may get a deputation of the shareholders at any moment, and you're not dressed.

TATIANA ALEXEYEVNA. Oh, yes, the

anniversary! I congratulate you, gentlemen. I wish you. . . . So it means that to-day's the day of the meeting, the dinner. . . . That's good. And do you remember that beautiful address which you spent such a long time composing for the shareholders? Will it be read to-day?

KHIRIN *coughs angrily.*

SHIPUCHIN. [*Confused.*] My dear, we don't talk about these things. You'd really better go home.

TATIANA ALEXEYEVNA. In a minute, in a minute. I'll tell you everything in one minute and go. I'll tell you from the very beginning. Well. . . . When you were seeing me off, you remember I was sitting next to that stout lady, and I began to read. I don't like to talk in the train. I read for three stations and didn't say a word to anyone. . . . Well, then the evening set in, and I felt so mournful, you know, with such sad thoughts! A young man was sitting opposite me—not a bad-looking fellow, a brunette. . . . Well, we fell into conversation. . . . A sailor came along then, then some student or other. . . . [*Laughs.*] I told them that I wasn't married . . . and they did look after me! We chatted till midnight, the brunette kept on telling the most awfully funny stories, and the sailor kept on singing. My chest began to ache from laughing. And when the sailor— oh, those sailors!—when he got to know my name was TATIANA, you know what he sang? [*Sings in a bass voice.*] "Onegin don't let me conceal it, I love Tatiana madly!" [*Roars with laughter.*]

KHIRIN *coughs angrily.*

SHIPUCHIN. Tania, dear, you're disturbing Kusma Nicolaievitch. Go home, dear. . . . Later on. . . .

TATIANA ALEXEYEVNA. No, no, let him hear if he wants to, it's awfully interesting. I'll end in a minute. Serezha came to meet me at the station. Some young man or other turns up, an inspector of taxes, I think . . . quite handsome, especially his eyes. . . . Serezha introduced me, and the three of us rode off together. . . . It was lovely weather. . . .

Voices behind the stage: "You can't, you can't! What do you want? *Enter* MERCHUTKINA, *waving her arms about.*

MERCHUTKINA. What are you dragging at me for? What else! I want him himself! [*To* SHIPUCHIN.] I have the honour, your excellency . . . I am the wife of a civil servant, Nastasya Fyodorovna Merchutkina.

SHIPUCHIN. What do you want?

MERCHUTKINA. Well, you see, your excellency, my husband has been ill for five months, and while he was at home, getting better, he was suddenly dismissed for no reason, your excellency, and when I went to get his salary, they, you see, deducted 24 roubles 36 copecks from it. What for? I ask. They said, "Well, he drew it from the employees' account, and the others had to make it up." How can that be? How could he draw anything without my permission? No, your excellency! I'm a poor woman . . . my lodgers are all I have to live on. . . . I'm weak and defenceless. . . . Everybody does me some harm, and nobody has a kind word for me.

SHIPUCHIN. Excuse me. [*Takes a petition from her hand and reads it standing.*

TATIANA ALEXEYEVNA. [*To* KHIRIN.] Yes, but first we. . . . Last week I suddenly received a letter from my mother.

She writes that a certain Grendilevsky has proposed to my sister Katya. A nice, modest, young man, with no means of his own, and no assured position. And, unfortunately, just think of it, Katya is absolutely gone on him. What's to be done? Mamma writes telling me to come at once and influence Katya. . . .

KHIRIN. [*Angrily.*] Excuse me, you've made me lose my place! You go talking about your mamma and Katya, and I understand nothing, and I've lost my place.

TATIANA ALEXEYEVNA. What does that matter? You listen when a lady is talking to you! Why are you so angry to-day? Are you in love? [*Laughs.*]

SHIPUCHIN. [*To* MERCHUTKINA.] Excuse me, but what is this? I can't make head or tail of it. . . .

TATIANA ALEXEYEVNA. Are you in love? Aha! You're blushing!

SHIPUCHIN. [*To his wife.*] Tanya, dear, do go out into the public office for a moment. I shan't be long.

TATIANA ALEXEYEVNA. All right.
[*Goes out.*]

SHIPUCHIN. I don't understand anything of this. You've obviously come to the wrong place, madam. Your petition doesn't concern us at all. You should go to the department in which your husband was employed.

MERCHUTKINA. I've been there a good many times these five months, and they wouldn't even look at my petition. I'd given up all hopes, but, thanks to my son-in-law, `Boris Matveyitch, I thought of coming to you. "You go, mother," he says, "and apply to Mr. Shipuchin, he's an influential man and can do anything," Help me, your excellency!

SHIPUCHIN. We can't do anything for

you, Mrs. Merchutkina. You must understand that your husband, so far as I can gather, was in the employ of the Army Medical Department, while this is a private, commercial concern, a bank. Don't you understand that.

MERCHUTKINA. Your excellency, I can produce a doctor's certificate of my husband's illness. Here it is, just look at it. . . .

SHIPUCHIN. [*Irritated.*] That's all right; I quite believe you, but it's not our business. [*Behind the scene,* TATIANA ALEXEYEVNA'S *laughter is heard, then a man's.* SHIPUCHIN *glances at the door.*] She's disturbing the employees. [*To* MERCHUTKINA.] It's strange and it's even silly. Surely your husband knows where you ought to apply?

MERCHUTKINA. Your excellency, I don't let him know anything. He just cried out: "It isn't your business! Get out of this!" And . . .

SHIPUCHIN. Madam, I repeat, your husband was in the employ of the Army Medical Department, and this is a bank, a private, commercial concern. . . .

MERCHUTKINA. Yes, yes, yes. . . . I understand, my dear. In that case, your excellency, just order them to pay me 15 roubles! I don't mind taking that to be going on with.

SHIPUCHIN. [*Sighs.*] Ouf!

KHIRIN. Andrey Andreyevitch, I'll never finish the report at this rate!

SHIPUCHIN. One moment. [*To* MERCHUTKINA.] I can't get any sense out of you. But do you understand that your taking this business here is as absurd as if you took a divorce petition to a chemist's or into a gold assay office. [*Knock at the door. The voice of* TATIANA ALEXEYEVNA *is heard,* "Can

I come in, Andrey?" SHIPUCHIN *shouts.*] Just wait one minute, dear! [*To* MERCHUTKINA.] What has it got to do with us if you haven't been paid? As it happens, madam, this is an anniversary to-day, we're busy . . . and somebody may be coming here at any moment. . . . Excuse me. . . .

MERCHUTKINA. Your excellency, have pity on me, an orphan! I'm a weak, defenceless woman. . . . I'm tired to death. . . . I'm having trouble with my lodgers, and on account of my husband, and I've got the house to look after, and my son-in-law is out of work. . . .

SHIPUCHIN. Mrs. Merchutkina, I . . . No, excuse me, I can't talk to you! My head's even in a whirl. . . . You are disturbing us and making us waste our time. . . . [*Sighs, aside.*] What a business, as my name's Shipuchin! [*To* KHIRIN.] Kusma Nicolaievitch, will you please explain to Mrs. Merchutkina. . . . [*Waves his hand and goes out into public department.*]

KHIRIN. [*Approaching* MERCHUTKINA, *angrily.*] What do you want?

MERCHUTKINA. I'm a weak, defenceless woman. . . . I may look all right, but if you were to take me to pieces you wouldn't find a single healthy bit in me! I can hardly stand on my legs, and I've lost my appetite. I drank my coffee to-day and got no pleasure out of it.

KHIRIN. I ask you, what do you want?

MERCHUTKINA. Tell them, my dear, to give me 15 roubles, and a month later will do for the rest.

KHIRIN. But haven't you been told perfectly plainly that this is a bank!

MERCHUTKINA. Yes, yes. . . . And

if you like I can show you the doctor's certificate.

KHIRIN. Have you got a head on your shoulders, or what?

MERCHUTKINA. My dear, I'm asking for what's mine by law. I don't want what isn't mine.

KHIRIN. I ask you, madam, have you got a head on your shoulders, or what? Well, devil take me, I haven't any time to talk to you! I'm busy. . . . [*Points to the door.*] That way, please!

MERCHUTKINA. [*Surprised.*] And where's the money?

KHIRIN. You haven't a head, but this. . . . [*Taps the table and then points to his forehead.*]

MERCHUTKINA. [*Offended.*] What? Well, never mind, never mind. . . . You can do that to your own wife, but I'm the wife of a civil servant. . . . You can't do that to me!

KHIRIN. [*Losing his temper.*] Get out of this!

MERCHUTKINA. No, no, no . . . none of that!

KHIRIN. If you don't get out this second, I'll call for the hall-porter! Get out! [*Stamping.*]

MERCHUTKINA. Never mind, never mind! I'm not afraid! I've seen the like of you before! Miser!

KHIRIN. I don't think I've ever seen a more awful woman in my life. . . . Ouf! It's given me a headache. . . . [*Breathing heavily.*] I tell you once more . . . do you hear me? If you don't get out of this, you old devil, I'll grind you into powder! I've got such a character that I'm perfectly capable of laming you for life! I can commit a crime!

MERCHUTKINA. I've heard barking

dogs before. I'm not afraid. I've seen the like of you before.

KHIRIN. [*In despair.*] I can't stand it! I'm ill! I can't! [*Sits down at his desk.*] They've let the Bank get filled with women, and I can't finish my report! I can't.

MERCHUTKINA. I don't want anybody else's money, but my own, according to law. You ought to be ashamed of yourself! Sitting in a government office in felt boots. . . .

Enter SHIPUCHIN *and* TATIANA ALEXEYEVNA.

TATIANA ALEXEYEVNA. [*Following her husband.*] We spent the evening at the Berezhnitskys. Katya was wearing a sky-blue frock of foulard silk, cut low at the neck. . . . She looks very well with her hair done over her head, and I did her hair myself. . . . She was perfectly fascinating. . . .

SHIPUCHIN. [*Who has had enough of it already.*] Yes, yes . . . fascinating . . . They may be here any moment. . . .

MERCHUTKINA. Your excellency!

SHIPUCHIN. [*Dully.*] What else? What do you want?

MERCHUTKINA. Y o u r excellency! [*Points to* KHIRIN.] This man . . . this man tapped the table with his finger, and then his head. . . . You told him to look after my affair, but he insults me and says all sorts of things. I'm a weak, defensely woman. . . .

SHIPUCHIN. All right, madam, I'll see to it . . . and take the necessary steps. . . . Go away now . . . later on! [*Aside*] My gout's coming on!

KHIRIN. [*In a low tone to* SHIP-UCHIN.] Andrey Andreyevitch, send for the hall-porter and have her turned out neck and crop! What else can we do?

SHIPUCHIN. [*Frightened.*] No, no! She'll kick up a row and we aren't the only people in the building.

MERCHUTKINA. Your excellency.

KHIRIN. [*In a tearful voice.*] But I've got to finish my report! I won't have time! I won't!

MERCHUTKINA. Your excellency, when shall I have the money? I want it now.

SHIPUCHIN. [*Aside, in dismay.*] A re-mark-ab-ly beastly woman! [*Politely.*] Madam, I've already told you, this is a bank, a private, commercial concern.

MERCHUTKINA. Be a father to me, your excellency. . . . If the doctor's certificate isn't enough, I can get you another from the police. Tell them to give me the money!

SHIPUCHIN. [*Panting.*] Ouf!

TATIANA ALEXEYEVNA. [*To* MER-CHUTKINA.] Mother, haven't you already been told that you're disturbing them? What right have you?

MERCHUTKINA. Mother, beautiful one, nobody will help me. All I do is to eat and drink, and just now I didn't enjoy my coffee at all.

SHIPUCHIN. [*Exhausted.*] How much do you want?

MERCHUTKINA. 24 roubles 36 copecks.

SHIPUCHIN. All right! [*Takes a 25-rouble note out of his pocket-book and gives it to her.*] Here are 25 roubles. Take it and . . . go!

KHIRIN *coughs angrily.*

MERCHUTKINA. I thank you very humbly, your evcellency. [*Hides the money.*]

TATIANA ALEXEYEVNA. [*Sits by her husband.*] It's time I went home. . . . [*Looks at watch.*] But I haven't done yet. . . . I'll finish in one minute and go away. . . . What a time we had! Yes, what a time! We went to spend the evening at the Berezhitskys. . . . It was all right, quite fun, but nothing in particular. . . . Katya's devoted Grendilevsky was there, of course. . . . Well, I talked to Katya, cried, and induced her to talk to Grendilevsky and refuse him. Well. I thought, everything's settled the best possible way; I've quieted mamma down, saved Katya, and can be quiet myself. . . . What do you think? Katya and I were going along the avenue, just before supper, and suddenly . . . [*Excitedly.*] And suddenly we heard a shot. . . . No, I can't talk about it calmly! [*Waves her handkerchief.*] No I can't!

SHIPUCHIN. [*Sighs.*] Ouf!

TATIANA ALEXEYEVNA. [*Weeps.*] We ran to the summer-house, and there ,. . . there poor Grendilevsky was lying . . . with a pistol in his hand. . . .

SHIPUCHIN. No, I can't stand this! I can't stand it! [*To* MERCHUTKINA.] What else do you want?

MERCHUTKINA. Your excellency, can't my husband go back to his job?

TATIANA ALEXEYEVNA. [Weeping.] He'd shot himself right in the heart . . . here. . . . And the poor man had fallen down senseless. . . . And he was awfully frightened, as he lay there . . . and asked for a doctor. A doctor came soon . . . and saved the unhappy man . .

MERCHUTKINA. Your excellency, can't my husband go back to his job?

SHIPUCHIN. No, I can't stand this! [*Weeps.*] I can't stand it! [*Stretches out both hands in despair to* KHIRIN.] Drive her away! Drive her away, I implore you!

KHIRIN. [*Goes up to* TATIANA ALEXEYEVNA.] Get out of this!

SHIPUCHIN. Not her, but this one . . . this awful woman. . . . [*Points.*] That one!

KHIRIN. [*Not understanding, to* TATIANA ALEXEYEVNA.] Get out of this! [*Stamps.*] Get out!

TATIANA ALEXEYEVNA. What? What are you doing? Have you taken leave of your senses?

SHIPUCHIN. It's awful? I'm a miserable man! Drive her out! Out with her!

KHIRIN. [*To* TATIANA ALEXEYEVNA.] Out of it! I'll cripple you! I'll knock you out of shape! I'll break the law!

TATIANA ALEXEYEVNA. [*Running from him; he chases her.*] How dare you! You impudent fellow! [*Shouts.*] Andrey! Help! Andrey! [*Screams.*] .

SHIPUCHIN [*chasing them*]. Stop! I implore you! Not such a noise? Have pity on me!

KHIRIN [*chasing* MERCHUTKINA]. Out of this! Catch her! Hit her! Cut her into pieces!

SHIPUCHIN [*shouts*]. Stop! I ask you! I implore you!

MERCHUTKINA. Little fathers . . . little fathers! . . . [*Screams.*] Little fathers!

TATIANA ALEXEYEVNA [*shouts*]. Help! Help! . . . Oh, oh . . . I'm sick, I'm sick!

Jumps on to a chair, then falls on to the sofa and groans as if in a faint.

KHIRIN [*chasing* MERCHUTKINA]. Hit her! Beat her! Cut her to pieces!

MERCHUTKINA. Oh, oh . . . little fathers, it's all dark before me! Ah! [*Falls senseless into* SHIPUCHIN'S *arms. There is a knock at the door; a* VOICE *announces* THE DUPUTATION.] The deputation . . . reputation . . . occupation . . .

KHIRIN [*stamps*]. Get out of it, devil take me! [*Turns up his sleeves.*] Give her to me: I may break the law.

A deputation of five men enters; they all wear frockcoats. One carries the velvet-colored address, another, the loving-cup. Employees look in at the door, from the public department. TATIANA ALEXEYEVNA on the sofa, and MERCHUTKINA in SHIPUCHIN'S arms are both groaning.

ONE OF THE DEPUTATION [*reads aloud*]. "Deeply-respected and dear Andrey Andreyevitch! Throwing a retrospective glance at the past history of our financial administration, and reviewing in our minds its gradual development, we receive an extremely satisfactory impression. It is true that in the first period of its existence, the inconsiderable amount of its capital, and the absence of serious operations of any description, and also the indefinite aims of this bank, made us attach an extreme importance to the question raised by Hamlet, 'To be or not to be,' and at one time there were even voices to be heard demanding our liquidation. But at that moment you become the head of our concern. Your knowledge, energies, and your native tact were the causes of extraordinary success and widespread extension. The reputation of the bank . . . [*coughs*] reputation of the bank . . .

MERCHUTKINA [*groans*]. Oh! Oh!

TATIANA ALEXEYEVNA [*g r o a n s*]. Water! Water!

THE MEMBER OF THE DEPUTATION [*continues*]. The reputation [*coughs*] . . . the reputation of the bank has been raised by you to such a height that we are now the rivals of the best foreign concerns.

SHIPUCHIN. Deputation . . . reputation . . . occupation. . . . Two friends that had a walk at night, held converse by the pale moonlight. . . . Oh tell me not, that youth is vain, that jealousy has turned my brain.

THE MEMBER OF THE DEPUTATION [*continues in confusion*]. Then, throwing an objective glance at the present condition of things, we, deeply respected and dear Andrey Andreyevitch . . . [*Lowering his voice.*] In that case, we'll do it later on. . . . Yes, later on. . . ."

[DEPUTATION *goes out in confusion.*]

CURTAIN

The Proposal

DRAMATIS PERSONAE

STEPAN STEPANOVITCH CHUBUKOV, *a landowner.*

NATALYA STEPANOVNA, *his daughter, 25 years old.*

IVAN VASSILEVITCH LOMOV, *a neighbour of* CHUBUKOV, *a large and hearty. but very suspicious landowner.*

The scene is laid at CHUBUKOV'S *country-house.*

ACT I

A drawing-room in CHUBUKOV'S *house.*

[LOMOV *enters, wearing a dress-jacket*

and white gloves. CHUBUKOV *rises to meet him.*]

CHUBUKOV. My dear fellow, Ivan Vassilevitch! I am delighted! [*Squeezes his hand.*] A surprise, my darling. . . . How are you?

LOMOV. Thank you. And how are you?

CHUBUKOV. We just get along somehow, my angel, thanks to your prayers, and so forth. Sit down, please do. . . . Why do you forget your neighbours, my darling? My dear fellow, why are you so formal in your evening dress, gloves, and so forth? Are you going anywhere?

LOMOV. No, I've come only to see you, honoured Stepan Stepanovitch.

CHUBUKOV. Then why are you in evening dress, my good fellow? As if you're paying a New Year's Eve visit!

LOMOV. Well, you see, it's like this. [*Takes his arm.*] I've come to you, honoured Stepan Stepanovitch, to trouble you with a request. Often have I already had the privilege of applying to you for help, and you have always, so to speak . . . I ask your pardon, I am becoming excited. I shall drink some water, honoured Stepan Stepanovitch. [*Drinks.*]

CHUBUKOV [*aside*]. He's come to borrow money! Never! [*Aloud.*] What is it, dear boy?

LOMOV. You see, Honour Stepanitch . . . I beg pardon, Stepan Honouritch . . . I mean, I'm awfully excited, as you will notice. . . . In short, you alone can help me, though I don't deserve it, of course . . .

CHUBUKOV. Don't beat around the bush, darling! Spit it out! Well?

LOMOV. One moment . . . this very minute. The fact is, I've come to ask the hand of your daughter, Natalya Stepanovna, in marriage.

CHUBUKOV [*joyfully*]. By Jove! Ivan Vassilevitch! Say it again—I didn't hear it all!

LOMOV. I have the honour to ask . . .

CHUBUKOV [*interrupting*]. My dear boy . . . I'm so glad. . . . Yes, indeed. [*Embraces and kisses* LOMOV.] I've been hoping for it for a long time. It's been my long desire. [*Sheds a tear.*] And I've always loved you, my angel, as if you were my own son. May God give you both His help and His love, and I did so much hope . . . What am I behaving in this idiotic way for? I'm giddy with joy, absolutely. Oh, with all my soul . . . I'll go and call Natasha.

LOMOV [*greatly moved*]. Honoured Stepan Stepanovitch, do you think she will consent?

CHUBUKOV. Why, of course, my darling . . . as if she won't consent! She's in love; she's like a lovesick cat. Be right back! [*Exit.*]

LOMOV. It's cold . . . I'm trembling all over, just as if I'd got an examination before me. The great thing is, to decide. If I give myself time to think, to hesitate, to talk, to look for an ideal, or for real love, then I'll never get married. . . . Brr! . . . It's cold! Natalya Stepanovna is an excellent housekeeper, not bad-looking, well-educated. . . . What more do I want? But I'm getting a noise in my ears from excitement. [*Drinks.*] And it's impossible for me not to marry . . . In the first place, I'm already 35—a critical age, so to speak. In the second place, I ought to lead a quiet and regular life. . . . I suffer from palpitations, I'm excitable and always getting awfully upset. . . . At this very moment my lips are trembling, and there's a twitch in my right eyebrow. . . . But the very worst of all is the way I sleep. I no sooner get into bed and begin to go off when suddenly something in my left side—gives a pull, and I can feel it in my shoulder and head. . . . I jump up like a lunatic, walk about a bit, and lie down again, but as soon as I begin to get off to sleep there's another pull! And this may happen twenty times. . . .

NATALYA STEPANOVNA *comes in.*

NATALYA STEPANOVNA. Well, there! It's you, and papa said, 'Go; there's a merchant come for his goods.' How do you do, Ivan Vassilevitch!

LOMOV. How do you do, honoured Natalya Stepanovna?

NATALYA STEPANOVNA. You must excuse my apron and *néglige* . . . we're shelling peas for drying. Why haven't you been here for such a long time? Sit down. . . . [*They seat themselves.*] Won't you have some lunch?

LOMOV. No, thank you, I've had some already.

NATALYA STEPANOVNA. Then smoke. . . . Here are the matches. . . . The weather is splendid now, but yesterday it was so wet that the workmen didn't do anything all day. How much hay have you stacked? Just think, I felt greedy and had a whole field cut, and now I'm not at all pleased about it because I'm afraid my hay may rot. I ought to have waited a bit. But what's this? Why, you're in evening dress! Well, I never! Are you going to a ball, or what?—though I must say you look better. . . . Tell me, why are you got up like that?

LOMOV [*excited*]. You see, honoured Natalya Stepanovna . . . the fact is, I've made up my mind to ask you to hear me out. . . . Of course you'll be surprised and perhaps even angry, but a . . . [*Aside.*] It's awfully cold!

NATALYA STEPANOVNA. What's the matter? [*Pause.*] Well?

LOMOV. I shall try to be brief. You must know, honoured Natalya Stepanovna, that I have long, since my childhood, in fact, had the privilege of knowing your family. My late aunt and her husband, from whom, as you know, I inherited my land, always had the greatest respect for your father and your late mother. The Lomovs and the Chubukovs have always had the most friendy, and I might almost say the most affectionate, regard for each other. And, as you know, my land is a near neighbour of yours. You will remember that my Oxen Meadows touch your birchwoods.

NATALYA STEPANOVNA. Excuse my interrupting you. You say, 'my Oxen Meadows. . . .' But are they yours?

LOMOV. Yes, mine.

NATALYA STEPANOVNA. What are you talking about? Oxen Meadows are ours, not yours!

LOMOV. No, mine, honoured Natalya Stepanovna.

NATALYA STEPANOVNA. Well, I never knew that before. How do you make that out?

LOMOV. How? I'm speaking of those Oxen Meadows which are wedged in between your birchwoods and the Burnt Marsh.

NATALYA STEPANOVNA. Yes, yes. . . . They're ours.

LOMOV. No, you're mistaken, honoured Natalya Stepanovna, they're mine.

NATALYA STEPANOVNA. Just think, Ivan Vassilevitch! How long have they been yours?

LOMOV. How long? As long as I can remember.

NATAYLA STEPANOVNA. Really, you won't get me to believe that!

LOMOV. But you can see from the documents, honoured Natalya Stepanovna. Oxen Meadows, it's true, were once the subject of dispute, but now everybody knows that they are mine. There's nothing to argue about. You see, my aunt's grandmother gave the free use of these Meadows in perpetuity to the peasants of your father's grandfather, in return for which they were to make bricks for her. The peasants belonging to your father's grandfather had the free use of the Meadows for forty years, and had got into the habit of regarding them as their own, when it happened that . . .

NATALYA STEPANOVNA. No, it isn't at all like that! Both my grandfather and great-grandfather reckoned that their land extended to Burnt Marsh—which means that Oxen Meadows were ours. I don't see what there is to argue about. It's simply silly!

LOMOV. I'll show you the documents, Natalya Stepanovna!

NATALYA STEPANOVNA. No, you're simply joking, or making fun of me. . . . What a surprise! We've had the land for nearly three hundred years, and then we're suddenly told that it isn't ours! Ivan Vassilevitch, I can hardly believe my own ears. . . . These Meadows aren't worth much to me. They only come to five dessiatins, and are worth perhaps 300 roubles, but I can't stand unfairness. Say what you will, but I can't stand unfairness.

LOMOV. Hear me out, I implore you! The peasants of your father's grandfather, as I have already had the honour of explaining to you, used to bake bricks for my aunt's grandmother. Now my aunt's grandmother, wishing to make them a pleasant . . .

NATALYA STEPANOVNA. I can't make head or tail of all this about aunts and grandfathers and grandmothers. The Meadows are ours, and that's all.

LOMOV. Mine.

NATALYA STEPANOVNA. Ours! You can go on proving it for two days on end, you can go and put on fifteen dress-jackets, but I tell you they're ours, ours, ours! I don't want anything of yours and I don't want to give up anything of mine. So there!

LOMOV. Natalya Ivanovna, I don't want the Meadows, but I am acting on principle. If you like, I'll make you a present of them.

NATALYA STEPANOVNA. I can make you a present of them myself, because they're mine! Your behaviour, Ivan Vassilevitch, is strange, to say the least! Up to this we have always thought of you as a good neighbour, a friend: last year we lent you our threshing-machine, although on that account we had to put off our own threshing till November, but you behave to us as if we were gipsies. Giving me my own land, indeed! No, really, that's not at all neighbourly! In my opinion, it's even impudent, if you want to know. . . .

LOMOV. Then you make out that I'm a land-grabber? Madam, never in my life have I grabbed anybody else's land, and I shan't allow anybody to accuse me of having done so. . . . [*Quickly steps to the carafe and drinks more water.*] Oxen Meadows are mine!

NATALYA STEPANOVNA. It's not true, they're ours!

LOMOV. Mine!

NATALYA STEPANOVNA. It's not true! I'll prove it! I'll send my mowers out to the Meadows this very day!

LOMOV. What?

NATALYA STEPANOVNA. My mowers will be there this very day!

LOMOV. I'll give it to them in the neck!

NATALYA STEPANOVNA. You dare!

LOMOV [clutches at his heart]. Oxen Meadows are mine! You understand? Mine!

NATALYA STEPANOVNA. Please don't shout! You can shout yourself hoarse in your own house, but here I must ask you to restrain yourself!

LOMOV. If it wasn't, madam, for this awful, excruciating palpitation, if my whole inside wasn't upset, I'd talk to you in a different way! [Yells.] Oxen Meadows are mine!

NATALYA STEPANOVNA. Ours!

LOMOV. Mine!

NATALYA STEPANOVNA. Ours!

LOMOV. Mine!

[Enter CHUBUKOV.]

CHUBUKOV. What's the matter? What are you shouting at?

NATALYA STEPANOVNA. Papa, please tell to this gentleman who owns Oxen Meadows, we or he?

CHUBUKOV [to LOMOV]. Darling, the Meadows are ours!

LOMOV. But, please, Stepan Stepanitch, how can they be yours? Do be a reasonable man! My aunt's grandmother gave the Meadows for the temporary and free use of your grandfather's peasants. The peasants used the land for forty years and got as accustomed to it as if it was their own, when it happened that . . .

CHUBUKOV. Excuse me, my precious. . . . You forget just this, that the peasants didn't pay your grandmother and all that, because the Meadows were in dispute, and so on. And now everybody knows that they're ours. It means that you haven't seen the plan.

LOMOV. I'll prove to you that they're mine!

CHUBUKOV. You won't prove it, my darling.

LOMOV. I shall!

CHUBUKOV. Dear one, why yell like that? You won't prove anything just by yelling. I don't want anything of yours, and don't intend to give up what I have. Why should I? And you know, my beloved, that if you propose to go on arguing about it, I'd much sooner give up the Meadows to the peasants than to you. There!

LOMOV. I don't understand! How have you the right to give away somebody else's property!

CHUBUKOV. You may take it that I know whether I have the right or not. Because, young man, I'm not used to being spoken to in that tone of voice, and so on: I, young man, am twice your age, and ask you to speak to me without agitating yourself, and all that.

LOMOV. No, you just think I'm a fool and want to have me on! You call my land yours, and then you want me to talk to you calmly and politely! Good neighbours don't behave like that, Stepan Stepanitch! You're not a neighbour, you're a grabber!

CHUBUKOV. What's that? What did you say?

NATALYA STEPANOVNA. Papa, send the mowers out to the Meadows at once!

CHUBUKOV. What did you say, sir?

NATALYA STEPANOVNA. Oxen Meadows are ours, and I shan't give them up, shan't give them up, shan't give them up!

LOMOV. We'll see! I'll have the matter taken to court, and then I'll show you!

CHUBUKOV. To court? You can take it to court, and all that! You can! I know you; you're just on the look-out for a chance to go to court, and all that . . . . You pettifogger! All your people were like that! All of them!

LOMOV. Never mind about my people! The Lomovs have all been honourable people, and not one has ever been tried for embezzlement, like your grandfather!

CHUBUKOV. You Lomovs have had lunacy in your family, all of you!

NATALYA STEPANOVNA. All, all, all!

CHUBUKOV. Your grandfather was a drunkard, and your younger aunt, Nastasya Mihailovna, ran away with an architect, and so on. . . .

LOMOV. And your mother was humpbacked. [Clutches at his heart.] Something pulling in my side. . . . My head. . . . Help! Water!

CHUBUKOV. Your father was a guzzling gambler!

NATALYA STEPANOVNA. And there haven't been many backbiters to equal your aunt!

LOMOV. My left foot has gone to sleep. . . . You're an intriguer. . . . Oh, my heart! . . . And it's an open secret that before the last elections you bri . . . I can see stars. . . . Where's my hat?

NATALYA STEPANOVNA. It's low! It's dishonest! It's mean!

CHUBUKOV. And you're just a malicious, double-faced intriguer! Yes!

LOMOV. Here's my hat. . . . My heart! . . . Which way? Where's the door? Oh! . . . I think I'm dying. . . . My foot's quite numb. . . . [Goes to the door.]

CHUBUKOV [following him]. And don't set foot in my house again!

NATALYA STEPANOVNA. Take it to court! We'll see!

LOMOV staggers out.

CHUBUKOV. Devil take him! [Walks about in excitement.]

NATALYA STEPANOVNA. What a rascal! What trust can one have in one's neighbours after that!

CHUBUKOV. The villain! The scarecrow!

NATALYA STEPANOVA. The monster! First he takes our land and then he has the impudence to abuse us.

CHUBUKOV. And that blind hen, yes, that turnip-ghost has the confounded cheek to make a proposal, and so on! What? A proposal!

NATALYA STEPANOVNA. What proposal?

CHUBUKOV. Why, he came here so as to propose to you.

NATALYA STEPANOVNA. To propose? To me? Why didn't you tell me so before?

CHUBUKOV. So he dresses up in evening clothes. The stuffed sausage! The wizen-faced frump!

NATALYA STEPANOVNA. To propose to me? Ah! [Falls into an easy-chair and wails.] Bring him back! Back! Ah! Bring him here.

CHUBUKOV. Bring whom here?

NATALYA STEPANOVNA. Quick, quick! I'm ill! Fetch him! [Hysterics.]

CHUBUKOV. What's that? What's

the matter with you? [*Clutches at his head.*] Oh, unhappy man that I am! I'll shoot myself! I'll hang myself! We've done for her!

NATALYA STEPANOVNA. I'm dying! Fetch him!

CHUBUKOV. Tfoo! At once. Don't yell!

Runs out. A pause. NATALYA STEPANOVNA *wails.*

NATALYA STEPANOVNA. What have they done to me! Fetch him back! Fetch him! [*A pause.*]

CHUBUKOV *runs in.*

CHUBUKOV. He's coming, and so on, devil take him! Ouf! Talk to him yourself; I don't want to. . . .

NATALYA STEPANOVNA [*wails*]. Fetch him!

CHUBUKOV [*yells*]. He's coming, I tell you. Oh, what a burden, Lord, to be the father of a grown-up daughter! I'll cut my throat! I will, indeed! We cursed him, abused him, drove him out, and it's all you . . . you!

NATALYA STEPANOVNA. No, it was you!

CHUBUKOV. I tell you it's not my fault. [LOMOV *appears at the door.*] Now you talk to him yourself. [*Exit.*]

LOMOV *enters, exhausted.*

LOMOV. My heart's palpitating awfully. . . . My foot's gone to sleep. . . . There's something keeps pulling in my side. . . .

NATALYA STEPANOVNA. Forgive us, Ivan Vassilevitch, we were all a little heated. . . . I remember now: Oxen Meadows really are yours.

LOMOV. My heart's beating awfully. . . . My Meadows. . . . My eyebrows are both twitching. . . .

NATALYA STEPANOVNA. The Meadows are yours, yes, yours. . . . Do sit down. . . . [*They sit.*] We were wrong. . . .

LOMOV. I did it on principle. . . . My land is worth little to me, but the principle . . .

NATALYA STEPANOVNA. Yes, the principle, just so. . . . Now let's talk of something else.

LOMOV. The more so as I have evidence. My aunt's grandmother gave the land to your father's grandfather's peasants . . .

NATALYA STEPANOVNA. Yes, yes, let that pass. . . . [*Aside.*] I wish I knew how to get him started. . . . [*Aloud.*] Are you going to start shooting soon?

LOMOV. I'm thinking of having a go at the blackcock, honoured Natalya Stepanovna, after the harvest. Oh, have you heard? Just think, what a misfortune I've had! My dog Guess, whom you know, has gone lame.

NATALYA STEPANOVNA. What a pity! Why?

LOMOV. I don't know. . . . Must have got twisted, or bitten by some other dog. . . . [*Sighs.*] My very best dog, to say nothing of the expense. I gave Mironov 125 roubles for him.

NATALYA STEPANOVNA. It was too much, Ivan Vassilevitch.

LOMOV. I think it was very cheap. He's a first-rate dog.

NATALYA STEPANOVNA. Papa gave 85 roubles for his Squeezer, and Squeezer is heaps better than Guess!

LOMOV. Squeezer better than Guess? What an idea! [*Laughs.*] Squeezer better than Guess!

NATALYA STEPANOVNA. Of course he's better! Of course, Squeezer is young, he may develop a bit, but on points, and pedigree he's better than anything that even Volchantesky has got.

LOMOV. Excuse me, Natalya Stepanovna, but you forget that he is overshot, and an overshot always means the dog is a bad hunter!

NATALYA STEPANOVNA. Overshot, is he? The first time I hear it!

LOMOV. I assure you that his lower jaw is shorter than the upper.

NATALYA STEPANOVNA. Have you measured?

LOMOV. Yes. He's all right at following, of course, but if you want him to get hold of anything . . .

NATALYA IVANOVNA. In the first place, our Squeezer is a thoroughbred animal, the son of Harness and Chisels, while there's no getting at the pedigree of your dog at all. . . . He's old and as ugly as a worn-out cab-horse.

LOMOV. He is old, but I wouldn't take five Squeezers for him. . . . Why, how can you? . . . Guess is a dog; as for Squeezer, well, it's too funny to argue. . . . Anybody you like has a dog as good as Squeezer . . . you may find them under every bush almost. Twenty-five roubles would be a handsome price to pay for him.

NATALYA STEPANOVNA. There's some demon of contradiction in you to-day, Ivan Vassilevitch. First you pretend that the Meadows are yours; now, that Guess is better than Squeezer. I don't like people who don't say what they mean, because you know perfectly well that Squeezer is a hundred times better than your silly Guess. Why do you want to say it isn't?

LOMOV. I see, Natalya Stepanovna, that you consider me either blind or a fool. You must realize that Squeezer is overshot!

NATALYA STEPANOVNA. It's not true.

LOMOV. He is!

NATALYA STEPANOVNA. It's not true!

LOMOV. Why shout, madam?

NATALYA STEPANOVNA. Why talk rot? It's awful! It's time your Guess was shot, and you compare him with Squeezer!

LOMOV. Excuse me; I cannot continue this discussion, my heart is palpitating.

NATALYA STEPANOVNA. I've noticed that those hunters argue most who know least.

LOMOV. Madam, please be silent. . . . My heart is going to pieces. . . . [Shouts.] Shut up!

NATALYA STEPANOVNA. I shan't shut up until you acknowledge that Squeezer is a hundred times better than your Guess!

LOMOV. A hundred times worse! Be hanged to your Squeezer! His head . . . eyes . . . shoulder . . .

NATALYA STEPANOVNA. There's no need to hang your silly Guess; he's half-dead already!

LOMOV [weeps]. Shut up! My heart's bursting!

NATALYA STEPANOVNA. I shan't shut up.

Enter CHUBUKOV.

CHUBUKOV. What's the matter now?

NATALYA STEPANOVNA. Papa, tell us truly, which is the better dog, our Squeezer or his Guess.

LOMOV. Stepan Stepanovitch, I implore you to tell me just one thing: is your Squeezer overshot or not? Yes or no?

CHUBUKOV. And suppose he is?

What does it matter? He's the best dog in the district for all that, and so on.

LOMOV. But isn't my Guess better? Really, now?

CHUBUKOV. Don't excite yourself, my precious one. . . . Allow me. . . . Your Guess certainly has his good points. . . . He's pure-bred, firm on his feet, has well-sprung ribs, and all that. But, my dear man, if you want to know the truth, that dog has two defects: he's old and he's short in the muzzle.

LOMOV. Excuse me, my heart . . . . Let's take the facts. . . . You will remember that on the Marusinsky hunt my Guess ran neck-and-neck with the Count's dog, while your Squeezer was left a whole verst behind.

CHUBUKOV. He got left behind because the Count's whipper-in hit him with his whip.

LOMOV. And with good reason. The dogs are running after a fox, when Squeezer goes and starts worrying a sheep!

CHUBUKOV. It's not true! . . . My dear fellow, I'm very liable to lose my temper, and so, just because of that, let's stop arguing. You started because everybody is always jealous of everybody else's dogs. Yes, we're all like that! You too, sir, aren't blameless! You no sooner notice that some dog is better than your Guess than you begin with this, that . . . and the other . . . and all that. . . . I remember everything!

LOMOV. I remember too!

CHUBUKOV [teasing him]. I remember, too. . . What do you remember?

LOMOV. My heart . . . my. foot's gone to sleep. . . . I can't . . .

NATALYA STEPANOVNA [teasing]. My heart. . . . What sort of a hunter are you? You ought to go and lie on the kitchen oven and catch blackbeetles, not go after foxes! My heart!

CHUBUKOV. Yes really, what sort of a hunter are you, anyway! You ought to sit at home with your palpitations, and not go tracking animals. You could go hunting, but you only go to argue with people and interfere with their dogs and so on. Let's change the subject in case I lose my temper. You're not a hunter at all, anyway!

LOMOV. And are you a hunter? You only go hunting to get in with the Count and to intrigue. . . . Oh, my heart! . . . You're an intriguer!

CHUBUKOV. What? I an intriguer? [Shouts.] Shut up!

LOMOV. Intriguer!

CHUBUKOV. Boy! Pup!

LOMOV. Old rat! Jesuit!

CHUBUKOV. Shut up or I'll shoot you like a partridge! You fool!

LOMOV. Everybody knows that—oh my heart!—your late wife used to beat you. . . . My feet . . . temples . . . sparks. . . . I fall, I fall!

CHUBUKOV. And you're under the slipper of your housekeeper!

LOMOV. There, there, there . . . my heart's burst! My shoulder's come off. . . . Where is my shoulder? . . . I die. [Falls into an armchair.] A doctor! [Faints.]

CHUBUKOV. Boy! Milksop! Fool! I'm sick! [Drinks water.] Sick!

NATALYA STEPANOVNA. What sort of a hunter are you? You can't even sit on a horse. [To her father.] Papa, what's the matter with him? Papa! Look, papa! [*Screams.*] Ivan Vassilevitch! He's dead!

CHUBUKOV. I'm sick! . . . I can't breathe! . . . Air!

NATALYA STEPANOVNA. He's dead. [*Pulls* LOMOV's *sleeve.*] Ivan Vassilevitch! Ivan Vassilevitch! What have you done to me? He's dead. [*Falls into an armchair.*] A doctor, a doctor! [*Hysterics.*]

CHUBUKOV. Oh! . . . What is it? What's the matter?

NATALYA STEPANOVNA [*wails*]. He's dead . . . dead!

CHUBUKOV. Who's dead? [*Looks at* LOMOV.] So he is! My word! Water! A doctor! [*Lifts a tumbler to* LOMOV's *mouth.*] Drink this! . . . No, he doesn't drink. . . . It means he's dead, and all that. . . . I'm the most unhappy of men! Why don't I put a bullet into my brain? Why haven't I cut my throat yet? What am I waiting for? Give me a knife! Give me a pistol! [LOMOV *moves.*] He seems to be coming round. . . . Drink some water! That's right. . . .

LOMOV. I see stars . . . mist. . . . Where am I?

CHUBUKOV. Hurry up and get married and—well, to the devil with you! She's willing! [*He puts* LOMOV's *hand into his daughter's.*] She's willing and all that. I give you my blessing and so on. Only leave me in peace!

LOMOV [*getting up*]. Eh? What? To whom?

CHUBUKOV. She's willing. Well? Kiss and be damned to you!

NATALYA STEPANOVNA [*wails*]. He's alive. . . . Yes, yes, I'm willing. . . .

CHUBUKOV. Kiss each other!

LOMOV. Eh? Kiss whom? [*They kiss.*] Very nice, too. Excuse me, what's it all about? Oh, now I understand . . . my heart . . . stars . . . I'm happy. Natalya Stepanovna. . . . [*Kisses her hand.*] My foot's gone to sleep. . . .

NATALYA STEPANOVNA. I . . . I'm happy too. . . .

CHUBUKOV. What a weight off my shoulders. . . . Ouf!

NATALYA STEPANOVNA. But . . . still you will admit now that Guess is worse than Squeezer.

LOMOV. Better!

NATALYA STEPANOVNA. Worse!

CHUBUKOV. Well, that's a way to start your family bliss! Have some champagne!

LOMOV. He's better!

NATALYA STEPANOVNA. Worse! worse! worse!

CHUBUKOV [*trying to shout her down*]. Champagne! Champagne!

CURTAIN

The Forced Tragedian

DRAMATIS PERSONAE

IVAN IVANOVITCH TOLKACHOV, *the father of a family*.
ALEXEY ALEXEYEVITCH MURASHKIN, *his friend*.
The scene is laid in St. Petersburg, in MURASHKIN'S *flat*.

ACT I

MURASHKIN'S *study. Comfortable furniture.* MURASHKIN *is seated at his desk. Enter* TOLKACHOV *holding in his hands a glass globe for a lamp, a toy bicycle, three hatboxes, a large parcel containing a dress, a bin-case of beer, and several little parcels. He looks round stupidly and lets himself down on the sofa in exhaustion.*

MURASHKIN. How are you, Ivan Ivanovitch! Glad to see you! What brings you here?

TOLKACHOV [*breathing heavily*]. My dear fellow . . . I want to ask you something. . . . I beg you . . . lend me a revolver till to-morrow.

MURASHKIN. What do you want a revolver for?

TOLKACHOV. I need it. Oh, little fathers! . . . give me some water . . . quickly! . . . I need it. . . . I've got to go through a dark wood to-night . . . do, please, lend me one.

MURASHKIN. Oh, you liar, Ivan Ivanovitch! What the devil have you got to do in a dark wood? You have some secret. I can see by your face that you are up to something. What's the matter with you? Are you sick?

TOLKACHOV. Wait a moment, give me time. . . . Oh little mothers! I am dog-tired. I feel as if I've been roasted on a spit. I can't stand it any longer. Don't ask me any questions or insist on details; just give me the revolver! I beg you!

MURASHKIN. Well, really! Ivan Ivanovitch, what a coward! The father of a family and a Civil Servant holding a responsible post! A disgrace!

TOLKACHOV. What sort of a father of a family am I! I am a martyr. I am a beast of burden, a slave, a rascal who keeps on waiting here for something to happen instead of starting off for the next world. I am a stick, a fool, an idot. Why am I alive? What's the use? [*Jumps up.*] What's the purpose of these continuous mental and physical sufferings? I understand being a martyr to an idea, yes! But to be a martyr to skirts and lamp-globes, no! I decline! No, no, never! I've had enough!

MURASHKIN. Don't yell, the neighbours will hear you!

TOLKACHOV. Let them; it's all the same to me! If you don't give me a revolver somebody else will, and there will be an end of me anyway! Ive made up my mind!

MURASHKIN. Hold on, you've pulled off a button. Calm down! I still don't understand what's wrong with your life.

TOLKACHOV. What's wrong? You ask me what's wrong? Very well, I'll tell you! I'll tell you all, and then perhaps relieve myself. Let's sit down. Now listen. . . . Oh, little mothers, I am out of breath! . . . Just let's take to-day as an instance. Let's take to-day. As you know, I've got to work

675

at the Treasury from ten to four. It's hot, it's stuffy, there are flies, and, my dear fellow, the very dickens of a chaos. The Secretary is on leave, Khrapov has gone to get married, and the smaller fry is mostly in the country, making love or occupied with amateur theatricals. Everybody is so sleepy, tired, and done up that you can't get any sense out of them. The Secretary's duties are in the hands of an individual who is deaf in the left ear and in love; the public has lost its memory; everybody is running about angry and raging, and there is such a hullaballoo that you can't hear yourself speak. Confusion and smoke everywhere. And my work is deathly: always the same, always the same—first a correction, then a reference back, another correction, another reference back; it's all as monotonous as the waves of the sea. One's eyes, you understand, simply crawl out of one's head. Give me some water. . . . You come out a broken, exhausted man. You would like to dine and fall asleep, but you don't!—You remember that you live in the country—that is, you are a slave, a rag, a bit of string, a bit of limp flesh, and you've got to run round and do errands. Where we live a pleasant custom has grown up: when a man goes to town every wretched female inhabitant, not to mention one's own wife, has the power and the right to give him a crowd of commissions. The wife orders you to run into the modiste's and curse her for making a bodice too wide across the chest and too narrow across the shoulders; little Sonya wants a new pair of shoes; your sister-in-law wants some scarlet silk like the pattern at twenty copecks and three arshins long. . . . Just wait; I'll read you.

[Takes a note out of his pocket and reads.] A globe for the lamp; one pound of pork sausages; five copecks' worth of cloves and cinnamon; castor-oil for Misha; ten pounds of granulated sugar. To bring with you from home: a copper jar for sugar; carbolic acid; insect powder, ten copecks' worth; twenty bottles of beer; vinegar; and corsets for Mlle. Shanceau at No. 82. . . . Ouf! And to bring home Misha's winter coat and goloshes. That is the order of my wife and family. Then there are the commissions of our dear f r i e n d s and neighbours—devil take them! To-morrow is the name-day of Volodia Vlasin; I have to buy a bicycle for him. The wife of Lieutenant-Colonel Virkhin is in an interesting condition, and I am therefore bound to call in at the midwife's every day and invite her to come. And so on, and so on. There are five notes in my pocket and my handkerchief is all knots. And so, my dear fellow, you spend the time between your office and your train, running about the town like a dog with your tongue hanging out, running and running and cursing life. From the clothier's to the chemist's, from the chemist's to the modiste's, from the modiste's to the pork butcher's, and then back again to the chemist's. In one place you stumble, in a second you lose your money, in a third you forget to pay and they raise a hue and cry after you, in a fourth you tread on the train of a lady's dress. . . . Tfoo! You get so shaken up from all this that your bones ache all night and you dream of crocodiles. Well, you've made all your purchases, but how are you to pack all these things? For instance, how are you to put a heavy copper jar together with the lamp-globe or the carbolic acid with the tea? How are you to make a combination of beer-bottles and this bicycle? It's the labours of Hercules, a puzzle, a rebus! Whatever tricks you think of, in the long run you're bound to smash or scatter something, and at the station and in the train you have to stand with your arms apart, holding up some parcel or other under your chin, with parcels, cardboard boxes, and such-like rubbish all over you. The train starts, the passengers begin to throw your luggage about on all sides: you've got your things on somebody else's seat. They yell, they call for the conductor, they threaten to have you put out, but what can I do? I just stand and blink my eyes like a whacked donkey. Now listen to this. I get home. You think I'd like to have a nice little drink after my righteous labours and a good square meal—isn't that so?—but there is no chance of that. My spouse has been on the look-out for me for some time. You've hardly started on your soup when she has her claws into you, wretched slave that you are—and wouldn't you like to go to some amateur theatricals or to a dance? You can't protest. You are a husband, and the word husband when translated into the language of summer residents in the country means a dumb beast which you can load to any extent without fear of the interference of the Society for the Prevention of Cruelty to Animals. So you go and blink at 'A Family Scandal' or something, you applaud when your wife tells you to, and you feel worse and worse and worse until you expect an apoplectic fit to happen any moment. If you go to a dance you have to find

partners for your wife, and if there is a shortage of them then you dance the quadrilles yourself. You get back from the theatre or the dance after midnight, when you are no longer a man but a useless, limp rag. Well, at last you've got what you want; you unrobe and get into bed. It's excellent—you can close your eyes and sleep. . . . Everything is so nice, poetic, and warm, you understand; there are no children squealing behind the wall, and you've got rid of your wife, and your conscience is clear—what more can you want? You fall asleep—and suddenly . . . you hear a buzz! . . . Gnats! [*Jumps up.*] Gnats! Be they triply accursed Gnats! [*Shakes his fist.*] Gnats! It's one of the plagues of Egypt, one of the tortures of the Inquisition! Buzz! It sounds so pitiful, so pathetic, as if it's begging your pardon, but the villain stings so that you have to scratch yourself for an hour after. You smoke, and go for them, and cover yourself from head to foot, but it's no good! At last you have to sacrifice yourself and let the cursed things devour you. You've no sooner got used to the gnats when another plague begins; downstairs your wife begins practising sentimental songs with her tenor friends. They sleep by day and rehearse for amateur concerts by night. Oh, my God! Those tenors are a torture with which no gnats on earth can compare. [*He sings.*] "Oh, tell me not my youth has ruined you." "Before thee do I stand enchanted." Oh, the beastly things! They've about killed me! So as to deafen myself a little I do this: drum on my ears. This goes on till four o'clock. Oh, give me some more water, brother! . . . I can't . . . Well, not having slept, you get up at six o'clock in the morning and off you go to the station. You run so as not to be late, and it's muddy, foggy, cold—brr! Then you get to town and start all over again. So there, brother. It's a horrible life; I wouldn't wish one like it for my enemy. You understand—I'm ill! Got asthma, heartburn—I'm always afraid of something. I've got indigestion, everything is thick before me . . . I've become a regular psychopath. . . . [*Looking round.*] Only, between ourselves, I want to go down to see Crechotte or Merzheyevsky. There's some devil in me, brother. In moments of despair and suffering, when the gnats are stinging or the tenors sing, everything suddenly grows dim; you jump up and race round the whole house like a lunatic and shout, "I want blood! Blood!" And really all the time you do want to let a knife into somebody or hit him over the head with a chair. That's what life in a summer villa leads to! And nobody has any sympathy for me, and everybody seems to think it's all as it should be. People even laugh. But understand, I am a living being and I want to live! This isn't farce, it's tragedy! I say, if you don't give me your revolver, you might at any rate sympathize.

MURASHKIN. I do sympathize.

TOLKACHOV. I see how much you sympathize. . . . Good-bye. I've got to buy some anchovies and some sausage . . . and some tooth-powder, and then to the station.

MURASHKIN. Where are you living?

TOLKACHOV. At Carrion River.

MURASHKIN. [*Delighted.*] Really? Then you'll know Olga Pavlovna Finberg, who lives there?

TOLKACHOV. I know her. We are even acquainted.

MURASHKIN. How prefectly splendid! That's so convenient, and it would be so good of you . . .

TOLKACHOV. What's that?

MURASHKIN. My dear f e l l o w, wouldn't you do one little thing for me? Be a friend! Promise me now

TOLKACHOV. What's that?

MURASHKIN. It would be such a friendly action! I implore you, my dear man. In the first place, give Olga Pavlovna my very kind regards. In the second place, there's a little thing I'd like you to take down to her. She asked me to get her a sewing-machine but I haven't anybody to send it down to her by. . . . You take it, my dear! And you might at the same time take down this canary in its cage . . . only be careful, or you'll break the door. . . . What are you looking at me like that for?

TOLKACHOV. A sewing-machine . . . canary in a cage . . . . siskins, chaffinches . . .

MURASHKIN. Ivan Ivanovitch, what's the matter with you? Why are you turning purple?

TOLKACHOV. [*Stamping.*] Give me the sewing-machine. Where's the birdcage? Now get on top yourself! Eat me! Tear me to pieces! Kill me! [*Clinching his fists.*] I want blood! Blood! Blood!

MURASHKIN. You've gone mad!

TOLKACHOV. [*Treading on his feet.*] I want blood! Blood!

MURASHKIN. [*In horror.*] He's gone mad. [*Shouts.*] Peter! Maria! Where are you? Help!

TOLKACHOV. [*Chasing him round the room.*] I want blood! Blood!

CURTAIN

LaVergne, TN USA
28 October 2009
162337LV00003B/32/A